Ireland

written and researched by

Margaret Greenwood, Geoff Wallis, Mark Connolly and Hildi Hawkins

with additional contributions by

Paul Gray and Max Wooldridge

www.roughguides.com

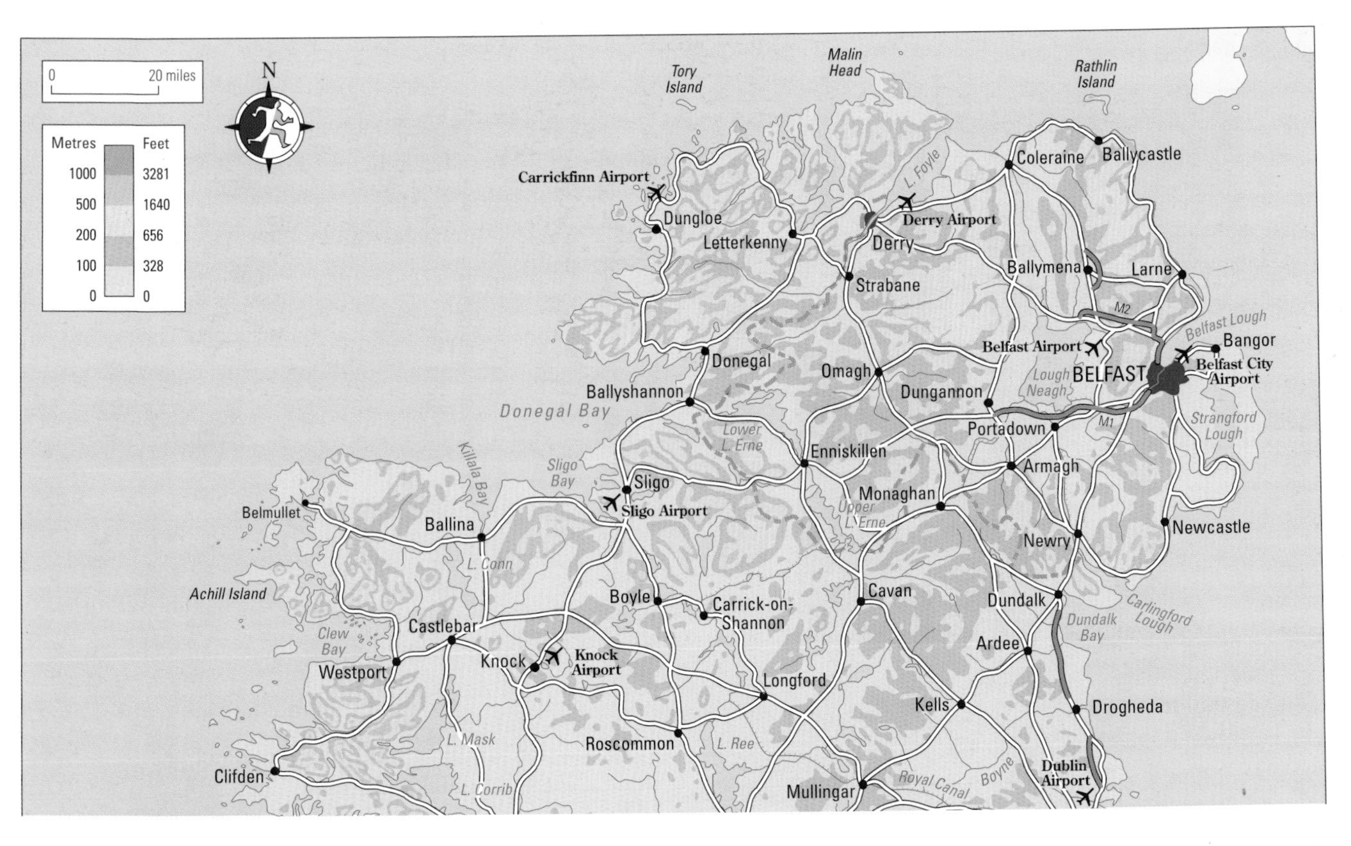
0
20 miles
Metres
Feet
1000
3281
500
1640
200
656
100
328
0
0
N
Tory Island
Malin Head
Rathlin Island
Carrickfinn Airport
Dungloe
Letterkenny
L. Foyle
Derry Airport
Derry
Coleraine
Ballycastle
Ballymena
Larne
Strabane
M2
Belfast Lough
Bangor
Belfast Airport
Belfast City Airport
BELFAST
Lough Neagh
Donegal
Omagh
Dungannon
Ballyshannon
Donegal Bay
Portadown
M1
Strangford Lough
Lower L. Erne
Enniskillen
Armagh
Killala Bay
Sligo Bay
Sligo
Sligo Airport
Monaghan
Upper L. Erne
Belmullet
Ballina
Newry
Newcastle
L. Conn
Achill Island
Boyle
Carrick-on-Shannon
Cavan
Dundalk
Carlingford Lough
Dundalk Bay
Castlebar
Clew Bay
Westport
Knock
Knock Airport
Ardee
Longford
Kells
Drogheda
L. Mask
Roscommon
L. Ree
Clifden
L. Corrib
Mullingar
Royal Canal
Boyne
Dublin Airport

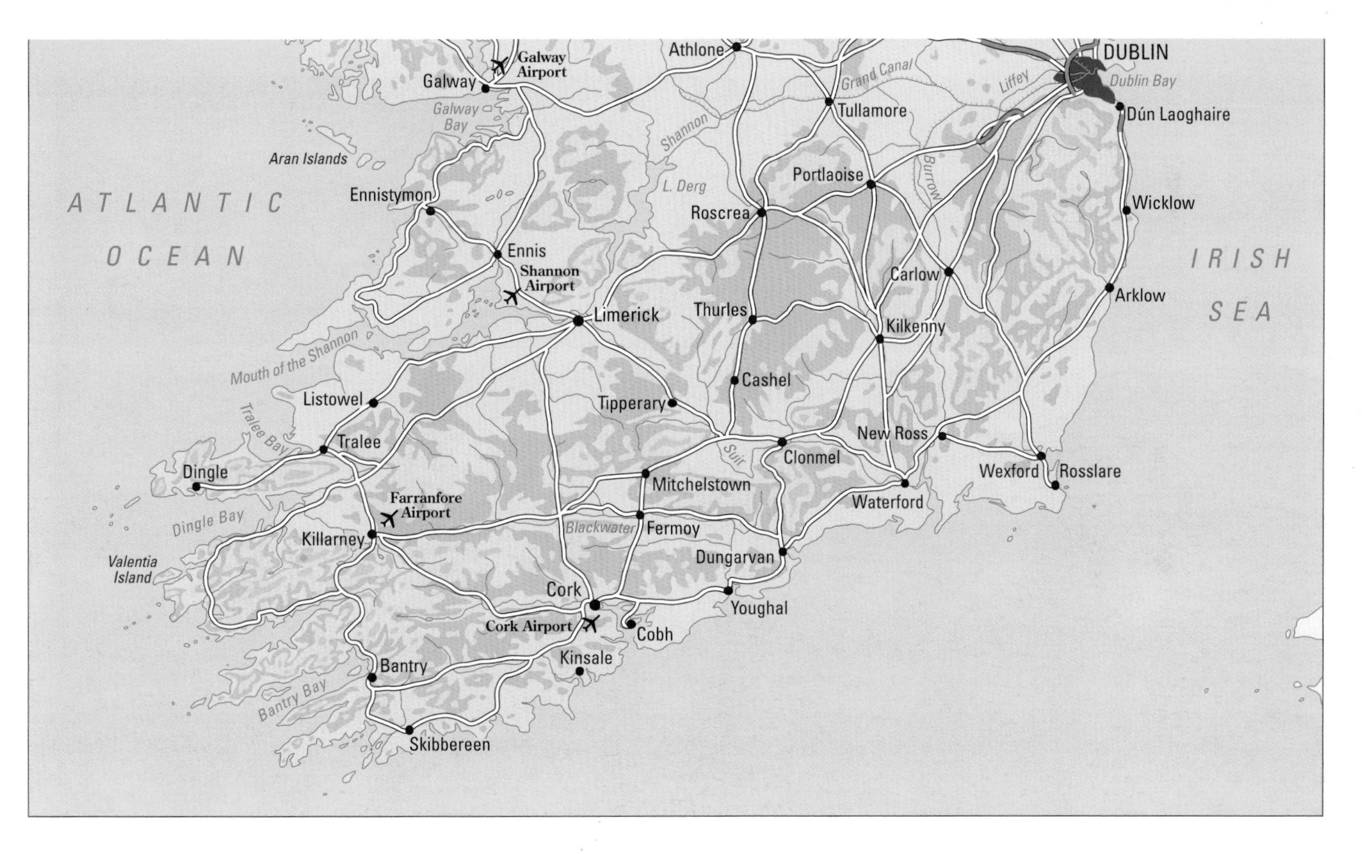

Athlone
DUBLIN
Galway Airport
Galway
Grand Canal
Liffey
Dublin Bay
Galway Bay
Tullamore
Dún Laoghaire
Shannon
Aran Islands
Portlaoise
Burrow
L. Derg
Ennistymon
ATLANTIC
OCEAN
Roscrea
Wicklow
Ennis
Shannon Airport
Carlow
IRISH
SEA
Arklow
Limerick
Thurles
Kilkenny
Mouth of the Shannon
Cashel
Listowel
Tipperary
Tralee Bay
New Ross
Tralee
Suir
Clonmel
Dingle
Wexford
Rosslare
Mitchelstown
Farranfore Airport
Waterford
Dingle Bay
Blackwater
Fermoy
Killarney
Dungarvan
Valentia Island
Cork
Youghal
Cork Airport
Cobh
Kinsale
Bantry
Bantry Bay
Skibbereen

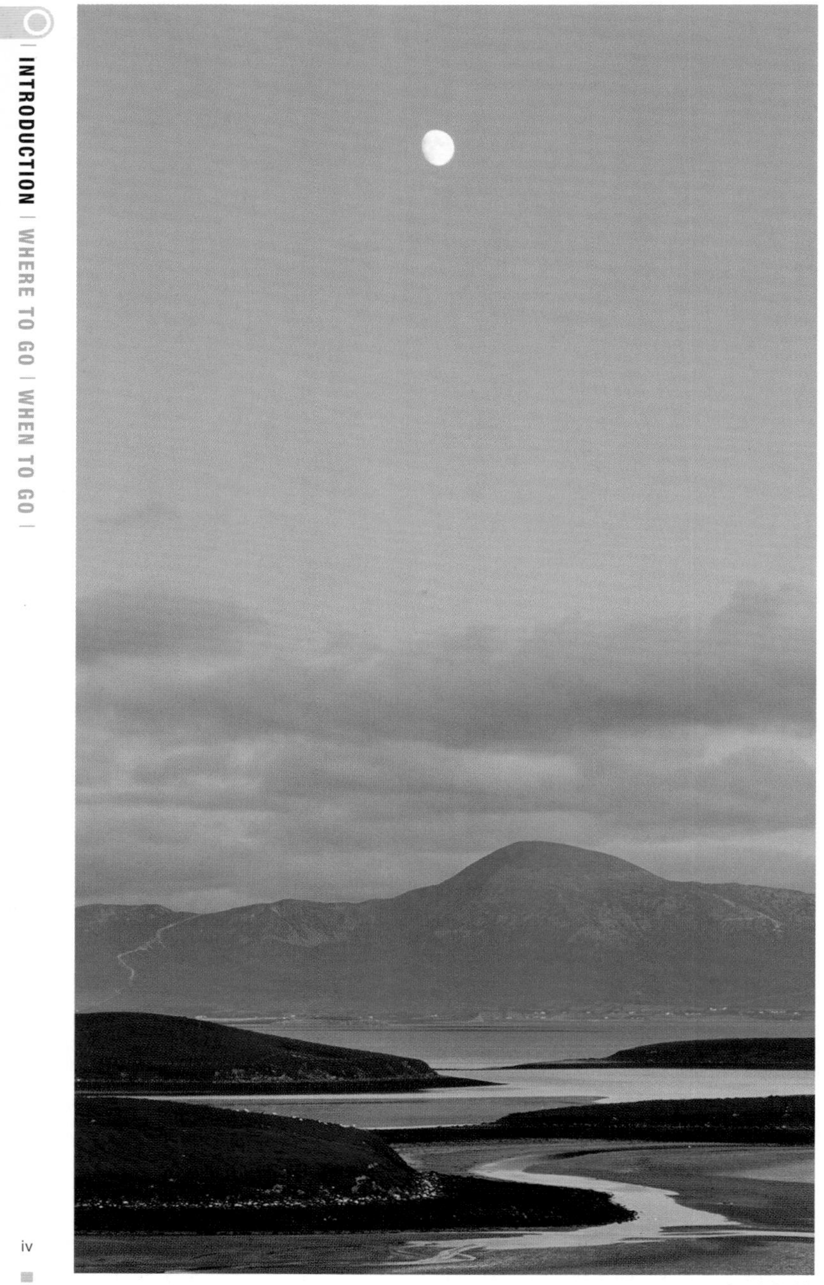

△ Croagh Patrick

Introduction to

Ireland

It's the undoubted lure of the landscape, along with the easy pace and rhythms of life, which draw the majority of visitors to Ireland. Once there, few are disappointed: the green, rain-hazed loughs and wild, bluff coastlines, the inspired talent for conversation and the place of music and language at the heart of Irish culture all conspire to ensure that the reality lives up to expectations. More surprising perhaps is just how much variety this very small land packs into its countryside. The limestone terraces of the stark, eerie Burren seem separated from the fertile farmlands of Tipperary by hundreds rather than tens of miles, and the harshly beautiful west coast, with its cliffs, coves and strands, looks as if it belongs in another country altogether from the rolling plains of the central cattle-rearing counties.

It's a place to explore slowly, roaming through agricultural landscapes scattered with farmhouses, or along the endlessly indented coastline. Spectacular seascapes unfold from rocky headlands where the crash of the sea against the cliffs and myriad islands is often the only sound. It is perfect if you want space to walk, bike or (with a bit of bravado) swim, or if you want to fish, sail or spend a week on inland waterways. In the smaller towns, too, the pleasures are unhurried: evenings over a Guinness or two in the snug of a pub, listening to the chat around a blood-orange turf fire.

In every part of the island are traces of a **culture** established long before the coming of Christianity while, in the depths of the so-called Dark Ages,

Fact file

- Ireland covers approximately 32,600 square miles (84,500 square km). The island is comprised of the Republic of Ireland and Northern Ireland, which is part of the United Kingdom. The Republic is a parliamentary democracy with an elected president as its head of state. While electing members of parliament to the UK Government in Westminster, Northern Ireland has its own devolved assembly responsible for certain local affairs.
- The total population of Ireland is around 5.6 million: over 3.9 million live in the Republic and around 1.7 million live in Northern Ireland. Over 50 percent of the Republic's population and 43 percent of Northern Ireland's are under the age of 30. The population of Dublin is 1,122,600; that of Belfast is around 277,000.
- In the Republic the vast majority of people – around 3 million – are Roman Catholic; the figure for non-Christian peoples is around 70,000. In Northern Ireland around 40 percent of the population are Roman Catholic, and around 45 percent are of Protestant and other Christian denominations.
- Irish is the first language of the Republic – at least according to the constitution. Around 43 percent of the population can speak it, and in Irish-speaking areas (the Gaeltacht) around 76 percent of the population do; nevertheless, in effect, English is the first language. In Northern Ireland around 90 percent of people have no knowledge of Irish at all.

△ Book of Kells

the Christian communities of Ireland were great centres of learning. Fortifications raised by the chieftains of the Celtic clans and the Anglo-Norman barons bear witness to a period of later turbulence, while the Ascendancy of the Protestant settlers has left its mark in the form of vast mansions and estates.

But the richness of Irish culture is not just a matter of monuments. Especially in the Irish-speaking Gaeltacht areas, you'll be aware of the strength and continuity of the island's oral and musical traditions. **Myth-making** is for the Irish people their oldest entertainment. The ancient classics are full of extraordinary stories – Cúchulainn the unbeatable hero in war, Medb the insatiable heroine in bed or Fionn Mac Cumhaill (Finn Mac Cool) chasing Diarmuid and Gráinne up and down the country – and tall tales, superstition-stirring and "mouthing off" (boasting) play as large a part in day-to-day life as they did in the era of the *Táin Bó Cúailnge*, Europe's oldest vernacular epic. As a guileless foreigner enquiring about anything from a beautiful lake to a pound of butter, you're ideally placed to trigger the most colourful responses. And the **speech of the country** – moulded by the rhythms of the ancient tongue – fired such twentieth-century greats as Yeats, Joyce and Beckett. Yet, while almost half of Ireland's population claims to be able to speak the Irish language, fewer than ten percent use it on a daily basis and a fair proportion of these only do so during school hours.

Music has always been at the centre of Irish community life. You'll find traditional music sessions in all the popular coastal counties (especially Antrim, Donegal, Sligo, Galway, Clare, Kerry, Cork and Waterford) and in the cities, too (particularly Dublin, Belfast, Cork and Galway); some of it might be of dubious pedigree, but the Gaeltacht areas, and others, can be counted on to provide authentic renditions. Side by side with the traditional circuit is a strong rock scene that has spawned Van Morrison, Thin

The fiddle

Rarely known by its classical-music synonym of violin, the fiddle has been the dominant instrument in Ireland's traditional music for the last hundred years or so. Its popularity lies in both its relative cheapness (compared to instruments such as the *uilleann* pipes and button accordion) and portability, while, in the hands of an adroit exponent, few instruments can match its versatility, particularly in providing scope for all the ornamentation, rhythm and colour so essential to the dance music tradition.

Undoubtedly, part of its popularity is owed to the stream of American 78rpm recordings made during the 1920s and 1930s by fiddlers such as Michael Coleman, James Morrison and Paddy Killoran who had all emigrated from County Sligo to the US. The tunes these musicians recorded can still be heard (sometimes even in the same order) at today's traditional sessions and the Sligo style certainly had an impact on music-making throughout Ireland.

Nevertheless, other local fiddle styles still survive, especially in County Donegal, where a more dynamic, driving kind of music can be heard, and in the Sliabh Luachra region encompassing parts of Cork, Kerry and Limerick where the style is more gentle and melodious. There are certainly plenty of modern fiddle virtuosos too, and amongst the most justifiably lauded are Frankie Gavin (of the band De Dannan), Paddy Canny, John Carty, Cathal Hayden, Mairéad Ní Mhaonaigh and Ciarán Tourish (both members of Altan), Paddy Glackin, Seán McGuire and the US-based Martin Hayes, Liz Carroll and Tommy Peoples.

Passage graves, portal tombs and stone circles

△ Newgrange

Ireland has around 1500 recorded examples of megalithic tombs dating from the Neolithic period. Passage graves and portal tombs are two of the most distinctive types. Built for communal burial by early farming communities, they point to the existence of highly organized societies dating from around 4000 BC.

The greatest concentrations of passage graves are found in the north and east of the country, tombs in which a long stone passage leads to the burial chamber and the whole is covered by a mound of earth and stone.

The spectacular site at Newgrange (see p.200) is the most famous of all – and with good reason. Around 5000 years old, the complexity of the site's construction and the sheer size of the boulders used are awe-inspiring. The meanings of its fabulous swirling spiral decorations are a source of continuing speculation, and possibly symbolize fertility, renewal and rebirth.

Portal tombs – or dolmens – are arguably the most dramatic of Ireland's megalithic monuments. Today they usually appear as two or three large upright stones supporting one huge sloping stone. Originally many would have been covered in earth, providing a monumental enclosed burial chamber. Especially striking examples include Browneshill dolmen in County Carlow, Poulnabrone dolmen in County Clare and Kilclooney dolmen, County Donegal.

Stone circles are also impressive, if not as old, dating from the Bronze Age. Over 200 stone circles have been found, and around 100 of these are in Cork and Kerry. While their precise purpose remains unknown, it is likely that all were associated with ritual monuments.

Lizzy, U2, Sinéad O'Connor and The Corrs, alongside up-and-coming young hopefuls such as Damien Dempsey and Gemma Hayes. And ever-present are the balladeers, fathoming and feeding the old Irish dreams of courting, emigrating and striking it lucky; there's hardly a dry eye in the house when the guitars are packed away.

The lakes and rivers of Ireland make it an **angler's dream**, and the country has some of the most beautiful (and demanding) **golf** courses in the world, but the sports that raise the greatest enthusiasm amongst the Irish themselves are speedier and more dangerous. **Horse racing** in Ireland has none of the socially divisive connotations present on the other side of the Irish Sea, and the country has bred some of the world's finest thoroughbreds. While association football is as popular as in most parts of the world now, **Gaelic football**, sharing elements of soccer and rugby (which itself has its hotbeds, notably in Limerick and Cork), still commands a large following. **Hurling**, the oldest team game played in Ireland, requires the most delicate of ball skills and the sturdiest of bones.

The essence of Ireland, however, is defined by its many profound **cultural contrasts**. Divided politically since 1921 – the Republic an independent state, Northern Ireland part of the UK – it has been ravaged by centuries of oppression and emigration. Drawn via the historic links of empire and economy to Britain, by political process to Brussels and by aspiration to variously Europe, Britain and the United States, Ireland's position on the very fringes of Europe has had a defining influence in the forging of its complex identities.

The **people** themselves bear witness to those same divisions and contrasts. Almost the entire population of Ireland still defines itself on religious grounds. Though churchgoing may have diminished dramatically in the Republic, the strength of the Roman Catholic Church there still has a tremendous impact on political decision-making. The North remains rigidly divided between Catholics and those following a variety of Protestant denominations, a division almost entirely mirrored by the political schism between Republicans/Nationalists and Unionists/Loyalists, a legacy of partition in 1921.

△ Inishmore, Aran Islands

During the 1990s, the **Republic's burgeoning economy**, accompanied by massive British and European investment in the North, gave rise to a new plutocracy whose wealth not only manifested itself in changing cityscapes (and numerous financial scandals) but in the building of palatial mansions fit to rival the Palladian edifices of the Plantation era. At the same time, the gap between rich and poor has been exacerbated by rising property prices and the cost of urban living. The arrival of refugees and asylum, seekers in the Republic has challenged perceived notions about Ireland's homogeneity and, while many Irish people have embraced the concept of a more pluralist multiculturalism, others have seen the newcomers as a threat, and this has resulted in a spate of racist attacks over the last few years.

But a country notoriously blighted by emigration is, at last, drawing people back with the lure of work, and a generation has grown to adulthood with expectations of making a life for themselves at home. The conspicuous new wealth of many makes itself felt in every quarter of Irish life, but most especially in **cities** like Dublin and Galway where a proliferation of new bars, cafés and restaurants reveals a determination to enjoy life to the full. The driving cosmopolitan energy of these cities is informed, in part,

△ Fishing harbour, Ring of Kerry

Much of the countryside of Ireland is intensely beautiful and thankfully unspoilt

by the complex array of experiences brought home by returning ex-pats, more familiar with the ways of London and New York, Melbourne and San Francisco, than with those of the Aran Islands.

Where to go

It's arguably the **Republic's west coast** that has the most appeal in terms of landscape. Dramatic and daunting peninsulas, breath-taking sea-cliffs and the expansive shorelines of the northern reaches contrast with the mystical lakes of the **Donegal** highlands. South from Donegal the coastline is just as strangely attractive: **Sligo** offers a compelling mix of spectacular bays and prime surf beaches; immediately inland lie exquisite lakes and the weird escarpment of Yeats's beloved Benbulben. **County Mayo** affords some of the most isolated seascapes in the country, backed by huge tracts of wind-racked bog, and further south you'll find the fabulous bog wilderness of **Connemara** in County Galway, and a coastline fringed with white-sand beaches set against violently jumbled peaks of quartz and granite.

South of Galway city, the coast strikes a less melodramatic tone as both the climate and the setting soften. The eerie limestone hills of the **Burren**, County Clare, rise from turquoise waters in fine weather; the spectacular **Cliffs of Moher** fall to treacherous beaches, and in the south of the county lies a mix of safe family beaches and exhilarating stack rocks and puffing holes.

County Kerry has some of the most striking scenery in the country, a heady mix of dramatic mountains, wonderful seascapes, fertile meadows, glassy lakes and fuchsia-fringed lanes. The wild coast that makes up the **Ring of Kerry** is firmly on the tourist trail, yet despite its popularity it's still easy enough to head down quiet paths and find something like seclusion. In the far southwest of the country the ragged peninsulas of **County Cork**, bound by barren rock, offer yet more fabulous views of the ocean, along with a handful of fine beaches and quiet sandy coves.

The west coast has some of the best of the islands too, offering a glimpse of the isolation that was once the way of life for remote island communities. The **Aran Islands** are perhaps the most famous: wind-swept expanses of limestone supporting some of the most extraordinary prehistoric sites

△ Ormond Castle, Carrick-on-Suir

in Europe. In the far northwest, rugged **Tory Island** has a vibrant local culture and its inhabitants possess an indomitable spirit, undiminished by the sometimes bitter weather. The **Blasket Islands** off the Kerry coast, now uninhabited in the winter months, were once home to a thriving Gaelic-speaking community and here too you can gain a sense of the harshness of existence in a savage, beautiful landscape. More daunting still is the sense of the past conjured up by a visit to the early Christian site on **Skellig Michael**, frequently inaccessible even today. Closer to land, **Cape Clear** off west Cork is exceptional in its bird life, the water and skies a riot of cormorants, auks and storm petrels.

The wild splendours of the west coast can be isolated and remote and are best enjoyed if you have a week or more to spend there. Elsewhere in the Republic lie coastal regions just as varied, if less dramatically charged. Cork's south coast offers quiet estuaries backed by mist-wrapped pastures, undulating headlands falling to gentle inlets and the historic harbours of **Kinsale**, **Cork city**, **Cobh** and **Youghal**. **County Waterford** also has some exceptional coastal scenery, with sandstone cliffs, broad sandy beaches and pleasant low-key resorts. In the extreme southeast, **Wexford's** broad estuaries are famously alive with birds, while its east coast offers miles of dune-backed beaches of golden sand.

The Republic's inland scenery can rarely compete with the romantic wildernesses of the west coast, though the **River Shannon**, with its string of huge lakes, and the pretty river valleys of the southeast have distinct charms of their own. The classical landscapes of **estates** planned and cultivated in the eighteenth century – and the mansions that they were designed to serve – are found throughout Ireland, and are especially typical of the fertile farmland of counties Dublin, Kildare, Laois, Offaly, Limerick and Waterford. In complete contrast, wide expanses of **peat bog** form much of the midlands and, while you are not likely to spend a lot of time here, the bogs, endangered habitats and home to rare plants, are worth exploring.

Landscape aside, the Republic's **archaeological** and **historic sites** are understandably top tourist attractions. The prehistoric sites of **Newgrange** in County Meath and **Dún Aengus** on the Aran Islands are exceptionally impressive, and there's a profusion of **stone circles** in County Cork, and of **cairns** and **tombs** in Sligo, Donegal, Clare and Wicklow. Superb early **Christian monuments** also abound: the **Rock of Cashel** and **Skellig Michael** are two of the most impressive sites. And in just about any part of the country, with the exception of the northwest, you can be sure of finding evocative ecclesiastical sites along the way – **Clonmacnois**, **Kilmacduagh**, **Glendalough** and **Monasterboice** are among the finest.

△ Monasterboice

The ancient cities of Dublin, Waterford, Limerick and Kilkenny also offer exceptional **medieval monuments** and, along with Cork, have the lion's share of the Republic's **museums and galleries**. The eclectic **Hunt Museum** in Limerick, the Viking and medieval collections of **Waterford Treasures** and the vast and varied displays of the **National Museum** and the **National Gallery** in Dublin are among the most exceptional of these.

Much of the countryside of **Northern Ireland** is intensely beautiful and thankfully unspoilt, with most of the major attractions lying at its fringes.

△ Beehive hut, Blasket Islands

To the north are the green **Glens of Antrim** and a coastline as scenic as anywhere in Ireland, with, as its centrepiece, the bizarre black basalt geometry of the **Giant's Causeway**, and, just offshore, the stark beauty of **Rathlin Island**. In the southeast, **County Down** offers the contrasting beauties of the serene **Strangford Lough** and the brooding mass of the **Mourne Mountains**. To the west, the inland counties of **Tyrone** and **Fermanagh** are dotted with **megalithic remains** and ruined **Plantation castles**. Tyrone's main attraction is the wild and desolate **Sperrin** mountain range, while Fermanagh has the peerless lake scenery of **Lough Erne**, a fabulous place for watersports, fishing and exploring island monastic remains. Elsewhere, near the huge, central **Lough Neagh**, lie the planned towns of the merchant companies who were entrusted with the resettlement of this region in the seventeenth century, and the rolling countryside of **south Armagh** that is almost unsullied except for lingering military installations. Evidence of the Plantation is also provided by a panoply of grand mansions, often set in sprawling, landscaped grounds, such as **Castle Coole** and **Florence Court** in Fermanagh, **Ardess House** and the **Argory** in County Armagh and **Mount Stewart** in County Down.

△ Hurling sticks

To get to grips with the history of the North, a visit to its **cities** is essential: **Belfast**, with its grand public buildings, was built on the profits of Victorian industry; **Derry** has shed the security barriers and barbed wire that formerly shrouded its medieval walled town; and the cathedral town of **Armagh**, set on seven hills, is where St Patrick established Christianity in Ireland. Further insights are provided by a tremendous selection of museums including Belfast's **Ulster Museum**, Derry's **O'Doherty Tower** and the **Ulster Folk and Transport Museum** in County Down.

The plethora of Irish festivals can make even the tiniest of villages come alive

Ireland's cities, both North and South, are also the easiest way to sample the richness of the country's **cultural life**: **Dublin** is an extraordinary combination of youthfulness and tradition, a modern European capital on a human scale. **Belfast** vies with Dublin in the vitality of its nightlife, while **Cork** and **Galway** have an energy and bustle that makes them a pleasure to visit. It's in the cities that you will find art, music and theatre year-round, but there are pleasures too in enjoying the arts in the more intimate venues of small towns. Even the tiniest of villages can come alive at any time of year in the plethora of **festivals** that mark out the seasons. Anything from comedy, theatre and storytelling to horse fairs, archaeology and opera might be the theme, offering visitors the chance to tap into the life of a place at a local level and experience the love of festivities and conversation that make Ireland such an engaging country to visit.

When to go

Ireland's **climate**, determined by the pressure-systems of the Atlantic, is notoriously variable, and cannot be relied upon at any time of the year. Each year produces weeks of beautiful weather – the problem lies in predicting when they are likely to arrive. In recent years **late spring** and **early autumn** have seen some of the best of the weather, with **May** and **September** often the most pleasant months due to the clear, and relatively dry, skies.

Geographically, the southeast is the driest and sunniest part of the country, and the northwest is the wettest. But the regional variations are not

△ Carrying a curragh to the sea, Inisheer, Aran Island

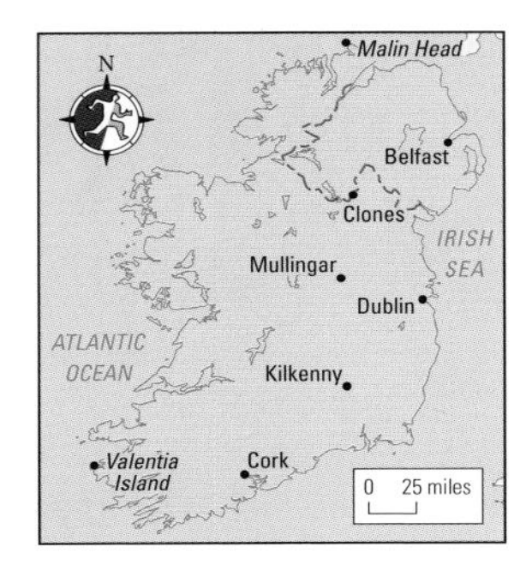

particularly pronounced, the overall climate being characterized by its **mildness** – the country benefiting from the warming effects of the Gulf Stream. Even in the wetter zones, mornings of rain are frequently followed by afternoons of blue sky and sun – and besides, a downpour on a windswept headland can be exhilarating, and provides as good a pretext as any for repairing to the local pub, the hub of Irish social activity.

Average maximum and minimum daily temperatures (°C) and monthly rainfall (mm)

	Jan	Feb	Mar	Apr	May	Jun	Jul	Aug	Sep	Oct	Nov	Dec
Belfast												
Max	7	7	8	10	13	15	17	17	15	11	8	7
Min	4	5	6	6	9	11	13	12	11	8	5	5
Rainfall	100	77	73	66	69	72	90	101	88	106	103	106
Clones												
Max	7	7	9	12	15	17	19	18	16	13	9	7
Min	1	1	2	3	6	9	10	10	8	7	3	2
Rainfall	91	68	77	56	67	68	60	85	83	97	86	91
Cork												
Max	9	9	11	13	16	19	20	20	18	14	11	9
Min	2	3	4	5	7	10	12	12	10	7	4	3
Rainfall	119	79	94	57	71	57	70	71	94	99	116	122
Dublin												
Max	8	8	10	13	15	18	20	19	17	14	10	8
Min	1	2	3	4	6	9	11	11	9	6	4	3
Rainfall	67	55	51	45	60	57	70	74	72	70	67	74
Kilkenny												
Max	8	8	10	12	15	18	20	20	17	14	10	8
Min	1	2	2	3	6	8	10	10	8	6	3	2
Rainfall	86	66	64	51	62	51	53	69	74	85	74	89
Malin Head												
Max	8	8	9	10	13	15	16	17	15	13	10	8
Min	3	3	4	5	7	10	11	11	10	8	5	4
Rainfall	114	76	86	58	59	64	72	91	102	118	115	103
Mullingar												
Max	7	7	9	12	15	18	19	19	16	13	9	8
Min	1	1	2	3	6	9	10	10	8	6	3	2
Rainfall	93	66	72	59	72	66	62	81	86	94	88	94
Valentia Island												
Max	9	9	11	12	14	16	18	18	17	14	11	10
Min	4	4	5	6	8	10	12	12	10	9	6	5
Rainfall	167	123	123	76	90	80	74	111	124	156	148	159

things not to miss

It's not possible to see everything that Ireland has to offer in one trip – and we don't suggest you try. What follows is a selective taste of the country's highlights: natural wonders and outstanding architecture, plus the best festivals and outdoor activities. They're arranged in five colour-coded categories, which you can browse through to find the very best things to see and experience. All highlights have a page reference to take you straight into the guide, where you can find out more.

01 **Killarney National Park** Page **388** • Stride out among spectacular lakes and the highest peaks in Ireland.

02 White Island Page **770** • Take the ferry to White Island to see the mix of a pagan and christian culture.

03 The Jack Yeats Collection in the National Gallery Page **94** • Arguably Ireland's greatest twentieth-century painter; the collection includes images of Dublin such as *The Liffey Swim*.

04 Dublin bars Page **129** • Enjoy the *craic* in Dublin's bars – traditional or contemporary – an integral part of city life.

05 Lough Gill Page **539** • The glassy tranquillity of Lough Gill was the inspiration for some of W.B. Yeats's most famous verse.

06 St Patrick's Day Page **48** • Ireland's favourite festival is equally enjoyable in big cities and out-of-the-way country places.

07 Surfing Ireland has some great spots for catching a wave: check out Lahinch page **438**, Portrush page **676** and Strandhill page **547**.

08 Georgian Dublin Page **92** • The city is at its most elegant around St Stephen's Green and Merrion Square.

09 Dún Aengus Page **478** • Visit the spectacular ring fort of Dún Aengus, Inishmore.

18 The Burren Page **439** • Explore these huge, stark terraces, which stretch out to the Atlantic Ocean.

19 The Rock of Cashel Page **314** • An extraordinary cluster of early ecclesiastical buildings, rising from a limestone outcrop amid the Tipperary plains.

20 Connemara Page **483** • Admire the wildlife and beautiful scenery of Connemara.

21 Murals Page **690** • Politics and art combine in Derry's renowned political murals.

22 The Book of Kells Page **85** • Ireland's most celebrated medieval manuscript, on display in Trinity College Library, Dublin.

23 Twelve Bens Page **492** • The rugged peaks of the Twelve Bens mountains offer some great walks.

24 Kinsale Page **356** • Historic Kinsale has a couple of forts, an intriguing museum and an astonishing number of first-rate restaurants.

| ACTIVITIES | CONSUME | EVENTS | NATURE | SIGHTS |

25
Sperrin Mountains
Page **755** • Hike through the wild, remote and beautiful Sperrins.

26 Galway Arts Festival Page **454** • The famous Macnas Parade fills the streets of Galway during the Arts Festival in July.

27 Traditional music Head to *The Cobblestone* in Dublin Page **132**, *Húdaí Beag* in Bunbeg Page **590** or *Ciarán's Bar* in Ennis Page **428** for excellent sessions.

28 Giant's Causeway Page **672** • Marvel at the eerie but entirely natural basalt formation of the Causeway.

Contents

Using this Rough Guide

We've tried to make this Rough Guide a good read and easy to use. The book is divided into five main sections, and you should be able to find whatever you want in one of them.

Colour section

The front colour section offers a quick tour of Ireland. The **introduction** aims to give you a feel for the place, with suggestions on where to go. We also tell you what the weather is like and include a basic country fact file. Next, our authors round up their favourite aspects of Ireland in the **things not to miss** section – whether it's great food, amazing sights or a special hotel. Right after this comes a full **contents** list.

Basics

The Basics section covers all the **pre-departure** nitty-gritty to help you plan your trip. This is where to find out which airlines fly to your destination, what paperwork you'll need, what to do about money and insurance, about Internet access, food, security, public transport, car rental – in fact just about every piece of **general practical information** you might need.

Guide

This is the heart of the Rough Guide, divided into user-friendly chapters, each of which covers a specific region. Every chapter starts with a list of **highlights** and an **introduction** that helps you to decide where to go, depending on your time and budget. Likewise, introductions to the various towns and smaller regions within each chapter should help you plan your itinerary. We start most town accounts with information on arrival and accommodation, followed by a tour of the sights, and finally reviews of places to eat and drink, and details of nightlife. Longer accounts also have a directory of practical listings. Each chapter concludes with **public transport** details for that region.

Contexts

Read Contexts to get a deeper understanding of what makes Ireland tick. We include a brief history, articles about **environment**, **architecture** and **music**, and a detailed further reading section that reviews dozens of **books** relating to the country.

Language

The **language** section gives useful background on the Irish language, plus information on courses. Here you'll also find a glossary of words and terms peculiar to the country.

Index + small print

Apart from a **full index**, which includes maps as well as places, this section covers publishing information, credits and acknowledgements, and also has our contact details in case you want to send in updates and corrections to the book – or suggestions as to how we might improve it.

Chapter list and map

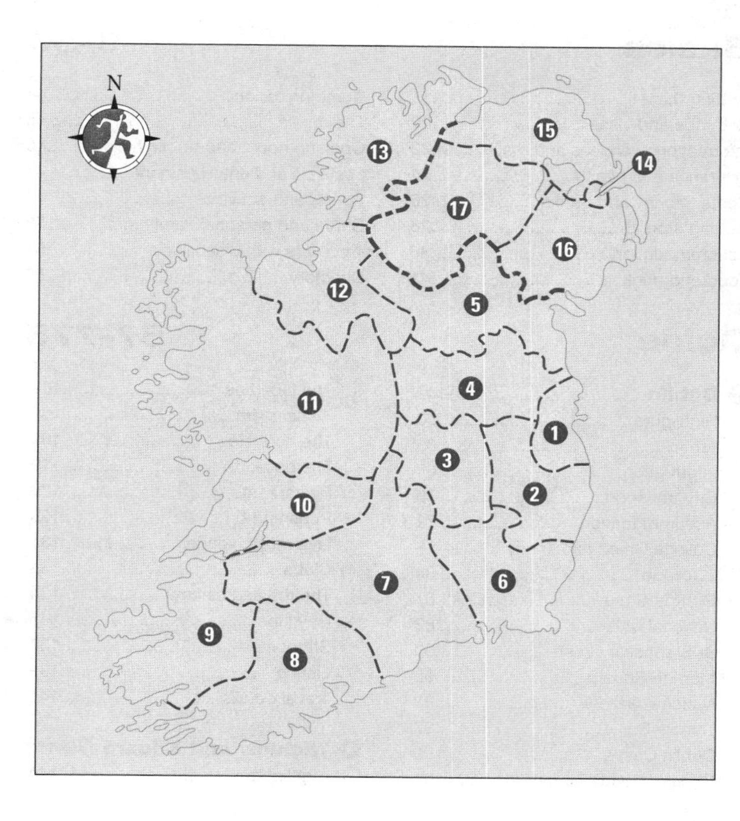

Contents

Colour section i–xxiv

Basics 9–56

Guide 57–775

Contexts 777–877

Language 879–888

Index and small print 889–903

Map symbols

maps are listed in the full index using coloured text

National border	Church
County border	Ruins
Chapter boundary	Statue
Motorway	Mountain range
Major road	Mountain peak
Minor road	Viewpoint
Pedestrianized roads	Waterfall
Footpath	Gardens
Railway	Tourist information
Wall	Post office
Ferry route	Hospital
River	Parking
Airport	Restaurant/bar
Place of interest	Building
Museum	Stadium
Castle	Church
Country house	Park
Tower	Cemetery
Abbey	Beach

Basics

Basics

Getting there

Dublin is the Republic of Ireland's transport hub, Belfast that of the North, and for travellers from the UK stiff competition between airlines means that there are generally plenty of good deals on flights available to both destinations. If the spectacular scenery of the west coast is the focus of your trip, it is well worth considering flying direct to one of Ireland's regional airports. For travellers from North America, Dublin and Belfast prove the most popular gateways, but again it is worth considering the provincial option of Shannon, an ideal point of arrival for the magnificent seaboard of the southwest. If you want to bring your own car, there are ferry routes from both the UK and northern France. Similarly, for foot passengers there are numerous train/ferry and coach/ferry deals available from the UK and northern France.

Air fares generally depend on the season, with the highest being from around the beginning of June through to September, when the weather is best, and from 12 December through to the start of January. Fares drop during the "shoulder" season – October to early December – and you'll get the best prices during the low season, January through May. If you are travelling from the UK it's worth looking out for promotional offers year-round, but especially during the winter months. No matter where you are travelling from, if you want to travel during the Christmas–New Year period, book at least two or three months ahead.

You can often cut costs by going through a **specialist flight agent** – either a consolidator, who buys up blocks of tickets from the airlines and sells them at a discount, or a **discount agent**, who in addition to dealing with discounted flights may also offer special student and youth fares and a range of other travel-related services such as travel insurance, rail passes, car rentals, tours and the like. Some agents specialize in **charter flights**, which may be cheaper than anything available on a scheduled flight, but departure dates are fixed and withdrawal penalties are high. You may even find it cheaper to pick up a bargain **package deal** from one of the tour operators listed overleaf and then find your own accommodation when you get there. A further possibility is to see if you can arrange a courier flight, although you'll need a flexible schedule, and preferably be travelling alone with very little luggage; in return for shepherding a parcel through customs, you can expect to get a very discounted ticket. You'll probably also be restricted in the duration of your stay. A couple of courier associations are listed on p.15.

If Ireland is only one stop on a longer journey, you might want to consider buying a round-the-world (RTW) ticket. Some travel agents can sell you an "off-the-shelf" RTW ticket that will have you touching down in about half a dozen cities; you may have to have the route tailor-made for you and prices depend on the number of stops and miles travelled. Figure on about US$1300 for a RTW ticket including Ireland from the US and A$2335 for a RTW ticket from Australia.

Whichever way you choose to book a flight, it pays to shop around and to be aware that many well-established airlines now offer flights at prices that compete with those specifically branded as low-cost airlines. The cost of air travel is prone to considerable variation and prices given throughout this section are for guidance only.

Booking flights online

Many airlines and discount travel websites offer you the opportunity to book your tickets **online**, cutting out the costs of agents and middlemen. Good deals can often be found through discount or auction sites, as well as through the airlines' own websites.

Online booking agents and general travel sites

Ⓦ**www.etn.nl/discount.htm** A hub of consolidator and discount agent Web links, maintained by the nonprofit European Travel Network.
Ⓦ**www.geocities.com/Thavery2000/** Has an extensive list of airline toll-free numbers and websites.
Ⓦ**www.flyaow.com** Online air travel info and reservations site.
Ⓦ**www.smilinjack.com/airlines.htm** An up-to-date compilation of airline website addresses.
Ⓦ**travel.yahoo.com** Incorporates a lot of Rough Guide material in its coverage of destination countries and cities across the world, with information about places to eat, sleep, etc.
Ⓦ**www.cheaptickets.com** Discount flight specialists.
Ⓦ**www.cheapflights.com** Bookings from the UK and Ireland only. Flight deals, travel agents, plus links to other travel sites.
Ⓦ**www.lastminute.com** Bookings from the UK only. Offers good last-minute holiday package and flight-only deals.
Ⓦ**www.expedia.com** Discount airfares, all-airline search engine and daily deals.
Ⓦ**www.travelocity.com** Destination guides, hot Web fares and good deals for car rental, accommodation and lodging. Provides access to the travel agent system SABRE, the most comprehensive central reservations system in the US.
Ⓦ**www.hotwire.com** Bookings from the US only. Last-minute savings of up to forty percent on regular published fares. Travellers must be at least 18 and there are no refunds, transfers or changes allowed. Log-in required.
Ⓦ**www.priceline.com** Name-your-own-price website that has deals at around forty percent off standard fares. You cannot specify flight times (although you do specify dates) and the tickets are nonrefundable, nontransferable and nonchangeable.
Ⓦ**www.skyauction.com** Bookings from the US only. Auctions tickets and travel packages using a "second bid" scheme. The best strategy is to bid the maximum you're willing to pay, since if you win you'll pay just enough to beat the runner-up regardless of your maximum bid.
Ⓦ**www.travelshop.com.au** Australian website offering discounted flights, packages, insurance, online bookings.
Ⓦ**www.gaytravel.com** Gay online travel agent, concentrating mostly on accommodation.

Flying from Britain

Flight time from London to the Republic is between an hour (to Dublin) and one hour thirty minutes (to Cork, Kerry, Knock, Shannon and Waterford). The main carriers are Aer Lingus, which flies from nine UK airports; its main Irish competitor Ryanair, which flies from thirteen; and British Airways, which departs from twelve. Northern Ireland is similarly well served: there are flights to Belfast from all of the London airports and there are also flights from fifteen regional airports. You can fly to Derry from Stansted, Manchester and Glasgow.

Competition between airlines is steep, especially on the main routes to Dublin, which means that there are often very cheap fares available. The best way to compare prices, which vary considerably, is online – and many of the companies will take a few pounds off if you book via their website too.

Return fares to Dublin and Belfast from both London and UK regional airports can be **very cheap** – Ryanair advertise a single Liverpool–Dublin fare for as little as £4.99 – though be aware that discount prices quoted in the press and on websites often exclude taxes, which can add £25–35 to the price. On the whole though, promotional offers aside, you can expect to pay from around £60 for return flights to Dublin from London, and prices do rise steeply at peak times, especially around bank holiday weekends. Flights from London to Irish regional airports can vary considerably: for example, a return flight from London Heathrow to Shannon with British Airways might cost in the region of £120, while Ryanair's Stansted–Shannon flight might cost around £70. Fares from **UK regional** airports to **Irish regional** airports tend to be dearer – but it's still worth checking what's on offer well in advance. A return Manchester–Cork flight with British Airways can cost as little as around £72. It is worth noting too that some routes from regional airports are not available every day.

If you want to bring a **bike** with you, most airlines will allow you to do so and don't charge (except Ryanair: £15 extra each way), as long as you don't exceed your baggage allowance. It makes sense to ask if the airline carries bikes before you buy your ticket. It is also worth informing them in advance and checking in early – particularly if you are travelling to a small regional airport or during peak times, since carrying bikes is subject to available space.

Airlines

Aer Arann Republic of Ireland ⓣ1890/462726 or from outside the Republic 00 353 1/814 1058, ⓦwww.aerarann.ie and ⓦwww.aerarannexpress.com. Daily service between London Luton and Galway. Services from Birmingham, Southampton and Bristol to Cork.
Aer Lingus UK ⓣ0845/084 4444, ⓦwww.aerlingus.ie. The main carrier to Ireland, flying from nine UK airports.
Air Wales UK ⓣ0870/013 3151, ⓦwww.airwales.co.uk. Flights from Cardiff and Swansea to Cork.
British Airways UK ⓣ0845/77 333 77, ⓦwww.britishairways.com. Major airline, flying from ten UK airports, with routes serving Belfast City, Dublin, Cork, Derry, Shannon and Knock.
BMI British Midland UK ⓣ0870/607 0555, ⓦwww.flybmi.com. Flights from Heathrow and East Midlands to Dublin, and from Heathrow to Belfast.
British European UK ⓣ0870/567 6676, ⓦwww.british-european.com. Flights from Bristol, Birmingham, East Midlands, Exeter, Gatwick, London City and Newcastle to Belfast; flights from Exeter to Dublin, Edinburgh to Cork and Birmingham to Shannon.
easyJet UK ⓣ0870/600 0000, ⓦwww.easyjet.com. Budget scheduled flights from Luton, Liverpool, Edinburgh, Bristol, Stansted, Gatwick and Glasgow to Belfast.
Euroceltic UKⓣ0870/040 0100, ⓦwww.euroceltic.com. Flights from Luton to Waterford.
Luxair ⓣ01293/596633, ⓦwww.luxair.lu. Flights from Manchester to Dublin.
Ryanair UK ⓣ0871/246 0000, ⓦwww.ryanair.com. Low-cost flights from Luton, Stansted, Gatwick, Teesside, Leeds Bradford, Manchester, Liverpool, Edinburgh, Birmingham, Bournemouth, Bristol, Cardiff, Glasgow and Prestwick to various Irish destinations including Dublin, Cork, Kerry, Knock and Shannon.

Flight and travel agents

Abbey Leisure UK ⓣ020/8861 5353. Middlesex-based company specializing in travel to Ireland.
Claddagh Travel UK ⓣ0121/382 4803 or ⓣ0121/200 3320. Birmingham-based travel agents specializing in Ireland.
Co-op Travel Care Belfast ⓣ028/9047 1717, ⓦwww.travelcareonline.com. Flights and holidays around the world.
Destination Group UK ⓣ020/7400 7045, ⓦwww.destination-group.com. Good discount airfares.
Flightbookers UK ⓣ0870/010 7000, ⓦwww.ebookers.com. Low fares on an extensive selection of scheduled flights.
Flynow UK ⓣ0870/444 0045, ⓦwww.flynow.com. Large range of discounted tickets.
North South Travel UK ⓣ & ⓕ01245/608291, ⓦwww.northsouthtravel.co.uk. Friendly, competitive travel agency, offering discounted fares worldwide – profits are used to support projects in the developing world, especially the promotion of sustainable tourism.
Premier Travel Derry ⓣ028/7126 3333, ⓦwww.premiertravel.uk.com. Discount flight specialists.
STA Travel UK ⓣ0870/160 0599, ⓦwww.statravel.co.uk. Worldwide specialists in low-cost flights and tours for students and under-26s, though other customers welcome.
Top Deck UK ⓣ020/7370 4555, ⓦwww.topdecktravel.co.uk. Long-established agent dealing in discount flights.
Trailfinders UK ⓣ020/7628 7628, ⓦwww.trailfinders.com. One of the best-informed and most efficient agents for independent travellers; produces a very useful quarterly magazine worth scrutinizing for round-the-world routes.
Travel CUTS UK ⓣ020/7255 2082, ⓦwww.travelcuts.co.uk. Canadian company specializing in budget, student and youth travel and round-the-world tickets.
Wannabeinireland.com ⓦwww.wannabeinireland.com. Online booking for accommodation, flights, ferries, car rental and insurance.

Tour operators

Drive Ireland 311 Tower Building, Water St, Liverpool L3 1AS ⓣ0151/231 1480, ⓦwww.drive-ireland.co.uk. Combined flight/accommodation/car-rental deals, plus walking, cycling, golf and horse-drawn caravan holidays.
Irish Ferries Holidays Corn Exchange Building, Ground Floor, Brunswick St, Liverpool L2 7TP ⓣ0870/517 1717, ⓦwww.irishferries.com. Huge range of flexible package holidays, including ferry and hotel, B&B and self-catering accommodation. Also offers golfing holidays.
Leisurebreaks 33 Dovedale Rd, Liverpool L18 5EP ⓣ0845/130 5200,

ⓦwww.irelandbreaks.co.uk. Leisure breaks, including ferry and accommodation packages, fly-drive deals and golf and angling holidays.
Saddle Skedaddle 110 Ouseburn Building, Albion Row, Newcastle upon Tyne, NE6 1LL ⓣ0191/265 1110, ⓦwww.skedaddle.co.uk. Five- to seven-day cycling tours in either west Cork and Kerry or in the Wicklow Mountains. B&B accommodation, and luggage van.
Sherpa Expeditions 131A Heston Rd, Hounslow, TW5 0RF ⓣ020/8577 2717, ⓦwww.sherpaexpeditions.com. Self-guided inn-to-inn walks in Kerry, and cycling tours in Kerry and Connemara.
Stena Line Holidays Stena Line Ltd, Charter House, Park St, Ashford, Kent TN24 8EX ⓣ0870/574 7474, ⓦwww.stenalinehols.co.uk. Full range of ferry, car-rental, hotel and self-catering packages.
Swansea Cork Ferries King's Dock, Swansea, West Glamorgan ⓣ01792/456116, ⓦwww.swansea-cork.ie. Activity holidays, self-catering packages in Cork and Kerry and go-as-you-please tours (you tell them where you want to go and they book hotels on your itinerary).
Tara Travel 245 High Rd, Ilford, Essex IG1 1NE ⓣ020/8514 5141, ⓦwww.taratravel.com. Fly- and ferry-drive packages, self-catering and coach tours.
Thomas Cook UK ⓣ0870/443 4457, ⓦwww.tcholidays.com. Long-established travel agency offering package holidays, including cruising, motoring, self-catering holidays and short breaks.

Ireland-based tour operators

Emerald Star The Marina, Carrick-on-Shannon, Co. Leitrim ⓣ078/20234, ⓦwww.emeraldstar.ie. Specialist boat-holiday operator offering cruising packages on the Shannon–Erne Waterway.
Go Ireland Killorglin, Co. Kerry ⓣ066/976 2094, ⓦwww.goactivities.com. Guided walking holidays in Connemara, Donegal, Kerry and other counties; guided and independent cycling tours; specialist golfing, horse-riding and fishing holidays.
Irish Cycling Safaris Belfield Bike Shop, UCD, Dublin 4 ⓣ01/260 0749, ⓦwww.cyclingsafaris.com. Well-organized guided tours for cyclists of all abilities in prime areas along the west coast from Cork to Donegal, with luggage van, and hotel/guesthouse accommodation.

Flying from the US and Canada

Ireland is easily accessible from the US by a number of airlines that offer direct flights to the major gateways of Dublin and Shannon. From Canada, direct flights are available from Toronto during the summer; during low season flights are via London. Ferries and cheap flights also make Ireland easily accessible as a part of a wider European travel itinerary.

Flying time from New York is approximately five hours thirty minutes direct to Dublin and seven hours to Belfast. Flying time from Los Angeles is approximately ten hours and thirty minutes to Dublin, and twelve hours to Belfast, with a stopover somewhere en route.

Aer Lingus, the national airline of the Republic, flies from Boston, Chicago, New York, Baltimore and Los Angeles to both Shannon and Dublin. The best low-season fares from the east coast to Dublin cost around US$265, and from Los Angeles around US$620. In high season these rise to around US$615 from the east coast, US$785 from Los Angeles. Flying to Shannon is worth considering if the focus of your trip is the west coast. Aer Lingus has special limited promotional fares, which crop up from time to time, most likely in the off season, and are advertised in national newspapers and on their website. As always, a reputable discount agent, such as Council Travel or STA, should be able to sift through all the available fares and find one that best suits your particular travel requirements.

Flying from Canada, Air Canada has flights from Toronto direct to Dublin (and then on to Shannon) from June to October, with a flight time of around six hours and 35 minutes. In the winter months, flights are via London. Typical return fares in low season are Can$1603, rising to Can$1298 in high season.

Air Canada's Toronto–Belfast route is via London year-round; prices in low season are around Can$1028, rising to around Can$1313 in high season.

Airlines

Aer Lingus ⓣ1-800/223-6537, ⓦwww.aerlingus.ie.
Air Canada ⓣ1-888/247-2262, ⓦwww.aircanada.ca.
American Airlines ⓣ1-800/433-7300, ⓦwww.aa.com.

British Airways ⓣ 1-800/247-9297, ⓦ www.britishairways.com.
Continental Airlines international ⓣ 1-800/231-0856, ⓦ www.continental.com.
Delta Air Lines international ⓣ 1-800/241-4141, ⓦ www.delta.com.
Royal Jordanian Airlines ⓣ 1-800/223-0470 or 212/949-0050, ⓦ www.rja.com.jo.

Courier associations

Air Courier Association ⓣ 1-800/282-1202, ⓦ www.aircourier.org or www.cheaptrips.com. Courier flight broker. Membership (1yr US$29, 3yr US$58, 5yr US$87) entitles you to discount flights and hotels.
International Association of Air Travel Couriers ⓣ 352/475-1584, ⓦ www.courier.org. Courier flight broker with membership fee of US$45 a year or US$80 for two years.
Now Voyager ⓣ 212/459-1616, ⓦ www.nowvoyagertravel.com. Courier flight broker and consolidator.

Flight and travel agents

Air Brokers International US ⓣ 1-800/883-3273, ⓦ www.airbrokers.com. Consolidator and specialist in round-the-world and Circle Pacific tickets.
Airtech US ⓣ 1-877/247-8324 or 212/219-7000, ⓦ www.airtech.com. Standby seat broker; also deals in consolidator fares and courier flights.
Council Travel US ⓣ 1-800/226-8624, ⓕ 617/528-2091, ⓦ www.counciltravel.com. Nationwide organization that mostly, but by no means exclusively, specializes in student and budget travel. Flights from the US only.
Educational Travel Center US ⓣ 1-800/747-5551 or 608/256-5551, ⓦ www.edtrav.com. Student/youth discount agent.
High Adventure Travel US ⓣ 1-800/350-0612 or 415/912-5600, ⓦ www.airtreks.com. Round-the-world and Circle Pacific tickets. The website features an interactive database that lets you build and price your own round-the-world itinerary.
New Frontiers/Nouvelles Frontières ⓣ 1-800/677-0720, ⓦ www.newfrontiers.com. French discount-travel firm based in New York City. Other branches in LA, San Francisco and Québec City.
Skylink US ⓣ 1-800/247-6659 or 212/573-8980, Canada ⓣ 1-800/759-5465, ⓦ www.skylinkus.com. Consolidator.
STA Travel ⓣ 1-800/777-0112 or 1-800/781-4040, ⓦ www.sta-travel.com. Worldwide specialists in independent travel; also student IDs, travel insurance, car rental, rail passes, etc.
Student Flights ⓣ 1-800/255-8000 or 480/951-1177, ⓦ www.isecard.com. Student/youth fares, student ID cards.
TFI Tours International ⓣ 1-800/745-8000 or 212/736-1140, ⓦ www.lowestairprice.com. Consolidator offering low-cost flights.
Travac ⓣ 1-800/872-8800, ⓦ www.thetravelsite.com. Consolidator and charter broker with offices in New York City and Orlando.
Travel Avenue US ⓣ 1-800/333-3335, ⓦ www.travelavenue.com. Full-service travel agent that offers discounts in the form of rebates.
Travel cuts Canada ⓣ 1-800/667-2887, US ⓣ 1-866/246-9762, ⓦ www.travelcuts.com. Canadian student-travel organization.
Travelers Advantage US ⓣ 1-877/259-2691, ⓦ www.travelersadvantage.com. Discount travel club; annual membership fee required (currently US$1 for three months' trial).

Tour operators

Adventures Abroad ⓣ 1-800/665-3998 or 604/303-1099, ⓦ www.adventures-abroad.com. Adventure specialists.
Backroads ⓣ 1-800/462-2848 or 510/527-1555, ⓦ www.backroads.com. Cycling and hiking tours, with superior accommodation.
BCT Scenic Walking ⓣ 1-800/473-1210, ⓦ www.bctwalk.com. Walking tours in Clare, Kerry and Connemara.
CBT Bicycle Tours ⓣ 1-800/736-2453, ⓦ www.cbttours.com. Cycling tours in the southwest of Ireland.
Classic Journeys ⓣ 1-800/200-3887, ⓦ www.classicjourneys.com. Cultural walking tours taking in Dublin and the southwest.
Contiki Tours ⓦ www.contiki.com. 18- to 35-year-olds-only tour operator. Coach tours covering a lot of ground, including Waterford, Blarney, Killarney, Galway and Dublin in one week.
Cross Culture ⓣ 1-800/491-1148 or 413/256-6303, ⓦ www.crosscultureinc.com. Offers hiking tours in Connemara and Kerry, and cultural tours that take in Powerscourt House, Dublin and Newgrange.
Euro-Bike & Walking Tours ⓣ 1-800/321-6060, ⓦ www.eurobike.com. Cycling tours in Cork and Kerry; walking tours of Connemara.
Global Exchange ⓣ 1-800/497-1994, ⓦ www.globalexchange.org. Political study tours looking at the conflict in the North, including meetings with grassroots progressive organizations.
Insight International Tours ⓦ www.inusa.insightvacations.com, ⓔ ivcontactus@aol.com. Coach tours covering a lot of ground and taking in

the top sites; accommodation in first-class hotels.
Wilderness Travel ⓣ1-800/368-2794, ⓦwww.wildernesstravel.com. Hiking tours, around 5–8hr a day, taking in coastal and mountain scenery, archeology and traditional music.

Flying from Australia and New Zealand

Travel to Ireland from **Australia** and **New Zealand** is generally via London, Amsterdam or Frankfurt. As flights take over twenty hours, it is well worth considering a stopover en route. There's considerable competition between airlines, so it's worth checking your options through travel agents and looking for special deals advertised in the press. Companies such as STA and Trailfinders offer good discounts and can also help with visas, travel insurance and tours. Internet agencies such as ⓦwww.sydneytravel.com and ⓦwww.travel.com.au will offer discounted fares online and are well worth visiting.

You might consider a round-the-world ticket from either Australia or New Zealand since these may work out cheaper than the standard fare and can offer greater flexibility. Again, checking your options is best done through a travel agent who will be able to cut through the intricacies of mileage, number of stops and seasons that determine the ticket price. Discount fares are always subject to availability, so it makes sense to book your flight well in advance.

Fares from Melbourne and Sydney start at around A$1500 (plus around A$180 tax), rising to A$2322–3300 in high season.

If you are travelling from New Zealand, you can expect to find fares from Auckland to Dublin from around NZ$2300 in low season, to NZ$2700 in high season, plus NZ$100–200 tax.

Airlines

Aer Lingus Australia ⓣ02/9244 2123, New Zealand ⓣ09/308 3351, ⓦwww.aerlingus.ie.
Aeroflot Australia ⓣ02/9262 2233, ⓦwww.aeroflot.com.
Air Malta Australia ⓣ02/9244 2011, ⓦwww.airmalta.com.
Air New Zealand Australia ⓣ13 24 76, New Zealand ⓣ0800/737 000, ⓦwww.airnz.co.nz.
Air Pacific Australia ⓣ1800/230 150, New Zealand ⓣ0800/800 178, ⓦwww.airpacific.com.
Alitalia Australia ⓣ02/9262 3925, ⓦwww.alitalia.com.
British Airways Australia ⓣ02/8904 8800, New Zealand ⓣ0800/274 847, ⓦwww.britishairways.com.
Cathay Pacific Australia ⓣ13 17 47, New Zealand ⓣ09/379 0861 or 0508/800 454, ⓦwww.cathaypacific.com.
Delta Air Lines Australia ⓣ02/9251 3211, New Zealand ⓣ09/379 3370, ⓦwww.delta-air.com.
Gulf Air Australia ⓣ02/9244 2199, New Zealand ⓣ09/308 3366, ⓦwww.gulfairco.com.
Japan Airlines Australia ⓣ02/9272 1111, New Zealand ⓣ09/379 9906, ⓦwww.japanair.com.
KLM Australia ⓣ1300/303 747, New Zealand ⓣ09/309 1782, ⓦwww.klm.com.
Qantas Australia ⓣ13 13 13, New Zealand ⓣ09/661 901, ⓦwww.qantas.com.au.
Scandinavian Airlines (SAS) Australia ⓣ1300/727 707 or 02/9283 9111, New Zealand agent: Air New Zealand ⓣ0800/737 000, ⓦwww.scandinavian.net.
Singapore Airlines Australia ⓣ13 10 11, New Zealand ⓣ09/303 2129, ⓦwww.singaporeair.com.
Virgin Atlantic Airways Australia ⓣ02/9244 2747, New Zealand ⓣ09/308 3377, ⓦwww.virgin-atlantic.com.

Flight and travel agents

Australian Pacific Tours Australia ⓣ1300/655 965, New Zealand ⓣ09/279 6077. Package tours and independent travel.
Budget Travel New Zealand ⓣ09/366 0061 or 0800/808 040, ⓦwww.budgettravel.co.nz.
Destinations Unlimited New Zealand ⓣ09/373 4033.
Flight Centre Australia ⓣ13 31 33, ⓦwww.flightcentre.com.au, New Zealand ⓣ0800/243 544 or 09/358 4310, ⓦwww.flightcentre.co.nz. Specializes in discount international airfares and holiday packages.
Irish Travel Agency/Eblana Australia ⓣ02/9232 8247. Airfares and packages to Ireland.
Northern Gateway Australia ⓣ08/8941 1394, ⓦwww.northerngateway.com.au.
STA Travel Australia ⓣ1300/733 035, ⓦwww.statravel.com.au, New Zealand ⓣ0508/782 872, ⓦwww.statravel.co.nz.
Student Uni Travel Australia ⓣ02/9232 8444, ⓔaustralia@backpackers.net.
Trailfinders Australia ⓣ02/9247 7666, ⓦwww.trailfinders.com.au.
Travel.com Australia ⓣ1300/130 482 or 02/9249 5444, ⓦwww.travel.com.au, New Zealand ⓣ09/359 3860, ⓦwww.travel.co.nz.

Tour operators

Explore Holidays Australia ⓣ02/9857 6200 or 1300/731 000, ⓦwww.exploreholidays.com.au. Accommodation and package tours.
Viator Australia ⓣ02/8219 5400, ⓦwww.viator.com. Bookings for hundreds of travel suppliers, including walking and cycling tours.

By rail

Prices of combined train and ferry tickets vary according to departure time and season, and whether your journey qualifies for one of the several special offers available or can be booked some time in advance. It's usually more expensive to travel on Friday, Saturday or Sunday and during peak periods: Easter, July and August, Christmas and bank holidays. Journey times are considerably quicker than coaches: London or Birmingham to Dublin takes from around seven to ten hours, Manchester to Dublin takes around five to eight hours and Glasgow to Belfast is roughly four to six hours – add another two hours if you are travelling from Edinburgh.

The best way to find out about the most economical deals available to you, is to call the National Rail Enquiry Service (see below) and ask them directly what your options are. An Irish Virgin Value return fare to Dublin from London, Watford or Milton Keynes costs £29 if booked fourteen days in advance and £49 if booked three days ahead; tickets are subject to availability, so booking well in advance is advisable. Return fares to Dublin from Belfast range between £50.50 and £74, from Manchester £45.50–69. An Edinburgh–Belfast return ticket costs between £38 and £52, the cheaper fare being an APEX ticket which needs to be booked 48 hours in advance; a Glasgow–Belfast return costs between £36 and £48.

If there are two of you travelling together, there are some very good deals on offer: Virgin's Dublin Duo, which can be booked up until 2pm before the day of travel, costs £82 return for two passengers; the same ticket from Birmingham costs £72, and from Manchester £67.

Anyone under 26 can buy a Young Persons Railcard (£18), although it's worth bearing in mind that the savings are not necessarily worthwhile in comparison with some of the cheapest available deals. The Young Persons Railcard is not valid with APEX tickets, and sometimes deals are less expensive than the cost of a standard ticket with a railcard. It makes sense to check out other options before buying one.

If you plan on visiting Ireland via Britain from elsewhere, it is worth checking out the special travel passes available; see p.29.

Rail contacts

Eurostar ⓣ0870/160 6600, ⓦwww.eurostar.com.
National Rail Enquiry Service UK ⓣ0845/748 4950, ⓦwww.rail.co.uk.
Northern Ireland Railways UK ⓣ028/9089 9411, ⓦwww.translink.co.uk.
Rail Europe UK ⓣ0870/584 8848, ⓦwww.raileurope.co.uk.
Trainseurope UK ⓣ020/8699 3654, ⓦwww.trainseurope.co.uk.

By ferry

Ferry routes from Britain and northern France provide access to Ireland via the country's six main ferry ports: Cork in the southwest, Rosslare in the southeast, Dublin and Dún Laoghaire on the east coast and in the North, Belfast and Larne. Nowadays, most ferry services are more like floating shopping precincts, with restaurants, fast-food outlets, bars and shops. Generally journeys are relatively quick and comfortable. There are also catamaran or high-speed services on some of the main routes: Holyhead to Dún Laoghaire and Dublin Port, Fishguard to Rosslare, Liverpool to Dublin, Cairnryan to Larne, Stranraer to Belfast, Troon to Belfast and Heysham to Belfast; and these cut sailing times almost in half. The Irish Sea can be rough at any time from October to April, so if you are travelling during this period, it is worth bearing in mind that in bad weather catamaran services are more likely to be cancelled than regular ferry services.

If you need a car when you get to Ireland, bringing your own is a convenient option. Ferry routes operated by the different companies are shown on p.19 and your choice is probably going to be determined by your point of departure.

Ferry prices vary enormously depending on the time of year, and even the day and hour you travel. Most ferry companies have peak seasons of July and August and also operate higher fares around bank holidays; many close altogether over the Christmas period. In summer, in particular, car and foot passengers should always book in advance or risk turning up and not getting on the boat. Generally, midweek crossings are cheaper throughout the year, and many companies offer special off-peak deals, one-, two-, three-, four- and five-day return tickets and various fares related to the number of passengers in a vehicle. In almost all cases, bicycles are carried free of charge. Generally, combined bus/ferry or train/ferry tickets are good value, and it is worth bearing in mind too that many of the ferry companies offer competitive combined ferry/accommodation deals. It makes sense to compare the prices and sailing times of ferries across different companies; the prices shown below will give you some idea of what to expect.

The main crossing points to the **Republic** from Britain are from Holyhead on the Isle of Anglesey in north Wales and from Fishguard and Pembroke in southwest Wales. For a car and driver Stena Line's single fares (Holyhead–Dún Laoghaire/Dublin Port or Fishguard –Rosslare) cost £79 off-peak, £144 peak on their standard services; the high-speed journeys cost £99 off-peak, £159 peak season; additional passengers cost £10, and walk-on adult single fares range between £19–23 single. Sailings between Swansea and Cork are operated by Swansea–Cork Ferries, with most sailings departing at 9pm and arriving at Ringaskiddy, Cork at 7am. Return fares for a car, driver and up to four adults cost from £155 (off-peak) to £378 (peak) and for foot passengers from £48 to £68; the fare for bicycles is £16 return. Although Pullman seats are provided, you might want to consider a cabin to make the most of the night crossing. These cost from £34 per crossing for a standard two-berth cabin.

Most of the departure points for **Northern Ireland** are in southwest Scotland. The quickest option is the Stena Line service from **Stranraer to Belfast** and single fares cost £90 low season to £120 high season for a car and driver; a six-day return costs between £149 and £189 on the same route. Foot passenger fares range from £14 to £19 single.

A little further north, P&O runs a fast ferry and standard service from **Cairnryan to Larne**, costing from around £180 to £240 return for a car and driver; additional passengers cost £28 extra and fares for foot passengers range between £30 and £42 return. Handy for those who live further north in Scotland or anyone first touring the Highlands, Seacat now operates a fast catamaran service from **Troon to Belfast**, costing from £299 to £499 return for a car, driver and four passengers. Foot passengers are charged from £22 to £40. Similar fares apply on its service from **Heysham** (on the Lancashire coast) **to Belfast**. P&O also runs a service from **Fleetwood to Larne** from a little further south, costing £130 to £180 return for a car, driver and one passenger; note that there are no foot passengers allowed on this route or on P&O's Mostyn–Dublin and Liverpool–Dublin routes. Finally, Norse Merchant Ferries operates a service from **Liverpool to Belfast**; return fares for a car and two adults cost from £130 to £230 for daytime crossings. Overnight sailings range from £340 to a hefty £450 in high season, though for this you get a cabin, dinner and breakfast. Foot passengers are charged from £50 to £70 with supplementary charges for cabins, if required. Advance booking is usually essential for this route.

A Round Ireland fare with Stena Line – which lets you use different routes for the outward and return journeys (Stranraer–Belfast, Holyhead–Dún Laoghaire/Dublin Port or Fishguard–Rosslare) costs a car and driver £149 off-peak, £279 peak season; the same journeys on their high-speed service cost £169 off-peak, £299 peak season. Norse Merchant Ferries offer a similarly flexible arrangement with their Explorer ticket, which gives travel from Liverpool to Belfast, returning via Dublin to Liverpool and costs between £150 and £375 return for a car and two passengers.

Travelling **from northern France** there are a number of options. Brittany Ferries operates a weekly sailing from Roscoff to Cork. The return trip costs €630, plus €200 for a four-berth cabin. Irish Ferries sails from Cherbourg and Roscoff to Rosslare. A one-way fare for a car and two passengers on both routes costs €229–539 depending on the season. P&O Irish Sea sails from Cherbourg to Dublin and the return fare for a car and two passengers, including a two-berth cabin, costs €1088.

Student reductions on ferries can be considerable and it is worth checking out special deals. For example, P&O offers a standard return for up to three students plus car from £130 on their Cairnryan–Larne route. Stena Line has single student foot-passenger fares of £10–15 on their Stranraer to Belfast route. Reductions are also available for **senior citizens**.

Ferry contacts

Brittany Ferries UK ⓣ0870/366 5333, ⓦwww.brittany-ferries.co.uk. Sailings from Roscoff, France to Cork once a week from April to early October.
Irish Ferries UK ⓣ0870/517 1717, ⓦwww.irishferries.com. Holyhead to Dublin Port; Pembroke to Rosslare; also services from Cherbourg and Roscoff in France to Rosslare. Continental services March to end Sept.
Norse Merchant Ferries UK ⓣ0870/600 4321, ⓦwww.norsemerchant.com. Liverpool to Belfast and Dublin.
P&O Irish Sea UK ⓣ0870/242 4777, ⓦwww.poirishsea.com. Cairnryan to Larne; Fleetwood to Larne (cars only); Mostyn to Dublin (cars only); Liverpool to Dublin (cars only); also sailings from Cherbourg in France to Rosslare and Dublin.
Sea Cat/Isle of Man Steam Packet Co. ⓣ0870/552 3523, ⓦwww.steam-packet.com and ⓦwww.seacat.co.uk. Ferries to Belfast from Heysham, Troon and the Isle of Man; ferries to Dublin from Liverpool and the Isle of Man.
Stena Line UK ⓣ0870/570 7070, ⓦwww.stenaline.co.uk. Fishguard to Rosslare; Holyhead to Dún Laoghaire and Dublin Port; Stranraer to Belfast.
Swansea Cork Ferries UK ⓣ01792/456116, ⓦwww.swansea-cork.ie. From Swansea to Cork.

By bus

Getting to Ireland by bus is a slog, but very cheap. The main service is provided by Eurolines, 52 Grosvenor Gardens, London SW1 0AU (ⓣ020/7730 8235 or 0870/514 3219, ⓦwww.gobycoach.com) which operates a daily and nightly service from London **to Dublin** via Birmingham and Holyhead throughout the year with extra departures from May to October and over the Christmas period. The trip takes between eleven and thirteen hours, depending on the speed of the ferry.

Eurolines ticket prices depend upon the age of the traveller and the season. Generally, peak season is July, August and the Christmas–New Year period. Standard return tickets are valid for six months; an APEX return is generally a little cheaper and is valid for one month, but you need to book seven days in advance and you also have to specify the outward and return journeys. Youth fares are available for 13- to 25-year-olds on all return tickets except APEX returns and the Minipass; travellers over 50 are eligible for senior fares, which cost the same as youth fares. Standard return adult and youth fares from London to Dublin cost £49 and £54 respectively during peak season, £42 and £47 off-peak. The Apex fare is £49 peak season and £39 off-peak. A host of **connecting services** is available from Dublin to just about anywhere with a main bus station in the Republic or the North and the return fare to all points beyond Dublin is identical: return fares from London via Dublin to Galway, Sligo, Ballina and Donegal all cost £62 adult, £57 youth during peak periods, £55 and £50 off-peak. The APEX fares on these journeys are £55 peak, £45 off-peak. Other Eurolines services to Dublin run daily from main National Express coach stations throughout the UK, including Leicester, Nottingham, Leeds, Manchester, Birmingham, Liverpool and Bristol.

If you are heading for the south of Ireland from southern England, the best routes are via Fishguard and Rosslare. London to Waterford return adult and youth fares cost £54 and £49 respectively during peak periods, £47 and £42 off-peak. For destinations via Rosslare beyond Waterford, including Killarney, Limerick and Tralee the return peak fares are £62 and £57, £52 and £50 off-peak. APEX fares on the same journeys cost £55 peak, £45 off-peak.

Travel from the UK to the North is via Stranraer. London to Belfast adult and youth return fares cost £64 and £59 in peak season respectively, £54 and £50 off-peak. The APEX fares for these journeys are £50 peak season, £40 off-peak.

The Minipass is a good option if you plan on touring around a lot once you arrive in Ireland. It is valid for ninety days and allows you to plan the pace of your journey as you go along. There are two routes on offer – both of which can be taken in either direction: the London–Dublin–Galway–Limerick–Killarney–Cork–London ticket costs £65; the London–Dublin–Galway–Donegal–Derry–Belfast–London ticket costs £75. In both cases you simply need to book the first leg of your journey; after that you can book the departure date of subsequent stages of your journey at coach stations in Ireland.

Tickets for coach travel to both the Republic and the North can be booked at any National Express agent, at London Victoria Coach Station, the Eurolines office, by phone, or online at ⓦwww.gobycoach.com. Bicycles cannot be carried on Eurolines services.

Red tape and visas

British nationals born in the UK do not need a passport to enter the Republic or the North, but it is useful to carry one in case you use the medical services, and for cashing travellers' cheques. If you don't take a passport, be sure to have some other form of convincing ID, and note that airlines increasingly require some form of official photo ID on flights between Britain and Ireland. British passport holders not born in Great Britain or Northern Ireland must have a valid passport or national identity document. If you are a British national of Indian, Pakistani, Bangladeshi, Far Eastern or African descent, it is advisable to take along your passport (or your birth certificate), in spite of the fact that, technically speaking, you don't need one.

If you are an EU national, you can enter the **Republic** with either a national ID card or, even better, a passport, and you are entitled to stay for as long as you like. Travellers from the US, Canada, Australia and New Zealand are required to show a passport and can stay for up to ninety days; if you want to stay beyond that, you'll need to apply to the Garda Registration Officer at the nearest police station. All other visitors to the Republic should contact the Irish embassy in their home country in advance as regulations vary. A comprehensive list of Irish consulates and embassies, along with visa information, is available on the Department of Foreign Affairs website: ⓦwww.irlgov.ie/iveagh.

In the **North**, British and Irish citizens need no ID or passport. Other EU nationals need either a national ID card or, even better, a passport, and are entitled to stay for as long as they like. US, Canadian, Australian and New Zealand citizens can enter the country for up to six months with just a passport. To extend a visit you need to apply for an extension of leave, before the six-month period expires, to the Immigration and Nationality Directorate, 40 Wellesley Rd, Croydon CR9 2BY (ⓣ0870/606 7766, ⓦwww.ind.homeoffice.gov.uk); to arrange a visit of more than six months prior to your arrival, contact the British embassy or high commission in your home country. Citizens of most other nationalities require a visa, obtainable from the British consular office in the country of application. To find out if you need a visa, either contact your nearest British embassy or high commission, or visit the British Foreign Office website: ⓦwww.fco.gov.uk.

Travellers coming into the Republic or the North directly from another EU country do not have to make a declaration to **customs** at their place of entry and can effectively bring in almost as much wine or beer as they like – although the general rule for imports of alcohol and cigarettes is that goods should be for personal use only. However, for travellers entering from outside the EU there are still restrictions – details of which are prominently displayed in all duty-free outlets – on tax- or duty-free goods. There are general import restrictions on a variety of articles and substances, from firearms to furs derived from endangered species, none of which should bother the average tourist. Visitors from mainland Britain can bring pet dogs and cats into the North and the Republic, although animals brought from elsewhere are subject to tight restrictions – go to ⓦwww.defra.gov.uk or ⓦwww.irlgov.ie/daff for the details.

Throughout Ireland most goods are subject to **Value Added Tax** (VAT), rated at 13.5 or 21 percent in the Republic (depending on the type of goods) and 17.5 percent in the North. Visitors from non-EU countries can save a lot of money through the **Retail Export Scheme**, which allows a refund of VAT on goods to be taken out of the country. Note that not all shops participate in this scheme – enquire before you make your purchase – and you cannot reclaim VAT charged on hotel bills or other services. In order to make a **claim** you have to leave the country within three months of purchase. Some shops offer the lower price directly to the customer, and all you are required to do is hand in a receipt to customs as you leave the country, but this procedure does vary, so check at the time of purchase. Information online can be found at ⓦwww.revenue.ie and ⓦwww.hmce.gov.uk.

Irish embassies abroad

Australia 20 Arkana St, Yarralumla, Canberra, ACT 2600 ⓣ02/6273 3022.
Britain 17 Grosvenor Place, London SW1X 7HR ⓣ020/7235 2171.
Canada 130 Albert St, Suite 1105, Ottawa, ON K1P 5G4 ⓣ613/233-6281.
New Zealand Handled by the embassy in Australia.
US 2234 Massachusetts Ave NW, Washington, DC 20008 ⓣ202/462-3939.

British embassies and high commissions abroad

Australia High Commission, Commonwealth Ave, Yarralumla, Canberra, ACT 2600 ⓣ02/6270 6666, ⓦwww.uk.emb.gov.au.
Canada High Commission, 80 Elgin St, Ottawa, ON K1P 5K7 ⓣ613/237-1530, ⓦwww.britainincanada.org.
Ireland 29 Merrion Rd, Dublin 4 ⓣ01/205-3700, ⓦwww.britishembassy.ie.
New Zealand High Commission, 44 Hill St, PO Box 1812, Wellington ⓣ04/924-2888, ⓦwww.britain.org.nz.
US 3100 Massachusetts Ave NW, Washington, DC 20008 ⓣ202/588-6500, ⓦwww.britainusa.com.

Information, websites and maps

There's no shortage of information published on Ireland, much of it free; it's well worth contacting the local office of the Bord Fáilte (Irish Tourist Board) and/or the Northern Ireland Tourist Board before you leave. Alternatively, the Internet has a wealth of sites, giving information not only on Ireland's history, culture and politics but also a range of practical advice on visiting the country.

Bord Fáilte and NITB offices outside Ireland, operating jointly as Tourism Ireland, are listed below. Once **in Ireland**, you'll find some kind of tourist office in nearly every town that has a reasonable number of tourists passing through, and many that don't, especially in Northern Ireland. These will be either a branch of Bord Fáilte or the NITB, or a locally run information centre, many of which open only for the summer. Most of these are listed in the relevant sections of the Guide and are usually extremely helpful, providing local maps and leaflets as well as information on where to stay (booking charge £1–2/€2–3). It has to be said, though, that most offices only give details on services which they have approved, thereby excluding some excellent hostels, campsites and private bus services, and they tend to be reluctant to show favouritism among hotels and restaurants, so always go to them for information, not advice. A Bord Fáilte or NITB recommendation implies a certain standard of service, however, so if you don't think your approved B&B comes up to scratch, they are the people you should complain to.

Tourism Ireland offices abroad

The NITB and Bord Fáilte now run a joint information service at the following addresses:

Australia Level 5, 36 Carrington St, Sydney NSW 2000 ⓣ02/9299 6177.

Britain Ireland Desk, British Visitor Centre, 1 Regent St, London SW1Y 4XT ⓣ0800/039 7000 and James Miller House, 7th Floor, 98 West George St, Glasgow G2 1PJ ⓣ041/572 4030.

Canada 2 Bloor St West, Suite 1501, Toronto, M4W 3E2 ⓣ01-800/223-6470.

New Zealand 6th Floor, 18 Shortland St, Auckland 1 ⓣ09/977 2255.

US 345 Park Ave, New York, NY 10154 ⓣ1-800/223-6470.

Websites

The Internet is an excellent point of reference before travelling to and when you are in Ireland, not only for accessing general information about the country, but also for researching and booking accommodation and activities. In Ireland itself (even in the supposedly remote west) an Internet point is never far away, though the further west you go the more expensive it tends to be.

General information

ⓦ**www.blather.net** An idiosyncratic site dealing with a range of Irish-related subjects, with a lively discussion forum.

ⓦ**www.indigo.ie** A huge site that lists everything from online recipes to cars, including up-to-date news headlines, entertainment details and a myriad of well-chosen links.

ⓦ**www.iol.ie**, ⓦ**www.browseireland.com**, ⓦ**www.doras.ie**, ⓦ**www.mayo-ireland.ie**, ⓦ**www.searc.ie**, ⓦ**www.touchtel.ie** These six excellent online resources collate and review sites relating to Ireland and offer good links, which makes them a good starting point for any online search or enquiry.

ⓦ**www.searc.ie** Offers an efficient, free service, answering any query you have about Ireland.

ⓦ**www.ireland.travel.ie** The official tourist-board site offering plenty of facts and information, though little practical advice.

ⓦ**www.discovernorthernireland.com** A site posted by the Northern Ireland Tourist Board outlining all officially approved tourist information.

ⓦ**www.local.ie** This site operates as a portal for local information about Ireland's cities, towns and villages.

ⓦ**www.corkkerry.ie**, ⓦ**www.ecoast-midlands.ie**, ⓦ**www.ireland-northwest.travel.ie** ⓦ**www.irelandwest.ie**, ⓦ**www.shannon-dev.ie/tourism**, ⓦ**www.southeastireland.com** The Republic's six regional tourist boards, all

offering plenty of information on local attractions.
Ⓦ**www.visitdublin.com** An exceptional site on Dublin run by the local tourist authority.

Architecture

Ⓦ**www.irish-architecture.com** A large site supplying information on all of Ireland's major buildings.

Genealogy

Ⓦ**www.irishorigins.com** A good starting point for anyone interested in tracing their Irish roots.

Irish cuisine

Ⓦ**www.irishfood.com** This site speaks for itself, covering in delicious detail traditional Irish recipes and the best places to eat in the country.

Music and entertainment

Ⓦ**www.ceili.ie** A good place to begin, if you want to track down information on traditional music and dance.
Ⓦ**www.entertainmentireland.ie** An up-to-date site listing concerts, festivals and special events throughout the country.

News

Ⓦ**www.irishnews.com** A must for anyone with an interest in the politics of Northern Ireland, this site also has links to travel information on the North, especially the Glens of Antrim.
Ⓦ**www.irishtimes.com** The best news site relating to Ireland and posted much earlier than the print version of the paper is available. It offers an efficient free email service, and features information on the live entertainment scene in Dublin with excellent up-to-the-minute listings.

Sport

Ⓦ**www.setanta.com** A site offering comprehensive sports coverage including the Irish sports of Gaelic football and hurling, with quirky features and up-to-date results.

Maps

A variety of large-scale **road maps** covering the whole of Ireland is available for general touring, such as the Michelin 1:400,000 (no. 405) or the AA 1:350,000. The four Ordnance Survey Ireland Holiday Maps, covering the north, west, east and south at a scale of 1:250,000, give more contour detail and are probably the best all-purpose maps on offer. These and others are widely available in Ireland.

For more detail, and for **walking**, the **Ordnance Survey** Discovery Series (1:50,000; a little over one mile: 1in) is generally the best option and now covers the whole island. Additionally, there are 1:25,000 maps on offer for certain tourist areas such as the Fermanagh Lakeland and Mourne Country. The old OS half-inch maps were surveyed in the nineteenth century and can be inaccurate over 1000ft, so a certain amount of caution is advisable if using them. Ordnance Survey maps for Ireland are available to purchase online at Ⓦwww.osi.ie and, similarly, those for Northern Ireland at Ⓦwww.osni.gov.uk.

For specialist interest maps it makes sense to check locally, as tourist boards or bookshops will often have something better than the above.

Map outlets

Britain

Blackwell's Map and Travel Shop 50 Broad St, Oxford OX1 3BQ ⓣ01865/793550, Ⓦwww.bookshop.blackwell.co.uk.
Daunt Books 83 Marylebone High St, London W1 ⓣ020/7224 2295.
Heffers Map and Travel 20 Trinity St, Cambridge CB2 1TJ ⓣ01865/333536, Ⓦwww.heffers.co.uk.
The Map Shop 30A Belvoir St, Leicester LE1 6QH ⓣ0116/247 1400, Ⓦwww.mapshopleicester.co.uk.
National Map Centre 22–24 Caxton St, London SW1 ⓣ020/7222 2486, Ⓦwww.mapsnmc.co.uk.
Newcastle Map Centre 55 Grey St, Newcastle upon Tyne, NE1 6EF ⓣ0191/261 5622.
John Smith and Sons 26 Colquhoun Ave, Glasgow G52 4PJ ⓣ0141/552 3377, Ⓦwww.johnsmith.co.uk.
Stanfords 12–14 Long Acre, London WC2 ⓣ020/7836 1321, Ⓦwww.stanfords.co.uk.
The Stationery Office Ltd 71 Lothian Rd, Edinburgh EH3 9AZ ⓣ0131/228 4181, Ⓦwww.thestationeryoffice.com.
The Travel Bookshop 13 Blenheim Crescent, London W11 2EE ⓣ020/7229 5260, Ⓦwww.thetravelbookshop.co.uk.

US and Canada

Adventuroustraveler.com US ⓣ1-800/282-3963, ⓦadventuroustraveler.com.
Book Passage 51 Tamal Vista Blvd, Corte Madera, CA 94925, US ⓣ1-800/999-7909, ⓦwww.bookpassage.com.
Distant Lands 56 S Raymond Ave, Pasadena, CA 91105, US ⓣ1-800/310-3220, ⓦwww.distantlands.com.
Elliot Bay Book Company 101 S Main St, Seattle, WA 98104, US ⓣ1-800/962-5311, ⓦwww.elliotbaybook.com.
Globe Corner Bookstore 28 Church St, Cambridge, MA 02138, US ⓣ1-800/358-6013, ⓦwww.globercorner.com.
Map Link 30 S La Patera Lane, Unit 5, Santa Barbara, CA 93117, US ⓣ1-800/962-1394, ⓦwww.maplink.com.
Rand McNally US ⓣ1-800/333-0136, ⓦwww.randmcnally.com. Around thirty stores across the US; dial ext 2111 or check the website for the nearest location.
The Travel Bug Bookstore 2667 W Broadway, Vancouver V6K 2G2, Canada ⓣ604/737-1122, ⓦwww.swifty.com/tbug.
World of Maps 1235 Wellington St, Ottawa, ON K1Y 3A3, Canada ⓣ1-800/214-8524, ⓦwww.worldofmaps.com.

Australia and New Zealand

The Map Shop 6–10 Peel St, Adelaide, SA 5000, Australia ⓣ08/8231 2033, ⓦwww.mapshop.net.au.
MapWorld 173 Gloucester St, Christchurch, New Zealand ⓣ0800/627 967 or 03/374 5399, ⓦwww.mapworld.co.nz.
Mapland 372 Little Bourke St, Melbourne, Victoria 3000, Australia ⓣ03/9670 4383, ⓦwww.mapland.com.au.
Perth Map Centre 1/884 Hay St, Perth, WA 6000, Australia ⓣ08/9322 5733, ⓦwww.perthmap.com.au.
Specialty Maps 46 Albert St, Auckland 1001, New Zealand ⓣ09/307 2217, ⓦwww.ubdonline.co.nz/maps.

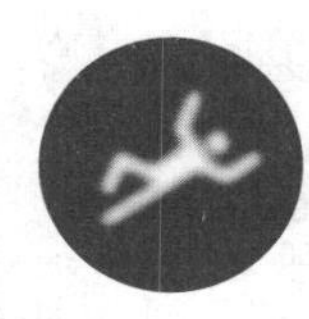

Insurance and health

As an EU country, Ireland has free reciprocal health agreements with other member states. There are no inoculations required for travellers to Ireland, nor any particular health hazards to beware of beyond those of taking care when travelling in an unknown place. Still, you're as likely to fall ill or have an accident here as anywhere else, so it's as well to make sure you're covered by adequate travel insurance.

Before paying for a new policy, however, it's worth checking whether you are already covered: some all-risks **home insurance policies** may cover your possessions when overseas, and many **private medical schemes** include cover when abroad. In **Canada**, provincial health plans usually provide partial cover for medical mishaps overseas, while holders of official student/teacher/youth cards in Canada and the US are entitled to meagre accident coverage and hospital in-patient benefits. Students will often find that their student health coverage extends during the vacations and for one term beyond the date of their last enrolment.

After exhausting the possibilities above, you might want to contact a specialist **travel insurance** company, or consider the travel insurance deal we offer (see box). A typical travel-insurance policy usually provides cover for the loss of baggage, tickets and – up to a certain limit – cash or cheques, as well as cancellation or curtailment of your journey. Most of them exclude so-called dangerous sports unless an extra premium is paid: in Ireland this could mean horse riding, scuba diving, wind-surfing, mountaineering and kayaking. Many policies can

Rough Guides travel insurance

Rough Guides offers its own travel insurance, customized for our readers by a leading UK broker and backed by a Lloyd's underwriter. It's available for anyone, of any nationality and any age, travelling anywhere in the world.

There are two main Rough Guide insurance plans: **Essential**, for basic, no-frills cover; and **Premier** – with more generous and extensive benefits. Alternatively, you can take out **annual multi-trip insurance**, which covers you for any number of trips throughout the year (with a maximum of sixty days for any one trip). Unlike many policies, the Rough Guides schemes are calculated by the day, so if you're travelling for 27 days rather than a month, that's all you pay for. If you intend to be away for the whole year, the **Adventurer** policy will cover you for 365 days. Each plan can be supplemented with a "Hazardous Activities Premium" if you plan to indulge in sports considered dangerous, such as skiing, scuba diving or trekking. For a policy quote, call the Rough Guide Insurance Line on UK freephone ⓣ0800/015 0906, US toll-free ⓣ1-866/220-5588, or, if you're calling from elsewhere ⓣ+441243/621046. Alternatively, get an online quote or buy online at ⓦwww.roughguidesinsurance.com.

be chopped and changed to exclude coverage you don't need – for example, sickness and accident benefits can often be excluded or included at will. If you do take medical coverage, ascertain whether benefits will be paid as treatment proceeds or only after return home, and whether there is a 24-hour medical emergency number. When securing baggage cover, make sure the per-article limit – typically under £500 – will cover your most valuable possession. If you need to make a claim, you should keep receipts for medicines and medical treatment, and in the event you have anything stolen, you must obtain an official statement from the police.

Visitors from **EU countries** are entitled to medical treatment in the **Republic** under the EU Reciprocal Medical Treatment arrangement. UK visitors are advised to collect a form E111 from any main post office: although this form is technically not a requirement for people from the UK, in reality it's essential to get the entitlement to free treatment and prescribed medicines (though this does not cover dental examinations, X-rays and so on). Even then, you can run into problems, and it makes sense to take your NHS card, too. Armed with these documents, check that the doctor you use is registered with the Health Board Panel, and make it clear you want to be treated under the EU's social security arrangements. Similarly if you are admitted to hospital, make it clear you want to be treated within the EU Reciprocal Medical Treatment scheme. The only other real problem is that in rural areas you may find yourself miles from the nearest doctor or hospital, and possibly even further from one prepared to treat you under the reciprocal arrangements. British citizens need no documentation to be treated in the **North**.

Citizens of **non-EU countries** will be charged for all medical services except those administered by accident and emergency units at health service hospitals. Thus a US citizen who has been hit by a car would not be charged if the injuries simply required stitching and setting in the emergency unit, but would if admission to a hospital ward were necessary. Health insurance is therefore extremely advisable for all non-EU nationals. Citizens of some countries may also enjoy a reciprocal agreement; in Australia, Medicare has such an arrangement with Ireland and Britain; check before you leave. And remember that whatever your legal rights, the local doctor may not necessarily know anything about them.

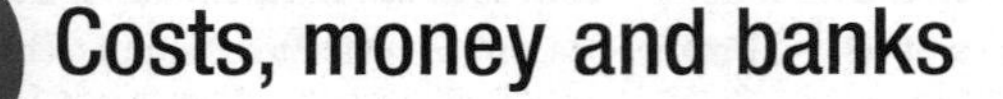

Costs, money and banks

The Republic of Ireland is one of twelve European Union countries who have changed over to a single currency, the euro (€), divided into 100 cents. The currency in the North is pounds sterling, as in Britain, though the notes are different and are not as readily accepted in mainland Britain. Exchange rates vary, but at the time of writing one pound sterling was worth €1.58 and $1.57; one euro was worth £0.63 and $0.99. For the best rates you should change money either in banks or bureaux de change; depending on whom they bank with, visitors may find withdrawing money directly from their accounts via an ATM the best option of all.

Costs

It may be a surprise to find that the **Republic** is not a cheap place to travel. The least expensive **accommodation** in a hostel bed will rarely cost less than €10 a night (€14 in Dublin), while bed and breakfast generally starts at around €25 per person sharing, €30 in Dublin (and single travellers can expect to pay a supplement ranging from 25 to 50 percent extra in many instances – hostels aside). Reckon on at least €7.50 for a basic, filling **meal**, around €20–30 for a restaurant dinner with wine, and on spending more than you expect on drink, partly because it's expensive and partly because so much social life and entertainment revolves around the pubs. In short, you're likely to spend an absolute minimum of €25 a day, even if you're being very careful, and it's easy to find yourself getting through €50 or more if you're staying in B&Bs and eating out. Prices in the **North** tend to be roughly similar for eating and drinking, though B&B accommodation, especially in country areas, may be a little cheaper than in the Republic.

If you are planning on visiting a lot of **historic monuments** in the **Republic**, it may be worth buying a **Heritage Card** (€19, senior citizens €12.70, children/students €7.60, family €45.70), valid for one year from the date of purchase. This gives you unlimited admittance to sites cared for by **Dúchas**, the Heritage Service, which runs many parks, monuments and gardens. Cards can be bought from the first Dúchas site you visit, or in advance by credit card (Ⓣ01/647 2461 or 1850/600601; further details on Ⓦwww.heritageireland.ie). Monuments for which the card is valid are indicated throughout this book; membership of An Óige also includes discounts on access to certain sites (see p.39). In the **North**, the **National Trust** offers a similar deal, but there are a lot fewer sights. If, however, you are also visiting Britain, membership (£32.50, under-25s £15, family £60, one-adult family £46) may be worthwhile. Contact the National Trust for Northern Ireland, Rowallane House, Saintfield, County Down BT24 7LH (Ⓣ028/9751 0721), or the National Trust Membership Department, PO Box 39, Bromley, Kent BR1 3XL (Ⓣ0870/458 4000, Ⓦwww.nationaltrust.org.uk).

Throughout the Guide, the full entry price for museums, art galleries and other sights has been given. Many places will also offer a **concessionary** price for children, students and those over 60, which is usually at least a third off the full amount.

Youth and student discounts

Once obtained, various official and quasi-official youth/student ID cards soon pay for themselves in savings. Full-time students are eligible for the **International Student ID Card** (ISIC; Ⓦwww.isiccard.com in the UK, or go to Ⓦwww.istc.org for more information), which entitles the bearer to special air, rail and bus fares and discounts at museums, theatres and other attractions. For Americans there's also a health benefit, providing up to $3000 in emergency medical coverage and $100 a day for sixty days in the hospital, plus a 24-hour hotline to call in the event of a medical, legal or financial emergency. The card costs US$22/£7.

You only have to be 26 or younger to qualify for the **International Youth Card**, which costs US$22/£7 and carries the same benefits. Both these cards are available in the US from Council Travel, STA, Travel CUTS and, in Canada, Hostelling International; in Australia and New Zealand from STA; and in the UK from STA (see pp.13, 15, 16 and 40 for addresses).

Several other travel organizations and accommodation groups also sell their own cards, good for various discounts. A university photo ID might open some doors too, but is not as easily recognizable as the ISIC and youth cards.

Credit and debit cards

The easiest way to draw out cash is with a **debit or credit card** directly from your account. Most sizeable towns throughout Ireland have at least one bank with an ATM cash dispenser, that will accept Visa and/or Mastercard and most also accept Plus and Cirrus. The majority of large department stores, petrol stations, hotels and upmarket restaurants in both the Republic and Northern Ireland accept the major credit cards – MasterCard, Visa and all cards carrying the Eurocard symbol, though Diners' Club and American Express are less widely accepted. However, credit cards are less useful in rural areas, where many smaller establishments, such as B&Bs, will not accept them.

Travellers' cheques

Another easy and safe way to carry your money is in **travellers' cheques**, available for a small commission from any major bank. The most commonly accepted travellers' cheques are American Express, followed by Visa and Thomas Cook – most cheques issued by banks will be one of these brands. You'll usually pay commission again when you cash each cheque, or a flat rate – though no commission is payable on Amex cheques exchanged at Amex branches and the same goes for Thomas Cook cheques exchanged at Thomas Cook branches. Make sure you keep the purchase agreement and a record of the cheques as you cash them, so you'll be able to get the value of all uncashed cheques refunded immediately if you lose them.

Banks

Almost everywhere banks are the best places to change money and cheques; outside banking hours you'll have to use a **bureau de change**, widely found in most city centres and at international arrival points (listed in the Guide). Avoid changing money or cheques in hotels, where the rates are normally very poor.

The main high-street **banks** in the **Republic** are Allied Irish Bank, Bank of Ireland and Ulster Bank. Most are open Monday to Friday 10am to 12.30pm and 1.30 to 4pm; banks in larger cities stay open all day and are open until 5pm one day a week, usually Thursday. It makes sense to change your money while in the cities since many small country towns are served by sub-offices open only on certain days of the week.

In the **North**, the main high-street banks are National Irish Bank (associated with HSBC), Ulster Bank (associated with NatWest), Northern Bank and Bank of Ireland. Main banks in large towns are open Monday to Friday 9.30am to 4.30pm, with some opening for longer hours and on Saturdays; outside the cities some may close between 12.30pm and 1.30pm. In very small villages banks may only open on two or three days a week – so, as in the Republic, aim to get your cash in the bigger centres.

Wiring money

Having money wired from home using one of the companies listed below is never convenient or cheap, and should be considered as a last resort. It's also possible to have money wired directly from a bank in your home country to a bank in Ireland, although this is somewhat less reliable because it involves two separate institutions. If you go this route, your home bank will need the address of the branch bank where you want to pick up the money and the address and telex number of the Dublin or Belfast head office, which will act as the clearing house; money wired this way normally takes two working days to arrive, and costs around £25/$40 per transaction.

Money-wiring companies

Thomas Cook US ⓣ1-800/287-7362, Canada ⓣ1-888/823-4732, UK ⓣ01733/318922, Republic of Ireland ⓣ01/677 1721, ⓦwww.thomascook.com.

Travelers Express Moneygram US ⓣ1-800/926-3947, Canada ⓣ1-800/933-3278, ⓦwww.moneygram.com.

Western Union US and Canada ⓣ1-800/325-6000, Australia ⓣ1800/501 500, New Zealand ⓣ09/270 0050, UK ⓣ0800/833 833, Republic of Ireland ⓣ1800/395 395, ⓦwww.westernunion.com.

Getting around

Travel between major centres in the Republic is generally straightforward, with reliable – albeit infrequent and slow – public transport operated by the state-supported train and bus companies Iarnród Éireann (Irish Rail) and Bus Éireann. There are, however, glaring anomalies, and you should never assume that two major, local towns are necessarily going to be connected. It pays to think and plan ahead. Once off the main routes this becomes particularly important since it's quite usual for small towns and villages to be served by a couple of buses a week and no more. Transport in the North is similarly infrequent in rural areas. Ulsterbus is generally regular and dependable, as is the (limited) train network.

Ireland's relatively quiet rural roads make car rental an attractive and increasingly popular option, allowing you to visit the more remote areas of the country. It is worth bearing in mind though that roads between major towns and cities can be horribly congested during rush hour. Scenic areas of the country are especially enjoyable by bike; again, increased traffic on main roads means that covering long distances can be more difficult. It's worth considering renting a bike and exploring a small area rather than taking your own with you. Bikes are available for rent in even the smallest villages and, once off the beaten track there's plenty of fine open country to enjoy.

By rail

In the **Republic**, Iarnród Éireann (Irish Rail; ⓣ01/836 6222, ⓦwww.irishrail.ie) operates **trains** between many major cities and the towns en route; on direct lines it's by far the fastest way of covering long distances, but the network is by no means comprehensive – Donegal, for instance, has no service at all. In general, train lines fan out from Dublin, with few routes running north–south across the country. So although you can get to the west easily by train, you can't sensibly use the train network to explore the west coast.

Train travel is not particularly cheap, either. On the Dublin–Galway route and the Dublin–Westport route it makes sense to avoid travelling on a Friday or a Sunday when fares are at their dearest. Generally a return ticket is much better value than a single. For example, a midweek return, valid for one month, between Dublin and Galway costs €32.50; the single fare is €22. On a Friday and a Sunday the return fare on this route rises to €38. It's always worth asking about any special fares that may be on offer.

In **the North**, Translink (ⓣ028/9066 6630, ⓦwww.translink.co.uk) provides both bus and train services, and while the network is not extensive, the service is efficient and reasonably cheap: a Belfast–Derry ticket will cost you £7.80 single, £12 return. The only service **between the Republic and the North** is the Dublin to Belfast express (€29 single, €43 return/£21 single, £31 return).

The cost of taking **bikes** on trains varies

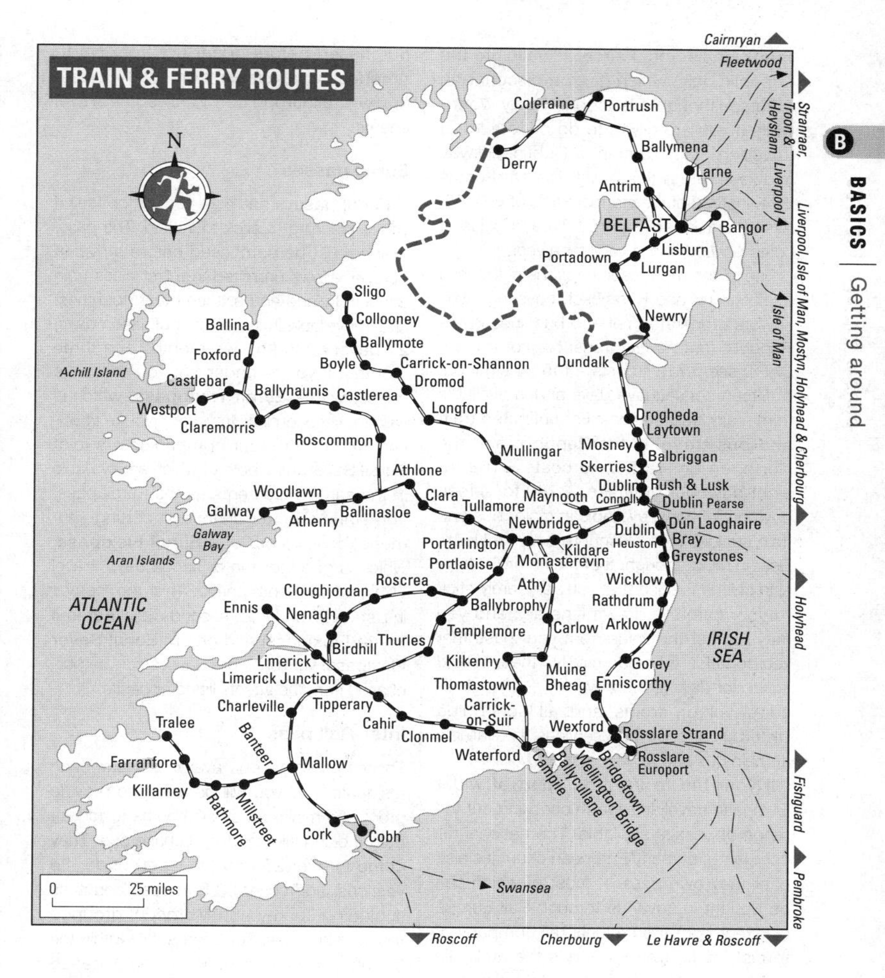

between €2.50 and €8 per single journey in the Republic. In Northern Ireland it costs a quarter of the single fare.

Students in possession of an ISIC card can buy a Travelsave stamp (€10 from any USIT travel agent in the Republic or online at ⓦwww.usitnow.ie) which gives discounts on rail fares. These vary depending on the route: travel from Dublin to Galway for example costs €15.50 single, €22.50 return and can be used on any day of the week. In the North students can buy a Translink Student Discount Card (£6; from bus and train stations in Northern Ireland) which entitles you to discounts of a third off standard train fares in the North and fifteen percent off bus fares over £1.60.

Rail passes

If you're considering purchasing a rail pass for travel within Ireland only bear in mind the limitations of the rail network; a combined bus and rail pass may prove more suitable. An Irish Rover Rail ticket, valid in the Republic and the North, costs €122 for five days out of fifteen. An Irish Explorer ticket, valid in the Republic only, costs €98 and gives five days of travel out of fifteen consecutive days. A further option open to 16–26-

year-olds is the Faircard (valid in the Republic only) which gives a discount on tickets, although it is probably only worthwhile if you are going to do quite a lot of travelling. For example, a Dublin–Galway midweek return ticket with the card costs €24, instead of the standard fare of €32.50. Available from any Iarnród Éireann office, it costs €10.50 and is valid for a year.

One of the most useful options is the Irish Explorer Rail and Bus ticket, covering intercity state-operated rail and bus lines in the Republic (but no city transportation except DART; see p.71); it costs €145 for eight out of fifteen consecutive days and is available from major train stations. For **unlimited train and bus travel** in the Republic and the North, an Emerald Card costs €168 for eight days out of fifteen, €290 for fifteen days out of thirty, available in major bus and train stations in the Republic and the North. Bear in mind, though, that the nature of travel in Ireland is such that you very rarely stick to your carefully drawn itinerary, and you may not get the value from your pass that you hope for. A Freedom of Northern Ireland ticket, for daily (£12) or weekly (£42) unlimited travel on trains and all scheduled Ulsterbus and Citybus services, is available at main bus and railway stations.

If your trip to Ireland is part of wider European travel, it is worth checking out the range of passes available. The national rail companies of many European countries also offer their own passes, most of which can be bought in advance through Rail Europe or direct from the national rail company or tourist office. Rail Europe is the umbrella company for all national and international rail purchases, and its comprehensive website (Ⓦwww.raileurope.com or Ⓦwww.raileurope.co.uk) is the most useful source of information on which rail passes are available; it also gives all current prices.

BritRail and Ireland passes

North American travellers also taking in Great Britain might benefit from the **BritRail and Ireland Pass**, which entitles the holder to five days' unlimited travel within a month (US$529 first class, US$399 standard) or ten days within a month (US$749 first class, US$569 standard). The pass, which must be purchased before departure from North America, is available from Rail Europe (Ⓦwww.raileurope.com) and some travel agents.

Eurail passes

A **Eurail pass** is not likely to pay for itself if you're planning to stick to Ireland. The pass, which must be purchased before arrival in Europe, allows unlimited free first-class train travel in Ireland and sixteen other countries, and is available in increments of fifteen days, 21 days, a month, two months and three months. If you're under 26, you can save money with a **Eurail Youthpass**, which is valid for second-class travel or, if you're travelling with one to four companions, a joint **Eurail Saverpass**, both of which are available in the same increments as the Eurail pass. You stand a better chance of getting your money's worth out of a **Eurail Flexipass**, which is good for ten or fifteen days' travel within a two-month period. This, too, comes in first-class, under-26/second-class (**Eurorail Youth Flexipass**) and group (**Eurail Saver Flexipass**) versions. The passes can be purchased from the agents listed opposite.

Inter-Rail pass

These passes are only available to European residents, and you will be asked to provide proof of a minimum of six months residency before being allowed to purchase one. They come in over-26 and (cheaper) under-26 versions, and cover 28 European countries (including Turkey and Morocco) grouped together in zones. For travel solely within the Republic they are expensive – an under-26 ticket for twelve days' rail travel costs £125, £149 for 22 days; for over-26s the corresponding prices are £182 and £219. If you intend on travelling to a number of European countries, the pass becomes a more useful option: sample rates for one month's rail travel within two zones are £265 standard, £189 under-26s.

Full details of the zones and rates can be found on the Inter-Rail website, where you can also book (Ⓦwww.inter-rail.co.uk).

Eurodomino pass

These are also only available to European residents. They are individual country passes providing unlimited travel in 28 European and North African countries. The passes are available for between three and eight days' travel within a one-month period; prices vary depending on the country, but include most high-speed train supplements. You can buy as many separate country passes as you want. There is a discounted youth price for those under 26, and a half-price child (age 4–11) fare. For example, for visitors from the UK travel for three days in Ireland costs £44 and £40 for under-26s; for eight days' travel the prices are £88 and £77 respectively. Tickets need to be bought before you leave your country of residence; further details are available at ⓦwww.raileurope.co.uk and purchases can be made by phone on ⓣ0870/584 8848.

Rail contacts

In Ireland

Iarnród Éireann Irish Rail ⓣ01/836 6222, ⓦwww.irishrail.ie. Train services in the Republic.
Translink ⓣ028/9066 6630, ⓦwww.translink.co.uk. Train services in Northern Ireland.

In the UK

Rail Europe ⓣ0870/584 8848, ⓦwww.raileurope.co.uk.
Discounted rail fares for under-26s on a variety of European routes; also agents for Inter-Rail, Eurodomino and other rail passes.

In North America

CIE Tours International US ⓣ1-800/243-8687, ⓦwww.cietours.com. Irish passes.
CIT Rail US ⓣ1-800/223-7987 or 212/730-2400, Canada ⓣ1-800/361-7799, ⓦwww.fs-on-line.com. Eurail passes.
DER Travel US ⓣ1-888/337-7350, ⓦwww.dertravel.com/rail. Eurail passes.
European Rail Services Canada ⓣ1-800/205-5800 or 416/695-1211, ⓦwww.europeanrailservices.com. Eurail passes.
Europrail International Canada ⓣ1-888/667-9734, ⓦwww.europrail.net. Eurail passes.
Online Travel US ⓣ1-800/660-5300, ⓦwww.eurorail.com. Eurail passes.
Rail Europe US ⓣ1-800/438-7245, Canada ⓣ1-800/361-7245, ⓦwww.raileurope.com/us. Official North American Eurail-pass agent.
ScanTours US ⓣ1-800/223-7226 or 310/636-4656, ⓦwww.scantours.com. Eurail passes.

In Australia and New Zealand

CIT World Travel Australia ⓣ02/9267 1255 or 03/9650 5510, ⓦwww.cittravel.com.au. Eurail and other European rail passes.
Rail Plus Australia ⓣ1300/555 003 or 03/9642 8644, ⓔinfo@railplus.com.au. Eurail and other European rail passes.
Trailfinders Australia ⓣ02/9247 7666, ⓦwww.trailfinder.com.au. All Europe passes.

By bus

Bus Éireann (ⓣ01/836 6111, ⓦwww.buseireann.ie) operates throughout the **Republic**, and its services are reliable, if infrequent. It's possible to travel by bus between all major towns, but routings can be complex, involving several connections, and hence very slow. Having said that, buses are generally twenty to fifty percent cheaper than trains. In addition **private local companies** operate in most Irish counties (the names, telephone numbers and routes of these companies are listed at the end of each chapter) and these can be cheaper still.

Useful timetable publications

The red-covered **Thomas Cook European Timetables** details schedules of over 50,000 trains in Europe, as well as timings of over two hundred ferry routes and rail-connecting bus services. Updated and issued every month, the main changes are in the June edition (published end of May) with details of the summer European schedules, and the October edition (published end of September) for the winter schedules. Some have advance summer/winter timings also. **Thomas Cook Overseas Timetable** is a blue-covered guide with public transport timetables for the rest of the world: comprehensive rail schedules and long-distance bus timetables for the US, Canada, Australia and Japan, as well as other countries with more selective coverage. It is updated every two months. Both are available from branches of Thomas Cook (see p.14).

Bus Éireann offers a number of passes, ideal if you want to explore the country at your own pace. Rambler tickets (€45 for any three days out of eight; €100 for any eight days out of fifteen; €145 for fifteen days out of thirty) all give unlimited bus travel throughout the Republic; **students** can get reductions on standard fares if they have an ISIC card with a Travelsave stamp (see p.29). It makes sense to pick up the relevant information for the area you intend to explore before you leave; remote villages may only have a couple of buses a week, so knowing when they are is essential.

Carrying a **bike** on a bus will cost you €7.62 single, regardless of length of journey, though be warned that the driver is under no obligation to take a bike and in any case usually has room for only one. Many buses show destinations in Gaelic rather than English, so it's worth checking this out before you set off.

Private buses, which operate on many major routes, are often cheaper than Bus Éireann, and sometimes faster. They're very busy at weekends, so it makes sense to book ahead if you can; during the week you can usually pay on the bus. Prices for parts of the journeys are often negotiable, and bikes can sometimes be carried if booked with your seat.

If you intend on travelling to Ireland from the UK by coach, it's worth considering buying a Eurolines Minipass which includes extensive travel within Ireland too (see p.20).

In the **North**, Ulsterbus, part of Translink (☎028/9066 6630, Ⓦwww.translink.co.uk), runs regular and reliable services throughout the six counties, particularly to those towns not served by the train network. Students can get a fifteen percent discount on standard bus fares over £1.60 with a Translink Student Discount Card (see p.29).

Details of bus services connecting principal towns and cities are given in "Travel details" at the end of each chapter in the Guide.

For details of **joint train and bus passes** see "Rail passes", p.29.

Bus contacts

Bus Éireann ☎01/836 6111, Ⓦwww.buseireann.ie. For bus services in the Republic

Translink ☎028/9066 6630, Ⓦwww.translink.co.uk. Ulsterbus for services in Northern Ireland and Citybus in Belfast.

By car

In order to **drive** in Ireland you must have a current driving licence. A licence from any EU country is equivalent to an Irish one. Visitors from non-EU countries need an International Driving Permit, and these can be obtained from motoring organizations before leaving for Ireland. If you're bringing your own car into the country you should also carry your vehicle registration or ownership document at all times. Furthermore, you must be adequately **insured**, so be sure to check your existing policy.

The **Republic's** roads remain relatively uncongested and having your own transport is ideal if you want to access the best of the landscape. It has to be said, though, that the economic boom of recent years has brought with it an increase in the number of cars on the road. Congestion on roads to and from the main cities – and especially Dublin and Galway – is a serious problem during rush hour (Monday to Friday between 8am and 9.30am and 5pm to 6.30pm). In addition, traffic tends to be especially bad for drivers heading out of Dublin any time after about 2pm on a Friday and into Dublin on a Sunday evening, and bank holidays can be similarly problematic. The urban congestion can also have a knock-on effect on more rural areas too.

The Republic remains (along with Britain) one of the few countries in the world where you drive on the left, a situation that can lead to a few tense days of acclimatization for many overseas drivers. Unleaded petrol is about €0.83–0.93 per litre and available just about everywhere. **Speed limits** are 30mph/50kph in built-up urban areas, 60mph/100kph on the open road and 70mph/110kph on the motorway. All passengers must wear **seat belts**, and motorbikers and their passengers must wear helmets. In remote areas, wandering cattle, unmarked junctions and appallingly potholed minor roads are all potential dangers, particularly for motorbikes. Other hazards to watch out for include drunk drivers late at night, a continuing problem in spite of high accident rates and a concerted police crackdown. A cause of some confusion are "passing lanes" or "slow lanes", indicated by a broken yellow line, where you can pull over to the left for the car behind to overtake. These should be used with care as many have poor surfaces and can suddenly end with little or no warning. Be careful if you take a car to Dublin – congestion is chronic, theft and vandalism rates are high, and you're best advised to leave your car in a supervised car park.

All signposts and place names are given in both Gaelic and English and while most signs give distances in kilometres (although you will see old black and white fingerpost signs giving distances in miles), speed limits are still denoted in miles per hour. Irish people still tend to think in miles and there is also such a thing as an "Irish mile" too – longer than the standard imperial measure – though this is rare and found only on very old signposts. In large towns a **disc parking** system is in operation: discs can be bought in newsagents or at roadside vending machines and have to be displayed on the vehicle when parked in a designated area; failure to display a disc will result in clamping or towing, especially in Dublin and Galway. In Dublin you will also find parking meters.

Roads in the **North** are, in general, notably superior to those in the Republic. Driving is on the left and the rules of the road are as in Britain: speed limits are 30–40mph/50–60kph in built-up areas, 70mph/110kph on motorways and 60mph/100kph on most other main roads. Car seat-belt and motorbike-helmet rules are the same as in the Republic (see opposite). All signposts and speed limits in Northern Ireland are given in miles. Cars bearing large red "R" (Restricted) plates identify drivers who have passed their driving test within the past twelve months and are meant to keep to low speeds. Although security is not as rigorous as it was during the IRA's campaign, controlled parking is still in effect in some towns; a parked car in a control zone is considered a security risk and may result in a security alert. **Petrol prices** in the North are about 79–84p a litre, so it's well worth filling your car's tank with petrol before you cross the border into the North, since the Republic's prices are so much cheaper. In the Republic, the **Automobile Association of Ireland** operates 24-hour emergency breakdown services. It also provides many other motoring services, including a reciprocal arrangement for free assistance through many overseas motoring organizations – check the situation with yours before setting out. You can ring the emergency number (☎1800/66 77 88) even if you are not a member of the respective organization, and they will put you in touch with a local garage. In the North, similar services are offered by the **Automobile Association** (AA) and the **RAC Ireland**.

Large international **car-rental companies**, such as Hertz, have outlets in all major cities, airports and ferry terminals in the **Republic**: they're expensive and, especially if you're travelling from North America, you'll probably find it cheaper to arrange things in advance. Booking a fly-drive or a train-sail-drive package is one of the cheapest ways to arrange car rental or, if you don't want to be so tied down, try an **agency** or **broker**, such as Holiday Autos or Autos Abroad, who will arrange advance booking through a local agent and can usually undercut the big companies considerably – and some of these give further discounts if you book online. It's also worth booking ahead online through a company such as GoIreland.com (ⓦwww.goireland.com).

If you haven't booked, then the smaller local firms can sometimes offer better deals than the well-known names. You must produce a full, valid driving licence (which you must have held without endorsement for at least two years). Most companies will only rent cars to people over 23 years of age, though you might find some that will rent to drivers over 21; it will generally be more expensive if they do. It's advisable to take out a collision damage waiver with your car rental – otherwise expect to be liable for hefty damages in the event of an accident. If you intend to drive **across the border**, you should inform your rental company beforehand to check that you are fully insured.

Renting a car in the **North** involves much the same cost – and age restrictions – as in the Republic. There are fewer outlets, but rental is available in all major cities and at Belfast and Derry airports. Again, the cheapest deals are those booked ahead, and here too you must inform the car-rental company if you plan to cross the border.

Car-rental agencies

Booking car rental before you travel is a convenient way of making the most of your time in Ireland, and it also gives you the opportunity to shop around for the best deal – which is well worth doing given the variation in prices.

In North America

Alamo US ⓣ1-800/522-9696, ⓦwww.alamo.com.
Auto Europe US ⓣ1-800/223-5555, Canada ⓣ1-888/223-5555, ⓦwww.autoeurope.com.
Avis US ⓣ1-800/331-1084, Canada ⓣ1-800/272-5871, ⓦwww.avis.com.
Budget US ⓣ1-800/527-0700, ⓦwww.budgetrentacar.com.
Hertz US ⓣ1-800/654-3001, Canada ⓣ1-800/263-0600, ⓦwww.hertz.com.
Kemwel Holiday Autos US ⓣ1-800/422-7737, ⓦwww.kemwel.com.
National ⓣ1-800/227-7368, ⓦwww.nationalcar.com.
Thrifty ⓣ1-800/367-2277, ⓦwww.thrifty.com.

In Britain

Autos Abroad ⓣ0870/066 7788, ⓦwww.autosabroad.co.uk.
Avis ⓣ0870/606 0100, ⓦwww.avisworld.com.
Budget ⓣ0800/181 181, ⓦwww.budget.co.uk.
National ⓣ0870/536 5365, ⓦwww.nationalcar.com.
Hertz ⓣ0870/844 8844, ⓦwww.hertz.co.uk.
Holiday Autos ⓣ0870/400 00 99, ⓦwww.holidayautos.co.uk.
Thrifty ⓣ01494/751600, ⓦwww.thrifty.co.uk.

In Ireland

Argus Republic of Ireland ⓣ01/490 4444, ⓦwww.argus-rentacar.com.
Avis Northern Ireland ⓣ028/9024 0404, ⓦwww.avis.co.uk, Republic of Ireland ⓣ01/605 7500, ⓦwww.avis.ie.
Budget Republic of Ireland ⓣ01/9032 7711, ⓦwww.budgetcarrental.ie or www.budget-ireland.co.uk.
Cosmo Thrifty Northern Ireland ⓣ028/9445 2565, ⓦwww.thrifty.co.uk.
Dan Dooley Republic of Ireland ⓣ06/253 103, ⓦwww.dan-dooley.ie.
Europcar Northern Ireland ⓣ028/9442 3444, Republic of Ireland ⓣ01/614 2800, ⓦwww.europcar.ie.
Hertz Republic of Ireland ⓣ01/676 7476, ⓦwww.hertz.co.uk.
Holiday Autos Republic of Ireland ⓣ01/872 9366, ⓦwww.holidayautos.ie.
McCausland Northern Ireland ⓣ028/9033 3777, ⓦwww.mccausland.co.uk.
SIXT Republic of Ireland ⓣ1850/206 088, ⓦwww.irishcarrentals.ie.

In Australia

Avis ⓣ13 63 33, ⓦwww.avis.com.
Budget ⓣ1300/362 848, ⓦwww.budget.com.
Hertz ⓣ13 30 39, ⓦwww.hertz.com.
National ⓣ13 10 45, ⓦwww.nationalcar.com.au.
Thrifty ⓣ1300/367 227, ⓦwww.thrifty.com.au.

In New Zealand

Avis ⓣ0800/655 111 or 09/526 2847, ⓦwww.avis.co.nz.
Budget ⓣ0800/652 227 or 09/976 2222, ⓦwww.budget.co.nz.
Hertz ⓣ0800/654 321, ⓦwww.hertz.co.nz.
National ⓣ0800/800 115 or 03/366 5574, ⓦwww.nationalcar.co.nz.
Thrifty ⓣ09/309 0111, ⓦwww.thrifty.co.nz.

Motoring organizations

In North America

American Automobile Association (AAA) ⓣ1-800/222-4357, ⓦwww.aaa.com. Each state has its own club – check the phone book for local address and phone number.
Canadian Automobile Association (CAA) ⓣ613/247-0117, ⓦwww.caa.com. Each region has its own club – check the phone book for local address and phone number.

In the UK and Ireland

AA UK ⓣ0800/44 45 00, ⓦwww.theaa.co.uk.
AA Travel Republic of Ireland ⓣ01/617 9999, ⓦwww.aaireland.ie.
RAC Republic of Ireland ⓣ1800/483 483, ⓦwww.rac.ie.
RAC UK ⓣ0800/55 00 55, ⓦwww.rac.co.uk.

In Australia and New Zealand

Australian Automobile Association ⓣ02/6247 7311.
New Zealand Automobile Association ⓣ09/377 4660.

Hitching

Hitching in the **Republic** is commonplace and if you are without transport of your own it is the best way to see Ireland's wild and remote places. The chief problem that you are likely to encounter is lack of traffic, especially off the main roads, and if you are travelling around one of the tourist-swamped areas of the west, you may find there's a reluctance to pick up foreigners. Wherever you are hitching to, be sure to leave yourself plenty of time.

For women, it's best to avoid hitching alone. The single women that you will see standing beside the road on the edge of small towns and villages are generally waiting to catch a lift off someone that they know – rural communities are small. Although it's probably safer than just about anywhere else in Europe, it goes without saying that hitching is never entirely risk-free.

Hitching a lift in the **North** is rather less straightforward and probably easiest for pairs of women who are obviously tourists. Men travelling alone or in pairs can still be viewed with suspicion and may find it impossible to get a lift. Men and women travelling together are at least in with a chance.

Cycling

If you are lucky enough to get decent weather, cycling is one of the most enjoyable ways to see Ireland, ensuring you're continually in touch with the landscape. Roads in some of the most spectacular areas are generally empty, though very poor surfaces may well slow you down. This said, roads between towns of any size and those in touristy areas are far less pleasurable – the huge increase in traffic in recent years has made cycling along main roads a lot more stressful. To get the best out of cycling in Ireland, plan your route so that you avoid them – there's plenty of superb scenery to enjoy.

Many airlines carry **bicycles** for free as long as you don't exceed your weight allowance; be sure to check the regulations in advance (charters may be less obliging) and let them know when you book your ticket that you plan to carry a bike. Always deflate the tyres to avoid explosions in the unpressurized hold.

If you don't want to cycle long distances, it's easy and relatively cheap to **rent a bike** in most towns in the **Republic** and at a limited number of places in the **North** (most outlets are listed in the text). Raleigh, who operate a rental scheme throughout the Republic are the biggest distributors (€20 per day, €80 per week, €100 if you drop the bike off somewhere other than where you picked it up, plus between €50–100 deposit); collection and delivery service rates vary, so check when you call to book the bike). You can call Raleigh's main office at Unit 1, Finches Park, Long Mile Rd, Dublin 12 (Ⓣ01/465 9659, Ⓦwww.raleigh.ie and Ⓦwww.eurotrekraleighgroup.com) to find out details of their agents throughout Ireland. Local dealers (including some hostels) are often less expensive. Wherever you rent your bike, it makes sense to check the tyres and brakes immediately and ask for a pump and repair kit before you set off. You should also consider the terrain: if you plan on mountain biking, make sure your machine has enough gears to cope. **Cycle helmets** are available for rent at some shops, but if you want to be certain of wearing one, bring your own along. Similarly, many outlets will rent out panniers.

In tourist spots at high season it's best to collect a bike early in the day (or book it the day before) as supplies frequently run out. If you arrive with your own bike, it's easy enough to carry it across long distances by train, less so by bus (see pp.28, 32). Local tourist offices will supply information on organized cycling tours, or contact Irish Cycling Safaris (see p.14).

Finally, a problem you may encounter – for some reason particularly in the west – is that of farmers' dogs chasing and snarling at your wheels. Should you be fortunate enough to be heading downhill at the time, freewheeling silently past cottages and farm entrances is perhaps the only humane way of minimizing the risk of savaged wheels and ankles.

Accommodation

Ireland offers a wide range of accommodation, from the spartan (camping for free in a farmer's field is often possible if you ask permission first) to the luxurious (many of Ireland's elegant old country houses take bed-and-breakfast guests). There's also a huge number of hostels, which vary enormously, but most have at least a bed and somewhere to cook, with some offering a great deal more. A notch up in price, in more or less the following order, come: bed and breakfasts (B&Bs), guesthouses, country houses and hotels. Price codes throughout this book indicate the cost of a double room in high season. In B&Bs and hotels, rates for single rooms are generally considerably higher than doubles per person and can range from twenty-five to fifty percent more.

Whatever your budget, remember that accommodation can be difficult to find in **Dublin** at any time of year and that in **July and August** accommodation in the cities and big tourist centres gets booked up well in advance. During **festivals** things get even more hectic. For the really big festivals – such as the Fleadh Cheoil na hÉireann and the Cork Jazz Festival (see p.48 for a full list of events) – there's often an extra accommodation office trying to cope with the overload, but you may still end up sleeping in a different town, or perhaps just revelling your way through to morning. The less famous festivals can be equally difficult for the spontaneous traveller. Since festivals take place all over Ireland throughout the summer, it's worth checking out where and when they are before you head off. Try Bord Fáilte's website ⓦwww.ireland.travel.ie, or call ⓣ0800/039 7000 in the UK and ask for a calendar of events to be sent to you free of charge.

Accommodation booking

Gulliver Ireland

Accommodation in the Republic and Northern Ireland can be booked in advance through the Tourist Board-approved agency, Gulliver Ireland. The cost of booking a room in a hotel, B&B or guesthouse using the service is €4 with subsequent bookings charged at €1.50. A ten percent nonrefundable deposit is taken from your credit card at the time of booking. There's a flat fee of €7 to reserve self-catering accommodation. All calls to these Gulliver Ireland numbers are free: from within the Republic of Ireland ⓣ1800/668 668, from the UK ⓣ0800/668 668 66, from the US ⓣ1-800/398-4376. A worldwide number is available subject to carriers accepting certain freephone numbers ⓣ00 800 668 668 66. You can use Gulliver Ireland to book online at ⓦwww.gulliver.ie or through the websites of the Irish tourist boards: ⓦwww.ireland.travel.ie and ⓦwww.discovernorthernireland.com. The same charges apply as for telephone bookings.

Bord Fáilte websites

Online booking is also available via one of a growing number of accommodation websites. Bord Fáilte is the official tourist board of the Irish Republic and its websites only feature accommodation registered either with it or with the Northern Irish Tourist Board.

ⓦ**www.hidden-ireland.com** Over thirty private country homes, chiefly in the Republic and generally chosen for their architectural merit and country-house atmosphere.

ⓦ**www.irelandhotels.com** Details of hotels and guesthouses of the Irish Hotels Federation; covers both the Republic and the North.

ⓦ**www.irelands-blue-book.ie** A small site detailing high-quality accommodation; produced by an association of country houses and restaurants in the Republic and Northern Ireland.

ⓦ**www.irishcottageholidays.com** Self-catering accommodation throughout the Republic.

Accommodation price codes

Throughout this book, prices of hotels, guesthouses and B&Bs have been graded with the codes below, according to what you can expect to pay for a double room in high season.

❶ Under €50/£30	❹ €90–110/£55–70	❼ €160–200/£100–125
❷ €50–70/£30-40	❺ €110–130/£70–80	❽ €200–250/£125–160
❸ €70–90/£40-55	❻ €130–160/£80–100	❾ Over €250/£160

Apartments and traditional-style cottages in clusters throughout the Republic.
Ⓦ **www.irishfarmholidays.com** Farmhouses offering B&B accommodation.
Ⓦ **www.nihf.co.uk** Website of the Northern Ireland Hotels Federation.
Ⓦ **www.nischa.com** Self-catering holiday homes in Northern Ireland, from cottages and chalets to castles and luxury apartments.
Ⓦ **www.townandcountry.ie** Comprehensive listing of B&Bs in the Republic and the North.
Ⓦ **www.visitdublin.com** The official website of Dublin Tourism, detailing accommodation in the capital.

Other websites

Ⓦ **www.accommodationireland.org** Health farms, pubs with rooms, gourmet restaurants taking guests, and activity holidays.
Ⓦ **www.tourismresources.ie** A wide-ranging site including The Friendly Homes of Ireland B&Bs, family-run hotels and castles, country houses and cottages to rent.

B&Bs, guesthouses and hotels

B&Bs in the **Republic** vary enormously, but most are welcoming, warm and clean, with huge breakfasts including cereal, massive fry-ups (of bacon, egg, sausage and tomato) and toast and tea; many B&Bs now also offer healthier alternatives. Afternoon tea can usually be arranged and can be delicious, with homemade scones and soda bread – it will cost you around €4 or €6. Evening meals in guesthouses tend to be expensive – from around €17 – and generally need to be pre-booked. Bord Fáilte is the Republic's official tourist board and its registered B&Bs are generally pretty good, though it's not an absolute guarantee. Don't assume that nonregistered places will be of a lower standard – inclusion in the Bord Fáilte guide is voluntary, and a fair few simply choose not to bother. Many historic buildings are run as B&Bs, and they can be surprisingly inexpensive. Many are managed by extremely good cooks, with some of the best and most inventive examples of new Irish cuisine on the menu.

You can expect to pay from around €25.50–32 per person sharing, €30–45 in Dublin. **Bookings** for registered B&Bs can be made through tourist offices (with a booking fee of €3 per establishment) – well worth considering at busy periods, or you can do it yourself by phone or online. Many phone numbers and addresses are given in the text of the Guide. The most useful of a number of accommodation guides available from Bord Fáilte is the *Town & Country Homes B&B Guide* (free of charge; telephone Ⓣ0800/039 7000). Bord Fáilte's website is perhaps the most comprehensive source of accommodation available online (see opposite). The Family Homes of Ireland is a smaller organization, their B&Bs tend to be slightly cheaper, and are particularly worth considering if you require single rooms; their brochure (€6) is available from The Family Homes of Ireland, Oughterard, Co. Galway (Ⓣ091/552000, Ⓦwww.family-homes.ie). Alternatively, finding accommodation is simple enough in just about any town or touristy village – simply go into a pub and ask.

In the **North**, B&B accommodation costs much the same as in the Republic, perhaps a pound or two cheaper in country areas. It's worth ringing ahead if you're planning to stay in Belfast, Derry or one of the main resorts during festivals or high season. Addresses and phone numbers for B&Bs in all of the main centres are given in the Guide. In addition the Northern Ireland Tourist Board's *B&B Northern Ireland* (free of charge; telephone Ⓣ0800/039 7000) gives extensive, highly detailed lists. You can also view accommodation online at ⓦwww.discovernorthernireland.com, the website of the Northern Irish Tourist Board.

Accommodation in a **farmhouse** or in a cottage in the Republic can be arranged through Bord Fáilte; for all their simple rooms and turf fires, many "Rent-an-Irish-Cottage" cottages cluster in tiny tourist villages, so it's worth checking out exactly what the set-up is if you're after real solitude. That said, some are very good value; the Family Homes of Ireland (see p.37) also offers a good range. If you are planning to travel to Ireland by ferry, it is also well worth checking out combined cottage and ferry deals from the major ferry companies.

Inns and **Travel Lodges** are a recent innovation providing good-quality, if often rather characterless, accommodation, and for families and small groups are often less expensive than B&Bs: a typical room sleeping from two to three adults costs around €75 per night, €96 in Dublin.

Hotels are generally more expensive, particularly in the cities; however, many of the swanky hotels will slash their tariffs at weekends, when the business types have gone home, or offer competitively priced low-season deals. In smaller towns and villages, hotels are not always so pricey and may well be a lively social focus – though not necessarily providing accommodation superior to good B&Bs. Virtually all hotels have bars and provide meals to residents and nonresidents alike.

Hostels

Hostel accommodation in Ireland has continued to grow hugely in breadth and quality recently, and staying in one certainly doesn't mean subjecting yourself to the rigours of old-fashioned hostelling. However, An Óige, the official Irish Youth Hostel Association in the Republic, and Hostelling International Northern Ireland (HINI), its counterpart in the North, still manage to satisfy spartan tastes in some of their more remote hostels. That said, they also have some excellent newly refurbished hostels in prime locations. Hostels in the more popular areas tend to fill up very quickly in July and August, so booking in advance is strongly advised. If you are new to hostelling and are not sure which type of room to go for, bear in mind the fewer in the dorm, the better the night's sleep. Some hostels offer bike rental, some food; details are given in the text.

Independent hostels

Independent hostels in both the Republic and the North are generally run along more relaxed lines than those of the youth hostel associations, and as well as having traditional dormitory accommodation, many have private, double and family rooms. Some new city hostels compare favourably in terms of comfort with B&Bs. The majority are members of the **Independent Holiday Hostels** (IHH) and are recommended by Bord Fáilte or the NITB, but you will also find some excellent (usually small) hostels that don't belong to An Óige, HINI or IHH; many of these are part of the Independent Hostel Owners organization (IHO). All independent hostels are privately owned, and reflect the character and interests of the owner. Some are tucked away in such beautiful countryside that they're worth staying in for the setting alone. Very often the atmosphere is cosy and informal: you can stay in all day if you want, and there are no curfews or chores. On the downside, such is their popularity that some hostels cram people in to the point of discomfort. July and August are particularly bad, especially in the major cities and on the west coast, as are festival times. If you're relying on staying in hostels it's worth booking in advance. The IHH book-a-bed-ahead scheme allows you to book at one IHH hostel for your next stop, usually for a charge of €1 per booking; the hostel owner will phone through your booking and on payment of €10 deposit will issue you with a ticket that guarantees your bed – you then simply pay the balance on arrival. In high season expect to pay anything from €19 to €35 for a dormitory bed in Dublin, and around €10–15 elsewhere; in the North prices vary from around £5.50–30 per person. Many hostels have double or twin rooms: expect to pay around €19–46 per person in Dublin and €13–20 elsewhere. Such is the degree of variation in price that it is worth getting a copy of hostel listings from the IHH and IHO before you set off if you are travelling on a tight budget. If you spend most of your time in out-of-the-way locations, you may find prices considerably cheaper. In the North, dormitory beds are generally priced between £7 and £10.50, and twin or double rooms cost much the same.

Many hostels are open all year round. Where this is not the case, we have specified in the text which months they open. If you are planning on using hostels extensively, it's worth checking their detailed lists in advance: for the IHH call ⓣ01/836 4700 or go to ⓦwww.hostels-ireland.com/ihi; for the IHO call ⓣ073/30130 or see ⓦwww.holidayhound.com or ⓦwww.backpackershostelsireland.com. In recent years a number of independent hostels have turned to providing accommodation for refugees, so it's worth phoning ahead to check that they still cater for backpackers.

An Óige and HINI hostels

An Óige and HINI hostels are run more traditionally: many are closed during the daytime and enforce evening curfews, at least officially. Thanks to competition from other hostels though, you'll find many far more flexible than the rule book would suggest, and the quality of accommodation in newly refurbished hostels can be exceptionally good. Smaller dorms and private rooms are available in certain hostels; some are worth visiting for the location (which can often make up for the lack of facilities) and others, especially in the mountains, may be the only place to stay.

In the Republic, An Óige membership – which includes membership of the umbrella organization, **Hostelling International** (HI), and therefore also membership of HINI – costs €15 for adults and €7.50 for under-18s, and can be obtained by visiting or writing to An Óige's main office in Dublin (see p.80). In Northern Ireland, HINI membership (including membership of HI and therefore An Óige) costs £10 for adults and £6 for under-18s. Visitors from elsewhere in the UK, and foreign nationals, are advised to join the HI organization in their country of residence as there are additional benefits. For example, if you buy membership before leaving home some ferry companies offer discounts on foot passenger fares, and certain car-rental companies offer reduced rates too. The members' handbook lists these along with discounts available at a range of historic sites, and in shops and visitor centres. If you do turn up at an An Óige hostel as a nonmember, you can buy a temporary membership card for €11, although this doesn't carry the benefits of full membership. Alternatively, you can pay a €2 supplement for each night that you stay, and after paying for six nights, you in effect acquire the temporary membership. In Northern Ireland nonmember supplements cost £1.50 per night.

An Óige and HINI hostel rates vary according to quality of facilities; **prices** in the **Republic** are around €12–14.50 for a dorm in high season; city hostels are generally the most expensive, especially in Dublin where the price rises to €19; the exception is the hostel at Glendalough which costs €19.50. In the **North**, charges for an overnight stay range around £8 to £11 for a dorm bed including linen. The *An Óige Handbook*, clarifies the intricacies of the system, lists every hostel in the association and gives details of HINI hostels; it's available from the address on p.40. An Óige also offers special accommodation-and-travel deals, which are well worth checking out in advance.

Hostelling organizations

Independent hostels

Independent Holiday Hostels of Ireland (IHH) ⓣ01/836 4700, ⓦwww.hostels-ireland.com.
Independent Hostel Owners (IHO) ⓣ073/30130, ⓦwww.holidayhound.com/ihi and ⓦwww.backpackershostelsireland.com.

Youth hostel associations

Youth Hostel Association (YHA) Trevelyan House, 8 St Stephen's Hill, St Albans, Herts AL1 2DY ⓣ0870/870 8808, ⓦwww.yha.org.uk and ⓦwww.iyhf.org. Annual membership £13; under-18s £6.50; family £26 (one-parent family £13); group £13; lifetime £190 (or five annual payments of £40).
Scottish Youth Hostel Association (SYHA) 7 Glebe Crescent, Stirling, FK8 2JA ⓣ0870/155 3255, ⓦwww.syha.org.uk. Annual membership £6;

under-18s £2.50; family £12; lifetime £60.
An Óige 61 Mountjoy St, Dublin 7 ⓣ01/830 4555, ⓦwww.irelandyha.org. Annual membership €15; under-18s €7.50; family €31.50; lifetime €75.
Hostelling International Northern Ireland (HINI) 22–32 Donegall Rd, Belfast BT12 5JN ⓣ028/9032 4733, ⓦwww.hini.org.uk. Annual membership £13; under-18s £8; family £25; lifetime £75.
Hostelling International-American Youth Hostels (HI-AYH) 733 15th St NW, Suite 840, PO Box 37613, Washington, DC 20005 ⓣ202/783-6161, ⓦwww.hiayh.org. Annual adult membership (18–55) US$25; seniors (55 or over) US$15; under-18s and groups of ten or more free. Lifetime US$250.
Hostelling International/Canadian Hostelling Association (HI-Canada) Room 400, 205 Catherine St, Ottawa, ON K2P 1C3 ⓣ1-800/663-5777 or 613/237 7884, ⓦwww.hostellingintl.ca. Rather than sell the traditional one- or two-year memberships, the association now sells one Individual Adult membership with a 28- to 16-month term. The length of the term depends on when the membership is sold, but a member can receive up to 28 months of membership for just Can$35. Membership is free for under-18s and you can become a lifetime member for Can$175.
Australia Youth Hostels Association 422 Kent St, Sydney ⓣ02/9261 1111, ⓦwww.yha.com.au. Adult membership A$52 (under-18s A$16) for the first twelve months and then A$32 each year after.
New Zealand Youth Hostels Association 173 Gloucester St, Christchurch ⓣ03/379 9970, ⓦwww.yha.co.nz. Adult membership NZ$40 for one year, NZ$60 for two and NZ$80 for three; under-18s free; lifetime NZ$300.

Camping

The cheapest way to sleep in Ireland is to **camp** rough, although the distinct possibility of rain, without the facilities of a campsite, may put you off. You'll also find that some of the terrain is very tricky, especially in the areas of bog and rock in Clare, Donegal, Galway and Mayo. In the Republic, there's usually no problem if you ask to camp in a field, and in out-of-the-way places nobody minds where you pitch a tent (the only place you definitely can't camp in the Republic is in a state forest – but these are usually dark pine woods and unsuitable for camping anyhow). You may find that the farmer will ask you for a euro or two if the field happens to be in a very touristy region such as Kerry, and if there's an organized site nearby you'll probably be directed to it. The cost of staying in **organized campsites** varies depending on the facilities offered, the number of people sharing and the size of the tent; expect to pay €6–10 per tent. In the North prices are higher; expect to page £6–£10 a tent, and more in some prime holiday locations. Lists of sites in the Republic and the North are available free of charge from Bord Fáilte (ⓣ0800/039 7000, ⓔinfo@campingireland.ie). It's also worth bearing in mind that many of the **hostels** will let you camp on their land for around €4–6 a night per person, with the use of kitchen facilities and showers.

Food and drink

Ireland has no real tradition of eating out, but the range and quality of food has increased enormously in recent years, especially at the top end of the market, and this edition of the Guide includes the most luxurious and expensive of eating places, along with more everyday establishments. Outside smart restaurants the best of Irish food is to be found in seafood bars on the west coast and in the all-too-rare vegetarian cafés dotted around the country. These aside, the fresh, though rather plain, selection of vegetables, meat and breads available in the shops make self-catering a reasonable option; in some areas these can often be enlivened by a fine selection of Irish cheeses. If your budget is restricted, the best bet is to avoid hefty restaurant prices by filling up with a hearty breakfast and/or a good lunch from a pub or coffee shop in the middle of the day, though an increasing number of pubs now serve food in the evening too.

Irish food is generally highly meat-oriented, and you don't have to be a vegetarian to find this wearing after a while. Having said that, meat in Ireland is generally of a good standard – lamb and steaks in particular, are excellent. You may also find that you begin to long for something which hasn't been roasted or fried.

If you're staying in B&Bs, you'll most likely be served the hearty, "traditional" Irish **breakfast** of sausage, bacon and eggs, which often comes accompanied by generous quantities of delicious soda bread. Many B&Bs, however, now offer less fattening alternatives, including everything from fresh fruit to smoked salmon. Country pub **lunch** staples are usually meat and two veg, with plenty of potatoes and gravy, although you can usually get sandwiches (sometimes excellent, but often with sliced white bread and processed cheese), and homemade soups can be very good too. Most larger towns have good, simple **coffee shops** (open daytime only) where you can get soup, sandwiches, cakes and scones, and a choice of one or two hot lunches. In the North expect enormous platters of meat, vegetables – most usually cabbage – and plenty of potatoes. It's worth remembering that many **hotels** in the Republic will offer food to nonresidents so you can usually find a sandwich and a cup of coffee at any reasonable hour, which can be especially worth remembering on Sundays. You can generally order a plate of sandwiches and a pot of tea or mug of coffee (usually instant) in pubs too – as long as it's before 6pm. This said, some rural backwaters offer no places to eat or drink at all – and many cafés and restaurants in tourist areas outside the cities close from September to May. If you are going to explore the best of the landscape, you'll probably need to take your own provisions.

Many traditional Irish dishes, served up in abundance in areas of rural Ireland, are based on the **potato**, and you certainly do get an awful lot of them – often in several different forms in the same meal. Potato cakes can be magnificent – a flour and potato dough fried in butter – as can potato soup. **Colcannon** – known as **champ** in the North – made up of cooked potatoes fried in butter with onions and cabbage, or leeks, is delicious. **Irish stew** of varying qualities will be available almost everywhere. **Barm brack**, a sweet yeast bread with spices and dried fruits, is thoroughly traditional; **carrot cake** is perhaps a more recent introduction and is seen in coffee shops and tea rooms throughout Ireland.

For Ireland's major **cities** it's a different story: with the Republic's economic boom came a return of a large number of Irish people previously living overseas, which has meant that increasingly inexpensive lunch and dinner menus may just as easily see **Mediterranean** influences as those of the traditional Irish farmhouse – and vegetarians can expect far more variety too. In the North, the range of food available in restaurants has significantly increased in both Belfast and Derry where even the smallest café now serves paninis or ciabatta bread.

Restaurants and self-catering

Once away from the pubs and coffee shops, food in Ireland is far more cosmopolitan than you might imagine – both in the cities and in some unexpected out-of-the-way places. Ireland's **gastronomic revolution**, which began around 1996 and has continued unabated ever since, has seen the development of a new Irish cuisine consisting of elegant meals, using local produce, that are often adaptations of traditional recipes. Some **guesthouses**, particularly if they're historic buildings, serve excellent food in what can be very grand surroundings, and a small number of high-quality vegetarian and wholefood cafés offer a good budget alternative with a growing interest in the delights of organic food. Some impressive **seafood restaurants**, particularly along the west coast and around Dublin Bay and Carlingford Lough, serve freshly caught fish and seafood along with home-grown vegetables. Bars on the west coast are also a good bet for excellent salmon and crab salads and sandwiches, and there are numerous seafood festivals held around the coast. Irish **oysters** are famous: the season opens with an oyster festival at Clarinbridge on Galway Bay. **Salmon** and trout can also be fabulous, although away from the coast fish-farming is the norm. Outside the large cities there's a great deal of variation in opening times, especially in low season, and it's advisable to phone ahead if you have a particular restaurant in mind.

Catering for yourself, at least some of the time, may be a good option. Produce available in Ireland is usually fresh and excellent, but – aside from in the cities and some tourist towns on the west coast – it is limited in range (you won't find exotic fruits and vegetables, for instance). Irish potatoes, cabbages and carrots are delicious, though they can be surprisingly hard to buy in remote rural areas where the population may be too small to support even a grocer's shop. Meat is very good; bread and scones are wonderful, with a particularly wide variety on offer in the North. If you're travelling around the coast, you can sometimes buy seafood cheaply direct from the fishermen; this can throw up more unusual treats – spider crabs and monkfish, for example – that you would be less likely to find in local fish shops. In many places you can gather your own mussels from the rocks, but be sure to check locally in case there's a sewage outlet nearby.

Dairy products, especially cheese, are excellent. The Irish cheese business has seen a definite upturn since the late 1980s, and now produces many delicious, often unpasteurized, cheeses. Look out for the creamy Cashel Blue, St Killian brie, and Gubbeen Farmhouse in west Cork as well as countless more idiosyncratic cheeses from smaller makers, many of whom like to experiment; you can often find them in grocer's shops and markets.

Drink

To travel through Ireland without visiting a **pub** would be to miss out on a huge chunk of Irish life, some would say the most important. Especially in rural areas, the pub is far more than just a place to drink but is also the communal heart of any Irish village, and often the cultural centre too. If you're after food, advice or company, the pub is almost always the place to head for; very also they'll also be the venues for local entertainment, especially traditional and not so traditional music (see "Festivals and entertainment", p.47). Talking is an important business here, and drink is the great lubricant of social discourse. In most big towns and cities you'll find bars heaving with life, and out in remote country villages it can be great fun drinking among the shelves of the ancient grocery shops-cum-bars you'll find dotted around. That said, it doesn't pay to arrive with too romantic a notion of what this actually means; there are plenty of miserable, dingy bars where the only spark of conviviality is the dull glow of the TV.

While women will always be treated with genuine (unreconstructed) civility, it's true to say that the majority of bars in country areas are a predominantly male preserve. In the

Pub opening hours

In the Republic, **opening hours** are Monday to Wednesday 10.30am to 11.30pm; Thursday, Friday and Saturday 10.30am to 12.30am; Sunday 12.30 to 11pm. In the **North** pubs are open Monday to Saturday 11.30am to 11pm, Sunday 12.30 to 10pm.

evening, especially, women travellers can expect occasional unwanted attention, though this rarely amounts to anything too unpleasant. Should your first encounters be bad ones, persist – the good nights will come, and will probably rank amongst the most memorable experiences of your trip. In the major cities and large towns things are a lot more balanced and women drinking in bars is totally the norm.

One recent significant change in Northern Ireland has been the arrival of the JD Wetherspoon chain of pubs in various towns and cities. Child-friendly and free of music and televisions, the pubs are changing drinkers' palates by introducing a range of real ales while also serving food all day at very reasonable prices.

What to drink

The classic Irish drink is, of course, the stout **Guinness** ("a Guinness" is a pint; if you want a half of any beer, ask for "a glass") which, as anybody will tell you, is simply not the same as the drink marketed as Guinness outside Ireland. For one thing, good Guinness has to be kept properly, something non-Irish pubs abroad tend not to do; it has to be poured gradually (the ultimate gaffe in a pub is to ask them to hurry this process); and even across Ireland you'll taste differences. A proper pint of Irish Guinness is a dream, far less heavy than you may be used to, though still a considerably filling drink. Other local stouts, like Beamish and Murphy's (both manufactured in Cork), make for interesting comparison: they all have their faithful adherents.

If you want a pint of English-style keg **bitter**, then Smithwicks is the most commonly available option, though it has none of the flavour of a decent real ale. In Dublin and the surrounding area, the Dublin Brewing Company has made some incursions into the ale industry with its range of very flavoursome draught ales (best sampled at *The Cobblestone* – see p.132) and a small, but increasing number of pubs in Northern Ireland now serve real ale. **Lager** is also increasingly popular: it's mostly Harp (made by Guinness), Heineken or Carling, but an increasing number of bottled Continental lagers are available. In recent years a number of **microbreweries** have popped up offering a range of beers – usually themed in some medieval fashion – made on the premises: generally there's a blond (lager), a red (ale) and a stout, with perhaps the addition of a wheat beer. Still really something of a novelty, these often have the advantage of being additive-free. Whatever your tipple, you're likely to find drinking in Ireland an expensive business at around £2.20 a pint in the North and anything from €3–4 in the Republic.

Irish **whiskeys** – try Paddy's, Powers, Jameson's or, from the North, Bushmills – also seem expensive, but in fact the measures are far larger than those you'll get in England or Wales. If you've come in from the cold you might like to try whiskey served warm with cloves and lemon – just ask for a hot whiskey. Asking for Scotch in an Irish pub is frowned on, and in any case anyone here will tell you that the Irish version is infinitely superior. **Poteen** (*poitín*), the subject of many an Irish song, is a powerful and illicitly distilled whiskey which varies enormously in quality – some being fit only to strip paint.

Wine is expensive in the Republic – expect prices in supermarkets to start at around €6.50 a bottle (and in small villages in the west you can expect to pay €8 at the very least), so if you are planning a self-catering holiday and travelling from Britain, it's worth bringing your own; in the North prices are similar to those in Britain.

Nonalcoholic drinks are limited to an uninspiring array of the usual soft drinks and bottled fruit juices. Among the most pleasant are Cidona (apple juice), plus a range of Irish mineral waters, some of which are available in a number of pleasantly unsweet, fruity flavours. Unless a bar is extremely busy, you can always get **coffee** (generally served with a dollop of full cream) or **tea**. You can usually get **Irish coffee** too (with whiskey and cream), which is delicious if not very traditional – it's generally believed to have been invented at Shannon airport, but the County Limerick village of Foynes has mounted a strong counter-claim (see p.331).

Communications

Post to or from Ireland is generally reasonably efficient, and you'll find fully automatic payphones in towns and villages, where national and international calls can easily be made. Internet access is available in most reasonably sized towns and in many hostels, and is detailed throughout the Guide.

Phones

A local **phone** call generally costs 40 cents minimum in the Republic, 20p in the North but, as you might imagine, long-distance daytime calls are very expensive. International calls are cheapest if dialled direct after 6pm. Cardphones, found in towns all over the country, are by far the most convenient way of making long-distance calls, avoiding the chugging of coins interrupting your call; they're also cheaper than coin-operated phones. Phonecards can be bought at newsagents and post offices – it's worth carrying one with you since cash-operated phones are rare in remote areas. If you make calls from a hotel or the like, expect a hefty premium charged on top of the normal price.

The **international dialling code** for the Republic is 353, and for Northern Ireland, as part of the UK, it's 44. If you're calling the North from the Republic, however, the code is 048 followed by an eight-digit number.

Mobile phones

If you want to use your mobile phone abroad, you'll need to check with your phone provider whether it will work abroad, and what the call charges will be. Unless you have a tri-band phone, it is unlikely that a mobile bought for use in the **US** will work outside the States and vice versa, with many only working within the region designated by the area code in the phone number, ie 212, 415, etc. Most mobiles in **Australia** and **New Zealand** use GSM, which works well in Ireland, though it's still advisable to check with your provider before travelling.

If you are coming from **Britain** your mobile phone should work in Northern Ireland, but it is likely that you will need to have your international access switched on in order to be able to receive calls in the Republic. It is best in both cases however to check with your service provider. You may also get charged extra for this depending on your existing package. You are also likely to be charged extra for incoming calls, as the people calling you will be paying the usual rate. If you want to retrieve messages while you're away, you'll have to ask your provider for a new access code, as your home one is unlikely to work.

Operator services

In the Republic:
Directory Enquiries within Ireland, including the North ☎11811
International Directory Enquiries ☎11818
Operator Assistance, including the North and Britain ☎10
International Operator Assistance ☎114
In the North:
Operator ☎100
Directory Enquiries ☎118500
International Directory Enquiries ☎153
International Operator Services ☎155

Post

From the **Republic**, post is generally reasonably efficient; allow at least three days for a letter to reach Britain, for example. An Post (the postal service) has three different charge bands: letters and postcards within Ireland or to Britain start from 41c; those going to any other European country 44c; cards or letters outside Europe 57c. Main post offices are open Monday to Friday 9am to 5.30pm, Saturday 9am to 1pm, and in cities and large towns until 5.30pm on Saturday. From the **North**, first-class mail to the rest of the UK costs 27p, postcards and letters to the rest of Europe start from 37p, and to the rest of the world postcards cost 42p and airmail letters start from 47p. Post office hours in the North are generally Monday, Tuesday, Thursday and Friday 9am to 5.30pm and Wednesday and Saturday 9am to 12.30pm – later on Wednesday and Saturday in large towns and cities.

The media

The most widely read newspapers in the Republic are the heavyweight *Irish Times* and the lighter *Irish Independent*, both high-quality papers. The *Times* is more upmarket; a liberal newspaper with good foreign-news coverage and plenty of feature material on home news and sport. A relative newcomer on the national scene, *The Irish Examiner* (formerly *The Cork Examiner*), is, if you include its former provincial incarnation, the oldest daily published newspaper in the country; it has a softer focus, with excellent local sports coverage. The *Star* is Ireland's daily tabloid, and Sunday sees the production of two more tabloids, *Ireland on Sunday* and the *Sunday World*, as well as several broadsheets, among which the liberal *Sunday Tribune* and the *Sunday Business Post*, which has a broader coverage than its name might suggest, are probably your best bets. If you want to dig a little deeper into the murky world of Irish politics, it's well worth picking up a copy of the satirical fortnightly magazine *The Phoenix*. British newspapers, some of which have Irish editions, are generally available the same day in Dublin and other cities. Mostly conservative and varying widely in quality, there's a local weekly paper in every county; some of the best are *The Kerryman*, *The Donegal Democrat* and *The Kilkenny People*.

In the **North**, all the main British papers are sold. Of the newspapers produced in Northern Ireland, the biggest seller is the evening paper, the *Belfast Telegraph*, which has a soft Unionist stance, while the morning papers are the *Irish News*, read by the Nationalist community, and the Unionist tabloid *News Letter*.

In the **Republic**, RTÉ (Radio Telefís Éireann) oversees three state-sponsored **television** channels. RTÉ 1 reflects the state broadcasting policy with an emphasis on public information, showing the best news and current affairs programmes, as well as long-standing favourites such as the home-grown soap, *Fair City*. Network 2 is more upbeat, with plenty of youth-oriented programmes, comedies and movies. The excellent Irish-language channel TG4 (Telefís na Gaeilge Cathair) is worth a look, especially as most of its programmes are subtitled in English. TG4 has done much to use the contemporary medium of television to reinvigorate the language, reflected in the often upbeat and visually progressive nature of its programming. The relatively new independent channel TV3 features mostly British and American soaps, films and sport. In most of the Republic, the four major British terrestrial TV channels are available on cable.

RTÉ also runs three national, English-language **radio** stations. RTÉ Radio 1 (FM 88.2–90.0, 95.2) is largely devoted to middle/high-brow cultural and political programmes; highlights include the extended news and current affairs slots, *Morning Ireland* (7–9am) and *Five Seven Live* (5–7pm), *Rattlebag*, a review of the arts at 2.45pm (repeated in the evenings) and *The Mystery Train* (from 7pm), in which whispering John Kelly presents a diverse but always interesting selection of music, from world to soul and back again. 2FM (FM 90.4–92.2, 97.0) is a popular music channel with a more light-hearted feel; in the mornings for a flavour of everyday Irish life tune into *The Gerry Ryan Show* from 9am to noon whose host has the ability to turn the most mundane subjects into highly entertaining radio. Lyric FM is a largely populist classical music station (FM 96–99, 102.7). Today FM (FM 100–102) was launched as an ambitious commercial attempt to rival the state-owned media, and although its daytime output is rather uninspiring, a few programmes in the evening are worth listening out for: *The Last Word* (5–7pm) mixes current affairs and satire, then from 7 to 10pm in *Pet Sounds* Tom Dunne trawls through his eclectic and, at times, idiosyncratic music collection, while the evening winds down (10pm–1am) to the dulcet tones of Kerryman Donal Dineen, an authority on contemporary electronic music.

In the **North** you get the BBC whose strongest programming is related to politics: look out for the current affairs programme *Spotlight* on BBC1 on Tuesday evenings, while *Talkback* (daily noon–1.30pm) on BBC Radio Ulster (FM 92.4–95.4), gives an insight into the complex sectarian politics of the North. Also well worth tuning into are Derry-based BBC Radio Foyle (FM 93.1) and the commercial station Q102.9 FM. The independent Ulster Television, the BBC's main rival, focuses on softer news issues; Northerners can also pick up RTÉ.

Opening hours and holidays

Business and shop opening hours in both Northern Ireland and the Republic are very similar to Britain's: approximately 9am to 5.30pm, Monday to Saturday. Many places in the towns stay open until 8pm or later, especially on Thursdays, and open on Sundays usually from noon until 6pm. The midweek half-day closing tradition survives in some of the smaller towns, though even then you're likely to find somewhere open.

In the Republic, however, particularly away from the bigger towns, hours are more approximate, with later opening and closing times. In rural areas you can generally find someone to sell you groceries at any reasonable hour, even if they have to open their shop to do it – and very often the village shop doubles as the local pub. For banking hours see "Costs, money and banks" on p.26. On the main **public holidays** (see opposite), in places outside the cities, virtually everything will be closed except the garages and pubs; on Good Friday in the Republic, even the pubs close. Should St Patrick's Day or Orange Day happen to fall on a Saturday or Sunday, the holiday is carried over to the Monday.

There's no pattern to the opening and closing of museums, archeological sites and the like, though many close altogether for at least one day a week; hours and prices are listed in the Guide. The bigger attractions will normally be open throughout the day, while smaller places may open only in the afternoon. Many sites outside the cities – especially houses or castles which are also private homes – are open only during the peak summer months. Churches, at least if they're still in use, are almost always open, and if they're locked there's usually someone living nearby (often the priest) who will have the keys; otherwise, opening times will follow religious activity fairly closely.

Public holidays

In the Republic:
New Year's Day
St Patrick's Day, March 17
Good Friday
Easter Monday
First Monday in May
First Monday in June
First Monday in August
Last Monday in October
Christmas Day
December 26 (St Stephen's Day)

In the North:
New Year's Day
St Patrick's Day, March 17
Good Friday
Easter Monday
First Monday in May
Last Monday in May
Orange Day, July 12
Last Monday in August
Christmas Day
December 26

Festivals and entertainment

Virtually every village and town in Ireland seems to have a festival of some kind or other each year, many centred around either the June or August public holidays. Whatever the pretext for the celebration, it's usually also an excuse for serious partying. Well-established ones like the Cork Jazz Festival and the Wexford Opera Festival are major international events, and getting tickets for top performances can be well nigh impossible without advance planning. The very word "festival" seems to act as a magnet for all sorts of musicians, and many events are wonderfully overwhelming. No matter the size of the town, there's rarely enough room for all that's happening, with music and dancing bursting out of the official venues into surrounding streets and bars. The biggest of the annual events are listed here, but pick up a calendar of events at any major tourist office and you'll soon get a picture of the huge range of celebrations.

Music

Apart from their sheer exuberance, the most enjoyable aspect of Irish festivals is, without doubt, the traditional music. Many festivals (the Irish for festival is *fleadh* – pronounced "fla") are devoted almost exclusively to this: the biggest of them is the Fleadh Cheoil na hÉireann (see p.49), which includes the finals of the All-Ireland music and dance contests.

However, if you can't make it to a festival, there's usually plenty going on in the pubs and bars, especially in high season in the popular tourist spots. Music in Irish pubs is legendary, and there's lots on offer, though only a relatively small proportion of it is "traditional". The national hybrid form of country and western, country and Irish, is extremely popular, with a host of regular gigs around the island. You'll still find that Irish staple, the showband, too, and there are a myriad of middle-of-the-road pop bands lurking in rural areas. Ballads are another well-developed Irish music form though the term "ballad" is a bit of a catch-all and open to countless interpretations – it's generally some form of dull crooning, often accompanied by just a guitar and monotonous beatbox. Brace yourself for the worst, and from time to time you'll be very pleasantly surprised.

The cream of pub music, however, has to be the traditional sessions of fiddles, flutes, accordions, *bodhrán* (a goatskin frame drum) and, occasionally, singing. Interest from abroad and the tourist industry has much to do with the resurgence of this musical culture – but this hardly matters, since the music can be phenomenal. The west coast (especially around Clare, Donegal, Galway, Kerry and Sligo) has the best of the traditional scene. There's plenty in all the major cities, and pointers to the best sessions are given in the text. However, venues may change for all manner of reasons and it's wise to ask around and keep your ears open for local tips.

Traditionally Sunday evening was the night for sessions, and in rural areas this is often still the case (a throwback to restrictions on holy days that meant partying on Saturdays had to stop at midnight), but increasingly Friday and Saturday have become just as important, and, in summer, you may find something happening any night of the week. Things generally don't get going till late, and a bar that's still empty at 10pm may be a riot of music by half-past. While it's all extremely convivial and relaxed, if you're a musician yourself and want to join in, then do so tactfully. The first thing to do is sit and listen for a while – to make sure you can play to a high enough standard and are familiar with the repertoire – and then work out who the leader is and ask. If you're not playing, don't crowd the musicians; the empty seats around them are reserved for others who may arrive later.

Comhaltas Ceoltóiri Éireann is an organization that exists purely to promote traditional music and culture, and evenings organized by them (not always in bars), though by their nature not spontaneous, are well worth looking out for. They are run by real enthusiasts, and the standard of playing is usually pretty high.

Major annual festivals and events

St Patrick's Day March 17; Ⓦwww.stpatricksday.ie. Celebrations all over Ireland, including a national festival in Dublin and major events in all the larger towns and cities, including Downpatrick, the supposed burial place of the saint (Ⓦwww.stpatricksdayfestival.com).

Irish Grand National April 1. National Hunt horse racing at Fairyhouse, Co. Meath.

Cork International Choral Festival Early May; Ⓦwww.corkchoral.ie. Includes the Fleischmann International Trophy competition and a host of choirs.

North-West 200 May. The island's biggest motorcycle road racing event takes place on a circuit at Portstewart, Co. Derry.

Wicklow Garden Festival May–July Ⓦwww.wicklow.ie. A host of gardens, both large and small, on view in Wicklow.

Fleadh Nua Late May; Ⓦwww.comhaltas.com. One of the country's biggest traditional music festivals, held in Ennis, Co. Clare.

Fleadh Amhrán agus Rince Mid-June; Ⓦwww.comhaltas.com. Major traditional music and dance festival in Ballycastle, Co. Antrim.

Irish Derby Late June. The major event in the Irish flat-racing season and other important horse races at the Curragh, Co. Kildare.

Irish Open Golf Championship Late June. Traditionally, the major golf tournament.

Willie Clancy Summer School Early July. One of the biggest traditional music events of the year, based in Miltown Malbay, Co. Clare.

James Joyce Summer School Mid-July; Ⓦwww.artsworld.ie/joyce_school. Strictly for Joyce buffs, Dublin.

Galway Film Fleadh Mid-July; Ⓦwww.galwayfilmfleadh.com. New Irish and international releases.

Orange Order Parades July 12. Unionists and Loyalists commemorate the Battle of the Boyne and close down much of Northern Ireland in the process.

Galway Arts Festival Mid-July; Ⓦwww.galwayartsfestival.ie. Festival of music, theatre and general partying – one of the best.

Boyle Arts Festival July/Aug. Smaller but popular version of the Galway festival, held in Co. Roscommon.

Galway Races July/Aug. Another important National Hunt race meeting which is very popular.

Yeats International Summer School July/Aug; Ⓦwww.yeats-sligo.com. This Sligo event has often courted controversy through its exploration of nationalistic themes.

Mary from Dungloe July/Aug. Ten days of music and other entertainment in Co. Donegal, usually featuring Daniel O'Donnell and culminating in a beauty contest (where one of the prizes is normally a date with the man himself).

Kilkenny Arts Festival Mid-Aug;

Ⓦ www.kilkennyarts.ie. Includes recitals, theatre, poetry readings and art exhibitions.

Puck Fair Mid-Aug. Three days of mayhem in Killorglin, Co. Kerry.

Rose of Tralee International Festival Late Aug; Ⓦ www.roseoftralee.ie. A massive event, centred round a beauty contest.

Fleadh Cheoil na hÉireann Late Aug; Ⓦ www.comhaltas.com. The most important of all the traditional music festivals, supposedly held in a different town every year (but more often than not in Listowel, Co. Kerry).

Oul' Lammas Fair Late Aug. Four hundred years old and still going strong, Ballycastle's traditional market fair is a major crowd-puller with music, dancing, sports and entertainment.

All-Ireland Hurling and Football Finals Sept. The biggest sporting events of the year, separated by a fortnight, held in Dublin.

Lisdoonvarna Matchmaking Festival Sept/Oct; Ⓦ www.matchmakerireland.com. Plenty of traditional entertainment accompanies the lonely-hearts side of the festivities.

Dublin Fringe Festival Sept/Oct; Ⓦ www.fringefest.com. Lively programme of theatre, dance, performance arts and comedy featuring more than three hundred events.

Dublin Theatre Festival Oct. Major drama festival encompassing around twenty productions.

Cork International Film Festival Early Oct; Ⓦ www.corkfilmfest.org. Established in 1956 and still going strong.

Wexford Opera Festival Oct/Nov; Ⓦ www.wexfordopera.com. A large gathering of international renown.

Cork Jazz Festival Late Oct; Ⓦ www.corkjazzfestival.com. Four days of jazz in all its forms.

Derry Halloween Carnival Oct/Nov; Ⓦ www.derryvisitor.com. Street theatre, music and mayhem, especially during the fireworks display on October 31.

Belfast Festival at Queen's Oct/Nov; Ⓦ www.belfastfestival.com. Major arts festival, Ireland's equivalent to Edinburgh, nowadays complete with its very own Fringe.

Foyle Film Festival Nov. The best of new Irish and international film in Derry.

Sports and activities

Ireland has two hugely popular indigenous amateur sports, hurling and Gaelic football, with important matches attracting big crowds and passionate support. Gaelic games occupy a special place in Ireland, as ancient sports whose renaissance was entwined with the Celtic revival movement and the struggle for independence. The Gaelic Athletic Association (GAA) fostered a network of local clubs that are still the heart and soul of many communities, with political clout in the provinces.

Said to have descended from a game played by the legendary warrior Cúchulainn, **hurling** is a fifteen-a-side stick game, a precursor of hockey, but much faster and more exciting, as it's played mostly through the air rather than on the ground. Like rugby, there's an H-shaped set of goalposts and each team aims to score as many points as possible by either hitting the leather, baseball-sized ball (*slíothar*) over the crossbar for one point or into the net below for three points. The game's skill lies in control of the broad, wooden hurley stick (*camán*); the *slíothar* is belted prodigious distances, caught and carried on the flattened end of the player's hurley stick. It's a game of constant movement and aggression that does not permit a defensive, reactive style of play. The main hurling season begins with local inter-county games in the early summer, progressing through provincial championships to reach its climax in the All-Ireland Hurling Final usually on the first Sunday in September at Croke Park in Dublin. Cork,

Kilkenny, Offaly and Tipperary are the most successful counties. Camogie, the women's version of hurling, is becoming increasingly popular, and is well worth watching, if there's a match in the area.

Gaelic football is played on the same pitches as hurling and shares the same scoring system and team size. It has similarities with both rugby and association football, as the round, soccer-sized ball can be kicked, caught and passed by either boot or hand. However, running with the ball is only allowed if a player keeps control by tapping the ball from foot to hand or bouncing the ball, and throwing is not allowed – the ball must be "hand-passed", volleyball-style. The main season, which runs from early summer, is organized like hurling's, culminating in an All-Ireland final at Croke Park usually on the third Sunday in September, a flavour of which can be gained from the excellent film shown as part of the Croke Park GAA Museum tour (see p.114). Whereas hurling's strongholds are in the southern counties of the island, footballing prowess is more widely spread – Kerry, Cork, Galway, Meath, Dublin and one of the northern counties are usually likely to make a challenge. Details of fixtures for hurling and Gaelic football can be obtained from the Gaelic Athletic Association (Ⓣ01/836 3222, Ⓦwww.gaa.ie).

Rugby union and soccer are also extremely popular and tickets for international matches are very much in demand, especially in the Republic. The international **rugby** team is a joint Republic-Northern Ireland side, with home matches played at Dublin's Lansdowne Road Stadium (Ⓣ01/647 3800, Ⓦwww.irfu.ie). The main event of the year is the Six Nations Championship, a series of international games against France, England, Scotland, Wales and Italy played in spring. **Soccer** is organized on a professional basis in both the North and the Republic, though the majority of players are semi-professional, with teams competing in the Irish League and League of Ireland respectively. Standards are not especially high, and Irish teams rarely progress beyond the preliminary rounds of the European competitions. Northern Ireland's international matches are played at Windsor Park, Belfast (see p.649), and the Republic's at Lansdowne Road. Both international teams draw the overwhelming majority of their players from the English and Scottish leagues. The Northern Ireland side had its heyday in the 1980s, culminating in their famous 1–0 victory over hosts Spain in the 1982 World Cup, while the Republic gained a high profile and creditable international reputation in the early 1990s under the managership of the Englishman "Big Jack" Charlton – it's undoubted high point was the 1–0 defeat of Italy during the 1994 World Cup Finals. However, the most popular clubs here (and in the North) are Manchester United and Liverpool. Glasgow Celtic and Rangers are also popular in the North with support following sectarian Catholic and Protestant divisions, respectively.

Uniting two Irish passions, horses and betting, **horse racing** is carried out with a relaxed good humour that you shouldn't miss. Racing is concentrated around the Curragh, a grassy plain in County Kildare (see p.168), where the classic flat-race course of the same name is located, along with Punchestown race course and many of Ireland's famous stud farms. The Irish Grand National is run at Fairyhouse in County Meath on Easter Monday, followed in April by the four-day Irish National Hunt Festival at Punchestown; at the Curragh, the Irish 1000 Guineas and 2000 Guineas are held in May, the Irish Derby in June, the Irish Oaks in July and the Irish St Leger in September. For details of Dublin's race course, Leopardstown, as well as Fairyhouse and Punchestown, see p.167; notable local meetings, such as those at Galway and Listowel, are described throughout the Guide. Just as much fun and more easily accessible is **greyhound racing**. Shelbourne Park (Ⓣ01/668 3502) in Dublin is the most prestigious venue, although there are sixteen tracks across the country. Information on meetings is available from Bord na gCon, the Irish Greyhound Racing Board (Ⓣ01/496 6016).

Cycling is a popular sport in Ireland, exemplified by the large crowds lining the route of the Irish sections of the 1998 Tour de France, a race won in 1987 by one of the country's sporting heroes, Stephen Roche. Another, Sean Kelly, was world number one from 1984 to 1988. On a more mundane level, pedalling is one of the best ways to appreciate the quiet pleasures of the Irish countryside, and bikes are available to rent all over the island, as detailed throughout the Guide. Signposted cycling trails in the Republic include the Beara (see p.374) and Kerry Ways (p.394), and the epic, 365-mile Táin Trail, which links sites associated with the *Táin Bó Cúailnge* saga in a figure-of-eight that stretches from Carlingford in County Louth, via Kells in County Meath, to Rathcroghan in County Roscommon (map guides available from local tourist offices or go to ⓦwww.midlandseastireland.travel.ie). In the North, similar cycling trails, including the Kingfisher route (see p.765) which also stretches into Leitrim and Cavan, come under the umbrella of the UK's ambitious National Cycle Network; for details, contact Sustrans, 89–91 Adelaide St, Belfast BT2 8FE (ⓣ028/9043 4569, ⓦwww.sustrans.co.uk).

There's an enormous number of **golf** courses here too, with major championships like the Irish Open in late June/early July. Both of the Irish tourist boards produce information on where you can play and have details of holiday packages and accommodation. Naturally, as this is an island, there are innumerable opportunities for sea **angling** and hundreds of lakes and rivers for fly- and game-fishing. In general, the best of the sea angling takes place on the south and west coasts and Bord Fáilte can help with information. The high spot of the fly-fishing season is the emergence of the mayfly around mid-May when anglers flock to the best brown-trout spots, such as Lower Lough Erne, County Fermanagh, Lough Derg, County Clare and the Corrib system, County Galway. There are plenty of other possibilities, however, and, again the tourist boards can assist.

The relatively sheltered waters of the east coast see most of the **sailing** activity, especially in Dublin Bay and further south around Arklow and Wexford; other excellent areas include west Cork and on Lough Derg, County Clare. The south and southwest are most popular for cruising, though the Cork coast offers many possibilities for yachting. The rougher waters of the west coast restrict the options to places more protected from the elements, such as Galway Bay or Killybegs, County Donegal. On the north coast, Lough Swilly is increasingly popular, while on the other side of the border, there are numerous boating possibilities on Strangford Lough. For further information contact the Irish Sailing Association (ⓣ01/280 0239). Inland waterways and sheltered coasts also offer **canoeing** and **kayaking** opportunities, ranging from day-trips and touring to rough- and white-water racing; go to ⓦwww.irishcanoeunion.com for advice and a comprehensive list of approved outdoor centres.

There are some fabulous beaches for **wind-surfing** and **surfing**, and their various spin-offs. Some of the best in the Republic are: Barleycove beach, County Cork; Inch Strand and Ventry on the south side of the Dingle Peninsula, County Kerry, and Brandon Bay, near Castlegregory on the north side, which hosts a leg of the wind-surfing world championships every October; Easky, County Sligo; and Bundoran and Rossnowlagh beaches, County Donegal. The Northern Ireland coast between Castlerock, County Derry and Portrush, County Antrim attracts hordes of board fanatics.

Situated in the path of the Gulf Stream, the Irish coast offers fantastic opportunities for **diving**; from protected harbours for beginners, to rocky cliff faces for the more experienced. There are plenty of places where you can learn to dive too. The Irish Underwater Council can provide details of clubs and courses (ⓣ01/284 4601).

The Ulster Way was the first waymarked **walking** trail in Ireland and it's still the longest, running a 560-mile circuit of Northern Ireland and linked to trails from Donegal and Cavan (see p.663, p.666 & p.774. Dozens of similar trails also exist in the Republic, ranging from linear mountain routes, such as the Wicklow Way (see p.151) and the Western Way (p.484), or around entire peninsulas, like the Sheep's Head (p.370), Beara (p.374), Kerry (p.394) and Dingle (p.406) Ways. Although the walks are waymarked, you should get hold of the relevant Ordnance Survey map, whether you're doing the whole or just part of the route. These walks are maintained in the

Walking safely

Though one of the joys of hill- and mountain-walking in Ireland is the sheer solitude of the experience, bear in mind that the lack of other people in your vicinity can be a significant drawback if a mishap occurs. The Irish climate can seem pretty mild, but the temperature drops two to three degrees Celsius for every thousand feet climbed and a strong wind can make it seem even colder. Mist and cloud can suddenly transform your surroundings too, so a pleasant day at sea level can rapidly become perilous higher up. If you're planning any walk, especially on high ground, consider the following:

1. Always plan your route carefully beforehand and ensure, especially, that it can be finished before nightfall. As a rough guideline, average walking speed is around two and a half miles an hour. A map is essential and, if you're unfamiliar with your route, carry a compass too. A torch, small first-aid kit and whistle are useful – the mountain distress signal is six blasts of a whistle per minute, followed by a pause.
2. Check weather forecasts in advance and, no matter the weather when you set out, ensure you have clothing suitable for changes – warm, wind- and water-proof. Walking boots are essential for all but the shortest and easiest of walks.
3. Always carry water and a reserve supply of high-energy food, such as chocolate or trail mix, and in winter, if possible, a hot drink.
4. Walking alone is inadvisable, except in populated areas or where there are plenty of other walkers. Even when walking in a group, it's advisable to let someone (your hostel or B&B for example) know where you're going and when you're likely to return. If you drive to your starting point, a note left visible in your car is another alternative.
5. Exercise caution when walking along cliff-tops – some apparently safe walks can become perilous in high winds. Streams in flood are particularly dangerous too, and bear in mind that most accidents occur on the way back when you're fatigued, especially on descents.
6. Take your mobile phone, if you have one – if an accident does happen and urgent assistance is needed, telephone ⓣ999 and ask for the Mountain Rescue, if you're on high ground, or the local police station.
7. Follow the Farmland Code of Conduct – remember that more often than not you'll be crossing someone's land, so respect the environment and leave everything as you found it, closing gates behind you.

south by the National Waymarked Ways Committee, 21 Fitzwilliam Square, Dublin (ⓣ01/240 7717), who maintain a very useful website, including a handy overview of each route, at ⓦwww.irishwaymarkedways.ie, and local tourist offices and councils have also produced map guides for many of the Ways. Other walking highlights include the ascents of Croagh Patrick in County Mayo (see p.499) and Carrauntoohil, for more experienced walkers, in County Kerry (see p.499 & p.500), and just about anywhere in Connemara (see p.483). Particularly useful walking guides are listed in "Contexts", p.877.

Though Ireland's mountain ranges are not especially high, there are numerous opportunities for **rock-climbing**, especially in counties Cork and Kerry – the latter's Macgillycuddy Reeks make up for their lack of height by spectacular settings. To the east, the Wicklow Mountains are hugely popular, while the craggy splendour and coastal setting of the Mourne Mountains in County Down are hard to beat. The Mountaineering Council of Ireland (ⓣ01/450 7376) publishes a compendious website (ⓦwww.mountaineering.ie), a magazine, *Irish Mountain Log*, and a number of guides.

The number of rare species visiting Ireland makes the country a **birdwatching** paradise. Again, the tourist boards can provide details, but the best contacts are Birdwatch Ireland in the Republic (ⓣ01/280 4322, ⓦwww.birdwatchireland.ie) and in the North the Royal Society for the Protection of Birds (ⓣ028/9049 1547, ⓦwww.rspb.org.uk).

Crime and personal safety

The Republic is one of the safest countries in Europe in which to travel. That said, don't let the friendliness of people as a whole lull you into a general carelessness; like anywhere else visitors are seen as easy targets for petty thieves (particularly in the bigger cities) and women especially should always take note of our advice in the Guide chapters on choosing accommodation. Theft is very common in Dublin and some areas of the city can be unsafe: it's a good idea to take local advice about safety on the streets from your hostel or B&B and in all of the cities to take care at night as you would in any other European country. Although the North has opened up a lot in the last few years, there is still a security presence, and you should be careful in certain city areas. Personal security and crimes against the individual are not a major worry except in certain areas of Dublin and Limerick.

In the Republic people generally have a healthy indifference to law and red tape, perhaps in part a vestige of pre-Independence days, when any dealings with the police smacked of collusion with the British. The **police** – known as **Garda** or Gardaí – accordingly have a low profile. In rural areas the low level of crime is such that policing is minimal and, should you need them, you might spend an entire afternoon waiting for the Garda to arrive. If you have any dealings with the Garda at all, the chances are that you'll find them affable enough. If you are unlucky enough to be a victim of crime you can contact Tourism Victim Support, Garda HQ, Harcourt Square, Dublin 2 (ⓣ01/478 5295). Rape crisis support is available from the Dublin Rape Crisis Centre (freephone ⓣ1800/778 888, ⓦwww.drcc.ie), and they can also direct you to other centres both in the Republic and the North. In the North, the freephone number is ⓣ0800/053 6813.

In the **North** the Police Service of Northern Ireland deals with all general civic policing and are the people you should go to if in difficulty. Police stations are heavily fortified and security inside is tight, but you'll find that police officers are helpful. Security measures have been considerably relaxed during the last few years. Permanent border controls are no longer operative and you will rarely see either a police roadblock or army foot patrol unless travelling through South Armagh and parts of Fermanagh and Tyrone. In the unlikely event that you do find yourself being quizzed about your movements and plans, simply be polite and co-operative and you should experience no problems.

Obviously, politics remains a sensitive subject in the North, and you should use your common sense about what you say to whom.

Emergencies

The emergency numbers in both the North and the Republic are ⓣ999 and 112.

Travellers with disabilities

The disabled traveller in Ireland is not well served, and wheelchair users in particular are likely to find the lack of ramps, lifts and wide doors inconvenient. With this in mind, it is well worth gathering as much information as you can before you travel. In the Republic there's been a move towards dealing with disabilities issues within the mainstream as far as possible: information and advice is provided by Comhairle, the government support agency for social services, though obviously they're more geared up for disabled Irish citizens than for travellers to Ireland. In the North, the Northern Ireland Tourist Board (see p.22) produces a number of useful publications for disabled visitors; the campaign and information group, Disability Action, is again more geared up for the needs of local disabled people, but their *A–Z Guide*, available in printed form or on their website, has plenty of useful contacts.

For **accommodation**, probably the most useful contact is RADAR, which produces an annual guide called *Holidays in Britain and Ireland* for £8 in the UK, £11 to Europe and £15 to other overseas destinations (includes postage); this information is now also available on a dedicated website, Ⓦwww.radarsearch.org, where they plan in the future to cover other holiday services and facilities. The NITB publish a guide to accessible accommodation in the North, while Bord Fáilte's yearly accommodation guides identify the wheelchair-accessible establishments in the Republic.

The main **transport** companies, Iarnród Éireann (Irish Rail) and Bus Éireann in the Republic, and the joint organization, Translink, in the North, have considerably improved their facilities for disabled travellers, with, for example, low-floor city buses and kneeling coaches on many routes. Go to the "About Us" sections of their websites for full details of their accessibility policies and facilities, or get in touch with them about specific routes and services (see "Getting around" pp.31 & 32 for contact details).

Most of the major **ferry companies** offer good reductions to disabled drivers coming from mainland Britain, but generally you need to be a member of the Disabled Drivers Association (DDA) or the Disabled Drivers Motor Club (DDMC); it's well worth enquiring about the reductions in advance as they tend to vary considerably according to season.

Contacts

In Britain and Ireland

All Go Here Ⓣ01923/840463, Ⓦwww.everybody.co.uk. Provides information on accommodation suitable for disabled travellers throughout the UK, including Northern Ireland.

Comhairle Hume House, Dublin 4 Ⓣ01/605 9000, Ⓦwww.comhairle.ie.

Disability Action Portside Business Park, 189 Airport Rd West, Belfast BT3 9EP Ⓣ028/9029 7880, Ⓦwww.disabilityaction.org.

Disabled Drivers Association National Headquarters, Ashwellthorpe, Norwich NR16 1EX Ⓣ01508/489449, Ⓦwww.dda.org.uk.

Disabled Drivers Motor Club Cottingham Way, Thrapston, Northamptonshire NN14 4PL Ⓣ0870/770 3333, Ⓦwww.ddmc.org.uk.

Holiday Care 2nd floor, Imperial Building, Victoria Rd, Horley, Surrey RH6 7PZ Ⓣ01293/774535, textphone Ⓣ01293/776943, Ⓦwww.holidaycare.org.uk. Holds a database of information on all aspects of holidays and travel in the UK and abroad for people with disabilities. Details of financial help for holidays available.

Irish Wheelchair Association Blackheath Drive, Clontarf, Dublin 3 Ⓣ01/818 6400, Ⓦwww.iwa.ie. Wheelchair rental (€30/week) and useful information on accessibility in Ireland.

RADAR (Royal Association for Disability and Rehabilitation) 12 City Forum, 250 City Rd, London EC1V 8AF ⓣ020/7250 3222, minicom ⓣ020/7250 4119, ⓦwww.radar.org.uk. A good source of advice on holidays and travel in the UK and Ireland, with a useful and well-organized website.

Tripscope Alexandra House, Albany Rd, Brentford, Middlesex TW8 0NE ⓣ0845/758 5641, ⓦwww.justmobility.co.uk/tripscope. This registered charity provides a national telephone information service offering free advice on UK and international transport for those with a mobility problem.

In the US and Canada

Access-Able ⓦwww.access-able.com. Online resource for travellers with disabilities.

Directions Unlimited 123 Green Lane, Bedford Hills, NY 10507 ⓣ1-800/533-5343 or 914/241-1700. Travel agency specializing in bookings for people with disabilities.

Mobility International USA 451 Broadway, Eugene, OR 97401 ⓣ541/343-1284, ⓦwww.miusa.org. Information and referral services, access guides, tours and exchange programmes. Annual membership $35 (includes quarterly newsletter).

Society for the Advancement of Travelers with Handicaps (SATH) 347 5th Ave, New York, NY 10016 ⓣ212/447-7284, ⓦwww.sath.org. Nonprofit educational organization that has actively represented travellers with disabilities since 1976.

Wheels Up! ⓣ1-888/389-4335, ⓦwww.wheelsup.com. Provides discounted airfare, tour and cruise prices for disabled travellers, also publishes a free monthly newsletter and has a comprehensive website.

In Australia and New Zealand

ACROD (Australian Council for Rehabilitation of the Disabled) PO Box 60, Curtin ACT 2605; Suite 103, 1st Floor, 1–5 Commercial Rd, Kings Grove 2208; ⓣ02/6282 4333, TTY ⓣ02/6282 4333, ⓦwww.acrod.org.au. Provides lists of travel agencies and tour operators for people with disabilities.

Disabled Persons Assembly 4/173–175 Victoria St, Wellington, New Zealand ⓣ04/801 9100 (also TTY), ⓦwww.dpa.org.nz. Resource centre with lists of travel agencies and tour operators for people with disabilities.

Directory

Children Children are generally liked and indulged in Ireland, even if there are few places actually designed to cater for them. Baby supplies are easily obtained, and children are generally welcome at B&Bs (though few have cots or special facilities), in pubs during the daytime, and almost everywhere else.

Contraceptives Throughout Ireland condoms can now be bought at pharmacies and supermarkets, while the pill is available on prescription only.

Electricity In the Republic electricity is 230V AC, in the North 240V AC. Plugs are British-style three square pins (just occasionally you may still find old round ones). North American appliances will need both a transformer and a plug adapter; Australian and New Zealand appliances only an adapter.

Laundry You'll only find laundries in the bigger towns and on large caravan/campsites. Hostels often have a washing machine for residents' use, and at many B&Bs they'll do your washing for you. Elsewhere it's worth taking along a tube of travel wash – designed to be used in hotel washbasins – which makes a lot less mess than powder.

Time Ireland is in the same time zone as Britain. Clocks are moved forward one hour at the end of March and back again at the end of October for daylight saving.

Tipping Tipping in restaurants in both the Republic and the North is at your discretion; if you are happy with the level of service and the meal, it is customary to leave an additional ten to fifteen percent of the total bill.

Toilets Public toilets are reasonably common in all the big towns, and generally acceptably clean, if no cleaner. Or you can pop into the local pub, and stop for a drink while there. The Irish labels to look out for are *Fir* (Men) and *Mna* (Women).

Work EU citizens are legally allowed to live and work in Ireland and most towns of any size will have a job centre advertising vacancies. Plenty of jobs are available in Dublin for waiting staff, especially in the Temple Bar area. Another option for travellers is seasonal work in resorts or perhaps helping out in a hostel in return for board and pocket money. You'll need to search locally.

Guide

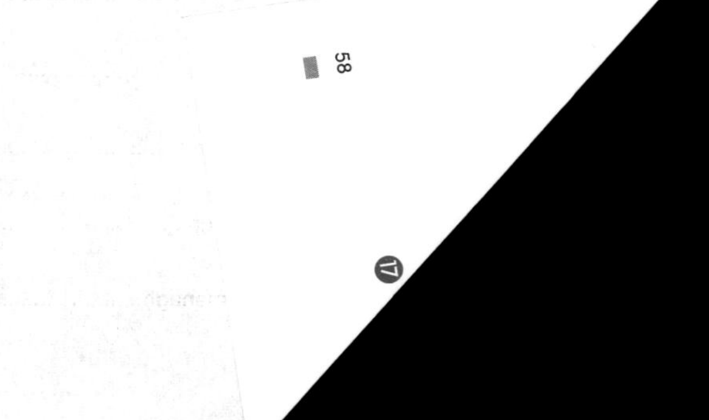

Guide

Dublin

CHAPTER 1 **Highlights**

* **Trinity College** Admire the illuminated Book of Kells and the magnificent Long Room, or just enjoy the architecture. See p.84

* **The National Museum** Stunning prehistoric gold and Christian treasures are the highlights of this well-presented collection. See p.89

* **The National Gallery** A graceful showcase, especially for Irish art and the vibrant Yeats collection. See p.93

* **The Chester Beatty Library** An elegant, world-renowned display of manuscripts, prints and objets d'art. See p.101

* **Kilmainham Gaol** Tour the city's most historic prison and visit the museum for fascinating insights into Republican history. See p.108

* **Bloomsday** Follow Joyce's Dublin novel nonpareil on this annual pilgrimage on June 16. See p.114

* **The Croke Park GAA Museum** The stunning stadium home of Gaelic games also houses one of Ireland's best museums. See p.114

* **The Cobblestone** A Mecca for traditional music fans and an atmospheric pub to boot. See p.132

Dublin

Dubliners are fiercely proud of their city, and while **DUBLIN** is the Republic of Ireland's capital, it is quite apart from, and can be dismissive of, the rest of the country – one Dublin wag once remarked with characteristic caustic humour that "the only culture outside Dublin is agriculture". Yet over the last dozen years or so young people from rural Ireland and all over Europe have gravitated towards the city to share in the wealth engendered by an economic boom not experienced since Dublin's much celebrated Georgian heyday. Dublin exudes the style and confidence of any cosmopolitan European capital – most apparent at night when Dubliners party with a panache verging on the reckless. The city's economic upturn has impacted on the city's rapidly changing urban landscape too, with restaurants, cafés, bars and clubs opening in abundance, and the city's famous pub scene is now matched by an equally celebrated club scene. On the downside, however, its reputation as one of the party capitals of Europe has attracted droves of "alco-tourists" who arrive in the city for booze-fuelled weekends; they have become such a problem that some areas of the city, such as Temple Bar, have actually banned stag and hen parties.

The continual drift of population from the land to the capital has meant that the urban/rural divide has started to wane but it has brought its fair share of problems too as Dublin is now bulging at the seams. Spend just a couple of days here and you'll come upon traffic congestion and inner-city deprivation as bad as any in Europe. The cost of living has risen enormously too and, according to a 2002 survey, Dublin is the third most expensive capital city in the European Union, with housing, food and drink prices especially high. The spirit of the city is also undergoing massive upheavals, with youthful enterprise set against a leaden traditionalism that harks back, as in the words of one popular folk song, to "Dublin city in the rare old times". However, the collision of the old order and the forward-looking younger generations is an essential part of the appeal of this extrovert and dynamic city.

If you approach Dublin by sea, you'll have an opportunity to appreciate its magnificent physical setting, with the fine sweep of **Dublin Bay** and the weird, conical silhouettes of the Wicklow Mountains to the south providing an exhilarating backdrop. Central Dublin is not big, and it's easy to find your way around. One obvious axis is formed by the **River Liffey**, which runs from west to east and acts not only as a physical, but also a social and, at times, psychological dividing line. The **northside**, distinctly working class, with some areas blighted by unemployment and drugs, stands in stark contrast to the affluent neighbourhoods of the **southside**.

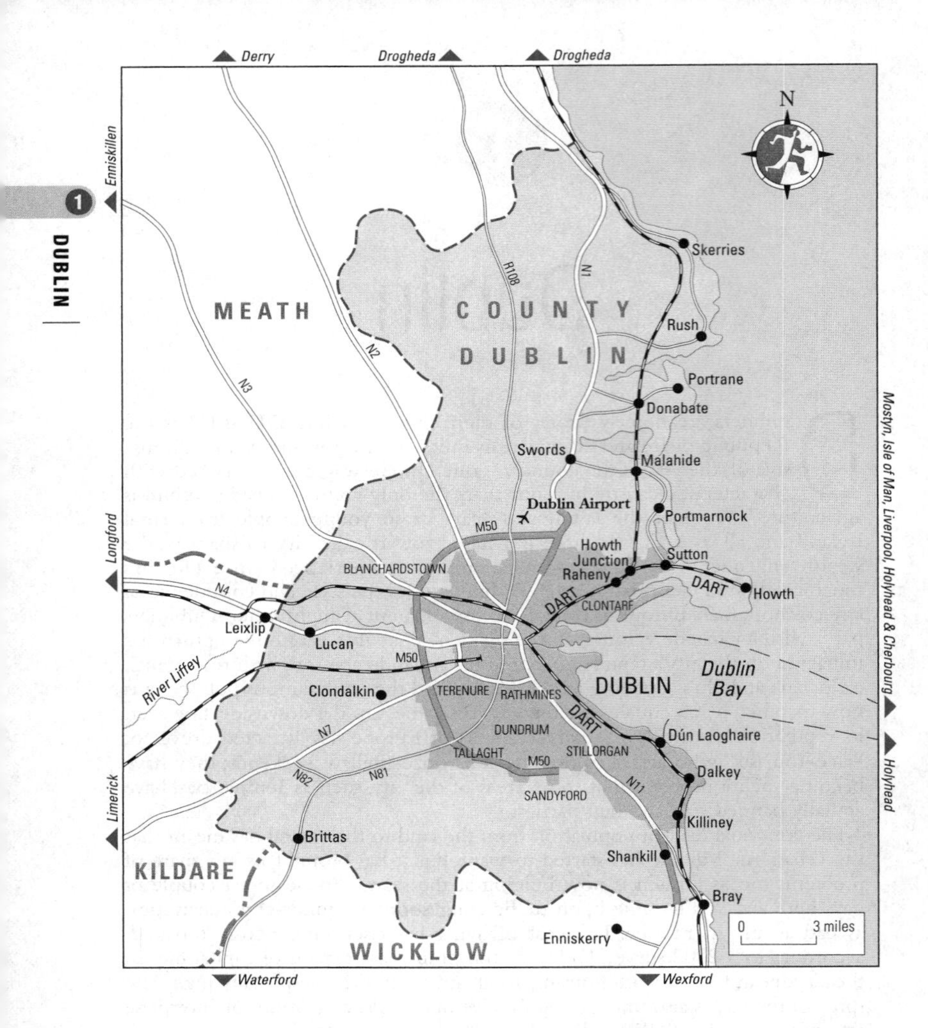

The transformation to the top of Europe's financial league has cast the city economically and culturally into the heart of the continent. This new-found cosmopolitan chic has its home in the vibrant **Temple Bar** area, "Dublin's Left Bank", with its numerous pubs, clubs, galleries and restaurants. However, for many visitors, the city's heart lies around the best of what is left of Georgian Dublin – the grand set pieces of **Fitzwilliam** and **Merrion** squares, and their graceful red-brick houses with ornate, fan-lit doors and immaculately kept central gardens, and the wide and decorous open space of St Stephen's Green. The elegant southside is also the setting for Dublin's august seat of learning, Trinity College and its famous library where you can see the exquisitely ornate *Book of Kells*; **Grafton Street**, the city's upmarket shopping area; and most of the city's museums and art galleries.

North of the Liffey, the main thoroughfare is **O'Connell Street**, on which stands the **General Post Office**, the scene of violent fighting in the Easter Rising of 1916. Further north, among Georgian squares older and seedier than the ones you'll see on the southside, are the **Dublin Writers' Museum** and the **Hugh Lane Municipal Art Gallery**. Heading west, you come to Dublin's biggest open space – indeed, one of the world's largest city parks – **Phoenix Park**, home of both the President's Residence and the zoo.

The urban sprawl quickly gives way to the genteel villages which punctuate the curve of Dublin Bay, from the fishing port of **Howth** in the north, to the southern suburbs of **Sandycove** with its James Joyce connections, **Dalkey**, made famous by the comic writer Flann O'Brien, and salubrious **Killiney**, now colonized by the rich and famous. Added to this is the fact that Dublin must be one of the easiest capitals to escape from, making it a good base for exploring the hills and coastline of Wicklow to the south and the gentler scenery to the north that leads up to the megalithic monuments of the verdant Boyne valley (see p.199).

Some history

Fort of the Dane
Garrison of the Saxon
Augustan capital
Of a Gaelic nation

Louis MacNeice
from *The Closing Album*, 1939

Although the earliest evidence of a settlement beside the Liffey is on Ptolemy's celebrated world map of 140 AD, which shows a place called Eblana on the site of modern Dublin, it is as a **Viking settlement** that Dublin's history really begins. The Norse raiders sailed up the Liffey and, destroying a small Celtic township, set up a trading post on the south bank of the river at the ford where the royal road from the Hill of Tara in the north crossed the Liffey on its way to Wicklow. The Vikings adopted the Irish name, Dubh Linn ("dark pool"), for their settlement, which soon amalgamated with another Celtic settlement, Baile Átha Cliath ("town of the hurdles", pronounced "ballya-aw-kleea", and still the Irish name for Dublin), on the north bank.

The next wave of invaders were the **Anglo-Normans**. In the twelfth century the beleaguered King of Leinster Dermot McMurrough requested help from Henry II to regain his throne lost in a power-struggle with the High King Rory O'Connor. In return for an oath of fealty, Henry dispatched the opportunistic Strongbow and a band of Welsh knights, who conquered Dublin, but, fearing they would become too powerful, Henry fixed a court there. The city was thereby established as the centre of British influence in Ireland and was the setting for the annual social and political gathering, known as the Seasons, which was to shape Dublin's role and character for the next seven centuries.

Because most of the early city was built of wood, only the two cathedrals, part of Dublin Castle, and one or two churches have survived from before the seventeenth century. What you see today, in both plan and buildings, dates essentially from the **Georgian period**. By this time, soldiers in the service of the English monarchs, who had been rewarded with confiscated land, had begun to derive income from their new estates. As they began to replace their original fortified houses with something more fashionable, they wished also to participate in the country's burgeoning economic and political life, which was centred on Dublin. Their town houses (along with those of the growing business and professional classes), and the grandeur of the public buildings erected during this period, embodied the new confidence of the **British ruling class**. However, this was a group that was starting to regard itself not as British, but as Irish.

In the second half of the eighteenth century, the wealth of this Anglo-Irish class was reflected in a **rich cultural life**; Handel's *Messiah*, for instance, was first performed in Ireland, while much of the architecture, furniture and silverware associated with the city dates from this period. Growing political freedom was to culminate in the parliament of 1782 in which Henry Grattan made a famous **Declaration of Rights**, modelled on the recent American example, which came very close to declaring Irish (by which he meant Protestant Anglo-Irish) Independence. A severely limited and precarious enterprise, the Irish bid for self-government was soon to collapse, with the abortive **1798 Rebellion** and the **Act of Union** which followed in 1801.

The Act of Union may have shorn Dublin of its independent political power, but the city remained the centre of British administration, in the shape of the vice-regent, and the Seasons continued to revolve around the Viceroy's Lodge (now the President's Residence) in Phoenix Park. Along with the rest of Ireland, Dublin entered a long **economic decline** and became the stage for much of the agitation that eventually led to Independence. The first step towards self-government came in 1829, when the Catholic lawyer (and Kerryman) Daniel O'Connell achieved limited Catholic emancipation, allowing Catholics to play some part in the administration and politics of their capital city and, in a signal victory, was elected Lord Mayor of Dublin. The city was also the centre of the **Gaelic League**, founded by Douglas Hyde in 1893, which encouraged the formation of an Irish national consciousness through efforts to restore the native language and culture. This paved the way for the **Celtic literary revival** under W.B. Yeats and Lady Gregory, and the establishment, in 1904, of the Abbey Theatre.

While political violence in nineteenth-century Dublin revolved around the Independence issue, it was social politics, most especially the fight for the establishment of trade unionism, that resulted, at the turn of the century, in Dubliners taking to the streets in protest. In 1913, this came to a head in the **Great Lock-Out**, when unemployed workers and their families died of hunger and cold. Open violence hit the streets during Easter Week of **1916** in the uprising that was the main event in the long struggle for Irish Independence. The prominent battles were fought in and around the centre of Dublin, and the insurgents made the General Post Office their headquarters (see p.110). The city's streets were once again the scene of violence during the brief **civil war** that broke out after the creation of the Irish Free State in 1921, when supporters and opponents of the **partition** of Ireland fought it out across the Liffey, and the Four Courts, one of Dublin's great Georgian buildings, went up in flames after being seized by opponents of the Anglo-Irish Treaty.

Since Independence, Dublin has been the capital of an old country yet a young nation, endeavouring to leave behind its colonial past. It's to this, as well as the appalling condition of many of the old tenements, that the destruction of much of the Georgian city can be attributed. A corollary of the demolition of the city's Georgian buildings in the 1960s was the decanting of Dubliners to inadequately planned suburban estates, which today are blighted by some of the worst social conditions in Europe. Since the mid-1980s, city planners have aimed to reverse this trend of inner-city depopulation, with new apartment blocks being built in previously run-down areas to cater for the city's burgeoning and increasingly affluent middle classes.

One of the outstanding architectural successes of recent years has been the **redevelopment** of the Temple Bar area, which has done much to enhance the image and atmosphere of the city. Indeed, Dublin now has a new feel to it, a sense that the legacy of its colonial relationship with Britain has finally been put to one side, as the capital, along with the rest of the Republic, looks increasingly to Europe and America rather than across the Irish Sea.

Arrival

Dublin's main **points of arrival** are all within easy reach of the city centre, with the bulk of tourist traffic entering either via the airport, 7 miles to the north, or the ferry terminals at Dublin Port, 2 miles east, and Dún Laoghaire, 9 miles south.

By air

Dublin Airport arrivals hall has a **tourist office** (daily: July & Aug 8am–10.30pm; Sept–June 8am–10pm), a bureau de change (open for arrivals and departures), various car-rental desks and an ATM. For airport information call ⓣ01/704 4222.

Buses into town leave from outside the arrivals exit. The cheapest choice (€1.65 single) is to catch the regular #16A bus to O'Connell Street or a #41, #41A, #41B or #41C bus to Eden Quay, near O'Connell Bridge (every 15–30min). Airlink buses #747 and #748 (Mon–Sat 5.45am–11.30pm every 10min, Sun 7.15am–11.30pm every 15–20min; €4.50 single, €7.50 return) to Busáras (the central bus station) go via Connolly Station, with some continuing on to Heuston Station, twenty minutes further along. Tickets can either be purchased at the CIÉ travel information desk in the arrivals hall or on board the bus, though you'll need the exact fare for the latter. Alternatively, the privately run Aircoach serves the main shopping areas and hotels (Mon–Sat 5.30am–11.30pm, Sun 6.30am–11.30pm every 15min; €5 single). If you're heading straight to accommodation that's near a DART (see p.71) station, a further option is to take Aerdart bus #A1 (Mon-Fri 5.45am–11.45pm, Sat & Sun 6.30am–11.45pm every 15min; €4.50 single), which connects with the DART rail service at Howth Junction. A **taxi** into the centre from the rank outside the arrivals exit should cost about €25, but can be much dearer during rush hour; cars are there to meet all incoming flights but be prepared to queue at peak times.

By bus

Dublin's main bus station, **Busáras**, is located on Store Street, and is within ten minutes' walk of O'Connell Street. Bus Éireann services from all parts of the Republic and Northern Ireland arrive here (timetable enquiries ⓣ01/836 6111), along with Airlink buses and coaches from Britain. City buses into the centre pass along Talbot Street, a block to the north and taxis can usually be hailed on Beresford Place, just to the south of the bus station. Busáras has a **bureau de change** (daily 8.45am–2.30pm & 3.30–7pm) and a **left-luggage** facility (Mon–Sat 8am–7.45pm, Sun 10am–5.45pm; €3.40).

For information on leaving the city see box on p.140

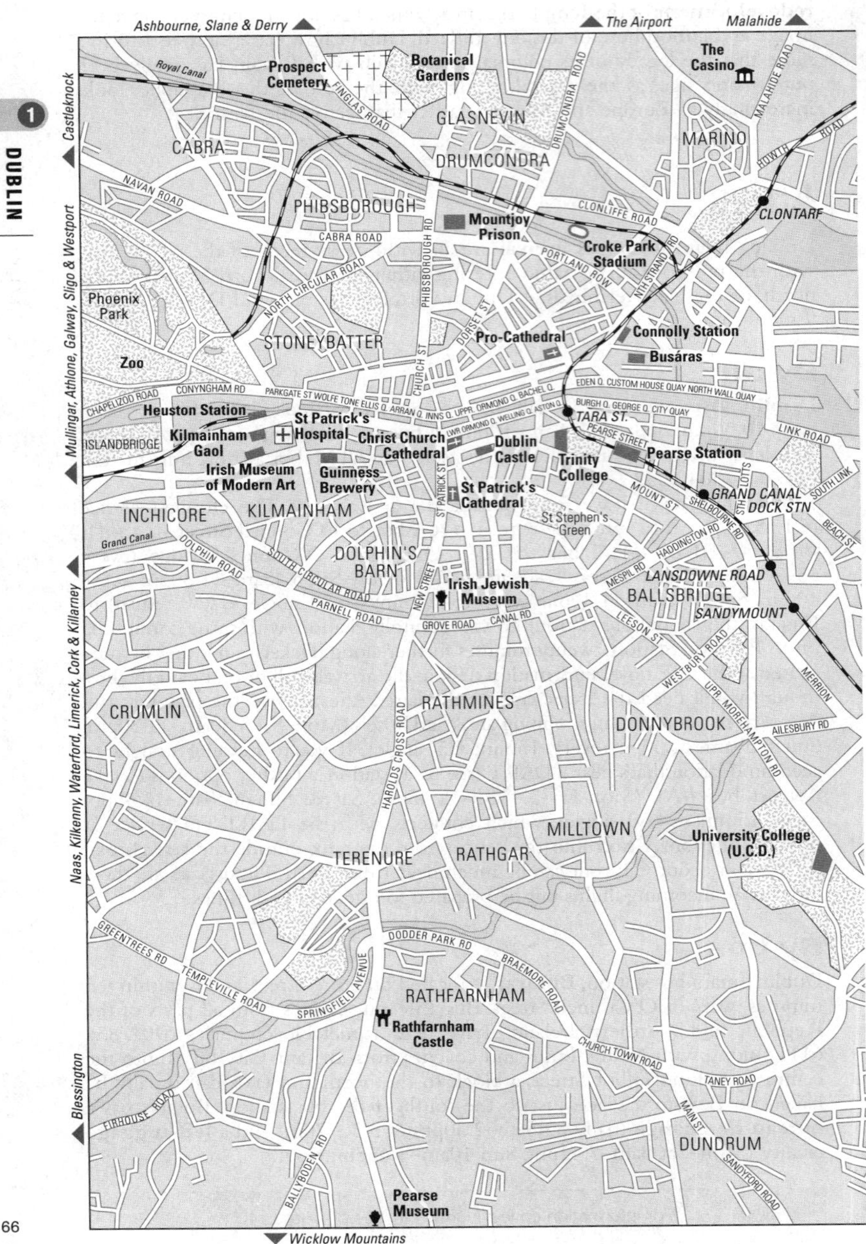
Ashbourne, Slane & Derry
The Airport
Malahide
Castleknock
Mullingar, Athlone, Galway, Sligo & Westport
Naas, Kilkenny, Waterford, Limerick, Cork & Killarney
Blessington
Wicklow Mountains
Royal Canal
Prospect Cemetery
Botanical Gardens
FINGLAS ROAD
GLASNEVIN
DRUMCONDRA ROAD
The Casino
MALAHIDE ROAD
MARINO
HOWTH ROAD
CABRA
DRUMCONDRA
NAVAN ROAD
PHIBSBOROUGH
Mountjoy Prison
CLONLIFFE ROAD
CLONTARF
CABRA ROAD
Croke Park Stadium
PORTLAND ROW
NTH STRAND RD
NORTH CIRCULAR ROAD
PHIBSBOROUGH RD
Phoenix Park
DORSET ST
Pro-Cathedral
Connolly Station
STONEYBATTER
Busáras
Zoo
CHURCH ST
EDEN Q. CUSTOM HOUSE QUAY NORTH WALL QUAY
CHAPELIZOD ROAD
CONYNGHAM RD
PARKGATE ST WOLFE TONE ELLIS Q. ARRAN Q. INNS Q. UPPR. ORMOND Q. BACHEL Q.
BURGH Q. GEORGE Q. CITY QUAY
Heuston Station
St Patrick's Hospital
LWR ORMOND Q. WELLING Q. ASTON Q.
TARA ST.
LINK ROAD
Kilmainham Gaol
Christ Church Cathedral
Dublin Castle
PEARSE STREET
ISLANDBRIDGE
Pearse Station
Irish Museum of Modern Art
Guinness Brewery
Trinity College
ST PATRICK ST
St Patrick's Cathedral
SOUTH LOTTS
GRAND CANAL DOCK STN
SOUTH LINK
INCHICORE
KILMAINHAM
MOUNT ST
SHELBOURNE RD
St Stephen's Green
BEACH ST
Grand Canal
DOLPHIN ROAD
DOLPHIN'S BARN
HADDINGTON RD
SOUTH CIRCULAR ROAD
NEW STREET
MESPIL RD
LANSDOWNE ROAD
Irish Jewish Museum
BALLSBRIDGE
PARNELL ROAD
SANDYMOUNT
GROVE ROAD
CANAL RD
LEESON ST
WESTBURY ROAD
MERRION
UPR. MOREHAMPTON RD
RATHMINES
CRUMLIN
HAROLDS CROSS ROAD
DONNYBROOK
AILESBURY RD
MILLTOWN
University College (U.C.D.)
TERENURE
RATHGAR
GREENTREES RD
DODDER PARK RD
BRAEMORE ROAD
TEMPLEVILLE ROAD
SPRINGFIELD AVENUE
RATHFARNHAM
Rathfarnham Castle
CHURCH TOWN ROAD
TANEY ROAD
FIRHOUSE ROAD
MAIN ST
DUNDRUM
BALLYBODEN RD
SANDYFORD ROAD
Pearse Museum

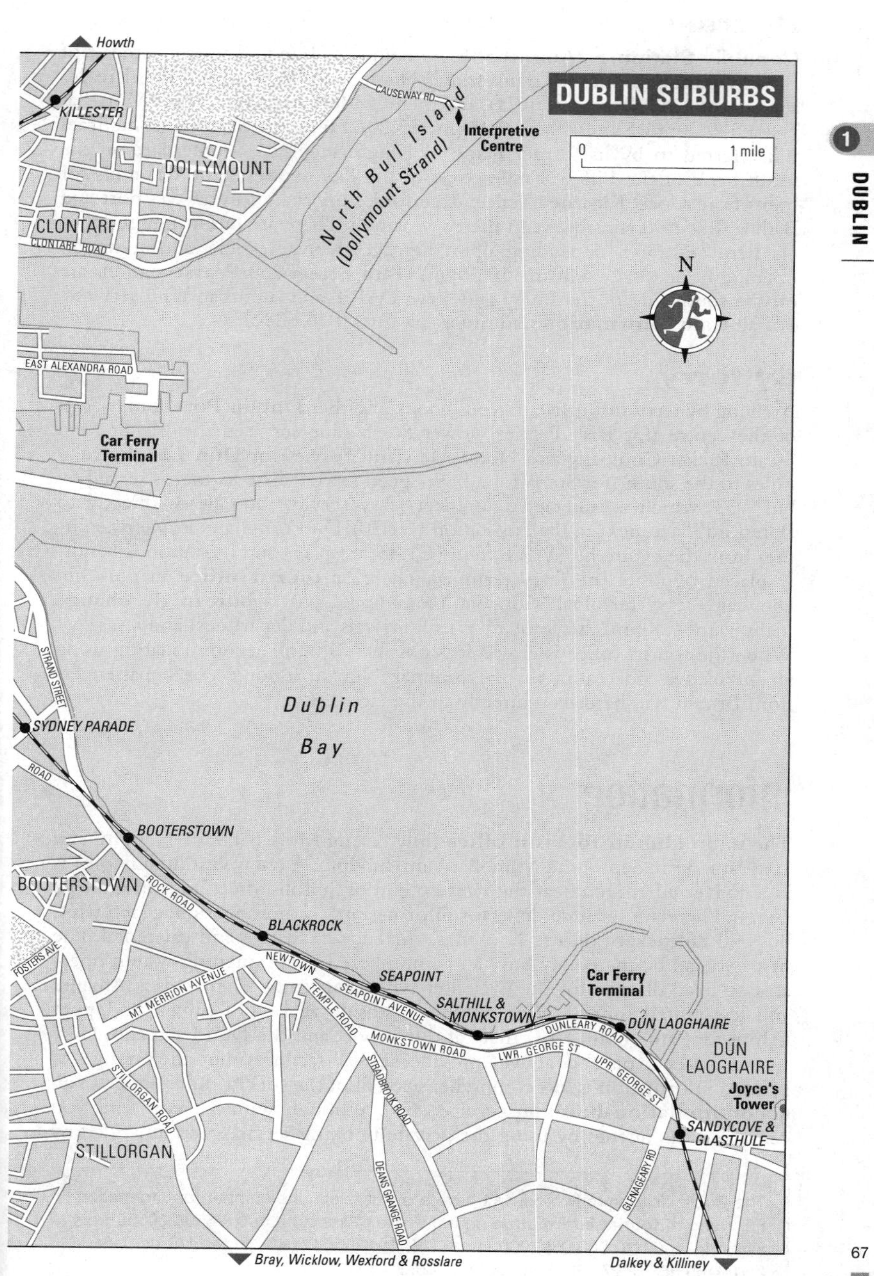

DUBLIN SUBURBS
0
1 mile
N
Howth
KILLESTER
CAUSEWAY RD
North Bull Island
(Dollymount Strand)
Interpretive Centre
DOLLYMOUNT
CLONTARF
CLONTARF ROAD
EAST ALEXANDRA ROAD
Car Ferry Terminal
STRAND STREET
SYDNEY PARADE
Dublin Bay
ROAD
BOOTERSTOWN
BOOTERSTOWN
ROCK ROAD
BLACKROCK
FOSTERS AVE
NEWTOWN
MT MERRION AVENUE
SEAPOINT
TEMPLE ROAD
SEAPOINT AVENUE
SALTHILL & MONKSTOWN
Car Ferry Terminal
DÚN LAOGHAIRE
DUNLEARY ROAD
MONKSTOWN ROAD
LWR. GEORGE ST
UPR. GEORGE ST
DÚN LAOGHAIRE
Joyce's Tower
STILLORGAN ROAD
STRADBROOK ROAD
SANDYCOVE & GLASTHULE
STILLORGAN
GLENAGEARY RD
DEANS GRANGE ROAD
Bray, Wicklow, Wexford & Rosslare
Dalkey & Killiney

By train

Connolly Station, on Amiens Street, a couple of hundred yards northeast of Busáras, is the terminus for trains from Belfast, Sligo, Wexford and Rosslare. It's also on the DART line (see p.71), and there is a **left-luggage** office (Mon–Sat 7.40am–9.20pm, Sun 9.10am–9.45pm; €3.20). **Heuston Station** (sometimes still referred to by its former name of Kingsbridge), its counterpart on the south bank of the Liffey, 2 miles west of the city centre, is the terminus for trains from Cork, Killarney, Tralee, Waterford, Limerick, Galway, Westport and Ballina. Bus #90 runs between the two termini. There are **left-luggage** lockers here (€1.50–5 depending upon luggage size) accessible during station opening hours (daily 6.30am–10.30pm). **Tara Street** and **Pearse** stations are on the south side of the Liffey and serve DART and suburban train services. For all **train information** and times call ⓣ01/836 6222.

By ferry

Arriving by ferry from Britain, you'll dock at either **Dublin Port**, 2 miles east of the centre (for Irish Ferries, slower Stena Line services, the Isle of Man Steam Packet Company and Norse Merchant Ferries) or **Dún Laoghaire**, 9 miles to the south (for Stena Line high-speed ferries). The former is served by bus #53, which is timetabled to meet ferry services and heads directly to Beresford Place, next to the bus station (€1.30). Dún Laoghaire is twenty minutes from the centre by DART train (€1.45; see p.71) and its station is handily placed opposite the ferry terminal. There's a **tourist office** in the Dún Laoghaire ferry terminal Mon–Sat 10am–6pm), plus a **bureau de change** (daily 9am–4.30pm, also for earlier/later arrivals and departures) and an ATM. When the tourist office is closed it is possible to book accommodation using an interactive video unit in the terminal. Note that some coach passengers from Britain will be driven directly to the city centre.

Information

The **main Dublin Tourism office** (July & Aug Mon–Sat 9am–6.30pm, Sun 10.30am–3pm; Sept–June Mon–Sat 9am–5.30pm; ⓦwww.visitdublin.com) is in a converted church near the western end of Suffolk Street, just off College Green. There are separate desks for information, accommodation, coach trips, bus and rail tickets, theatre bookings, currency exchange and car rental. The first two can be incredibly busy and a numbered ticket queuing system operates, so head directly for the dispenser when you enter. There's also a smaller and less-visited tourist office on the northside at 14 O'Connell St Upper (Mon–Sat 9am–5pm). The offices at the airport and the Dún Laoghaire ferry terminal (see p.65 and above) provide similar facilities, but their range of printed information is less comprehensive. All of the tourist offices operate an **accommodation-booking** service (€3), although with a credit card you can avoid the queues by using the private booking service recommended by

> The Dublin Tourism office doesn't have a direct telephone number for information. For **general tourist information** on the whole of Ireland ring ⓣ1850/230330 from within Ireland, ⓣ0800/0397000 in the UK, ⓣ1800/2236400 in the US or Canada and ⓣ00 353 6697 92083 from other countries.

Bord Fáilte for the same price (Ⓣ1800/6686 6866; also available from many countries outside Ireland – use the international access code and substitute your own national freephone code for 1800 – from the UK call Ⓣ00 800/6686 6866, from the US call Ⓣ011 800/6686 6866 or Ⓣ00 353/6697 92082). If you're heading to the North, there's an excellent branch of the **Northern Ireland Tourist Board** at 16 Nassau St (Mon–Fri 9am–5.30pm, Sat 10am–5pm; Ⓣ1850/230230, Ⓦwww.discovernorthernireland.com).

A downtown alternative to Dublin Tourism is the **USITNow** discount student travel agency on Aston Quay, opposite O'Connell Bridge (Mon–Wed & Fri 9.30am–6.30pm, Thurs 9.30am–8pm, Sat 9.30am–5pm; Ⓣ01/602 1600, Ⓦwww.usitnow.ie). USITNow can book you a B&B during the summer, and runs its own hotel and hostel; like the tourist centre it can get busy and operates a ticket waiting system. Their notice board is useful if you're looking for work or a flat-share, and there are flyers for hostels, clubs and other points of interest.

A good way to get up-to-the-minute local information is to pick up a copy of *The Event Guide* (Ⓦwww.eventguide.ie), a freesheet which provides concise **listings** of gigs, clubs, exhibitions and tourist sites; it's available from the tourism offices and various bars, cafés and shops around the city. The other major listings guides are *In Dublin* (€2.48), available at most newsagents, with lots of information on clubs and style, and a listings section that also covers exhibitions and theatre, and *Hot Press* (€3.17), Ireland's recently revamped rock, politics and style magazine, which is the best place to find music listings. All three are published fortnightly. Daily cinema and theatre listings appear in the *Irish Times* and the *Evening Herald*.

Bus and walking tours

If you're only in Dublin for a short time or just want a quick feel for the city's landmarks, you could take one of the many **city tours** on offer. We've quoted adult prices below, but most of the operators give discounts to children, senior citizens or students. Tickets can be purchased at the beginning of the tour or in advance at any Dublin Tourism office.

Open-top bus tours

These guided bus tours all cover almost exactly the same routes, operating as hop-on-hop-off services with stops at or near all the main sites, including Parnell Square, Trinity College, St Stephen's Green, Dublin Castle, the cathedrals, the Guinness Storehouse, the Museum of Modern Art, Phoenix Park and Collins Barracks.

Dublin Bus Ⓣ01/873 4222, Ⓦwww.dublinbus.ie. A daily guided "Dublin City Tour" with commentary, which commences outside the company office on O'Connell Street Upper. Tours run every fifteen minutes from 9.30am until 4.30pm, then half-hourly until 6.30pm. Tickets (€10) are valid all day and include discounts to attractions.

Guide Friday Ⓣ01/676 5377, Ⓦwww.guidefriday.com. A "Discover Dublin" guided tour with commentary, which runs from outside the Dublin Tourism office on O'Connell Street Upper every ten minutes from 9.30am until 5.30pm between May and September, with reduced frequency and earlier finishing times during the rest of the year. The route doesn't include the Irish Museum of Modern Art. Tickets (€12) are valid all day and include discounts to attractions and a reduction of €2 on the company's tours to sites outside Dublin.

Irish City Tours Ⓣ01/872 9010, Ⓦwww.irishcitytours.com. Operates from outside 12 O'Connell St Upper. Between mid-July and the end of September, tours run every ten minutes from 9.30am to 5.30pm. From April until mid-July and in October, frequency is every fifteen minutes between 9.30am and 5pm; between November and March, services stop at 4pm. Tickets (€12) are valid for 24 hours and give discounts to certain attractions.

Land and water tours

If you're travelling with children, **Viking Splash Tours** (Ⓣ01/855 3000, Ⓦwww.vikingsplashtours.com) offer the most innovative and enjoyable tour option, aboard reconditioned World War II amphibious vehicles known as "Ducks", which take you on a road-tour around the city's major sites before splashing into the water at the Grand Canal Harbour and heading for home; the complete tour lasts one hour and a quarter. Ten tours depart daily (Feb–Nov; call for details) from Bull Alley, next to St Patrick's Cathedral; tickets (€13.50) are available adjacent to the departure point at 64–65 Patrick Street and you can also reserve over the phone with a credit card.

Walking tours

Conducted by graduates from Trinity College, the excursions on offer from **Historical Walking Tours** (Ⓣ01/878 0227, Ⓦwww.historicalinsights.ie) bring history alive, with well-chosen locations and witty insights into not only Dublin but Ireland's history. Tours start at the College front gate (May–Sept daily 11am & 3pm, plus Sat & Sun noon; Oct–April Fri–Sun noon), and tickets for the two-hour tour cost €10.

The **Literary Pub Crawl** (Ⓣ01/670 5602, Ⓦwww.dublinpubcrawl.com), tours Dublin boozers with literary connections, using professional actors to perform extracts from some of Ireland's greatest works. It's a great way to spend an evening, elevated by poetry and pints, and there's a literary quiz to test your memory. Starts upstairs at *The Duke* on Duke Street (April–Oct Mon–Sat 7.30pm, Sun noon & 7.30pm; Nov–March Thurs–Sat 7.30pm, Sun noon & 7.30pm). Tickets for the two-and-a-quarter-hour tour cost €10.

Another evening roam through Dublin's pubs, the **Musical Pub Crawl** (Ⓣ01/478 0193, Ⓦwww.musicalpubcrawl.com), features two musicians recounting the story of traditional Irish music by performing songs and tunes while visiting half a dozen bars in the vicinity of Temple Bar. It's fun and informative, though as the musicians move with the party you are left in doubt as to the point of changing pubs at all. Tours, which last two and a half hours, start upstairs at *Oliver St John Gogarty's* in Temple Bar (May–Oct daily 7.30pm; Nov & Feb–April Fri & Sat 7.30pm); arrive early to be sure of a ticket (€9).

The **1916 Rebellion Walking Tour** (Ⓣ01/676 2493, Ⓦwww.1916rising.com) offers an expert and insightful two-hour stroll around some of the sites associated with the uprising, the guides recounting the events of the week which led up to the fateful Easter Sunday. Tours (mid-April to mid-Oct Mon–Sat 11.30am & 2pm, Sun 1pm) commence at *The International Bar* on Wicklow Street, and last approximately two hours; tickets €10.

City transport

It's customary to say that the way to get to know Dublin is to walk and the city's size makes this a practical possibility, but roaming the streets can quickly become a tiring slog. Luckily there's an extensive and reasonably priced local **bus network** that makes it easy to hop on a bus whenever you want. Buses start running between 6am and 6.30am, and the last city-centre buses leave town around 11.30pm. The minimum fare on the daytime bus system is €0.75, rising to a maximum of €1.65, and since all buses are "exact fare only" it's worth carrying a lot of change (the driver will issue you with a ticket in lieu of change, which you can redeem at the Dublin Bus office). If you don't know which stop to go to in the first place, either ask a bus inspector – there usually seems to be one around, dispensing directions – or invest in a bus timetable, which includes a **Dublin bus map**, for €2.50 from Dublin Bus, 59 O'Connell St Upper (Mon–Fri 8.30am–5.30pm, Sat 9am–1pm; ⓣ01/873 4222); you can also obtain a free bus map of the city centre and individual route timetables here. Finding your way around the bus system can be confusing, although most stops have timetables and routes for the buses that stop there.

A one-day Rambler bus-only pass costs €4.50, and three-day (€8.80), five-day (€13.90) and seven-day (€16.50) passes are also available. If you're not using buses every day, the best bet is a Rambler Handy Pack (€14) containing five individual one-day passes. A one-day bus-and-rail pass (including suburban services and the DART) costs €7.20; a three-day version is better value still at €13.30. Passes are available from the Dublin Bus office and most newsagents . After 11.30pm the Nitelink service comes into operation with buses running out to the suburbs from Westmoreland Street, D'Olier Street and College Green (Mon–Wed 12.30am & 2am, Thurs–Sat every 20min from 12.30–4.30am). Tickets on most routes cost €4 or €6 for some of the longer routes. Note that travel passes are not valid on Nitelink services and that there is no service on Sundays, so if you're out late on a Saturday night, you may need a taxi (see below). Dublin Bus also runs **city tours** and cheap **trips** outside Dublin to places the regular services don't visit, so it's worth enquiring about these.

The other useful city transport service is the **DART**, the Dublin Area Rapid Transport system (ⓣ01/703 3523), which links Howth to the north of the city with Bray to the south in County Wicklow, via such places as Sandycove, Monkstown and Dún Laoghaire. DART services are quick, efficient and easy to use, and the stretch that runs along Dublin Bay from Dalkey to Killiney gives you such an amazing view that it's worth taking the train just for that. It's not expensive – the maximum single fare is €2.95 – but if you're considering taking more than one or two trips, it's worth buying a travel pass. The DART runs from Monday to Saturday 6.30am to 11.20pm and on Sundays from 9.20am to 11.30pm and is accessible to wheelchair users, though in some stations there is a pronounced gap between the platform and the coach.

Because most public transport stops before midnight, Dubliners are forced to rely on an oversubscribed **taxi** service. Limited deregulation has helped alleviate the problem, but long post-midnight lines at designated ranks remain a frustrating feature of the city's night scene. The best-served city-centre ranks are situated opposite the St Stephen's Green Shopping Centre, Dame Street (opposite the main gate of Trinity College), Abbey Street Lower (on the right-hand side going up O'Connell Street from the bridge) and outside *The Gresham* hotel on O'Connell Street Upper, or close to *Jurys and The Towers* hotel in Ballsbridge. You can also book taxis by phone: some of the more reliable firms include ABC Taxis (ⓣ01/285 5444), Checker Cabs (ⓣ01/834 3434), Eurocabs (ⓣ01/872 2222) and Metro Cabs (ⓣ01/668 3333). If you know you'll need a taxi after 11pm it's worth booking one.

If you're brave enough to face the often hair-raising habits of Dublin drivers, a **bike** can prove a useful way of getting around, though the cost of insurance has cut down the number of companies renting them out. Cycle Ways, 185 Parnell St (ⓣ01/837 4748), charges €20 per day and €80 for a week's rental.

Accommodation

As Dublin's popularity as a tourist destination increases, so too does the variety and quality of **accommodation** offered in the city. New hotels and hostels continue to appear in both the centre and previously unfashionable areas.

Generally, prices are cheaper on the northside and anywhere out of the centre. **Hotels** in Dublin are mostly expensive and sometimes no more comfortable than good guesthouses, but if you're travelling out of season, it's worth checking reductions, which can be considerable. Also, many swanky hotels drop their tariffs at the weekends when the business types have gone home. **B&Bs** are plentiful and of a high standard in the suburbs, but central B&Bs can be overpriced. If you're determined to be right at the heart of the action, and you are on a fairly limited budget, various well-organized official and private **hostels** are the cheapest option; most have some private rooms. Dublin Tourism's main office in Suffolk Street (see p.68) has lists of most places that are available, though there are many good options that, for various reasons, neither have nor want tourist-board recommendation. In summer it is highly advisable to book ahead, and imperative to do so on weekends. There are also a couple of **campsites** on the outskirts of Dublin.

Hotels and B&Bs

Dublin's **hotels** are on the whole rather pricey, but if you are looking for luxury, Georgian elegance and good food, there are many to choose from, especially in Temple Bar and in the vicinity of St Stephen's Green. **B&Bs** abound in Dublin, with the cheapest central options clustered around Connolly Station, especially on Gardiner Street, on the northside. While this area has the advantage of proximity to the centre, it is prone to car theft and it's worth considering whether or not secure car parking is available. The tree-lined Victorian suburbs of Clontarf, Drumcondra and Glasnevin to the north of the centre are reasonable places to stay and only a short bus hop from the action, or you might consider the seaside setting of Howth further north. In the south there are more salubrious, and more expensive, guesthouses in the Ballsbridge area, though nearby Sandymount has cheaper options, still within easy walking distance of the centre or a short bus ride away. Further south, there are some excellent options along the coast at Dún Laoghaire, Dalkey and Killiney. The best balance between price and quality generally involves staying further out in the suburbs, given the relatively small scale of the city and the excellent bus service.

The City Centre

Temple Bar and around

Adams Trinity 28 Dame Lane ⓣ01/670 7100, ⓔadamshtl@indigo.ie. A small and welcoming hotel tucked behind Dame Street with comfortable rooms equipped with Victorian reproduction furniture and double-glazed windows. Breakfast is served in a gallery overlooking the bar, but there is no private lounge. The hotel offers good weekend reductions, especially on its triple rooms, which can be ideal for families. Closed Dec 24–27. ❻

Bewley's Principal 19–20 Fleet St ⓣ01/670 8122, ⓦwww.bewleysprincipalhotel.com. Cosy, friendly and recently refurbished three-star hotel next to the excellent Palace Bar on the edges of Temple Bar. There's a comfortable lounge and breakfast is served in a gallery overlooking the café below. Some rooms have air-conditioning and secure parking is available nearby. Closed Dec 23–27. ❼

Central Hotel 1–5 Exchequer St ⓣ01/679 7302, ⓦwww.centralhotel.ie. This refurbished nineteenth-century establishment (part of the Best Western group) is located amongst the red-brick buildings of Victorian Exchequer Street and makes

△ James Joyce Statue

a perfect base for exploring the city. Bright colours throughout give the hotel a cheery feel. A pleasant lounge features contemporary Irish paintings. Of the two fine bars, *The Library* is popular with locals seeking a sanctuary from the increasingly hectic streets outside. ❼

The Clarence 6–8 Wellington Quay ⓣ01/407 0800, ⓦwww.theclarence.ie. Originally opened in 1852, and now owned by U2, *The Clarence* was once renowned as a popular clerical hangout. Its ultra-stylish rooms and penthouse suites are now more likely to provide temporary home to rock stars. Rooms feature Egyptian linen, candles and video recorders. Rates do not include breakfast, but food is available from the award-winning *Tea Rooms* restaurant. ❾

Harding Hotel Copper Alley, Fishamble St ⓣ01/679 6500, ⓦwww.hardinghotel.ie. Attractive two-star USITNow hotel facing Christ Church Cathedral which offers a good-value flat rate of €92 for its twin, double and triple rooms, all en suite. The wood-panelled bar/restaurant *Darkey Kelly's*, named after the keeper of a notorious eighteenth-century brothel on Copper Alley, often has live rock music at night, making this a lively place to stay. Closed Dec 23–27. ❹

Jurys Inn Christchurch Christchurch Place ⓣ01/454 0000, ⓦwww.jurysdoyle.com. Looking more like an office block than a hotel, *Jurys Inn* lies opposite Christ Church Cathedral and within easy reach of St Patrick's Cathedral, the Guinness Brewery and the Irish Museum of Modern Art. While not as comfortable as other branches in the city, the standards here are quite high, and the flat rate for rooms (which accommodate up to three adults or two adults and two children) is good value for groups on a budget. Price excludes breakfast. Closed Dec 24–26. ❹

The Temple Bar 13–17 Fleet St ⓣ01/677 3333, ⓦwww.towerhotelgroup.ie. A modern hotel, ideally placed for exploring the Temple Bar area. Rooms are larger than average, though the front rooms can suffer from street noise. Breakfast is served in a light-filled, glass-roofed dining room. Triples are available; under-12s stay free; reductions for weekend breaks. Closed Dec 24–27. ❼

Westin Dublin Westmoreland St ⓣ01/645 1000, ⓦwww.westin.com. Opened in September 2001, this swish, five-storey temple of excellence hides behind the nineteenth-century facade of the old Allied Irish Bank building, just north of Trinity College. Its 163 bedrooms are designed with character and are elegantly equipped, while the bar is housed in the former bank's vaults, and the lounge has a stunning glass roof. ❾

The southside

Buswell's 23–27 Molesworth St ⓣ01/614 6500, ⓦwww.quinnhotels.com. A superb Georgian town house offering comfortable, three-star accommodation in a prime, quiet location near Leinster House. Although tastefully modernized, the hotel retains its charm and style with ornamental fireplaces, antique furnishings and cosy bedrooms. Closed Dec 24–28. ❼

Fitzwilliam 41 Fitzwilliam St Upper ⓣ01/662 5155, ⓔfitzwilliamguesthouse@eircom.net. A plush twelve-bedroom guesthouse occupying a splendid Georgian building on the corner of Baggot Street Lower, with a restaurant, bar and en-suite rooms with TV and phone. The breakfasts are of a high standard, and are all the more enjoyable when served in the opulent Grand Salon on the first floor. ❻

Harrington Hall 70 Harcourt St ⓣ01/475 3497, ⓦwww.harringtonhall.com. Deservedly popular and elegantly furnished Georgian guesthouse, with 28 comfortable, well-equipped en-suite rooms with soundproofing. Superb breakfasts are served in a bright and airy basement. Secure parking. Closed Dec 23– Jan 1. ❾

Kilronan Guesthouse 70 Adelaide Rd ⓣ01/475 5266, ⓦwww.dublinn.com. Excellent, family-run Georgian guesthouse in a quiet setting within walking distance of St Stephen's Green. Ten en-suite bedrooms with plenty of facilities and, best of all, very comfortable beds. Private car parking and splendid breakfasts. ❻

Le Méridien Shelbourne 27 St Stephen's Green North ⓣ01/663 4500, ⓦwww.shelbourne.ie. Dublin's most prestigious hotel, and a society watering-hole with elegantly furnished interiors and a buzzing social scene (afternoon tea in the Lord Mayor's Lounge is a Dublin tradition). It was here, in room 112, that the Irish constitution was drafted in 1921. The rooms are incredibly chic, with many of the older ones displaying pieces from the hotel's impressive antique collection. Those to the front of the hotel offer fine views over St Stephen's Green, but can be a little noisy. There's an excellent restaurant, a popular bar, swimming pool and health club. Rates do not include the fifteen percent service charge. ❾

Leeson Inn 24 Leeson St Lower ⓣ01/662 2002, ⓦwww.leesoninn.com. This elegant four-storey Georgian town house just off St Stephen's Green has en-suite bedrooms, are thoughtfully designed around original period sash windows, with natural colours and contemporary furnishings. Breakfast is a continental-style buffet. Friendly staff. Attractive low-season rates (❺) available; as is parking. Closed Dec 23–28. ❻

Longfields 9–10 Fitzwilliam St Lower ⓣ01/676 1367, ⓦwww.longfields.ie. A small, friendly hotel, right in the heart of Georgian Dublin, *Longfields* has the feel of a country guesthouse with an air of gentility characterized by period furnishings in both the rooms and public areas. Renowned also for its excellent gourmet restaurant, *Kevin Arundel@Number 10*. Closed Dec 24–27. ❼

The Merrion Merrion St Upper ⓣ01/603 0600, ⓦwww.merrionhotel.com. This five-star hotel, complete with top-hatted doorman, is housed in four restored eighteenth-century town houses opposite the government buildings, and offers every modern amenity, including its own spa and pool. The restored garden wing houses one of the most important collections of contemporary Irish art in the country. The elegant bedrooms feature crisp linen bedsheets, fax, Internet access, a mini-bar and a safe and have en-suite Italian marble bathrooms. ❾

Mont Clare Merrion Square ⓣ01/607 3800, ⓦwww.ocallaghanhotels.ie. Close to the National Gallery this smart hotel has a contemporary interior and generously proportioned, well-furnished rooms with cool marble bathrooms. Facilities include room service, valet parking and fitness centre. Good weekend discounts available. ❾

Number 31 Leeson Close, off Leeson St Lower ⓣ01/676 5011, ⓦwww.number31.ie. A stylishly converted stable block forms the sitting and breakfast areas of this fine, secluded Georgian guesthouse, the former home of architect Sam Stephenson. The sunken lounge, turf fires and ethnic rugs give it the air of a country retreat in the heart of the city. Comfortable rooms, excellent breakfasts and great hospitality. ❾

Staunton's on the Green 83 St Stephen's Green East ⓣ01/478 2300, ⓦindigo.ie/~hotels. An elegant Georgian house overlooking St Stephen's Green, offering stylish accommodation with private garden to the rear. The reception rooms are fine Georgian period pieces, and, while the bedrooms do not reflect the house's former elegance, they are very comfortable. Family-friendly with discounts for children. Closed Dec 24–27. ❼

The northside

Anchor Guest House 49 Gardiner St Lower ⓣ01/878 6913, ⓦwww.anchorguesthouse.com. All rooms in this tastefully refurbished Georgian house are en suite, with TV and phone. Limited parking is available, but ring ahead as on-street parking in this area is not recommended; discounts for children. ❹

Celtic Lodge Guesthouse 82 Talbot St ⓣ01/677 9955, ⓔcelticguesthouse@eircom.net. Housed in a converted Victorian residence on a busy, somewhat dowdy street only two minutes' walk from O'Connell Street, this businesslike guesthouse has brightly decorated and comfortably furnished en-suite bedrooms, all with TV. Breakfast is served in an even brighter canteen and there is also a bar downstairs. ❺

Charleville Lodge 268–272 North Circular Rd, Phibsborough ⓣ01/838 6633, ⓦwww.charlevillelodge.ie. A family-run guesthouse in a Victorian terrace near Phoenix Park with well-furnished and extremely comfortable bedrooms. The owners can arrange a round of golf, if you fancy bringing your clubs. Baby-sitting service and parking available. Closed Dec 20–28. ❺

Chief O'Neill's Smithfield, Smithfield Village ⓣ01/817 3838, ⓦwww.chiefoneills.com. This hotel is dedicated to a Chicago police commissioner (the eponymous Police Chief O'Neill) who compiled one of the most important collections of traditional Irish music at the end of the nineteenth century. However, there's nothing traditional about this ultra-stylish, progressively designed hotel with bedrooms bearing cool light and lines and lots of hi-tech gadgetry. Similarly styled lounges and bars occupy the lower floors and are used for live-music shows at the weekends. Closed Dec 24–26. ❾

Clifden Guesthouse 32 Gardiner Place ⓣ01/874 6364, ⓦwww.clifdenhouse.com. Set in an old Georgian street just off Mountjoy Square, the *Clifden* has extremely helpful owners and fourteen pleasant en-suite rooms (single, double, twin, triple and family), each with TV. Child discounts and mid-week reductions are available, as is a baby-sitting service and private car parking. ❺

The Gate 80–82 Parnell St ⓣ01/872 2500. Taking its name from the nearby theatre, this is a popular northside hotel, thanks to its score of comfortable en-suite bedrooms, all equipped with TV, and extremely economical prices. Family-friendly. Closed Dec 24–Jan 1. ❸

The Gresham 20–22 O'Connell St Upper ⓣ01/874 6881, ⓦwww.gresham-hotels.com. Dating from 1817, this is Dublin's oldest hotel, and one of the classiest, comprising 288 luxury bedrooms and six even more luxurious penthouse suites (one of which once housed film-star couple Richard Burton and Elizabeth Taylor for two months). The grandiose lobby, with its crystal chandeliers, decorative stuccowork and potted palms, makes the perfect spot for afternoon tea. Comfortable, recently refurbished rooms (some with oversize beds), and a huge range of amenities including restaurant and bar, room service, valet parking and a well-equipped business centre. Family-friendly. ❾

Hotel Isaacs Store St ⓣ01/855 0067, ⓦwww.isaacs.ie. The upmarket sister to *Isaacs Hostel* (see p.80), situated right next to Busáras, offering 58 brightly furnished en-suite rooms, all with TV, its own Italian restaurant, *Il Vignardo*, and the associated *Isaac Butt* pub (see p.132) next door. Prices rise by €10 at weekends. Closed 23–27 Dec. ❻

Jurys Inn Custom House Custom House Quay ⓣ01/607 5000, ⓦwww.jurysdoyle.com. Formerly a run-down dock area, the north quays are now flourishing with the Financial Services Centre as their hub and, not surprisingly, this branch of *Jurys* is business focused with fax and modem lines in the larger rooms. It also offers rooms that can accommodate up to four people, at a reasonable flat rate, which makes it a good family option, though breakfast is not included in the price. Closed Dec 24–26. ❹

Marian Guesthouse 21 Gardiner St Upper ⓣ01/874 4129. The best budget B&B near the city centre with six basic rooms, shared bathrooms and a garden. A clean and friendly place with good breakfasts and no exploitive price hikes or single supplements at peak times. Single rooms cost little more than dorm beds in nearby hostels. ❷

Morrison Ormond Quay Lower ⓣ01/887 2400, ⓦwww.morrisonhotel.ie. A minimalist *tour de force*, this is one of Dublin's most stylish new hotels. Perfectly proportioned throughout, its decor, with John Rocha as design consultant, utilizes natural Irish materials with dark ash-brown fittings and cream stone floors. If you've recently won the lottery, the penthouse is utterly stunning. Aside from offering aesthetic bliss, bedrooms have en-suite bathrooms, plus mod cons including CD players and ISDN links. On site are a very mellow bar and the *Halo* restaurant (see p.129). Closed Dec 24–27. ❾

Ormond Quay Ormond Quay Upper ⓣ01/872 1811, ⓦwww.ormondquayhotel.com. A historic hotel, formerly inhabited by priests, barristers and, on the odd occasion, their clients (the Four Courts is nearby). Joyce makes mention of the hotel in *Ulysses*, comparing the staff to Sirens, a theme used in the hotel's bar/restaurant. The hotel also has its own art gallery and the bright, comfortable bedrooms, many overlooking the river, are adequately insulated from the constant stream of traffic along the busy quays. ❻

Othello Guesthouse 74 Gardiner St Lower ⓣ01/855 4271, ⓔothello1@eircom.net. One of the area's longest-established guesthouses, with pleasant window-boxes and floral displays to boot. Twenty-two en-suite bedrooms with TV and telephone. Family rooms are available at good rates, and the Irish breakfast is very good. Secure parking available; child-friendly. Closed Dec 23–26. ❹

The Townhouse 47–48 Gardiner St Lower ⓣ01/878 8808, ⓦwww.gtrotter.indigo.ie. A snazzily refurbished Georgian house, once the home of playwrights Dion Boucicault and Lafcadio Hearn, and definitely the classiest guesthouse on the northside. All rooms are en suite with TV, fridge and tea-maker. Fine healthy breakfast; secure parking; higher rates at weekends; hostel attached (see p.80). ❻

The southern suburbs

Ballsbridge and Sandymount

8 Dromard Terrace Off Seafort Ave, Sandymount ⓣ01/668 3861 (Mrs Maureen Bermingham). This is a fine, traditional family-run guesthouse in an ivy-covered period house near the beach in Sandymount, which has no aspirations beyond offering comfortable, clean rooms, good breakfasts and a warm welcome. A good choice for either a single traveller, or a family on a budget as there are child reductions; the owners also arrange baby-sitting. Closed Nov–March. ❶

Aberdeen Lodge 53–55 Park Ave, off Ailesbury Rd, Ballsbridge ⓣ01/283 8155, ⓦwww.halpinsprivatehotels.com. Close to the Sydney Parade DART station near Merrion Road, this large Edwardian house offers all the comforts expected from a stylish hotel. All the rooms are well equipped, but those with a private Jacuzzi offer the ultimate in comfort. Gardens, secure parking and baby-sitting service available. ❻

Anglesea Town House 63 Anglesea Rd, Ballsbridge ⓣ01/668 3877, ⓕ668 3461. More like a country manor than a city town house, this is a congenial place with a warm welcome from the irrepressible proprietor, Helen Kirrane. The house is Edwardian, and the bedrooms, which retain a period feel (most have the original fireplaces intact), are comfy and spacious. The breakfast, made from home produce, is rightly regarded by many to be the best in the city. Reductions for seniors and children. Closed Dec 15– Jan 8. ❸

Berkeley Court Lansdowne Rd, Ballsbridge ⓣ01/660 1711, ⓦwww.jurysdoyle.com. The glass and concrete exterior disguises the inner elegance of this five-star hotel, set in its own grounds, in the heart of fashionable Dublin 4. Huge chandeliers light the elegant foyer, while the rooms are large and brightly painted, with marble-tiled bathrooms. ❾

Camelot 37 Pembroke Park, Ballsbridge ⓣ01/668 0331.One of several excellent options in a pleasant street that's only a 5min bus ride from the centre (#10 and #46A), *Camelot* has friendly owners, well-appointed en-suite rooms, all with TV, excellent breakfasts and parking on the forecourt. ❸

Jurys Ballsbridge and The Towers Pembroke Rd, Ballsbridge ⓣ01/660 5000 or 01/667 0033, ⓦwww.jurysdoyle.com. Formerly two hotels, despite *Jurys* and *The Towers* amalgamation they both retain a distinct identity. *Jurys* is a huge, modern complex whose comfortable, spacious, though somewhat bland rooms, have become popular with the business community. *The Towers* has a warmer ambience, more suited to holidaymakers; rooms here are larger, and the wood finish, warm colours and comfy furniture give it a homely feel. ❾

Merrion Hall 54 Merrion Rd, Ballsbridge ⓣ01/668 1426, ⓦwww.halpinsprivatehotels.com. Sister establishment to the equally high-standard *Aberdeen Lodge*, though set on a busy main road. Bedrooms are spacious, and there is a comfy sitting area. Parking is limited, so it's a good idea to call ahead and reserve a space. Children are welcome, and there is a pleasant garden. ❹

Montrose House 16 Pembroke Park, Ballsbridge ⓣ01/668 4286. Some rooms in this elegantly furnished town house are almost suite-like in size. Most are en suite, with TV, and there are plenty of books available if you're short of reading matter. Breakfast is taken communally around one big table. On-street parking requires a disc purchasable from a nearby machine. ❷

Mount Herbert Herbert Rd, Ballsbridge ⓣ01/668 4321, ⓦwww.mountherberthotel.ie. A large hotel made up of several Victorian houses, and one of the less expensive options in this upmarket southside neighbourhood. The rooms are basic, though brightly painted, and all have TV and en-suite bathrooms. The house offers a play area for children. The restaurant serves hearty, if a little uninspiring, food. ❼

Pembroke Townhouse 90 Pembroke Rd, Ballsbridge ⓣ01/660 0277, ⓦwww.pembroketownhouse.ie. Situated on stylish Pembroke Rd, this guesthouse has all the amenities of a good hotel (pool, Jacuzzi, gym, tennis and golf), while retaining personal service. It's advisable to book early as it can fill up with business groups. ❻

St Jude's Guesthouse 17 Pembroke Park, Ballsbridge ⓣ01/668 0928, ⓕ668 0483. This well-kept house offers comfortable en-suite accommodation in a quiet location; all rooms have TV and there's parking on the forecourt. The excellent breakfast is taken in a pleasant downstairs room. ❸

Schoolhouse 2–8 Northumberland Rd, Ballsbridge ⓣ01/667 5014, ⓔschool@schoolhousehotel.iol.ie. Set in a former derelict schoolhouse that was traditionally a landmark near the city's Grand Canal, this tastefully refurbished hotel offers modern, well-furnished rooms. The restaurant here is first rate, and a busy bar (especially on Sunday afternoons) spills patrons out into the gardens in summer. ❾

Stonehaven 9 Claremont Rd, Sandymount ⓣ & ⓕ01/668 2028. Cosy, ivy-clad Victorian town house in Sandymount village, ten minutes' walk from the sea and Lansdowne Road DART station. The house has three comfortable and neatly furnished en-suite rooms, well maintained by a friendly owner. Open March–Nov. ❸

Dalkey and Killiney

The Court Killiney Bay, Killiney ⓣ01/285 1622, ⓦwww.killineycourt.ie. Large Victorian-style hotel set in pleasant grounds close to the DART station. The rooms are basic but comfortable (try to secure one with a view of the sea) with en-suite bathrooms and TVs. Check for weekend or family reductions. The hotel boasts two restaurants, one of which specializes in fish dishes. ❺

Fitzpatrick Castle Killiney ⓣ01/284 0700, ⓦwww.fitzpatrickhotels.com. A former stately home perched on the edge of Killiney Hill. Not surprisingly, many of the rooms offer fine, bay views, but for a real panorama head up the hill behind the hotel. The spacious rooms exude elegance, many with four-poster beds and antique furnishings, and the hotel has an excellent family-friendly policy with good child reductions and creche facilities. Breakfast is not included in the price. ❼

Tudor House Off Castle St, Dalkey ⓣ01/285 1528, ⓔtudorhousedalkey@hotmail.com. Listed manor house set in its own grounds, offering six individually and stylishly decorated en-suite rooms with views over Dublin Bay. Elegant throughout, this family-owned establishment offers real seclusion from the Dublin bustle. ❺

Dún Laoghaire

Gresham Royal Marine Royal Marine Rd ⓣ01/280 1911, ⓦwww.gresham-hotels.com. Built in 1870, the *Gresham Royal Marine* is a definite throwback to the nineteenth century, when Dún Laoghaire was a chic holiday resort. Although recently modernized, the hotel retains much of its former elegance: from the marble-floored foyer to the splendid bay-window suites with four-poster beds and antique furniture. The other rooms are a little more mundane, though many have magnificent bay views. ❼

Kingston Adelaide St ⓣ01/280 1810, ⓦwww.kingstonhotel.com. Don't be put off by the dreary facade of this large Victorian hotel as the inside is both welcoming and comfortable. The pale-green rooms, while not luxurious, are adequate, and many overlook the sea. This is a family-friendly hotel that can prove a bargain if you book one of the rooms that sleep five people. ❹

Lynden 2 Mulgrave Terrace ⓣ01/280 6404, ⓔlynden@iol.ie. A friendly family-run Georgian guesthouse five minutes' walk from the car-ferry terminus with four comfortable rooms (two en suite). The helpful owners offer a value-for-money service, including early-morning breakfasts for those catching the ferry. Secure parking available. ❶

Windsor Lodge 3 Islington Ave ⓣ01/284 6952, ⓔwinlodge@eircom.net. Ideally located on a small street leading from the coast, near to Sandycove & Glasthule DART station, this non-smoking house with four en-suite rooms is especially suitable for families, as it offers a child service and generous concessions for older children. Secure parking. ❷

The northern suburbs

Clontarf, Drumcondra and Glasnevin

69 Hollybank Rd Drumcondra ⓣ01/837 7907. If you are coming from the airport turn right at the popular *Fagan's* pub, onto the quiet red-brick terrace to reach this guesthouse, run by Kathleen Hurney. The house is cheery and rooms are bright; only two rooms are en suite. Reductions for children. Non-smoking. ❷

Clontarf Castle Castle Ave, Clontarf ⓣ01/833 2321, ⓦwww.clontarfcastle.ie. This superbly renovated four-star hotel, occupying a castle which dates back in part to 1172, not only contains exquisitely and individually designed bedrooms, but a swimming pool, two bars and a bistro. To cap it all, service is highly efficient and friendly. ❽

Egan's Guesthouse 7–9 Iona Park, Glasnevin ⓣ01/830 3611, ⓦwww.eganshouse.com. *Egan's* has long been regarded as one of the best northside guesthouse options. It is family-run, and situated on a very quiet road in a maze of red-brick houses. There is car parking to the front of the house, and children are welcome. Breakfast is not included. ❹

Hedigan's 14 Hollybrook Park, Clontarf ⓣ01/853 1663, ⓔhedigans@indigo.ie. Fine detached, listed Victorian house just off Howth Road next to Clontarf Golf Club. *Hedigan's* is well furnished, with rooms themed according to different countries, and offers secure parking, child-minding facilities, a small playground and reductions for children and pensioners. ❹

The White House 125 Clontarf Rd, Clontarf ⓣ01/833 3196, ⓔinfo@family-homes.ie. On the city centre bus route, this is a very friendly guesthouse near Dublin Bay with comfortable rooms that offer excellent value for money. Booking early is advisable between June and August . The breakfast served here is particularly substantial. ❷

Howth

Hazelwood 2 Thormanby Woods, off Thormanby Rd ⓣ & ⓕ01/839 1391. A large modern bungalow set in its own extensive grounds, one mile from the seafront near Howth Golf Club. Four en-suite, non-smoking bedrooms with fifty-percent child discounts; plenty of parking space. ❷

King Sitric's Fish Restaurant East Pier ⓣ01/832 5235, ⓔinfo@kingsitric.ie. A piscivore's ultimate fantasy, with eight well-appointed en-suite rooms, all with sea views, slap bang by the harbour and above one of the area's finest seafood restaurants (see p.129). Closed Christmas and the last two weeks in January. ❼

Margaret & Michael Campbell Highfield, Thormanby Rd ⓣ01/832 3936. Up towards The Summit, this late Victorian guesthouse has three rooms with TV, two of them en suite (the front rooms offer views of Malahide). Families are especially welcome. Child discounts; cot available. ❷

Gay-friendly accommodation

Frankie's 8 Camden Place ⓣ01/478 3087, ⓦwww.frankiesguesthouse.com. Near both Grafton St and Temple Bar this long-established gay guesthouse is a friendly place, though the rooms are on the small side. ❸

The Horse and Carriage 15 Aungier St ⓣ01/478 3537. Largest pink hotel in the city, but don't expect frills or value for money, though there are considerable reductions for double rooms between Sunday and Thursday. The price includes admission for men to the Incognito sauna in the basement. ❸

Inn on the Liffey 21 Ormond Quay Upper ⓣ01/677 0828. As the name suggests this guesthouse is found on the northern banks of the River Liffey. The en-suite rooms are mostly small, though there are triples, and some offer fine views of the river itself. Male customers receive free admission to the Dock next door, one of the city's most popular saunas. ❸

Hostels

Dublin's newer **hostels** tend to market themselves as budget accommodation rather than hostels (they seem to feel that there is something slightly pejorative about the term) and it is fair to say that there is a difference between these and old-fashioned hostels, not only in the price and generally higher standard of accommodation, but also in their emphasis on the individual rather than the communal; many have private and double rooms but often no sitting room. The hostels in the centre, especially around Temple Bar, tend to be very lively, so if you need a good night's rest it would be advisable to take one further out. The price of a dorm bed in Dublin is generally around double the rate you might expect to pay elsewhere in Ireland in high season (see Basics p.38), though breakfast is usually included, and the price code given in the listings here refers to the cost of a twin-bedded or double room in high season. All hostels in these listings are members of the Independent Holiday Hostels of Ireland association (IHH; see p.38) unless otherwise stated. IHH hostels guarantee that twenty per cent of their standard dorm beds will be available at the lowest figure given in the high-season price ranges below.

The southside

Ashfield House 19–20 D'Olier St ⓣ01/679 7734, ⓔashfield@indigo.ie. Spacious, clean and friendly 104-bed hostel occupying a converted church near Trinity College. Consists mostly of small four- or six-bed dorms with seven double rooms, en-suite facilities throughout plus a kitchen and laundry. ❹

Avalon House 55 Aungier St ⓣ01/475 0001, ⓔinfo@avalon-house.com. Friendly, traditional 281-bed hostel in a former medical school five minutes' walk from St Stephen's Green and Temple Bar, with sixteen double rooms (❹), mostly en suite. Pleasant café – excellent for hanging out and meeting people – plus a large self-catering kitchen, tip-top security and Internet access. ❸

Barnacles Temple Bar House Temple Lane ⓣ01/671 6277, ⓦwww.barnacles.ie. Custom-built 149-bed hostel right in the heart of Temple Bar and extremely popular as a result, so book early. Excellent en-suite rooms (sleeping four to twelve), as well as a dozen doubles. Efficient and friendly staff. ❸

Brewery Hostel (IHO) 22–23 Thomas St West ⓣ01/473 8600, ⓔbrewery@indigo.ie. Housed in a converted library, a 10min walk along Thomas Street from Christ Church, the *Brewery* is friendly and offers good value for its en-suite rooms. The unfashionable location often means that it still has some of its 52 beds free when other hostels are full. Four doubles are also available. ❹

Kinlay House Christchurch 2–12 Lord Edward St ⓣ01/679 6644, ⓔkinlay.dublin@usitworld.com. Cheerful and relaxed 196-bed USITNow hostel near Christ Church Cathedral, which can be a little noisy due to both traffic and high-spirited guests. There are thirteen doubles, and there's a café and kitchen on site; bike rental and laundry are available. ❷

Oliver St John Gogarty's 18–21 Anglesea St ⓣ01/671 1822, ⓔolivergogartys@hotmail.com. Comfy and stylish, this hostel is situated next to the eponymous pub in the heart of Temple Bar and, like the pub itself, is hugely popular. Offers doubles, triples, and four-bed rooms as well as six- and ten-bed dorms (128 beds in the whole hostel), and snazzy one- to three-bedroom rooftop apartments (❻) with kitchen, TV and washing machine. ❷

The northside

Abbey Court 29 Bachelors Walk, O'Connell Bridge ⓣ01/878 0700, ⓔinfo@abbey-court.com. Just north of O'Connell Bridge this is a modern, blue-fronted, well-equipped and friendly hundred-bed hostel. The mostly small rooms are all en suite with excellent showers and fitted with a swipe-card security system and storage cages under every bed. There are also eight doubles. Laundry, kitchen and Internet facilities are all available. ❸

Abraham House 82–83 Gardiner St Lower ⓣ01/855 0600, ⓔstay@abraham-house.ie. A large, well-run 191-bed hostel with plenty of doubles, *Abraham House* is handy for both Busáras and Connolly Station. Facilities include a kitchen, laundry, bureau de change, efficient showers and secure parking. Bus #41 from the airport stops outside. ❹

Celts House 32–33 Blessington St, just off Dorset

St ⓣ01/830 0657, ⓔres@celtshouse.iol.ie. The bright-yellow Georgian door marks the mood of this friendly hostel on a quiet cul-de-sac north of O'Connell Street. There are only 38 beds, including a few doubles, which makes this a cosier alternative to some of the larger hostels. Prices are very competitive, but breakfast is not included. ❷

Dublin International Youth Hostel (An Óige) 61 Mountjoy St ⓣ01/830 1766, ⓔdublininternational@anoige.ie. Way up near the Black Church and Dorset Street Upper (bus #41 from the airport and #19 and #19A from O'Connell Street Lower and Upper), the northside headquarters of An Óige, is a well-equipped 369-bed hostel in an ex-convent. Generally cheaper for a dorm bed (€16–€18) than IHH or IHO hostels, though non-members of An Óige or Hostelling International pay a nightly surcharge of €2, and you need to bring or rent a sleeping sheet.

Globetrotters Tourist Hostel 46 Gardiner St Lower ⓣ01/873 5893, ⓔgtrotter@indigo.ie. Well-run, comfortable 250-bed hostel connected to *The Townhouse* B&B (see p.76) whose cosy, tasteful dorms sleep six to ten people and have security-coded doors and individual bed lights. The breakfast is the best you'll get in any Dublin hostel and the decor and standards are higher than the norm, plus there's a garden for summer lounging. Eighty-two well-equipped doubles also available. ❹

Goin' My Way 15 Talbot St ⓣ01/878 8484, ⓔgoinmyway@esatclear.ie. Small, family-run, value-for-money hostel above a clothes shop, close to O'Connell Street and the river. Breakfast is not included, but there is a kitchen for guests' use. Due to its midnight curfew this is one of Dublin's quieter hostels. Forty-two beds but just two doubles are available. ❶

Isaacs Hostel 2–5 Frenchman's Lane ⓣ01/855 6215, ⓔhostel@isaacs.ie. Well-run, modern 235-bed hostel housed in a former wine warehouse, just around the corner from Busáras. Comfortable dorms and excellent doubles, as well as a laundry, Internet facilities, a bureau de change and bike storage. There's a room lockout from 11am–2.30pm. Breakfast isn't included, though there's an excellent café on site. ❸

Jacob's Inn 21–28 Talbot Place ⓣ01/855 5660, ⓔjacobs@isaacs.ie. Just north of Busáras, this 295-bed sister hostel to *Isaacs* offers comfortable and stylish budget accommodation. Staff are friendly and security is first-rate with swipe cards and spacious lockers. Breakfast is not included, but there's a kitchen and a café, Internet facilities and a bureau de change; a dozen en-suite double rooms are available. ❸

Litton Lane 2–4 Litton Lane ⓣ01/872 8389, ⓔlitton@indigo.ie. Just off Bachelors Walk, by O'Connell Bridge, this well-equipped 96-bed hostel is housed in a former warehouse which also served time as a major recording studio. Comfortable dorms as well as three cosy double rooms and well-kept showers plus laundry facilities, kitchen and parking. ❷

Mount Eccles Court 44 North Great George's St ⓣ01/873 0826, ⓔinfo@eccleshostel.com. Housed in two converted listed buildings (with most of their original features intact) on a fine Georgian street, ten minutes' walk from the Busáras. Breakfast is served in a well-equipped basement kitchen where the walls have been stripped to their original stonework. The comfortable dorm bunks are generally cheaper than other northside options and the four doubles are reasonably priced too. There are 115 beds in total. ❷

Paddy's Palace 5 Beresford Place, off Gardiner St Lower ⓣ01/888 1758, ⓔpaddyspalace@dublin.com. Part of the *Paddywagon* backpacker-tours empire, this is a small, plain, but very airy and economically priced 42-bed hostel whose kitchen and some rooms overlook the Liffey. Dorms are entered by swipe card, some are en-suite, and there are also a few economically priced doubles available. Internet facilities and organized tours on offer. ❷

Dún Laoghaire and Monkstown

Belgrave Hall 34 Belgrave Square, Monkstown ⓣ01/284 2106, ⓦwww.dublinhostel.com. The best out-of-town option, offering fine communal dorm accommodation and a few comfortable doubles in a magnificent building in Monkstown, popular with Irish guests studying at the nearby traditional music academy. Both dorms and doubles are spacious and some have period furniture. Bike rental and laundry. Bus #7 and #7A from O'Connell Street and College Green or DART to Seapoint. Fifty beds. ❷

Marina House 7 Old Dunleary, Dún Laoghaire ⓣ01/284 1524, ⓔinfo@marinahouse.com. Dublin's smallest hostel (just thirty beds), housed in a renovated stone building next to the DART line and near to Salthill and Monkstown station; handy too for the Dún Laoghaire ferry terminal, just five minutes' walk away. Well-furnished and cosy, beds are very reasonably priced, but there's only one double. Laundry facilities. ❸

Student accommodation

As an alternative to staying in a hostel or B&B, you can rent **student accommodation** during the summer holidays (mid-June to mid-Sept). These generally offer better facilities for self-catering than hostels, with a camaraderie arising from the fact that so many of the guests are foreign students attending courses – which makes it imperative to book months ahead.

Dublin City University Larkfield Apartments, DCU Campus, off Ballymun Rd, Glasnevin ⓣ01/700 5736, ⓦwww.dcu.ie. Definitely the most affordable of the campus options, though a little way out of town (bus #11, #13 and #19 from O'Connell Street). There are 270 en-suite bedrooms, consisting of fifty singles (€42 per night) and two hundred doubles (€70 per night) with breakfast served in the restaurant, plus use of a nearby sports centre and laundry.

Mercer Court Mercer St Lower ⓣ01/478 2179, ⓦwww.mercercourt.ie. Part of the Royal College of Surgeons and just two minutes from Grafton Street, this offers excellent en-suite single (€62 per night) and double rooms (€104 per night) with a TV and direct-dial telephone. Also has self-catering three- and four-bed apartments (€785–920 per unit per week) which sleep up to five people.

Trinity College College Green ⓣ01/608 1177, ⓦwww.tcd.ie. Not cheap, but the setting is unique and utterly central, offering a range of standard or en-suite accommodation in either single, twin or four-bed rooms in one of the many halls of residence on campus. Shared kitchen and lounge, breakfast taken in the restaurant. Per person prices range from €37.50 per night for a standard double to €59.50 per person per night for an en-suite double.

University College Dublin Village Off Stillorgan Rd, Belfield ⓣ01/269 7111, ⓦwww.ucd.ie. A complex of modern single rooms (€35 per night) and four-bed apartments (€110 per night) with shared kitchens, dining areas and shower rooms. Located on the UCD campus, about four miles south of the centre (bus #46 from Fleet Street).

Camping

There are two **campsites** on the outskirts of Dublin, one in Clondalkin, the other between Killiney and Bray. Both are mainly aimed at caravanners, and relatively few backpackers use them for the simple reason that by the time you've taken fares into account it's unlikely to be any cheaper than staying in a hostel in Dublin – and involves far more effort.

Camac Valley Tourist Caravan & Camping Park Corkagh Regional Park, Naas Rd, Clondalkin ⓣ01/462 0644, ⓦwww.irishcamping.com. On the southwestern edge of Dublin, off the Naas road (bus #68 from Aston Quay; 40min). An attractive setting of landscaped grounds within a national park, with views of the Wicklow Mountains. Open all year.

Shankill Caravan & Camping Park Off Dublin Rd, Shankill ⓣ01/282 0011, ⓔshankhillcaravan@eircom.net. South of Killiney and some ten miles from the centre, near the Shankill DART station; direct buses are the #45 and #84 from Eden Quay or #46 from Fleet St; 45min). Handy for the Dún Laoghaire ferry terminal and not far from the sea and secluded beaches. Open all year.

The City

Dublin is divided into north and south with the River Liffey acting as a physical, social and at times psychological dividing line. Traditionally the southside has been regarded as the wealthier end of town, and certainly it does possess the majority of the city's historic sites, as well as being the home of the newer,

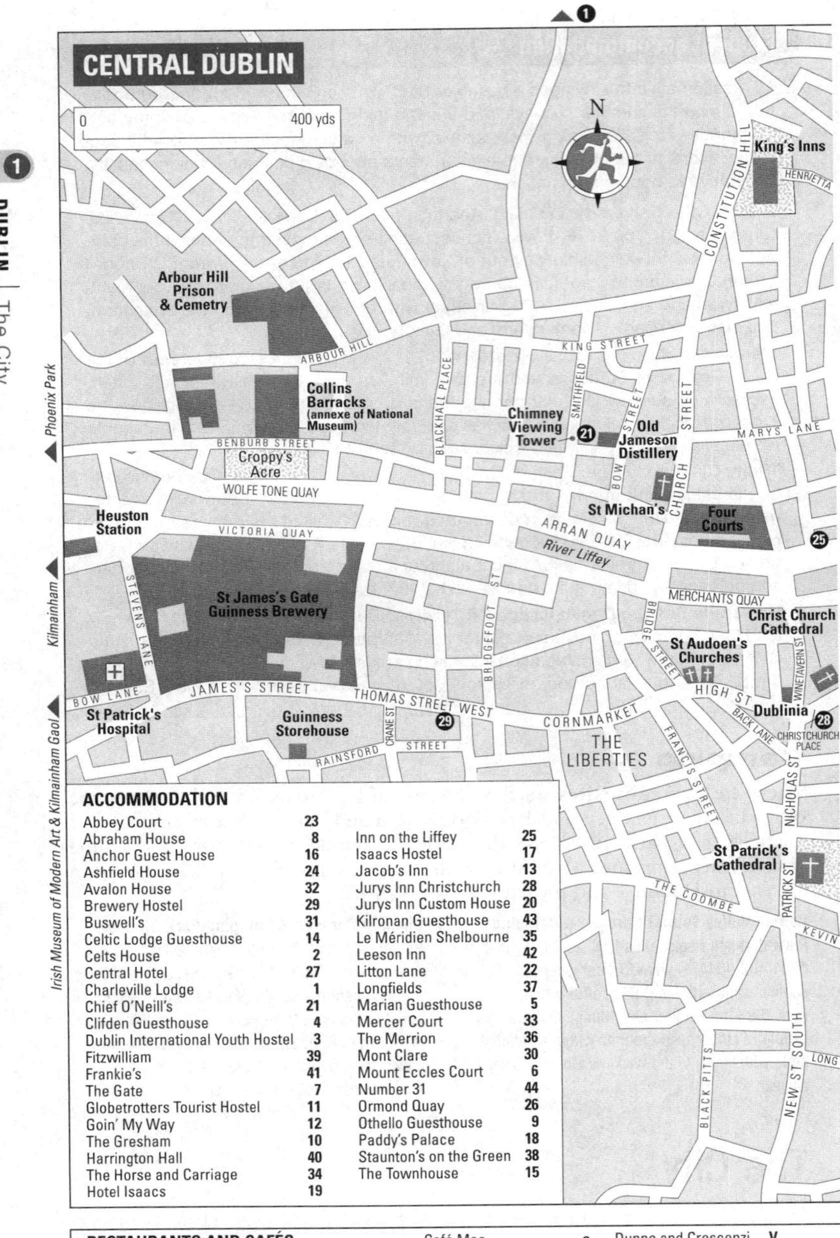

RESTAURANTS AND CAFÉS

101 Talbot	D	Bond	E	Café Mao	c	Dunne and Crescenzi	V		
AYA	U	C-Bar	F	Chapter One	B	Ely Wine Bar	j		
Beshoff's	C	Café-Bar-Deli	O	Cobalt Café and Gallery	A	Fitzer's	Y/Z		
Bewley's Oriental Café	H/X	Café Java	a	Cornucopia	M	Fresh	T		
				Diep le Shaker	k	Gotham Café	b		

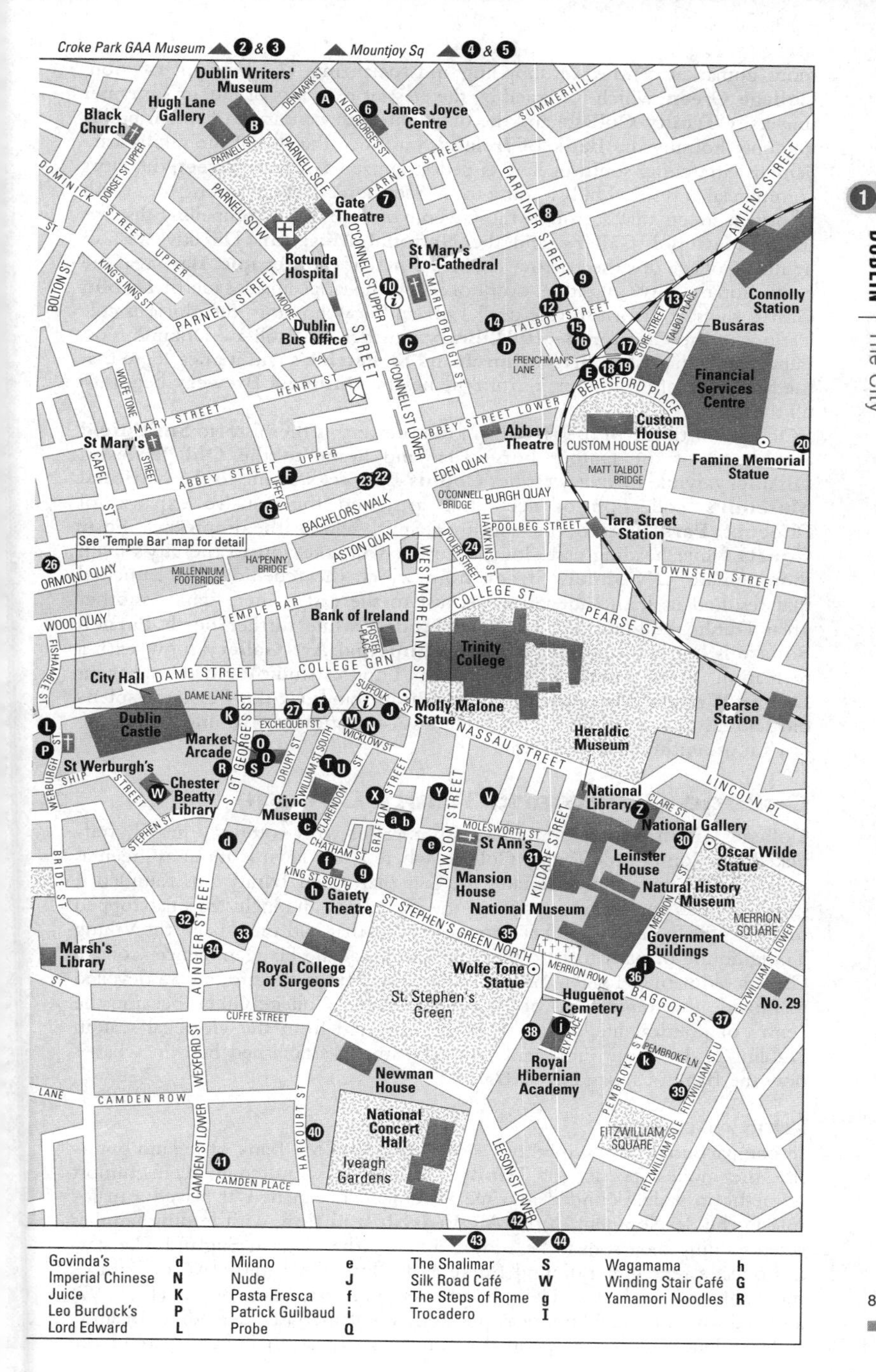

Croke Park GAA Museum 2 & 3
Mountjoy Sq 4 & 5
Dublin Writers' Museum
Hugh Lane Gallery
Black Church
James Joyce Centre
Gate Theatre
Rotunda Hospital
St Mary's Pro-Cathedral
Dublin Bus Office
Connolly Station
Busáras
Financial Services Centre
Custom House
Custom House Quay
Abbey Theatre
Famine Memorial Statue
Matt Talbot Bridge
Tara Street Station
St Mary's
See 'Temple Bar' map for detail
Ha'penny Bridge
Millennium Footbridge
Bank of Ireland
Trinity College
City Hall
Dublin Castle
Market Arcade
Molly Malone Statue
Pearse Station
Heraldic Museum
National Library
National Gallery
Oscar Wilde Statue
Leinster House
Natural History Museum
St Werburgh's
Chester Beatty Library
Civic Museum
St Ann's
Mansion House
National Museum
Gaiety Theatre
Government Buildings
Merrion Square
Marsh's Library
Royal College of Surgeons
Wolfe Tone Statue
St. Stephen's Green
Huguenot Cemetery
No. 29
Royal Hibernian Academy
Newman House
National Concert Hall
Iveagh Gardens
Fitzwilliam Square
Summerhill
Parnell Street
Parnell Sq
Gardiner Street
Amiens Street
Dominick Street Upper
Dorset St Upper
Bolton St
King's Inns St
Parnell Street Upper
Moore St
O'Connell St Upper
O'Connell St Lower
Marlborough St
Talbot Street
Talbot Place
Store Street
Frenchman's Lane
Beresford Place
Henry St
Mary Street
Wolfe Tone
Capel St
Abbey Street Upper
Abbey Street Lower
Liffey St
Eden Quay
O'Connell Bridge
Burgh Quay
Bachelors Walk
Poolbeg Street
Hawkins St
D'Olier Street
Aston Quay
Westmoreland St
Townsend Street
Ormond Quay
Wood Quay
Temple Bar
College St
Pearse St
Foster Place
Fishamble St
Dame Street
College Grn
Dame Lane
Suffolk St
Exchequer St
Wicklow St
Nassau Street
Drury St
William St South
Clarendon St
Grafton Street
Dawson Street
Kildare Street
Molesworth St
Clare St
Lincoln Pl
Werburgh St
Ship Street
Stephen St
S. Gt George's St
Chatham St
King St South
St Stephen's Green North
Merrion St
Merrion Row
Baggot St
Fitzwilliam St Lower
Bride St
Aungier Street
Cuffe Street
Ely Place
Pembroke St
Pembroke Ln
Fitzwilliam St U
Fitzwilliam Sq E
Fitzwilliam Sq W
Wexford St
Camden Row
Lane
Harcourt St
Camden St Lower
Camden Place
Leeson St Lower
43
44
Govinda's d
Imperial Chinese N
Juice K
Leo Burdock's P
Lord Edward L
Milano e
Nude J
Pasta Fresca f
Patrick Guilbaud i
Probe Q
The Shalimar S
Silk Road Café W
The Steps of Rome g
Trocadero I
Wagamama h
Winding Stair Café G
Yamamori Noodles R

more upmarket centres for shopping and socializing. The busy intersection, **College Green**, which is framed by the elegant exteriors of Dublin's premier university **Trinity College** and the old eighteenth-century parliament building, now housing the **Bank of Ireland**, was once the site of the Viking parliament. Stretching south of here is pedestrianized **Grafton Street**, the city's commercial and social hub, leading to **St Stephen's Green**; among the stylish Georgian streets that surround the Green, you'll find the compelling displays of the **National Gallery** and the **National Museum**. Directly west of Trinity College are the narrow, cobbled lanes of the **Temple Bar** area, the centre for the city's nightlife, overlooked by the imposing facade of **Dublin Castle**, the seat of British rule until 1921 and now home to the glorious collections of the **Chester Beatty Library**. Further west still are Dublin's most important cathedrals, **Christ Church** and **St Patrick's** and it's near here that the rich smell of malting grain from the nearby **Guinness Brewery** begins to fill the air.

On the northside of the river from the brewery is the historic **Smithfield** area, scene of the famous horse sales and home to the **Old Jameson Distillery**, while further west lies **Collins Barracks**, home to the **National Museum's** collection of decorative arts, and the massive expanse of **Phoenix Park**. Just to the south of Smithfield is the impressive **Four Courts** while heading east along the river will take you to the city's main thoroughfare, **O'Connell Street**, from which the rebellion was launched that resulted in Irish Independence. Just to the east of here stands another great Dublin building, the **Custom House**, while further north **Parnell Square** is home to the **Hugh Lane Municipal Art Gallery** (now with a recreation of the painter Francis Bacon's London studio) and the adjacent **Dublin Writers' Museum**. To the northeast stands **Croke Park**, the splendid stadium home of the Gaelic Athletics Association, containing one of the city's most enthralling museums.

College Green and Trinity College

College Green is something of a misnomer for what is today a heavily trafficked junction outside Trinity College, where a tiny lawn is about as green as it gets. The name commemorates the fact that when Trinity was founded it stood on open common land outside the walled city and included a flat-topped mound, 40ft high and 230ft in circumference, that had once been the Viking Thingmount, or parliament (otherwise known as the Haugen, hence College Green's old name, Hoggen Green). In Georgian times the ground was levelled to provide the foundations of Nassau Street, and College Green became the centre of political life, as power briefly diverted from the viceregal seat in Dublin Castle to the Protestant Irish Parliament, established here in what is now the Bank of Ireland in 1782.

Trinity College

In comparison with the mighty Classical facade of the Bank of Ireland opposite, the modest portico of **Trinity College** (Ⓦwww.tcd.ie) seems almost domestic in scale. Founded in 1592 by Queen Elizabeth I, it played a major role in the development of the **Anglo-Irish tradition**, with leading families often sending their sons to be educated here rather than in England. The statues outside represent Edmund Burke and Oliver Goldsmith, two of Trinity's most famous graduates. The philosopher and statesman Burke (1729–97) adopted an interesting political position, simultaneously defending Ireland's Independence and insisting on the country's role as an integral part of the

British Empire; Goldsmith (1728–74) was a noted wit and poet (see box on p.224). Other illustrious alumni include Jonathan Swift, author of *Gulliver's Travels* and many other satirical works (see box on p.106), and Wolfe Tone, leader of the United Irishmen and prime mover of the 1798 Rebellion (see p.786), as well as Bram Stoker, of *Dracula* fame, the playwright J.M. Synge, all-round wit Oscar Wilde and playwright and novelist Samuel Beckett.

Until recently, Trinity's Anglo-Irish connections gave it a strong **Protestant bias**. At its foundation, the college offered free education to Catholics who were prepared to change their religion, and right up to the 1970s – long after the rule on religion had been dropped by the college itself – Catholics had to get a special dispensation to study at Trinity or risk excommunication. Nowadays, roughly seventy percent of the student population is Catholic, and Trinity is just one of Dublin's three universities: University College Dublin is based just south of Donnybrook and forms part of the National University of Ireland; and Dublin City University is in Glasnevin.

As an architectural set piece, Trinity takes some beating. Its harmoniously composed eighteenth- and nineteenth-century buildings are ranged around cobbled quadrangles in a grander version of the arrangements at Oxford and Cambridge (the cobbles apparently have to be relaid every seven years as the land, reclaimed from the sea, subsides). The college served as an English university in the film *Educating Rita*.

As you enter the college via the **Front Gate**, the first buildings to catch your eye, facing one another across the cobbled square, are the **Chapel** and the **Examination Hall**, both designed by the Scottish architect Sir William Chambers who never actually visited Ireland. The Examination Hall's elegant, stuccoed interior makes a fine setting for the concerts sometimes held here (check the notice boards by the main gate) while the room's chandelier once adorned the old Irish Parliament building on the other side of College Green. Beyond the chapel on the left is the **Dining Hall**, built by the German architect Richard Cassels in 1742 and totally restored after a fire in 1989. The bell tower, or **Campanile**, in the middle of the square, was put up in 1853 and is believed to mark the site of the priory which long predated the university. A startling element of colour is introduced by the red brick of the **Rubrics**, student accommodation dating from the early 1700s and one of Trinity's oldest surviving buildings.

The Old Library and the Book of Kells

The other early survivor is the famous **Old Library** (June–Sept Mon–Sat 9.30am–5pm, Sun 9.30am–4.30pm; Oct–May Mon–Sat 9.30am–5pm, Sun noon–4.30pm; closed for ten days over Christmas and New Year; €7), which receives a free copy of every book published in Britain and Ireland and also contains a famous collection of priceless Irish manuscripts, above all the celebrated **Book of Kells**. Some 200,000 of the total collection of three million books are held here and the rest are stored off site, where over half a mile of new shelving is needed every year to accommodate new volumes.

On the ground floor of the library is a well-conceived and informative exhibition entitled **"Turning Darkness into Light"** which offers background on the Book of Kells (and other manuscripts such as the Book of Armagh and the Book of Durrow) in the context of early Christianity and the art of illumination – ranging from Ogham (the earlier, Celtic writing system of lines carved on standing stones) to Ethiopian books of devotions. The Book of Kells itself probably originated around 800 AD at the monastery on Iona (off the west coast of Scotland), which had been founded around 561 by the great Irish scholar, bard and ruler St Columcille (St Columba in English). During the Viking raids of the ninth century, the book was taken to the monastery of Kells in County Meath for safekeeping and, after a chequered history – during which it spent some time buried underground and some thirty of its pages disappeared – it was brought to Dublin in the seventeenth century. Totalling 680 pages, the Book of Kells consists of the four gospels of the New Testament, written in Latin. The book was re-bound in the 1950s into four separate volumes, of which two are on show at any one time: one open at a completely illuminated page, the other at a text page, itself not exactly unadorned, with patterns and fantastic animals intertwined with the capitals.

Less famous but no less significant than the Book of Kells is the **Book of Durrow**, the first of the great Irish illuminated manuscripts, dating from between 650 and 680 AD. It's noticeable in all these early manuscripts that the depictions of the human form make no attempt at realism – St Matthew in the Book of Durrow, for instance, is apparently wrapped in a poncho, with no hands. The important thing is the pattern, which is derived from metalwork (as in the amazing Ardagh Chalice and Tara Brooch, which you can see in the nearby National Museum). The characteristic spirals are always slightly asymmetrical – apparently a trick to ensure that the eye doesn't tire – and it's believed that the ornamentation in general had a symbolic meaning, although its full significance is not known.

After examining the manuscripts, you climb the stairs to the magnificent **Long Room**, built by Thomas Burgh between 1712 and 1732 and enlarged, with a barrel-vaulted ceiling, in 1860. Besides fascinating temporary exhibitions of books and prints from the library's collection, the Long Room also displays a gnarled fifteenth-century harp, the oldest to survive from Ireland, and an original printing of the 1916 Proclamation of the Irish Republic, made on Easter Sunday in Liberty Hall.

The Dublin Experience, Douglas Hyde Gallery and beyond

In summer, visitors to the college tend to be steered towards the **Dublin Experience**, in the Arts and Social Sciences Building opposite the Old Library, an audio-visual show that takes you through over one thousand years of Dublin history in 45 minutes. It's unlikely that it will give, as it claims, a "complete orientation to the city", but if you're footsore and still have money in your pocket, it may warrant a visit (late May to Sept daily 10am–5pm, hourly shows; €4.20, combined ticket with Old Library €10). The arts block also contains a cheap sandwich and coffee bar and the **Douglas Hyde Gallery** (Mon–Wed & Fri 11am–6pm, Thurs 11am–7pm, Sat 11am–4.45pm; free), an experimental art venue that's usually worth checking out.

On the other side of Fellows' Square stands the 1960s Brutalist-style Berkeley Library, named after Kilkenny-born George Berkeley, who studied at Trinity from the age of 15 and remained a tutor here until he was 28 in 1713. A philosopher, theologian and educationalist, he later became Dean of Derry and Bishop of Cloyne. In front of the library sits a suitably intriguing modern sculpture, *Sphere within a Sphere* by Arnaldo Pomodoro, though its magic is somewhat diminished by its local nickname, "the half-eaten Malteser". Just beyond the Berkeley Library, the School of Engineering occupies a former **museum**, designed by Benjamin Woodward (who enlarged the Old Library) and carved with monkeys, owls and parrots by the O'Shea brothers, whom Woodward invited to carve freely like medieval artists, but then fired after the College authorities expressed displeasure with their work.

The Bank of Ireland

Across the junction from the college, the massive **Bank of Ireland** played an even more central role in the history of Anglo-Irish Ascendancy. When originally begun in 1729 by Sir Edward Lovett Pearce, it was envisaged as a suitably grand setting for the parliament of a nation, as the Anglo-Irish were coming to regard themselves, although Jonathan Swift, for one, had some typically tart opinions as to its worth:

As I stroll the city, oft I
Spy a building large and lofty
Not a bow-shot from the college
Half the globe from sense and knowledge.

The Ascendancy's efforts to achieve self-government culminated in the famous Grattan Parliament of 1782, in which **Henry Grattan** – whose gesturing statue stands outside on College Green – uttered the celebrated phrase "Ireland is now a nation". The Protestant, Anglo-Irish Parliament endorsed the country's Independence unanimously.

This period of nominal self-government was, however, short-lived; with the passing of the Act of Union in 1801, Ireland lost both its Independence as a nation and its parliament (which acquiesced by voting itself obediently out of existence). With its original function gone, the building was sold to the Bank of Ireland for £40,000 two years later. Though not exactly geared up for coach parties, the bank does admit sightseers during normal banking hours (Mon–Wed & Fri 10am–4pm, Thurs 10am–5pm, guided tours Tues 10.30am, 11.30am & 1.45pm). In a room at the back is the atmospheric former **House of Lords**, with its coffered ceiling, oak surrounds and eighteenth-century Waterford glass chandelier, where you can see two 1733 Thomas Baille tapestries celebrating Protestant victories of the previous century: the Siege of Derry in 1689 and the Battle of the Boyne in 1690. Around the corner on Foster Place stands an armoury added during the Napoleonic Wars which now acts as an **arts centre**. It is also the venue for an exhibition on the "**Story of Banking**" which explains the role of the Bank of Ireland in the economic development of the country (Tues–Fri 10am–4pm; €1.50).

Grafton Street to the National Museum

Just to the south of College Green stands Jean Rynhart's famous statue of Molly Malone, affectionately nicknamed the "tart with the cart" due to its brazen decolletage and what Molly reputedly got up to while wheeling her barrow of cockles and mussels through streets broad and narrow. Her famous cry "Alive, alive-o" could well describe **Grafton Street**, the vibrant stretch of pedestrianized road that runs from here up to St Stephen's Green. The streets that surround Grafton Street frame Dublin's quality shopping area, where, in designer clothing stores and chic cafés, affluent Dubliners flaunt and dispose of their new-found prosperity. East of here is Kildare Street, an elegant legacy of the city's eighteenth-century wealth on which stands **Leinster House**, a Georgian town house which is now home to the Irish Parliament.

Grafton Street

Grafton Street is unabashedly commercial. Visit Dublin's leading department store, **Brown Thomas**, for some classy retail therapy, or try the similarly upmarket shops in **Powerscourt Townhouse**, an imaginative conversion of an eighteenth-century mansion set back a little on Clarendon Street. Since its pedestrianization, Grafton Street has become the best place to catch street entertainers – and there are plenty to choose from, ranging from string quartets to groups of guitar-playing kids.

Unmissable in Grafton Street is the Egyptian mosaic facade of **Bewley's Oriental Café** (see p.126), a Dublin institution where all classes mingle over tea, coffee, all-day fried breakfasts, cakes and sticky buns. Founded by the Quaker Bewley family in the 1840s as a (then) teetotal bulwark against the demon drink, it almost folded in 1986, provoking such a national outcry that the government had to step in until a buyer was found.

While in the vicinity, it's worth checking out the **Dublin Civic Museum** (Tues–Sat 10am–6pm, Sun 11am–2pm; free), just west of Grafton Street at 58 William St South. Though it's mainly devoted to temporary exhibitions, on anything from barges to Irish tenors, permanent features include historical views of the city, old shop signs and the 1877 bylaws of St Stephen's Green, denying entry to persons "in an intoxicated, unclean or verminous condition" and "any dog which may be reasonably suspected to be in a rabid state".

Dawson Street

Dawson Street, just east of Grafton Street, is altogether quieter than its neighbour, and is home to some of Dublin's better **bookshops** (see p.137) as well as a number of august institutions. Chief among these is the **Mansion House**, a delicate building of 1710 weighed down by heavy Victorian wrought iron. This has been the official residence of the Lord Mayor since 1715 and was also where the *Dáil Éireann*, the Irish Parliament, met in 1919 to ratify the Independence proclamation of 1916. The Mansion House isn't generally open to the public, but in any case there's not a great deal to be seen inside.

Further along is **St Ann's Church**, whose amazingly ornate Italianesque facade comes as a real surprise when you catch sight of it along South Anne Street. Inside, behind the altar, are wooden shelves that were originally designed to take loaves of bread for distribution among the poor of the parish under the provisions of a 1720s bequest. It's worth checking out the lunchtime and evening concerts of classical music at the church – call ⓣ01/676 7727 for details.

Leinster House

Moving east again, you'll come to **Kildare Street**, the heartland of the Dublin establishment. Its most imposing building is undoubtedly **Leinster House**, built in 1745 for the Duke of Leinster. At that time, the fashionable area of Dublin was north of the river, and there were those who mocked the duke for building in the south on what was then a greenfield site. The Kildare Street facade, facing the town, is built to look like a town house; the other side, looking out on to what is now Merrion Square, resembles a country residence.

The mansion was converted into the **Irish Parliament** in 1922 after the establishment of the Irish Free State. Despite calls to fulfil Daniel O'Connell's dream of restoring the former Grattan Parliament (see p.786), the provisional government at the time deemed Leinster House easier to defend. Beset by enemies at home and abroad, they felt, as Kevin O'Higgins confessed, like "eight young men standing amidst the ruins of one administration with the foundation of another not yet laid, and with wild men screaming through the keyhole".

While the president is the head of state, legislative and executive powers are vested in the Parliament (Oireachtas na hÉireann; ⓦwww.irlgov.ie), which has two chambers: Dáil Éireann (House of Representatives) and Seanad Éireann (Senate). The Dáil (pronounced "doil") has 166 representatives (Teachtaí Dála or TDs), elected by proportional representation, whereas the sixty senators are selected by various authorities including the prime minister or Taoiseach (pronounced "tea-shock") and the universities.

Parliament generally sits from mid-January to July (breaking for Easter), and October until Christmas, on Tuesdays at 2.30pm, and Wednesdays and Thursdays at 10.30am. To visit Leinster House you should telephone ⓣ01/618 3000, preferably two weeks in advance, and ask for the Captain of the Guard or the PR office; free **tours** are then arranged subject to the political diary and the number of people wishing to attend at any given time. The sedate Senate meets in a semicircular blue salon in the north wing; the Dáil sits on the other side of the building and is more of a bear-pit. There are also tours of the adjacent Edwardian administrative block, **Government Buildings** (entrance on Merrion Square), on Saturdays from 10.30am to 3.30pm. Although tours are free, you'll need to get a ticket, available on the day from the ticket office in the National Gallery; the tour lasts forty minutes and takes in the Taoiseach's office, the ceremonial stairs and the cabinet room.

The National Library and Heraldic Museum

The **National Library** (Mon–Wed 10am–9pm, Thurs & Fri 10am–5pm, Sat 10am–1pm; free; ⓦwww.nli.ie) was built in the late nineteenth century, along with the National Museum, to flank Leinster House. It's chiefly worth visiting for its associations – almost every major Irish writer from Joyce onwards has used it at some time. On the ground floor, temporary exhibitions feature anything from old Irish maps to the diaries of Joseph Holiday, describing Dublin's theatrical life. Ask for a visitor's pass to enter the stately domed **Reading Room** on the first floor, scene of one of the great set pieces of *Ulysses* – Stephen's extravagant speech on Shakespeare. If you want to trace your ancestors, visit the **Genealogy Room** (Mon–Fri 10am–4.45pm, Sat 10am–12.30pm; free) where professional genealogists are on hand to give you advice about how to access parish, land and state records.

At the bottom of Kildare Street stands the former **Kildare Street Club**, a Venetian-Gothic red-brick edifice with whimsical figures carved on its pillars – including monkeys playing billiards and a mole with a lute. Once an Anglo-Irish gentlemen's playground, it now houses the Alliance Française and the **Heraldic Museum** (Mon–Wed 10am–8.30pm, Thurs & Fri 10am–4.30pm, Sat 10am–1pm; free), which contains such items as Sir Roger Casement's Order of St Michael and George, the lord chancellor's purse, and the mantle and insignia of the Order of St Patrick.

The National Museum

With its prehistoric gold, medieval treasures and Viking finds, as well as material covering the 1916–21 period and a small but impressive Egyptian collection, the **National Museum** (Tues–Sat 10am–5pm, Sun 2–5pm; free; ⓦwww.museum.ie) is one of the city's essential sights. The collection has grown a great deal from its origins as a donation by the Royal Irish Academy in 1891, and in 1994 the museum acquired the Collins Barracks (see p.117) which now houses artefacts covering social, political and military history, and the decorative arts.

In the main hall, **Ór: Ireland's Gold** gathers together a stunning collection of gold from the Irish Bronze Age (c. 2500–700 BC). Look out especially for the lunulae (crescent-shaped collars made from thin sheets of beaten gold), the twisted bars known as torcs and the Tumna Hoard of nine gold balls, which were probably strung together to form an extravagant necklace.

The adjacent **Treasury** holds many of the museum's better-known ecclesiastical objects, including the elaborate **Ardagh Chalice**, found in County Limerick in 1868 and dating from the eighth century. Perhaps the finest example of Irish metalwork, however, is the **Tara Brooch**, both sides of which bear intricate patterns that may have inspired those in manuscripts such as the Book of Kells. One of the more recent finds is the **Derrynaflan Hoard**, a legacy of the metal-detecting fad which gripped Ireland in the 1980s. This collection of eighth- and ninth-century objects, including a silver chalice and paten, was discovered in February 1980 in County Tipperary by amateur treasure hunters.

The museum's other must-sees are the fascinating exhibitions upstairs on **Viking Age Ireland** (c. 800–1150) and **Medieval Ireland** (c. 1150–1550). In the former you'll find the ornate **Cross of Cong**, made to enshrine a fragment of the True Cross given by the pope to the king of Connacht in 1123 which was later lost. Medieval Ireland covers the period of the first English colonists, their withdrawal to the area around Dublin known as "the Pale" after 1300, and the hybrid culture that developed all the while. To illustrate the reorganization of the Church, a mass of finely decorated, but distinctly strange shrines are on show, including examples for all three of Ireland's patron saints: the Shrine of St Patrick's Tooth, the Shrine of St Brigid's Shoe and the Shrine of the Cathach, containing a manuscript written by St Columcille (St Columba).

St Stephen's Green

Walk to the top of Kildare Street and you'll emerge on the north side of **St Stephen's Green**, the focus of central Dublin's city-planning. It's a decorous expanse, with little bandstands and pergolas, laid out as a public park in 1880 by Lord Ardilaun (Sir Arthur Edward Guinness). It was an open common until 1663, and was only completely surrounded by buildings in the eighteenth century; unfortunately, very few of these have survived, and their replacements speak eloquently of the failure of 1960s planning regulations. The **gardens** are a popular place to while away some time on a sunny day and boast a great range of **statues**, which bear testimony to the city's varied history and cultural life. Maps pinpointing their locations are situated at the main entrances; notable among them is the statue at the northeast corner in memory of Wolfe Tone, backed by slabs of granite and nicknamed "Tone-henge".

The north side of the square, known in the eighteenth century as the "Beaux Walk" because of the dandies who used to promenade there, is dominated by the **Shelbourne Hotel**. Fittingly, the *Shelbourne*, which boasts that it has "the best address in Dublin", continues to be a focus for the upper echelons of the city's social life. It's worth bearing in mind that, as with all Irish hotels, you can wander in for a drink and something to eat in the airy, chandeliered lobby at any time of day, even if you're not staying. The hotel's afternoon teas (from 3pm) are wonderful, but the lobby and bars really come into their own in the evening, when they're great for celebrity spotting.

Just past the hotel at the start of Merrion Row, lies the **Huguenot Cemetery**, which dates from 1693. The Huguenots – French Protestants who fled persecution under Louis XIV, after the repeal of the Edict of Nantes in 1685 took away the religious privileges they had previously enjoyed – enriched cultural life all over Europe with their craftsmanship (their silverwork was particularly valued). Ireland was no exception, and this quiet burial place, with its understated French headstones, seems a particularly fitting tribute to their quietly industrious way of life; for more on the Huguenots in Dublin see p.107.

Linked to the east side of the Green by Hume Street is **Ely Place**, where you can see some of the best-preserved Georgian domestic buildings in Dublin. Here also is the modern **Royal Hibernian Academy of Arts Gallagher Gallery**, one of Ireland's most important galleries for contemporary art (Tues–Sat 11am–5pm, Thurs 11am–8pm, Sun 2–5pm; free; Ⓦ www.royalhibernianacademy.com).

Newman House

On St Stephen's Green South, nos. 85–86 are collectively known as **Newman House** (hourly guided tours June–Aug Tues–Fri noon–5pm, Sat 2–5pm; €4), after Cardinal Newman, the first rector of the Catholic University of Ireland. Founded in 1854 to provide a Catholic equivalent to Trinity College, the institution provided education for generations of Catholics who would otherwise have been obliged to study abroad or submit to the Protestant hegemony of Trinity; James Joyce, Pádraig Pearse and Eamon de Valera were among its alumni. The university later moved out to Belfield, changing its name to University College Dublin (UCD) on the way.

Newman House is fabulously decorative. **Number 85** was originally Clanwilliam House, a miniature Palladian mansion built by Cassels in 1738 for Captain Hugh Montgomery so he could entertain while in town for the "season". Inside, the **Apollo Room** on the ground floor is decorated with superb stuccowork by the Swiss-Italian Franchini brothers, including the nine muses on the walls, a rabbit and two cherubs over the doorway and a fine figure of Apollo himself above the fireplace.

Upstairs is the **Saloon**, with its coffered ceiling and allegorical relief of good government and prudent economy. When the Jesuits acquired the building in 1883, they covered the naked female bodies on the ceiling with what look like furry bathing costumes, to protect the morals of their students; the garments were removed when the house was restored in the 1980s, but one was left *in situ* to show how bizarre they appeared. At the back of the house is an extension in the Gothic style, used as a **Physics Theatre**, where Joyce once lectured to the "L & H" (Literary and Historical Society) and which features in *Portrait of the Artist as a Young Man*.

Number 86 is a larger house built in 1765 for Richard "Burnchapel" Whaley, a virulent anti-Catholic who earned his sobriquet by torching chapels in County Wicklow. His son, Buck Whaley, was a founder of the Hellfire Club. The Saloon has flowing Rococo plasterwork by Robert West and is known as the **Bishops' Room**, having been used for meetings of the university's committee. On the top floor are the **classroom** where Joyce studied from 1899 to 1902, and the **bedroom** of the poet and Jesuit priest Gerard Manley Hopkins, who was Professor of Classics from 1884 until his death in 1889, a miserable period during which he wrote what are called the "Terrible Sonnets".

Beside Newman House stands the Byzantine-style **University Church**, whose opulent interior is adorned with marble quarried from five different sites in Ireland (definitely worth seeing) and is regarded as a chic location for weddings. **Iveagh House**, further along, was the first building that Cassels designed in Dublin, a stately pedimented building which now houses the Department of Foreign Affairs.

The Shaw birthplace

A short walk up Harcourt Street, which heads south from the southwest corner of St Stephen's Green, will bring you to Harrington Street. Turn right, then left into Synge Street, a modest street of patchy Georgian houses, for the **birthplace of George Bernard Shaw** (May–Sept Mon–Sat 10am–5pm, Sun &

George Bernard Shaw

Born in Dublin in 1856, **George Bernard Shaw** was technically a member of the privileged Ascendancy, but his father's failed attempt after leaving the civil service to make money as a grain merchant, meant that Shaw grew up in an atmosphere of genteel poverty and, by the age of 16, he was earning his living in a land agency. His mother left his father for her singing teacher and took her two daughters with her to London; Shaw soon joined them and set about the process of educating himself. Subsidized by his mother's meagre income as a music teacher, he spent his afternoons in the British Museum's reading room and his evenings writing novels. He also became a vegetarian, a socialist and a public speaker of some note.

Shaw's novels were unsuccessful, but his plays were a different matter entirely: underlining the flamboyant young man's wholehearted involvement with his new London environment, he was acclaimed the most important British playwright since the eighteenth century. However, Shaw recognized his foreignness as being a big part of his success: "the position of foreigner with complete command of the same language has great advantages. I can take an objective view of England, which no Englishman can." In the 1890s, influenced by the new drama pioneered by Ibsen, he began to write plays hinged on moral and social questions rather than romantic or personal matters. In play after play – his best-known dramas include *Man and Superman*, *Caesar and Cleopatra*, *Major Barbara*, *St Joan* and *Pygmalion*, from which the musical *My Fair Lady* was adapted – he expounds a progressive view of humanity. For Shaw, the "life-force" is evolving toward an ever-higher level, and his plays successfully mix the accompanying moral fervour with high social comedy. As well as a dramatist, he was an active pamphleteer, critic, journalist and essayist, on subjects ranging from politics and economics to music. After the ecstatic reception of *St Joan*, Shaw was awarded the Nobel Prize for Literature in 1925 – which he initially refused as he didn't want money or recognition, but he relented and donated the money to the newly formed Anglo-Swedish Literary Foundation. In his old age, he was famous almost as much for his dandified persona and espousal of vegetarianism as his writing. He died in 1950 in Ayot St Lawrence in Hertfordshire, England.

bank holidays 2–6pm; €5.50; bus #16, #19 or #122 from O'Connell St or Dame St). For playwright Shaw (see box above) this house, where he lived until he was 10, was not exactly a cause for celebration; Shaw remembered that "neither our hearts nor our imaginations were in it" and recalled the "loveless" atmosphere. You certainly get a vivid impression of the claustrophobic surroundings of the house and its tiny, neat garden. The terse inscription on the facade, "Bernard Shaw, author of many plays", is as Shaw wished.

Merrion Square and Georgian Dublin

East from St. Stephen's Green stand Merrion and Fitzwilliam squares which, along with the surrounding streets, form the heart of what's left of the city's **Georgian heritage**. Representing the latest of the city's Georgian architecture – Mountjoy and Parnell squares, north of the river, are almost all that's left of the earlier Georgian city – their worn, red-brick facades are a brilliant example of confident urban planning, riding on the back of the immense wealth generated in the eighteenth century. The overall layout, in terms of squares and linking streets, may be formal, but there's a huge variation of detail: height, windows, wrought-iron balconies and ornate doorways are all different, but the result is a graceful meeting of form and function that's immensely beguiling.

The apogee of the Georgian area, **Merrion Square** was laid out in the 1770s. Its spacious terraced houses have belonged to diverse famous citizens

– Daniel O'Connell, the Wildes, W.B. Yeats and Nobel prize-winning physicist Erwin Schrödinger – and a stroll past their commemorative plaques gives a marvellous sense of the cultural legacy of the place. There's nothing, however, to recall the British Embassy at no. 39 Merrion Square South, burnt out in 1972 by a crowd protesting against the Bloody Sunday massacre in Derry. Today, the buildings are mainly occupied by offices, but enough people still live here for the square to retain something of a residential feel. The park in the centre is a real pleasure to walk through, with its thickets of low-flowering shrubs, tulip-filled borders and manicured lawns, and on summer Saturdays and Sundays the railings are used by artists flogging their wares. A remarkable statue of **Oscar Wilde** languishes against a rock near the northwest corner of the square, in a pose of outrageous insouciance. Wilde's childhood home is opposite at no. 1; it's been heavily restored as the base of the American College Dublin. Several of the rooms are open to the public (Mon, Wed & Thurs 10.15am & 11.15am; €2.54), but it's really only of interest if you're mad about Wilde. Looking along the south side of the square, you experience one of the set pieces of early-nineteenth-century Dublin's architecture: the hard outlines, pepper-pot tower, Ionic columns and pediment of **St Stephen's Church**.

The National Gallery

On the west side of Merrion Square, the **National Gallery** (Mon–Sat 9.30am–5.30pm, Thurs until 8.30pm, Sun noon–5.30pm; free, €3 donation suggested; ⓦwww.nationalgallery.ie) houses a fine collection of European art, dating from the fifteenth century to the present, which will happily engage you for half a day. The gallery's old building, divided into **Beit**, **Milltown** and **Dargan** wings with its entrance on Merrion Square West, has now been joined by the **Millennium Wing**, whose lofty, skylit atrium gives access to the gallery from Clare Street, opposite the back corner of Trinity College. The resulting layout, however, can be confusing and some further reorganization is planned, including a new National Portrait Gallery on the Dargan Wing's mezzanine. The best way to get a handle on it all is to follow the gallery's division of the collection into Level 1 and Level 2, each spreading across all four wings.

Level 1 is given over largely to **Irish painting**, including a marvellous **Yeats Museum** in the Dargan Wing and a twentieth-century section in the Millennium Wing. Highlights of **Level 2** include works by Caravaggio, Velázquez, Rubens and Vermeer, a fascinating room devoted to art in eighteenth-century Rome and an excellent survey of French art from Poussin to the Cubists; Level 2 of the Millennium Wing is dedicated to major international temporary exhibitions. In the **Print Gallery** (Beit Wing mezzanine) various temporary shows are held throughout the year, and watercolours by **Turner** are exhibited every January (when the light is low enough for these delicate works). In a prime location under the Millennium Wing's glass roof, *Fitzer's* run a good **restaurant** and a cheaper **café**.

When you arrive you can pick up a free leaflet with a **floor plan**, but if it is still all too much for you, head for the Shaw Room (Dargan Wing Level 1) to hook up with one of the free **guided tours** (Sat 3pm & Sun 2pm, 3pm & 4pm).

Level 1: Irish art

The ground floor of the Milltown Wing covers **Irish art 1700–1900**, a period when many Irish painters found employment in England. Notable among the exiles was **Nathaniel Hone the Elder**, who became a founder member of the Royal Academy. His most famous painting, *The Conjurer* (Room 16), is a vicious satire of the RA's president, Sir Joshua Reynolds, whose practice of borrowing from Old Master paintings is characterized by Hone as plagiarism. In Room 17, the emotionally charged extravagances of Romanticism are all too evident, but you can also follow the interest in individuality that gradually took over during the nineteenth century, as painters began to take people from all social strata for their subjects. In **William Mulready**'s *The Toy Seller*, for example, the artist explores the racial interaction between a black toy seller and a wealthy white woman. Many artists of the second half of the nineteenth century drew their inspiration from France and the Impressionist and post-Impressionist movements. This development is exemplified in Room 19, in paintings such as **Walter Osborne**'s *Apple Gathering at Quimperlé*, which demonstrates his preoccupation with atmospheric light and colour, and **Roderic O'Conor**'s vibrant, Gauguin-influenced *Farm at Lezaven, Finistère*.

From Room 19, the best plan is to press on with **modern Irish art** via a short detour into the Millennium Wing. Garish and confrontational, **William Orpen**'s satirical *The Holy Well* (Room 4) stands out here, depicting villagers of the west tearing off their clothes to seek succour at the well, while a lone figure derides their faith. Under the influence of Orpen, many Irish artists largely ignored Modernism but continued to produce vigorous work in the academic tradition, as evidenced in Room 3. **Sean Keating**'s *Allegory* is a particularly affecting piece here, produced in 1922 when civil war was tearing Ireland apart. Notable in Room 1 is *The Family* by **Louis le Brocquy**, conveying the sense of alienation in the years after World War II; the work, which was recently bought by an Irish businessman for nearly €3 million and donated to the gallery in exchange for tax breaks, was flatly rejected by Dublin's Municipal Gallery of Modern Art when offered free of charge in the 1950s.

Level 1: The Yeats Museum and British art

Over in the grandiose Shaw Room in the Dargan Wing, there's a splendid statue by Paul Troubetzkoy of George Bernard Shaw, who left one third of his residual estate to the gallery, the "cherished asylum" of his youth. Standing taut with intellectual rigour it announces the entrance to the **Yeats Museum**. Though dedicated to **Jack B. Yeats** (1871–1957), the small museum also covers the work of the talented family from which he came, including portraits of Irish notables such as playwright J.M. Synge by Jack B.'s father, John Butler Yeats. However, it's Jack B.'s paintings that really steal the show, mapping the development of his art as it moved away from representation and became increasingly more abstract, fluid and vivid. Look out especially for later works such as *The Singing Horseman* and *For the Road*, spirited paintings in which the subject appears to be trying to break free from the canvas, and *Grief*, a chaotic abstraction of anguish.

The ground floor of the Beit Wing is largely devoted to **British art**, most of it from the eighteenth century. In Rooms 10 and 9, superb large-scale portraits by **Reynolds**, **Gainsborough** and **Hogarth** vie for attention.

Level 2: Spanish and Italian art

Upstairs in the Beit Wing, the highlight of the gallery's **Spanish art** collection is *Kitchen Maid with the Supper at Emmaus*, the earliest known picture by **Velázquez** (c. 1617–18; Room 33) – Christ and his disciples are in the background and attention is focused on the Moorish maid, her startled pose perhaps suggesting that she too might convert to Christianity.

You can quite happily avoid making the acquaintance of the anonymous

German and Netherlandish masters in Room 31, as the collection of **Italian art** beyond is far more compelling. In Room 30, *SS Cosmas and Damian*, a panel by **Fra Angelico**, the fifteenth-century Florentine master, shows the medical saints miraculously surviving trial by fire, while in Room 29 there's a superb **Mantegna**, *Judith with the Head of Holofernes*, painted in monochrome to simulate a marble relief. In the same room, look out for **Filippino Lippi**'s lively *Portrait of a Musician*, in which the subject carefully tunes his lyre to illustrate the inscription on the back, "never start before the time". Progressing into Room 28 and the sixteenth century, you'll come face to face with **Tintoretto**'s wizened *Portrait of a Venetian Senator*, bracketed by a pair of **Titians**: the delicately composed *Supper at Emmaus* and a severe portrait of the diplomat and writer Baldassare Castiglione. Room 27 contains some fine examples of the Bolognese School of painting of the sixteenth and seventeenth centuries, which left behind Mannerism for more spontaneous handling of emotions. Especially notable are the sharply observed *Portrait of a Man* by **Annibale Carracci**, one of the school's prime movers, and *Jacob Blessing the Sons of Joseph* by **Guercino**, who demonstrates here his outstanding feel for colour and naturalism.

Room 25 covers "Art in Rome in the eighteenth century" with plenty of local interest. Among some diverting views of Rome and various Irish gentlemen who had themselves immortalized in the Eternal City, don't miss **Reynolds**' fascinating *Parody of Raphael's "School of Athens"*, which purveys some familiar Irish stereotypes to ridicule the Grand Tourists.

From Room 25 it makes sense to continue the Italian theme into 42 and 43, before going Dutch and Flemish in Rooms 37 to 41. The highlight of Room 42 is **Caravaggio**'s *The Taking of Christ*. The violence of the act is conveyed in the powerful movement of the soldiers' gestures, with Christ a figure of spiritual stillness at the centre; Caravaggio portrayed himself as a passive spectator on the right of the picture, holding a lamp. In Room 43, among several harmoniously restrained cityscapes by **Canaletto** and his nephew **Bellotto**, the dynamic, symbolically fraught *Allegory of the Immaculate Conception* by **Tiepolo** is striking.

Level 2: Dutch and Flemish art

Backtracking through the Caravaggio Room, you'll find the highlight of the **Dutch collection** in Room 40: **Vermeer**'s *Woman Writing a Letter, with her Maid*, one of only 35 accepted works by the artist, with his characteristic use of white light from the window accentuating the woman's emotions. A painting of *The Finding of Moses* on the wall behind provides a reminder to trust in Divine Will to resolve matters. Otherwise, the best of the Low Countries is in Room 37, with its collection of **Flemish art**. Your eye is most likely to be drawn here to *A Boy Standing on a Terrace* – in this, the most elaborate of his portraits of children, **van Dyck** skilfully juxtaposes the young Genoese nobleman's haughty, grown-up stance with the vulnerability of his cherubic expression.

Level 2: Baroque masters and French art

Lofty Room 44 in the Dargan Wing is where oversized, and generally overstuffed, **Baroque** masters have found their setting. Only *St Peter Finding the Tribute Money* by **Rubens** demands attention, a beautifully observed portrayal of middle-aged men in robust discussion.

From here, take the left-hand set of stairs up to Room 48 to get a chronological take on the excellent collection of **French art**. Among several fine paintings by **Poussin**, the master of restrained Classicism, *The Lamentation over the Dead Christ* stands out: this unusually emotive work, heightened by the use of intense colours, was painted by the ageing artist as a meditation on death.

Room 46 injects a sense of realism with the Barbizon School, who left their Paris studios to paint directly from nature, taking their inspiration from the seventeenth-century Dutch landscapists and providing some of their own for the Impressionists who followed. Works by **Millet**, **Corot** and **Courbet** amply illustrate what this meant in practice, while **Couture**'s *La Peinture Réaliste* is a satirical counter-attack on the theory from the Classical establishment: with his behind parked on a sculpted head of Jupiter, the Realist sketches a pig's head, with an old lantern, a shoe and a cabbage on the wall for further inspiration.

To finish off, Room 45 gives a whirlwind tour of Impressionism and the movements that came in its wake. Both **Claude Monet**'s *Argenteuil Basin with a Single Sailboat* and **Alfred Sisley**'s *The Banks of the Canal du Loing at St-Mammès* beautifully capture the transitory effects of light. Those that followed attempted to reintroduce structure as a key element, most successfully in the vibrant, emotive colours of Fauvist **Kees van Dongen**'s *Stella in a Flowered Hat* and Expressionist **Emil Nolde**'s *Two Women in a Garden*. By the time of **Picasso**'s exuberant *Still Life with a Mandolin* and fellow-Cubist **Juan Gris**' melancholic *Pierrot*, structure has firmly won the day.

The Natural History Museum

On the same side of Merrion Square as the National Gallery, the **Natural History Museum** (Tues–Sat 10am–5pm, Sun 2–5pm; free) preserves the essence of Victorian museums like a fly in amber, being virtually unchanged since the explorer and missionary Dr David Livingstone delivered the inaugural lecture in 1857. A statue of a rifle-toting naturalist with his foot on an animal skull on the lawn – Surgeon Major T.H. Park, the first Irishman to travel the breadth of Africa – presages the orgy of taxidermy and taxonomy within. The ground-floor **Irish Room** opens with three skeletons of the giant Irish deer, which had the largest-ever antler span (12ft) and became extinct around 9000 BC. Upstairs, the **World Collection** on the first floor includes taxidermic rhinoceroses, moose and other appealing creatures, as well as the Barrington Collection of birds, many of which were hapless enough to crash into Irish lighthouses. The **lower gallery** on the second floor, the last resting place of a stuffed dodo, is the best spot to view the skeletons of two whales stranded on Irish shores. The third-floor **upper gallery** includes the amazing Blaschka Collection of glass models of marine creatures.

No. 29 Fitzwilliam Street Lower

An assiduous reconstruction of a Georgian town house at the southeast corner of Merrion Square, **No. 29 Fitzwilliam Street Lower** (Tues–Sat 10am–5pm, Sun 2–5pm, closed last three weeks of Dec; €3.15) is well worth visiting. An engaging and informative guided tour explains the kind of society developed by the political and merchant classes of late-eighteenth-century Dublin and explores the minutiae of bourgeois life. The tour kicks off in the basement, where water was filtered for drinking and coal and wine were stored in the cellar. Next door to the pantry the housekeeper's room has a small window, through which she could keep a close eye on light-fingered servants (who slept in slums elsewhere). Gracious living began upstairs, where you'll see such contraptions as a lead-lined wine cooler and a belly-warmer for soothing gastric complaints. The nursery contains a doll's house and a bed for the governess, who was hired to instruct the daughters (boys went to boarding school) in such ladylike arts as embroidery; the governess's needlework samplers on the wall were the Georgian equivalent of a curriculum vitae.

Fitzwilliam Square, south of Merrion Square along Fitzwilliam Street, is another elegant example of a late Georgian square – it was built between 1791 and 1825 – with some of the city's finest Georgian doors and fanlights. The dwindling number of residents still hold keys to the central garden.

Baggot Street and the Grand Canal

Running east from Grafton Street and across Fitzwilliam Street, **Baggot Street** – with its multitude of lively pubs – starts out Georgian, but the street plan is pretty soon broken by the great black metal and glass bulk of the Bank of Ireland building, enlivened only by a few brightly coloured metal Constructivist sculptures. Just beyond the bank, you reach the Grand Canal, one of Dublin's two constructed waterways – the other, the Royal Canal, runs through the north of the city. True Dubliners, or "Jackeens", are said to be those born between the two waterways.

The **Grand Canal** was the earlier and more successful of the two waterways: started in 1756 and reaching the Shannon by 1803, it carried passengers and freight between Dublin, the midland towns and the Shannon right up to the 1960s, despite competition from the railways. Its total length, including stretches of the rivers Barrow and Shannon, was 340 miles. The potential for tourism in re-opening the canals has only been realized over the last decade; consequently some patches are clean, free-flowing and beautiful while around the bend the vista is a picture of economic decline. Perhaps the best stretch of the canal to visit is the section around Baggot Street Bridge, where the water is fringed by trees. Baggot Street and a Dublin institution, the late, lamented **Parson's bookshop**, were haunts of many of Dublin's celebrated writers in the 1950s, including the poet and novelist Patrick Kavanagh and the playwright Brendan Behan. Kavanagh lived in a flat nearby in Pembroke Road and produced a "journal of literature and politics" entitled *Kavanagh's Weekly*, written largely by himself (with a few contributions from Behan and Myles na Gopaleen, aka Flann O'Brien). It ran to a total of thirteen issues before folding, with pieces about anything and everything – professional marriage makers, visits to the bookies, weeks when nothing happens. After Kavanagh's death in 1967, his home on Pembroke Road was found to contain little more than a bed, and his friends erected a plain memorial **seat** opposite the *Mespil Hotel* on the Mespil Road side of Baggot Street Bridge in accordance with his wish: "O commemorate me with no hero-courageous/Tomb – just a canal-bank seat for the passer-by". Sadly, the seat's wood is now decaying and the life-size **statue of Kavanagh**, musing on a bronze bench on the other side of the canal, is tarnished by verdigris.

The Grand Canal reaches the River Liffey at Ringsend (about a mile north-east of Baggot Street Bridge), through its original locks, constructed in 1796. You can find out more about the history and use of all of Ireland's canals and waterways at the **Waterways Visitor Centre** (June–Sept daily 9.30am–5.30pm; Oct–May Wed–Sun 12.30–5pm; €2.50), a little upstream from the Grand Canal Dock (bus #2 or #3 from O'Connell St or Townsend St; DART to Grand Canal Dock Station).

Temple Bar

The main thoroughfare west from College Green is **Dame Street**. Immediately north, the area between the modern Central Bank and the Liffey is known as **Temple Bar**. Until the dissolution of the monasteries in 1537, the land on which Temple Bar stands was the property of the Augustinian order. Originally built on marshy land reclaimed from the Liffey, Temple Bar owes its name not to the friars, but to Sir William Temple, who bought the plot in the late sixteenth century. During the eighteenth century, the place was a centre for Dublin's low life, in the shape of brothels and pubs (the pubs are still there), while in the nineteenth century it attracted the small businesses and tradesmen who altered its character.

Bought up in the 1960s by CIÉ (formerly the state transport company), which wanted to build a new central bus terminal to replace the one on the other side of the river, Temple Bar suffered for many years from a benign sort of planning blight. With its old warehouses and cobbled streets preserved by default, it gained a name as the city's arty quarter, as studios and shops were rented out on short leases. After the bus station idea was abandoned in the 1980s, they were joined by art galleries, restaurants and cultural centres. However, in recent years the area has been extensively redeveloped – including the new shopping district that's bizarrely tagged "Old City" on the west side of Parliament Street – and has lost much of its bohemian and anarchic appeal. All the same, Temple Bar still remains one of the liveliest and most interesting parts of town, often compared with Covent Garden in London or Les Halles in Paris. With its emphasis now firmly placed on the bacchanalian, it's not surprising that the area really comes to life at night, as revellers spill out from bars onto the narrow streets for impromptu street parties.

The heart of Temple Bar

You won't have to wander far off Dame Street to find an arts centre of some kind in Temple Bar. Off Temple Lane, once known as Dirty Lane, is ultramodern Curved Street, flanked by the **Arthouse**, a multimedia centre for the arts (recently closed due to financial difficulties, its future is uncertain), and the state-of-the-art **Temple Bar Music Centre**, a major gig venue (see p.132) that's also home to recording and television studios. A passageway links to Eustace Street, where you'll find **The Ark**, a cultural centre for children (Ⓣ01/670 7788 or Ⓦwww.ark.ie for details of its programmes and festivals of music, theatre, literature, visual arts and new media), and the coolly minimalist **Irish Film Centre** (see pp.135 & 127). Its two screens show art-house and special-interest films, and its bar and restaurant attract a trendy crowd.

On the other side of Eustace Street, **Meeting House Square**, named after the Quaker meeting hall, hosts a Saturday food market (see p.138) as well as a wide variety of free outdoor cultural events throughout the summer. Facing onto the square are the **Gallery of Photography**, which shows contemporary photoworks from around the world (Ⓣ01/671 4654, Ⓦwww.irish-photography.com), and the **National Photographic Archive** (Ⓣ01/603 0200, Ⓦwww.nli.ie), which puts on exhibitions from the photographic collections of the National Library.

Turning right from Eustace Street or Meeting House Square will take you along Temple Bar itself to the **Original Print Gallery** (Ⓣ01/677 3657, Ⓦwww.originalprint.ie), where you can catch the work of emerging and established Irish and international printmakers; and to **Temple Bar Gallery and Studios** (Ⓣ01/671 0073), one of the largest of its kind in Europe, with thirty studios for contemporary artists and a cutting-edge exhibition space. **Temple Bar Square** just beyond hosts a lively book market on Saturdays and Sundays.

If you turn left instead of right at the top of Eustace Street, along Essex Street East, you'll find the **DESIGNyard** (see p.138), a showcase for contemporary

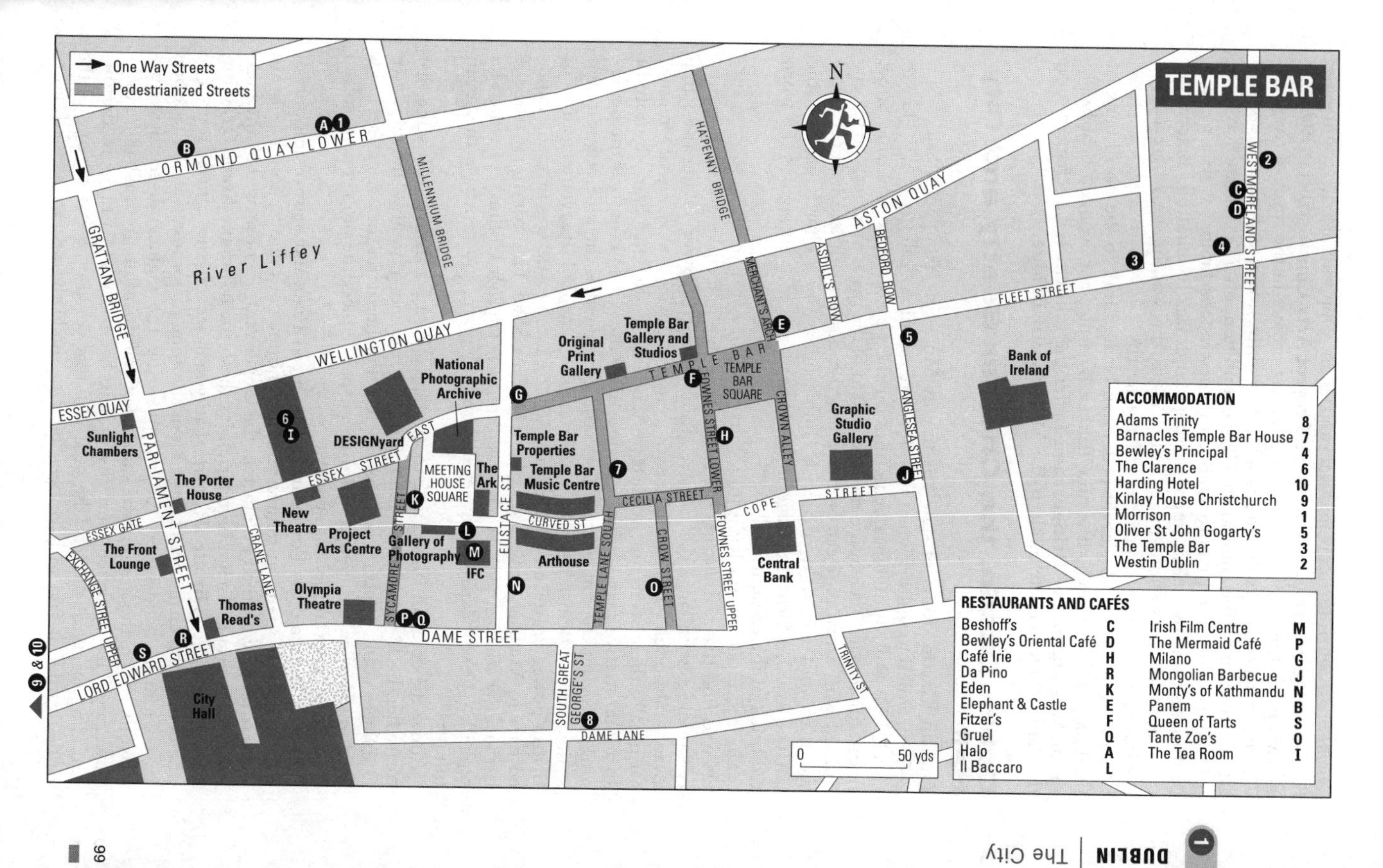
TEMPLE BAR
One Way Streets
Pedestrianized Streets
N
ORMOND QUAY LOWER
GRATTAN BRIDGE
River Liffey
MILLENNIUM BRIDGE
HA'PENNY BRIDGE
ASTON QUAY
WELLINGTON QUAY
ESSEX QUAY
PARLIAMENT STREET
ESSEX STREET EAST
ESSEX GATE
EXCHANGE STREET UPPER
LORD EDWARD STREET
CRANE LANE
SYCAMORE STREET
EUSTACE ST
CURVED ST
MEETING HOUSE SQUARE
TEMPLE BAR
TEMPLE BAR SQUARE
TEMPLE LANE SOUTH
CECILIA STREET
CROW STREET
FOWNES STREET LOWER
FOWNES STREET UPPER
MERCHANT'S ARCH
CROWN ALLEY
COPE STREET
ASDILL'S ROW
BEDFORD ROW
ANGLESEA STREET
FLEET STREET
WESTMORELAND STREET
DAME STREET
SOUTH GREAT GEORGE'S ST
DAME LANE
TRINITY ST
Sunlight Chambers
The Porter House
The Front Lounge
Thomas Read's
City Hall
DESIGNyard
New Theatre
Project Arts Centre
Olympia Theatre
Gallery of Photography
IFC
National Photographic Archive
The Ark
Temple Bar Properties
Temple Bar Music Centre
Arthouse
Original Print Gallery
Temple Bar Gallery and Studios
Graphic Studio Gallery
Central Bank
Bank of Ireland
0 50 yds
9 & 10
ACCOMMODATION
Adams Trinity 8
Barnacles Temple Bar House 7
Bewley's Principal 4
The Clarence 6
Harding Hotel 10
Kinlay House Christchurch 9
Morrison 1
Oliver St John Gogarty's 5
The Temple Bar 3
Westin Dublin 2
RESTAURANTS AND CAFÉS
Beshoff's C
Bewley's Oriental Café D
Café Irie H
Da Pino R
Eden K
Elephant & Castle E
Fitzer's F
Gruel Q
Halo A
Il Baccaro L
Irish Film Centre M
The Mermaid Café P
Milano G
Mongolian Barbecue J
Monty's of Kathmandu N
Panem B
Queen of Tarts S
Tante Zoe's O
The Tea Room I

jewellery as well as furniture and interior design. Opposite lies the bright-blue flagship of the contemporary art scene, **Project Arts Centre** (Ⓣ01/679 6622, Ⓦwww.project.ie), which began life as an art project in the foyer of the Gate Theatre, but now hosts theatre, dance, film and live music as well as the visual arts. Further up on the same street, U2 spent millions on *The Clarence* hotel (see p.74) and have turned it into Dublin's coolest establishment, with a rooftop penthouse used by celebs such as Björk and Jack Nicholson. Before the Custom House moved downriver in the 1780s, this was the site where a crane used to unload ships – hence Crane Lane, nearby.

From Temple Bar, two elegant pedestrian bridges lead to the north bank of the Liffey (see p.61), which is now flanked by a pleasant, wooden boardwalk: the arching **Ha'penny Bridge**, named after the toll which was charged until the early 1900s; and the modern, flat **Millennium Bridge**.

Dublin Castle, the Chester Beatty and City Hall

Dublin Castle (tours of state apartments Mon–Fri 10am–5pm, Sat & Sun 2–5pm, closed to visitors when used for state occasions, call Ⓣ01/677 7129 to check; €4; Ⓦwww.dublincastle.ie.) lies on the opposite side of Dame Street from Temple Bar. Once inside the Lower Yard of the castle precinct, you're confronted with a real pig's ear of architectural styles: an ugly modern tax office stands to your left; an over-precise Gothic fantasy of a church of 1803, the Chapel Royal, adorns the ridge straight ahead; and to your right is the worn red brick of the castle itself.

The castle dates from King John's first Dublin court of 1207, so it's a surprise to find that today it has the appearance of a graceful eighteenth-century building, with only the massive stone **Record Tower** giving the game away – although, in the nineteenth century, this too was heavily rebuilt. Originally there were four such towers, but the castle later became more of an administrative than a military centre. After the Act of Union at the beginning of the nineteenth century the castle continued as the viceroy's seat, and as the heart of British rule, the place stands as a symbol of seven centuries of British power in Ireland. On January 16, 1922, the castle was formally handed over to Michael Collins and the Irish Free State. The story goes that the last viceroy complained, "You're seven minutes late, Mr Collins", to which he replied, "We've been waiting seven hundred years, you can have the seven minutes."

Above the ceremonial entrance to the Upper Yard is a **figure of Justice** that turns her back to the city, illustrating, it was said, just how much justice Dubliners could expect from the English. Furthermore, the scales she holds used to tilt when it rained; to ensure even-handedness, the problem was solved by drilling holes in the scale-pans.

The castle hosted the European Parliament in 1990, and massive amounts of EU funds were spent on refurbishing it in honour of the occasion. The **State Apartments**, with their entrance in the Upper Yard, are now used by the president to entertain foreign dignitaries. It's these, including the **State Drawing Room** and the **Throne Room**, that you'll see on the official tour. The grandeur of the furnishings takes a bit of adjusting to; for instance, all the rooms have Donegal hand-tufted carpets mirroring the eighteenth-century stuccowork, which, though superb examples of craftsmanship, are really quite overpowering. This opulence must always have been in stark contrast to the surrounding reality of the city: the high wall that you'll notice at the end of the castle's garden is said to have been built to shield the delicate sensibilities of

Queen Victoria from the appalling condition of the slums on Stephen Street.

Excavations for the new conference centre built in 1990 revealed perhaps the most interesting part of the tour, the **Undercroft**. Here you can see remains of an earlier Viking fort, part of the original thirteenth-century moat plus the base of the **Powder Tower**, a section of the old city wall and the steps that used to lead down to the Liffey. It's unfortunate that similar care for the city's past was not practised two blocks north of the castle on **Wood Quay**, the site of Viking and Norman settlements that yielded amazing quantities of archaeological finds (on show in the National Museum). The excavations were never completed and there's undoubtedly more to be discovered on the site, but despite a lot of argument the corporation of Dublin was able to go ahead and put up two massive Civic Offices, known to one and all as "The Bunkers", destroying what may have been the most important early Viking archaeological site in Europe.

The Chester Beatty Library

Beyond the Lower Yard lies the pretty castle garden: now adorned with a swirling motif taken from the passage grave at Newgrange (see p.200), it marks the site of the "Dark Pool" (Dubh Linn) which gave the city its English name. Overlooking the garden from the renovated eighteenth-century Clock Tower Building, the **Chester Beatty Library** preserves a dazzling collection of books, manuscripts, prints and *objets d'art* from around the world (Tues–Fri 10am–5pm, Sat 11am–5pm, Sun 1–5pm, guided tours Wed 1pm & Sun 3pm & 4pm; free; Ⓦwww.cbl.ie). Superlatives come thick and fast here: as well as one of the finest Islamic collections in existence, containing some of the earliest manuscripts from the ninth and tenth centuries, the library holds important biblical papyri, including the earliest surviving examples in any language of Mark's and Luke's Gospels, St Paul's Epistles and the Book of Revelation. Elegantly displayed in hi-tech galleries, the artefacts are used to tell the story of religious and artistic traditions across the world with great ingenuity, a formula which won the CBL the European Museum of the Year award in 2002. It's well worth timing your visit to coincide with lunch at the excellent *Silk Road Café* – see p.127.

The collection was put together by the remarkable **Sir Alfred Chester Beatty**, a mining magnate born in New York in 1875 into a family of Ulster-Scots, English and Irish ancestry. At about the same time as he moved to London in 1911, Beatty began collecting, buying only works of the utmost rarity and highest quality, and always comparing them against similar material in the British Museum or the Bibliothéque Nationale in Paris. Although he became a naturalized British subject in 1933 (and was later knighted), after World War II Beatty grew disillusioned with Britain under the new Labour government, holding in contempt what he saw as their socialist bureaucracy and, in particular, their strict foreign exchange rules. He cut a deal with the Irish government to gain exemption from their currency limits (then sixty guineas, whereas Beatty liked to travel with no less than $10,000), from import taxes on his artistic purchases and from estate duties on his collection after his death. In the early 1950s, Beatty moved himself and his works to Dublin, in 1957 he was made the first honorary citizen of Ireland, and when he died in 1968 he was given a state funeral and bequeathed his collection to the state.

Most of the CBL's vast holding is accessible only to scholars via the reference library, with just two percent on show in the public **galleries** at any one time – though that's more than enough to keep you occupied for a few hours. Consequently, and to protect the delicate artefacts, the examples on display are changed every six months, but the gist of the exhibition's narrative remains the same. The second-floor gallery covers "Spiritual Traditions", the first floor "Artistic Traditions", with each divided into Western, Islamic and Eastern sections; exhibits range from sixteenth-century biblical engravings by Albrecht Dürer to one of the world's largest collections of intricately carved rhino-horn cups, and from gorgeously illustrated books of Persian poetry to serene Burmese statues of the Buddha.

City Hall

In front of the castle on Lord Edward Street is **City Hall** (Mon–Sat 10am–5.15pm, Sun 2–5pm), one of the finest examples of Georgian architecture in the city. Built between 1769 and 1779 as the Royal Exchange, it has been occupied by Dublin Corporation since 1852 and is still the venue for council meetings. It's definitely worth walking in to view the gleamingly restored Neoclassical rotunda, where creamy Portland-stone columns, interspersed with statues of Daniel O'Connell and other worthies, are bathed in wonderful natural light from the dome. Check out also the exquisite plasterwork and the Arts and Crafts murals tracing Dublin's history. The civic coat of arms on the floor shows three burning bastions, symbolizing resistance to invaders, but the motto *Obedientia Civium Urbis Felicitas* ("Happy the City whose Citizens Obey") suggests that rebellion was a greater worry for Dublin's rulers. In 1922, as headquarters of the provisional government during the civil war, City Hall witnessed the lying-in-state both of Arthur Griffith, the first president, and, just a week later, of the assassinated Michael Collins – for which the twenty-foot-high statue of O'Connell was dramatically swathed in black robes.

The vaults beneath the rotunda now shelter a branch of the excellent *Queen of Tarts* café (see p.127) and **The Story of the Capital** (€4), a fascinating multimedia journey through Dublin's history and politics. The story is told through exhaustive display panels, slick interactive databases and videos, as well as specially commissioned artworks such as *Utopian Column*, a stack of glass plates engraved with historical scenes and flooded with light.

The cathedrals and around

The area west of Dublin Castle is the site of the **original Viking settlement** and represents the most ancient part of the city: the old Tholsel, or town hall, used to stand here, as did the original Four Courts. Today, this historic place is remarkable for its strange combination of urban desolation and renewal (generous tax concessions are ensuring that there's plenty of new building), and the massive, over-restored grey bulks of not one but two **cathedrals**. Both date originally from the twelfth century: Christ Church from 1172 and St Patrick's, designed to supersede it, from 1190. The reason that both have survived appears to be that Christ Church stood inside the city walls, and St Patrick's outside. Both cathedrals remain dedicated to the Church of Ireland, their great forms once a symbol of the dominance of the British, but now manifestations of what is very much a minority religious denomination.

Christ Church Cathedral

In medieval times, **Christ Church** (Mon–Fri 9.45am–5pm, Sat & Sun 10am–5pm; €3; Ⓦwww.cccdub.ie) would have soared above the city's wooden houses from its commanding site on Dublin Hill, but today the view is generally obscured by buildings, and the cathedral has been isolated from its surroundings by the traffic system. Dublin's first (wooden) cathedral was founded here by Sitric IV ("Silkenbeard"), first Christian king of the Dublin Norsemen, in 1038; that church was demolished by the Norman Richard de Clare – Strongbow – who started work on a new stone cathedral in 1172. This building didn't fare very well either: it was built on inadequate foundations on a peat bog, and the south wall fell down in 1562, pulling down half the cathedral. The rest continued as a church (and a tavern and market) but steadily deteriorated until the distiller Henry Roe lavished £230,000 to finance its restoration in the 1870s. Architect George Street transformed the cathedral's outward appearance by adding flying buttresses, but the interior preserves more of its original character.

Close to the entrance lies the curious **tomb of Strongbow**. The original was destroyed by the collapse of the south wall, but was substituted with an effigy of an earl so that Dublin landlords could resume their practice of collecting rents around it. Elsewhere in the nave, look out for the Civic Pew for Dublin's Lord Mayor, and on the other side the State Pew, used by the Irish president, which still bears the royal arms of the Stuarts. The **choir** contains fine oak stalls for the canons and choristers, and the lofty archbishop's throne. Turning back to face the nave, you'll be startled by the "leaning wall of Dublin" – ever since the south wall collapsed, the north wall has leaned outwards. Beyond the choir on the wall of Laud's Chapel is a heart-shaped iron casket containing the heart of Archbishop Laurence O'Toole, the patron saint of Dublin, who died in Normandy and was canonized in 1225.

Descend the stairs by the south transept to reach the **crypt**, the purest remnant of the twelfth-century cathedral (you can still see parts of the timber frame used during construction); formerly a storehouse for the trade in alcohol and tobacco, it's one of the largest crypts in Ireland and Britain. Part of the crypt is taken up with the **Treasures of Christ Church** exhibition (Mon–Fri 9.45am–5pm, Sat 10am–4.45pm, Sun 12.30–3.15pm; €3, pay at the turnstiles), which contains a miscellany of manuscripts and church crockery. Look out for a ropey-looking tabernacle and pair of candlesticks made for James II on his flight from England in 1689, when, for three months only, Latin Mass was again celebrated at Christ Church (the existing cathedral paraphernalia was hidden by quick-thinking Anglican officials under a bishop's coffin).

Twisting downhill along the east side of the cathedral, **Fishamble Street** was the main thoroughfare of Viking Dublin. Between the *Handel Hotel* and the *Chorus Café*, a white arch and a low red-brick wall are all that's left of **Neal's Music Hall**, where Handel conducted the combined choirs of Christ Church and St Patrick's in the first performance of his *Messiah* in 1742. Swift's verdict was, "Oh, a German, a genius, a prodigy". Excerpts from the *Messiah* are performed here on the anniversary of the event (April 13, throughout the day). In the private garden beyond the white arch, Handel's reward is a statue of himself conducting in the nude, perched on a set of organ pipes.

Dublinia

Like many of Dublin's larger monuments, Christ Church keeps drawing in the crowds with multimedia evocations of history. Styling itself as "a bridge to the medieval past", **Dublinia** (April–Sept daily 10am–5pm; Oct–March Mon–Sat 11am–4pm, Sun 10am–4.30pm; €5.75, €7 for combination ticket with Christ Church Cathedral; Ⓦ www.dublinia.ie) offers a series of presentations on medieval Dublin, including a reconstruction of a merchant's house and a quayside, and a panoramic model of Dublin c. 1500. Some of the Viking and Norman artefacts dug up at nearby Wood Quay are also on display here. The exhibition occupies the ex-Synod Hall of the Church of Ireland, connected to the cathedral by an elegant and famous bridge across which visitors exit the exhibition.

St Audoen's

Just to the west of Dublinia, on the corner of Bridge Street, stand two churches dedicated to St Audoen (in French, Ouen, seventh-century bishop of Rouen and the patron saint of Normandy). The monumental but largely uninteresting nineteenth-century Catholic version overshadows its neighbour, **Protestant St Audoen's**, which was built around 1190 and is now partly administered by Dúchas, the Heritage Service, as an intriguing tourist site (May Sat & Sun 9.30am–5.30pm; June–Sept daily 9.30am–5.30pm; €1.90; Heritage Card). There are still services every Sunday at 10.15am – the church has been continuously used for worship for over eight centuries, longer than any other in Dublin.

The most fascinating aspect of a visit is seeing the physical evidence of how the church's fortunes waxed and waned over the centuries. As it prospered through close association with the city's guilds, St Audoen's expanded in stages around its original single-naved church, including the addition, in 1431, of **St Anne's Guild Chapel**, making a two-aisled nave. The latter is now the main exhibition area, with interesting displays on the parish and the guilds.

Before the Reformation, St Audoen's had been the most prestigious parish church among Dublin's leading families, who sought to worship and be buried here. Afterwards, however, many members of the all-important Guild of St Anne refused to become Protestant and the congregation declined. By the nineteenth century St Audoen's had retreated to its original single nave, by the simple expediency of removing the roofs from the other parts of the church and letting them rot. You can now poke around the open-air **chancel** and **Portlester Chapel**, where, before the building was declared a national monument, locals would hang their washing out to dry.

A guide will escort you into the present (and original) parish church. The big crowd-pleaser here is the **Lucky Stone**: this unprepossessing ninth-century grave slab has been credited with all manner of powers – glowing, groaning, rolling and even assuming human form – and has been worn down to a smooth sheen over the centuries with supplicants stroking and kissing it for luck.

Behind the Protestant church, steps descend to thirteenth-century **St Audoen's Arch**, the only remaining gate in the **Norman city walls** – a dramatic, though heavily restored remnant stretching for two hundred yards along Cook Street, 22ft high and tipped with battlements.

St Werburgh's Church

Werburgh Street, which leads south from Christ Church to the back of St Patrick's, was the site of Dublin's first theatre; today, it's home to *Leo Burdock's*, the legendary fish-and-chip shop (see p.127) as well as **St Werburgh's Church**. Founded by the Normans in 1178, its plain exterior, with peeling paint in motley shades of grey, conceals a flamboyant and elegant 1759 interior built in the height of Georgian style, which is well worth seeing should you manage to gain entry (Sun 10am for Church of Ireland services). Lord Edward Fitzgerald, one of the leaders of the 1798 Rebellion, is buried in the Fitzgerald vault; Major Henry Sirr, who captured him for the British, is interred in the churchyard. Also, John Field, the early-nineteenth-century Irish composer and pianist who is credited with having invented the nocturne, later developed by Chopin, was baptized here, and in the church records there is mention of one "Molly Malone, fishmonger" who died in 1734.

St Patrick's Cathedral

Like Christ Church, **St Patrick's** (March–Oct daily 9am–6pm; Nov–Feb Mon–Fri 9am–6pm, Sat 9am–5pm, Sun 10am–3pm; €3.50; Ⓦ www.stpatrickscathedral.ie) was restored by the Victorians, though it seems closer to its origins than Christ Church and is altogether quirkier, thanks to its array of odd memorials. The cathedral stands on one of Dublin's earliest Christian sites, where St Patrick is said to have baptized converts in a well (c. 450).

Once inside, most visitors make a beeline for the **graves of Jonathan Swift and Stella**, Swift's long-term partner, beneath brass tablets in the nave, just to the right of the entrance. On the nearby wall of the south aisle are a bust of Swift and his epitaph, translated from the Latin:

Here is laid the body of
Jonathan Swift, Doctor of Divinity,
Dean of this Cathedral Church,
Where fierce indignation can no longer
Rend the heart.
Go, traveller, and imitate, if you can
This earnest and dedicated
Champion of liberty.

There's also a copy of a tribute to Swift by his friend Alexander Pope, with whom he planned to share a home in retirement. Among other Swift memorabilia in this area are his pulpit and table, his death mask and a cast of his skull: both his and Stella's bodies were exhumed by Victorian phrenologists, studying the skulls of the famous.

To the left of the entrance, you can't miss the gigantic **Boyle monument**, which teems with painted figures of the fifteen children borne by Katherine Fenton, the "dearest, dear wife" of Richard Boyle, Earl of Cork. Erected in 1632, it originally stood near the altar but was moved after the viceroy objected to churchgoers being forced to pray "crouching to an Earl of Cork and his lady. . . or to those sea nymphs his daughters, with coronets upon their heads, their hair dishevelled, down upon their shoulders". The earl got his revenge years later by engineering Viceroy Wentworth's execution. His seventh son, **Robert Boyle**, famous for formulating Boyle's Law on the relationship between the pressure, volume and temperature of gases, is given a niche of his own on the monument.

At the junction with the north transept is a curious **wooden door**, which once belonged to the cathedral's chapterhouse. In 1492, so the story goes, a quarrel arose between soldiers of the earls of Kildare and Ormond. Ormond barricaded himself in the chapter house, whereupon Kildare, eager to end hostilities, cut a hole in the door and stuck his arm through, inviting Ormond to shake hands. Peace was restored, and so the expression "chancing your arm" entered the English language.

The chapterhouse is now the **south transept**, containing various opulent funerary monuments – that of Archbishop Marsh (see p.106) is the finest surviving carving by Grinling Gibbons in Ireland. In one corner of the transept is a small tablet dedicated by Swift to his manservant, Alexander McGee, "in memory of his discretion, fidelity and diligence in that humble station". McGee's discretion in the libel case arising from *The Drapier's Letters* (purportedly written by a humble tailor) saved Swift from financial ruin.

Returning to the south aisle you'll find memorials to eminent Irish Protestants of the twentieth century, starting with a bust of Erskine Childers

Jonathan Swift

Born at Hoey's Court near Dublin Castle in 1667, **Jonathan Swift** could read by the age of 3, and at 15 was accepted as a student at Trinity College. On graduating, he worked for the diplomat Sir William Temple (after whom Temple Bar is named) and subsequently for the Church of England, hoping to secure "a fat deanery or a lean bishopric". This ambition clashed with his activities as a political pamphleteer, from 1704 onwards; as his pen had been deployed on behalf of the Tories, the incoming Whig administration of 1714 bore a grudge against Swift, who felt it wise to return to Dublin and take up the post of Dean of St Patrick's, which he had accepted the previous year.

Back home his commitment to Ireland and his social conscience grew, as expressed in a series of anonymous **tracts** during the 1720s. An early advocate of economic independence, Swift's *Proposal for the Universal Use of Irish Manufactures* argued that the Irish should burn all English imports, except coal. *The Drapier's Letters* exposed shady business deals, and *A Modest Proposal* bitterly suggested that the Irish poor could solve their problems by selling their babies to the rich, as food. He is now chiefly known for *Gulliver's Travels*, a dazzlingly diverse satire now too often misperceived as a children's story.

Besides his increasingly vitriolic writings, Swift was famous for his eccentricities and his mysterious relationship with **Esther Johnson**, known as **"Stella"**. The daughter of Sir William Temple's housekeeper, she was variously rumoured to have been Swift's niece or sister, his secret bride or his platonic companion. Whatever the truth, Swift was heartbroken by her death in 1728, finishing his *Journal to Stella* in the darkened cathedral on the nights following her burial.

His final years were overshadowed by a malady causing giddiness, which Swift mistook for symptoms of insanity. Eventually he did go mad, hailing the viceroy as "you fellow with the Blue String" and assaulting two clergymen in a carriage. In his will, he left money to build a mental hospital, St Patrick's on Bow Lane West, which was one of the first in Europe when it opened in 1749.

Given Swift's reputation as a Dubliner and a patriot, he was astonishingly rude about both, calling Dublin "the most disagreeable place in Europe, at least to any but those who have been accustomed to it from their youth", in which case "a jail might be preferable"; and averring that "no man is thoroughly miserable unless he be condemned to live in Ireland."

(Irish president 1973–74). The adjacent plaque in Irish honours Douglas Hyde, the founder of the Gaelic League, who became Ireland's first president. At his funeral service in 1949, former government colleagues waited outside St Patrick's in their cars, adhering to a ruling which forbade them to enter a Protestant cathedral.

Marsh's Library

Beside St Patrick's Cathedral, a crenellated wall with an arched gateway surrounds a Georgian edifice half faced in stone to match the cathedral. This is **Marsh's Library** (Mon & Wed–Fri 10am–12.45pm & 2–5pm, Sat 10.30am–12.45pm; €2.50; Ⓦ www.marshlibrary.ie), the oldest public library in Ireland, opened to "All Graduates and Gentlemen" in 1707. Its founder, Archbishop Narcissus Marsh – of whom Swift remarked that "no man will be either glad or sorry at his death" (Swift believed that it was Marsh's fault he had not risen higher in his ecclesiastical career) – was a scholar and scientist who translated the Old Testament into Irish and first used the word "microphone" in his own works on acoustics. The core of the library is the collection of Edward Stillingfleet, Bishop of Worcester, whose entire accumulation of

10,000 books Marsh bought for £2500; donations by other clerics and bibliophiles have boosted the tally to 25,000 printed books and 300 manuscripts.

Built by Sir William Robinson (who restored Dublin Castle), Marsh's is a charming example of an eighteenth-century scholar's library, consisting of two L-shaped rooms whose oak bookcases have carved and lettered gables crowned by a bishop's mitre, and three alcoves, or "cages", where readers were locked in with rare books. A case displays books owned by Swift, including a *History of the Great Rebellion*, with pencilled notations disparaging the Scots. The bindery for the conservation and repair of antique books (featured in *Ulysses*) has had the odd task of treating bullet-marks, as Marsh's Library was peppered by shots aimed at the nearby Jacob's Biscuit Factory during the Easter Rising.

The Liberties, the Guinness Brewery and Kilmainham

Northwest of the library is the area known as **The Liberties**, which was once outside the legal jurisdiction of the city and settled by French **Huguenot** refugees escaping religious persecution in their own country. They set up home and poplin- and silk-weaving industries in the southern part of The Liberties known as the Coombe (there is now a street named after it). The ten thousand Huguenots who arrived between 1650 and the early eighteenth century had a great civilizing effect on what was then a small and underdeveloped city: they founded a horticultural society and encouraged the wine trade. The Liberties have maintained the characteristics of self-sufficiency that the Huguenots brought with them, and there are families able to trace their local roots back for many generations. Nowadays, The Liberties are still a hotchpotch of busy streets full of barrows and bargain and betting shops, but Government tax incentives and low property prices have encouraged speculators to build blocks of high-security luxury apartments, which sit oddly among the urban jumble.

The main road leading west of Christ Church (High Street leading eventually to James's Street), is interspersed with grim corporate housing and deserted factories, and dominated by the **Guinness Brewery**. The brewery was used as one of the sets in Fritz Lang's *Metropolis*, with huge dark chimneys belching smoke and tiny figures hurrying along grimy balconies. For all the seediness of its surroundings, however, Guinness is one of Ireland's biggest commercial successes. Founded in 1759, the St James's Gate Brewery covers 64 acres and has the distinction of being the world's largest single beer-exporting company, exporting some three hundred million pints of the famous stout a year; 2.5 million pints are brewed here every day.

Unfortunately, you can't go round the brewery, but the recently developed **Guinness Storehouse** just off Rainsford Street, parallel to Thomas Street West, houses an exhibition centre containing a replica brewery, pub, restaurant, gift shop and various exhibition rooms (daily 9.30am–5pm; €12; bus #51B, #78A or #206 from Aston Quay, and #123 from O'Connell St or Dame St). The best of the exhibition rooms are on the upper floors of the airy, seven-storey building, and feature displays on Guinness advertising from the animal cartoons and painful puns of John Gilroy to the more obscure modern masterpieces. The self-guided tour ends in the *Gravity Bar* on the seventh floor with panoramic views of Dublin and the surrounding countryside and what is arguably the best Guinness in Dublin – arguably because the honour traditionally went to *Mulligan's* in Poolbeg Street (see p.130), which still has its devotees.

The Royal Hospital Kilmainham and the Irish Museum of Modern Art

Continuing further west, Thomas Street West becomes James's Street and, where the latter joins Bow Lane West, you'll walk past Swift's Hospital, now known as St Patrick's, on your way to the **Royal Hospital Kilmainham** (just five minutes' walk further west up Irwin Street). The hospital was extensively and well restored between 1980 and 1984, and the result is that Ireland's first Classical building, dating from 1680, is a joy to look at, from the outside at least. The name doesn't imply a medical institution of any kind: it was built as a home for wounded army pensioners, like Chelsea Hospital in London or Les Invalides in Paris. The plan is simple: a colonnaded building around a central courtyard, the sober stone arcading creating a lovely, unadorned rhythm.

Initially the use of the hospital to house the **Irish Museum of Modern Art** (Tues–Sat 10am–5.30pm, Sun noon–5.30pm, guided tours Wed & Fri 2.30pm & Sun 12.15pm; free; Ⓦwww.modernart.ie; bus #51B, #78A, #123 and #206), which opened in 1991, caused a great deal of controversy. This was not least because its interior was stripped of existing decor and painted white to provide gallery space of the correct, "modern" kind of conversion, which led one commentator to quote Flann O'Brien's novel *At Swim-Two-Birds* whose characters include a man born at the age of 25 with a consciousness but no history. As the gallery evolved, acquiring a permanent collection and thus a character and "history" of its own, most of the criticism dissipated and the former hospital has proved to be a very successful and popular exhibition space. There are no permanent exhibitions in the museum, only temporary shows, often half a dozen or more at a time, some being sited in the newly converted Deputy Master's House outside the museum's east wing (consult *In Dublin* or *The Event Guide* for current exhibitions). In the basement under the north wing is an excellent restaurant and a well-stocked bookshop.

Kilmainham Gaol

Outside the hospital, a small formal garden runs down to the Liffey, and a long, tree-lined avenue leads west towards the front gates, beyond which looms the grim mass of **Kilmainham Gaol** on Inchicore Road (April–Sept daily 9.30am–4.45pm; Oct–March Mon–Fri 9.30am–4pm, Sun 10am–4.45pm; €4.40; Ⓦwww.heritageireland.ie; Heritage Card). Built in 1792, the gaol was completed just in time to hold a succession of Nationalist agitators, from the United Irishmen of 1798, through Young Irelanders, Fenians and Land Leaguers (including Parnell and Davitt) in 1883, to the leading insurgents of the 1916 Easter Rising – Pádraig Pearse and James Connolly were executed in the prison yard. Éamon de Valera, subsequently three times prime minister and later president, was the very last prisoner to be incarcerated here; he was released in July 1924.

The complex is a great introduction to the history of Republicanism in Ireland, though don't expect any revisionism here, as the history has a real green tint. Not all the prisoners were political and an indication of the severity of punishments is given by a document recording a sentence of seven years' transportation for stealing a piece of printed calico. The **guided tours** (every half-hour and included in the admission price) give an emotionally coloured impression of the place, climaxing in the low lighting of the chapel, where, on May 4, 1916, Joseph Plunkett, one of the leaders of the Easter Rising of 1916, was married by candlelight to Grace Gifford while twenty British soldiers stood to attention, bayonets fixed. They were married at 1.30am, separated and he was executed at 3.30am, after being allowed just ten minutes in his wife's company. Until the executions of most of the leaders of the Easter Rising, the insurrection commanded little popular support in Dublin. The rebels had held notable buildings, among them the General Post Office (see p.110) and the Jacob's factory, for five days until British artillery pounded them into submission. It was only after the leaders of the rebellion, most especially James Connolly, already seriously wounded, were executed at Kilmainham (he had to be tied to a chair so they could shoot him) that a wave of support gathered behind the Nationalist cause – leading, ultimately, to the withdrawal of British troops, the partition of Ireland and civil war. Also on show is the yacht *Asgard* used by the Republican Erskine Childers and his wife Molly to run guns into Ireland in 1914.

O'Connell Street and around

Crossing over O'Connell Bridge you reach O'Connell Street, the northside's main thoroughfare and once the most grandiose of Dublin streets. However, before wandering up what is still the city's busiest, although less salubrious, centre for shopping, it's worth taking a detour eastwards along Eden Quay to the famous **Abbey Theatre** and the elegant **Custom House**. To the north lies **Parnell Square**, home to the **Hugh Lane Municipal Art Gallery** and **Dublin Writers' Museum**, and the nearby area is replete with associations with the novelist **James Joyce**. To O'Connell Street's northeast is the less salubrious **Mountjoy Square** and, a little further out, **Croke Park**, the massively redeveloped stadium of the Gaelic Athletics Association.

The Abbey Theatre

Not far along Eden Quay, turn left up Marlborough Street to the Abbey Theatre on the corner of Abbey Street Lower (see also p.134). Ireland's national theatre, it was opened in 1904 (nearly twenty years before Independence), with co-founders and Celtic literature revivalists W.B. Yeats and Lady Gregory as its first directors. The Abbey soon gained worldwide prestige for its productions of Irish playwrights such as Sean O'Casey, J.M. Synge and W.B. Yeats, but at home it also generated great controversy – even riots. O'Casey's *The Plough and the Stars* (1926), which questioned the motivations of the by-now haloed martyrs of 1916, so undercut and discredited the romanticized vision of Ireland that Yeats had helped to create – and the Nationalists had encouraged – that Dubliners took to the streets to protest. Today the new Abbey (its predecessor was destroyed by a fire in 1951) holds two theatres, the main one devoted to the Irish classics and new works by writers such as Brian Friel and Frank McGuinness, while the smaller Peacock Theatre often shows new experimental drama.

The Custom House

It's easy enough to overlook the **Custom House** (mid-March to Nov Mon–Fri 10am–12.30pm, Sat & Sun 2–5pm; Dec to mid-March Wed–Fri 10am–12.30pm, Sun 2–5pm; €1), lying in the shadow of the metal railway viaduct that runs parallel to O'Connell Bridge, east along the river. But, as one of the great Georgian masterpieces built by James Gandon, it's an impressive reminder of the city's eighteenth-century splendour. It is principally Gandon's public buildings that put Dublin ahead of other great, and better-preserved, Georgian cities such as Bath and Edinburgh. The Custom House was the first of them, completed in 1791, taking ten years to build and costing the unheard-of sum of £500,000. Nine years later the Act of Union made it redundant by transferring customs and excise to London. In 1921 the building was set alight by Sinn Féiners and totally gutted. Initial rebuilding by the new Irish government later that decade radically altered its internal structure and some significant changes were made to its facade; however, further reconstruction work in the 1980s sought to restate the splendour of Gandon's initial design. Since its restoration, the building has housed government offices.

The Custom House displays some of the most elaborate **architectural detailing** in the city: its embankment facade, 120 yards long, is flanked by arcades culminating in pavilions crowned with the arms of Ireland; around the building are fourteen heads representing Ireland's rivers (the Liffey is a goddess, above the main door), and cattle heads symbolizing the beef trade; the Four Continents (Africa, America, Asia and Europe) decorate the rear portico; and the 125-foot-high dome, modelled upon Wren's design for Greenwich Hospital, is topped by a figure of Commerce. Inside the displays on transport and revenue collection in Ireland are pretty insipid, but it's worth paying the entrance fee to enjoy the beauty of Gandon's original decor.

The best view of the building is from the other side of Matt Talbot Bridge, from where you can admire the long, regular loggia, portico and dome, all reflected in the muddy waters of the Liffey. This elegance conceals a story of personal ambition and dirty tricks. The building was originally planned by John Beresford, chief commissioner of revenue, and his friend Luke Gardiner. A large stone in the bed of the Liffey was preventing some boats from reaching the old customs point, further upstream, and this was ostensibly the argument for building a new one; Beresford and Gardiner's prime reason for backing the scheme on the other hand was that it served their own purposes to shift the commercial centre of the city east from Capel Street to the area where O'Connell Street now stands. Their plans were opposed through parliamentary petitions, personal complaints, even violence, and the hostile party was delighted to discover that the site for the new building was the muddy banks of the Liffey where, they thought, it would be impossible to build foundations. Gandon, however, confounded the scheme's critics by building the foundations on a layer of pine planks – which seems to have done the job.

O'Connell Street

Most things of historical interest on O'Connell Street – now lined by fast-food restaurants, shops, cinemas and modern offices – have long since been submerged under the tide of neon lights and plate glass, but one major exception is the **General Post Office** (Mon–Sat 8am–8pm, Sun 10am–6.30pm), which stands at the corner of Henry Street. It was opened in 1818, and its fame stems from the fact that almost a century later it became the rebel headquarters in one of the most significant battles in the fight for Independence in 1916 (see box opposite). The entire building, with the exception of the facade, was destroyed in the fighting; it was later restored and reopened in 1929. From the street you can still see the scars left by bullets: inside, the reconstructed marbled halls are also worth a look. In the window is one of the finest sculptures anywhere in the city – *The Death of Cúchulainn* by Oliver Sheppard. The exquisite bronze sculpture was commissioned in 1935 and represents the moment when the raven rests on the shoulder of Cúchulainn, the mythical warrior, before he finally dies.

O'Connell Street itself is reputedly one of Europe's widest, and there's a paved stretch down the middle with a series of **statues**. Until 1966 one of them, directly in front of the GPO, depicted Nelson on top of a column; it was blown up by IRA sympathizers in March 1966 (you can inspect the statue's

The Easter Rising

The **Easter Rising** of 1916, which resulted in pitched battles in the streets of Dublin, is remembered as one of the key events leading to Irish self-government. In fact, at the time, it seemed to most contemporary observers to be a botched and inconclusive event. Leaders of the **Irish Republican Brethren**, a Republican group dating from 1858, secretly planned a nationwide uprising for Easter Sunday 1916, using the strength of the much larger **Irish Volunteers**, a generally Nationalist body founded in 1913. The insurrection was to be staged with the help of a shipment of arms from Germany that was to be picked up by Sir Roger Casement (a British official who became a fervent Republican; see p.667). Things began to go wrong almost immediately: the arms arrived a day too early, and the British apprehended Casement and hanged him.

So secret had the preparations for the uprising been that the Irish Volunteers' leader, Eoin MacNeill, knew nothing of them. A week before Easter, the extremist plotters, led by **Pádraig Pearse**, showed MacNeill a forged order, purporting to come from the British authorities at Dublin Castle, for the suppression of the Irish Volunteers. MacNeill consented to give the order for the uprising. Then, the day before it was due to happen, he learned that the document was a forgery, and placed advertisements in the Sunday papers cancelling the insurrection and ordering Volunteers not to participate. Pearse and his allies, however, simply postponed the action until the next day: Easter Monday. They took, among other public buildings, the General Post Office (GPO) in O'Connell Street, and Pearse walked out onto the steps of the GPO to read the historic Proclamation of the Irish Republic (see p.790). Fighting continued for five days before being suppressed by the British authorities.

It was not the rising itself, but the British reaction to it, that was significant for the Republicans. The authorities executed a total of fifteen leaders of the rebellion, including Pearse and another patriot, James Connolly, at Kilmainham Gaol (see p.108 and 791). The result in the eyes of the public, however, was to turn these men into martyrs for the Republican cause. When, a year later, the British attempted to introduce conscription to the trenches of World War I, the public mood turned sharply away from any form of compromise with British rule and towards demands for full Independence, which was finally achieved in 1921.

head in the Collins Barracks (see p.117). The city's millennium year saw a notoriously expensive new addition: an angular recumbent woman bathed by a fountain representing Joyce's Anna Livia, the personification of the River Liffey, and quickly nicknamed "the floozie in the Jacuzzi", or "the whore in the sewer" (this rhymes in a Dublin accent). This, however, has now been removed to make way for another contentious statue, the *Monument of Light*. This huge 393ft illuminated stainless steel spike said to represent the city's hope for the new millennium; Dubliners have been outdoing each other yet again to devise a suitable sobriquet, with "the stiletto in the ghetto" proving to be the most popular so far.

Two areas of interest lie either side of O'Connell Street. Beside the GPO, Henry Street leads to **Moore Street Market**, where you'll find some of the disappearing street life that people are apt to get misty-eyed about, a bustling place whose brightly coloured stalls and banter provide plenty of fun. On the opposite side of O'Connell Street is Cathedral Street, which leads to the Greek Revival **St Mary's Pro-Cathedral** (daily 8am–6.30pm, Sun until 7pm), which was built between 1816 and 1825 and remains Dublin's most important Catholic church. Due to fears that the originally planned position on O'Connell Street would incite anti-Catholic feeling among the English, the cathedral is hidden away here. Consequently, getting a good view of its six Doric columns – based on the Temple of Theseus in Athens – is nigh on impossible. Every Sunday at 11am the Palestina Choir, established in 1902, can be heard. John McCormack, the respected and popular tenor, began his career here in 1904.

The final statue at the top end of O'Connell Street commemorates the nineteenth-century politician Charles Stewart Parnell (see p.788), quoting his famous words:

No man has a right to fix the boundary to the march of a nation.
No man has a right to say to his country, "Thus far shalt thou go and no further".

Parnell Square

At the top of O'Connell Street, behind Parnell's statue in the square named for him, stands the **Rotunda Maternity Hospital**, built in 1752. This was the very first purpose-built maternity hospital in Europe. The barber-surgeon Bartholomew Mosse funded the enterprise by organizing events including fancy dress balls, recitals and concerts – one of these was the first performance of Handel's *Messiah*, which took place on April 13, 1742. There's a superb chapel with a stucco ceiling by Bartholomew Cramillion, and the Rotunda Room itself houses The Ambassador (see p.131), once a cinema but now a music venue. Part of the remainder of the building is still a maternity hospital, while another section – the old Assembly Rooms – houses the **Gate Theatre**, which was opened by the legendary actor Micheál Mac Liammóir and his lover Hilton Edwards in 1929 (see also p.135). Behind the Rotunda, bordering on Parnell Square, is all that remains of the pleasure gardens, yet another of Dr Mosse's successful fund-raising ventures. This little open space is now a **Garden of Remembrance** for all those who died in the Independence struggle, with a sculpture by Oisín Kelly of the *Children of Lir* (see box on p.218). **Parnell Square**, originally called Rutland Square, was one of the first of Dublin's Georgian squares and still has its plain, bright, red-brick houses, broken by the grey-stone mass of the **Hugh Lane Municipal Art Gallery** (Tues–Thurs 9.30am–6pm, Fri & Sat 9.30am–5pm, Sun 11am–5pm; free; Ⓦ www.hughlane.ie; buses passing from the centre include #10, #11, #13, #16, #19 and #22). Originally the town house of the Earl of Charlemont, built for him by the Scottish architect Sir William Chambers in 1762, it was the focus of fashionable Dublin – the northside of the square was known as Palace Row – before the city centre moved south of the river. Chambers was also the architect of the delightful Casino, built to embellish the aesthetic Lord Charlemont's country house a few miles away at Marino (see p.122).

The house works well in its revised role as an art gallery, with plenty of good lighting and an intimate scale that complements the pictures. The gallery was set up in 1908 with funds donated by Sir Hugh Lane (nephew of Lady Gregory of Abbey Theatre fame), who died when the *Lusitania* was torpedoed in 1915. He left his collection – centred around the French Impressionists – to "the nation", and with Ireland's Independence the problem arose of which of the two nations he might have meant. In 1960 the two governments agreed to exchange halves of the collection every five years, but in 1982 the British government put in a claim for the lot. The matter was finally settled, with half the collection permanently in residence at Hugh Lane. It makes interesting viewing, with work from the pre-Raphaelites onwards via works by Degas and Renoir to more modern Irish painters such Roderic O'Conor; of particular note is a stained glass window by Harry Clarke, who was also responsible for the Birds of Paradise window in the Westmoreland Street *Bewley's* (see p.126). At the building's rear lies a recently opened wing devoted to Irish-born artist **Francis Bacon** (same hours; €7.60) consisting of a reconstruction of his cluttered London studio using the original contents and a startling collection of five unfinished paintings. There are sometimes free recitals on Sunday lunchtimes (see *The Event Guide* for details), and downstairs there's a good-value café/restaurant.

Two doors down, at nos. 18 and 19, a pair of modest Georgian houses are the home of the **Dublin Writers' Museum** (Mon–Sat 10am–5pm, Sun 11am–6pm; €5.50). There's certainly plenty of material to draw on: apart from its three Nobel laureates – George Bernard Shaw, W.B. Yeats and Samuel Beckett – Dublin nurtured a host of other writers, including Joseph Sheridan le Fanu, Jonathan Swift, Sean O'Casey, Brendan Behan and, of course, James Joyce (see box overleaf). However, the exhibits are on the dull side – there's a predictable range of memorabilia, including Brendan Behan's typewriter and press card – and the free audio guide does little to enliven the proceedings. The exhibition begins with a reference to early Irish poetry and the English poet Edmund Spenser's *Faerie Queen*, written while Spenser was living in County Cork, weaves rapidly through Jonathan Swift's *A Modest Proposal* of 1729 and the romantic fiction of the mid-nineteenth century to Oscar Wilde and the playwright George Bernard Shaw. Joyce shares a cabinet with Sean O'Casey – this really is a whistle-stop tour – and the exhibits wind up with material on Samuel Beckett, Brendan Behan and the comic writer Flann O'Brien. Upstairs is a fine 1760s library with rather oppressive colour added in the nineteenth century, now somewhat sententiously dubbed the Gallery of Writers. A good **bookshop** stocks an intelligent selection of books, including contemporary authors, and a **café** offers a modest selection of salads; the **Chapters restaurant** below the museum is excellent, and if you are in the area, you could do worse than try their pre-theatre menu. Next door is the **Living Writers' Centre**, with work rooms, a couple of apartments, a lecture room, and an ongoing programme of literary lectures and seminars: phone the museum for further details.

Mountjoy Square

As you head northeast along Denmark Street toward Mountjoy Square you'll notice that the streets, although a little run-down, are being slowly regenerated. Appropriately enough given the presence of the Writers' Museum, the area also has plenty of **literary associations**: Belvedere College in Great Denmark Street is where James Joyce went to school; Sean O'Casey wrote all his plays for the Abbey Theatre – *The Shadow of a Gunman*, *Juno and the Paycock*, *The Plough and the Stars* and *The Silver Tassie* – at 422 North Circular Rd (a few streets north of the square); and Brendan Behan grew up nearby at 14 Russell St.

Mountjoy Square itself is Dublin's earliest Georgian square, now in an advanced state of decay. Although there are some signs of revitalization, there's little left of the elegance described by Thomas Cromwell in his *Excursions through Ireland* in 1820 "Taste and opulence have united to embellish; the streets in the vicinity are all built on a regular plan; the houses are lofty and elegant; and neither hotels, shops, nor warehouses, obtruding upon the scene, the whole possesses an air of dignified retirement – the tranquillity of ease, affluence and leisure. The inhabitants of this parish are indeed almost exclusively of the upper ranks."

James Joyce

Author of *Ulysses* (1922), the ultimate celebration of his native city, **James Joyce** was born in 1882, but spent most of his adult life in voluntary exile from Ireland. After an impoverished childhood, he went to University College, a place of learning then staffed by Jesuit priests, where he led a dissolute life and began to experiment with writing short pieces of prose which he called "epiphanies". In 1904 he started writing the short stories that were eventually published as *Dubliners*. On June 10 of that year, Joyce met Nora Barnacle, and arranged to meet her again on June 16; it's on this latter day that the entire epic narrative of *Ulysses* is set. They were eventually married some 27 years later.

With the exception of two brief visits to Dublin in 1909, when he attempted to set up a chain of cinemas, and a final visit in 1912, Joyce never again lived in Ireland. All the great works, including *A Portrait of the Artist as a Young Man* (1916) and his late masterpiece, *Finnegans Wake* (1939), were written in various European cities – Zürich, Paris, Trieste – where Joyce and his family eked out a penurious existence supported mostly by donations from rich patrons. At the time of Joyce's death in 1941, *Ulysses* was banned in Ireland, condemned as a pornographic book; it was not published in the Republic until the 1960s.

Joyce once remarked that he was "more interested in the street names of Dublin than in the riddle of the universe", and boasted that Dublin could be rebuilt from scratch using the information contained in his books. The **Bloomsday** pilgrimage, held every year on June 16, draws people from all over the world to meet in Dublin where they retrace the action of the novel. It starts at the Martello tower at Sandycove (see p.120) and progresses through the streets of Dublin, stopping at *Davy Byrne's* pub (see p.130) where Leopold Bloom's lunch of a glass of Burgundy and a Gorgonzola and mustard sandwich is served, followed by the National Library (see p.89), the *Ormond Quay Hotel* (see p.76) and all the other locations made iconic by this great novel.

For serious Joyceans, the **James Joyce Centre** at 35 North Great George's St (Tues–Sat 9.30am–5pm, Sun 12.30–5pm; €4.50; Ⓦwww.jamesjoyce.ie), not far from the Dublin Writers' Museum, has a museum with documents of his life and work and an excellent bookshop. The centre also has information on lectures, walking tours and Bloomsday events.

Croke Park GAA Museum

Half a mile east of Mountjoy Square, just outside the boundary formed by the Royal Canal, is Ireland's premier sports stadium, **Croke Park**, home of the Gaelic Athletic Association and its impressive **museum** (May–Sept daily 9.30am–5pm; Oct–April Tues–Sat 10am–5pm, Sun noon–5pm; open to New Stand ticket-holders only on match days; €5; Ⓦwww.gaa.ie; bus #3, #11, #11A, #16, #16A or #123 to Clonliffe Road). Somewhat surprisingly, considering the amateur status of the matches played here, the redeveloped stadium has the fourth-largest capacity in Europe (following Barcelona's Nou Camp, Real Madrid's Bernabeu and the San Siro in Milan), holding some 85,000 spectators. The stadium is intended for use exclusively for the playing of Gaelic games (hurling and Gaelic football), though it has in the recent past, much to the horror of cultural traditionalists, hosted pop concerts. One such concert was almost cancelled when a band attempted to fly the flags of the world, because included amongst them was a Union Jack.

This mixture of sport and politics lies at the core of the GAA's history. Croke Park was the scene of one of the bloodiest atrocities in modern Irish history when, on November 11, 1920, the notorious Black and Tans entered the ground during a match and opened fire on the players and the crowd killing twelve, including Gaelic football captain Michael Hogan after whom one of the stands is named. The **museum** is situated under the impressive New Stand, and the exhibition as a whole, most especially the fascinating film *National Awakening*, reflects the political and cultural as well as the sporting history of the organization. There is plenty of interactive entertainment for kids, although anyone will struggle to master the intricate skills of hurling on their first attempt. The tour ends with the exhilarating film *A Day in September*, which captures the excitement, colour and passion, both on and off the field on All Ireland finals day. Tours of the museum and stadium are available daily at 12.30pm and 3pm, but call ⓣ01/855 8176 for information on weekend availability.

The King's Inns, St Michan's and the Four Courts

Leaving Parnell Square at the northwest corner and following Granby Row round brings you to the deconsecrated **Black Church** (or St Mary's Chapel of Ease) in St Mary's Place – a sinister, brooding building with spiky finials. Legend has it that St Mary's and other similar massive Protestant churches built during the 1820s were designed so that they could be turned into defensive positions should the Catholics attack. As you walk southwest down Dorset Street Upper and into Bolton Street, you're confronted with a scene of urban deprivation: rubbish blowing in the gutters, broken glass, barred shop windows. Running off Bolton Street is Henrietta Street; dowdy as it is now, it was once the most fashionable street in Dublin and was one of the first sites of really big houses in the city, two of which (nos. 9 and 10, at the far end) were designed by Sir Edward Lovett Pearce. These adjoin the impressive **King's Inns** – home of the Irish Bar – designed in 1795 by James Gandon, architect of the Four Courts and the Custom House. During the daytime you can walk through the courtyard to the Inns' garden from which the grandeur of Gandon's building can be truly appreciated. At the west end of the garden is the exit to Constitution Hill. It was from here that St Patrick admired the city he had just converted to Christianity, though the great saint's view was not blocked by the tower blocks that litter the modern-day hill. Walking along Constitution Hill into Church Street you reach St Michan's Church.

St Michan's Church

Though it doesn't look much now – only the tower and a few other fragments are original – **St Michan's Church** (April–Oct Mon–Fri 10am–12.45pm & 2–4.45pm, Sat 10am–12.45pm; Nov–March Mon–Fri 12.45–3pm, Sat 10am–12.45pm; €3; bus #134 from Abbey St Lower), founded in 1095, is the oldest building on the northside. The reason it's on the tourist trail is that the crypt's combination of dry air and constant temperature, together with methane gas secreted by rotting vegetation beneath the church, keeps corpses in a state of mummified preservation: some of the "best" are on display, with skin, fingernails and hair all clearly identifiable, sometimes after as long as seven hundred years. Depending on the mood of the guide, different crypts are opened. Among the dead are a nun, a crusader and a thief – this last identified as such because of a missing hand, amputated as penance for an earlier offence. One of the crypts contains the death mask of United Irish leader, Wolfe Tone, and the bodies of two of his compatriots, the Sheare brothers. None of the bodies was originally stored in the church, and how this odd collection of corpses got here is still a mystery. St Michan's also boasts an early eighteenth-century organ, still with its original gilding on the case, which Handel reputedly admired and played during a visit to Dublin.

The Four Courts

Towards the river and east of St Michan's Church are the Four Courts, another of Gandon's majestic architectural pieces. A solid example of Georgian architecture and urban planning, the **Four Courts** were built between 1786 and 1802, as the seat of the High Court of Justice of Ireland and a chambers for barristers. From the outside the Four Courts have a dour grey perfection. Inside, the courts – Exchequer, Common Pleas, King's Bench and Chancery – radiate from a circular central hall. The building holds particular historical significance in that it was here that former comrades turned their guns on one another following the 1921 treaty; it was completely gutted and legal documents dating back to the thirteenth century destroyed, when shelled by pro-treaty forces led by Michael Collins, who received the unwelcome reassurance from Winston Churchill that "the archives of the Four Courts may be scattered, but the title deeds of Ireland are safe." If you're curious to observe a trial, the courts are open to the public (all year except Aug & Sept Mon–Fri 11am–1pm & 2–4pm).

Smithfield and around

A short walk west along Arran Quay from the Four Courts takes you into the cobbled expanse of **Smithfield**, a traditional public space where, for over three hundred years, horse fairs have taken place. In the 1980s the area became infamous as the meeting point for prostitutes and their clients until the idea was mooted to develop the square as Dublin's next cultural centre. Seemingly quixotic at the time, these plans have in many ways been realized by the building of the complex on its eastern edges known as **Smithfield Village**, which includes **Chief O'Neill's Hotel** (see p.75), the **Old Jameson Distillery** and the **Chimney Viewing Tower**.

The square itself cast off its former scruffy image when architect Garry Ní Eanaigh's visionary plans were realized: the 400,000 cobbles were lifted, hand-cleaned and replaced, and the square is now lit by twelve imposing 85-feet-high braziers which cast a six-foot flame skyward. Now the city's largest civic space, though bearing an uncanny resemblance to an unfinished football stand, it was here that U2 received the Freedom of Dublin in 2000, the highest honour that Dublin Corporation can bestow. Less dramatically, on the first Sunday of the month, the travelling community's traditional horse sales still take place. Deals on the filthy ponies are finalized by spitting into the palm and clapping the hands together. There's nothing remotely glamorous about this entirely male activity, but the event does possess a certain fascination. Most of the buyers and sellers are travellers, once known as itinerants, and before that gypsies, people who speak their own dialect, known as shelta. In fact, shelta has nothing to do with Romany (the most common theory is that the travellers are of purely Irish origin, and took to the roads at the time of the Famine), but the travellers do share with gypsies an impressive knowledge of horses. There's great concern, however, that the sales, which date back to 1664, may not form part of the vision for the square.

Old Jameson Distillery

Housed in the former distillery of Ireland's favourite whiskey, the tour around the **Old Jameson Distillery** (daily 9.30am–6pm, tours every 30min; €6.50) extols the virtues of Irish whiskey, or *uisce beatha* (pronounced "ishke baha") in

Irish, literally translated as "the water of life", from which the English word whiskey is derived. The exhibits explain the modern-day malting, fermenting and maturing processes, while claiming that it is not only the Scotch spelling of the word (whisky, without the "e") but the product itself that is a corruption of the real (Irish) whiskey. It is alleged that the famous "peaty" taste of Scotch is caused by their use of cheaper fuel and that Scotch is only distilled twice, while the purer, smoother, life-giving water from Ireland is distilled three times. The blatant plugging of the Jameson product and the fact that whiskey is not actually distilled here (the rich aroma which pervades the building is, in fact, synthetic) can be forgiven at the end of the tour when you get to test a tot or two from around the world and compare them with the excellent Jameson product.

Chimney Viewing Tower

Directly outside the entrance to *Chief O'Neill's Hotel* stands the old 52-metre distillery chimney, originally constructed in 1895 and recently redeveloped as a **viewing platform** (Mon–Sat 10am–5.30pm, Sun 11am–5.30pm; €6; tickets from the hotel gift shop). A glass-panelled lift whisks you up to the top of the chimney whose impressive vantage point allows you to take in this architectural hotchpotch of a city from the huge expanse of green that is Phoenix Park (see below), to the regular, maze-like streets of nearby Stoneybatter, and eastwards to the grey-blue waters of the docks where the Liffey finally spews into the Irish Sea. As no maps are provided it's advisable to take your own.

Collins Barracks

A few roads west of Smithfield towards Phoenix Park stand **Collins Barracks**, a series of imposing grey-stone buildings formerly known as the Royal Barracks. Founded in 1701, their chief claim to fame is as the oldest continuously occupied purpose-built barracks in the world, with the largest drill square in Europe – it could hold six regiments. The Barracks now hold the **decorative arts collection of the National Museum** (Tues–Sat 10am–5pm, Sun 2–5pm; free). The eclectic collection ranges from the exotic to the mundane, and highlights are the excellent Curator's Choice room where museum curators from throughout Ireland have submitted items of particular interest, and the Irish Silver Room which demonstrates the craftsmanship of early Irish silversmiths. To the north is **Arbour Hill Cemetery** (Mon–Sat 9am–4.30pm, Sun 9.30am–noon; free) where fourteen of the executed 1916 leaders are buried, while to the south of here is a railed-in plot of grass known as the **Croppy's Acre** where a monument marks the spot where some of the executed rebels of 1798 are buried.

Phoenix Park

If you have walked through the urban confusion of the northside, the open spaces of **Phoenix Park**, Dublin's playground – which begins a few minutes' walk west of Collins Barracks – will come as a welcome relief. The name is a corruption of the Irish *fionn uisce*, or "clear water", as a fresh-water stream flows through its grounds. A series of pillars stand across the road and suddenly you're surrounded by grand, clipped hedges and tended flowerbeds in what is one of the largest city parks in the world – it's more than twice the size of London's Hampstead Heath or New York's Central Park. The park originated as priory lands, which were seized after the Reformation in the seventeenth century and made into a royal deer park. The Viceroy's Lodge – now Áras an Uachtaráin, the President's Residence – is here, as well as a 205 foot obelisk erected in 1817 in tribute to the **Duke of Wellington**. Wellington was born in Dublin, but was less than proud of his roots – when reminded that he was Irish by birth, the duke replied tersely "being born in a stable doesn't make one a horse."

The park was also the scene of two politically significant **murders** in the late spring of 1882. Two officials of the British parliament, Lord Frederick Cavendish, the chief secretary, and T.H. Burke, the undersecretary, were killed by an obscure organization known as "The Invincibles", in reaction to long-standing bitterness over the landlord-and-tenant relationship in post-Famine Ireland. The murders, however, were at first directly connected with the Anglo-Irish politician Charles Stewart Parnell's ongoing agitation for reform on behalf of the Irish tenancy (see p.788). Parnell believed that in order to disassociate himself with the claims he would need to withdraw from public life, but his obvious sincerity in denouncing them, and the effect that the event had on British policy towards reforming the tenancy issue, was in fact to make his position in Ireland stronger than ever.

Phoenix Park also contains Dublin's **zoo** at the southeast corner of the park (Mon–Sat 9.30am–6pm, Sun 10.30am–6pm; €9.80; bus #10 from Aston Quay, and buses #25, #25A, #26, #66 and #67 from Wellington Quay), the second oldest in Europe – it was opened in 1830. Its claim to fame used to be that this is where the MGM lion was bred; the zoo now has a programme for breeding endangered species for subsequent release into the wild.

Towards the park's northern extremity, near the Ashtown Gate exit, is the **Phoenix Park Visitor Centre** (Jan to late March & Nov–Dec Sat & Sun 9.30am–4.30pm; late March daily 9.30am–5pm; April–May daily 9.30am–5.30pm; June–Sept daily 10am–6pm; Oct daily 10am–5pm; €2.50; Ⓦwww.heritageireland.ie; Heritage Card). Set in the stables of what was once the home of the papal nuncio, this is a mildly interesting diversion. While the exhibits in the centre are a little dull, there is a good video on the history of the park and a short tour of the adjacent restored **Ashtown Castle** (a slender seventeenth-century tower house), which was only discovered in 1978 when the papal nuncio's residence, which had been built around it, was demolished. It is from here that free tours of **Áras an Uachtaráin** (President's Residence) leave on Saturdays every hour between 10.30am and 4.30pm (come early in summer as there are a limited number of places). The old duelling grounds, or **Fifteen Acres**, are also to be found in the park – now the venue for Gaelic football, cricket, soccer and, occasionally, polo – as well as a racecourse where a **flea market** is held every Sunday from noon onwards. The quality of what's available can vary tremendously, and there seems no way of knowing what it will be like until the day.

Accessed by White's Gate, on the park's northwestern fringe, lies one of the most splendid buildings in the city, **Farmleigh** (Easter–Oct Sun & bank holidays: house 11am–4pm; grounds 10am–5pm; free; bus #37 from Abbey St Lower to Castleknock Gate), set in equally impressive grounds and well worth making a special effort to see. Originally constructed in 1752 for the Trench family, the building was purchased by Edward Cecil Guinness, the first Earl of Iveagh, as a rustic residence offering easy access to his brewery. James Franklyn Fuller (who also designed Ashford Castle at Cong, County Mayo for Sir Arthur Guinness) was employed to extend the house in the 1880s, and the Guinness family remained in residence until the death of the third earl in 1992. The house was then purchased by the Irish government as a state guesthouse and, consequently, **tours** may not be available if a visiting delegation is in residence (call Ⓣ01/815 5900 to check in advance).

Informative guided tours take you through several of the ground-floor rooms including the **hall**, featuring a pair of debtors' chairs in which the sitting pauper's legs would be trapped until he or she had agreed to pay their debts, and the **library**, which now contains four thousand items on loan from the Iveagh Collection, including a first edition of *Ulysses* and books dating back to the twelfth century. The **Blue Room** causes a double-take, thanks to an unusual fireplace actually situated below a window, while the real treat is the **ballroom**, added in 1897, whose Irish oak floor was constructed of wood originally intended for Guinness barrels. Delicate linen portières frame doors that lead out to a massive, plant-stocked and astonishingly warm conservatory. Behind the house there's a tearoom in the stable block and a beautiful walled garden.

The outskirts

Even without going as far as the Wicklow Mountains, whose unlikely, conical outlines you encounter every time you look to the south, there are a number of rewarding trips beyond the city centre which are well worth making time for. The best of these are out along Dublin Bay, using the regular DART services. These trains will take you southwards to **Sandycove** and the James Joyce Tower; to the pretty village of **Dalkey**, with its incongruously continental atmosphere; and to the hills between Dalkey and **Killiney**, where the views across Dublin Bay are magnificent. Although the journey north on the DART is nothing like as spectacular as the southward trip, it ends up at the popular seaside resort of **Howth**, with its rugged hill and long views south and north. Further out, **Malahide** and its castle, and Georgian Newbridge House at **Donabate** are accessible by commuter train. Buses run to (or at least near) the worthwhile stops closer in to the city on the northside – the National Botanic Gardens and the historic cemetery at **Glasnevin**, the exquisite Casino at **Marino** and **North Bull Island** nature reserve.

Dún Laoghaire and Sandycove

Taking the DART south out of Dublin, you very quickly have the feeling that you're leaving the grime of the city far behind. Almost immediately, the track starts to run along the coast, past **Booterstown Marsh**, a designated bird sanctuary, and out to **DÚN LAOGHAIRE** (pronounced "dunleary"), where high-speed ferries from Britain dock. Formerly known as Kingstown, Dún Laoghaire manages to retain some of its flavour as a superior kind of Victorian resort, with wide, tree-lined avenues, promenades and wedding-cake architecture. Its port is still the base for lightships and **yacht clubs** (contact the Irish National Sailing School for details: ⓣ01/284 4195, ⓦwww.inss.ie). The **East Pier** has all the requisites for an edifying constitutional, a popular pastime among locals on Sundays in particular: a bandstand, a lifeboat memorial, a compass pointer and an anemometer for measuring wind speed (one of the first in the world when installed in 1852).

Sandycove

A short way along the seafront from the East Pier, Dún Laoghaire merges into **SANDYCOVE**, a quiet suburb whose most famous son was **Roger Casement**, the British diplomat turned Irish rebel. Casement made his name as a consul championing the rights of indigenous tribes in the Belgian Congo and the Peruvian Amazon, and retired with a knighthood, convinced that Irish freedom was his next cause. In 1914 he travelled to Berlin to enlist German support and returned by U-boat shortly before the Easter Rising, but was soon captured. Charged with high treason, Casement was stripped of his honours and hanged at Pentonville prison in London. Unfortunately, his legacy has been overshadowed by an unseemly, essentially homophobic argument about his sexuality: Republicans, unable to accept the graphic details of homosexual activities in his "Black Diaries", have maintained that the diaries were forged by British secret services, but recent forensic examination has established, hopefully once and for all, that they are genuine. See the box on p.667 for more on Casement.

Today, Sandycove is more widely associated with James Joyce, who for a brief period lived in the suburb's Martello tower. Originally it was just one of 21 **Martello towers** built against the threat of French invasion between 1804 and 1806 (the name comes from Cape Mortella in Corsica, where the British navy captured a tower of this type in 1794). The walls of these towers are over 7ft thick and each has an armoured door 12ft off the ground as its sole means of entry, making the towers almost impregnable. The towers proved an unnecessary precaution, however, given that the French never fired a shot in Ireland. You'll see other Martello towers at Dalkey, Bray, Howth and Sandymount.

Sandycove's **James Joyce Tower** (April–Oct Mon–Sat 10am–1pm & 2–5pm, Sun 2–6pm; €5.50) is named not so much for its association with his life – Joyce spent barely a week here in September 1904, a month before running off with Nora Barnacle – but more because it features so prominently in the opening chapter of *Ulysses*. The characterization of "stately, plump Buck Mulligan" was Joyce's revenge on his host, Oliver St John Gogarty. On the sixth night of Joyce's stay, a fellow guest, Samuel Chenevix Trench, had a nightmare about a panther and fired some shots into the fireplace; Gogarty seized the gun and shot down a row of saucepans above Joyce's head, shouting, "Leave him to me!" Joyce took the hint and left promptly. The tower is now a museum and the starting point of the Bloomsday pilgrimage.

All of the items on show are donations to the museum, which was opened in 1962 by Sylvia Beach, who first published *Ulysses*. An edition illustrated by Matisse vies for attention with a plaintive letter from Joyce to Nora, accusing her of "treating me as if I were simply a casual comrade in lust", and such odd exhibits as a pandybat of the kind with which Joyce was beaten for "vulgar language" at school. In the first-floor guardroom, Gogarty's abode has been re-created complete with a life-size ceramic panther representing Trench's *bête noire*. The spiral staircase emerges onto the rooftop gun-platform where Buck Mulligan does his ablutions at the start of the novel.

From here you can see right over the back yard of **Geragh**, a Constructivist seaside villa that Michael Scott, architect of Busáras, built for his family in the 1930s. Beyond it lies a knobbly brown headland with a famous bathing place known as the **Forty Foot Pool** (so called not for the pool's size but because of a forty-feet-deep fishing hole off the coast here). The pool was long reserved for male nude bathing: nowadays both sexes can use it but "Togs must be worn" – though nude bathers still get away with it before 9am. If you're tempted to join them, bear in mind the water temperature only varies by about 5°C throughout the year, so you'll find it pretty chilly.

Dalkey and Killiney

Just down the coast from Sandycove is the charming seaside town of **DALKEY** (pronounced "dawky"), immortalized in Flann O'Brien's satirical novel *The Dalkey Archive*. On sunny days, the narrow streets and cliffside villas here have an almost Mediterranean lushness that makes Dublin itself seem a little cold and grey. Historically, Dalkey has thrived on comparisons with the capital: for two hundred years, it was the only natural harbour on the east coast of Ireland. Goods unloaded here filled Dalkey's warehouses and swelled its coffers, until the dredging of the Liffey in the sixteenth century wiped out its business and Dalkey dwindled to a village. In time, though, Dalkey's beauty ensured that fresh comparisons were made, as well-to-do Dubliners built seaside homes and the advent of the railway brought day-trippers with it. Today, its nostalgic old quarter merges into a commuter-belt hinterland under the cover of forested slopes and azaleas.

From Dalkey DART station it's a short walk down Railway Road to Castle Street, distinguished by two fortified warehouses from the fifteenth century, when Dalkey was dubbed the "Port of the Seven Castles". **Goat Castle**, across the way from **Archibold's Castle**, serves as Dalkey's town hall, with a **visitor centre** (Sat & Sun 11am–5pm, April–Oct also Mon–Fri 9.30am–5pm; €5) that features detailed exhibits on the town's history, set within the castle's impressive interior. If you're making the fifteen-minute walk from Sandycove to Dalkey, you'll pass a third fortification, **Bullock Castle**, built by the Cistercians in 1180 to protect Bullock fishing harbour.

From Castle Street you can take a lovely walk down **Coliemore Road**, past Georgian houses and Victorian villas, to Coliemore Harbour facing **Dalkey Island**, 300yd offshore. In summer there are daily **boat trips**, weather permitting, to the island, although it is advisable to phone in advance as even when the weather is fine the service can be a little erratic (Ⓣ01/283 4298; €5 return). First inhabited 8500 years ago (the dwelling sites are marked by thickets of nettles), the island was known in Gaelic as Deiliginish (from which Dalkey derives), a name which recalls a spiked wooden fort (*dealg* means "thorn" or "spike") that once existed there. Here you'll find another Martello tower and the ruins of the medieval St Begnet's Oratory on the far side of the saddle-shaped island.

From Coliemore Harbour you can head south towards Killiney along the cliffside **Vico Road** to view the fabulous coastline. Steps and a path ascend steeply from Vico Road to **Dalkey Hill**, which is definitely worth climbing. There's an easier route off Sorrento Road via Knocknacree Road and Torca Road. On the latter road, Shavians can track down **Torca Cottage**, where George Bernard Shaw spent much of his boyhood; the house is privately owned, but a plaque on the wall acknowledges Shaw with his words, "The men of Ireland are mortal and temporal but the hills are eternal." En route to the summit, with its crenellated former telegraph station and fine views over Dublin Bay, you'll pass Dalkey **quarry**, from where the granite blocks that form the walls of Coliemore Harbour and the great piers of Dún Laoghaire were hewn.

To give your lungs a further workout, follow the partly wooded ridge up to **Killiney Hill**, where a stone obelisk enjoys even more glorious views, north to Howth and south to Killiney Bay and the Wicklow Mountains. From here, you can quickly descend to the park gate on Killiney Hill Road and refreshment at the cosy *Druid's Chair* pub; and then head down Victoria Road and Vico Road through the leafy and exclusive borough of **KILLINEY**, to reach the Killiney DART station in around fifteen minutes. The wide grey beach in front of the station runs the length of the four-mile bay to Bray (see p.157).

Glasnevin, Marino and North Bull Island

The suburb of **GLASNEVIN**, a couple of miles north of O'Connell Street (take bus #13, #19 or #19A, or from Abbey St Middle #134), has two main attractions. As you head off Botanic Road on to Glasnevin Hill you'll see the gates of the **National Botanic Gardens** (summer Mon–Sat 9am–6pm, Sun 11am–6pm; winter Mon–Sat 10am–4.30pm, Sun 11am–4.30pm; free; call ⓣ01/857 0909 for details of the opening hours of the glasshouses), founded by an act of the Irish Parliament in 1795. Ireland's mild climate makes it an excellent place for growing exotic species, and Glasnevin's Botanic Gardens were the first in the world to raise orchids from seed, and the first in Europe to grow pampas grass and the giant waterlily. Some 20,000 species and varieties flourish over nineteen hectares of gardens, rockeries and arboreta by the River Tolka, and in cast-iron glasshouses that are early masterpieces of the genre. The **Curvilinear Range** was fabricated from 1843 onwards by Richard Turner, a Dublin ironmaster who built the Palm House at Kew Gardens in London; its newly restored ironwork is sublime. The new **Alpine House** is a worthy addition to Turner's legacy, while the Palm House and Orchid House are due to open early in 2004 after extensive renovation.

Fifteen minutes' walk from the Botanic Gardens (down Glasnevin Hill and Botanic Road, before turning right into Prospect Way and Finglas Road) lies the entrance to **Glasnevin Cemetery**, aka **Prospect Cemetery** (Mon–Sat 8am–4.30pm, Sun 9am–4.30pm, guided tours Wed & Fri 2.30pm; free; ⓦwww.glasnevin-cemetery.ie), which started out as a burial place for Roman Catholics in 1832. Its jungle of patriotic iconography – shamrocks, high crosses and harps – are eerily surveyed by the watchtowers in the walls from which sentries would endeavour to deter body snatchers in the nineteenth century. The cemetery is, in many ways, a good place to end a trip to Dublin as so many of the city's important historical figures are buried here. The 160-foot-high round tower by the entrance is a monument to Daniel O'Connell, whose corpse was interred in its crypt in 1869, having been brought home from Genoa in 1847 (in fact, not all of his body is here: his heart was buried in Rome). Similar pomp attended the burial of Parnell – he asked to be buried in a mass grave among the people of Ireland, beside which a huge granite boulder carries his name (to the left of the round tower). Other political figures among the 1.2 million dead at Glasnevin include Roger Casement (see p.667), Michael Collins, Arthur Griffith, Jim Larkin, Countess Markievicz and Éamon de Valera; from the arts, Gerard Manley Hopkins, Maud Gonne MacBride, Brendan Behan, Alfred Chester Beatty (see p.101) and Phil Lynott of Thin Lizzy. After a trip to the graveyard, drop in for a pint at nearby *Kavanagh's* (commonly known as *The Gravediggers*), one of Dublin's finest old pubs, where mourners have sought solace since 1833.

The Casino at Marino

MARINO, just off the Malahide Road 3 miles north of the city centre (#20B bus from Eden Quay and many others up the Malahide Road, or DART to Clontarf then a 15min walk), is the home of the eighteenth-century **Casino**, one of the most delightful pieces of Neoclassical lightheartedness you could hope to see anywhere. The bus will let you off next to some playing fields, from where the Casino, exuberantly decorated with urns and swags of carved drapery, is clearly visible to the left.

Needless to say, the Casino (guided tours: Jan–March, Nov & Dec Sat & Sun noon–4pm; April Sat & Sun noon–5pm; May & Oct daily 10am–5pm;

June–Sept daily 10am–6pm; €2.50; Heritage Card) has nothing to do with gambling. Commissioned by the Earl of Charlemont (whose town house in Parnell Square is now the Hugh Lane Municipal Art Gallery), it was built between 1757 and 1778 by Sir William Chambers, the leading architect of the day, as a summer residence which would accompany the existing Marino House as repositories for some of the priceless works of art Charlemont had brought home from his grand tour of Europe. Marino House was demolished long ago, but the Casino, restored in 1984, survives in perfect condition, crowded with witty and unlikely architectural features: the urns, for example, conceal chimneys.

If you're catching a bus back into town, try to sit upstairs on the left-hand side. As it turns from the Malahide Road into Fairview, you can see Marino Crescent, an elegant row of Georgian town houses, once nicknamed "Ffolliot's revenge" after a painter who built the crescent out of spite to block the view from Marino House to the sea. Ffolliot's final twist of the knife was to make the backs of the houses, which faced Marino House, an unsightly jumble of chimneys, ill-placed windows and sheds.

North Bull Island

In fine weather it's pleasant to stroll along **Dollymount Strand**, the three-mile beach on the seaward side of **North Bull Island**, now designated a UNESCO Biosphere Reserve (DART to Raheny, then a 30min walk; or bus #130, from Abbey St Lower or from Clontarf Road near Marino, to Dollymount, then a 30min walk). Originally no more than a sandbank visible at low tide, the island grew in the tidal shadow of the North Bull Wall, which was built along with the South Bull Wall in 1821 at the suggestion of Captain Bligh, of HMS *Bounty* fame, to prevent Dublin harbour from silting up. Besides golfers and day-tripping Dubliners, the island provides winter accommodation for up to 40,000 migrating birds of more than fifty species, including a sixth of the world's population of Brent geese. As well as a rich and varied flora, the grasslands behind the mudflats sustain foxes, shrews, badgers, rabbits and one of the few remaining large indigenous mammals, the much-harassed Irish hare. You can find out more at the **interpretive centre** (Mon–Thurs 10.15am–1pm & 1.30–4pm, Fri 10.15am–1.30pm, Sat & Sun 10.15am–1pm & 1.30–5.30pm; closes 4.30pm Sat & Sun in winter) by the beach in the centre of the island, at the end of the causeway road from the mainland.

Howth

A rugged peninsula at the northernmost point of Dublin Bay and the end of the DART line, **HOWTH** derives its name from the Old Norse *hofuth*, or "cape", and is pronounced to rhyme with "both". While the DART gives you a glimpse of the northern coast of the peninsula, the #31B bus (from Abbey St Lower or Howth Rd near Marino) crosses the summit, with views right across Dublin Bay to the Wicklow Mountains, and even the Mourne Mountains on fine days.

Howth **village** is a sleepy place of steep streets and dramatic views. Poised above Harbour Road but accessible by Church Street, the Gothic shell of **St Mary's Abbey** dates from the fourteenth to the sixteenth centuries and traces its origin to the first church founded by the Norse king Sitric, in 1042. You can see a fair bit of the interior without going to the trouble of obtaining the keys from no. 3 Church Street opposite, but you will need them to view the fifteenth-century double tomb of Lord and Lady Howth. St Mary's offers a fine view of Howth harbour and Ireland's Eye, and there's **food** and log fires to be enjoyed at the sixteenth-century *Abbey Tavern*, on Abbey Street below, or excellent fish and chips at *Beshoff's* on Harbour Road (for details of Howth's famous *King Sitric's Fish Restaurant*, see p.129). Windy walks along the harbour's east pier are a popular way to blow away the Guinness-induced cobwebs, giving you the chance to stare out at **Ireland's Eye**, a rocky island and sea-bird sanctuary that shelters the ruins of a sixth-century monastery and a Martello tower. During the summer, **boats** from the east pier (Ⓣ01/831 4200 or 087/267 8211; €8 return) run across to Ireland's Eye when they have enough takers. It was at the west pier, in July 1914, that the Irish Volunteers succeeded in landing nine hundred rifles and 25,000 rounds of ammunition from Erskine Childers' yacht *Asgard*, which you can see at Kilmainham Gaol.

To the west of the harbour, **Howth Castle**, built in 1564 and now the oldest inhabited house in Ireland, is a weather-beaten and battlemented veteran of numerous restorations. For many years the St Lawrence family kept open house at meal times, a custom said to have arisen from an incident in 1575, when Grace O'Malley, the "Uncrowned Queen of the West", was turned away because the family was at dinner, and reacted by kidnapping their eldest son and holding him until Lord Howth promised to keep his gates open at meal times in the future. Although the castle isn't open to the public, you can wander along to a barn in the grounds that enthusiasts have turned into a **National Transport Museum** (June–Aug Mon–Fri 10am–5pm, Sat & Sun 2–5pm; Sept–May Sat & Sun 2–5pm; €2.50), with vehicles from buses to fire engines, armoured cars and a Hill of Howth tram. In spring, don't miss the rhododendron glades behind the Deer Park golf club, where four hundred species flourish in the peaty soil below Mud Rock. Just downhill is a prehistoric dolmen, its gigantic 91-ton capstone balanced on a dozen smaller rocks.

On a fine day you can enjoy Howth's famous **Cliff Walk**, with imposing rockscapes and superb **views** south past the mouth of the Liffey to the Wicklow Mountains, and north to the flatlands of the Boyne. The footpath runs for some 5 miles (allow 2hr 30min) almost right around the peninsula to Shielmartin Road, where you can catch bus #31A to Sutton Cross near Sutton DART station or all the way back to Abbey Street; bus #31B runs parallel and above for much of the way, along Carrickbrack Road, so you can bail out of the walk if you feel like it. You first head out east from the harbour along Balscadden Road to the Nose of Howth, before the path turns south, crossing the slopes above the cliffs, which are covered in colourful gorse and bell heather in season, towards the **Baily Lighthouse** on the southeast point. Built in 1814 on the site of a Celtic fort (*baile*), it was, until March 1997, the last manned lighthouse on Ireland's coastline. The path along the south-facing coast of the peninsula is the most spectacular part of the walk, providing close-up views of cliffs, secluded beaches and rocky islands. If all that doesn't sound strenuous enough, you could add on a long detour to the peninsula's highest point, which despite sporting a large radio mast offers panoramic views: leave the Cliff Walk to the north of the Baily Lighthouse and head up through the area known as The Summit, which has a pub and a café, to the actual summit, the 510 ft **Ben of Howth**.

Malahide and Donabate

A few kilometres up the coast from Howth, the old feudal estate of **MALAHIDE** lends its name to a commuter village of pretty houses and quiet streets sloping gently down to a yachting marina (bus #42 from Beresford

Place or Marino, or suburban train from Connolly Station or Howth Junction). It's a fifteen-minute walk from the station through pretty Malahide Demesne to a cluster of tourist attractions, chief among them **Malahide Castle** (guided tours Mon–Sat 10am–12.45pm & 2–5pm, Sun 11am–12.45pm & 2–6pm; Nov–March closes 5pm Sun; €5.50), a twelfth-century tower house that was modified and expanded over the eight hundred years that it was owned by the Talbot family. Its charm lies in its disparate styles, as it evolved from a defensive to a domestic building while retaining the look of a romantic turreted castle. If you're in need of refreshment pay a visit to the recommended tearoom and restaurant.

The **first room**, whose stone walls are hidden by dark sixteenth-century panelling carved in swirling floral patterns, was the principal room in the tower house. The panels on one wall incorporate copies of Raphael's Vatican frescoes of Adam and Eve, and Joseph and his brothers. You then pass on through the **drawing rooms** of the west wing, with their beautiful Rococo cornices, to the family **bedrooms** upstairs, featuring an eighteenth-century four-poster bed which is said to have belonged to the actor David Garrick. From there you descend to the **Great Hall**, whose oak hammer-beam ceiling and minstrels' gallery date from 1475. A picture of the Battle of the Boyne is flanked by portraits of the Earl of Tyrconnell, "Fighting Dick" Talbot, who led the Jacobites, and other family members who fought with him. The tour ends in a small **library** with Flemish floral wall-hangings and an exquisite inlaid table. In 1928, many of the papers of James Boswell (the great-grandfather of Emily Boswell, who married the fifth Lord Talbot) were found here, including an unexpurgated draft of his *Life of Johnson*.

Having seen the castle, most visitors make a beeline for the **Fry Model Railway** (April–Sept Mon–Sat 10am–5pm, Sun 2–6pm; €5.50), installed in the old Corn Store nearby. The nation's largest model rail layout (covering 287 square yards), it represents Ireland's transport system in all its diversity, from canal barges to the DART and ferry services.

Pride of place in the Craft Courtyard behind the model railway goes to **Tara's Palace and the Museum of Childhood** (April–Oct Mon–Sat 10am–1pm & 2–5pm, Sun 2–6pm; Nov–March Sat & Sun 2–5pm; €2, with proceeds going to Irish children's charities). Downstairs is a display of toys from 1720 to 1960, including a rare travelling dolls' house, while the first floor shelters Tara's Palace, a meticulous re-creation of an eighteenth-century mansion at one-twelfth scale.

Finally, there's the twenty-acre **Talbot Botanic Gardens**, which contain a walled garden, conservatory and five thousand species from Australia, New Zealand and Chile (May–Sept daily 2–5pm; €3; guided tours Wed 2pm).

A stop northward from Malahide on the suburban train is **DONABATE**, a trim commuter village that is graced by **Newbridge House** (April–Sept Tues–Sat 10am–1pm & 2–5pm, Sun 2–6pm; Oct–March Sat & Sun 2–5pm; €5.50). This solid brownstone edifice with a fine Georgian interior was built around 1737 for Charles Cobbe, archbishop of Dublin from 1742 to 1765. It remained in the Cobbe family until 1985, when the estate was sold to the county council (though the Cobbes retain an apartment upstairs). From the station, it's a fine fifteen-minute walk across Newbridge Demesne to reach the house. Guided tours include the family's **Museum of Curiosities**, containing all sorts of weird artefacts from around the world, including an intricate Kashmiri sari box and some ostrich eggs laid in Dundalk. The house remained unelectrified until the 1960s, when it was wired up for the filming of *The Spy Who Came in from the Cold*. There's also a coffee shop and a **traditional farm**

(€1.50), home to various breeds of sheep, fowl, pigs and cattle, and work is afoot in the grounds to restore the nineteenth-century walled fruit and vegetable garden.

Cafés and restaurants

Dublin may not be the gastronomic capital of the world, but the phenomenal expansion in the range of **places to eat** since the 1980s means that almost any preference is now catered for. Today, Dubliners are far more sophisticated in their tastes than twenty years ago and the rise in expectations and standards looks set to continue.

Many restaurants, bistros and upmarket cafés offer a **lunch-time** set menu of two to four courses for about half the cost of their evening fare, and on Sundays there are plenty of sustaining brunches on offer. Alternatively, you could see what pubs are serving up; carvery lunches, seafood, steaks, hearty Irish stew and nourishing soups are typical, but you can find more exotic dishes at trendier bars on the southside. For **dinner**, many establishments have an early-bird menu before 7pm or so, which is often excellent value compared to what you'd pay later on.

In the listings below, **prices** are indicated by the terms "Cheap" (under €10 for a main course); "Moderate" (€10–15); "Expensive" (€15–20); and "Very expensive" (over €20).

Cafés and quick meals

The distinction between **cafés** and restaurants is often arbitrary: some of the places reviewed here are licensed and open in the evenings; a few establishments listed under "Restaurants" opposite offer a lighter, café-style menu at lunch time; and many of the newer places that call themselves cafés are actually restaurants (or at least bistros) in all but name. This section is essentially a run-through of the best places to eat if what you want is a quick, unpretentious bite. All are in the centre of Dublin, the majority of them on the southside.

Beshoff's 14 Westmoreland St (daily 11am–11pm) & 6 O'Connell St Upper (Mon–Wed 11am–9pm, Thurs–Sun 11am–10pm). Superior fish and chips with counter service and functional tables. Cheap.

Bewley's Oriental Café 78 Grafton St (Mon–Sat 7.30am –9pm, Sun 8am–8pm) & 11–12 Westmoreland St (daily 7.30am–7.30pm, Thurs until 8pm). A Dublin institution, serving everything from hearty hot breakfasts and lunches to sticky buns and cakes. The Grafton Street branch (which plays host to lunch-time plays and cabaret evenings – see p.134) has lost some of its atmosphere now that it's mostly self-service, while Westmoreland St *Bewley's* has a busy, lived-in atmosphere, along with wooden pews and cosy fireplaces. Cheap.

Café Irie 11 Fownes St Lower, Temple Bar. Hippy café that stuffs its bagels, pitta and plain doorsteps with a tempting variety of copious fillings. Salads available if that all sounds too starchy, as well as healthy breakfasts until 11.30am during the week and all day at the weekend. Daily 9am–8.30pm. Cheap.

Café Java 5 South Anne St. Popular breakfast, lunch-time and coffee stop, offering such light meals as poached eggs with bacon, or chicken with yogurt. Mon–Fri 7am–7.30pm, Sat 8am–6.15pm, Sun 9am–6.15pm. Cheap.

Cobalt Café and Gallery 16 North Great George's St. Converted Georgian town house offering a light menu including sandwiches and cakes. Perfect for a refresher after visiting the James Joyce Centre. Mon–Fri 10am–5pm, Sat 11am–4.30pm. Cheap.

Cornucopia 19–21 Wicklow St. A small, friendly buffet café of long standing, well regarded by veggies. Mon–Sat 8.30am–8pm, Thurs until 9pm. Cheap.

Dunne and Crescenzi 14 Frederick St South. A cosy and very popular Italian café, with croissants and spot-on coffee for breakfast, and for the rest of the day, all manner of Italian sandwiches and excellent *antipasti*. Mon, Tues & Sat 9.30am–7pm, Wed–Fri 9.30am–10pm. Cheap.

Fresh 2nd Floor, Powerscourt Townhouse Centre. A great vegetarian and vegan menu, using organic ingredients wherever possible: soups, salads, pasta, veggie tarts, curries, baked potatoes, pulse dishes and hotpots; and organic wines, fresh juices and smoothies. Ten percent discount for students. Mon–Sat 10am–6pm, Thurs until 8pm. Cheap.

The Gotham Café 8 South Anne St. This buzzy, child-friendly café just off Grafton Street does a global menu that includes great pizzas and salads, Louisiana crab cakes and Thai vegetable curries. Mon–Sat noon–midnight, Sun noon–11.30pm. Cheap/Moderate.

Govinda's 4 Aungier St. Great little vegetarian café serving dahl and rice, samosas, salads, pizzas and burgers, as well as daily specials such as pasta and moussaka. Mon–Sat noon–9pm. Cheap.

Gruel 67 Dame St. Styling itself as a "soup kitchen", this offshoot of the *Mermaid Café* next door (see p.128) doles out a daily-changing menu of excellent sandwiches, salads and soups. Mon–Fri 7.30am–7.30pm, Sat 10.30am–5.30pm. Cheap.

Irish Film Centre 6 Eustace St, Temple Bar. One of the coolest hangouts in Temple Bar, with quick meals ranging from sandwiches, fish and chips and lasagne to fish cakes and goat's-cheese salad, with lots of veggie options. Daily 12.30–3.30pm & 5.30–9pm. Cheap.

Leo Burdock's 2 Werburgh St. Dublin's best-loved fish-and-chippie (takeaway only), near Christ Church Cathedral. Mon–Sat noon–midnight, Sun 4pm–midnight. Cheap.

Nude 21 Suffolk St. Funky canteen-style café serving up hot and cold wraps – try the delicious beef burrito – panini, salads, soups and some weird and wonderful juices and smoothies, to eat in or take away; ample choice for vegetarians. Mon–Sat 8am–9pm, Sun 10am–7pm. Cheap.

Panem 21 Ormond Quay Lower. Minuscule, stylish café serving excellent French and Italian snacks – fresh soups, filled focaccia, a couple of daily pasta specials and sweet and savoury croissants. Mon–Fri 8.30am–5pm, Sat 9am–5pm. Cheap.

Probe Market Arcade, South Great George's St. Funky little spot with wooden booths and cheerful staff, serving Mexican food, spicy Irish stew, baked potatoes and sandwiches. Ten percent discount for students. Mon–Wed & Fri 11am–6pm, Thurs & Sat 11am–7pm. Cheap.

Queen of Tarts 4 Cork Hill, on Lord Edward St. Small, laid-back patisserie-cum-café with an overflow branch in the vaults of City Hall opposite. Bagels and croissants for breakfast; ham, spinach and cheese tarts, Greek salad and all sorts of sandwiches for lunch; and delicious cakes baked fresh on the premises to keep you going between times. Mon–Fri 7.30am–6pm, Sat 9am–6pm, Sun 10am–6pm. Cheap.

Silk Road Café Chester Beatty Library, Dublin Castle. Well worth a visit in its own right, this stylish museum café spills over into the Library's skylit atrium. Mostly Middle Eastern food – lamb moussaka and lasagne, falafel, spinach and feta filo pie and plenty of other veggie options, and very good salads. Tues–Fri 10am–5pm, Sat 11am–5pm, Sun 1–5pm. Cheap.

The Steps of Rome 1 Chatham Court, Chatham St. Just off Grafton Street, this tiny, crammed café with a wine licence serves excellent pizzas made by friendly staff. You'll be lucky to get a table, but if you don't, their takeaway slices are a treat. Mon–Sat 11am–11pm, Sun 11am–10pm. Cheap.

Winding Stair Café 40 Ormond Quay Lower. With crepes, sandwiches, cakes and very good coffee, this secondhand book emporium's café is good enough to stand on its own merits, and has large windows overlooking the Ha'penny Bridge. Mon–Sat 9.30am–6pm, Sun 1–6pm. Cheap.

Restaurants

The majority of Dublin's **restaurants** are on the south side of the river in the city centre, with a tight concentration in Temple Bar. Wherever they're situated, it's always worth booking in the evenings. The places listed below are open daily for lunch and dinner except where noted.

Restaurant **chains** worth mentioning are the reliable, moderately priced *Fitzer's*, which offers daily-changing menus and lots of choice for vegetarians from its branches on Temple Bar Square (Ⓣ01/679 0440), at 51 Dawson St (Ⓣ01/677 1155) and in the National Gallery (Ⓣ01/661 4496); and *Milano*, 19 Temple Bar (Ⓣ01/670 3384) and 61 Dawson St (Ⓣ01/670 7744), part of the British *Pizza Express* chain, which dishes up superior pizzas at affordable prices and stays open until midnight.

Temple Bar

Da Pino 38–40 Parliament St ☎01/671 9308. One of the best of the many Italian restaurants in Temple Bar, offering spaghetti carbonara, *zuppa di cipolla* and other classic dishes. The welcome is warm and the decor sympathetic. Cheap/Moderate.

Eden Sycamore St ☎01/670 5372. Chic, upmarket but congenial restaurant in the heart of Temple Bar, with seats out on the square during the summer. The menu offers classic Irish cuisine with a Mediterranean twist. Expensive.

Elephant & Castle 18 Temple Bar ☎01/679 3121. The panache and informality of the *E&C* has had a huge influence on the culinary scene in Dublin. Imagine a neighbourhood diner that just happens to be in the coolest part of town, and does gourmet burgers, breakfasts or late-night meals with a Cajun-Creole or Pacific-Rim spin. Big queues on Sundays when clubbers celebrate their hangovers with brunch. Cheap/Moderate.

Il Baccaro Meeting House Square ☎01/671 4597. Lively, informal cellar restaurant serving traditional rustic Italian food. Mon–Fri & Sun 6–11pm, Sat noon–3pm & 6–11pm. Cheap/Moderate.

The Mermaid Café 69–70 Dame St ☎01/670 8236. Airy, chic restaurant with unfussy contemporary furnishings and helpful service. Great food from an eclectic menu, and there's an equally well-travelled wine list. Expensive.

Mongolian Barbecue 7 Anglesea St ☎01/670 4154. On the strength of this cheery theme-restaurant, you can't help feeling that if the Mongols had eaten this well at home, they wouldn't have bothered to maraud across half of Asia. All-you-can-eat noodle stir-fries, composed from a wide range of exotic ingredients and cooked on the spot. Moderate.

Monty's of Kathmandu 28 Eustace St ☎01/670 4911. Authentic Nepalese restaurant serving up delicious dishes such as chicken gorkhali, cooked with yoghurt, chilli, coriander and spices. Closed Sun lunch. Moderate.

Tante Zoe's 1 Crow St ☎01/679 4407. The first Cajun-Creole restaurant to open in Temple Bar, *Tante Zoe's* remains popular for continuing to serve decent food at affordable prices, and for managing to be fun. Moderate.

The Tea Room *The Clarence*, 6–8 Wellington Quay ☎01/670 7766. Stunning design provides a perfect backdrop to the eclectic menu, ranging from shellfish lasagne to *magret* of duck. Very expensive.

The rest of the southside

AYA 48 Clarendon St ☎01/677 1544. Japanese restaurant with Dublin's first sushi conveyor belt as its focal point. There's plenty of regular seating too, for more substantial dishes such as salmon teriyaki. Moderate/Expensive.

Café-Bar-Deli 12–13 South Great George's St ☎01/677 1646. A former *Bewley's Café* that's been smartly updated without losing its character. The menu of simple food, well done, is a winner, with some interesting starters, pastas, pizzas, Mediterranean salads and mouthwatering desserts. Cheap/Moderate.

Café Mao 2–3 Chatham Row, Chatham St ☎01/670 4899. Slick, trendy spot presenting great dishes from around Asia, including such tempting creations as grilled, marinated squid with watermelon. Moderate.

Diep le Shaker 55 Pembroke Lane, off Pembroke St Lower ☎01/661 1829. Dublin's best and swankiest Thai restaurant, with prices that won't break the bank – though drinks are expensive – and a menu that's strong on seafood. Closed Sat lunch and Sun. Moderate.

Ely Wine Bar 22 Ely Place ☎01/676 8986. Popular, congenial wine bar serving wholesome and unpretentious snacks and main dishes to accompany over fifty wines by the glass, as well as some top-notch beers. Closed Sun. Moderate.

Imperial Chinese Restaurant 12A Wicklow St ☎01/677 2580. A large room often buzzing with Chinese customers, who generally rate it as the best restaurant in the city centre, this place offers superb dim sum (served daily 12.30–5pm). Moderate.

Juice 73–83 South Great George's St ☎01/475 7856. Chic and vegetarian without a sweaty sandal in sight. The imaginative dinner menu might offer mushroom Wellington and aduki-bean Juiceburgers; simpler and cheaper dishes are served at lunch time. Cheap/Moderate.

Lord Edward Seafood Restaurant 23 Christchurch Place ☎01/454 2420. Dublin's oldest seafood restaurant, above a pub opposite Christ Church Cathedral, this is a venerable club-like institution dedicated to simple cooking with the very freshest fish. Closed Sat lunch and Sun. Moderate/Expensive.

P.D.'s Woodhouse 1 Coliemore Rd, Dalkey ☎01/284 9399. A friendly, cosy steakhouse where meat and fish grilled over oak wood is the speciality, and they don't ignore veggies – try the delicious halloumi kebabs. Mon–Sat 5.30–11pm, Sun 4–9.30pm. Moderate/Expensive.

Patrick Guilbaud *Merrion Hotel*, 21 Merrion St Upper ☎01/676 4192. An elegant French restaurant with bags of cachet, not to mention two Michelin stars. Formal and showy in the evenings, "Paddy Giblets" loosens his collar just a little at

lunch time, when the €28 set menu represents amazing value. Closed Mon & Sun. Very expensive.
The Shalimar 17 South Great George's St ☎01/671 0738. Choose between tandooris, biryanis and other classic Punjabi dishes upstairs, or a simpler keema or kofta in the basement balti house – both with lots of options for veggies. Cheap/Moderate.
Trocadero 3 St Andrew St ☎01/677 5545. Pleasant and friendly trattoria with excellent food, including a very popular pre-theatre menu. It's one of Dublin's oldest Italian restaurants, and the walls are hung with plaudits in the form of signed photographs of visiting showbiz luminaries. The place really comes into its own late at night when it fills up with theatre folk. Mon–Sat 5pm–12.30am. Moderate/Expensive.
Wagamama King St South ☎01/478 2152. Ultra-healthy Japanese-style meat and vegetarian noodle dishes served in a near-clinical atmosphere of long benches, crisp lighting and clean air. Best for noodle soups, dumplings and a wide variety of wholesome juices. Cheap/Moderate.
Yamamori Noodles 71–72 South Great George's St ☎01/475 5001. Trendy, fun Japanese restaurant in the heart of publand, with delicious noodles, soups, teriyaki, tempura, sushi and sashimi. Moderate.

The northside

101 Talbot 100–101 Talbot St ☎01/874 5011. Conveniently close to the Abbey Theatre, with a lovely spacious dining room where flavoursome dishes with Mediterranean and Middle Eastern influences keep meat-eaters and vegetarians coming back. Tues–Sat 5–11pm. Moderate.
Bond 5 Beresford Place ☎01/855 9244. Great, innovative food and a must for wine buffs, as you can choose your own bottle from over two hundred well-priced wines in the cellar. Closed Sat lunch & Sun. Expensive.
C-Bar Epicurean Food Hall, 13–14 Liffey St ☎01/865 6663. Small, tiled fish and seafood bar on the north side of Ha'penny Bridge, where the imaginative cooking is seriously good, and the service friendly and efficient. Mon–Wed 12.30–6pm, Thurs noon–9pm, Fri & Sat 12.30–7pm. Moderate.
Chapter One 18–19 Parnell Square North ☎01/873 2266. A formal restaurant with an excellent reputation for modern Irish cooking, housed in the atmospheric cellars of the Dublin Writers' Museum. Excellent-value deals at lunch time or before a show at the nearby Gate Theatre. Closed Sat lunch, Sun & Mon. Very expensive.
Halo *Morrison Hotel*, Ormond Quay Lower ☎01/887 2421. Cutting-edge interior design sets the scene for the fresh, crisp flavours of Asian-fusion cuisine, using Irish ingredients, especially seafood, wherever possible. Lunch-time set menus bring the price down. Very expensive.
King Sitric's Fish Restaurant East Pier, Howth ☎01/832 5235. Excellent seafood restaurant with panoramic sea views, specializing in fish landed at the nearby pier, oysters, mussels and lobsters. The €20 two-course lunch menu is a bargain. Mon–Fri 12.30–2.15pm & 6.30–10pm, Sat 6.30–10pm; May–Sept Mon–Sat also noon–3pm. Expensive/Very expensive.

Pubs and bars

Good puzzle would be cross Dublin without passing a pub

James Joyce, *Ulysses*

Pubs are an integral part of Dublin's social life and an essential part of any visit. The charm of most of Dublin's older pubs derives from the fact that they're simple, no-nonsense places, the better ones unchanged for decades, where you can get a good pint of Guinness and the people are friendly. There are over eight hundred pubs and bars in the city, so what follows doesn't try to be anything like a comprehensive, or even a representative, guide. Instead it's a small – and very personal – selection of Dublin's traditional pubs and new drinking places.

It's worth knowing that many of the pubs listed under "Live music venues" (see p.131) are great for a drink in their own right, notably *The Brazen Head*, *The Cobblestone*, *Hughes's Bar* and *O'Donoghue's*. And plenty of bars in Dublin have late licences, as noted in the reviews below, which allow them to stay open until 2.30am or so, usually from Thursday to Saturday. For details of Dublin's highly entertaining pub tours see p.70.

Temple Bar

Front Lounge 33 Parliament St. The spacious interior is always full of the city's most beautiful people. Gay-friendly, great cappucinos, but can get very crowded at weekends. Fri & Sat until 1.30am.

The Palace Bar 21 Fleet St. Wood and glass interior, crowded and friendly pub much loved by Dubliners.

The Porter House 16–18 Parliament St. Dublin's first microbrewery serves a wide selection of excellent and playfully monikered beers, attracting both curious locals and visitors enticed by the bright, bustling interior. Check out a sample tray of all nine beers for €9, a great way to establish your chosen pint before settling in. Live music every night and good food. Fri & Sat until 2am.

Thomas Read's and The Oak 1 Parliament St. Two contrasting, interconnected bars. The former is a lively establishment, serving a globe-spanning selection of bottled and draught beers to its youngish regulars. *The Oak* next door is a more introverted spot, cosy, traditional and dark-panelled. Fri & Sat until 2.30am.

The rest of the southside

4 Dame Lane 4 Dame Lane ⓣ01/679 0291. Announced by burning braziers just along the lane from the *Stag's Head* (see opposite), this airy, minimalist bar/club probably has the stylistic edge over its bare brickwork and wood rivals. There're good tunes, anything from hip-hop and jazz to chilled ragamuffin, and a dance floor upstairs. Daily until 2.30am, admission charge after 11pm.

The Chocolate Bar Old Harcourt Street Train Station, Harcourt St. Nestling in the armpit of one of Dublin's most stylish nightclubs, POD (see p.133), this Gaudí-inspired watering-hole is where young hip Dubliners congregate to swig alcopops and imported bottled beers.

Davy Byrne's 21 Duke St, off Grafton St. Davy Byrne's "moral pub" receives a particularly honourable mention in Joyce's epic novel as the place where Leopold Bloom takes a break from his famous perambulation across Dublin for a Gorgonzola sandwich and a glass of Burgundy. Over the years it's been extensively redecorated as a lounge bar in a mix of Art Deco and other vaguely Modernist styles, but it's still a good place for a quiet drink and perhaps a plate of seafood.

Doheny and Nesbitt 5 Baggot St Lower. Archetypal Dublin pub – the tiny, atmospheric, smoke-filled front room looks as if it has hardly changed for a hundred years. Always packed, but there are cosy snugs at the back, and at weekends, a slightly less hectic lounge open upstairs.

The Globe 11 South Great George's St. Outrageously popular with the sassy and fashion-conscious twenty-somethings of Dublin, this loud and lively bar is invariably packed at weekends, and busy every night. It's pleasantly wood-panelled and discreetly lit, which makes it the perfect chill-out room for *Rí-Rá* (see p.133).

Grogan's 15 William St South. Smoky, eccentric haunt of literary types down through the years, where conversation dominates. Good drinks at relatively reasonable prices; head here if you like your beer without the frills.

The International Bar 23 Wicklow St. Another great drinking establishment that has changed little over the decades. Upstairs hosts comedy, music and theatre in a small, informal venue.

Kehoe's 9 South Anne St, off Grafton St. Until a few years ago the family whose name adorns this wonderful old establishment lived upstairs, reputedly the last resident publicans in the city centre. To the collective relief of Dublin's more discerning drinkers, the new owners have scarcely touched the mahogany interiors, and there are few happier places to be than in the innermost seat of the tiny snug, with a pint settling on the table in front of you.

The Long Hall 51 South Great George's St. Dark and wonderfully ornate Victorian pub, with friendly staff and a good pint of Guinness.

McDaid's 3 Harry St, off Grafton St. A literary pub, this is where Brendan Behan used to drown his talent in Guinness. It remains more or less intact, and despite now selling its own T-shirts, it's still popular with locals, with overspill seating upstairs for when the crush gets too mighty.

Messrs Maguire 1–2 Burgh Quay. Microbrewery pub that's not quite as classy as *The Porter House* (see above), but well worth trying out. Centrally located overlooking the river, with numerous floors and mezzanines off a grand, winding staircase. Mon, Tues & Sun until 12.30am, Wed–Sat until 2.30am.

Modern Green Bar 31 Wexford St. Handy for *Mono* (see p.133), this lively, friendly student bar does exactly what it says on the tin, with a splash of primary red paint thrown in. Bright, simple booths and good DJs most nights of the week.

Mulligan's 8 Poolbeg St. *Mulligan's* traditionally served the best Guinness in Dublin; many people now acknowledge that honour to have passed to the Guinness Storehouse (see p.107), but this place still has its partisans.

O'Neill's 2 Suffolk St. This rambling pub with plenty of quiet corners has been a home from home for generations of students and lecturers from nearby Trinity College. Also much favoured as a lunching spot by office workers, who come for the sandwiches and healthy portions of buffet food.

SoSuMe 64 South Great George's St. Generations of tellers who worked in this lofty former bank are no doubt turning in their graves at its oriental-themed reincarnation, whose punning name belongs firmly to the Celtic Tiger. But it's a lively enough spot, and the theme, with its Buddhas, dragons and botanical prints, is attractive but not too in-your-face. Wed–Sat until 2.30am, Sun until 1am.
Stag's Head 1 Dame Court, a tiny turning off Dame Street almost opposite the Central Bank. Hard to find – a mosaic set in the pavement on Dame Street alerts you to the tiny alleyway it's located in – but worth it when you get there: inside it's all mahogany, stained glass and mirrors. Good pub lunches, too, and a friendly atmosphere.
Toners 139 Baggot St Lower. Dark, cosy pub with a refreshingly plain interior. Snugs, with glazed partitions, for making and breaking confidences.

The northside

Dice Bar Queen St, just off Arran Quay. Part-owned by Huey from the Fun Lovin' Criminals, the *Dice Bar* is an ice-cool New York-style place, though it can get wild later in the evening. Long, black bar and black banquettes, lit by church candles, and nightly DJs, playing anything from soukous to lounge funk. Thurs–Sat until 2.30am.
Pravda Liffey St Lower. Trendy superbar on the north side of Ha'penny Bridge which might have pleased even Papa Stalin, with its huge Revolutionary murals and industrial theme. Decent food available. Fri & Sat until 2.30am.
Ryan's Parkgate St, across the river from Heuston Station. Another pub famous for its cosy, wood-lined snugs and the quality of its Guinness; considered the finest Victorian pub in Dublin.

Live music venues

Dublin's **music scene** is volatile, so if you're after something in particular – jazz, folk, traditional – the best place to check is the fortnightly listings magazine *The Event Guide* (see p.69). *Hot Press* (see p.69), the national music paper, is another useful source of information. Depending on the size of the venue and the nature of the act performing, tickets generally cost between €10 and €30. There are also a number of open-air events during the summer, commencing in early May with the Heineken Green Energy Festival with gigs at Dublin Castle, followed later in the year by one-off gigs at places such as the Lansdowne Road Stadium, and the Royal Dublin Society (RDS) Showgrounds, both in Ballsbridge. **Traditional music** is once again flourishing in Dublin with a number of pubs and bars offering sessions. These usually commence at around 9.30pm and are almost always free (apart from, of course, the cost of your pint). Listings of these can be found in the monthly *Irish Music* magazine (€2.48 from newsagents) or ask for advice in Claddagh Records (see p.138).

Major venues

The Ambassador Parnell St. Credit-card bookings via Ticketmaster ⓣ01/1890/925100, ⓦwww.ticketmaster.ie. Up-and-coming venue in a former cinema at the top of O'Connell Street, whose programme veers towards alternative and leftfield US acts; prices tend to be slightly higher than at other Dublin venues.
The National Stadium South Circular Rd ⓣ01/453 3371. Frequently used medium-size venue holding 1000–2000 people, depending on whether or not the seats are taken out.
Olympia Theatre 72 Dame St ⓣ01/677 7744, ⓦwww.olympia.ie. This wonderful old Victorian theatre is frequently used to stage live music performances. Established international and Irish acts tend to play early-evening sets, with late-night gigs on Fridays and Saturdays, known as "Midnight at the Olympia", often featuring funk or R&B bands.
Point Theatre North Wall Quay ⓣ01/836 3633. The venue of choice for most visiting superstar acts, the cavernous Point Theatre is a huge and charmless converted warehouse on the north bank of the Liffey, about one mile east of O'Connell St, with a capacity of 3000–5000, depending on whether the show is seated or standing.
The SFX 28 Sherrard St Upper ⓣ01/855 4673.This 1500-capacity hall is one of Dublin's oldest and most popular rock venues, and has hosted some of the city's best rock and pop gigs over the last two decades.

Temple Bar Music Centre Curved St ⓣ01/670 9202, ⓦwww.tbmc.ie. This custom-built facility includes an impeccable, if slightly antiseptic venue for audiences of up to 650, and has a policy determinedly geared towards innovation and experimentation when it comes to booking acts.

Vicar Street 58–59 Thomas St West ⓣ01/454 6656, ⓦwww.vicarstreet.com. Despite its rather downtown location opposite John's Lane Church, *Vicar Street* has acquired an estimable reputation for its staggeringly varied programme of gigs, from cool jazz to alt.country, via traditional music and indie rock, and the occasional comedian. *Vicar Street*'s little brother, *The Shelter* next door, offers less well-known names.

Other venues

Break for the Border Stephen St ⓣ01/478 0300. This enormous Western-themed restaurant attracts hundreds of good-natured punters in pursuit of rock, indie and dance music, drink and the opposite sex.

Eamonn Doran's 3A Crown Alley, Temple Bar ⓣ01/679 9114. A large, rather soulless joint, but young bands can be heard here most nights, sometimes two or three per evening.

The International Bar 23 Wicklow St ⓣ01/677 9250. Somewhat of an old-fashioned pub venue, the *International* still hosts some great music, usually of the good-time and raunchy variety, including the regular "Dirty Jazz Club" (Tues) and a blues night (Fri). Also noted for the comedy nights upstairs (Mon, Tues & Thurs).

Irish Film Centre Bar 6 Eustace St ⓣ01/679 5744. The place to go on Friday and Saturday nights if you want to quietly savour the best jazz and blues in the city. After 11.30pm, when the film-goers have departed, the main foyer converts into the perfect venue, where a relaxed and discerning crowd listens to renowned local and international artists.

The Isaac Butt Store St ⓣ01/855 5884, ⓦwww.theisaacbutt.com. Nightly gigs from mostly unknown bands and singers, ranging from hard-boiled grunge to candy-sweet pop.

J.J. Smyth's 12 Aungier St ⓣ01/475 2565. *J.J.*'s offers a feast of contemporary jazz (one of Ireland's best-known saxophonists, Richie Buckley, regularly plays here), a weekly Irish blues club (Tues) and gigs from the more rumbustious end of the rock spectrum.

Slattery's of Rathmines 217 Rathmines Rd Lower ⓣ01/497 2052. Large and popular bar, a little way south of Portobello Bridge, offering a variable programme of rock, country, traditional music, jazz and blues; usually free.

Whelan's 25 Wexford St ⓣ01/478 0766, ⓦwww.whelanslive.com. With its welcoming 350-capacity, two-level room, this is perhaps the city's best place to see live music up close.

Traditional music pubs and venues

The Brazen Head 20 Bridge St Lower. Laying claim to the title of Dublin's oldest pub, *The Brazen Head* opens its doors to musicians every night, though the quality of the sessions can be extremely variable, even if the surroundings are grand.

The Cobblestone 7 King St North ⓣ01/872 1799, ⓦwww.musiclee.ie. Arguably the best traditional music venue in Dublin (and, some would claim, in Ireland too), this dark, cosy wooden-floored bar at the north end of Smithfield offers high-quality sessions nightly and on Sunday afternoons, while regular concerts (€8–10) featuring some of Ireland's best-known singers and musicians are staged upstairs several nights a week.

Hughes's Bar 19 Chancery St. Tucked away behind the Four Courts, this renowned bar attracts the cream of the city's traditional musicians to its nightly sessions. Fridays can draw a large crowd, so arrive early to grab a seat.

The Merchant Merchants Quay. It always helps when the landlord is a traditional music lover himself, which is definitely the case in this popular bar on the corner of Bridge Street Lower – high-quality sessions most nights of the week.

Monto O'Shea's Hotel, 19 Talbot St ⓣ01/836 5670. Dublin's newest traditional music venue, specializing in gigs by some of the country's bigger names in traditional music (tickets usually costing around €10), *Monto* has already garnered a reputation for the quality of its programme.

O'Donoghue's 15 Merrion Row. The centre of the folk and traditional music revival which began in the late 1950s, *O'Donoghue's* will forever be associated with The Dubliners. Nightly sessions draw a considerable crowd, partly because the bar is a notable landmark on the tourist trail.

Clubs

Dublin's **club** scene is ever-changing, so you should check the latest listings in *The Event Guide*, *In Dublin* or the monthly club-oriented freebie *The Slate* (available in record stores) to see which club nights are still in operation. There are two distinct club scenes in Dublin. The first (and the one listed here) is an eclectic collection scattered around the city centre, many of which offer special interest and theme nights. Most are hard to get into – that's part of their cachet – and expensive at the weekends. The second, and distinctly less appealing, is based in and around Leeson Street, southeast of St Stephen's Green. The clubs here do, however, serve a purpose: a string of basement places that are busy after everything else has shut, these are the clubs to hit at two or three in the morning if you're really desperate to go on partying. Most have no entry fee but serve very expensive drinks – they're at their dubious best Thursday to Sunday from around 1am till dawn.

Gaiety Theatre King St South ⓣ01/677 1717, ⓦwww.gaietytheatre.com. At weekends Dubliners throng to the beautiful old *Gaiety Theatre*, some enticed by the attraction of the city's latest serving bars – all five of them! Each night features live bands (Fri salsa and jazz, Sat rock) and DJs playing an assortment of music. Fri & Sat 11.30pm–4am.

Lillie's Bordello Adam Court, off Grafton St ⓣ01/679 9204. Rock stars – would-be, has-been and actual – quaff and bitch with supermodels in the velour-bedecked *Lillie's Bordello*. Regulars get priority and rarely pay the reasonably hefty entrance fee (€15), but if you beat the after-pub crowd, act relaxed and don't look too dishevelled you should get in easily enough. Mon–Sun 11pm till late.

Mono 26 Wexford St ⓣ01/478 0766, ⓦwww.clubmono.com. Ultra-cool recently redesigned bar and club with an extensive programme of club nights, including Messy (Sun) with resident funk DJs, Saturday (Sat) for house lovers, Bliss (Wed) for fans of dance-floor anthems, Cushi (Thurs) for drum 'n' bass and, perhaps best of the lot, Motion (Fri) featuring guest DJs, deep house, techno and progressive trance. Nightly 10.30pm–2.30am.

POD Old Harcourt Street Train Station, Harcourt St ⓣ01/478 0225, ⓦwww.pod.ie. The phenomenally popular POD (short for "Place Of Dance") is a match for anything that New York, Berlin or Tokyo has to offer, boasting ultramodern decor and a tooth-loosening sound system. The clientele are intimidatingly chic, and the door policy, especially at weekends, can be tough. Dress to impress and get there early. Wed–Sat 11pm–2.30am.

Redbox Old Harcourt Street Train Station, Harcourt St ⓣ01/478 0225, ⓦwww.pod.ie/redbox.html. Far more plush than other similar-size dance venues in the city, Redbox is a tailor-made, lovingly designed 1000-capacity hall located upstairs from the POD, but with a more relaxed and less style-conscious atmosphere. Features probably Dublin's largest student night (Thurs) and major DJs (Fri & Sat) playing techno and house, plus occasional live gigs on other nights of the week. Thurs–Sat 10.30pm–2.30am.

Renard's Setanta Centre, 35 Frederick St South ⓣ01/677 5876, ⓦindigo.ie/~robbief/renards/find.html. Popular with Dublin's small but self-important music and media pack, who tend to inhabit the upstairs VIP area. Claustrophobes may find the ground-floor bar preferable to the sweaty basement dance floor playing everything from commercial dance to hardcore funk. Mon–Sun 9pm–3am.

Rí-Rá 1 Exchequer St ⓣ01/677 4835. The records spun at Rí-Rá (pronounced "ree-raw") can range from plain commercial disco through world music to hard funk, depending on night and mood: this club manages to be both informal and fashionable and draws an eclectic and friendly crowd. Thurs–Sun 11.15pm–3am.

Spy Powerscourt Townhouse Centre, Clarendon St ⓣ01/677 0067. Stylishly designed, ultra-cool club spanning three floors, equally enjoyed by lounge lizards and dance-floor divas. Be seen in the Monochrome Bar, loll in the Pink Room or just get down to a wide variety of DJs and music. Mon–Sat 9pm–3am.

Switch 23 Eustace St, Temple Bar ⓣ01/668 2504. DJs nightly, both downstairs and in the bar of this sometimes frenzied venue. Phunk'dUp (Sat) is a huge, justifiably popular night of house and tough techno with a strong, underground atmosphere. Nightly 11pm–3am.

Temple Theatre Temple St North ⓣ01/874 5088, ⓦwww.templetheatre.ie. Housed in an enormous restored church and spread over three floors, the Temple Theatre was clearly inspired by UK mega-clubs like Cream and Ministry of Sound, and has had some difficulty finding its feet not least because of its unfashionable location. Nonetheless, the Rhythm Corporation (Fri) has become an R&B mainstay, bringing DJs over from the UK and Europe, and the Temple is trying to repeat the formula with Space (Sat). Fri & Sat 9/10pm–3am.

Tivoli Theatre 135–138 Francis St ⓣ01/670 3771. The city's current "in" venue, the Tivoli has a state-of-the-art 360-degree sound system and a hefty techno flavour and often books top local and international DJs for Influx (Sat). Genius (Tues) aims at student techno lovers while the wildest night is undoubtedly Foot Fetish (Fri). Sun, Tues, Fri & Sat 10.30pm–very late.

Tomato Harcourt Hotel, 60 Harcourt St ⓣ01/478 3677. Popular three-room venue, offering a more downmarket alternative to nearby POD and Redbox, with a range of different club nights and DJs throughout the week, including the Spark indie night (Wed), Cheeze (Thurs) and FM104 (Fri) both for commercial dance music. Nightly 9pm–3am.

Theatre and cinema

As befits a city with a rich literary past, **theatre** flourishes in Dublin. The traditional diet of Irish classics at the "establishment" theatres is now spiced by experimental or fringe programmes at newer, smaller venues. Highlights of the year include the **Dublin Theatre Festival** in early October and the **Dublin Fringe Festival** which runs from late September to mid-October (see p.49 for more on them both). Theatres generally operate from Monday to Saturday; evening performances usually begin at 7.30pm or 8pm, and there may be matinees, too. Credit-card booking is widely available – expect to pay €10–20 per ticket for fringe theatre, €15–30 for mainstream. Bookings can also be made through Ticketmaster (ⓣ01/456 9569 or 1890/925100, ⓦwww.ticketmaster.ie). If you're budget-conscious, it's worth enquiring about any low-cost previews and occasional cut-price Monday- and Tuesday-night shows, while students (with ID) and OAPs can sometimes find good concessionary rates.

Dublin has numerous **cinemas** showing mainstream films. Most of them are in the suburbs, but there's a couple near the top of O'Connell Street: the Savoy on O'Connell Street Upper itself (programme info ⓣ01/874 8487, booking ⓣ01/874 6000, ⓦwww.filminfo.net) and UGC on Parnell Street (programme info ⓣ01/872 8400, booking ⓣ01/872 8444). For more interesting fare, the Irish Film Centre and The Screen Cinema, reviewed below, are the chief venues; the outdoor summer screenings in Meeting House Square organized by the Irish Film Centre are also well worth checking out. All cinemas operate a policy of cheap seats before 5pm (6.30pm in some cases), seven days a week, during which time tickets cost €3.50–5.50 – after this they cost €5–8; student discounts are also often available.

For details of what's on, check the *Irish Times*, the *Evening Herald*, *The Event Guide* or *In Dublin* (see p.69).

The Abbey Theatre Abbey St Lower ⓣ01/878 7222, ⓦwww.abbeytheatre.ie. This is the National Theatre of Ireland (see also p.109), founded by W.B. Yeats and Lady Gregory in 1903 and was the first theatre in the English-speaking world to be state-subsidized (since 1925). The original building was destroyed by fire in the 1950s and replaced by the current, much-detested pile in 1966 – it's slated for redevelopment or, more likely, relocation sometime in the future. It tends to show international and Irish classics (by Synge, Sheridan, O'Casey, Wilde, etc), plus new offerings by contemporary playwrights such as Brian Friel, Marina Carr, Bernard Farrell and Tom Murphy. See also Peacock Theatre opposite.

Andrew's Lane Theatre Between St Andrew and Exchequer streets ⓣ01/679 5720. Situated just off Dame Street, the main theatre here puts on generally mainstream plays and musical works, while the studio upstairs presents a mix of fringe and amateur theatre.

Bewley's Café Theatre 78 Grafton St ⓣ086/878

4001. On the second floor above the café (see p.126), you can often catch an innovative, small-scale production while eating your lunch (€10 including soup and a sandwich); there's also regular evening cabaret (€10–13), at which you can buy wine, soft drinks, tea and coffee.
Crypt Arts Centre Dublin Castle ⓣ01/671 3387, ⓦwww.cryptartscentre.org. A small venue in the crypt of the Chapel Royal, managed by a company called *íomhá Ildánach* (roughly translated as "varied image") who stage a number of plays throughout the year, generally fringe pieces.
Focus Theatre 6 Pembroke Place ⓣ01/676 3071. Founded by the late Deirdre O'Connell, a student of Lee Strasberg at the Actors' Studio in New York, this diminutive but important venue stages powerful international modern drama.
Gaiety Theatre King St South ⓣ01/677 1717, ⓦwww.gaietytheatre.com. An old-style playhouse with velvet curtains and gilded boxes, which hosts everything from opera and Irish classics to musicals, concerts and other family entertainments. Late on Fridays and Saturdays it becomes a nightclub (see p.133).
Gate Theatre 1 Cavendish Row, Parnell Square ⓣ01/874 4045, ⓦwww.gate-theatre.ie. Founded in the 1920s by Micheál Mac Liammóir and Hilton Edwards in an eighteenth-century building leased from the Rotunda Hospital, the Gate has a reputation for staging adventurous experimental drama as well as established classics, in a small, elegant auditorium.
Irish Film Centre 6 Eustace St ⓣ01/679 3477, ⓦwww.fii.ie. Art-house cinema with two screens, a good bar (see p.132) and restaurant (see p.127) and a film-related bookshop. Films include new, low-budget Irish works as well as a good range of world and gay cinema.
The Lambert Puppet Theatre 5 Clifton Lane, Monkstown ⓣ01/280 0974, ⓦwww.lambertpuppettheatre.com. Dublin's only puppet theatre, producing shows of very high quality every Saturday and Sunday at 3.30pm. Great for kids, though there are also performances for adults during the International Puppet Festival in September.
Olympia Theatre 72 Dame St ⓣ01/677 7744, ⓦwww.olympia.ie. This old-style music hall has been through many incarnations since it opened in 1749, with a roll-call of luminaries from Charlie Chaplin to Noel Coward. Nowadays it hosts musicals, stand-up comedy shows and medium-size gigs (see p.131), as well as dramatical crowd-pleasers.
Peacock Theatre 26 Abbey St Lower ⓣ01/878 7222, ⓦwww.abbeytheatre.ie. The Abbey's smaller, sister theatre, in the basement, produces new drama in both Irish and English, and can often be a goldmine for new talent.
Project Arts Centre 39 Essex St East ⓣ01/679 6622 or 1850 260027, ⓦwww.project.ie. Renowned for its experimental and often controversial Irish and international theatre, this flagship of the contemporary art scene also hosts dance, film, music and performance art.
The Screen Cinema D'Olier St ⓣ01/672 5500. A fairly old-fashioned, low-key venue with three screens; a good place to catch art-house as well as mainstream films.
Tivoli Theatre 135–138 Francis St ⓣ01/454 4472. A modern theatre in The Liberties, the Tivoli shows everything from mainstream drama and musicals to comedy and dance, as well as hosting club nights (see opposite).

Gay life

As attitudes to homosexuality in Dublin have become increasingly liberal over the last decade, so the capital's **gay** community has grown in confidence, and a small but vibrant scene has established a niche in the city's social life. The number of permanent fixtures on the scene is small but growing; most of the real action happens on the gay nights in the straight venues. Most **pubs** around Temple Bar and South Great George's Street have a mixed clientele and a keen eye on the pink euro, while several mainstream **clubs** have theme nights and gay events.

A good starting point for finding out the latest **information** on gay events and venues in Dublin is OUThouse, 105 Capel St (Mon–Fri noon–6pm; ⓣ01/873 4932, ⓦwww.outhouse.ie), a drop-in centre with a café and a small library. Alternatively, you can ring Gay Switchboard Dublin (Mon–Fri & Sun 8–10pm, Sat 3.30–6pm; ⓣ01/872 1055) or Lesbian Line (Thurs 7–9pm;

☎01/872 9911). It's also a good idea to get a copy of the excellent freebie *GCN* (Gay Community News), which has detailed listings of upcoming events and can be found in the gay-friendly Books Upstairs (see opposite) opposite the main gate of Trinity College or in clubs and bars. Alternatively, check out the listings page of *In Dublin* (see p.69) or Ⓦwww.gay-ireland.com.

Pubs and bars

Dublin's small number of **gay bars** aren't just meeting places but fully-fledged entertainment centres, offering a broad range of different events throughout the week from quizzes and singalongs to dance-floor delights.

Front Lounge 33 Parliament St. More a mixed than an exclusively gay venue, its atmosphere is certainly camp, which appeals to quite a large gay crowd. Entertainment includes karaoke (Tues), lounge music (Wed) and DJs at the weekend. Fri & Sat until 1.30am.

The George 89 South Great George's St. Ireland's first gay pub when it opened twenty years ago, *The George* is a characterful place which offers a range of entertainment, including pre-club DJs, as well as serving good meals during the day. Upstairs has a small dance floor where you'll hear house and funk. Upstairs Wed–Sun until 3am. Downstairs bar Wed–Sat until 2.30am.

Gubu 7–8 Capel St. This brightly decorated, relaxed mixed bar hosts probably Dublin's most alternative cabaret, G-Spot (Wed), compered by the awesome Busty Lycra, featuring comedy, drag acts and more. Other events include a regular eighties disco (Fri). Fri & Sat until 1am.

Out on the Liffey 27 Ormond Quay Upper. More relaxed than *The George*, this pub is popular with gays and lesbians alike and hosts events (quizzes, karaoke, etc). Thurs–Sat until 2am.

The Wig and Pen 131 Thomas St West. The newest bar on the gay scene has proved a real hit with both men and women, with a happy hour most nights 6–8pm. Often has DJs playing house, techno and funk at the weekend and other entertainment during the week. Sunday night is men only.

Clubs

As yet Dublin has no single dedicated venue for **gay clubbers**, who rely on usually weekly events in mainstream clubs. Some of these, however, such as H.A.M. (see below) are now almost scene institutions. Entry prices are usually pretty reasonable and you should expect to pay around €8–10. Regularly updated details of club nights can be found at Ⓦwww.pink-pages.org/clubs .html.

Baby at *Mono*, 26 Wexford St ☎01/478 0766, Ⓦwww.clubmono.com. Recently relaunched techno night in a revamped venue, featuring resident DJs and a very sociable mixed crowd – a good place to meet people. Mon 11pm–3am.

Candy Club at *Soho*, Earl of Kildare Hotel, corner of Nassau and Kildare streets ☎01/220 1320, Ⓦwww.clubcandy.net. Four fun nights, including the ever-popular Lollypop (Tues) and Super Handbag (Thurs) both of which favour commercial dance classics from the eighties. Often has regular drinks promotions and giveaways; neat dress code. Sat, Sun, Tues & Thurs 11pm–3am.

H.A.M. (Homo-Action Movies) at *POD*, Old Harcourt St Train Station, Harcourt St ☎01/478 0225, Ⓦwww.pod.ie. Weekly gay night at one of Dublin's trendiest clubs, drawing a regular and often extravagant, mostly male crowd. The music is usually heavily oriented towards funky house and the Art Deco anteroom is for chilling out and watching the movie, often of the action-man variety. Totally queer door policy – definitely an occasion for dressing up. Fri 11pm–3am.

Hilton Edwards at *Spy*, Powerscourt Townhouse Centre, Clarendon St ☎01/677 0067. One of Dublin's plushest clubs, spread over three floors, *Spy* hosts an enjoyable homosocial Sunday night, devised by the originators of H.A.M.: resident DJs playing tracks with a techno edge and an extremely cool lounge. Sun 10pm–3am.

Libida at *Chief O'Neill's Hotel*, Smithfield, Smithfield Village ☎01/817 3838. Popular lesbian night with various DJs specializing in high-energy commercial dance, cool Latin tracks and slower sets, plus spotlight dancers on the stage and occasional live bands in swish, modernist surroundings. Last Sat of the month 10.30pm–2am.

Muffins at *Molloy's Café Bar*, 13 High St ☎01/677 3207. Women-only night in an elegant bar just west of Christ Church Cathedral, featuring three floors of DJs, playing everything from commercial dance to Latin grooves, and a chill-out room. First & third Sat of the month 8.30pm–2am.

Sharpshooter at *Eamonn Doran's*, 3A Crown Alley, Temple Bar ☎01/679 9114. Advertises itself as "Dublin's queer indie night", though the upbeat crowd can be pretty mixed and sometimes struggles to fill this rather cavernous club. Tues 11pm–2am.

Slam at *Switch*, 23 Eustace St, Temple Bar ☎01/668 2504. A long-standing Monday-night event, playing no-frills, commercial house to a friendly, often exuberant crowd. Mon 11pm–2am.

Shopping

Around Grafton Street and O'Connell Street, the business of buying and selling rates second only to pub life for vigour, humour and sheer panache. Although many of the store chains – Next, Marks & Spencer, Waterstone's – will be familiar to British visitors, the relatively small size of the city means that shopping in Dublin is as much about seeing, being seen and socializing as it is about actually purchasing anything, making it both a spectator and participant sport of the highest order. The **O'Connell Street** area represents the more ordinary, high-street end of the market, with cut-price shops, chain stores and a boisterous street market concentrated on nearby Henry and Moore streets. Clery's, the august department store, and Eason's bookshop are two of the highlights; the ILAC centre, behind Moore Street, is probably the nadir.

South of the river are the smarter outlets and the tourist shops, as well as the kaleidoscopic and rapidly changing range of "alternative" boutiques that characterizes the fashionable **Temple Bar** area (the place to go for club gear and street fashions). Pedestrianized **Grafton Street** contains Dublin's swankiest department store, Brown Thomas. Just off Grafton Street, the 200-year-old Powerscourt Townhouse has been converted into a covered mall, with plenty of expensive clothes shops.

As a visitor, you'll find it difficult to escape the range of shops touting "typically" **Irish goods** aimed at tourists, mainly wool, ceramics and crystal. You may well come away with the impression that these are universally depressingly overpriced, but there are some exceptions, and you can occasionally pick up some real bargains.

Bookshops

General bookshops include Eason's, 40–42 O'Connell St Lower (beside the GPO) and 27–29 Nassau St; Waterstone's at 7 Dawson St; and Ireland's leading independent bookstore Hodges Figgis, across the road at 56–58 Dawson St, which has a particularly extensive stock of **Irish books**, a good remainder bookshop downstairs and a pleasant café on the first floor. Probably the best place to try for specialized Irish books, however, is Cathach Books, 10 Duke St (☎01/671 8676), which also has many rare first editions. Dublin Bookshop, 24 Grafton St, is one of the better mainstream bookshops, while Books Upstairs, 36 College Green (opposite the gates of Trinity College), is still Dublin's major alternative bookshop and has a good selection that includes feminist and gay fiction, women's studies, poetry and cinema, magazines and reviews. Greenes, 16 Clare St, an academic, topsy-turvy secondhand bookshop is also worth a look, and The Winding Stair, 40 Ormond Quay, is an excellent and pleasantly shabby secondhand bookshop with an unhurried café where you can peruse your finds, before or after purchase. If it's sci-fi, fantasy or horror you're after then Forbidden Planet, 36 Dawson St, is the place to find it, while Connolly Books, 43 Essex St East, stocks a wide range of books on the political sciences.

Clothes

Brown Thomas, Grafton Street, offers smart designer wear from Irish labels such as Paul Costelloe, Louise Kennedy and John Rocha, while the Irish Fashion Design Centre (Powerscourt Townhouse Centre), Clarendon Street, has a changing range of stalls by young designers who work mainly in natural materials such as linen, silk and wool. For secondhand clothes try Eager Beaver, 17 Crown Alley, Temple Bar, and The Harlequin, 13 Castle Market or Flip, Sharp's Ville and The Real McCoy, all in a row at 4–6 Fownes St Upper, Temple Bar, which specialize in Americana, jackets, shirts and jeans.

Irish goods

Kilkenny, 6 Nassau St, originally set up by the government to promote good design, is now privately run and stocks high-quality Irish goods such as clothes (mainly linen and knitware) and crystal and ceramics, which come significantly reduced in price in the sales. Nearby Kevin & Howlin, 31 Nassau St, specializes in Donegal tweed clothes and accessories. For knitted clothing made only from natural fibres, try Cleo, 18 Kildare St. A range of jewellery and Irish ceramics can be found in the Powercourt Townhouse Centre, while The Blarney Woollen Mills, College Park House, Nassau Street, offers a more traditional range of Irish crystal and china, plus the obligatory woolly pullovers and linen blouses; again, some bargains if you are prepared to sift. House of Ireland, 37–38 Nassau St, has fancy Irish crystal ranging from Belleek to Waterford, as well as the sweetly sentimental Lladro ceramics. At 41 Ormond Quay Lower, The Dublin Woollen Company sells a huge range of cut-price Irish knitwear, tweeds and lace. Talented local jewellers showcase their work at the DESIGNyard, 12 Essex St East, Temple Bar, where you can also commission works, and if the jewellery on display there fails to impress, the stunning collection on display at Angles, 10 Westbury Mall, off Harry Street, surely will. Weir and Sons, 96 Grafton St, has antique silver and jewellery plus a good selection of Irish crystal. If you are keen on genealogy, Clans of Ireland, 2 Kildare St, is able to trace the location and significance of most Irish family names. The Historical Picture Company, 5 Ormond Quay Lower, has a vast range of nostalgic and historical photographs from every county in Ireland, organized by town and village.

Markets

Moore Street Market (Mon–Sat 10am-6pm), just off O'Connell Street Upper, is one of the last and certainly the most colourful of Dublin's markets, selling mainly fresh produce. The Liberty Market, Meath Street (Thurs–Sat 10am–5pm) is a covered market whose stalls stock a multiplicity of essential items and tat, while Temple Bar Market, Meeting House Square (Sat 10am–5pm) offers a wide range of organic products. The Market Arcade, between South Great George's Street and Castle Street (Mon–Sat 10am–6pm, Sun 1–6pm) offers everything from secondhand clothes, books and CDs to olives. Of the suburban markets, the best is at Blackrock, just off Main Street (Sat 11am–5.30pm, Sun noon–5.30pm), easily accessible by DART and with a range of stalls selling crafts, clothes, books, CDs and plants.

Records and CDs

Claddagh Records, 2 Cecilia St, Temple Bar, stocks the most extensive range of traditional Irish and world music while Celtic Note, 12 Nassau St, has a reasonable assortment too and often has live music at lunch time. Back in Temple Bar, Road Records, 16B Fade St, specializes in indie and alt.country CDs;

Freebird, 1 Eden Quay, has a broad stock of new and secondhand music from rock to techno. The best place for secondhand records is Final Vinyl, 40A Camden St Lower. For local and international dance music head to Disque, 29 Wellington Quay. The chain stores are represented by HMV on Grafton and Henry streets, Tower Records on Wicklow Street and the Virgin Megastore on Henry Street.

Listings

Airlines Aer Lingus, 41 O'Connell St Upper or 13 St Stephen's Green ⓣ01/886 8888 reservations, ⓣ01/886 6705 flight enquiries, ⓦwww.aerlingus.com; BMI British Midland ⓣ01/407 3036 reservations, ⓣ01/814 4259 flight enquiries, ⓦwww.flybmi.com; British Airways ⓣ1800/626747, ⓦwww.british-airways.com; Ryanair ⓣ01/609 7800, ⓦwww.ryanair.com.
Banks Banking hours are Mon–Fri 10am–4pm, Thurs until 5pm. Main high-street banks are the Allied Irish, the Bank of Ireland, Northern Bank and Ulster Bank; branches throughout the city centre. ATMs are widely available across the city.
Bicycle rental Bicycles can be rented from Cycle Ways, 185 Parnell St ⓣ01/837 4748.
Car rental Argus at the airport and at the Dublin Tourism Centre, Suffolk St ⓣ01/490 4444, ⓦwww.argusrentals.com; Atlas at the airport ⓣ01/844 4589, ⓦwww.atlascarhire.com; County Car Rentals at the airport and at the Dublin Tourism Centre, Suffolk St ⓣ01/235 2030; Dan Dooley, 42–43 Westland Row ⓣ01/677 2723, ⓦwww.dan-dooley.com; SixT at the airport ⓣ1850/206088, ⓦwww.irishcarrentals.com; plus a range of other desks at the airport.
Dentists In the case of dental emergencies, contact the Eastern Health Board, Dr Steeven's Hospital, Dublin 8 ⓣ01/679 0700 or 1800/520520.
Embassies Australia, Fitzwilton House, Wilton Terrace ⓣ01/676 1517; Canada, 65 St Stephen's Green ⓣ01/478 1988; New Zealand (honorary consul), 37 Leeson Park ⓣ01/660 4233; UK, 31 Merrion Rd ⓣ01/205 3700; US, 42 Elgin Rd ⓣ01/668 8777.
Emergencies Call ⓣ999 or 112 for emergency medical aid, fire services or police.
Exchange American Express Foreign Exchange in Dublin Tourism's main office, Suffolk St (Mon–Sat 9am–5pm), Thomas Cook, 118 Grafton St (Mon–Sat 9am–5.30pm, Thurs until 8pm) and the General Post Office, O'Connell St (Mon–Sat 8am–8pm), give a fair rate, although the best exchange rates are given by banks (see p.27).
Ferry companies Irish Ferries ⓣ1890/313131, ⓦwww.irishferries.com; Isle of Man Steam Packet Co. (Seacat) ⓣ1800/551743, ⓦwww.seacat.co.uk; Norse Merchant Ferries ⓣ01/819 2999, ⓦwww.norsemerchant.com; P & O ⓣ1800/409049, ⓦwww.poirishsea.com; Stena Line ⓣ01/204 7777, ⓦwww.stenaline.ie.
Gaelic football and hurling Most of the major games of the season are played at Croke Park (ⓣ01/836 3222, ⓦwww.gaa.ie), which is also home to the excellent GAA museum – see p.114. In football, the All-Ireland Final occurs on the third or fourth Sunday in September and has been won by Dublin on 22 occasions (a record beaten only by Kerry). The Dubs have a poor record at hurling, however, so the crowd at the All-Ireland Final on the first or second Sunday in September mainly consists of out-of-towners. You'll be hard pushed to get tickets for either of the finals, but you're quite likely to get in for earlier rounds at "Croker" – expect to pay around €15 to stand, and sing, on the famous Hill 16, €35 to sit in the stands. For more on Gaelic football see p.50.
Gay Switchboard ⓣ01/872 1055 (Mon–Fri & Sun 8–10pm, Sat 3.30–6pm) and Lesbian Line ⓣ01/872 9911 (Thurs 7–9pm).
Helplines Rape Crisis Centre ⓣ01/661 4911 or 1800/778888; Samaritans ⓣ1850/609090; Victim Support ⓣ01/878 0870.
Horses You shouldn't leave Dublin without experiencing Irish horse racing. Dublin's nearest large racecourse is Leopardstown (ⓣ01/289 3607, ⓦwww.leopardstown.com), in the southern suburb of Foxrock (bus #114 from Blackrock DART station, plus special buses on race days from Eden Quay). Races are held at weekends throughout the year and on Wednesday evenings in summer, the main events being the four-day Christmas Festival starting on St Stephen's Day (Dec 26), and the Hennessy Cognac Gold Cup in February. The Irish Grand National is held on Easter Monday at Fairyhouse (ⓣ01/825 6167, ⓦwww.fairyhouseracecourse.ie), 15 miles northwest of Dublin, followed in April by the four-day Irish National Hunt

Departures from Dublin

Buses to the airport either pass along O'Connell St (#16A) or set off from Eden Quay (#41, #41A, #41B or #41C). The Airlink bus departs from Busáras on Store St. For the ferries, take the DART service to Dún Laoghaire, or a bus (#53) to Dublin Port from Beresford Place. Buses to all parts of the country (Bus Éireann) leave from Busáras or the streets immediately around (Abbey St Lower, Talbot St). Enquiries regarding city buses are handled at the Dublin Bus office located at 59 O'Connell St Upper (Mon 8.30am–5.30pm, Tues–Fri 9am–5.30pm, Sat 9am–1pm; ⓣ01/873 4222) while the Bus Éireann information desk is at Busáras (ⓣ01/836 6111). Officially approved private buses are generally cheaper: ask to see the bus information file at the tourist office. Unofficial buses may be cheaper still; they leave from various points around the city, especially on Friday and Sunday evenings. Check the *Evening Herald* for advertisements – weekend buses generally need advance booking. **Trains** to the limited parts of Ireland served by the national train system leave from Heuston Station (still sometimes known by its old name of Kingsbridge) on the southside (Cork, Waterford, Limerick, Killarney, Tralee, Athlone, Galway, Westport, Ballina, Claremorris) or Connolly Station (aka Amiens St Station) on the northside (Belfast, Newry, Portadown, Dundalk, Sligo, Arklow, Wexford, Rosslare Harbour). Mainline commuter trains serving coastal towns north and south of Dublin call at Connolly, Tara Street and Pearse stations. For train information call ⓣ01/836 6222.

Festival at Punchestown (ⓣ045/897704), 25 miles southwest of Dublin near Naas. Flat-racing classics are held at the Curragh, 30 miles southwest of the capital – see p.168. Bus Éireann and Iarnród Éireann (see p.31) lay on race-day transport to Fairyhouse, Punchestown and the Curragh. Showjumping, like racing, has less of an elitist image than in Britain. The Dublin Horse Show at the Royal Dublin Society (RDS) pavilion in Ballsbridge in August is the most prestigious international event, with top riders competing in the Nations Cup, and prizes in ninety different classes of jumping and dressage. More than 1500 horses compete, before an aggregate audience of 100,000. Though day-tickets might be available, you'd be wise to book ahead (ⓣ01/240 7213, ⓦwww.rds.ie). The RDS is accessible by DART to Sandymount or by bus #5, #7 or #45.

Hospitals Beaumont Hospital, Beaumont Rd ⓣ01/837 7755; Mater Misericordiae, Eccles St ⓣ01/830 1122; St James's, James's St ⓣ01/453 7941; and St Vincent's, Merrion Rd ⓣ01/269 4533. All have accident and emergency departments. In emergencies dial ⓣ999 or 112 for an ambulance.

Internet cafés *Central Cybercafé*, 6 Grafton St ⓣ01/677 8298, ⓦwww.centralcafe.ie; *Global Internet Café*, 8 O'Connell St Lower ⓣ01/878 0295, ⓦwww.global.cafe.ie; *Planet Cyber*, 13 St Andrew St ⓣ01/670 5183.

Laundries Most self-service laundrettes are open Mon–Fri 8am–8pm, with earlier closing on Saturday. Central ones include All American, Wicklow Court, South Great George's St ⓣ01/677 2779; and Wash to Iron, 45 Francis St ⓣ01/473 1876. For dry-cleaning a central option is Craft Cleaners, 12 Baggot St Upper ⓣ01/668 8198.

Left luggage There are left-luggage offices at Busáras (Mon–Sat 8am–7.45pm, Sun 10am–5.45pm) and Connolly Station (Mon–Sat 7.40am–9.20pm, Sun 9.10am–9.45pm) and lockers at Heuston Station (daily 6.30am–10.30pm).

Lost property For items lost on Dublin Bus call ⓣ01/703 1312; at the airport ⓣ01/814 4483; for those left on trains, Connolly Station ⓣ01/703 2363 or Heuston Station ⓣ01/703 2102.

Pharmacies Dame St Pharmacy, 16 Dame St ⓣ01/670 4523, and O'Connell's, 55 O'Connell St Lower ⓣ01/873 0427, are open daily until 10pm.

Photography For rapid developing try One Hour Photo, 110 Grafton St ⓣ01/677 4472; 6 St Stephen's Green ⓣ01/671 8578; and the ILAC Centre, Henry St ⓣ01/872 8824.

Police The main Garda station for the Dublin region is in Harcourt Square ⓣ01/666 6666. In emergencies dial ⓣ999 or 112.

Post offices The General Post Office is on O'Connell St Lower (Mon–Sat 8am–8pm, Sun 10am–6pm; ⓣ01/705 8833 or 01/872 8084). Another handy post office is situated in St Andrew St, near Dublin Tourism, Suffolk St ⓣ01/705 8256.

Telephones For cheap-rate international calls, go to Talkshop, 20 Temple Lane South, Temple Bar ⓣ01/672 7212.

Travel agents USIT (youth/student travel), 19–21 Aston Quay ⓣ01/602 1600 for Europe and the US, ⓣ01/602 1700 for the rest of the world; Thomas Cook, 118 Grafton St ⓣ01/677 1721; CIÉ Tours (Irish tour organizer), 35 Abbey St Lower ⓣ01/703 1888; Trailfinders (long-haul flights), 4–5 Dawson St ⓣ01/677 7888.

Travel details

Services listed are for Mon–Sat; trains and buses are less frequent on Sun.

Trains

Dublin Connolly to: Arklow (4 daily; 1hr 45min); Belfast (8 daily; 2hr–2hr 10min); Dundalk (7 daily; 50min); Newry (8 daily; 1hr 10min); Rosslare (3 daily; 3hr 10min); Sligo (3 daily; 3hr 15min); Wexford (3 daily; 2hr 30min).

Dublin Heuston to: Athlone (7 daily; 1hr 40min); Ballina (3 daily; 3hr 40min); Claremorris (3 daily; 3hr); Cork (9 daily; 2hr 40min–3hr 20min); Galway (5 daily; 2hr 45min); Killarney (6 daily; 3hr 40min); Limerick (11 daily; 2hr 20min–3hr); Tralee (4 daily; 4hr); Waterford (4 daily; 2hr 30min); Westport (3 daily; 3hr 50min).

Buses

Dublin Busáras to: Belfast (7 daily; 3hr); Cork (6 daily; 4hr 30min); Derry (6 daily; 4hr 30min); Donegal (5 daily; 4hr 30min); Enniskillen (5 daily; 3hr 40min); Galway (13 daily; 3hr 30min); Killarney (5 daily; 6hr); Limerick (6 daily; 3hr 30min); Sligo (4 daily; 4hr); Waterford (6 daily; 2hr 45min); Westport (3 daily; 5hr).

In addition to Bus Éireann, scores of private companies connect Dublin with the rest of the country. Routes are too numerous to detail here – we've listed the most useful in the text of the relevant chapters.

2

Wicklow and Kildare

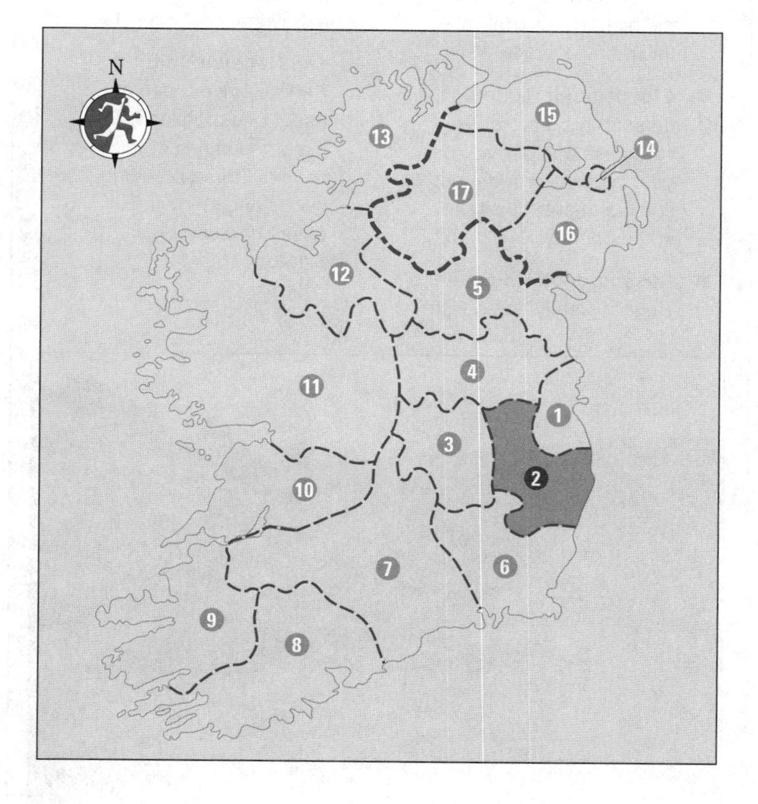

CHAPTER 2

Highlights

* **Walking in the Wicklow Mountains** Wild and desolate terrain, traversed by the Wicklow Way, within easy reach of Dublin. **See p.148**

* **Powerscourt** Beautiful ornamental gardens and the highest waterfall in Ireland. **See p.149**

* **Glendalough** Hidden deep in this remote valley lies one of the best-preserved and most spiritual monastic sites in the country. **See p.152**

* **Russborough House** An elegant stately home with a small but remarkable – and much-coveted – collection of paintings. **See p.161**

* **Castletown House** Just west of Dublin, a Palladian mansion and grounds of unrestrained extravagance. **See p.164**

* **The National Stud, Kildare town** Learn all about one of Ireland's major industries at this national horse-breeding centre and enjoy the quirky gardens. **See p.168**

2

Wicklow and Kildare

Wicklow and Kildare, to the south and west of Dublin, provide a welcome respite from the capital's urban bustle. As central counties of the Pale region (the area of land around Dublin most successfully controlled by the Anglo-Normans and then the British, both are heavily resonant with the presence of the Anglo-Irish, yet scenically they are in complete contrast with each other. **County Wicklow** has some of the wildest, most spectacular mountain scenery in Ireland, as well as impressive monuments: the early Celtic monastery of **Glendalough** and the Neoclassical splendours of the great houses of **Russborough** and ruined **Powerscourt**. **County Kildare**'s charms are more understated: a gently undulating landscape of farmland punctuated only by the great horse-racing plain of **the Curragh**, where the **National Stud** and adjacent ornamental gardens are well worth making time to see. Here, too, there are signs of the shifting patterns of settlement and land ownership – Celtic high crosses and pedimented buildings, such as the extravagant stately home of **Castletown**.

The proximity of both counties to Dublin makes **transport** fairly easy. The Dublin city rail network, the DART, will take you southwards as far as the seaside resorts of Bray and Greystones on the Wicklow coast; the main line continues to the bustling small towns of Wicklow and Arklow. The major tourist centres in inland County Wicklow are served, albeit infrequently, by buses. In County Kildare the major N7 and N4 roads and their roughly parallel railway lines offer access to many sites.

The scenic beauties of County Wicklow attract a lot of visitors and the positive spin-off is that a good range of **accommodation** is on offer, as well as an increasing number of excellent **restaurants**. It's worth bearing in mind, however, that hostels and B&Bs tend to be concentrated in just a handful of villages – especially in mountainous areas – and advanced booking is advisable during the summer months and over bank-holiday weekends. Kildare is less visited, although here too a few pioneers offer good food and accommodation in beautiful surroundings; nevertheless, you'll generally find yourself relying on the standard B&B trade.

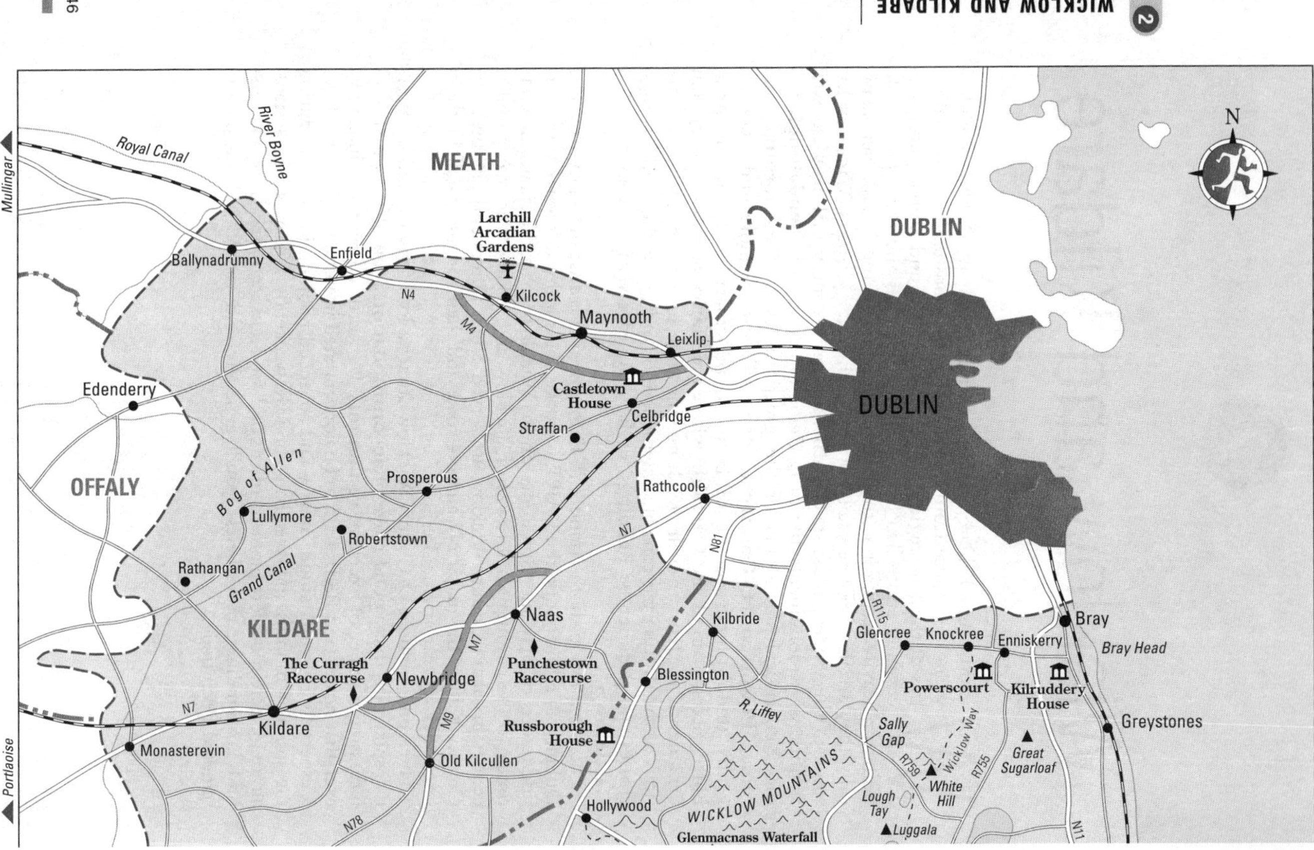
N
MEATH
DUBLIN
DUBLIN
OFFALY
KILDARE
Mullingar
Portlaoise
Royal Canal
River Boyne
Larchill Arcadian Gardens
Ballynadrumny
Enfield
N4
Kilcock
M4
Maynooth
Leixlip
Castletown House
Celbridge
Edenderry
Straffan
Bog of Allen
Prosperous
Lullymore
Robertstown
Rathcoole
N7
N81
Rathangan
Grand Canal
Naas
M7
Kilbride
R115
Glencree
Knockree
Enniskerry
Bray
Bray Head
The Curragh Racecourse
Newbridge
Punchestown Racecourse
Blessington
Powerscourt
Kilruddery House
Kildare
M9
Russborough House
R. Liffey
Sally Gap
Wicklow Way
Greystones
Monasterevin
Old Kilcullen
R759
R755
Great Sugarloaf
White Hill
WICKLOW MOUNTAINS
Lough Tay
Hollywood
N78
Glenmacnass Waterfall
Luggala
N11

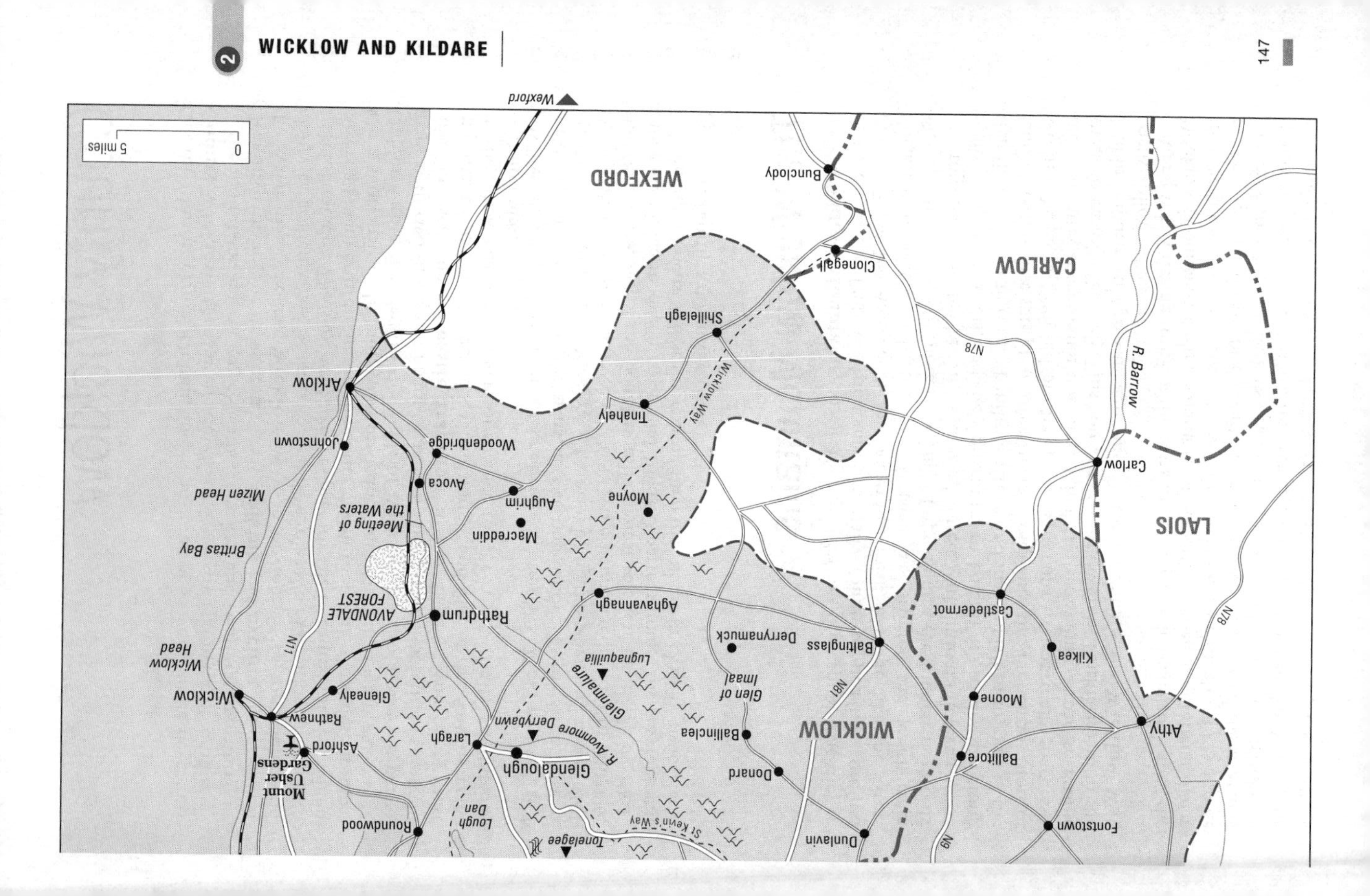

WICKLOW
WEXFORD
CARLOW
LAOIS
Wicklow
Wicklow Head
Brittas Bay
Mizen Head
Mount Usher Gardens
Ashford
Rathnew
Roundwood
Glenealy
N11
AVONDALE FOREST
Meeting of the Waters
Johnstown
Arklow
Lough Dan
Laragh
Rathdrum
Avoca
Woodenbridge
Glendalough
Derrybawn
Macreddin
Aughrim
Tonelagee
R. Avonmore
Glenmalure
Lugnaquilla
Aghavannagh
Moyne
Tinahely
St Kevin's Way
Ballinclea
Derrynamuck
Glen of Imaal
Wicklow Way
Shillelagh
Donard
Dunlavin
N81
Baltinglass
Bunclody
Clonegall
N9
Ballitore
Moone
Castledermot
N78
Kilkea
Fontstown
Carlow
R. Barrow
Athy
Wexford
0
5 miles

County Wicklow

Get on a bus in central Dublin, and in an hour or so you can be deep into **County Wicklow** (Ⓦwww.wicklow.ie or Ⓦwww.wicklowtoday.com), high in the mountains among gorse, heather, bracken and bent grass, breathing in clear air with no one in sight. It's great **walking** and **cycling** country, with the waymarked, six-day **Wicklow Way** an obvious focus for hiking, and plenty of golden sandy beaches for gentle strolls; Wicklow Tourism produce a useful booklet, *The Wicklow Walking Guide* (for sale in tourist offices), which covers all manner of hiking in the county, with route maps and descriptions. On a short trip to Ireland, you could do a lot worse than simply combine Dublin with a few days in the wilds of Wicklow. It's also a place to get to grips with two of the dominant themes of Irish history, sometimes strangely superimposed: the **monastic tradition** in the shape of one of its most important and charismatic sites, Glendalough; and that of the **Anglo-Irish**, at the great seats of Powerscourt and, to the west of the mountains, Russborough.

Wherever you go, apart from a few obvious centres like **Wicklow** town and **Arklow**, you're struck by the sparseness of population. It's the same story as elsewhere in Ireland, and Wicklow is far from being the worst sufferer: in 1841 the population of the county was 126,431, the Famine reduced it to 100,000, then steady seepage of the population brought it to a low of 58,473 by 1961. Since then it has recovered to around 100,000, partly through the development of commuter towns, as first the railway, then the suburban DART service, have penetrated further down the coast.

The Wicklow Mountains

The **Wicklow Mountains**, so clearly viewed from the capital that they're often called the Dublin Mountains, are really round-topped hills, ground down by the Ice Ages, with the occasional freakish shape like the Great Sugarloaf Mountain, where a granite layer has arrested the weathering. Despite their relatively modest height – Lugnaquillia, the highest peak,only just tops 3000ft – they're wild and uninhabited, with little traffic even at the main passes. Given this, and their proximity to Dublin, it's hardly surprising that they were traditionally bandit territory, and that the last insurgents of the land agitation that spread all over Ireland following the French invasion of County Mayo in 1798 hid out here; the mountains were virtually inaccessible until after the ensuing uprisings, when the army built a road to enable them to patrol effectively. This you can still follow, from Rathfarnham in the Dublin suburbs to Aghavannagh, high in the mountains; the **Wicklow Way** partly follows the road, too.

Along with offering some of the east's most wild and desolate landscapes, the Wicklow Mountains shelter a number of powerful historic monuments. Deep in a remote valley, the medieval monastic site at **Glendalough** evokes a sense of the sequestered lives of the early Christian monks who lived there. Stately **Powerscourt House**, with its beautiful gardens, grand facade and charred yet glorious interior, stands as a fitting symbol for the passing of the Anglo-Irish Ascendancy, and **Avondale House**, set in a landscaped estate on the southeast side of the mountains, tells the story of one of Ireland's greatest nineteenth-century statesmen, Charles Stewart Parnell.

Public **transport** will get you to Powerscourt and the neighbouring village of **Enniskerry**, and one bus a day continues up the valley of Glencree to allow you to join the Wicklow Way at the An Óige hostel at **Knockree**. Further south, Glendalough and its service town **Laragh**, along with the lofty village of **Roundwood**, are all accessible from Dublin on the St Kevin's bus service and make good bases from which to explore the mountains. One bus a day on the Dublin–Arklow route detours inland from Wicklow to **Rathdrum** and the intensely pretty **Vale of Avoca**, on the southern edge of the mountains. The nearest village to Avondale, Rathdrum also has a station on the Dublin–Wexford rail line. Of course, you'll get the most out of the mountains and their many opportunities for walking if you have your own transport, but otherwise it's worth considering one of the many **tours** on offer, which can be booked through Dublin Tourism on Suffolk Street. One of the best companies is **Wild Coach Tours** (Ⓣ01/280 1899, Ⓦwww.wildcoachtours.com), who offer fun, sociable all-day tours of the wilds of Wicklow (8.50am; €28), taking in Glendalough and stupendous scenery, and afternoon tours to Powerscourt (1.30pm; €20). Tours from Dublin run daily all year round, and pick up from the *Shelbourne*, St Stephen's Green, Dublin Tourism on Suffolk Street and the *Gresham Hotel*, O'Connell Street Upper; the prices include all admission charges.

Enniskerry and Powerscourt

Nestled in the foothills of the Wicklow Mountains twelve miles south of Dublin, the village of **ENNISKERRY** originally belonged to the **Powerscourt Estate** (Ⓦwww.powerscourt.ie), which was owned by a dynasty founded by one of James I's generals, Richard Wingfield. The great house, half a mile south of Enniskerry's main square, is one of the largest Palladian mansions in Ireland, but its real attraction is the magnificent formal gardens which are blended into the backdrop of the Great Sugarloaf and other Wicklow peaks (gardens daily: March–Oct 9.30am–5.30pm; Nov–Feb 9.30am–dusk; €6; house daily: March–Oct 9.30am–5.30pm; Nov–Feb times may vary; €2.50; combined ticket for gardens & house €8).

The grey-stone **house**, with its twin copper domes, was designed by Richard Cassels for the first Viscount Powerscourt and took a decade to build (1731–41). Although it still looks impressive from afar, inside only shadows of its former glory remain. It was gutted by fire in 1974 (on the eve of a party to celebrate the completion of extensive renovation), but you can at least get some sense of its past grandeur from the smoky brickwork remains of the double-storey ballroom. Photographs of the room before the fire, with its classical columns and lavish gilded decoration, survive and are on display in the exhibition by the house's entrance, where you can also take in an interesting audiovisual display on the history of Powerscourt.

In front of the house the great **stone terrace**, with its winged figures of Fame and Victory, was designed in 1843 by Daniel Robertson, who used to be wheeled about the site in a barrow, clutching a bottle of sherry. When his creative powers were exhausted and the bottle was empty, he'd call it a day. In the 1850s, the seventh viscount began the terraced **Italian Gardens**, which accompany a grand staircase leading down to the circular **Triton Lake** with its central eponymous statue (based on Bernini's fountain in the Piazza Barberini in Rome) firing a jet of water one hundred feet skywards. From here the view up the terraces towards the house is staggering – colossal amphitheatre populated by winged horses and assorted statuary.

At the far end of the terrace the land falls away sharply, enhancing the beauty of the North American conifers planted by Robertson, which can be viewed by climbing the **Pepper Pot Tower**. Below lies a very fragrant Edwardian **Japanese Garden** of azaleas, Chinese Fortune Palms and Japanese maples, built on reclaimed bogland. Skirting the Triton Lake, you can carry on to the **Pet Cemetery**, where the graves of family dogs and horses are accompanied by that of a cow who produced seventeen calves and over 100,000 gallons of milk during her lifetime. The ceremonial entrance to the **walled garden** beyond is the gilded ironwork Bamberg Gate, which originally belonged to Bamberg cathedral in Bavaria. Back at the house, the **terrace café** makes an ideal spot from which to enjoy views over the gardens to the Wicklow Mountains.

The famous **Powerscourt Waterfall** (daily: summer 9.30am–7pm; winter 10.30am–dusk; €3.50) lies three miles from the house: turn right as you exit the main gate and follow the signs along the road. At almost four hundred feet, it's the highest in Ireland, leaping diagonally down the rockface into a valley where it joins the River Dargle.

Practicalities

To get to Enniskerry from Dublin, take the #44 **bus** from Hawkins Street (off Burgh Quay), or the DART **train** to Bray and then the #185 bus or one of the hourly Alpine Coaches shuttle buses (Ⓣ01/286 2547), which also run to Powerscourt Estate and the waterfall. There are a couple of **places to stay** on the square in Enniskerry village: the recently renovated *Powerscourt Arms Hotel* provides comfortable accommodation (Ⓣ01/282 8903, Ⓕ286 4909; ❹), while *Ferndale B&B* (Ⓣ01/286 3518; ❷) is a lovely, relaxed alternative with antique furniture and a great breakfast menu.

Although there are very few **places to eat** in the village itself, *Poppies Country Kitchen* serves tasty homemade pies, quiches, salads and daily specials, as well as a tempting array of cakes and puddings, and is open until 6.30pm in summer. Eighteenth-century *Johnnie Fox's Pub*, three miles northwest of Enniskerry at **Glencullen**, is a time-honoured watering-hole, where Daniel O'Connell was a regular when he lived in the village. Such a heritage attracts a fair share of coach parties these days, but it's still worth negotiating the back roads to get there, not least for the seafood specialities on the menu; if you want to be sure to eat here, book a table (Ⓣ01/295 5647).

To Glencree and south through the mountains

Lying about four miles west of Enniskerry, the tiny village of **KNOCKREE** is home to an An Óige **hostel** (Ⓣ01/286 4036; ❶), with dorms and private rooms, to service walkers on the **Wicklow Way** (see box opposite), which passes through its grounds. Once a day, Alpine Coaches (Ⓣ01/286 2547) from Bray DART station via Enniskerry pass within a mile of Knockree, before continuing to **GLENCREE** at the head of the lush valley. There's a cemetery for German servicemen who died in Ireland during the two World Wars, and a reconciliation centre for people affected by the conflict in the North, but the only reason the ordinary visitor is likely to be at Glencree is to join the military road into the mountains.

South of the village the road climbs past the dramatic twin tarns of Lough Bray Lower and Upper (accessible by boggy paths opposite a car park) and then

The Wicklow Way

The Wicklow Way is Ireland's first officially designated long-distance walk. Following a series of sheep tracks, forest firebreaks and bog roads – above 500m for most of the way – the walk leads from Marlay Park in the Dublin suburbs up into the Wicklow Mountains. It cuts across the Glencree valley, traverses the bleak, boggy hillside below Djouce Mountain, and pushes on to Glendalough, before passing through Glenmalure and skirting Lugnaquillia, the highest Wicklow peak; the walk finally ends up after 130km at Clonegall on the Wexford–Carlow border. The whole route is waymarked with yellow signs and can be walked in five to six days.

Marlay Park is accessible via the #16 bus from O'Connell Street in Dublin city centre, for those who want to walk the whole route. If you're short of time, the best part to walk is probably the 29-kilometre section from **Knockree to Glendalough**, which can be done in one very long day or preferably two, with a short detour to overnight at Roundwood. The path goes past the waterfall at Powerscourt and reaches its highest point at White Hill (632m), from which you can get a view of the mountains of North Wales on a fine day. Take the Alpine Coach from Bray DART station to get to Knockree (see opposite), and pick up St Kevin's bus service at Glendalough for the return journey.

Low as they are, the Wicklow Mountains are notoriously treacherous, and it's well worth investing in the Ordinance Survey's *Wicklow Way*, a booklet of 1:25,000 **maps** with accompanying text opposite, or EastWest Mapping's *The Wicklow Way Map Guide*, a similar publication with 1:50,000 maps plus details of accommodation. Both are available in bookshops and local tourist offices. EastWest also produce *Wicklow Way Walks*, a booklet of 26 short, circular walks based on the Way. OS map nos. 56 and 62 cover almost the whole route, with nos. 50 and 61 picking up the extremities. Some sections of the Wicklow Way have changed recently, but the latest advice on routes and conditions is available from the Wicklow Mountains National Park **information point** in Glendalough (see p.154).

There are three An Óige hostels along the Wicklow Way – at Knockree (see opposite), Glendalough (see p.154) and Glenmalure (see p.155) – as well as plenty of other **places to stay**, many of which will collect you from or deliver you to parts of the route, or ferry your bags to your next resting place, if given prior notice. Accommodation in Enniskerry, Roundwood and Laragh/Glendalough is detailed in the text. On the southern part of the Way, the following B&Bs (listed north to south) all provide transport and packed lunches and/or evening meals by prior request:

Butler's Byrne Rednagh Hill, near Aughrim Ⓣ & Ⓕ0402/36644; open all year. ❷
Kyle Farmhouse Kyle, near Tinahely Ⓣ0508/71341, Ⓦwww.kylefarm.f2s.com; camping possible; open April–Oct. ❷
Jigsaw Cottage Moyne, near Tinahely Ⓣ & Ⓕ0508/71071, Ⓦwww.wickloway.ie; camping possible; open March–Oct. ❷
Sunindale Coolafunshoge, near Tinahely Ⓣ & Ⓕ0402/38170; open all year. ❷
Rosbane Farmhouse Rosbane, near Tinahely Ⓣ0402/38100; camping possible; open all year. ❷
Park Lodge Clonegall Ⓣ055/29140; open March–Dec. ❷

The upmarket *Ballyknocken House* at Glenealy (see p.160) and *Brooklodge Hotel* at Macreddin (see p.157) will also provide transport to and from the Wicklow Way.

Outfits offering **guided walking tours** of the Wicklow Way include Footfalls, Trooperstown, Roundwood (Ⓣ0404/45152, Ⓦwww.walkinghikingireland.com), and the National Adventure Centre at Tiglin (Ⓣ0404/40169), halfway between Laragh or Roundwood and Wicklow, which also has rock-climbing and kayaking courses and An Óige hostel accommodation (Ⓣ & Ⓕ0404/49049).

through ever wilder terrain close to the source of the Liffey towards one of the two main passes in the Wicklow Mountains, the **Sally Gap**. From here the military road (R115) continues south through spectacular countryside down to Laragh and Glendalough. If you fancy stretching your legs along the way, pull in at the car park a mile and a half south of the Sally Gap, cross the road and follow the rough, boggy path for 45 minutes or so to the prominent summit of **Luggala** or Fancy Mountain; from here, you'll be rewarded with precipitous views straight down to Lough Tay (see below) and a panorama to the south and west of Lough Dan and the major Wicklow peaks. Beyond Luggala, the military road runs over rough country until it joins the Glenmacnass River – at this point there's the extraordinary, extended **Glenmacnass Waterfall**.

The R759 heading southeast of the Sally Gap winds its way past Lough Tay, and several roadside car parks, down to Sraghmore, a couple of miles north of Roundwood. Dramatic **Lough Tay** – whose scree sides plunge straight into the water from the summit of Luggala – is owned by Garech a'Brún, a member of the Guinness family who is also the man behind Claddagh Records in Dublin. Just to the south of here, linked by the Cloghoge River with its gentler woodlands, is **Lough Dan**. This is private land, but visitors are normally welcome to descend through the pillared gates towards Lough Tay, turning left before reaching the lake onto a track that leads down to Lough Dan after about an hour. In the other direction you can walk from one of the car parks above Lough Tay north up the Wicklow Way for about fifteen minutes to the memorial to J.B. Malone (one of the pioneers of Irish hill-walking and of the Way itself) for the finest view of the ensemble, and on to the top of White Hill in another twenty minutes for further scenic delights.

Roundwood

The swifter, less mountainous route via the R755 to Glendalough from Dublin or Bray, as well as the R759 from Sally Gap, will bring you to **ROUNDWOOD** (one of the stops on the St Kevin's bus service; see p.153), a pleasant enough village, which claims to be the highest in Ireland though it's not in the heart of the mountains. Roundwood is just a mile from the Wicklow Way as it passes south of Lough Dan and, Glendalough and Laragh aside, is one of the few places to get a range of food and accommodation in this part of the county.

Bike rental is available from Footfalls (see box on p.151) or Johnny Price's Garage, Main Street (Ⓣ01/281 8128). You can get **B&B** accommodation here at *Tochar House* (Ⓣ01/281 8247; ❷), a good, central option. Slightly further out are two other recommended B&Bs: *Woodside* (Ⓣ01/281 8195; ❶), a mile and a half along the Dublin road, and *Ballinacor House* (Ⓣ01/281 8168; ❶), a mile along the road towards Glendalough. The village also has a smart, well-equipped **campsite** (Ⓣ01/281 8163, Ⓔroundwoodcaravancamp@yahoo.co.uk; May to mid-Sept). Among **eating** choices in Roundwood, there's bar food at *The Coach House*, or you might try *The Roundwood Inn* (Ⓣ01/281 8107), a seventeenth-century coaching inn which is noted for its excellent, but pricey food in the restaurant (for which you'll need to book), and great bar meals. However, for a wider range of accommodation, and for readier access to lonelier and more impressive scenery, your best bet is probably to head on down to Laragh, six miles southwest of here.

Glendalough and Laragh

Deeper into the Wicklow Mountains lies **GLENDALOUGH**, the "valley of the two lakes", a magical setting for one of the best-preserved **monastic sites** in Ireland. Despite the car parks and the coach parties, there remains a sense of peace and spirituality here making it easy to imagine how the hermits and monks once lived. The Glendalough visitor centre, its adjacent car park and the main monastic site are reached first, on the eastern side of the **Lower Lake**, while further west up the valley is the larger and more impressive **Upper Lake**, with its wooded cliffs and waterfall plunging vertically into the water, as well as more ruins, the national park information point and another car park. On the main road in, just over a mile to the east of the visitor centre, lies the small village of **LARAGH**, which has most of the area's amenities, notably accommodation. **Transport** to Laragh and Glendalough from Dublin is easy: St Kevin's bus service (Ⓣ01/281 8119; €15 return) runs daily from outside the Royal College of Surgeons, St Stephen's Green at 11.30am, via Bray and Roundwood, returning from Glendalough at 4.15pm.

The monastery's foundation is attributed to **St Kevin**, a descendant of the royal house of Leinster who studied under three holy men before retreating to Glendalough to fast and pray in solitude. His piety attracted followers, and in 570 he became abbot of a monastic community. As a centre of the Celtic Church, the monastery was famous throughout Europe for its learning. It was sacked by the Vikings, Normans and English and was finally dissolved during the Reformation. However, as the pope decreed that seven pilgrimages to Glendalough would procure the same indulgence as one to Rome, pilgrimages continued until 1862, when a local priest banned gatherings thanks to the activities of the pilgrims, whose abstemious devotions on St Kevin's Day (June 3) were often followed by more licentious behaviour.

The Lower Lake sites

The **visitor centre** (daily: mid-March to mid-Oct 9.30am–6pm; mid-Oct to mid-March 9.30am–5pm; €2.50) features photographic displays and a video setting Glendalough in the context of ancient monasteries elsewhere in Ireland, as well as a model of how the monastery probably looked when it was at the height of its activity. The centre's entry price also includes an informative **guided tour** of the site, which is well worth taking.

You enter the main monastery grounds (same hours; free) through a double stone archway that was once surmounted by a tower. The nearest ruin is the site's largest structure, the impressive **cathedral**, dating from the early ninth century, whose roofless nave and chancel contain numerous grave slabs. Among the tombs outside stands **St Kevin's Cross**, one of the best remaining relics from the period, consisting of a granite monolith decorated with an eighth-century carving of a Celtic cross superimposed upon a wheel; it's thought to have been left unfinished, in that, unusually, the quadrants of the cross have not been pierced. Nearby is a small twelfth-century **Priest's House**, above the door of which are three barely discernible carved figures, thought to represent Kevin and two abbots. Further downhill is the two-storey **St Kevin's Church**. The steeply pitched roof and bell-turret so resemble a chimney that the building is also known as St Kevin's Kitchen, although it was probably an oratory. The most impressive structure is the hundred-foot-high **Round Tower**, which served as a belfry, watchtower, treasury and place of refuge – the doorway high above the ground would have been reached by a ladder that could be pulled up in times of danger. Further west, outside the enclosure, you'll see the remains of **St Mary's Church**, which is believed to have been the first building in the lower valley, and may mark the site of Kevin's grave. Downhill from St Kevin's Church is a footbridge, on the far side of which is the hollowed-out **Deerstone**, named after a legend claiming that tame deer squirted their milk into it to feed the motherless twins of one of Kevin's followers.

The Upper Lake sites

You can drive to the Upper Lake car park along the north side of the valley, but it's far preferable to walk from the Deerstone along the signposted **Green Road** (part of the Wicklow Way), a scenic track that skirts the south side of the Lower Lake. After twenty minutes or so, this will bring you to the tiny, ruined **Reefert Church** (which dates from the late tenth century and whose small cemetery is thought to contain the graves of local chieftains), and the start of a path to **St Kevin's Cell**, where the remains of a typically Celtic, corbel-roofed, "beehive" hut mark the spot where he slept on a promontory overlooking the Upper Lake. He later moved into a cave halfway up the cliff – dubbed **St Kevin's Bed** – to avoid the advances of a maiden called Kathleen. She eventually found his hiding place and, awaking one morning to find her beside him, he reacted with the misogyny characteristic of the early Church fathers by throwing her into the lake, where she drowned. (Kevin himself is said to have died in 617 or 618, at the age of 120.) The cave is only accessible by boat from the far shore of the lake in summer.

Walks around Glendalough

At the eastern end of the Upper Lake, the Wicklow Mountains National Park **information point** (April & Sept Sat & Sun 10am–6pm; May–Aug daily 10am–6pm; ⓣ0404/45425) has details of local walking routes and conditions. *Twelve Walks in Glendalough* by Paddy Dillon and *Exploring the Glendalough Valley* published by Dúchas are useful guides to the trails in the area, and a couple of good routes here are covered by Joss Lynam's *Easy Walks near Dublin*.

The recently laid-out **St Kevin's Way** follows what was the main pilgrim path to Glendalough in medieval times, from the west and the fertile midlands. Waymarked with yellow pilgrim symbols, the eighteen-mile trail runs along country tracks and quiet roads from Hollywood, near the N81 south of Blessington, climbing to the **Wicklow Gap**, 1500ft above sea level in the shadow of Tonelagee (2677ft), before following the descent of the Glendasan River for four miles to the Glendalough visitor centre. *St Kevin's Way*, a booklet by Peter Harbison and Joss Lynam, covers the route with comprehensive maps and text.

The easiest to follow and most satisfying short hike is on the south side of Glendalough valley, where it's possible to climb 1500-foot **Derrybawn** in around an hour, for spectacular views. Follow the Wicklow Way south from the national park information point past the Poulanass Waterfall, before eventually peeling left off the waymarked forest track up a narrow path, which climbs steeply to the edge of the forest and then straight up to Derrybawn's ridge and summit cairn.

Glendalough practicalities

There's a small **tourist information** kiosk in Glendalough (May to first week Sept Mon–Sat 10am–1pm & 2–5.30pm, may be subject to variation; ⓣ0404/45688). **Accommodation** in Glendalough itself is limited and it's advisable to book up in advance: *Luganure*, Lake Road (ⓣ0404/45563; ❷), is a comfortable B&B in a great location overlooking the tranquil scenery between Glendalough and the lakes; the large Victorian *Glendalough Hotel* (ⓣ0404/45135, ⓦwww.glendaloughhotel.ie; closed most of Jan; ❺) occupies a similarly scenic location near the visitor centre, with well-furnished bedrooms and lovely views. For budget travellers, the recently refurbished An Óige hostel, *Glendaloch International* (ⓣ0404/45342, ⓕ45690; ❶) is a haven of comfort and can provide breakfast and evening meals; en-suite and family rooms are available, as are **bike rental** and **Internet access**. Unless you are staying in the hostel, the only place to **eat** in Glendalough is in the hotel restaurant or bar.

If you're into quiet solitude and spiritual rejuvenation, you might be interested in the **hermitages** at St Kevin's Parish Church on the road towards Laragh. These very basic self-catering huts, with bathrooms and kitchenettes, need to be pre-booked through the parish priest, Sean O'Toole (Ⓣ & Ⓕ0404/45140, Ⓔglendalough2000@eircom.net; ❷).

Laragh practicalities

Laragh sports a wide choice of **places to stay**, a selection of which are listed below. **Places to eat** are thin on the ground, however: *Lynham's* is probably one of the best places, where you can dine in the smart restaurant, or the lively bar with its roaring fires in winter and outside tables by the river in summer; *The Wicklow Heather* is a popular, moderately priced family restaurant offering steaks, chops and stews; and the tea rooms at the Woollen Mills, about half a mile out of Laragh on the Rathdrum road, occupy a particularly pretty location and serve scones, desserts and sandwiches.

Accommodation

Glen Ailbhe In the village Ⓣ0404/45236. A friendly B&B next to the post office, offering good-quality accommodation in brightly coloured rooms, all en suite. ❷

Glendale In the village Ⓣ & Ⓕ0404/45410, Ⓔmerrigan@eircom.net. Welcoming accommodation in a modern bungalow on the R755 towards Roundwood. ❷

Glendalough River House Off the Rathdrum road in the same complex as the Woollen Mills, about half a mile out of Laragh Ⓣ & Ⓕ0404/45577, Ⓔglendaloughriverhouse@hotmail.com. Comfortable B&B in a converted eighteenth-century mill house, occupying a superb, tranquil, riverside location with fabulous views. ❸

Lynham's Hotel In the village Ⓣ0404/45345, Ⓦwww.lynhamsoflaragh.com. Airy, tasteful, modern hotel overlooking the Glenmacnass River; half-board deals offered. ❻

Tudor Lodge Half a mile from the village on the Rathdrum road Ⓣ & Ⓕ0404/45554, Ⓦwww.tudorlodgeireland.com. Spacious, modern, half-timbered B&B offering comfortable accommodation in a beautiful spot. ❷

Valeview On the road towards Glendalough Ⓣ & Ⓕ 0404/45292, Ⓔlisa.mc@oceanfree.net. Recommended for its smart rooms, good breakfasts and great views. ❷

Glenmalure and the Glen of Imaal

South and west of Glendalough, the country rises, becoming wilder and more desolate, dominated by **Lugnaquillia**, the highest mountain in the Wicklow range at 926m. The military road offers a scenic route branching off the R755 just south of Laragh and continuing southwest; walkers have the option of following the Wicklow Way out of Glendalough, skirting Derrybawn mountain and scaling 2000-foot Mullacor before descending into the next glen.

Whether on foot or by car, you'll arrive in dark and lonely **GLENMALURE**, which was the scene of a decisive victory by the Wicklow Irish under Fiach MacHugh O'Byrne over the English under Elizabeth I. One of the 1798 barracks, now ruined, stands at the point where the military road hits the glen. It's a symbol of decay that somehow sets the tone for the entire valley, with its enclosed, mysterious feel and steep scree sides which scarcely afford a foothold to the heather. The road northwest up the valley eventually peters out in a car park, but a track continues up to the very basic An Óige Glenmalure **youth hostel** (Dublin office Ⓣ01/830 4555; late June to Aug daily; Sept to late June Sat only), which stands at the head of the valley just above the point where the river rushes over a weir. From here it's possible to follow a track further up the valley, over the Table Mountain, and down into the Glen of Imaal.

By comparison with Glenmalure, the **Glen of Imaal** is almost inviting, still wild and desolate but lighter and more open. However, half of it is used as an army shooting range – look out for the red flags to show when the range is in use and therefore off limits. There's an An Óige **youth hostel** at **BALLINCLEA** (Ⓣ & Ⓕ045/404657; March–Nov daily; Dec–Feb weekends only), just over two miles southeast of Donard on the north side of the glen.

At **DERRYNAMUCK**, on the southeast side of the valley, stands a whitewashed, thatched cottage where Michael O'Dwyer, one of the last insurgents of 1798, took refuge when trapped by the British, and subsequently escaped because Samuel McAllister drew the enemy's fire and died in his place. It's now run by Dúchas as a folk museum, the **Dwyer McAllister Cottage** (mid-June to mid-Sept daily 2–6pm; free).

Avondale House, the Vale of Avoca and Macreddin

South of Laragh, the **Vale of Clara** leads to **RATHDRUM**, a quiet village on the Dublin–Wexford rail route and the once-daily Dublin–Arklow bus route. Here the *Old Presbytery* **hostel** (IHH; Ⓣ0404/46930, Ⓔthehostel@hotmail.com; ❶) offers comfortable accommodation in dorms or twin and family rooms, and **camping** is possible at *Avonmore Riverside Caravan and Camping Park* (Ⓣ0404/46080). There's also a small **tourist office** in the market square (Mon–Fri 9am–5.30pm, July & Aug also Sat 1.30–5.30pm; Ⓣ0404/46262).

About a mile and a half south of Rathdrum lies Avondale, where you can visit **Avondale House** (mid-March to Oct daily 11am–5pm; €4.45; grounds open daily all year, free), which was home to one of Ireland's most influential and important politicians. **Charles Stewart Parnell**, born here in 1846, was hailed as the "uncrowned king of Ireland" until his career – and his campaign for home rule – was brought to an end by the scandal of his love for a married woman, Kitty O'Shea (see p.788 for more on Parnell). The **house**, designed in 1779 by the celebrated English architect John Wyatt, is a modest, box-shaped building. Inside, there's a delicate, Wedgwood-like blue dining room with plasterwork by the famous Franchini brothers (who decorated Dublin's Newman House), a striking vermilion library (Parnell's favourite room), and, in the entrance hall, an elegant minstrels' gallery from where Parnell, a nervous orator, used to practise his political speeches. The Avondale estate has been in the possession of the Irish Forestry Board, Coillte, since 1904, and the **grounds** are used for silvicultural experiments. Several trails of up to an hour in length have been laid out through the forested parkland, with its rare tree species and fine views of the Avonmore River. There's a café, and plenty of picnic tables in the estate.

The scenic **Vale of Avoca**, which begins two miles south of Avondale, can be excessively crowded with coach tours heading for the mills. Don't be put off though as its beauty is genuinely rewarding, with thickly wooded slopes on either side of the river. The Vale kicks off at the **Meeting of the Waters**, the confluence of the Avonmore and Avonbeg rivers, where *The Meetings* **pub** takes pride of place. Picturesquely located with its own gardens and picture windows, the pub serves decent food and is known for its traditional music sessions (summer Mon–Sat evenings, plus an outdoor *ceili* on Sun afternoons; winter Sat & Sun evenings; Ⓣ0402/35226).

A couple of miles downstream the pretty village of **AVOCA** still trades on its role as the location for the now-defunct BBC TV series *Ballykissangel*.

There's more to it than that though, most notably in the form of its famous **mill**, where you can watch the weavers at work (daily 9.30am–6pm; free; Ⓦwww.avoca.ie). The weavers are housed in a group of whitewashed buildings with steep grey roofs, where the fly-shuttle looms that caused mass unemployment when they were introduced in 1723 appear as picturesquely traditional. There's an excellent, inexpensive lunch room and, of course, a shop selling the fruits of the looms as well as other good-quality clothes and crafts. In the centre of the village, the small library (Ⓣ0402/35022) provides **tourist information** and **Internet access**. At Avoca, you're only six miles from Arklow and routes up and down the coast, but if you're inclined to stay, there are plenty of **B&Bs** in the vicinity, notably *Keppels Farmhouse* (Ⓣ0402/35168, Ⓦwww.keppelsfarmhouse.com; April–Oct; ❷), a comfortable and relaxing dairy farm signposted two miles south of the village.

Venturing further afield, you might well be tempted to **stay** or **eat** at the *Brooklodge Hotel* at **MACREDDIN**, to the west of Avoca, two miles north of Aughrim (Ⓣ0402/36444, Ⓦwww.brooklodge.com; ❽). The enterprising owners have redeveloped this picturesque village, which had fallen into decline in the late nineteenth century, with a modern country-house-style hotel, the excellent and innovative *Strawberry Tree Restaurant*, which uses only organic, free-range and wild ingredients, a pub with its own microbrewery, an equestrian centre and craft and organic food stores. The first Sunday of every month sees a big organic food fair in the afternoon, with barbecues and music.

The Wicklow coast

County Wicklow's most outstanding scenery is undoubtedly inland, but the **coast** offers a handful of pleasant, if unassuming, towns, bracing walks and some very fine beaches, notably at **Brittas Bay**, between Wicklow and Arklow. By **train**, the DART service from Dublin runs as far as Greystones; to get to Wicklow town or Arklow, catch the Wexford train.

Travelling south from Dublin, the first major town you'll come to is **Bray**, which, although very much a dormitory suburb, retains something of its Victorian resort character and offers the finest walk along this coast, across Bray Head to the village of **Greystones**. Halfway down the county's seaboard, **Wicklow** town enjoys a fine setting and a good choice of places to stay and eat. If you have your own transport, this would make a good base for exploring the coast and mountains, getting the nod over its more industrialized cousin **Arklow** to the south.

Bray and around

BRAY, a resort first developed in the 1850s when the railway was extended south of Dún Laoghaire, now welcomes hordes of visitors taking the DART from Dublin on summer weekends with a seafront full of video arcades, B&Bs and fast-food shops. Inevitably the town has lost some of its genteel Victorian charm, but it does boast a superb sand and shingle **beach** and there are fine walks to be had up around **Bray Head**, a knob of rock pushing into the sea, where a massive cross, erected to mark the holy year of 1950, serves as a reminder that you are still in Catholic Europe.

The **Bray Heritage Centre**, in the Old Court House on Main Road (Mon–Fri 9.30am–4.30pm, until 5pm June–Aug, Sat 10am–3pm; €3), focuses on local history and the engineer William Dargan (1799–1867), who brought the railway to the town and is thus considered the founder of modern Bray. Probably a more interesting diversion though, especially if you have children, is the **National Sea-Life Centre** on the seafront (Mon–Fri 10am–4pm, Sat & Sun 10am–5pm; reduced hours in winter; €8, children €5.50; ⓣ01/286 6939), a hi-tech aquarium specializing in Irish marine life that is both entertaining – the touch pool, full of crabs and starfish, is a particular favourite – and educational, with a strong emphasis on the need for conservation.

The **tourist office** can be found at the heritage centre (same hours; ⓣ01/286 6796) and will provide details of the three-day Jazz Festival in May, the three-day International Festival of Music and Dance in early August and October's Oscar Wilde Autumn School, a celebration of the author and wit's life, work and times. **Internet access** is available at Starnet (ⓣ01/286 1520), above Star Leisure on the seafront. Bray's outstanding **restaurant** option is the *Tree of Idleness* (ⓣ01/286 3498; Tues–Sun evenings), fifteen minutes' walk along the seafront from the DART station. This award-winning Greek Cypriot establishment serves the freshest seafood, wonderful moussaka, smoked lamb and suckling pig, complemented by great service, wine list and desserts. Also on the seafront is a branch of Temple Bar's *Porterhouse* **pub**, serving beers from their own microbrewery and good food.

There's an excellent two- to three-hour **walk** from Bray seafront south across Bray Head all the way to **GREYSTONES**, a small commuter town at the end of the DART line. You can follow the comparatively flat cliff path that runs above the rail tracks for most of the way, giving close-up views of rocky coves and slate pinnacles, lashed by magnificent waves on windy days. Alternatively, take on the steep climb over the top of Bray Head for great views of Killiney Bay and the cone-shaped hills inland known as Little Sugarloaf and Great Sugarloaf, with a distant backdrop of the Wicklow Mountains: the route ascends rapidly from the end of Bray seafront through pine woods and over gorse slopes to a large cross, 600ft above sea level; from here a track winds across the ridge below the 782ft summit of Bray Head, before it turns sharply left, down to join the cliff path which will bring you into Greystones. The village supports several pubs serving food, as well as *The Hungry Monk*, a fine traditional **restaurant** that's especially popular for Sunday dinner (or "linner" as they call it), served any time between noon and 8pm.

The leeward side of Bray Head partakes of the softness of Wicklow, the "Garden of Ireland", where trees and plants from five continents flourish in gardens that throw open their gates during the **Wicklow Gardens Festival** (May to late July). A full list of the gardens and viewing days is available from the Bray tourist office; the easiest to reach is the seventeenth-century French-style **garden of Killruddery House** (April–Sept daily 1–5pm; €4.50), off the Southern Cross Route on the edge of Bray (bus #84 from Main Street or a twenty-minute walk from Strand Road). By paying €2 extra you can tour Killruddery House itself (May, June & Sept daily 1–5pm), the Tudor Revival seat of the Earls of Meath, which was a famous hunting-lodge for generations.

Wicklow and around

WICKLOW, seventeen miles south of Bray, is the first place that wholly escapes the influence of Dublin as you go down the coast. It's an easy-going, ramshackle county town of solidly built houses in bright marine pastels, enlivened by its fine setting: the Vartry River broadens into a lough here before flowing into the Irish Sea, cutting off a narrow strip of land, **the Murrough**, that's rich in bird life, notably wintering swans and geese. On the south side of the river mouth, a knoll encrusted with some meagre piles of stone constitutes all that's left of **Black Castle**, one of the fortifications built by the Fitzgeralds in return for lands granted them by Strongbow after the Anglo-Norman invasion of 1169, and all but demolished by the O'Byrnes and O'Tooles in 1301. It's possible to walk round **Wicklow Head** beyond the castle, and find exhilarating views of the open sea and, northward, the weird silhouettes of the Great and Little Sugarloaf mountains, to the sandy **beaches** that begin at Silver Strand, a couple of miles from town, and stretch all the way down through Brittas Bay (see p.160) to Arklow. There's also sociable, if unglamorous, swimming near the harbour breakwater closer to the centre of town.

Two minor squares, linked by Main Street, form the town's core: **Fitzwilliam Square**, where you'll find the tourist office (see below); and **Market Square**, where a spirited memorial to the 1798 rebel Billy Byrne grabs your attention. Byrne, born into a wealthy Catholic family, led rebels from south and central Wicklow during the 1798 Rebellion, but was eventually executed at Gallow's Hill in Wicklow town (for more on the rebellion see p.786). Around fifty yards from Market Square on Kilmantin Hill stands **Wicklow's Historic Gaol**, originally built in 1702 to hold prisoners under the repressive penal laws, and now converted into a tourist attraction (mid-March to Sept daily 10am–6pm, tours every 10min; €5.80), offering a very lively re-creation of the life of the prison, which looks at the part it played in the lives of those involved in the 1798 Rebellion, and those transported from here to the Penal Colonies.

Practicalities

The **tourist office** is on Fitzwilliam Square (June–Sept Mon–Fri 9am–6pm, Sat 9.30am–5.30pm; Oct–May Mon–Fri 9.30am–1pm & 2–5.30pm; ⓣ0404/69117). Bus **tours to Glendalough** and other sights in the Wicklow Mountains depart from here daily at 11am (sometimes twice daily in summer; €15). **Internet access** is available at the Community IT Access Centre on Abbey Street (ⓣ0404/62663, ⓦwww.witc.org).

A wide range of **accommodation** is on offer in Wicklow and the surrounding area (see below), and you can **camp** near the beach at Silver Strand, about two miles south of town (ⓣ0404/67615; June–Sept). Options for **eating** in Wicklow are also good. *The Bakery Restaurant*, Church Street, just off Fitzwilliam Square (ⓣ0404/66770; closed Mon–Sat lunchtimes) is one of the best places, specializing in seafood dishes such as scallops with Thai dressing, in a cosy bistro-style setting. They offer good-value early-bird menus (Mon–Thurs & Sun 6–8pm) and cheap brunches on Sunday. Other choices include two good Italian restaurants, *Vesuvius* behind the tourist office (ⓣ0404/64877; Tues–Sun evenings) and the simpler *Casa Pepe* (ⓣ0404/67075), a cheap and lively pasta and pizza joint on Main Street, as well as the self-explanatory *Square Steakhouse* on Market Square (ⓣ0404/66422; closed Sat lunchtime, Sun & Mon). For top-quality – and expensive – modern Irish cuisine, make a reservation at *Hunter's Hotel*, listed overleaf.

Several **pubs** serve decent food: *Phil Healy's*, a congenial place on Fitzwilliam Square; *The Old Court Inn* on Market Square; or for a more interesting range of dishes and outdoor seating in summer, the welcoming *Old Forge*, on Abbey Street, the continuation of Main Street towards the west end of town. For traditional music try *O'Connor's* on Abbey Street on Thursdays, *The Bayview Hotel*, Main Street, on Sundays and Mondays, or *The Bridge Tavern*, Bridge Street, which claims to have live music every night.

Accommodation

Ballyknocken House Glenealy, around five miles southwest of Wicklow town on the Rathdrum road ⓣ0404/44627, ⓦwww.ballyknocken.com. Elegant, ivy-clad 1850s farmhouse, furnished with antiques and set in an attractive garden. Table d'hôte dinners and walking programmes available. ❹

The Grand Hotel Abbey St ⓣ0404/67337, ⓦwww.grandhotel.ie. A large, traditional, recently refurbished three-star hotel in the town centre. Cosy fires in the lobby and large, comfortable bedrooms, all en suite with TV. Reduced rates for short breaks. ❺

Greenhill House 2 Ballyguilemore, Greenhill Rd ⓣ0404/67111, ⓔgreenhillhouse@eircom.net. Spacious, tastefully decorated rooms, with or without their own bathrooms, and great breakfasts in a welcoming B&B, with spectacular views from its lofty perch above the town centre. ❷

Hunter's Hotel Rathnew, around two miles west of Wicklow town ⓣ0404/40106, ⓦwww.hunters.ie. Comfortable rooms furnished with antiques in this lovely old coaching inn, which was once a haunt of the nineteenth-century politician Charles Stewart Parnell. Today it's particularly renowned for its excellent restaurant serving lunch, afternoon tea and dinner, and for the riverside gardens. ❼

Kilmantin House Kilmantin Hill ⓣ0404/67373. A centrally located B&B, right next door to Wicklow's Historic Gaol. Bright, cheery rooms with stripped-pine floors and airy colour schemes. All en suite with TV. ❷

Wicklow Bay Hostel Marine House, The Murrough (IHH; ⓣ0404/69213 or 61174, ⓔinfo@wicklowbayhostel.com; Feb–Nov). A big, breezy hostel, close to the town centre but overlooking the sea, that's well run by friendly staff. Dorms, four-bed and twin rooms are available (linen included). Bike rental is also on offer here. ❶

Brittas Bay and Mount Usher Gardens

Heading south of Wicklow towards Arklow on the R750, you'll come to a string of attractive white-sand **beaches** backed by rolling dunes. The one at **Brittas Bay**, just north of Mizen Head and around eight miles from Wicklow, is particularly good – don't be put off by the caravan site, there's plenty of seclusion to be found. If you want to get to Brittas Bay by public transport, any bus on the inland N11 to Arklow will put you off at Jack White's Crossroads, from where it's a half-hour walk to the beach.

In the other direction, horticultural enthusiasts should make for **Mount Usher Gardens** (mid-March to Oct daily 10.30am–6pm; €5; ⓦwww.mount-usher-gardens.com), on the N11 three miles inland just south of Ashford, where a profusion of rare trees, shrubs and flowers, including the finest eucalyptus specimens in Europe, grow in an informal style in the woodlands and meadows. The gardens straddle the Vartry River, which is broken up here by a remarkable series of nineteenth-century weirs, watercourses and miniature suspension bridges.

Arklow

If the poetry and passion of Van Morrison's *Streets of Arklow* have brought you here, you may well be disappointed. While it's an ideal point from which to access the picturesque Vale of Avoca (see p.156), the town itself is chiefly a commercial centre wrapped around an old port. **ARKLOW** (ⓦwww.arklow.ie) has a long and prosperous history based on fishing, shipbuilding and the export of copper ore, pyrites and even gold, mined further up the valley. While no longer a major port, shipbuilding continues to be important – *Gypsy Moth IV*, Sir Francis Chichester's prize-winning transatlantic yacht now moored at Greenwich in London, was built at John Tyrrell's yard here. For some historical background, stop off at the **Maritime Museum** in St Mary's Road, between the railway station and Upper Main Street (summer Mon–Sat 10am–1pm & 2–5pm; €5). A delightfully haphazard collection of local finds, it claims a history for Arklow that goes back to Ptolemy's celebrated second-century map of the world. It also emerges that Arklow was a major centre for arms-smuggling during the upheavals of 1798. The museum houses such curiosities as a whale's tooth and eardrum and a model ship made with 10,700 matchsticks.

Arklow's **beach**, white sand like the rest of this part of the coast, is sandwiched between the docks and a gravel extraction plant – you may prefer to head north to Brittas Bay (see opposite), or three miles south to the sheltered, sandy **Clogga Beach**.

Practicalities

The **tourist office** (June–Sept Mon–Sat 10am–1pm & 2–5.30pm; Oct–May Mon–Fri variable hours; ⓣ0402/32484) is located in the Coach House on Upper Main Street. Accommodation should be easy enough to find, with plenty of **B&Bs** – try *Vale View*, Coolgreaney Road (ⓣ & ⓕ0402/32622, ⓔpat.crotty@ifi.ie; March–Oct; ❷), a comfortable Edwardian house with fine views from its rooftop sun lounge, or *Valentia* on the same road (ⓣ & ⓕ0402/39200, ⓦwww.geocities.com/valentiahouse; ❷). *Avonmore House* **hostel**, Ferrybank (IHH; ⓣ0402/32825 or 33855 after 6pm, ⓔavonmorehouse@eircom.net; ❶; June–Sept), a handy short walk from the town centre, offers decent budget accommodation in dorms, twins or family rooms. The best **place to eat** is the *New Riverwalk Restaurant* (ⓣ0402/31657; closed Mon–Sat lunchtimes), overlooking the Avoca at River Walk, off Main Street, which offers dishes such as Wicklow lamb with mint and red wine jus, as well as a long list of daily seafood specials. There are lots of **pubs**, most of which serve food and have some kind of entertainment on offer, including traditional Irish music, discos and the odd pub quiz: *Oscar's* and the more sedate *Mary B*, both on Lower Main Street, are worth trying.

Blessington and Russborough House

BLESSINGTON's marvellous location close to the shining waters of the **Blessington lakes** and, beyond them, the spectacular heights of the Wicklow Mountains, makes it a good base for exploration for those with their own transport. Three miles south of the village stands the classic Palladian structure of **Russborough House** (April & Oct Sun 10.30am–5.30pm; May–Sept daily 10.30am–5.30pm; €6), designed, like Powerscourt House and Leinster House in Dublin, by the German architect Richard Cassels (with the assistance of Francis Bindon). The house, with its 700-foot-long facade and fine rococo stuccowork by the Franchini brothers, was constructed for Joseph Leeson, son of a rich Dublin brewer who became MP for Rathcormack and then **Lord Russborough** in 1756. In its grandiose extravagance, Russborough House epitomizes the great flowering of Anglo-Irish confidence before the Act of Union deprived Ireland of its parliament, much of its trade and its high society.

The chief reason why Russborough is so firmly on the tourist trail is its collection of **paintings**. The German entrepreneur Alfred Beit (1853–1906), co-founder with Cecil Rhodes of the De Beers Diamond Mining Company, poured the fortune he derived from that enterprise into amassing works of art. His nephew, Sir Alfred Beit, acquired Russborough in 1952, and donated many of the collection's most valuable paintings to the National Gallery in Dublin in 1988. Only a fraction of his extraordinary collection of Dutch, English, Flemish and Spanish masterpieces is on display at Russborough at any one time (the bulk is at the National Gallery), but you're likely to see works by artists such as Hals, Gainsborough, Goya and Rubens.

Russborough has been **burgled** four times, first in 1974, when an Englishwoman, Rose Dugdale, stole nineteen paintings to raise money for the IRA (her booty, worth £18 million, was recovered undamaged from a farmhouse in County Cork a week later). The house was again broken into in May 1986 in an operation orchestrated by one of Dublin's most notorious criminals, Martin Cahill; the robbery subsequently became a central element in John Boorman's 1997 film *The General*, which takes its title from Cahill's nickname. Most of the paintings taken in this second heist have since been retrieved, but Russborough was burgled again in 2001, possibly by an associate of Cahill's, when a Gainsborough portrait was stolen for the third time, along with a work by Bellotto. Both were recovered in September 2002, only days before a fourth break-in, which netted five pictures including two by Rubens. Nowadays, visitor security is understandably tight, and the 45-minute guided tour limits study of the paintings in detail, but for all that the house is still well worth a visit.

The **lake** in front of Russborough provides the house with an idiomatically eighteenth-century prospect. The impression is a false one, however – it's actually a thoroughly twentieth-century reservoir, created by damming the Liffey, which provides Dublin with twenty million gallons of water a day.

Practicalities

Blessington is about an hour from central Dublin on the hourly #65 **bus** from Eden Quay. There's a central **tourist office**, set back from the main street opposite the church (summer Mon–Fri 10am–3pm; ⓣ045/865850), which has information on possibilities for **outdoor pursuits**. A wide range – including canoeing, wind-surfing, sailing, pony-trekking and abseiling – is available at Blessington Sports, on the south side of town (ⓣ045/865092, ⓦwww.blessingtonsports.com). **Bike hire** is available at Hillcrest Hire, Main Street (ⓣ045/865066).

Haylands House, Dublin Road, at the north end of town (ⓣ045/865183, ⓔhayland@eircom.net; ❷), offers **B&B** in a spacious bungalow with an impressive garden. The village also sports a comfortable **hotel**, *Downshire House* (ⓣ045/865199, ⓦwww.downshirehouse.com; ❻), which occupies a pink-painted Georgian house with a large, secluded garden on the main street. A few miles out of town, there's the An Óige *Baltyboys* **hostel**, on the wooded shores of the lake (ⓣ045/867266; Dec–Feb closed weekdays). Blessington also has a decent choice of **places to eat**. Pride of place goes to the *Old Schoolhouse*, Kilbride Road (just off the main street near *Downshire House*; ⓣ045/891420; closed Mon), a relaxing setting for delicious Italian dishes such as chicken with pistachio and pesto cream sauce. Otherwise, the informal *Courtyard Restaurant* next to the tourist office is a good spot for sandwiches, snacks and more substantial meals; also on Main Street, *O'Connor's* serves good bar food during the day and posher fare in the evening in its restaurant (closed Mon).

County Kildare

Although **County Kildare** (Ⓦwww.kildare.ie) lacks the spectacle of the Wicklow Mountains, or the extraordinary range of ancient monuments of the lush Boyne Valley to the north, it has a quiet charm of its own. The **landscape** is a calm one of rolling farmland for the most part, with open grasslands and rough pasture, just touching the drab stretches of the monotonous **Bog of Allen** in the northwest. This is ancient countryside, marked by a string of **Celtic crosses** at Moone, Old Kilcullen and Castledermot. But you're also constantly made aware that you're in Pale country – with big, stone, estate walls bordering many of the fields and Georgian proportions in the buildings, as well as more obvious attractions such as the magnificent **Castletown House** at Celbridge; the **Grand Canal**, which traverses the county and has a walkable towpath; and the pin-neat **National Stud** at Kildare town with its fabulous horses and ornamental gardens.

Because of its proximity to Dublin, there are few problems with **transport** in County Kildare, although it's worth avoiding driving in or out of Dublin during rush hour as delays are common; Friday afternoons coming out of the capital and Sunday or Bank Holiday evenings returning are particularly bad. In the north of the county, Dublin city **buses** serve Castletown House, the motley attractions of **Straffan** and the university town of **Maynooth**, which is also on the N4 and the main **rail** line to the west. Buses to Limerick and Cork ply up and down the N7 via **Kildare** town, with the rail line running close beside the road for most of the way.

Maynooth, Castletown House and around

There really isn't all that much to detain you in **MAYNOOTH**, pretty though it is (pronounced "ma-nooth", with the stress on the second syllable; frequent trains from Dublin's Pearse, Tara Street and Connolly stations and #66 buses from Wellington Quay). The town is renowned chiefly for its seminary, **St Patrick's College**, which, in addition to training priests, now houses a branch of the National University of Ireland. Visitors are welcome to tour the college's forbidding grey quadrangles, leavened by Virginia creepers and ornamental gardens, and can buy a useful historical guide (€4) at the Reception Area. Fans of Victoriana will be especially interested in the second quad, which is by Pugin in Gothic Revival style, and the adjoining chapel, notable for its huge stained-glass rose window and finely carved oak choir stalls. The grandiosely titled **National Science Museum** (May–Sept Tues & Thurs 2.30–4.30pm, Sun 2–6pm; free) hosts a bizarre collection of bishops' copes, harps and induction coils, the latter invented by Nicholas Callan, who was professor of natural philosophy here in the early nineteenth century.

The substantial ruins beside the entrance to the college are of the thirteenth-century **Maynooth Castle** (June–Sept Mon–Fri 10am–6pm, Sat & Sun 1–6pm; Oct Sun 1–5pm; 45min guided tours €1.90; Heritage Card), one of the two main strongholds of the Anglo-Norman Fitzgerald family who ruled

Kildare and, effectively, most of Ireland from the thirteenth century until the coming of the Tudor monarchs (their other castle is at Kilkea, in the south – see p.172). Maynooth's formal town-planning is based around **Carton House**, a Georgian gem by Richard Cassels which lies at the other end of the main street. It's unlikely that you'll need to stay in Maynooth, but it does boast a very good **restaurant**, *Lemongrass*, in the *Glenroyal Hotel*, Straffan Road (☎01/629 0915), which serves all manner of east and southeast Asian food – including good-value lunchtime bento boxes, containing a variety of taster dishes – in smart, modern surroundings.

Castletown House

Few places give a better impression of the immense scale on which the Anglo-Irish imagination was able to work than **Castletown House** (Easter–Sept Mon–Fri 10am–6pm, Sat & Sun 1–6pm; Oct Mon–Fri 10am–5pm, Sun 1–5pm; Nov Sun 1–5pm; €3.80; Heritage Card), designed in 1722 for the Speaker of the Irish House of Commons, William Connolly, by the Italian Alessandro Galilei. You enter the grounds through the village of **CELBRIDGE**, around four miles southeast of Maynooth and thirteen miles west of Dublin (bus #67 or #67A from Wellington Quay), planned to lend importance to the house itself. Exhibiting the strictest Classicism, the house faces out over the Liffey, giving little away except for a rigidly repeated succession of windows. It's the only thing about the design that is restrained, though, for Castletown, from the very beginning, was built for show.

William Connolly was a publican's son from Donegal, who made his fortune by dealing in forfeited estates after the Battle of the Boyne, as legal adviser to William III, and was acknowledged as the richest man in Ireland by the 1720s. Castletown was begun in 1722, in a somewhat haphazard fashion, and the interior was still unfinished when Connolly died seven years later. Work on the house didn't resume until his nephew Tom Connolly inherited it in 1758; the actual driving force, however, was Tom's wife, Lady Louisa, who was only 15 years old when she assumed responsibility for the job, which carried on into the 1770s. Castletown was eventually sold by the Connolly family in 1965, and would have been demolished to build houses if the property developer owners hadn't gone bust. Desmond Guinness stepped in to buy the house on behalf of the Irish Georgian Society, and it was finally transferred to State care in 1994 to undergo a £5 million restoration programme.

The guided tour starts in the **Main Hall**, where some of the characteristically ornate stuccowork of the Italian Franchini brothers is on view, and moves on to the pine-panelled **Brown Study**, the only room to retain the house's original plain decorative style. During the 1760s, Sir William Chambers, the architect of Somerset House and the Kew Gardens pagoda in London, was commissioned by Lady Louisa to remodel much of the ground floor and his designs remain intact on the walls of the **Red Room**, which are covered in torn French damask, and in the viridescent silk decoration and use of gilded fillet in the adjacent **Green Room**. The **Print Room**, next door, is the only surviving example in Ireland of the eighteenth-century fad for gluing prints of the works of old masters onto walls. A splendid yellow and blue silk canopied bed dominates the **State Bedroom**, beyond.

The grand cantilevered **staircase**, with what's thought to be the first set of brass banisters in Ireland, has more wonderful plasterwork by the Franchini brothers on the walls. Upstairs the highlight is the **Long Gallery**, with its Pompeiian murals and gilded sconces bearing busts of poets and philosophers,

△ Powerscourt Estate, County Wicklow

the decor somewhat marred by grotesque glass chandeliers from Murano, near Venice. One oddity here is a pair of doors on the south wall, only one of which is real – the false one exists simply to provide symmetry.

From the gallery's windows you can see the **Connolly Folly**, two miles to the north. This bizarre structure consists of a 130-foot-high obelisk, balanced precariously on the top of a stack of arches, and was commissioned by Katherine Connolly as a memorial to her husband, William. She also commissioned the **Wonderful Barn**, three miles northeast of the house, a weird conical tower with an external stairway, which can be seen from the N4 motorway just west of the Leixlip junction. Both projects were set up to provide relief work for estate labourers hit by the famine-ridden winter of 1739. Unfortunately, the land on which they stand is privately owned and so not accessible to the public.

Straffan

About four miles southwest of Celbridge, the village of **STRAFFAN** is home to the diverse attractions of **Lodge Park Heritage Centre**. Housed in a neat Victorian church (the former Great Southern and Western Railway Church of St Jude) that's been brought stone by stone from Inchicore in Dublin, the **Steam Museum** (April, May & Sept Sun 2.30–5.30pm; June–Aug Tues–Sun 2–6pm; Ⓦwww.steam-museum.ie; €4) offers a benign view of the driving force behind the Industrial Revolution. There are miniature models of steam trains and four – amazingly quiet – working steam engines, plus a series of wall panels offering a rather rose-tinted account of how steam advanced the way forward to our modern world. They also reflect Ireland's uneven industrialization – in 1838 the North had more steam horsepower than the rest of Ireland put together. In bucolic contrast is Lodge Park's recently restored eighteenth-century **walled garden** (June & July Tues–Fri & Sun 2–6pm; Aug Tues–Fri 2.30–5.30pm; €4), which encloses such features as a salad parterre, an orchard, topiary and a greenhouse containing an unusual collection of plants from around the world.

A big hit with children is nearby **Straffan Butterfly Farm** (June–Aug daily noon–5.30pm; €4.50): huge exotic butterflies fly freely, while giant insects, reptiles and tarantulas remain safely behind glass.

Larchill Arcadian Gardens

If you're exploring this area by car, **Larchill Arcadian Gardens** (May–Sept daily noon–6pm; €6.50), three miles north of Kilcock, are well worth a detour. Painstakingly restored, Larchill is the only surviving example in Ireland or England of a *ferme ornée*, a type of garden (literally an "ornamental farm") that represents a midway point between the true landscaped garden and the rigorously formal style of garden that preceded it. These attained a degree of fashionableness amongst wealthy landowners during the latter half of the eighteenth century, inspired by the influence of Marie Antoinette at Versailles.

A fifteen-minute circular walk through avenues of beech trees links ten Classical and Gothic **follies**, the most notable of which are the fortified island named **Gibraltar** and the curious **Foxes' Earth**. The latter was built on the instruction of a dedicated fox-hunter, Mr Watson, who, convinced he would be reincarnated as a fox as retribution, wanted to be sure of a bolt-hole from the hounds in his next life – it appears today as a grass-covered mound with tunnels for escape, topped by a cluster of rubble-rough columns. The ten acres of **parklands** are stocked by rare breeds of farm animals, especially sheep, some of which are kept in a string of recently constructed buildings which form a new *ferme ornée*. An attractive **walled garden** holds a variety of unusual plants, as well as a herb garden and a pergola, and these new projects are explained in the pleasant **tearoom**, where there's interesting material on the conservation project here.

Kildare, the Curragh and around

The main Limerick road, the N7, provides a relatively swift – rush hour aside – but rather dull drive from Dublin to **Kildare** town and the **Curragh**; to speed things up further, there's a new stretch of motorway, the M7, which begins just before Naas and will, by the end of 2003, bypass the notorious bottleneck of Kildare town. The chief attraction at **NAAS** (pronounced "nace") is **Punchestown Racecourse** (Ⓣ045/897704), whose main meeting is the four-day Irish National Hunt Festival in April, when the racecourse itself is greatly celebrated for its flowering gorse. A close second is **Mondello Park** motor-racing circuit (Ⓣ045/860200; Ⓦwww.mondellopark.com), which holds races most weekends from March to October. If you're not content with simply spectating, for €199 you can experience the thrill of driving a racing saloon or single-seater around the track. Foodies are more likely to be tempted by the branch of Maynooth's excellent oriental **restaurant**, *Lemongrass*, on Abbey Street (Ⓣ045/871544).

Newbridge, a nineteenth-century town which grew up around the British barracks here, is similarly unmemorable. But after Newbridge the road heads over the grassy plain of the Curragh, and you're into racing country proper.

Kildare town

KILDARE town is a solid, respectable place centred on a sloping triangular square, which is overlooked by the massive, squat Church of Ireland **Cathedral of St Brigid**. Brigid founded a religious house here on a major pagan site, in 490, and it became an important monastic centre of art, learning and culture – the Book of Kildare, for example, produced here in the seventh century but now lost, had been dictated by an angel, according to the twelfth-century scholar, Giraldus Cambrensis, and was as magnificent as the Book of Kells. The present church (Mon–Sat 10am–1pm & 2–5pm, Sun 2–5pm) dates originally from the thirteenth century, though the north transept and choir were burned to the ground in the Confederate War of 1641, and the Victorian reconstruction of 1875 is pseudo-medieval. Its **round tower** (€3), probably twelfth century, is the second highest in Ireland at 107ft and has a particularly elaborate doorway 12ft up; nineteenth-century battlements conceal the original conical roof and afford a fine panorama – rolling farmland to the south, the Bog of Allen to the north and the Curragh to the east. On the north side of the church is the restored **fire temple**, where a fire is lit every year on St Brigid's feast day (Feb 1) – Brigid had cannily preserved the pagan cult of fire, which her nuns observed here until the Reformation in the sixteenth century.

Practicalities

The **tourist office** (May–Sept Mon–Sat 9.30am–5.30pm, Sun noon–6pm; Oct–April Mon–Fri 10am–5pm; Ⓣ045/521240) and its mildly interesting **heritage centre** (same hours; €2.54) are in the nineteenth-century Market House right in the middle of the main square. **Internet access** is available across the road at the library, which keeps eccentric hours (☎045/520235). The best **accommodation** option in town is the comfortable, pristine-white *Singleton's B&B*, just north of the square at 1 Dara Park, Station Road (☎045/521964; ❷); otherwise try the en-suite rooms at the *Silken Thomas* pub on the square (☎045/522232; ❷, breakfast not included). It's also possible to stay in some luxury at the Curragh Racecourse itself, four miles east of town, in the *Standhouse Hotel* (☎045/436177, Ⓦwww.standhousehotel.com; ❼), which has been recently renovated and expanded from its original eighteenth-century building to include modern facilities such as a swimming pool and gym. For **eating**, the *Silken Thomas* does good bar food and has a restaurant alongside, and there are a couple of good upmarket options: *Kristianna's Bistro* on the square (☎045/522985; closed Thurs lunchtime), which specializes in seafood, and *Annamars*, 200yd up Station Road (☎045/522899; closed Tues–Sat lunchtimes & Mon), where the French chef's inspiration runs to dishes such as monkfish wonton with caesar salad. Just off the square on Claregate Street stands *Mahon's*, a smartly kept old-time **pub** done out in cosy dark woods and green leather; or try *Nolan's*, beside the cathedral, a slightly scruffier place with welcoming snugs and occasional traditional music.

The Curragh and the National Stud

The Curragh, which stretches east from Kildare to the River Liffey, with its racecourse and dozens of stud farms, is the centre of the Irish racing world. First thing in the morning you can see strings of slim racehorses exercising on the five-thousand-acre plain, the largest area of semi-natural grassland in Europe. Breeding and training them is one of Ireland's major money-spinners, and much of it is centred on the Curragh. For an idea of the scale of the operation, Goff's Kildare Paddocks at Kill, which sells over half of all Irish-bred horses, processes an annual turnover of around €50 million.

Security considerations mean that none of the working stud farms are open to the public. The best place to see the perfectionism that attends the breeding and training of these valuable horses is the **National Stud**, based at Tully on the south side of Kildare, signposted from the centre of town (mid-Feb to mid-Nov daily 9.30am–6pm, last admission 5pm; guided tours on the hour from 11am; ☎045/521617, Ⓦwww.irish-national-stud.ie; €8.50). You can easily walk out to it from the town, though the entrance is not the obvious one (through the main gates that you pass on the road from Dublin); instead, follow the signs from the centre for the stud. Access to the adjacent St Fiachra's Garden and the Japanese Garden (see opposite) is included in the price of the ticket.

The National Stud itself consists of neat white buildings set in green lawns as close-cropped and well groomed as a Derby-winner's coat, a spick-and-span monument to the greater glory and perfectability of horses. Established in 1900 by Colonel William Hall-Walker, who believed that horoscopes affected horses' form, the stud enjoyed a marvellous record of success, and in 1915 was bequeathed to the British Crown, which rewarded Hall-Walker by creating him Lord Wavertree. When finally transferred to the Irish State in 1944, it became the National Stud.

Colonel Hall-Walker's belief in the stars is reflected in the **stallion boxes**, built in the 1960s according to his astrological principles, with lantern roofs allowing moon and stars to exert their influence on the occupants. There's a brass plaque on each door giving the stallion's name and details of his racing

A day at the races

You don't have to know anything about horses to enjoy a day at the races. Racegoing is extremely popular in Ireland, with less of the snobbery that's attached in Britain – and it's not as expensive, starting at around €13.

The major Irish flat-racing classics are all held at the **Curragh Racecourse** (Ⓣ045/441205, Ⓦwww.curragh.ie): the Irish 1000 Guineas and 2000 Guineas in May, the Irish Derby in June, the Irish Oaks in July and the Irish St Leger in September. Other major meetings near Dublin are held at Punchestown (see p.167), Leopardstown and Fairyhouse. Details of race meetings can be found in all the daily papers, at Ⓦwww.racemeetings.com, from tourist offices or in the specialist press: *Irish Field* (published Sat morning) and the *Racing Post* (daily).

You can take special **bus and train** services to get to the Curragh from Dublin on race days, the former from Busáras (contact Bus Éireann on Ⓣ01/836 6111), the latter from Heuston to the racecourse's own station, with a return ticket plus admission to the course costing €20 (contact Iarnrod Éireann on Ⓣ01/836 6222).

career. The National Stud's **museum** is an enjoyably chaotic account of the history of horses and horse racing which contains, among other bizarre exhibits, the skeleton of the 1960s champion racehorse, Arkle. The high point of the visit though has to be the **horses** themselves: you can admire top stallions at close quarters, stroll between perfect paddocks of grazing thoroughbreds and, between February and June, watch mares with their foals.

Within the grounds of the National Stud are two highly distinctive gardens: the Japanese Garden and St Fiachra's Garden (both with the same opening hours as the National Stud). The beautiful **Japanese Garden** was laid out on a drained bog, between 1906 and 1910, by Colonel Hall-Walker and two Japanese gardeners. Part of the Edwardian craze for all things Japanese, it's planned to represent the "life of man" – man, emphatically, it has to be said, rather than woman. In a weird kind of enumerated metaphysical joyride, you're led from birth to death via the Tunnel of Ignorance (no. 3) and the Parting of Ways (no. 6), where you're invited to choose between a life of philandering bachelorhood or marriage. Choosing marriage, you step across stepping stones to the Island of Joy and Wonder (no. 7) and meet your wife at the engagement bridge (no. 8; easily confused with the Red Bridge of Life, no. 17) and so on. Finally you pass through the Gateway to Eternity (no. 20), and it's time to go.

The nearby **St Fiachra's Garden** is similarly engaging. St Fiachra was an Irish monk of noble birth who travelled throughout Ireland and Scotland in the early seventh century before founding a hermitage at Breuil in France. Fiachra urged his followers to undertake manual labour, cultivate gardens and thus aid the poor; after his death he became the French patron saint of gardeners. St Fiachra's Garden seeks to present some sense of the natural environment which inspired the spirituality of the sixth- and seventh-century monastic movement in Ireland, through a series of motifs gleaned from that history. The resulting landscape of still pools and rushing water, monumental limestone and sculpted grassy banks makes for a suitably peaceful place. At the centre of the ensemble stands a re-creation of the stone monastic cells found on Skellig Michael, off the Kerry coast (see p.399); once inside you can make up your own mind about the hoard of twinkling Waterford crystal embedded in the floor, which is claimed to be "like the delicacy of the human soul, pure and undefiled".

ı of Allen

ıllen, around the village of **Rathangan** six miles northwest of the beginning of what was a great belt of bogland stretching the country to the Shannon and beyond. It has figured in Irish nd since prehistoric times, though these days only small pock-... **LULLYMORE**, five miles northeast of Rathangan, at the foot of the Hill of Allen, site of the legendary Fionn Mac Cumhaill's palace, offers a good opportunity to get to grips with the life of the bogs, past and present. The place – its name means "great dairy pasture" – is an island in the bog where St Patrick reputedly appointed Eve, an early convert, to run a training college for monks.

Peatland World (Mon–Fri 9.30am–6pm, plus April–Oct Sun 2–6pm; ⓣ045/860133; €5), housed in the eighteenth-century stable block of Lullymore House, provides a comprehensive introduction to Irish bogs and includes exhibitions on conservation, energy production and plant and animal life, together with a history of the area and the estate itself. Future plans for the centre include letting visitors make peat briquettes to take home, and afternoon walking trips onto the bogland.

Further insights into the area's history are provided by the nearby **Lullymore Heritage and Discovery Park** (Easter–Oct Mon–Fri 9.30am–6pm, Sat & Sun noon–6pm; rest of year by appointment ⓣ045/870238; €6), set in wooded parkland, with reconstructions of a Mesolithic campsite, a Neolithic farmstead, an exhibition on early Christian history, and displays covering social history from the eighteenth century onwards.

All about bogs

Ten thousand years ago, after the last Ice Age, the melting glaciers and ice sheets left central Ireland covered by shallow lakes. As time went by the lake and lakeside vegetation grew and died and partly decomposed in a continuing cycle that changed these lakes to fens, and eventually into domed **bogs**. Ireland now has the finest range of peatlands in Europe.

Bogs have been cut away and used for **fuel** for centuries, and there are plenty of songs and stories that bear witness to the importance of the bog in folk history. Estimates of the amount of raised bog that has been lost over the centuries vary widely, from 300,000 to 600,000 hectares. Today there are only 300,000 hectares of raised bog remaining, making it an **endangered habitat**. It was during the 1930s in particular that depletion rates began to accelerate as the work of the newly founded Turf Development Board got under way. Whatever the exact statistics though, it is likely that the large commercial bogs will be exhausted within fifty years.

It is only recently that the Irish have awoken to the **great natural importance** of the boglands. Not only are they home to rare plants, from mosses to bilberries, but they provide a habitat for birds. The bog gases also act as preservatives, and the bogs of Ireland have yielded archaeological evidence of botanical and human history up to 9000 years old in the form of pollens and plant remains, gold and silver artefacts, dug-out canoes and human bodies. For more on bogs, see "Contexts" p.807, or visit the Irish Peatland Conservation Council's website at ⓦwww.ipcc.ie.

Canal country

Monuments to eighteenth-century confidence in Irish trade, the **Royal and Grand canals** flow from Dublin through County Kildare and on into the Irish heartland. While Ireland had experienced a minor industrial revolution in the mid- to late-eighteenth century, when mines, mills, workshops and canals were created, the Act of Union precluded further development. By walking along the towpaths, or cruising on the Grand Canal, you can see how industrialization affected – and failed to affect – the landscape.

The **Grand Canal** was a monumentally ambitious project, running from Dublin to Robertstown, where it forks. The southern branch heads down for 29 miles through Rathangan and the attractive Georgian town of Monasterevin before joining the River Barrow at Athy, effectively extending the waterway as far south as Waterford; the western branch runs up to Tullamore in County Offaly and on to join the great natural waterway of the Shannon at Shannon Harbour, a total of 71 miles from Dublin. As late as 1837 the Grand Canal was carrying over 100,000 passengers a year; it continued to be used for freight right up to 1960.

ROBERTSTOWN, ten miles due north of Kildare and six miles east of Lullymore where the ways divide, is particularly evocative of canal life. The village boasts pleasant walks along the towpath and a canal stop complete with the *Grand Canal Hotel* (Ⓣ045/870005; no accommodation), which has a **restaurant** and a small **exhibition** on the history of the canal and the hotel, and arranges leisurely **barge tours** for large groups (€150 for 1hr or €300 for 3hr). If you want to navigate the Grand Canal through County Kildare yourself, **barge rental** is available, for around €700–1200 per week depending on the season, from: Lowtown Marina, Robertstown (Ⓣ045/860427, Ⓦwww.lowtownmarina.com); Canalways, Rathangan (Ⓣ045/524019, Ⓦwww.canalways.ie); and Leisure Afloat in Levitstown, just south of Athy (Ⓣ056/64395, Ⓦwww.leisureafloat.com).

The **Royal Canal** brushes the northern part of County Kildare near Maynooth before heading up to Mullingar and joining the Shannon, ninety miles and many tortuous meanderings later, at Cloondara, north of Lough Rea, for access to the northwest. With the recent reopening of the Shannon–Erne Waterway (see pp.252 and 554), these southern waterways are linked once more with the Fermanagh Lakes in the North, as they were in the nineteenth century. The canals are flanked by a series of pleasantly undeveloped – and easy-to-follow – **trails**, the Royal Canal Way, the Grand Canal Way and the Barrow Way. Go to Ⓦwww.kildare.ie for full details and descriptions of the routes as they pass through Kildare.

South Kildare

At **Old Kilcullen**, seven miles south of Naas, three **high crosses** set in green, rolling farmland mark the site of an early Celtic monastery, and nearby stands an evocative **round tower** damaged during the 1798 Rebellion. Further south along the N9, there are more monuments to Ireland's ancient heritage at **Moone** and **Castledermot**, and on the R418 at **Kilkea**, just southeast of the genteel heritage town of **Athy**; but first it's well worth stopping off at the village of **Ballitore** about seven miles south of Old Kilcullen.

Ballitore

BALLITORE is an old Quaker village where the Anglo-Irish political philosopher **Edmund Burke** (1729–97) was educated before going to Trinity College, Dublin. The **Ballitore Quaker Museum** (June–Sept Wed–Sat noon–5pm, Sun 2–6pm; Oct–May Tues–Sat noon–5pm; free) above the village library, which is housed in the old Friends Meeting House, gives a vivid picture of what Quaker life would have been like here: each member of the industrious community plied a trade, and their sober, business-like approach made Ballitore a model village by comparison with the general squalor and poverty of surrounding places. But the dominant impression given by the copperplate handwritten letters on show is the sheer boredom of life in a place where any stranger was cause for excitement. Up towards the main road is the walled **Quaker graveyard**, whose plain, dignified tombstones seem suitable monuments to the qualities of the dead. *Griesmount* (ⓣ0507/23158, ⓔgriesemount@eircom.net; March–Nov; ❸), a fine Georgian house and garden a little way from the village centre, offers a place to **stay** amidst Ballitore's peaceful simplicity.

A couple of miles south at the village of Timolin is the **Irish Pewtermill** (Mon–Fri 10am–2.30pm; ⓣ0507/24164); although you can see pewter being cast (usually in the mornings), the place is primarily a retail experience, selling mostly jewellery and tableware.

Moone, Castledermot and Kilkea

Back on the N9, the small village of **MOONE**, three miles south from Ballitore, once formed a link in the chain of monasteries founded by St Columba, and the garden of Moone Abbey contains the ruins of a fourteenth-century Franciscan friary and a ninth-century **cross**. Rich in naive and strangely orderly carving, the cross is particularly interesting. The east side depicts Daniel in the lions den, the sacrifice of Isaac, Adam and Eve and the Crucifixion; on the west are the twelve apostles, the Crucifixion and St John; and on the north, other carvings – including a number of figures and animals. The *Moone High Cross Inn* (ⓣ0507/24112; ❸) is a friendly, rambling old pub here, with a good range of bar **food**, plus a more ambitious menu in the restaurant, and five en-suite **bedrooms**.

Five miles further south at **CASTLEDERMOT** there's more to see: two tenth-century granite high crosses, plus a bizarre twelfth-century Romanesque doorway standing by itself in front of an ugly modern church and a truncated round tower. Castledermot also boasts the substantial remains of a thirteenth-century Augustinian abbey, an example of how the European monastic orders muscled in on the indigenous Irish Church. Cosy **accommodation** in an old school and excellent set **dinners** (reservations essential) are available at *Doyle's Schoolhouse Country Inn* on the main street (ⓣ & ⓕ0503/44282; closed Nov–Easter; ❸).

Kilkea Castle, the Fitzgeralds' second Kildare stronghold (after Maynooth), stands a couple of miles up the Athy road (R418) from Castledermot. Originally built in 1180, it was modified in the seventeenth century, and most of it is a mid-nineteenth-century restoration, though it still looks impressive enough. Massively refurbished again in the 1980s, it's now a luxury **hotel** (ⓣ0503/45156, ⓦwww.kilkeacastle.ie; ❼) boasting a swimming pool, gym and eighteen-hole golf course. There's a more reasonably priced **B&B** option at *Kilkea Lodge Farm* (ⓣ & ⓕ0503/45112, ⓔmigreene@indigo.ie; dinner available by prior arrangement; ❸), a stone-built farmhouse with a riding centre attached.

Athy

On the border with County Laois, five miles north of Kilkea and close to the point where the Grand Canal meets the River Barrow, sits **ATHY** (rhymes with "sty", emphasis on the last syllable). It's one of those places where a bucketful of imagination is required to envisage it as it once was: prosperity has turned a formerly handsome Georgian town with a fine main square into something much more ramshackle. Georgian fanlights sit oddly with a bizarre modern church: the church is apparently supposed to make reference to a dolmen, although the Sydney Opera House seems a stronger influence. Athy's designation as a heritage town, however, is bringing its historical resonances to life. By the riverside stands the square tower of the fifteenth-century **White's Castle**, built by Sir John Talbot, Viceroy of Ireland, to protect the ford across the River Barrow and the inhabitants of the Pale from the dispossessed Irish beyond. The early eighteenth-century town hall houses a **heritage centre** (March–Oct Mon–Sat 10am–6pm & Sun 2–6pm; Nov–Feb Mon–Sat 10am–6pm; €2.50), with a comprehensive exhibition covering the 1798 Rebellion, the Famine, the part played by Athy men in World War I and the life of Antarctic explorer Sir Ernest Shackleton, who came from nearby Kilkea. The town hall is also where you'll find the **tourist office** (same times; ⓣ0507/33075, ⓔathyheritage@tinet.ie). Aside from some leisurely **strolls** along the Grand Canal and visiting the heritage centre, the town's unlikely to detain you for too long – except to **eat** or **stay** at *Tonlegee House* (ⓣ0507/31473, ⓦwww.tonlegeehouse.com; ❺), signposted off the Kilkenny road, a solidly built Georgian mansion that surveys the countryside just beyond Athy's suburban sprawl and has a restaurant noted for its imaginative menu.

Travel details

Trains

Arklow to: Rathdrum (3–6 daily; 20min); Rosslare Europort (3 daily; 1hr 40min); Wexford (3 daily; 1hr 15min); Wicklow (3–7 daily; 30min).
Dublin Connolly to: Arklow (3–6 daily; 1hr 30min); Rathdrum (3–6 daily; 1hr 15min); Wicklow (3–6 daily; 50min).
Dublin Heuston to: Kildare (20–30 daily; 30min).
Maynooth to: Dublin Pearse (via Connolly & Tara Street; 5–16 daily; 30min); Longford (3 daily; 1hr 30min–2hr); Mullingar (4 daily; 40min).
Wicklow to: Arklow (3–6 daily; 30min); Rathdrum (3–5 daily; 25min); Rosslare Europort (3 daily; 2hr 20min); Wexford (3 daily; 2hr).

Buses

Bus Éireann
Arklow to: Avoca (1 daily; 15min); Rathdrum (1 daily; 30min); Rosslare Europort (11 daily; 2hr); Waterford (3 daily; 1hr 45min); Wexford (11 daily; 1hr 20min); Wicklow (4 daily; 30–50min).
Dublin to: Arklow (17 daily; 1hr 30min–2hr 20min); Ashford (6 daily; 1hr 20min); Athy (5–7 daily; 1hr); Avoca (1 daily; 2hr 5min); Castledermot (7–10 daily; 1hr 30min); Kildare (at least hourly; 1hr–1hr 30min); Rathdrum (1 daily; 1hr 50min); Straffan (1–5 daily; 45min); Wicklow (7–8 daily; 1hr–1hr 30min).
Kildare to: Cork (6 daily; 3hr 30min); Limerick (hourly; 2hr 40min).
Wicklow to: Arklow (3 daily; 30–50min); Avoca (1 daily; 35min); Rathdrum (1 daily; 20min); Rosslare Europort (2 daily; 2hr 20min); Wexford (2 daily; 2hr).

St Kevin's bus service
ⓣ01/281 8119
Dublin to: Glendalough, via Bray and Roundwood (2–3 daily; 1hr 30min).

Laois and Offaly

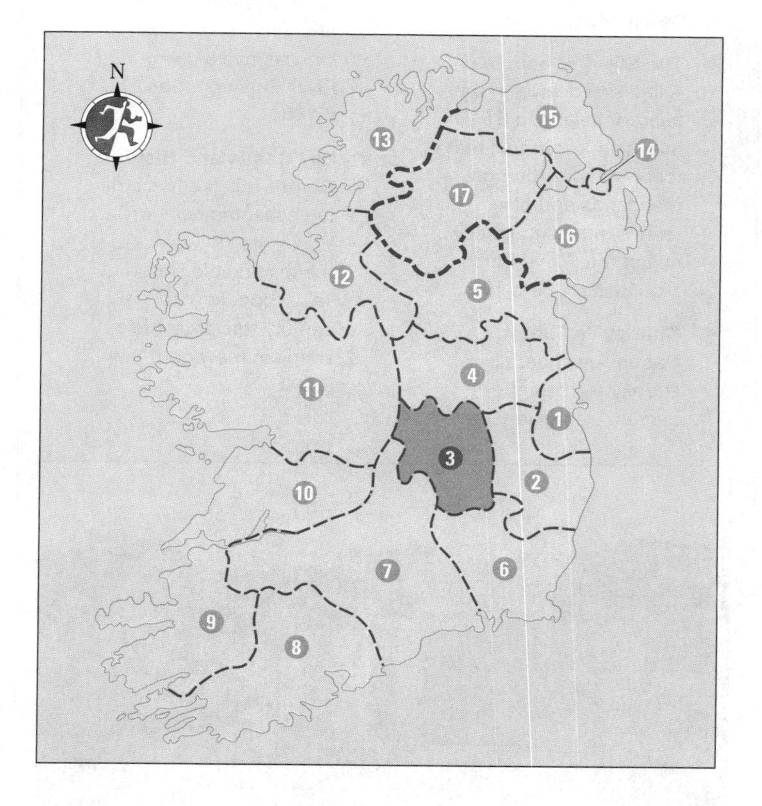

CHAPTER 3 Highlights

* **Morrissey's Bar** Sit with a pint and soak up the atmosphere at this enormous grocer's shop and pub in Abbeyleix, complete with pew seats, a brazier and old adverts for beer and tobacco. See p.180

* **The Slieve Bloom Way** A little-used jewel in the heart of Ireland, a 31-mile signposted trail that follows tracks through moorlands and pine forests in a complete circuit of the Slieve Bloom Mountains. See p.182

* **Charleville Forest Castle** A wonderfully spooky eighteenth-century Georgian-Gothic mansion with castellated turrets, shady trees and clinging ivy. See p.185

* **Clonmacnois** The royal city and burial place of the last king of Ireland, Clonmacnois comprises an impressive complex of churches and high crosses overlooking the River Shannon. See p.186

* **Birr Castle and Historic Centre** Still the home of the eccentric Earls of Rosse, its showpiece is the remarkable Rosse Telescope, for nearly a century the largest telescope in the world. See p.190

3

Laois and Offaly

If you've come to Ireland for the scenery, the wild remote places or the romance of the far west, then the central counties of **Laois and Offaly** probably don't hold a great deal to entice you. But this quiet and unremarkable part of the country between Dublin and the Shannon is an excellent place to get to know another Ireland, one not yet much hyped by the tourist authorities. The gentle, verdant landscape bears the marks of a complex pattern of settlement by the Celtic Church, Viking invaders, the Anglo-Normans and especially the British whose planted settlements in the counties attempted to keep the Pale secure (see p.781). As a result of the Act of Union in 1801 and the subsequent destruction of Ireland's foreign trade, the land has remained untouched by the Industrial Revolution and thus virtually unchanged over the past two hundred years.

Getting around Laois and Offaly is straightforward – the main N7 trunk road and the main rail line to Limerick slice straight through Laois, while the industrial centre of Tullamore makes an obvious transport hub, by both road and rail, for Offaly. There's an increasing number of accommodation possibilities – some comfortable, mid-price hotels and even the odd hostel – but, with the exception of the Celtic monastery at Clonmacnois, the area is only visited by a small number of tourists, and it's wise to plan overnight stops in advance.

County Laois

Laois, or Leix in the more old-fashioned orthography (pronounced "leash"), is one of Ireland's least-visited counties. Most people know it only for the maximum security jail at Portlaoise, or as an ill-defined area you pass through on the way to Limerick. While most Irish counties have a strong identity, Laois seems oddly accidental. To the east it's more or less bordered by the **River Barrow**; to the north, it forms a large part of the **Slieve Bloom** mountain range (though some of that is in County Offaly); but to the west and south, with no distinct geographical features to mark its borders, Laois quietly gives way to its more prominent neighbours Tipperary and Kilkenny. The county smarts from an image problem that's summed up by the adage that its landscape is like the local accent – flat and boring. That unjust reputation seems at last to be fading, as its quiet charms and proximity to Dublin attract a variety of people escaping the pressures of life in the capital.

Some history

Until the mid-sixteenth century, Laois remained under its traditional chiefs, the O'Mores, Fitzpatricks, O'Dempseys and O'Dunnes, and posed an increasing threat to the British in the Pale. In 1556, a new county was carved out of these tribal lands, settled – or "planted", in the terminology of the time – and named Queen's County (to Offaly's King's County). A new town, **Maryborough**, named after Mary Tudor, was established at what is now Portlaoise. None of this pacified the O'Mores, but eventually transplantation succeeded where mere plantation had failed. The troublesome clans of Laois were exiled to County Kerry, and Laois was left free for the colonizers. Because Laois came under British control so early, there are none of the huge estates here that were later dished out by Cromwell and Charles II to loyal followers in the far west. Rather, smaller landholdings and planned towns were interspersed with some settlements of dissenting religious groups – such as the Quakers and French Huguenots. These groups, unlike the Catholic population, which was being persecuted at the time, were able to find the freedom of worship they desired here. All this makes for an intimate – if unspectacular – landscape, reflecting a history of colonialism typical of the former British Empire.

Portlaoise and around

PORTLAOISE is best known for its top-security **jail** and mental hospital – they're both on the same street, known to locals as Nuts 'n' Bolts Road. The prison was founded in 1547, when the O'Mores held the fortress of Dunamase to the south, as a fortification under the name of Fort Protector. The town itself is pretty unremarkable, though it does have a useful **tourist office** situated on James Fintan Lawlor Avenue (Mon–Sat 9.30am–5.30pm; ⓣ0502/21178) offering information on the whole county; it's reached by car by taking the bypass and stopping at the car park beside the new shopping mall, or, more easily, on foot by walking along Main Street and turning right down the small alley beside *Dowling's Cafe*. There's an adequate **hotel**, *O'Loughlin's*, on Main Street (ⓣ0502/21305, ⓔoloughlins@eircom.net; ❷–❻), though it's advisable to continue to Abbeyleix (see p.180) where the accommodation is generally of a higher standard. You'll have no trouble finding somewhere to **eat**, however: possibilities range from the hospitable home cooking and open fires of the *Kitchen* café/restaurant in Hynds Square, a small courtyard off Main Street (ⓣ0502/62075), to the excellent *Kingfisher* Indian restaurant, a little further down Main Street (ⓣ0502/62500), in a fine converted red-brick building that once acted as the town's bank. There are plenty of drinking options: the town boasts 22 pubs in all. You could also head a few miles out of town on the Dublin road to the thatched *Treacy's*, supposedly the oldest family-run pub in Ireland (founded in 1780), which now sits somewhat uncomfortably on an island between a motorway and a main road, but still fulfils its role of serving travellers on the long haul from Dublin to the west.

Around Portlaoise

The most impressive site in the vicinity, physically and historically, is the **Rock of Dunamase**, three miles east on the Stradbally road (N80) – the easiest way

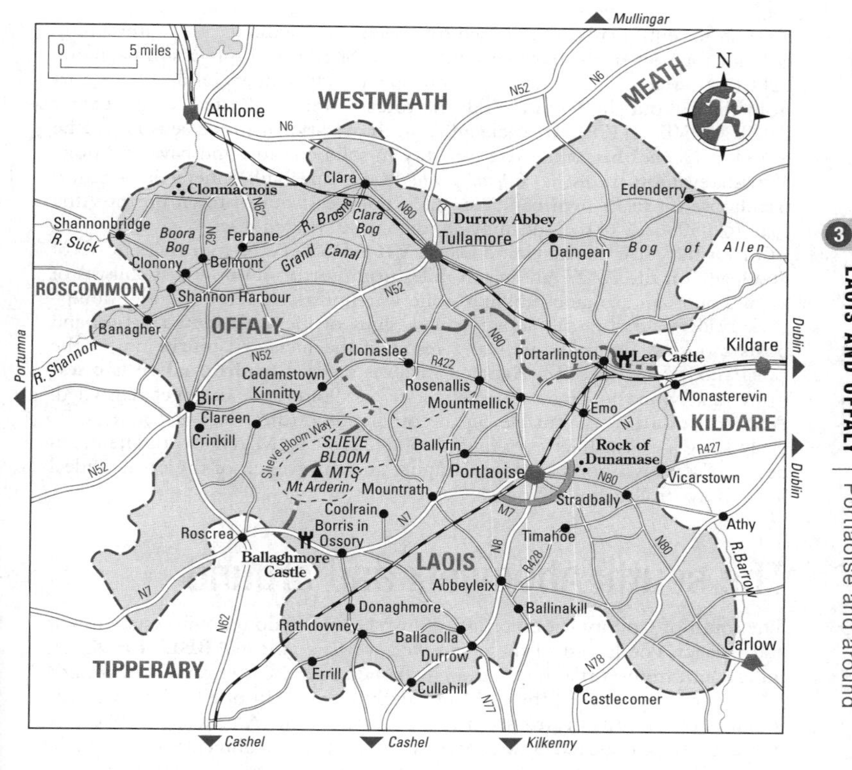

to reach it from Portlaoise is by car; follow the signs from the roundabout at the end of the cobbled Main Street. An extraordinary, knobbly mound encrusted with layer upon layer of fortifications, it's a great place for gazing out, beyond the flat surrounding countryside, to the Slieve Bloom Mountains to the north and the Wicklow Mountains in the east. There are suggestions that Dunamase was known to Ptolemy under the name of Dunum, and to the Celts as Dun Masc. It was valuable enough to be plundered by the Vikings in 845. Today, the hill is crowned by a ruined castle of the twelfth-century King of Leinster, Dermot MacMurrough. He invited Strongbow to Ireland to marry his daughter, Aoife, and included Dunamase in her dowry. The castle was taken back into Gaelic control by the bellicose O'More family at the end of the fourteenth century, though they surrendered their lands to the Cromwellian forces under Charles Cook in 1641. In 1645 Dunamase again fell into Catholic hands for a brief period before its destruction by Cromwell's army in 1650. The earthworks five hundred yards to the east of the fortress are still known as Cromwell's lines.

STRADBALLY (literally "street-town"), three miles southeast of Dunamase, is home to a **narrow-gauge railway** at Stradbally Hall, where a nineteenth-century steam locomotive, formerly used in the Guinness Brewery in Dublin, runs six times a year. The town has a **Steam Museum** (Easter–Oct Mon–Fri 11am–1pm & 2–4pm; €2; ⓣ0502/25444, ⓦwww.irishsteam.ie), renovated and restored by the Irish Steam Preservation Society. Although of particular interest to enthusiasts, the museum's mechanical exhibits are entertaining enough for non-steam buffs too. In August, Stradbally hosts a steam-engine rally that attracts all manner of steam-operated machinery and vintage cars from throughout the country (call the tourist office in Portlaoise for further details ⓣ0502/21178). At weekends a lively traditional music session can be found in *Dunne's* bar, while you can **stay** in solid comfort and have traditional Irish evening meals at *Tullamoy House*, a stone-built nineteenth-century farmhouse set in its own parkland, three miles east out of town on the Athy road (ⓣ05986/27111, ⓔtullamoy@indigo.ie; ❷; March–Oct).

Once a busy halt on the Grand Canal, **VICARSTOWN**, four miles north of Stradbally on the R427 (about ten miles from Portlaoise) now just consists of a few houses and some crumbling stone warehouses clustered round a hump-back bridge, although it's showing new signs of life with rented barges and boats mooring along its quays as a result of the increased tourist use of the canal. *Turley's* bar (aka *The Anchor Inn*) hosts spirited **traditional music** sessions on Monday nights – they start at 9pm and can get crowded. **Accommodation** is available on the other side of the water at *Crean's*, officially known as *The Vicarstown Inn* (ⓣ0502/25189; ❷; March–Sept). The green beside *Turley's* is a good spot for camping and this stretch of the canal is ideal for a lively stroll before dinner.

The south: Abbeyleix and around

The south of County Laois consists of lush farmland, dotted with estate towns and villages. The largest of these and well worth a visit is **ABBEYLEIX**, ten miles south from Portlaoise on the N8, named after a Cistercian abbey founded here by a member of the O'More family in 1183. In one of those periodic bursts of enthusiasm that seem to be a mark of the Ascendancy, Abbeyleix was entirely remodelled by Viscount de Vesci in the eighteenth century and relocated on the coach road away from the old village to the southwest.

Abbeyleix has an excellent **heritage centre** (May–Aug Mon–Fri 9am–5pm, Sat & Sun 1–5pm; €3; ⓣ0502/31653, ⓦwww.laois.local.ie/abbeyleix), housed in the old National School Building just off Main Street, which has exhibits on the town's history and examples of the craft of carpet-weaving that once was an important part of the local economy. Unfortunately, the attractive pedimented eighteenth-century **Abbeyleix House** (just outside town on the Rathdowney road), which was designed by James Wyatt, isn't open to the public, and the gardens are open just two Sundays a year. In the village, the famous **Morrissey's Bar** (ⓣ0502/31281), an enormous grocer's shop and pub combined, probably hasn't changed in fifty years, with pew seats and a brazier and old adverts for beer and tobacco. It's a great place to sit and soak up the atmosphere. Across the road from *Morrissey's* are the **Sensory Gardens** of Dove House Convent. Inside the convent's ivy-clad walls, the gardens provide a sanctuary from the busy street and specially devised walks lead you round striking flowerbeds which exude an intoxicating combination of smells.

Accommodation is plentiful in the area: the friendliest B&B is offered at *Olde Manse* (ⓣ0502/31423; ❷), while next door is the creeper-covered B&B *Preston House* (ⓣ0502/31432; ❷–❻), which boasts good-quality rooms and excellent home cooking in the adjoining restaurant. Just out of town on the main Cork road is the comfortable, though characterless, modern *Manor Hotel* (ⓣ0502/30111, ⓔinfo@abbeyleixmanorhotel.com; ❷–❸), which hosts **traditional music** sessions most Wednesday nights in July and August.

Around Abbeyleix

Two and a half miles southeast of Abbeyleix is **BALLINAKILL**, a pretty Georgian village on a sloping main street, and just north of the town, the gardens of **Heywood House** (daily dawn to dusk; free; phone ahead for guided tours ⓣ0502/33563) are worth a look for their re-creation of a distant Italian idyll. The gardens were drawn up by the English garden designer Gertrude Jekyll and the architecture, complete with gazebos and sunken terraces, is by Sir Edwin Lutyens, architect to the British Empire. The house was burned down early last century but has been fully restored.

DURROW, back on the N8, six miles south of Abbeyleix, is yet another planned estate town, grouped around a green adjoining **Castle Durrow**, built in 1716. It was – its medieval gateway notwithstanding – the first great Palladian house of the area and is now a convent, but you can walk up the drive and see it from the outside. The town was owned by the Duke of Ormond, who had it adopted by County Kilkenny; it took an act of parliament to get it returned to what was then Queen's County in 1834. The *Castle Arms* (ⓣ0502/36117; ❷–❻), facing the green, is one of the few places to **stay** (it also does lunches and dinners), while sturdy **home cooking** can be found at the *Copper Kettle*, two doors up.

The extreme **southwest** corner of County Laois consists of quiet farming land punctuated by small villages such as Cullahill, Rathdowney and Erill, full of neat colour-washed houses. **Cullahill**, four miles southwest of Durrow, and its castle (up the road opposite the *Sportsman Inn*) are of little interest in themselves, but if you walk through the farmyard next to the castle and look at the stone protruding high up on the southern wall, you'll see a fine example of a Sheila-na-Gig (an ancient fertility symbol; see box on p.195). The unassuming village of **BALLACOLLA**, two miles northwest of Durrow, has few sights to speak of but offers some cosy, and reasonably priced accommodation options. Excellent **hostel** accommodation (IHH; ⓣ0502/34032) is available in a converted grain loft on a working farm just outside the village itself; take the right turn at the bottom of the village (R434) to the welcoming, family-friendly farm. Nearby is the *Foxrock Inn* (ⓣ0502/38637, ⓦwww.foxrockinn.com; ❷) a convivial pub with fine B&B accommodation; from the R434 take a right in the middle of the village and from there follow the Foxrock signposts to the small hamlet of Clogh.

DONAGHMORE is little more than three pubs, a Protestant church and a mill. Its **Workhouse and Agricultural Museum** at some distance from the village itself (ⓣ0505/46212) gives some idea of the less picturesque aspects of the area's past. The austere and evocative building functioned as the parish workhouse between 1853 and 1886 and its very size indicates the scale of the problem of rural poverty. Families were frequently broken up on admission and no one was allowed to leave the premises; on average two of the eight hundred inmates died every week, to be buried in the mass grave behind the workhouse. The building's history is continued with a series of documents relating to the Donaghmore Co-operative, which was founded in 1927. Unfortunately, many of them – one of the cases has an order for sandwiches at a hotel in Birr – are of little more than local interest. The museum practises a strenuous self-censorship over the intervening period, during which the buildings were used as a British army barracks, at one stage housing the notorious Black and Tans.

For a glimpse of the other end of the social spectrum you can visit **Ballaghmore Castle** (by appointment only; €5; ⓣ0505/21453) on the Laois/Tipperary border (take the R435 north to where it meets the main N7 road and the castle is on the right, two miles west of the town of Borris-in-Ossory). Formerly guarding the outer reaches of the Fitzpatrick lands, the castle has been single-handedly renovated by the current owner, and it can be rented for weddings, private parties or as accommodation (€1500 per week, €750 for a weekend). As with many of the castles in the area, a Sheila-na-Gig can be found three-quarters of the way up the southern wall.

Slieve Bloom

North Laois is dominated by the **Slieve Bloom Mountains** – Bloom is an anglicized version of Bladhma, the name of a Celtic warrior who once sought refuge in the area – which bring some welcome variation to this flat county. Although the highest point, the Arderin Mountain, in the southern half of the range, only reaches to 1735ft, the range is ruggedly desolate enough to give a taste of real wilderness. The **Slieve Bloom Way**, a little over 31 miles in length, takes you on a complete circuit of the mountains – across moorland, woods and bog, along part of one of the old high roads to Tara and through the bed of a pre-Ice Age river valley. Along the way, dense conifer plantations attempt to survive, way above the natural tree line. If your time is limited and you have a car, the best place to start is probably at the northern end of the range at **Glen Barrow**'s car park (three miles west of Rosenallis). Skirting the mountains, the road from Mountmellick (R422), as it passes through Clonaslee and Cadamstown (strictly speaking in County Offaly), offers easy access to some pleasant walking, particularly at **Cadamstown**. Here a waterfall's icy waters are used for bathing by hardy locals, with the tweely named *My Little Tea and Craft Shop* (actually the front room of a cottage) providing a revitalizing feed afterwards. If you don't have a car, you can catch the Dublin–Portumna **bus** at Birr or Portarlington and start walking at **Kinnitty** (a couple of miles south of Cadamstown) a delightful upland village, which has an excellent **pub**, *The Slieve Bloom*, with a pretty beer garden. A section of the Slieve Bloom Way passes Arderin Mountain, the summit of which offers a breathtaking panorama of the midland counties; the old custom of trekking to the summit in summer has recently been revived so, if you're here on the last Sunday of July, ask around for details. The Slieve Bloom Walking Centre (Ⓣ0509/37299, Ⓔardmorehouse@eircom.net) can also advise on maps, walks and guided tours.

Excellent **accommodation** options in this area include Victorian *Ardmore House*, as you enter Kinnitty (Ⓣ0509/37009; ❷), offering old-fashioned comforts and fine home cooking. Comfortable and stylish, **Kinnitty Castle**, on the road between Kinnitty and Cadamstown (Ⓣ0509/37318, Ⓔkinnittycastle@eircom.net; ❻–❼), is a unique Gothic Revival castle standing in 650 acres of parkland in the Slieve Bloom foothills. If none of the above suits, you may want to base yourself in Birr (see p.190) or you could head for the Slieve Bloom's southeastern foothills. Here, in **COOLRAIN**, *Pine House Farm* (Ⓣ0509/37029; ❶–❷) makes an ideal base for walking, while the *Village Inn* (Ⓣ0502/35216; ❷) is good for traditional music. Alternatively, check in at **Roundwood House** (Ⓣ0502/32120, Ⓔroundwood@eircom.net; ❻; closed Jan), just outside Mountrath, a mid-eighteenth-century Palladian mansion now run as a guesthouse. Built by a Quaker who made his fortune in America, it's a doll's house of a building decorated in vibrantly authentic Georgian colours, with a double-height hall boasting a Chippendale Chinese-style staircase. It's a relaxed, unceremonious sort of place, devoted to the virtues of good food and conversation.

Mountmellick, Portarlington and around

Mountmellick and Portarlington, in the northeast of County Laois, are typical of settlements that grew up independently of the great houses; both were communities of outsiders. **MOUNTMELLICK**, six miles north of Portlaoise on the N80, was founded in the seventeenth century by Quakers. Cultured and prosperous in its heyday – it was home to 27 different industries including brewing, distilling, soap- and glue-making and also iron foundries – Mountmellick now lacks its former elegance. It was also famous for **Mountmellick work**, white-on-white embroidery that used the forms of flowers and plants to create elegant designs. Displays on this, and on the town's Quaker heritage, can be found in the renovated Codd's Mill which now acts as the town's **heritage centre** (daily 9am–5pm; ⓣ0502/24525); take the first right after Market Square to the Portlaoise road, and the heritage centre along with the fine *Old Mill* **restaurant** next door are on the right.

PORTARLINGTON, six miles northeast of Mountmellick along the R423, was founded in 1667 by Sir Henry Bennett, Lord Arlington, and settled by a group of Huguenot refugees in the late seventeenth century. They built elegant Georgian houses with large orchards and gardens, which once grew fruit such as peaches and apricots; particularly fine mansions are to be seen in Patrick Street. Names such as Champ and Le Blanc on the tombstones of St Michael's Church, still known as the French Church, are testimony to the town's heritage. Huguenot menfolk used to sit outside the Tholsel, or Market House, in Market Square, sipping the exotic new beverage, tea, from porcelain cups. A channel was dug to encircle the town, already surrounded on three sides by the River Owenmass, with water. This was to protect the inhabitants from the displaced Irish, who had been forced to relocate to the nearby bogs. Today, the town's heritage is celebrated each July in a French week, complete with snail-eating competition. The **People's Museum** (free) in the Catholic Club on Main Street, has exhibits ranging from 4000-year-old axe-heads to twentieth-century artefacts.

There are few eating options in the town but for a quick **snack** try *Matthews* café on Main Street, which as well as serving good coffee has a fine collection of books and pamphlets relating to local history.

Lea Castle and Emo Court

Set on the banks of the tranquil River Barrow, between Portarlington and Monasterevin, the ivy-clad ruins of **Lea Castle**, with its towered keep and outer walls leading down to the river, are an impressive sight. To reach the castle leave Portarlington on the main Dublin road and once you've passed the turning for Killenard, shown by a sign a mile along on the right, take the next left; to access the castle, walk through the farmyard near the road. Alternatively you can head along a pleasant river walk beginning in the village of Monasterevin, four miles to the east. The castle dates back to the thirteenth century when it was the stronghold of Maurice Fitzgerald, a member of the powerful Anglo-Norman family who controlled this area. In 1315 it was burned by Edward Bruce (brother of King Robert Bruce of Scotland), who had been invited to Ireland by the Irish chieftains to create trouble for the

Anglo-Normans. The castle later provided refuge for Silken Thomas, another Fitzgerald, after he rebelled against Henry VIII, and in 1650, like most castles in the area, it fell foul of Oliver Cromwell's forces after they had taken Dunamase.

One of the few really big estates in County Laois is Neoclassical **Emo Court**; take the R419 from Portarlington (or if approaching from Portlaoise turn off the N7 at New Inn). The estate was designed by James Gandon for Sir Henry Bennett around 1790, although it was not finished until the mid-nineteenth century, by which point Gandon's plans had been somewhat neglected. It's a massive domed building that has been well restored after years of neglect when it was run as a Jesuit seminary. The **house** is now administered by the Office of Public Works and is open for guided tours (mid-June to mid-Sept Mon–Sat 10.30am–5pm, Sun 11am–5.30pm; €2.50; Heritage Card). You can also wander through the extensive **gardens** and **grounds** (dawn to dusk; free). Nearby **Coolbanagher Church** is a modest and graceful building also designed by Gandon, but unfortunately is only open for services.

County Offaly

A low-lying region bounded to the northwest by the meandering Shannon and its flood plain, and in the south by the foothills of the Slieve Bloom range, County Offaly is dominated by its bogs: from Boora, Blackwater and Clara bogs in the west to the Bog of Allen in the northeast, stretching over into County Kildare (see p.170). North Offaly is traversed by the Grand Canal, which connects to both the Shannon and Barrow rivers, and on which you'll find the county town, **Tullamore**. Although only worth a short visit it makes a good starting point for a river trip, as does relaxed **Banagher**, further west on the Shannon. Also on the Shannon's banks, in the far north of the county, lies **Clonmacnois**, one of the most important Celtic monastic sites in Ireland. **Birr**, further south, an elegant Georgian town with a fascinating castle, makes an excellent base for exploring the river's flood plain and indeed the whole of the county.

Tullamore and around

Coming from either direction, from the Bog of Allen to the east or Boora Bog to the west, the bright lights and solid buildings of **TULLAMORE**, astride the Grand Canal, seem welcoming. The town's Victorian ambience makes it feel more English than Irish: the capital was moved from Philipstown – now Daingean – to Tullamore in 1834, following decades in which the British pushed the boundaries of King's County (both county and capital were planted in Mary Tudor's reign and named after her husband, Philip II of Spain) ever further westward. One aspect of its history that Tullamore is attempting to exploit is its whiskey, Tullamore Dew, which was once distilled here, though the factory has since moved to Clonmel (County Tipperary). The story behind the smoothest of Irish whiskeys is celebrated by a painfully dull exhibition which doesn't justify the entrance fee, despite the fact that the price includes a complimentary whiskey. The exhibition is housed in the **heritage centre**, on Bury Quay (May–Sept Mon–Sat 9am–6pm, Sun 10am–5pm; Oct–April Mon–Sat 10am–5pm, Sun noon–5pm; €4.45; ⓣ0506/25015), a fine converted warehouse, which has a pleasant basement bar and café; to get there from the main street, walk down Rahan Road, turn right and head towards the canal.

The main reason for visiting Tullamore, however, is **Charleville Forest Castle** (April–May Sat & Sun 2–5pm; June-Sept Wed–Sun 11am–4pm; Oct–March by appointment; €5; ⓣ0506/21279), an extraordinary Georgian-Gothic mansion built in 1779 to the designs of Francis Johnston. The surrounding estate is wonderfully spooky, with a Gothic element suggestive of a horror movie – castellated turrets, shady trees and clinging ivy – while the house, surrounded by an inner wall topped by urns, is a secretive, eerie place. With its splendid old trees, leafy walks and grotto, you'll find plenty of diversions. To get there, take the Birr road west out of Tullamore (N52), and Charleville's gates are on the right as you leave the town – about ten minutes' walk.

Practicalities

Tullamore's **tourist office** (May–Sept Mon–Sat 9am–6pm, Sun noon–5pm; Oct–April Mon–Sat 10am–5pm, Sun noon–5pm; ⓣ0506/52617) is housed in the heritage centre on Bury Quay. If you want to **stay**, you could try one of the numerous B&Bs in town, such as the comfortable and friendly *Oakfield House*, on Rahan Road (ⓣ0506/21385; ❷), or *High House* (ⓣ0506/51358; ❷), which serves decent food at reasonable prices. More upmarket *Tullamore Court Hotel* (ⓣ0506/46666, ⓦwww.tullamorecourthotel.ie; ❼–❽) offers wholesome meals, while traditional hospitality and hearty cuisine are available at the excellent *Beechlawn Farmhouse* (ⓣ0506/53099; ❶) in Daingean, a little way out of Tullamore along the canal. Cabin cruisers can be rented from Celtic Canal Cruisers (ⓣ0506/21861). **Bike rental** is available from Buckley Cycles (ⓣ0506/52240) on Canal Place near Bury Quay.

Durrow Abbey

Four miles north of Tullamore on the N52, beyond some handsome wrought-iron gates to the left of the road, lies the site of **Durrow Abbey** (daily 9am–1pm; free), one of the monasteries founded by the energetic St Columcille (better known as St Columba), and the place where the Book of Durrow – an illuminated late-seventh-century copy of the Gospels, now exhibited in Trinity College Library, Dublin – was made.

A long avenue leads you to a typically Irish juxtaposition: a grand Georgian mansion next to a medieval church, which stands on the site of the monastery. A notice at the main gates gives directions to the high cross and tombstones, and ahead of you are the well-tended grounds of the house. Within the disused churchyard is a rather eerie atmosphere: the masonry is strangled with ivy, and gravestones lean crazily on uneven ground.

Along the Shannon: Clonmacnois to Banagher

Western Offaly is dominated by a boggy landscape and the **Shannon**, the first virtually impassable, the other for centuries a means of transportation and communication. Exploring the *eskers* (raised paths above the bog) of this drowsy, bog and water landscape has a quiet appeal if you hit good weather. Equally appealing, and increasingly popular, are boat trips, following the gentle flow of the meandering Shannon downstream to Clonmacnois, Banagher and further west to the sea. It's excellent **cycling** country too with intriguing ruins dotting the landscape and roads that have for centuries been the only passages through the bog.

Although the remarkable monastery at **Clonmacnois**, in the northwest of the county, has made it onto the bus-tour itinerary, visitors generally climb straight back on board and head for the west. The area remains for the most part pleasantly unfashionable and untouristy. That said, there's an increasing range and number of places to **stay** in the area as the Shannon-based tourist industry expands, the best being located in the relaxed Georgian town of **Banagher**, which sits on the banks of the river.

Clonmacnois

Of all the ancient sites along the Shannon, **Clonmacnois**, early Celtic Ireland's foremost monastery, in the northwest of Offaly, is by far the most important. Approaching from Shannonbridge to the south, the first evidence of its whereabouts is a stone wall leaning precariously towards the Shannon. This is actually a remnant of a thirteenth-century Norman castle, built to protect the river crossing, and has nothing whatsoever to do with the monastery.

The **monastic complex** (daily: end of May to mid-Sept 9am–7pm; mid-Sept to end of May 10am–6pm; €4.40; Heritage Card) – a huddle of wind- and rain-swept remains on an open plain on a bend of the Shannon – can feel swamped at times by the volume of tourist traffic being processed by the new visitor centre. It's advisable to stay nearby and visit the complex in the evening, when it's less busy and the site is at its most tranquil. Clonmacnois was not just a monastery, but a **royal city** and burial place for the kings of Connacht and Tara, including the last High King of Ireland, Rory O'Conor, who was buried here in 1198. It stood at what was then the junction of *Escir Riada*, the great road from Dublin to the west, and the Shannon, and – as the bookshrines, croziers and other richly decorated artefacts on show in the National Museum in Dublin testify – it was also an artistic centre of the highest order. The twelfth-century Book of the Dun Cow, now in the Royal Irish Academy Library in Dublin, is only one of many treasures made here. Founded by **St Kieran** around 548, the monastery was largely protected by its isolation: surrounded by bog, Clonmacnois could only be reached by boat or by the road that ran along the *eskers*. It withstood Irish, Viking and Norman attacks, but in 1552 the English garrison at Athlone looted the monastery and left it beyond recovery. However, plenty remains: a cathedral, eight churches, two round towers, high crosses, grave slabs and a thirteenth-century ring fort.

Clonmacnois is still a pilgrimage site – St Kieran's festival is in September – and the video is a rather romantic hagiography, detailing the saint's peregrinations through ancient Ireland before he settled at Clonmacnois.

More important is the **exhibition**: all the site's carved crosses – it has the richest collection in Ireland – have been moved inside to protect them from County Offaly's incessant wind and rain. The early-tenth-century **Great Cross**, over 12ft high, is unusual in that it includes a secular scene representing the monastery's foundation and scenes from the Passion; it is believed to commemorate King Flann and Abbot Coman. The **South Cross**, dating from the ninth century, is decorated with flower and animal motifs.

The **cathedral**, scarcely bigger than its gaunt, grey companions, was built in 904 by King Flann and Abbot Coman Conailleach and rebuilt in the fourteenth century by Tomultach MacDermot; the sandstone pillars of the west doorway may have been incorporated from the earlier church.

To the right of the cathedral is the small church **Teampall Doolin** (*teampall* derives from the Irish word for "church") which carries the elaborate coat of arms of Edmund Dowling of Clondarane, who restored the building in 1689. The adjacent **Teampall Hurpan** was actually added in its entirety in the seventeenth century. **Teampall Kieran**, on the other side of the cathedral, is the reputed burial place of the founding saint, as well as where he allegedly built the site's first church; the ruined **Teampall Kelly** probably dates from the twelfth century.

Away from the main group of buildings is **O'Rourke's Tower**, a round tower 60ft high, erected just after the cathedral and blasted by lightning in 1134. On the outer boundary of the site, by the Shannon, are **Teampall Finghin**, with another round tower, dating from 1124, and **Teampall Connor**, which was founded early in the eleventh century by Cathal O'Connor and used as a parish church from around 1790.

The **Church of the Nunnery**, away from the main enclosure, is signposted but difficult to find, and most people lose heart before they reach it. Follow the path across the site and bear left along the lane and you'll find the church a little further along on the right, complete with two lovely Romanesque arches in a field by the Shannon, exuding a feeling of peace. If your arrival at Clonmacnois does happen to coincide with a bus party, this is certainly the place to come.

Practicalities

Next to the monastery is the Clonmacnois **tourist office** (daily: May, Aug & Sept 10am–5.30pm; June & July 9am–7pm; ⓣ0906/74134). For comfortable B&B **accommodation** and a friendly reception try *Kajon House* (ⓣ0905/74191; ❷), which has en-suite rooms and can be found a mile from Clonmacnois on the Shannonbridge Road. Nearby a picturesque whitewashed nineteenth-century **cottage**, with red windows and a peat roof, has been restored and can be rented (ⓣ0905/74149; ❷). To reach the **camping** spot nearby, take the winding road from the monastery (follow signs for the Transport Museum), where, near Clonfalough Church, you'll find the tranquil *Glebe Camping Park* (ⓣ0902/30277; Easter to mid-Oct). The admission fee to the complex includes an audio-visual presentation and a guided tour, as well as access to the interpretive centre, exhibition and coffee shop.

The **boats** you'll see moored at Clonmacnois, incidentally, are all private; to rent a craft, you'll have to go downstream to Banagher or Athlone. About five miles east of Clonmacnois, just off the main N62 Athlone–Roscrea road, the An Dún **Transport and Heritage Museum** (May–Sept daily 10am–5.30pm; €4; ⓣ0902/30106) has a small collection of lovingly tended vintage cars, plus agricultural vehicles and an odd assortment of butter churns, televisions and typewriters. There's also a pleasant coffee shop.

Shannonbridge and around

From Clonmacnois, the road south skirts the Boora Bog to the tiny village of **SHANNONBRIDGE.** This is the point where counties Offaly, Roscommon and Galway meet and the River Suck joins the Shannon: hence the strategically placed and massive artillery fortification dating from Napoleonic times. There are a couple of **B&Bs** here, including *Racha House*, right in the middle of the village (ⓣ0905/74249; ❷), and *Laurel Lodge* (ⓣ0905/74189; ❷), a mile out of town towards Banagher, both of which rent out bikes and boats. For food, try the *Bog Oak* restaurant (ⓣ0905/74224) or the *Shannonside Diner* which does snacks and light **meals**; there's a music **pub** – *Killeen's Tavern* – on the main street.

Just outside the town on the Tullamore road (R357), at the Irish Peat Board (Bord na Mona)'s Blackwater power-generating plant, is the **Clonmacnois and West Offaly Railway**, which will take you on a five-mile circular tour on narrow gauge through the Blackwater Bog. Unlike Clara Bog (see opposite), Blackwater Bog is being exploited hell-for-leather; you can't miss the power station with its thin chimneys belching brown smoke into the air. The irony of touring the bog under the auspices of the organization that's itself helping to destroy it won't be lost on anyone. The tour, which lasts some 45 minutes, leaves every hour on the hour (April–Oct daily 10am–5pm; Nov–March by request only; €5.50; ⓣ0905/74114, ⓦwww.bnm.ie) and is preceded by a 35-minute video on the flora and fauna you're about to see.

Also nearby, just south of Shannonbridge, and of particular interest if you have children to entertain, is the **Ashbrook Open Farm and Agricultural Museum** (April–Sept daily 10am–7pm; €3), with plenty of farm animals, donkeys, rare birds and farm implements. Five miles further south (take the R357 and turn at Clonony), **Shannon Harbour** is where the River Brosna and the Grand Canal meet the Shannon after their journey right across Ireland: at the junction, the entire landscape seems to become water. **Clonony Castle**, two miles further inland, is a ruined sixteenth-century tower house with a nineteenth-century reconstructed barn – to the side of which are buried Anne Boleyn's sisters, Elizabeth and Mary.

Banagher and around

Another couple of miles downstream from Shannon Harbour, **BANAGHER** consists of one long street sloping down to the Shannon, fortified on the Connacht side by a Martello tower. Since the construction of a marina, the town has turned itself into a relaxed and elegant tourist centre and is a great place from which to explore the river and surrounding area. In 1841 Anthony Trollope was sent here as a Post Office surveyor, and it was also where he wrote his first book, *The Macdermots of Ballycloran*. Charlotte Brontë spent her honeymoon in Banagher. Two houses on the main street are worth note for their wayward local variant on Classical architecture: pepper-pot towers, inside which everything curves – doors, fanlights, pediments, the lot.

Cloghan Castle, two miles from Banagher and signposted from the centre, is a massive Norman tower house with Georgian additions, inside an equally massive enclosure (by appointment only; group tours €25; ⓣ0509/51650). St Cronan founded a monastery on the site in the seventh century and the castle was continuously inhabited for the next eight hundred years. You can also **stay** here (❸) and eat breakfast – included in the price – in the magnificent dining hall, warmed in winter by a massive fire.

Also signposted from Banagher, is **Victoria Lock**, a local beauty spot, where the Shannon runs into two separate channels. Trollope's biographer, James Pope-Hennessy, found the vegetation "so rich and wild, so tangled and impenetrable", that he was moved to compare it to Jamaica or Dominica. It's certainly a beautiful place; beneath the lock, released from artificial constraints, the river spills over once more across its flood plain.

Practicalities

One of the pepper-pot tower houses, dated around 1760, has been transformed into a first-rate **hostel**, *Crank House* (IHH; ⓣ0509/51458). It also houses a **tourist office** (March–Oct Mon–Fri 9.30am–8pm, Sat & Sun 9.30am–5pm) as well as the regional offices of Crann, an organization dedicated to the preservation of Ireland's woodlands, and a fine **coffee shop** (daily 7am–9pm). There's B&B **accommodation** across the road at the startlingly pink *Old Forge* (ⓣ0509/51504; ❷) and further up the main street near the post office, a comfortable, friendly hotel, *The Brosna Lodge* (ⓣ0509/51350; ❷–❻).

For daytime eating, *The Water's Edge* offers **coffee and snacks** – and a fine view of the pitch-and-putt course on the opposite bank. *Flynn's* on Main Street (ⓣ0509/51312) is a family-run **bar and restaurant** in business since 1914; it serves traditional Irish fare and also sandwiches. *The Vine House* restaurant and music bar (ⓣ0509/51463), close to the river, has a courtyard garden and a reasonably priced menu specializing in seafood. *The Brosna Lodge*'s restaurant, *Snipes*, is good but slightly pricier. There's a handful of **bars** – the *Shannon Hotel*, on the main street, often holds music sessions and there's also a pleasant garden where you can sit outside in good weather; *J.J. Hough's*, on Main Street (ⓣ0509/51893), is a good old "singing pub" where drinkers are openly encouraged to take the mike and there's often traditional music at weekends. You can **rent canoes** from Shannon Adventure Canoeing Holidays (ⓣ0509/51411) and **boats** from Carrick-Craft (ⓣ0509/51189) to cruise up the Shannon: boats range from a Clare Class cruiser, which will sleep up to eight, to much smaller vessels costing €390 for a week that sleep just an intimate couple and a cat. Short cruises on the river are available on Thursdays and Sundays on board the *River Queen*, an enclosed launch with a full bar (ⓣ0509/51112; €8, or €6 per person for groups of over twenty).

Clara Bog

Banagher is a good base for exploring **Clara Bog**, a vast and relatively unspoiled tract of raised bog. Bórd na Móna planned to develop it for industrial-scale peat-cutting and began draining the eastern section in the early 1980s, but in 1987 public pressure resulted in its takeover by the Office of Public Works. The bog features rare species of lichen, moss and the uniquely adapted plants that are able to survive in the intensely acid environment – including, in the hollows and pools, the carnivorous sundews and bladderworts that like to supplement their diet with unwary insects. Check the Banagher tourist office for more information on walks into the bog or the Shannon flood plain.

Birr and around

BIRR is a perfect example of a mid-sized town planned round a great house – in this case, Birr Castle, home of the Parsons family (the town used to be known as Parsonstown), later elevated to the Earls of Rosse. Here, eighteenth-century urban planning has resulted in a truly delightful Georgian town, with wide streets and finely detailed, fan-lit houses. After decades of neglect, the potential of Birr's heritage has been realized, but although it has enjoyed some cosmetic pampering, it still retains the earthy vitality of a busy county town. Birr's claim to be the centre-point of the country is not unwarranted and the town is highly recommended as a base for exploring the county or simply as a stopover to break up a journey south or west. Habitation at Birr dates back to the sixth century, when there was a monastery here; an Anglo-Norman castle was succeeded by an Irish stronghold of the O'Carrolls and then, after the place was granted to Sir Laurence Parsons in 1619, it became an English garrison town. The development of the Georgian town dates from the time of another Laurence, who succeeded to the title Earl of Rosse in 1740 and immediately began to "improve" the town, fired by the architectural enthusiasm he'd gained on his Grand Tour.

The Town

Birr is a heritage town and by far and away its greatest attraction – and fast becoming one of Ireland's – is **Birr Castle and Historic Centre** (March–Oct daily 9am–6pm; Nov–Feb 10am–4pm; €7; Ⓦwww.birrcastle.com), which allows visitors a glimpse into the life and home of one of Ireland's most interesting, intelligent and eccentric families, the Earls of Rosse, who still live here. The greatest attraction on display is the impressive **Rosse Telescope**, built in 1845 by the third earl; it was then, and remained for three-quarters of a century, the largest telescope in the world – a reflector with a diameter of 72in. The instrument was used by the fourth earl to make the first accurate measurement of the surface of the Moon and to catalogue the spiral nebulae. The telescope has been restored and a replica of the six-foot mirror in the mirror box has been installed. At regular intervals visitors can use the telescope, which is the centrepiece of the castle's gardens. The telescope forms the subject base of the **Historic Centre**, housed in the stable block of the Demesne, which also celebrates the scientific achievements of other family members: there is the Lunar Heat Machine invented by the fourth earl, the steam turbine invented by his younger brother Charles and an early darkroom used by the photographer, Mary Rosse, wife of the third earl. This talent for invention had its downside though when a family friend and talented microscopist, Mary Ward, became the first motor fatality in Ireland when she was run over in the grounds by an experimental, steam-powered car.

While the formal gardens boast the largest box hedges in the world, a visit to the **Demesne** is highly recommended. It offers acres of wild-flower meadows with over a thousand species of shrubs and trees from all over the world, punctuated by a large artificial lake and a crystal-clear river spanned by a charming suspension bridge. Visitors are free to explore the Demesne and formal gardens at their leisure until dusk. The centre also has a pleasant **coffee shop** in the courtyard of the stable block.

Practicalities

Birr's **tourist office** is located in Market Square (May–Sept daily 9.30am–5.30pm; Ⓣ0509/20110) and can advise on the town's accommodation. *Spinners Town House* (Ⓣ0509/21673, Ⓦwww.spinners-townhouse.com; ❷) in Castle Street, an elegant **B&B** carved out of old warehouse buildings grouped around an elegant enclosed courtyard, is the best place to stay in town. Accommodation is in fourteen cosy rooms with bare wooden floors, and the rate includes a delicious, cooked breakfast served on warm days in the courtyard. Almost opposite is the modern *Maltings Guest House* (☎0509/21345; ④) a large complex with en-suite rooms. The three-star *Dooly's Hotel* in Emmet Square (☎0509/20032, Ⓦwww.doolyshotel.com; ③–④), is an old coaching inn and is one of the focal points of the town's social life, thanks in no small part to its award-winning restaurant; it also has its very own nightclub, *Melba's*. *Dooly's* is where the Galway Hunt acquired the nickname of the Galway Blazers after a hunt in 1809, when their overenthusiastic celebrations resulted in the gutting of the building by fire.

Spinners Bistro (☎0509/21673), almost opposite the castle entrance, is a quirky place with an eclectic menu featuring good vegetarian options, that changes regularly and always features fresh local ingredients. You'll get sturdy evening **meals** and B&B accommodation at *The Stables*, Oxmantown Mall (☎0509/20263; ②–⑥), and good, if very rich, food is served at *The Thatch* (☎0509/20682), a bar and restaurant three minutes out of town at Crinkill – take the Portumna road from Market Square and it's signposted at the split in the road. The walls of *The Thatch* are hung with some fascinating photographs of the military architecture of the old British army barracks at Birr which were blown up in 1922. An alternative is the *Riverbank Restaurant* (☎0509/21528), a mile from Birr, which overlooks the Little Brosna River and the old stone bridge that will take you over into County Tipperary – again, take the Portumna road from Market Square, but follow the signposts for Portumna itself. There's also a good Chinese restaurant, *Kong Lam* (☎0509/21253), in Bridge Street. As for **pubs**, you'll get a friendly welcome at *Craughwell's*, in Castle Street (just down from *Spinners Town House*), which often has traditional music (Fri) and barbecues; or try *Kelly's* on Green Street, where you can sit outside on the street and watch the world go by.

Around Birr

If you're thinking of doing some **walking**, a mile out on the Roscrea road (N62), is the Slieve Bloom Interpretive Centre (daily 10am–6pm), which offers some rather dry background on the hills' flora and fauna, land use, architecture and legend. It doubles as the Birr Outdoor Education Centre (☎0509/20029), which runs courses in kayaking, wind-surfing, rock climbing and so on. For **horse riding**, ring the Birr Riding Centre (☎0509/20551).

Finally, there's a little excursion for ghostbusters. A few miles southeast of town beyond **Clareen**, as the land rises towards the Slieve Bloom Mountains, the fifteenth-century remains of **Leap Castle** (☎0509/31115) fortify the valley between Leinster and Munster. Before it was destroyed in 1922, it enjoyed the sinister reputation of being the most haunted house in Ireland, and was particularly famous for an unusual, smelly ghost, which was described by both Yeats and his contemporary Oliver St John Gogarty.

Travel details

Trains

Portlaoise to: Cork (9 daily; 2hr); Dublin (8 daily; 1hr); Limerick Junction (13 daily; 1hr).

Tullamore to: Dublin (8 daily; 55min); Galway (5 daily; 1hr 45min).

Buses

Birr to: Athlone (1 daily; 50min); Cork (1 daily; 3hr 30min); Dublin (2 daily; 4hr).

Portlaoise to: Abbeyleix (2 daily; 20min); Dublin (6 daily; 1hr 45min); Durrow (1 daily; 30min).

J.J. Kavanagh
Ⓣ056/31106
Abbeyleix to: Dublin (5 daily; 1hr 30min).
Monasterevin to: Dublin (5 daily; 1 hr 30min).
Mountrath to: Dublin (5 daily; 1hr 30min).
Portlaoise to: Dublin (5 daily; 1hr 45min).

Paddy Kavanagh
Ⓣ0902/74839
Athlone to: Clonmacnois (summer 1 daily; 30min).

Kearns Coaches
Ⓣ0509/22244
Banagher to: Dublin (1 daily; 3hr 30min).
Birr to: Dublin (3 daily Mon, Fri & Sun, 2 daily Tues–Thurs & Sat; 2hr 20min).
Tullamore to: Dublin (2 daily; 1hr 40min).

Meath, Westmeath and Longford

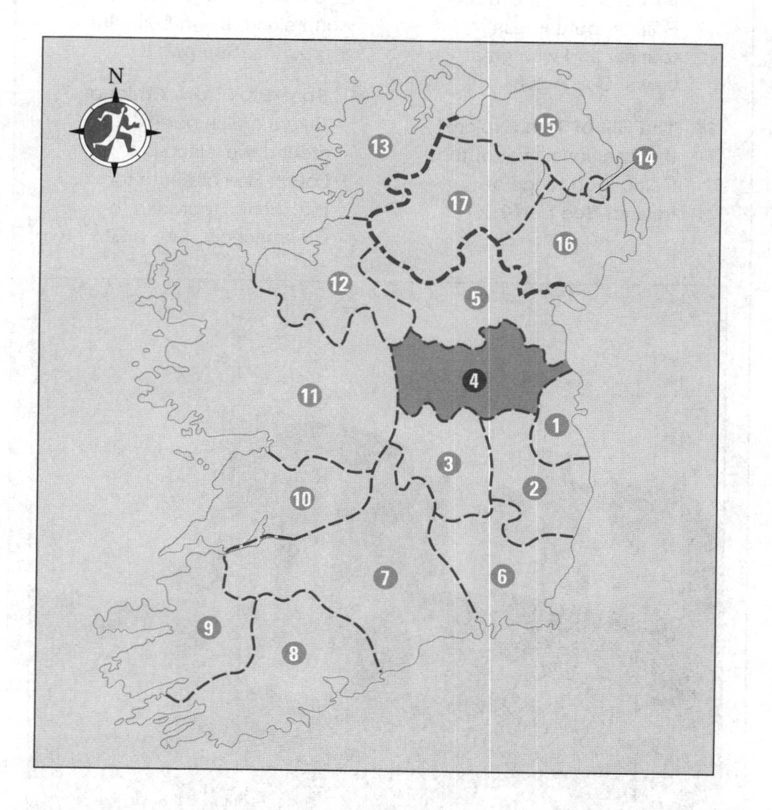

CHAPTER 4 **Highlights**

* **Brú na Bóinne** Don't miss the extraordinary prehistoric passage graves of Newgrange and Knowth. **See p.199**
* **Loughcrew Cairns** These prehistoric mounds are slightly less impressive than Brú na Bóinne, but far less touristy and with great views. **See p.208**
* **The Hill of Tara** Explore the traditional seat of the Celtic High Kings of Ireland. **See p.210**
* **Trim** A historic town boasting the largest Anglo-Norman castle in Ireland, a fine old pub and other medieval remains. **See p.212**
* **Tullynally Castle** One of the grandest and most romantic country houses in Ireland, set in beautiful grounds. **See p.218**
* **Boat-trips from Athlone** Take a cruise north around the islands of Lough Ree or south for the scenic approach to Clonmacnois. **See p.223**

Meath, Westmeath and Longford

Stretching from Dublin and the coast to the heart of Ireland, the counties of **Meath, Westmeath and Longford** epitomize green and rural Ireland, yet provide a total contrast to the west of the country. It's a region neglected by most visitors, whose impression is one of monotonously similar countryside. But if you slow down and target a small area for more detailed exploration, you'll discover far more. In the east there's a wealth of remains of an exceptionally long, rich history, including the great **ritual landscapes** flanking the River Boyne. Further west, you're into the lush, **agricultural backbone** of Ireland; it's not spectacular country, but as dense in historical resonance as anywhere else, and largely untouristy, with a slow pace and plain style of living that have a steady charm of their own.

Although it does touch the coast, **County Meath** (*Midhe*, middle) is primarily an inland county, whose exceptionally rich farmland unfurls lazily around its major river, the **Boyne**, and its tributaries. Along these waterways, Meath can boast by far the richest bounty of historical remains in Ireland. This history starts in the Stone Age, with some of the oldest buildings in the world at **Brú na Bóinne** and the **Loughcrew Cairns**, and other important Neolithic remains still being discovered. Celtic Ireland is said to have been ruled from **Tara**, in Meath, and from **Uisneach** in Westmeath, while Christian Ireland has left a wealth of early monastic remains, magnificent tenth-century high crosses, and the celebrated illuminated manuscript known as the Book of Kells. The largest Norman fortress in Ireland can be seen at **Trim**, and later castles

Sheila-na-Gig

Sheila-na-Gig sculptures (the term itself is thought to be a corruption of the Irish *síla na gcíoch*, "Sheila of the teats") are nude female figures, generally represented face on with their legs splayed and hands placed behind the thighs, the fingers opening a grossly oversized vulva. They were thought to be either the symbol of a fertility cult or used to ward off the evil eye, though quite how they managed the latter is not explained. They mainly appear in the walls (usually near the main entrance door) of castles and churches, built between 1200 and 1600. To a lesser extent they are also found in round towers and on standing stones and bridges. They are also known in other parts of the British Isles, and even France, but the majority of them by far are in Ireland.

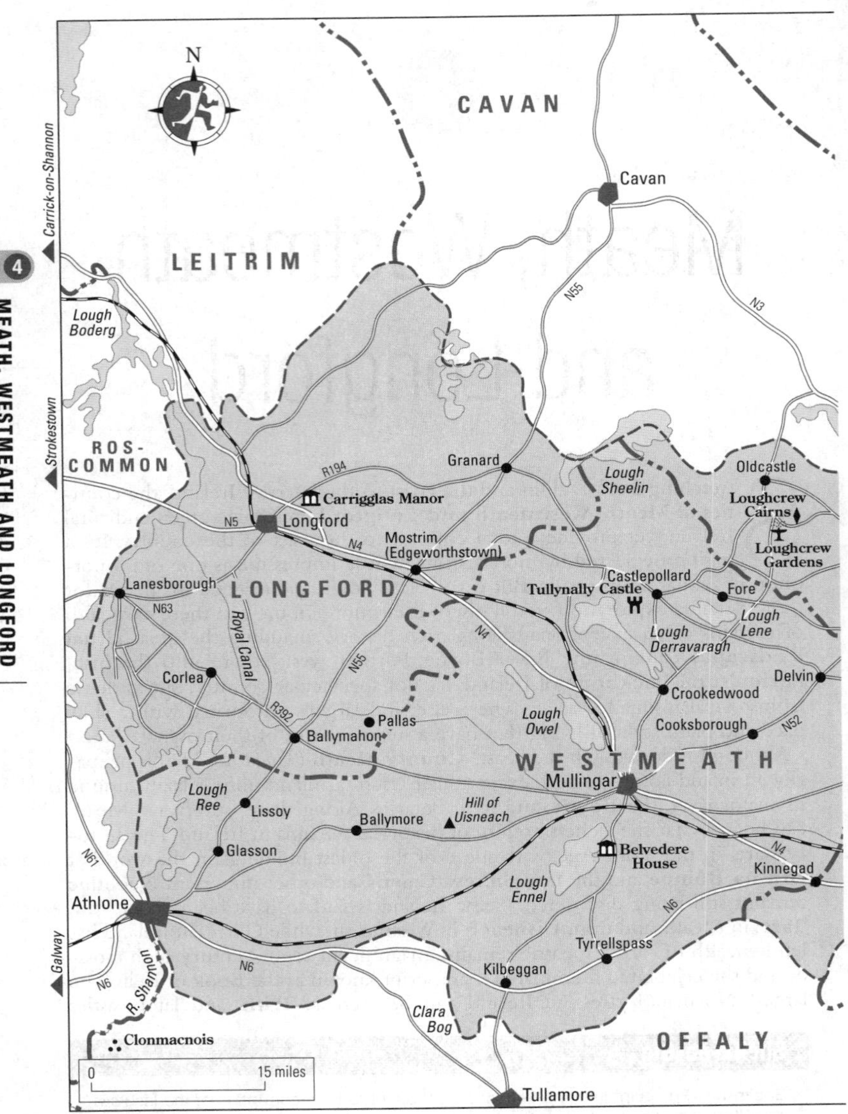

and mansions – from the Plantation period when the county was wholly confiscated and extensively developed – are everywhere, though only a few, notably **Slane Castle**, are open to the public.

County Westmeath is characterized by its lakes – Lough Sheelin, Lough Lene, Lough Derravaragh, Lough Owel and Lough Ennell cut down through its heart – which go a long way to compensate for the falling off in historical

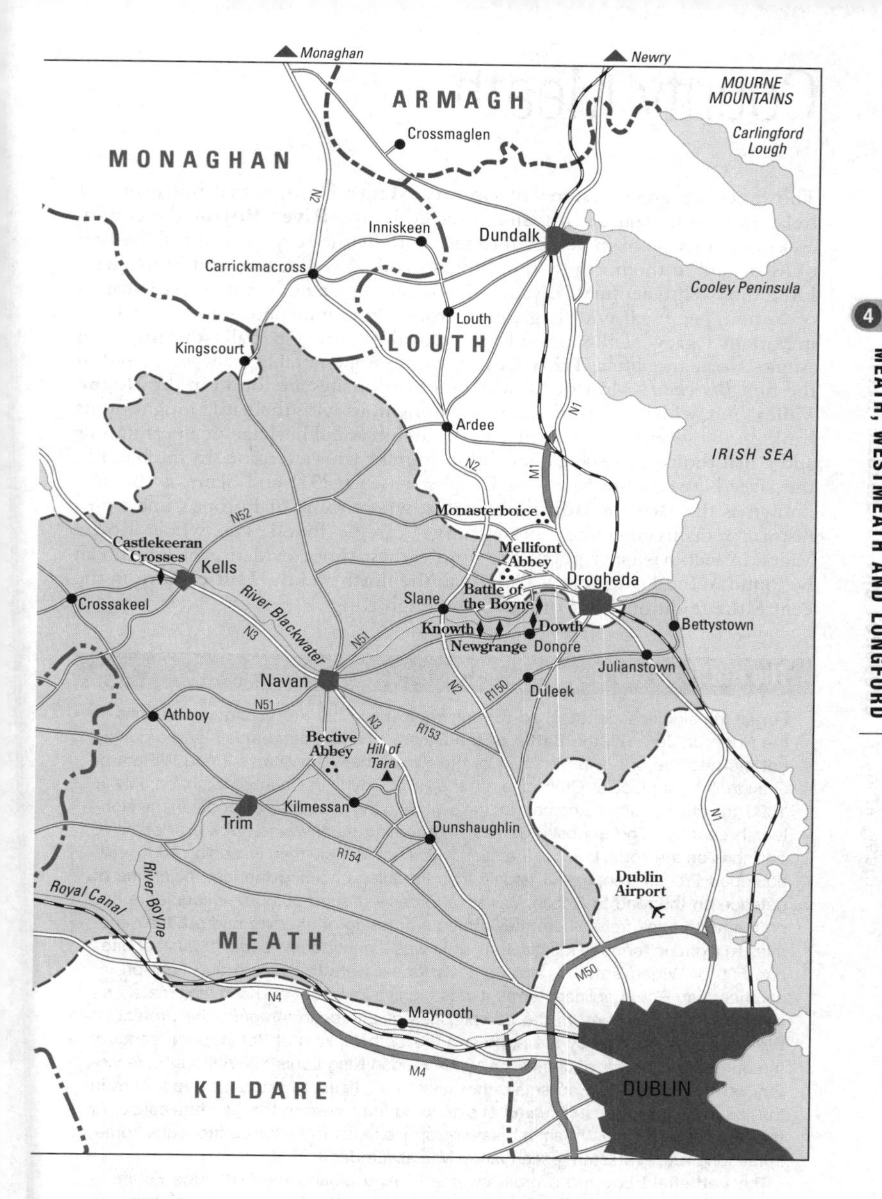

and scenic splendour. In the south it becomes increasingly flat, easing into the bogland of northern Offaly, while in the west the border is defined by Lough Ree and the River Shannon. The Shannon also forms the western border of **County Longford**, which is about all the county has going for it. There's nothing wrong with the place in a dull and placid sort of way, but placid and dull is what it is, and you're unlikely to want to stay long.

County Meath

The sweeping, green pastures of **County Meath** illustrate that this is one of Ireland's richest areas of farmland. Bisected by the **River Boyne**, the county consists of a fertile plain bordered to the south by the Royal Canal and the Bog of Allen, and to the north by the drumlins and lakes of Cavan and Monaghan. From the twelfth century onwards, Meath became one of the most settled areas of Ireland, peppered with large, prosperous farms and solid houses. The most important legacy of this period are its castles, most especially the imposing Anglo-Norman edifice, **Trim Castle**, whose impenetrable walls were used in the film *Braveheart*. Most of Meath's other major sites are found in the **Boyne Valley**, and, while the river's name is synonymous with the battle fought on its banks in the seventeenth century, it's the architectural heritage of a period four and a half thousand years earlier that first grabs your attention. In the bend in the river between the towns of Drogheda (see p.231) and Slane, is the area known as the **Brú na Bóinne** complex, where some of Europe's finest prehistoric remains, including **Newgrange**, can be found. The whole Boyne Valley, in fact, has been populated from earliest times, evidence of which can be found in the **Loughcrew Cairns** in the north and the **Hill of Tara** in the centre, the traditional seat of the Celtic High Kings.

The Battle of the Boyne

For all the significance attached to it now (including big Protestant celebrations in the North on July 12), the **Battle of the Boyne** was just one battle – and arguably not the decisive one – in the "War of the Kings" between James II and William of Orange. It took place at Oldbridge, on the River Boyne in County Meath, on July 1, 1690 (the change of date came with the switch to the Gregorian calendar in the eighteenth century). The deposed James II, retreating southwards, took up defensive positions on the south bank of the river, with some 25,000 men (including 7000 well-equipped French troops, but largely Irish irregulars) holding the last major line of defence on the road to Dublin. William's forces – around 36,000 – occupied a rise on the north bank from where they forced a crossing of the river and put their enemies to flight. In terms of losses, the battle was a minor one – some 1500 Jacobites and 500 of William's men – and James's forces were to regroup and fight on for another year. But in political terms it was highly significant and can legitimately be seen as a turning point. In the complexities of European struggle, the Protestant William was supported by the pope and the Catholic king of Spain, both fearful of the burgeoning power of James's ally, the French King Louis XIV. Although the victory on the battlefield was small, the news gave heart to William's supporters in Europe while making Louis fearful of extending further aid to the Jacobite cause. At the same time, it gave William a breathing space to establish his control back home: in the long run, Protestant ascendancy was assured.

The **battlefield** covered a great swathe of land around the Oldbridge Estate, a couple of miles west of Drogheda on the south bank of the Boyne. Dúchas, the Heritage Service, now runs thirty-minute guided tours of the site (May–Sept daily 10am–6pm; free); to get there, head two miles north from the village of Donore on the south bank, or head west from Drogheda on the N51 and cross the Obelisk Bridge.

There are several **tours** available from Dublin to Meath's main sights and, given the limitations of public transport, they're well worth considering. Try to book a day or two in advance during high season – the tourist offices in Dublin (see p.68) can do this for the operators listed below. Bus Éireann (Ⓣ01/836 6111, Ⓦwww.buseireann.ie) runs excursions from Busáras to Newgrange and the Boyne Valley (mid-Jan to March & Nov to mid-Dec Thurs & Sat; April–Sept Mon–Thurs, Sat & Sun; €20). From the end of March to the end of October, Gray Line (Ⓣ01/676 5377, Ⓦwww.grayline.com) runs half-day tours to Newgrange (Mon, Tues & Sat; €24) and Knowth (Thurs; €22), as well as full-day tours (€38) to Newgrange (Fri). Over the Top Tours (Ⓣ01/838 6128 or freefone reservations only Ⓣ1800/424252, Ⓦwww.overthetoptours.com) operates minibus trips (€25) that are specifically designed to reach the places not covered by the larger tourist coaches, including a daily, full-day tour to the Hill of Tara, the Hill of Slane, Mellifont (see p.237) and Monasterboice (see p.238). Pick-up points for both Gray Line and Over the Top include the tourist office in Suffolk Street.

Brú na Bóinne

Brú na Bóinne comprises an extraordinary landscape of forty or so related prehistoric monuments, tucked in a curve of the river five miles west of Drogheda between the villages of Tullyallen and Slane. The three most important of them, **Dowth**, **Knowth** and **Newgrange**, are what are known as **passage graves** – high round mounds raised over stone burial chambers. They predate the pyramids by several centuries, and although there's no comparison in terms of size or architecture, there are certain parallels. Just as the fertility of the Nile floodplain helped create the great Egyptian culture, so the lands of the River Boyne and its watershed had some of the richest soil in Europe around 3000 BC (along with considerably higher temperatures than today), and what may have been the most advanced Neolithic civilization in Europe flourished here. Physically, the tombs' size and solidity are what impress most; beyond the massive, bare stones there's not much to be seen, but there's plenty of scope to try and disentangle the various theories about these structures, to work out who built them, where the people came from and where they went.

All access to the site is channelled through the **Brú na Bóinne Visitor's Centre** on the southern side of the river, clearly signposted from Drogheda and Slane town centres; if you're coming from Dublin without your own **transport**, catch a suburban train from Pearse Street, Tara Street or Connolly stations to Drogheda, then bus #163, or consider hooking up with a coach tour (see above). The visitor centre is a well-organized place that provides background information on the construction, artwork and religious significance of the tombs and also contains a reconstruction of a passage grave (daily: March, April & Oct 9.30am–5.30pm; May & mid- to end Sept 9am–6.30pm; June to mid-Sept 9am–7pm; Nov–Feb 9.30am–5pm); here too is a Bord Fáilte **tourist office** (same hours; Ⓣ041/988 0305). Tour buses (last tours 1hr 30min before closing) run from the visitor centre to Knowth (closed Nov–April) and Newgrange (year-round); the third site, Dowth, remains closed to the public while lengthy excavations are carried out. A ticket which includes entrance to the visitor centre and a shuttle bus to Newgrange costs €5 while the same for Knowth is €3.80 (both include a 45min guided tour; Heritage Card). Tickets for both Newgrange and

Knowth (plus the visitor centre) cost €8.80; if for some reason you only want to go to the visitor centre, that'll cost you €2.50.

It would be an understatement to say that the visitor centre is controversial and there has been much argument about how best to preserve the tombs. One of the main arguments for building the centre was that, with the increase in numbers visiting the site, a scheme had to be devised to protect it from destruction; however, since its opening and the intense marketing of Brú na Bóinne the amount of visitors has increased enormously, though the number of people allowed to visit the Newgrange tomb is limited to six hundred per day. Consequently, long **delays** for the Newgrange tour are common, especially in high season, a problem further compounded by the fact that you can't book a tour in advance of your arrival. While the sites themselves, especially Newgrange, are extremely impressive, the overcrowding and slight theme-park approach tends to detract somewhat from a true appreciation of their significance. The best advice is to come as early in the day as possible, book a place on one of the tours and, if you have transport, spend the intervening time exploring the surrounding area. If you want to visit a comparable yet unexploited site head north to the Loughcrew Cairns complex (see p.208).

Newgrange

The **Newgrange** tumulus is an artificial mound built between 3500 and 2700 BC, when stone was the only material available for use as tools. The mind boggles at the effort required to transport the building materials, which amounted to 450 giant boulders and over one million sackfuls of small stones – a task believed to have taken forty years. Though evidently important, its purpose remains unclear: a burial place, a cenotaph, a solar temple or a kind of astronomical chart have all been suggested as functions.

To confuse matters, the mound is surrounded by later additions, such as the **Great Circle** of massive standing stones, of which a dozen of the estimated 35 originals remain upright. There is also a series of concrete **slabs** and wooden **stakes**, the former representing the remains of a satellite passage grave which has largely been destroyed over the centuries, the latter marking the centre-point of deep pits whose purpose remains unknown.

The grass-covered mound itself covers about an acre. Around 250ft in diameter and rising gradually to a height of just over 40ft at its centre, it has the look of a grounded, green flying saucer. The white quartz **retaining wall** gives some hint of the power this stone must have had for the builders, since the nearest source is the Wicklow Mountains. The base is girdled by a ring of 97 granite **kerbstones** weighing between four and eight tons apiece. These were quarried in the Mourne Mountains of County Down – it's estimated that it would have taken eighty men four days to drag one from the quarry to the river, from where it was transported by boat to Newgrange.

The most important feature, and one which distinguishes Newgrange from Dowth and Knowth, is the **roof-box** above the entrance, containing a slit through which the light of the rising sun penetrates the tomb on the **winter solstice** (December 21). At 8.58am, the rays start edging their way slowly up the passage, to illuminate the chamber at the far end with an orange glow, which fades away fifteen minutes later. Guided tours feature a speeded-up "re-creation" of this phenomenon, using electric light; there's a nine-year waiting list to witness the real event, though the effect is almost as good a couple of days before or after the solstice.

The **passage** extends for twenty yards into the tumulus (about a quarter of its depth), sloping gently upwards so that the floor of the chamber at the end is the same height off the ground as the roof-box. The **chamber** is roughly cross-shaped with a corbelled roof of huge slabs that stands exactly as it did some five thousand years ago, without renovation or repair. The stones are carved all over with superbly intricate decorations, apparently abstract but perhaps with some more precise meaning (see box below). When the chamber was excavated in 1967 the charred bones of four or five people were found, which some take as proof that only priests and rulers were buried here – others argue that is where bodies were merely laid out before being interred elsewhere (a theory given credence by the discovery of hundreds of cremated remains in other tumuli).

Knowth

Major excavations have been going on at **Knowth** since 1962, but since the mid-1990s about a third of the complex has been opened to the public. Though there's less to see for visitors here, the discoveries have already surpassed what was excavated at Newgrange. At Knowth alone, about 250 decorated stones have been found: over half of all known Irish passage-grave art.

Newgrange – myth and supposition

The name Newgrange derives from "new granary", simply because that was its function at one stage in its history. This hardly seems an adequate description for one of the most important Stone Age sites in Europe, however, and an alternative derivation, "the Cave of Gráinne", is considerably more satisfying, if less accurate. The site has many associations with **myth**. First among these concern the **Tuátha Dé Danann**, the first Irish gods who descended from the sky and inhabited the land before the Celts. Dagda (chief of the gods) gained possession of the mound by making love to Boand (the white cow goddess who later deliberately drowned herself at the source of the Boyne so as to invest the river with her divinity), first tricking Boand's husband Elcmar by sending him on an errand for a day which took him nine months. From their union was born **Oengus**, also called *Mac ind Oc* (The Youthful Son). In ancient literature Newgrange is *Brugh Mac ind Oc*, the Brugh of Oengus. Oengus also appears later in the **Fenian Cycle** as the succourer of Diarmuid and Gráinne, carrying the fatally wounded body of Diarmuid to Newgrange "to put aerial life into him so that he will talk to me every day". Other legends make the local mounds the tombs of the Kings of Tara although radio-carbon dating, pinpointing the third millennium BC, disproves this fairly convincingly.

What does emerge is just how little concrete information there is on the people who created Newgrange. Perhaps the most tempting of the more off-beat **theories** regarding the meaning of the monuments is that of the American Martin Brennan in his book *Stars and Stones* (1983). He claims that the scrollwork, lozenges and lines on the stones, which most archaeologists see as abstract decoration, perhaps with religious significance, are in fact all part of a single incredibly involved **astronomical chart** which includes not only Newgrange itself, but the rest of the Brú na Bóinne complex and even sites as far-flung as Loughcrew (see p.208) and those in the Curlew Mountains in south County Sligo. In his book he claims that the scrollwork all relates to a calibration system based on the diameter of the earth. Brennan insists that the Newgrange monument is not only the largest but also the oldest such system in the world, predating and far outranking in sophistication the instruments of the Greek astronomers. It is not a theory you are likely to find espoused by your guide, but it does have its convincing aspects. In the end, though, you have to ask why, if they were so sophisticated, is this the only evidence that survives?

Several periods of occupation by different cultures have been identified, from the **Neolithic**, when the original passage tombs were built (around 3200 BC), through occupation by the Beaker People (2000–1800 BC) – so-called because of a distinctive beaker left with each of their dead – and a late **Celtic** settlement in the early centuries AD. Early **Christian** occupation has been identified from the eighth to twelfth centuries, bringing a glut of souterrains (underground passages and chambers), followed by **Norman** usage during the twelfth and thirteenth centuries.

The main passage tomb is about twice the size of that at Newgrange – with a tunnel over 100ft long leading to the central chamber – and even more richly decorated. There's also a smaller second passage tomb within the main tumulus, and up to seventeen **satellite tumuli**. Structurally the main mound is similar to the one at Newgrange, with a cruciform chamber, high corbelled roof and richly decorated stones. However, unlike Newgrange, evidence (such as bronze and iron workings) has been found here of settlement around the mound, while the discovery of a circle of large holes suggests that a woodhenge might once have stood here.

Dowth

The **Dowth mound** – roughly 50ft high and 200ft in diameter – was closed for excavation and conservation work at the time of writing, but you can wander about and see the outside. It's reached by taking the first left off the N51 after the Battle of the Boyne site, a minor road which trails the north bank of the river. When you get to the site, the signs of earlier excavations and of pillaging (in the nineteenth century some of the stones were removed for roadmaking) are immediately apparent; there's a crater in the top of the mound and a large chunk burrowed out of the side. Around one hundred kerbstones, perhaps half of which can be seen today, originally marked the edge of the tumulus, and inside are two passage tombs and an early Christian chamber. The passages are similar in construction to those at Newgrange, as is the decoration of the standing stones which form the walls of the passage, and the ten-foot-high corbelled roof. One distinction between the two sites, however, is the sill stones placed across the passage floor and at the entrance to the chamber.

The name Dowth derives from the Irish for "darkness", and the main chamber faces west to the setting sun (the minor chamber looks southwest, directly towards Newgrange). In myth, the site was built when the Druid Bresal, attempting to build a tower that would reach heaven, contracted all the men of Erin for a single day. His sister worked a spell so that the sun would not set until the mound was built, but the two then committed incest, destroying the magic and causing the sun to set: thereafter the sister declared "Dubad (darkness) shall be the name of that place forever." Today, as the sun sets at the winter solstice, its rays enter the tomb (at about 3pm), lighting up the tall stone slab at the back and then moving across to illuminate a recess in which is a decorated stone precisely angled to catch this moment, before finally sinking below the horizon.

Slane and around

SLANE village, set on a steep hillside running down to the Boyne a mile or so west of Knowth, is an enchanting little place which packs a surprising amount of interest. The scene is set at the village centre, where four three-storey eighteenth-century houses stand at the four corners of a crossroads, each virtually identical (with arched entrance courtyards to the side) and built of rough-cut grey limestone. The story goes that they were built by four spinster sisters who wanted to keep an eye on one another's comings and goings.

Down by the river, the Georgian theme is continued in the fine **mill**, built in 1766, across the road from which stands a large Gothic gate to **Slane Castle** (mid-May to mid-Aug Mon–Thurs & Sun noon–5pm; €7), whose lands stretch out westwards along the river. The castle, which was built from 1785 onwards but has only recently reopened after an enormous fire in the spring of 1992, is a classically ordered mass of mock battlements and turrets with a neo-Gothic library. The best architects of the day – Wyatt, Johnston and Gandon – were involved in the design, and the grounds were laid out by Capability Brown. Inside, there's a substantial art collection and many mementos of King George IV, who is said to have spent the last years of his life involved in a heady liaison with the Marchioness Conyngham: some claim that this relationship accounts for the exceptionally fast, straight road between Slane and Dublin. Once a year the castle opens its gates to half of young Ireland for massive, open-air rock concerts promoted by the entrepreneurial Henry Conyngham, Lord Mountcharles, who has a warm relationship with Ireland's rock stars – including U2, who recorded *The Joshua Tree* in one of the rooms at Slane.

Walking north from the crossroads, uphill, you can climb to the top of the **Hill of Slane**, where **St Patrick** lit his Paschal Fire at Easter 433, announcing the arrival of Christianity in Ireland. This was in direct defiance of Laoghaire, High King of Tara, who had ordered no fire-making until Tara's own hillside was set alight. Fortunately for St Patrick, Laoghaire was promptly converted, welcoming the new religion throughout the country. The summit commands magnificent views of the whole Boyne Valley. Near the top, the ruined **Friary Church** (1512) and separate college building are worth investigating. The church has a well-preserved **tower**, with a very narrow and steep flight of sixty-odd steps: if you make it up you're rewarded with a broad panorama of the eastern counties, though Slane itself is all but hidden from view. In the graveyard there is a very unusual early Christian tomb with gable-shaped end-slabs. This is supposed to be the final resting place of **St Erc**, one of Laoghaire's attendants who became Patrick's greatest friend and servant, and was later made Bishop of Slane by him.

Practicalities

Comfortable budget **accommodation**, with dorms, private rooms and bike rental, can be found at *Slane Farm Hostel*, which is well signposted both from the village and opposite the castle gates (Ⓣ041/988 4985, Ⓔpaddymacken@eircom.net; ❶). B&B is offered at *Boyne View* (Ⓣ041/982 4121; ❷), one of a row of stone cottages overlooking both the river and the grandiose entrance lodge of the castle. Handily placed in the centre of the village, the stone-fronted *Conyngham Arms Hotel* (Ⓣ041/988 4444, Ⓦwww.conynghamarms.com; ❹) has comfortable rooms and also serves reasonably priced lunches and evening **meals**. Inexpensive though delicious food is also served at *Boyle's Tea Rooms* on Main Street.

The Ledwidge Museum

A mile or so east out of Slane is the **Francis Ledwidge Museum** (April–Sept daily 10am–6pm; Oct–March Mon, Fri, Sat & Sun 10am–3.30pm, but hours may vary – ⓣ041/982 4544; €2.50). This stone-built labourer's cottage was the birthplace, in 1887, of the poet Francis Ledwidge, who died on a battlefield in Flanders on July 31, 1917. His poems were written on a small scale, and the museum reflects this: a modest, almost spartan house with the poetry daintily hung in miniature picture frames. The lines inscribed on a stone plaque outside the cottage were written when Ledwidge heard of the death of his Irish poet friend Thomas MacDonagh, who was executed by the British for his involvement with the Easter Rising of 1916 – it's an echo of MacDonagh's own poetic translation of Cathal Buidhe's *Mac Giolla Ghunna* (The Yellow Bittern):

He shall not hear the bittern cry
In the wild sky, where he is lain,
Nor voices of the sweeter birds
Above the wailing of the rain.

Duleek

DULEEK, five miles southeast of Slane, is an historic little place founded by St Patrick, who settled St Ciaran here to build the first stone church in Ireland and found a monastic settlement; it was also an early bishopric. The ruined **St Mary's Priory** you see today was probably founded in the twelfth century, and was abandoned after Henry VIII's dissolution of the monasteries: there are some fine tombs in the roofless building, and nearby a squat, tenth-century **high cross**. In the town square is a **wayside cross** of a different nature, erected by Genet de Bathe in 1601 as a memorial to William, one of her husbands, and one of the finest examples of a type of cross that crops up all over Ireland.

Good B&B **accommodation** and home-produced food are available at the historic house of Annesbrook, signposted a short way out of town (closed Oct–March; ⓣ041/982 3293, ⓦwww.annesbrook.com; ❸). William Thackeray in his *Irish Sketchbook* (1842) wrote uninspiringly about Annesbrook, but its most striking asset, the Ionic pedimented portico, has an interesting tale attached. The stately entrance is said to have been hastily affixed onto the box-shaped house for a visit from George IV, the first king to arrive from England after the departure of William and James. The portico was felt to be a necessary addition to bring the house up to the standards expected by royalty. The north wing, housing a Gothic dining room, was also built in the king's honour, but he preferred to dine in the garden.

Navan and around

At **NAVAN** the River Blackwater meets the Boyne. It's an historic crossroads – important in the days when the waterways were the chief means of transport – and also a modern one. The N3 comes up from Dublin, past Tara (see p.210) to follow the course of the Blackwater to Kells and to the Loughcrew Mountains in the northwestern corner of Meath; the N51 arrives from Drogheda and Slane to continue into Westmeath, its interest diminishing rapidly as you go; and to the south you could take the R161 to Bective Abbey and Trim (see p.212).

Although it offers access to a lot of places and has a **tourist office**, centrally placed on Ludlow Street (March–Nov Mon–Sat 9.30am–1pm & 2–5.30pm; ⓣ046/907 3426), Navan itself has little to detain you. There are plenty of

B&Bs in and around the town, should you wish to **stay**, such as the excellent *Athlumney Manor* (Ⓣ046/9071388, Ⓦwww.athlumneymanor.com; ❷), less than a mile out of town on the Duleek road. A good upmarket option is the modern *Newgrange Hotel* on Bridge Street (Ⓣ046/9074100, Ⓦwww.newgrangehotel.ie; ❻, weekend specials available) with a fine **restaurant**, *The Bridge*, serving up dishes like caramelized duck with tomato polenta, and a less formal café. You'll find a good cheap lunch at *Poppy Seed*, on Ludlow Street opposite the tourist office, and more upmarket dinners at *The Loft* on Trimgate Street (Ⓣ046/907 1755), a fun, relaxed place serving salads, seafood and grilled meats, or *Hudson's Bistro* (Ⓣ046/9029231) on Railway Street, which has an eclectic menu with good vegetarian choices. *Ryan's* on Trimgate Street is a smart, spacious **pub** that's very popular on weekday lunchtimes for its soups, panini and wraps.

Athlumney Castle

One local sight worth going out of your way for is **Athlumney Castle**, about a mile's walk from the centre of town – head over the bridge, then turn first right following the signs. Just as you come up to the ruin, veer right into Loreto Convent (once the castle's outbuildings) where you can pick up the keys. The castle, a fifteenth-century tower house to which a Jacobean manor house was added in the early seventeenth century, has four floors in excellent condition, the first of which has a secret chamber down the stairs in the wall. The last occupant of the mansion was Sir Lancelot Dowdall, a Catholic who, on hearing of the defeat of James II, decided to set his home alight rather than see it fall into the hands of William's army. According to the story, he crossed the river and stood all night watching it burn before heading into permanent exile. The interior shows large gaping fireplaces and a horseshoe stone-oven on the bottom floor which would have been the area of the kitchens, and still has many impressive mullioned windows as well as a magnificent oriel window overlooking the modern road.

Kells and around

Following the Blackwater upstream from Navan, the obvious place to make for is **Kells**, ten miles up the N3 Dublin–Cavan road. En route, you'll pass the site of the **Tailteann games** (on the hill above Teltown House), a little over halfway. Here, games and ancient assemblies sacred to the god Lugh took place in the first days of August. As late as the twelfth century the games were still being recorded, and right up to the eighteenth century a smaller celebration took place, in which locals rode their horses across the river for the benefit of the sacred qualities of its waters. Christianity eventually put paid to most of the rituals, but there is still talk of what were known as the **Teltown marriages**, where young couples would join hands through a hole in a wooden door, live together for a year and a day, and then be free to part if they so wished. Today only a few impressions in the soil remain, and certainly if you have visited Tara, or intend doing so, there's little to be gained in stopping here.

Kells

KELLS itself is a place of monastic antiquities but is most famous for what is not here: the magnificent illuminated manuscript known as the **Book of Kells**, now housed in Trinity College, Dublin. The **monastery** was founded by St Columcille in the sixth century, and from about 807 it became the leading Columban monastery in Ireland, when the monks from the original foundation on the Scottish island of Iona fled here from repeated Viking raids. It is probable that the Book of Kells was actually made on Iona and that they brought it with them when they moved. The new home was little safer than the original one and was attacked time and again by Danes and later the Normans: in the twelfth century the monastic order's headquarters moved on to Derry, and by the time of the dissolution there was little left to suppress. Most of what you see in Kells today is eighteenth century or later, though the town's layout still etches out the concentric ridges of the early monastery's plan.

When you arrive, the **heritage centre** on Navan Road (May–Sept Mon–Sat 10am–5.30pm, sometimes closed for lunch 1–2pm, Sun 1.30–6pm; Oct–April Tues–Sat 10am–1pm & 2–5pm, Sun 1.30–6pm; €4) is a good place to start your explorations, located in the old courthouse that was designed by Francis Johnston, architect of Dublin's GPO, in 1801. There's a well-made audio-visual on the history of the town, as well as a facsimile of the Book of Kells and touch screens for accessing its pages on CD-ROM. In front of the heritage centre stands the fine **Market Cross** which used to stand in the central market square. It was said to have been placed there by Jonathan Swift, but was damaged when the school bus driver ran into it and has recently been moved here. One of the more macabre episodes in the history of the original cross was during the 1798 Rebellion when it was used as the gallows from which local rebels were hanged.

Next head for the modern bell tower of **St Columba's Church**, which stands on the site of the monastery and is where most of the relics are to be seen. The **Round Tower** in the churchyard is known to have been here before 1076, for in that year Murchadh Mac Flainn, who was claiming the High Kingship, was murdered within the tower. It's a little under 100ft high, with five windows near the top, and missing only its roof. Near the tower is the **South High Cross**, heavily eroded but still the best and probably the oldest of the crosses in Kells, carved as ever with scenes from the Bible. On the south face appears: Adam and Eve, Cain and Abel, the three children in the fiery furnace, and Daniel in the lions' den. On the left arm of the wheel Abraham is about to sacrifice Isaac, and on the right are St Paul and St Anthony in the desert; at the top is David with his harp and the miracle of the loaves and fishes. There are two other complete crosses in the churchyard, and the stem of a fourth, the **Broken Cross**, behind the church back-entrance. This has several identifiable panels: on the near side, the baptism of Christ, the marriage feast at Cana, David with his harp again, and the presentation in the Temple; on the other side, a self-conscious Adam and Eve, and Noah's Ark.

St Columcille's House, thought to have been an oratory built by the Columban community, can be found just outside the churchyard walls at the north end – coming out of the main gates take a sharp left uphill, but first obtain the keys from Mrs Carpenter at the chocolate-brown house just after the stop sign (or ask the heritage centre to phone ahead). It's a beautifully preserved building – thick-walled and high-roofed – and peculiarly in character with the terrace of nineteenth-century workers' houses alongside which it stands. A modern entrance has been broken in at ground level, when originally the door would have been about eight feet off the ground in the west wall (reached, for security, by a removable ladder); at the top of the building were three tiny attic rooms, reached now by a metal ladder, which were probably where the residents slept and also a hideout in times of trouble.

Practicalities

Kells' **tourist office** is in the heritage centre (same hours and phone number). For accommodation, the *Headfort Arms* **hotel** (ⓣ046/9240063, ⓦwww.headfortarms.com; ❻) at the beginning of the Navan road is a reasonable choice, and there are two very good **B&B** options: *White Gables* (ⓣ046/924 0322, ⓔkelltic@eircom.net; ❷), a cosy house with a garden and excellent breakfasts, right by the heritage centre; and *Boltown House* (ⓣ046/9243605, ⓦwww.hiddenireland.com/boltown; closed Christmas & Jan; ❹), a lovely eighteenth-century farmhouse where fine dinners are served given advance notice, about five miles west off the Oldcastle road. Kells' **hostel** (IHH; ⓣ046/9249995, ⓔhostels@iol.ie; March–Nov; ❶), which has dorms, twins and family rooms, is part of the *Carrick House* pub, at the top of Carrick Street, a steep street of pastel-coloured flat-fronted houses that leads out of the centre of town.

You'll get tasty **food** during the day at *Pebbles*, a café/lunch room at the bottom end of New Market Street. In the evening, choose between *Vanilla Pod* at the *Headfort Arms*, which serves dishes such as wild mushroom risotto in minimalist-chic surroundings; and *The Ground Floor* on Bective Square on the south side of the centre (ⓣ046/924 9688), a relaxing bistro – sister establishment of Navan's *The Loft* – serving salads, seafood and grilled meats. Good **pubs** are surprisingly scarce, but one that's worth a visit is *O'Shaughnessy's* on Market Street (opposite the gates of St Columba's Church), which has a roster of live music including ballads. The song *The Isle of Inishfree* was written here by D. Farley, the former owner who was also once superintendent at Dublin Castle.

The Castlekeeran crosses

From Kells the N3 follows the Blackwater northwest into County Cavan. A considerably more interesting route takes the R163 Oldcastle road (the one that passes alongside the round tower) towards the Loughcrew cairns (see p.208). Only a mile out of Kells a very worthwhile short detour takes you up a winding road to the right that leads, after about another mile, to the **Castlekeeran crosses**. Entry is signposted through the yard of a creamy-orange farmhouse and across a field which will take you into the old monastery enclosure.

Hardly anything of the monastery, known as **Díseart Chiaráin** (Hermitage of Ciaran) has survived, although you can pick out a partially earth-covered

Ogham

Ogham was an early Irish script which was widely used from around the fourth to the seventh century AD, after which it was gradually replaced by Latin script. Even at the height of its popularity ogham co-existed with Latin writing: it was used primarily on stones and monuments, while Latin script was found in manuscripts. It is thought that the script was once used for secret communication, part of a signalling or gesture system for magical or cryptic purposes; it can also be found in parts of Devon, Wales and Scotland. As late as the nineteenth century some isolated peasant communities still used ogham script if they needed to write anything down – it had the advantage that no one from outside would be able to interpret it. On standing stones, the edge is used to help define the characters. Five strokes above the line give you five letters; five below another five letters. Five strokes that cross the line make five more letters and five oblique strokes five more: to these a few less obvious symbols are added to make up the alphabet.

arch. The high crosses here, three of them plus a fourth in the middle of the river, are older than those at Monasterboice and Kells and far simpler, but their greatest charm lies in the fact that you'll probably be quite alone as you contemplate them. The only decoration on the crosses are some fringing patterns and boss protruberances in the "armpits", tops and wheel centres. The story of the cross in the River Blackwater tells how St Columcille was caught red-handed by St Ciaran as he carried the cross off to his own monastery. In his shame he dropped the cross where he stood and fled back to Kells. There is also an early Christian grave slab in the graveyard, and a very good example of an ogham stone (see box on p.207). The inscription here reads *covagni maqi mucoi luguni*, but although the letters can be made out nobody seems to know what these words actually mean.

The Loughcrew Cairns, gardens and Oldcastle

Sliabh Na Cailliighe, the Mountains of the Sorceress, virtually cut off the furthest, northwesterly tip of County Meath, and from the top there's a wonderfully disparate view, with the Cavan lakelands in one direction and the undulating flow of earthy Meath in the other, blending in the far distance into the mountains of Wicklow and Slieve Bloom. Three major groupings of Neolithic cairns, known as the **Loughcrew Cairns**, were constructed on these summits, no doubt chosen to be seen from afar. The first group (coming from the east) is known as the **Patrickstown Cairns** and has been so thoroughly despoiled, largely for building material in the nineteenth century, that no significant trace remains. The other two summits have one major cairn each: **Cairn T on Carnbane East**, the highest point at (910ft), and **Cairn L on Carnbane West**. Each has a handful of satellite mounds, though these represent only a fraction of what must once have been here. The sites are not easy to get to – you'll need your own transport and still face a hefty walk at the end – but they are well worth the effort. Little known as they are, the Loughcrew Cairns are almost as impressive as the Newgrange mounds (certainly when you take into account the sheer number) and you'll almost certainly be free to explore them entirely alone, and with as much time as you want.

The Oldcastle road runs beneath the northern flank of the mountains, and about four and a half miles before Oldcastle you'll see a broken signpost pointing off to the left. Follow this road for a mile and then take the right turn (signposted) that clearly heads towards the hill complex. Cairn T and Cairn L are now administered by Dúchas, the Heritage Service, with **guides** on hand to accompany you inside the former and give you the key to the latter (mid-June to mid-Sept daily 10am–6pm; call ⓣ041/988 0300 about gaining entry out of season; €1.20; Heritage Card). Bring a torch to get the most out of what lies inside.

Carnbane West

On your way to the **Carnbane West** grouping you'll notice **Cairn M** off to your left on a high peak – this hasn't much of interest and it's not really worth the hike. **Cairn L**, with its wide ring of kerbstones, was explored by Martin Brennan in 1980, after years of relative neglect by archaeologists, and it is his astronomical theories which are in part set out below. They are far from being generally accepted, but they do at least attempt to answer some of the questions about the sites.

Cairn L has an asymmetrical chamber with a white **standing stone**, over 6ft high, positioned at the back right. It is probable that the mound was built as a majestic housing for this one special stone. According to Brennan its function is found in the rising sun on two of the cross-quarter days (the days halfway between the solstices and the equinoxes) November 8 and February 4, when a flash of light enters the tomb from the rising sun at about 7.40am and catches the top of the standing stone. If you have a torch, you can study the decorated slab by the basin to the left of the stone, facing away from the entrance; at the bottom, according to Brennan, you can see a pictorial representation of this astronomical event.

Brennan sees **Cairn H** as a warning of the November cross-quarter day. The rising sun begins to penetrate its chamber from mid-October onwards, with the backstone being touched in November, and then from about the third onwards the sun leaves Cairn H and moves on to Cairns M and L for November 8. **Cairn F** kicks off another alignment series. The sun begins to enter in late April, ready to mark another cross-quarter day on May 6, when the rays of the setting sun centre on **Cairn S**. Cairn S is also aligned for the final cross-quarter day, August 8. By August 16 they enter F again, and from there move on to **Cairn I** to warn of the autumn equinox. If Brennan's theories are correct (critics tend to claim that if you look long enough, and pick enough times and days, you can prove almost anything this way), then cairns I, T, F and S form the longest such sequence of alignments known.

Carnbane East

At **Carnbane East** Brennan sees three mounds functioning as solar dials. **Cairn T** deals with the spring and autumn equinoxes (March 23 and Sept 22). In its cruciform chamber is a large backstone liberally patterned with chevrons, ferns, petals and moon and sun signs. At the spring equinox a shaped patch of light passes across various of the designs, to focus on the large radial sun sign in the centre of this stone. At the autumn equinox the sun makes a more leisurely progress, rising at about 7.11am, and striking the backstone just over half an hour later. Once again it crosses the sunwheel emblem. Of the satellite mounds, **Cairn S** is said to mark the cross-quarter days on May 6 and August 8, while **Cairn U** is synchronized with Cairn L to mark November 8 and February 4. Whatever you make of Brennan's theories in the end, he has at least opened an important new area of exploration; and in the undeniable light of Newgrange's connection with the equinox there are few people any more who would contend that these structures were simply tombs and nothing more.

Loughcrew Gardens and Oldcastle

While you're in the area, it's worth visiting **Loughcrew Gardens** (April–Aug daily noon–6pm; Sept–Nov & Jan–March daily noon–4pm; €5; Ⓦwww.loughcrew.com), signposted on the southwestern side of Sliabh Na Cailligh e and three miles south of Oldcastle. These painstakingly restored gardens encompass a seventeenth-century yew walk and nineteenth-century lawns, herbaceous borders, fountains and a grotto, as well as signposted woodland walks. There's a **café** serving teas, coffees and light meals, or you could press on to *The Fincourt* (Ⓣ049/854 1153, Ⓦwww.fincourt.com; ❸) in **OLDCASTLE**, a pleasant, family-run country **pub**, specializing in seafood meals and offering tasteful **accommodation**.

Tara and around

South of Navan on the N3 Dublin road is one of the most famous historic and mythical sites in Ireland, **Tara**, and its eponymous hill. Not far west of the hill, the remains of **Bective Abbey** are beautifully located on the River Boyne and make a pleasant detour on the way to Trim (the R161 from Navan to Trim is just by the abbey).

Tara

TARA, the home of the High Kings of Ireland and source of so many of the great tales, looks nowadays like nothing so much as a neatly kept nine-hole golf course: a gently undulating swath of green marked out by archaeological plaques. Imagining the palace, whose wood-and-wattle structures have entirely disappeared, leaving only scars in the earth, isn't easy. But it's an effort worth making, for this was a great royal residence, already thriving before the Trojan War and still flourishing as late as the tenth century AD. The origins of the site are lost in prehistory, but it probably had a religious significance, gradually growing from the base of a local priest-king to become the ritual seat of the High Kings. Its heyday came in the years following the reign of the legendary Cormac Mac Art in the third century AD, when five great highways converged here, and by the time of the confrontation of St Patrick with King Laoghaire in the fifth century, its power was already declining. The title of High King was not, on the whole, a hereditary one: rather the kings were chosen, or won power, on the battlefield. They were not necessarily local, or even permanently based here, but all evoked the spirit of Tara as the basis of their power.

In later history, there was a minor battle at the site during the 1798 Rebellion, and in 1843 **Daniel O'Connell** held a mass "Monster" meeting – said to have attracted as many as a million people – as part of his campaign against union with Britain.

You'll find the **site** signposted just off the N3; if you want to stay at Tara, there's **B&B** in a modern, non-smoking bungalow with standard and en-suite rooms, at *Seamróg*, right next to the site (ⓣ046/902 5296; May–Sept; ❷). The path to the site leads through the yard of the old Church of Ireland, which is now used as a **visitor centre** (May–Oct 10am–6pm; ⓣ041/988 0300 about admission out of season; €1.90; Heritage Card), with a romantic but reasonably sophisticated audio-visual show that gives some background to Tara's history and also, more valuably, shows a number of aerial views that do a lot to make sense of the design. The most remarkable feature of the church itself is a bright stained-glass window by the well-known Dublin artist Evie Hone, which was installed in 1935 to commemorate the 1500th anniversary of the visit of St Patrick to the site and thus the coming of Christianity to Ireland. St Patrick challenged the then High King at Tara, Laoghaire, by lighting his paschal (Easter) flame on the nearby Hill of Slane in defiance of the holy fire at Tara, thereby demonstrating the ritual sympathies of the new religion with the old. Once you are on top of what is actually very rich pasture, the power of the setting immediately becomes clear, with endless views that take in whole counties, their patchwork fields and a huge sky.

The Banquet Hall, Gráinne's Fort and the Sloping Trenches

The **Banquet Hall** on the northern hill slope consists of two parallel banks between which runs a long sunken corridor, 750ft long and 90ft wide. It's traditionally held to have been a huge hall into which thousands of men from all over Ireland would have thronged on ritual occasions, but this is now known to be fantasy. The actual meaning of the banks, however, remains unclear; they may perhaps have been part of a ceremonial entrance to the site.

Northwest of the Banquet Hall is a smaller group of earthworks, the first of which is **Gráinne's Fort**. Surrounded by a fosse and bank, with a low mound at its centre, this was probably once a burial mound or maybe a house site, and has become associated with the opening of the tragic love tale of the *Pursuit of Diarmuid and Gráinne*. Gráinne was the daughter of Cormac Mac Art, who had arranged to marry her to his aged commander-in-chief, Finn Mac Cool. Instead, she fell in love with Diarmuid, one of Mac Cool's young warriors, and the two of them fled together, relentlessly pursued by the spurned Mac Cool. Their various hiding places lie strewn throughout Ireland, marking practically every geological oddity in the country.

Further west lie the **Sloping Trenches**, created, according to legend, when Cormac Mac Art as a youth in disguise corrected the judgements of the then king, Lugaid MacCon (Mac Art was something of an Irish Solomon figure); in consequence half the house where the false judgements had been given slipped down the hill, creating the sloping trenches. The southern part of the trenches witnessed the murder of the princesses of Tara, some thirty of them, in a massacre whose total casualties were said to have been three thousand, by Dúnlaing, King of Leinster, in 222 AD.

The major mounds

South of the Banquet Hall lies the main group of mounds, the most prominent of which is the fort known as the **Rath of the Synods**, so called because of the various church synods said to have been held here by Ss Patrick, Brendan, Ruadhan and Adamnan, although little archaeological evidence has been found relating to this function. Two gold torques were found here in 1810, but much of the site, which appears to have originally been a ring fort defended by three concentric banks, has been destroyed over the years – partly by the graveyard which encroaches on it, but more especially by a group of British Israelites who early last century rooted around trying to find the Ark of the Covenant. More serious archaeologists have discovered four stages in the rath's construction, starting with a flat-topped mound in the centre known locally as the **King's Chair**. There were timber palisades on the banks, and in the middle a house where five burnt bodies were found, along with Roman artefacts which suggest trading links between Tara and the Romans in Britain or Gaul.

The **Mound of the Hostages** is the most prominent of the mounds and also the most ancient. It contained a passage grave to which entrance is now barred, though you can look in to see the markings on the upright slab at the threshold. About forty Bronze Age cremated burials were found inside, many in large urns which were then inverted over the remains. Eating vessels and knives had been left with them, and an elaborate necklace of amber, jet, bronze and faience was found round the neck of a 15-year-old boy, the only body not cremated. A wealth of goods from the passage-grave culture (carbon-dated 2000 BC) were also discovered, making it the most comprehensive find rescued from any tumulus in Ireland. The mound, once again, is associated with Cormac Mac Art: here he is said to have imprisoned hostages taken from Connacht, who subsequently died within the chamber.

The **Royal Enclosure**, immediately to the south, is a large area surrounded by a bank and ditch, within which are two ringforts, the Royal Seat and Cormac's House. In the centre of Cormac's House is the so-called Stone of

Destiny, a standing stone moved from elsewhere on the site and re-erected here in memory of those who died in 1798. According to one tradition this was the stone used in the inauguration of the High Kings, which would roar three times to signify its approval of the coronation. The final remaining rath on the site is the **Enclosure of King Laoghaire**, who is said to be buried here standing upright and dressed in his armour.

Bective Abbey

West along the minor roads from Tara, **Bective Abbey** is a beautiful example of medieval Cistercian architecture, set in idyllic surroundings by an old bridge over the river. The abbey was once a considerable power in the land, and its abbot held a peer's seat in the English Parliament – one of only fifteen granted to the whole of the Pale. At this time the Church as a whole owned as much as a third of the county of Meath. The buildings you see date from a variety of different periods, sometimes bewilderingly so, but its basics are clearly identifiable.

Of the original abbey, founded in 1146 by Murcha O Maelechlainn, King of Meath, nothing at all survives. In the late twelfth century, the abbey was completely rebuilt, perhaps in time to accept the disinterred body of Hugh de Lacy in 1195 (see below). Of this second abbey you can still see the **chapter house** with its central column, part of the **west range** and fragments of the cruciform **church**. In the fifteenth century, this church was shortened on the west side, and a new, smaller **cloister** erected, of which the south and west sides remain. The **tower** at the entrance over the porch is in excellent shape, and you can also see the layout of the fortified mansion that was built after the abbey's dissolution in 1543.

Trim

Five miles southwest of Bective Abbey, **TRIM** is surprisingly little visited but can boast the remains of the largest Anglo-Norman castle in Ireland, ruins of various abbeys and a host of other medieval remains. The obvious place to start exploring is **Trim Castle** (May–Oct daily 10am–6pm; €3.10 including 45min guided tour of the keep, €1.20 excluding the keep) – used as a location for Mel Gibson's 1995 film *Braveheart* – right in the centre of town and approached either from the riverside walk or via the gate at the end of a modern causeway off Castle Street. The first castle on the site was a motte-and-bailey construction put up by **Hugh de Lacy** in 1173 after he had been granted the lordship of Meath by Henry II. Within a year this was attacked by Rory O'Connor, King of Connacht, and destroyed. A new castle was begun in the late 1190s, too late for Hugh de Lacy who, in the meantime, had been beheaded with an axe by an Irish labourer in Durrow. It was this second attempt that eventually grew to become the finest, and largest, castle in Ireland.

The stronghold became known as King John's Castle after John spent a day or two in Trim in 1210 – though in fact he didn't even lodge there – but it has stronger associations with Richard II, who incarcerated his ward Prince Henry of Lancaster (later Henry IV) here for a time. In look and feel this is very much an English medieval castle, with a 486-yard **curtain wall** enclosing some three acres, ten D-shaped **towers**, various **sally gates** (small openings in the wall for surprise sorties) and, most impressive of all, a massive, square, 70-foot-high **keep** with 11-foot-thick walls. One unusual, and not altogether successful, feature of the keep was the addition of a side chamber on each face (three out of

△ High Cross at Kells, County Meath

four survive); this experiment was not repeated elsewhere as it greatly increased the number of places which could be attacked, and hence which had to be defended. Here, though, it hardly mattered given the solidity of the outer wall. Hardly anything is left inside the keep, but you can make out the outlines of two great halls and, above these, the main bedrooms.

Outside, the curtain wall runs round only three sides of the keep – on the fourth, the deep-running river was relied on as adequate cover. As you walk around, take in especially the **Dublin gate**, with its well-preserved barbican and two drawbridges, and the impressive section of the wall between here and the river, near the end of which is an underground chamber thought to have been used as a **mint** in the fifteenth century.

Across the river

On the opposite bank of the river from the keep stands **Talbot's Castle**, a beautiful three-storey fortified manor house that's still in private hands (admission is possible on certain days in June, July & Sept – call ☎046/9431213 for details). It was built in 1415 by the Lord Lieutenant of Ireland, Sir John Talbot, on the site of an Augustinian abbey, St Mary's; remains of the earlier building are incorporated into the lower floors of the castle. Queen Elizabeth I formulated a plan to convert it into Ireland's first university, but instead it was established as a Latin school whose most famous scholar was Arthur Wesley, later (having changed his name to Wellesley) the Duke of Wellington. Wellington entered parliament as MP for Trim and, despite his contempt for his Irish roots, was responsible as prime minister for passing the Act of Catholic Emancipation. Behind Talbot's Castle rises the **Yellow Steeple**, the belfry of St Mary's Abbey destroyed by Cromwell's attack in 1642 and so called because of the glint of its ruined stones in the sunset, and nearby is **Sheep Gate**, the only remaining piece of the fourteenth-century town walls.

Also on this side of the river, but about a mile east of town on Lackanash Road, off the Dublin road, are the ruins of thirteenth-century **SS Peter & Paul Cathedral**. The cathedral, which was the largest Gothic church in Ireland, burned down over five hundred years ago, but its remains preserve a surprising amount that is worth seeing, especially in the nave and chancel. The wall of the attached Augustinian priory acts as a soundpost to create a natural echo that is eerily brilliant in its clarity and closeness, and nearby in the cemetery, look out for the famous sixteenth-century tomb of the **Jealous Man and Woman**, Sir Lucas Dillon and his wife Lady Jane Bathe, their effigies separated by a sword (Lady Jane is said to have had an affair with her husband's brother). The rusty pins you'll see left in the stone tresses are thanksgiving offerings for the rainwater caught here that is reckoned to cure warts.

Just across the river is the **Hospital of St John the Baptist**, another fine thirteenth-century ruin. It was run by the so-called Crutched (or Crossed) Friars, the *Fratres Cruciferi*, whose habits were marked with a cross in recognition of the fact that they had tended the Crusaders. The gorgeous Norman **St Peter's Bridge** between the cathedral and the hospital is reckoned to be the second oldest bridge in Ireland, but at this stage in your wanderings, it's probably more rewarding to know that *Marcy Regan's*, at the north end of the bridge, claims to be the **second oldest pub** in the land.

Practicalities

Buses stop on Haggart Street outside Tobin's newsagents on the north side of the river. The seasonal **tourist office** is currently looking for new premises in the centre of town (June–Sept 10am–1pm & 2–5.30pm; ⓣ046/9437111). The **heritage centre** on Mill Street (Mon–Wed, Fri & Sat 10am–5pm, Sun noon–5.30pm; €3.20; ⓣ046/9437227) houses an informative audio-visual display, *The Power and the Glory*, on the town's medieval history and a crafts shop, and can help with tourist information off season.

For **B&B** accommodation try *Crannmor House* (ⓣ046/9431635, ⓦwww.crannmor.com; ❷), a solid Georgian country house with fine gardens, a mile north of town on the Dunderry road. A more upmarket option is the attractively renovated early-eighteenth-century *Highfield House* on Maudlins Road, just off the Dublin road (ⓣ046/9436386, ⓔhighfieldhouse@eircom.net; ❸), with fine views of Trim Castle. The town's **hostel**, *Bridge House* (IHH; ⓣ046/9431848, ⓔsilversue@eircom.net), is off Bridge Street and apart from communal accommodation has a couple of good-value private rooms (❶). When it comes to **eating**, you can get sandwiches and light meals from the *Salad Bowl Delicatessen* on Market Street, bar food at *Brogan's* on the High Street, or fancier cuisine from *Franzini O'Brien's*, an excellent café-bar on French Lane, off Market Street.

Counties Westmeath and Longford

Heading west, as you leave the Boyne valley behind, historical interest diminishes rapidly as you cross into **Westmeath**. Topographically similar to Meath, Westmeath consists of rich pastures used primarily for beef and dairy farming. **Mullingar**, the central town, is a traditional stopover for people on their way west towards Mayo and Sligo. If you wish to spend a night in the county, however, you might be better off journeying on to the historical town of **Athlone**, where the main Galway road meets the River Shannon as it flows through Lough Ree on its long journey south. While Athlone is the centre for cruising the Shannon, the main attractions of Westmeath lie in the lakes in the north of the county, around **Castlepollard**, an area well worth visiting. Although **County Longford** has little to offer in terms of either dramatic scenery or conventional tourist attractions, its rolling, fecund countryside does have a certain modest charm, and the area is beginning to attract young, affluent Dubliners who are buying up and renovating the county's many abandoned cottages (the result of generations of emigration).

Mullingar and around

MULLINGAR, the chief town of Westmeath, is a raucous, wheeling-and-dealing provincial capital, constantly choked with traffic. While it's the centre of a rich cattle-rearing area and its preoccupations are essentially rural,

Mullingar is a far cry from the sleepy towns further west, and you get the impression that this big trading centre has much stronger connections with Dublin to the east. In 1951 Mullingar hosted a traditional music festival which evolved into the annual celebration of Irish music, the **Fleadh Cheoil** (Festival of Music), which only took place once again in the town, in 1963, and now moves from town to town throughout the country. You're unlikely to be bowled over by the beauty of the place, but Mullingar is a good base for exploring the county and a convenient stopover on the journey west.

One of the few points of interest is the **cathedral**, an uninspiring Neoclassical structure whose tapering twin towers, which look like melting candles, are visible from the south of town. Inside, behind the side altars of St Patrick and St Anne, are two well-known mosaics by the Russian artist Boris Anrep. To get into the **Ecclesiastical Museum** – whose contents include many wooden penal crosses and the vestments of St Oliver Plunkett – ask the tourist office to arrange a visit with Sister Waldron.

Practicalities

Mullingar is on the main Dublin–Sligo **train** line; **buses** arrive at and depart from beside the *Bacon & Banana Café* on Austin Friars Street to Dublin, Sligo, Athlone and Galway. The **tourist office** occupies Market House on Pearse Street, the westerly continuation of Austin Friars Street (May–Aug Mon–Sat 9am–6pm; Sept–April Mon–Fri 9.30am–1pm & 2–5.30pm; ⓣ044/48650). There's an **Internet café** at *Net Express*, Millmount Road (ⓣ044/49645, ⓦwww.netexpress.ie).

There are plenty of places to **stay** in Mullingar, including *Hilltop* (ⓣ044/48958, ⓦwww.hilltopcountryhouse.com; closed Dec & Jan; ❷), a highly recommended B&B a mile or so northeast of the centre on the Delvin road, and the moderately luxurious *Greville Arms Hotel* on Pearse Street, where they also serve good food (ⓣ044/48563, ⓦwww.grevillearms.com; ❻); a wax effigy of James Joyce stands in the bar, a reminder of a mention of Mullingar somewhere in *Stephen Hero*. If you have transport you could consider travelling about five miles out of town for both accommodation and **food**: *Woodville House* (ⓣ044/43694, ⓦwoodvillehouse.com; ❸) has fine rooms and excellent country cooking – take Lynn Road past the greyhound track and then the first left after O'Brien's garage. Among eating places in town, *Gallery 29* on Oliver Plunkett Street is the best café (closed Sun & Mon), while the bright and welcoming *Oscar's*, opposite at no. 21, is a mostly Italian restaurant with a good local reputation. Congenial **pubs** include *Hughes's*, with live music, mostly traditional, on Wednesday evenings, and *Canton Casey's*, both on Pearse Street; and *Temple Bar* on Mount Street, which has traditional music sessions on Sunday mornings.

Lough Ennell and Belvedere House

Lough Ennell, with its low-lying, rushy shoreline, is not an especially dramatic expanse of water, but it is an easy place to go bathing, boating or fishing, especially if you base yourself at the *Lough Ennell* **campsite** (ⓣ044/48101; April–Sept), which lies three miles out of Mullingar on the Tullamore road, or in any of the **B&Bs** that cluster around the lough – one secluded and rather stately establishment close to the water is *Lynnbury*, two miles out on the Tullamore road (ⓣ044/48432; ❷).

If you do stay here, you'll be well placed for making the short trip to **Belvedere House and Gardens** (May–Aug Mon–Fri 9.30am–6pm, Sat &

Sun 10.30am–7pm; Sept & Oct daily 10.30am–6pm; Nov–April daily 10.30am–4.30pm; €6; Ⓦwww.belvedere-house.ie), on the Tullamore road just before the turning to the campsite. The house was designed by Richard Cassels and built in 1740 by Lord Belfield, the first Earl of Belvedere, as a hunting and fishing villa. Much of Belfield's life seems to have been spent feuding with his younger brothers, George and Arthur. In 1736 he married the 16-year-old Mary Molesworth, but within a few years of building Belvedere House he accused her of having an affair with Arthur, and virtually imprisoned her for 31 years at another of his houses. She was eventually released by her son on his father's death in 1774, still protesting her innocence. Meanwhile Arthur had fled to Yorkshire, but when he returned to Ireland in 1759 the earl sued him for adultery and Arthur, unable to pay, spent the rest of his life in jail. An argument with his other brother was responsible for one of the first sights you'll come across in the gardens south of the house, the **Jealous Wall**. This folly is said to be Ireland's largest purpose-built ruin, and was constructed to block the view of Tudenham House, where George lived, from the earl's own home. Considerable expense went into the construction, including the employment of an Italian architect to design the authentic-looking Gothic facade.

In the **house** itself, the Rococo plasterwork of the drawing- and dining-room ceilings is well worth a look, as is the curved balustrade staircase in the entrance recess. Otherwise, the **gardens** are the main attraction. In front of the house three terraces run down to the lake's shore and, behind, woodland stretches along the northeast shore of Lough Ennell. There's also a walled garden, gazebo, ice house and stables, where there is a **coffee shop** for refreshments.

Kilbeggan

At **KILBEGGAN**, south of Lough Ennell and heavily advertised for miles around, is **Locke's Distillery Museum** (daily: April–Oct 9am–6pm; Nov–March 10am–4pm; €4.20; Ⓦwww.lockesdistillerymuseum.com). The mill-wheel is still working and the entrance fee includes a free sample which certainly enhances the tour. The building is suffused with a tantalizing malty smell and there is a small bar that sells some exceptional *uisce beatha* – the Irish for whiskey – which literally means "the water of life"; try the peaty Connemara single malt for a real treat. The building that looks like a small coal-tip is actually a whiskey warehouse reputedly modelled on a Syrian palace. A pleasant restaurant adjoining the museum serves good food, in front of an open fire in winter. The town is also well known for its **racecourse**, which hosts evening meetings between May and August (Ⓣ0506/32176, Ⓦwww.kilbegganraces.com).

Northern Westmeath

A good portion of the interest of Westmeath lies in the northeast, around the Fore Valley, Lough Lene and Lough Derravaragh. Certainly this is the most beautiful part of the county by some way. It's easily approached from Meath, from the area of Oldcastle and the Loughcrew cairns, or from Mullingar. Coming from Mullingar you'll pass through **CROOKEDWOOD**, near the scenic lower end of **Lough Derravaragh**, set among steep wooded hills that stand out immediately in such flat country. There are two main attractions to detain you here: an excellent restaurant (see overleaf) and a fine church, **St Munna's**. This beautifully restored fifteenth-century tower-fortified church lies a mile and a half up the road to the right of the village pub; fifty yards before is a butterscotch-coloured bungalow on the left, where you can pick up the key. From the church you can spot a motte on the hill slope, behind which is the Georgian house whose rustic cellar contains the superlative **restaurant**, *Crookedwood House* (Tues–Sat evenings & Sun lunch; ⓣ044/72165, ⓦwww.crookedwoodhouse.com; ❻), which is far better than you would normally hope to find in such an obscure location, and which also offers equally impressive **accommodation**.

Castlepollard and Tullynally Castle

Towards the northern end of Lough Derravaragh, **CASTLEPOLLARD** is the most convenient base from which to explore the whole area, a picturesque village with a vast triangular green surrounded by carefully tended eighteenth- and nineteenth-century dwellings. Many visitors come here for the fishing – mainly roach, pike and trout – on Lough Derravaragh. There are a number of **B&Bs**, of which the *Pollard Arms* (ⓣ044/61194; ❸) is probably the most attractive.

The biggest draw in the immediate vicinity is **Tullynally Castle** (gardens May–Aug daily 2–6pm; guided tours of castle mid-June to end July daily 2–6pm; gardens €5, gardens & castle €8), whose entrance can be found half a mile from Castlepollard down the road to Granard (alongside the gable of the *Derravaragh Inn*). From the gatehouse a drive leads across another half-mile of rolling parkland to the castle itself. The home of ten generations of the Anglo-Irish Pakenham family – the Earls of Longford – it's one of the largest and most romantic castles in Ireland, a vast conglomeration of architectural styles (largely Gothic Revival) with four towers and a long stretch of battlements.

The Children of Lir

Throughout Ireland, physically atmospheric places are the setting for ancient tales or myths, and Lough Derravaragh is no exception. In this case the legend is that of the **Children of Lir** (*oidheadh cloinne Lir*), one of the most tragic of all Irish fables.

Lir had married the daughter of Bodb Derg, King of Connacht. Her name was Aebh and she bore him twins, Fionula and Aodh, and then two more children, Fiachra and Conn. Aebh died and Lir then married her sister, Aoife, who very quickly became jealous of Lir's love for her sister's children. She took them to Lough Derravaragh, and with the help of a druid changed them into swans, condemned to spend three hundred years on Derravaragh, another three hundred years on the Sea of Moyle, the waters between Ireland and Scotland, and a final three hundred on Inis Glóire off Erris Head, County Mayo. In a last-minute pang of remorse she granted them one mercy: that they could have human voices and make the most beautiful music for all humans to hear. When Lir learned of what had happened, he was enraged and changed Aoife into an ugly grey vulture. Meanwhile the sons of Bodb Derg, Fergus and Aed, set out to search for the Children of Lir with a host of the *Tuátha Dé Danann*. They eventually found them suffering on the Sea of Moyle, but were helpless to save them from the spell. Left to their destiny the children flew towards Inis Glóire, stopping on the way to search for their father's palace on the plains of Armagh, but finding that only earth mounds remained as they were now six hundred years old. At the end of the allotted span they died, finally returning to a very aged human form for their last few breaths, and were buried at the onset of the Christian era on Inis Glóire.

Three hundred years ago the castle was no more than a tower house set amidst the ancient oakwoods which grow around Lough Derravaragh. The park was first laid out in 1760, very much along the lines you see today, by the first Earl of Longford; his wife founded the family **library** of more than eight thousand volumes which features on the tour. Their son returned from the French wars to greatly expand the castle to the Gothic designs of Francis Johnston, whose work crops up throughout Ireland. The second earl's other claim to fame is to have refused his daughter Kitty's hand in marriage to the young man later to become the Duke of Wellington – they eventually married regardless. One of Kitty's brothers, Edward, fought as Commander-in-Chief of the British Army in America in 1814, and died leading his troops in the attack on New Orleans. His body was sent home pickled in a barrel of rum. In 1840 the third earl added a further 600ft of battlements, a servants' hall for forty and an immense **Victorian kitchen** which also features on the tour. Later Pakenhams have been less militarily inclined than their forebears: one, Charles Pakenham, forsook the army in the nineteenth century to found the Irish Passionist order of priests; and the last Lord Longford was well known in Britain for his liberal writings and involvement in prison reform.

In the castle **grounds**, winding paths lead through the woodland to lakes, walled gardens and follies, including the recently added Chinese garden complete with pagoda and Tibetan water garden of waterfalls and streams. The most rewarding walk of all is a forest path which takes you around the perimeter of the spearhead-shaped demesne, with excellent views back onto the castle. A **café** in the castle courtyard offers teas, coffees and homemade cakes.

The Fore Valley

East of Castlepollard towards the Meath border, the **Fore Valley** is an area of exceptional natural beauty. It's easy hiking country with a wealth of small-scale interest, especially in the **Seven Wonders of Fore**. These supposed "wonders" are all based on quite ordinary things which you can find in the valley, but in this perhaps lies the lasting strength of their reputation. The Seven Wonders are: the water that will not boil; the wood that will not burn; the monastery built on a quaking sod; the mill without a race; the miraculous emplacement of the lintel stone above the door of St Fechin's Church; the water that flows uphill; and the Anchorite's Cell in the Greville-Nugent family vault.

The village of **FORE** sits at the eastern end of the valley and is the best place to start, discovering the wonders as you walk west. You'll need to pop into the *Seven Wonders* **pub** anyway to pick up the key for the Anchorite's Cell, and there's plenty of ready advice in here or in the *Fore Abbey* **coffee shop** for anyone planning to head down the valley. **B&B** is available at *Hounslow House* (Ⓣ044/61144, Ⓔeithnehealyhounslow@mailandnews.com; ❷; closed Nov–March), about half a mile from the village and well signposted.

The Seven Wonders

On the valley plain you'll immediately spot the ruined Benedictine priory built on reclaimed bogland (the third wonder), and en route to it you'll pass the first two. The **wood that will not burn** consists of a dead branch of a tree, now landscaped into a viewing spot; the idea of piercing its bark with coins is also a recent invention. The **well of unboilable water** is handily close by.

The **priory** was founded by the De Lacys around 1200, and its remains are the most substantial reminder of the Benedictine order left in Ireland. It was fortified in the fifteenth century; the towers also served as living quarters. There's a plan in the cloister of the various periods' additions, and some subtly sensitive restoration has been undertaken so that although it's very much a ruin, there's a strong monastic feel to the walls and halls. If you intend to ascend the **tower** at the chancel end, beware that its spiral staircase seems to wind around the diameter of a dinner plate and, above all, that the steps finish in midair; it should certainly not be attempted in poor light.

On the far hillside from here, the lower of the two buildings is the tenth-century **St Fechin's Church**, which marks the site of the original monastery founded in 630 by St Fechin himself, at one time housing over three hundred monks. Note the rare Greek cross on the massive **lintel stone** (which weighs over two tons and was only moved by the miraculous intervention of the saint, hence wonder five), resting on two boulder-sized jambs. From here a ridged path takes you up to the tiny fortified church known as the **Anchorite's Cell** (wonder seven), decoratively hugged by a low-lying, castellated perimeter wall. The most famous hermit who lived here was Patrick Beaglan, who broke his neck trying to climb out of the window in 1616, thereby fulfilling his vow to stay in the cell till his death. The Romanesque doorway leads into a barrel-vaulted, sandstone interior.

The **water that flows uphill** (wonder six) refers to another of St Fechin's miracles; and the river flowing out of Lough Lene up at the head of the valley does look as if it's flowing upwards. The **mill without a race** (wonder four) is signposted two hundred yards downstream from here.

The heart of Ireland: Uisneach to Athlone

As you head west from Mullingar towards Athlone on the R390, you'll approach the middle of Ireland, a spot traditionally identified as the **Hill of Uisneach**. About a mile before Killare (ten miles or so from Mullingar) there are two signposts pointing off the road up to the hill. Follow the second, more westerly one, climb the hill steeply, veering a little to the left, and after crossing a few fields you'll come to the **Catstone** (so called because it resembles the pose of a pouncing cat). More historically known as the *Ail na Mearainn* (the "Stone of Divisions"), it's a massive boulder (now fragmented a little) set into a circular indentation in the hillside. The stone was said to mark the very centre of Ireland and the division of the five provinces of old. A further and longer walk up the slope will bring you to the summit of a flat-topped hill, barely 250ft above the neighbouring land yet able, on a clear day, to command a view of parts of twenty of the thirty-two counties of Ireland.

Here, it is recorded, the palace of **King Tuathal Techtmar** stood in the second century AD, and here some claim that the High Kings of Ireland ruled for the two centuries preceding the arrival of St Patrick in 433 AD, when the seat moved back to Tara. On the hill there are two spurs with traces of earthworks, but these are neither easy to find nor to make out if you do, so it's probably easier to accept the history without evidence. Excavations were made here in the late 1920s, but came up with surprisingly little. No pottery was found, nor any significant trace of permanent occupation. Instead there were great **beds of ashes** which suggested that the place was used for elaborate feasts and ceremonials rather than for defence or peaceful habitation. This accords with the tales of the great pagan festival of *Bealtaine* (Bel's Fire) that was said to be held here in the opening days of the month of May, when vast fires were lit and cattle sacrificed. It was both a religious festival and a market, where traders from the Mediterranean would arrive with their silks and spices in exchange for Irish tools and materials. *Bealtaine*, incidentally, is now the Irish word for the month of May.

Athlone and around

The Hill of Uisneach may be the traditional centre of Ireland, but the busy, thriving town of **ATHLONE** is a more convincing modern contender. Here, east meets west and north meets south at the midpoint of the River Shannon. This position is its greatest asset, with access by boat upstream to the islands and shores of **Lough Ree**, and downstream to the magnificent early Christian site of **Clonmacnois** (see p.186). Details of these cruises, as well as alternative means of transport to Clonmacnois, are given below.

Not surprisingly, perhaps, given its position, Athlone has quite an interesting history attached, and at least one important legend. The name *Áth Luain*, the "Ford of Luan", came from (or may perhaps have inspired) the **Snám Dá Én** ("Swim of Two Birds"), a tale that tells of Estiu, wife of Nár. She had a lover called Buide who used to come and visit her in the form of a bird with his foster-brother Luan. The magic of their song lulled all around to sleep, allowing the lovers to enjoy their trysts undisturbed. Nár, however, questioned a druid about the coming of the birds and on learning the secret he set out for the place on the Shannon (near Clonmacnois) where Buide and Luan could be found and shot both of them with one cast of his sling. Buide was killed instantly, but Luan managed to fly as far north as the ford that marks Athlone today, where he dropped dead from the sky. An alternative derivation of the name comes from the *Táin*, which describes how the remains of the white bull (*Finnbennach*) were deposited throughout the countryside as he died. His loins were left at a place that came to be known as *Áth Luain*, the "Ford of the Loins".

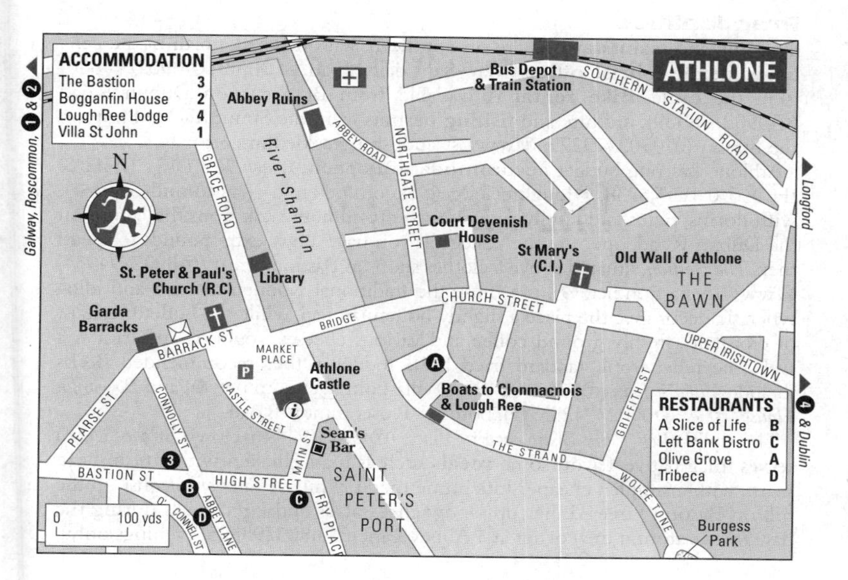

In straight historical terms, this ford on the Shannon has always been strategically important. The first castle was erected in 1129 by Toirdelbach Ó Conchobhair, King of Connacht, and replaced in 1210 by the **Norman castle** which still stands today. It saw action many times, above all in the seventeenth century during the Cromwellian Wars and the Jacobite invasion. The former put a swift end to the predominantly Catholic nature of the town, placing most of the land and political power in the hands of Protestants. The later battles of 1690 and 1691 saw probably the most vicious fighting in the **War of the Kings**, as the Williamites captured first the Leinster part of town and, after 12,000 cannonballs had reduced much of it to rubble, the Connacht side.

The Town

Aside from the castle the few really distinguished old buildings that survive can be found off Church Street in the **Court Devenish** area. Finest of them is **Court Devenish House**, a seventeenth-century Jacobean mansion now resting ruined in private grounds. Nearby the ruins of the likewise seventeenth-century **abbey** offer perhaps the most peaceful spot in town, and there's an intriguing corridor of tombstones leading off the Abbey Road into its graveyard.

The one place really worth visiting, if only briefly, is **Athlone Castle Visitor Centre** on the west bank of the river (May–Sept daily 10am–4.30pm; €4.55). Within the castle's imposing grey walls is a diverse range of displays, including folk and local history collections, with two fine examples of Sheila-na-Gig sculptures (see box on p.195). There are also sections on the sieges of Athlone in 1690 and 1691, on the flora and fauna of the Shannon and on one of the finest lyric tenors ever recorded, **John Count McCormack**. Said to have been born in the Bawn area, the old market quarter up behind Devenish Gate Street, McCormack was rewarded for his work for Catholic charities by being made a Count of the Papal Court in 1928. The display features his own 78rpm gramophone, which travelled all over the world with him so that he could use it to test out the quality of his new releases

Practicalities

The **bus** and **train stations** are on Southern Station Road, north of the centre, while the **tourist office** (May–Sept daily 10am–4.30pm; ⓣ0902/94630) is in the castle. **Bike rental** is available from Buckley's on Dublin Road (ⓣ0902/78989), rod hire and **fishing** permits from the Strand Tackle Shop on the Strand (ⓣ0902/79277, ⓦwww.strandfishingtackle.8m.com).

Athlone has one budget **accommodation** option: *Lough Ree Lodge* (IHH & IHO; ⓣ0902/76738, ⓔloughreelodge@eircom.net; mid-May to mid-Sept; ❶), with dorms, twins and family rooms, a twenty-minute walk from the centre on the Dublin Road, opposite the college. If you have a few extra pounds to spend then *The Bastion*, situated above a clothes shop on Bastion Street (ⓣ0902/94954, ⓦwww.thebastion.net; ❷), is a must: the traditional wooden interior and idiosyncratic decor give the place a slightly bohemian feel, while the buffet breakfast of croissants, freshly ground coffee and various cheeses, yoghurts and fruit is a welcome relief from standard fried B&B fodder. Other recommended B&Bs include *Villa St John* (ⓣ0902/92490, ⓔvillastjohn@eircom.net; ❶) and *Bogganfin House* (ⓣ & ⓕ0902/94255; ❶), both on Roscommon Road.

The stylish *Left Bank Bistro* on Fry Place (ⓣ0902/94446; closed Sun & Mon) serves imaginative, flavoursome **meals** such as roast chicken with Tuscan bean mash, with a simpler, cheaper lunchtime menu, while *A Slice of Life* just up the hill on Bastion Street dishes up sandwiches, salads and light meals during the day. *Tribeca*, around the corner at 1 Abbey Lane (ⓣ0902/98805; evenings only), is a welcoming spot for good, thin-crust pizzas, pasta, burgers and the like. The *Olive Grove* (☎0902/76946) restaurant on the east side of the bridge serves decent Greek and other Mediterranean food at reasonable prices.

The best **pub** is *Sean's Bar*, tucked away behind the castle and easily identified by its four Ionic columns. It claims to be the oldest pub in Ireland and has popular **traditional music** sessions every night except Friday and Saturday, plus Sunday lunchtimes.

Trips to Lough Ree and Clonmacnois

Try to make time for one of the excellent **cruises** along the River Shannon while you're in Athlone. Trips head either south for the scenic approach to **Clonmacnois** (see p.186) via the Shannon Callows, an important bird conservation area noted especially for the corncrakes who spend the summer there (about 4hr 30min round trip, including 1hr 30min at Clonmacnois); or north around the islands of **Lough Ree** (90min). These include Hare Island, site of a Viking encampment which has yielded considerable amounts of treasure, and you may catch a glimpse towards the north of the lake of Inchclearaun, which took its name (*Inis Clothrand*) from Clothru, sister of Medb, the goddess of war and fertility. Legend has it that Medb murdered Clothru so that she could wed and bed her husband Ailill and rule Connacht from the island. Medb's life was to end in the waters by the island when Clothru's son Furbaide hurled a piece of cheese from his sling that entered Medb's forehead and struck her dead while she was bathing, thus avenging the murder of his mother.

Viking Tours (☎0902/73383 or 086/262 1136, Ⓦwww.vikingislandtours.com), which involve sailing in a replica longboat, with Viking costumes for kids to dress up in, are especially enjoyable for families. In summer (roughly May–Sept) they depart from the Strand in front of the Strand Tackle Shop, where tickets can be bought, every day for Lough Ree (€8) and several times a week for Clonmacnois (€14), according to demand. The MV *Ross* (☎0902/72892) operates from the Jolly Mariner Marina on the north side of town and cruises Lough Ree daily from June to August (€8). The same people offer self-drive **live-aboard boats** through Athlone Cruisers Ltd (same phone number; Ⓦwww.iol.ie/wmeathtc/acl) and, in the absence of public buses from Athlone, run a daily summertime **bus to Clonmacnois** and back (€13). The third option for a trip to Clonmacnois would be a **taxi** from Athlone Cabs, Dublin Road (☎0902/74400; €25, including 1hr waiting time).

Goldsmith country

The N55 rushes north from Athlone along the eastern shore of Lough Ree, crossing the Royal Canal into the area known as **Goldsmith country**, which straddles western Westmeath and southern Longford. The area gets its name from its geographical associations with the works of the eighteenth-century poet, playwright and novelist, Oliver Goldsmith (see box overleaf). It's pretty, small-scale countryside, gently rolling and ready-made for cycling through landscaped villages and along aromatic fuschia-lined lanes.

Three miles out of Athlone, **GLASSON** – identified as "Sweet Auburn", the subject of Goldsmith's celebrated anti-enclosure poem *The Deserted Village*, and sometimes spelt "Glassan" – owes its orderly layout of creamy-grey pebbledash cottages to enclosure: it was built by the neighbouring Waterstown estate to provide accommodation for the artisans needed to tend the massive estate with its ten-acre formal garden. The estate was divided by the Land Commission in the 1920s, and the house, designed by the eighteenth-century architect Richard Cassels, was sold for scrap. As you head north along the N55, there's a profusion of brown "Goldsmith country" signs. Only the front and end walls of Goldsmith's childhood home, the parsonage at **Lissoy**, remain, and still less of the school he attended, or of the "busy mill" that may be the one mentioned in the poem; *The Three Jolly Pigeons*, a congenial pub with traditional sessions on Wednesday and Sunday in summer, claims to have the millstone. **Forgney Church**, where Goldsmith's father worked as curate until 1730, was rebuilt in 1810 and is usually locked. Goldsmith's supposed birthplace at **Pallas** has a rather spooky shrine erected by members of the Oliver Goldsmith Society in 1974: a larger-than-life statue of the writer enclosed behind bars in a sort of grotto-prison, as if his poetic spirit is too dangerous to be let out into the world. It's curious to imagine what Goldsmith's mocking soul would have made of such funereal pomposity.

Glasson is the best **place to stay** in Goldsmith country. There's a scattering of B&Bs – try *Benown House* in the village (Ⓣ0902/85406, Ⓦwww.glasson.com; ❷). *Grogan's Pub* is a popular local watering-hole and does fine bar food, while the good, rather elaborate *Village Restaurant* (Ⓣ0902/85001) specializes in seafood. Back down the road towards Athlone you'll find excellent contemporary Irish cooking at the *Wineport Lodge* restaurant on the shores of Lough Ree (Ⓣ0902/85466).

Oliver Goldsmith

Best known for his prose, including the comedy *She Stoops to Conquer* and the novel *The Vicar of Wakefield*, **Oliver Goldsmith** (1728–74), the son of a Church of Ireland parson, was probably born in Pallas, ten miles north of Glasson in County Longford. When he was 2, he and his family moved to the parsonage at Lisson, just a couple of miles north of Glasson. Goldsmith was also active as a poet, and in travelling through this depopulated landscape, his epic anti-enclosure poem, *The Deserted Village*, conjures up the reality of the short-lived heyday of the Anglo-Irish society of which he was a part:

Sweet was the sound, when oft at evening's close
Up yonder hill the village murmur rose;
There, as I passed with careless steps and slow,
The mingling notes came softened from below.

But now the sounds of population fail,
No cheerful murmurs fluctuate in the gale,
No busy steps the grassgrown foot-way tread,
For all the bloomy flush of life is fled.

The poem is a protest against an oppression of the rural poor all over the British Isles, not just Ireland; whether it can really be traced to Glasson village is uncertain, but its mood of nostalgic regret for a golden childhood past undoubtedly gives it some points of contact with the local landscape. The treasure-hunt for locations mentioned in the poem, all signposted and almost all in ruins, can prove oddly evocative of an absent population – removed not by enclosure but by much more recent economic pressures. The poem also points out some of the internal contradictions of the self-confident Georgian building mania: Goldsmith's lament is for a landscape that disappeared with the building of the great Georgian houses – many of which, like Waterstown at Glasson itself, have now disappeared.

A weekend Goldsmith summer school is held in the area in June, when academics gather and discuss his works; details can be obtained from John O'Donnell on Ⓣ086/829 4093 or at Ⓔlinesend@iol.ie.

Longford and around

The town of **LONGFORD** has little of special interest but makes a good base for visiting the county's few attractions. There's a **tourist office** on Dublin Street (July–Sept Mon–Sat 9am–6pm; ⓣ043/46566), and **accommodation** is plentiful, including the recently renovated *Longford Arms* on Main Street (ⓣ043/46296, ⓦwww.*longfordarms.ie*; ❻), which has a leisure centre and does good food in its restaurant and coffee shop. There are also numerous B&Bs, most of them on the Dublin road, such as *Viewmount House* (ⓣ043/41919, ⓔviewmt@iol.ie; ❸), though it may be worth travelling three miles north of town to the hamlet of Newtonforbes to stay in the comfort of Mandy Etherton's *Olde Schoolhouse* (ⓣ043/24854, ⓦwww.inet-sec.com/mandy.htm; ❷). The best **places to eat**, both on Ballymahon Street, are the *Torc Café*, for sophisticated sandwiches, organic pastas and great cakes during the day, and the *Aubergine Gallery Café* (ⓣ043/48633), for contemporary dishes such as aubergine, feta and olive bruschetta in the evening.

Carrigglas Manor

Chief of the surrounding attractions is **Carrigglas Manor** (May–Sept Mon, Tues, Fri & Sat 11am–3pm; €8.80, gardens and costume museum only €5; ⓦwww.carrigglas.com). Situated just three miles northeast of Longford on the R194 towards Granard, it's the seat of the descendants of a Huguenot family, the Lefroys. As you go up the avenue, the stableyards with their classically pedimented and rusticated archways, built by James Gandon in 1790, are on the left. They now house a tearoom and a **costume and lace museum**, whose costumes date mainly from the mid-eighteenth century and were found going mouldy in trunks in the castle.

The castle itself is perhaps best described as Tudor-Gothic Revival, and extremely handsome it is, too. It was built in 1837 by Thomas Lefroy, possibly the model for Darcy in *Pride and Prejudice*, as at one stage he enjoyed a romantic liaison with Jane Austen. The **tour** of the building is directed by the present Lefroys, who have succeeded in restoring the place to a state which reflects its former majesty. It takes in the dining room, with its set of 1825 Waterford glasses and original ironstone china; the drawing room with its Dutch furniture, one cabinet of which contains an original tea and breakfast set of 1799; a fastidiously well-stocked library; and family portraiture on virtually every wall. All this is explained and expanded on in detail by the present occupier.

Corlea Trackway Visitor Centre

It's well worth making an archaeological detour to the **Corlea Trackway Visitor Centre** (April–Sept daily 10am–6pm; €3.10; Heritage Card), nine miles south of Longford on the R392 Mullingar–Lanesborough road. This low, mustard-coloured cruciform building is aligned with a buried *togher*, an Iron Age trackway of oak planks that was discovered by turf cutters in 1985. A twenty-yard stretch of this has been excavated and preserved in an air-conditioned chamber, while the rest still lies beneath the bog. The largest of its kind to have been uncovered in Europe, the road dates from 148 BC, and its evolution and the way of life in the bog is examined in a number of displays, while the guided tour includes a walk outside in the bog and a video of the archaeological dig.

Travel details

Trains

Athlone to: Dublin Heuston (8 daily; 1hr 40min–2hr); Galway (4–5 daily; 1hr 10min); Westport (3 daily; 2hr).
Longford to: Dublin Connolly (4 daily; 2hr); Sligo (3–4 daily; 1hr 30min).
Mullingar to: Dublin Connolly (4 daily; 1hr 15min); Sligo (3–4 daily; 2hr).

Buses

Athlone to: Castlebar (1–4 daily; 1hr 30min); Cork (1–2 daily; 4hr 30min); Drogheda (1–2 daily; 2hr 30min); Dublin (13 daily; 2hr); Dundalk (1–2 daily; 3hr 15min); Galway (9 daily; 1hr 45min); Longford (hourly; 1hr); Mullingar (4 daily; 1hr); Navan (1–2 daily; 2hr); Roscommon (1–4 daily; 35min); Sligo (2–5 daily; 2hr 15min–3hr); Waterford (1–2 daily; 4hr); Westport (1–4 daily; 2hr 45min).
Dublin to: Kells (hourly; 1hr); Longford (10 daily; 2hr 15min); Navan (hourly; 1hr); Slane (5–9 daily; 45min); Trim (15 daily; 1hr 15min).
Mullingar to: Athlone (4 daily; 1hr); Drogheda (1–2 daily; 1hr 40min); Dublin (10 daily; 1hr 30min); Dundalk (1–2 daily; 2hr 15min); Galway (1–2 daily; 3hr); Longford (6–8 daily; 40min); Navan (1–2 daily; 1hr); Sligo (3–4 daily; 2hr 30min).

Louth, Monaghan and Cavan

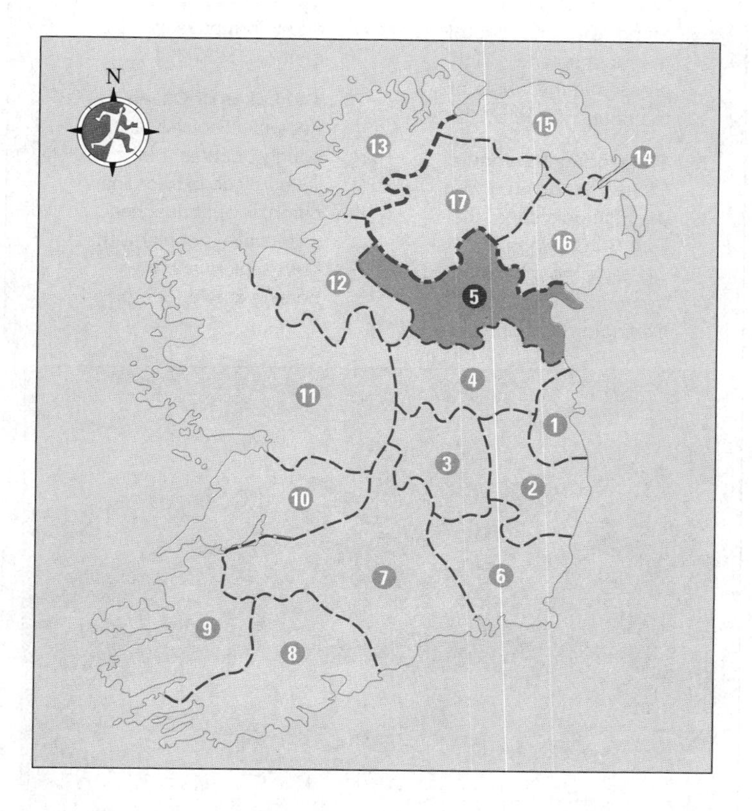

CHAPTER 5 Highlights

* **Drogheda** One of Ireland's liveliest towns, rich in antiquities and with atmospheric bars. **See p.231**

* **Monasterboice** Not only does Monasterboice have Ireland's tallest round tower, but two of the most splendid high crosses in the whole of the country. **See p.238**

* **The Cooley Peninsula** Closely associated with the Irish epic saga, the *Táin Bó Cúailnge*, Cooley's mountains offer tremendous views of Carlingford Lough, while Carlingford itself has some terrific restaurants. **See p.243**

* **Inniskeen** The birthplace of one of the country's greatest poets, Patrick Kavanagh, celebrates its scion through an excellent and informative resource centre. **See p.251**

* **The Lakes of Cavan** Known collectively as Lough Oughtes and linked by an extraordinary complex of atmospheric waterways, popular with both anglers and the boating crowd. **See p.254**

Louth, Monaghan and Cavan

Louth, Monaghan and Cavan all share a border with Northern Ireland and, like their neighbours in the North, bear many of the marks of the plantation. Not surprisingly, the people of these three counties (both Protestant and Catholic) still share a strong affinity with their northern neighbours. As border counties, they have also sheltered Republican activity during the Troubles, and, despite the peace process, the communities are still largely polarized along staunch political lines.

The most northerly county in the Leinster province, Louth is also Ireland's smallest county and much of its life centres on the diverse towns of Drogheda, Dundalk and Ardee, making travel around the area relatively easy. Much of its coastline has limited attraction and inland, rolling drumlin country hardens in the northeast becoming mountainous. Here, on the Cooley Peninsula, lies the most exciting part of the coast between Dublin and the border. The peninsula is also the setting of one of the richest and oldest legendary tales of Irish literature, the *Táin Bó Cúailnge* (Cattle Raid of Cooley).

The Ulster-province counties of Monaghan and Cavan sit side by side as if one were a physical imprint of the other – Monaghan all small hills, Cavan all small lakes. County Monaghan is renowned for being drumlin country – rashes of rounded hills that diminish as you head west into Cavan where the land breaks up into a crazy pattern of tiny lakes. Both landscapes have their charms, both their practical difficulties. If you're walking or cycling in either county, a compass can be very useful; although the terrain isn't inaccessible or dangerous, you should be aware that there's such a network of winding, crisscrossed roads – the minor ones often riddled with potholes – that you can very easily get lost. In Monaghan, the drumlins all look similar, while the myriad lakes of Cavan enforce constant twists and turns. The lakes, however, now offer a more leisurely means of travel; since the reopening in 1994 of an old canal system, you can sail through Cavan along the Shannon–Erne Waterway.

Although the border with Northern Ireland has sharpened political and social definitions, there is a sense in which it has also sheltered both Cavan and Monaghan. You'll probably be struck by the unspoilt nature of the landscape; while slow, rural ways are as prevalent in other Irish counties, the sharp

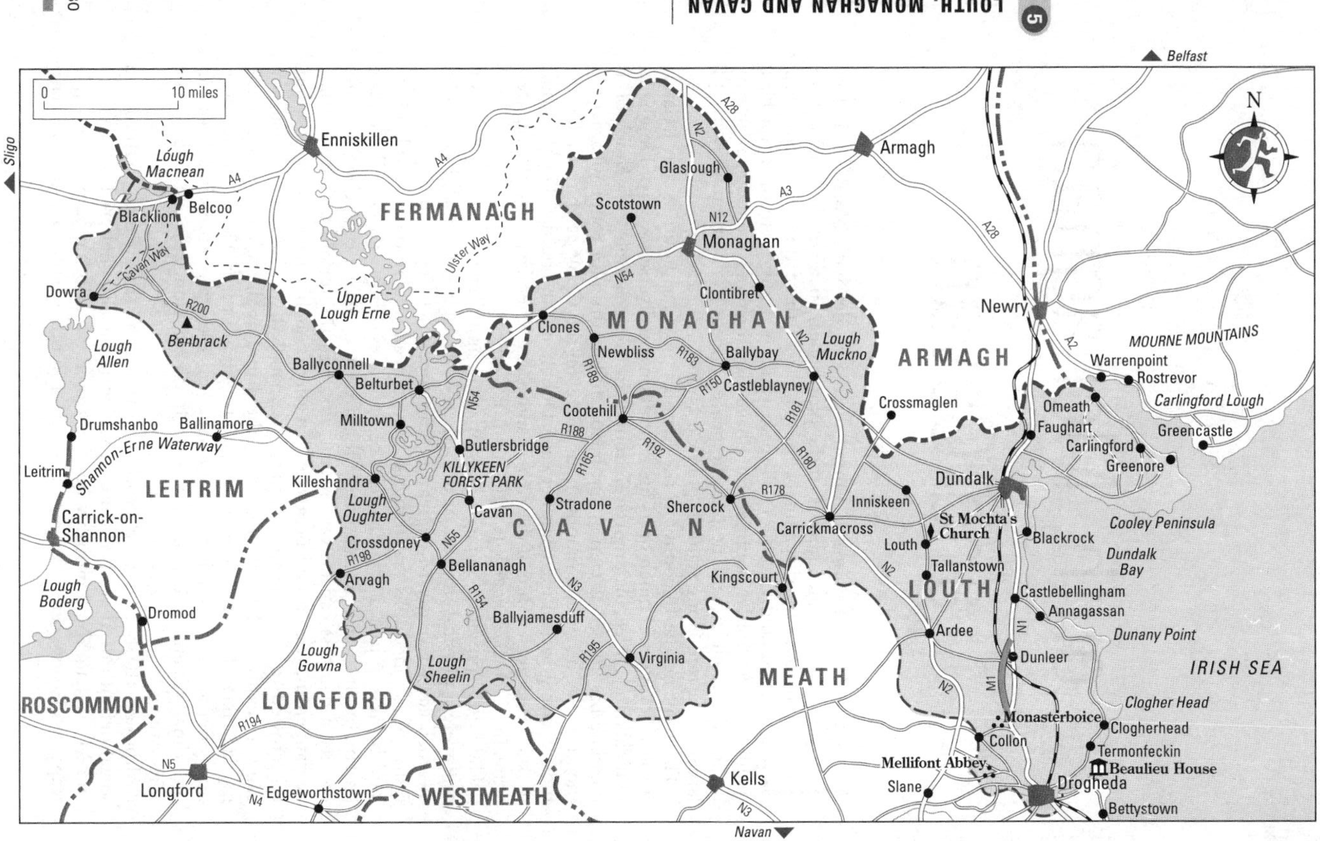
0 10 miles
N
Belfast
Sligo
Navan
Enniskillen
Armagh
Lough Macnean
A4
Blacklion
Belcoo
FERMANAGH
Glaslough
Scotstown
A3
N12
N2
A28
Monaghan
Ulster Way
Cavan Way
Dowra
Upper Lough Erne
N54
Clontibret
MONAGHAN
Newry
MOURNE MOUNTAINS
R200
Benbrack
Lough Allen
Clones
Newbliss
R183
Ballybay
Lough Muckno
ARMAGH
A2
Warrenpoint
Rostrevor
Ballyconnell
Belturbet
R189
R150
Castleblayney
Crossmaglen
Omeath
Carlingford Lough
Milltown
Cootehill
R181
Faughart
Greencastle
Drumshanbo
Ballinamore
R188
Butlersbridge
R192
R180
Carlingford
Shannon-Erne Waterway
Greenore
Leitrim
LEITRIM
Killeshandra
KILLYKEEN FOREST PARK
R165
Dundalk
Lough Oughter
Cavan
Stradone
Shercock
R178
Inniskeen
Carrickmacross
St Mochta's Church
Cooley Peninsula
Carrick-on-Shannon
CAVAN
Louth
Blackrock
Crossdoney
N55
Dundalk Bay
R198
Bellananagh
Tallanstown
Arvagh
Kingscourt
N2
LOUTH
Castlebellingham
Lough Boderg
R154
N3
Annagassan
Dromod
Ballyjamesduff
Ardee
N1
Dunany Point
Lough Gowna
R195
Virginia
Dunleer
Lough Sheelin
MEATH
IRISH SEA
M1
ROSCOMMON
LONGFORD
Clogher Head
Monasterboice
Clogherhead
R194
Collon
Termonfeckin
N5
Mellifont Abbey
Beaulieu House
Longford
Kells
Slane
Drogheda
Edgeworthstown
N4
WESTMEATH
N3
Bettystown

contrast with the industrialization and development over the border makes them more striking here, and an unhurried ordinariness constitutes much of these counties' appeal. They are not gaily painted for tourists, nor visibly quaint, and there's a dour Scottish severity in many of the towns and villages, particularly in Monaghan – clear evidence of the Ulster planters. But as you explore, you'll find both Cavan and Monaghan have an understated and quiet charm.

County Louth

The main Dublin–Belfast road (N1) and the rail line provide rapid access to **County Louth** and its principal town, Drogheda, and on to Dundalk and the North. Bisecting Drogheda is the River Boyne, whose verdant valley is home to the most important cluster of megalithic monuments in the country including **Monasterboice**, **Mellifont**, and, nearby in County Meath, Bú na Bóinne (see p.199). The **Boyne** is not only important in prehistory but modern history too, as it was here, in 1690, that if not the most significant, then certainly the most celebrated battle in Irish history took place, when the forces of Protestant King William of Orange defeated those of Catholic King James. The battle is celebrated annually on the streets of Northern Ireland on July 12, the climax of the now infamous "marching season" (see p.198).

The historic town of **Drogheda** is also closely associated with seventeenth-century English politics, most especially Oliver Cromwell, whose New Model Army (ironically the first republican army in Ireland) breached the city's walls in 1649 and massacred its royalist garrison with typical zeal. The county is also famous for mythological as well as actual warfare, as it was here that the hero of Ulster, Cúchulainn, single-handedly defeated the forces of the rest of Ireland in the great Irish epic the *Táin Bó Cúailnge* (Cattle Raid of Cooley); much of the county, from the inland town of **Ardee** where Cúchulainn eventually killed his best friend Ferdia, to the Cooley mountains where most of the battles took place, are closely associated with the story. The **Cooley Mountains** cover much of the Carlingford Peninsula, the furthest point north on the Republic's eastern seaboard, and from here it's hard to believe that the towns of Rostrevor and Warrenpoint on the other side of the lough are, in fact, under another dominion. This sense of Louth as a crossing point between the Republic and the North is most keenly felt in the town of **Dundalk** which, despite the peace process, still exudes the slightly forbidding air of a border town and is seen as the home of hawkish Republicanism.

Drogheda and around

DROGHEDA, clustered on either side of the river and tightly contained between two hills, is an enjoyable place in its own right, easily accessible and surprisingly unused to tourism, but with enough sights and entertainment to warrant a stay. The precise grey stone of which the town is built, combined with its post-industrial decay, give it a slightly forbidding air, but it has a certain vitality nonetheless. The architectural legacy of successive civilizations forms the main attraction. The ancient **Millmount mound** and the **Boyne** valley have key significance in Celtic history and mythology, but the story of Drogheda as a town really began with the Vikings, who arrived in 911 AD and founded a separate settlement on each bank. By bridging the ford between these two, the Danes gave the place its name – Droichead Átha, "the bridge of the ford". By the fourteenth century, the walled town was one of the most important in the country, where the parliament would meet from time to time; remnants of **medieval walls** and **abbeys** lie like splinters throughout the town. As ever, though, most of what you see is from the eighteenth century or later, reflecting the sober style of the Protestant bourgeoisie after the horrific slaughter of Drogheda's defenders and inhabitants by Cromwell. The important surviving buildings of this age – the Tholsel, courthouse and St Peter's Church – have mellowed romantically and stand among the nineteenth-century flowering of triumphal churches, celebrating the relaxation of the persecuting stranglehold on Catholicism, and the riverside warehouses and huge rail viaduct that welcomed the industrial boom years. More recent development, with riverside laneways and suburban housing estates, has affected the flavour of the place very little: the past somehow seems more powerful here than the present.

Arrival, information and accommodation

Drogheda is an easy place to find your way around. The **Bus Éireann** depot is on Donore Road, on the south bank of the river, and is also where you'll find the **tourist office** (Mon–Sat 10am–1pm & 2–5pm, also March–Oct Sun 11.45am–5pm; ⓣ041/983 7070; ⓦwww.drogheda-tourism.com). There's also a small tourist information office at Millmount (Mon–Fri 9.30am–1pm & 2–5.30pm). The **train** station is also on the south side, a short way east of town just off the Dublin road. **Taxis** line up in the centre on Laurence Street.

The town has several **hotels**, including the elegant, Victorian *Boyne Valley Hotel & Country Club*, Dublin Road (ⓣ041/983 7737, ⓦwww.boyne-valley-hotel.ie; ❻), set in landscaped gardens southeast of town on the N1, and the well-appointed and central *Westcourt Hotel*, West Street (ⓣ041/983 0965, ⓦwww.westcourt.com; ❺). Though **B&B** accommodation is plentiful in the area, most is situated a couple of miles or so from the town centre. Exceptions include *Maple House*, 59 Maple Drive (ⓣ041/983 3502, ⓕ983 2244), a comfortable guesthouse, five minutes east of the town centre and *Orley House*, Bryanstown, Dublin Road (ⓣ041/983 6019, ⓦwww.orleyhouse.com; ❷), a modern town house, just off the N1 near the train station. Alternatively, *River Boyne House* (ⓣ041/983 6180, ⓕ982 4592; ❷) offers good service two miles out of town in Oldbridge, an isolated rural location near the Boyne battlefield. **Hostel** accommodation is provided by the *Green Door Hostel*, 47 John St, just across from the bus station (ⓣ041/983 4422, ⓦwww.greendoorhostel.com); it's a friendly place with comfy bunks and double rooms. There is also a fine, farm-hostel a little way out in Slane (see p.202). If you want to **rent a bike** try Bridge Cycles, 4 North Quay. **Internet** access is available at the Write *Access* cybercafé, 47 West St (daily 10am–10pm; €4 per hour).

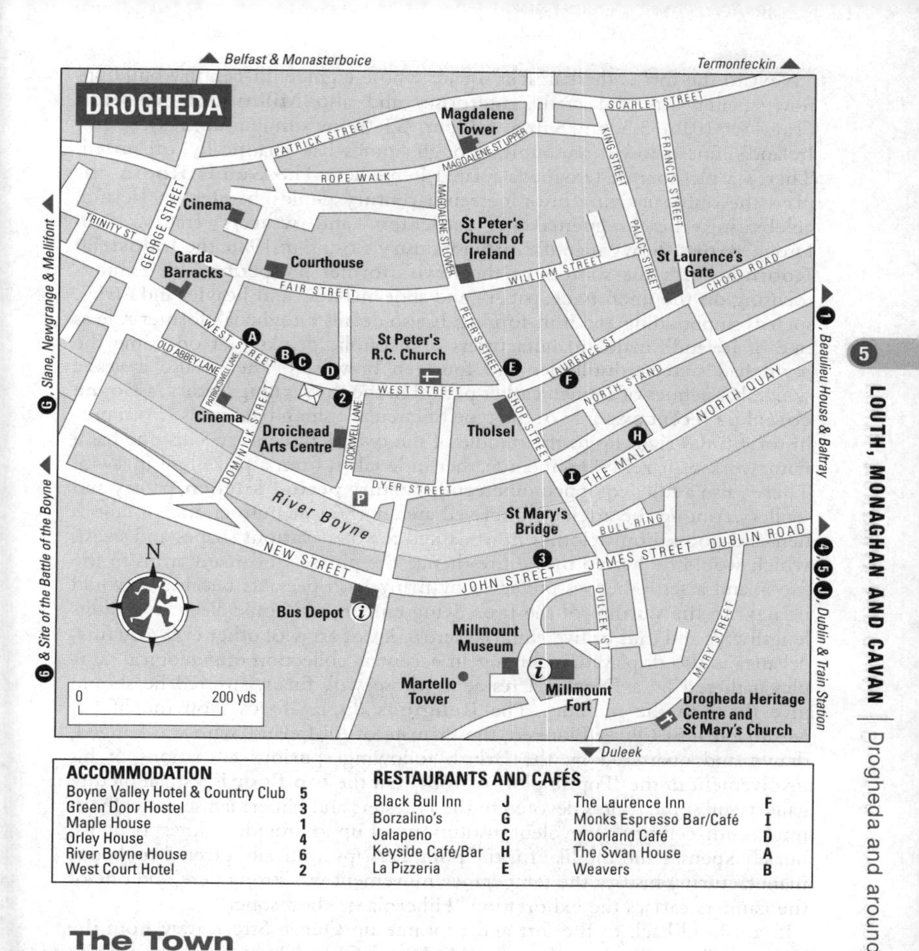

The Town

Millmount hill, south of the river on the Meath side of town, is the best place to begin exploring Drogheda. The quickest way up here on foot is via the narrow flight of steps directly opposite **St Mary's Bridge**, very near the spot where the original bridge was built by the Danes. From the hill you can enjoy an unimpeded panorama, with the bulk of the town climbing up the northern hill slope opposite, clearly revealing how the original medieval street pattern offered scant room for expansion over the succeeding centuries. Millmount's **Martello tower** (key from the museum) was severely damaged by bombardment during the 1922 Civil War, but in any event it is the earthen mound on which it stands that gives the place its real importance. The strategic value of the site was recognized from the earliest times and was chosen by the Anglo-Normans for their motte in the twelfth century, and later a castle was built, standing until 1808 when it was replaced by the tower and military barracks you see today.

Next to the fort is the barracks square whose eighteenth-century buildings now shelter arts and crafts enterprises and also **Millmount Museum** (Tues–Sat 10am–5.30pm, Sun 3–4.30pm; €3; www.millmount.net), one of Ireland's finest town museums, though somewhat chaotically organized. There's a plethora of Drogheda-related items here. The **Guilds Room** displays the only surviving pre-nineteenth-century Guilds' banners in Ireland, celebrating the broguemakers', carpenters' and weavers' trades. With Drogheda's last heavy manufacturing industry closing in 1986, the **Industrial Room** records the sources of the town's former prosperity with exhibits focusing on the linen trade, paper- and shoe-making, and heavier industries, such as shipbuilding and iron-forging. It also details Drogheda's former role as one of Ireland's major manufacturers of alcoholic drinks – at one time the town had sixteen distilleries and fourteen breweries. There's also a vessel which has echoes of a much earlier period in the town's long history: a **Boyne coracle**, a recent example of the type of circular fishing boat in use from prehistoric times right up to the middle of the twentieth century. This one has a framework of hazel twigs and a leather hide taken from a prize bull in 1943. There's also a fully equipped nineteenth-century **period kitchen**, pantry and scullery. Among the artefacts displayed are an 1860 vacuum cleaner; a tailor's hen-and-goose irons (clothes irons named for their various shapes and sizes), which would be heated in the fire (hence the phrase "too many irons in the fire"); and a settle-bed, as preferred by many Irish peasants because it would be next to the warmth of the fire's dying embers and could sleep two adults lengthways and four or five children across. A vast array of other everyday miscellanea is also displayed, including an eccentric collection of geological samples gathered by a Drogheda resident whose wife finally insisted he should give them to the museum. The **Religious** display focuses on the life of Meath-born St Oliver Plunkett, the Primate of All Ireland, who was hanged, drawn and quartered by the British following spurious allegations of his involvement in the "Popish plot" of 1681. On the **top floor** is a small picture gallery and some rooms devoted to the Foresters and Hibernian societies, both nineteenth-century benevolent institutions set up to provide sickness benefits, burial expenses and the like for the poor. Perhaps ironically, given Drogheda's manufacturing history, the temperance movement was strong here, and one of the banners carries the exhortation "Hibernia be thou sober".

If you head back to the fort and continue up Queen Street away from the river, you'll come to Mary Street and St Mary's Church, which now houses the **Drogheda Heritage Centre** (Mon–Fri 10am–5pm, Sat noon–5pm, Sun 2–5pm; €3). The centre caused a furore locally on its opening by displaying the death mask of the town's arch-nemesis, Oliver Cromwell, whose forces breached the city's walls right at this very point in 1649. While the exhibits are far from inspiring, the low-budget video does offer a surprisingly revisionist account of the town's traumatic history, and there is a fine coffee shop attached.

The northside

The steep streets of the town's northside run up the hill which is topped by the fifteenth-century **Magdalene Tower** – formerly the belfry tower of an extensive Dominican friary, founded in 1224 by Lucas De Netterville, Archbishop of Armagh. The tower rises above a Gothic arch where the transept and nave would have met; inside, a spiral staircase reaches up into its two storeys, but since it is railed off from public access it's probably seen to best advantage from a distance. In March 1395, **Richard II**, King of England, received within the priory the submission of the Ulster chiefs; in 1467, Thomas, Earl of Desmond, a former Lord Chief Justice, was found guilty of treason and beheaded here (his Act of Parliament for a university in Drogheda expired with him).

Lower down, the spire that leaps out from the centre of town belongs to the heavily Gothic-styled nineteenth-century **St Peter's Roman Catholic Church** on West Street, the town's main thoroughfare. It's an imposing building, with a grand double flight of steps, but it's the presence of a martyr's head, on view in a tabernacle-like box that forms part of a small shrine down the left-hand aisle, that transforms the place into a centre of pilgrimage. The severed head is a searing reminder of the days of religious persecution. It once belonged to **Oliver Plunkett**, Archbishop of Armagh and Primate of All Ireland in the seventeenth century, when Drogheda was the principal seat in Ireland. On July 1, 1681, Plunkett was executed in London for treason: as the Lord Chief Justice of England explained, "the bottom of your treason was your setting up your false religion, than which there is not anything more displeasing to God." His head and mutilated members were tossed onto a fire and, though rescued, but were not brought back to Ireland until 1721, a time when persecution had somewhat subsided. Plunkett was canonized in 1975, after miracles were said to have occurred in his name in southern Italy.

Walking east along West Street and turning up Peter's Street you'll find the town's other St Peter's Church (this time Church of Ireland). The original church on the site was a thirteenth-century wooden structure and it is said that many of the town's inhabitants perished here in a fire as they sought refuge from Cromwell's forces. The present church was erected in 1753, and a porch and spire, designed by the eminent Irish architect Francis Johnston, were added in 1793.

Heading south of here towards the docks, the back alleys and stone warehouses, once relics of Drogheda's short-lived industrial heyday and of the local brewing and milling trades, are being done up by a new breed of entrepreneur to cater for the housing demands of Irish yuppies, known locally as "Celtic Cubs", profiting from the Celtic Tiger. The docks themselves are beginning to show evidence of new life, too, though the depleted commercial shipping fleet anchored on the lethargic Boyne is a far cry from the sixty Viking ships which are said to have wintered here. The docks do, however, boast one of the finest old pubs in the country, **Carbery's**. A local, family-run institution for over a century, in the evening or early morning (it is allowed to open at 7.30am to cater for the dockers and the men off the boats) the faint orange glow from the lanterns or fire inside the pub makes a welcome landmark and sign of life.

Eating, drinking and entertainment

Drogheda might not be a culinary hotspot, but it has plenty of choices for **meals** throughout the day. *Weavers* on West Street is an excellent pub for a cheap lunch, and is always crowded; *Jalapeno*, a few doors down, serves filling sandwiches and is also good value. *The Swan House* on West Street is a good Chinese restaurant, with cheap takeaway and sit-down meals; while *La Pizzeria*, on Peter Street, is very popular with locals (daily 6–11pm except Wed; ⓣ041/983 4208). The *Westcourt Hotel* on West Street does a good early-bird menu, while the *Moorland Café*, 97 West St, is a popular spot in the day. *The Laurence Inn*, Laurence Street, offers one the town's most economical lunch-time options. Near the docks are two of Drogheda's trendier hangouts, *Monks*

Espresso Bar/Café, and the *Keyside Bar/Café*, both of which serve excellent coffee and well-prepared, if overpriced, food. On the outskirts of town, on the Dublin road, is the *Black Bull Inn* which has excellent bar food, while on the opposite side of town, a short way out on the old Slane road, is *Borzalino's*, serving traditional Italian meals.

As far as entertainment goes, many of Drogheda's **pubs** are rich in character. *Carbery's* on the North Strand is probably the best-known gathering place on this part of the east coast. *Clarkes*, on the corner of Fair and Peter streets, is quiet, old-fashioned and popular with the local literary set during the week, but a much more fashionable meeting place on Saturday nights. *The Pheasant Pub* on Duleek Street often has traditional music. *Peter Matthews* on Laurence Street (known locally as *McPhail's*) is frequented by a younger crowd and has lots of toffee-brown woodwork, partitions and alcoves, and a back room for music (4–5 nights weekly). *Bar Redz*, 79 West St, has a Wednesday night **traditional music** session, while the *Westcourt Hotel* offers a variety of music (Thurs–Sat).

Entertainment outside the pubs is limited. Your best bet is to check out what's happening at the Droichead Arts Centre (ⓣ041/983 0188) in Stockwell Lane off West Street, which regularly hosts plays, poetry readings and exhibitions. Drogheda's two Omniplex **cinemas** (ⓣ041/984 4007, ⓦwww.filminfo.net) are in the Abbey and Boyne shopping centres. The town's two most popular **clubs** are *Fusion*, George Street, and *The Soda Club*, Trinity Street, both offering several nights a week of DJs and occasional live bands.

Beaulieu House

Downstream from the town's docks, the **viaduct** carrying trains on the Dublin–Belfast line spans a 200-foot-deep gorge. Continuing east from *Carbery's* pub for a mile or so along the Baltray road will bring you to this impressive feat of nineteenth-century engineering by Sir John MacNeill. Beyond the viaduct and cement works you reach some pleasant woodland. Part of this belongs to **Beaulieu House** (May to mid-Sept Mon–Thurs 9am–1pm, closed public holidays; gardens open until Nov; house and gardens €5, gardens only €2.50), a private domain that claims to have been Ireland's first unfortified mansion, built between 1660 and 1666 after Cromwell's departure, when the land was confiscated from the family of Oliver Plunkett and given to Sir Henry Tichbourne, whose descendants reside there today. The house has a hipped roof in the artisan style and an almost perfectly preserved interior. Most rewarding of all is a fabulous picture gallery, with a collection ranging from contemporary portraits of William and Mary on tall canvases by the court painter Van der Wyck to an intense collection of early-twentieth-century Irish art. The exquisitely designed walled garden, thought to be one of the first of its kind in Ireland, is well worth visiting in its own right.

Mellifont and Monasterboice

A few miles north of Drogheda lie two of the great historical sites that characterize this part of the country: the **monasteries of Mellifont and Monasterboice**. To get to Mellifont from Drogheda (five miles), turn off the road to Collon at Monleek Cross; alternatively turn off the Slane–Collon road at the signpost. There is no direct bus service to Mellifont, though an infrequent service from Drogheda to Collon will drop you off at Monleek Cross, from which it's a two-mile walk. Mullen's taxis (Ⓣ041/983 3377) will take you for €15 each way. Monasterboice, six miles from Drogheda, can be reached from the main N1 Dublin–Belfast road, or by continuing up the Drogheda–Collon road and following the signs to the right. The Drogheda–Dundalk bus will stop at the *Monasterboice Inn* on request, from which it's a signposted fifteen-minute walk to the monastery.

Mellifont Abbey

Mellifont (May–Oct daily 10am–6pm; €1.90; Heritage Card) was, in medieval times, one of the most important monasteries in Ireland, the motherhouse of the Cistercian order and a building of exceptional beauty and grandeur. The ruins you see today do no justice to this former glory, but they're still pretty impressive.

At its foundation in 1142 – the inspiration of St Malachy, Archbishop of Armagh, who did much to bring the early Irish Church closer to Rome – Mellifont was the first **Cistercian monastery** in Ireland. Malachy's friend St Bernard, then abbot of the Cistercian monastery at Clairvaux in France, did much to inspire the work, and sent nine of his own monks to form the basis of the new community. The abbey took fifteen years to build, and you can gauge something of its original size and former glory by imagining the gargantuan pillars that once rose, finishing high among a riotous sprouting of arches and vaulted ceilings, from the broad stumps remaining today. For nearly four hundred years Mellifont flourished, at its peak presiding over as many as 38 other Cistercian monasteries throughout the country, until in 1536 all of them were dissolved by Henry VIII.

One hundred and fifty monks fled from Mellifont, and the buildings were handed over to Edward Moore, ancestor of the Earls of Drogheda, who converted the place into a fortified mansion. In 1603 the last of the great Irish chieftains, **Hugh O'Neill**, was starved into submission here before eventually escaping to the Continent in the Flight of the Earls. Mellifont, meanwhile, went into gradual decline. It was attacked by Cromwellian forces, and then used as William's headquarters during the Battle of the Boyne, before eventually falling so far as to be pressed into service as a pigsty in the nineteenth century.

The ruins

Today the remains rarely rise above shoulder height, with the striking exception of the Romanesque octagonal **lavabo**, built around 1200, whose basins and water jets provided washing facilities for the monks. The rest of the ruins can be easily identified on the map provided, their ground plan almost perfectly intact. You enter through the **north transept**, which originally had five chapels, three in its eastern and two in its western aisle. Two of the three on the eastern side had apsidal ends, an unusual feature in medieval Ireland, seen here presumably because of the French influence on the builders. The chancel area, or **presbytery**, has the remains of an ornate arch and sedilia where the priests celebrating Mass would sit. The entire **nave** would have been paved in red and blue tiles, some inscribed with the words "Ave Maria" and others decorated with the fleur-de-lis emblem; the **pillars**, too, would originally have been painted in brilliant colours and topped with flowery capitals. At the river end of the nave is a **crypt** – an unusual position which served to level the site on which the church was built. The **chapter house**, beyond the south transept, was once the venue for the daily meetings of the monks. It now houses a collection of medieval **glazed tiles**, moved here from around the site for safety.

Behind the lavabo is the south range, where the **refectory** would have been, and back towards the road you'll find the **gatehouse**, the only surviving part of a high defensive wall that once completely ringed the monastic buildings. Also within the grounds are another ruined church up on the slope (converted to a Protestant one in 1542) and a building that was converted by An Óige into a youth hostel. This is now permanently closed, a shame since the setting is delightful, with the River Mattock gliding through gently wooded country.

Monasterboice

Monasterboice (Mainistir Buite, "Buite's monastery") is a tiny enclosure (dawn to dusk), but it contains two of the finest high crosses, both dating from the tenth century, and one of the best round towers in the country. The squat cross nearer to you as you enter is reckoned the finer of the two, and its high-relief carving has certainly worn the centuries better. It is known as **St Muiredach's Cross** after the inscription in Irish at the base of the stem – *Or do Muiredach i Chros*, "A prayer for Muiredach by whom this cross was made." The boldly ornate stone picture panels retell biblical stories and were designed to educate and inspire the largely illiterate populace. Some of the subjects are ambiguous and open to a certain amount of conjecture (William Wilde, father of Oscar, argued that many relate as strongly to events associated with Monasterboice as to the Bible), but most have been fairly convincingly identified.

Part of the enjoyment of visiting Monasterboice lies in trying to decipher the meaning of the images represented. The story begins at the bottom of the **east face** of the cross, nearest the wall, with Eve tempting Adam on the left and Cain slaying Abel on the right. Above this in ascending order are David and Goliath alongside King Saul and David's son Jonathan, Moses striking a rock with his staff to conjure water for parched Israelites, and finally, the Wise Men bearing gifts to Mary and the baby Jesus. The centrepiece of the wheel is the **Last Judgement**, with the risen multitudes begging for entry to Heaven. The **west face** of the cross is largely devoted to the **life of Christ**. At the bottom is his arrest in the Garden of Gethsemane, with Roman soldiers and the treacherous kiss of Judas. This is followed by three figures clutching books – possibly representing the dispelling of the doubts of St Thomas. The third panel shows the Risen Christ returned to meet St Peter and St Paul. The hub of the wheel shows the Crucifixion, surmounted by Moses descending from Mount Sinai with the Ten Commandments. The flanks of the cross are also decorated. On the **north side** are St Anthony and St Paul, Christ's scourging at the pillar, and the **Hand of God** (under the arm of the cross) warning mankind. On the **south side** is the Flight of the Israelites from Egypt and also possibly Pontius Pilate washing his hands. All this is capped at the top as if under the roof of the church and surrounded with abstract or uninterpretable embellishment.

The **West Cross**, the taller of the two and near the round tower, is made up of three separate stone sections, all of them much more worn and almost indiscernible in places, though there's a handily placed display board offering guidance. The **east face** shows David killing the lion, then Abraham preparing to sacrifice his son Isaac. Above this is Moses discovering the idolatrous worship of the golden calf. The other three panels are hard to identify, though on the right arm of the wheel you can see the upside-down Satan being speared by St Michael. The **west face** begins with the **Resurrection**, and the **Baptism of Christ** is shown on the second panel. The four three-figure panels below the wheel, which again is dominated by the Crucifixion, are difficult to identify.

The round tower and churches

Behind the West Cross stands possibly the tallest **round tower** in Ireland, 110ft high even without its conical peak. Round towers were adopted between the ninth and eleventh centuries by monks throughout the country as a defence against continued Viking attack. They needed no keystone that enemies could pull out for speedy demolition, their height created a perfect lookout post and the entrance would be several feet from the ground, allowing a ladder to be drawn in when they were under attack. The only drawback was that if a lighted arrow were to pierce the inner floorboards the whole column would act as a chimney, guaranteeing a blazing inferno. Sadly, you can't go into the tower, which has been closed for safety reasons.

Finally within the enclosure are two thirteenth-century **churches**, the north and the south church. They probably had no real connection with the monastic settlement, which had almost certainly ceased to function by then, and there's little of great interest within their ruined walls.

North to Dundalk

The main reason to head northwards into County Louth, apart from reaching the border, is to get to the mountains of the **Cooley Peninsula**. Apart from the peninsula, the area has a few attractions worthy of a detour. There are various possible routes: the main Drogheda to Belfast road, the N1, is the fastest, speeding directly towards the border, passing Monasterboice, and skirting Dundalk. An alternative inland route is to head towards Collon on the less busy N2 and north to **Ardee**, the supposed scene of the heroic battle between Cúchulainn and Ferdia, then north to **Louth** village and **St Mochta's House**, and on to **Dundalk** from there. These roads give excellent, unhindered cross-country views of County Louth, especially the drumlins rising inland towards counties Cavan and Monaghan. The final, more scenic option, suitable if you want to dawdle along or if you're cycling, is to take the bay road out of Drogheda and follow the coast north through the villages of **Termonfeckin**, **Clogherhead** and **Annagassan**, joining the main N1 road once again in the attractive village of Castlebellingham.

The coastal road: Termonfeckin to Blackrock

TERMONFECKIN (Tearmann Feichin, "St Feckin's sanctuary") is a placid country village lying in a wooded dip half a mile from the shore. The village has a small tower-house **castle** and a tenth-century **high cross** in the graveyard of St Feckin's Church. The castle (keys available from the bungalow across the cul-de-sac) dates from the fifteenth and sixteenth centuries and features a corbelled roof. The only **accommodation** in the village is at *Highfield House* (March–Oct; ⓣ041/982 2172; ❷), an elegant farmhouse, dating from 1725 and set beside the sea.

Heading north from Termonfeckin, you pass through the glum beach resort of **Clogherhead**, from where the road takes you north to **Port Oriel**, a tiny fishing harbour tucked hard into the coast's rock face that enjoys good mackerel fishing off the pier in summer. It's only a little way beyond here, as you approach the village of **ANNAGASSAN** (Áth na gCosán, "ford of the paths") that the signposts designating the "scenic route" – the coastal road – begin to earn their keep, with the mountains of Cooley and Mourne, one range south of the border, the other north, spectacularly silhouetted against the sky. *The Glyde Inn* in Annagassan has food and is a nice reclusive spot to take time out for refreshment. There's little else to see around the village, although local archaeological explorations have provoked controversy by claiming to have revealed the first permanent Norse settlement in Ireland, predating even Dublin. As you continue northwards across the humpback stone bridge, you'll see rowing boats laid out along the bulging ramparts of the canalized river as it meets the sea, making for an attractive scene.

Inland from these villages, just off the M1 motorway on the N1 road, lies the village of **DUNLEER**, formerly a traditional stop on the Belfast to Dublin route. The town has little to offer in terms of tourist attractions, except for **White River Mill**, a traditional water mill, where wheat has been ground for at least three hundred years (enquire at the house beside the mill to view). B&B **accommodation** is available at the red-brick *Bramble Lodge*, Main Street (Ⓣ041/685 1565, Ⓔmcondra@esatclear.ie; ❷). For **food** you could follow the locals to the *Grove* restaurant where you can get a substantial economically priced meal.

Travel a further five miles north on the N1 and you will arrive at **CASTLEBELLINGHAM**. Despite the main Dublin–Belfast road blundering right through the middle, Castlebellingham remains a pretty village. You can take refuge from the traffic down by the **mill** where there's a turning gable-end water wheel powered by the River Glyde. Further upstream stands the *Bellingham Castle*, a sugary, castellated hotel (Ⓣ042/937 2176, Ⓦwww.bellinghamcastle.com; ❺) whose restaurant specializes in steaks and seafood. Moving northwards again, the next significant turning off the N1 (right) takes you to **BLACKROCK** and later allows you to bypass most of Dundalk. Blackrock itself is an overstretched ribbon of Victorian seaside villas along a mudflat beach. It does, though, offer a handsomely crystalline view across **Dundalk Bay** and on to the Cooley Peninsula, by now looming very close. If you want to stay here, then *Blackrock House*, Main Street (Ⓣ042/932 1829, Ⓔblackrockhse@eircom.net; ❷), provides comfortable en-suite accommodation with some rooms overlooking the bay.

Ardee to Dundalk

The inland route that follows the N2 from Collon to Ardee is far less travelled, with less to see along it, and really requires that you have your own transport. On the way to Ardee, you'll pass by one of the most atmospheric places to stay in the region, *Smarmore Castle* (Ⓣ041/685 7167, Ⓦwww.smarmorecastle.com; ❺), three miles south of the town. Dating back in part to 1320, the castle has undergone recent renovation and offers splendidly-furnished and spacious en-suite accommodation in very pleasant grounds.

Almost exactly halfway between Drogheda and Dundalk, **ARDEE** is a traffic-clogged place, though it has some evidence of the Plantation era, with fortified buildings along the main street and a memorial **statue** to a landlord, erected by his thankful tenants in 1861. The thirteenth-century **castle** on the main street was built here because the town was at the northern edge of the Pale, and from here the Anglo-Irish made forays into Ulster, or were themselves periodically forced onto the defensive.

For a quick sandwich or coffee Caffrey's bakery is the best bet, while *Gables Restaurant* (Ⓣ041/685 3789) does an immensely filling set dinner for around €30. For **B&B** accommodation try *Carraig Mór*, one mile south of Ardee on the N2 road, a comfortable, family-run house (Ⓣ041/685 3513, Ⓦwww.carriagmor.com; ❷), but if you want something a little special then head to *Red House* (Ⓣ041/685 3523, Ⓦhomepage.tinet.ie/~redhouse; ❻), a country residence just a little way up the N52 Dundalk road with indoor swimming pool, sauna, tennis courts and a croquet lawn.

A short diversion from Ardee takes you to the so-called **Jumping Church** at Kildemock. To get there head east from the junction at the southern end of Ardee's main street and turn right after about a quarter of a mile – the small, ruined church lies a mile further down this road. It gets its name from its end wall having shifted three feet from its foundations, which, according to local lore, it did to exclude the grave of an excommunicated person. Less romantic accounts tell of a severe storm taking place in 1715 at around the time the wall jumped, but either way it's a remarkable sight, with the wall shorn clear of its foundations yet still standing (albeit at a 35-degree angle). In the graveyard are simple, foot-high stone markers, some of the earliest grave slabs for the poor.

Ardee is a major road junction, and moving on you could head northeast to Dundalk, northwest to Carrickmacross or southwest to Kells (see p.205). Heading north, however, is an interesting route along the minor roads to **LOUTH** village: keep on the N2 at the northern end of Ardee and take an immediate right along the R171 to Tallanstown, where you'll need to turn right again for Louth. The village isn't much in itself (and certainly doesn't seem to merit sharing a name with the county), but in **St Mochta's Church** it does have one thing well worth seeing – turn left towards Carrickmacross and immediately right onto the Inniskeen road. According to legend the church was built in a night to give shelter to its founder, **St Mochta**, who died in 534. Originally part of a monastery, and dating probably from the late twelfth century, it has a beautifully crafted, vaulted roof reached by a constricted stairway. In its early years the church was plundered many times; these days they obviously feel safer, since the church is left open to any passing visitor. Fourteenth-century **Louth Abbey** is accessible through the graveyard back up the road, from where, if you look west, you'll notice a motte on the nearby hill.

Dundalk

Although **DUNDALK** has a reputation as a tough border town, home to uncompromising Republicanism, it still has enough interest to justify a visit. Industrial estates on the outskirts show signs of a burgeoning recent prosperity, a reflection of the town's strategic position economically on the main transport routes from Dublin to Belfast. Starting life in legendary prehistory as a fort guarding a gap in the mountains to the north (Dún Dealga, the "Fortress of Dealga"), it became in turn a Celtic, Norse, Anglo-Norman, Jacobean and finally Williamite stronghold. This defensive tradition seems still to hang over the town, and it never seems a place where you – or for that matter the locals – can feel fully at ease.

As far as sights go, the outstanding one is the nineteenth-century Neoclassical

courthouse, whose open Doric portico leads into an airy, classically proportioned interior. In the plaza outside, the Guardian Angel or motherland statue is unequivocally dedicated to "the martyrs in the cause of liberty who fought and died in the struggle against English Tyranny and foreign rule in Ireland" – a far cry from the monument of gratitude in Ardee. **St Patrick's Cathedral** in Francis Street is also worth a look while you're here: its cornucopia of embellished towers, turrets and crenellated walls is a reasonably successful imitation of King's College Chapel, Cambridge. Inside are some rich mosaics using gold pieces in abundance to depict biblical stories. **Louth County Museum** (Tues–Sat 10.30am–5.30pm, Sun 2–6pm; €3.80), in a warehouse next to the tourist office on Jocelyn Street, uses a variety of artefacts and documents to tell the stories of local industries, from coopering to cigarettes. The museum is an uneasy mix of high-tech display and poorly labelled exhibits, but there is a wealth of material here. During the 1960s, Heinkel bomber cockpits were sent over to Dundalk to be made into bubble cars – you'll find a 1966 model on the first-floor landing. The top two floors house an exhibition that focuses on the area's rich Stone Age history. Dundalk's oldest building is **Kelly's Tower**, a four-storey Franciscan bell tower, dating from the middle of the thirteenth century, on the corner of Mill Street and Castle Road. The tower was sacked in 1315 by Edward Bruce and again, in 1538, by Lord Deputy Grey.

Practicalities

The regional **tourist office**, which also hosts touring art exhibitions, occupies a restored tobacco warehouse on Jocelyn Street (June to mid-Sept Mon–Fri 9am–1pm & 2–6pm, Sat 9.30am–1pm & 2–6pm; mid-Sept to May Mon–Fri 9.30am–1pm; ⓣ042/933 5484). The Council Arts Office in the Market Square (Mon–Fri 9am–5pm; ⓣ042/933 2276) provides up-to-the-minute details of music and theatre. The **bus** station (ⓣ042/933 4075) is on Long Walk, off Market Square, and the **train** station (ⓣ042/933 5521) is on Carrick Road, half a mile west of the town centre.

For a town that's barely on the tourist trail, Dundalk has more **accommodation** than might be expected. Among the best of the town's numerous B&Bs are *The Townhouse*, 5 Roden Place (ⓣ042/932 9898, ⓔthetownhouse@eircom.net; ❷), a Georgian house near the centre, and *Pinewoods* (ⓣ042/932 1295, ⓔolmurphy@eircom.net; ❷), two miles out of town on the main Dublin road. The central *Hotel Imperial*, Park Street (ⓣ042/933 2241, ⓔinfo@imperialhoteldundalk.com; ❺), is much more comfortable inside than its drab facade would suggest. There are also out-of-town alternatives, including the modern *Fairways Hotel*, Dublin Road (ⓣ042/932 1500, ⓦwww.fairways.ie; ❻), and the excellent *Ballymascanlon Hotel* (ⓣ042/937 1124, ⓦwww.globalgolf.com/ballymascanlon; ❻) set in 130 acres of parkland on the fringes of the Cooley Peninsula.

Eating well and cheaply is not a Dundalk speciality, but there are plenty of fast-food places around the centre of town. Better fare can be had at *Quaglino's* (ⓣ042/933 8567), specializing in modern Irish and Italian food, and *McKeown's Pub*, both on Clanbrassil Street, or at *La Cantina*, River Lane (ⓣ042/932 7970) off Park Street (evenings only). Despite being the home of one of Ireland's biggest international music successes, The Corrs, Dundalk has little to offer by way of musical entertainment. **Pubs** that are well worth visiting include *Toale's* on Crowe Street, a sawdust-on-flagstone hideout (due for refurbishment at the time of writing), where you can sometimes catch traditional music. *McManus's* pub, Seatown, has old-fashioned snugs to drink in, while *Pádraig Ó Donngaile*, on the same street, is another cosy spot. *Café Metz* on Francis Street is the fashionable hangout in town, while there are several more old-style pubs on Park Street: *Mr Ridley's*, *The Phoenix* and *McDaid's*.

Faughart

From Dundalk, the border lies just eight miles on up the N1. Opposite the turning for the Cooley Peninsula, a couple of miles outside Dundalk, is a lesser road that leads a short distance inland to **FAUGHART**. A small place of little modern interest, it is said to be the birthplace of **St Brigid**, patron of Ireland, whose four-armed rush-cross is often to be found on the walls of rural Irish households. In the local churchyard you can see her holy well and pillarstone, as well as the grave of **Edward Bruce**, who was defeated here in 1318 after being sent to Ireland by his brother (Robert the Bruce) to divert the English away from the Anglo-Scottish border. There is a stone nearby which according to legend was used for his decapitation.

The Cooley Peninsula

You come to **Cooley**, east of Dundalk, for the raw beauty of its mountains, to walk and to experience a life where the twenty-first century rarely intrudes. Indeed when you get up among the bare hilltops, the peninsula's links with legend (see box on p.245) seem at least as strong as its grip on modern reality.

Approached from Dundalk, the road leaves the N1 to trace the southern slopes of the Cooley Mountains, passing through drab countryside on the way, and then cutting across country to Greenore, **Carlingford** and **Omeath** on the north shore. It is here, facing the Mourne Mountains across **Carlingford Lough**, that the most beautiful scenes lie, with forested slopes plunging steeply towards the lough. The southern slopes are gentler and lazier, making a far more sedate progress to the water's edge.

Before you reach any of this, however, only about a mile down the peninsula road, there's a short and rewarding detour. From the back of the *Ballymascanlon Hotel* (see opposite), a footpath leads to the **Proleek Dolmen** whose massive capstone balances with far more elegance than its 46 tons ought to allow; to reach the dolmen take the path that runs from the hotel car park through the courtyard of whitewashed cottages along the fringes of the hotel's golf course. On the path just before the dolmen, a Bronze Age wedge-shaped **gallery grave** can be seen, though be aware when visiting it of stray balls from the golf tees behind.

Carlingford

Aside from being the more scenic, the peninsula's north shore is also the best place to base yourself for **hill-walking** and the easiest for finding food and a bed. Sitting at the foot of Sliabh Foy mountain, the former fishing village of **CARLINGFORD** on the southern shore of the lough, is a neatly ordered place with a network of narrow, whitewashed, terraced streets, often with naive murals, which has developed into an upmarket resort, with overinflated accommodation and restaurant prices to match. The development is not immediately apparent – it's discernible on the surface perhaps mainly as a sprinkling of crafts shops – and the place retains real charm as well as some excellent places to eat and drink.

St Patrick is said to have landed in Carlingford briefly on his way to introduce Christianity to Ireland (he finally ended his journey further north, in County Down), and the settlement is ancient enough to have been raided by the Vikings. The oldest visible remain is the D-shaped ruin of **King John's Castle**, down by the main road on the water's edge. King John is said to have visited in 1210, and the Anglo-Norman castle, guarding the entrance to the lough, may be even older than that. It has its counterpart across the water at Greencastle. The village retains a distinctly medieval feel, and there are a couple of solid fifteenth-century buildings: the **Mint**, in a narrow street off the square, is a fortified town house with an impressive gate tower; **Taafe's Castle**, which stood on the shore when it was built but is now some way from it, is impressively crenellated and fortified but sadly not open to the public. The best and safest **beaches** in the area are at Gyles Quay and Shelling Hill.

Practicalities

Carlingford has a small **tourist office** (Mon–Fri 10am–1pm & 2–5.30pm, Sat & Sun 11am–1pm & 2–5.30pm; ⓣ042/937 3888, ⓦwww.carlingford.ie) housed in a small building in the car park by the main road entrance to the village. The tourist office can provide advice on the many **walks** available in the hills above Carlingford and usually has an extensive range of maps and related material on sale.

There's plenty of accommodation in the village, but, at peak times, it's advisable to take advantage of the tourist office's €2 accommodation-booking service. **B&Bs** close to the lough shore include the superb *Ghan House* (ⓣ042/937 3682, ⓦwww.ghanhouse.com; ❻), an eighteenth-century building with an exceptionally good restaurant (see overleaf). More modest, but still very comfortable are *Barnavave House* (ⓣ042/937 3878; ❷) and the adjacent *Shalom* (ⓣ042/937 5151, ⓦwww.jackiewoods.com; ❷). Alternatively, there's *Viewpoint*, Omeath Road (ⓣ042/937 3149; ❸), whose modern, motel-like flatlets enjoy good views from a little way up the hill. *Mourne View*, Belmont (ⓣ042/937 3551, ⓔmourneview@iolfree.ie; ❷), is a friendly place right at the foot of the mountains, signposted from the main Dundalk road. The recently renovated *McKevitt's Village Hotel* on Market Square (ⓣ042/937 3116, ⓦwww.mckevittshotel.com; ❺) provides a little more luxury, while *Jordan's Townhouse*, Newry Street (ⓣ042/937 3223; ❺), is exquisitely comfortable. Carlingford's **hostel**, on

Táin Bó Cúailnge (The Cattle Raid of Cooley)

The Cooley Peninsula is heavily associated with the **Táin Bó Cúailnge**, as many of the episodes in this great **Celtic epic** were played out in its mountains. The story's plot (set around 500 BC) concerns the Brown Bull of Cooley (Donn Cúailnge) which is coveted by Medb, Queen of Connaught, in her envy of her husband Ailill's White Bull (Finnbenach). In their efforts to capture the bull, Medb and Ailill, who come from the west, effectively declare war on the east in general, and Ulster in particular. All the men of Ulster – save one, Cúchulainn – are struck by a curse which immobilizes them through most of the tale, leaving our hero to face the might of Medb's troops alone. The action consists largely of his (often gory) feats, but the text is also rich in topography and place names, many of them still clearly identifiable. The earliest written version of the legend appears in the twelfth-century Book of the Dun Cow, and the saga's rich language has been captured in Thomas Kinsella's English translation and has also formed the basis for a 1973 concept album by the traditional-rock pioneers Horslips.

Tholsel Street (Ⓣ042/937 3100, Ⓦwww.carlingfordadventure.com; closed mid-Dec to mid-Jan) caters for the cheaper end of the market, but as this is part of the **Carlingford Adventure Centre**, you may have to reserve a bed early as it is often booked by groups taking part in the centre's land- and water-based activities.

The village has plenty of very good, if somewhat pricey, places to **eat**. The undoubted peach is *Ghan House* (Fri & Sat 7–9.30pm, Sun 5.30–7.30pm) which serves modern Irish cuisine, using ingredients from its own gardens, and has eight-course gourmet nights (approximately once a month). *The Oystercatcher Bistro* (Ⓣ042 937 3922) in the centre of the village will please seafood lovers, and nearby, *The Anchor Bar* (aka *PJ's*), on the corner near the Mint, is an old grocery store and bar which serves pub grub and oysters in season, which here seems to mean most of the year.

Omeath

At **OMEATH**, five miles west of Carlingford, the lough has narrowed dramatically, so that the sedate towns of Warrenpoint and Rostrevor on the Mourne mountain slopes across the border seem only a handshake away (see p728 & 727). As a village, Omeath, with its widely scattered dwellings, is far from typical of the east coast – it was until recent years the last remaining Gaeltacht village of any significance in this part of the country and has a strong singing tradition. Some of these songs have been collected by the Armagh singer Pádraigín Ní Uallacháin (see p.744) in her recently released album *An Dealg Óir*. In summer there's a handy passenger **ferry service**, which also takes bikes, between Omeath and Warrenpoint (June–Sept daily 1–6pm, tides permitting, 5min; €5 return). **B&B** is available at *Delamare House* (Ⓣ042/937 5101, Ⓔeileenmcgeown@eircom.net; ❷), a comfortable modern dormer bungalow and there's also the *Omeath Park Hotel* (Ⓣ042/937 5116, Ⓔtwinrose@iolfree.ie; ❺), half a mile out on the western side of the village at the end of a long driveway up the hillside, offering some degree of luxury as well as a gym and swimming pool.

County Monaghan

Monaghan is first and foremost **drumlin** country. Drumlins are softly rounded mounds of land left by retreating glaciers at the end of the last Ice Age, and the exceptional number of these small hills packed together in County Monaghan serves as a very good example of what textbooks call "basket of eggs" topography – a reference to the land's appearance from on high; at ground level the soil is poor and the land is broken up into small units which are difficult and uneconomic to farm. The drumlins are grass-covered, and light hedgerows stitch their way across them, marking out the fields. Initially it's a charming scene, but it soon becomes a little repetitive. Small lakes provide occasional relief and are excellent for fishing, but they're nothing like as numerous as in Cavan.

The feel of this countryside has been captured in the poetry and prose of **Patrick Kavanagh**, rated by many as Ireland's finest poet after Yeats. He was born in Inniskeen in the south of the county, and his writing evokes the poor quality of peasant life – and also something of the monotony of the rural landscape.

Particularly in the north of the county, the terrain has led to an insane criss-crossing of lanes: a compass is a good idea, as is an up-to-date map. It makes for good walking if you're not in too much of a hurry and in these hilly areas you can wander undisturbed for miles along the labyrinth of ancient tracks and lanes. If you're equipped with the Ordnance Survey of Ireland's Discovery series map #28, it's relatively easy to seek out the sites of court tombs, forts and cairns from the Bronze Age. Many of them, thanks to the underdevelopment of the land, have remained virtually untouched. The best megalithic sites in the region are the Lisnadarragh wedge tomb, Dún Dubh, at Tiravera and the Tullyrain triple ring fort near Shantonagh.

Monaghan town

You're most likely to find yourself in **MONAGHAN** town (Muineachán, "place of thickets") while on your way to somewhere else, but the actual fabric of the place makes for an interesting passing visit. Monaghan town epitomizes the impact of the Plantation upon the region. The planning of seventeenth-century settlers, the prosperity of the eighteenth-century linen industry (largely the achievement of Scots Presbyterians) and the subsequent wealth and status of the town in the following century are all very much in evidence. Monaghan's layout comprises three central squares linked by a chain of lanes, which is rather unusual for a Plantation town. At the town's very centre is the **Diamond** – the name given to most of these Ulster "squares" – in the middle of which stands a grandiose Victorian drinking fountain, the kind of memorial strongly reminiscent of any nineteenth-century industrial British city, and strangely out of place in rural Ireland. When the fountain was placed here, the earlier seventeenth-century Scottish settlers' cross, with its multifaceted sundial, was shifted a short distance along Dublin Street to Old Cross Square, where it still stands.

Alongside the Diamond is **Church Square**. Here a Classical courthouse, a solid Victorian bank and a very pretty Regency Gothic church, large and spacious, stand together, conferring a strong sense of civic dignity. The town's former importance as a British garrison town is quite clear, and a large obelisk commemorates a Colonel Dawson killed in the Crimean War. Everything about the place suggests a conscious attempt at permanency, with buildings apparently placed with a view to posterity. Even the rounded corners of the most mundane of the structures, and their boldly arched entrances, both features unique to Monaghan, suggest strength and pride.

Beyond Church Square, at the top of Market Street, is the pretty, arched **Market House** built in 1792; a solid, graceful building of well-cut limestone, with finely detailed decoration of carved oak leaves and oak apples. In the opposite direction, Dublin Street leads down to **Old Cross Square**, whose cross once stood in the Diamond. At no.10 stands the house of Monaghan's most famous son, **Charles Gavan Duffy** (actually born in Dublin in 1816, but a town resident for more than thirty years) – a Nationalist who was instrumental in the founding of both the Young Ireland Movement and the Irish

Tenant League. He was also the editor and co-founder, along with Thomas Davis, of *The Nation*, a paper which was to disseminate politically sensitive ideas. Duffy emigrated to Australia in 1856, becoming Prime Minister of Victoria in 1871 and, subsequently, in 1877, Speaker of the Australian Assembly. He died in Nice, France, in 1903.

Southeast of the centre and a short distance along the N2 Dublin road, standing high up on a hill, **St Macartan's Catholic Cathedral** commands views over the whole town and surrounding countryside. Completed in 1892, it's a Gothic Revival building of hard grey sandstone, with a tall spire and a spacious interior, complete with an impressive hammer-beam roof. As you stand on the steps looking out over the surrounding land you get a real feeling of its era – it's a most successful nineteenth-century statement of religious liberation and pride.

As well as being a busy commercial and administrative centre, Monaghan looks after the county's vigorous and sometimes violent history at the **Monaghan County Museum** on Hill Street (Tues–Sat 10am–1pm & 2–5pm; free). This fine building houses a permanent collection of archaeological material, prehistoric antiquities, examples of traditional local crafts, domestic utensils and paintings, prints and watercolours from the late eighteenth century to the present day. The museum's most prized artefact is the **Cross of Clogher**, a processional cross dating from around 1400. Contemporary art exhibitions are also held here. The **Heritage Centre**, St Louis Convent, Broad Road (Mon, Tues, Thurs & Fri 10am–noon & 2–4pm, Sat & Sun 2.30–4.30pm; €1.50), tells the story of the religious order of St Louis, with an intelligent display meticulously put together by one of the sisters; you're guided through it with a cassette recording.

Practicalities

The **tourist office** is in Market House in Market Street (May–Oct Mon–Fri 9am–5pm, Sat 10am–5pm; ⓣ047/81122, ⓦwww.monaghantourism.com). The **bus** station (ⓣ047/82377) is on North Road, five minutes' walk from Church Square in the centre of town. Bus Éireann (ⓣ047/82377) links Monaghan with all major towns in the Republic and with Armagh, Belfast, Derry, Omagh and Strabane in the North. McConnon's (ⓣ047/82020) operates a private daily bus service to Dublin, picking up in Church Square (Mon–Sat) and from behind the courthouse (Sun). There are several decent **B&Bs**, including *Ashleigh House*, 37 Dublin St (ⓣ047/81227; ❸), and *The Cedars*, Clones Road (ⓣ047/82783; ❷ closed Nov–Feb). Upmarket alternatives include: *The Hillgrove Hotel*, Old Armagh Road, near the cathedral (ⓣ047/81288, ⓦwww.quinnhotels.com; ❻), which is smart, spacious and welcoming and offers comfortable rooms; and the *Four Seasons Hotel & Leisure Club*, out towards Armagh in Coolshannagh (ⓣ047/81888, ⓦwww.4seasonshotel.ie; ❼) which has its own pool and gym.

Decent **cafés** in Monaghan include *Corr's Corner Restaurant*, Church Square, and *Nostalgia*, opposite the tourist office in Market Street. Several places serve bar **meals**: *Andy's Bar*, 12 Market St (ⓣ047/82277), is especially good and serves wholesome lunches daily in the bar as well as more exotic fare in its restaurant (Tues–Sun 6–10pm); *McConnon's Olde Cross Inn*, Olde Cross Square, is another good option; and carvery lunches are available at *The Hillgrove Hotel*. Otherwise, there is a limited choice of places to eat in the evening: the moderately priced, informal Italian restaurant *Mediterraneo* at 58 Dublin St (ⓣ047/82335; closed Tues) offers fish, pizza and pasta; and *Cooper's*, Market Street, is a bar/restaurant serving modern European cuisine.

You won't have to go far to hear **music** in the evenings. In Dublin Street, *The Brewery* (aka *McKenna's*) has heavy rock bands three to four nights a week and the *Shamrock Bar* has live music at weekends. *An Poc Fada*, North Street, is a lively bar with a range of musical entertainments, including live bands and DJs. The hippest places include the *Havana Bar*, 6 Glaslough St, which has music and DJs at weekends and *Club Max* at the Four Seasons Hotel (Wed, Fri & Sat). Monaghan has some very active local **theatre** groups: check out The Garage Theatre, St Dawnet's Complex, Armagh Road (Ⓣ047/81597, Ⓦwww.monaghanvec.ie), to find out what's on. Latest film releases are shown at The Diamond Screen cinema, the Diamond (Ⓣ047/84755). There's an international rhythm and blues **festival** over the first weekend in September, usually starting on the Thursday night (Ⓣ047/71114 for further information).

Around County Monaghan

Most of Monaghan's towns and villages have very clear origins in the seventeenth and eighteenth centuries. The influence of Scottish planters and English colonists is obvious in the number of planters' Gothic and Presbyterian churches, and in the planned towns and the landscaped estates developed around conveniently picturesque lakes. Stark, stern architecture reflects the character of the hard-working and hard-driving settlers who came here determined to extract prosperity from farming, and from the linen industries which they introduced. Probably the most extreme examples of such discipline are the dour, austere stone cottages of **Glaslough**, cold and orderly, in the north of the county. Monaghan's cultural identity, like Cavan's, is deeply rooted in Ulster history. Heading south of Monaghan town towards Dublin both **Castleblaney** and **Carrickmacross** are lively enough small towns, blending rural ways with modern development, while the village of **Iniskeen**, the birthplace of Patrick Kavanagh, is well worth visiting for insights into the poet's importance. To Monaghan town's southwest, the hilltop market town of **Clones**, almost on the border with Fermanagh, still evinces much of its Plantation origins. The county is generally well served by buses, though their frequency diminishes away from the routes along main roads.

Glaslough

There are just a few reasons for pushing six miles northeast of Monaghan to the eerie, chill-grey village of **GLASLOUGH** ("green lake"), and the best of these is *Castle Leslie* (Ⓣ047/88109, Ⓦwww.castleleslie.com; ❾), a majestic aristocratic pile, crammed with fabulous antiques. Book in and you leave the twenty-first century behind: there are no phones, TVs or room service, just wonderfully relaxed hospitality and a sense of fading splendour. Previous guests have included Yeats, George Moore (see p.851), Winston Churchill (a cousin of the Leslie family) and Mick Jagger, and the castle recently received major press coverage as the location for Paul McCartney's wedding reception. If an overnight stay is beyond your budget, you can sample some of the atmosphere if you book in for dinner (around €45 per head). Less expensive and very agreeable **B&B** accommodation is available in the village itself at the *Pillar House Hotel* (Ⓣ047/88125; ❺) and just around the corner from here is *The Olde Bar*, also in the village (Thurs–Sat only) a tiny **pub**, seemingly unchanged for decades.

Castleblayney

Unless you're heading for Glaslough or the North, there are two main routes out of Monaghan town: west to the pleasant town of Clones or south to Carrickmacross. On the latter route you'll pass first through **CASTLE-BLAYNEY**, fourteen miles from Monaghan, whose two proud broad streets hinge upon a fine Georgian courthouse at what was once the market square. Castleblayney was built by English colonists to serve the needs of a large estate, beautifully situated beside Monaghan's largest lake, **Lough Muckno**, and this is still the town's finest asset. The English picked their spot wisely: it's a particularly attractive demesne of mixed woodlands and gentle slopes beside placid waters. The estate is now the Lough Muckno Leisure Park, with clearly sign-posted walks around beautiful grounds; access is just behind the courthouse. The park tends to attract families and anglers in search of peace and quiet, but it's also home to the Muckno Adventure Centre (March–Oct; ⓣ086/313 1612), where you can hire canoes, sailing dinghies and sailboards. There's more water-based excitement to be had at Muckno Waterski Club (ⓣ087/666 0077), and plenty of coarse angling available at the lough and in the series of small lakes roundabout.

Castleblayney's sprucest **accommodation** is provided by the *Glencarn Hotel and Leisure Centre*, Monaghan Road (ⓣ042/974 6666, ⓕ974 6521; ❺), set beside Lough Muckno Forest Park and housing a range of leisure facilities. B&Bs include *Rockville House* (ⓣ042/974 6161, ⓔrockvillehouse@hotmail.com; ❷), a mile south out of town at the beginning of the Dundalk road, and *Blittogue House* (ⓣ042/974 0476, ⓔblittogue.house@ireland.com; ❷), a further half-mile up the Dublin road. There are several **places to eat**: during the day *Joan's Pantry*, Main Street, serves inexpensive, wholesome meals; *The Comet*, Main Street, has good bar food and a restaurant for evening meals; and the location of the down-to-earth *Hope Castle Bar and Restaurant* (ⓣ042/974 9450) takes some beating, over-looking the lake within the grounds of the forest park – they serve generous helpings of pub grub and their evening menu is only a little more expensive. *The Hope Castle* also sees plenty of the local **nightlife**, with bands several nights a week during the summer months – mainly country, ballads and so forth, plus bluegrass on Fridays. *The Phoenix Bar*, Muckno Street, has live music at weekends and other places to try include *The Comet* or *The Kitchen*, a Gothic theme bar on Main Street, while the *Glencarn Hotel* has its own nightclub featuring DJs and occasional star-name Irish live acts.

Carrickmacross and around

CARRICKMACROSS, ten miles south of Castleblayney, is the county's second most important town, boosted in the nineteenth century by a prosperous lace-making industry, whose modern products can be viewed in the Lace Gallery on the Market Square. Today Carrickmacross is a rather modest place with just one broad main street: a Planters' Gothic church stands at one end, and a fine mid-nineteenth-century courthouse at the other. In between lies a bustling array of pubs, shops and Georgian houses, and today's lacemakers have their tiny showcase in the nineteenth-century market buildings at the lower end of the main street. The town's most renowned modern son is the comedian Ardal O'Hanlon (best known as Father Dougal in the Channel 4 TV series *Father Ted*), whose debut novel *The Talk of the Town* satirizes life in a thinly disguised Carrickmacross.

Just outside town, landscaped parkland of sumptuous oaks and beeches surrounds **Lough Fea**. Further out, some six miles down the Kingscourt road, is the **Dún an Rí Forest Park** (actually in County Cavan) with more fine wooded walks. Accommodation options range from the massive and expensive *Nuremore Hotel*, south of town on the N2 (Ⓣ042/966 1438, Ⓦwww.nuremore-hotel.ie; ❾), with its own eighteen-hole golf course, to a few B&Bs near the centre of Carrickmacross. The best of these is *Breffni House*, O'Neill Street (Ⓣ042/966 1361, Ⓔfarneywines@eircom.net; ❷), a comfortable place, two minutes' walk in the Dundalk direction from Main Street. Alternatively, head for *Eureka* at 27 Ard Rois Ave (Ⓣ042/966 2009; ❷), a friendly, low-key, bungalow B&B. The best place to **eat** in town is *The Fiddler's Elbow*, Main Street, a busy bar with a reasonably priced and innovative restaurant menu. Opposite here, one of the county's few **traditional music** sessions can be found in *The Tavern* on Fridays during the summer months.

Inniskeen

INNISKEEN (Inis Caoin, "pleasant river-meadow"), six miles east of Carrickmacross, is the birthplace of **Patrick Kavanagh**. There's a small plaque bearing some of his verse in the village, and the house he lived in is well signposted – but you can't go in and it's an entirely uninteresting building. Kavanagh is buried in the graveyard of St Mary's Church, which is also home to the **Patrick Kavanagh Rural and Literary Resource Centre** (Tues–Fri 11am–4.30pm, plus mid-March–Sept Sat 2–6pm & June–Sept Sun 2–6pm; €4; Ⓦwww.patrickkavanaghcountry.com), which has a wealth of Kavanagh-related memorabilia and displays on his work, including a series of a dozen specially commissioned paintings based upon his epic poem *The Great Hunger*. The centre also runs occasional writers' weekends. If you're in need of refreshment try the aptly named *Poet's Rest* coffee shop next door. Iniskeen is the starting point for the first phase of the **Monaghan Way**, a waymarked walking trail which will run from here to Glaslough and eventually circumnavigate the entire county (Ⓣ042/974 5173 for details). The way is still in development but is scheduled to open in 2003. The only **accommodation** in the village is provided by *Gleneven Guest House* (Ⓣ042/937 8294, Ⓔglenevenguesthouse@iol-free.ie; ❷), a hundred yards or so towards Dundalk from the Kavanagh Resource Centre.

Clones

Around twelve miles southwest of Monaghan, **CLONES** (pronounced "clo-nez", from Cluain Eois, "Eos's meadow") is a busy, friendly market town, barely half a mile from the border. Situated on top of a hill, its streets give a good perspective over the surrounding countryside. The town – as it appears today – dates from 1601 when the English took it over and started to develop it. It's very obviously an Ulster town, with large Presbyterian and Methodist churches to rival the usual Catholic and Church of Ireland offerings. The solemn and impressive **St Tiernach's Church** (Church of Ireland) gives out onto the fine Diamond, and there is some evidence of eighteenth-century prosperity in the town's handful of Georgian houses. There are also traces of Clones' earlier identity, the most impressive being the weathered, deeply carved **high cross** which stands in the Diamond. Depicted on it are Adam and Eve, Abraham's near sacrifice of Isaac, Daniel in the lions' den and, on the north side, the Adoration of the Magi, the miracle at Cana and the miracle of the loaves and fishes. Though worn, there's still a strong impression of the richness of the carving. In the sixth century St Tiernach founded a monastery at Clones. It became an Augustinian **abbey** in the twelfth century, and the tumbled-down

△ Patrick Kavanagh

traces of this can be seen in Abbey Street, along with those of a round tower dating from the ninth century. Just on the edge of town, above Cara Street, is the site of an ancient rath (a hill fort) which later became the base for a twelfth-century Anglo-Norman motte-and-bailey castle, subsequently burned down by local chieftains. **Ulster Canal Stores** (July & Aug daily 9am–5pm; Sept–June Mon–Fri 9am–5pm), down by the canal on Cara Street, the distribution centre for goods arriving via the Ulster Canal which linked Belfast to Lough Erne, via Lough Neagh. These days, the Stores provide local information and have exhibitions on the area's history, including lace-making and the old canal.

Nowadays, the town's chief claims to fame are as the setting for Patrick McCabe's *The Butcher Boy* (see p.866), and as the home of Barry McGuigan, the former world-champion featherweight boxer – there are a couple of photos of him in *The Lennard Arms Hotel*, which also offers extremely comfortable **B&B** (Ⓣ047/51075; ❷) and has a bistro (Thurs–Sat). Other accommodation options include *Creighton's Hotel* in Fermanagh Street (Ⓣ047/51055; ❸) and the very welcoming *Clonkeen Cottage* (Ⓣ047/51268, Ⓔclonkeencottage@hotmail.com; ❷), a mile out of town on the Rosslea road. Classy, country-house accommodation can be found at *Hilton Park* (April–Sept; Ⓣ047/56007, Ⓦwww.hiltonpark.ie; ❾), set in its own landscaped park, three miles down the Scotshouse road from the Diamond. Just outside Newbliss, around five miles southeast of Clones, is *Glynch House* (Ⓣ047/54045, Ⓔmirth@eircom.net; ❸), an eighteenth-century mansion offering accommodation and evening meals.

Packed with lively **pubs**, Fermanagh Street is the place to head for an evening's entertainment. *The Paragon* has DJs (Fri–Sun) while *Papa Joe's* offers karaoke and live music at weekends. *Under the Bar* has a very cosmopolitan interior, while, contrastingly, *The Tower* is an old-fashioned long bar. *An Bonnan Buí* is a raucous, old boys' pub and *Treanors* offers the only hope of a **traditional music** session. Clones also houses the GAA's second largest stadium (after Croke Park), **St Tiernach's Park**, north of the town off Rosslea Road, which stages the Ulster province's **Gaelic football finals** in July.

County Cavan

Long neglected by most holidaymakers, **County Cavan** is slowly becoming more popular, thanks to the major redevelopment of the old Ballinamore–Ballyconnell Canal, linking the mighty Shannon waterway, which serves all four provinces of the country, and the Lough Erne lake system, which flows to the northwest. The project extended the original canal and renamed it the **Shannon–Erne Waterway**, weaving together streams, rivers and lakes through 39 miles of wild, unspoilt countryside, free of cities and major industries. It is now possible to sail the length of the Shannon, then along the canal, through the Erne system to Belleek, County Fermanagh, a total of 239 miles.

In former times, the region was even more water-ridden, boggy and forested than it is today. This complex of lake and bog was extremely difficult for foreign invaders to penetrate and control, and also made the land less desirable.

The county is renowned for its **fishing**, and a conservative tourism is growing which neither scars the land nor disturbs the peace. Forest parks have been developed to give anglers access to the heart of the lake complex. Everywhere, the stillness is profound. If you want to enjoy this largely untouched part of the country by bicycle, you could follow the **Kingfisher Cycle Trail**, a long-distance cycle path (200 miles), linking Cavan with Fermanagh and Leitrim in the north and west, and Clones, County Monaghan to the east – for further information see p.765. **Cavan** town itself is an agreeable enough place but has little of inherent interest, and if you want to explore the county's lakes and waterways **Belturbet** makes a far better base. Around **Lough Oughter** the village of **Killeshandra** is visited for its traditional music while there are notable ecclesiastical remains at **Kilmore**. There are few diversions in the south of the county, though the **county museum** in **Ballyjamesduff** amply rewards a detour.

Cavan town, Lough Oughter and Ballyjamesduff

CAVAN town (An Cabhán, "the hollow") grew up around an abbey, but nothing remains of this beyond an eighteenth-century tower beside the burial place of Owen Roe O'Neill. The town is quite subdued, with only two primary thoroughfares: Main Street is the principal artery of shops and bars, while Farnham Street has an older character with some very nice stone Georgian houses, a Classical courthouse of warm sandstone and a huge Catholic cathedral, built in the 1940s, that surprisingly succeeds in confirming status and a sense of place without being overbearing.

The **tourist office** on Farnham Street (April–Sept Mon–Fri 9am–5pm, Sat 9am–1pm; Ⓣ049/433 1942, Ⓦwww.cavantourism.com) will offer information on the county in general; there's little to see in the town itself. Cavan is very much the **transport** centre of the county, and Bus Éireann (Ⓣ049/433 1353) connects it with all major towns in the Republic and the North. The private Wharton's Buses (Ⓣ049/433 7114) also operate a daily service to Dublin, leaving from outside the *Lakeland Hotel*, Bridge Street.

There is a handful of places to stay in and around the town: **B&B** is available at *McCaul's Guesthouse*, 10 Bridge St (Ⓣ049/433 1327; ❸), right in the town centre, and at the equally comfortable *Oakdene*, 29 Cathedral Rd (Ⓣ049/433 1698; ❸), five minutes' walk west of the cathedral on Farnham Street. Alternatively, there's the welcoming and good-value *Lisnamandra House*, in a peaceful rural setting four and a half miles out of Cavan and just outside Crossdoney on the R198 (Ⓣ049/433 7196; ❸); it offers pleasant accommodation and very appetizing breakfasts. *The Farnham Arms Hotel* on Main Street (Ⓣ049/433 2577; ❺) provides pleasant and comfortable accommodation, and their bar and restaurant are open to nonresidents. The town's plushest **accommodation** is provided by *Hotel Kilmore*, Dublin Road (Ⓣ049/433 2288, Ⓦwww.quinnhotels.com; ❻).

Eating options in general are fairly limited, but there are a number of good spots for **bar food** on Main Street, including: *An Síbín*, an airy, old-fashioned place; the loud and popular *Blackhorse Inn*; and the *Fiddlers Flute*, which serves good-value evening meals. *Café Mona*, on Thomas Ashe Street, offers a bountiful range of salads and sandwiches while, just across the way on Main Street,

Internet access is available at *Ego*, also a popular lunch-time spot for light meals. There's no shortage of viable watering-holes: *An Cruíscín Lán*, 82 Main St, draws a young crowd, attracted by the DJs and live music (Thurs–Sat), as does *An Síbín* (DJ on Fri nights); if you are looking for a bar with character and a mixed crowd, try *Louis Blessings* on Main Street. *The Farnham Arms Hotel* has a **traditional music** session (Wed) and also houses *Club O.T.O.* (Thurs–Sun) for fans of contemporary dance anthems and chart hits. Other spots for music can be found on Dublin Road: *Meadow View* has a Monday-night traditional music session and rock at the weekends and *The Lavey Inn* offers live music (Sat & Sun). For rod hire, licences and information on **fishing**, visit *Sports World*, 11 Town Hall St (ⓣ049/433 1812).

Lough Oughter

A major focus of scenic interest in County Cavan is the complex of tiny lakes that riddle the north of the county. They're known collectively as **Lough Oughter** and form part of Upper Lough Erne. The land here is so fretted with water that its very fabric seems to be disintegrating. Contours are provided by very low, unassuming hills while the waters are edged with reeds, spindly silver birch and alder. Everything is on a small scale, but the landscape has a subtle attraction nonetheless, and the roads, making their way through the labyrinthine network of lakes, are quiet and empty. It makes little sense to head for a particular point in Lough Oughter – it's hard to tell when you've got there anyway – and the best plan is probably just to enjoy the gentle confusion.

The nicest of the little towns serving visitors, especially those interested in fishing, are Cavan town itself and, ten miles north, Belturbet. In between, just four miles north of Cavan, there's also the pretty village of **Butlersbridge**, with a popular bar, *The Derragarra Inn* – touristy but serving good food throughout the day. **BELTURBET** (Béal Tairbirt, "mouth of the isthmus") itself sits prettily on a hill beside the River Erne and is an angling and boating resort with a marina and cruiser station. Weekly **cabin cruiser rental** is available with Emerald Star Line, and you can sail from here and drop the boat off in Carrick-on-Shannon (ⓣ071/962 0234; €650–€3050 per week depending upon size and season). Well signposted from the town centre, and just five minutes' walk away, **Belturbet Railway Station** (April–Sept daily 9.30am–5pm; Oct–March closed weekends; €2.50; ⓦwww.belturbet-station.com) has undergone restoration, which began some forty years after its closure in 1959. Inside there's a small exhibition describing the history of the Cavan and Leitrim Railway and the station itself, but steam-train enthusiasts would probably gain more enjoyment from a visit to the actual working railway at Dromod (see p.557). For **B&B**, try the comfortable and friendly *Church View*, 8 Church St (ⓣ049/952 2358; ❷), up behind the library, off the main road. Near the main street, *The Seven Horseshoes* is a popular, if a little pricey, spot for lunches and evening **meals** or, alternatively, there's the *Erne Bistro* by the river offering modern European cuisine and regular music. There are also a number of lively **bars** on the main street, including the *Erne Lounge Bar* which has music, from jazz to country, most nights of the week.

Heading round the lough there are a few sights of interest. About a mile south of Milltown, you'll find **Drumlane Church and round tower**. A monastery was founded here by St M'Aodhog in the sixth century, and Augustinians from Kells took the place over in medieval times. The church itself is plain and roofless, but its setting beside a lake, and its size in such an intimate landscape, are impressive. The earliest parts of the building are thirteenth century, but it was substantially altered in the fifteenth century, the period from which the carved heads outside the doorways and windows date. The round tower is eleventh century and of good, clean stonework.

Continuing south, **KILLESHANDRA** (Cill na Seanrátha, "church of the old fort"), on the west side of Lough Oughter, is a village of little attraction itself, but is one of the few places to hear **traditional music** in the county. *Dickie's* has a Thursday-night session, and the *Shamrock Inn*, which also offers **B&B** (Ⓣ049/433 4139; ❸) has one on Sunday nights. You can also stay at the *Loughbawn Hotel* (Ⓣ049/433 4404; ❷) whose restaurant is just about the only place in the village offering evening meals.

The **Cathedral Church of St Fethlimidh** (June–Sept Fri–Sun 2–6pm; free) at **KILMORE** (An Chill Mhór, "the great church"), on the R198 three miles southwest of Cavan town, dates from 1860 and features an impressive array of stained-glass windows depicting biblical scenes; occasional choral and musical recitals are held here during the year (Ⓣ049/433 1918 for details). Set in the wall is an impressive twelfth-century Romanesque doorway, moved here from a monastery that stood on Trinity Island, three miles to the west in Lough Oughter. Its deep, chunky carving is superbly intricate. In the cathedral grounds a large sycamore tree stands by the grave of William Bedell, Bishop of Kilmore from 1629 to 1642. Responsible for the translation of the Old Testament into Irish (an original copy of which is on display inside the cathedral), Bedell was imprisoned in Clough Oughter Castle (the remains of which lie on an island three miles southeast of Killeshandra) during the 1641 Rebellion and died a year later. Follow the narrow road that runs for about three miles north from Kilmore to the hamlet of **Garthrotten**, and you can enter *Killykeen Forest Park*, a self-catering complex with accommodation in wooden chalets (Ⓣ049/433 2541). There is access to woodland **walks** and **fishing**, and **horse riding** is available at Killykeen Equestrian Centre (Ⓣ049/436 1707).

Ballyjamesduff

BALLYJAMESDUFF is eleven miles south of Cavan town, just off the N3. James Duff himself, the Earl of Fife, was an early Plantation landlord of the area, and one of his descendants, Sir James Duff, commanded English troops during the suppression of the 1798 Rebellion, making the more sombre Irish version of his name, "Black Séamus", rather appropriate to local ears. The town is the location for the **Cavan County Museum** (Tues–Sat 10am–5pm, plus June–Sept Sun 2–6pm; €3). The impressive collection covers all aspects of the county's history and many of the post-eighteenth-century exhibits on display came from Mrs Phyllis Faris's mammoth and eclectic "Pighouse Collection" of domestic artefacts and memorabilia in Killeshandra. Items include the Killycluggin Stone, dating from 200 BC, decorated in classic Celtic La Tène artwork and replicas of Celtic stone idols dating from the second century BC to the second century AD. Among the exhibits from the medieval period there's the Lough Errol dugout boat (900 AD) and a couple of impressive Sheila-na-Gigs. Surprisingly, the history of Cavan's emigrants yields Sioux girdles and headdresses, and there's extensive coverage of the GAA footballing history of the county, including the 1947 All-Ireland Senior Gaelic football final between Cavan and Kerry which took place in New York as a special commemoration of the centenary of the Great Famine. Also represented here is the songwriter Percy French who lived and worked in the county for a time as an inspector of drains – one of his more famous comic songs is "Come Back Paddy Reilly to Ballyjamesduff".

West Cavan

To the northwest of Milltown and Killeshandra, **west Cavan** sticks out like a handle, tracing the line of the border. It's quite different from the rest of the county – wilder and higher, with peat-covered hills, granite boulders and mountain streams. In this inhospitable bleakness, it has more in common with the wilds of Donegal than the more subtle Cavan lakeland.

About six miles from Belturbet is **BALLYCONNELL** (Béal Atha Conaill, "Conall's ford mouth"), two miles west of which is the independent **hostel**, *Sandville House Hostel* (all year, but advance booking advised Nov–March; ⓣ049/952 6297; ⓦhomepage.eircom.net/~sandville). Housed in an airy, converted barn alongside a large Georgian house, it's a tranquil spot, and there are bikes for rent and space for tents. If you've got your own helicopter, you might fancy landing on the helipad at the *Slieve Russell Hotel, Golf & Country Club* (ⓣ049/952 6444, ⓦwww.quinnhotels.com; ❾), a huge edifice a couple of miles back towards Belturbet which has its own pool, gym, tennis courts and an eighteen-hole PGA championship golf course. More modest **B&B** accommodation options in the area include the welcoming *Rossdean* (ⓣ049/952 6358; ❷), five hundred yards down the Belturbet road, and *Hillcrest House*, Slievebricken (ⓣ049/952 6475; ❸), a mile down the Killeshandra road. Ballyconnell has a surprising number of **eating** places, all situated on Main Street. *Pól Ó D* is an exceptional modern Irish restaurant serving lunches and dinners (Wed–Sat 6.30–9.30pm) – a three-course evening meal costs €30 per head without wine). Alternatively, there's excellent pub grub available at *The Angler's Rest* (both at lunch time and in the evening) or massive pub lunches in *The Ballyconnell Inn*. The *Bayleaf Café* specializes in chips with everything, but is very good value.

Right up in the northwestern corner of the county, the **Cavan Way** is a signposted walk of seventeen miles that takes you through rugged terrain from Dowra to Blacklion, where it meets the southwestern end of the Ulster Way. Small maps of the route can be picked up in tourist offices. From the heights above Blacklion there are spectacular views over Lough MacNean and the Fermanagh lakeland, to the Sligo and Leitrim mountains in the west, and on a clear day to the heights of south Donegal. Along the route, The Shannon Pot is the source of Ireland's mightiest river and figures heavily in Irish myth, though it's little visited.

DOWRA and **BLACKLION** themselves are tiny places: the former a remote place on the young Shannon before it fills Lough Allen, the first of many lakes; the latter a border crossing point which takes its name from a pub which once stood here. Blacklion has the better facilities, including **B&B** at *Lough Macneann House*, on Main Street (ⓣ071/985 3022; ❹; restaurant open July–Sept Mon–Sat; Oct–June Thurs–Sun); dinner in their award-winning bistro costs around €40. Nearby, *Olive Grove* (ⓣ071/985 3443, ⓔolivegrove59@hotmail.com; ❸) offers comfortable accommodation and organic ingredients in its wholesome lunches. Blacklion is on the main Enniskillen–Sligo bus route and there's also a more frequent service to Enniskillen from Belcoo, just over the bridge on the other side of the border. Dowra has only a Saturday bus service, just a few bars and a couple of shops.

Travel details

Trains

Drogheda to: Belfast (4–7 daily; 1hr 35min); Dublin (8–25 daily; 40min); Dundalk (4–7 daily; 25min); Newry (4–7 daily; 45min).
Dundalk to: Belfast (4–7 daily; 1hr 10min); Drogheda (4–7 daily; 25min); Dublin (4–7 daily; 1hr 5min); Newry (4–7 daily; 20min).

Buses

IBus Éireann

Cavan town to: Ballyconnell (5–6 daily; 30min); Belfast (1–4 daily; 2hr 55min); Belturbet (5–6 daily; 20min); Clones (2–4 daily; 30min); Dublin (4 daily; 1hr 40min); Enniskillen (5–6 daily; 1hr 10min); Monaghan (2–4 daily; 1hr).
Dowra to: Drumshanbo (1 Sat; 25 min); Sligo (1 Sat; 1hr 15min).
Drogheda to: Athlone (1–2 daily; 2hr 35min); Collon for Mellifont (3 Mon–Sat; 10min); Donore for Newgrange (4–7 daily; 10min); Dublin (6–26 daily; 1hr); Dundalk (3–6 daily; 35min); Termonfeckin (5 Mon–Sat; 20min).
Dundalk to: Athlone (1–2 daily; 3hr 15min); Carlingford (5 Mon–Sat; 40min–1hr); Carrickmacross (5 Mon–Sat; 35min); Drogheda (3–6 daily; 35min); Inniskeen (5 Mon–Sat; 20min); Newry (2–4 daily; 25min).
Monaghan town to: Armagh (1–4 daily; 35min); Belfast (1–3 daily; 2hr); Carrickmacross (8–12 daily; 40min); Castleblayney (8–12 daily; 20min); Cavan (2–4 daily; 1 hr); Clones (5–7 daily; 20min); Derry (5–6 daily; 2hr); Dublin (8–12 daily; 2hr); Glaslough (2 Tues & Sat; 20min); Letterkenny (5–7 daily; 1hr 50min).

Ulsterbus

Blacklion to: Enniskillen (3 Mon–Sat; 25min); to Sligo (3 Mon–Sat; 1hr).
Clones to: Enniskillen (2–5 daily; 50min).

McConnon's Buses

Monaghan town to: Dublin (1–2 daily; 2hr).

Wharton's Buses

Cavan town to: Dublin (1 daily; 1hr 50min).

Wexford, Carlow and Kilkenny

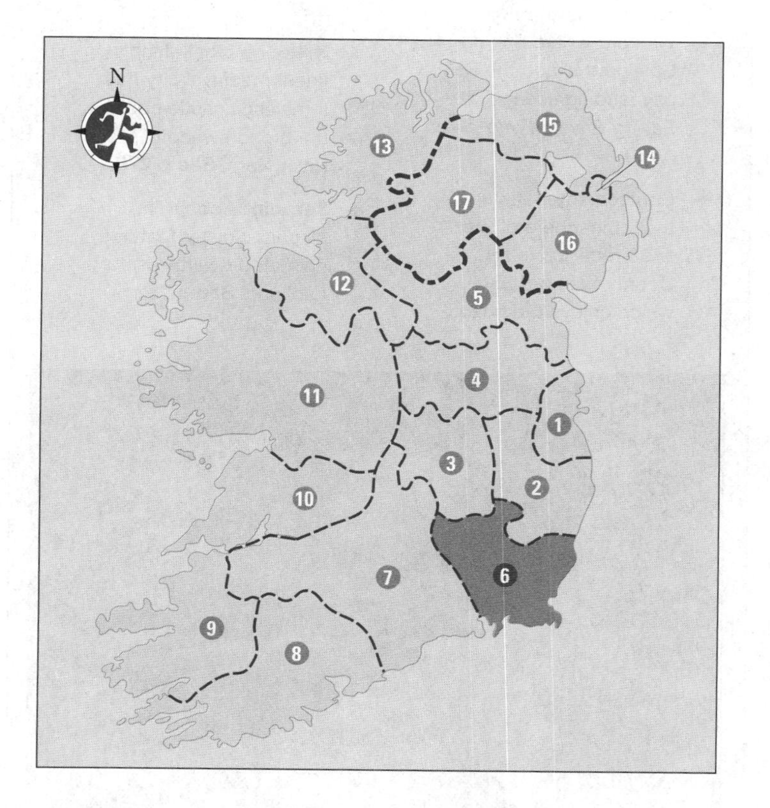

CHAPTER 6 **Highlights**

* **Wexford** Founded by the Vikings, the town is especially worth seeing during the world-famous Opera Festival. **See p.264**

* **Curracloe** Check out the excellent sandy beaches north of Wexford where Steven Spielberg filmed the D-day landing scenes of *Saving Private Ryan*. **See p.267**

* **Enniscorthy** Soak up the atmosphere of the 1798 rebellion in this County Wexford town, which enjoys the beautiful backdrop of Vinegar Hill. **See p.272**

* **The South Leinster Way** Pack your walking boots and explore valleys and open farmland skirting the bleak heights of Mount Leinster. **See p.274**

* **Kilkenny city** Ireland's finest medieval city has a majestic castle above the broad sweep of the River Nore. **See p.276**

* **Jerpoint Abbey** The elegant cloister features animated twelfth-century carvings. **See p.282**

6

Wexford, Carlow and Kilkenny

The southeast of Ireland is not the most obvious of areas to visit, especially if this is your first time in the country. There are none of the wild wastes of rock, bog and water, nor the accompanying abandoned cottages that tell of famine, eviction and emigration, so appealing to romantic tastes. It is, however, Ireland's sunniest and driest corner, and what the region does have to offer – whether you're spending a couple of days passing through, or if you simply haven't the time for more distant wanderings – is worth savouring. On the whole, the region's attractions are frustratingly widely scattered, but its medieval and Anglo-Norman history is richly concentrated in the ancient city of **Kilkenny** – the region's only really touristy town – and the lush countryside around it shelters some powerful medieval ruins. **Wexford** town's conviviality makes up for its disappointingly scant traces of a vigorous Viking and Norman past; in **Carlow** town, sadly, this isn't the case. While the extreme east is dull and low-lying, and the Blackstairs Mountains open and empty, the southeast is characterized overall by a history of rich cultivation

Inland, the region is shaped by three majestic rivers: the Nore, the Barrow and the Slaney, and by the empty Blackstairs Mountains which form a rough natural boundary between the counties of Wexford and Carlow. The three rivers roll through rich, lush pastures and pretty wooded valleys, past medieval Christian ruins and little towns and villages. This landscape is at its prettiest in the hills and valleys of the **Nore** and **Barrow**, just north of New Ross, and south of Kilkenny town, perfect countryside for leisurely cycling and easy **walking** – an option made all the more attractive by the hostels at New Ross and Kilkenny. The signposted **South Leinster Way** meanders through the heart of this countryside to some of the choicest spots, before heading north-east to the less intimate country of Carlow and the Blackstairs Mountains.

Head for **the coast** and, to the east, superb sandy beaches stretch practically the entire length of County Wexford. While the south coast is less suitable for swimming, its sand banks, shallow lagoons and silted rivers offer great opportunities for wildlife enthusiasts: prime spots for **birdwatching** include the Wexford Slobs (around the town itself), the lakes of Lady's Island and Tacumshane, the Saltee Islands off Kilmore Quay and the Hook Head Peninsula. This low-lying southern coastal region also provides an excellent

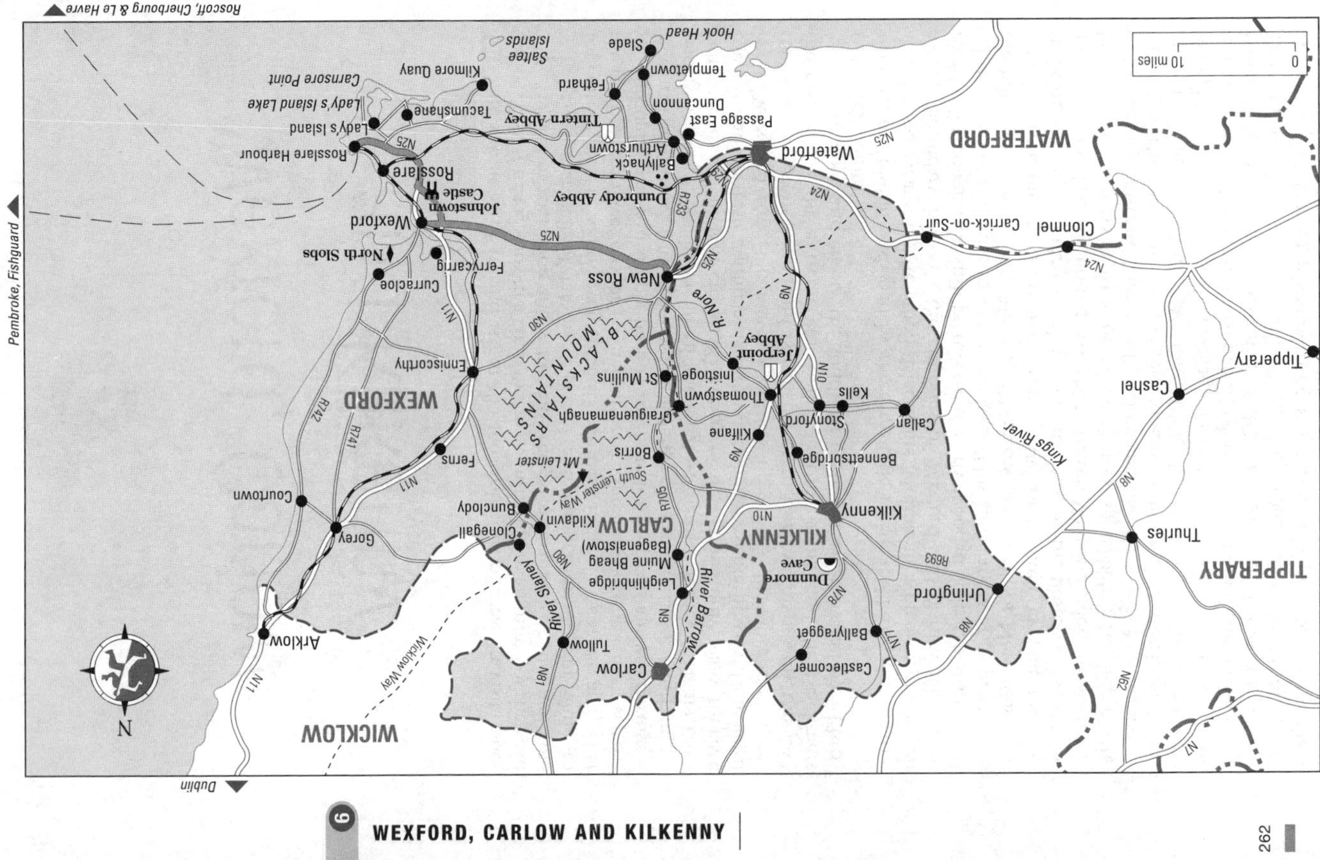

Pembroke, Fishguard
Roscoff, Cherbourg & Le Havre
Dublin
N
WICKLOW
WEXFORD
CARLOW
KILKENNY
WATERFORD
TIPPERARY
BLACKSTAIRS MOUNTAINS
Arklow
Courtown
Gorey
Ferns
Enniscorthy
Curracloe
North Slobs
Ferrycarrig
Wexford
Johnstown Castle
Rosslare
Rosslare Harbour
Lady's Island
Lady's Island Lake
Carnsore Point
Tacumshane
Kilmore Quay
Saltee Islands
Tintern Abbey
Fethard
Slade
Hook Head
Templetown
Duncannon
Passage East
Arthurstown
Ballyhack
Dunbrody Abbey
New Ross
Waterford
Carrick-on-Suir
Clonmel
Cashel
Tipperary
Thurles
Urlingford
Castlecomer
Ballyragget
Dunmore Cave
Kilkenny
Bennettsbridge
Callan
Kells
Stonyford
Thomastown
Jerpoint Abbey
Inistioge
R. Nore
Kilfane
Graiguenamanagh
St Mullins
Borris
Mt Leinster
South Leinster Way
Wicklow Way
Bunclody
Clonegall
Kildavin
Muine Bheag (Bagenalstow)
Leighlinbridge
Carlow
Tullow
River Slaney
River Barrow
Kings River
N11
N80
N81
N9
N10
N78
N77
N8
N62
N7
N24
N25
N30
R741
R742
R705
R693
R733
10 miles
0

quick route west to Waterford, since there's a car ferry from Ballyhack across to Passage East on the other side of Waterford Harbour.

Some history

The settled, developed character of this southeastern corner of Ireland owes much to its history of invasion, settlement and trade. The **Vikings** wrought havoc, but they also built the port of Wexford, which developed steadily, all the while assimilating ideas and peoples from overseas, ensuring the continual cultural influence of Europe. The arrival of mercenaries from Wales, for instance, was common throughout the medieval period, and after Henry II had consolidated the Anglo-Norman victories, Strongbow settled fellow Welshmen in the region: a dialect handed down from these people, known as *yola*, survived in the far southeast of County Wexford right into the nineteenth century.

But it was the power of the English Crown that was to have by far the greatest influence on the character of the region. The towns of Wexford, Carlow and Kilkenny still bear the marks of their **Anglo-Norman** past in city walls and ruined castles; the well-tended surrounding farmland similarly reflects centuries of English settlement. The Anglo-Norman takeover of the southeast was swift, and would have been total were it not for the fiercely Gaelic enclave of counties Carlow and Wexford. There the MacMurrough Kavanaghs became the scourge of the English in Ireland, and they continually thwarted the Crown's attempts to control the entire region. It was Art MacMurrough who defeated Richard II in battles that lost the king not only control of Ireland, but his English throne, too. Only after the arrival of Cromwell was the power of the MacMurroughs broken once and for all.

Colonization was thereafter pursued vigorously: the proximity of the Pale – and of England itself – meant that the Crown's influence was always far stronger here than in the remote west. The English found this area easier to control and administer, and during the growing unrest of the eighteenth century the region remained relatively tranquil. Surprisingly then, by far the most significant uprisings of the 1798 Rebellion took place in counties Wexford and Carlow. For nationalists, the bloodshed and heroics of that summer are central to the region's history and legend.

Counties Wexford and Carlow

Though the ancient Viking town of **Wexford** bills itself as a tourist centre, you're unlikely to spend more than a day or so here unless you have a car. Sadly, little evidence remains of the town's long and stormy history, and the place is most enjoyable for its small but lively **cultural scene**. The **wildfowl reserves** of the North Slobs are easily accessible, and some marvellous **beaches** are to be found nearby, stretching the length of County Wexford's shoreline north to the popular resort of Courtown. Inland, historic towns like **New Ross**, **Enniscorthy** and **Ferns** merit a visit if you're passing through. To see the best of the south coast, head for quaint **Kilmore Quay**, or rent a bike and explore the isolated and intriguing **Hook Head Peninsula**.

County **Carlow** is less likely to feature on your itinerary, as there's little in the way of sights. The county is at its prettiest along the River Barrow, which for much of its length forms the boundary between Carlow and Kilkenny. The **South Leinster Way** trudges at its most lonesome and desolate through the northern half of the Blackstairs Mountains; Carlow town, situated on the Dublin–Kilkenny train route, barely warrants attention.

Wexford town and around

Apart from the Viking legacy of narrow, quirky lanes, **WEXFORD** town retains few traces of its past, and only the quays suggest that it was once an important trading centre. In fact, the harbour, in business from the ninth century, has now silted up, and Wexford has lost its trade to its old rival Waterford. That's not to say, though, that the town's history stopped with the fall of the Vikings. Settled by the Normans in the twelfth century, it became an English garrison town, brutally taken by Cromwell in 1649 (he had 1500 Wexford citizens put to death). In the 1798 Rebellion, the town saw brave rebel fighting against the English Crown (backed by a mainly Protestant yeomanry), which was fearful that the port might be used as a landing place by the French. The uprising lasted longer in Wexford than in most places, but the rebels were finally put down, and the Crown was quick to exact retribution. Wexford, though, plays down its contribution to Republicanism and has emerged as a positive, forward-thinking place. It is internationally famous for its prestigious **Opera Festival**, while a more mainstream draw are the town's estimated 93 **bars**, reason enough to give Wexford at least a night.

Arrival and information

Wexford's **train** and **bus stations** (☎053/22522) are located in Redmond Place at the north end of the quays, just past the bridge over the estuary – the bridge takes you out to the campsite, the wildfowl reserve (see p.267) and the beaches of the county's east coast. **Bike rental** is available nearby at The Bike Shop, 9 Selskar St (☎053/22514; €11 per day). Wexford town centre runs southeast from Redmond Place, parallel to the estuary. The **tourist office** (April, May & Sept Mon–Sat 9am–6pm; July & Aug Mon–Sat 9am–6pm & Sun 11am–5pm; Oct Mon–Sat 9.30am–5.30pm; Nov–Jan & March, Mon–Fri 9.30am–1pm & 2–5.30pm; ☎053/23111) is located towards the south end of town in a break in the quays known as The Crescent. The Viking Shuttle Bus (☎053/21053) to Johnstown Castle and Kilmore Quay departs from outside the tourist office. **Harbour trips** run throughout the summer (€7) and can be booked at the *Kirwan House* hostel (see opposite). Padraig's Launderette is right next door to the hostel. **Internet access** is available at Bridge IT, 87 North Main St (☎053/42880).

Accommodation

Wexford has a good range of **accommodation** on offer, although bear in mind that rooms all over town are at a premium during the Opera Festival (see box on p.266). You can camp at Ferrybank Camping and Caravan Park (closed Nov–Easter; ⓣ053/42987), immediately over the bridge from Commercial Quay – and there's a swimming pool next to the campsite.

Bilrene 91 John St ⓣ053/24190. A cosy, welcoming family home offering B&B in standard rooms only. ❷

The Blue Door 18 George St ⓣ053/21047, ⓦindigo.ie/~bluedoor. Beautifully kept, spacious Georgian town house just off Main Street offering very good en-suite B&B accommodation. Despite its central location, rooms are very quiet. ❷–❹

Kirwan House 3 Mary St ⓣ053/21208, kirwanhostel@eircom.net. A fairly small, well-organized IHH hostel run by a convivial crowd. Two twin rooms are available, and dorms are mixed; linen is included. Bikes for hire and harbour trips can be booked here; launderette next door. ❷

McMenamin's Townhouse 3 Auburn Terrace, Redmond Rd ⓣ053/46442. A very cosy B&B near the station noted for its excellent breakfasts; rooms are en suite and no smoking. ❷

St Aidan's Mews Lower John St ⓣ053/22691. Plain, unpretentious B&B run by a friendly family offering standard rooms only; inexpensive single rooms available. ❷

Talbot Hotel Trinity St ⓣ053/22566, ⓦwww.talbothotel.ie. A very pleasant three-star hotel, tastefully decorated with original modern art, with a warm and traditional atmosphere. Facilities include a leisure club and pool. Located at the end of the quays; some bedrooms overlook the mouth of the bay. It's worth enquiring about special weekend and midweek deals. ❹–❻

Westgate House Westgate ⓣ053/22167, ⓦwww.wexford-online.com/westgate. The elegant sitting room of this B&B is furnished with elaborately carved antiques and crystal chandeliers; the rooms too are nicely decorated. It's a handy place for the train station. ❷

Whites Hotel George St ⓣ053/22311, ⓔinfo@whiteshotel.iol.ie. A comfortable three-star hotel right in the centre of Wexford. Although many of the bedrooms occupy a fairly characterless modern extension, the hotel itself is well run and welcoming and has a health and fitness club. ❷–❹

The Town

Set on the south side of the broad, featureless Slaney estuary, Wexford town sits behind its quays, which run on relentlessly. A waterfront promenade and marina cheer things up, and along **The Crescent**, a statue of **John Barry**, a local who founded the American Navy during their War of Independence, strides against the buffeting wind with cloak billowing. Parallel to the quays runs Wexford's lengthy Main Street, lined with bright shop fronts and creaking bars, a narrow and winding route that gives some idea of the medieval town's layout, and a place of some charm. Once you've seen it, there is little else left to explore. A monument to the 1798 Rebellion briefly draws your attention to the **Bull Ring** (part of Main Street), also scene of a massacre by Cromwell that left all but four hundred of the population dead. A lane up behind *The Cape Bar*, famous for being both a pub and an undertaker's, leads to the Cornmarket and the parallel streets of the small town centre.

The **Westgate**, built around 1300, is the sole survivor of the medieval walled city's original five gates, and is now designated as West Gate Heritage Tower (summer only Mon–Fri 9am–5pm; €3); you can watch a short film here on the town's history. Nearby are the remains of **Selskar Abbey** (wrecked by Cromwell), where Henry II spent an entire Lent in penitence for the murder of Thomas à Becket in Canterbury Cathedral.

Eating and drinking

There's no shortage of places to get a decent meal in Wexford. The town boasts a vast selection of **pubs** and bars, many featuring live music on one or more days of the week. For late-night drinking and dancing try *The Backroom* (Thurs–Sat; €4–8) behind the Centenary Stores in Charlotte Street.

The Wexford Opera Festival and the art scene

The long-established and hugely successful annual **Wexford Opera Festival** lasts for three weeks every October and draws people from all over the world. Each year the festival rescues three lesser-known operas by famous composers and presents them in the intimate setting of the Theatre Royal. Seasoned opera lovers find the festival a delight because of the sheer energy of the enterprise: a world-class festival on a shoestring budget in a friendly little town. Alongside the three major pieces are lunchtime recitals, choral and orchestral concerts, theatre, traditional music and immensely popular "Opera Scenes" in which well-known operas are presented in ninety-minute versions, with the principal characters accompanied by a pianist. It's advisable to book months in advance for tickets: the box office usually opens in June and you can get information on ticket availability and programmes from the festival office at any time (Ⓣ053/22400, Ⓦwww.wexfordopera.com).

Even out of festival time, Wexford has a lively cultural life, largely generated by a couple of **theatre** venues: the Theatre Royal on the High Street (Ⓣ053/22144, Ⓦwww.wexfordopera.com), and the Wexford Arts Centre (Ⓣ053/23764) housed in an eighteenth-century market house and town hall in Cornmarket. The Theatre Royal hosts visiting companies including light opera and touring theatre groups, and the Wexford Arts Centre offers a healthy turnover of exhibitions and hosts performance artists, dance groups, drama and music. It's also worth calling into Abstract Studios, 90 South Main St (up a little laneway), a small gallery that promotes the work of emerging artists, local and otherwise.

Restaurants

Asple's The Crescent. Big airy pub attracting a mixed sociable crowd. The bar food is a cut above average and this is one of the few places to get an inexpensive meal early evening.

Cappuccino's 23 North Main St. Cheap and jolly café, serving Mediterranean-inspired snacks and cramming in the customers. Hot ciabatta melts, filled pittas, omelettes, burgers and baguettes are amongst the reasonably priced dishes on offer.

Dragon Heed Redmond Place Ⓣ053/21332. Generally considered the best Chinese restaurant in town, with a friendly, family atmosphere. Also does takeaways.

Heavens Above 112 South Main St Ⓣ053/21273. Exquisite food makes this place a firm favourite, even though the seating is not especially comfortable. A varied menu encompassing pan-fried salmon with ginger and sun-dried tomatoes, steaks, suckling pig, a handful of vegetarian options and around 350 wines on its list. Closed Sun.

La Riva Crescent Quay Ⓣ053/24330. Lovely, intimate restaurant serving great food. Typical main courses include rack of lamb with roast vegetables; prawns with garlic, chilli and ginger; and baked monkfish with parmesan and cream sauce.

Mange 2 100 South Main St Ⓣ053/44033. Stylish yet cosy restaurant sporting abstract art on blood-red walls, and offering an eclectic contemporary menu. Closed Mon.

The Sky and the Ground 112 South Main St. One of Wexford's most popular pubs, full of character and serving excellent bar food.

Tim's Tavern South Main St Ⓣ053/23861. A regular local pub/restaurant with a lived-in feel and a bar menu which offers staples such as liver and bacon, and beef and Guinness casserole, while the restaurant is noted for cutlets, stews and steaks.

Pubs and bars

The Cape The Bull Ring. Bar/undertaker run by an affable family, and as good a place as any to raise the spirits.

The Centenary Stores Charlotte St. A lively pub attracting a young crowd, and a great spot to catch traditional music on Monday and Wednesday evenings, and Sunday morning, with a folk/blues mix on Tuesdays.

The Crown Bar Monke St. A pleasant bar, dating from 1841, tucked down a peaceful side street. A good place for a quiet pint five nights a week; live rock music on Thursdays and easy listening on Tuesdays.

The Sky and the Ground 112 South Main St. Immensely popular bar favoured by tourists and locals alike. The interior's kitted out with old enamel ads for beer, baccy and booze – you could be forgiven for thinking that it's been here for years. Great atmosphere, and traditional music every night except Saturday.

The Thomas Moore Tavern Cornmarket. Traditional bar with a good fire in the corner. Named after the poet who, in 1836, came here "in the zenith of his imperishable fame to render honour to the mother he venerated and loved", as an inscription outside will tell you. Things haven't really revved up much since then and this place is another ideal choice for a quiet pint.

Around Wexford town

Within a few miles of Wexford lie plenty of attractions to justify staying around for a day or so. Some, like the Wildfowl Reserve at the endearingly named **North Slobs**, are of specialist interest. Others, though, could claim anyone's time – not least the excellent sandy beaches at Curracloe to the north, or the resort town of Rosslare to the south. The mudflats sheltered behind the sea walls of the Slaney estuary, known as the North Slobs, are home to the Wexford Wildfowl Reserve. The Slobs are the main wintering grounds for a third of the world's population of Greenland white-fronted geese, Bewick's swans, pintails and blacktailed godwits; you can also see spotted redshanks, gulls and terns. At the reserve there's a **visitor centre** (daily: April–Sept 9am–6pm; Oct–March 10am–5pm; free), a wildfowl collection, a research station, hides, lookout towers and identification charts, all freely accessible.

To reach the North Slobs, take the Gorey road (R741) north out of Wexford over the bridge, and it's signposted on the right after about two miles. Just two and a half miles inland from Wexford, the **Irish National Heritage Park** at **FERRYCARRIG** (March–Oct daily 9.30am–6.30pm, closing times may vary; €6.35; Ⓦwww.inhp.com) plots nine thousand years of social change using full-scale models of settlements, homesteads and burial places, from the Stone Age through to Norman times. It's a great place to clarify your knowledge of Ireland's **ancient history**, and helps make sense of the numerous archaeological remains dotted throughout the country. The park is also being developed as a **nature reserve**, and the environment has been carefully nurtured to provide the appropriate settings. It works well, so that as you walk through the Mesolithic campsite, the shaggy lichen on the hazel trees, the mud and the reeds all help evoke a primeval bog, while the Viking shipyard nestles convincingly on the estuary's banks. Access by public transport is very difficult, but a taxi from Wexford costs around €6, or you could always rent a bike.

Irish Agricultural Museum

Four miles southwest of Wexford, off the Rosslare Road, the **Irish Agricultural Museum** (April, May, Sept & Oct Mon–Fri 9am–12.30pm & 1.30–5pm, Sat & Sun 2–5pm; June–Aug Mon–Fri 9am–5pm, Sat & Sun 11am–5pm; Nov–March Mon–Fri 9am–12.30pm and 1.30–5pm, closed Sat & Sun; €4) is set in the gardens of Johnstown Castle, a Gothic Revival castellated mansion. The museum, which is signposted "Research Centre", has good, clear displays on all aspects of rural life, encompassing domestic objects, farming machinery, carts and carriages, reconstructed workshops and much on dairy farming. In addition, the grounds have mounds of rhododendrons, ornamental lakes, hot houses, dark woodlands and walled gardens – all very spruce and well maintained. Three Viking Shuttle buses to Johnstown Castle depart daily from outside the tourist office.

The beaches

The southeast has more sunshine than any other part of Ireland, and as the entire coastline of the county to the north of Wexford town is made up of safe and sandy **beaches**, the region is a popular spot in summer for families and caravanners. From **CURRACLOE**, near Ballinskar, five miles northeast of town (take the R742), superb, sandy dunes stretch away into the far distance. Curracloe Beach stood in for Omaha Beach in the harrowing opening scenes of Steven Spielberg's World War II epic about the D-Day landings, *Saving Private Ryan*. *Kirwan's Farmhouse* near Curracloe Beach, on the R742 coast road between Blackwater and Kilmuckridge (April–Oct; ⓣ053/30168, ⓔkirwans-farmhouse@eircom.net; ❷) offers a warm welcome. Curracloe is a good point from which to access the **Wexford Coastal Path**, which covers the east and south coastline of the county from Kilmicheal Point above Gorey down to Ballyhack. Though the little villages roundabout are overloaded in July and August, the sands themselves aren't. Unfortunately, without your own transport you'll be reliant on the Bus Éireann services from Wexford to Curracloe, which run highly infrequently.

Roughly six miles southeast of Wexford is the huge sandy beach at **ROSSLARE**, the county's other main seaside resort, not to be confused with Rosslare Harbour, another five miles further south. Right on the edge of the beach, the best hotel in the southeast, four-star *Kelly's* (ⓣ053/32114, ⓦwww.kellys.ie; ❻), has excellent sporting facilities, outdoor hot tubs and an impressive collection of modern Irish art. Campers can pitch their tents among the caravans at Burrow Holiday Park (mid-March to early Nov; ⓣ053/32190, ⓔburrowpk@iol.ie).

Rosslare Harbour

ROSSLARE HARBOUR serves ferries to Cherbourg and Roscoff in France, and Fishguard and Pembroke Dock in South Wales. There's a tourist office at the harbour terminal (May–Sept open to meet all incoming ferries except the 6.30am arrival; ⓣ053/33622), or, especially handy if you are driving, there's the Rosslare Kilrane tourist office, just over a mile north of the harbour along the N25 (April–Sept daily to meet all sailings, except the 6.30am; Oct–March Tues–Sun restricted opening hours; ⓣ053/33232).

Ferries aside, there's not much to the place. If you do need to stay, head for St Martin's Road, the village's main street, which is dotted with several decent **B&Bs**: *Ailsa Lodge* (ⓣ053/33230, ⓦwww.ailsalodge.com; ❷), *Clifford House* (ⓣ053/33226; ❷), *Oldcourt House* (ⓣ053/33895, oldcrt@gofree.indigo.ie; ❷) and *Rock Villa* (ⓣ053/33212; ❷) are all of a similar standard. You'll find an An Óige **hostel** nearby on Goulding Street (ⓣ053/33399). You can **camp** for free down in the dunes by the beach or travel the three miles to Kilrane to the *Holiday Inn Caravan and Camping Park* (closed Oct–late May; ⓣ053/31168).

Rosslare Harbour travel information

Rosslare Harbour is the arrival point for ferries from Pembroke and Fishguard in Wales, and Cherbourg and Roscoff in France. It's worth noting that the train station here is called Rosslare Europort.

Bus Éireann ⓣ053/33114. For local and national bus services, with direct links to Cork, Dublin and Limerick, see "Travel details" at the end of this chapter.

Irish Ferries ⓣ053/33158, ⓦwww.irishferries.ie. Services to Cherbourg (April–Jan 1–2 weekly; 19hr); Pembroke Dock (year-round, 2 daily; 4hr); and Roscoff (April–Jan 1–3 weekly; 16hr 30min).

Irish Rail ⓣ053/33114. Rosslare Europort to Dublin (3 daily; 3hr 30min) and Wexford (3 daily; 30min).

Stena Line ⓣ053/33115, ⓦwww.stenaline.co.uk. Ferry service to Fishguard (year-round, 2 daily; 3hr 30min); Lynx catamaran to Fishguard (year-round 3–4 daily; 1hr 40min).

The south coast

In the southeast corner of Ireland, the sea has made inroads into an otherwise flat region, forming small lagoons popular with wind-surfers at **Tacumshane** and **Lady's Island**, both also venues for bird enthusiasts. Lady's Island itself sits mid-lagoon at the end of a causeway and has been a place of religious devotion for centuries: an annual pilgrimage to Our Lady is still made here on August 15. On the island are the remains of an Augustinian priory and a Norman castle, both built in the thirteenth century, but the spirit of the place has been destroyed by a large, modern church building that has been tacked onto the side. West of here lies the quaint fishing village of **Kilmore Quay**, a good choice for accommodation and the departure point for trips to view the colonies of puffins on the **Saltee Islands**. The **Hook Head Peninsula**, around twenty miles further west, offers fine beaches, bracing walks and atmospheric castle and abbey ruins. There are few eating options for travellers in the area, but *The Lobster Pot* bar and restaurant at **Carne**, six miles south of Rosslare Harbour, is a great exception, serving delicious seafood meals.

Kilmore Quay and the Saltee Islands

KILMORE QUAY comes as a real surprise after the largely dull countryside that precedes it. A small fishing and holiday village of thatched cottages and whitewashed walls, with a good sandy beach, it's attractively situated around a stone harbour wall, looking out at the nearby Saltee Islands. County Wexford's **Maritime Museum** is housed in an old lightship alongside the marina (May–Sept daily noon–6pm; April & Oct Sat & Sun noon–6pm; €2).

The village hosts a **seafood festival**, usually in the second week of July – a fine excuse to eat plenty of seafood. One of the most popular seafood restaurants, only a short walk from the harbour is *The Silver Fox* (Ⓣ053/29888). The village also has a handful of good bars, including *Kehoe's*, right in the middle of the village opposite the church, which has excellent bar food year-round and singalongs during the summer. *Walkers*, down by the harbour, is probably one of the best fish-and-chip shops in Ireland.

Kilmore Quay is also the point of departure for visiting the uninhabited **Saltee Islands**, one of Ireland's most important bird sanctuaries, especially for puffins, razorbills, cormorants, shags, gannets, kittiwakes and auks. In the nesting period of late spring and early summer, there are thousands of them; by the end of July they have all left – so time your trip carefully. **Boat trips** to the islands may be available during the summer – contact Declan Bates of *The Saltees Princess* (Ⓣ053/29684) or Dick Hayes (Ⓣ053/29704), who organizes deep-sea angling trips at around €20per day.

B&B accommodation can be found at the quaint, thatched *Curlew Cottage* (Ⓣ053/29772; ❷) and at *Harbour Lights* (Ⓣ053/29881; ❷), a short walk from the harbour. For a smart guesthouse there is *Quay House* (Ⓣ053/29988, Ⓦwww.quayhouseguesthouse.com; ❶), conveniently situated on the road into the village. A **hostel** and **camping** are available at *Kilturk Independent Hostel* (IHH; closed Oct–April; Ⓣ053/29883), a quiet spot about a mile outside the village on the R739.

The Hook Head Peninsula

Heading west from Kilmore Quay, the R736/R733 will take you to the **Hook Head Peninsula**, which forms the eastern side of Waterford Harbour. Only when you reach the peninsula does the flat coastline begin to undulate and the scenery becomes more attractive. Just five miles from the evocative ruin of **Tintern Abbey** is **Arthurstown**, the first village on the peninsula that you'll encounter, and about half a mile further on is the pretty **Ballyhack**, a tranquil spot beside the estuary and the place to catch the ferry across to County Waterford. South of both lies the popular seaside town of Duncannon, but it is really beyond here, on the head of the peninsula, that the eerie, windswept character of the Hook is best enjoyed.

Arthurstown and Tintern Abbey

ARTHURSTOWN, on the estuary near the neck of the peninsula, is a tiny village offering a handful of good B&Bs, namely *Clogheen* (Ⓣ051/389110; ❷), the comfortable *Arthur's Rest* (Ⓣ051/389192; ❷) and spacious *Glendine House* (Ⓣ051/389258, Ⓦwww.glendinehouse.com; ❷–❹). There's also an An Óige **hostel** (closed Oct–May; Ⓣ051/389411) in the old coastguard station – ring ahead to book. *Waterfront Restaurant* (Ⓣ051/389534; closed Mon) has a good reputation. About five miles east of Arthurstown (take the R733), near the muddy Bannow Bay, scene of the first Norman landing in 1169, stand the ruins of **Tintern Abbey** (June–Sept daily 10am–6pm; €1.90; Heritage Card), built in 1200 by William Marshall, Earl of Pembroke. Another fine Cistercian edifice, it owes its existence in this unprepossessing spot to a vow made by the earl while he was caught in a storm off the south coast. Praying that he might be saved, he promised to build an abbey wherever his boat came ashore. The presbytery is based on the foundation's more famous namesake in Wales.

Ballyhack and Dunbrody Abbey

Just half a mile to the north of Arthurstown lies the little village of **BALLYHACK**. From here a useful year-round **car ferry** service runs regularly across the harbour to Passage East in County Waterford, taking just ten minutes (see p.300). Setting off the picturesque scene is **Ballyhack Castle**, a fine five-storey, sixteenth-century tower house. You can climb about halfway up the tower and enjoy a strong sense of its stout proportions (June–Sept Mon–Fri 10am–1pm & 2–6pm, Sat & Sun 10am–6pm; €1.20). The village's upmarket **seafood restaurant**, *The Neptune* (Ⓣ051/389284), is held in high regard, while *Byrne's* is a pleasant quayside spot for a drink.

The magnificent ruin of **Dunbrody Abbey** (daily: April–June & Sept 10am–6pm; July & Aug 10am–7pm; €1.90) stands at the widening of the Barrow estuary, to the northeast of town off the R733. A thirteenth-century Cistercian foundation, it was altered in the sixteenth century after the dissolution of the monasteries, when the large central tower and adjacent buildings were added.

Duncannon to Slade

Unfortunately, the pretty, wooded coastline south of Ballyhack, down to Duncannon, is privately owned, and you can't walk along it. **DUNCANNON** itself is a holiday town, pleasant enough, with a rocky coast to the south that protects its big, sandy Blue Flag beach. Up on the headland, eerie **Duncannon Fort** (May to mid-Sept daily 10am–5.30pm; €2.50) dates back to 1586, when the Spanish Armada was expected to attack. Constantly added to since then, one of its grislier sights is the reputed dungeon of the Croppy Boy – tortured for his part in the 1798 Rebellion and hero of a well-known rebel song. Facilities in Duncannon are minimal: for **accommodation**, try *Sandunes* B&B, in a great location beside the beach (Ⓣ051/389250; ❷). If you're **camp-**

ing, ask to use a local field. A couple of bars serve sandwiches and burgers, and *The Strand Seafood Bar* does an all-day menu.

From Duncannon, the countryside opens out and gives way to the strange emptiness of the peninsula that is quite magical. Little sandy bays lie concealed behind low cliffs, and there are lovely views across to the broad and beautiful Waterford coastline. Although the Hook Head Peninsula promotes itself as a tourist area, caravans and kids mostly keep to the areas around Duncannon and Fethard to the east, and there are plenty of isolated spots to be found. A couple of particularly fine, **sandy beaches** are Booley Strand, two miles south of Duncannon, and beyond that the smaller Dollar Bay.

At the peninsula's tip the shoreline is rockier, the limestone rich with fossils, and the land, flat and desolate, just slips away into the sea. The extremity is marked by a **lighthouse** (March–Oct daily 9.30am–5.30pm; €4.75; Ⓦwww.thehook-wexford.com), said to be the oldest in Europe – the first on this site was built in the twelfth century. This part of Hook Head is favoured by ornithologists who come to watch the bird migrations, and if you're lucky you can sometimes spot seals. Crashing spray and blow-holes make it a dangerous and dramatic place in a storm – and you certainly shouldn't swim here at any time. For a bracing coastal walk, pick your way east along the coast as far as Slade (see below), about one and a half miles away.

The nearest shop to Hook Head is three and a half miles away at the Texaco petrol station at the Fethard–Duncannon junction. Along the Duncannon road, *The Templars Inn* in Templetown (Ⓣ051/397162), about three miles from the tip, has a seafood **restaurant** and bar food. The *Hotel Naomh Seosamh* (Ⓣ051/397129; ❷–❹) in Fethard, is the real hub of social activity in the area, serves great food both in the bar and restaurant, and has decent **accommodation**.

Tucked away on the east flank of the peninsula, the evocatively crumbling harbour of **SLADE** is a quiet, beautiful place: fishing boats cluster around its quays and slipways, stacked lobster pots lean against a fifteenth-century castle, and the whole place is built from stone a nutty-brown colour: rich, rusty and warm. To look around the castle, take the lane that runs alongside it and ask at the farm.

New Ross

First impressions of **NEW ROSS**, 21 miles west of Wexford on the N25, are not encouraging: a glamourless old port of grubby wharf buildings. However, the place isn't without character, thanks mostly to the river that has long given access to the heart of the Wexford and Kilkenny countryside, and the clutter of narrow lanes that does much to preserve the human scale of the place. In addition, the quayside itself has been greatly enhanced by the presence of the historic tall-ship *Dunbrody*, a magnificent reconstruction of the original *SS Dunbrody*, a three-masted famine ship that took thousands of emigrants to new lives in America and Canada. On board is an interactive visitor centre and a comprehensive database of all Irish immigration into the US from 1820 to 1920 (open daily all year round; Ⓦwww.dunbrody.com). It's worth climbing the steep back alleys to the top of town for views over the river and hills, and exploring the thirteenth-century ruins of St Mary's Church, with its graceful, Gothic windows and medieval tombstones in the chancel.

New Ross's **tourist office** (mid-June to Aug Mon–Sat 10am–6pm; Ⓣ051/421857) is located on the quays. Bus Éireann buses to Waterford leave from outside the Mariner's Inn, also on the quays. Options for **accommodation** include comfortable *Riversdale House*, Lower William St (March–Nov; ⓣ051/422515, ⓦwww.riversdalehouse.com; ❷), a short walk from the centre of town. Friendly *MacMurrough Farm Hostel* (IHH; ⓣ051/421383, ⓔmachostel@eircom.net) is a comfortable cottage hostel in a beautiful setting a couple of miles out of town; it makes a particularly good base for cyclists from which to explore the Nore and Barrow river valleys (see p.282). To get there, ask for directions to Kelly's Statoil petrol station on the ring road; the hostel is signposted down the lane alongside.

Down on the quays, *John V's* has an excellent reputation for midday and evening **meals**, while good-value bar food is also served at *The Ship* on North Street, and there's no shortage of coffee shops along South Street. For something different, reserve a table at the *Galley Restaurant* on Bridge Quay (ⓣ051/421723), which, from Easter to October, runs **boat trips** up the Barrow and Nore as far as Inistioge and St Mullins and along the Suir to Waterford.

You can sometimes catch live bands at *Crosbies*, while traditional music can be heard on a Friday night during summer at *Mannion's*, a cheerful country pub, about a mile out from the centre along the N30 Enniscorthy road.

The **arboretum** five miles south of New Ross, known as the J.F. Kennedy Memorial Park (daily: April & Sept 10am–6.30pm; May–Aug 10am–8pm; Oct–March 10am–5pm; €2.50; Heritage Card), contains a collection of around five thousand species of trees and shrubs and affords expansive views of the surrounding countryside. Kennedy's great-grandfather was born close by in Dunganstown, and the place is often frequented by Americans in search of presidential roots. The road south of here will take you to the coast and the Hook Head Peninsula (see p.269).

Enniscorthy and North Wexford

The market town of **ENNISCORTHY**, fourteen miles north of Wexford on the N11, is well worth visiting for the **National 1798 Visitor Centre** (Mon–Sat 9.30am–5pm, Sun 11am–5pm; €5; ⓦwww.1798centre.com), arguably the best interactive centre in Ireland and a must for anyone with an interest in the history of the eighteenth century and the political complexities of contemporary Ireland. Drawing on a rich array of audio-visual techniques, the exhibition brings to life the events surrounding the 1798 Rebellion in Ireland, and sets it in the wider context of revolution in France and the struggle for independence in America. One of the highlights is a tremendously effective audio-visual dramatization of a debate between the English radical Thomas Paine and the Anglo-Irish conservative Edmund Burke.

For a more traditional presentation of the events of 1798 and for material on the 1916 uprising, call in at the **County Museum** (March–Sept daily 10am–6pm; Oct–Feb Sun 2–5pm; €4), housed in a Norman castle overlooking the town. It's crammed with a wonderful mixture of local objects, from an ogham stone to a sedan chair. Across the river, covered in mustard and yellow gorse, lies **Vinegar Hill**, the site of the rebels' main encampment during the 1798 Rebellion – and the scene of their final slaughter by Crown forces. Enniscorthy hosts the enjoyable week-long "Strawberry Fair", usually held over the last week of June, or, the first week of July (ⓣ054/33256), which combines music and street entertainment with the pleasures of soft fruit. The modern *Enniscorthy Holiday Hostel*, Railway Square (IHH; ⓣ054/37766) offers family **rooms**, doubles (❶), dorms and bike hire.

The uplands to the north and west of Enniscorthy are bald and spartan. There's little in the way of sights on this side of the Blackstairs Mountains, though if you're heading north, **FERNS**, seven miles from Enniscorthy, makes a good lunch stop. One-time seat of the kings of Leinster, it's now a little scrap of a village, top-heavy with history: it was here that Dermot MacMurrough was attacked by Tiernán O'Rourke – whose wife he had abducted fourteen years earlier. MacMurrough sought help from Henry II in France, who lent him Richard Fitzherbert de Clare (Strongbow), and thus an adultery led to the Norman invasion of Ireland. An abbey was founded in Ferns in the sixth century, and you can see its remains in St Edan's churchyard and the adjacent field. Most impressive, though, are the ruins of the thirteenth-century castle, with its pair of towers – which you can climb – and two curtain walls (opening times and admission charges to be confirmed; ⓣ056/24623). When you're feeling peckish, head for *The Courtyard* in the village, which does superb bar food. Decent budget accommodation and camping are to be found at **BUNCLODY**, about twelve miles north of Enniscorthy, at *The Bunclody Hostel* (closed Oct–Feb; ⓣ054/76076). The village itself is pretty unremarkable, but it is on the Dublin–Waterford bus route, and just three miles from **CLONEGALL** at the southerly end of the Wicklow Way – the hostel will pick you up from here on request.

Quite the nicest family seaside town in the area is **COURTOWN**, around 25 miles north of Wexford (turn off the N11 onto the R742 at Gorey) and plumb in the middle of another excellent, long stretch of sand. A short walk from the beach, *Harbour House* (mid-April to Oct; ⓣ055/25117, ⓦwww.harbourhouseguesthouse.com; ❷) is a well-run B&B.

GOREY, four miles inland from Courtown, is the main shopping centre for the north Wexford coast, a very cheerful place of brightly coloured stores and plenty of interesting bars. Whether you're stopping here or not, you're likely to get caught up passing through Gorey as it's a notorious traffic bottleneck jammed with the heavy traffic travelling from Rosslare Harbour and Wexford to Dublin. Formerly the residence of the Earls of Courtown, sumptuous *Marlfield House* (ⓣ055/21124, ⓦwww.marlfieldhouse.com; ❾) can't be beaten in the area if you want to rest and dine in style; it's set amidst 36 acres, with woodland walks and lovely flower gardens.

Carlow town and around

For centuries, the town of **CARLOW**, 35 miles northeast of Wexford, was an Anglo-Norman stronghold at the edge of an otherwise fiercely Gaelic county. As such, it has a bloody history, with its most terrible battle during the 1798 Rebellion, when over six hundred rebels were slaughtered. Today there's nothing to suggest its former frontier status, and this small, busy town is distinguished only by a fine Classical courthouse with a portico modelled on the Parthenon, an elegant Regency Gothic cathedral – one of the first Catholic churches to be built after Catholic Emancipation in 1829 – and the remains of the once proud Norman **castle**, which lie beside the river at the west end of town. Otherwise, there's plenty on local military, religious and folk history in the **museum**, housed in the town hall on Centaur Street (Tues–Fri 11am–5pm, Sat & Sun 2–5pm; €2).

You can get more local information, including a free map and historical guide, from Carlow's **tourist office** at the junction of Tullow and College streets (May–Sept Mon–Sat 9.30am–5.30pm; Oct–April Mon–Fri 10am–5.30pm; ⓣ0503/31554). **Bike rental** is available during the summer from A.E. Coleman, 19 Dublin St (ⓣ0503/31273; €7per day), and you can rent a Canadian canoe from Charlie Horan (ⓣ0509/31307 or 087/529700; two-person canoe €40 per day) to paddle down the River Barrow. Those interested in getting to grips with the intricacies of **Celtic brewing techniques** should book in for a tour of the Carlow Brewing Company, lodged up beside the train station. The beers produced here are based on traditional Celtic recipes and include a wheat beer, red ale and, of course, stout. The short tour explains the process and offers the chance to sample a glass or two; it's best booked the day before as opening times vary (ⓣ0503/34356; €4).

B&Bs in Carlow include *Westlow*, Green Lane (ⓣ0503/43964; ❷), and *Redsetter Guesthouse*, 14 Dublin St (ⓣ0503/41848; ❷), both of which are a good standard. Several more accommodation options are out on Kilkenny Road; one of the best of these is *Barrowville Town House* (ⓣ0503/43324, ⓦwww.barrowvillehouse.com; ❷), an elegant Regency building set in a mature garden, just a short walk from the town centre. Nearby lies *Ottersholt Riverside Lodge* (IHH; ⓣ0503/30404; ❶), a rambling old hostel offering budget accommodation in dorms and twin rooms, and camping down by the river.

You'll find the best places to **eat and drink** on Tullow Street: *Tully's* is an appealing bar and a handy spot for lunch, and *Buzz's*, across the street, offers hearty home-cooked lunches and manages to combine laid-back stylishness with a no-nonsense lived-in atmosphere. Coffee shops serving light lunches, also in Tullow Street, include *Bradbury's* and *Muffins*. Both *Buzz's* (late closing Thurs–Sat till 1am) and *Tully's* are lively spots during the evening, and *Teach Dolmen*, at 76 Tullow St is the best place to catch impromptu traditional music sessions on Thursdays.

Two miles east out of town on the R726 road is arguably County Carlow's most impressive sight: the **Browneshill Dolmen**. It's enormous, possibly the largest Neolithic stone formation in Europe, dating from 2500 BC, and the burial place of a local king or prince.

Seven miles south of Carlow on the N9 lies **LEIGHLINBRIDGE**, a pretty riverside village. A good place to stop for lunch here is *The Lord Bagenal Inn*, an old and characterful bar popular for its **bar food** and family atmosphere.

Borris and the South Leinster Way

Ten miles south from Leighlinbridge, along the R705, is tiny **BORRIS**, which you're most likely to visit if you're travelling through the county by car or walking the South Leinster Way. It's not especially attractive, aside from its fresh air and one broad (fast) main road, the R705, that sweeps down towards a striking backdrop formed by the ash-mottled Blackstairs Mountains, but it's as good a place as any to stop in the area. Mrs Susan Breen in Church Street does decent, inexpensive **B&B** (ⓣ0503/73231; ❷) and *The Step House*, 66 Main St (ⓣ0503/73209; ❷), is a fine Georgian guesthouse. You can camp by the disused train line and get your provisions from *O'Shea's* bar and shop.

The Green Drake Inn serves snacks and lunches every day till 6pm, and more expensive **meals** until 9.30pm. Considering its size, there's a lot going on in Borris, with live music several nights of the week, mostly in the singalongs and ballads category: try *The Green Drake Inn* (Wed is Irish night, Sun for music and dancing), *O'Connors* or *O'Shea's*. This last doubles up as a hardware store so you

△ Jerpoint Abbey, County Kilkenny

can sup your pint leaning on a bacon slicer, keeping a weather-eye on the hacksaws and sink plungers dangling from the ceiling.

East of Borris, the **South Leinster Way** leaves the intimate landscape of the valleys, crossing the open farmland of south Carlow and eventually skirting the bleak height of Mount Leinster. The way finally descends to the lonely cluster of houses which makes up Kildavin, six miles or so from Mount Leinster on the main Carlow–Enniscorthy road.

County Kilkenny

County Kilkenny offers the finest of the southeast's countryside. Mostly it's intensely pretty, rich farmland, especially to the north of New Ross around the confluence of the Nore and Barrow rivers. **Medieval ruins** are scattered all over the county, but they reach their richest concentration in ancient **Kilkenny city** – a quaint but bustling place. The delightful surroundings make it ideal for biking around the river valleys and their medieval ruins, most notably **Kells Priory** and **Jerpoint Abbey**. The cycling is easy: off the main roads there's little traffic, and the minor roads that stay close to the rivers are especially scenic. Alternatively, the heart of this rich, historical farmland can be crossed on foot. As they head south, the Nore and Barrow rivers flow through gentle valleys of mixed woodland. The **South Leinster Way** provides unstrenuous walking, passing through pretty **riverside villages** – Inistioge, Graiguenamanagh, and nearby Borris and St Mullins – before heading north towards the **Blackstairs Mountains**. To access the area from Kilkenny hitching is probably your best bet, as there's just one bus a week, on Thursday, from Kilkenny to Inistioge. Alternatively, you could see the region from the **cruises** that operate from the river port of New Ross (see p.271).

Kilkenny city and around

KILKENNY is Ireland's finest medieval city. Above the broad sweep of the River Nore sits the castle, while a pretty, humpbacked stone bridge leads up into narrow, cheerful streets lined by carefully maintained buildings. Kilkenny's earliest settlement was a monastery founded by St Canice in the sixth century, but all that remains from those days is the round tower that stands alongside the cathedral. The city's layout today owes more to its medieval history. Following continual skirmishes between local clans, the arrival of the **Normans** in 1169 saw the building of a fort by Strongbow on the site of today's castle. His son-in-law, William Marshall, consolidated Norman power in Kilkenny, maintaining the fortified city and keeping the indigenous Irish in an area of less substantial housing, beyond its walls – of which only the name "Irishtown" remains. In 1391, the Butler family acquired Kilkenny Castle and so ensured the city's loyalty to the English Crown.

In the mid-seventeenth century, Kilkenny virtually became the capital of Ireland, with the founding of a parliament in 1641 known as the

Confederation of Kilkenny (see p.784). This attempt to unite resistance to the English persecution of Catholics was powerful for a while, though its effectiveness had greatly diminished by the time Cromwell arrived – in his usual destructive fashion – in 1650. Kilkenny never recovered its former prosperity and importance. The disgrace of the Butler family in 1715, coupled with English attacks upon the rights of Catholics through the Penal Laws, saw the city decline still further, though the towering mill buildings on the river banks are evidence of a considerable industrial history.

Enough medieval buildings remain to attest to Kilkenny's former importance, however, and in a place brimming with civic pride, there's been a tasteful push towards making the town a major tourist attraction. Kilkenny is sometimes known as "the marble city" because of the limestone mined locally, which develops a deep black shine when polished. Echoing this, the town's bar and shop signs all gleam with black and brown lacquer, the names cut in deeply bevelled, stout gold lettering.

Arrival, information and accommodation

The **train station** (Ⓣ056/22024) lies just off the north road out of the city on Dublin Street. Bus Éireann services (Ⓣ056/64933) depart from both the train station and Patrick Street; privately operated **buses** generally depart from The Parade outside Kilkenny Castle. Note that in Irish the city is called Cill Chainnigh, and this is what it says on the front of buses. You can get free maps of the city and plenty of other information from the tourist office in Rose Inn Street (May & June Mon–Sat 9am–6pm; July & Aug Mon–Sat 9am–7pm, Sun 11am–1pm & 2–5pm; Sept 9am–6pm, Sun 11am–1pm & 2–5pm; Oct–April Mon–Sat 9am–5pm; Ⓣ056/51500, Ⓔinfo@southeasttourism.ie).

Kilkenny is well served by **B&Bs**, although in the summer the city gets crowded, and at festival time (see p.281) you'll need to book in advance. *Tree Grove Campsite* (booking required mid-Nov to Feb; Ⓣ056/70302, Ⓣtreecc@iol.ie), about a mile south out of town along the R700, is a well-equipped and well-run site if you want to **camp**.

Berkeley House 5 Lower Patrick St Ⓣ056/64848, berkeleyhouse@eicom.net. Comfortable guesthouse in generously proportioned period town house, right in the centre of town. All rooms are en suite with TV and tea- and coffee-making facilities. ❺

Blanchville House Ⓣ056/27197, Ⓦwww.blanchville.ie. Fine Georgian house set in rich farmland, about five miles east out of town. Comfortable rooms with private bathrooms also offer lovely views of the surrounding countryside. There's a tennis court and billiard room for guests to use. Dinner is available but you need to book before noon. Closed Nov–Feb. ❺

Bregagh Guesthouse Dean St Ⓣ056/22315. Large, detached comfortable family house set back from the road, right in the town centre. All rooms are en suite. ❸

Celtic House 18 Michael St Ⓣ056/62249. Beautifully decorated, spic and span B&B offering spacious rooms, all of which are en suite. Quiet location, yet a 5min walk from the town centre. ❸

Danville House New Ross Rd Ⓣ056/21512, Ⓔtreecc@iol.ie. A delightful eighteenth-century Georgian mansion set in beautiful gardens of grassy lawns and mature trees; located about one mile south of town along the R700 and next door to the *Tree Grove Campsite*. The house is full of interesting antiques and the rooms are pleasant and airy. ❸

Dunromin Dublin Rd Ⓣ056/61387, Ⓔvaltom@oceanfree.net. Excellent and wonderfully welcoming B&B in a nineteenth-century family home. All rooms are en suite. ❸

Foulksrath Castle Jenkinstown Ⓣ056/67674. An Óige hostel located eight miles north of town along the N77. Buggy's Buses run from Kilkenny Castle to Jenkinstown; call Buggy's for timetable details (Ⓣ056/41264) or ask at the tourist office. The setting – a sixteenth-century fort in lush meadows – makes up for the inconvenience of getting out here. Dorm-room accommodation only is available.

Hibernian Hotel 1 Ormonde St Ⓣ056/71888, Ⓦwww.kilkennyhibernianhotel.com. An elegant hotel in the shadow of Kilkenny Castle, featuring bedrooms, suites and penthouses. Access to private leisure centre and pool as well as the *Contemporary Bar* and excellent *Jacob's Cottage* restaurant. ❽

Kilkenny River Court Hotel John St Ⓣ056/23388, Ⓦwww.kilrivercourt.com. Comfortable, traditionally styled accommodation, superbly situated on the banks of the river; some of the deluxe rooms have views of the castle. Facilities include pool, gym and riverside bar. ❽

Kilkenny Tourist Hostel 35 Parliament St Ⓣ056/63541, Ⓔkilkennyhostel@eircom.net. Right in the town centre and run by a friendly crowd, this IHH hostel is by far the nicest budget accommodation in town. There's a bright, airy kitchen and sitting room; clean and spacious dorms and private rooms are available. ❶

Majella Waterford Rd Ⓣ056/21129. Welcoming B&B in a modern bungalow about half a mile from the city centre. Good breakfasts and pleasant interiors. Open May–Oct. ❸

The City

Kilkenny is focused on the hill and its **castle**. Climbing from the river up Rose Inn Street brings you to the tourist office (see above), housed in the sixteenth-century **Shee Alms House**, one of the very few Tudor almshouses to be found in Ireland. A walking tour of the city leaves from here six times a day (€3); enquire at the tourist office for exact times. At the top of Rose Inn Street to the left is the broad stretch known as **The Parade**, which leads up to the castle. Formerly used for military and civic ceremonies, it now serves as a bus park in summer. To the right, the High Street – graced with the eighteenth-century **Tholsel**, once the centre of the city's financial dealings and now the town hall – soon becomes the busy main thoroughfare of Parliament Street, then continues, crooked and intriguing, with little medieval slips and alleyways ducking off it, through Irishtown towards the **cathedral**.

Of all the surviving buildings from the prosperous Tudor commercial period, the finest is **Rothe House** on Parliament Street (April–June & Sept–Oct Mon–Sat 10.30am–5pm, Sun 3–5pm; July & Aug Mon–Sat 10am–6pm Sun 3–5pm; Nov–March Mon–Sat 1–5pm, Sun 3–5pm; €3). Home to the **Kilkenny Archeological Society museum** and a **costume** gallery of waistcoats, bonnets and gowns from the eighteenth century onwards, the building itself is a unique example of an Irish Tudor merchant's home dating back to 1594, and comprises three separate houses linked by interconnecting courtyards. There is also a genealogical research centre here for those wanting to trace their roots locally.

Also on Parliament Street you can visit **Kilkenny Brewery** (June–Aug Mon–Fri at 3pm). Although you won't get a tour, they do at least show a video of the production process, followed by tasting in the cellar bar. It's free, but only fifty tickets are available each day; these can be picked up in advance at the security gate.

Kilkenny Castle

It's the **castle** (April–May daily 10.30am–5pm; June–Sept daily 10am–7pm; Oct–March Tues–Sat 10.30am–12.45pm & 2–5pm, Sun 11am–12.45pm & 2–5pm; guided tours only; €4.40), an imposing building standing high and square over the river, that really defines Kilkenny. Dating originally from the twelfth century, it was much added to in the seventeenth and nineteenth centuries. While the furnishings and paintings suggest a civilized wealth and domesticity, the scale and grandeur of the rooms, with their deeply recessed windows and robust fireplaces, signify a much cruder political power. The biggest surprise is the flimsy wooden hammer-beam roof of the picture gallery, covered with the folksy, Pre-Raphaelite decoration of John Hungerford Pollen – plenty of gold and burnt umber plant life smudging its way across the ceiling.

Also within the castle is the **Butler Gallery**, housing exhibitions of modern art, and a tearoom (summer only), in the castle's former kitchen – you don't have to pay the castle entrance fee to visit either the Butler Gallery or the tearoom. The eighteenth-century stables, opposite the castle, have been converted into the Design Centre, an outlet for high-quality Irish crafts, and an excellent cafe.

The cathedral, Round Tower, churches and brewery

The other must in Kilkenny is **St Canice's Cathedral** (Easter–Sept Mon–Sat 9am–1pm & 2–6pm, Sun 2–6pm; Oct–Easter Mon–Sat 10am–1pm & 2–4pm, Sun 2–4pm; €3). It was built in the thirteenth century, and the purity and unity of its architecture lends it a grandeur beyond its actual size. Rich in carvings, it has an exemplary selection of sixteenth-century monuments, many in black Kilkenny marble, the most striking being effigies of the Butler family. The **Round Tower** next to the cathedral (same hours; €1.90 to climb tower) is all that remains of the early monastic settlement reputedly founded by St Canice in the sixth century; there are superb views from the top – ask anyone working in the church or churchyard for access (if you want to climb the tower during June, July & August be there before 5.30pm; arrangements are more flexible at other times).

Kilkenny is littered with the remains of other medieval churches. The **Black Abbey**, founded by Dominicans in 1225, has been carefully restored and contains some unusual carvings and sepulchral slabs. On the other side of town, **St John's Priory** has only a roofless chancel, a fine seven-light window and a medieval tomb. Thirteenth-century **St Francis' Abbey** stands in ruins by the river.

Eating, drinking and entertainment

Kilkenny is a very lively small city, and while there's not a huge number of places to **eat**, there is at least a reasonable range. **Bars** are as alluring in Kilkenny as anywhere in Ireland, you won't be hard pushed to find some kind of music here either, and in June it hosts the fabulous comedy festival, **The Cat Laughs**. It's a small enough town to enjoy sampling a few bars before choosing your favourite; if you want to check out pubs and entertainment generally it's worth taking a look at Ⓦwww.kilkennycraic.com.

Cafes and restaurants

Café Sol William St Ⓣ056/64987. Arguably the best place to eat in Kilkenny, whether you want a quick lunch or a leisurely evening meal. The emphasis is on fresh, local ingredients; there's plenty of fish on the menu and always some good vegetarian options. Closed Sun year-round and Wed evenings in winter.

The Gourmet Store 56 High St. A deli that makes an excellent takeaway sandwich.

Italian Connection Parliament St Ⓣ056/64225. A firm favourite for inexpensive pizza and pasta as well as veal and fish dishes, in a convivial atmosphere.

Kilkenny Design Centre The Parade. The centre's café serves excellent homemade soups, salads and quiches.

Langton's 69 John St. Large, briskly run bar noted for its award-winning bar meals: homemade burgers, grilled cutlets and vegetarian stir-fry are typical evening fare.

Lautrec's Brasserie 9 St Kieran St Ⓣ056/62720. Bustling, friendly bar-bistro serving good pizza and pasta dishes. Open for dinner every day, Sun–Thurs 6–10pm, Fri & Sat 6–11pm.

M.L. Dore 65 High St. Cafe serving inexpensive sandwiches, salads and hot dinners. Open daily from breakfast till 10pm, Sun till 9pm.

Pordylo's Butterslip Lane, off High St Ⓣ056/70660, Ⓔpordylos@eircom.net. Serves international cuisine and varied fare such as red snapper, lamb shanks and ostrich steaks. Open 6–11pm seven days.

Restaurant Rinuccini 1 The Parade Ⓣ056/61575. Excellent and expensive Italian-Irish restaurant specializing in fish, game and homemade pasta dishes. Not especially spacious, but generally considered the classiest place in town.

Zuni 26 Patrick Street, Ⓣ056/23999, Ⓦwww.zuni.ie. Top restaurant with an open-plan kitchen that serves contemporary Irish cuisine. Open for dinner Tues–Sun 6.30–10pm. Guest rooms are available (❻).

Bars and music venues

Anna Conda Parliament St. Cosy, friendly little pub with new beer garden attracting locals and visitors alike. The atmosphere is relaxed, except for Saturdays when it tends to be hectic. Traditional music is played on Mon, Wed & Sat.

The Cat Laughs 50 Dean St. Newspapers, chess, coffee and croissants give this pub something of a cosmopolitan air. It's a venue for occasional theatre and comedy acts.

John Cleere's Parliament St. Traditional Irish and folk music on Mondays, an open jam session on Wednesdays, occasional bands at weekends and a tiny theatre where they sometimes lay on drama and comedy.

Kyteler's Inn St Kieran St. A pub which is something of a tourist attraction, but a must if you've an

interest in all things medieval. It was once the home of Dame Alice Kyteler, a woman accused of witchcraft and rumoured to have murdered four husbands. She escaped to France, but her maid, the unfortunate Petronella, was burned at the stake in her place.
Maggie Holland's St Kieran St. An old-style bar with a good atmosphere, and excellent traditional/folk sessions most of the year on Wednesdays and Thursdays.
Pumphouse Parliament St. A cosy old pub with a nice fire in the winter and a very lively atmosphere during the summer. Traditional music from Mondays to Wednesdays; rock bands during the summer at weekends.
Ryan's Friary St. A laid-back, friendly spot with great traditional music sessions on Thursdays.
Tynan's Bridge Bar beside John's Bridge. A quaint little old pub and a pleasant spot for a quiet pint.
Widow McGrath's Parliament St. Hosts live music at weekends and can be very lively indeed. Sit out in the beer garden in summer to enjoy the barbecues held on Tuesdays.

Entertainment

Other entertainment is fairly easy to come by in summer. The *Kilkenny People*, published on Wednesday, lists what's on in the city and the surrounding villages; and it is worth checking out the Watergate Theatre, Parliament St (Ⓣ056/61674, Ⓦwww.watergatekilkenny.com), which hosts a wide range of touring companies, including theatre, ballet and music. One event to try to coincide with is the **Kilkenny Arts Festival**, a ten-day event, usually run over the last two weeks in August (Ⓣ056/63663). The emphasis is on classical music, but alongside this is a fringe festival of literary readings, art exhibitions and jazz and folk sessions. **The Cat Laughs** (Ⓣ056/63416), a comedy festival held at the beginning of June, brings together comedians from all over the world – many of them trying out new material before heading for Edinburgh in August. Events are held in pubs, clubs and theatres. The programme comes out a month beforehand and is available from tourist offices, while information is available at Ⓦwww.thecatlaughs.com.

Listings

Bank Allied Irish Bank, 3 High St. *M.L. Dore* restaurant will cash travellers' cheques, personal cheques and currency, and operates Western Union till 10pm daily. Ulster Bank has an ATM upstairs in the Market Cross Shopping Centre.
Bike rental J.J. Walls, 86 Maudlin St Ⓣ056/21236. Rental is €9 per day, €40 per week.
Books For Irish-interest books, maps and guides, try Dubray Books, Market Cross Shopping Centre or the Book Centre in the High St – the latter also has a wide selection of foreign newspapers.
Camping supplies Kilkenny Camping and Watersports, Kilkenny Arcade (upstairs), High St Ⓣ056/64025.
Hospital St Lukes, Freshford Rd Ⓣ056/51133.
Internet access Compustore, Unit 12, Market Cross Shopping Centre, off High St Ⓔcstorekk@iol.ie.
Laundry Bretts, Michael St Ⓣ056/63200.
Pharmacy Boots, 36 & 37 High St; Michael O'Connell, High St.
Police Ⓣ056/22222.
Post office High St (Mon–Sat 9am–5.30pm, Tues opens 9.30am).
Swimming pool Michael St Ⓣ056/21380.
Trains Irish Rail Ⓣ056/22024.
Travel agent Mannings Travel, High St (closed 1–2pm; Ⓣ056/22950).

Dunmore Cave

The main point of local interest is undoubtedly **Dunmore Cave** (mid-March to mid-June & mid-Sept to Oct daily 10am–5pm; mid-June to mid-Sept daily 10am–7pm; Nov to mid-March Sat, Sun & public holidays 10am–5pm; check opening times with the tourist office; €2.50), situated seven miles north of Kilkenny (take the N77 then the N78) on an isolated limestone outcrop of the Castlecomer plateau. Alternatives to driving there include renting a bike in Kilkenny, or taking Buggy's Bus from The Parade.

In 1967, Viking coins and the skeletons of 46 women and children were found among the stalactites and stalagmites. It's thought that the Vikings attacked the native Irish, and the women and children hid in the caves for protection. The plan obviously failed, but the fact that the skeletons showed no broken bones suggests that the victims starved to death, were lost or that the Vikings tried to smoke them out.

The Nore and Barrow valleys

Two rivers, the **Nore** and the **Barrow**, flowing magnificently through rich countryside, have long been of immense importance to the southeast. Formerly they were the chief means of communication, bringing prosperity to the heart of the region: the Nore brought trade to medieval Kilkenny, the Barrow to Carlow. Today they are treasured for their considerable beauty and are a real treat for anglers. The surrounding countryside is extremely pretty, and can be enjoyed on bike or on foot – the South Leinster Way dips down into some of the choicest spots. Plan a leisurely route, and you can meander through picturesque ancient villages and take in exceptional medieval ruins. There's a concentration of high-quality craft workshops here too – including those of Jerpoint Glass and the potter Nicholas Mosse – pick up a leaflet on the Kilkenny Craft Trail from the tourist office for further information.

The Nore Valley

The **Nore Valley** is deservedly renowned for its beauty, the river rolling through lush pastures and past some appealing ruins. It is perhaps at its finest as it broadens to the south of Kilkenny, where, along the tributary King's River eight miles south of the city (take the R697 or the N10 and turn off at Stonyford), sits medieval **KELLS**. Set amidst lush pastureland, the tiny village is an unexpected sight: its broad bridge is majestically out of scale, an ancient stone watermill stands on the river bank, and the encompassing deep hollow is flecked with mallows, marsh marigolds, docks and irises. Hard by, the magnificent ruin of **Kells Priory** – founded in 1193 – sits like a perfect scale model of a medieval walled city, a clean iron-grey against the surrounding green fields. The ruins consist of a complete curtain wall with square towers and fortified gatehouse, and the remnants of the fourteenth- and fifteenth-century church form one of the most impressive and largest medieval sites in Ireland. This town has nothing to do with the Book of Kells, which is associated with Kells in County Meath, though ironically enough the remains at that far more famous site are considerably less exciting than these.

Signposted from Kells, two miles to the south, are **Kilkree Round Tower** – just one of the many round towers scattered around this part of the country – and the nearby high cross, decorated with much-eroded biblical carvings. Alternatively, you can take the road east out of Kells and past Stonyford to placid **Jerpoint Abbey** (☎ 056/24623, daily: March to May & mid-Sept to mid-Nov 10am–5pm; June to mid-Sept 9.30am–6.30pm; last two weeks of Nov 10am–6pm; €2.50; Heritage Card). The abbey follows a typical Cistercian layout around an elegant, cloistered garden, and is built of warm, oat-coloured stone, and is generally visited for its tombs and twelfth-century carvings – especially the animated figures in the cloister.

You can **stay** at the very pleasant *Abbey House* guesthouse (☎056/24166; open all year; ❹), which is directly opposite the abbey, or at *Nore Valley Park* (closed end Oct to Feb; ⓣ056/27229), about two miles south of Bennettsbridge, which is a neat, family-oriented campsite with a farm alongside.

Thomastown and Inistioge

A mile north of Jerpoint lies **THOMASTOWN**. Formerly a medieval walled town of some importance, it's now simply a picturesque country town on the Kilkenny–Waterford train line. Minimal ruins of the walls, a castle and a thirteenth-century church (with some weathered effigies) remain, and in the Catholic church you'll find the high altar from Jerpoint.

A restored medieval tower, *The Tower House*, on Low St (ⓣ056/24500; ❷) offers good quality **B&B**, as does *Belmore*, Jerpoint Church, an eighteenth-century hunting lodge a mile south of town in a picturesque spot (ⓣ056/24228, belmorehouse@eircom.net; ❷). Several places serve pub **lunches**, and *The Watergarden* tearoom, run by the local Camphill Community, makes a refreshing place for a break, combining a delightful, small ornamental garden with a craft workshop. There's also a couple of interesting little bars tucked away on Logan Street – *Carroll's* and *O'Hara's*.

Heading north, it's worth stopping off to visit **Kilfane Glen** and its **woodland garden** (April–June & Sept Sun 2–6pm; July & Aug daily 11am–6pm; €5), a steep glen, complete with cottage *orné*, waterfall and hermit's grotto. It's an example of the Romantic craze for constructing "wild" landscapes in the back garden, although it's something of a rarity in Ireland. To get to the glen, turn right two miles north of Thomastown on the N9 (before you get to Kilfane), then right again, following the signposts. In **KILFANE** itself, a ruined church holds the fourteenth-century **Cantwell Effigy**, an impressive piece of stone-carving of a knight in full armour.

INISTIOGE, a few miles southeast of Thomastown on the R700, boasts a tree-lined square beside a fine stone bridge. The village is dotted with crumbling stonework, and little eighteenth- and nineteenth-century houses climb the steep lane that twists away from its centre. The grounds of the local estate, Woodstock, are open to the public if you fancy a stroll overlooking the neighbouring countryside, but the house itself was burnt down in 1922 after it had been occupied by the Black and Tans (see p.791). Alternatively, there's a very pleasant walk along the riverbank signposted from the centre of the village.

For **accommodation**, the beautifully situated *Kookaburra House* B&B is on Rock Road (closed Sept–May; ⓣ056/58519; ❷) – head over the bridge towards New Ross, turn left, and follow the lane for just under a mile. *The Circle of Friends* (ⓣ056/58800) – named after the film starring Minnie Driver that was shot in the village – is a fairly formal **restaurant** with an interesting menu; they also have a good café downstairs serving homemade snacks, cakes and sandwiches.

The Barrow Valley

The Barrow River flows through some of the most picturesque spots in the southeast, which makes it particularly popular with boating enthusiasts; narrow boats can be hired in Graiguenamanagh from Valley Boats, Barrow Lane (ⓣ0503/24945). For walking, the stretch of the South Leinster Way northeast from Inistioge is particularly pretty and offers a couple of pleasant places to rest up. The dusty little market town of **GRAIGUENAMANAGH** (you can also reach here by road from Inistioge and Thomastown) stands in a lovely spot beside the River Barrow, with herons fishing in the rushing weir.

The town's great age is indicated by the central **Duiske Abbey** which dominates Graiguenamanagh. Founded in 1204, it was the largest Cistercian abbey in Ireland at that time, and although much has been altered and added to outside (including a nineteenth-century clock tower and pebble-dashed walls), the thirteenth-century interior has been lovingly preserved. Besides some original fleur-de-lis tiling and a fine effigy of a knight in chain mail, most impressive is the superb Romanesque processional doorway to the right of the organ – heavily decorated and one of the best to have survived the Reformation. In the churchyard, near the steps outside the south transept, are a couple of ninth-century stone crosses, and a sixth-century font from Ullard stands outside the north wall of the chancel. The **Abbey Centre** nearby (June–Aug Mon–Fri 10am–1pm & 2–5pm, Sat & Sun 2–5pm; Sept–May Mon–Fri 10am–1pm & 2–5pm) displays interesting contemporary religious art exhibitions.

Graiguenamanagh is also a good point from which to walk up **Brandon Hill** (1703ft). The walk is along forest tracks for much of the way, none of it particularly steep, opening out onto a heathery summit and wonderful views. Follow the South Leinster Way route from town, and when you reach the hill follow the route which is waymarked as the Brandon Way. Alternatively, for a more sheltered and leisurely walk, you can follow the Way north from here along the Barrow to Borris (see p.274).

The best place to **stay** and **eat** in Graiguenamanagh is the plush *Waterside* B&B and restaurant (Ⓣ0503/24246; ❼), a beautifully restored stone building overlooking the river. More modestly priced B&B accommodation is offered at the *Anchor Bar* (Ⓣ0503/24207; ❷), which also serves food daily; and also at *Woodside*, Ballynakill (Ⓣ0503/24765; ❷), about a mile out on the New Ross road. An extensive dinner menu and good, inexpensive daytime snacks are available in *Monks Refectory Restaurant* (closed Mon & Tues; Ⓣ0503/24988).

St Mullins

Five miles south down the towpath along the River Barrow from Graiguenamanagh, or the R729, and into County Carlow, is **ST MULLINS**, tucked away among wooded hills, with the open heights of the Blackstairs Mountains beyond. Strolling through the village, you'll come across the scant remains of a monastery, founded in 696 AD by St Moling, Bishop of Ferns and Glendalough, and alongside them in the churchyard are the base of a round tower and a very worn stone cross. Down beside the stream, at the back of the ruins, a path leads to St Moling's Well, while near the centre of the village stands a defensive earthwork, looking like a sturdy pudding just shaken from its bowl.

Blanchfield's **pub** does regular soup and sandwiches and *Teac Moling* offers **B&B** in a very pretty spot beside the river (Ⓣ051/424665; ❹). The nearest shop is at Glynn, one and a half miles away.

Travel details

Trains

Carlow to: Dublin (9 daily, 3 Sun; 1hr 15min); Kildare (9 daily, 3 Sun; 30min); Kilkenny (4 daily; 45min).
Kilkenny to: Carlow (4 daily; 30min); Dublin (4 daily; 1hr 45min).
Rosslare Harbour/Europort to: Dublin (3 daily; 3hr 15min).
Wexford to: Dublin (3 daily; 2hr 30min–3hr); Rosslare Harbour/Europort (3 daily; 30min).

Buses

For more information on privately run bus routes contact the following companies who operate in this area: Buggy's ⓣ056/41264; J.J. Kavanagh ⓣ056/31106.

Buggy's and Bus Éireann

Carlow to: Dublin (7 daily; 1hr 30min).
Kilkenny to: Clonmel (6 daily; 1hr); Dublin (6 daily; 2hr).
New Ross to: Dublin (3 daily; 2hr 45min).
Rosslare Harbour/Europort to: Cork (3 daily; 4hr); Dublin (9 daily; 3hr 15min); Limerick (4 daily; 4hr 15min); Waterford (6 daily; 1hr 15min).
Wexford to: Dublin (10 daily, 7 Sun; 2hr 45min); Rosslare Harbour/Europort (10 daily, 7 Sun; 30min).

J.J. Kavanagh

Kilkenny to: Dublin (2–5 daily; 2hr).

7

Waterford, Tipperary and Limerick

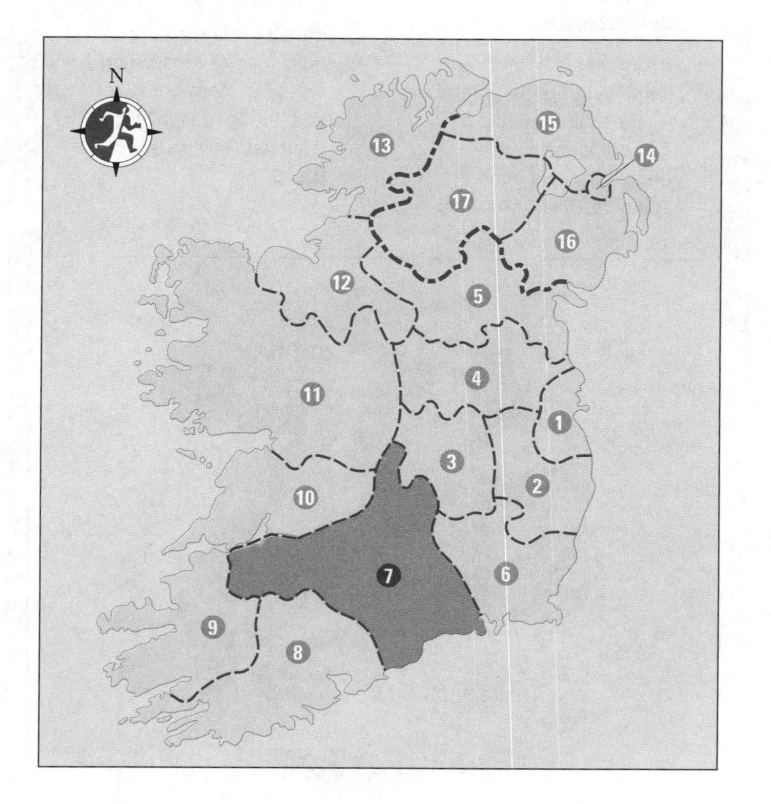

CHAPTER 7

Highlights

* **Waterford Treasures** A superb array of Viking artefacts and early royal charters are the show-pieces of this excellent museum detailing the history of this beautifully located city on the banks of the River Suir. **See p.296**

* **Ardmore** On Waterford's southwest tip, this pretty village, with a medieval cathedral and tower, has beautiful views over Ardmore Bay. **See p.302**

* **The Rock of Cashel** Spectacular collection of Christian buildings set atop a natural limestone outcrop jutting out of the surrounding Tipperary plains. **See p.314**

* **Hunt Museum** Limerick's finest attraction: a marvellous collection of fascinating artefacts, some of which rival those of Dublin's National Gallery. **See p.325**

Waterford, Tipperary and Limerick

Fertile, undulating farmland typifies the landscapes of **Waterford**, **Tipperary** and **Limerick**, generating prosperity, but offering, in the main, a fairly bland experience for the visitor. Parts of the countryside are exceptions to this rule and these, along with some interesting historical sites, are well worth making time to explore. Arrive in Ireland at Shannon Airport and Limerick city makes a good first stopover; arrive via Rosslare Harbour in the southeast of the country and you are likely to pass through County Waterford if you are heading for the scenic splendours of Cork and Kerry, and through all three of the counties in this chapter if you're making your way to the music of Clare.

County Waterford has a great deal more to offer than it is generally given credit for. All along the Waterford coast, rolling green hills spread down to a fine shore of cliffs interspersed with expansive bays and secluded beaches. Inland, rich farming country gives way to the desolate, boggy Comeragh and Knockmealdown mountains, offering good opportunities for easy, scenic walking. The county even boasts its own tiny Gaeltacht (Irish-speaking) community at **Ring**, one of the best areas on the south coast to hear traditional Irish music. Waterford city is perhaps most famous for the high-quality crystal that is made there, but its prime draw has to be **Waterford Treasures**, a superb museum with a wealth of Viking and medieval artefacts.

Straddling Waterford's border with **County Tipperary**, the **Knockmealdown Mountains** offer attractive walking opportunities, as do the **Galty Mountains**, and the landscape reaches its most sumptuous in the velvety slopes of the **Glen of Aherlow**. Scenery aside, Tipperary's farming towns have little to offer the visitor. At the very heart of the county, though, is a site of outstanding interest – the **Rock of Cashel**. A spectacular natural formation topped with Christian buildings from virtually every period, it's effectively a primer in the development of Irish ecclesiastical architecture. The historic sites at **Cahir** and **Carrick-on-Suir** are also well worth taking in.

County **Limerick** has relatively little to tempt you and is often just somewhere visitors pass through on their way to Clare and Kerry. Industrial and depressed, **Limerick city** has a luckless reputation. Nonetheless, recent efforts to regenerate the city do seem to be teasing out strands of elegance and interest in its weather-worn Georgian streets and there's a renewed vibrancy to its

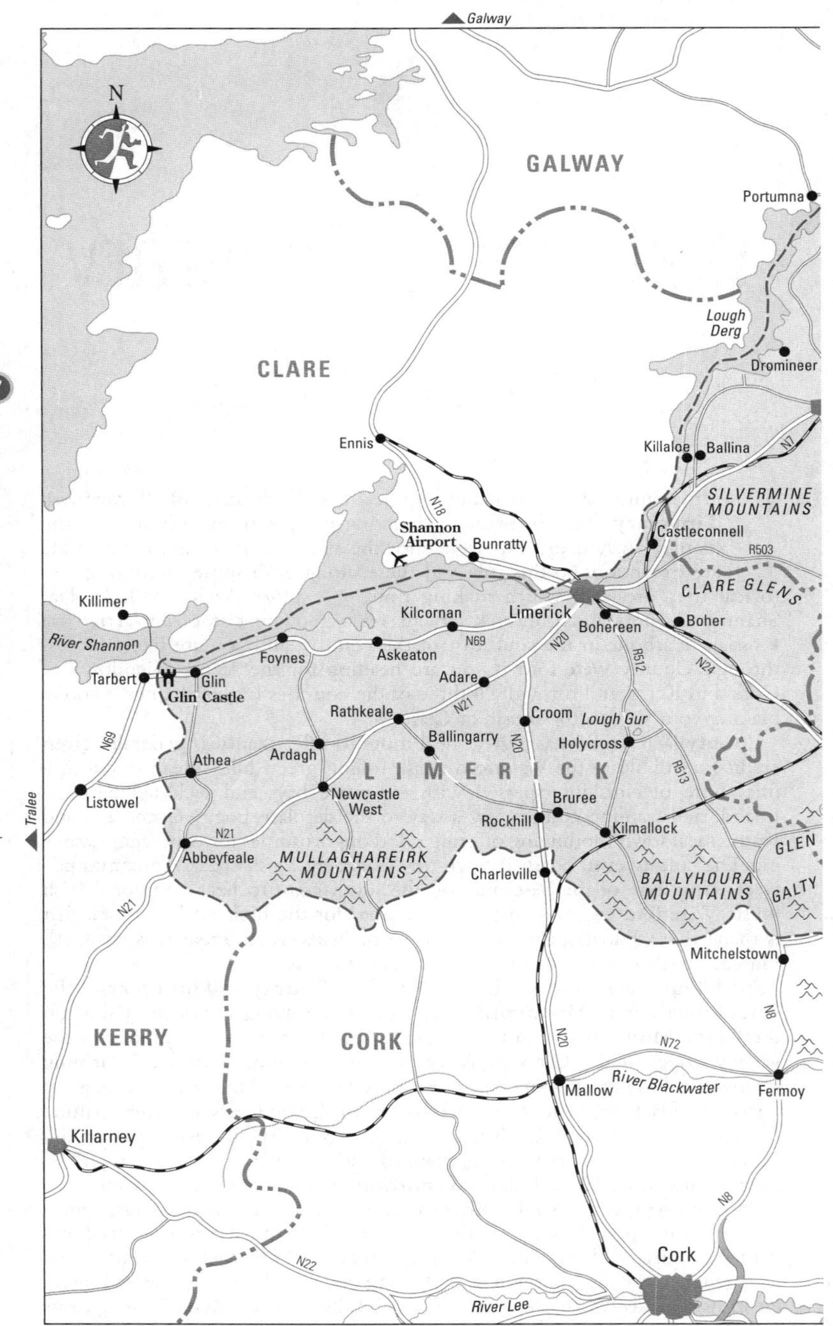
Galway
N
GALWAY
Portumna
CLARE
Lough Derg
Dromineer
Ennis
Killaloe
Ballina
N7
SILVERMINE MOUNTAINS
N18
Shannon Airport
Bunratty
Castleconnell
R503
CLARE GLENS
Killimer
Limerick
Kilcornan
Bohereen
Boher
River Shannon
Foynes
Askeaton
N69
N20
R512
N24
Tarbert
Glin
Glin Castle
Adare
N21
Rathkeale
Croom
Lough Gur
N69
Ballingarry
N20
Holycross
Ardagh
R513
Athea
LIMERICK
Listowel
Newcastle West
Bruree
Tralee
Rockhill
Kilmallock
N21
GLEN
Abbeyfeale
MULLAGHAREIRK MOUNTAINS
Charleville
BALLYHOURA MOUNTAINS
GALTY
N21
Mitchelstown
N8
KERRY
CORK
N20
N72
Mallow
River Blackwater
Fermoy
Killarney
N8
Cork
N22
River Lee

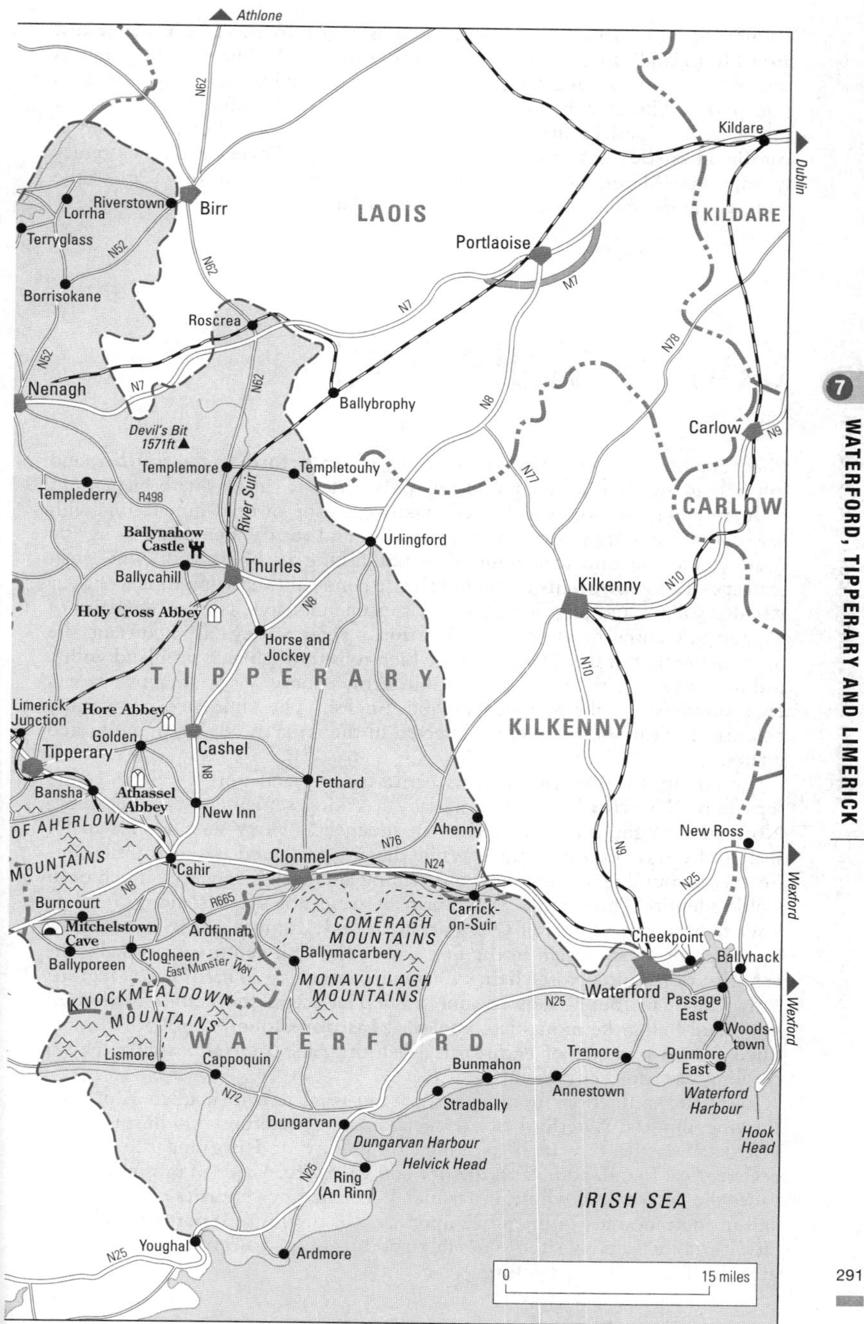
Athlone
Dublin
Wexford
Wexford
LAOIS
KILDARE
CARLOW
KILKENNY
TIPPERARY
WATERFORD
Birr
Riverstown
Lorrha
Terryglass
Borrisokane
Roscrea
Nenagh
Kildare
Portlaoise
Carlow
Kilkenny
Ballybrophy
Devil's Bit 1571ft
Templemore
Templetouhy
Templederry
Ballynahow Castle
Thurles
Ballycahill
Urlingford
Holy Cross Abbey
Horse and Jockey
River Suir
Limerick Junction
Hore Abbey
Golden
Tipperary
Cashel
Fethard
Bansha
Athassel Abbey
New Inn
GLEN OF AHERLOW
GALTEE MOUNTAINS
Ahenny
Clonmel
Cahir
Burncourt
Mitchelstown Cave
Ardfinnan
Carrick-on-Suir
COMERAGH MOUNTAINS
Ballyporeen
Clogheen
East Munster Way
Ballymacarbery
MONAVULLAGH MOUNTAINS
KNOCKMEALDOWN MOUNTAINS
Lismore
Cappoquin
New Ross
Cheekpoint
Ballyhack
Waterford
Passage East
Woodstown
Tramore
Dunmore East
Bunmahon
Annestown
Stradbally
Waterford Harbour
Hook Head
Dungarvan
Dungarvan Harbour
Helvick Head
Ring (An Rinn)
IRISH SEA
Youghal
Ardmore
N62
N52
N7
M7
N78
N8
N77
N9
N10
R498
N24
N76
R665
N25
N72
0
15 miles

cultural life. More importantly, Limerick is home to the **Hunt Museum**, arguably Ireland's most important collection outside Dublin, and the town is notable too as the setting for the international bestselling novel, *Angela's Ashes* (see p.874). The rich pasture of County Tipperary continues into County Limerick and perhaps its greatest attraction is the exceptional number of **medieval castles** and towers that dot the landscape. There's also an extremely important Mesolithic-to-Neolithic site at **Lough Gur**, in the heart of the county, and the famously quaint village of **Adare**.

County Waterford

Photographs rarely do justice to the beauty of **Waterford**. In the **south**, grand hills rise gradually from coast and valley, their slopes cloaked with plantations of fir trees. The smoothly sculpted **coastline** is one of bold dimensions with low cliffs giving views over large, open bays and **sandy beaches**. Along the coast you'll also find a handful of quaint fishing harbours and some great seascapes. The **mountains** in the **north** rise gently above the prettiness of their wooded valleys, and offer long walks with stupendous views over the plains of Tipperary. Central to the county, Waterford's **river valleys** are luxuriant, the finest being that of the **Blackwater**, which rolls through rich farmland with a real majesty. Here, it's easy to see why the fertile county was so attractive to foreign invaders – Viking, Norman and English. The influence of wealthy colonists is clear, their opulence reflected in the remains of elegant, cultivated estates.

The county of Waterford and its namesake city and port developed quite separately. **Waterford city** was initially a Viking settlement that became a Norman stronghold and thrived as an independent city-state with a major share of Ireland's European trade. While the city prospered as a mercantile centre, the surrounding county lived off farming and fishing, retaining much of its Celtic identity. The Vikings and Normans were not the first newcomers to leave their mark: the area of **Old Parish** around Ardmore gets its name as the arrival point of St Declan in the first half of the fifth century, supposedly the very first of Ireland's proselytizing Christians, preceding St Patrick. The region's early Christian foundations became influential across the country, the most important being the monastic complex at **Lismore**, founded in 636. It flourished first as a centre of ecclesiastical learning, and later as a secular power rivalling Waterford city itself.

Today the distinctions between urban and rural remain marked. Alongside thriving, modern Waterford city, pockets of ancient cultures and histories survive, such as the tiny Irish-speaking community of **Ring** and the historic ecclesiastical foundations of **Ardmore** and **Lismore**. An air of prosperity pervades the county as a whole, in farmland enriched by centuries of cultivation and in the renewed commercial importance of the historic port of Waterford city. It's easily accessible, too – notably good main roads serve city and county, great for long-distance **cycling**.

Waterford city

WATERFORD's appearance from the River Suir is deceptively grim: the bare and open stretch of water with its ugly grey wharves and cranes holds no suggestion of the lively city that lies beyond its dull quays. This is the commercial capital of the southeast, and it retains buildings from Viking and Norman times, as well as from the eighteenth century – all periods of past eminence. The web of narrow streets that grew up as the focus for commercial activity in the city's earliest days holds the modern city together in compact dynamism. While Waterford has had the modern infrastructure of a mercantile, rather than a rural, centre for decades, the city has developed socially and economically even within the last ten years, and the large number of students here has generated an increasingly upbeat social scene.

Waterford is basically a modern European port wrapped around an ancient Irish city. The **historic town** can happily be explored in a day or so, and the **nightlife** also warrants some sampling. Despite its size the city has some excellent bars, a limited but growing number of decent and imaginative places to eat and the burgeoning rock-music scene of an optimistic, albeit small-scale, urban environment. Alongside the city's modernity, though, there's plenty that's

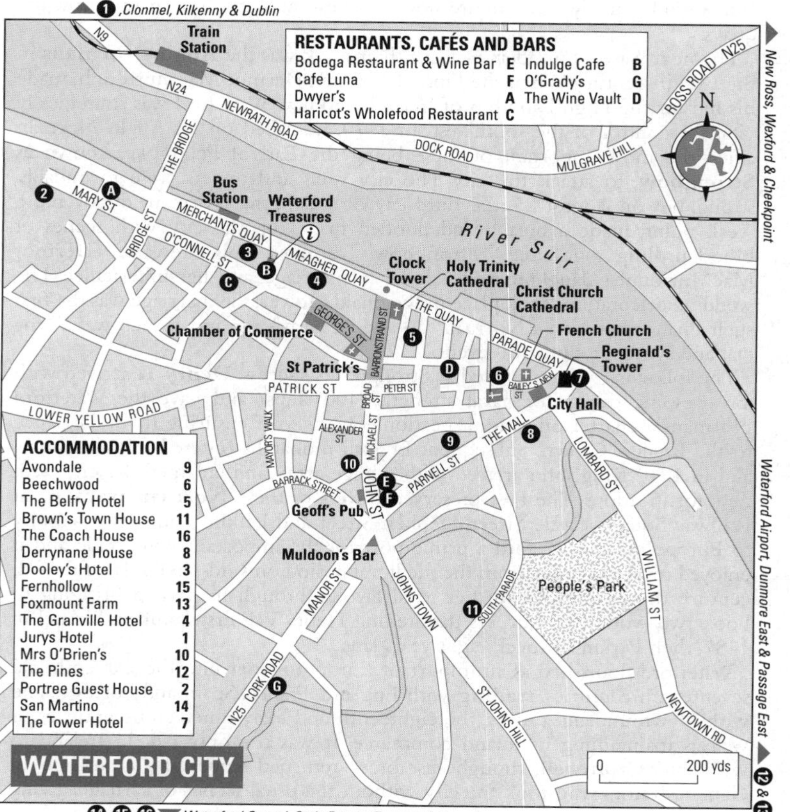

traditional, most obviously the place of the pub as a focal point of social activity, and the persistence of music as an integral part of city life.

Some history

Waterford is the oldest continuous urban settlement in Ireland. Reliable recorded history of the city starts with the tenth-century **Viking** settlement, since which the deep, navigable **River Suir** has been the source of the city's importance. Far inland, and therefore easily defended, Waterford was also perfectly positioned for the internal trading routes of the Barrow and Nore rivers, reaching into the heart of the southeast's rich farmland. The layout of the city retains its Viking roots, the very long quays and adjacent narrow lanes forming the trading centre. Waterford was the most important Viking settlement in Ireland, and its inhabitants were so feared that even the bellicose local Celtic Déisí had to pay them tribute – failure to pay Airgead Sróine (Nose Money) resulted in having your nose chopped off. **Reginald's Tower** dates from this time, as do some of the remains of the city walls. Nearby, two well-preserved stone arches inside *The Reginald* bar were in fact "sallyports", through which ships entered the fortified city from what is now The Mall, but was then a tidal pool that was only diverted in the eighteenth century. In the late 1980s and early 1990s, over a fifth of the Viking city was excavated and a wealth of artefacts found – many of them are now on show in Waterford Treasures on the quays.

The next wave of invaders to leave their mark was the **Anglo-Normans** in the twelfth century. When the king of Leinster, Dermot MacMurrough, made his bid for the High Kingship of Ireland, he knew Waterford was strategically vital for control of the southwest. In 1170, he called on his Anglo-Norman allies, the most important of these being the Earl of Pembroke, known as **Strongbow**, to attack the city. The city walls and towers were formidably strong, but on August 25, the third day of attack, the Normans discovered a weak point, made a breach and flooded in, taking the city with scenes of bloodcurdling violence. Strongbow received his reward: Dermot MacMurrough's daughter Aoife's hand in marriage, and her inheritance. The wedding celebrations took place in Reginald's Tower; the marriage was the first such alliance between a Norman earl and an Irish king, and as such was a crucial and symbolic historical event.

The following year, surprised at Strongbow's success, **Henry II** arrived with an awesome display of naval strength (400 ships) and gave the Waterford Normans a charter offering protection – his way of ensuring their allegiance to the English Crown. Subsequent English monarchs fostered this allegiance, and in 1210 King John arrived with a huge army and enlarged the city with new fortifications. The best-preserved towers of these **Norman walls** are at Railway Square, Castle Street, Stephen Street and Jenkins Lane. Its proximity to Europe made Waterford a prime port for the important wine trade and it enjoyed royal patronage from the medieval period onwards. In the late fifteenth century the city reaped further royal favour through its part in bringing to book two would-be usurpers threatening Henry VII: first Lambert Simnel in 1487, then Perkin Warbeck eight years later.

Waterford flourished as an important European **port** into the sixteenth and seventeenth centuries, **trading** with England, France, Spain and Portugal, and with Newfoundland during the eighteenth and early nineteenth centuries, as well as maintaining its inland commerce. It was the only city in Ireland to withstand **Cromwell**, though his forces returned under the command of General Ireton, who took the city without the usual scenes of carnage, giving its citizens honourable terms. Abundant testimony to the city's eighteenth-century prosperity is evident in both ecclesiastical and secular architecture. However, Waterford is nowadays most famous for its **crystal**, first produced here in 1783. The factory closed in 1851 but reopened in 1951 and is now one of the city's major employers, as well as being a popular draw for tourists.

Arrival and information

Roads from the north and the east converge on the river at the **train station**, on Dock Road (Ⓣ051/873401); the city – and the **bus station**, on Merchants Quay (Ⓣ051/879000) – lie over the bridge to the south. Regular daily trains connect Waterford to Clonmel, Tipperary, Limerick, Wexford, Kilkenny and Dublin. In addition to regular Bus Éireann services, Rapid Express Club Travel (Ⓣ051/872149) operates a cheap **bus service** to Dublin; buses leave from outside the Bank of Ireland, Parnell Street. Scheduled **flights** from London arrive at Waterford Regional Airport in Killowen eight miles south of the city (Ⓣ051/875589). There's no bus between the airport and the city: a taxi will cost you around €15.

The **tourist office** is in The Granary (Jan–March & Oct–Dec Mon–Fri 9am–5pm; April–June & Sept Mon–Sat 9am–6pm; July & Aug Mon–Sat 9am–6pm, Sun 11am–5pm; Ⓣ051/875823), roughly midway along the quays that run along the south side of the river. As well as providing a wealth of information about the city and surrounding region, it offers an accommodation-booking service for a small fee.

Accommodation

Waterford's **accommodation** ranges from grand hotels overlooking the river to comfortable, family-run B&Bs. At present there are no registered hostels in the city, and should you come across any advertised, you are strongly advised to talk with staff in the tourist office before booking in.

Avondale 2 Parnell St Ⓣ051/852267. A comfortable city-centre B&B in a Georgian town house. ❷

Beechwood 7 Cathedral Square Ⓣ051/876677. Standard B&B in a centrally located family home overlooking Christ Church Cathedral. ❷

The Belfry Hotel Conduit Lane Ⓣ051/844800, Ⓦwww.belfryhotel.ie. Centrally located family-run modern hotel with a business-like atmosphere. ❺–❻

Brown's Town House 29 South Parade Ⓣ051/870594, Ⓦwww.brownstownhouse.com. A pleasant Victorian town house decorated with modern Irish paintings and located in a quiet residential street. ❸

The Coach House Butlerstown Castle, Butlerstown Ⓣ051/384656, Ⓔcoachhse@iol.ie. Comfortable B&B, unsurprisingly in a converted coach house, around three miles south from Waterford, off the N25. ❹

Derrynane House 19 The Mall Ⓣ051/875179. Inexpensive, simple B&B in the city centre. The Mall can be noisy, so ask for a room to the rear. ❷

Dooley's Hotel The Quay Ⓣ051/873531, Ⓦwww.dooleys-hotel.ie. One of Waterford's most renowned hotels, still family run. Comfortable, three star and in a prime city-centre location next to The Granary overlooking the river. ❹–❻

Fernhollow Cork Rd, Ballinaneeshagh Ⓣ051/358128. Pleasant and comfortable B&B two miles out of the centre, just past the glass factory. ❷

Foxmount Farm Passage East Rd Ⓣ051/874308. Four miles from town, off the Dunmore Road, this farmhouse B&B also does excellent evening meals. ❷

The Granville Hotel Meagher Quay Ⓣ051/305555, Ⓦwww.granville-hotel.ie. Grandiose historic hotel whose former guests include Daniel O'Connell and Charles Stewart Parnell. Swish, elegant interiors and a prime location on the quays make it one of the most prestigious hotels in town. ❺–❽

Jurys Hotel Ferrybank Ⓣ051/832111, Ⓦwww.jurysdoyle.com. Overlooking the River Suir and the city, this rather characterless modern hotel, set in 38 acres of grounds, has its own leisure centre. ❹–❽

Mrs O'Brien's 2 New St ⓣ051/875764. Inexpensive accommodation in a city-centre family home; breakfast not provided. ❷
The Pines Knockboy, on the Dunmore road ⓣ051/874452, ⓔbjackman@eircom.net. Clean, comfortable B&B serving excellent breakfasts, two miles from the city centre. Closed Dec. ❷
Portree Guesthouse Mary St ⓣ051/874574. Impersonal but with helpful staff, this is a comfortable, central guesthouse in a quiet side street and offers en-suite rooms. It seems to be popular with stag-night parties so can be noisy at weekends. Close to the bus and train stations. ❸
San Martino Ballinaneeshagh ⓣ051/374949. Decent no-smoking B&B just past the glass factory. ❷
The Tower Hotel The Mall ⓣ051/875801, ⓦwww.towerhotelgroup.ie. Large, but rather charmless, modern three-star hotel right in the centre of town; facilities include a leisure centre and pool. ❹

The City

Waterford is centred on a wedge of Georgiana, between the eighteenth-century shops and houses of **O'Connell and George's streets**, which run behind the modern quays, and the faded splendour of **Parnell Street** and **The Mall** with their fine doorways and fanlights. The city's prime attraction is **Waterford Treasures**, which stands on Merchants Quay, housing an extraordinary collection of Viking and medieval artefacts. Head east along the quays from here for about 200yd and you'll pass the nineteenth-century clock tower and a turning into Barronstrand Street, which runs through the city's main shopping area and through a couple of changes of name to John Street, with its great concentration of fast-food joints and bars. Continue along the quays from the clock tower and after about 400yd you will reach **Reginald's Tower** (originally Ranguald's Tower), the most impressive medieval building that survives in Waterford. The area of tangled laneways between here and The Mall contains some of the city's finest juxtapositions of medieval and eighteenth-century architecture, including **Christ Church Cathedral**, which dates from 1770. The splendours of that era are remembered too at **Waterford Crystal**, the world-famous glass factory one and a half miles from the city centre, a trip to which is vigorously promoted throughout the region.

Waterford Treasures

The Granary, on Merchants Quay, is a nineteenth-century warehouse that has been converted to hold the tourist office and, behind this, the city's chief visitor attraction – **Waterford Treasures** (daily: April, May & Sept 9.30am–6pm; June–Aug 9.30am–9pm; Oct–March 10am–5pm; €6; ⓣ051/304500). This first-rate museum covers the history of the city from the Viking period to the present day through a variety of audio-visual presentations, and a superb array of Viking artefacts and early royal charters. **Viking finds** include elaborately carved antler combs, intricately fashioned bracelets, lathe-turned wooden bowls, weaponry, ceramics and leather footwear. The twelfth-century kite brooch is a work of incredible intricacy and there are gold and silver needles and pins of a similar age. There's plenty from the **Anglo-Norman period** too, including a mid-thirteenth-century yew bow stave – the only complete medieval bow in the British Isles; and a late-fifteenth-century cannon – the oldest in Ireland – which clearly shows the hooped construction typical of the time. Also on show is the city's magnificent collection of medieval, Tudor and Stuart royal charters. One of the highlights here is the extraordinary Great Charter Roll of 1372, Ireland's most important late-medieval decorated manuscript, rich in illustrations of English monarchs, governors of Ireland, medieval mayors and the earliest known depiction of an Irish city.

The collection is rich in content and it's well worth using the audio guide in order to dip in and out of the areas you want to learn about in depth. Refreshingly, the interpretation on offer has a markedly contemporary and international perspective, debunking commonly held notions that the Vikings were little more than marauding hooligans as well as presenting a balanced picture of just how beneficial Waterford's relationship with the English Crown was.

City Hall and the Chamber of Commerce

Christ Church apart, it's in the city's secular architecture that the best of the eighteenth century is realized. The cathedral looks down over The Mall, with its **City Hall** (Mon–Fri 10am–5pm), built in 1788 by the ubiquitous John Roberts. Its spacious entrance hall was once used as a meeting place and merchants' exchange; if you are interested in seeing the Waterford crystal chandeliers in the council chambers and the Waterford Room, ask at the desk. By far the finest eighteenth-century architectural detail in the city, though, is the beautiful cantilevered oval staircase inside the lilac-coloured **Chamber of Commerce** in George's Street (Mon–Fri 9am–5pm, access by appointment only; ⓣ051/872639). Built in 1785, with fine decorative stuccowork, it, too, is the work of John Roberts.

Christ Church and Holy Trinity cathedrals

The Church of Ireland **Christ Church Cathedral**, a short stroll up Bailey's New Street from the French Church, forms the prime architectural landmark of Georgian Waterford. Built in 1773 by John Roberts, who did much work in Waterford for both Catholics and Protestants, it's a nicely proportioned building with a fine steeple, a spacious interior and an elaborate Baroque stucco ceiling; it stands on the site of a Viking church which was enlarged during the medieval period and survived up until 1770. The monuments inside the cathedral are worth a look, in particular that of James Rice (one-time lord mayor of Waterford), dating from 1482, a gruesome effigy of a corpse in an advanced state of decay, with various creatures crawling in and out of the carcass. The story of Waterford city from the time of the Norman invasion to the present day is relayed in a 45-minute sound-and-light presentation (April, May, Sept & Oct Mon–Fri at 11.30am, 2.30pm & 4pm; June–Aug Mon–Sat at 9.30am, 11.30am, 2.30pm & 4pm, Sun 2.30pm & 4pm; voluntary donation of €3 is requested – all proceeds go towards the cathedral's conservation and restoration).

If you want to see more of Roberts' work, visit Holy Trinity Cathedral in Barronstrand Street off The Quay, and St Patrick's Church off George's Street. Originally built in 1793, **Holy Trinity Cathedral** was greatly altered during the nineteenth century to become the swirling, ornate extravaganza it is today. That the same architect could work on the Protestant and then the Catholic cathedral is evidence of the measure of religious tolerance enjoyed by Waterford's citizens at the time. This is further borne out in the little church of **St Patrick's**, tucked away up a lane off George's Street. Built in the mid-eighteenth century, it remained a Catholic church throughout penal times and as such is unique. It seems that mercantile strength gave Waterford considerable cultural independence, and Catholics were allowed to hold services here – in stark contrast to the suppression that went on in the rest of the country. Funding came from the sons of Waterford merchants who settled in Spain during the eighteenth century, and dark and dolorous paintings hang either side of the altar, revealing a strong Spanish influence.

Reginald's Tower and the French Church

Waterford's most historic building is **Reginald's Tower** (daily: Easter to May & Oct 10am–5pm; June–Sept 9.30am–6.30pm; €1.90; Heritage Card; ☎051/304220), around half a mile east along the quays from Waterford Treasures. A large cylindrical late-twelfth-century tower, its design is similar to the Scottish broch, with a concealed stairway built within its massive wall; the original Viking tower that stood here was built in 1003. It was the most substantial of the seventeen defensive towers that encircled the city in medieval times. During its life it has been used as a mint, a prison and a military store. Inside, a display details its history and that of the powerful Waterford Vikings, their struggles with the Anglo-Normans and the subsequent arrival of the English Crown. Much of this material is covered in a far more lively manner in the Waterford Treasures exhibition, but it's still worth visiting Reginald's Tower to absorb some sense of the power of its various former incumbents.

Wander up Bailey's New Street, just behind Reginald's Tower, and you soon come to Waterford's other important medieval building, the **French Church**, on Greyfriars (key from Reginald's Tower). Founded by Franciscans in 1240, the church served as an almshouse in the sixteenth century, and from 1693 to 1815 was used as a place of worship by French Huguenot refugees, whom the city sheltered in their exile from persecution at home. It's now a solid, roofless ruin with a complete tower and fine east triple-lancet window. Stones at the base of the outer windows are decorated with comic carved figures, and the church contains some interesting carved burial slabs, including that of Sir Neal O'Neill, who accompanied James II in his flight from the Battle of the Boyne.

Waterford crystal

If you want to find out more about Waterford crystal, which is for sale all over town, you should make a trip out to the **Waterford Crystal Glass Factory** for one of its **guided tours** around the glass-cutting and blowing workshops (March–Oct daily 8.30am–4pm; Nov–March Mon–Fri 9am–3.15pm, booking ahead advisable; €6; ☎051/332500). This is interesting if you've never seen the process before, and a fair way to work up an appetite on a wet day, but not the "absolute must" the publicity tends to suggest. The factory is a mile and a half from the city centre on the N25 towards Cork; check at the tourist office for times of buses from the city centre.

Eating

Finding something to **eat** in Waterford is unlikely to prove a problem. There's no shortage of **bar food**: try *Dooley's Hotel*, The Quay; *T.H. Doolan's*, also a live music venue (see opposite), on George's Street; or *Egan's* on Broad Street. For late-night cafés and fast food, head for John Street. The following listings cover the range:

Bodega Restaurant & Wine Bar 54 John St ☎051/844177. Relaxed wine bar serving plenty of specials such as scallops fricassee and wild salmon with couscous.

Cafe Luna 53 John St. A popular spot for inexpensive ciabatta, baguettes, croissants and hot specials. Mon–Wed 8.30am–midnight, Thurs–Sun 8.30am–3.30am.

Dwyer's 8 Mary St ☎051/877478. Despite a rather uninspiring exterior and location, this is one of the best restaurants in Waterford. It offers classic French cooking using the best local produce. Closed Sun.

Haricot's Wholefood Restaurant 11 O'Connell St ☎051/841299. Cheerful, inexpensive café with a cosy country-kitchen atmosphere. This long-time favourite guarantees a varied menu of flavoursome and satisfying meals. Mon–Fri 9am–8pm, Sat 9.30am–6pm.

Indulge Cafe The Granary, behind the tourist

office and occupying the same building ⓣ051/860977. One of Waterford's best spots for snacks and lunches, this is a stylish licensed café with a relaxed atmosphere. Serves huge and inexpensive dishes such as chicken and mushroom pie, chicken calzone, steak sandwiches and home-made burgers. Mon–Sat 9am–9pm.
O'Grady's On the Cork road before the Waterford Glass Factory ⓣ051/378851. A friendly restaurant open for lunch and dinner, serving local rock oysters and scallops and dishes such as crab cakes, monkfish tails in a light curry sauce and lemon sole with gazpacho sauce. B&B accommodation also available (❹).
The Wine Vault High St ⓣ051/853444, ⓦwww.waterfordwinevault.com. Classy and moderately priced bistro-restaurant, with a warm, convivial atmosphere, serving excellent contemporary Irish food as well as dishes such as chunky Mediterranean fish soup and honey-roast duckling. Mains from about €12. Mon–Sat lunch & dinner.

Nightlife and entertainment

The Garter Lane Arts Centre (Mon–Sat 10am–6pm; ⓣ051/855038, ⓦwww.iol.ie/~glac), housed at 5 and 22A O'Connell St, has a theatre showing both drama and film, and a good current-events notice board. It's the place to catch a performance by the Waterford-based Red Kettle Theatre Company as well as various other touring companies. The centre also hosts painting and sculpture exhibitions of contemporary Irish artists. Waterford's other theatre is the **Theatre Royal**, on The Mall (ⓣ051/874402), which stages the city's **Light Opera Festival** in September, an international competition for amateur musical societies (ⓦwww.waterfordfestival.com). The Regional Technical College on the main Cork Road is used for **classical music** recitals, generally advertised in the tourist office.

Waterford has a fair-sized student population and, not surprisingly, there is no shortage of lively **bars**, many with live **music** on offer, from traditional through rock to the astonishing array of tribute bands on the circuit.

Barr's Mayor's Walk. Cosy little pub attracting a discerning, off-beat clientele; there's space to think while you drink.
Geoff's 8–9 John St. The place to catch up on what's happening around town. Antiquated wooden benches and lots of space for the mixed, predominantly young, crowd.
Jack Meades Pub Halfway House. Despite being four miles east of the city along the road towards Cheekpoint, this is a very popular bar, noted for its traditional music.
Kitty Kerin's Barrack St. A pleasant bar and a good spot to catch traditional Irish music four or five nights a week.
M.Walsh 11 George's St. Ancient, old-fashioned bar and off-licence with a grocery-shop front stocked with pop bottles and sweets.
Muldoon's On the corner of Manor and Parnell streets. Large pub, popular with locals for the late bar (until 1.30am), its upstairs nightclub, *Merlins*, and varied entertainment – from excellent traditional music (Sun) to tribute bands (midweek).
Preachers John St. The club behind the Pulpit Bar. Arguably the liveliest club in town and certainly the most bizarre with its lavish Gothic-fantasy interior. Generally, the music is mainstream chart. Closed Mon.
Rhythm Room On the corner of Manor and John streets. Fairly casual club, playing mainstream chart and dance music, popular with students during the week and locals at weekends.
T.H. Doolan's 31–32 George's St. Big pub full of old carved fireplaces and dusty folk memorabilia. A good spot to catch traditional music, which is played here most nights.

Listings

Dental emergencies South Eastern Health Board, Community Care, on the Cork road ⓣ051/876111. Mon–Fri 9am–5pm.
Hospital Waterford Regional Hospital, Dunmore Rd ⓣ051/873321.
Internet access Waterford e-Centre, 10 O'Connell St ⓣ051/878448 ⓔecentre@eircom.net.
Laundry Boston Cleaners, Alexander St.
River cruises Galley River Cruises offers trips to New Ross, including lunch, afternoon tea or evening meal (June–Aug; ⓣ051/421723).
Travel agents USIT Youth and Student Travel Office, 36–37 George's St ⓣ051/872601.

The Waterford coast

Waterford's coastline offers good sandy beaches and some breathtaking coastal walks. The open grandeur of bays like Dungarvan is offset by the intimacy of hidden coves and scenic fishing ports. The best of the beaches are at **Woodstown**, **Dunmore East**, **Tramore**, **Annestown** and **Ardmore** – where you'll also find the vestiges of early Christian history. Major seaside towns are connected to Waterford by regular bus services; Suirway buses provide a limited service to some of the choicest spots, but you may well find that the best are walked, cycled or slowly hitched to. The coastal area also offers some of the best traditional music in the southeast of Ireland, most notably at **Ring**, home to a small Irish-speaking community.

Passage East, Cheekpoint and Woodstown

The tiny fishing village of **CHEEKPOINT**, east of Waterford on the N29, sits at the confluence of the rivers Suir, Nore and Barrow, and its chief draw is the excellent seafood at the *Suir Inn*. Also worth trying is *McAlpin's* bistro (Ⓣ051/382119; Tues–Sat 6–10pm), an old cottage a few doors up from the *Suir Inn*, serving Irish dishes. Immediately east of Waterford city, at the neck of its long harbour, the pretty ferry village of **PASSAGE EAST** nestles under craggy hills, the estuary slopes aflame with wild gorse. The **ferry** here connects with Ballyhack in County Wexford (Passage East Car Ferry, Ⓣ 051/382480; €6.50 single, €9.50 return) – a particularly useful route east for cyclists, especially if you're making for Rosslare or want to stay on the coast. If you need **accommodation**, try the *Cois Abhann* (Ⓣ051/382190; ❸). Across the water, less than a mile from Ballyhack, there's an An Óige hostel at Arthurstown (Ⓣ051/389411; June–Sept). Coastal paths south of Passage East afford views over the estuary to the Hook Head, County Wexford. The long sandy beach flanked by deep woodland at **WOODSTOWN**, just over two miles south of Passage East, takes some beating if you're looking for a quiet stroll or a gentle dip.

Dunmore East

Further around the Waterford coast, **DUNMORE EAST** settles snugly between small, chunky sandstone cliffs topped by masses of rambling golden gorse. The main street follows a higgledy-piggledy contour from the safe, sandy cove beside which the east village sits, towards a busy harbour full of the rippled reflections of brightly coloured fishing boats and cradled by the crooked finger of the harbour wall. From here, the ruddy sandstone cliffs make bold ribs around the coast. This is still a very active fishing harbour, but has also cashed in on its charm, with obviously new thatched houses sneaking in alongside the originals.

Quaint as it is, Dunmore East has become very much a playground for affluent Waterford citizens, and there are three large **hotels** to cater for them – including the *Haven* (Ⓣ051/383150, Ⓦwww.thehavenhotel.com; ❷–❹). More moderately priced accommodation is offered by a number of **B&Bs**, including *Church Villa* (Ⓣ051/383390; ❷) on Dock Road and *Copper Beech* (Ⓣ051/383187; ❷) and *Carraig Liath* on Harbour Road (Ⓣ051/383273; ❷–❸). For camping, there's *Strand Caravan Park* (Ⓣ051/383174; June to mid-Sept).

Eating is expensive here, and the café down by the beach is just about the only place where you'll get a cheap meal. You could also try *The Melting Pot* which serves simple, tasty food with great views across the harbour (11am–5pm). Good pub food is available at *The Ocean Hotel* (☎051/383136), by the sandy beach in the east village. *The Strand Inn* (☎051/383174), also beside the beach, has a very good fish restaurant and offers decent, more moderately priced bar food, while the upmarket *Ship* restaurant dishes up excellent meals (☎051/383141; 12.30–2pm & 7–10pm) such as turbot with parsley crust and blueberry *crème brûlée*.

For **kayaking** and **wind-surfing**, contact The Adventure Centre (☎051/383783). The Centra supermarket on Dock Road operates a bureau de change.

Tramore to Dungarvan

Nine miles west of Dunmore East, **TRAMORE** caters for a different type of holidaymaker and a different kind of bank balance. It's a busy, popular seaside resort serving families from Waterford and Cork, and has plenty of amusements, caravans and a huge sandy beach. **B&Bs** are concentrated along Tivoli Road: try the hospitable *Sea Court* (☎051/386244; March–Oct; ❷) or the smart *Tivoli House* (☎051/390208; closed Dec 20–Jan 1; ❷). For wholesome **food** such as venison and local fish try *Hartley's Bistro* (☎051/390888), 21 Queens St, which also has music in the bar at weekends. The Vic Deli, on Lower Main Street, sells speciality baked breads: the tomato and fennel seed bread and banana breads are excellent. *O'Shea's* (☎051/381246) on Strand Street is probably the liveliest and most popular **bar** in Tramore, with plenty of middle-of-the-road bands and good bar food.

The wild and splendid coast west of Tramore is one of tussocky grassland, hidden coves and sheer cliffs. Really just a handful of houses, **ANNESTOWN**, six miles from Tramore, is famous for being the only village in Ireland without a pub. It's said that there were once numerous bars catering for the local barracks, but that such was the brawling, the local landowner decided that enough was enough and took away all the licences. There's a cosy **B&B** at *Wee Bluin* (☎051/396344; ❷), or you can enjoy fabulous views at *Annestown House*, a fine early-nineteenth-century building where you can expect cosy log fires and excellent breakfasts (☎051/396160; ❹).

Seven miles further along the coast you'll come to the neat, pretty village of **STRADBALLY**. A road leads one mile from here through deep deciduous woods to the fabulous **Stradbally Cove**, a secluded sandy beach flanked by craggy oak- and ash-covered slopes. The nineteenth-century *Park House* farmhouse (☎051/293185; March–Nov; ❷) is an option if you want to **stay** overnight. Rather more popular, **CLONEA STRAND**, four and a half miles further along the coast and two miles east of Dungarvan, is a broad sandy beach with plenty of space for the holidaymakers at *Casey's Caravan and Camping Park* at its western end. For more comfort, try the nearby *Clonea Strand Hotel* (☎058/42416, Ⓦwww.clonea.com; ❷–❻), the pool and bar of which are also open to non residents.

DUNGARVAN, the major coastal town of County Waterford, has a confident, buoyant air and enjoys a magnificent setting. A wonderful view over the broad bay opens up as you descend to the town, surrounded by open heights topped by pine forests. The **tourist office** is at the Court House, opposite *Lawlors Hotel* on Meagher Street (May–Sept Mon–Sat 9.30am–6pm; Oct–April Mon–Fri 9.30am–5.30pm; ☎058/41741). For **accommodation** try *Powersfield House* on Ballinamuck Road (☎058/45594; ❸–❹), half a mile from

Dungarvan on the Lismore road. It offers excellent evening meals (Thurs–Sat 7–10pm), including grilled vegetable and goat's cheese pizza, roast aubergine soup, and roast duck with plum and date cake. *The Tannery* (☎058/45420) 10 Quay St, serves up some interesting specialities such as tournedos of pork and also local goat's cheese, while *The Parrish* (☎058/45700; noon–7pm) 41–42 Mary St, does high-quality and good-value soup and sandwiches. You may well come across first-rate **traditional music** too: *Bridgie Terries* at a spot known as the Pike, four miles out of town on the N25 towards Waterford, is especially recommended. On the whole, though, the area of greater interest and charm lies immediately to the west.

Ring (An Rinn)

RING, or An Rinn as it is known in Irish, is a pocket of Irish tradition hidden away on the modern Waterford coast, signposted off the N25 about six miles outside Dungarvan. It's a tiny **Irish-speaking community** of about 1500 that has somehow survived in what is otherwise one of Ireland's more developed counties, and all the more remarkable given the "West Brit" flavour of much of the county's coast. The language thrives as do other traditions, notably music and set dancing.

Like many Irish-speaking areas, the community consists of farms and a handful of bars spread over a wide area, with no real centre. This can be frustrating if you don't have transport, as you have to rely on hitching to and from some of the best **bars** – the real draw here, as there's little to see, other than the way of life. *Mooney's* is the first pub on the way into Ring if you are travelling from Dungarvan. It's a great spot for traditional music, and the owners will let you **camp** in their field. Another bar for good pub food and traditional music is *An Seanacai* (☎058/46285), just off the N25, about six miles west of Dungarvan (Thurs & Sat). The **Oyster Festival** over the first weekend in August is a real high point in Ring's music calendar: book accommodation in advance over this period or take a tent. At other times, you should have no trouble finding a bed at the pleasant little **hostel**, *Ceol na Mara* – the owners also offer **B&B** in their spacious nineteenth-century house (☎058/46425, ⓔdesibeau@eircom.net; ❷). Other options include the welcoming, well-run *Aisling*, Gurtnadiha, (☎058/46134; ❷), in a fabulous spot overlooking Dungarvan harbour, or *Helvick View* (☎058/46297; ❶). For **food**, try the *An Carn* restaurant, (☎058/46611) serving dishes such as local mussels with garlic and crisp breadcrumbs. They also have accommodation (❸) – the rooms at front of the house have good views out across the sea.

When the tide's out, you can walk a few miles west of the quayside towards Dungarvan, and out along a **sand spit**. Alternatively, you could walk along the cliffs at **Helvick Head** to gain splendid views of the sculpted coastal cliffs and of the mountains inland.

Ardmore

The delightful village of **ARDMORE**, fourteen miles southwest of Dungarvan, is steeped in history and full of character. The fifth century saw the arrival here of St Declan, at least thirty years before St Patrick arrived in Ireland, and the surrounding area of **Old Parish** is so called because it's supposedly the oldest parish in Ireland. In Ardmore itself, a medieval **cathedral** and **round tower** stand on the site of the saint's original monastic foundation, commanding stunning views over Ardmore Bay. The long, low twelfth-century cathedral has massive buttresses, its stoutly rounded doors and windows confirming the proud – albeit now roofless – Romanesque solidity of the building, while the slender round tower, tall and fine with a conical roof, stands alongside in poignant contrast. Inside, there are stones with early ogham inscriptions, but the most exceptional carvings are on the west external wall. Here, Romanesque arcading, originally from an earlier building, has been set beneath the window, with boldly carved scenes showing the Weighing of Souls, the Fall of Man, the Judgement of Solomon and the Adoration of the Magi: truly impressive, and unique in quality and design. **St Declan's Oratory**, supposedly his burial site, also stands in the graveyard. Earth from the saint's grave is believed to protect against disease.

The village down below, which gets busy in summer, consists of a pleasant row of cottages, a few pubs, a shop and a handful of cafés, with a couple of excellent sandy beaches nearby. Myth has it that when St Declan arrived here from Wales, his bell and vestments were magically carried by the large stone that now sits on the beach. This would explain why the boulder is completely different geologically from the surrounding land – though the Ice Age seems a more likely, if comparatively mundane, explanation. Another improbable tale is that crawling under the stone cures rheumatism, although getting underneath looks rather unmanageable.

Walking through the village to the east, up the hill you come to a path which leads to the ancient **St Declan's Well** and a steeply gabled **oratory**. It's an atmospheric spot, with fresh water springing beside three primitive stone crosses, where pilgrims used to wash, and a stone chair. From here, there's a fine walk around the headland along rocky cliffs for five miles or so, as far as Whiting Bay, a quiet spot with a small sandy beach; alternatively there's a waymarked path that takes you over three miles and brings you back down by the round tower. For longer rambling you can take **St Declan's Way**, a 55-mile route which links Ardmore with Cashel in County Tipperary.

Ardmore has a small number of modestly priced hotels, the best of which is probably *The Round Tower* on College Road (ⓣ024/94494, ⓔrth@tinet.ie; ❸–❺); **B&B** can be had at *Byron Lodge* (ⓣ024/94157; ❷; April–Oct), and there's also the excellent little *Ardmore Beach Hostel* on Main Street (ⓣ024/94501; ❷), with dorms and family rooms. The **caravan** and **camping** site is just beside the beach, and there's a **laundry** on Main Street. The welcoming *Paddy Mac's* **pub** does good bar **food**, and has occasional **traditional music** sessions during the summer. For inexpensive but filling meals there's the cosy *Cup and Saucer* café and nearby *White Horses Restaurant* (May–Sept Tues–Sun 11am–11pm; Oct–April Fri–Sun 11am–11pm) serves good-quality lunches and evening meals.

Cappoquin, the Blackwater Valley and around

Typical of the outstanding beauty of inland County Waterford is the stretch of the Blackwater Valley around Cappoquin, 38 miles west of Waterford city and 19 miles north of Ardmore, where the river makes a sharp westward turn towards County Cork, skirting the southerly limit of the Knockmealdown Mountains (see p.309). **CAPPOQUIN** itself is prettily situated on a wooded hillside overlooking the river, but despite its beautiful location the village seems strangely neglected, and there's little attempt to cater for visitors beyond a few

B&Bs used mainly by a handful of fishermen at holiday times. If you want to **stay**, try the friendly *Riverview House* (☎058/54073; ❶), which is a good, central option. You'll get inexpensive home-cooked **food** at *The Saddlers Teashop* (Mon–Sat 8am–6pm), including marvellous breads baked at Barron's Bakery (☎058/54045) next door – its old stone ovens are still fired by hand. *Richmond House* (☎058/54278, Ⓦwww.amireland.com/richmond; ❷–❺), an eighteenth-century Georgian country house on the way to Lismore is good for a more extravagant meal – four courses for about €35 – and also luxurious B&B.

Although there's little to detain you in the village, the surrounding countryside is lovely. Walk half a mile east, take the right fork by the statue of the Virgin, and you come to the **Glenshelane river-walk**. This follows the minor River Glenshelane through its deep valley banked by pine trees and, after about three miles, brings you to **Mount Melleray**, a Cistercian monastery that welcomes visitors in search of solitude. The trail eventually opens out, affording great views of the Knockmealdown and Galty mountains of Tipperary. The walk's a good taster for the varied terrain of the major long-distance walk just north of here in County Tipperary, the East Munster Way (see box on p.307).

Lismore

Set in the lovely broad plain of the Blackwater Valley, three miles west of Cappoquin, the heritage town of **LISMORE** has a significant ecclesiastical history. There's not much sign of this rich history today, but nevertheless the town does somehow manage to preserve a quiet reverence for its past. Lismore is dominated by the romantic towers and battlements of **Lismore Castle**, the Irish home of the Duke of Devonshire and his family – and not open to the public – whose pale, white-grey stone, set with mullioned windows, rises magnificently on the hill from glorious woodlands and sumptuous **gardens** (end of April to end of Sept daily 1.45–4.45pm; €4; ☎058/54424, Ⓦwww.lismorecastle.com). The castle itself is a successful mid-nineteenth-century imitation of a Tudor castle, remodelled by Joseph Paxton (who designed London's Crystal Palace) around the remains of the medieval fort that originally stood here. Its long occupation by the Anglo-Irish aristocracy (and less permanent colonists, including Sir Walter Raleigh) explains why so much of the layout of the park and farmland around here is reminiscent of wealthy English shires.

However, it is to a much earlier period than the castle's that Lismore owes its reputation. In 636 AD St Carthage founded a **monastic complex** for both monks and nuns in Lismore, and the place so flourished as a centre of learning that in the next century, under the influence of great teachers such as St Colman, it became an important **university city**. This growth continued into the twelfth century, despite three hundred years of sporadic pillage by first Vikings, then Normans. Lismore held great political as well as religious power, and the rivalry between the sees of Lismore and Waterford, which reflects the split histories of Waterford city and county, was only resolved in 1363 when the two dioceses were united.

Invaders continued to attack the city and in the late sixteenth century the medieval cathedral was almost totally destroyed by Queen Elizabeth's army. Its site is now occupied by the Church of Ireland **St Carthage's Cathedral**. Although built in 1633, its overall appearance is early-nineteenth-century Neo-Gothic, the tower and ribbed spire having been added in 1827 by James Pain, and the windows of the nave reshaped at the same time. It's a lovely building, sitting in a cobbled churchyard of ancient yews and limes. Inside is some interesting stonework, including the McGrath family tomb, dating from 1548, which has carvings of the apostles, mystical beasts and skulls. The chunky carving of a bishop holding an open book set in the back wall is probably from the ninth-century monastic settlement. In the south transept, just on your left as you enter, there's some striking stained glass by Edward Burne-Jones, the English Pre-Raphaelite.

Practicalities

Lismore's main street sits on the south side of the river, and it's here in the heritage centre in the courthouse that you'll find the **tourist office** (mid-March to Aug daily 9.30am–6pm; Sept & Oct Mon–Sat 9.30am–6pm, Sun noon–5.30pm; Nov to mid-March Mon–Sat 9.30am–5.30pm; ⓣ058/54975, ⓦwww.lismoreheritage.com). There's **B&B** in the centre of town at *Alana* in Chapel Street, just up behind the tourist office (ⓣ058/54106; ❸); at *Ballyrafter House Hotel*, Vee Road (ⓣ058/54002, ⓔballyrafter@waterfordhotel.com; ❹), a fine Georgian guesthouse set in mature gardens and popular with fishermen; and at *Beechcroft*, Deerpark Road, half a mile out of town (ⓣ058/54273; ❷). Converted Georgian coach houses provide **hostel** accommodation at *Kilmorna Farm* (ⓣ058/54315); breakfasts and evening meals are served on request, and they also have room for **camping**.

Eating places are limited to a few pubs along Main Street: *Madden's* (ⓣ058/54148) serves fresh modern Irish dishes and has a constantly changing menu; for more traditional good-value pub grub such as vegetable soups and liver-and-bacon casserole try *Eamonn's Place* (ⓣ058/54025). As for **drinking**, the town has some fascinating ancient bars, a delight to explore in themselves, though there's not much beyond this trip into the past by way of entertainment. Try *Foley's*, *O'Brien's* or *Madden's*, once the "local" for castle guests, such as Fred Astaire.

Towards the Comeragh Mountains

The road north from Lismore towards Cahir is typical of this area's gorgeous river valleys, stuffed with rhododendrons, bracken, beech trees, oaks and feathery pines. The walls are covered with spongy mosses and young ferns. About three miles along the road you can pick up a path leading to higher ground and more open spaces scattered with sheep and fir trees. The path goes through the **Knockmealdowns**, round the huge peat-covered mound of Sugarloaf Hill and after five miles leads to a viewing spot known as **The Vee**. From its steep, heathery V-shaped sides there's a tremendous view of the perfectly flat vale below with its patches of fields and of the town of Cahir at the foot of the Galty Mountains. From here you can push on to Cahir in County Tipperary or make for the independent An Óige **hostel**, *Mountain Lodge*, at Burncourt (ⓣ052/67277; March–Sept). If you want to continue walking, you can pick up the **East Munster Way** (see box on p.307) at The Vee. From here it descends to Clonmel, County Tipperary, around seventeen miles further on, taking in the scenic wooded Nier Valley.

At their most scenic from the Nier (also spelt "Nire") Valley, the Comeragh Mountains, which form the county's central uplands, appear for the most part as heathery, boggy open moorland. The valley runs from below Knockaunapeebra west to **BALLYMACARBERY**. Walks into the mountains take you up to a fine series of corrie lakes, encircled by high cliffs. Ballymacarbery makes a good base from which to explore the area on foot: *Clonanav Guesthouse* (ⓣ052/36141; ❺) offers **B&B** and *Hanora's Cottage*

(ⓣ052/36134, ⓦwww.hanorascottage.com; ⑥–⑦; closed Dec 24–Jan 1) is a comfortable stay with good breakfasts and great dinners. There's usually traditional music on a Tuesday and Wednesday at *Melody's* bar. The village is also a good stopover for walkers on the East Munster Way, which crosses the Nier three miles west of Ballymacarbery.

County Tipperary

Tipperary is the largest of Ireland's inland counties, and also the richest. The county's wealth comes from the central **Golden Vale**, a flat limestone plain shared with eastern Limerick that's prime beef and dairy cattle territory. This enormous stretch of farming land is abutted on most borders by crops of mountain ranges, the most beautiful of which are the **Galty Mountains** and the **Glen of Aherlow**. These are all in the south of the county, and it's this area, without doubt, that packs in the most excitement. The curling course of the Suir, Tipperary's principal river, sweeps by much of what there is to see. But for many, Tipperary's attractions hang on one site alone. The **Rock of Cashel** is the county's most dramatic feature by far; its limestone sides rising cliff-like, 200ft above the level ground, crowned with the high walls and towers of splendid medieval ecclesiastical architecture.

Made familiar to many by the World War I marching song *It's a Long Way to Tipperary*, the county was actually picked simply for the rhythmic beat of its name. In fact, Tipperary isn't particularly far from anywhere in southern Ireland, and this is probably its greatest advantage: you can catch the few worthwhile sights on your way through, and still be on the south or west coast within a few hours.

Carrick-on-Suir and around

Tucked in Tipperary's southeast corner, at the foot of the mountain slopes of neighbouring County Waterford, **CARRICK-ON-SUIR** is a quiet market town raised a cut above the rest by what is perhaps Ireland's most beautiful Elizabethan mansion: similar examples abound in England but are a rarity here. Set at the very eastern end of the main street, **Ormond Castle** (guided tours mid-June to Sept daily 9.30am–6.30pm; €2.50; Heritage Card; ⓣ051/640787) was built by Thomas, tenth Earl of Ormond ("Black Tom"), in anticipation of a visit from Queen Elizabeth I. Tributes to her are incorporated in the decoration throughout, above all in a fresco over the entrance way and in the superb stuccowork of the long gallery. A stunning mansion, with mullioned windows running the length of the building, it's the only major example in Ireland of a completely unfortified dwelling to date from the sixteenth century. It adjoins the remains of an earlier castle built in 1309; the two rectangular towers, currently undergoing renovation, date from the mid-fifteenth century. There's a collection of magnificent royal charters here, too: the oldest dates from 1661

The East Munster Way

The **East Munster Way** runs from Carrick-on-Suir for 43 miles west to the village of Clogheen, eight miles south of Cahir. The first stretch is easy walking alongside the River Suir as far as **Clonmel**. From here the Way climbs the heathery, wooded slopes of the Comeraghs, to descend three miles west of Ballymacarbery and the Nier Valley (see p.305). The path soon follows the flank of the Knockmealdown Mountains, affording fine views of the plain below, and winds up at the tiny village of Clogheen, six miles west of Ardfinnan. The walk involves long distances rather than steep, dramatic inclines, and for most of the way you're within a mile or so of habitation. Nevertheless, solitary walkers should bear in mind that much of the route is out of sight of the lowlands, and distress signals won't be noticed. The relevant Bord Fáilte Information Sheet, giving route guidelines for this section of the way, is Carrick-on-Suir–The Vee, Information Sheet no. 26J, and you'll need OS **maps** nos. 74 and 75, 1:50,000.

and granted James Butler the title of Duke of Ormond. Some historians also claim that Anne Boleyn was born here. Regardless of the mansion's splendours, however, it is as the birthplace of the champion cyclist **Sean Kelly** that the town is most proud – and the tiny main square at the west end of the main street has been renamed in his honour.

Tourist information (June–Sept Mon–Sat 10am–5pm, Sun 2–5pm; Oct–May Mon–Fri 10am–5pm; ⓣ051/640200) can be found in the heritage centre, just off Main Street. **Accommodation** is fairly limited: in the centre of town are *The Bell and Salmon Arms Hotel*, 95–97 Main St (ⓣ051/645555; ❹), and *Fatima House* B&B, John Street (ⓣ051/640298; ❷). There's also B&B at *Hillcrest* (ⓣ051/640847; ❷), a mile out on the N24 opposite the Sean Kelly Sports Centre. You can **camp** at *Carrick-on-Suir Caravan and Camping Park*, Ballyrichard, Kilkenny Road (ⓣ051/640461; March–Oct), one mile out of town. Cyclists heading for the **hostel** outside Clonmel (see p.308) are better off leaving the main road at Carrick-on-Suir and heading across country via Rathgormuck.

You'll find good **bar food** at *The Carraig Hotel* on Main Street (daily until 9.30pm). As for **entertainment**, *The Bell and Salmon Arms Hotel* has a bright modern bar attracting a young crowd, with open Irish sessions (Mon & Wed), live rock and pop bands (Sun) and discos (Fri & Sat in summer). For a quiet pint, try the bar of the *Carraig Hotel*.

Five miles north of Carrick, **AHENNY** has two beautiful high crosses in its graveyard. They're thought to be eighth century, and are excellent examples of the transitional style between the early Christian plain shaft crosses and the highly ornate didactic crosses of Monasterboice and Kells.

Clonmel and around

CLONMEL, thirteen miles upstream from Carrick-on-Suir, is far and away Tipperary's prettiest centre. It's a genteel kind of place and retains something of its flavour as an early coaching town. It was the birthplace in 1713 of Laurence Sterne, philosopher and literary comic genius, and it's not at all difficult to imagine Shandyesque shenanigans in the fine Georgian inns around town. A hundred years later Clonmel became the principal base for Bianconi, the most successful coach business in the country. The company's founder,

Bianconi, came from Lombardy in Italy and ran his so-called Bians from what is now *Hearn's Hotel* on Parnell Street.

The town is a beautiful place to breeze through: you can't miss Clonmel's finest building, the sorely dilapidated **Main Guard** sagging at the eastern end of O'Connell Street. Predating Dublin's Royal Hospital and modelled in the Classical style, it is the oldest public building in Ireland and is still undergoing full renovation. The facade visible today was built by James Butler, first Duke of Ormond, as a courthouse for the Palatinate of the County of Tipperary, and it bears two panels showing coats of arms dated 1675.

Other examples of period architecture include the nineteenth-century **St Mary's Roman Catholic Church**, with ziggurat tower and portico, in Irishtown, out past the Tudor-style nineteenth-century **West Gate**; the Greek Revival-style **Wesleyan Church** on Wolfe Tone Street; and the **Old St Mary's Church of Ireland** with its octagonal tower and tower house. All of these are impressive from the outside; none offer much if you venture in. The **County Museum** in Emmet Street (Tues–Sat 10am–1pm & 2–5pm; free; ⓣ052/25399) records local history in a collection of maps, newspapers, postcards and prints of Bianconi's coaches; it also has a small gallery of fine paintings and hosts temporary exhibitions.

At Richmond Mill, opposite SuperQuinn supermarket, there's a **Museum of Transport** (June–Sept Mon–Sat 10am–6pm, Sun 2.30–6pm; €3; ⓣ052/29727) housing two rooms of gleaming nostalgia, including Rolls, Jags and Fords from the 1930s onwards and a 1965 VW Karman Ghia.

Practicalities

Clonmel's **tourist office** is located in Sarsfield Street (July & Aug Mon–Fri 9.30am–7pm, Sat 9.30am–2pm; Sept–June Mon–Fri 9.30am–1pm & 2–5pm; ⓣ052/26500). There are a few **B&Bs** in the centre of town and plenty more further out. The central *Mr Bumbles*, Kickham Street (ⓣ052/29188; ❶), offers travel-lodge-style accommodation, and *Fennessy's Hotel*, Gladstone Street (ⓣ052/23680; ❷), is a traditional hotel with bright, comfy rooms and a good breakfast menu. For B&Bs outside the centre, follow the Cork road out of town for a mile and you'll find several signposted up a road that forks to the left, including the friendly and well-run *Benuala* (ⓣ052/22158; ❷) and *Hillcourt* (ⓣ052/21029; ❷). Worth the extra journey is the welcoming farmhouse B&B at *Ballyboy House* (ⓣ052/65297; ❷), five miles south on the R671 at Clogheen. But the nicest place to stay for miles around is undoubtedly *Kilmaneen Farmhouse* between Ardfinnan and Newcastle on the R670 (ⓣ052/36231, ⓦwww.kilmaneen.com; ❷; Easter to end of Sept). It's a remote gem in a little-visited part of the county, a working dairy farm with splendid walks starting right from its doorstep. The nearest **hostel** is *Powers the Pot* at Harneys Cross, five and a half miles up the slopes of the Comeragh Mountains (ⓣ052/23085). It's popular with **campers**, and there's a cosy bar on site. At 1200ft this claims to be the highest house in the country, and it's certainly on the threshold of excellent hill-walking country.

There are several good places to **eat** in Clonmel. At lunchtime *Angela's* on Abbey Street (Mon–Sat until 6pm), off behind the Main Guard, serves good-value, tasty vegetarian meals, and *Niamh's* deli and coffee shop on Mitchell Street, is a good spot for light snacks. For pub lunches there's the hugely popular *Mulcahy's* on Gladstone Street – they serve on into the evening, and there's a restaurant attached if you don't want to eat in the bar. *Tom Skinny's*, also on Gladstone Street (noon–midnight) is a cheerful place serving excellent pizzas, while *Mr Bumbles* on Kickham Street has one of Clonmel's more stylish and informal restaurants (☎052/29188).

Good **pubs** for music include *Kitty O'Donnell's* near the station, and *Lonergan's* on O'Connell Street. *Fennessy's Hotel* has a cosy bar with occasional sessions. Good for a quiet pint are *Chawke's* on Gladstone Street, and *Phil Carroll's* "antique bar" on Parnell Street, both full of character.

Keen anglers will be interested to hear that **fishing** off the quay is free; otherwise you can get salmon and trout licences from Kavanagh's Sports Shop, Westgate. If you want to find out about **walks** in this lovely area, head to the tourist office for advice, OS maps and copies of the *East Munster Way Map and Guide*.

Fethard

Leaving Clonmel, you could either head southwest to the plain between the Knockmealdown and Galty mountains (see below); or northwest for Cashel, in which case the route via **FETHARD** is the most rewarding. A touchingly plain place to travel through, and rarely sought out by tourists, Fethard has a number of forgotten medieval remains, set at the back of the town towards the river. One of these is a ruined **Templars' Castle**, access to which is through the *Castle Inn* (contact the publican). Other remains of **old friaries** and **Iron Age raths** can be found in the surrounding land. There's also a **Folk Farm and Transport Museum** at the beginning of the Cashel road (Sun noon–6pm, otherwise by appointment; €2.50; ☎052/31516). For **refreshments**, *P.J. Lonegan's* home-cooked lunches are worth stopping off for and *McCarthy's* has a good restaurant and is a fine place for a drink.

The Knockmealdown and Galty mountains

Well worth exploring, the **Galty Mountains** make up one of the most scenic inland ranges in Ireland. The Glen of Aherlow makes an excellent base in the heart of it all. The **Knockmealdowns** are less interesting, but offer easier hill-walking. The valley plain between the two mountain ranges, which runs for about ten miles east of Mitchelstown (over the border in County Cork, is not much in itself, but the **Mitchelstown cave** is well worth a visit. Starting from Clonmel you've a choice of two routes west: the main roads via Cahir, or the lesser R665, which cuts straight across to Mitchelstown.

The Glen of Aherlow

Tucked away four miles south of Tipperary town, the luxuriant and majestic **Glen of Aherlow** runs for eight miles beneath the northern slopes of the Galty Mountains, a breathtaking place to drive through. One of the nicest places to **stay** in the glen is *Ballinacourty House* (☎062/56000; ❷; closed Dec & Jan), offering accommodation in converted seventeenth- and eighteenth-century haylofts that look out over an extremely pretty, cobbled courtyard; there's also a **wine bar**, a moderately priced **restaurant** and a **campsite** within the grounds. Alternatively, you could try *Homeleigh Farm House* (☎062/56228; ❶), which offers welcoming B&B, **fishing** and **pony trekking**; or nearby *Aherlow House Hotel* (☎062/56153; ❷–❸), which makes a fine place to stay, offering comfortable rooms in one of the most scenic locations in the county – nonresidents can enjoy soups and sandwiches and stunning views from their terrace bar. For walkers, there's the An Óige **hostel**, the *Ballydavid Wood* (☎062/54148; March–Nov); try to arrive in daylight for this one – though meticulously signposted, the route has enough twists and turns to get you lost. It's a short day's trek from the *Mountain Lodge* hostel (☎052/67277; March–Sept), a spacious, Alpine-style old shooting lodge, offering the bare necessities (including gas lighting) on the southern slopes of the Galty Mountains. However, the forest trail between the two hostels is not waymarked and is little used, so if you do want to walk, it's advisable to contact the hostel manager about your estimated time of arrival.

Cahir

You're unlikely to miss **CAHIR**. The town sits on a major crossroads on the routes between Clonmel, Cork, Cashel and Tipperary. Its **castle** (daily: mid-March to mid-June & mid-Sept to mid-Oct 9.30am–5.30pm; mid-June to mid-Sept 9am–7.30pm; mid-Oct to mid-March 9.30am–4.30pm; €2.50; Heritage Card; ☎052/41011), set on a rocky islet in the River Suir, beside the road to Cork, is Cahir's outstanding attraction – even the name Cahir means "fort". In essence the building is Anglo-Norman, and goes back to the thirteenth and fifteenth centuries, though the virgin appearance of the outer shell is deceptive, with a good deal of the brickwork dating back to the eighteenth and nineteenth centuries. The Irish chieftain Conor O'Brien was the first to build a fortress on the rock; but it was the Anglo-Norman Butlers, the Earls of Ormond, who made this into one of the most powerful castles in the country. The Earl of Essex showered the castle with artillery fire in 1599; it got off lightly during the Cromwellian and Williamite invasions, and gradually fell into ruin until rejuvenated, along with other town buildings, by the Earl of Glengall in the mid-nineteenth century. In modern times, the interior has been uniformly whitewashed and spartanly furnished.

Entrance to the castle is along the side rampart, bringing you into the confined space of the **middle ward**, dominated by the three-storey thirteenth-century **keep**. The keep itself consists of a portcullis, vaulted chambers and a round tower containing a prison, accessible through a trap door. Down to the left, you pass through a **gateway** topped by machicolations, musket loops to either side, where sixteenth-century invaders could have been bombarded with missiles or boiling oil. Beyond is the much larger **outer ward** and, at its far end, the **cottage** built by the Earl of Glengall. The cottage now houses a video theatre where a twenty-minute film enthuses rhapsodically on the antiquities of southern Tipperary.

In the **inner ward**, two corner towers overlook the road to Cork. The larger was probably designed to be independently defensible once the keep had fallen, and it dates from a mixture of periods: the straight, stone stairs are thirteenth century; the stone vaulting over the ground-floor main room fifteenth to sixteenth century; and renovation work in the Great Hall, whose stepped battlements reflect sixteenth-century style, is nineteenth century. The smaller, square tower at the other end of the ward and the curtain wall date from the nineteenth century, though with medieval bases. Just to the left of this second tower, steps lead to the bottom of the **well tower**, which enabled the castle to safeguard its water supply during a siege. The informative **guided tour** of the castle is well worth taking.

Another building worth seeing in Cahir is the **Swiss Cottage** (mid-March & mid-Oct to Nov Tues–Sun 10am–1pm & 2–4.30pm; April Tues–Sun

△ Cahir Castle

10am–1pm & 2–6pm; May to mid-Oct daily 10am–6pm; €2.50; Heritage Card; ⓣ052/41144), a pleasant one-mile walk along the river from the castle or a short drive out of Cahir on the Clonmel road. Probably designed by John Nash, it was built in 1810 to provide the Earls of Glengall with a lodge of romanticized – and fashionable – rustic simplicity, from which to enjoy their hunting, shooting and fishing. With its thatched roof and ornate timberwork it certainly looks the part, and its status as a unique period piece makes it a popular attraction.

Practicalities

Buses from Waterford and Dublin drop you off outside the *Crock of Gold*, a small café/restaurant across from the castle, while those from Cork and Limerick stop outside the tourist office; there's a timetable posted in the window. The **tourist office** (April–Sept Mon–Sat 9am–6pm; July & Aug also Sun 11am–5pm; ⓣ052/41453) is in the car park beside the castle. From the castle you can see another castellated mansion on the hill further along the Cork road: the *Carrigeen Castle* (ⓣ052/41370; ❷), once the rather picturesque town prison and now a **B&B**. More conventional alternatives are signposted off the N24 Clonmel road, a short walk from the centre: *Killaun* (ⓣ052/41780; ❷) and *Silver Acre Guesthouse* (ⓣ052/41737; ❷). Basic **budget accommodation** and **camping** are available at the welcoming IHH-run *Lisakyle Hostel* (ⓣ052/41963; March–Oct), one mile out of Cahir beyond the Swiss Cottage and there are other hostel options in the nearby Glen of Aherlow (see p.310). You can camp among the fruit trees at *The Apple Farm* (ⓣ052/41459; Easter–Sept), four miles out of Cahir along the Clonmel road.

Standard **café** fare is served at the coffee shop above the *Crock of Gold*, opposite the castle, and at *Roma's Café*, on the Dublin side of the square. You can get pasta, pizzas and Irish food at the *Italian Connection* (daily until 11pm). For good **pub lunches** try the *Galty Inn* on the square or *The Castle*, opposite its namesake. **Traditional music** is minimal, but sometimes takes place at *Morrissey's*, opposite the castle, while *Irwin's*, on the square, has a mix of traditional music and ballads (Thurs); the tourist office can also tell you where to head.

Ardfinnan to the Mitchelstown Cave

Along the R665 from Clonmel to Mitchelstown, is **Ardfinnan**, where a beautiful fourteen-arched stone bridge crosses the Suir and a private castle stands on the hillside opposite. Follow the foot of the Knockmealdowns for several miles and you'll come to Clogheen, where there's the best turn-off route into the mountains, towards the terrific scenic point known as The Vee (see p.305).

Continuing along the R665, you'll come next to **BALLYPOREEN**, whose moment of glory came on June 3, 1984, when **Ronald Reagan** made a prodigal return – his great-grandfather was supposedly born here in 1810. You can read all about it and look at photos of the visit in a specially built centre at the crossroads, opposite the *Ronald Reagan* pub.

Eight miles from Mitchelstown itself, the massive pre-glacial underworld of the **Mitchelstown Cave** (daily 10am–6pm; €4.40; ⓣ052/67246) – signposted north from Ballyporeen down the interlacing lanes of the valley, or south off the N8 – are, aside from walking, the main attraction in the area. By far the most extensive and complicated cave system in Ireland (a couple of miles in all), it has remained, considering its scale, very uncommercial. The whole underground system was discovered in 1833, when a labourer lost his crowbar down a crevice, though there are records from much earlier of the cave being used as a hiding place, most famously to shelter the Earl of Desmond after his unsuccessful rebellion in 1601.

The cave was formed by the action of rainwater on the limestone over millions of years, and the fantastical stone formations grew out of the calcium carbonate (dissolved limestone) deposited by the dripping water, hardening as it evaporated into gigantic encrustations of stalactites and stalagmites. The temperature in the caves is around 54°F – this can feel chilly in summer, so bring a sweater. Tours only take in a few of the major cavities but are nonetheless worth taking.

Cashel and around

Just eleven miles north of Cahir on the road to Dublin, **CASHEL** grew around, and is completely dominated by, the spectacular **Rock of Cashel**, a limestone outcrop topped by a splendid array of medieval buildings. No tourist bus will bypass the site – so an early-morning or late-afternoon visit will make an important difference to your first impressions. In deep contrast to the ecclesiastical splendour of the Rock is a visit to the tiny **Bothán Scóir** – a unique one-roomed peasant dwelling. The **GPA Bolton Library** will appeal to antiquarian book lovers, and the museum at **Cashel Folk Village** will appeal to anyone interested in Irish social history.

A view of the Rock in the dwindling light of dusk is one of Ireland's most memorable sights; consider this along with the town's position around 95 miles from the ferry ports at both Dublin and Rosslare Harbour and there's a very strong argument for stopping over in Cashel if you are heading to the west coast.

Arrival, information and accommodation

Buses set down in the main street. Cashel's **tourist office** (May, June & Sept Mon–Sat 9.15am–6pm; July & Aug daily 9.15am–6pm; ⓣ062/61333) sits in the market house in the middle of the main street. The **Cashel of the Kings heritage centre** (ⓣ062/62511) alongside gives an overall picture of the history of the town, in particular its ecclesiastical buildings.

There are several central **B&Bs** to choose from and a handful of more spacious establishments can be found out along the Dulla road. The tourist office can suggest others in the area. For **hostel** accommodation, you could try one of two IHH-run places: the excellent and very central *Cashel Holiday Hostel* at 6 John St (ⓣ062/62330, ⓔcashelho@iol.ie; ❷); or the equally impressive, but more rural *O'Brien's Holiday Lodge* (ⓣ062/61003), on Dundrum Road, located in a converted stone barn a short walk from Cashel. To get to the latter, turn right at the bottom of Main Street and follow the road towards Dundrum; it's signposted off here. *O'Brien's* also offers excellent **camping** facilities with superb views of the Rock.

Abbey House 1 Dominic St ⓣ062/61104. Centrally located B&B in a quiet street near St Dominic's Friary. All rooms are en suite. Closed Dec & Jan. ❷

Ballyowen House Dulla, one mile north of Cashel on the N8 ⓣ062/61265. Excellent, family-operated B&B in an eighteenth-century country house. Fine dinners served too. ❷

Georgesland On the Dulla road ⓣ062/62788. Spacious modern farmhouse in a rural setting, within a mile of town. All rooms are en suite and non-smoking, with very comfortable beds. ❷

Rahard Lodge On the Dulla road ⓣ062/61052. Roomy and pleasant modern farmhouse, just a mile out of town with en-suite bedrooms and non-smoking policy. Open March–Nov. ❷

Rockview House ⓣ062/62187. B&B in a family home situated up a steep lane off the top of the main street, with views of the Rock from the rooms. ❷

Rockville House ⓣ062/61760. Another decent B&B near St Dominic's Friary, a short walk from both the Rock and the centre of town. En-suite rooms and a quiet location. Open mid-March to Oct. ❷

Thornbrook House On the Dulla road ⓣ062/62388, ⓔthornbrookhouse@eircom.net. Spacious B&B in an antique-furnished, large and modern bungalow, within a mile of town. Rooms are all non-smoking, and some are en suite. Open April–Oct. ❷

The Rock of Cashel

Approached from the north or west, the **Rock of Cashel** (daily: mid-March to mid-June 9am–5.30pm; mid-June to mid-Sept 9am–7.30pm; mid-Sept to mid-March 9am–4.30pm; €4.40; Heritage Card; ⓣ062/61437, ⓔrockofcashel@ealga.ie) appears as a spectacular mirage of fairytale turrets, crenellations and walls rising bolt upright from the vast encircling plain. It's a tour operator's dream: on one piece of freak limestone outcrop stands the most beautiful and complete Romanesque church in the country, a gargantuan medieval cathedral, a castle tower house, an eleventh-century round tower, a unique early high cross and the exquisite fifteenth-century Hall of the Vicars – medieval Irish architecture wrapped up in a morning's investigation. Two more medieval priories lie at its feet.

In **legend** the Rock was formed when the Devil, flying overhead with a large stone in his mouth, suddenly caught sight of St Patrick standing ready to found his new church on the site, and in his shock dropped the Rock (in the northeast of the county, a striking gap in a mountain range is known as the "Devil's Bit"). The Rock is also the place where St Patrick is supposed to have picked a shamrock in order to explain the doctrine of the Trinity – God the Father, Christ the Son and the Holy Ghost as three beings of the one stem – since which time the shamrock became Ireland's unofficial emblem.

The Hall of the Vicars

Approaching the Rock from Cashel town, you come first to the **Hall of the Vicars**, built in the fifteenth century to cater for eight vicar meistersingers, who assisted in the cathedral services but were later dispensed with because of growing resentment over the power and land that their privileged office entailed. The **upper floor** of the building is divided between the main hall, with screens and a minstrels' gallery, and what would have been the dormitories. The **ground floor**, a vaulted undercroft, today contains the original **St Patrick's Cross**, a unique type of high cross. It once stood outside, where there's now a replica. Tradition has it that the cross's huge plinth was the coronation stone of the High Kings of Munster, the most famous of whom was Brian Boru, killed in his tent by a fleeing Viking at the Battle of Clontarf. The cross is simpler than other high crosses, with a carving of Christ on one side and St Patrick on the other. It has an upright supporting its left arm and is without the usual ring-wheel in the centre. It may be that originally the upright and its missing counterpart represented the two thieves crucified with Jesus, and it is also possible that it was never intended as a freestanding cross in the first place, but for erection on a wall.

Cormac's Chapel

Cormac's Chapel, built between 1127 and 1134, is the earliest and most beautiful of Ireland's surviving Romanesque churches, with intricate decoration that is as spectacular as it is unique. The architecture has clear continental influences – the twin square **towers**, for example, were probably engineered by monks sent from Regensburg in Germany. The **tympana**, or panels, above the grandiose north door (more than likely the original entrance, now leading blindly into the flank of the cathedral) and the south door – today's entrance – are also rare in Irish church architecture. Above the north door is depicted a curious carved scene of a large beast ensnaring a smaller one, itself on the point of being speared by a macho centaur in a Norman helmet. The north door is set in six orders of pillars, creating a tunnel-vaulted **porch**, which is sheltered by an outer stone roof porch. Each arch is crowned with capitals, human heads, fantastic beasts, flutings and scallops.

The small size of the chapel is typical of Irish architecture of this period, as are the lack of aisles and the steeply pitched stone roof – you'll find similar-looking buildings at Glendalough and Kells, though Cormac's Chapel is larger than those. The wall opposite you as you walk in has a tall triple arcade, in the centre of which is a large round-headed **window** that would once have lit up the whole interior, illuminating all the painted colour – of which a little remains up at the altar and just above the chancel arch. The **sarcophagus** at the foot of this wall, although fragmented, has an exquisite Scandinavian Urnes design of interlacing serpents and ribbon decoration. It's said to have been the tomb of King Cormac, and is certainly old enough to be so.

The cathedral and the Round Tower

The cathedral, although Anglo-Norman in conception with Gothic arches and windows, is a purely Irish-built endeavour. Begun in the thirteenth century, it is a graceful limestone building and features a series of tall, high-set lancet **windows**, and also some good examples of quatrefoil, or four-petalled, windows, especially above the lancets in the choir space. You'll notice that some of the lancets have been shortened – probably as a measure of fortification. The **choir** is longer than the nave and both are without aisles: the nave was shortened to make room for the **castle tower**, built most obviously for refuge, and also as an archiepiscopal residence. A wooden-floored hall would once have been above the nave (the corbels are still apparent), accessible from the castle tower.

The **central tower**, at the meeting of the transepts, is also on a grand scale and was not built until the fourteenth century. It's supported by four Gothic arches rising from very wide piers, their shafts sweeping beautifully into the concave bottom. Access to the tower is by winding stairs from the south transept (this may not be open to the public, so ask). **Passages** also ran through the nave and choir walls, supposedly for the outcasts or lepers of the community, so that they could watch the holy ceremonies without being seen themselves. The **transepts** have shallow chapel altars with some tomb and piscina niches. In the north transept, panels from sixteenth-century altar-tombs survive – one with an intricately carved retinue of saints, the others more broken but still exquisite.

Some 92ft high, the nearby **Round Tower** is the earliest building on the Rock. Its tapering features have led to suggestions that it dates from as early as the tenth century, though the officially accepted date is early twelfth century. It's not a typical tower; the entrance door was originally 12ft above the ground, and various levels of windows ensure views in all directions.

Around the Rock

From the grounds of the Rock you can look down at **Hore Abbey**: although it's easy enough to get to if you don't mind jumping the wall – and an escape from the crowds – you can see it just as well from up here. The thirteenth-century abbey was the last Cistercian daughter monastery of Mellifont to be completed before the Reformation, and was probably built by those working on the Rock's cathedral. Originally a Benedictine foundation, it converted after its abbot had a wild dream that his Benedictine monks were plotting to cut his head off; he expelled them and donned the Cistercian habit in 1269. There's yet another abbey ruin, **St Dominic's**, below the south side of the Rock, in the town, but this has even less to offer in terms of things to see.

A path known as the **Bishop's Walk** leads from the Rock's rampart entrance down into town through the back garden of the **Palace Hotel**. The Palace was built in Queen Anne style by Archbishop Theophilus Bolton in 1730 as a mansion for the Archbishops of Cashel (hence the Bishop's Walk to the Rock). It has a simple, red-brick front and a cut-stone rear. Cashel owes much to this particular archbishop; it was he who saw the value of Cormac's Chapel and put his wealth into its restoration at a time when the Rock's antiquities were degenerating rapidly. A further legacy is the **GPA Bolton Library** (late May to Sept daily 11am–4.30pm; €2.50), opposite the hotel and set in the grounds of the slender-spired eighteenth-century **St John's Protestant Cathedral**. Its manuscripts (from as early as the twelfth century), rare maps and wealth of literary treasures were principally Bolton's own bequest when he died in 1744. Well worth a visit, a selection of the books and maps are on display, which changes bi-monthly.

Also worth seeing is the **Bothán Scóir**, a one-roomed peasant dwelling dating from around 1600, the only one of its kind in Ireland. It is situated half a mile out of town on the Clonmel road and can only be visited on request (☎062/61360). If you find no one at the cottage, go to 6 Ard Mhuire, the first cul-de-sac on the right as you head back down the hill towards town, and enquire about visiting. Bothán means "hut", scóir is "score", referring to the score notched up on a tallystick as the peasant worked the 180 days of the year demanded by the landlord in payment for rent of the cottage and a patch of land. The soot-black thatch, the chimneyless roof, the half-door and the jamb wall – layer upon layer of authentic detail – tell a history of systematic oppression and thorough misery.

If you have the time to delve further into Cashel's social history, **Cashel Folk Village** (March & April daily 10am–6pm; May–Oct daily 9.30am–7.30pm; €2.50), in a lane behind the tourist office, is recommended. Crammed with interesting exhibits, the collection includes a gruesome traditional butcher's shop guaranteed to turn you vegetarian and a fascinating museum of Republican history.

Eating and drinking

You'll have no trouble finding places to eat in Cashel. There are several **coffee shops** on Main Street and good-value **meals** are served at *The Bakehouse*. For pub food try *Kearney's Castle Hotel* or *Hannigan's*, both on Ladyswell Street, the top end of the main road. *Spearman's*, 97 Main St, serves good, wholesome meals, but if you feel like splashing out, head for *Chez Hans* on Dominick Street (☎062/61177; closed Sun & early Jan) which serves top-notch meals in the unlikely setting of a former Wesleyan chapel.

A great deal of **music** is laid on in the summer – from rock, through country and western, to singalong and traditional Irish. This last tends to move around, but Cashel is a very small town, so if there's something going on, it won't be hard to find. Likely spots worth checking out include three on Main Street: *Feehan's*, *Con Gleeson's* and the cosy *Dowling's*.

Tipperary town

Twelve miles from Cashel and less than five from the border of Limerick, stands **TIPPERARY** town, at the northern side of the Glen of Aherlow. Like many of these namesake county towns, Tipperary is much less important than it sounds. If you've already visited Clonmel, it will come as something of a shock – compared to Clonmel's yuppy prosperity, Tipperary feels somewhat down at heel. The town has bold **statues** sculpted in granite here and there, most notably one to its literary local son, Charles J. Kickham, entitled *Poet, Novelist but above all Patriot*.

You might want to stop over briefly to take in the small and intriguing **museum** (Mon–Sat 9.30am–5pm; free) hidden away in the foyer of the town swimming pool, by the Cashel road exit. A tiny store of memorabilia, it exhibits photos, letters and weaponry from the warring years of 1919 to 1923, especially relating to the old IRA. Tipperary was a particular hot spot during the Anglo-Irish and Civil War strife, especially through its famous son, **Seán Tracey**, whose battalion fired the first shots of the Anglo-Irish War (1919–21). There are letters he wrote to his family from prison, some talking about the honour the British had bestowed on him by taking the trouble to get him captured, others of a more domestic nature. A violin belonging to Joseph Mary Plunkett (one of the poets executed in the 1916 rising) hangs beside revolvers, pistols and land mines. Most striking of all, perhaps, are the photographs of the young officers shown clenching their revolvers, either posturing defiantly or looking slightly abashed.

Practicalities

Tipperary is a small town and you won't have any trouble finding your way around. **Buses** from Limerick will drop you in Abbery Street, right in the centre of town. The **tourist office** is on James's Street (May–Sept Mon–Sat 9am–6pm; ⓣ062/33466). If you plan to stay in town, try *Central Accommodation*, 45 Main St (ⓣ062/51117; ❷), a **B&B** run by a friendly family. If this is full, there are several pleasant alternatives about a mile out of town on the Galbally road, including *Clonmore House* (ⓣ062/51637; ❷) and *Riverside House* (ⓣ062/51219; ❷; March–Oct).

Places to **eat** are very much geared up to cater for locals working in town, though there's decent bar food at *Kiely's Bar* and *The Kickham House*, both on Main Street. *The Kickham House* is the best place to look for **traditional music** (Tues); other watering-holes include *Corney's* on Davitt Street, which has a mix of traditional and country and western music at weekends, and *The Churchwell Tavern*, also in Davitt Street, where you can sometimes hear rock bands.

Thurles and around

North of Cashel, both the Suir itself and the attractions along its banks wane. The river passes through the larger towns of **Thurles** and **Templemore**, though its source in the Devil's Bit Mountain falls short of the little town of **Roscrea**. Thurles is on the main Limerick–Dublin train line; Roscrea is more easily accessed by bus, being on the main bus route between those two cities.

THURLES is of very little interest in itself, but if you're passing through and in need of refreshment you might want to check out the *Dwan Brewery &*

Restaurant in The Mall off Liberty Square, a modern microbrewery giving the town's social scene something of a lift and offering a markedly contemporary bar-food menu. Just four miles south of town, **Holy Cross Abbey** sits beside a broad stretch of the Suir and is worth a quick stop (church: year-round; cloister and ranges: mid-April to Oct Mon–Sat 10am–6pm, Sun 11am–6pm). Founded in 1180, restored significantly in the fifteenth century and then left derelict for four hundred years, the abbey was totally restored between 1971 and 1985 and is now a thriving parish church as well as a tourist attraction. You really need to see photographs of the period before restoration to appreciate the significance of this – they suggest that every other ruin you've seen could be as easily converted. Holy Cross always had singular importance as a centre of pilgrimage, however, claiming to possess a piece of the **True Cross**. The splinter was reckoned to have been given to Murtagh O'Brien, King of Munster, by Pope Paschal II in 1110. At the turn of the seventeenth century both O'Donnell and O'Neill, the Ulster chiefs, stopped off to venerate this relic on their way to Kinsale to meet the French – no doubt hoping they'd be rewarded with a victory over Elizabeth I.

The **interior** of the church has been fully restored, though there's been no particular attempt at period accuracy; virtually every wall and pillar has been whitewashed, and all the pews have been varnished. Nevertheless, it's rewarding to see the stone ribbing of the vaulted roofs and most particularly the undamaged fifteenth-century **sedilia** in the chancel area, the finest in the country. The sedilia, recessed stone seats for the celebrants of the Mass, are of a hard limestone shaped into cusped arches and crowned with crockets, showing decorative frieze-work as well as the English royal crest and the escutcheon of the Earls of Ormond. In the transept to the left of the nave, you'll find one of Ireland's rare medieval **frescoes**, this one showing a Norman hunting scene painted in browns, reds and greens. The **exterior** of the church has a startling full-length slate roof, which reaches down to the cloister pillars. There's an informal **tourist information centre** with variable opening hours, a coffee shop and a religious crafts shop within the abbey complex.

Ballynahow Castle

If you're cycling or driving north towards Thurles you might also think of taking in **Ballynahow Castle**, a circular castle tower built by the Purcell family in the sixteenth century. To get there from Holy Cross, take the road directly opposite the Protestant church, not the Thurles route (even though the signpost says so). From Thurles itself, it's out on the Nenagh road, right at the Jet petrol station, and after another mile the castle stands next to a farmhouse – *Ballynahow Castle Farm* where you can pick up the key; the farm also offers **B&B** (Ⓣ0504/21297; ❷; March–Oct). You enter the castle at the lowest of its five storeys, the circular design giving the feel of entering into an igloo, with the corbelled roof curving round almost to the floor. There are many little rooms hidden within the walls and, although undecorated and entirely bare (and quite dark), most of it is in an excellent state of preservation and it is very atmospheric.

Roscrea

ROSCREA sits on a low hillock between the Slieve Bloom Mountains to the northeast and the Devil's Bit to the southwest. It's a charming place, with streets running down the hill slopes. However, where the rest of Ireland has secluded river sites and spacious countryside for its abbey ruins, Roscrea has the main Dublin–Limerick road roaring through the middle of **St Cronan's Monastery**. On one side of the road is the round tower, with a garage shed built into the side of it and the top third removed by the British in 1798. Immediately opposite, virtually on the pavement, is the west gable of **St Cronan's Church**, its yellow sandstone carved out in a twelfth-century Romanesque style reminiscent of Cormac's Chapel in Cashel. The rest of the church was pulled down in the nineteenth century and the stone used as building material elsewhere. **St Cronan's Cross**, just to the right of the gable, must have been a beauty once, but now it's severely weather-beaten and hacked. Up by the centre of the town is the large, sturdy-looking **Gate Tower Castle** dating from the thirteenth century and across the courtyard stands the imposing eighteenth-century **Damer House**, a good example of pre-Palladian architecture. Tours of both house and castle are available (April–Oct daily 10am–6pm on the hour from 10am, last tour 5pm; €3.10; Heritage Card; ⓣ0505/21850).

Nenagh

NENAGH is usually jam-packed with heavy traffic trying to plough its way through on the main Dublin–Limerick road. It has one singular historical remain, a colossal round **castle keep** with walls 20ft thick, its five storeys reaching a height of 100ft and topped with nineteenth-century castellations. Totally gutted within, this final retreat tower was originally one of five round towers which, linked by a curtain wall, formed a Norman stronghold. Founded by Theobald Walter, a cousin of Thomas à Becket, it was occupied by the Butlers, then captured in turn by the O'Carrols of Eile and Cromwell, went back to James II and then to and fro between Ginckel (King William's chief general) and O'Carrol in the Williamite war. And there the fighting stopped until many centuries later when a farmer, wanting to get rid of a nest of sparrows that were feeding on his crops, stuck some gunpowder in the walls of the keep and blew another hole in the fortress. A few reinforced concrete steps help you to get near the top, but there's little to be seen.

Across the road from the keep, the Nenagh **heritage centre** (Easter–Oct Mon–Fri 9.30am–5pm; €2.50) is set in the old jail, now a Convent of Mercy school. Housed in the octagonal Governor's House, up the driveway, it has a display room housing temporary exhibitions, a mock-up of an old schoolroom with a four-foot mannequin nun, and a re-created old post office, bar and telephone exchange. In the basement are the usual agricultural items and a faithfully reproduced but clinical-looking forge. Back at the entrance arch, the cells of the jail have their original hefty iron cell doors, and you can also see the former exercise yard, tiny and cluttered.

Buses from Dublin and Limerick stop right in the centre of town; some also stop at the train station, which is on the Thurles side of town, a short walk from the town centre. The **tourist office** is on Connolly Street (mid-May to mid-Sept Mon–Sat 9.30am–1pm & 2–5.30pm; ⓣ067/31610). There's reasonably priced **B&B** at *Williamsferry House*, on Fintan Lawlor Street (ⓣ067/31118; ❷), and *Sun View*, on Ciamaltha Road (ⓣ067/31064; ❷), quite close to the bus and train stations, and you can get excellent home-cooked meals at *Country Choice Deli & Coffee Bar*, 25 Kenyon St; the shop stocks superb Irish cheeses.

County Limerick

To an even greater extent than Tipperary, everyone passes through County Limerick, and hardly anyone stays. Once here, you're tantalizingly close to the much more rewarding counties of Cork, Kerry and Clare, and frankly you're not likely to linger. Urban, industrial Limerick has none of the breezy west-coast spirit so appealing just about everywhere else along this seaboard. Nevertheless, it is well worth making time to visit the superb **Hunt Museum** which has collections to rival that of the National Gallery in Dublin, and this, along with a handful of good restaurants and bars, makes the city worth considering as a stopover. **Lough Gur** lies thirteen miles south of the city, a Mesolithic-to-Neolithic lake and hill enclave of preternatural beauty, well worth the detour off the N20 Cork road. It can also which can also be reached by public transport.

For **cyclists**, Limerick's terrain is more variable than it's usually given credit for. In its western-to-southwestern corner, the upland bears a likeness to barren stretches of Donegal, whereas the northern estuary stretch is indeed only slightly undulating. More so than any other county, the land in Limerick is dotted with an array of **tower castles**, some inhabited but most in ruins or no more than stumps.

Historically, Limerick's most notable period arrived with the Norman strongholds, the most dominant family being the Fitzgeralds, also known as the Earls of Desmond – virtually all of Limerick's significant ruins were once this clan's power bases. They quickly became Gaelicized and ruled as independent monarchs, pulling very much away from English rule. The inevitable confrontation with Britain came to a head at the end of the sixteenth century, when in 1571 the Geraldine uprising against Elizabeth I sparked off a savage war, which brought about their downfall and destroyed in its wake much of the province of Munster.

Limerick city and around

Squarely on the path of all the major routes across the country, and situated pretty much at the head of the Shannon estuary, the city of **LIMERICK** seems a logical place to make for, but it's a disappointment. Though it's the Republic's third city, and heavily industrialized, it somehow falls significantly short of being a metropolis, yet also lacks the attractions of a typically relaxed western seaboard town. Unemployment and economic hard times have left their mark; it doesn't always seem a friendly place and certain areas can feel positively intimidating at night. Even so, recent efforts to clean up Limerick's image are starting to pay off. On a fine day the area around **King John's Castle** affords some sense of the city's medieval history and the Georgian Custom House is home to the excellent **Hunt Museum** – reason enough to give Limerick some time.

The city is famous too as the setting for Frank McCourt's international best-seller *Angela's Ashes* – a memoir that received a mixed reception locally for its portrayal of a Limerick childhood of grinding poverty. Lively walking tours are popular with tourists wanting to tap into the experiences at the heart of the book.

Sport in Limerick: the Garryowen

Limerick seems to be one of the most sport-obsessed places in Ireland: horse racing, Gaelic football, soccer, hurling and rugby are all avidly followed, with the last two having particularly strong local traditions. In rugby, the region passed into immortality with the invention in the 1920s of the **Garryowen**, a move named after a district of Limerick city which also lent its name to one of Ireland's finest rugby clubs. The Garryowen, a high kick up-field pursued by a charging team who hope to hit the opposition as they catch the ball, is the equivalent of Rugby League's "up-and-under".

The city you see today is predominantly Georgian, but nevertheless has three distinct historical areas: **Englishtown**, the oldest part of the city, built on an island in the Shannon with the castle as its focal point; **Irishtown**, which began to take shape in the thirteenth and fourteenth centuries; and within this **Newtown Pery**, the modern centre, a jumble of beautiful but rather dilapidated Georgian terraces and garish fast-food joints.

Some history

Limerick, located at the lowest fording point of the Shannon, was first settled by the **Vikings**, who sailed up the Shannon in the tenth century to Inis Sibhton (now Kingstown in Englishtown), an island by the eastern bank formed by a narrow bypass from the main stream now known as Abbey River. Here they established a port, and for a hundred years war after war raged between them and the native Irish. The Vikings were frequently defeated and were finally crushed nationally in 1014 at the Battle of Clontarf, at the hands of Brian Boru, the High King of Ireland. Limerick itself was attacked soon after and burned to the ground. Most of the Vikings didn't actually leave, but from then on they were gradually assimilated into the Gaelic population. The fate of Limerick itself didn't improve much, however, as over the next hundred years the Irish fought amongst themselves, burning the town to the ground time and again.

Some kind of stability was established with the arrival of the **Normans** at the end of the twelfth century. They expanded and fortified the town, King John arriving in 1210 to inaugurate King John's Castle, one of his finest. High walls were built that were now to keep the Gaels out, and because of this exile the first suburb across the Abbey River began to grow into **Irishtown**. There was trouble again with the visits of Edward Bruce in the fourteenth century; but the real emasculation of the city began with the onslaught of Cromwell's forces under the command of his son-in-law, Ireton, in the late 1640s. It was concluded when the city rallied to the Jacobite cause in 1689.

Following James II defeat at the Battle of the Boyne in 1690, most of his supporters surrendered quickly – except for the ones at Limerick. As the Williamites advanced, the Jacobite forces within Limerick castle resolved to fight it out under the command of their Irish champion **Patrick Sarsfield**, Earl of Lucan and second in overall command of the Jacobite army. Although the walls of a medieval castle had little hope of withstanding seventeenth-century artillery (one of James's French generals declared that they would not stand up to a bombardment of apples), Sarsfield gained time by sneaking out, with five hundred of his troops, for a surprise night attack on William's supply train. He succeeded in totally destroying the munitions, while William sat waiting for them in front of the castle walls. However, when the Williamites returned the following year, Sarsfield could finally hold out no longer, and he surrendered on October 3, 1691, to the terms of a **treaty** that's so sore a historical point that it's still stuck in the minds of most Limerick people today.

The treaty terms were divided into military and civil articles. Militarily, Jacobites were allowed to sail to France, which most of them did, along with Sarsfield himself (he died on the battlefield at Landon in Belgium, two years later); the civil agreement promised Catholics the religious and property rights they'd once had under Charles II. Within a couple of months the English reneged on this part of the treaty, and instead enforced extreme **anti-Catholic measures**. There followed civil unrest on such a scale that the city gates were locked every night for the next sixty years, and the betrayal has never been forgotten – it alone may explain the roots of today's element of Republican support in the city. The concordat was supposedly signed upon the Treaty Stone that rests on a plinth at the western end of Thomond Bridge. For many years, although this was used as a stepping stone for mounting horses, small pieces continued to be gouged out as souvenirs.

It was not a promising start for the modern city, and there are those who claim that festering resentment has stunted Limerick's growth ever since. Being also lumbered with a geographical setting that gives it the Irish name luimneach "a barren spot of land" has not helped. One redeeming factor has to lie in its humour; how else could its corporate motto read "An ancient city well studied in the arts of war".

Arrival and information

Limerick is the nearest big city to **Shannon Airport** (☎061/471444; see p.425) – ten miles away off the Ennis Road. Airport buses (☎061/313333; €5) run approximately every thirty minutes in the morning, hourly in the afternoon and irregularly after 6pm; a taxi costs around €20–25 from Limerick city to the airport (☎061/313131). The **train** (☎061/315555) and **bus** (☎061/313333) stations are next door to each other on Parnell Street in Newtown Pery; however, some buses arrive at Penney's Store on the corner of Lower Cecil Street and Henry Street rather than the bus station.

The excellent **tourist office** (July & Aug Mon–Fri 9am–6.30pm, Sat & Sun 9.30am–3.30pm; Sept–June Mon–Fri 9.30am–5.30pm; ☎061/317522) is at Arthur's Quay, near where the river branches merge and you cross over into Englishtown: most easily found by following O'Connell Street north towards the Custom House (Hunt Museum). The tourist office's city map also has useful information and phone numbers. **Walking tours** of the city are organized by St Mary's Action Centre, 44 Nicholas St (☎061/318106; phone ahead to book in low season). Their Historic Walking Tour (daily 11am & 2.30pm; €5) focuses on Englishtown; it's a colourful account steeped in murder, treachery and passion, and really does bring this, the oldest part of Limerick, to life. Alternatively, the **Angela's Ashes** Walking Tour (departs daily from the tourist office at 2.30pm; €5) takes in some of the same area in an account of slum life in early-twentieth-century Limerick, lavishly embellished with extracts from Frank McCourt's book, full of humour and pathos. For **bike rental** try Emerald Cycles, 1 Patrick St (☎061/416983) or The Bike Shop, O'Connell Avenue (☎061/315900). **Internet** access is available at Websters at 44 Thomas St (☎061/312066).

Accommodation

There is a good range of **accommodation** in Limerick, particularly for budget travellers. If you have a car, secure parking in the centre is a consideration. Some areas of town are far better lit than others at night; for women travelling

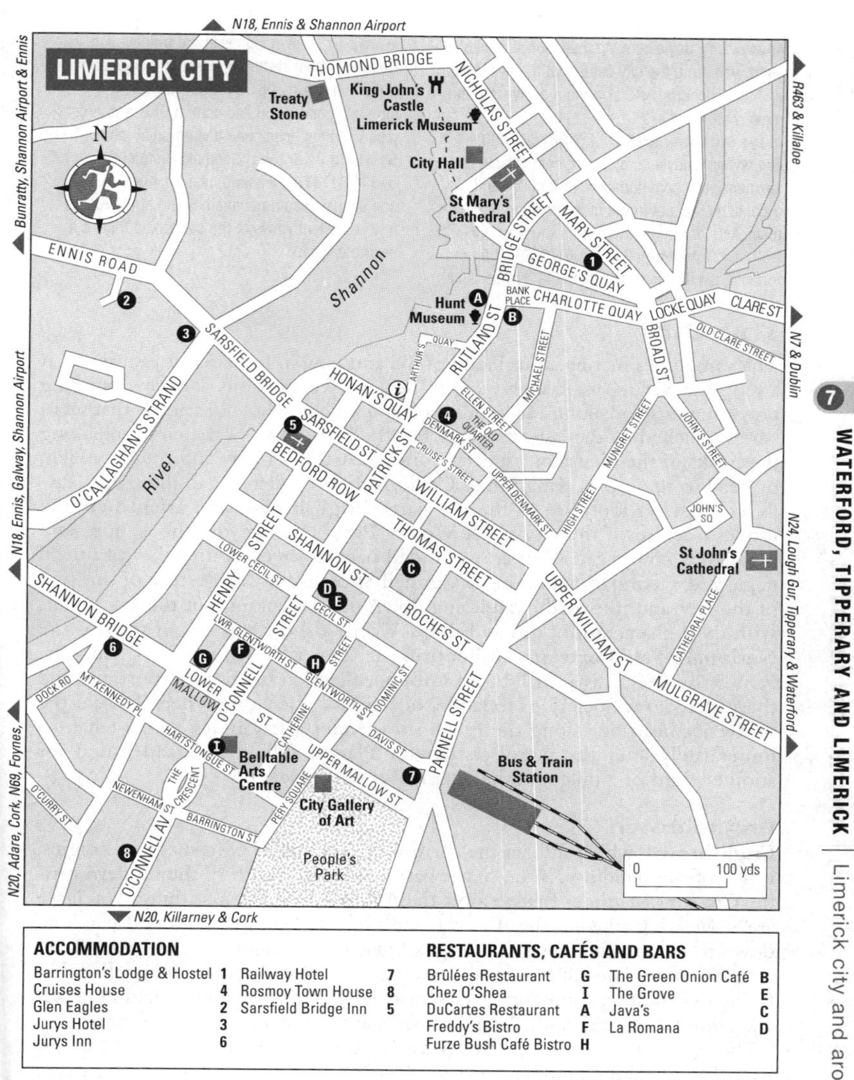

alone the following places are probably the least threatening: *Barrington's Lodge and Hostel*, the *Sarsfield Bridge Inn*, *Cruises House* and the B&Bs on the Ennis road.

Barrington's Lodge and Hostel (IHH) Barrington House, George's Quay ⓣ061/415222. Very well run hostel with secure parking. There's a large number of twin and four-bed/family rooms available.

Cruises House Denmark St ⓣ061/315320. Pleasant and functional city-centre guesthouse. All rooms have TVs and are en suite. Closed Christmas and New Year weeks. ❷

Glen Eagles 12 Vereker Gardens, off the Ennis road ⓣ061/455521. A short walk from town, this B&B is in a family home on a quiet cul-de-sac. Open March–Nov. ❷

Jurys Hotel On the Ennis road ⓣ061/327777,

Ⓦ www.jurysdoyle.com. A small four-star hotel, a short walk from the city centre, with a gym, pool and tennis courts. Ask for a room away from the main road. ❹–❻
Jurys Inn Lower Mallow St Ⓣ 061/207000, Ⓦ www.jurysdoyle.com. Smart, comfortable and inexpensive accommodation for families and groups, though not in the most inspiring part of town. Ask for a room away from the road. ❹–❻
Railway Hotel Parnell St Ⓣ 061/413653. A comfortable, family-run hotel located in a rather lacklustre part of town, opposite the train station. ❷
Rosmoy Town House 1 Alexandra Terrace, O'Connell Ave Ⓣ 061/314556. Warm and welcoming , this good-value and central B&B is in an elegant Victorian house and has en-suite rooms. ❷
Sarsfield Bridge Inn Sarsfield Bridge Ⓣ 061/317179. Pleasant, modern, purpose-built and simple accommodation. Some of the rooms have excellent views of the castle and there's a secure car park. ❷–❹

The City

The sometimes incongruous blend of old and new in Limerick is testimony to a city discovering itself after years of neglect. Renovations and new building programmes stand alongside buildings – and indeed whole districts – that seem barely touched by the last fifty years. For the best **views** of the city walk along the banks of the Shannon, especially around Arthur's Quay and the City Hall, or head to the top of King John's Castle. Although virtually all the sights (easily covered on foot) are in the old parts, **Englishtown** and **Irishtown**, the modern centre of the city is **Newtown Pery** – where the shops, pubs and restaurants congregate – an area of broad parallel streets scattered with fine, if neglected, Georgian buildings. O'Connell Street is the chief artery of this part of the city, and it's worth wandering down here, checking out the side streets with their characterful pubs and shops. Worth a short trip out of town is the **National Self-Portrait Collection** at Limerick University (Mon–Fri 9am–5pm; free). It is a small but absorbing collection of Irish self-portraits, and the Watercolour Society of Ireland Collection is also housed here. To find the university, head out along the Dublin road; after a few miles, take a left turn immediately after the petrol station for Plassey; follow the road round for another third of a mile and the entrance is on the left.

Englishtown

Englishtown, which still has the narrow curving streets of its medieval origins, if few of the buildings, is the oldest part of the city, north of the modern centre. Crossing Matthew Bridge, over the Abbey River, the first things you'll see are St Mary's Cathedral ahead of you and the City Hall to your left. If you look down to the embankment of George's Quay on the right, your eye should just catch two very fine but **armless torsos**, metal-sculpted and set upon tall plinths facing one another some forty paces apart. This gruesome representation of war takes you by surprise and it's an unusually strong statement for Limerick.

The Church of Ireland **St Mary's Cathedral** (June–Sept Mon–Sat 9am–1pm & 2.30–5pm; Oct–May Mon–Sat 9am–1pm; suggested donation €1.27) was built at the end of the twelfth century, but only the Romanesque doorway facing the courthouse, the nave and parts of the transepts remain from this period. The chancel, windows and the rest of the transepts date from the fifteenth century. The cathedral's unique feature is its **misericords**, the only set in Ireland: made of black oak with reptilian creatures and cockatrice, griffin, sphinx and wild boar, they are carved in bold relief. The area around St Mary's has had a very successful face-lift in recent years. As you leave the cathedral, walk down to the courthouse and stroll around City Hall – a modern affair of glass and pink tubing – to appreciate the rushing river and Limerick's buoyant new civic pride. Follow the Shannon up towards Thomond Bridge and just before you get there you'll find yourself diverted up **Castle Lane**, a reconstruction of an "authentic" eighteenth- and nineteenth-century Irish streetscape – bounded on the north by the outer wall of King John's Castle. The buildings to your right are actually all new, but create a "historic" atmosphere as you progress to Nicholas Street. Housed in one of these buildings is the **Limerick Museum** (Tues–Sat 10am–1pm & 2.15–5pm; free; ⓣ061/417826), which holds the city maces, civic sword and charters granted by Charles I along with pieces of local lace work. Also on show are: coins which date as far back as the Viking period; historic maps showing the old walled Englishtown and Irishtown; memorabilia of various Fenian uprisings (notably a Pádraig Pearse letter from the Easter Rising of 1916); and Stone, Iron and especially Bronze Age implements. Many of the Mesolithic items (circa 7000–4000 BC) are from the Lough Gur area, and it's worth looking at the excavation photographs of this site before you visit it.

Nearby, on Nicholas Street, overlooking the river at Thomond Bridge, stands **King John's Castle** (daily: mid-April to Oct 9.30am–5.30pm; Nov to mid-April 10.30am–4.30pm; €6.35; ⓣ061/360788, ⓦwww.shannonheritage.com). Don't be put off by the entrance hall, a senseless addition of overwhelming vacuity that negates any feeling of power as you approach what is in fact one of the most impressive Anglo-Norman castles in Ireland. Built in the early thirteenth century, the castle was originally a five-sided fortress with four stout round towers. The towers were shortened at a much later stage to accommodate artillery positions, although one was actually replaced as a bastion in 1611. Instruments of medieval siege warfare enliven the castle yard and you can climb the battlements for superb views. You can also watch an interesting twenty-minute film of the history of Limerick in the museum. There's a much more detailed history of the Normans in Ireland in the **interpretive centre**. Beneath all of this are the foundations of pre-Norman dwellings – the finds of recent excavations. Despite it all, the castle is probably most impressive from the outside, as you stare up at the cliff-like immensity of its walls alongside Thomond Bridge.

The famous **Treaty Stone** stands opposite the castle, on the far side of Thomond Bridge, on Clancy Strand. In recent years it has been moved – only about twenty yards – and sandblasted clean. This, if you want to read symbolic significance into it, can be seen as an attempt to loosen a burden that was preventing the city from developing.

Irishtown

Cross back over Matthew Bridge to reach **Irishtown** and the bustle of the modern city centre along Rutland Street and then Patrick Street. Without doubt the most distinguished building in this part of town is the **Custom House**, an eighteenth-century structure of harmonious Classical balance, and home to the excellent **Hunt Museum** (Mon–Sat 10am–5pm, Sun 2–5pm; €5; ⓣ061/312833, ⓔinfo@huntmuseum.com). This astonishing collection – spanning nine thousand years, from the Stone Age through to the twentieth century – is the personal collection of John Hunt (1900–76), an English antiques dealer who went on to become an expert on medieval art, advising on internationally important collections such as those of William Burrell in Glasgow and the Aga Khan. One of the highlights of the collection is the bronze and enamel **Antrim Cross**, one of Ireland's most important examples of ninth-century early-Christian metalwork and thought to be a precursor of the high cross designs at Monasterboice and Kells. Other highlights include the eleventh-century Beverley crozier, made of exquisitely carved walrus tusk; the dazzling fifteenth-century O'Dea mitre and crozier; and the late Bronze Age Ballyscullion cauldron. Many of the artefacts are kept in drawers which visitors are free to open and include a thirteenth-century Limoges enamel and drawings by Giacometti.

A series of lanes – Ellen Street, Denmark Street and Cruise's Street – run off the main thoroughfare, Patrick Street, just a couple of hundred yards from the museum. They are worth exploring for their sprinkling of contemporary design shops and fashionable café-bars. The back streets beyond here are somewhat less appealing, the only feature of note being **St John's Cathedral**, a nineteenth-century Gothic Revival monstrosity whose spire of 280ft is the tallest in the country. Outside stands a memorial to Patrick Sarsfield, unsuccessful Jacobite defender of the city.

Newtown Pery

Patrick Street soon becomes O'Connell Street, Limerick's main, busy, but run-down commercial strip. Further south along it, however, the Georgian buildings are better preserved and The Crescent at the far end of the street is rather fine, especially when lit up at night. Just before The Crescent, on the left, is the **Belltable Arts Centre** (☎061/319709), whose gallery space shows a diverse range of contemporary art with twelve exhibitions a year. The centre also stages theatre (see p.326). To the east of here lie more examples of Limerick's Georgian architecture, and the interior of one such elegant home can be explored at **2 Pery Square** (for details contact St Mary's Action Centre, see p.322), along with an exhibition on the history of Limerick and, in the stable block to the rear, a reconstruction of the damp, cramped slumhome that Frank McCourt detailed so vividly in *Angela's Ashes*. Alongside Pery Square is the People's Park in which stands the **City Gallery of Art** (Mon–Fri 10am–6pm, Thurs until 7pm, Sat 10am–1pm) whose emphasis is on international contemporary art, with a lesser focus on Irish work. It also houses the city's permanent collection of paintings from the eighteenth century to the present day, and includes work by Yeats and Sean Keating.

Eating, drinking and entertainment

A welcome sign of Limerick's regeneration is the rate at which good new cafés and pubs are appearing. The following list will give you some useful starting points. There's an abundance of **bars**, and in recent years Limerick has revived its reputation as a musical centre – particularly for contemporary and rock **music**. Again, a selection of bars and places to hear music can be found below.

Cafés and restaurants

Brûlées Restaurant 21 Henry St ☎061/319931. A converted Georgian town house given a crisp, contemporary look. The menu includes such delights as glazed chilli quail followed by pan-seared fillet steaks. Tues–Fri 12.30–2.30pm & 6.30–10pm, Sat 6.30–10pm.

Chez O'Shea 74 O'Connell St ☎061/316311. Modern Irish cooking with fish brought in daily from Galway Bay. Dishes such as beef Wellington and seafood stew also available. Starters from €5, mains from €15. Next to the Belltable Arts Centre.

DuCartes Restaurant Hunt Museum, Custom House basement, Rutland St ☎061/312662. A stylish spot overlooking the river and Limerick's marina and extremely popular for its excellent, inexpensive home-cooked lunches, teas and snacks. Opening hours same as museum.

Freddy's Bistro Theatre Lane ☎061/418749. Down an alley off Lower Glentworth St. Expensive bistro serving steaks and seafood. Tues–Sun 5.30pm until late.

Furze Bush Café Bistro Corner of Glentworth and Catherine streets. Delightful bistro serving delicious crepes, sandwiches and salads. Lunch only Mon–Wed, dinner Mon–Sat, closed Sun.

The Green Onion Café Rutland St ☎061/400710.

Funky jazz café/restaurant with an imaginative and reasonably priced menu offering such dishes as Moroccan spiced vegetables with pulses, Italian spicy sausage with tagliatelle, and numerous off-beat sarnie combos. Daily until 10pm.

The Grove Cecil St. Health-food shop that does good bar-stool lunches and takeaways.

Java's 5 Catherine St. Little café, with bags of atmosphere. Hot lunches, all-day breakfasts plus bagels, baguettes and butties all generously stuffed with tasty homemade fillings. Good value. Mon–Wed 9am–midnight, Thurs–Sat 9am–3am, Sun 11am–midnight.

La Romana 36 O'Connell St ⓣ061/314994. Warm, convivial and unpretentious Italian restaurant. The food is moderately priced and a notch better than you might expect from the location. Flavoursome and satisfying Italian standards.

Bars and music venues

An Síbín, Royal George Hotel, O'Connell St. Traditional music and country singalongs every night June–Oct.

Castle Lane Tavern Off Nicholas St. Brand new pub cunningly disguised as a medieval hostelry. Purpose-built to cater for tourists visiting the castle, it's generally full of locals. On a warm evening the grassy slope to the rear is worth considering as a place to enjoy the fading light over the Shannon. Solid bar food is also served.

Doc's The Granary Bank Place. Upbeat bar in brick-vaulted granary courtyard; generally attracts a studenty crowd.

Dolan's 3–4 Dock Rd ⓣ061/314483. Limerick's top traditional music venue, with sessions every night all year round.

Dolan's Warehouse 4 Alphonsus St, behind Dolan's bar ⓣ061/314483, ⓦwww.dolans-pub.ie. A great venue for live bands – from soul and R&B, to traditional Irish and tribute bands. There's also a big screen for viewing major sporting events. Doors open at 9pm.

James Gleeson The White House Bar, 52 O'Connell St. Ancient ale house, full of character – and characters; packed, but warm and friendly.

The Locke 3 George's Quay. Head for this pleasant bar, one of Limerick's oldest, with its easy sociable atmosphere, rather than the larger bar that's been added alongside. A good spot to catch traditional Irish music (Sun & Mon) and ballads and folk (Tues). Particularly pleasant on a fine evening, as you can sit outside.

Kurova Milk Bar 3 Ellen St. Trendy late-night bar playing Latin jazz sounds; especially popular at weekends, when the sets go on into the early hours. Baguettes, tortillas and sandwiches are also available. Mon–Wed & Sun 11am–11pm, Thurs–Sat 11am–4am.

Nancy Blake's Upper Denmark St. Lively pub with traditional music (Mon–Wed & Sun) and a pleasant beer garden.

The Outback at the back of Nancy Blake's. A great venue for live bands, chiefly rock.

The Works Bedford Row. Popular club playing mainly charts, dance and indie music until 2am.

Theatre and classical music

For full, current listings of theatre and classical concerts pick up a copy of the *Limerick Corporation Arts Calendar* at the tourist office. The **Belltable Arts Centre**, 69 O'Connell St (ⓣ061/319709), hosts an interesting mix of performances, including some by local and international touring companies. The **University Concert Hall** at Limerick University (ⓣ061/331549) is the largest purpose-built concert hall in Ireland and the best place to catch classical music; pick up their events listings at the tourist office and see p.323 for directions to get there.

The Clare Glens and around

The **Clare Glens** on the Limerick–Tipperary border is a beautiful area of flowing falls, parts of which you can swim in: it makes a great day's excursion from Limerick for cyclists. Head for Moroe (sometimes spelt Murroe), about ten miles east of the city; Clare is two miles north of this. A circular ride of some twenty miles could take this in, along with **Glenstal Abbey** and the village of **Castleconnell**, a well-known Irish-music and Irish-language centre in a scenic setting on the banks of the Shannon some seven miles from Limerick.

Lough Gur and around

Leaving Limerick city for Cork the main route is the N20, a fast and efficient but rather dull route south. If you have time to stop along the way, the smaller R512 road has considerably more to offer – above all **Lough Gur**, site of a wealth of Mesolithic and Neolithic finds and one of County Limerick's chief attractions. Seventeen miles south of Limerick city, the lough looks as though its waters have been accidentally spilt onto the Limerick soil. It's the only significant lake in the county and comes as a rare treat in the midst of an otherwise lacklustre terrain. The area that surrounds the lake has been an extraordinarily rich source of archaeological finds – though what exists now is an extremely frugal sketch of what took place five thousand years ago. The lake is C-shaped, with a marshy area to the east that would complete the full circle.

In the middle of this circle is a small rise known as **Knockadoon**, whose slopes are studded with faint remains of earthworks showing ring forts and hut foundations dating from 3500 to 1000 BC. The length of its less secure marshy side is naturally forested and guarded at either end by two **medieval tower houses**, Bouchier's Castle and Black Castle. Mary Carbery's nineteenth-century book, *The Farm by Lough Gur*, gives a vivid contemporary account of life by the lough – the farm still stands up the road from the Neolithic huts known as the Spectacles.

Lough Gur must have been the perfect setting for a **Neolithic settlement**. The lake provided fish, and the gentle hillsides produced berries, nuts and trappings for animal hunting, as well as protection from the elements – and detection. When the lake was partly drained in the middle of the nineteenth century, and its level dropped by three yards, prehistoric artefacts were found in such quantities that stories tell of whole cartloads being hauled away. Evidence of this is seen in the amount of museums around the world that display archaeological finds from Lough Gur. The most famous discovery was a bronze shield from 700 BC, perfect in its concentric rings of bosses but for a hacking in two places by the reed-cutter who discovered it. The finds here pair well with the Neolithic discoveries made in Meath; this was once a Neolithic living community, whereas the Brú na Bóinne site is concerned with ritual and burial. Today there's abundant **birdlife** on the lake; the grazing cattle, antlered goats and lack of modern buildings give you a strong intimation of life five thousand years ago.

Heading further south towards the border with Cork, the cottage in which Eamon de Valera grew up, just outside **Bruree**, is worth a quick visit.

The interpretive centre and stone circle

The simplest approach to Lough Gur is to come off the R512 at Holycross. Follow the road to the northernmost section of the lake, keeping an eye out for a wedge-shaped **gallery grave**. The grave, typically, shows a long gallery space where the bodies of eight adults and four children from around 2000 BC were found. The gallery has parallel double walls of stone slabs filled in with rubble and what's called a septal slab at its back. The road then circles on round the marsh to an **interpretive centre** (mid-May to Sept daily 10am–6pm; €3; ⓣ061/85186). Housed in replica Neolithic huts, the centre attempts to give some idea of what life was like for the early inhabitants. From it, the chief attractions on Knockadoon are easily accessible on foot.

A quarter of a mile north of the Holycross turn-off, the first thing you'll see is a gargantuan **stone circle** close to the main road, the most substantial of the area's prehistoric remains. Possibly the grandest example in the country, it has a ring of standing stones marking out an almost perfect circle. A posthole was found at the centre which must have held a stake, from which, with a length of cord attached, the circle could be struck. Some of the stones are massive and are bolstered within their earth sockets by smaller boulders, which were then covered. Flints, arrowheads, blades and bowls were found within the enclosure, but little has been learned about the site's exact function. A circle of this size clearly demanded a good deal of social organization and a strong sense of purpose, and its most likely use was religious rituals.

The castles and Knockadoon

If you're walking, an alternative approach to Knockadoon is across the stone causeway that leads from near the gallery grave to **Black Castle**. Possibly thirteenth century, the castle is now weighed down by a swarthy camouflage of nettles, brambles and trees. It was once quite extensive, with a high curtain wall and square towers, and acted as a principal seat for the Earls of Desmond. The pathway north to **Bouchier's Castle** has three Neolithic hut remains at various degrees up the hill slope. If you're intent on seeing them, you'll have to forage around among the wooded thickets. Bouchier's Castle itself is a typical fifteenth-century Desmond tower house of five storeys; but it's privately owned and can't be visited.

Turning westwards from the Black Castle towards the lakeshore, you'll see various ring forts and hut traces on the bare grassy slopes. It's not much, but even this scant evidence is enough to conjure up the image of a thriving Stone Age community on **Knockadoon**. Rather than continue round along the bank of the lake, it's best to take this opportunity to cross back along the hilltop centre, where, from a point known as M, you can get penetrating views into Kerry and Cork, with Limerick spreading towards them in a swath of low hills. **Crock** and **Bolin islands** in the lake are both *crannógs* which the mainland has now caught up with. They were built by laying down a ring of boulders, then the inner space

Eamon de Valera

Eamon de Valera founded the Fianna Fáil (Soldiers of Destiny) party in 1926 and is familiarly known as the "big man" or "Dev" to a population for whom he's been the most influential political instigator since the birth of the Free State in 1922. He acted as premier of Ireland from 1932 to 1948, 1951 to 1954 and 1957 to 1959, and assumed the honorary role of president from 1959 to 1973. This makes up a sizeable chunk of the Republic's history, and his grip on the nation has left an ambivalent attitude to his worth and integrity.

De Valera was the only leader of the 1916 Easter Rising to survive. His initial death sentence was commuted to imprisonment because of his American dual nationality – he was born in New York, and at the time the British were sensitive to American neutrality in World War I. He escaped from prison in England and was unconstitutionally elected the first president of the Irish Republic in 1919; his almost miraculous survival had marked him out as the man to lead Ireland out of seven hundred years of British domination. The Republic immediately declared war on Britain, and when two years of struggle forced the British to negotiate, de Valera's was the leading rebel voice against the signing of the Anglo-Irish Treaty in 1921. He wanted to hold out for an all-Ireland Free State, rather than accept only 26 counties out of 32, as was laid down in the Treaty. This stance divided the Irish and provoked the Civil War of 1921 to 1923. The one war he succeeded in keeping the Irish out of was World War II, at the end of which he had the gall to send official commiserations to the Reichstag on Hitler's death, so profound was the bitterness of his battle with the British.

was filled with earth and brushwood. **Garret Island** is a natural island with some stone remains of another Desmond castle.

Bruree

A small cottage just outside **BRUREE** (four miles west of Kilmallock) was the childhood home of **Eamon de Valera** (see box on p.329), and has now been turned into a modest memorial of the family's household possessions, including a bulky trunk that was used for their return from exile in New York. The cottage is signposted nearly a mile down the road to the right at the eastern end of Bruree village – get the key from the house on the right, a hundred and fifty yards further down the road. At the western end of Bruree village itself is the old schoolhouse, which has been turned into a **museum and heritage centre** (Tues–Fri 10am–5pm, Sat & Sun 2–5pm; €4), stocked with memorabilia of the former premier and president, plus a few rural items of general interest.

South and west of Limerick

The road southwest to Killarney is the most interesting route out of Limerick, catching the prim English beauty of thatched cottages in **Adare**. The road west to Tralee, the N69, is the least interesting of the three major routes across County Limerick. It runs parallel to the Shannon estuary but mostly through flat alluvial land, without the compensation of having the waters alongside except for the last few miles into Glin.

Adare

Famously picturesque **ADARE** has cultivated nearly as many antiques shops as pubs. In peak season, it will more than likely be infested with tourists taking photos of the wayside cottages that sit in a neat row, their quaint deep-brown thatch hanging in low fringes. The cottages represent the nineteenth-century ideal of romanticized rusticity, as realized by the third Earl of Dunraven (1812–71), landlord and master of Adare Manor and an eternal improver of circumstances for his tenants. Given that Adare is now probably regarded as the prettiest village in Ireland, it's hard to believe that before the earl's improvements it was one of the grottiest. The cottages today are pure upmarket thatch, with pricey restaurants and crafts shops.

Adare Manor House, to the north of the village, is a huge, near-fanatical assemblage of castellations and turrets in limestone, built by the earl to Gothic Revival designs in 1832. This castle has only recently passed into private hands as a grand hotel, the *Adare Manor* (Ⓣ061/396566, Ⓦwww.adaremanor.com; ❽–❾), which offers luxurious accommodation, swimming pool and eighteen-hole golf course. The River Maigue flows by the estate a little further up, at the head of the village, and although an exciting-looking triumvirate of **medieval buildings** beckons, a golf course steers its course next to all of them, inhibiting any close inspection. This is not such a shame as the Desmond castle is completely bricked up and deemed unsafe, and the fifteenth-century friary which appears far better preserved, was extensively restored as late as the mid-nineteenth century. These are perhaps easiest viewed from the bridge.

Back in the village there are ecclesiastical sites, too, starting with an **Augustinian Priory** just by the bridge. Beautifully preserved, the priory still serves as the local Church of Ireland church, its interior as close as any to the old medieval model. The **Trinitarian Abbey**, halfway down the main street, was founded in 1230 for the Trinitarian Canons of the Order of the Redemption of Captives, and is the only house of this order in Ireland. Today, it's Adare's Catholic church, with one of its turrets at the back a deserted columbarium.

Buses from Limerick stop in the main street. Adare's **tourist office** (June–Sept Mon–Fri 9am–7pm, Sat & Sun 9am–6pm; ⓣ061/396255) is in the main street alongside the **heritage centre** (same times; €4). There are numerous **B&Bs** in the village, including *Berkeley Lodge* (ⓣ061/396857; ⓔberlodge@iol.ie; ❷), *Avona* (ⓣ061/396323; ❷) and *Church View House* (ⓣ061/396371; ❶), situated on Station Road. You can get decent **meals** at *The Arches Restaurant* on Main Street; for snacks try the café in the same building as the tourist office. *Bill Chawke's* and *Collin's Bar* both have **traditional music** sessions one evening a week during the summer while *Lena's Bar* on Main Street has traditional music every Wednesday night.

Five miles southwest of Adare, the pleasant village of **BALLINGARRY** has an excellent IHH hostel, *Trainor's* (ⓣ069/68164; March to mid-Oct). The village is also home to an excellent upmarket restaurant of some renown, *The Mustard Seed* (ⓣ069/68508; closed March), which offers imaginative country-house cooking using plenty of organic and local produce.

Newcastle West

From Adare the N21 continues into Rathkeale, after which a signpost points to Ardagh, the ring fort where the wonderful Ardagh Chalice was found in 1868 (it's now in the Dublin National Museum). The site here is unimpressive, however, and it's not really worth dragging yourself off the main road. Press on, instead to **NEWCASTLE WEST** to look at the **Desmond Banqueting Hall** (mid-June to mid-Sept daily 9.30am–6.30pm; €1.90). The hall is on the main square and very little fuss is made of it, but it's part of a scattered and hidden complex of ruined buildings – a keep, a peel tower, a bastion and curtain wall. Even though this was once the principal seat of the Fitzgeralds, the town hasn't harnessed its history to its advantage. The hall is in a near-perfect state of preservation, and ready for an inspired restoration. At present, apart from a marriage fireplace said to have been imported from Egypt, it's all bare.

There are several small **B&Bs** in town – try Mrs Burke on Bishop Street (ⓣ069/62287; ❶); you can also get food and rooms at the *Courtney Lodge Hotel* (ⓣ069/62244; ❷–❹). For traditional music sessions every Friday night (June–Oct) try *Danaher's Bar* on Maiden Street and *The Shamrock Bar* on South Quay.

Glenquin Castle is another well-preserved but entirely deserted tower house, about five miles south of Newcastle West, just outside the village of Killeady. To find it follow the N21 from Newcastle West towards Abbeyfeale; the road to the castle is signposted after a few miles on the left by a petrol station. It has very good views of the countryside, but is really only worth a stop if you're passing by anyway. If you have children in tow, you might prefer to visit **Springfield Castle Deer Centre** (summer daily 1–6pm) outside Dromcollogher, about ten miles south of Newcastle West. There are pets for children to handle, and a tractor trailer takes you on a tour past herds of deer, so tame they feed from your hand.

Along the estuary

A good mile off the N69 at Kilcornan, five miles from Adare, is the excellent **Celtic Theme Park and Gardens** (mid-March to Nov daily 9am–6pm; €4; ⓣ061/394243). Don't let the words "theme park" put you off – there's not a drop of moulded plastic in sight. The hour or so stroll through the park takes in a string of features associated with ancient Ireland – a stone circle, dolmen, holy well and twelfth-century church. While some are replicas, others, most notably the lake dwelling and the (unexcavated) ring fort, are original, and overall this is a very sensitive blending of ancient landscape with imitation. Back up by the tearoom, there's an attractive formal garden, with fine scented flowers, a tranquil lily pond and walkways between silver birch and blackthorns.

Back on the N69, the road passes a few more tower houses on the right and the Curraghchase Forest Park on the left before reaching **ASKEATON**. Here, there's an Anglo-Norman **friary** next to the River Deel, just off the main road at its second entry to Askeaton from the east. The friary was founded by the fourth Earl of Desmond, Gerald the Poet, in 1389. It now seems particularly hidden away, and has one of the loveliest cloisters you'll come across and some excellent window tracery. From the dormitory above, you can pick out the towering remains of the **castle**, penned in towards the centre of the town. Worth a quick scout around, it has a large banqueting hall, very similar to the better example in Newcastle West, its vaulted ground-floor chambers remaining just within the walls. A very dodgy-looking fifteenth-century end tower stands upon a rock in the centre of what was once an island in the River Deel. The castle's present decay does little to suggest its one-time Anglo-Norman prominence, when it flourished in the hands of the Earls of Desmond, until the Earl of Essex crushed them during the sixteenth century.

FOYNES is a moderately busy village, with a **flying-boat museum** (April–Oct daily 10am–6pm; €4.40; ⓣ069/65416, ⓔfamm@eircom.net) which celebrates the town's past as an aviation centre. In the late 1930s and early 1940s, Foynes, as Limerick's only link to the sea, was the terminus for a transatlantic flying-boat service. Here in 1942, chef Joe Sheridan made the first Irish coffee to warm up some damp and miserable passengers. Every July his now-famous concoction is celebrated with an **Irish Coffee Festival**. Moving on, the forested hillsides that now appear mark a pleasant route along the estuary as far as Glin on the Limerick–Kerry border.

Travel details

Trains

Services listed are for Mon–Sat; trains and buses are less frequent on Sun.

Limerick to: Cahir (1 daily; 1hr 15min); Carrick-on-Suir (1 daily; 2hr); Clonmel (1 daily; 1hr 35min); Dublin (8–13 daily; 2hr 40min); Rosslare Harbour/Europort (1 daily; 3hr 50min); Tipperary (1 daily; 50min).

Waterford to: Dublin (3–6 daily; 2hr 45min); Limerick (1 daily; 3hr).

Buses

Bus Éireann

Cahir to: Waterford (6–8 daily; 1hr 15min).

Cashel to: Cahir (summer 7 daily, winter 3 Mon–Sat, 2 Sun; 15min); Cork (3 daily; 1hr 35min–2hr); Mitchelstown (4 daily; 45min).

Limerick to: Cahir (6–7 daily; 1hr 35min); Cork (14 daily; 1hr 50min); Dublin (13 daily; 3hr 30min); Shannon Airport (frequent service; 45min); Tipperary (6–10 daily; 50min); Waterford (6–7 daily; 2hr 5min).

Nenagh to: Dublin (13 daily; 2hr 40min); Limerick (13 daily; 1hr 20min).

Roscrea to: Dublin (10 daily; 2hr 20min); Limerick (13 daily; 1hr 15min).

Waterford to: Dublin (7–10 daily; 3hr 30min); Tramore (frequent service; 25min).

Rapid Express ⓣ051/872149

Waterford to: Dublin (9 daily; 3hr).

Suirway ⓣ051/382209

Waterford to: Dunmore East (4 daily; 30min); Passage East (3 daily; 30min); Woodstown (3 daily; 30min).

Cork

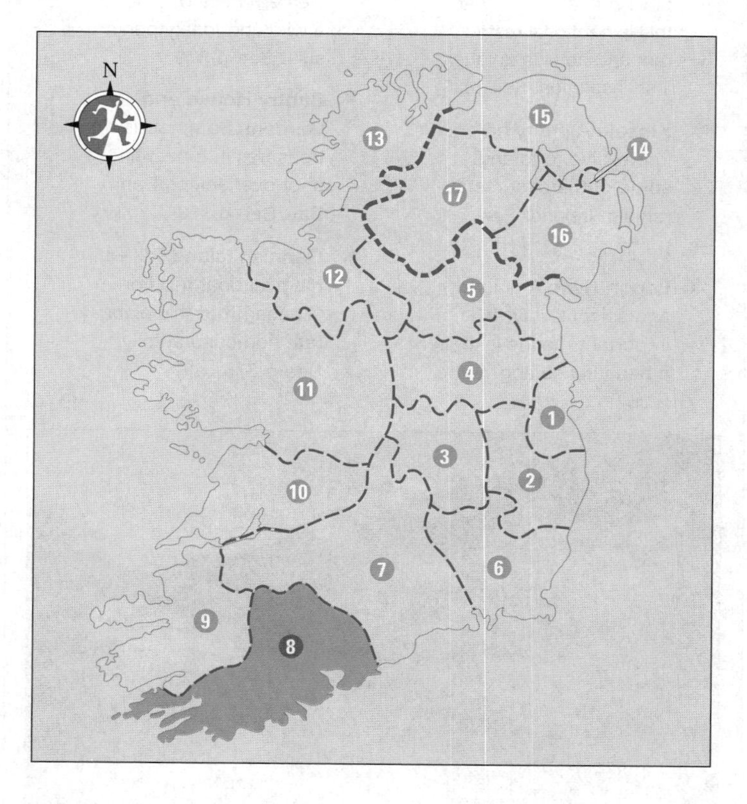

CHAPTER 8 **Highlights**

- **Fota House** An extravagantly decorated mansion, brought to life by imaginative displays and set in impressive grounds. See p.348
- **Ballymaloe House** For a blow-out, eat or stay at this exceptional restaurant and hotel, a uniquely Irish institution. See p.351
- **Kinsale** A pretty harbour, impressive forts and some of the best restaurants in Ireland. See p.356
- **Lough Hyne** A unique and scientifically important marine lake, in a beautiful setting. See p.364
- **Clear Island** Hop on the ferry for rich birdwatching and easy walking. See p.367
- **The Sheep's Head Way** The shortest and easiest walking route in south-western Ireland, around a wild and lonely peninsula. See p.370
- **Bantry House and Gardens** Sumptuous art treasures in a beautiful spot overlooking Bantry Bay. See p.373
- **Garinish Island** Take a magical boat trip from Glengarriff to this elaborate horticultural folly. See p.375

Cork

Cork, Ireland's largest county, is the perfect place to ease yourself gently into the exhilarations of Ireland's west coast. **Cork city**, a major port on the estuary of the River Lee and the south's self-proclaimed cultural capital, manages to be at one and the same time a relaxed and a spirited place. There are no spectacular sights, but Cork is one of Ireland's most pleasurable and accessible cities. Around Cork city, maritime history is still more richly distilled in the small ports of **Cobh**, **Youghal** and – most of all – **Kinsale**, all suggestive of a prosperity that Ireland could have had throughout the eighteenth and nineteenth centuries were it not for the strangulation of its overseas trade by Britain. On the other side of this coin are the riches of the Anglo-Irish legacy, most in evidence in the far west of the county at **Bantry House** with its outrageously sumptuous art treasures.

In the main, the charms of the Cork countryside are those of a gently rural backwater, but as you head west along a fabulously indented coastline of hidden bays and coves to the wild peninsulas of the extreme southwest, or through the ravine of Gougane Barra high above **Glengarriff** and **Bantry Bay**, the soft contours of a comfortable and easy prettiness slip away to reveal beauty of a more elemental kind. There's not as much of this as you might find in, say, Kerry, but in the **Caha Mountains** careering north from Bantry Bay, the scintillating cliffs of **Mizen Head** or the seascapes of **Sherkin and Clear islands**, teeming with birdlife, Cork has scenery as exciting and dramatic as you'll find anywhere.

Public transport around the county is fairly extensive if infrequent. Bus Éireann covers the whole of Cork except for the extreme west of Mizen Head and the Beara Peninsula. Major towns have daily connections, but small towns and villages off the main roads are served less frequently, so if you're relying on public transport it's worth taking details of times and days of services you are likely to want while in a major bus station. On certain routes private buses provide the only transport; see "Travel details" at the end of this chapter for all the details. The intricate landscape of west Cork, in particular, is best explored at a slow pace, making it ideal country for **walking** or **cycling**, both of which pursuits are served by waymarked routes on the Beara Peninsula and the Sheep's Head Peninsula.

Cork city

CORK city – the second city of the Republic – is built on an island, the two channels of the River Lee embracing it either side while nineteenth-century

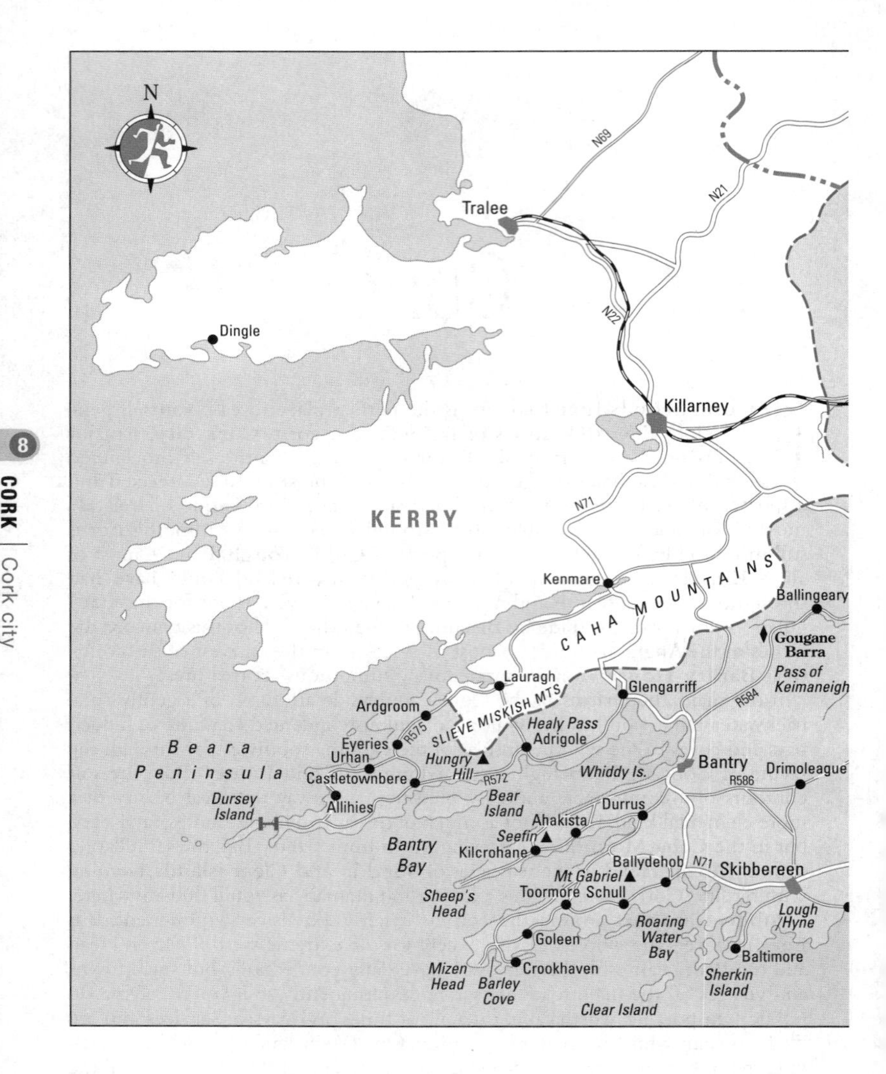

suburbs sprawl up the surrounding hills. This gives the city centre a compactness and sharp definition. It's a place of great charm, with a history of vigorous intellectual independence, and when approached from rural Ireland, it has a surprisingly cosmopolitan feel.

Evidence of Cork's history as a great mercantile centre is everywhere, with grey stone quaysides, old warehouses and elegant and quirky bridges spanning the river. Many of the city's streets were at one time waterways: St Patrick's Street had quays for sailing ships, and on the pavement in Grand Parade you can still see moorings dating from the eighteenth century. Important port though Cork may be, however, it doesn't feel overridingly commercial, and the Lee is certainly not the river of an industrial town. The all-pervading presence

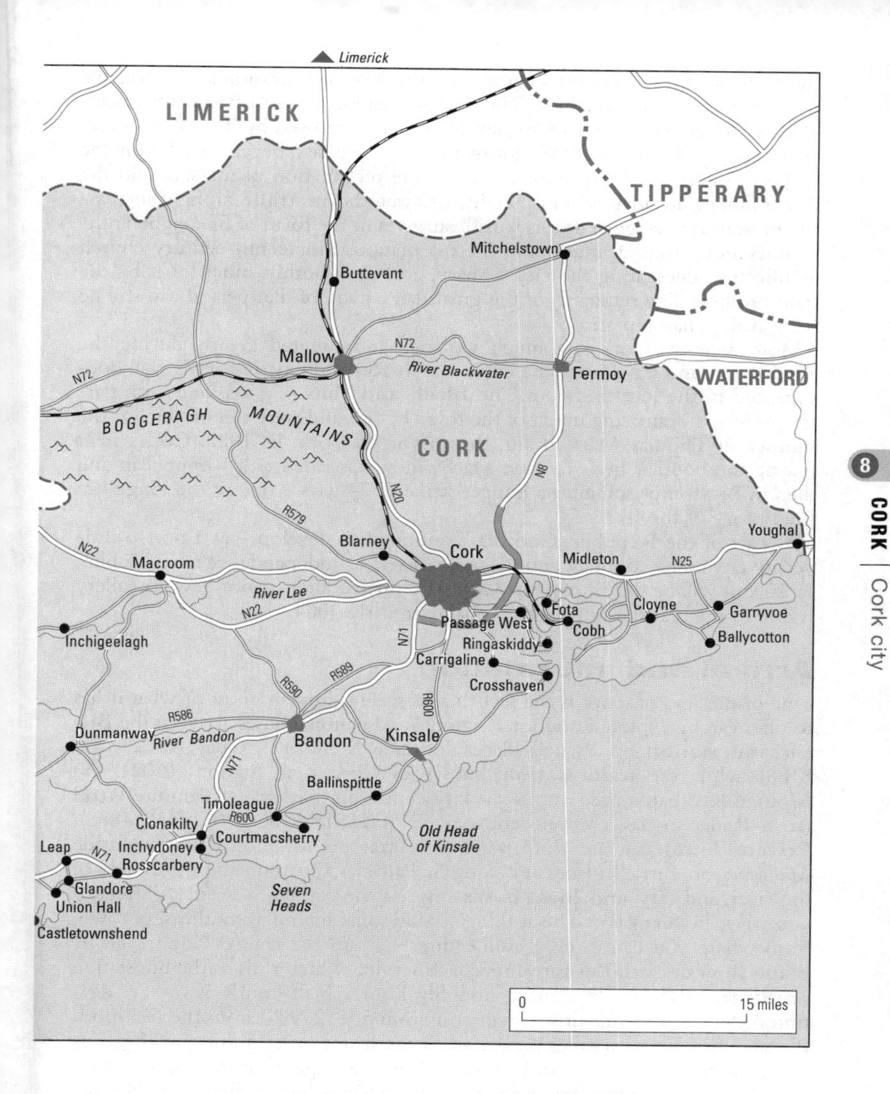

of its waters reflects the light, so that even on the cloudiest of days there is a balmy, translucent quality to the atmosphere.

Some history

Cork (Corcaigh, "marshy place") had its origins in the seventh century when St Finbarre founded an abbey and school on the site where the impressive nineteenth-century Gothic St Finbarre's Cathedral stands today. A settlement grew up around the monastic foundation, overlooking a marshy swamp where the city centre now stands. In 820 the Vikings arrived, bringing their usual violence and destruction, and wrecked both abbey and town. They built a new settlement on one of the islands in the marshes and eventually integrated with the native Celts. The twelfth century saw the Norman invasion and Cork, like other ports, was taken, in 1172. The new acquisition was fortified with massive stone walls, which survived Cromwell but were destroyed by Williamite forces at the Siege of Cork in 1690. From this time the city began to take on the shape recognizable today. Expansion saw the reclamation of marshes and the development of canals within the city, and waterborne **trade** brought increasing prosperity. Evidence of this wealth survives in the form of fine eighteenth-century bow-fronted houses and the ostentatious nineteenth-century church architecture decorating the city – sharp, grey and Gothic, much of it by the Pain brothers. The remnants of the great dairy trade of that period can still be seen in the Shandon area.

More recently, Cork saw much violence and suffered greatly during the Anglo-Irish and Civil wars: the city's part in **Republican** history is well documented in the local museum. The **Black and Tans** reigned here with particular terror, destroying much of the town by fire, and were responsible for the murder of Thomas MacCurtain, the mayor of Cork, in 1920. Cork's next mayor, the popular hero Terence MacSwiney, was jailed as a Republican and died in Brixton prison after a hunger strike of 74 days – one of the longest in the history of the IRA.

As part of the Republic, Cork has continued to develop – as a port, a university city and a cultural centre – and to assert its independence from Dublin. In 2005 it will be the **European City of Culture**, and a major new art gallery is due to open at the university, probably in early 2004.

Arrival and information

One of the joys of Cork is the fact that its scale is human: most of what it has to offer can be explored on foot. Regional and national buses arrive at the **Bus Éireann station** on Parnell Place alongside Merchant's Quay (ⓣ021/450 8188), while the **train station**, known as Cork Kent Station (ⓣ021/450 6766), is less than a mile out of the city centre on the Lower Glanmire Road (Irish Rail also has a travel centre at 65 St Patrick's St, ⓣ021/450 4888). **Private buses** operate from various central points, mostly from outside *Mulligan's* on Parnell Place and along St Patrick's Quay on the north side of the river, and **city and local buses** stop on the central St Patrick's Street. If you arrive by **ferry** you'll be at Ringaskiddy, some ten miles southeast of town, from where you can catch a connecting bus into the centre. Coming in by **plane** you can catch Bus Éireann's coach service, which runs to the bus station on Parnell Place in 25 minutes roughly hourly (half-hourly Mon–Fri daytimes). A taxi from the airport will cost around €12, €20 from the ferryport. If you're driving remember that, as in all the major cities, a disc **parking** system is in operation; discs can be bought from newsagents or the tourist office. There's a useful multistorey car park on Coal Quay beside the Opera House.

The **tourist office** on Grand Parade supplies the usual wide variety of information and tacky souvenirs, and can also book accommodation (June Mon–Sat 9am–6pm; July & Aug Mon–Sat 9am–6pm, Sun 10am–5pm; Sept & Oct Mon–Sat 9.15am–5.30pm; Nov–May Mon–Fri 9.15am–5.30pm, Sat 9.30am–4.30pm; ⓣ021/427 3251). In summer, literary **walking tours** of the city head off from the *Imperial Hotel* on South Mall every Tuesday and Thursday, finishing up with a pint of Beamish at *An Spailpín Fánac* (mid-May to mid-Sept; ⓣ021/488 5405; €6.50). There's also a choice of open-top bus tours, both of which can be booked at the tourist office: Guide Friday departs from opposite the tourist office to take in the city centre as well as Cork City

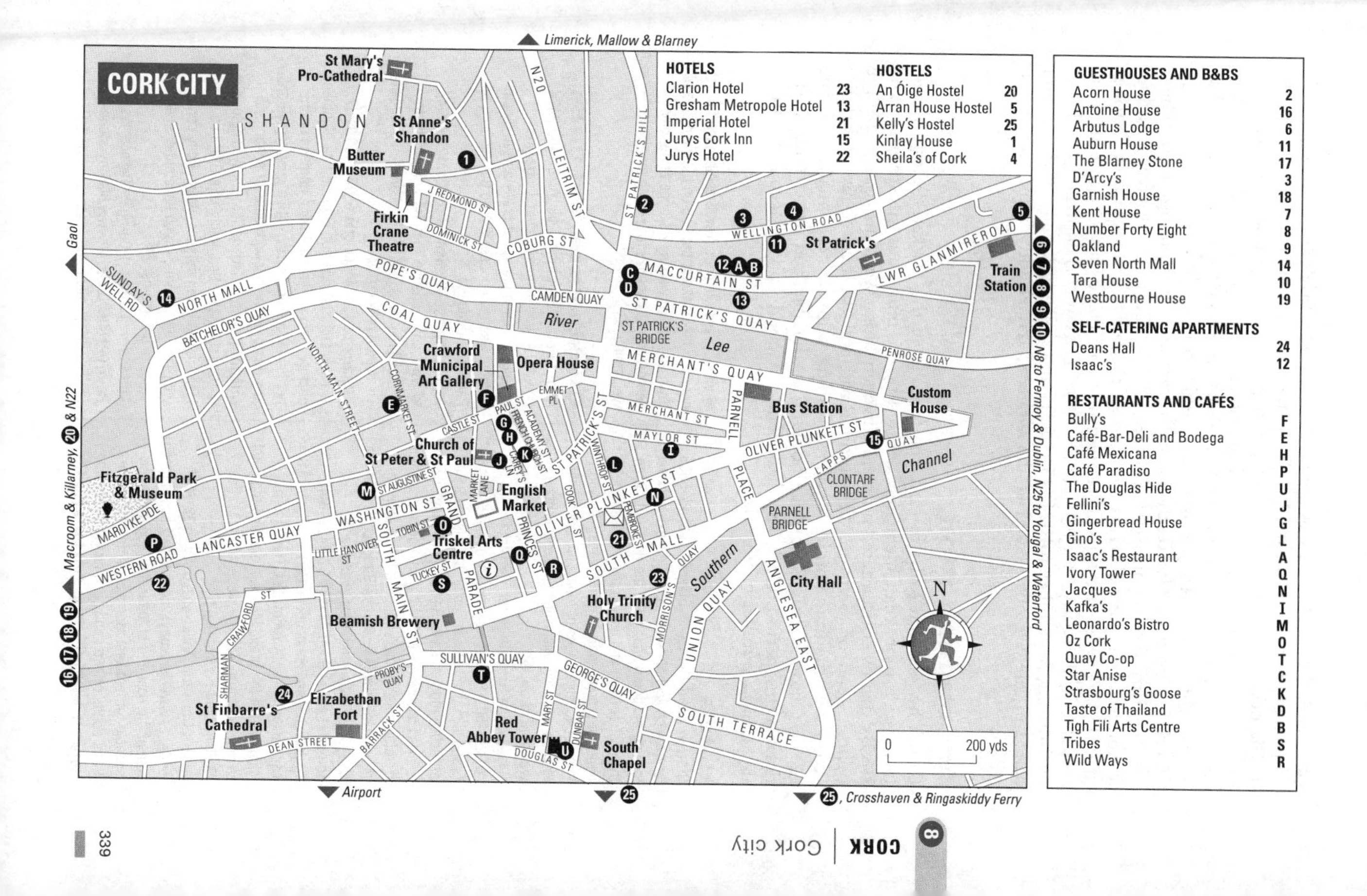
CORK CITY
Limerick, Mallow & Blarney
Gaol
16, 17, 18, 19, Macroom & Killarney, 20 & N22
Airport
25
25, Crosshaven & Ringaskiddy Ferry
6, 7, 8, 9, 10, N8 to Fermoy & Dublin, N25 to Yougal & Waterford
HOTELS
Clarion Hotel 23
Gresham Metropole Hotel 13
Imperial Hotel 21
Jurys Cork Inn 15
Jurys Hotel 22
HOSTELS
An Óige Hostel 20
Arran House Hostel 5
Kelly's Hostel 25
Kinlay House 1
Sheila's of Cork 4
GUESTHOUSES AND B&BS
Acorn House 2
Antoine House 16
Arbutus Lodge 6
Auburn House 11
The Blarney Stone 17
D'Arcy's 3
Garnish House 18
Kent House 7
Number Forty Eight 8
Oakland 9
Seven North Mall 14
Tara House 10
Westbourne House 19
SELF-CATERING APARTMENTS
Deans Hall 24
Isaac's 12
RESTAURANTS AND CAFÉS
Bully's F
Café-Bar-Deli and Bodega E
Café Mexicana H
Café Paradiso P
The Douglas Hide U
Fellini's J
Gingerbread House G
Gino's L
Isaac's Restaurant A
Ivory Tower Q
Jacques N
Kafka's I
Leonardo's Bistro M
Oz Cork O
Quay Co-op T
Star Anise C
Strasbourg's Goose K
Taste of Thailand D
Tigh Fili Arts Centre B
Tribes S
Wild Ways R
St Mary's Pro-Cathedral
SHANDON
St Anne's Shandon
Butter Museum
Firkin Crane Theatre
J REDMOND ST
DOMINICK ST
COBURG ST
LEITRIM ST
N20
ST PATRICK'S HILL
WELLINGTON ROAD
St Patrick's
LWR GLANMIRE ROAD
Train Station
MACCURTAIN ST
SUNDAY'S WELL RD
NORTH MALL
POPE'S QUAY
CAMDEN QUAY
ST PATRICK'S QUAY
River
Lee
ST PATRICK'S BRIDGE
BATCHELOR'S QUAY
COAL QUAY
PENROSE QUAY
MERCHANT'S QUAY
Crawford Municipal Art Gallery
Opera House
NORTH MAIN STREET
CORNMARKET ST
EMMET PL
PAUL ST
CASTLE ST
FRENCH CHURCH ST
ACADEMY ST
CAREY'S LN
MERCHANT ST
PARNELL PLACE
Bus Station
Custom House
MAYLOR ST
OLIVER PLUNKETT ST
QUAY
Channel
Church of St Peter & St Paul
ST PATRICK'S ST
WINTHROP ST
LAPPS
CLONTARF BRIDGE
Fitzgerald Park & Museum
ST AUGUSTINE ST
MARKET LANE
English Market
COOK ST
PEMBROKE ST
MARDYKE PDE
WASHINGTON ST
GRAND PARADE
TOBIN ST
PRINCES ST
PARNELL BRIDGE
LANCASTER QUAY
Triskel Arts Centre
SOUTH MALL
Southern
QUAY
WESTERN ROAD
LITTLE HANOVER ST
TUCKEY ST
SOUTH MAIN ST
MORRISON'S QUAY
UNION QUAY
ANGLESEA EAST
City Hall
Holy Trinity Church
N
CRAWFORD ST
Beamish Brewery
SHARMAN
SULLIVAN'S QUAY
PROBY'S QUAY
GEORGE'S QUAY
St Finbarre's Cathedral
Elizabethan Fort
BARRACK ST
Red Abbey Tower
MARY ST
DUNBAR ST
SOUTH TERRACE
DEAN STREET
DOUGLAS ST
South Chapel
0 200 yds

Gaol and the public museum on the west side (May–Sept 6 daily; €11; ⓦwww.guidefriday.com); and Bus Éireann covers the city centre and runs out to Blarney, with stops at the bus station on Parnell Place and opposite the tourist office (June to mid-Sept 2 daily; €8). For those short on time, Bus Éireann runs a variety of coach tours from Cork in the summer – contact the bus station (ⓣ021/450 8188) or the tourist office for details.

Cork is a great city for **festivals**, the biggest and most prestigious of which are the **film festival** in early October (ⓣ021/427 1711, ⓦwww.corkfilmfest.org) and the **jazz festival** over one of the last two weekends in October (ⓣ021/427 8979, ⓦwww.corkjazzfestival.com). There's also an international choral festival in early May (ⓣ021/430 8308, ⓦwww.corkchoral.ie), a folk festival during September (ⓣ021/431 7271) and a fringe festival of drama and dance in late October, based at the Granary, Triskel and Firkin Crane (see p.346).

Accommodation

Cork's **hotels** tend to be towards the top end of the market; the mid-range, however, is more than adequately covered by the numerous **guesthouses** and **B&Bs**, mainly concentrated near the university along Western Road, and at the opposite end of town on Wellington Road and the busy Lower Glanmire Road, near the train station. If you're planning your stay to coincide with one of the October festivals, advance booking is advisable, and prices tend to rise during this period. Cork also has plenty of good budget accommodation, including a number of **hostels**.

Hotels

Clarion Hotel Morrison's Quay ⓣ021/427 5858, ⓦwww.choicehotelscork.com. Ugly exterior overlooking the south channel of the river, but inside the style is fresh and contemporary. Comfortably appointed rooms with en-suite baths, TVs and Internet access. Suites of rooms including galley kitchen also available. Quiet yet central; good weekend deals. ❼

Gresham Metropole Hotel MacCurtain St ⓣ021/450 8122, ⓦwww.gresham-hotels.com. Grand Victorian hotel, recently refurbished in an attractive modern style. Residents have full use of a lavish leisure centre, with gym, pool and saunas. If traffic noise bothers you, ask for an internal room away from MacCurtain Street or St Patrick's Quay. Good weekend rates available. ❻

Imperial Hotel South Mall ⓣ021/427 4040, ⓦwww.imperialhotelcork.ie. Cork's oldest hotel, central and recently renovated. The foyer retains glimmers of the grand Victorian era, and the hotel is noteworthy, too, as the place where Michael Collins spent his last night. ❺

Jury's Cork Inn Anderson's Quay ⓣ021/427 6444, ⓦwww.jurysdoyle.com. Smart accommodation at the east end of the island, especially reasonable for families; rooms accommodate either three adults or two adults and two children. ❹

Jury's Hotel Western Road ⓣ021/427 6622, ⓦwww.jurysdoyle.com. A well-established formal hotel, on the banks of the Lee on the west side of town and within walking distance of the city centre, which manages to be both smart and welcoming. ❼

Guesthouses and B&Bs

Acorn House St Patrick's Hill ⓣ021/450 2474, ⓦwww.acornhouse-cork.com. Large, well-appointed rooms and great breakfasts in a comfortable Georgian house, just up the hill from St Patrick's Bridge. ❸

Antoine House Western Rd ⓣ021/427 3494, ⓦwww.antoinehouse.com. B&B of a high standard, all rooms en suite with phones and satellite TV; secure parking. ❸

Arbutus Lodge Montenotte ⓣ021/450 1237, ⓦwww.arbutuslodge.net. Elegant, late-eighteenth-century town house, set in fine gardens on the northeast side of the city, with a good restaurant and an appealing bar with outdoor seating. ❻

Auburn House 3 Garfield Terrace, Wellington Rd ⓣ021/450 8555. Beautifully kept B&B in a quiet location within ten minutes' walk of city centre, with TVs in all rooms, which have either shared or en-suite bathrooms. ❷

The Blarney Stone 1 Carriglee Terrace, Western Rd ⓣ021/427 0083, ⓦwww.blarney-stone-guesthouse.com. Newly refurbished Victorian guesthouse, with TVs and phones in all rooms, optional Jacuzzis, and off-street parking. ❸

D'Arcy's 7 Sidney Place, Wellington Rd ⓣ021/450 4658, ⓦwww.darcysguesthouse.com. It's worth paying a little more to stay in this beautiful Georgian town house, with spacious rooms, some offering fine views over the city, and excellent breakfasts. ❸

Garnish House Western Rd ⓣ021/427 5111, ⓦwww.garnish.ie. Good-quality guesthouse offering an impressive breakfast menu, including porridge with Irish whiskey and spiced grapefruit with cinnamon toast; some rooms have a Jacuzzi. Studios and suites available; off-street parking. ❹

Kent House 47 Lower Glanmire Rd ⓣ021/450 4260. B&B in a family home offering en-suite and standard non-smoking rooms. Handy for the train station. No car parking. ❷

Number Forty Eight 48 Lower Glanmire Rd ⓣ & ⓕ021/450 5790. Comfortable, smart B&B in a Victorian town house with good breakfasts. No parking. ❷

Oakland 51 Lower Glanmire Rd ⓣ021/450 0578. Regular B&B in a terraced eighteenth-century house offering both standard and en-suite rooms. ❷

Seven North Mall 7 North Mall ⓣ021/439 7191, ⓔ sevennorthmall@eircom.net. Upmarket guesthouse in a fine, listed eighteenth-century town house, centrally located on the north side of the river. Excellent breakfasts; secure car park. ❹

Tara House 52 Lower Glanmire Rd ⓣ021/450 0294. Regular B&B with standard and en-suite rooms; TVs throughout. ❷

Westbourne House 2 Westbourne Villas, Western Rd ⓣ021/427 6153. Pleasant, traditional B&B about a mile from the centre; all rooms are en suite and non-smoking throughout; secure parking. ❷

Hostels

An Óige Hostel 1 Redclyffe, Western Rd ⓣ021/454 3289. Recently refurbished hostel with en-suite facilities throughout; very comfortable, spacious and well run. Bus #8 from St Patrick's Street; two and four-bedded rooms, bike rental and meals available.

Arran House Hostel Lower Glanmire Rd (IHO) ⓣ021/455 1566. Small town house near the train station with comfortable bunks, kitchen, laundry and bike lock-up and rental; twin and family rooms available.

Kelly's Hostel 25 Summerhill South, off Douglas St (IHO) ⓣ021/477 2124, ⓔkellyshostel@hotmail.com. Small, friendly and colourful hostel. Cable TV dominates the common room. Laundry facilities and bike rental. Dorm, twin and family rooms available.

Kinlay House Shandon (IHH) ⓣ021/450 8966, ⓦwww.kinlayhouse.ie. Very clean, friendly and efficiently run hostel, with laundry facilities. Price includes breakfast. Dorms, singles and twin rooms. Internet access and bike rental also available.

Sheila's of Cork Belgrave Place, Wellington Rd (IHH) ⓣ021/450 5562, ⓦwww.sheilashostel.ie. A central, friendly and well-run hostel with good cooking and laundry facilities, breakfast, sauna, bike rental and Internet facilities, and en-suite twin rooms available.

Self-catering apartments

Deans Hall Crosses Green, nr St Finbarre's Cathedral ⓣ021/431 2623, ⓦwww.deanshall.com. Student accommodation let to visitors in the summer. Central, clean, well-equipped three-bedroom (€125/night, €580/week) and five-bedroom (€180/night, €620/week) apartments with TV, phones and large living areas, set around a landscaped courtyard; laundry facilities on site. Rooms also available on a B&B basis (❷). Open mid-June to early Sept.

Isaac's 48 MacCurtain St ⓣ021/450 8388, ⓦwww.isaacs.ie. Well-appointed two-bedroom (€120/night, €550/week in high season) and three-bedroom (€150/night, €650/week in high season) apartments in this former hostel, each with fully fitted kitchen, spacious living/dining area, TV and phone. Hotel rooms (❺) also available.

The City

Cork has no really spectacular sights, but it's a fine place to wander around, with many evocative remnants of a great mercantile past. The city centre is essentially the island, with its quaysides, pretty bridges and the narrow alleys of the city's medieval core, plus a segment to the north of the River Lee that has MacCurtain Street as its central thoroughfare, and the lanes leading up to Shandon. The ambience and sense of place are enjoyable in themselves, and for those with a taste for it – and with shoe leather to spare – there's plenty of nineteenth-century **Gothic church architecture** to see along the river banks, giving the city a rhythmic architectural cohesion. Both Pugin and Pain are very much in evidence, Pugin in the brilliant Revivalist essay of the Church of St Peter and St Paul just off St Patrick's Street in the centre, and Pain in the Church of the Most Holy Trinity on Father Matthew Quay, with its handsome lantern spire, and in St Patrick's Church out to the northeast on Lower Glanmire Road. Best of all is William Burges's **St Finbarre's Cathedral** (Mon–Sat: April–Sept 10am–5.30pm; Oct–March 10am–12.45pm & 2–5pm; free; ⓣ021/496 3387 to book a guided tour), obsessively detailed, with its impressive French Gothic spire providing a grand silhouette on the southwest shoulder of the city.

The island

St Patrick's Street (aka Patrick Street) and **Grand Parade** form the modern commercial heart of the city, with a healthy smattering of modish boutiques and major chainstores cohabiting quite happily with modest traditional businesses. To the north of St Patrick's Street lie the pedestrianized laneways of **French Church Street**, **Carey's Lane** and **Paul Street**, busy with restaurants, cafés and boutiques; tucked away to the south are the pungent food stalls of the covered **English Market**, which is well worth wandering through even if you don't need to stock up your larder. Stronger stimulation is provided across Grand Parade at the **Beamish Brewery** on South Main Street, where they've been brewing porter, or stout, since the seventeenth century. Their tours (April–Oct Tues & Thurs 10.30am & noon; Nov–March Thurs 11am; €5; ⓦwww.beamish.ie) end up, not surprisingly, with a sample of the black stuff.

The city's major set-piece sight – and for what it's worth, the second most important gallery in the Republic – is the **Crawford Municipal Art Gallery**, next to the Opera House in Emmet Place on the north side of Patrick Street (Mon–Sat 10am–5pm; free). Its permanent collection of Irish art, though far from compulsory viewing, could happily while away an hour and more of your time, and the gallery hosts some interesting temporary exhibitions of Irish and international art as well as an excellent café (see p.344). Renovations of the gallery are ongoing, and many works, including paintings by Walter Osborne and Louis le Brocquy, are yet to come out of storage.

The lion's share of the collection is housed on the first floor, where, in the landing area, *Ulysses and a Companion Fleeing the Cave of Polyphemus* (1776), a complex allegory by Cork's greatest and most troubled painter, **James Barry**, takes pride of place. Barry depicted himself as the companion, with his friend and patron, the statesman Edmund Burke, as Ulysses, raising his index finger to counsel caution – to no avail. The outspoken nationalist Barry was the only artist ever to achieve expulsion from London's Royal Academy, and was ostracized as a result. Opposite hangs a fascinating *View of Cork*, painted in around 1780 by **Nathaniel Grogan**. You can pick out the waterway that is now Patrick Street, the 1724 Custom House (with a Union Jack in the courtyard), which is now the gallery you're visiting, and the Dutch-style houses on the quays, evidence of Cork's role in expanding Anglo-Dutch trading influence in the North Atlantic.

Among some sentimentally cloying nineteenth- and twentieth-century works, the Gibson Galleries beyond shelter fine representative works by **Jack B. Yeats** and **Sean Keating**. Look out for the former's *Returning from the Bathe, Mid-day*, painted in 1948 and typical of his expressionist late work, a joyful melange of bright, summery colours and swift brush-strokes. Though obviously posed in a studio, Keating's *Men of the South* (1921) achieves the restrained grandeur of a classical frieze, depicting a grim-faced IRA column waiting to ambush British soldiers.

The eastern, downstream end of the island is the more clearly defined: many of its quays are still in use, and it's here that you get the best sense of the old port city. In the west the island peters out in a predominantly residential area. Heading in this direction, though, you can follow the signs off Western Road for **Fitzgerald Park**, home of the **Cork Public Museum** (June–Aug Mon–Fri 11am–1pm & 2.15–6pm, Sun 3–5pm; rest of year Mon–Fri 11am–1pm & 2.15–5pm, Sun 3–5pm; closed bank holiday weekends; free), about a mile out of the city centre; it is easily combined with a trip to Cork Gaol (see below). Primarily a museum of Cork's history, it has an excellent commentary on the role of local characters and events in the Republican movement. There are exhibits of archaeological and geological finds, too, and sections on local trades and crafts, notably silverware and glassware.

Shandon and the northside

North of the River Lee is the area known as **Shandon**, a reminder of Cork's status as the most important port in Europe for dairy products in the eighteenth and nineteenth centuries. To get there, head up John Redmond Street, or simply aim for the giant fish atop the church tower. The most striking survival is the nineteenth-century Doric portico of the **Cork Butter Exchange**, while the old **butter market** itself sits like a generously proportioned butter tub in a cobbled square and now houses the Firkin Crane Theatre. The fascinating story of the trade and its impact on the development of the city is told in the adjacent **Butter Museum** (May–Sept daily 10am–1pm & 2–5pm; €3). The museum begins with dairy culture in early Ireland, as illustrated by a keg of bog butter: on remote grazing lands, milk was churned into butter on the spot and preserved in the bogs for later use; to this day, such kegs are often turned over by peat-cutters, who'll swear the butter is still edible. In the eighteenth century, thanks to its fertile hinterland and its position on the largest natural harbour in the northern hemisphere, Cork became the main provisioning port in the Atlantic for both the British Navy and trade convoys, with most Cork butter ending up in the West Indies. In the following century, the city managed to ride out the general agricultural collapse precipitated by the Napoleonic Wars and the Famine, by gearing the butter trade to the English market through rigorous controls – the butter-market building you see outside was where barrels were washed and weighed at this time, to avoid underhand practices by farmers. The story is brought up to date with a video on the successful development of the Kerrygold brand by tycoon and museum sponsor, Tony (now Sir Antony) O'Reilly.

This part of town is also worth a visit for the pleasant Georgian church of **St Anne's Shandon**, easily distinguishable from all over Cork city by its weather vane – an eleven-foot salmon. The church is perhaps most famous for its bells, which feature in the verse of Father Prout, a nineteenth-century fictional character devised by an ex-Jesuit to satirize the Church. You can climb its tower (daily: May–Sept 10am–6pm; Oct–April 10am–5pm; €5) for excellent views and ring the bells – a good stock of sheet tunes is provided.

To the west of here is an area known as Sunday's Well, and **Cork City Gaol** (daily: March–Oct 9.30am–6pm; Nov–Feb 10am–5pm; €5; Ⓦ www.corkcitygaol.com). It's a good thirty minutes' walk from the city centre, up the hill from North

Mall. A lively taped tour takes you through the prison, focusing on social history in a way that is both engaging and enlightening. It's occasionally threaded with characters of national importance, all vividly brought to life by a dramatic audio-visual finale. The gaol also houses the **Radio Museum Experience** (same times and price) which uses similarly engaging techniques to convey the tremendous importance of the development of the wireless. The museum also has a large collection of early radios, a wealth of popular archival recordings and a strangely affectionate and evocative reconstruction of the first radio station in Cork. There's a pleasant walk from here to Fitzgerald Park: turn right as you leave the prison, left, right and then left down a flight of steps and over the Shaky Bridge.

Eating

Cork doesn't have a wide range of cuisines for you to choose from – the main influence is Mediterranean – but it does have a high standard of food on offer; many **cafés** and **restaurants** serve dishes made from organic local produce, and there are plenty of seafood and vegetarian options. Places like the *Ivory Tower*, *Café Paradiso*, *Isaac's* and, above all, the *Crawford Gallery Café* epitomize the creativity of Cork's culinary scene, and their influence permeates the city's more affordable establishments. The best eating places come in a wide variety of guises, with all manner of hybrid café-bistros, bar-restaurants and café-galleries. The easiest way to distinguish them is by cost: the prices of the places listed below are indicated by the terms "Cheap" (under €10 for a main course); "Moderate" (€10–15); and "Expensive" (over €15).

If you're self-catering or just fancy a takeaway picnic on a sunny day, the **English Market**, located between Grand Parade and Princes Street with entrances off both, is a wonderful place to share in the city's enthusiasm for all things culinary. Here, the cosmopolitan rubs shoulder with the decidedly unpretentious; stalls specializing in the finest olive oils and cheeses jostle for space among the racks of tripe and bacon.

The island

Bodega and Café-Bar-Deli Cornmarket St. The *Bodega* bar has opened a branch of the successful Dublin restaurant in its extension, offering the same winning formula of simple food well done – some interesting starters, pastas, pizzas, Mediterranean salads and mouthwatering desserts. *Café-Bar-Deli* is only open Wed–Sun evenings at the moment, but *Bodega* takes its bar food from the *CBD* menu every evening, as well as offering lunch Mon–Fri, brunch Sat & Sun and cheap deals such as pizza and beer for €10 Wed–Fri early evenings. Cheap–moderate.

Bully's 40 Paul St ☎021/427 3555. Plain, simple wine bar serving burgers, pizzas, fresh pasta and fish; popular with families. Cheap–moderate.

Casanova 1st Floor, Triskel Arts Centre, Tobin St ☎021/427 5777. Congenial bar-trattoria, with attractively simple decor and cool sounds, serving a limited menu of excellent, authentic Italian food – try the linguine with mussels or the stuffed aubergines – as well as a good range of Italian wines and beers. Moderate.

The Crawford Municipal Art Gallery Café Emmet Place ☎021/427 4415. The gallery café is an affordable offshoot of *Ballymaloe House* near Cloyne, famous for taking traditional Irish cooking to new heights (see p.351). You can lunch on snacks such as delicious pâté and salad, more substantial dishes like confit of duck or push the boat right out with three courses (soup, main course and dessert) for €18. And after a short spin round the gallery, you might well find yourself tempted back for tea and cake. Mon–Sat 10am–5pm. Cheap–moderate.

The Farm Gate Café Upstairs in the English Market, Princes St. Great for affordable lunches and teas: lots of salads, savoury tarts, pastas and plenty of seafood, with the emphasis on using fresh, local produce; in line with tradition, they also serve tripe and *drisheen* (a kind of black pudding). Listen to the pianist (Mon, Wed & Fri lunchtime) as you eat and watch the market below. Closed Sun. Cheap–moderate.

Fellini's Carey's Lane. Comfortably dishevelled café atmosphere with papers to read and seating inside and out; soups, salads, sandwiches, coffees and teas. One of the few places open all day on a Sunday, when it's a popular spot for brunch. Cheap.

The Gingerbread House Paul St. Large, efficient but laid-back self-service café, great for soaking up the Paul Street scene. Cheap, filling and tasty pizza slices, tartlettes, doorstep sandwiches, soups and coffees. Daily till 10pm. Cheap.

Gino's Winthrop St. Good cheap pizzas and home-made ice cream. Cheap.

The Ivory Tower The Exchange Buildings, 35 Princes St ⊕021/427 4665. The place to go to treat yourself: an adventurous menu specializing in wild and organic food. Exquisite. Five-course set menu €50. Closed Mon & Tues. Expensive.

Jacques Phoenix St, a lane off Pembroke St by the GPO ⊕021/427 7387. Imaginative restaurant with excellent reputation; mouthwatering food with a Mediterranean influence. Mon–Fri for lunch, Tues–Sat for dinner (early-bird two-course menu 6–7pm). Expensive.

Kafka's 7 Maylor St. Great veggie and non-veggie breakfasts, and a huge range of tasty baguettes, burgers, sandwiches and coffee. Handy for the bus station. Closed Sun. Cheap.

Leonardo's Bistro 97 South Main St ⊕021/427 9969. Informal bistro-restaurant with a convivial atmosphere serving a good range of pizza, pasta, tortillas, enchilladas, steaks, fish and fajitas. Lunch cheap–moderate; dinner moderate–expensive.

Café Mexicana Carey's Lane ⊕021/427 6433. Largely authentic Mexican restaurant with relaxing, warm decor and a party atmosphere. Moderate.

Oz Cork Grand Parade ⊕021/427 2711. No kangaroo steaks, but the Australian theme is evident in the brightly coloured tiles that decorate this cheap and popular café-bistro and in the variety of world cuisine on offer: pasta, noodles, burgers, panini and salads, as well as gourmet coffees and teas. Cheap.

Café Paradiso 16 Lancaster Quay, Western Rd ⊕021/427 7939. Busy, informal restaurant serving excellent and innovative Mediterranean-influenced vegetarian and vegan cuisine. Closed Sun & Mon. Moderate lunches; expensive dinners.

Strasbourg's Goose 17–18 French Church St ⊕021/427 9534. Lively, informal restaurant popular with a mixed young crowd; casual, pavement café atmosphere, and absolutely no anxieties about serving chips and beer with all sorts of dishes, including steaks, fish and homemade burgers. Moderate.

Tribes Tuckey St. Smoky coffee bar for caffeine diehards. Over thirty varieties of coffee, and many herbal teas. Open late (till 4am Thurs–Sat); closed Sun. Cheap.

Wild Ways 21 Princes St. Friendly organic sandwich shop and coffee bar, offering good breakfasts, and delicious wraps, rolls and soups for lunch. Closed Sun. Cheap.

Off-island

The Douglas Hide 63 Douglas St ⊕021/431 5695). The pun (Douglas Hyde was founder of the Gaelic League, who became Ireland's first president) should give it away – the most civilized bar in Cork, with fine art on the walls, laid-back ambience and top-notch food, such as spicy Moroccan chicken, goat's cheese and strawberry salad, and fish and pasta of the day. Worth booking ahead, especially at weekends. Dinner Tues–Sun, lunch Mon–Fri & Sun. Moderate.

Isaac's MacCurtain St ⊕021/450 3805. Deservedly popular restaurant with a buzzy atmosphere. Light, delicious, mostly Mediterranean-style food, with a good range of salads, grilled meats, curries, pizzas and pasta. High emphasis on local and organic produce. Moderate.

The Quay Co-op 24 Sullivan's Quay ⊕021/431 7026. Spacious self-service café above a health-food store, serving delicious, large vegetarian and vegan meals (and catering for many other dietary requirements), great salads, soups, puddings, breakfasts and teas. Mon–Sat 9am–9pm. Cheap.

Star Anise Bridge St ⊕021/455 1635. Well-regarded, bright orange café-restaurant serving excellent modern food such as cod tempura and slow-cooked lamb. Tues–Fri breakfast and lunch, including a wide range of energy juices; Tues–Sat dinner. Cheap daytimes, expensive evenings.

A Taste of Thailand 8 Bridge St ⊕021/450 5404. Cosy, dimly lit Thai restaurant, where the dishes themselves aren't all that authentic, but the flavours certainly are – try the tasty beef salad with mangoes and crispy noodles. Moderate.

Tigh Fili Arts Centre Thompson House, MacCurtain St. Calm and congenial art gallery/café serving vegetarian snacks and lunches. Soup, sandwiches, pastas and quiches, plus delightful cakes. Cheap.

Nightlife and entertainment

Cork has several **all-round venues** for entertainment and the arts. The hub of alternative artistic activity is the **Triskel Arts Centre**, down narrow and dingy Tobin Street, between Grand Parade and South Main Street (Ⓣ021/427 2022, Ⓦwww.iol.ie/triskel). It has changing exhibitions of contemporary art, a cinema showing arthouse films, and a continuous programme of gigs, DJ nights, comedy, drama, performance art and poetry readings. It's also an excellent source of information about what's on in the city. The leading mainstream theatre is **Cork Opera House** in Emmet Place (Ⓣ021/427 0022, Ⓦwww.corkoperahouse.ie), which puts on high-quality drama, jazz and pop concerts, dance, opera and comedy; the attached **Half Moon Theatre** (Ⓦwww.halfmoontheatre.ie) has a more eclectic programme of drama, comedy and music, and, among a largely uninspiring selection of mainstream discos, is the city's most interesting **club** venue, with a wildly varied weekly roster of DJs and live acts. The Granary, Mardyke (Ⓣ021/490 4275), offers a range of small-scale **drama** productions, while the Firkin Crane Theatre at the Institute for Choreography and Dance, O'Connell Square, Shandon (Ⓣ021/450 1673), is the best spot to catch classical and contemporary **dance**. **Classical concerts** are held at the School of Music, on Union Quay, and the City Hall, Anglesea Street, and the excellent **arthouse cinema**, Kino, on Washington Street (Ⓣ021/427 1571) screens films throughout the year. For information on film, drama and music performances, ask at the tourist office or consult the *Irish Examiner*, available in newsagents, or the free monthly leaflet, *Whazon* (Ⓦwww.whazon.com), available in cafés and arts venues around the city.

There are plenty of good watering-holes in the city, and if all you want is a drink, you won't need a guide to find somewhere – though a couple of the city's older **pubs** (mentioned below) are worth seeking out for their atmosphere. Many bars have **music**, traditional or otherwise: the following list should give some good pointers on where to find the best of this. Wherever you end up, this is not a difficult town in which to enjoy yourself.

Pubs and bars

An Bodhrán 42 Oliver Plunkett St. Atmospheric small pub, all bare wood and stone, with live traditional music, mostly ballad sessions, every night.

An Brog Oliver Plunkett St. Dark, grungy, sprawling and packed with students, who come for the late bar (till around 1.30am every night) and the DJs at weekends.

An Spailpín Fánac 28 South Main St. Rambling, scruffy bar with live music every night except Thurs, mostly traditional sessions but also singer-songwriters (some with an admission charge).

Bodega Cornmarket St. Cork's most stylish bar, with a wonderfully bold, barn-like interior that pulls in a friendly, mixed and surprisingly unpretentious crowd. DJs Fri & Sat (late bar till 2am) with dancing in the upstairs room Sat, rotating art exhibitions and great food – see p.344.

Counihan's Pembroke St, by the GPO. Two styles under one large roof: welcoming, old-fashioned, tile-floored pub downstairs, with trad on Sun nights and a bright, trendy bar upstairs with comfy sofas.

The Douglas Hide 63 Douglas St. Laid-back bar with a refreshingly unpretentious contemporary interior and a friendly atmosphere; open-mike session and resident acoustic band Mon night.

Franciscan Well 12A North Mall. Micro-brewery on the site of a thirteenth-century Franciscan monastery. Lager, ale, stout and wheat beer produced on the premises, and there's a good selecton of bottled beers too. The no-frills beer yard to the rear is a pleasant option in summer, with barbecues on Thurs evenings. Trad sessions Mon nights.

Fred Zeppelin's 8 Parliament St. Live gig and DJ venue for all styles of music; it has a touch of the bikers' hangout about it, but attracts a mixed clientele. Tues is open-mike night for singer-songwriters. Happy hour Mon–Fri & Sun till 8pm.

Gable's 32 Douglas St. Regular bar with good Asian and veggie food, and traditional music and singing on Wed, Thurs and Sun.

The Lobby Union Quay, by Parnell Bridge Ⓣ021/431 1113, Ⓦwww.lobby.ie. This is one of Cork's top venues and a great spot to catch live

music year round. Free traditional sessions (Tues & Fri) and acoustic (Mon & Wed) take place in the bar downstairs, and all manner of gigs upstairs, mostly singer-songwriters, but also occasional jazz and indie rock (Wed, Thurs, Fri & Sat), for which there's a cover charge. *Charlie's* next door hosts popular traditional sessions on Sun afternoon.
The Long Valley Winthrop St. Excellent traditional bar; something of a one-off and a locals' favourite, with sessions upstairs Fri & Sat.
The Ovens 18 Oliver Plunkett St. This old, wood-panelled bar has been tastefully revamped, and it's still a friendly place for a quiet drink or to watch some sport.
The Roundy 1 Castle St. Fashionable and stylish bar on this landmark (rounded) corner with Grand Parade, offering corner-hugging, leather-clad bench seating, regular DJs and a wide range of beers.
Scott's Oliver Plunkett St, corner of Caroline St. Generic slick and airy modern bar, but pleasant enough, with big leather sofas and decent bar food. The club upstairs plays mainstream pop Thurs–Sat, mellower R'n'B and soul on Sun.
The Vineyard Market Lane, off Patrick St. Stylish, airy interior decorated with iconic Irish characters from Beckett to Bacon; also serves sandwiches and lunches (except on Sun) and hosts regular salsa and tango nights.

Listings

Airlines Aer Lingus ⓣ021/432 7155; British Airways ⓣ1800/626747; Ryanair ⓣ01/609 7800.
Airport information ⓣ021/431 3131.
Banks Branches of the Allied Irish Bank and Bank of Ireland on Patrick St and Bridge St.
Bike rental CycleScene, 396 Blarney St ⓣ021/430 1183; Rothar Cycles, 55 Barrack St ⓣ021/431 3133.
Bookshops The Cork Bookshop, Carey's Lane; Eason's, 113/115 Patrick St; Liam Russell, Oliver Plunkett St; Mercier Bookshop, Academy St; Waterstones, 69 Patrick St. Good Yarns in the English Market sells new and secondhand books and does book exchange.
Bureau de change At the tourist office and at *Sheila's Hostel.*
Car rental Besides the big multinationals at Cork Airport, there are several smaller and usually cheaper local outfits, including Car Rental Ireland, 43 MacCurtain St (ⓣ021/496 3456) and Monahan Rd (ⓣ021/496 2277), and Great Island Car Rentals, 47 MacCurtain St (ⓣ021/450 3536 or 481 1609).
Ferry companies Brittany Ferries, 42 Grand Parade ⓣ021/437 8401; Swansea–Cork Ferries, 52 South Mall ⓣ1800/620397; see "Getting there" in "Basics" for full details.
Gaelic football and hurling Cork is one of the few counties that's strong on both Gaelic games, with one of the country's major stadiums at Parc Ui Chaoimh, 1 mile east of the centre off Centre Park Rd. For fixtures, consult the *Irish Examiner* or phone ⓣ021/496 3311.
Gay information Cork Gay Community Development Company (ⓣ021/427 8470) runs a helpline (Wed & Fri 7–9pm ⓣ021/427 1087) and *The Other Place*, a simple café and resource centre at 8 South Main St (Mon–Sat 11.30am–5pm), which also hosts a nightclub Fri–Sun nights. Linc, 11A White St (ⓣ021/480 8600), is Cork's lesbian resource centre, with drop-ins on Tues (noon–4pm) & Thurs (8–10pm), and a film club on the first Tues of the month. Cork's gay bars are *Loafers*, 26 Douglas St, with a beer garden and women's night on Thurs, and *Taboo*, Faulkner's Lane, off Patrick St, and gay and lesbian accommodation is available at *Roman House*, 3 St John's Terrace (ⓣ021/450 3606), and *Emerson House*, 2 Clarence Terr (ⓣ086/834 0891).
Helplines Rape Crisis Centre, Camden Place ⓣ1800/496496; Samaritans, Coach St ⓣ021/427 1323.
Hospital Cork University Hospital, Wilton Rd ⓣ021/454 6400.
Internet access Internet Exchange, Paul St and Wood St, off Washington St (ⓣ021/425 4666, ⓦwebworkhouse.com) and 8 Winthrop St (ⓣ021/427 3090); and at the hostels.
Laundry Cork Launderette Service, 14 MacCurtain St, next door to the Everyman Palace theatre ⓣ021/450 1421.
Left luggage At the Bus Éireann station (Mon–Fri 8.35am–6.15pm, Sat 9.30am–6.15pm, plus Sun 9am–6pm in summer; €1.90 for the first day, €1.25 for each subsequent day) and at the hostels.
Music The Living Tradition, 40 MacCurtain St (ⓣ021/450 2040, ⓦwww.thelivingtradition.com), sells a great range of Irish and world music on CD and cassette, as well as sheet music and traditional instruments such as *bodhráns* and tin whistles.
Pharmacy Phelan's Late Night Pharmacy, 9 Patrick St ⓣ021/427 2511.

Swimming pool Gus Healy Swimming Pool, Douglas Rd ⓣ021/429 3073.
Taxis ABC ⓣ021/496 1961; Blue Cabs ⓣ021/439 3939; Cork Taxi Co-op ⓣ021/427 2222; and there's a rank on Patrick St.

Travel agents USIT have two offices in Cork: at 66 Oliver Plunkett St (ⓣ021/427 0900), and UCC Student Travel, near The Boole Library, University College (ⓣ021/490 2293).

East Cork

The varied coast of **East Cork** encompasses islands, mudflats, lagoons, beaches and cliffs as it meanders its way to Youghal, thirty miles or so distant on the Waterford border, and there are plenty of points of interest as you pass through. A trip across the harbour to **Fota Island**, with its wild animals and eighteenth-century Classicism, and **Cobh**, a pretty harbour town on Great Island, will allow you to get back in the evening early enough to take advantage of Cork's nightlife. On the way to the quaint port of **Youghal** – with its colourful maritime history and scenic location – there are a string of places worth a brief stop, including **Midleton**, the home of Jameson whiskey, and the beaches at **Ballycotton** and **Garryvoe**.

Fota and Cobh

A visit to Fota and Cobh can easily be managed in a day by **train** from Cork, the journey taking you across the mudflats of an estuary teeming with birdlife. **Fota House** (Mon–Sat 10am–6pm, Sun 11am–6pm; €5, parking €2; ⓦwww.fotahouse.com), an elegant, mostly early-nineteenth-century hunting lodge, has only recently been reopened to the public, and the painstaking restoration work is ongoing, with hopes of soon opening the upper floors and coach house. For the moment, visits are confined to the minimally furnished but extravagantly decorated ground floor, where good audio-visuals convey the reminiscences of gardeners and housekeepers who worked on the estate, the history and architectural quirks of the house and the conservation of the arboretum, along with a plant catalogue. The highlights are the **entrance hall**, a beautifully symmetrical space divided by striking ochre columns of *scagliola* (imitation marble), and the ceiling of the **dining room**, with its gilded plasterwork birds and musical instruments and delicately painted cherubs and floral motifs. Before visiting the **servants' quarters** and their impressive octagonal game larder, be sure to catch the AV in the study, which explains such features as the gaps at the top of the windows of the butler's servery – so that food smells would tantalize the poor servants rather than the house guests. There's a nice little café in the billiards room, where you can refresh yourself before pressing on to the estate's **arboretum** (same times as house; free). Laid out in the mid-nineteenth century, it's one of the most important in Europe and at its best in April and May. There's a great variety of rare and exotic flowering shrubs and trees here, including some magnificent Lebanese cedars, a Victorian fernery and a lush, almost tropical lake.

The adjacent **Fota Wildlife Park** (mid-March to Oct Mon–Sat 10am–6pm, Sun 11am–6pm; Nov to mid-Dec & Jan to mid-March Sat 10am–6pm, Sun 11am–6pm; €7; ⓦwww.fotawildlife.ie) is a small, pleasant park, renowned for its success in breeding cheetahs, which, along with apes, giraffes, red pandas and zebras, wander about the landscaped former estate of Fota House.

Cobh

Rejoining the train at Fota takes you out to **COBH**, which is held in a quaint cup of land with steep, narrow streets climbing the hill to **St Colman's Cathedral**. This Neo-Gothic monster dominates the town, its entrance giving marvellous views out across the great curve of the bay to Spike Island. Thanks to its fine natural harbour, Cobh has long been an important **port**: it served as an assembly place for ships during the Napoleonic Wars and was a major departure point for steamers carrying emigrants to America during the nineteenth century and convicts to Australia. The first-ever transatlantic steamer sailed from here in 1838, and the *Titanic* called in on her ill-fated voyage. Cobh was also the last port of call for the *Lusitania* before she was sunk off the Old Head of Kinsale (see p.357); many of the victims' bodies were brought back to Cobh for burial and a monument to the dead stands in Casement Square. Cobh's dramatic maritime history is retold at its excellent **heritage centre** at the train station, the **Queenstown Story** (daily: March–Oct 10am–6pm; Nov–Feb 10am–5pm; €5; Ⓦwww.cobhheritage.com). If your appetite for salty tales and memorabilia still hasn't been sated, get along to the **Cobh Museum** (Easter–Oct Mon–Sat 11am–1pm & 2–6pm, Sun 3–6pm; €1.50), housed in a nineteenth-century Presbyterian church on the west side of the town centre. Today the port is still used by a substantial fishing fleet. From September to February, when it is awash with fishermen, the town's character changes completely.

First and foremost, though, Cobh is a holiday resort, and a historic one at that. Ireland's first yacht club was established here in 1720, and from 1830 onwards the town was a popular health resort, imitative of English Regency resorts like Brighton, a style reflected in its architecture. The main square is flanked by brightly painted Victorian town houses, and the place has a robust cheerfulness – though none of the cosmopolitan flavour of harbours further west. It attracts holidaying Irish families and offers pitch and putt, tennis, swimming and a stony beach. The **International Sailing Centre** on East Beach (Ⓣ021/481 1237, Ⓦwww.sailcork.com) runs courses in sailing, canoeing and wind-surfing. There's a **regatta** weekend in mid-August, and the third week in July sees the **Ford Week** of yachting across the harbour in Crosshaven (alternate summers; for latest details, check with the tourist office); best observation points are reckoned to be Ringabella, Fennel's Bay, Myrtleville or Roche's Point. Any other time in the summer you can at least take a **harbour boat trip** through Marine Transport Services, Atlantic Quay (Ⓣ021/481 1485; €5).

Practicalities

Cobh's helpful **tourist office** (summer Mon–Fri 9.30am–5.30pm, Sat & Sun 11am–5pm; winter Mon–Fri 9.30am–5.30pm, Sat & Sun 1–5pm; Ⓣ021/481 3301, Ⓦwww.cobhharbourchamber.ie), which also offers **Internet access**, shares the old yacht club in the town centre with the **Sirius Art Centre** (Ⓣ021/481 3790), home to some interesting art exhibitions, literature events and classical and traditional concerts. The engaging and enterprising Michael Martin (Ⓣ021/481 5211, Ⓦwww.titanic-trail.com) runs *Titanic*-themed **walking tours** (daily 11am, starting from the *Commodore Hotel*; 75min; €7.50) and ghost walks (every Fri 9.30pm from *Pillars Bar*, 75min; €7.50).

Hostel accommodation is available at *Beechmount* (IHO; Ⓣ021/481 2177, Ⓦwww.beechmounthostel.com), where breakfast is included in the price and you can **rent bikes**. Pick of the scores of **B&Bs** include *Ardeen*, 3 Harbour Hill (Ⓣ021/481 1803; ❷), with great views from its lofty position near the cathedral and good child reductions; *Ard na Laoi*, a smartly kept house opposite

Cork harbour ferry

If you want to head west from Cobh along the coast towards Kinsale and beyond, or if you want to cut around twenty minutes' driving time off your return to Cork city, you can take a five-minute **ferry** to Glenbrook near Passage West from Carrigaloe, a couple of miles north of Cobh as you head back up towards the N25. Services start at 7.15am from Carrigaloe and run about every ten minutes till the last ferry at 12.15am from Glenbrook (car €4.50 return, €3.50 single; adult €0.70 each way; bikes carried free).

and *Seafield*, in a grand period house to the west of the centre on Lower Road (Ⓣ021/481 1563; ❷). Next to the heritage centre stands *Waters Edge* (Ⓣ021/481 5566, Ⓦwww.watersedgehotel.ie; ❼, half-board deals available), a tastefully decorated **hotel**, where the spacious bedrooms have seafront verandas and the recommended *Jacobs Ladder* **restaurant** specializes in seafood and local produce. The latter's main competition comes from the **Titanic Bar & Restaurant**, but this one's almost a tourist sight in itself: lottery winner Vincent Kearney spent his loot on recreating the *Titanic*'s Verandah Café, complete with ivy trellises and Villeroy and Bosch tiling, in the building from which the ill-fated liner's last passengers embarked. The menu features dishes such as "Titanic Surf'n'Turf", beef fillet and prawns on lemon and saffron couscous, while downstairs the ornate, wood-panelled bar has simple food and a lovely waterside deck.

Midleton, Cloyne and Ballycotton Bay

The cheery market town of **MIDLETON**, about ten miles east of Cork, is best known for being the home of Jameson Irish whiskey. The **Old Midleton Distillery** tour is a highly polished promotional affair, culminating in a whiskey-tasting session (daily: March–Oct 10am–6pm, last admission 4.30pm; Nov–Feb tours at 11.30am, 2.30pm & 4pm; €5.70), and there's an on-site **tourist office** (summer Mon–Fri 9.30am–5.30pm, Sat & Sun 9.30am–1pm & 2–5.30pm; Ⓣ021/461 3702). The town and the surrounding area are building a reputation for **crafts** workshops – check out the Courtyard Craft Centre, 8 Main St (Ⓣ021/463 4644), where you can also pick up a copy of the *East Cork Creates* leaflet. The best **place to eat** is *The Farm Gate*, Coolbawn, off the west side of Main Street near the distillery (Ⓣ021/463 2771; closed Mon–Wed evenings & all Sun), a deli and restaurant selling and serving fresh local produce – which is also on sale at the Saturday-morning farmers' market, held behind the courthouse off Main Street. For accommodation, try the **hostel** *An Stór*, Drury's Avenue (IHH; Ⓣ021/463 3106; ❶), a converted mill off Main Street, offering dorms, twin and family rooms, as well as **bike rental**.

Four miles to the south is the sleepy, historic village of **CLOYNE**. One of Ireland's earliest Christian foundations, the monastery of St Colman, was established here in the sixth century. In medieval times the village that grouped around it continued to be of religious importance with the establishment of the See of Cloyne, a diocese which extended well into County Limerick. Reminders of this era, though, are few. There's a fine tenth-century **round tower**, from where, 100ft up, there are superb views (key from Cathedral House; €1.25), and you can also visit the Church of Ireland **St Colman's Cathedral**, a large building of warm, mottled stone originally built in 1250 but disappointingly restored in the nineteenth century. Inside is the alabaster tomb of George Berkeley, the famous philosopher who was bishop here from 1734 to 1753.

Off the Cloyne–Ballycotton road lies **Ballymaloe House** (☎021/465 2531, Ⓦwww.ballymaloe.com; ❼, half-board deals available), the most famous **restaurant** in Ireland, serving exceptional modern Irish cuisine using carefully sourced local ingredients. There's much more to this grand enterprise than just a restaurant: **accommodation** in the vine-covered, originally fifteenth-century manor house and adjacent courtyard mixes country-house style with contemporary features, and there's a heated outdoor pool, five-hole golf course and tennis court in the extensive grounds. Attached to the house is a daytime café and shop, selling crafts and, of course, kitchenware; the **cookery school** (☎021/464 6785, Ⓦwww.cookingisfun.ie) runs prestigious twelve-week certificate courses as well as a host of short courses; and you can even visit the cookery school's restored nineteenth-century **gardens**, featuring the largest formal herb garden in Ireland and a Celtic maze (April–Sept daily 11am–6pm; €5).

Five miles on from Cloyne, **BALLYCOTTON** is a pleasant enough spot, with a little quayside, fine cliff walks for miles to the west and a beach half a mile away. There's fine guesthouse **accommodation** at *Spanish Point Restaurant* (☎021/464 6177; closed Jan to mid-March; ❸): bright and airy, it's in a terrific spot and has a beautiful conservatory/dining room overlooking **Ballycotton Bay**. North around the bay are the holiday villages of **Shanagarry** and **Garryvoe**. Garryvoe **beach** is very long and sandy, but it's beset by caravans advancing upon the shore and very busy during high season. To the east of here the bay is flat and of interest only to birdwatchers, its reed-infested estuary now a protected **bird sanctuary**.

Youghal

YOUGHAL is an ancient port at the mouth of the River Blackwater, where the counties of Cork and Waterford meet. In a small way it combines the richness of the Blackwater towns with the prettiness of Kinsale and Cobh, and can boast a string of clean sandy beaches to the west of town. A quiet, picturesque resort, popular with holidaying Irish families, Youghal has a colourful history and some fine architecture to remember it by; even if you're en route elsewhere, it's worth stopping off to take in some of the character of the place.

Some history

Youghal's walls were first built by the Norman settlers who established the town, but those which stand today were erected by Edward I in 1275. From medieval times the town prospered as one of Ireland's leading ports, trading with the Continent – particularly France – and with England. Political disturbances and trade restrictions imposed on Irish ports by the English Crown, however, meant the town's growth began to slow in the mid-sixteenth century. It fell into the hands of the Earl of Desmond, and in 1579 the "Rebel" Earl (rebelling against Elizabeth I) sacked and burned the place. After Desmond's death, Youghal was part of the 40,000 acres granted to Walter Raleigh during the Munster Plantations, with which Elizabeth hoped to control Ireland. Raleigh, though, had little interest in Youghal – though legend has it that he introduced the potato to Ireland here – selling his land to Richard Boyle, the "Great" Earl of Cork (and father of the scientist), who then greatly developed the town as he did all his newly acquired land. When Cromwell reached New Ross in 1649, the English garrison at Youghal went over to the Parliamentarian side, and so the town escaped destruction. Nonetheless, the port maintained its relative decline, though there is enough fine eighteenth-century architecture still standing to make it clear that a small but affluent class of merchants continued to prosper.

The Town

Youghal's most famous landmark is the **clock tower**, bridging the long, curvy main street, a superbly proportioned Georgian structure of warm, plum-coloured stone, which doubled as a prison. Steps leading off the tower climb the steep hill through little lanes to the top of the town, where the walls and turrets of the old defences still define the shape of the compact harbour.

The most charming buildings lie, in the main, on the landward side of North Main Street and in the lanes that run behind it. On North Main Street itself the **Red House**, built in 1710, is a fine example of domestic architecture, clearly showing the Dutch influence of the original merchant owner. Here, too, are seventeenth-century almshouses, built by Richard Boyle to house Protestant widows, and opposite stands **Tyntes Castle**, a fifteenth-century tower house that is now sadly dilapidated. Lanes off to the west of this end of Main Street lead to the Elizabethan **Myrtle Grove**, known as "Raleigh's House" as it was part of the extensive estates granted to him by Elizabeth I, one of the oldest unfortified houses in Ireland and, sadly, no longer open to the public.

Nearby, you'll find the **Collegiate Church of St Mary's**, a large, simple, thirteenth-century building, one of the few of such age still in use in Ireland. The building has been much altered over the centuries, but still has interesting medieval tombs and effigies. Particularly notable are the thirteenth-century monuments in the south transept (entrance is by a little door to the left as you walk up towards the church, or by the main door when open). Wrecked when the town was sacked by Desmond's men in 1579, they were later restored by Boyle, with the addition of effigies in seventeenth-century costume.

Towards the south end of town, just off Main Street and signposted from the tourist office, is **Fox's Lane Museum** (July & Aug Tues–Sat 10am–1pm & 2–6pm; rest of year open by prior appointment, call ⓣ024/91145; €2.50), which displays with illuminating clarity and imagination a collection of domestic gadgetry – everything from sausage-makers to petrol-fuelled irons and cucumber straighteners.

Practicalities

The very helpful **tourist office** and the attached heritage centre which recounts the port's history since the ninth century (€2), are on Market Square, just behind the harbour (June–Aug Mon–Fri 9am–6.30pm, Sat & Sun 9.30am–5pm; March–May, Sept & Oct Mon–Fri 9am–5.30pm, Sat & Sun 9.30am–5pm; Nov–Feb Mon–Fri 9am–5pm; ⓣ024/20170). There is an interesting **walking tour** of the town, which sets off from the tourist office (1hr 30min; June–Aug Mon–Sat at 11am; at other times, tours for groups of four or more can be arranged; €4.50). The tourist office also provides details of the town's summertime **festival**, which features a music weekend with street entertainment in late June, and a maritime weekend with raft races and more street music in late July, as well as the heritage week in late September, when art shows, story-telling and a flower festival accompany an international historical conference.

You'll find plenty of **B&Bs** along the main streets and around the quayside – try the elegant Georgian *Avonmore House* (ⓣ024/92617, ⓔavonmoreyoughal@eircom.net; ❷) or the well-maintained *Attracta* (ⓣ024/92062; April–Oct; ❷,

△ Cork city

with good child reductions), both on South Abbey, or *Roseville*, an attractive detached house and garden with good breakfasts, on New Catherine Street (Ⓣ024/92571, Ⓔrosevillebandb@eircom.net; ❷). There are more out on the Cork Road, including *Green Lawn* (Ⓣ024/93177; ❷), about two miles south of the centre. **Dorms**, as well as family and twin rooms, are available at *Evergreen House*, The Strand (IHH & IHO; Ⓣ024/92877, Ⓦwww.evergreenireland.com; ❶). For **hotel** accommodation, and for many of your other needs (see below), the outstanding choice is the spacious and tastefully decorated luxury bedrooms at *Aherne's*, on North Main Street (Ⓣ024/92424, Ⓦwww.ahernes.com; ❼), in the centre of town.

There's no shortage of **places to eat** in Youghal. *The Coffee Pot*, on North Main Street, just near the clock tower, serves coffee, cakes and good-value meals during the day, and at no. 61 on the same street, *Pak Fook* is a popular, spick-and-span Chinese restaurant, with a takeaway branch opposite (Ⓣ024/90668). The excellent restaurant at *Aherne's* is renowned for its fresh seafood, or you can choose from a scaled-down menu by the open fire in its very congenial **bar**. You'll find **music** of some sort in Youghal's pubs several nights a week during the summer, and at the weekends throughout the year; for the latest information, check the tourist office's weekly calendar of events. *The Nook* on North Main Street hosts sessions on Tuesday nights in summer and the *Walter Raleigh Hotel* at the south end of town offers traditional music, dancing and story-telling nights on Mondays and Thursdays in July and August; *Molly's* towards the south end of the main street boasts DJs and live bands. If you just want a quiet pint, head for the *Moby Dick* pub on the quays – Youghal was used as a location for the film of the same name, and inside you'll find memorabilia and photographs from the making of the film.

Inland Cork

The wide expanse of **inland Cork** can't compete with the extravagant beauty of the coast, but it does provide a couple of quick, scenic routes west, mostly through gentle, lush pastoral land. The main tourist attraction is the famous historic town of **Blarney**, which makes a pleasurable stop on your way westwards or a handy day-trip from Cork city. Further inland, the **Boggeragh Mountains** and the route from **Macroom** to Bantry provide opportunities for gentle walking.

Blarney

BLARNEY is an easy six miles west of Cork city; buses leave the bus station roughly hourly. The town itself functions chiefly as a tourist service centre and, naturally, there are plenty of **places to eat** here: try *The Muskerry Arms* or the bar, grill or restaurant at the Woollen Mills. *Blair's Inn* (Ⓣ021/438170), about four miles west of Blarney on the R579, is difficult to reach without your own transport, but is especially noted for its food and a lovely riverside location. The **Blarney Woollen Mills**, one of Blarney's original industries, is the place to find quality Irish goods – especially clothing – in traditional wools and linens. Alongside is a **tourist office** (daily 9.30am–5.30pm, winter closed Wed; Ⓣ021/438 1624).

The **castle** (May & Sept Mon–Sat 9am–6.30pm, Sun 9.30am–5.30pm; June–Aug Mon–Sat 9am–7pm, Sun 9.30am–5.30pm; Oct–April Mon–Sat 9am–6pm or sunset, Sun 9.30am–sunset; €7), a fine stronghold built in 1446 by Dermot McCarthy, King of Munster, is sadly now synonymous with the whole "Blarney phenomenon". The **Blarney Stone** has been kissed by visitors for over a hundred years, the legend being that to do so gives you the gift of eloquent and persuasive speech. The most famous version of how the legend came about tells of one McCarthy – King of Munster and Lord of Blarney – who, supposedly loyal to the colonizing Queen Elizabeth I, never actually got around to fulfilling any of the agreements between them, always sidetracking her emissaries with drinking, dancing and sweet talk. He was said to be able to talk "the noose off his head". In her frustration the queen is said to have eventually cried out "Blarney, Blarney, what he says he does not mean. It is the usual Blarney." The stone itself is a four foot by one foot limestone block set in the battlements 83ft above the ground, so kissing it requires a head for heights. If you want to, you'll have to join the queue (it can take an hour) in the castle keep from which you can watch everyone else (one at a time) being dangled backwards by the shins over the battlements aided by two strong men. This also gives you time to consider whether or not you really want to join in. According to a less challenging legend, the stone is half of the Stone of Scone on which Scottish kings were crowned, given to Cormac McCarthy by Robert the Bruce in gratitude for the support of four thousand men at the Battle of Bannockburn (the rest is at Edinburgh Castle). Views from the top of the castle are superb.

In the castle grounds, **Rock Close** is a nineteenth-century folly, a rock garden supposedly built around druidic remains. It is a pity that myths, authentic or not, are such big business around here, because without the hype these ancient yews and oaks could create a potent atmosphere.

Macroom and the routes west

The secondary roads west of Cork city run up the Lee Valley, through scenic countryside and a number of small villages. **MACROOM** (Ⓦwww.macroom.ie), the only place of any size on the N22 between Cork and Killarney, serves as a stopping-off point for tourists and music enthusiasts heading west. Several bars offer **meals**; or you can head for *Café Muesli* off South Square, a homely café-restaurant serving mostly Italian dishes, with lots of options for veggies. The opulent *Castle Hotel* (Ⓣ026/41074, Ⓦwww.castlehotel.ie; ❺) on Main Street is a good **overnight** option, if your budget will stretch that far, offering a leisure centre with pool and gym, bar, café and restaurant. For cheaper B&B, try *Richaldine House*, close to the centre on the N22 Killarney road (Ⓣ026/41966; ❷), with comfy, en-suite rooms and good child reductions. The **Boggeragh Mountains** to the north of the Lee Valley appear as high, rolling moorland, unspectacular compared with other ranges in Cork and Kerry but particularly rich in archaeological remains: stone circles, standing stones, wedge tombs and ring forts. A leaflet to help you locate these sites, *Antiquities of the Boggeragh Mountains*, is available from the **tourist office** on the central square in Macroom (May–Sept generally daily 10am–5pm, closed for lunch; Ⓣ026/43280).

The stretch of road (R584) beyond Macroom southwest to Bantry Bay is a far quieter one than the route out of Cork; it leads into the mountains and to one of the county's last remaining Gaeltacht regions, Muskerry (*Múscraí*). Fine scenery accompanies you all the way, especially as the road runs along Lough Allua; the little village of **INCHIGEELAGH** at the eastern end of this ribbon lake shelters a small IHO **hostel**, *Tír na Spideoga* (Ⓣ026/47151, Ⓦwww.euroka.com/spideoga; ❶), with private rooms, camping and meals available. Beyond here the route southwest takes you through the steep, rocky Pass of Keimaneigh, on the north side of which lies **Gougane Barra Forest Park** and a corrie lake, the source of the River Lee. An island on this lake, now the site of small, modern chapel, was the location of St Finbarre's sixth-century hermitage before he founded his monastery at Cork city downstream. It's an area famous for its beauty and popular for day-trips, and there are several sign-posted nature trails through the park, notably *Slí Easa* (Way of the Waterfall), with magnificent views of the entire glen and the enclosing mountain wall.

Alternatively, taking the road southwest of Cork city to Bandon and then west to **DUNMANWAY** brings you to very promising country of deserted hills and lakes, on the way to Skibbereen or Bantry. Dunmanway is a plain country town, but just outside it the excellent IHH-run **hostel**, *Shiplake Mountain Hostel* (Ⓣ & Ⓕ023/45750, Ⓔshiplakehostel@hotmail.com; ❶), occupies a traditional farmhouse in a beautiful setting. As well as gypsy caravans for couples and families, camping and delicious vegetarian food, *Shiplake* offers bike rental, maps of local walks and luggage transport for walkers and cyclists. To find it take Castle Road next to the *Market Diner* out of town, follow it for two and a half miles in the direction of Coolkelure and turn right at the hostel sign – or phone for a pick-up.

Kinsale

KINSALE (Ⓦwww.kinsale.ie), eighteen miles south of Cork city, has retained much of the flavour of its rich maritime history and has much in common with the formerly affluent ports of Youghal, Cork and Cobh. With its pretty harbour and impressive forts, the opportunities it offers for watersports and its reputation as the gourmet centre of the southwest, Kinsale has become an extremely successful tourist town. For the most part development has been tasteful, though the pace of change is swift and a garish scar of pastel-coloured apartments disfiguring the hillside illustrates the threat commercialism poses to Kinsale's historic character. Still, despite the crowds and the cars, there is plenty of interest in the life, landscape and history to keep you here.

Some history

Originally a fishing town, Kinsale's sheltered harbour has made it a place of strategic importance in Irish, and English, history. The town received its first royal charter from Edward III in 1333, but it was of little importance up until the **Battle of Kinsale** in 1601, a disastrous defeat for the Irish which signalled the end of the Gaelic aristocracy as a power for the English to reckon with. A Spanish fleet stood in the bay ready to support the Irish cause against Elizabeth I's forces, but was unable to make useful contact with O'Neill and O'Donnell attacking from the north. So the battle was lost, and although resistance to English rule continued, six years later came "the flight of the Earls" – when the Irish nobility fled to the Continent, giving up the fight for their own lands.

It was also at Kinsale that **James II** landed with French support in an attempt to regain his throne in 1689, and it was later the port of his final departure from Ireland after the Battle of the Boyne. The town was an important naval base for the English Crown in the seventeenth and eighteenth centuries, and the sixteenth-century tower house in Cork Street – Desmond Castle – became known as "The French Prison" when it was used to hold as many as six hundred French prisoners during the Napoleonic Wars.

It was off the Old Head of Kinsale that the ocean liner, the **Lusitania**, en route to Liverpool from New York, was torpedoed by a German submarine in 1915, killing 1198 people. It remains a controversial incident: Germany claimed there was ammunition on board; the US said it contained only civilians. Whatever the truth, it has been seen as a catalyst for America's entry into World War I.

Information and accommodation

The **tourist office** is next to the bus depot and cinema in the centre of town (daily 9.30am–5.30pm, winter closed Wed; ⓣ021/477 2234). **Bike rental** is available at The Hire Shop, 18 Main St (ⓣ021/477 4884). Both the Outdoor Education Centre (ⓣ021/477 2896), around two miles south of town on the harbour, and Oysterhaven Activity Centre (ⓣ021/477 0738, ⓦwww.oysterhaven.com), three miles east of Kinsale on Oysterhaven Bay, offer **sailing**, **wind-surfing** and **kayaking**.

There are plenty of good places to **stay** in Kinsale, but even so you're strongly advised to book ahead during July, August and the gourmet festival in early October (see p.358). You can **camp** at *Garrettstown House Holiday Park* (ⓣ021/477 8156; May to mid-Sept) at Ballinspittle, six miles southwest of Kinsale.

Blindgate House Blindgate ⓣ021/477 7858, ⓦwww.blindgatehouse.com. Bright, stylish guesthouse decorated with natural fabrics and contemporary furniture and offering great breakfasts and a quiet garden to relax in. 5min walk west of the town centre. ❻

Guardwell Lodge Guardwell ⓣ021/477 4686, ⓦwww.guardwelllodge.com. The budget accommodation in this smart, modern, pine-floored building runs the gamut: dorms, singles, doubles, twins and family rooms, all en-suite. Kitchen, dining room and cosy lounge with Internet access. ❶

Hilltop B&B Sleaveen Heights ⓣ021/477 2612. Comfortable modern bungalow overlooking the town and harbour. All rooms en suite, with tea and coffee, TVs and hairdryers in rooms. It's a 2min walk into the centre; the B&B is signposted off the R600 to Cork. ❷

The Lighthouse The Rock ⓣ021/477 2734. Cosy B&B in a flurry of antique lace and Victorian furniture; no-smoking en-suite bedrooms. A steep walk up the hill behind the museum. ❸

Long Quay House Long Quay ⓣ021/477 3201, ⓔlongquayhouse@eircom.net. Beautiful, creeper-clad Georgian house in the centre of town offering good-quality B&B. All of the spacious bedrooms have en-suite facilities; many have baths. Closed mid-Nov to Xmas. ❸

Old Bank House 11 Pearse St ⓣ021/477 4075, ⓦwww.oldbankhousekinsale.com. Top-quality Georgian guesthouse: the lounge and drawing room are furnished with antiques, while prints and illustrations decorate the walls. Highly comfortable throughout; all the bedrooms have en-suite bathrooms. Their extensive breakfast menu includes kippers, smoked mackerel and scrambled eggs. Quiet, despite the central location. ❼

Seagull House Cork Street ⓣ021/477 2240, ⓦwww.seagullhouse.com. A plain old-style B&B, next door to Desmond Castle. En-suite double rooms; there is one standard single room available. Closed Nov–Feb. ❷

Walyunga Sandycove ⓣ021/477 4126, ⓦwww.walyunga.com. Spacious and very welcoming non-smoking bungalow, with landscaped gardens and outstanding sea and valley views. Excellent breakfasts served on the panoramic patio in good weather. Closed Nov–Feb. ❷

The town centre

The town's history is recorded in the **museum** (Wed–Sun 10.30am–1pm & 2–5.30pm, closes 4.45pm in winter; hours may vary – ⓣ021/477 2044 or check with the tourist office; €2.40), bang in the centre of town above the old market (1600) with its Dutch-style facade (1704). It's an intriguing jumble of stuff, including memorabilia from the *Lusitania* disaster, sixteenth-century royal charters and maps, local craftwork, personal effects of the eighteenth-century giant of Kinsale and a variety of bizarre local inventions that never got further than the local museum. Here, too, is the musty old courthouse that had remained much the same from the eighteenth century up until 1915, when the inquest into the sinking of the *Lusitania* was held here and Kinsale suddenly became the focus of the world's press; after the inquest it was decided that the courtroom should be left as a memorial.

Desmond Castle (mid-April to mid-June Tues–Sun and bank holidays 10am–6pm; mid-June to early Oct daily 10am–6pm; €2.50; Heritage Card) offers little to see beyond its simple, sturdy structure, although the tour is worth taking since the guides are instructive and entertaining. In the castle is a small **wine exhibition** which details the history of the "wine geese", those families that fled Ireland after the Battle of Kinsale in 1601 and also those who left after the departure of James II in 1690, and who went on to establish vineyards and wine trading routes around the world. Nearby **St Multose Church** has traces of a medieval structure, and in the church porch are the town stocks dating back to the eighteenth century.

Around the harbour

South of the centre, a tongue of land curls from the west into the harbour, protecting the town from harsh winds. On this promontory, the ivy-clad ruins of **James Fort**, a ruddy-coloured castle built by the English king James I in the early seventeenth century, is fun to clamber over. It's worth checking with the tourist office whether the ferry which used to run out here from the *Trident Hotel* marina during the summer has resumed service.

Better preserved is **Charles Fort** (1677) on the opposite side of the harbour, two miles southeast of town at **SUMMERCOVE** (mid-March to Oct daily 10am–6pm; Nov to mid-March Sat & Sun 10am–5pm; €3.10; Heritage Card). There's a very pleasant walk out here from Kinsale that takes you alongside the harbour: to find it, follow the minor coast road east for a quarter of a mile to *The Spaniards* pub at Scilly, and look out for a path down towards the sea. The star-shaped outer walls of Charles Fort, barely touched by weather or gunfire, seem pretty innocuous, but they conceal a formidable war machine. Within is an awesome system of barracks, ramparts and bastions, impressive testimony to the complexity and precision of seventeenth-century military science. The barracks were occupied until 1922, when the British left and handed the fort over to the Irish government. Today they remain largely intact, with only the barracks' missing roofs to give the place an eerily deserted feel. *The Bulman* pub at Summercove serves very good **bar food** and makes the ideal place to recharge the batteries before making the pleasant stroll back into town.

Eating

Kinsale is a well-known gourmet centre and even has a **gourmet festival** (☎021/477 2382), which is generally held in early October – if you plan to stay or eat here at this time, book well in advance. Kinsale also has two excellent **delis**: The Quay Food Co. on Market Quay stocks organic produce, Irish cheeses, coffee, preserves and olives, and Kinsale Gourmet Store (see *Fishy Fishy Café* below) is similarly enticing.

Crackpots 3 Cork St (☎021/477 2847). A fairly informal but upmarket bistro-restaurant with plenty of interesting artwork and – as the name suggests – ceramics. Varied menu that might offer parmesan polenta cake and prawns in sweet chilli sauce. Early-bird menu €18.50 until 7.30pm. Wed–Sun evenings.

Dino's Pier Rd. Waterfront chipper of good repute, with plenty of tables if you want to eat in.

Fishy Fishy Café At the Kinsale Gourmet Store

Guardwell. Deli and fishmongers with a much-vaunted café, and outdoor tables, that's one of the best places to enjoy a great range of fresh seafood – including mussels, crab, lobster and clams. Mon–Sat till 4.30pm.
Jim Edward's Market Square. Pleasant, central pub with a posh restaurant, though you might as well stick to the excellent seafood on the bar menu: try the chowder or cod in smoked salmon sauce with great chips.
Mango Tree Café Market Quay. Small, bright orange café, offering delicious wraps, panini and salads, as well as good coffees and desserts.
Max's Wine Bar Main St ⓣ021/477 2443. Cosy, upmarket spot with a small conservatory, where meat and vegetarian dishes make an appearance alongside seafood offerings such as skewered monkfish with ginger and lime. Snack lunches and an early-bird menu also available. Closed Tues & Nov–March.
The White House The Glen. Excellent, inexpensive bar food with dishes such as chicken fajitas and salmon in brandy, prawn and cream sauce featuring alongside the catch of the day.

Drinking

Kinsale has the complement of convivial **bars** that you might expect in a historic town turned tourist centre, and the place is so compact that most of them are within a couple of minutes' walk of each other. *The Grey Hound*, just off Market Square, is especially appealing and has a quaint old interior which originally came from England. The rambling, atmospheric *Shanakee* (*An Seanachai*) in nearby Market Street is a regular venue for live music and DJs; or head for *The 1601* on Pearse Street, a tidy, friendly spot with folk music Wednesday and Sunday. *The Spaniards* in Scilly, a mile away around the east side of the harbour, is a welcoming pub with good bar food which also has plenty of live sessions – the walk out there is a pleasant one along a minor road that dips down beside the shoreline. Pick up a copy of the weekly *Kinsale Newsletter* at the tourist office to check out what else is on around town.

The Seven Heads Peninsula

Between Timoleague, around thirteen miles west of Kinsale, and Clonakilty, six miles further on, lies the **Seven Heads Peninsula**, a delightful area with a pretty indented shoreline and, in summer, a wonderfully balmy atmosphere. While the peninsula has none of the drama of landscapes further west, it does have a quiet, understated charm that can be quite disarming after the hectic tourism of Kinsale. It's a fine place too for birdwatching and leisurely cycling. Both the town of **Clonakilty** and the village of **Timoleague** make good bases from which to explore this part of the county; the little coastal village of **Courtmacsherry** offers a quieter option still.

Timoleague and Courtmacsherry

TIMOLEAGUE is a small village, set inland on the muddy estuary of the Arigideen River and dominated by the extensive remains of a **Franciscan abbey** which was sacked in 1649. Despite its size, the village boasts a handful of good **bars**, including *Charlie Madden's*, where you stand a good chance of finding some sort of live music at weekends, and *Dillon's*, a relaxing, informal **bar-restaurant** which serves excellent, reasonably priced food in the evenings (closed Mon & Tues). About a mile west of town, *Lettercollum House* offers atmospheric **B&B** in a spacious nineteenth-century former convent set in wooded grounds (ⓣ023/46251, ⓦwww.lettercollum.ie; ❷). If you want to stay in the village itself, try *Panorama B&B*, Chapel Hill (ⓣ & ⓕ023/46248; ❷), which provides very comfortable accommodation and excellent views. There's also good **camping** around two miles out of Timoleague along the R600 towards Clonakilty at *Sexton's Camping* (Ⓣ023/46347; March–Sept). Some of Ireland's finest smoked salmon (both wild and organically reared), as well as excellent smoked chicken and rashers, can be bought at Ummera smokehouse, a couple miles north of Timoleague at Inchy Bridge (Ⓣ023/46644 for directions; Ⓦwww.ummera.com).

At the broad mouth of the estuary, the village of **COURTMACSHERRY** is a safe, quiet family resort. It's certainly tranquil – when asked what happens here one local reckoned "the tide comes in and the tide goes out again". That's somewhat exaggerated: if you're feeling rich you can go **deep-sea angling** or **shark fishing** (Courtmacsherry Sea Angling Centre; Ⓣ023/46427); **horse riding** can be arranged through the pleasant, family-run *Courtmacsherry Hotel* (Ⓣ023/46198, Ⓦwww.courtmacsherryhotel.com; ❸); and there's **windsurfing**, **canoeing** and **sailing** at the leisure club in front of the hotel. For **B&B**, *Woodpoint* (Ⓣ023/46427, Ⓔcsal@iol.ie; ❷) is a good, en-suite option, with evening meals available.

On the west side of the tip of the Seven Heads Peninsula, there's an excellent **restaurant** at Dunworley Bay: *Otto's Creative Catering* (reservations essential on Ⓣ023/40461, bring your own wine; evenings only, plus Sun lunch; Ⓦwww.ottos-creative-catering.com; ❹) prepares contemporary Irish cuisine, using top-quality organic and wild seafood and meats, and vegetables from their own garden. They also run a cookery school and have a couple of en-suite **bedrooms** if you want to make a night of it.

Clonakilty

The busy little town of **CLONAKILTY** (Ⓦwww.clonakilty.ie) makes a good base from which to explore the Seven Heads Peninsula and the beautiful shoreline to the south of here. The town itself is a pleasantly unassuming place, with plenty of live music in its pubs, but is most famous as the birthplace of the Republican leader **Michael Collins** (see also pp.791 and 792).

Just over two miles east of Clonakilty, off the R600 towards Timoleague, is the eclectic but highly recommended **Arigideen Valley Heritage Park** (mid-June to mid-Sept Mon–Sat 10.30am–5pm; Sun & off season by appointment, Ⓣ023/46107, Ⓦwww.reachireland.com). Engaging hour-long guided tours (€5), full of anecdotes, particularly about his distant relative Michael Collins, are led by Mr Crowley; features include an archaeology trail, with replicas of monuments such as standing stones commonly found in West Cork, and the 1921 Trail, a representation of Collins's ambush site. On top of this there's story-telling for kids, a Michael Collins slide show and talk (Mon & Thurs evenings in summer), and guided hill walks and Michael Collins tours (by appointment). Aficionados will also want to visit the the scant remains of **Collins's birthplace**, which was burnt out by the Black and Tans in 1921, about four miles west of Clonakilty on the N71 towards Rosscarbery.

A couple of more ancient historical sites might also appeal. In the grounds of the agricultural college at the east end of town, the recently excavated Lisnagun Christian **ring fort** is the only one in Ireland to be reconstructed on its original site, with defensive walls, a thatched central house, souterrains, replica weapons, utensils and clothing – all of which create a vivid picture of tenth-century life (closed for redevelopment at the time of writing, but due to reopen in summer 2003). Just over a mile north of town are the remains of the Templebryan **stone circle** – four of the original nine stones still stand, along with a central white quartzite pillar; to find it head out of town up MacCurtain Hill.

Clonakilty makes a good base from which to explore the crazily indented coastline roundabout, which is especially enjoyable by bike. Quiet, low-lying roads follow the shore offering tranquil cycling and plenty of opportunities for birdwatching with numerous waders searching for food in the sand. **Inchydoney Beach**, about two and a half miles south, is especially fine, though check that the red flag isn't flying before swimming, as there can be strong currents here. Around three miles southwest of Inchydoney, the impressive ruins of the eighteenth-century Castle Freke mansion make a good focus for a walk. The surrounding demesne is varied with oak, beech and conifer woodland; walks here offer fine views over Rosscarbery Bay.

If poor weather rules out any of this outdoor exploration, you could do worse than holing up in the **West Cork Regional Museum** (June–Oct Mon–Sat 10.30am–5.30pm, Sun 2.30–5pm; €2.50) at the west end of Clonakilty's main street (here Western Road), which covers the area's contribution to the War of Independence and Clonakilty's once-prosperous linen industry, alongside a host of agricultural implements.

Arrival, information and accommodation

There's a **tourist office** in the town centre at 25 Ashe St (Mon–Sat 9.30am–1pm & 2–5.30pm; ⓣ023/33226). **Internet access** is available at Hi-Tec Computing, 10–12 Astna St (ⓣ023/34557); for **bike rental** try MTM Cycles, 33 Ashe St (ⓣ023/33584).

Recent years have seen an increase in the range of **accommodation** on offer in Clonakilty, particularly towards the top end of the price range. **Camping** is available a mere five hundred yards' stagger from the pubs at *Desert House*, near the shore (Easter & May–Sept; ⓣ023/33331); head east out of the village and turn right at the roundabout.

Bay View Old Timoleague Rd ⓣ023/33539, ⓦwww.bayviewclonakilty.com. Very welcoming, non-smoking B&B at the east end of town, with decent reductions for children. Bright and cheerful decor; all rooms en suite. Closed Nov–Feb. ❷

Clonakilty Old Brewery Hostel Old Brewery Lane (IHO) ⓣ023/33525, ⓔwytchost@iol.ie. Excellent hostel accommodation in a quiet yet central location off Emmet Square; private rooms are available, along with facilities for wheelchair users. ❶

The Lodge and Spa Inchydoney Island ⓣ023/33143, ⓦwww.inchydoneyisland.com. Luxury retreat, beautifully sited on Inchydoney Beach, offering a range of treatments, including a fully equipped thalassotherapy (seawater) spa, and a fine restaurant. ❾

Nordav Fernhill Rd, off Western Rd ⓣ & ⓕ023/33655. Comfortable, quiet, en-suite B&B in a detached house with pleasant gardens. Family suite and studio apartment also available. Closed Oct–March. ❷

O'Donovan's Hotel Pearse St ⓣ & ⓕ 023/33250, ⓦwww.odonovanshotel.com. Traditional town-centre family-run hotel, and the hub of much social activity during the summer months. Previous guests include Marconi, Parnell and Michael Collins. ❹

Quality Hotel and Leisure Centre On the road towards Rosscarbery ⓣ023/35400, ⓦwww.qualityhotelclon.com. Modern hotel on the edge of town; facilities include bar, restaurant, leisure centre, pool and multiplex cinema. Weekend deals available. ❺

Wytchwood Off Emmet Square ⓣ023/33525, ⓔwytchost@iol.ie. A Georgian house with a walled garden offering welcoming, comfortable and tranquil B&B right in the town centre. Non-smoking and en-suite throughout. Cycle hire and route information. ❷

Eating, drinking and nightlife

The town has several decent **places to eat**: the cosy *An Súgán*, 41 Wolfe Tone St, does good bar food; *Fionnuala's*, 30 Ashe St (ⓣ023/34355), is an inexpensive and cosy Italian restaurant, serving mostly pizzas and pastas; and the well-run, popular *Cobra Tandoori and Balti Restaurant* (ⓣ023/35957) and the more atmospheric, Pakistani *Shama* (ⓣ023/36945) are in keen sub-continental competition on opposite sides of Ashe Street. Clonakilty is noted for its **black puddings** (a sausage made from the blood of pigs with a warm peppery flavour), and you may well find it dished up at breakfast in your hotel or B&B; if you're self-catering, and fancy giving it a go, it's well worth it – you'll be able to get some at any one of the local butchers.

Finally, there are plenty of excellent old **bars**: for music *De Barra's* on Pearse Street is probably the most popular place, with traditional or folk music more or less every night. As well as a beer garden, *An Teach Beag* (behind *O'Donovan's Hotel*) has traditional music every night during July and August, and at weekends throughout the year, with occasional set dancing. *O'Donovan's Hotel* hosts regular live bands with a late bar at *The Venue* nightclub.

West towards Skibbereen

The coastline beyond Clonakilty is a beautiful stretch of little bays and creeks, sandy coves and tidal loughs. There are tiny lagoons here and there, isolated along the shore from the main body of the sea, providing placid contrast to the furling white ocean spray. The main N71 runs west to Skibbereen, with a maze of country lanes running south from it to the heavily indented shore.

The broad bay at **ROSSCARBERY** has lost a great deal of its ethereal beauty since the building of the modern and hideously large *Celtic Ross Hotel* (Ⓣ023/48722, Ⓦwww.celticrosshotel.com; ❻), where facilities include a pool, sauna and gym. If you want to stay in more discreet surroundings, try the family-run *Curraheen Lodge* (Ⓣ023/48498; March–Oct) **hostel** about one mile west of here – it offers quiet camping and bike rental too; to find it, turn left opposite the pleasant *Courthouse Bar*, and then take the second lane on the left. Rosscarbery's pretty village square is tucked up a lane on the north side of the main road, and here you'll find a handful of **bars** and **places to eat**, including *O'Callaghan Walshe* (May–Oct every evening, weekends only during the winter; Ⓣ023/48125), an intimate, expensive **restaurant** renowned for its fresh seafood. A particularly atmospheric **B&B** in the area is *Castle Salem* (Ⓣ023/48381, Ⓦwww.castlesalem.com; Feb–Nov; ❷), two and a half miles away, a seventeenth-century farmhouse in an extraordinary setting of deep green rolling fields; it's signposted off the N71 after about one mile west of Rosscarbery. There's plenty of history too – the house adjoins a fifteenth-century **castle**, accessible via a doorway off the main stairs, and **William Penn**, founder of Pennsylvania, is known to have stayed here.

Heading on from Rosscarbery, take the minor R597 towards Glandore and look out for signs to the **Drombeg stone circle**. Dating from the Bronze Age, the seventeen stones that make up this circle are particularly impressive for their fine location – overlooking fields that fall to the sea. Nearby is a **fulacht fiadh** – a cooking site from the same era, where troughs of cold water would have been heated by hot stones thrown into them from a fire. Back on the R597, about a mile before Glandore, the road passes the neat little *Meadow* **campsite** (Ⓣ028/33280; mid-March to Sept).

There's a fleeting outrageous glamour to **GLANDORE** with its turquoise-blue waters and deep-green slopes, and there can be no better way to absorb the scene than with a plate of seafood and a cool drink from *Hayes Bar* overlooking the bay. Accommodation is thin on the ground, but *Bay View* is a pleasant, recently refurbished **B&B** with great views (Ⓣ028/33115; ❷). The nearest **hostel** is just outside **UNION HALL**, a quaint village across the deep inlet from Glandore: *Maria's Schoolhouse* (IHH; Ⓣ028/33002, Ⓦwww.geocities.com/mariasschoolhouse; mid-March to Oct) is a bright and cheery place, with comfy armchairs and big log fires; twins and family rooms, as well as excellent vegetarian and non-vegetarian meals are available, and the hostel also organizes **bike rental** and pick-ups from Leap. Waterfront **B&B** is available at *Seascape* (Ⓣ028/33920; ❷), a large, attractive, grey-stone house with a pretty terrace overlooking the bay, and nearby *Ardagh House* (Ⓣ & Ⓕ028/33571; ❷), which also has a pleasant, brightly painted, upmarket **restaurant** serving dishes such as John Dory with orange butter. Based at Union Hall, Atlantic Sea Kayaking (Ⓣ028/33002, Ⓦwww.atlanticseakayaking.com) runs **sea kayaking** trips along the West Cork coast.

LEAP (pronounced "Lep"), a small village straddling the N71 just north of Union Hall and Glandore, is best known for *Connolly's* bar, the best **live music venue** in west Cork, with a great range of bands year round: rock, reggae, traditional, bluegrass – just about anything that makes it out of Dublin will be on here. For the latest, details check out *Connolly's* website (Ⓦwww.connollysofleap.com). For those looking to stay in the village, *Highfield* B&B is the best place to try (Ⓣ028/33273, Ⓔhighfieldleap@eircom.net; ❶).

Skibbereen and around

Cheerful **SKIBBEREEN** (Ⓦwww.skibbereen.ie), smartly painted and set on the River Illen, is the main service and administrative centre for this part of west Cork. This traditional role is still remarkably alive: on Wednesdays the cattle market operates, drawing crowds from the surrounding country, and every Friday afternoon there's the regular country market. For travellers, it's a good place to stock up or to stop over – there are plenty of supermarkets, a smattering of good eating places, and plenty of pubs.

The **West Cork Arts Centre** on North Street (Mon–Sat 10am–6pm; Ⓣ028/22090) is worth checking out. It hosts monthly exhibitions which can be first-rate, as well as staging occasional music and dance performances. The excellent **heritage centre**, on Upper Bridge Street (mid-March to mid-May & mid-Sept to Oct Tues–Sat 10am–6pm; mid-May to mid-Sept daily 10am–6pm; €4), displays two very different exhibitions. "The Great Famine Commemorative Exhibition" offers a vivid and sobering account of the Famine of the 1840s: Skibbereen was particularly badly affected and around ten thousand victims lie buried nearby. The ninety-minute **Skibbereen Trail**, marked by bronze plaques and detailed in a leaflet available from the heritage centre, takes in some of the Famine sites. The second of the two exhibitions celebrates the abundant marine life of nearby Lough Hyne (see p.364) and sets out to explain the survival of a range of species – from corals, anemones and sea-squirts to gobies and sea slugs – in this unique marine lake.

Practicalities

The **tourist office** (June & Sept Mon–Sat 9am–6pm; July & Aug daily 9am–7pm; Oct–May Mon–Fri 9.15am–5.30pm; Ⓣ028/21766) is on North Street and will help with accommodation. You can get **Bus Éireann** information from O'Cahalanes in Bridge Street, and **rent bikes** from the hostel and from N.W. Roycroft and Son in Ilen Street (Ⓣ028/21235).

Among **B&Bs**, *Sunnyside*, 42 Mardyke St (Ⓣ028/21365, Ⓔsunnysideskibb@eircom.net; ❷), is a comfortable, run-of-the-mill, central option; distinctly out of the ordinary is *Bridge House*, Bridge Street (Ⓣ028/21273; ❷), an eccentric Victorian-styled B&B stuffed with antiques, swags and china dolls. There's a good IHH **hostel**, *The Russagh Mill Hostel*, a mile out on the Castletownshend road (closed Nov to mid-March; Ⓣ028/22451, Ⓦwww.russaghmillhostel.com; ❶), with dorm, twin and family rooms in a beautifully renovated mill house. Mick Murphy, the hostel manager, is happy to talk to visitors about his Everest climb in 1993, rents out bikes, and leads **hill-walking**, **climbing** and **abseiling** activities as well as **kayaking** on Lough Hyne most days. **Campers** should make for *The Hideaway* (Ⓣ028/22254; May–Sept), half a mile out on the Castletownshend road.

There are plenty of decent **places to eat** in town: *Il Forno*, 12 Bridge St, serves tasty, reasonably priced pizzas and pastas, with good veggie options, and you can tuck into good budget meals during the day at *The Stove* on Main Street. Moving upmarket, *Kalbo's Bistro*, 48 North St (Ⓣ028/21515), has an informal café atmosphere and offers inexpensive filled baguettes and home-cooked lunches and a varied and enticing but fairly pricey evening menu. *Ty Ar Mor* on Main Street (Ⓣ028/22100; closed Oct & Nov; tourist menu €30, gastronomic menu €40) concentrates on Breton-style seafood, specializing in lobsters, oysters and huge plates of *fruits de mer*.

For a wholly memorable meal, make a reservation at *Island Cottage* (mid-May to mid-Sept Wed–Sun evenings; Ⓣ028/38102, Ⓦwww.islandcottage.com; set menu €30), a delightful and exceptional restaurant on **Heir Island**; to get there you'll need to drive or cycle along the N71 towards Ballydehob for three miles, then follow the signs down the small peninsula for about another three miles to Cunnamore, from where a small boat will ferry you across to the restaurant in five minutes.

There's no shortage of **bars** in Skib: *Baby Hannah's*, 42 Bridge St, is a lively young place and hosts singer-songwriters and other live music; for traditional music there's *Sheehy's* on the square, or you might try *The Corner Bar* at 37 Bridge St.

Castletownshend

Around five miles southeast of Skibbereen at the end of the R596 lies **CASTLETOWNSHEND**, a delightful little village worth making a quick detour to see. The village clings to a steep lane, a tree in the middle of the road sending what traffic there is gingerly either side, and ends abruptly at a tiny stone quay. It's an eerie, twee place, and appropriately enough was once the home of Edith Somerville of Somerville & Ross fame, authors of the *Irish RM* stories. Their graves are to be found in St Barrahane's churchyard. There's little else to see here, but there is good seafood on the bar menu at *Mary Ann's*, an attractive little pub worth seeking out. If you're interested in gardens, stop off at **Liss Ard** (Mon–Fri 10am–4.30pm; free; Ⓦwww.lissardresort.com), around a mile out of Skib on the Castletownshend road, where a 200-acre plot beside Lough Abisdealy contains innovative features such as a sky garden and talking stones, and you can walk along one- or two-hour trails designed for peace and contemplation.

Lough Hyne

If you head out of Skib on the Baltimore road and take the turning on your left after about three miles, you'll soon find **Lough Hyne** (pronounced *Ine*), a land-locked salt lake, linked to the ocean only by a very slender channel, known as the rapids, down which the receding tide returns to the sea. The lough, surrounded by hillsides dripping with lush, moist greenery, is a unique phenomenon, of great interest to marine biologists, as detailed in the Skibbereen heritage centre (see p.363). From the head of the lake steep slopes, easily climbed, rise to panoramic views: eastwards along the coast to Kinsale, west across the length of the Mizen Peninsula, and out across to Sherkin and Clear islands.

Baltimore and the islands

The approach to **Baltimore** takes you through a landscape that is disarmingly low-key. Instead of some dramatic climax at this, the most southerly point of Ireland, the land seems simply to be fading away: rocky terrain and scrawny vegetation accompany the windy, listless estuary, untidy with lumps of land that seem to have been tossed at random towards the sea. But as the ocean comes into full view this tailing-off is put into spectacular context, with the island-speckled expanse of Roaringwater Bay culminating in **Sherkin and Clear islands**.

Baltimore

For all the development of holiday homes jostling around **BALTIMORE**, the quayside at the heart of the place still retains the engaging bustle and spirit of an old fishing harbour, the sixteenth-century O'Driscoll stronghold visible above the new houses. Combining traditional fishing activities with tourism, Baltimore makes a good base from which to explore this part of the coast. It's popular too with the yachting crowd and the port is particularly busy during the **regatta** held on the last two weeks in July and the first weekend in August. Baltimore serves as the main departure point for **ferries** to **Sherkin Island** (5–10 daily; 10min; €7 return; ⓣ028/20218) and **Clear Island** (summer 4 daily; winter 1–3 daily; 45min; €11.50 return; ⓣ028/39135 or 086/266 2197), as well as **Schull** on the Mizen Head Peninsula (see p.369).

Arrival and information

The crafts shop in a hut down by the quay dispenses **tourist information** daily in summer (ⓣ028/20347). As well as the scheduled Bus Éireann, there is a private service that operates between Skibbereen and the harbour at around 10–10.30am – check the exact schedule locally. For **changing money**, the post office and *Bushe's Bar* by the harbour have bureaux de change. Aquaventures (ⓣ028/20511, ⓦwww.aquaventures.ie) runs **diving** trips, while the Atlantic Boating Service (ⓣ028/22734, www.atlanticboat.ie) offers **water-skiing** and **boat rental**.

Accommodation

Baltimore is a small and attractive place **to stay**, so that, while there is a good range of accommodation on offer, it is nevertheless advisable to book in advance if you want to stay during July and August or over bank holiday weekends.

Baltimore Bay ⓣ028/20600, ⓦwww.youenjacob.com. Good-quality, spacious guesthouse accommodation right by the harbour above *La Jolie Brise* café, where most rooms have great sea views. ❸

The Baltimore Harbour Hotel ⓣ028/20361, ⓦwww.bhrhotel.ie. Comfortable, modern hotel overlooking pleasant gardens and the bay, where all rooms have en-suite bathrooms and TVs. Facilities include a leisure centre with pool, gym and steam room and children's activities in high summer. Good discounts for weekend breaks. Closed Jan. ❻

Bushe's Bar ⓣ028/20125. Comfortable, simple accommodation. Rooms overlooking the harbour are more expensive, but all have en-suite baths and TVs. A continental self-service breakfast is provided in the bedrooms. ❶

Casey's Hotel About a mile from the harbour on the main road in from Skibbereen ⓣ028/20197, ⓦwww.caseysofbaltimore.com. A tremendous small, family-run hotel: the comfortable rooms are decorated with original artwork, and all come with en-suite baths and satellite TV. The very pleasant residents' lounge affords views over a tranquil inlet. Lively bar and very good seafood restaurant. Discounts mid-week. ❻

Channel View ⓣ028/20440, ⓔchannelview@eircom.net. Comfortable, en-suite B&B accommodation in a spacious bungalow overlooking the bay. Closed Nov–Feb. ❷

Fastnet House B&B ⓣ028/20515, ⓔfastnet-house@eircom.net. The house was built in 1820 and the new owners have set about renovating it in an attractive rustic style, complete with stripped floors, open fires and bare-stone walls. Comfortable B&B accommodation; all rooms have en-suite facilities. ❷

Rolf's Hostel Signposted to the left off the main road, around half a mile after *Casey's Hotel* (IHH) ⓣ028/20289. Something of a favourite with its cosy cottage atmosphere, gardens and fine café-restaurant; dorms, twin, double, triple and family rooms are top-notch. *Rolf's* also offers bike rental, laundry facilities and a well-equipped kitchen, as well as self-catering cottages. ❶

Eating, drinking and entertainment

For its size, Baltimore offers a very good range of places to **eat**, and you can expect the quality to be high. For excellent barfood there's *Bushe's Bar*, by the harbour, and *Casey's Hotel*, about a mile out on the main road; the latter also has an excellent restaurant noted for its seafood, local farm produce and vegetarian options, with great sea views. *Café Art* at Rolf's hostel encourages relaxed dining: tasty pastas, Mediterranean salads, stir fries and seafood are on offer, and no one minds if you sit down for a full meal or take just one course – or even just a drink in the wine bar; the garden is an especially nice place to eat in fine weather. *La Jolie Brise*, with outdoor tables right down by the harbour, is a day-and-night café serving inexpensive breakfasts, excellent pizzas and Sherkin Island oysters; the same owners run *Chez Youen* around the corner (ⓣ028/20136), a formal white-tablecloth affair where set menus range from €30 for three courses to €50 for a huge seafood platter. The Australian-run *Customs House Restaurant* (ⓣ028/20200; Wed–Sat evenings mid-March to Sept, plus Sun in peak season) specializes in seafood and organic produce and has an excellent reputation for good-value haute cuisine.

Baltimore has a lively **pub scene** during the summer: *Declan McCarthy's* and, again, *Bushe's Bar* are a couple of lively spots overlooking the harbour; *McCarthy's* hosts traditional, folk and ballad sessions several nights a week in summer. *Casey's Hotel* has a cosy characterful bar with traditional music on Saturdays and during the summer on Wednesdays and Sundays, too.

Sherkin Island

Tiny **Sherkin Island** (ⓦwww.sherkinisland.ie) is a delightfully pretty place: the considerable remains of a fifteenth-century Franciscan friary nestle down by the quayside, and little fuchsia-spattered lanes lead across the island to fine sandy beaches in the west. There are the remains of an O'Driscoll stronghold, too, and the annual O'Driscoll clan gathering in June is a hectic five-day event spread between Sherkin Island, Clear Island and Baltimore.

The place can get busy with day-trippers on bank holidays and during July and August. If you want to stay you can get **B&B** at *Cuinne House* (ⓣ028/20384; ❷), with spacious standard and en-suite rooms and evening meals available, and the all-en-suite *Horseshoe Cottage* (ⓣ028/20598; closed Christmas to mid-March; ❷). *The Islander's Rest* (ⓣ028/20116,

Ⓦwww.islandersrest.ie; ④) offers 21 slightly more upmarket, en-suite bedrooms with great views, as well as **bar food**, which is also served at *The Jolly Roger* pub opposite. You can buy supplies at the Abbey Store and post office.

Clear Island

Clear Island (Oileán Chléire; Ⓦwww.oilean-chleire.ie), also known as Cape Clear, offers rather more to do, and is worth visiting for the ferry trip alone. There's an important ornithology station here, and on the 45-minute boat ride out to the island, it becomes obvious that the place is paradise for **wildlife** enthusiasts: the bay is alive with seabirds and with luck you may see seals and, in warm weather, basking sharks. With even more luck you might find your boat raced by a playful dolphin or two, dodging around the bows and leaping out of the ocean to crash back down right alongside the ferry.

The hilly, rocky, three-mile-wide island seems to have been pinched in the middle where two inlets, **North Harbour** and **South Harbour**, almost meet. In the south, steep and inaccessible cliffs rise from the water; the North Harbour is perfectly sheltered. Roads climb up from here through hills covered in the coarse grass that seems to spread over everything, including old walls and houses long derelict. Sea pinks cling to rocky outcrops, and honeysuckle clambers wherever it can. The island's high points give spectacular views back across the archipelago to the mainland.

The **bird observatory** at North Harbour (Ⓣ028/39181) has been here since 1959 and has complete records going back to that time. When it was set up, by an amateur group, this station was a pioneer of the constant observation of seabirds, and its work has done much for the knowledge of migratory patterns. Clear Island is one of the most important places for seabirds in Ireland, including some genuine rarities – especially plentiful are storm petrels, shearwaters, black guillemots and choughs. If you are new to birdwatching, but fancy learning more, call in at the observatory and see what's happening, though bear in mind that late spring and October are the best times for birdwatching.

Clear Island is also an isolated remnant of the **Gaeltacht** and Irish is still spoken by about one hundred and thirty islanders. During the summer, Irish youngsters are sent here to practise the language and at the end of August the island holds an international story-telling **festival**, with concerts, workshops and plenty of music (Ⓣ028/39116, Ⓦwww.indigo.ie/~stories). The island also prides itself on being the birthplace of **St Kieran**, who supposedly preceded St Patrick by thirty years, but the holy well and stone that are attributed to him stand in a sadly unromantic spot by the road at North Harbour. By far the best of Clear Island's historic ruins is **Dún an Óir** ("Fort of Gold"), an O'Driscoll fort, impressive on a high, narrow splinter of rock which is now an island at high tide – sadly inaccessible, though you can see it as you walk down the hill from the heritage centre, or from the two-hundred-foot cliffs to the south. The **heritage centre** (June–Aug daily 2–5.30pm; €2.50), a steep, one-mile walk from North Harbour (follow the sign for the church), is a tiny museum of the whole domestic, fishing and seafaring history of the island.

There's a small **tourist office** at North Harbour (Mon–Fri 9.30am–1pm & 2–4pm; Ⓣ028/39119), and **Internet access** is available at the nearby library. Chuck Kruger leads historical and archaeological **guided walks** of the island (Ⓣ028/39157), while Geoff Oliver takes nature walks (Ⓣ028/39193). If you intend **to stay** anytime between July and October, you would be advised to arrange accommodation before sailing. There are a number of **B&Bs**: *Cluain*

Mara, available through *Ciaran Danny Mike's* pub (Ⓣ028/39153, Ⓔcodriscoll@eircom.net; self-catering cottages also available; ❷), is good value and run by a friendly family; alternatively, you might try *Ard na Gaoithe*, the Glen, up the steep laneway behind the youth hostel (Ⓣ028/39159; ❷). The An Óige **hostel** at South Harbour (closed Nov–May; Ⓣ028/39198) is fairly basic, but the staff are friendly and it does offers kayaking, archery and snorkelling. **Camping** is available on a terraced site overlooking South Harbour; if you bring food over from the mainland, bear in mind that the island has difficulties in dealing with refuse, so avoiding bringing (and leaving) glass and plastic containers is helpful.

The island has three **pubs** within five minutes' walk of each other: *The Club*, beside North Harbour, where you may well find music in the summer months, *Cotter's Bar*, offering simple food a short walk from here, and *Ciaran Danny Mike's*, just at the brow of the hill overlooking South Harbour, which serves very good home-cooked **meals** and has a **restaurant** alongside. *An siopa beag* underneath *The Club* is the island's one grocery store, with a **bureau de change**; inside is a **coffee bar** serving drinks, filled rolls, crepes and, in the evenings, takeaway pizzas. A chip van parks at North Harbour in summer.

Mizen Head Peninsula

The **Mizen Head Peninsula** is a beautiful, remote finger of land poking its way west, offering superb sandy **beaches**, notably at **Barley Cove**, and stunning cliff scenery, getting wilder the further west you go. It's an area rich in **archaeological sites**, from Bronze Age wedge graves contemporary with the first copper mining of Mount Gabriel, through Iron Age and early Christian ring forts, down to medieval castles – pick up a copy of the leaflet *Antiquities of the Mizen Peninsula* from the tourist office in Cork city if you want to locate these sites. The whole of the peninsula's empty northern coast consists of sheer cliffs and stupendous views – an impossible route for hitching, but great for those with transport. The south coast of the peninsula is more travelled, with small towns of **Ballydehob**, **Schull** and **Crookhaven**, while the main tourist attraction is in the signal station at the very tip, the **Mizen Head Visitor Centre**.

Ballydehob

BALLYDEHOB, a small town of brightly coloured streets at the neck of the peninsula, was once known as the hippie capital of the west because it was said to have more "blow-ins" than locals. Heavily colonized in the 1960s, it still has traces of their influence, like health-food shops and resident artists, and remains a liberal place compared to others of its size. For all this, it's a sleepy town with just a handful of crafts and antiques shops worth exploring and a large number of pubs. Ballydehob's nearest **beach** is three miles away at Audley Cove: a secluded pebbly cove, with lovely views of the islands.

For **B&B**, try the pleasant *Dun an Oir* (Ⓣ028/37272, Ⓔstaball@eircom.net; April–Oct; ❷) or *The Old Crossing* (Ⓣ028/37148; ❷), which enjoys fantastic views of the surrounding countryside – follow the lane alongside *Levi's* bar on Main Street to find it. The *12 Arch* **hostel** on Church Road (Ⓣ & Ⓕ 028/37232; ❶) offers dorms and twin rooms, laundry facilities and bike rental. Among **places to eat**, *Annie's Restaurant* (closed Sun & Mon; Ⓣ028/37292), on Main Street, is renowned for its seafood, and the same people serve lunches during the day at *Clara's* on Main Street. *Hudson's* combines a wholefood shop with a vegetarian, mostly organic café, serving ciabattas, pizzas and daily specials such as halloumi on garlic mushrooms. Interesting old **bars** include *Levi's*, a bar-grocery opposite *Annie's*, and *O'Sullivan's*, a few doors up from *Annie's*.

Schull

SCHULL is perhaps the most obvious place to stay on the peninsula, an attractive seaside market town with plenty of cheery amenities aimed at holidaying families and the yachting fraternity. Schull's sheltered, bulb-shaped harbour looks out over Carbery's Hundred Islands, while the aircraft-tracking station on **Mount Gabriel** stands 1339ft above sea level to the north, offering wonderful views. To make this walk from Schull (9 miles there and back) head up Gap Road past the convent and you'll find a clear track all the way. From the top you can continue around the north side of the mountain, to return through Rathcool and Glaun. As you walk, beware of unguarded mine shafts: this rough and rocky land was heavily mined for copper in the nineteenth century, and is still dotted with Cornish-style mining chimneys.

Schull is at its liveliest during its **sailing events**. The international sailing festival for children is usually held the second week in July, when the town is awash with nautical teenagers, and the yachting set proper swamp the town for the regatta held in Calves week (following the August bank holiday weekend, usually the first week of the month). At these times accommodation can be difficult, and phoning ahead is advisable.

Schull boasts a **planetarium**, developed by a local German resident in the village's community college. It's generally open only in the summer (May–Sept), at Easter and over bank holidays, with a detailed programme of starshows (€4.50) – call ⓣ028/28315 or 28552 for details.

Practicalities

On Main Street, *Adele's Restaurant* offers very comfortable **B&B**, including good continental breakfasts (ⓣ028/28459, ⓦwww.adelesrestaurant.com; ❷), or try *Stanley House*, about half a mile north of the village, a no-smoking house with en-suite rooms, a pleasant garden and good single rates (ⓣ028/28425, ⓔstanleyhouse@eircom.net; March–Oct; ❷). Five minutes' walk from the village centre is *Schull's Backpackers' Lodge* (IHH; ⓣ028/28681, ⓦwww.schullbackpackers.com; ❶), an attractive, clean, well-run wooden **hostel** surrounded by trees and offering dorms, single, double (some en-suite) and family rooms, where you can also **camp** and access the **Internet**.

As for **eating**, *Adele's Restaurant & Coffee Shop* in Main Street does very good and moderately priced homemade lunches and evening meals, and also has an excellent bakery. *The Courtyard*, on Main Street, serves tasty, inexpensive lunches in its coffee shop and has a good deli selling fresh bread from its brick-built steam oven, as well as local cheeses, oils and pickles. You can get superior fish and chips down at the harbour, and very good **bar food** at the *Bunratty Inn*. Schull's swankiest restaurant, the French-run *La Coquille* (ⓣ028/28642), offers only a short menu fleshed out with daily seafood specials, but still manages to be hit-and-miss, and generally overpriced.

Schull's pubs have **music** year round – look out for posters around town. Your best bets for sessions or just a relaxing **drink** are *The Courtyard*, *The Bunratty Inn* or *An Tigin* on Main Street, all of them cosy in winter, with beer gardens for the summer. The town also has a **bank**, and Fuchsia Books on Main Street is a good place to while away a rainy afternoon.

In summer, the *Karycraft* **ferry** runs from Schull to Clear Island (June–Aug 3 daily; Sept 2 daily; 45min; €12 return) and operates cruises around the Fastnet Rock (July & Aug 2 weekly; June & Sept 1 weekly; 2hr 30min; €13); and the *Eventide* crosses to Sherkin Island and Baltimore in around an hour (June 1 daily; July & Aug 3 daily; €12 return). For information on all these sailings, contact Kieran Molloy (ⓣ028/28278 or 086/237 9302). If you fancy taking to the water yourself, contact Schull Watersports Centre, The Pier (ⓣ028/28554), which organizes **sea-angling trips**, **dinghy rental** and **wind-surfing**; **diving** is organized by Divecology (ⓣ028/28946). **Horse riding** can be arranged with *The Colla House Hotel* on Colla Road (ⓣ028/28105). **Bike rental** is available from the hostel and from Cotter's Yard on Main Street (ⓣ028/28165).

Goleen, Crookhaven and Mizen Head

Around ten miles southwest down the peninsula from Schull is **GOLEEN**. Here on the harbour you'll find the delightful upmarket **restaurant** and **B&B**, *Heron's Cove* (ⓣ028/35225, ⓦwww.heronscove.com; ❸), where if you don't want a full meal you can still enjoy chowder, cakes and creek life. Beyond lies **CROOKHAVEN**, the nearest resort to the peninsula's best beach, the long, dune-backed, sandy strand at **Barley Cove**, whose rolling breakers make it a favourite with surfers. On the Goleen–Crookhaven road here is Barley Cove Holiday Park (ⓣ028/35302; Easter & May to mid-Sept), a large and well-equipped caravan and **camping park** with a café-takeaway, tennis courts and bikes for rent. In Crookhaven itself, you'll find welcoming **B&B** at *Galley Cove* (ⓣ028/35137, ⓦwww.galleycovehse.com; March–Nov; ❷), a modern bungalow on the main road into the village, with fine views of the sea and Fastnet lighthouse.

The most spectacular scenery on the peninsula is reserved for **Mizen Head** itself – sheer, vertiginous cliffs, where the famous signal station, linked by a little arched bridge, is accessible via the **visitor centre** (mid-March to May & Oct daily 10.30am–5pm; June–Sept daily 10am–6pm; Nov to Mid-March Sat & Sun 11am–4pm; €4.50; ⓦwww.mizenhead.net). A plethora of exhibits here includes a navigation simulator and the keepers' former kitchen and bedroom; there's a café, and you might be lucky enough to catch sight of dolphins, whales or basking sharks.

Sheep's Head

The peninsula north of Mizen, **Sheep's Head**, has an ancient feel to it: barren land almost entirely devoid of people. There are only a couple of tiny villages here, and traffic is sparse, so don't try to hitch if you're going to need to return in a hurry. It's an ever-changing landscape, where surges of harsh granite rise from sweet green fields, fuchsias and honeysuckle scramble over greystone walls, and gorse and heather colour wild heathland. The north coast looks down on the magnificent Bantry Bay, backed by the wild Caha Mountains, and offers cyclists a wonderful descent towards Bantry. There are also fabulous panoramic views over County Cork, the Beara Peninsula, and County Kerry from the top of **Seefin**, Sheep's Head's highest hill (1136ft); there's no clear path, but you can head for the summit in around 45min from the north-coast road two miles or so north of Kilcrohane. All of this can best be enjoyed by pedalling the easy-to-follow, fifty-mile **Sheep's Head Cycle Route**, or by walking the 55-mile **Sheep's Head Way**, both of which are clearly signposted circuits of the peninsula via Bantry, Kilcrohane, Ahakista and Durrus; the latter is relatively easy walking, can be done in four days and is marked on OS Discovery Series map number 88 or the 1:50,000 map that comes with the locally available *Guide to the Sheep's Head Way*.

DURRUS, little more than a handful of pubs and shops at the head of the peninsula's south coast, is the largest village here. If you want to stay, there's pleasant, en-suite **B&B** at *Avoca House* (Ⓣ027/61511, Ⓔavoca@emara.com; ❷), with evening meals available; *Ivo's* nearby serves inexpensive **bar food**. Moving way up the scale and two miles southwest down the R591 towards Crookhaven, *Blairs Cove House* (Ⓣ027/61127, Ⓦwww.irelands-blue-book.ie; ❽) combines spacious luxury accommodation in beautiful grounds overlooking Dunmanus Bay, with an excellent restaurant, renowned for its buffet-style starters and grilled meats. *Dunbeacon* **campsite** (Ⓣ027/61246, Ⓔcamping@fishpublishing.com; closed mid-Oct to Easter), a mile or so further down the same road, is a relaxing, low-key affair. Midway down Sheep's Head, minuscule **AHAKISTA** has a narrow slip of sandy beach backed by trees. *The Tin Bar* here serves food, including summertime barbecues, and hosts traditional music sessions. One and a half miles beyond Ahakista, *Reenmore Farmhouse* **B&B** offers standard and en-suite rooms and evening meals (Ⓣ027/67051, Ⓔjenniebarry@oceanfree.net; closed Nov–March; ❷).

KILCROHANE, three and a half miles southwest of Ahakista, has a **post office**, a couple of **bars** serving food, and basic **accommodation** at *Carbery View Hostel* (Ⓣ027/67035). On the less populous north side of the Sheep's Head, there's an outstanding **B&B** at Glenlough West, seven miles southwest of Bantry on the Goats' Path Route: the welcoming, all-en-suite *Sea Mount Farmhouse* (Ⓣ027/61226, Ⓔseamountfarmhouse1@eircom.net; closed Oct–March; ❷) provides magnificent views of Bantry Bay, fine home baking, evening meals and plenty of useful information about exploring the area.

Bantry

The beauty of **BANTRY** is its setting at the head of ever-turbulent **Bantry Bay**, which stretches thirty miles from the town to the ocean. The deep, churning blue waters of the bay, backed by the dramatic heights of the Beara's Caha Mountains, form as dramatic a backdrop as any in Ireland. If the tide's out, it's well worth taking a short stroll along the stony shore from the north end of the harbour to fully appreciate all of this. Alternatively, take the steep road that runs up to Vaughan's Pass from the back of the town, as this also affords spectacular views over the bay.

For centuries these sheltered waters attracted attempts from abroad to invade. In 1689, a French fleet sailed up the bay to assist James II, but was forced to return after an indecisive battle with Williamite forces. A century later, in 1796, **Wolfe Tone** arrived with another French fleet – and this time with revolutionary ideals – to try to overthrow British rule. Channel storms, however, had already reduced the fleet from 43 ships to sixteen by the time it arrived, and the remaining vessels spent six days in the bay unable to land, even though, as Tone said, "we were close enough to toss a biscuit on shore." After this failure they were forced to turn back. Richard White, a local landowner, was rewarded for his loyalty to the English Crown at the time of the invasion by being made Baron Bantry. **Bantry House**, with its fabulous interior and gardens, still belongs to the same family and constitutes a major reason to visit the town.

There's some irony in the fact that it also houses the 1796 French Armada Exhibition so that you can ponder the exhilarating ideals of revolution in the lavish, aristocratic setting that Tone would have swept away had the venture been successful.

Arrival, information and accommodation

Bus Éireann **buses** have their stop outside *Murphy's Bar* (information inside) on the quays; private buses drop off on Wolfe Tone Square (usually just referred to as the square). At the east end of the square is the uninspiring **tourist office** (March–June, Sept & Oct Mon–Sat 9.30am–5.30pm; July & Aug daily 9am–6pm; sometimes closed Wed & for lunch; ⓣ027/50229). **Bike rental** is available at Kramer's, Glengarriff Road (ⓣ027/50278). **Internet access** at Fast.net, Main Street (ⓣ027/51624).

There's a good, if small, range of **accommodation** in Bantry and the surrounding area, and it's advisable to book ahead in July and August and during the **mussel festival** over the second weekend in May – plenty of music, street entertainment and, of course, seafood – or the prestigious ten-day **West Cork Chamber Music Festival** held at Bantry House generally at the beginning of July (ⓣ027/52788 or ⓦwww.westcorkmusic.ie for details of this and other classical music concerts in and around Bantry). The **hostel**, *Bantry Independent Hostel*, is on Bishop Lucey Place (ⓣ027/51050), a short signposted walk from the square. It's a friendly, welcoming place with a big garden and the kind of atmosphere that makes you want to linger. At Ballylickey, four miles from Bantry along the road towards Glengarriff, is *Eagle Point Caravan and Camping Park* (closed Oct–April; ⓣ027/50630, ⓦwww.eaglepointcamping.com), a superbly situated site right on the edge of the bay; you can swim from their pebbly beach and there are excellent wild mountain walks roundabout.

Atlanta House Main St ⓣ027/50237, ⓦwww.atlantaguesthouse.com. Traditional, good-value, family-run guesthouse right in the heart of Bantry, with en-suite bathrooms, TVs and phones in all the bedrooms. ❷

Bantry House ⓣ027/50047, ⓦwww.bantryhouse.ie. One of the finest stately mansions in Ireland in a superb location overlooking the bay, yet still a family home. The interior is furnished with antiques and works of art, and musical concerts are often held here. Dinner is available (enquire when booking). Closed Nov–Feb; closed 2003, reopening 2004. ❽

Dunauley Seskin ⓣ027/50290, ⓦwww.dunauley.com. Located just under a mile out along the steep road towards Vaughan's Pass, this very comfortable and welcoming no-smoking B&B offers some of the most spectacular views in Cork. The excellent breakfast menu includes smoked salmon and scrambled eggs, stewed fruits and Irish cheeses. Rooms with views are slightly more expensive than those without, but are well worth the extra money. Closed Oct–April. ❸

The Mill Newtown ⓣ027/50278, ⓔbbthemill@eircom.net. Half a mile along the Glengarriff road, this spacious bungalow is comfortably furnished, with stripped pine floors and every inch of wall covered with vibrant paintings; all bedrooms are en suite and non-smoking. Closed Nov–March. ❷

Sunville Newtown ⓣ027/50175. Modern bungalow B&B about half a mile out on the road towards Glengarriff. Standard and en-suite rooms available; non-smoking bedrooms; good reductions for children. Closed Nov–April. ❷

Westlodge Hotel ⓣ027/50360, ⓦwww.westlodgehotel.ie. All rooms at this large, purpose-built, modern hotel have en-suite bathrooms, TVs, radios and tea- and coffee-making facilities, and there's a leisure centre, with pool, gym, tennis and squash courts the major draws. Organized family activities June–Aug. Self-catering cottages also available. The hotel is located about a mile out of town on the southbound N71. ❼

The Town

Bantry gathers itself around the expansive, bayside **Wolfe Tone Square**, distinguished by a pretty Regency Gothic church, a statue of St Brendan staring out to sea and a rather refined one of Wolfe Tone himself further inland. In the immediate surrounds are lush wooded slopes – a safe haven tucked between the ravages of the sea and the wilds of the rocky mountains. The **Sheep's Head Way** starts here, passing through the grounds of Bantry House before heading west for the low hills of the Sheep's Head Peninsula (see p.370); if you have your own transport, you could also easily reach Gougane Barra from Bantry (see p.371). The town itself is the chief fishing port and commercial centre for the area, and a market is held in the square every Friday.

Bantry House (March–Oct daily 9am–6pm; closed 2003, reopening 2004; house €5.50, armada exhibition and gardens €4; Ⓦwww.bantryhouse.ie) nowadays provides an elegant vision of the rarefied life led by the Anglo-Irish aristocracy. It is sumptuously decorated and packed with art treasures. Much of the furniture is French Napoleonic, and there are Gobelin tapestries and Aubusson carpets; the sheer variety of artefacts, many of them from the second earl's European wanderings in the nineteenth century is exceptional. The setting is superb: ordered landscaped gardens look down over the bay, calmly asserting the harmony of the aristocratic order, unruffled by the ruggedness of the surroundings. **The Bantry 1796 French Armada Exhibition Centre** (March–Oct daily 9am–5pm), housed in one of the courtyards, gives a blow-by-blow account of Wolfe Tone's failed mission. You can see artefacts recovered from the wreck of the frigate *La Surveillante*, scuttled on Whiddy Island in 1797 and rediscovered in 1982.

Another aspect of the past is remembered with relish by the ladies who run the **Bantry Museum**, behind the fire station on Wolfe Tone Square (July & Aug Mon–Fri 11am–3pm, but likely to vary – try contacting the tourist office; €1). The museum is the collection of the local history society – domestic paraphernalia, old newspapers and everyday trivia of every sort – which the curators willingly elaborate on with an entertaining blend of history and gossip. The modern library, at the top of Bridge Street, was built in 1974 and, at first glance, looks like some sort of spaceship, though the design was in fact inspired by a prehistoric dolmen: as adventurous a piece of public architecture as you'll find in the west of Ireland, it's let down by a white facade that already seems thoroughly tacky.

One final thing worth going out of your way to see is the fine, early Christian **Kilnaruane Pillar Stone** just out of town. Its worn carvings depict four men rowing, an apostle and the Cross; two of the men are thought to represent SS Paul and Anthony, and the boat is considered to be an early representation of a currach. Follow the main road south out of town and take the first turning on the left past *The Westlodge Hotel*: the stone is in a field 500 yards further on the right.

Eating, drinking and entertainment

There are a handful of decent places to **eat** in Bantry, but if the weather's fine and the tide's out, getting together a **picnic** and heading out around the northern shoreline is probably your best option. This aside, *The Snug* on the square serves excellent cheap **bar food** (last orders 8.45pm daily); *Ó S'ocháin* in Bridge Street is a cheery **café** serving hearty lunches and seafood platters and stays open in the evening during the summer; and *The Brick Oven* on the square serves very good **pizza**, salads and baguettes. *The Pantry Bistro* (Ⓣ027/52181) on New Street, above a fish shop and opposite the supermarket, has a welcoming, informal atmosphere and a varied menu that might include pasta, burritos and salads during the day and moderately priced Mediterranean-style meals in the evening. For more upmarket evening meals

Road bowling

One local sport worth looking out for is **road bowling**, a game peculiar to west Cork and played around Bantry on Sundays. A 28oz iron ball is thrown along country roads, and the winner of the game is the person who moves the ball over a prescribed distance (usually two and a half miles) with the fewest throws. Unsurprisingly, a fair amount of betting goes on too. If you come across handfuls of grass that have been dropped along a lane at intervals, it generally means a game has been or is being played along that route – clumps of grass are used as markers.

in a relaxed setting try the seafood at *O'Connor's* (Ⓣ027/50221) on the square, where mussels are the speciality.

Regular **pubs** are plentiful: *The Anchor Bar*, with a good, friendly mix of locals and visitors, or *Ma Murphy's*, a cosy bar-grocery with a beer garden, are convivial places to start, both on New Street. For traditional **music** and ballad sessions, try *Crowley's* on Wednesday, Friday and Sunday nights or *The 1796 Bar* on Thursdays, both on the square.

The Beara Peninsula

The **Beara Peninsula** (Ⓦwww.bearatourism.com), barren and remote, seems to have an energy all of its own, bounding in great ribs of rock thirty miles out into the ocean. In good weather it can be outrageously beautiful, especially in the extreme west, but the weather is notoriously changeable and when the mists roll in and the wind rises there are precious few places to shelter from it all. It is a fine place for tough cycling and energetic hiking, though you need to be prepared: careful planning of routes, particularly the descent, is vital. Alternatively, you could try the **Beara Way**, a signposted walk of 125 miles (9–11 days), following old roads and tracks from Glengarriff west along the southern side of the peninsula (via Adrigole, Castletownbere, Bere Island and Allihies) to Dursey Island, then along the north side (via Eyeries, Ardgroom and Lauragh) to Kenmare and back down to Glengarriff; or the roughly parallel, waymarked, 86-mile **Beara Way Cycle Route**. Route guides are available locally, and the Ordnance Survey 1:50,000 Discovery map 84 covers nearly the whole peninsula; Cork Kerry Tourism produce a free "Services Guide" to walking and cycling routes in the area, but accommodation shouldn't be a problem on the Beara, unless you're walking at a snail's pace. Everywhere along the peninsula you are accompanied by fine views of the mountains and the sea, and there are occasional sandy **beaches** on either side; take local advice before swimming, as currents can be treacherous.

Glengarriff and around

Around nine miles northwest along the main N71 road from Bantry and cradled between the Caha Mountains and Bantry Bay, **GLENGARRIFF** is an oasis of greenery. South-facing and sheltered by the mountains, it has a peculiarly gentle climate; oak and holly woodlands hug the shoreline while occasional palms flourish in hotel gardens. This picturesque juxtaposition has been exploited since the nineteenth century, when sensitive Victorians became alerted to the beneficial effects of the uniquely mild atmosphere in this pocket of lushness. The landscape – and the gift shops – still pull in the coach parties, but the village's popularity also means there's a decent range of places to stay, making it a good base for exploring some of Cork's wildest and most beautiful countryside or for just hopping over to see the horticultural delights of **Garinish Island**.

The surrounding mountains are wonderfully rugged; huge areas of barren rock show odd patches of scrawny, rough vegetation, and then the occasional seam of brilliant deciduous woods. As well as the Beara Way and Cycle Route, there are plenty of opportunities in the immediate vicinity of Glengarriff for exploration on foot or by bike (or a combination of both). To the west of the village, the short climb up to **Lady Bantry's Lookout** (30–45 min return) is rewarded with panoramic views of the bay, while the adjacent **forest park** of pine trees and ancient oaks is crossed by waymarked nature trails and cycle routes. Further west again, about six miles from Glengarriff, lies **Barley Lake**, a beautiful armchair or corrie lake that can be circled in around an hour. Hostellers can get advice at *Murphy's* (which also has information about the local three-day walking festival over the bank holiday weekend in early May), or you can pick up a leaflet of suggested walks at one of the two **tourist offices** in the main street: Bord Fáilte's (June to mid-Sept hours variable, but generally daily 10am–5pm, closed for lunch; ⓣ027/63084) or the privately run office next to *Murphy's* (daily: high summer 9am–9pm; shoulder season 10am–6pm; closed mid-Nov to Feb; ⓣ027/63201). **Bike rental** is available in the summer from Jem Creations (ⓣ027/63113), by the main junction in the village; if that sounds too much like hard work, contact Glengarriff Cabs about their **tours** of the area ⓣ027/63060. Note that there are no banks in Glengarriff, but most shops have **bureaux de change**.

Murphy's (IHH; ⓣ027/63555, ⓦwww.glengarriffhostel.com; ❶) is a well-run and cheerful **hostel**, with double and family rooms, the best showers in the west, Internet access and plenty of useful information about what to do in the area; if this is full, try the sporadically open *Wanda Hostel* (ⓣ027/63595) by the central junction. Comfortable **B&Bs** include the central, well-kept *Conimar* (ⓣ027/63405; ❷) and the good-value, all-en-suite *Cottage Bar and Restaurant* (ⓣ027/63226, ⓦwww.cottagebar.com; ❶), which offers excellent half-board deals and has some self-catering cottages. For traditional **hotel** accommodation, head for *Casey's* (ⓣ027/63010; ❸), a friendly and recently refurbished nineteenth-century establishment in the centre of the village; upmarket digs are available at the lavishly renovated *Eccles Hotel* (ⓣ027/63003, ⓦwww.eccleshotel.com; ❻) at the east end of town. You can **camp** in some comfort at *Dowling's* (ⓣ & ⓕ027/63154; closed Nov–Easter), about a mile out of Glengarriff on the Castletownbere road (R572).

Casey's Hotel does very good bar **food**, and such delights as monkfish with saffron and dill sauce in its smart restaurant, while the *Cottage Bar and Restaurant* is a good bet for good-value traditional food. During the day, *The Village Kitchen* underneath *Murphy's Hostel* does everything from breakfasts and cakes to soups, bagels and sandwiches plus excellent hot meals. Glengarriff's **bars** are very lively during July and August; there's usually music at *The Blue Loo* or *Johnny Barry's*.

Garinish Island (Ilnacullin)

In 1910, the MP Annan Bryce bought **Garinish** (aka Ilnacullin) from the British War Office and conceived a plan to turn his island – then mostly bare rock – into an oasis of exotic plantlife. All the topsoil had to be imported and the resultant growth delicately nurtured for decades, before and after the island passed into public ownership in 1953. The end product is hugely impressive: flowers and shrubs from all over the world flourish here, and through much of the year – but especially from May to August – the place is ablaze with colour, in vibrant contrast to the desolate mountains of the Beara a stone's throw across the water. The island's centrepiece is a formal Italianate garden, surrounded by a walled garden and wilder areas, a Grecian temple with magnificent views of the Caha Mountains and an early-nineteenth-century Martello tower. There's a one-hour self-guided trail around the gardens, and serious horticulturalists should pick up the Heritage Service's guidebook, which includes detailed plant lists.

The **island trip** is quite something, but undeniably pricey. The ten-minute trip out there past basking seals costs €10 return, either with Harbour Queen Ferries (which also runs fishing trips and harbour cruises; Ⓣ027/63116) from opposite the *Eccles Hotel*, or with the Blue Pool Ferry (Ⓣ027/63333), based next to *Murphy's Hostel*. The price you pay the boatmen does not include admission to the island, which is administered by Dúchas, the Heritage Service (March & Oct Mon–Sat 10am–4.30pm, Sun 1–5pm; April Mon–Sat 10am–6.30pm, Sun 1–6.30pm; May, June & Sept Mon–Sat 10am–6.30pm, Sun 11am–6.30pm; July & Aug Mon–Sat 9.30am–6.30pm, Sun 11am–6.30pm; €3.10; Heritage Card).

Adrigole

About fifteen miles west along the coast from Glengarriff is **ADRIGOLE**, a handful of houses stretching over a few miles with no real centre but with access down to a couple of good beaches. The West Cork Sailing Centre offers **sailing**, **powerboating** and **kayaking**, and is based down by the harbour at the Boathouse (Ⓣ027/60132, Ⓦwww.westcorksailing.com), which doubles as a café-bistro serving the full gamut from coffee and cakes to substantial dishes, such as fish of the day with lemon dressing and pickled cucumber. Just to the west of the junction for the Healy Pass is a shop, a pub and an IHH **hostel**, *Hungry Hill Lodge* (Ⓣ027/60228, Ⓦwww.hungryhilllodge.com; closed Jan & Feb; ❶), with twin and family rooms, meals, camping and bike rental available. A couple of miles back towards Glengarriff, Mrs O'Sullivan offers standard and en-suite **B&B** rooms at *Beachmount* (closed Nov–Feb; Ⓣ & Ⓕ027/60075; ❷), as well as cooked meals and a pleasant garden. It's all wild and wonderful walking country: made famous by the Daphne du Maurier book of the same name, **Hungry Hill** rises to 2251ft (signposted from the main road 4 miles west of Adrigole), a tough climb rewarded by fabulous views, hidden lakes and waterfalls, while the steep, scenic road through the **Healy Pass** leads north to Lauragh in County Kerry (see p.405).

Castletownbere

Beara communities have always relied heavily on fishing; **CASTLETOWN-BERE** (sometimes referred to as Castletown Berehaven or just Castletown), the peninsula's main town, is no exception. Set on Ireland's second largest natural harbour, it's periodically awash with Spanish and Portuguese sailors. To serve them there's a good selection of cafés and restaurants, well-stocked shops, a bank with an ATM, a chip shop and some enjoyable pubs. Essentially, the town serves as a useful place to pick up provisions or rest up if you're travelling through the area. It's also the home of the **Beara Arts Festival** in late July and early August (Ⓣ027/70765) and the point of departure for **ferries** to Bere Island (June–Aug 6–8 daily; Sept–May 4–6 daily; Ⓣ027/75014, Ⓦwww.murphysferry.com), which shelters the harbour.

If you want to learn more about the Beara's mostly maritime history, head for the entertaining, well-designed **Call of the Sea** visitor centre on the northeast side of town on North Road (mid-May to mid-Sept Mon–Fri 10am–5pm, Sat & Sun 1–5pm; €4). It covers the themes of smuggling and copper-mining, keeping watch from lighthouses and Martello towers, fishing and the naval history of Bantry Bay, through videos, hands-on activities and lively, anecdotal display boards put together by the Beara Historical Society. A coastal walk west from Castletownbere takes you past a **stone circle** about a mile from town, and on to the ruins of **Dunboy Castle** – where an Irish and Spanish force was besieged and overcome by the English in 1602 – and **Puxley Mansion**, the eerie, dilapidated shell of a Victorian Gothic mansion, burnt down by the IRA in the 1920s. This was the home of the Puxley family, who made their money out of copper-mining; their story, and that of the mines, was used by Daphne du Maurier in *Hungry Hill*. The setting is idyllic: a placid inlet behind Castletownbere harbour fringed by rich woodlands, with stunning views of the wild mountains – expect to be charged €0.70 per person, €2.50 for a car, to enter the grounds.

There's a **tourist information** hut on the square (Mon–Fri 10am–1.30pm & 2–5pm; ⓣ027/70054). **B&B** options include, at the west end of town, the pleasant *Old Presbytery* (ⓣ027/70424, ⓔmarywrigley@eircom.net; April–Sept; ❸), hung with some interesting paintings by Allihies artists, and *Knockanroe* (ⓣ027/70029; March–Nov; ❶). *The Old Bank* (ⓣ027/70252, ⓔoldbankseafoodrest@ireland.com; ❷), near the centre on Main Street, offers decent B&B (and a seafood restaurant) in a grand, old bright-red building and is a good source of local information, and about a mile east of town there's *Rodeen* (ⓣ027/70158, ⓦwww.welcome.to/rodeen; March–Oct; ❷), a family home set in beautiful sub-tropical gardens overlooking the bay. **Hostel** accommodation, as well as en-suite twin and family rooms, are on offer at both *Harbour Lodge* (ⓣ027/71043, ⓔharbourlodge@eircom.net; ❶), a converted convent in the centre of town, and *Beara Hostel* (ⓣ & ⓕ027/70184), two miles west of Castletownbere on the road towards Allihies, which also has a large **campsite** and offers breakfast, evening meals and bike rental.

One of the best inexpensive places to **eat** is *The Old Bakery*, West End; serving excellent home-cooked food, it's a welcome refuge on a rainy day with plenty of art books and board games to while away the time. Seafood features prominently on the menu at *Niki's*, on Main Street, a cosy all-rounder that also does breakfast. *The Copper Kettle* on the square (closed Sun) dishes up tasty baguettes, soups, salads and seafood platters during the day, and there's **Internet access** upstairs at Beara Computers. Your best bet for dinner, or a blow-out Sunday lunch, is probably *The Mariner* to the west of the square (ⓣ027/71111; closed Mon), an upmarket but informal spot with dishes such as salmon with green beans and chorizo and good veggie options. If all that doesn't suffice, provisions are available at all hours from *MacCarthy's* shop-cum-bar – one of the nicest places to **drink**, with traditional sessions on Thursdays. You're also likely to find music at *Twomey's*, which runs set dancing on Fridays. **Bike rental** is available from the Supervalu supermarket (ⓣ027/20070). If you want to explore this coastline from the water, try **sea kayaking** with Frank Conroy (ⓣ027/70692, ⓦwww.bearaoutdoors.com).

On to Dursey Island and the north side of the peninsula

Moving on from Castletownbere, you can head down to the remote, tiny villages at the end of the peninsula, a few houses, a shop and a pub being the typical set-up. This extreme of the peninsula saw some development in the nineteenth century when copper was mined, but little remains beyond the unguarded shafts; beware of these if you're walking. Signposted to the left off the road around five miles west of Castletownbere (then about another half a mile on) is the remote **Garranes Farmhouse Hostel** (ⓣ027/73147; ❶), clinging to a beautiful, ravaged coastline. The hostel, which also offers single and double rooms, is next to the **Buddhist Dzogchen Beara Retreat Centre** (same number), and hostellers are welcome to join meditation classes. Phoning ahead is advised since the hostel can be full of people on retreat at any time of the year.

The quietest of the islands to be visited off the Cork coast is **Dursey Island**, situated at the very tip of the peninsula and fringed by high cliffs. Dursey's attractions include fabulous views, solitude and the thrill of taking a very dodgy-looking cable car across the narrow and treacherous sound. You can walk its seven-mile stretch of the Beara Way for endless views westward over the ocean, with three great lumps of rock in the foreground: the Cow, the Calf and the Bull. For a day-trip, you need to get to the very end of the R572 in the morning: the **cable car**, which takes about fifteen minutes, only operates during certain periods of the day (roughly Mon–Sat 9–11am, 2.30–5pm and 7–8pm; Sunday times depend on when and where Mass is being held). If you want to stop over on the island you'll need to pitch a tent, as Dursey has just a few houses, none offering B&B, and there's no pub or shop. On the mainland at Garnish near the cable-car station, there's a **B&B**, *Windy Point House* (closed Nov–March; ⓣ & ⓕ027/73017; ❷), which also offers tea and snacks, evening meals and bike rental, and a **hostel**, *Dursey View Lodge* (ⓣ086/822 6275).

Continuing round the peninsula on the R575, you'll come to tiny **ALLIHIES**, which was formerly a major mining centre – a copper-mining museum is planned for the old Protestant church at the west end of the village. Nowadays it has four pubs, a shop, a summer-only tourist information kiosk, a sandy beach, a handful of places to stay and, in fine weather, superb views. For **B&B**, *Sea View House* (ⓣ027/73004, ⓔseaviewg@iol.ie; ❷) on the main street offers very comfortable en-suite rooms and good breakfasts. There are a couple of **hostels**: the comfy, central *Village Hostel* (IHH; ⓣ027/73107, ⓦwww.allihieshostel.com; ❶) is a delightful place with dorms, twins and family rooms, and has a good bookshelf and bikes to rent, but you'll need to book ahead in the summer; the An Óige hostel (closed Oct–May; ⓣ027/73014) is about a mile from the centre and is rather more basic, though adequate nonetheless and beautifully secluded – follow the Beara Way signs from the south end of the village if you are walking. You can **camp** by the beach at *Anthony's* small site. There's **bar food** in *O'Neill's*, and you may come across some kind of folk music either here or in any of the three other pubs.

Heading further along the north side of the Beara towards Lauragh (see p.405) and Kenmare, the fine scenery continues, with peerless views of the Kerry mountains to the north. About four miles before reaching Eyeries you can get simple **hostel** accommodation at **URHAN** post office (ⓣ027/74005 or 74036). Phoning ahead is strongly advised, especially in July and August. There's nothing here but a shop, a pub with bar food, a little beach and fabulous views to enjoy. **EYERIES** itself is a brightly painted village with some pleasant pubs serving bar food and the friendly little *Ard Na Mara* **hostel** (closed Oct–April; ⓣ027/74271 or 74406, ⓔelizgibson@eircom.net; ❶), a spacious bungalow with dorms, twins and family rooms in a beautiful spot overlooking the sea, where you can also **camp** – to find it walk around half a mile along the road east from the pubs and it's signposted off to the left.

Phoning ahead is strongly advised. There is en-suite **B&B** in the village at *Coulagh Bay House* (Ⓣ027/74013; closed Jan; ❶), and on the Castletownbere road at the well-equipped and tastefully appointed *Inches* (Ⓣ027/74494, Ⓦwww.eyeries.com; ❷), which also offers self-catering apartments, evening meals with seafood a speciality and lifts for walkers to and from the Beara Way.

Around two miles north of Eyeries just off the main road stands the tallest **ogham stone** in the world, over seventeen feet in height. Two miles further on, the small village of **ARDGROOM** enjoys beautiful scenery, backed by the Slieve Miskish mountains and set beside a rushing river. It makes a very pleasant stopover if you're walking the Beara Way or want to fish for brown trout in nearby Glenbeg Lake. **B&B** is available at *O'Brien's* (Ⓣ027/74019; ❷) in the main street, and you can get food and occasional music at *The Village Inn* or *The Holly Bar*.

Travel details

Trains

Cork to: Cobh (7–16 daily; 25min); Dublin Heuston (7–8 daily; 3hr 10min); Fota (7–16 daily; 15min); Rosslare Harbour/Europort (Mon–Sat 1 daily; 5hr).

Buses

Bus Éireann

Bantry to: Dunmanway (4–10 daily; 40min); Macroom (1 on Sat; 1hr 40min); Kenmare, via Glengarriff (2 daily in summer; 1hr 10min); Kilcrohane (2 on Sat; 45min); Killarney, via Glengarriff (2 daily in summer; 2hr 20min).

Castletownbere to: Kenmare, via the north side of the Beara (summer Mon–Sat daily; 1hr 20min).

Cork to: Ballycotton (1–3 daily; 1hr 20min); Ballydehob (2 daily; 2hr); Bantry (4–7 daily; 1hr 50min–2hr 20min); Blarney (hourly; 20–30min); Castletownbere (6–8 weekly; 3hr); Clonakilty (6–9 daily; 1hr); Courtmacsherry (5 weekly; 1hr 20min); Dublin (6 daily; 4hr 30min); Dunmanway (4–8 daily; 1hr 15min); Galway (hourly; 4hr 15min); Glengarriff (2–3 daily; 2hr); Goleen (1–2 daily; 3hr); Killarney (5–8 daily; 2hr 30min); Kinsale (3–12 daily; 40min); Limerick (hourly; 2hr); Macroom (6–15 daily; 1hr 20min); Midleton (Mon–Sat hourly, 4–5 on Sun; 30min); Schull (2 daily; 2hr 30min); Skibbereen (5– 9 daily; 2hr); Timoleague (5 weekly; 1hr 15min); Tralee (2 weekly; 2hr 30min); Waterford (hourly; 2hr 15min); Youghal (hourly; 50min).

Skibbereen to: Baltimore (Mon–Fri 3–5 daily, plus 4 on Sat in summer; 20min).

Bantry Rural Transport

Ⓣ027/52727

Bantry to: Ballydehob (Mon–Fri 2 daily; 30min); Durrus (at least 10 weekly; 45min–1hr 40min); Kilcrohane (6 weekly; 1hr); Schull (4 weekly; 1hr); Skibbereen (4 weekly; 1hr).

Harrington's Buses

Ⓣ027/74003

Castletownbere to: Cork (1 daily except Thurs; 2hr).

O'Donoghue's Buses

Ⓣ027/70007

Castletownbere to: Bantry, via Glengarriff (1–2 daily except Wed; 1hr 10min); Cork (Thurs 1 daily; 2hr 45min).

O'Sullivan's Buses

Ⓣ027/74168

Castletownbere to: Cork (1 daily; 2hr 30min).

Kerry

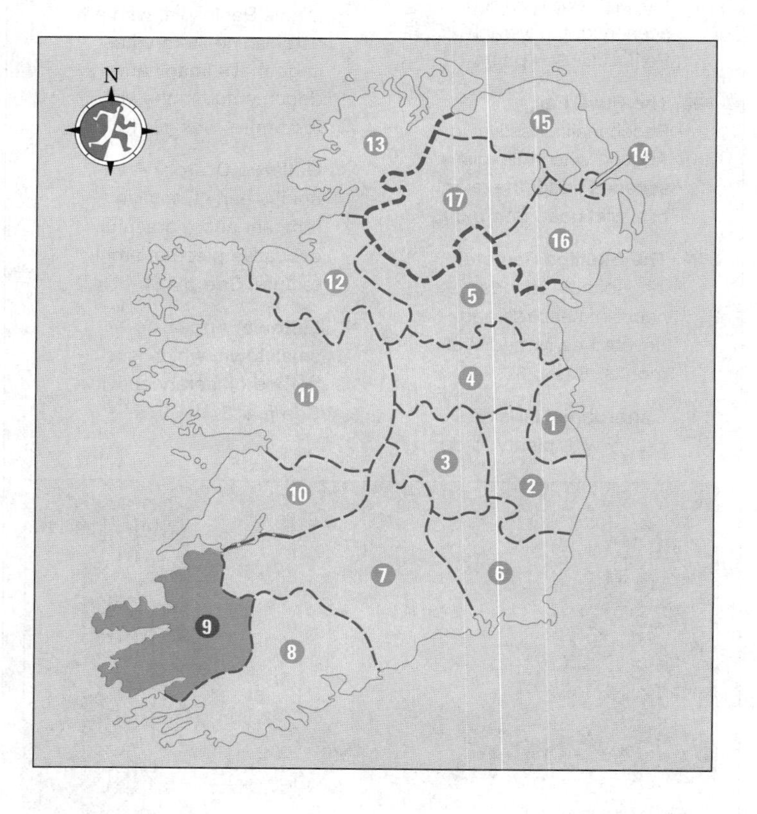

CHAPTER 9

Highlights

- **Killarney National Park** Beautiful – and popular – landscape of mountains and lakes, that can be explored by boat, bike and on foot. See p.388

- **The Kerry Way** A 130-mile walking route through the wild, awe-inspiring scenery of the Iveragh Peninsula. See p.394

- **The Puck Fair** Bacchanalian festival in August, when Killorglin secedes under the reign of a wild goat. See p.395

- **The Skelligs** Remote, inhospitable islands, haunt of seabirds and devoted early medieval monks. See p.399

- **Caherdaniel** Hillside village with plenty to do and a great beach. See p.402

- **Kenmare** An agreeable base with a great selection of places to eat, sleep and drink. See p.403

- **The Blaskets** Lonely islands off the scenic Dingle Peninsula, with an astonishing literary heritage that's imaginatively documented in the visitor centre. See p.413

- **Gallarus Oratory** A unique early Christian remnant and a graceful, evocative piece of architecture. See p.414

- **Listowel** Appealing small town, which is a hotbed of literary activity. See p.418

Kerry

If you've come to Ireland for the scenery and the remoteness, you'll certainly find them in **County Kerry**: miles and miles of mountain and moorland where the heather and the bracken are broken only by the occasional lake; smooth hills whose fragrant, tussocky grass is covered with sea pinks, speedwells, thrift and red campion, and that fragment into jagged rocks as they reach the sea. The ocean looks enormous, and you can stand in the sunshine and watch a storm coming in for miles before you have to run for cover. The only catch is that a good part of the county is very much on the tourist trail. However, the plus side of Kerry's long tradition of welcoming tourists is that it's very easy country to travel in, with plenty of accommodation and food in all price brackets, and, during the summer at least, transport is pretty good – though with some notable exceptions.

Broadly speaking, Kerry can be divided into four areas: the Dingle Peninsula; the Iveragh Peninsula, encircled by the Ring of Kerry, with Killarney in its hinterland; the Kenmare River, between the Iveragh Peninsula and, to the south, the Beara Peninsula, most of which lies within County Cork; and northern Kerry, from Tralee to the Shannon. Each section is quite distinct and has its partisans. By far the most visited area – indeed the most visited in the whole of Ireland – is **Killarney and the Ring of Kerry**. Deservedly famous for the beauty of its lakes and mountains, this region is, predictably, geared up for tourism, and the principal roads and sights are often overburdened with visitors. Luckily, however, the real wilds are never far away, and whether you head for the mountains or the sea you can soon lose yourself and feel remote from modern civilization. The **Dingle Peninsula** is on a smaller scale than Iveragh, but equally magical: peppered with monastic remains, it has a contemplative atmosphere that makes you understand why people talk about the mystic quality of the west. Around **Kenmare** things are different again, with a tamed, genteel feeling about the scenery – and about the amenities, which include a sophisticated range of restaurants, hotels and bars. To the **north**, flat, fertile farming land makes for less exciting scenery, but the county town of **Tralee** and **Listowel**, self-styled literary capital of Ireland, have their compensations.

Killarney and around

KILLARNEY has been commercialized to saturation point and has little in the way of architectural interest, but the real reason for coming here is without

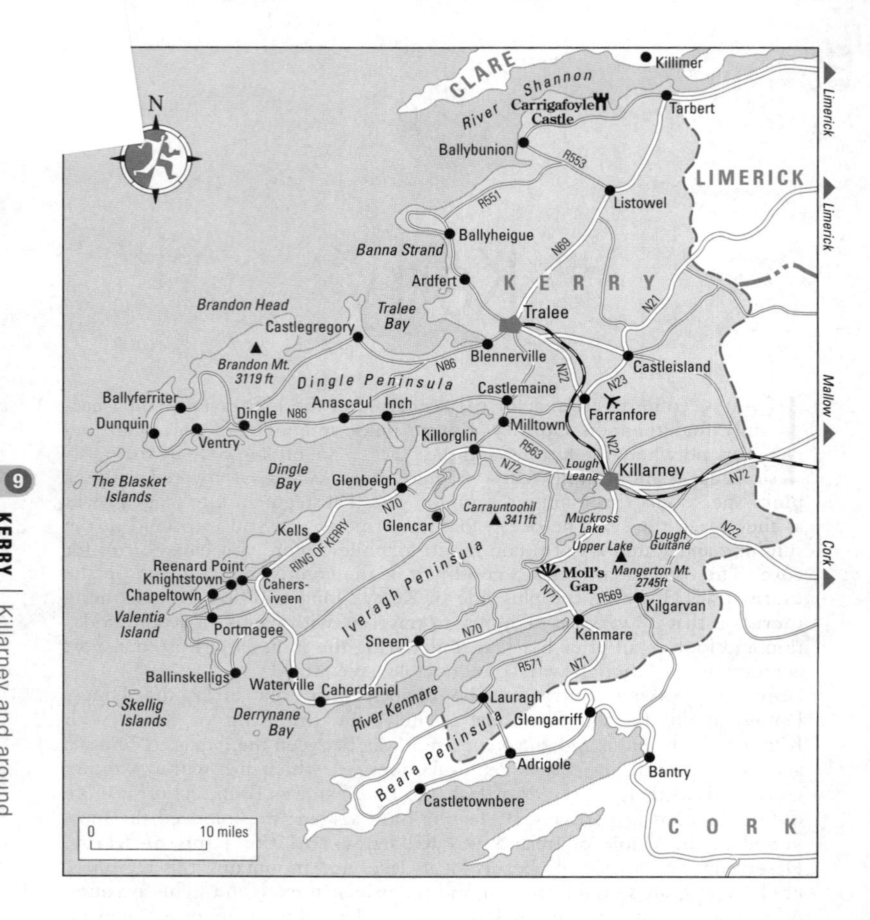

doubt the surrounding landscape. Its three spectacular **lakes**, Lough Leane (the Lower Lake), Muckross Lake (the Middle Lake) and the Upper Lake, are only the appetizer. Behind them loom **Macgillycuddy Reeks**, which have a grandeur out of all proportion to their height: rarely exceeding 3000ft, they're still the highest mountains in Ireland. Much of this wonderful scenery is contained within the **Killarney National Park**.

Arrival, getting around and information

Kerry's **airport** (ⓣ066/976 4644, ⓦwww.kerryairport.ie) is on the N23 about a mile northeast of the village of Farranfore, which itself lies eight miles north of Killarney on the N22 Tralee road; for details of airlines and flights, see p.12 of Basics. Farranfore village is on the Killarney–Tralee rail line. Buses between Castleisland and Killarney stop at the airport roughly every two hours; a taxi into Killarney centre will cost around €15. Killarney's **train station** off East Avenue Road, and **bus station** on nearby Fair Hill, are both pretty central. Even if you're not planning to bike round the Ring of Kerry, cycling is a great way of seeing Killarney's immediate surroundings, and makes good sense because local transport is almost non-existent. **Bike rental** outlets include O'Sullivan's Cycles and Outdoor Store, Bishop's Lane, New Street (Ⓣ064/31282), with a branch on Beech Road opposite the tourist office; Trailways Outdoors Centre, College Street (Ⓣ064/39929, Ⓦwww.trailwayskillarney.com), which also runs fishing trips; and several of the hostels. **Car rental** is available through Avis, with a desk in the tourist office (Ⓣ064/36655, Ⓦwww.avis.ie); Hertz, 28 Plunkett St (Ⓣ064/34126, Ⓦwww.hertz.com); and Randles, Muckross Road (Ⓣ064/31237), all of which have desks at the airport.

The extremely helpful **tourist office**, on Beech Road (June Mon–Sat 9am–6pm, Sun 10am–1pm & 2–6pm; July & Aug Mon–Sat 9am–8pm, Sun 10am–1pm & 2–6pm; Sept–May Mon–Sat 9.15am–1pm & 2.15–5.30pm; Ⓣ064/31633), offers a wealth of information about Killarney and the surrounding area, a good stock of local guides and maps for sale, a foreign exchange and Western Union money transfer, and is a good place to make bookings for a number of bus and walking tours including trips to the Dingle Peninsula, the Gap of Dunloe and around the Ring of Kerry. **Internet access** can be had at *Café Internet*, 18 New St, with a side order of coffee and snacks. Killarney Riding Stables, one mile west of town on the Killorglin road (Ⓣ064/31686, Ⓦwww.killarney-reeks-trail.com), offer **horse riding** in the national park, as well as on the six-day Reeks Trail.

Accommodation

Although there's plentiful **accommodation** of all sorts, the town gets very crowded in high season and it's worth visiting the tourist office or better still calling ahead to make advance bookings. There are a number of options for **camping** nearby, including *Fleming's White Bridge* (Ⓣ064/31590, Ⓦwww.killarneycamping.com; mid-March to Oct) just a mile east of Killarney (follow the N22 Cork road, turning right for Ballycasheen); *Flesk Muckross Caravan and Camping Park* (Ⓣ064/31704; April–Sept), a mile south from Killarney on the N71 Kenmare road and handy for both the Kerry Way and Muckross House; and *White Villa Farm* (Ⓣ064/32456, Ⓦwww.killarneycaravanpark.com; Easter to mid-Oct), a small site about two miles east of town on the N22 Cork road.

An Óige Hostel Aghadoe road Ⓣ064/31240. A large, well-run hostel that has been recently refurbished. About three miles northwest of town towards Killorglin it's located in beautiful countryside, and is well situated for walking in the mountains. Dorms sleeping up to eight are available, and there are comfortable twin (❶) and family rooms. A free shuttle bus service to and from the bus and train stations, cooked meals, Internet access and bike rental are available here.

Arbutus Hotel College St Ⓣ064/31037, Ⓦwww.arbutuskillarney.com. One of Killarney's oldest, this is a charming, traditional hotel with a spacious antiques-furnished lobby and a homely atmosphere. Some of the spacious bedrooms have canopy beds, and all offer TV and tea- and coffee-making facilities. Half-board deals available. ❻

The Copper Kettle Lewis Rd Ⓣ064/34164, Ⓦwww.copperkettlekillarney.com. Comfortable B&B accommodation near the town centre with a variety of rooms that have pleasant, rustic-styled interiors; one room has an en-suite Jacuzzi bath. Discounts for *Rough Guide to Ireland* readers. ❷–❹

Fair View House Michael Collins Place, off College St Ⓣ064/34164, Ⓦwww.fairviewkillarney.com. Top-quality, tastefully appointed guesthouse in the centre of town (with parking) that offers a range of en-suite rooms. All rooms have satellite TV, video and tea- and coffee-making facilities; some rooms are wheelchair-accessible. Discounts for *Rough Guide to Ireland* readers. ❷–❺

Gleneagle Hotel About a mile south of town on the Kenmare road Ⓣ064/36000, Ⓦwww.gleneagle-hotel.com. Huge complex that's good for families with a wide range of entertainments, restaurants, bars and leisure facilities, including a 25-metre pool. ❻

Killarney Royal Hotel College St Ⓣ064/31853, Ⓦwww.killarneyroyal.ie. A family-run, traditional town-house hotel with a warm welcome. All the rooms have air-conditioning, excellent furnishings and en-suite bathrooms, and there are some superior suites available. The generously proportioned sitting room has an elegant fireplace with a turf fire. Weekend deals available. ❼

Neptune's Bishop's Lane, off New St ⓣ064/35255, ⓦwww.neptunes-hostel.com (IHH). A friendly hostel which manages to successfully combine size with intimacy and offers lots of information about the area. Family rooms, twins, doubles (❶) and dorms, as well as Internet access and bureau de change, are available.

Northwood House Muckross View ⓣ064/37181, ⓦwww.northwoodhouse.com. Newly built, palatial, non-smoking house on a quiet road near the centre with fine views of the surrounding countryside. En-suite bedrooms with TV and tea- and coffee-making facilities. ❷

Peacock Farm Hostel Seven miles out of town by Lough Guitane, signposted off the road to Muckross ⓣ064/33557, ⓔpeacockhostel@eircom.net (IHH & IHO). A relaxed hostel with lovely airy rooms that overlook a stunning, rugged mountain location: an ideal place to unwind. Breakfast is available, but bring your own food to cook in the evening. Free lifts to and from Killarney are available. Closed Oct–March.

Rosslands Ross Road ⓣ064/36139, ⓦwww.rosslands.com. Pleasant B&B in a quiet, modern bungalow with a fine garden, 800yd from the centre on the south side of town. En-suite rooms with satellite TV and video. Discounts for *Rough Guide to Ireland* readers. ❷

Súgán Hostel Lewis Rd ⓣ064/33104 (IHO). Small, cosy, cottage-style hostel right in the centre of town. The owner is a musician who welcomes others who want to play, and sessions take place frequently in the summer. Dorms are cheerful and small, and two private rooms (❶) are available. You can rent bikes from here and there is plenty of information about what's on around town.

Valley View Farmhouse Lough Guitane Road ⓣ064/31206, ⓔvalleyview1@eircom.net. You'll be well looked after and enjoy tranquillity and great views on this working farm, five miles south-east of town near Lough Guitane. Most rooms en-suite; pick-ups from town available. Closed Nov–April. ❷

The Town

The town is essentially one main street – High Street which runs into Main Street – and a couple of side roads – New Street and Plunkett Street, which runs into College Street – all full to the brim with souvenir shops, cafés, pubs, restaurants, B&Bs and guesthouses. Pony traps are lined up against walls, while their weather-beaten owners talk visitors into taking trips through the surrounding countryside. These can be expensive and you might want to consider taking a combined pony and trap and boating trip as an alternative (see p.368).

The town's Irish name, Cill Áirne (which means "Church of the Sloe"), does not imply a settlement of any great antiquity, and the Cromwellian Survey of 1654 found no town or village of that name in existence. By 1756, however, a burgeoning **tourist trade**, fed by the growing Romantic attraction to lakes and mountains, had created Killarney: "A new street with a large commodious inn was designed to be built here, for the curiosities of the neighbouring lake have of late drawn great numbers of curious travellers to visit it," records a contemporary survey. The local landowner, Lord Kenmare, quickly spotted commercial opportunities and granted free leases for new inns and houses, building four major roads to connect his creation with the outside world. That said, Killarney doesn't look particularly planned, and the only building of any distinction is the high Gothic Revival **cathedral** at the west end of town, built by Augustus Pugin in 1855. A particularly florid Victorian interpretation of medieval architecture, the cathedral inspires both respect and derision, but is certainly worth seeing. During the Famine, when building work ceased for five years, the covered area served as a hospital for victims of starvation and disease; the tree on the lawn marks a mass grave from this period. On a rainy day, you might find some diversion, especially if you have kids, in the **Museum of Irish**

Transport, Scott's Gardens, off College Street or East Avenue (daily: March–Oct 10am–6pm; Nov–Feb 11am–4pm; €4, children €2), which shelters bicycles, motorbikes, vintage cars, fire engines and associated memorabilia, or at **Killarney Model Railway**, near the tourist office on Beech Road (Jan to mid-March & Nov Sat & Sun 10.30am–6pm, mid-March to Oct & Dec daily 10.30am–6pm; €4, children €2), where you can take in the landmarks of Europe in just over a mile of track.

Eating, drinking and entertainment

Places to **eat and drink** are thick on the ground in Killarney, and the only time when you might need to book ahead is over bank holiday weekends. Given the number of visitors to Killarney, it's not surprising that there's plenty of **entertainment** laid on, particularly throughout the summer. Although the widely publicized "traditional" Irish music can seem pretty spurious when you are surrounded by bus loads of other tourists, it sounds great nonetheless. Most of the pubs listed below have some form of music several nights a week during the summer months; in winter this dies down to weekends only in many instances, with the exception of the *Grand Hotel*.

In May and July there's **racing** at Killarney's racecourse on Ross Road, which, like any Irish race meeting, is well worth a detour. The *Gleneagle Hotel* organizes **Summerfest** over ten days in late June and early July, featuring big-name concerts – the likes of Elton John and Westlife – and plenty of street entertainment. The tourist office can give details of **Gaelic football** matches; major matches are held at Fitzgerald Park on Lewis Road, while local side, Dr Croke's, All-Ireland club champions in 1992, have their stadium across the road. The Rally of the Lakes brings hordes of motor fanatics to Killarney over the first weekend in May. Rally drivers roar along the roads around the lakes, so if you want to enjoy the mountains in peace, this is probably a weekend best avoided.

Restaurants and cafés

The Bean House 8 High St. A pleasant café which serves all the usuals: toasted sandwiches, soups, salads, cakes, herb teas and good coffees.

The Bricín 26 High St ⓣ064/34902. A reliable, homely restaurant serving traditional Irish food, notably filled boxties (potato pancakes), as well as more eclectic dishes such as prawns in a calvados cream sauce. There's plenty of choice for veggies. Early-bird menu until 6.30pm. Mon–Sat evenings only.

The Caragh 106 New St ⓣ064/31645. A restaurant and bar whose winning combination of filling hot dinners of roast lamb, Irish stew and pan-fried trout, served up with delicious pints of stout, make it extremely popular with families.

The Cooperage Old Market Lane, off Main St ⓣ064/37716. A stylish, modern interior and contemporary menus make this popular with a fashion-conscious young crowd and one of the more interesting places to eat in Killarney, with plenty of fish and game specialities; a simpler, cheap menu operates at lunchtime. Closed Sun lunch.

Cronin's 9 College St. A bright and cheerful café offering great-value filling meals such as shepherd's pie, lasagne, and smoked-salmon salads.

Gaby's Seafood Restaurant 27 High St ⓣ064/32519. One of Killarney's best seafood restaurants, with a warm and welcoming atmosphere. Lobster and wild salmon dishes feature prominently. This place is very popular and booking is advised. Mon–Sat evenings only.

The Old Presbytery Cathedral Place ⓣ064/30555. Attractive, upmarket restaurant in a quieter part of town near the cathedral, dishing up delights such as wild salmon with crispy bacon and bearnaise sauce.

Bars and music

Buckley's *Arbutus Hotel*, College St. A comfortable traditional bar catering for all age groups, this is a great spot for traditional music.

Courtney's Plunkett St. Appealingly plain, bare-wood bar, serving decent food and popular among a 20-something crowd for its DJ sessions, especially on Sun nights.

The Danny Man New St. A cavernous bar catering for the hordes of tourists who arrive in town looking for traditional Irish music. The bands who perform here tend to be heavily amplified, and a lively holiday atmosphere is guaranteed.

The Granary Beech Rd, opposite the tourist office. Stylish, modern, purpose-built bar-venue, furnished with blonde wood and leather banquettes, and serving an interesting selection of good food (not Mon). Frequent gigs – singer-songwriters, blues, indie rock and traditional – as well as set dancing (Tues) and late-night DJs (Fri & Sat).

The Killarney Grand (aka *Sheehan's*), Main St. A large but often-crowded bar, popular with locals and tourists, with nightly live entertainment: ballads or traditional music between 9 and 11pm, with a cover charge for bands and a club after 11pm; on Wednesday evenings there's set dancing.

O'Connor's High St. A quaint old-style bar attracting a good mix of locals and tourists. Look out for comedy performances by The Mug (a one-man story-telling show) in the theatre upstairs.

O'Meara's 12 High St. Large, lively bar attracting a fairly young crowd. Live music is performed here (4 nights weekly during summer, and weekends in winter) ranging from singer-songwriters and blues through to the occasional traditional session.

Killarney National Park and the Gap of Dunloe

The jaw-dropping landscape on the town's southwestern doorstep is now protected by the 24,700-acre **Killarney National Park**, which includes the three lakes, Leane, Muckross and Upper, while the glacial breach known as the **Gap of Dunloe** runs roughly parallel to the park's western border. The **National Park Visitor Centre** (mid-March to June, Sept & Oct daily 9am–6pm, July & Aug daily 9am–7pm; free) at Muckross House provides information about all aspects of the park, including a twenty-minute audio-visual on the landscape, flora and fauna, and there's an information point (July to mid-Sept daily 9.30am–6.30pm) at Torc Waterfall. The Ordnance Survey of Ireland produce a detailed, 1:25,000 **map** of the national park.

There's all manner of tours and transport available, including rented bikes (see p.385) and boats (see below). Two-hour **guided walks** through the park set off from the Shell petrol station opposite the cathedral every morning at 11am (€7; Ⓣ064/33471, Ⓦwww.kerrygems.ie/killarneywalks). **Jaunting cars** (pony traps) tout for business at several destinations, including Muckross House and Kate Kearney's Cottage (for the Gap of Dunloe), charging anything from €25 to €70 for up to four people. It's worth haggling with the "jarveys" – as the drivers are known – but as a rough guide, a fifty-minute trip through the Muckross Estate should cost around €35. The only jarvey currently registered with the tourist office, giving you some comeback if you have a complaint, is Paul Tangney based on the Muckross road (Ⓣ064/33358 or 087/532770). Several tour operators, including Dero's, Main Street (Ⓣ064/31251, Ⓦwww.derostours.com), and Gap of Dunloe Tours, *O'Connors Pub*, 7 High St (Ⓣ064/30200, Ⓦwww.castlelough-tours.com), offer full-day **combination tours**, which take you by bus to the starting point of Kate Kearney's Cottage, from where you walk or ride a jaunting car through the Gap; then after a lunch stop at Lord Brandon's Cottage you take a boat ride through the three lakes to Ross Castle, and finally a bus brings you back into town (€21 per person, €38.50 with jaunting car). Simpler **bike-on-boat tours** (you cycle through the Gap of Dunloe and sling your bike on a boat between Lord Brandon's Cottage and Ross Castle) can be arranged through the hostels, Trailways (see p.385) or Gap of Dunloe Tours, who also run a **bus to Muckross House** and back once a day.

Knockreer Estate, Ross Castle and Lough Leane

The gates of the old Kenmare Estate, now known as the **Knockreer Estate**, are just over the road from the cathedral, giving immediate access to the

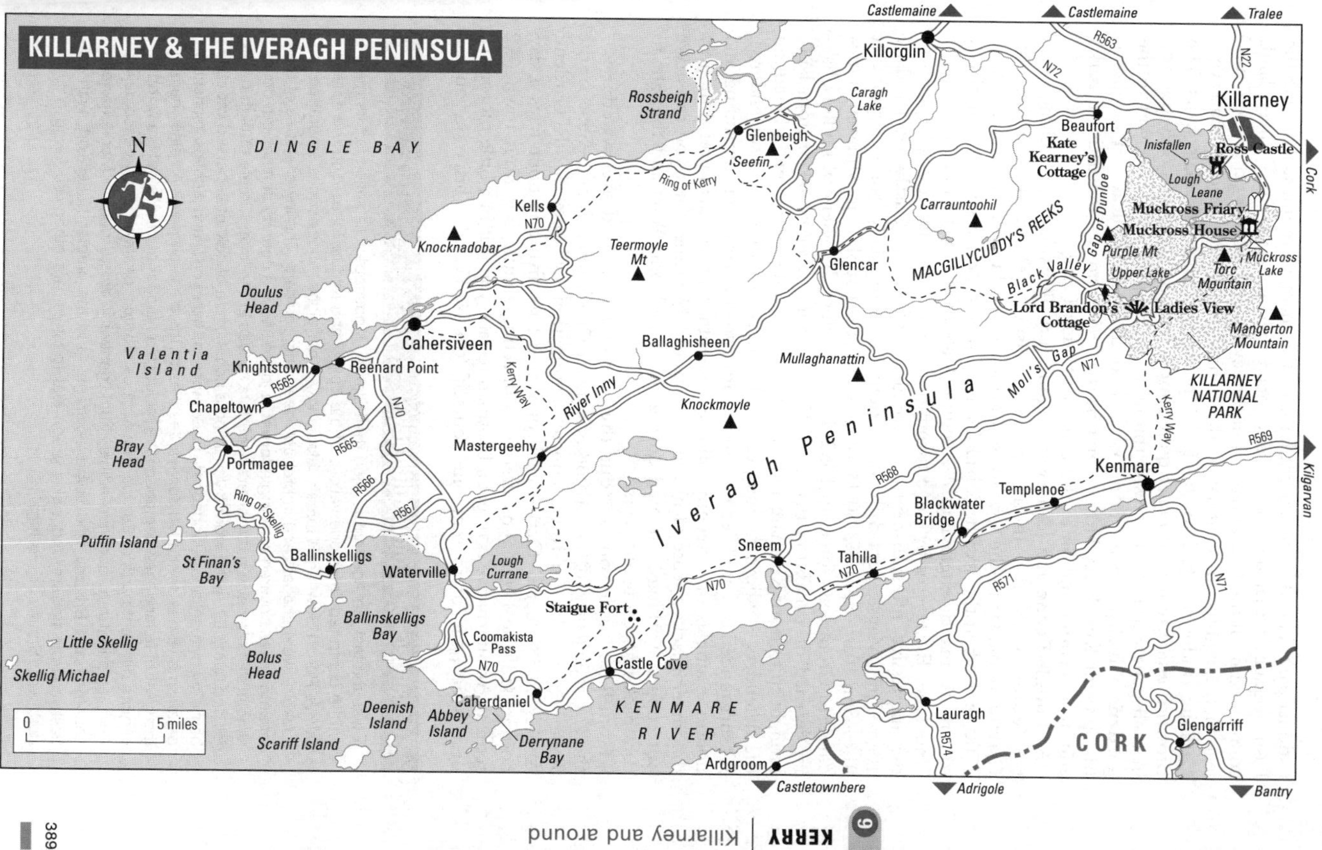
KILLARNEY & THE IVERAGH PENINSULA
N
DINGLE BAY
Rossbeigh Strand
Killorglin
Caragh Lake
Glenbeigh
Seefin
Ring of Kerry
Kells
N70
Knocknadobar
Teermoyle Mt
Glencar
Carrauntoohil
MACGILLYCUDDY'S REEKS
Black Valley
Killarney
Beaufort
Kate Kearney's Cottage
Gap of Dunloe
Inisfallen
Lough Leane
Ross Castle
Muckross Friary
Muckross House
Purple Mt
Upper Lake
Torc Mountain
Muckross Lake
Lord Brandon's Cottage
Ladies View
Mangerton Mountain
KILLARNEY NATIONAL PARK
Kerry Way
Moll's Gap
N71
N72
N22
R563
Castlemaine
Castlemaine
Tralee
Cork
Kilgarvan
R569
Kenmare
Templenoe
Blackwater Bridge
R568
Mullaghanattin
Iveragh Peninsula
Knockmoyle
Ballaghisheen
River Inny
Kerry Way
Doulus Head
Cahersiveen
Valentia Island
Knightstown
Reenard Point
R565
Chapeltown
Bray Head
Portmagee
R565
R566
R567
Mastergeehy
Ring of Skellig
Puffin Island
St Finan's Bay
Ballinskelligs
Waterville
Lough Currane
Staigue Fort
Sneem
Tahilla
N70
N70
Coomakista Pass
N70
Castle Cove
Ballinskelligs Bay
Little Skellig
Skellig Michael
Bolus Head
Deenish Island
Abbey Island
Caherdaniel
Derrynane Bay
Scariff Island
KENMARE RIVER
Ardgroom
Lauragh
R574
R571
N71
CORK
Glengarriff
Castletownbere
Adrigole
Bantry
0
5 miles

national park. The Browne family, Earls of Kenmare, were unusual among the Irish peerage in that they never renounced their Catholic faith. Given lands confiscated from the O'Donoghues in the seventeenth century, they were subject in the eighteenth century to the penal laws which decreed that every Catholic landowner had to divide his property among his male heirs. The Brownes' estate remained intact quite simply because there was only one son in each generation. A short walk through the grounds will bring you to the **gardens**, which blaze in spring with rhododendrons, azaleas and magnolias (the present Knockreer House, built in the 1950s, houses the national park's education centre), and on to the banks of Lough Leane.

At **Lough Leane**, the scenery is magnificent: tall wooded hills plunge into the water, with the mountain peaks rising behind to the highest, Carrauntoohil, far to the southwest. Ireland's last wild wolf was killed here in 1700, and when the weather's bad (as it often is) there's a satisfying similarity to early Romantic engravings. A lakeshore walk of just over a mile through the Knockreer Estate – or by car, a turning off the N71 Kenmare road – leads to the impressive fifteenth-century stronghold of **Ross Castle** (April daily 10am–5pm; May & Sept daily 10am–6pm; June–Aug daily 9am–6.30pm; Oct Tues–Sun 10am–5pm; €3.80; Heritage Card), the last place in Munster to succumb to Cromwell's forces in 1652. The story goes that General Ludlow, having learned of a tradition that Ross Castle would never be taken from land, brought ships from Kenmare and sailed them up from Castlemaine, whereupon the defenders – whom nothing else had budged – immediately surrendered. It's surrounded by a fortified enclosure with two circular towers remaining, and houses examples of sixteenth- and seventeenth-century furniture; somehow the interior lacks a sense of its medieval history. Near the water you can make out copper workings, last used during the Napoleonic Wars and thought to date back four thousand years.

From Ross Castle you can **tour the lake** in large glassed-over waterbuses – the *Lily of Killarney* (Ⓣ064/31068 or contact Dero's Tours; March–Sept) or the *Pride of the Lakes* (in town, contact Destination Killarney, Scotts Gardens, Ⓣ064/32638; March–Oct) – each of which runs five one-hour trips a day, costing €8; the latter also offers a connecting shuttle bus from town (€2 return). An alternative is to get a boatman to take you out in a little motorboat or rowing boat, or to rent one yourself (Ⓣ064/32252). This way, you can

The landscape around Killarney

It was the last Ice Age that formed the Killarney landscape. Glaciation left its mark on the contorted limestone valleys of the Lower and Middle lakes, and the nearby Devil's Punch Bowl and Horses' Glen show other signs – huge rocks smoothed to sucked-sweet shapes, and improbably teetering boulders. The lower slopes of the mountains are covered with virgin **forest**, a joy to see in a country that has cut down almost all its trees. A great diversity of flora thrives in the local climate of high rainfall and humidity. In the woods you'll find a rich mixture of oak interspersed with bilberry, woodrush and woodsorrel, plus mosses, liverworts and lichens (sensitive organisms whose continued survival testifies to the clean air here). As elsewhere in the west of Ireland the vegetation here includes a number of **plants** generally found in quite different parts of Europe. The famous arbutus, or strawberry tree (so called from its bright-red, and non-edible, fruit), generally grows only in Mediterranean countries and Brittany, and some saxifrages and the greater butterwort, with its fleshy purple flowers and sickly green leaf rosettes, are otherwise found only in northwest Spain and Portugal.

get as far as Lord Brandon's Cottage (with or without a bike – see p.393), or land on and explore the island of **Inisfallen**, the biggest and most enchanting of the thirty-odd small islands that dot Lough Leane. The monastery founded here in the seventh century was an important scholastic centre for a thousand years. Brian Boru, the eleventh-century High King and victor over the Vikings at Clontarf in 1014, was reputedly educated here, and the twelfth-century Annals of Inisfallen, now in Oxford's Bodleian Library, are an important source document for early Irish history. Wandering round the island is a delight: heavily wooded, it's also scattered with monastic buildings – nothing from the original seventh-century foundation, but there's a small Romanesque church and a ruined twelfth-century Augustinian priory. Eighteenth-century tourists were clearly aware of Inisfallen's charms: Lord Kenmare used to give parties for his influential friends here, and the gap in the wall of the Romanesque church is where he installed a bay window when the building was converted into a banqueting house. The picturesque ruin you see now is the result of further tinkering, around 1840.

Muckross Estate

The road south from Killarney to the **Muckross Estate** passes through unlovely territory dominated by huge modern hotels – if you're cycling, take the earliest turning right into the park that's available, to escape the busy main road. The first place to head for, here at the northern end of the estate, is **Muckross Friary** (mid-June to early Sept daily 10am–5pm; free), not only for the ruin itself – one of the best preserved in Ireland, part Norman, part Gothic, though sadly despoiled by Cromwell's troops – but also for its calm, contemplative location, and the fact that it, like Ross Castle, hints at something pre-dating Killarney's tourist history. Founded as a Franciscan institution by MacCarthy Mor in the mid-fifteenth century, it was suppressed by Henry VIII; the friars returned again, but were finally driven out by Cromwell's army in 1652.

You can continue through the estate on foot or by bike, but car drivers will have to stick to the main road, where signposts direct you to **Muckross House** (daily: mid-March to June 9am–6pm; July & Aug 9am–7pm; Sept & Oct 9am–6pm; Nov to mid-March 9am–5.30pm; €5, joint ticket including farms €7.50; Heritage Card), a solid, nineteenth-century Neo-Elizabethan mansion designed by the Scottish architect William Burn. Craftspeople demonstrate their trades, both in the basement of the house, where you can watch weavers, and in the nearby crafts centre, where there's more weaving, book-binding and a pottery. On the other side of the car park are the three **traditional working farms** where you can chat to actors playing out the roles of farmers and their wives (mid-March to April & Oct Sat, Sun & bank holidays 1–6pm; May daily 1–6pm; June–Sept daily 10am–7pm; €5, joint ticket including the house €7.50; Heritage Card). The excellent **café-restaurant** in the crafts centre provides a good refuge from the rain, but the **gardens** (open all year; free) – well known for their rhododendrons and azaleas and their pretty rock garden – are the place to be when the weather is fine.

Muckross Lake and the Upper Lake

The estate gives access to well-trodden paths along the shores of **Muckross Lake**, and it's here that you can see one of Killarney's celebrated beauty spots, the **Meeting of the Waters**, about an hour's walk from Muckross House. This highly picturesque spot, where Lough Leane, Muckross Lake and the outflow from the Upper Lake meet, has a profusion of indigenous and flowering subtropical plants – eucalyptus, magnolia, bamboo and an arbutus, or strawberry

△ Dún Beag, Dingle Peninsula

tree, on the left of the Old Weir Bridge. Motorboat trips on Muckross Lake can be arranged at the Muckross House Boathouse (Ⓣ087/278 9335). On the south side of the lake is the massive shoulder of Torc Mountain, shrugging off the spectacular 60ft **Torc Waterfall**; the climb up the side of the mountain is worth doing, if only for the view across to Macgillycuddy Reeks. On a good day, the Slieve Mish Mountains on the far side of Dingle Bay are visible.

About two miles south of here is the **Upper Lake** which is also incredibly beautiful, although it too is still firmly on the tourist trail. The main road running along one side up to **Ladies' View** (site of a café, bar and crafts shop) is where many queue up to admire the scenery – which is, in fact, truly amazing, including the Gap of Dunloe and the wild and desolate Black Valley to the west. Just before reaching Ladies' View on the main road, there's a signposted path, part of the Kerry Way, to Lord Brandon's Cottage (see below); beyond Ladies View, spectacular vistas continue at least as far as **Moll's Gap**, where the Avoca crafts shop and its good café mark the parting of the Kenmare road and the R568 to Sneem.

The Gap of Dunloe

Although the **Gap of Dunloe** – a narrow defile formed by glacial overflow that cuts the mountains in two – is one of Killarney's prime tourist attractions, with an almost-continuous stream of jaunting cars in high summer, it's possible to find a modicum of solitude if you're willing to use your legs.

At the foot of the road leading to the Gap stands **Kate Kearney's Cottage**, a pub and restaurant which caters for the large number of tourists who climb down from pony and trap rides here during the summer months. Moderately priced meals and sandwiches are on offer, and this is the last place for food and water before **Lord Brandon's Cottage** (open approximately June–Aug), seven miles away over the other side of the Black Valley, which serves teas, scones and sandwiches. The best time to walk the four and a half miles from the cottage up the valley is late afternoon, when the jaunting cars have gone home and the light is at its most magical. The road, which is closed to motor traffic, winds its way up the desolate valley between cliffs and waterfalls – Macgillycuddy Reeks are to your right, and to your left is the Purple Mountain, so called because in late summer it's covered in purple heather – past a chain of icy loughs and tarns, up to the top, where you find yourself in what feels like one of the most remote places in the world: the **Black Valley**. Named after its entire population perished during the potato famine, and now inhabited by a mere handful of families, the Black Valley makes you begin to feel that you've left mass tourism behind. The fact that it was the very last valley in Ireland to get electricity is some measure of its isolation, and there are no pubs or shops here. There is, however, a **hostel** run by An Óige (closed Dec–Feb; Ⓣ064/34712; ❶), where you can also get meals. Moving on, you can either carry on down to the Upper Lake or pick up the Kerry Way westwards (see box overleaf).

The Iveragh Peninsula: the Ring of Kerry

The **Ring of Kerry** is often used as a substitute name for the **Iveragh Peninsula**, but more properly it refers to the 110-mile road that encircles this vast, scenic leg of land. The route can be driven in a day, and most tourists view its spectacular vistas without ever leaving their bus or car. Consequently, anyone straying from the road or waiting until the buses knock off in the afternoon will be left to experience the long, slow twilights of the Atlantic seaboard in perfect seclusion. Part of the excitement of travelling round the Kerry coast comes from the clarity with which its physical outline stands out against the vast grey expanse of the Atlantic. Every gully, bay, channel and island is as distinct as it is on the map, giving a powerful sense of place amidst the isolation.

Cycling around the peninsula can be done in three days (not counting any diversions), and a bike will let you get onto the largely deserted mountain roads; just be sure your machine has lots of gears, and you have plenty of energy – the combination of gradients and strong winds can be gruelling. The waymarked, 134-mile **Ring of Kerry Cycle Route** (map guide available from local tourist offices) of necessity follows the main road for around a third of its journey, but includes a long, scenic loop through Ballinskelligs, Portmagee and Valentia Island and covers the north coast of the peninsula and the area around Killarney almost entirely on minor roads. **Buses** serve the entire circuit from late May to mid-Sept only (2 daily), returning to Killarney from Sneem via Moll's Gap; the rest of the year buses from Killarney, via Killorglin, only go as far as Waterville (Mon–Sat 1 daily), and there's one bus a week (Fri) from

The Kerry Way and Carrauntoohil

The **Kerry Way**, 133 miles long, is a spectacular, waymarked long-distance footpath that starts in Killarney, takes in the Muckross Estate, Torc Waterfall, the Upper Lake and the Black Valley before crossing to Glencar, then goes right around the Iveragh Peninsula through Glenbeigh, Cahersiveen, Waterville, Caherdaniel, Sneem and Kenmare – a sort of walkers' Ring of Kerry. More than most of Ireland's long-distance footpaths, it's resonant of the culture, as well as the nature, of the area and consists largely of green roads, many of them old drovers' roads or "butter roads" (along which butter was transported) and routes between Kerry's ancient Christian settlements. You'll need OS 1:50,000 map numbers 78 and 83, and Cork Kerry Tourism produce a useful *Kerry Way Map Guide*. The whole thing can be done in nine or ten days, or, with careful study of bus timetables, you could do day-walks along the Way beyond Glenbeigh in summer, or on the section between Glenbeigh and Waterville in winter. All the usual precautions need to be taken seriously in a region where gales blowing in off the Atlantic can make the weather change rapidly.

You should really fix up **accommodation** beforehand. There's an An Óige hostel in the **Black Valley** (see p.393), roughly eight hours' walk from Killarney. Next stop is the *Climbers' Inn* (☎066/976 0101, Ⓦwww.climbersinn.com; March–Oct; ❸), which has recently changed hands but still offers both B&B and hostel accommodation en suite, hidden among woodlands at **Glencar**; good meals and summertime traditional music are laid on in the bar, and they're planning to open a shop. Accommodation in **Glenbeigh**, **Cahersiveen**, **Waterville**, **Caherdaniel**, **Sneem** and **Kenmare**, which should be enough to get you all the way round the Kerry Way, is detailed in the text.

Experienced walkers may well be tempted off the Kerry Way to tackle Ireland's highest peak, **Carrauntoohil** (3411ft). Two of the finest approaches are described in *Best Irish Walks* by Josh Lynam: the Coomloughra Horseshoe, a seven-hour, occasionally vertiginous circuit (3750ft of ascent in total), starting from the bridge at Breanlee on the Killorglin–Glencar road, which also takes in the second and third highest peaks, Beenkeragh (3280ft) and Caher (3250ft); and a tough, nine-hour MacGillicuddy Reeks ridge walk (6000ft of ascent in total), beginning at Kate Kearney's Cottage, bagging six peaks over 3000ft and ending at the Breanlee bridge.

Kenmare to Sneem. Hitching is unreliable as traffic simply may not exist away from the main roads.

In the account below, we've covered the Ring of Kerry **anticlockwise**, which gives you a gradual introduction to the wild grandeur of the coastline scenery, starting out with the Dingle Peninsula and the dim shapes of the Blasket Islands visible in the distance. Coach tours from Killarney, which ply the Ring in flotillas in summer, are required to travel anticlockwise: you can weigh up the disadvantages of getting stuck in a convoy – plenty of time to admire the views – against meeting the buses on the many blind corners.

Killorglin to Glenbeigh

The first stop on the way out from Killarney is the pleasantly unexceptional riverside town of **KILLORGLIN**, whose main claim to fame is the **Puck Fair**, held over three days in mid-August (Ⓣ066/976 2366), a bacchanalian event with a wild goat captured and enthroned as king of the town, plenty of entertainment, dancing and drinking, plus a traditional horse fair. These rituals honour the wild goats which, stampeding through the town, warned residents of the approach of Cromwell's army. The fair's pagan origins, however, date back to the Celtic festival of Lughnasa, three days of feasting and ritual sacrifices to celebrate the beginning of harvest.

For B&B **accommodation**, comfortable *Riverside House* on Ballykissan Road (Ⓣ066/976 1184, Ⓦwww.riversidehousebnb.com; March–Nov; ❷), and homely *Orglan House*, with fine views and delicious breakfasts, five minutes' walk from town on the Killarney road (Ⓣ066/976 1540, Ⓔorglanhouse@eircom.net; April–Oct; ❷), are good options. Just over a mile away on the N70 Tralee road, *Laune Valley Farm Hostel* (IHH & IHO; Ⓣ066/976 1488, Ⓔlaunehostel@eircom.net; ❶) offers dorms, private rooms and cooked meals, while the well-equipped *West's* caravan park and campsite (Ⓣ066/976 1240, Ⓦwww.westcaravans.com; Easter–Sept) is a mile out on the Killarney road.

Inexpensive, hearty bar **food**, including seafood specials, is served day and night at the pleasant *Kerry's Vintage Inn*, Upper Bridge Street, and the popular, but pricey, *Nick's Restaurant* (Ⓣ066/976 1219) comes recommended. Most of your daytime appetites (though not on Sundays) can be satisfied at *Broadbery's* on The Square (Ⓣ066/976 2888), a café, restaurant and wine bar which serves speciality platters, from Irish parma ham to Kerry seafood, and lots of veggie dishes – there's an attached deli and art exhibitions for good measure. For such a small town, Killorglin has some excellent **bars**: the lively *Kerry's Vintage Inn* holds traditional music sessions on Thursday to Sunday evenings during the summer and on the two weekend nights in the winter; *The Old Forge Inn* is an atmospheric bar on the steep main street, attracting a young crowd; and *Coffey's*, at the bottom of the main street beside the bridge, is a plain old bar with traditional music on Thursday. All manner of **outdoor activities**, including wind-surfing, canoeing and rock-climbing, are available seven miles west off the Ring of Kerry at Cappanalea Outdoor Education Centre (Ⓣ066/976 9244). **Bike rental** is available at O'Shea's on Lower Bridge St (Ⓣ066/976 1919).

In **GLENBEIGH**, eight miles southwest along the N70 from Killorglin, almost everything is given over to tourism – despite plenty of accommodation, the town illustrates the disadvantages of sticking rigidly to the Ring. However, there are wonderful views all along the coastline and across to Dingle, and a spectacular Blue Flag beach, Rossbeigh Strand, which hugs a three-mile-long spit of land, just a mile away to the west; you can arrange **horse riding** on the

South Kerry and the Fianna

Many legends of the **Fianna**, a band of warriors led by **Fionn Mac Cumhaill** who served the High King in the third century, are set in South Kerry. One of them tells of how, near Killarney, Niamh, a golden-haired beauty on a white horse, persuaded Fionn's son Oisin to come away to her kingdom. Where the magical wave Tonn Toime roars between Inch and Rossbeigh, they galloped out across the sea to Tír na Nóg, the Land of Eternal Youth. After a blissful three hundred years, Oisin borrowed Niamh's magical horse to visit his homeland, with a warning not to dismount. Unable to find any of the Fianna in Kerry, he rode north to Dublin and found a band of puny men trying to shift a boulder. Leaning down to help, he broke a girth and landed on the ground a very old man. Before he died, St Patrick persuaded him to convert to Christianity.

beach through Burke's Horse Trekking Centre (ⓣ087/237 9110). For **accommodation**, try the family-run *Oaktree Lodge* B&B (ⓣ066/976 8606) at the end of the main street, or the upmarket *Towers Hotel* (ⓣ066/976 8212, ⓦwww.towershotel.com; ❺), an old-fashioned staging post with a modern extension on the main junction; campers should head for *Glenross Caravan and Camping Park* (ⓣ066/976 8451, ⓦwww.killarneycamping.com; May to mid-Sept), which also has **bikes** to rent, on the east side of the village. *Sweeney's* at the *Towers* is a lively, cosy **bar**, which serves sandwiches, salads and plenty of seafood, and hosts traditional and other live music every night in the summer; a wider choice of marine life is offered on the hotel **restaurant**'s set menu in the evenings. By taking the road up past **Caragh Lake**, you'll find some of Kerry's best mountain scenery. If you're on a generous budget and are looking for luxury and good food, you could stay here at the *Caragh Lodge*, a mid-nineteenth-century country house in beautiful gardens on the shores of the lake (ⓣ066/976 9115, ⓦwww.caraghlodge.com; ❼). Alternatively, you could carry on up to the three small lakes of Coomnacronia, Coomaglaslaw and Coomasaharn (good trout fishing, but you'll need a licence). The lack of trees that contributes to the feeling of austerity in this area was not an original feature of the landscape; Sir William Petty, Cromwell's surveyor general, had an iron mine at Blackstones and felled the forests to fuel a smelter.

Cahersiveen and around

At **Kells Bay**, eight miles west of Glenbeigh, the road veers inland for Cahersiveen, giving you an opportunity to take a detour down to the coast. On the way you'll pass *Caitín's* pub and **hostel** near the village of Kells (IHO; ⓣ066/947 7614, ⓦwww.patscraftshop.com), which can rustle up cooked meals and has family rooms. Any of the turnings right will lead eventually to the sea, past bright fuchsia hedges, with little or no traffic. "One wonders, in this place, why anyone is left in Dublin, or London, or Paris, when it would be better one would think, to live in a tent, or a hut, with this magnificent sea and sky, and to breathe this wonderful air, which is like wine in one's teeth," wrote J.M. Synge of the Kerry landscape, and here, for the first time, you begin to understand how the Ring inspires such hyperbole.

CAHERSIVEEN (sometimes spelt Caherciveen or Cahirsiveen, but always pronounced with the stress on the last syllable) was said by Daniel O'Connell, its most famous son, to be the only town established in Ireland after the Act of Union. With its one long, narrow street – at various points named East End, Church Street, Main Street and New Street – it's the main shopping centre for the western part of the peninsula, giving itself over cheerfully to the tourist trade in summer. It's worth having a peek at the **heritage centre** in the fearsome, castle-like **Barracks** (June–Sept Mon–Fri 10am–5pm, plus July & Aug Sat 10am–5pm & Sun 2–5pm; €4), which contains a concise history of the town, covering O'Connell and the Fenian uprising of 1867; it was the latter that prompted the construction of these heavily fortified quarters for the Royal Irish Constabulary. The **tourist office** in the old library on the main street (June–Sept Mon–Fri 9am–5pm; ⓣ066/947 2531) can give you directions to a number of attractive spots on the nearby Doulus Head peninsula that are accessible on foot or by bike, including a ruined fifteenth-century castle, a couple of well-preserved stone forts and White Strand; **bikes** can be rented from Casey's on the main street (ⓣ066/947 2474). Not far from here is the magnificent **Daniel O'Connell Memorial Church**, highly unusual in that it is dedicated to a statesman rather than a saint, an indication of the high regard in which the Liberator was held (for more on O'Connell see p.787).

On Valentia Road at the west end of town you can get **B&B** at *Castleview* (ⓣ066/947 2252; May–Oct; ❶), where you can choose between standard and pricier en-suite rooms, or the smart and imposing *San Antoine* (ⓣ066/947 2521, ⓔsanantoine@eircom.net; ❷). If you also fancy **riding** through the countryside or galloping along a beach, try *The Final Furlong Farmhouse Accommodation and Stables* (ⓣ066/947 3300, ⓔfinalfurlong@eircom.net; March–Oct; ❷), just over a mile out on the Glenbeigh road. There's a small, friendly **hostel** on the main street, *Sive*, 15 East End (IHH & IHO; ⓣ066/947 2717; ❶), with camping and private rooms available. For **camping**, however, you'd be better off at the waterfront *Mannix Point Camping and Caravan Park* on the west side of town (ⓣ066/947 2806, ⓦwww.campingkerry.ruralbiznet.com; mid-March to Sept), run by expert on the locality Mortimer Moriarty, who organizes music sessions in the cosy campers' sitting room.

As for **food**, you can get home-baked bread, cakes, salads and hot meals, including meaty and vegetarian breakfasts, at *Aoife's Cupan Eile*, and very good, reasonably priced bar food (not Sun evenings) at the welcoming *An Bonnán Buí* (both on Main Street). Chargrilling, Basque dishes and seafood are the diverse – often combined – specialities of *QC's*, a stylish, nautical-themed bar-restaurant at 3 Main St (ⓣ066/947 2244; in winter Thurs–Sun evenings only). Good coffee and **Internet access** are available at *Java-site.ie* on West Main Street (ⓣ066/947 2116). There are plenty of characterful **bars**, notably the *East End Bar* opposite the hostel, which has traditional music Tuesday and Thursday nights, and the aforementioned *An Bonnán Buí* (music Wed & Thurs, plus other nights in summer). Cahirsiveen holds a lively **music festival** (ⓣ066/947 3772, ⓦwww.celticmusicfestival.com) over the bank-holiday weekend at the beginning of August, which has attracted big names such as Sinead O'Connor and The Hothouse Flowers.

From **REENARD POINT**, three miles west of Cahersiveen, a ferry shuttles across to Knightstown on Valentia Island (April–Sept every 15min until about 10pm; ⓣ066/947 6141; cars single €5, return €7; cyclists single €1.50, return €2). There's also excellent, reasonably priced seafood here at *The Point Bar* – it's hugely popular, so you may well have to wait to be served. If you need **B&B**, *Sea Breeze* (ⓣ066/947 2609; ❷) has stunning views over the island.

Portmagee and Ballinskelligs

Beyond Cahersiveen, the main road takes the bulk of the traffic inland again towards Waterville, giving you an opportunity to explore the quiet lanes that lead out towards Valentia Island and the peninsula's end. **PORTMAGEE** nestles beside a small harbour at the northwest corner of the peninsula, its handful of bars and coffee shops providing welcome refuge on a blustery day. The village's small but interesting **Skellig Heritage Centre** (April–Sept daily 10am–7pm; Oct to mid-Nov Tues–Thurs, Sat & Sun 10am–5.30pm; Ⓦwww.skelligexperience.com; €4.40), just across the bridge on Valentia Island, provides information on Celtic monastic life, lighthouses and lighthouse-keeping, seabirds and aquatic life, and an audio-visual show on Skellig Michael. The centre also has a café with fine views of Portmagee, and runs **cruises** around, but not onto, Skellig Michael (1hr 45min; €21, including admission to the visitor centre; usually 3pm daily, plus others subject to demand, but Ⓣ066/947 6306 to check); and up to Knightstown and around the harbour, which is likely to be the only way out onto the water hereabouts when the weather is rough (1hr; €17, including the visitor centre; subject to demand). Back in the centre of Portmagee, you can get tastefully decorated **accommodation** – ask for a room overlooking the harbour – and good **food**, either in the restaurant or the lively, friendly bar, at *The Moorings* (Ⓣ066/947 7108, Ⓦwww.moorings.ie; ❸); there's also music on Friday (with set-dancing classes) and Sunday nights.

The often single-track and very steep road south of here is part of the **Ring of Skellig**, a quiet, scenic route round the peninsula via wild and exposed **St Finan's Bay** – which is the unlikely home of the high-quality Skellig Chocolate Factory (visitors welcome to taste and buy; Ⓣ066/947 9119). From the highest point of the road between Portmagee and St Finan's Bay, you can climb the hill on the seaward side of the saddle in twenty minutes or so for the most spectacular views out to the Skellig Islands, across to the Dingle Peninsula and the Blaskets, and inland to the Iveragh mountains. Monks from the Skelligs retreated to Ballinskelligs Abbey on the south side of the peninsula in the thirteenth century; today **BALLINSKELLIGS** (Baile an Sceilg) is a focus of the Gaeltacht (Irish-speaking area) on the Iveragh Peninsula (Slí Uích Ráthach), drawing large numbers of schoolchildren and students of Irish in the summer. The village is small but sprawling – there's an An Óige **hostel** (closed Oct–May; Ⓣ066/947 9229), with cooked meals available and a shop, the *Ballinskelligs Inn*, a pub with a deli and a lovely sandy Blue Flag beach with fabulous views across Ballinskelligs Bay to the mountains behind Waterville. The striking thatched roundhouse at the north end of the village is an art gallery and café, attached to the Chill Rialaig retreat for artists, who each donate a work of art for sale here.

Valentia Island

VALENTIA, an island now linked to the mainland by bridge, is Europe's most westerly harbour, and standing at Bray Head on the island's tip, there's nothing but ocean between you and Newfoundland, 1900 miles away. Valentia's significance is out of all proportion to its size: the first-ever transatlantic telegraph cable was laid from here in 1857 – though permanent contact wasn't established until 1866 – and for years it had better communications with New York than with Dublin. To add to the island's fame, in 1992 the oldest fossilized footprints in the northern hemisphere were discovered near the northerly lighthouse, nearly 400 million years old and belonging to a marine tetrapod that pre-dated the dinosaurs.

Almost every scrap of land on the seven-by-two-mile island has been cultivated, forming a rolling patchwork of fields stitched with dry slate walls. Valentia's position in the Gulf Stream gives it a mild, balmy climate, and the abundance of fuchsias grown by the inhabitants in local hedgerows only enhances its domesticated, old-fashioned atmosphere.

Arrival and accommodation

Access is by summertime ferry from Reenard Point (see p.397) to Knightstown, or from Portmagee on the south side of the island via the Maurice O'Neill Bridge (site of the Skellig Heritage Centre – see opposite). There's no public transport at all on the island, and accommodation is at a premium during the summer season. **B&Bs** include, in Knightstown, *Spring Acre*, across from the pier with good single rates (Ⓣ066/947 6141, Ⓔrforan@indigo.ie; March–Oct; ❷), and *Altazamuth*, a well-appointed place just inland from the waterfront where you can **rent bikes** (Ⓣ066/947 6300; ❷); and *Glenreen Heights*, Knightstown Road, about a mile away towards Chapeltown (Ⓣ066/947 6241, Ⓦhomepage.eircom.net/~glenreen; ❶), which offers standard and pricier en-suite rooms and evening meals. The An Óige **hostel** has space for thirty at the Coastguard Station in Knightstown, though services are spartan (closed Oct–May; Ⓣ066/947 6154), while en-suite dorms and B&B rooms, as well as **camping**, are available in the former grandeur of the *Royal Pier* (IHO; Ⓣ066/947 6144, Ⓔroyalpier-val@ireland.com; ❷). The island's other hostel, the *Ring Lyne* (IHO; Ⓣ066/947 6103; ❶), with private rooms, bar and restaurant, lies midway between the bridge and Knightstown at Chapeltown.

Around the island

KNIGHTSTOWN is the focal village on the island and, facing Cahersiveen across the harbour, affords fine panoramic views of the Iveragh mountains. A pretty waterfront with a scattering of sprucely painted cottages is dominated by the Victorian *Royal Pier Hostel*, while the main street has a few well-stocked shops and a post office with free maps of the island. *The Schooner* at the *Royal Pier*, where the beer garden enjoys the finest views of the mainland, and *Boston's Bar* both serve **food**, and the spruce *Knightstown Coffee Shop* does espressos, cakes, soup and sandwiches. It's hard to miss the trademark pink paint of *Fuchsia* (Ⓣ066/947 6051), an upmarket restaurant with courtyard seating, offering main courses such as cajun salmon and a daily vegetarian special.

From Knightstown, take the Kilmore road which affords a fine view to the north of Valentia's empty harbour, the Beginish Islands and tiny **Church Island**. This mere rock supports the ruins of an eighth-century cell, once inhabited by a solitary monk, a soulmate of the brotherhood on the nearby Skellig Islands, whose only company was the seabirds. On a clear day you can also make out the sheer cliffs of the Blasket Islands west of the Dingle Peninsula. A turning off this road leads to the incongruously exotic subtropical gardens of **Glanleam House** (April–Oct daily 11am–5pm; €4), former seat of the local magnate, the Knight of Kerry. Near the island's northernmost tip and highest point is the **Valentia Slate Quarry**, which has furnished slate for the Houses of Parliament in London and the Paris Opera House; it's a noisy, gaping cavern, dripping with icy water and topped by a much-revered Grotto of the Virgin, with lofty vistas over the sea. Further exciting views are provided by the spectacular cliffs to the west of here, and the ruined lookout tower on **Bray Head**, at the southwestern end of the island.

The Skellig Islands

From Valentia you get a tantalizing view across eight miles of sea to the **Skellig Islands** (Na Sceilg), apparently no more than two massive rocks. **Little Skellig** is a bird sanctuary, home to forty thousand gannets, and landing isn't permitted, but you can visit Great Skellig, or Skellig Michael as it's also called, and climb up to the ancient monastic site at the summit.

Skellig ferries

A trip to the Skelligs really demands fine weather; if it looks changeable be prepared for a very rough ride. Either way, boats need to be booked at least the day before – only around 250 people are allowed on the island each day, and it's not uncommon to have to wait several days before the boats will sail because of bad weather – and it's worth phoning the boatman about conditions on the morning of your trip. Bear in mind too that it is possible to get stranded on the island if the weather breaks. The trip is only feasible if you are able-bodied since landing on the island involves climbing a vertical ladder up onto the quay, and there are 650 steps to the top; the alternative is a cruise around the islands from the Skellig Heritage Centre (see p.398). It's advisable to take warm clothing, walking shoes, waterproofs and a picnic lunch as there is nowhere to get any food or drink. Ferries, costing €35 per person, operate between May and September (sometimes with extra departures at the back end of April and in October) from several points around the Kerry coast. Operators include: Joe Roddy and sons from Ballinskelligs (the shortest crossing to Skellig Michael at around 45min), who will pick up from Waterville (☎066/947 4268 or 087/284 4460); Seán Murphy (☎066/947 6214 or 087/236 2344) and Eoin Walsh (☎066/947 6327 or 087/283 3522), who sail from Knightstown, via Reenard Point and Portmagee; and Patrick Casey (☎066/947 2437 or 087/239 5470) from Portmagee, who will pick up in Cahirsiveen. Boats depart between 10 and 11am and should allow you at least two hours on the island.

There are several **departure points for the Skelligs** around the Kerry coast (see box above); the trips are not cheap but if the weather's good they make a fascinating and dramatic voyage. Once at sea, boats are followed by wheeling seagulls and, if you're lucky, puffins, too, from the nature reserve of Puffin Island, further north. You'll pass the huge, jagged arch of rock that forms Little Skellig, where gannets with six-foot wingspans career overhead or make headlong dives into the sea for fish.

Skellig Michael looms sheer from the ocean, a gargantuan slaty mass with no visible route to the 715-foot summit. From the tiny landing stage, however, you can see steps cut into the cliff face, formerly a treacherous path for the monks. Nowadays there's also a broad path leading to Christ's Saddle, the only patch of green on this inhospitable island. From here, it narrows and leads on to the arched stone remains of **St Fionan's Abbey** (560 AD). Among the ruins are six complete beehive cells – drystone huts that have survived centuries of foul weather. The island is dedicated to St Michael, guardian against the powers of darkness and patron of high places, who helped St Patrick drive the last of the venomous serpents over the seven-hundred-foot cliffs to perish in the sea. Contrasted with Valentia, it's a wild, cruel place, an awesome sanctuary of devotion, even if the monks didn't remain here all year round to feel the violence of the elements. The Viking invasion of the island in the ninth century lived long in folk memory, inspiring a Skellig monk to write:

Bitter and wild is the wind tonight
Tossing the tresses of the sea to white
On such a night as this I feel at ease
Fierce Northmen only course the quiet seas.

Waterville

WATERVILLE (*An Coireán*) may be touristy, but it manages to avoid being tacky. Popular as a Victorian and Edwardian resort and angling centre, and later

Waterville in legend: Noah's children in Ireland

Waterville and Ballinskelligs Bay form the setting for one of the more wayward Irish legends. When the biblical Flood was imminent, so the story goes, Noah's son **Bith** and his daughter **Cessair** found that there was no room for them in the Ark. So they and their retinue set sail for Ireland which, Cessair was advised, was uninhabited, free of monsters, reptiles and sin, and would therefore escape the Flood. However, although 49 women survived to land along with Cessair in 2958 BC, only two men besides Bith made it. The three men divided the women between them, but when Bith and Ladra, the pilot, died, Fintan, the last man, was overwhelmed and, to his eternal shame, ran away – upon which Cessair, who loved him, died of sorrow.

frequented by the likes of Charlie Chaplin, it still has an air of consequence that sits oddly with the wild Atlantic views. Its few bars and hotels aside, the town is chiefly notable as one of the best bases on the Ring for exploring the mountainous country inland, with minor roads heading up the Inny Valley to Ballaghisheen and on to Glencar. There's a small **tourist office** (summer Mon–Sat 10am–6pm; ⓣ066/947 4646) in the crafts centre on the north side of town, and B&B **accommodation** at the *Old Cable House* (ⓣ066/947 4233, ⓦwww.old-cable-house.com; ❷) and *Ashling House*, Main Street (ⓣ066/947 4247; mid-March to mid-Oct; ❷). The *Butlers Arms Hotel* (closed late Oct to March; ⓣ066/947 4144, ⓦwww.butlerarms.com; ❼) offers sea-views and a welcoming atmosphere. *Peter's Place Hostel* (no phone), on the seafront at the south end of town, is small and cosy, and its jovial owner may rustle you up a meal. Seven miles away up the Inny Valley near Mastergeehy (Maistir Gaoithe), the dorms and private rooms of the *Bru na Dromoda* hostel (IHH & IHO; ⓣ066/947 4782, ⓔmaistirgaoithe@tinet.ie; mid-May to Oct; ❶) are on the Kerry Way and well placed for exploring the mountainous interior of the Iveragh Peninsula. Most of the bars and hotels do food, one of the best being *The Lobster Bar* on the front, and for inexpensive home cooking including plenty of veggie options, try the welcoming *An Corcán* nearby. Skelligs Surf School (ⓣ066/947 8992, ⓦwww.skelligsurf.com), next to *Peter's Place*, offers **surfing** lessons and surfboard, bodyboard and wetsuit rental, as well as **Internet access**.

From Waterville, it's a long haul by bike or on foot further round the Ring of Kerry up to the **Coomakista Pass**, but the effort is well worth it for the breathtaking views from the Beenarourke viewing point over the mouth of the Kenmare River, and the three rocks called the Bull, the Cow and the Calf off the end of the Beara Peninsula – most spectacular when the weather's good; when it rains you can see the squalls being driven in across the ocean. Unfortunately you can't hope to avoid lots of other tourists here.

Derrynane Bay to Sneem

Tucked away behind the southernmost point of the Iveragh Peninsula, about six miles south of Waterville, is **Derrynane Bay** (pronounced "Derrynaan"), home of the family of Daniel O'Connell, the Catholic lawyer and politician who negotiated limited Catholic emancipation in 1829. On the west side of the bay, **Derrynane House** (April & Oct Tues–Sun 1–5pm; May–Sept Mon–Sat 9am–6pm, Sun 11am–7pm; Nov–March Sat & Sun 1–5pm; €2.50; Heritage Card), remodelled by the "Liberator" himself, is absolutely simple – a square slate tower and roughly elegant rooms, now displaying relics of O'Connell's life and career. The O'Connells were an old Gaelic family who'd made their money trading and smuggling – the west of Ireland had a long tradition of trade with Europe in wine, spices and silks. Daniel O'Connell's uncle bequeathed him a fortune, giving him the financial independence necessary to devote himself to politics. Discrimination against Catholics was widespread and closely experienced by Daniel: another uncle was shot dead because he would not give up his fine horse, as the law demanded of Catholics.

The thickly wooded parklands around the house, accessible on a signposted trail, have been declared a national historic park, and give onto wide, flat, sandy beaches, with two miles of dunes, good swimming and the possibility of an atmospheric stroll across to Abbey Island with its graveyard and ruined abbey. At the inlet on the western side of the island causeway, Derrynane Harbour Watersports Centre (Ⓣ066/947 5266) offers canoeing, sailing, wind-surfing and other waterborne **activities**. From here you can pick your way west for around a mile along a beautiful Mass Path to Bealtra Pier; follow the lane uphill from the pier and turn onto the Kerry Way heading east back towards Derrynane House, for a very satisfying circular **walk** of a couple of hours or so.

The little village of **CAHERDANIEL** (Cathair Donál), overlooking Derrynane Bay from its eastern flank, makes a very good base and there's excellent **hostel** accommodation, including private rooms, right in the centre at the *Traveller's Rest Hostel* (IHO; Ⓣ & Ⓕ066/947 5175; ❶). Also in the centre, next to *The Blind Piper*, *Kerry Way* offers plain but comfortable **B&B** (Ⓣ066/947 5227, Ⓦwww.activity-ireland.com; ❷), as well as various **activities** on land and sea, including diving, hill-walking and rock-climbing. Most other accommodation is outside the village to the west, including *Derrynane Bay House*, less than a mile from Caherdaniel on the main road (Ⓣ066/947 5404, Ⓦwww.ringofkerry.net; closed Christmas to mid-March; ❷), offering fine views and cooked dinners; the touristy *Scarriff Inn* (Ⓣ066/947 5132, Ⓦwww.caherdaniel.net; closed Nov–Feb; ❷), three miles away on the N70, providing rooms with seaviews and good **food** in the bar or restaurant to the hordes of coach parties passing by; and the attractive, upmarket *Iskeroon* (Ⓣ066/947 5448, Ⓦwww.iskeroon.com; ❹), down the lane by the *Scarriff Inn* on a pebbly beach. For **camping**, head a mile east of the village to *Wave Crest Caravan Park* (Ⓣ066/947 5188, Ⓦwww.wavecrestcamping.com; mid-March to mid-Oct), a fabulous spot overlooking the sea with a summertime **tourist information** point, or to *Glenbeg* on a sandy beach just beyond (Ⓣ066/947 5182; mid-April to Sept). Caherdaniel hosts a market for crafts and local produce in the village hall on Friday mornings in summer, and has a small shop, a petrol station and a couple of lively **pubs**, *Freddy's* and *The Blind Piper* – in the latter you can get very good food at the bar or in the upstairs restaurant and there's fine traditional music in the summer on Wednesday and Saturday evenings.

The immediate area has plenty of ancient forts and standing stones. Continuining east around the Ring of Kerry towards Sneem, a sign points left to **Staigue Fort**, near the village of Castlecove; there's a small visitor centre (Easter–Sept daily 10am–9pm; €2) near the junction, attached to a coffee shop and friendly bar with outdoor tables. After two and a half miles up a rough lane (some of it part of the Kerry Way), you'll come to a very well-preserved ring fort, possibly 2000 years old, and probably a residence of the kings of Munster (the local landowner charges €1 for "trespassing").

Spectacularly set on the Sneem River with 2245-foot Knockmoyle as a backdrop, **SNEEM** has attracted its fair share of tourist shops and cafés. Its houses are washed in different colours – reputedly so that drunken residents can find their way home – which lends the village a somewhat unreal, picture-book prettiness. Good local fishing is advertised by the salmon-shaped weathercock on the Protestant church. You'll probably want to push on to more interesting Kenmare, but if you do decide to **stay** here, you could try *Avonlea House* (ⓣ064/45221; April–Nov; ❶), *Old Convent House* (ⓣ064/45181; ❷) or *Rockville House* (ⓣ064/45135; March to mid-Nov; ❷); there's a **campsite**, *Goosey Island* (ⓣ064/45577; mid-April to mid-Oct), on the river bank in the centre of the village.

The approach to Kenmare along the estuary is unexciting, seemingly more in character with the Beara Peninsula opposite than with wild Iveragh, and you'll have a more scenic journey back to Killarney if you take the mountain road direct from Sneem. The two routes join up again at the spectacular **Moll's Gap**, north of Kenmare (for information on the route between Moll's Gap and Killarney, see p.393).

Kenmare and around

With its delicatessens and designer boutiques, **KENMARE** (ⓦwww.neidin.net) feels like a prosperous foreign enclave, and you're almost as likely to hear English or German tones here as Irish. Neatly organized on an X-plan (laid out by the first Marquess of Lansdowne in 1775), the town is pleasantly cosmopolitan: besides the resident foreigners, it's the natural crossing-over point for everyone travelling up from Cork.

Kenmare was founded by **Sir William Petty**, Cromwell's surveyor general, to serve his mining works beside the River Finnihy. Petty was extremely active in (and benefited greatly from) the dealings in confiscated properties that went on after the Cromwellian wars. Many soldiers were paid by the impecunious government in land, but not all of them wanted to settle in Ireland and so sold their land to dealers – such as Petty. His acquisition of land all over Ireland, including roughly a quarter of Kerry, was surely helped by his commission to survey the country on behalf of the government, when he investigated two-thirds of the Irish counties in the amazingly short period of fifteen months. Petty's other achievements were no less remarkable: a professor of medicine at Oxford at 27, he was also a professor of music and founder member of the Royal Society in London; an early statistician, economist and demographer; and politically astute enough to get yet more land and a knighthood out of Charles II, even though he had earlier served Cromwell faithfully. In Kerry, he laid the foundations of the mining and smelting industries, encouraged fishing and founded the enormous Lansdowne Estate which once surrounded the town; many of its buildings still remain today.

Evidence of a much more ancient settlement are the fifteen stones which make up the **stone circle** just outside the centre of town on the banks of the river; go up by the right of the market house that faces the park, and past some estate houses. Then walk up the lane at the cul-de-sac sign, and a few yards after it meets another lane coming in from the left you'll find the circle, behind a high ditch.

Practicalities

Buses stop in Main Street which runs down to the square, where you'll find the **tourist office** (April, May, Sept & Oct Mon–Sat 9.15am–1pm & 2.15–5.30pm; June–Aug daily 9am–6pm; ⓣ064/41233). The attached **heritage centre** (same hours; free) has a wealth of detail on the history of

Kenmare, particularly on the lace-making industry that was introduced here by the Church during the nineteenth century. Rather less engaging is the photograph of Margaret Thatcher that grimaces at you on the way in – apparently the former British Prime Minister is fiercely proud to have descended from a Kenmare washerwoman.

Bike rental is available from Siopa Rothar, opposite the *Fáilte Hostel* on Shelbourne Street, and **Internet access** from the nearby post office or *Moeran's* pub. If you want to see Kenmare from the water, Seafari (Ⓣ064/83171) runs **cruises** from the pier five times a day in high season, with the hope of seeing whales, dolphins and seals; they also offer **kayaking**, **sailing** and **wind-surfing**. Kenmare Bay Diving (Ⓣ064/42238) does beginners' three-hour **diving** courses, as well as trips and courses for the more experienced.

Accommodation

Plenty of good **accommodation** is available in the Kenmare area, but only a limited amount in the centre of town, so if you're travelling in high season or on a bank holiday it's worth booking in advance. The *Ring of Kerry* **campsite** is located at Reen (Ⓣ064/41648; April–Sept), three miles west of town towards Sneem.

Druid Cottage 1 mile out on the Sneem road Ⓣ064/41803. A solid nineteenth-century house, which has been pleasantly renovated and offers excellent hospitality. En-suite and standard rooms are available. Feb–Nov. ❷

Fáilte Shelbourne St Ⓣ064/42333 (IHH). Large, clean and well-run hostel right in the town centre. There are twin (❶) and family rooms as well as dorms. Closed Nov–March.

Hazelwood Killaha, two miles out of town towards Lauragh Ⓣ064/41420, Ⓔrawson@eircom.net. This excellent-value B&B is set in a stunning location overlooking the Kenmare River. The atmosphere is relaxed and the vegetarian and traditional Irish breakfasts are superb. There's a delightful woodland walk to a private beach, and they can arrange horse riding. Closed Nov & Dec. ❶

Park Hotel At the top of Main St Ⓣ064/41200, Ⓦwww.parkkenmare.com. A famous, and phenomenally expensive, luxury hotel built in the late nineteenth century in a fabulous location overlooking the Kenmare estuary. The extensive facilities include a fitness centre, tennis and croquet. ❾

Rose Cottage The Square Ⓣ064/41330. Very comfortable and welcoming old-fashioned cottage, with pretty garden and en-suite rooms, bang in the centre of town. ❷

Sheen Falls Lodge Ⓣ064/41600, Ⓦwww.sheenfalls.ie. Top-notch, five-star hotel, overlooking the eponymous waterfall in a 300-acre estate across the Kenmare River. The arm-long list of facilities includes swimming pool, fitness centre, tennis and horse riding. Weekend specials available. Closed Jan. ❾

Shelburne Lodge Killowen, Cork Rd Ⓣ064/41013, Ⓕ42135. Grand, beautifully decorated upmarket guesthouse, with great breakfasts – the owner also runs *Packie's* restaurant. ❺

Silver Trees Killowen Rd Ⓣ064/41008, Ⓔhodnettc@eircom.net. A friendly, efficient and rather plush B&B, five minutes' walk from the centre, opposite the golf course on the road towards Kilgarvan. Rooms, which all have their own bathroom and TV, are spacious and comfortable, and the breakfast, whether Continental or a full Irish fry-up, is definitely worth getting up for. Closed Nov–March. ❷

Eating and drinking

Kenmare is an affluent tourist town and, while this means there's a good range of **places to eat**, prices tend to be quite expensive – and you can really blow a gasket if you book in at the excellent restaurants in the *Park Hotel* or *Sheen Falls Lodge*. You will have no problem finding a decent pub to **drink** in and catch some traditional Irish music: as well as *The Square Pint*, reviewed below, places worth trying include *The Wander Inn* and *Crowley's* on Henry Street, and *Moeran's* at the top of Main Street.

An Leath Phingin 35 Main St ☎064/41559. Excellent Italian-Irish restaurant with a cosy cottage interior, serving fresh pasta, stone-oven pizzas and oak-wood fired barbecued meats. Temporarily closed at the time of writing, but will hopefully reopen.

Jam Henry St. Very successful update of a traditional, self-service bakery-café. Good cakes, *pains au chocolat* and scones, and excellent coffee, as well as delicious filled croissants, sandwiches, quiches and shepherd's pie.

Mickey Ned's The Square ☎064/40200. Manhattan comes to downtown Kenmare: this 150-year-old pub has been radically and stylishly updated in metropolitan minimalist mode, by former All-Ireland-winning Kerry football captain, Mickey Ned O'Sullivan. Reasonably priced, contemporary main courses and various panini are served every day at the bar downstairs, as well as in the upstairs restaurant, along with extra dishes such as scallops with pernod-creamed spinach and angel-hair pasta (lunch Sat & Sun, dinner Tues–Sun in summer, Thurs–Sat in winter). Regular traditional music, jazz and DJs.

Mulcahy's 16 Henry St ☎064/42383. Crisp, modern decor and sophisticated, pricey dishes with global influences, including sushi and a daily veggie special. Evenings Mon & Wed–Sun.

Packies Henry St ☎064/41508. Homely, upmarket restaurant with a good reputation, under the same management as *The Purple Heather*, cooking up dishes such as rack of lamb with rosemary and garlic on herbed lentils. Tues–Sat evenings.

The Purple Heather Henry St. A traditional pub that serves good bar food. The interesting menu includes homemade chicken-liver paté with Cumberland sauce, crab salad and Cashel blue cheese sandwich with walnut salad.

The Square Pint The Square. This very pleasant bar has a contemporary interior, late-night licence every night and serves daytime food; there's traditional music every night in summer, at least once a week in winter, plus DJs at weekends, with plans for a club to open at the back.

Wharton's Chipper Main St. A good-value fast-food option, with seating upstairs. Traditional fish and chips: the fish is fresh and the chips homemade.

The Beara Peninsula

Cross the river from Kenmare and you're on the **Beara Peninsula**, which Kerry shares with Cork (see p.374). Beara has its followers, but after the wildness of the rest of Kerry, it can at first seem over-lush and polite; head west towards the end of the peninsula, however, or uphill on the scenic N71 towards Glengarriff, and the terrain soon becomes more windswept and lonely.

Turn right after the bridge out of Kenmare, and the road runs through heavily wooded country alongside the Kenmare estuary; after about seven miles there's a signpost to the left for **Inchiquin Lake**. Following this, you soon quit the luxuriant vegetation as the bumpy road ascends rapidly to the lake, affording exhilarating views of the countryside left behind. A waterfall tumbles down from a second lake, and on the far side of Inchiquin Lake is **Uragh Wood**, one of the last surviving remnants of the ancient sessile oak woods that once covered most of Ireland. The entire valley is packed with **plants**: large-flowered butterwort covers the meadows in spring, and you can find Irish spurge, saxifrage, arbutus and other flora specific to the southwest here. At the lake itself, the surrounding hills seem to act as some kind of intensifier focused on a tiny stone circle by the side of the water – bringing to mind the theory that these prehistoric monuments indicate earth forces. There's salmon, sea trout and brown trout fishing in both lakes, but, as always, check the licence position before you start.

Following the main road for **LAURAGH**, twelve miles southwest of Kenmare, you're still in the enormous estate once owned by Petty. The gardens at **Derreen House** (April–Oct daily 11am–6pm; €4), for a long time one of the Irish residences of Petty's descendant, the Marquess of Lansdowne, are open to the public and stocked with plants that clearly luxuriate in the mild sea climate, including such exotica as tree ferns and bamboo, plus rhododendrons and camellias. Head westwards from Lauragh and you're soon over the border into

e way to Ardgroom; south towards Adrigole, the road climbs spec-
ɔve Glanmore Lake to the Healy Pass – again, the county border –
ing views in both directions. There's a small **campsite**, *Creveen*
4/83131, Ⓦwww.creveenlodge.com; Easter–Oct), about a mile
uragh, and further on, the friendly but fairly basic An Óige
ıke **hostel** in an old school beside the lake (closed Oct–May;
Ⓣ064/83181).

The Dingle Peninsula

The **Dingle Peninsula** (Ⓦwww.dingle-peninsula.ie) is a place of intense, shifting beauty. Spectacular mountains, long sandy beaches and the staggering splinter-slatted mass of rocks that defines the extraordinary coast at Slea Head all conspire to ensure that, remote though it is, the Dingle Peninsula is firmly on the tourist trail. The upland scenery is at its most dramatic at **Mount Brandon**, which rises to 3119ft and affords splendid opportunities for hiking. The steep Conor Pass road that runs south of here between Dingle town and the peninsula's northern coast is much loved by cyclists determined to prove their stamina. There are very fine beaches all around the peninsula: at the tiny village of **Inch** three miles of sand stretches out into the ocean; **Castlegregory** on the Maharees Peninsula acts as a magnet for wind-surfers and surfers; and as you travel west, both the inland and coastal scenery intensifies, with superb beaches at **Ventry** (the best place for safe swimming), **Murreagh** and **Ballyferriter**, as well as on the Blasket Islands, to name but a few.

There's plenty of myth and history too: the peninsula has one of the greatest concentrations of Celtic ruins in Ireland. Ring forts, beehive huts, oratories and stone crosses are prevalent here and the vigour of the Christian culture that set out from here to evangelize and educate the rest of Europe is almost palpable. The best of these ancient monuments lie at the west end of the peninsula and include **Dún Beag**, just outside the tiny village of Ventry, the early Christian **Gallarus Oratory** and the medieval church of **Kilmalkedar**, northwest of Dingle town. The now uninhabited **Blasket Islands** once generated a wealth of Irish literature, and indeed the western half of the peninsula (which is called Corca or Chorca Dhuibhne in Irish) remains a *Gaeltacht* region; **courses in Irish** language and culture can be arranged at Feileastram Teo, *An Portán*, Dunquin (see p.413), and through the museum in Ballyferriter (see p.414). The peninsula has a place in film history too: *Ryan's Daughter* was filmed here, as were parts of *Far and Away,* starring Tom Cruise. For all its popularity as a tourist destination, the Dingle peninsula remains magical. On a fine day exhilarating views stretch out as far as the monastic settlement on Great Skellig, off the Iveragh Peninsula to the south; but it can be more exciting still in the rain, when the cloud shifts down over the land and you find yourself in a white mist through which the dim shapes of oratories and beehive huts loom.

Probably the best way to soak up this landscape is to walk all or part of the waymarked, 112-mile **Dingle Way**, which begins in Tralee, heads west to Camp, then loops round the rest of the peninsula, via long, sandy beaches, the steep north face of Mount Brandon and most of Dingle's major sites and villages. The whole thing is best done in seven days, catching a bus out to Camp on the first day to avoid repeating the stretch between there and Tralee; **accommodation** in Anascaul, Dingle, Dunquin, Ballydavid, Cloghane and

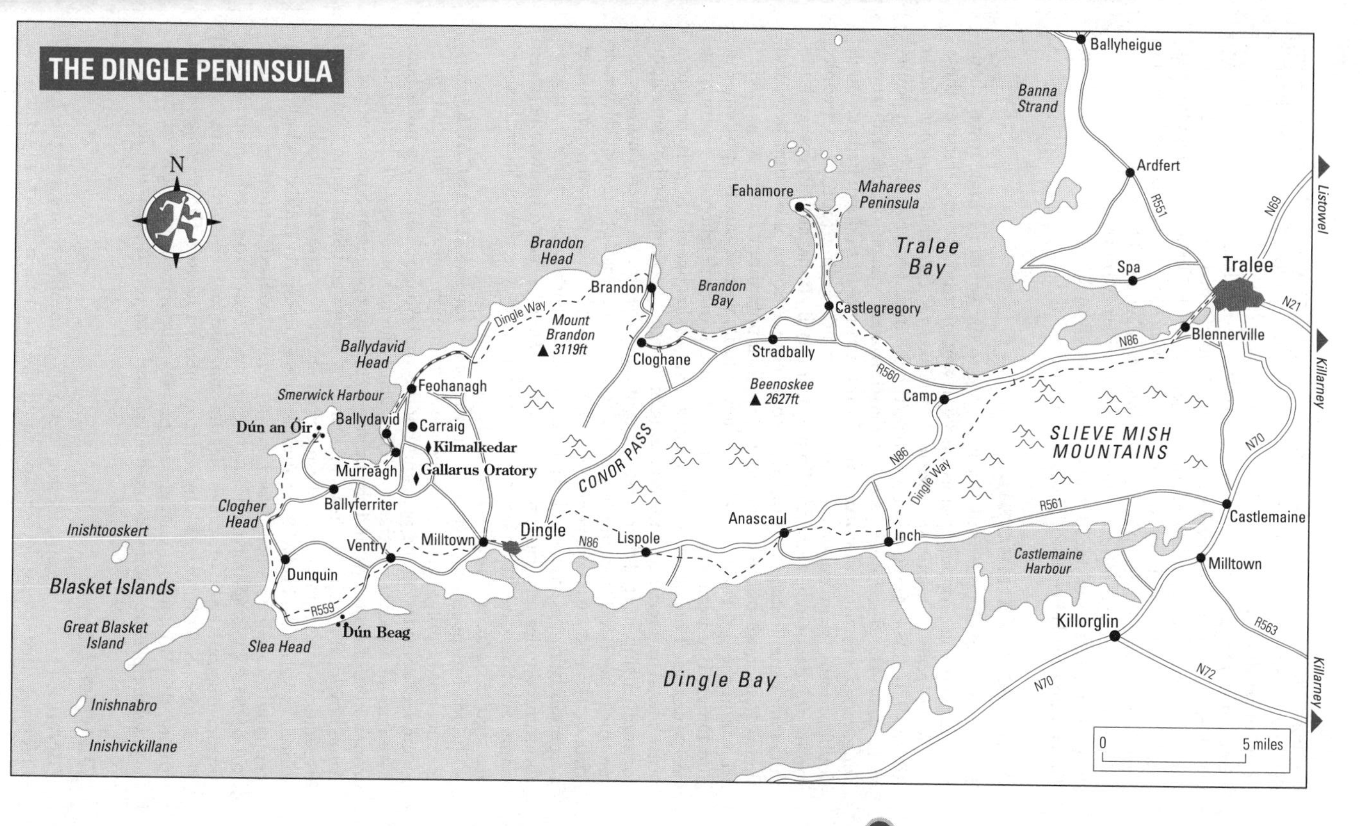
THE DINGLE PENINSULA
N
Ballyheigue
Banna Strand
Ardfert
R551
Listowel
N69
Spa
Tralee
N21
Killarney
Blennerville
N86
Tralee Bay
Maharees Peninsula
Fahamore
Castlegregory
Brandon Bay
Brandon Head
Brandon
Dingle Way
Mount Brandon
3119ft
Cloghane
Stradbally
Beenoskee
2627ft
R560
Camp
Ballydavid Head
Feohanagh
Smerwick Harbour
Dún an Óir
Ballydavid
Carraig
Kilmalkedar
Murreagh
Gallarus Oratory
CONOR PASS
SLIEVE MISH MOUNTAINS
N70
Clogher Head
Ballyferriter
Inishtooskert
Dingle
Milltown
Ventry
Lispole
Anascaul
Inch
R561
Castlemaine
Dunquin
Blasket Islands
R559
Great Blasket Island
Dún Beag
Slea Head
Castlemaine Harbour
Milltown
Killorglin
R563
N72
Dingle Bay
Inishnabro
Inishvickillane
0
5 miles

Castlegregory is detailed in the text. OS 1:50,000 **map** no. 70 covers most of the route, with the eastern end of the peninsula on no. 71, and Cork Kerry Tourism produces a useful 1:50,000 map-guide.

Getting to Dingle is easy by **bus** from Tralee, with at least three services a day via Camp and Anascaul; there's a weekly service from Tralee to Castlegregory and Cloghane, and summertime buses from Killarney to Dingle via Castlemaine and Inch. Travel west of Dingle town is less straightforward – buses leave Dingle for Dunquin via Ballyferriter Monday and Thursday three times daily, and during the summer months they depart Monday to Saturday (1–2 daily) and go via Slea Head; three buses run from Dingle to Ballydavid on Tuesday and Friday, one stopping at Gallarus.

Inch and Anascaul

Though most of the peninsula's delights are to the west of Dingle town, there are a few notable stopping points on your way in from the east. First of these is *The Phoenix Organic Vegetarian Restaurant & Farmhouse Accommodation* (ⓣ066/976 6284, ⓦwww.kerryweb.ie/thephoenix; Oct–Easter by appointment only; ❶), three miles west of **Castlemaine** village on the Killarney–Dingle road, providing **accommodation** that ranges from dorm beds, through double rooms (standard or en suite), to a chalet sleeping four to six people; rooms are decorated with furnishings from Bali, India and Egypt and the restaurant's menu strikes a similarly exotic note. You can also camp here, and there's Irish music and set dancing in *The Anvil* pub, about a mile away. There's a break in the shoreline at **INCH**, where a long, narrow sandbar pushing out into Dingle Bay attracts wind-surfers and surfers. In the eighteenth century, the beach was used by wreckers who, on stormy nights, would tie a lantern to a horse's head and leave the horse grazing; mariners mistaking the bobbing light for another ship steered their vessels aground on the strand. There's non-smoking, en-suite **B&B** accommodation about a mile east of here at *Waterside* (ⓣ066/915 8129, ⓔwatersideinch@hotmail.com; March–Oct; ❷). For **hostel** accommodation, as you head west take a sharp right after *Foley's* pub; after about three miles turn right for the *Bog View Hostel*, situated midway between Camp and Anascaul (ⓣ066/915 8125; closed Sept–May). Back in Inch, there are regular traditional music sessions at *Foley's* pub.

The road turns inland, five miles further west, towards **ANASCAUL**, a single street of brightly painted houses, pleasant enough but with a curiously safe, inland feel considering the proximity of the wild Atlantic coast. Two **pubs** here have famous associations: the magician Dan Foley's shocking-pink bar, familiar from a host of postcards, and the atmospheric and congenial *South Pole Inn*, so named by local man Tom Crean, a veteran of Scott's and Shackleton's Antarctic expeditions – it's hung with polar memorabilia, serves good food and hosts traditional sessions on Friday and Saturday. There are several **B&Bs**, including the centrally located, en-suite *Anchor House*, where cooked dinners are available (ⓣ066/915 7382, ⓔdropanchor@tinet.ie; mid-March to Oct; ❷), and slightly further out on the road to Dingle, the standard and en-suite rooms of *Four Winds* (ⓣ066/915 7168; ❶). In addition there's a **hostel**, *Fuchsia Lodge* (IHH; ⓣ066/915 7150, ⓔfuchsia@eircom.net; ❶), about two miles east of the village, where private rooms, cooked meals and bike rental are available.

Dingle town

DINGLE (An Daingean) doesn't offer a huge amount to see, but the town is a pleasant place to stay, devoted to fishing and tourism, and certainly makes the best base for exploring the peninsula. There are plenty of opportunities to get out onto the water from here and many fine walks accessible from the town centre; the Dingle Way actually passes right through the centre. Though crammed with pubs, little restaurants and B&Bs, Dingle somehow never feels too crowded, and even if you don't like the way it has geared itself up for tourism, you'll be glad when the weather's bad that there are plenty of cosy spots to hole up in. The town services the tiny communities west of here, so if you are heading on it makes good sense to stock up on supplies.

Information and accommodation

The **tourist office** in Strand Street (year-round, hours variable, ranging from winter Mon, Tues & Thurs–Sat 10am–1pm & 2.15–5pm, to high summer Mon–Sat 9am–7pm, Sun 10am–6pm; ⓣ066/915 1188) has an accommodation service and plenty of information on the surrounding area; perhaps the only drawback is the very long queues that you can expect during high season. Fascinating **archaeological tours** of the peninsula by minibus are run in the summer by Sciúird Tours based at *Kirrary B&B* (see below; 2 daily, 2hr 30min; €15). For **Internet access**, head for the *Dingle Internet Café* on Main Street (ⓣ066/915 2478).

Dingle offers a very good range of **hostels, B&Bs** and **hotels**. It is advisable to book ahead during July and August, either directly or through the very helpful tourist office. **Camping** is possible at *Ballintaggart House* and *Rainbow Hostel* (see below).

An Capall Dubh Green St ⓣ066/915 1105. Tasteful, upmarket, non-smoking B&B – and self-catering – accommodation around a quiet courtyard in the centre of town. ❹

Ballintaggart House Racecourse Rd, one mile east of Dingle (IHH). ⓣ066/915 1454, ⓦwww.dingleaccommodation.com. This hostel, built in the eighteenth century as a hunting lodge, is one of the best around, boasting huge roaring fires, plenty of space and wonderful views. Private rooms (❶) have excellent en-suite power showers. Camping and Internet access are available and there's a regular free pick-up service from town. Closed Nov to mid-March.

Benners Hotel Main St ⓣ066/915 1638, ⓦwww.dinglebenners.com. A traditional town-centre hotel where the lobby and bar have a pleasantly lived-in feel, and the bedrooms are newly refurbished in a warm rustic style. Half-board deals available. ❽

Boland's Goat St, at the top of Main St ⓣ066/915 1426, ⓔbolanddingle@eircom.net. A well-run B&B in a central location, with guest lounge and conservatory breakfast room. All rooms are en suite with phones, TV and tea- and coffee-making facilities. Closed Dec & Jan. ❸

Brosnan's Cooleen ⓣ066/915 1146. A B&B located just a short walk from the centre of town down the laneway opposite the Esso station. Bedrooms are pleasant, with stripped floors and en-suite facilities, although there's no use of the sitting room. ❸

Captain's House The Mall ⓣ066/915 1531, ⓔcaptigh@eircom.net. Central, en-suite B&B, with TV and phones, quirkily furnished with items collected on the captain's voyages. Breakfast, including homemade bread and jam, is served in the conservatory, which overlooks the picturesque garden and stream. ❸

Dingle Skellig Hotel ⓣ066/915 0200, ⓦwww.dingleskellig.com. A large and modern four-star hotel situated right down by the bay. Facilities include a pool, gym, kids' club and creche. Enquire about the good weekend deals. ❽

Grapevine Dykegate St ⓣ066/915 1434. A friendly, welcoming and well-run hostel off Main St in the centre of town.

Greenmount Guesthouse Upper John St ⓣ066/915 1414, ⓦwww.greenmounthouse.com. This spacious and award-winning guesthouse is set in a great location overlooking the harbour. All rooms are en suite and have TVs and phones. ❹

Kirrary B&B Avondale St ⓣ066/915 1606, ⓔcollinskirrary@eircom.net. Pleasant, non-smoking B&B in a very central spot which offers a homely atmosphere, good breakfasts and a lovely garden. Rooms are either en suite or with shared bathroom. Archaeological tours (see available) and bike rental available. ❷

O'Coiléain B&B Holyground ⓣ066/915 1937, ⓔarcheo@eircom.net. A congenial family home, in an excellent central location, with fresh, porary interiors and a lovely garden. All are en suite. ❷

ɔw Hostel 1 mile west of town ⓣ066/915 ⓦwww.net-rainbow.com. Sociable, family-run hostel, with landscaped gardens, large kitchen, double rooms (❶) and small dorms, camping and Internet access. Free lifts from the bus stop in town.

The Town

The solidity of the town's colour-washed houses suggests this was a place of some consequence, and Dingle was indeed Kerry's leading port in the fourteenth and fifteenth centuries. It later became a centre for **smuggling**, and at one stage during the eighteenth century (when the revenue from smuggling was at its height) even minted its own coinage. Contemporary reports describe the stone houses with balconies and oval windows, imparting a Spanish feel to the town. In the nineteenth century, Dingle was the focus of a uniquely successful attempt to woo the Kerry Catholics from their faith, when in 1831 the Protestant curate T. Goodman began preaching in Irish, establishing schools on the peninsula and building houses as inducements for converts; these still stand at the edge of town. Proof of the robustness of Catholicism, especially since Independence, can be seen at Díseart Institute of Education and Celtic Culture on Green Street: in this former convent of the enclosed order of Presentation Sisters, twelve **stained-glass windows by Harry Clarke**, one of the foremost artists in the medium in the last century, are now on show to the public (Mon–Sat 10am–5pm; free); commissioned in 1922, they depict scenes from the life of Christ in opulent detail. Díseart also hosts an interesting variety of **courses**, talks and exhibitions on Irish and Celtic culture (ⓣ066/915 2476, ⓦwww.diseart.ie).

Dingle's hugely impressive natural harbour is where **Fungi the dolphin**, one of Dingle's main tourist attractions, likes to play. It may sound silly, but there are people who talk of their meetings with this solitary, 663lb bottlenose dolphin in the terms of a religious conversion, and others travel hundreds of miles just to see him. If you want to go for an early-morning dip with him, check out Flannery's beside the tourist office (ⓣ066/915 1967; two-hour boat trip €15, wetsuit hire €20) – boats depart at 8am and you will need to be measured for a wet suit the day before. There are also boat trips out to see him (ⓣ066/915 2626; €10). Alternatively, you can walk down to the coast via the lane alongside the *Skellig Hotel* and watch him from the shore – Fungi often comes in this far.

There are plenty of other ways to get out onto – and into – the water from Dingle, most of them bookable through the Water-based Activities Office next to the tourist office (ⓣ066/915 0768): late-afternoon, two-hour Eco Tours **cruises**, which head along the coast, the guide explaining the flora, fauna, geology and history of the peninsula as you go (€25); trips across Dingle Bay to **Valentia Island** (according to demand, but usually twice a day in summer; €30 return); and ferries to **Great Blasket** (see p.413). **Surfboards** and wetsuits can be rented from Finn McCool's in Green Street, and **diving** can be arranged at the Dingle Marina Diving Centre (ⓣ066/915 2422). Back on land, you can go **riding** at Coláiste Íde Stables, two miles west of Dingle at Burnham (ⓣ066/915 9100, ⓦwww.colaisteidestables.com), and **bikes** can be rented from Foxy John's hardware store/pub on Main Street and *Kirrary B&B*.

If all these nautical pursuits have whetted your curiosity, head for **Dingle Oceanworld** (Mara Beo) on the waterfront (May & Sept daily 10am–6pm; June daily 10am–7pm; July & Aug daily 10am–8.30pm; Oct–April Mon–Sat 9am–4.45pm, Sun 10am–4.45pm; €7.50; ⓦwww.dingle-oceanworld.ie). As well as an important centre for marine conservation, Oceanworld is a richly detailed aquarium, where you can stick your hands in the touch tank, observe sharks, stingrays and eels at close quarters and walk underneath a variety of fish from around the Irish coast in the tunnel tank.

Eating and drinking

For its size, Dingle has a high proportion of upmarket restaurants, a number of them noted for seafood. More affordable meals are available in several pubs and a handful of cafés.

Adam's Main St. Characterful old-style bar with an up-beat atmosphere serving inexpensive and delicious homemade soups, open sandwiches, and fresh crab salads.

An Cafe Liteartha Dykegate Lane. Wholly unpretentious bookshop-café that stocks both Irish- and English-language editions (politics and local interest are both well represented). The no-nonsense food focuses on delivering very cheap tea, coffee, soup, scones and sandwiches (ham, cheese, beef). The laid-back atmosphere makes this a great place to chill.

The Chart House The Mall, down by the roundabout ☎066/915 2255. Informal, friendly, upmarket restaurant with a fine reputation for its imaginative menus, which might feature turbot with citrus basil couscous and pan-fried guinea fowl, as well as a daily seafood special. Call ahead for a reservation. Closed Tues & Wed.

Doyle's Seafood Restaurant John St ☎066/915 1174. There's great seafood to be had all around the Kerry coast, and in Dingle *Doyle's* is the most famous place to sample the delights of the deep – but you'll have to dig deep into your pockets to sample such dishes as caramelized scallops in ginger and coriander cream sauce. Evenings only.

The Global Village Main St. True to the name, the menu revolves around a wide-ranging mix of influences gleaned during the proprietor's world travels. Breakfasts are tasty, lunches light and inexpensive. Evening meals are a little pricey.

Half Door John St ☎066/915 1600. Relaxing, white-tablecloth restaurant with excellent cooking, mostly seafood, a good wine list including carafes and glasses, and friendly, efficient service. It's pricey, but there's a very good-value three-course set menu – which will oblige you to leave room for delicious desserts such as apple and pear crumble.

John Benny's Strand St. Regular smoky pub catering for tourists, and generally very busy. Plenty of filling pub grub, including Irish stew, fresh fish, vegetarian options, sandwiches and homely puddings.

Murphy's Ice Cream Strand St. Delicious homemade ice cream, as well as other great desserts, excellent coffee and Continental breakfasts.

Out of the Blue Opposite the tourist office on Strand St ☎066/915 0811. Simple seafood deli and restaurant with outside tables, dishing up excellent, fresh, reasonably priced dishes such as plaice with crabmeat and vegetable stir-fry.

The Oven Doors and Dingle Tea Rooms Holyground. Handy café and pizza restaurant right in the town centre serving tea and scones, salads and fabulous cakes along with its inexpensive pizza menu. Open till 8.30pm, depending on business.

Nightlife and entertainment

Life in the evenings is centred on Dingle's many **pubs**, which between them offer **traditional music** sessions on just about any night you choose during the summer, and at weekends during the winter. *An Droichead Beag* at the bottom of Main Street is probably the best place to start at any time with music most nights year round and set-dancing classes on Wednesdays; *An Conair* a couple of doors away has traditional music on Sundays year-round (more often in summer) and a beer garden; and *John Benny's* hosts traditional, folk or ballads four nights a week in summer, with set dancing on Mondays. **Special events** here include the compulsive Dingle Races in early August, the Dingle Regatta for traditional currachs later in the month and a varied music festival in early September, featuring folk, jazz and traditional music – contact the tourist office for details.

ɘntry and ancient monuments

ıe first village of interest west of Dingle is tiny **VENTRY** (Ceann Trá) five ıııles further on, once the main port of the peninsula and another fine natural harbour: a wide curve of sandy beach beneath the enormous, gnarled shoulder of Mount Eagle, dropping almost sheer to the sea with only a precarious ledge for the road.

It's in the inhospitable surroundings on the stretch out from Ventry to Slea Head that the main concentration of **ancient monuments** can be found. What follows here can only be an introduction to the major sites; the minor ones alone could take weeks to explore. A good local **map**, such as the one available at the tourist office, is essential for exploring minor sites, while several excellent guides to the peninsula (available at bookshops in Dingle town) exist for real enthusiasts, who should also consider signing up for one of Sciúird's archaeological tours (see p.409).

First off there's the spectacular **Dún Beag** (dating from the eighth or ninth century AD), a scramble down from the road towards the ocean about three to four miles out from Ventry (entry €2). A promontory fort, its defences include four earthen rings, with an underground escape route, or souterrain, by the main entrance. It's a magical location, overlooking the open sea and the Iveragh Peninsula, the drama of its setting only increased by the fact that some of the building has fallen off into the sea.

Between Dún Beag and **Slea Head**, the hillside above the road is studded with stone beehive huts, cave dwellings, souterrains, forts, churches, standing stones and crosses – over five hundred in all. The huts can be deceptive – they were still being built and used for storing farm tools and produce until the late nineteenth century, so not all of them are as old as they look. But, standing among genuinely ancient buildings like the two **beehive hut sites** of the Fahan group (entry to each €2) and looking south over a landscape that's remained essentially unchanged for centuries, the Iveragh Peninsula and the two Skellig Islands in the distance, you do get a strong sense of the past.

Ventry itself consists of a sprinkling of houses with, at the east end of the bay, a shop, post office, pub and a few **accommodation** options. Up the lane past the post office are *Ceann Trá Heights* (ⓣ066/915 9866, ⓔventry@iol.ie; mid-March to Oct; ❷) and *The Plough* (ⓣ066/915 9727, ⓔplough@iol.ie; ❷), two B&Bs which are worth trying. The very comfortable *Bally Beag Hostel*, signposted from the main road at the turning for Ballyferriter (ⓣ066/915 9876, ⓔbalybeag@iol.ie), offers dorms, family and twin rooms (❶), as well as bike rental, laundry facilities and lifts to and from Dingle. *Penny's Pottery* has a good **café** (summer only) for inexpensive coffee, cakes, quiches, salads and baguettes, while *The Skipper* is a highly recommended seafood **restaurant** near the post office (ⓣ066/915 9900). Also recommended is *The Stonehouse* café and restaurant (ⓣ066/915 9970) opposite the entrance to Dún Beag, which offers reasonably priced lunchtime dishes such as crab with Mediterranean salad and a more sophisticated menu in the evenings. At the west end of Ventry is *Páidi Ó Sé's*, a **bar** owned by the Kerry Gaelic football manager, which is noted for traditional music sessions and serves food.

Just west of Ventry is the **Celtic and Prehistoric Museum** (May–Sept daily 10am–6pm; phone at other times, ⓣ066/915 9941; €4), a small, up-beat, family-run museum which boasts a large nest of dinosaur eggs, beautiful Celtic jewellery and the only intact woolly mammoth skull in Ireland – complete with huge curling tusks and affectionately named Milly. There's a pleasant tearoom here too, and a shop selling local crafts and all manner of fossils. **Surfing** and **wind-surfing** at Ventry can be arranged through Jamie Knox (Ⓣ066/713 9411, Ⓔjamieknox@tinet.ie), **horse riding** through Long's (Ⓣ087/225 0286, Ⓦwww.longsriding.com).

The Blasket Islands and Dunquin

At Slea Head, five miles west of Ventry, the view opens up to include the desolate, splintered masses of the **Blasket Islands** (Na Blascaodaí), officially uninhabited since 1953, though there are still summer communities on the islands. The weather in Blasket Sound can be treacherous – two of the Armada's ships were shattered to matchwood when they came bowling round the Head in September 1588 – but, inhospitable as they seem, the islands were once the home of thriving communities. The astonishing body of **Irish literature** that emerged from these tiny islands (Maurice O'Sullivan's *Twenty Years A-Growing*, Peig Sayers's *Peig* and Tomás O'Crohan's *Island Cross-Talk*) gives a vivid picture of the life of the islanders which, although remote, was anything but unsophisticated. Ironically, these literary works describe life among people who could neither read nor write, yet their oral tradition emerges as being far from primitive. The islands' story is told with great imagination at the Great Blasket heritage centre, **Ionad an Bhlascaoid Mhóir**, at Dunquin (Easter to June, Sept & Oct daily 10am–6pm; July & Aug daily 10am–7pm; €3.10; Heritage Card). Though the building doesn't look like much as you approach, inside is a beautiful museum space, brought to life with excerpts from the island writers, and including a moving section on Great Blasket's abandonment in 1953 and the migration of many islanders to Springfield, Massachusetts – where they still receive the *Kerryman* newspaper from Tralee every week. There's a good **café** for lunch too, with fine views of the islands.

In the summer, **boats** bound for **Great Blasket** (An Blascaod Mór) leave the pier just south of Dunquin in good weather between around 10am and 5pm for €20 return (Easter–May & Sept to mid-Oct hourly, June–Aug every half-hour; Ⓣ066/915 6422, Ⓦwww.blasketferries.com); there are also between two and five ferries a day, according to demand, from Dingle (€30 return; Ⓣ066/915 1344 or 087/672 6100). Whether or not you choose to stay over, Great Blasket's delights are simple ones: sitting on the beaches and staring out to sea, tramping the many footpaths that crisscross the island or trying to spot a seal. If you want to swim be careful as currents are very strong – and the water will be icy. Three of the old houses have been renovated and turned into a **hostel** (April–Sept; Ⓣ086/848 6687, Ⓦwww.greatblasketisland.com); there's no electricity on the island, but the hostel has cooking facilities and hot showers. There's also a **café** (same months), serving soup, cakes, pies, open sandwiches and daily specials, with a wine licence and evening meals, mostly vegetarian, available on request. If you want to **camp** on the island you'll need to be prepared – take food (there's no shop, just the café), water carriers for the well and bags to carry refuse home. It's advisable to check the long-term weather forecast with the boatmen in advance, as it's possible to be stranded for days if the weather breaks.

There's a comfortable An Óige **hostel** on the mainland at **DUNQUIN** (Dún Chaoin), with plenty of dorm, twin (❶) and four-bed rooms, a drying room and cooked meals available (Ⓣ066/915 6121). *Kruger's* **pub** (closed Oct–Feb; Ⓣ066/915 6127; ❷) is the hub of local activity, with food and traditional music in summer, and offers **B&B**. Across from here *An Portán* **restaurant** (Ⓣ066/915 6212, Ⓦwww.anportan.com; ❷) enjoys a good reputation and also offers B&B and Irish-language courses. About ten minutes' walk up the hill from here lies the *Dunquin Pottery Café*, one of the best places in Dunquin for daytime eating (the other being the heritage centre) which affords spectacular views out across the Blaskets. *Tig Áine* (Ⓣ066/915 6214), about two miles north round Clogher Head from Dunquin at An Ghráig, is a laid-back summertime café, crafts shop and weaver's workshop where you can enjoy soups, sandwiches, salads and cakes overlooking the sea and a delightful garden. Just beyond here is the pottery and shop of one of Ireland's leading potters, Louis Mulcahy (Ⓣ066/915 6229, Ⓦwww.louismulcahy.com).

Ballyferriter

A couple of miles further on, largely Irish-speaking **BALLYFERRITER** (Baile an Fheirtearaigh) is a lively little village during the summer, though it can be bleak out of season. Its beach, the beautiful Wine Strand, is a great spot for swimming in fine weather. The little lanes running northwards from the village lead to impressive 500ft hilltop walling at Sybil Head and the Three Sisters rock (with the Norman ruins of Castle Sybil built within an older promontory fort), and to Smerwick Harbour and **Dún an Óir** (the Golden Fort). In September 1580 at Dún an Óir, a band of Italian, Spanish, English and Irish supporters of the rebellion in Munster, backed by papal funds in support of Catholic Ireland against Protestant England, were defeated by the English. The rebels were massacred – men, women and children – as a warning to others.

In Ballyferriter itself **Corca Dhuibhne Regional Museum** (April–Sept daily 10am–5.30pm; other times by appointment; Ⓣ066/915 6100, Ⓦwww.corca-dhuibhne.com; €1.90), for all its modest means of presentation, has excellent material on the geology and archaeology of the Dingle Peninsula and is an ideal place to make sense of the surrounding landscape. In addition to providing plenty of information on local prehistoric sites it also has fine examples of cross slabs bearing ogham inscriptions. There's a good café at the museum, which as part of the Dingle Peninsula Development Co-operative also organizes courses in Irish language and culture.

Also in the village centre are various **accommodation** and **food** options, all within a stone's throw of each other. *Tigh Pheig* is a genial pub which serves good food and hosts traditional music and set dancing on Thursday nights. Very pleasant en-suite B&B is available at *Murphy's Bar* (Ⓣ066/915 6224; ❷), and there's hostel accommodation at *An Cat Dubh* (The Black Cat), just outside Ballyferriter on the road to Dunquin (IHO; Ⓣ066/915 6286), which also has a grocery shop attached.

The Gallarus Oratory, Kilmalkedar and Mount Brandon

The single most impressive early Christian monument on the Dingle Peninsula is the **Gallarus Oratory**, around three miles east of Ballyferriter, signposted off the road to Ballydavid. The most perfectly preserved of around twenty such oratories in Ireland, it looks almost too good to be true, though apparently it hasn't undergone any great restoration programmes. Though the oratory can't be dated with any great certainty, it's thought to have been built between the ninth and twelfth centuries (Christian architectural activity dates from the late sixth or early seventh century, but it wasn't until the ninth century that churches began to be built of stone rather than wood), and with its gracefully curved, upturned-boat shape, to represent a transition between the round beehive huts elsewhere on the peninsula and the later rectangular churches. The problem with this construction (and the reason why so many similar buildings have fallen down) is that the long sides tend to cave in – if you look carefully at the Gallarus Oratory, you can see it's beginning to happen here, too. Adjacent to the oratory is the **Dingle Activities Information Centre** (ⓣ066/915 5143), which provides local information especially on walking, and *Teach an Aragail* **campsite** (same number; May–Sept).

The next architectural stage can be seen a mile to the northeast of here in the rectangular church at **Kilmalkedar**. Its nave dates from the mid-twelfth century, and the corbelled stone roof was a direct improvement on the structure at Gallarus. The site marks the beginning of the Saint's Road, dedicated to **St Brendan**, patron saint of Kerry, which leads to the top of **Mount Brandon** – the route taken by pilgrims to St Brendan's shrine. If you want to follow this tough but historically resonant route up the mountainside, it's marked on the Ordnance Survey map number 70. Alternatively, there's a less challenging hike that skirts around the south of the mountain and leads to Cloghane (see p.416).

Carraig and Ballydavid

The tiny village of **Murreagh** (An Mhuiríoch), a couple of miles north of the Gallarus Oratory, lies at the north end of a fabulous sandy beach. Take the road from here north towards **CARRAIG**, half a mile away, and you will come to *Ard na Carraige* (ⓣ066/915 5295; May–Sept; ❷), a very comfortable and welcoming **B&B**. There are a number of other places to stay in Carraig itself: *Tigh an Phóist* **hostel**, beside the church and a well-stocked shop (IHH; closed Nov–March; ⓣ066/915 5109, ⓔs.nichon@indigo.ie), offering dorms, private rooms (❶) and bike rental, and nearby *Nic Gearailt* B&B (ⓣ066/915 5142, ⓔmnicgear@indigo.ie; March–Oct; ❷) which offers decent accommodation and a splendid breakfast menu that might include smoked salmon, mackerel and pancakes, as well as evening meals. The nearest pubs from Carraig are about two miles away, in Ballydavid or north of the village towards Feohanagh, but there's **music and set dancing** at Teach Siamsa twice weekly during the summer (contact Siamsa Tire in Tralee for details – see p.417).

Around the coast from Murreagh lies **BALLYDAVID** (*Baile na nGall*), backed by the mass of Mount Brandon and offering fine walks. A couple of bars stand at Ballydavid pier overlooking the magnificent sweep of the bay: *Begley's* (ⓣ066/915 5123; ❷), which offers fairly basic **B&B**, and the cosy *Tigh TP* (ⓣ066/915 5444) which has a good range of **meals** on offer both in the bar and in the restaurant alongside. North of the village on the way to Feohanagh, *Gorman's Clifftop House & Restaurant* (ⓣ066/915 5162, ⓦwww.gormans-clifftophouse.com; ❹) offers upmarket B&B, fine dining and great views from its cliff-top perch. Ballydavid also has a post office and a small shop. **Brandon Creek** (signposted Cuas), just east of Ballydavid Head, is one of a number of contenders for St Brendan's sixth-century departure point, when he sailed off to discover the Islands of Paradise in the western ocean and, arguably, America.

The Conor Pass and the north side of the peninsula

The interior of the Dingle Peninsula is dominated by two mountains, Mount Brandon and Beenoskee, separated by the spectacular **Conor Pass**, which runs northeastwards from Dingle town. This mountainous terrain is excellent walking country; not only are there countless relics of the Celtic Church and earlier to explore, but the area is dotted with a series of lakes that give the tussocky landscape some focus. The best base for walking is **CLOGHANE** (An Clochán), a tiny village flanked by lovely beaches on the eastern flank of Mount Brandon: signposted archaeological and walking trails crisscross the area, and the *Cloghane and Brandon Walking Guide* is available from the small, summer-only tourist office in the village (Ⓣ066/713 8277). There's good bar **food** and **rooms** at *O'Connor's* pub (Ⓣ066/713 8113, Ⓔoconnorsguesthouse@tinet.ie; ❷), which has space for camping, or you can stay at *Mount Brandon House* **hostel** (IHO; Ⓣ066/713 8299, Ⓦwww.mountbrandonhostel.com), which has private rooms (❶), small dorms and a café.

There's another **hostel** five miles east of Cloghane overlooking the long sandy beach of **Brandon Bay**, the *Conor Pass Hostel* in the hamlet of Stradbally (IHH; closed mid-Oct to mid-March; Ⓣ066/713 9179). The **Maharees Peninsula**, stretching north from Stradbally and the adjacent village of **CASTLEGREGORY**, is an exposed, beach-girt spit of land separating Brandon Bay and Tralee Bay, affording what's reckoned to be some of the best **wind-surfing** in the world – it's good in all wind directions, with a variety of spots suitable for all levels of ability, and its status has been endorsed by the Professional Windsurfers' Association who hold the wave final of their world tour here every October; there's a good break for **surfers**, too. Jamie Knox is the best contact for information in Castlegregory, as well as for board and wet-suit hire, and other watersports (Ⓣ066/713 9411, Ⓔjamieknox@tinet.ie); boards and wetsuits can also be rented from Celtic Wave on Strand Street (Ⓣ087/667 8525), just along from the **Castlegregory Visitor Information Centre** (Mon–Fri 9.30am–4.30pm; Ⓣ066/713 9422). **Diving** trips and courses are run by Waterworld from their base at Scraggane Pier, three miles north of Castlegregory (Ⓣ066/713 9292, Ⓔdive@iol.ie).

Back on Strand Street in town, *Fitzgerald's Euro-Hostel* (Ⓣ066/713 9133; ❶) has **dorms** and private rooms above a shop and bar. En-suite **B&B** is available at the smart, well-run *Fuchsia House* nearby (Ⓣ066/713 9000, Ⓔfuchsia-house@kerryview.com; ❷), and at *Suan na Mara*, a welcoming place with tasteful rooms and excellent breakfasts, outside of town at Lisnagree, halfway along the road to Camp (Ⓣ066/713 9258, Ⓦwww.kerry.ie/suanmara; mid-March to Oct; ❷). Also in this direction is the well-signposted, beachfront *Anchor* **campsite** (Ⓣ066/713 9157; Easter–Sept). Surfies refuel on sandwiches, pancakes, salads, tortillas and good coffees at *Hang Time* **café** above Celtic Wave, or there's a reasonably priced **restaurant** with good vegetarian options, *The Milesian*, in a cosy stone cottage round the corner on Main Street. On the west side of town, *Ned's* **pub** has bar food all day, a beer garden and regular traditional sessions.

Tralee and around

TRALEE has had quite a face-lift of late, and chief among its new attractions is **Kerry the Kingdom** in the Ashe Memorial Hall, Denny Street (mid-March to Oct daily 9.30am–5.30pm; Nov & Dec 11.30am–4.30pm; €8), which incorporates a comprehensive but rather dry run-through of the history of Ireland and Kerry since the Stone Age in the Kerry County Museum; the Irish Medieval Experience, a kind of ghost-train ride through recreated scenes of mid-fifteenth-century Tralee complete with artificial smells; and some interesting long-term temporary exhibitions – "Antarctica" is the current theme, at least till the end of 2003. Other attractions include the **Tralee to Blennerville Steam Railway** (May–Sept Tues–Sun hourly; €4; occasional closures so call ahead to check ⓣ066/712 1064), which is part of the famous Tralee–Dingle line (1891–1953), and the largest working windmill in Ireland and Britain, the **Blennerville Windmill**, at the other end of the train journey or about a mile southwest of town along the N86 (April–Oct daily 10am–6pm; €4, combined train and windmill ticket €7), which has its own exhibition, craft workshops and the usual tourist trinkets.

The **National Folk Theatre of Ireland** has its home at the Siamsa Tíre Theatre beside the tourist office (ⓣ066/712 3055, ⓦwww.siamsatire.com), though their excellent performances don't draw the same crowds as the **Rose of Tralee International Festival**. Held in the last week of August, with much accompanying merriment and followed immediately by the raucous Tralee Races, this is a beauty contest in which women, including foreigners who can demonstrate some credible Irish connection, compete for the dubious honour of being Rose of Tralee; details are available from the Festival Office, Ashe Memorial Hall, Denny Street (ⓣ066/712 1322, ⓦwww.roseoftralee.ie). There's also an Easter **arts festival**, based at Siamsa Tíre, including theatre, music and street entertainment (ⓣ066/712 9934).

Tralee practicalities

The **bus** station (ⓣ066/712 3566) and **train** station (ⓣ066/712 3522) are located next to each other, about a five-minute walk northeast of the town centre. The helpful **tourist office** (May, June, Sept & Oct Mon–Sat 9am–6pm; July & Aug Mon–Sat 9am–7pm, Sun 9am–6pm; Nov–April Mon–Fri 9am–1pm & 2–5pm; ⓣ066/712 1288) is in the Ashe Memorial Hall beneath Kerry the Kingdom. Tralee has innumerable **B&Bs**, among them *Leeside*, a welcoming place with good breakfasts on Edward Street, Oakpark (ⓣ066/712 6475, ⓔdowlingsbandb@hotmail.com; March–Nov; ❷), and *Ardroe House*, Oakpark Road, with en-suite and standard rooms and good child reductions (ⓣ066/712 6050; May–Sept; ❷), both about half a mile northeast of the centre beyond the train station. There's no shortage of **hostels** either: try the friendly and cosy *Lisnagree Hostel* (IHH; ⓣ066/712 7133; May to mid-Oct; ❶), out towards the general hospital on Ballinorig Road, the central *Courthouse Lodge*, 5 Church St, with **Internet access** (IHH; ⓣ066/712 7199, ⓦwww.courthouselodge.20m.com; ❶), or the grand, nineteenth-century *Collis-Sandes House*, set in spacious grounds with room for **camping** a mile northeast of the centre on Oakpark Road (phone for pick-up from town; IHH; ⓣ066/712 8658, ⓦwww.colsands.com; ❶). There's also a well-equipped campsite at *Woodlands Park*, Dan Spring Road (ⓣ066/712 1235; Easter–Sept), ten minutes' walk south of the centre of town. You can **rent bikes**, including mountain bikes, from Tralee Gas Supplies in Strand Street (ⓣ066/712 2018). Slattery's, 1 Russell St (ⓣ066/718 6240, ⓕ718 6222), organize **horse-drawn caravan** holidays around Killarney or the Dingle Peninsula. Finding a decent place to **eat** in Tralee isn't a problem. During the day, head for *Coffee and Spice*, Barrack Lane off The Mall, a deli-café serving gourmet sandwiches, soup, cakes and good coffee, or *Brat's Place*, nearby on Milk Market Lane, a plain and simple veggie café that cooks up a small range of dishes for lunch, such as stuffed pancakes and aubergine and mozzarella cake. For bar food try *Val's*, an attractive modern pub on Bridge Street which does good-value light meals and daily specials at lunchtime, with pricier bistro meals in the evening. *The Cookery*, a French-influenced restaurant with a friendly, cottagey atmosphere, is your best bet for a sit-down dinner (ⓣ066/712 8833; Tues–Sat evenings). Tralee is a lively town and there are plenty of **pubs** which form the hub of evening entertainment; for **traditional music**, the top spots are *Seán Og's* on Bridge Street (at least 4 nights a week throughout the year), *Turner's*, 22 Castle St (at least 3 nights a week throughout the year), and *Baily's Corner*, Ashe Street (Tues, plus Wed in summer).

Ardfert and Banna Strand

More worthy of your time than anything in Tralee itself is the ruined twelfth- to seventeenth-century **cathedral** at **ARDFERT**, five miles to the northwest (early May–late Sept daily 9.30am–6.30pm; €1.90; Heritage Card). In a landscape littered with ruined ring forts, castles and churches, Ardfert was the site of a monastery founded by St Brendan in the sixth century, and later became the centre of the Anglo-Norman Church in Kerry. As well as the cathedral with its Romanesque west doorway and fine east window, there are two smaller fifteenth-century churches on the site.

It's worth continuing beyond Ardfert to **Banna Strand** for the spectacular view over Tralee Bay, and its association with Sir Roger Casement, to whom there's a monument. In April 1916, on the eve of the Easter Rising, Casement was captured by local police as he attempted to land at Banna Strand from a German submarine. He was tried and executed for high treason in 1916, and his body was returned from England to Ireland in 1965 to be reinterred with full military honours (for more on Casement see p.667). You can carry on north up the coast towards Tarbert from here – round the cliffs of Kerry Head and through the traditional seaside resorts of Ballyheigue and Ballybunion, famous for its seaweed baths – for more great vistas south over Tralee Bay and north across the mouth of the Shannon.

Castleisland and Crag Cave

The faster route – the N21 – to Limerick runs east inland via Newcastle West from Tralee. On this road **CASTLEISLAND** offers shops and places to stop for a drink or a bite to eat. Nearby **Crag Cave** (mid-March to June & Sept–Nov daily 10am–6pm; July & Aug daily 10am–6.30pm; €5.50; Ⓦwww.cragcave.com) is an impressive limestone cave system extending a couple of miles underground. If you're passing, the thirty-minute guided tour is enjoyable, with plenty of weirdly sculpted stalactites and stalagmites to keep you amused.

Listowel and Tarbert

The Banna Strand coastal road aside, the landscape of North Kerry is unexciting – undulating farmland rolling up to the Shannon. The main road from Tralee heads up through **LISTOWEL** (Ⓦwww.listowel.com), however, a congenial market town that has a high degree of literary distinction, boasting a number of fine writers and a four-day festival of literary workshops and meetings, held over the bank-holiday weekend at the beginning of June (Ⓣ068/21074, Ⓦwww.writersweek.ie). Arguably, the town's most famous writer is the late John B. Keane, known for works such as *Man of the Triple Name*, an amusing account of North Kerry matchmaking during the 1930s and 1940s; *Sive*, a tragedy based on a similar theme; and *The Field*, a dramatization of a shocking murder that took place in this region in the 1950s.

In the town square stands **Seanchaí**, the new **Kerry Literary and Cultural Centre** (April–Sept daily 10am–6pm; Oct–March Mon–Fri 10am–5pm, weekends by appointment, ⓣ068/22212; €5; ⓦwww.kerrywritersmuseum.com). The centre includes rooms devoted to local writers Keane, Brian McMahon, Maurice Walsh, George Fitzmaurice and Brendan Kennelly, which have been imaginatively designed, with recorded extracts, to reflect the personality of each. There are some interesting audio-visuals, featuring Kerryman Eamon Kelly, Ireland's most famous story-teller (or *seanchaí*, pronounced "shanakee"), and various writers explaining how the landscapes of North Kerry have inspired them. In July and August, the centre hosts a show of traditional music, dance and story-telling on Tuesday and Thursday evenings (€7), and there are literary lectures and workshops throughout the year. Listowel's other main venue is **St John's Theatre and Arts Centre** (ⓣ068/22566), based in the former church in the middle of the square, which hosts drama, dance, all kinds of music and art exhibitions; in July and August, guided walking tours of the town depart from the theatre (Mon–Fri 6pm). In the same months, there are lively, free theatre performances in the *John B. Keane* pub on William Street (Tues & Thurs; also Thurs year-round), *Lynch's* on the square (Mon) and *The Mermaids* on William Street (Wed). In the third week of September, Listowel comes to life again for the annual **Listowel races**, when farming people from far and wide, their harvest in, take time off to eat, drink and lose money on the horses.

Further information can be had from the **tourist office**, in St John's Church on the square (June–Sept daily 10am–1pm & 2–6pm; ⓣ068/22590), where you can also get the latest news on Dúchas's renovation of Listowel Castle, next to the literary centre, and the redevelopment of the highly unusual Lartigue steam monorail. There's plenty of **accommodation** here, ranging from the old-world comfort of the *Listowel Arms* on the square (ⓣ068/21500; ❻) and *Allo's* luxury guesthouse, decorated with antiques and marble bathrooms on Church Street (ⓣ068/22880, ⓔallosbar@eircom.net; ❹), to simpler B&Bs such as *The North County House*, 67 Church St (ⓣ068/21238, ⓔbryanmonica1@eircom.net; ❷), and *Ashford Lodge*, Tarbert Road (ⓣ068/21280, ⓔashfordlodge@unison.ie; ❷). There's a good, cheap **café** at the literary centre, and decent **bar food** is available at *The Mermaids.* For a blow-out dinner – or a better-value lunch – head for *Allo's* characterful bar and **bistro**, where you can feast on dishes such as leg of venison in cider gravy.

Northbound from Listowel the main road continues to **TARBERT** on the Shannon estuary, and from there trails the river inland (through County Limerick) towards Limerick and Shannon Airport. There's a comfortable **hostel**, *The Ferry House*, on the square (IHH; ⓣ068/36555, ⓦwww.ferryhostel.com), with dorms, private rooms (❶) and meals available. Immediately north of the town, the twenty-minute **car ferry** across the estuary provides a useful short cut into County Clare; there's no other river crossing west of Limerick (June–Sept every 30min, Oct–May hourly; car €13 single, €20 return; foot passenger/cyclist €3 single, €5 return; ⓣ065/905 3124, ⓦwww.shannonferries.com). If you have time to spare on your onward journey and your own transport, it's worth detouring west down the estuary for about five miles to the ruined fifteenth-century **Carrigafoyle Castle**, which seems to rise miraculously from the water, joined to the land by a causeway.

Travel details

Trains

Killarney to: Cork (3–4 daily, often with a change at Mallow; 2hr 30min); Dublin (4 daily, some with a change at Mallow; 4hr–4hr 30min); Farranfore (4–7 daily; 25min); Tralee (4–7 daily; 45min).

Buses

Dingle to: Ballydavid (Tues & Fri 3 daily; 20–40min); Dunquin (summer Mon–Sat 1–2 daily, winter Mon & Thurs 3 daily; 45min).
Kenmare to: Bantry, via Glengarriff (2 daily in summer; 1hr 10min); Castletownbere (summer Mon–Sat daily; 1hr 20min); Lauragh (summer Mon–Sat daily, winter 1 on Fri; 40min); Sneem (1 on Fri; 35min).
Killarney to: Bantry, via Glengarriff (2 daily in summer; 2hr 20min); Caherdaniel (summer 1–2 daily; 2hr); Cahersiveen (summer 1–3 daily, winter Mon–Sat 1 daily; 1hr 30min); Cork (hourly; 2hr); Dingle (summer 2–5 daily; 1hr 45min–2hr 30min); Dublin (5–6 daily, change at Limerick; 6hr); Farranfore airport (6 daily; 20min); Kenmare (summer 2–3 daily, winter Mon–Fri 1 daily; 45min); Killorglin (4–5 daily; 30min); Limerick (6–8 daily; 2hr); Ring of Kerry (summer 1–2 daily; 4hr 45min); Tralee (11–16 daily; 40min–1hr); Waterville (summer 1–3 daily, winter Mon–Sat 1 daily; 1hr 45min).
Tralee to: Ardfert (1–3 daily; 15min); Cloghane (weekly; 1hr 10min); Cork (8–10 daily; 2hr 15min–2hr 45min); Dingle (3–8 daily; 1hr 20min); Dublin (6–7 daily, change at Limerick; 6hr); Killorglin (4–6 daily; 40min); Limerick (8–9 daily; 2hr 15min); Listowel (8–10 daily; 40min).

Clare

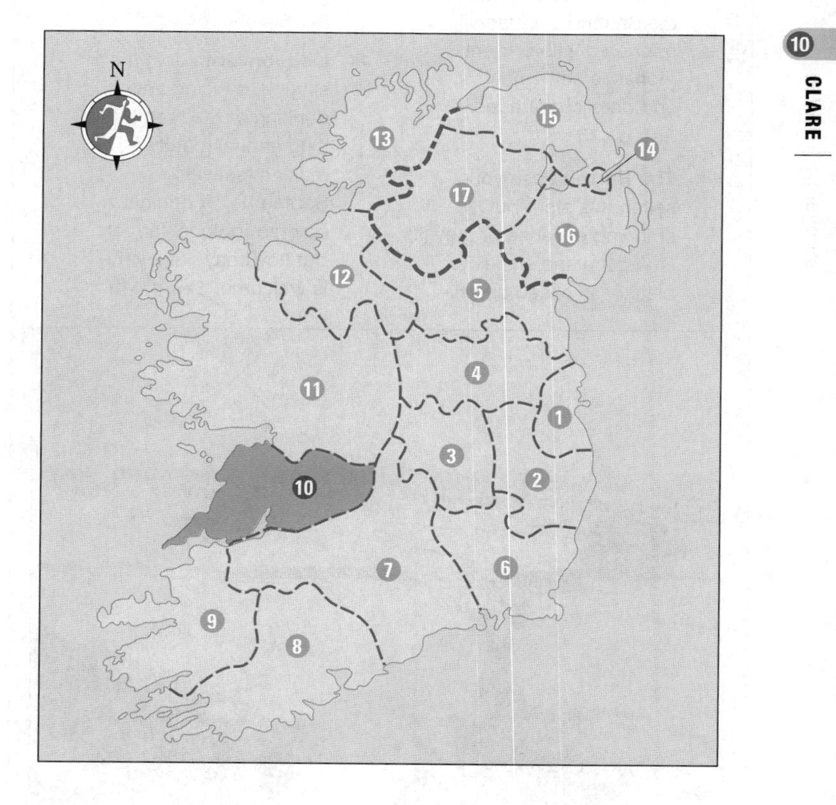

CHAPTER 10 **Highlights**

* **Ennis** County Clare's bustling capital is well worth an overnight stay to sample the abundance of traditional music. **See p.425**

* **Scattery Island** Peaceful and uninhabited island in the Shannon estuary, peppered with ancient monastic settlements and derelict cottages. **See p.435**

* **The Burren** Lose yourself in this stark but stunning expanse of grey limestone and shale, its bleakness eased by brilliantly coloured wild flowers growing up through the rocks. **See p.439**

* **The Cliffs of Moher** Six hundred and sixty feet of dramatically ravaged rock face towering over the Atlantic. **See p.442**

* **Lisdoonvarna** Join the singing, dancing and drinking at the month-long annual match-making festival in September; it originally catered for local farmers but nowadays everyone is welcome. **See p.446**

Clare

Physically, **County Clare** is clearly defined, with Galway Bay and the Shannon estuary to the north and south, massive Lough Derg forming its eastern boundary, and the Atlantic to the west. Strangely, although plenty of people visit, the county is sometimes glossed over by travellers as simply land between the magnificent scenery of Kerry and Galway. It's true that it doesn't have the scenic splendour of either of these, and for many, the north of the county is too bleak to be attractive. Nonetheless, Clare has a subtle flavour that, once tasted, can be addictive.

Clare has earned itself two epithets: "the banner county" and "the singing county". It was called "the banner county" originally because of the part played by its men in the Battle of Ramillies and more recently because of its courageous **political history**, particularly in the fight for Catholic emancipation. The second epithet reflects the strong **musical traditions** that are still very much alive in the county and constitute a major reason for coming here. Throughout the summer you will find sessions in pubs and in *teach cheoils* (pronounced "chuck key 'ole"); the latter hosts more sober entertainments, with tea and brown bread rather than stout for refreshment, and very fine musicians too. To find out what's going on, pick up a copy of the *Shannon Region Traditional Irish Music Pubs* leaflet from any tourist office or check out *The Clare Champion*, and, above all, ask around. Pub sessions very often start late in the evening so don't give up on a bar just because it's half past nine and nothing is happening. A great session can seemingly spring from nowhere, and is liable to prove a wholly memorable experience. Don't underestimate the popularity and excitement of Clare's festivals either. If you have yet to experience "the *craic*", you are sure to find it here.

Both of Clare's titles, "the banner county" and "the singing county" – the strong and the gentle – suggest something of the character of the place and are echoed in the contrasts of the landscape. The **Burren** heights in the north are startlingly stark and barren, while **Ennis**, the county's capital, is surrounded by low, rolling farmland. Fabulous cliff scenery stretches for miles round Clare's southern extreme at Loop Head and is spectacularly sheer at the **Cliffs of Moher**, further north. In between are small seaside towns and villages and wonderful sandy beaches, most dramatic at **Lahinch** – famous for its surf. In the east, **Lough Derg** affords opportunities for watersports, and there are panoramic views from the slopes of the Slieve Bernagh and Slieve Aught mountains across to the mountains of Tipperary.

This varied countryside holds plenty of specialist interest. The Burren is a major attraction for geology and botany enthusiasts, and is also rich in ring forts, dolmens and cairns in the north. The legacy of later communities is found throughout the county, in the thickly sprinkled medieval monastic remains and the tower houses of the O'Brien and Macnamara clans.

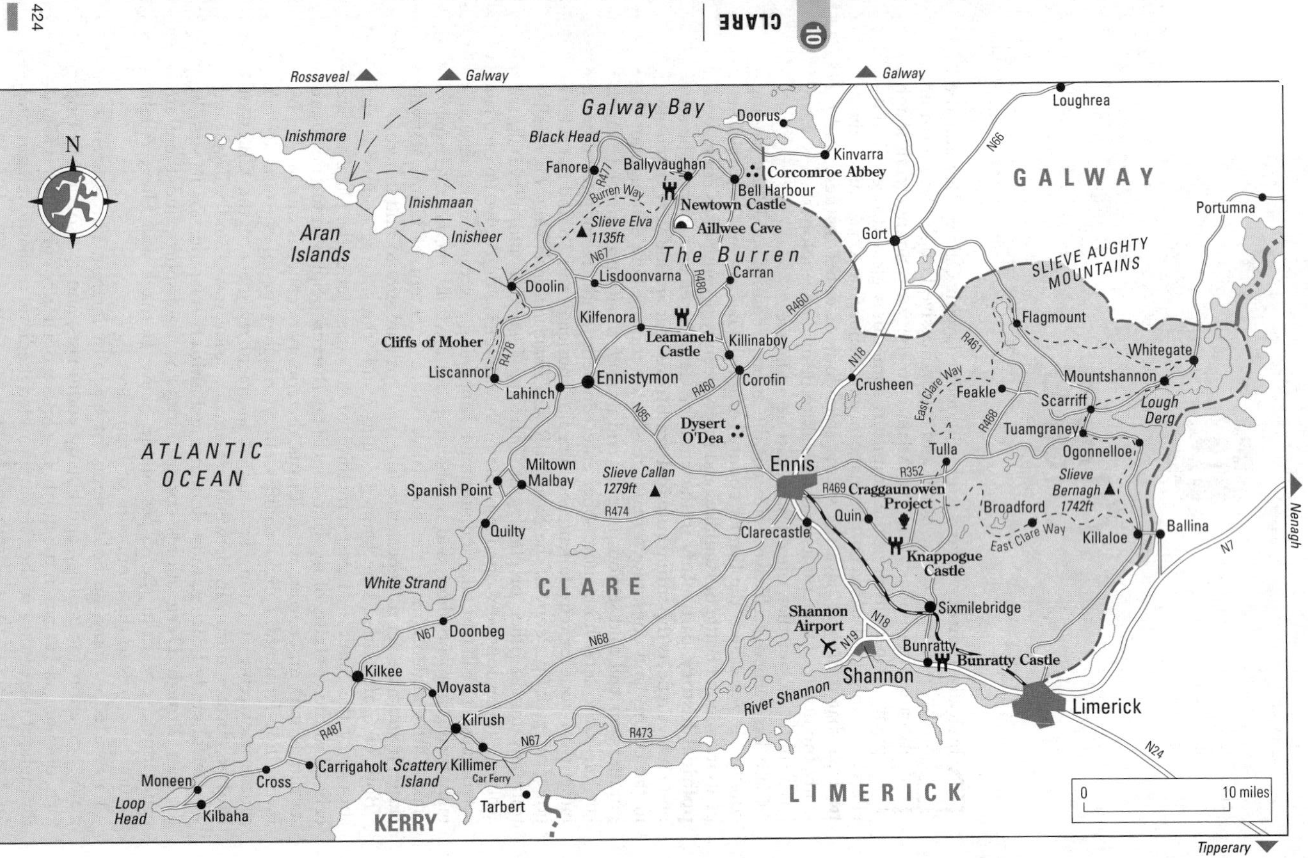
Rossaveal
Galway
Galway
Galway Bay
Doorus
Kinvarra
Loughrea
N66
GALWAY
Portumna
Inishmore
Inishmaan
Inisheer
Aran Islands
Black Head
Fanore
R477
Ballyvaughan
Burren Way
Corcomroe Abbey
Bell Harbour
Newtown Castle
Aillwee Cave
Slieve Elva 1135ft
The Burren
Gort
SLIEVE AUGHTY MOUNTAINS
N67
Doolin
Lisdoonvarna
R480
Carran
Kilfenora
Leamaneh Castle
Killinaboy
R460
Flagmount
R461
Whitegate
Cliffs of Moher
R478
Liscannor
Lahinch
Ennistymon
Corofin
N18
Crusheen
East Clare Way
Feakle
Mountshannon
Scarriff
Lough Derg
N85
Dysert O'Dea
R468
Tuamgraney
Ogonnelloe
ATLANTIC OCEAN
Tulla
Ennis
R352
Slieve Bernagh 1742ft
Miltown Malbay
Spanish Point
Slieve Callan 1279ft
R469
Craggaunowen Project
Quin
Broadford
R474
Quilty
Clarecastle
East Clare Way
Killaloe
Ballina
Nenagh
N7
Knappogue Castle
White Strand
CLARE
Sixmilebridge
Shannon Airport
N18
N67
Doonbeg
N68
N19
Bunratty
Bunratty Castle
Shannon
Kilkee
Moyasta
River Shannon
Limerick
Kilrush
R487
R473
N67
N24
Carrigaholt
Scattery Island
Killimer
Car Ferry
Moneen
Cross
LIMERICK
Loop Head
Kilbaha
Tarbert
KERRY
0
10 miles
Tipperary

Shannon Airport

Arriving at **Shannon International Airport** (☎061/471444) you're most likely to want to head for **Limerick**, barely fifteen miles to the southeast, where you can get bus and train connections to just about anywhere in the country. **Ennis**, a similar distance to the north, is also easily accessible and a pleasant place to stop over if you plan to spend some time in County Clare or want to break your journey before you head further north. Alternatively, Bunratty is worth considering as a closer overnight option. From the airport, Bus Éireann **buses** (☎061/313333) run around twenty services daily to Bunratty (20min), around fourteen daily to Ennis (45min) and around twenty daily to Limerick (45min). A **taxi** (☎061/471538) from Shannon Airport to Bunratty will cost about €15, and to Ennis or Limerick about €25. If you just want to find a bed for the night, you could stay at one of the **B&Bs** in Shannon town, all around a five-minute drive from the airport. Try *35 Tullyglass Crescent* (☎061/364268; ❷) overlooking the River Shannon, or *Avalon*, 11 Balleycaseymore Hill (☎061/362032, Ⓦwww.avalonbnb.net; ❷).

Shannon Airport **tourist office** (daily for all major flights; ☎061/471664) is extremely helpful and will book accommodation for you for the usual charge. There's a **Bus Éireann** and **Irish Rail** information point (April–Oct), and an **airport information desk**, open to serve all flights – if there's no one there, pick up the phone and dial 0. For Aer Lingus enquiries call ☎061/471666. The **airport bank** is open daily from 6am until 5.30pm, though it sometimes closes early if there are no flights.

Ennis

A bustling market town and the commercial capital of County Clare, **ENNIS** is little more than a handful of busy lanes laced together, with a nineteenth-century cathedral, a stout monument to Daniel O'Connell and a medieval friary. You could probably walk from one side of Ennis to the other in half an hour, and you can certainly see all it has to offer in a single afternoon – but it's worth staying longer for the plentiful **traditional music**. Ennis also makes an excellent base from which to explore the church ruins and tower houses dotted about the surrounding countryside, although you'll need your own vehicle as public transport is minimal.

Arrival, information and accommodation

There are direct bus connections between Ennis and **Shannon Airport** (see box above), which is thirteen miles away in the south of the county and is the major airport on the west coast, with flights to Dublin, the UK, Europe and the US. The **bus** (☎065/682 4177; if closed, phone the office in Limerick) and **train stations** (☎065/684 0444, Ⓦwww.irishrail.ie) sit alongside one another, a ten-minute walk from the town centre – follow Station Road, which runs off O'Connell Street from beside the cathedral. The very helpful **tourist office** is tucked away on Arthur's Row, signposted off O'Connell Street near the Daniel O'Connell monument (July & Aug Mon–Sat 9am–6pm; Sept–June Mon–Sat 9.30am–5.30pm; ☎065/682 8366).

For a small town, Ennis has a good range of accommodation. It's worth bearing in mind that if you're planning to stay over a weekend, especially in the summer, it's best to book ahead.

The Abbey Tourist Hostel Harmony Row ☎065/682 2620, Ⓦwww.abbeytouristhostel.com. This large and well-run hostel is situated in a prime location, just across the river from the friary. Private rooms are also available. Closed Christmas. ❶–❷

Avonlea Francis St ☎065/682 1632. A pleasant B&B with en-suite rooms, only a short walk from the town centre. ❷

Cloneen Clon Rd ☎065/682 9681. Just a five-minute walk from Ennis, this welcoming B&B offers standard and en-suite accommodation in a comfortable non-smoking house. Open April–Oct. ❷

Glenfarne 10 Ard Aoibhinn, Clare Rd ☎065/684 4922. Comfortable and family-run B&B in a quiet cul-de-sac off the Ennis–Limerick road, about half a mile out of town. TV and tea- and coffee-making facilities in each room. Open March–Oct. ❷

Newpark House Tulla Rd ☎065/682 1233, Ⓔnewparkhouse.ennis@eircom.net. Located about half a mile out of Ennis on the R352 (turn right opposite the *Roselevan Arms*). A welcoming B&B in a striking seventeenth-century mansion set in wooded grounds. Open Easter to end of Oct. ❷

Old Ground Hotel O'Connell St ☎065/682 8127, Ⓦwww.flynnhotels.com. This is one of Ennis's oldest hotels with a beautiful ivy-clad entrance, pleasant gardens and plenty of traditional character. There's an elegant dining room and a welcoming bar. Good weekend rates available. ❺–❼

Queens Hotel Abbey St ☎065/682 8963, Ⓦwww.irishcourthotels.com. Modern hotel in the centre of Ennis next door to *Cruises* pub and restaurant and overlooking the thirteenth-century Franciscan abbey ❹–❼

Rockfield Station Rd ☎065/682 4749. A decent budget B&B in a central location, a short walk from Ennis cathedral, offering some en-suite rooms and some with shared bathrooms. ❷

The Temple Gate Hotel The Square ☎065/682 3300, Ⓦwww.templegatehotel.com. A comfortable, town-centre hotel styled around the Gothic architecture of the old convent it partially occupies. All rooms are en suite and have TV and tea- and coffee-making facilities. ❹–❼

The West County Hotel Clare Rd ☎065/682 3000, Ⓦwww.lynchotels.com. A comfortable and modern hotel about three quarters of a mile south of the centre. Facilities include three pools, a gym and a children's play centre. ❸–❺

The Town

The finest monument in town, **Ennis Friary**, lies right in the historic centre (April, May, mid-Sept & Oct Tues–Sun 10am–5pm; June to mid-Sept daily 10am–6pm; €1.20; Heritage Card; ☎065/682 9100, Ⓔennisfriary@ealga.ie). Established by the O'Briens, kings of Thomond, in 1242, most of the existing building dates from the fourteenth century. At that time, it had three hundred and fifty friars and over six hundred pupils and was considered the finest educational institution in Ireland for the clergy and upper classes. In parts it remains striking: graceful lancet windows fill the east end of the chancel, while adjacent convent buildings include cloister ruins and a stoutly barrel-vaulted chapter house. There is good **sculpture**, too: look out for the small square carving on the jamb of the arch between the nave and transept, which shows a half-length figure of Christ with his hands bound; the relief of St Francis with cross-staff and stigmata at the east end of the nave; and the carved corbels beneath the south tower showing the Virgin and Child and an archbishop. The real sculptural highlight, however, is the fifteenth-century **MacMahon Tomb** (now incorporated in the Creagh Tomb), embellished with fine alabaster carvings of the Passion.

Despite the beauty of the friary, Ennis today seems more proud of its later history, as capital of the unyielding "banner county" and a bastion of Nationalism. A monument to **Daniel O'Connell** solidly dominates the old narrow streets that meet in O'Connell Square. In 1828, County Clare returned O'Connell to Westminster by such a huge majority that he had to be allowed to take his seat, despite the fact that he was a Catholic, which should have barred him at the time; he went on to force through parliament the Catholic Emancipation Act. It was in Ennis, too, that **Parnell** made his famous speech advocating the boycott in the land agitations of the late nineteenth century. **De Valera** was TD for the county from 1917 to 1959 (and Taoiseach for much of that time) and is remembered in a memorial outside the courthouse.

The **Clare Museum** alongside the tourist office on Arthur's Row (Jan–Feb Mon–Fri 9.30am–1pm & 2–5.30pm; March–May Mon–Sat 9.30am–1pm &

2–5.30pm; June–Sept daily 9.30am–5.30pm; Oct–Dec Mon–Sat 9.30am–1pm & 2–5pm; €3.50; ⓣ065/682 3382, ⓦwww.clarelibrary.ie) is well worth a visit, housing a large number of antiquities on loan from the National Museum in Dublin. A permanent exhibition entitled the **Riches of Clare** illustrates the story of this remarkably diverse county, encompassing weaponry from the Bronze Age through to that of the IRA, Clare's links with the Spanish Armada and the development of the submarine, and a number of interesting letters and telegrams from Daniel O'Connell (seeking support in the forthcoming election) and de Valera, including the telegram he sent his wife on being elected to parliament. Also among the exhibits are: a thirteenth-century bell from Corcomroe Abbey (see p.446) and material from the Poulnabrone dolmen (see p.447), including an arrow-pierced human hipbone, arrow heads and beads.

Ennis's **cathedral**, an austere nineteenth-century building with a sharp spire, stands at the far end of O'Connell Street. An enjoyable way to kill time in the town is to wander the ancient lanes that run from O'Connell Street to the old market place (where a Saturday vegetable and livestock market is held), and from Parnell Street down to the post office field, a riverside meadow right in the town centre. You could also follow the river a short way up from Woodquay to the newly renovated mill chase.

It's also worth considering taking a **tour of the Burren** from Ennis, particularly if you are short of time and without transport; ask at the tourist office for details.

Eating and drinking

There are a handful of exciting places to **eat** in Ennis, although it has to be said that most of the rest have a fairly workaday character. For general provisions, the small O'Connell Street shopfront of Dunne's Stores hides an enormous, and well-stocked, supermarket behind.

Bistro on the Lane 6 Chapel Lane, off Parnell St ⓣ065/684 0622, ⓔjhughesbistroonthelane@oceanfree.ie. A new and promising restaurant featuring mouth-watering dishes including grilled aubergine with roast vegetables and pan-seared wild Fergus salmon on buttered leeks.

Hal Pino's 7 High St ⓣ065/684 0011, ⓦwww.halpinos.com. Contemporary cuisine such as tiger-prawn kebabs and roast whole baby poussin with a melange of exotic fruits. Open daily 5–10.30pm and also Fri noon–2.30pm.

Henry's Deli & Coffee Shop Abbey St car park. Cheap and cheerful sandwich bar and coffee shop serving tasty sandwiches filled with delicious cheeses, relishes and Mediterranean salads. Closed Sun.

McCanny's 17/18 Salt House Lane ⓣ065/682 3686. In a side road off Parnell St, this popular seafood restaurant serves up particularly good salmon, swordfish and monkfish. Open daily noon–3pm & 6–10pm.

Numero Uno 3 Old Barrack St ⓣ065/684 1740. This tiny, cheap and cheerful pizza café offers eat in or takeaway and is open until 1am Fri & Sat.

Old Ground Hotel O'Connell St ⓣ065/682 8127. A traditional hotel bar whose wood-panelled walls hung with oil paintings generate a comfortably conservative atmosphere. Decent bar meals are served from Monday to Saturday, and typical dishes include stuffed pork, fried fish and braised beef in Guinness. Lighter meals of soup and sandwiches are served on a Sunday.

Punjab 59 Parnell St ⓣ065/684 4655. One of the best Indian restaurants in the west of Ireland, and reasonably priced too. Lunchtimes are exceptionally good value.

Ruby Tuesday's Merchants Square ⓣ065/684 0474. An inexpensive, family restaurant with a broad range of meals on offer – burgers, pastas, chicken and fish – and a BYO policy.

The Sherwood Inn Ennis Shopping Centre, Francis St. The place to go when funds are low for a cheap and hearty breakfast or lunch. Open until 6pm.

Temple Gate Hotel The Square ⓣ065/682 3300. Spacious medieval-theme bar which offers good-value carvery lunches at midday, and bar meals in the evening.

Tiger Lilies Abbey St. Modern bistro serving dishes such as roast saddle of lamb and baked whole sea bass.

Nightlife and entertainment

Ennis may not have the best selection of restaurants in the west, but when it comes to music, it takes some beating. **Glór**, Irish Music Centre, Friar's Walk (Mon–Sat 9.30am–5.30pm, plus evening concerts; ⓣ065/684 3103, ⓦwww.glor.ie), is a proud new national centre for the performance of Irish traditional music, with year-round concerts and a busy programme between June and August featuring the best of local and national artists. It was set up in 2001 to provide visitors and locals alike with authentic and good-quality Irish music, not just a watered-down product aimed at tourists. It is also well worth checking out **Cois na hAbhna** (ⓣ065/682 2347), a centre for local traditional music enthusiasts, located less than half a mile out on the Gort road. The centre offers *céilí* dancing on Tuesdays and informal traditional music and set dancing on Wednesdays at 8.30pm. On alternate Saturdays from June to September they have Oíche Ceilidh evenings of song and dance. Sessions organized by Cois na hAbhna also move around the county, so it's worth watching out for them in smaller towns roundabout; call into the tourist office for details.

The town also has two major traditional music festivals, the **Fleadh Nua**, which takes place over the last weekend in May (ⓣ065/682 8366), and the fabulous **Guinness Traditional Music Festival** (ⓣ065/682 8366), which is usually held over the second weekend in November and draws top musicians. The Knotted Chord, Cook's Lane, off O'Connell Street, is a music shop specializing in traditional Irish, folk and world music, and there's **what's-on information** posted on the wall; it's also worth checking out ⓦwww.knotted-chord.com.

For such a small town, Ennis has a surprising number of **bars** with **music** sessions. For traditional music try: *Fawl's Bar*, 69 O'Connell St (summer Fri); *Kerin's Bar*, Lifford, a short walk along Newbridge Road (summer Fri); *P.J. Kelly's Bar*, 5 Carmody St (summer Sat & Sun); *Cruises*, Abbey Street (nightly); and *Ciarán's Bar*, 1 Francis St (summer Thurs–Sun). You might also find traditional music in *O'Halloran's*, High Street; *Paddy Quinn's*, 7 Market St (Sat), and *Knox's Bar*, Abbey Street (summer Wed). *Brandon's*, O'Connell Street, is one of the liveliest young bars, offering a mixture of traditional (Mon & Wed), a DJ (Thurs), rock, blues or cajun (Fri and Sat) and a varied selection on Sundays. They also have a singers' club upstairs (first and third Wed of every month), where anyone is welcome to do any kind of performance including stand-up. *El Paso's*, Parnell Street, is a huge, Western-theme bar with pop, folk and ballads four or five nights a week, and *Alexander Knox*, Abbey Street, attracts a young crowd with pop and rock (Mon & Wed–Fri). For clubs, try *The Sanctuary* located behind *Cruises* on Abbey Street (chart music), or *The Boardwalk* (rock, world, cajun mix), behind *Brandon's* on O'Connell Street.

Around Ennis

Ennis sits in a low-lying strip of land that runs from a deep inlet of the Shannon River right up to south Galway. To the east of the town lie lush fields edged by white-grey walls and clumps of wild flowers: pinks, purples and yellows of willow herb and ragwort, the strong white horns of bindweed and even the occasional orchid. Further out, the land breaks into little lakes and rivers before becoming gently hilly where it meets the Slieve Bernagh Mountains.

This gentle farmland makes for easy **cycling**, and your trip can be punctuated by village pubs and plenty of characterful historical sites. The best of these include the evocative fifteenth-century **Quin Abbey**, imposing medieval **Knappogue Castle** and the **Craggaunowen Project**, which includes a reconstruction of a Bronze Age lake dwelling. Northwest of Ennis lies the fifteenth-century **Dysert O'Dea Castle**, and thirteen miles south of the county capital stands **Bunratty Castle**, arguably the most impressive of the region's medieval strongholds. It is worth bearing in mind though that the N18 Galway–Limerick road is horribly busy, a nightmare for cyclists as drivers adopt motorway attitudes on what is in fact quite a narrow road.

Quin Abbey and Knappogue Castle

One of the most pleasant routes is east of Ennis to **Quin Abbey** (June–Sept Mon–Fri 10.30am–6pm, Sat & Sun 11.30am–5pm; free), the area's best-preserved Franciscan friary, founded in 1433. The main church building is graceful, its slender tower rising clear over the high, open archway between chancel and nave and making a distinct outline against the green of the surrounding pastures. Climb up a floor to the first storey and you can look down on the abbey's complete cloister with its arches and buttresses. For all the uplifting beauty of the tower, the abbey seems to have been built on a human scale, to function as a place in which to live and worship rather than to impress and dominate.

On the other hand, the massive walls of **Knappogue Castle** emanate an awesome sense of power. Leave Quin and continue two miles south on the L31 to reach this huge sixteenth-century tower house (April to early Oct daily 9.30am–5.30pm; €3.81; Ⓣ061/360788). It was built by the Macnamaras in 1467, but they lost it to Cromwell, who then used it as his HQ – thereby, no doubt, saving it from the major damage he inflicted elsewhere. During the Restoration, the Macnamaras managed to regain ownership of the castle and hung onto it until 1800. It's been beautifully restored, and inside are boldly carved sixteenth-century oak fireplaces and stout oak furniture. At odds with the overall flavour of Knappogue, the nineteenth-century domestic additions are furnished in eighteenth-century style: beautifully appointed with Irish Chippendale furniture and Waterford crystal. The main body of the castle is used for medieval banquets (April–Oct twice nightly 5.30–8.45pm, subject to demand).

The Craggaunowen Project

The second left turning, two miles south of Knappogue, brings you to the **Craggaunowen Project**, situated on the edge of a reedy lake under a wooded hillside (May–Oct daily 10am–6pm; €6.65; Ⓣ061/360788, Ⓦwww.shannonheritage.com). This is based around another fortified tower house, the ground floor of which houses a collection of sixteenth-century European wood-carvings. The project itself aims to re-create a sense of Ireland's ancient history, with reconstructions of earlier forms of homes and farmsteads: a ring fort and a *crannóg*, or artificial island, for example. Young workers experiment with old craft techniques, using replicas of wooden lathes, kilns and other traditional devices, and double up as guides if asked.

The most adventurous, and certainly the most famous, of the working replicas here is Tim Severin's **Brendan**, a curragh (leather-hulled boat) in which he and four crew successfully sailed across the Atlantic in 1976, to prove that the legend of St Brendan could be true. St Brendan's story – he was supposedly the first European to reach America – is recorded in a ninth-century manuscript, and the design of the *Brendan* is based on its descriptions, along with the features of curraghs still used off Ireland's west coast. The result is a remarkable vessel of oak-tanned oxhides stretched over an ash-wood frame. Craggaunowen also has an actual Iron Age road, excavated at Corlea Bog, County Longford and moved to this site. Made of large oak planks placed across runners of birch or alder, it must have formed part of an important route across difficult bog. For refreshment, there's a **tea shop**, serving delicious homemade cakes.

Bunratty Castle

Bunratty Castle (June–Aug daily 9am–6.30pm; Sept–May daily 9.30am–5.30pm; combined ticket for castle and Folk Park €9.50; ⓣ061/360788, ⓦwww.shannonheritage.com), thirteen miles south of Ennis and handily situated on the N18 Ennis–Limerick road, stands on the north bank of the Shannon on what was once an island. The Vikings of Limerick recognized the site's strategic importance for protecting trade, and so they fortified it – you can still see the moat. The first castle on the site was built by Normans but they lost control and, in 1460, the Macnamaras built the castle that stands today. It's exceptionally impressive: the fine rectangular keep has been perfectly restored and now houses a large collection of furniture, tapestries, paintings and ornate carvings from all over Europe, spanning the fourteenth to the seventeenth centuries. In the castle grounds stands **Bunratty Folk Park** (daily: June–Aug 9am–6.30pm; Sept–May 9.30am–5.30pm) a complete reconstruction of a nineteenth-century village, hilariously mocked in Pete McCarthy's *McCarthy's Bar*. Although extremely touristy, both castle and folk village are well worth taking time over, and you can break up your visit in the excellent **tearoom** or the **pub** within the Folk Park.

The nearby *Durty Nelly's* (ⓣ061/364861) is a favourite tourist **bar**, with **traditional music** sessions every Thursday night, and is regularly overrun by bus parties. *The Bunratty Castle Hotel* (ⓣ061/478700, ⓦwww.bunrattycastlehotel.com; ❹–❻), offers comfortable accommodation in traditional Georgian-style rooms and serves excellent bar food in *Kathleen's Irish Pub*, though again coach parties can mean a long wait to be served. Follow Lower Road, which runs between Bunratty Castle and *Durty Nelly's*, for *Bunratty Caravan and Camping Park* (ⓣ061/369190; April–Oct), a serviceable **campsite**. On this road you'll also find numerous good-quality **B&Bs** including *Bunratty Villa* (ⓣ061/369241, ⓦwww.bunrattyvilla.com; ❷), a handy ten-minute walk from the castle; *Innisfree* (ⓣ061/369773; ❷); *Bunratty Heights* (ⓣ061/369324; ❷); and, about a mile from the castle, the friendly *Castleside* (ⓣ061/369390; ❷).

Three miles east of Bunratty the village of **Cratloe** is renowned for its oak-wooded hills overlooking the Shannon and Fergus estuaries and is a particularly good spot from which to start some lovely walks. Contact the tourist office in Ennis for more information (see p.425).

Dysert O'Dea

Alternative routes from Ennis can take you north through low-lying country fretted with rush-bordered lakes, their banks dotted with O'Brien strongholds. Six miles north is **Dysert O'Dea**, the site of the ancient monastic foundation of St Tola (d. 737) and the scene of an important battle in 1318 when the O'Briens defeated the De Clares of Bunratty, thus preventing the Anglo-Norman takeover of Clare. To get there, take the road for Ennistymon out of Ennis, then after two miles take the right fork for Corofin and it's up a road to the left. At the site you can wander around the remains of a twelfth- to thirteenth-century Romanesque church with a richly carved south doorway and carvings of grotesque animal heads and human faces. Of particular interest is the twelfth-century **White Cross of Tola**, with carvings of Christ and a bishop in high relief, Daniel in the lions' den, as well as intricate patterning. The **O'Dea Castle** nearby houses an archaeological centre (May–Sept daily 10am–6pm; €4; ⓣ065/683 7401) from where a history trail starts out that takes in the high cross, ring forts and an ancient cooking site. Travelling north of Dysert O'Dea, you'll come across an abundance of little lakes, offering good **fishing**.

Lough Derg

The west bank of **Lough Derg** is a seam of beautiful countryside set between bald, boggy mountains and the great expanse of the lake. It forms the county's eastern boundary and, isolated by the heights of the Slieve Bernagh and the Slieve Aughty mountains, has a different character from the rest of Clare. The lough's wealth of fish and bird life, and the quaint villages on either shore, have long made it popular with a wealthy lough-cruising set, whose exclusive brand of tourism supports the fairly conservative and well-kept villages. The hunting, shooting and fishing crowds are well catered for and tend to dominate the character of local pubs, but the historic town of **Killaloe** and the village of **Mountshannon** make attractive bases, offering accommodation, bars and opportunities for watersports. There are also pockets renowned for their traditional music sessions, notably the tiny villages of **Feakle** and **Ogonnelloe**, attracting predominantly local crowds.

The main road north varies the scene, at times clinging to the lakeshore, at others gaining higher ground and panoramic views over the lough, its islands and the mountains of Tipperary. **Access** to the area is via Limerick. Bus Éireann runs a very limited service: from Limerick to Killaloe, Scarriff, Tuamgraney (Mon–Sat), Mountshannon and Whitegate (Sat only). For timetable information, phone ⓣ061/313333. Hitching isn't such a good idea in the Slieve Bernagh and Slieve Aughty mountains to the west where roads are empty, and this isn't ideal cycling country either, as the roads are deceptively steep and unsheltered. However, if you are keen to cycle, you can arrange **bike rental** through the Killaloe tourist office.

Killaloe

At **KILLALOE**, the Shannon narrows again after the lough for the final stretch of this great river's journey to the sea. An old stone bridge still spans the waters at this traditional crossing point. The old part of Killaloe centres on **St Flannan's Cathedral**. It is a plain thirteenth-century building, impressive in its solid simplicity, with a low square tower and straight, strong buttresses. Just inside the entrance is a heavily decorated Romanesque doorway from an earlier church, and alongside it the huge **Thorgrim Stone**, unique in its ogham and runic inscriptions (ogham is a form of the Latin alphabet associated with

The East Clare Way

The **East Clare Way** is a long-distance walking route through a less visited, but no less scenic, part of the county. It passes through a green and rugged corner of Clare, taking in rivers, lakes, woodlands and boglands. It's a circular walk and the latter stages can be broken up with **boat trips** out onto Lough Derg from Mountshannon, or, in fine weather, swimming from the lakeshore (ask locally about currents). The circular route begins at Killaloe and goes through Broadford, O'Callaghan's Mills, Tulla, Feakle, Flagmount, Whitegate, Mountshannon, Ogonnelloe and back to Killaloe. The longest stage is Flagmount to Whitegate – some 21 miles.

Access: There is a limited bus service from Limerick to Killaloe and Scarriff (Mon–Sat). You can also catch a bus from Limerick to Mountshannon, Whitegate, Broadford and O'Callaghan's Mills (Sat only), and to Tulla (Wed).

Accommodation: B&Bs at Killaloe, Tulla and Ogonnelloe, and hotel accommodation in Feakle and Mountshannon; these are small communities, so it makes sense to book accommodation in advance.

Overall distance: 112 miles.

Highest point: Cragnamurragh, 1729ft.

Maps and guides: *East Clare Map Guide*, available from the tourist office in Ennis; OS map Nos. 58 & 65, 1:50,000 (1.25 inches to 1 mile).

early Christianity; the runic forms are Scandinavian in origin), which is probably the memorial of a Viking convert. In the churchyard the stout Romanesque **St Flannan's Oratory** dates from the twelfth century and is complete with barrel-vaulted roof. Well signposted just over a mile north of town, on the western shore of Lough Derg, stands the earthern fort **Beal Boru**, possibly the site of Brian Boru's palace "Kincora", which was either here or in Killaloe itself. Another great way to spend your time in Killaloe is to get out onto the water; see below for details of **cruises** and **boat rental**.

Practicalities

The **tourist office**, in Lock House on The Bridge (May–Sept daily 10am–6pm; ⓣ061/376866), can help with accommodation. Alternatively you could opt for one of the central **B&Bs**, such as *Kincora House*, Church Street (ⓣ061/376149; ❷), a lovely old town house with antiquated furnishings, or *Lyon's B&B* (ⓣ061/376652; ❷), just next door. For a really great location check in at *The Lakeside Hotel* (ⓣ061/376122, ⓦwww.lakesidekillaloe.com; ❹–❻). **Camping** beside the lake is possible at the *Lough Derg Holiday Park* (ⓣ061/376329; May to late Sept), just three miles north of Killaloe along the Scarriff road.

One-hour **lough cruises** on the *Derg Princess* leave from beside the tourist office (May–Sept daily noon & 2.30pm; €7), and the *Spirit of Killaloe* (ⓣ086/814 0559) departs from the pier at Ballina, across the bridge in Tipperary (July & Aug daily 1pm, 2.30pm & 4pm). To **rent boats** with outboard engines that can take up to four adults, call in at Whelan's Foodstore, Main Street (ⓣ061/376159). You can rent wind-surfs, canoes, wetsuits and dinghies from **Killaloe Activity Centre** (ⓣ061/376622), situated two miles out along the road towards Scarriff.

You'll find a few pubs serving decent **food** both in Killaloe and across the bridge in Ballina: *Crotty's Courtyard Bar*, Bridge Street, Killaloe, is a popular spot with a fabulous collection of old signs, a cheery beer-yard and bar food until 10pm in summer; across the bridge, *Gooser's* is a rather pricier place for good-quality bar food, while the nearby *Simply Delicious* café serves cheap meals that are just that. Many **pubs** have some kind of **music** at weekends during the summer – usually a traditional/country mix. For set dancing and traditional music head for *The Anchor Inn*, Bridge Street (summer Wed); *Molly's*, across the bridge in Ballina, usually has traditional music (summer Thurs).

In **OGONNELLOE**, two and half miles north of Killaloe, *The Piper's Inn* is noted for its traditional music sessions (summer Wed–Sun) and offers reasonably priced **B&B** (ⓣ061/375544; ❶). The village is also on the East Clare Way (see box opposite).

Scarriff, Mountshannon and around

The villages along the scenic road north of Killaloe are all very small. Hotels here generally cater to the top end of the market, and amenities for other visitors are sparse. That said, it's still very beautiful countryside, especially the lakeside area up as far as Mountshannon. Traditional music here is very much alive, and there are some excellent opportunities to get out onto the water.

SCARRIFF is a little farming town set high up in rough, open country overlooking the lough. It's a handy place to pick up provisions. There's a couple of pubs serving **bar food**. For **traditional music** sessions in the summer check out *McNamara's Bar* (ⓣ065/921020) on Wednesday nights as well as Friday and Saturday nights at the *Merriman Tavern* (ⓣ061/921011).

FEAKLE, about six miles to the west, is another small village, but has a far busier social calendar. There are excellent **traditional music** sessions throughout the year in *Lena's Bar* (ⓣ061/924277) every Thursday evening and in *Pepper's Bar* (ⓣ061/924322) on Wednesday nights in summer. Feakle also hosts an **International Traditional Music Festival** (ⓣ061/924288), which is usually held during the second weekend in August. Accommodation can be problematic and unless you bring a tent and ask to **camp** at a farm, your choices are limited to *The Smyth Country Lodge Hotel* (ⓣ061/924000; ❹–❻), which offers cosy log fires, comfortable rooms and is popular with people on fishing holidays and *Laccaroe House* (ⓣ061/924150; ❶), a B&B with en-suite rooms, located about a mile from *Pepper's* along the road to Scarriff.

Nine miles southwest of Feakle sits the similarly quiet village of **TULLA**. You are most likely to be here if you are walking the East Clare Way, or if you want to sample some of the **traditional music** to be had in *Torpey's* bar (Sun). Accommodation is limited to a few **B&Bs**: *Cragville* (ⓣ065/683 5110; ❷) in the village, and the welcoming Toonagh House (ⓣ065/683 5316; ❷), two and half miles away, off the Ennis road.

The best spot to stay right by the lake, Killaloe and Portumna aside, is **MOUNTSHANNON**, about five miles northeast of Scarriff. It's among the prettiest of the villages and has a couple of cosy pubs and some good places to eat. Good **bar food**, and sometimes traditional music in the summer, are to be had at *Cois na hAbhna*, while meals are served all day at *An Cupán Caífé* (ⓣ061/927275), a relaxed, small bistro with a cosy atmosphere. Places to **stay** include the *Mountshannon Hotel* (ⓣ061/927162; ❹–❽), and, slightly further out heading north of the village, *Derg Lodge* (ⓣ061/927180 or 927319; ❷) and *Oak House* (ⓣ061/927185; ❷), which has its own private beach. **Watersports** enthusiasts will find reasonably priced canoeing, wind-surfing, sailing and motor-boat rental, from May to October, at the nearby *Lakeside Watersport Caravan and Camping Park* (ⓣ061/927225).

Southwest Clare

The southwest of the county features glorious sandy beaches, stunning cliff scenery and a couple of popular family holiday resorts. Arguably the best of the resorts is **Kilkee**, a traditional holiday town full of character, with a superb beach and within easy reach of the spectacular scenery of the **Loop Head peninsula**. **Kilrush**, the only other place of any size, can't compete in terms of setting, but it does offer plenty of opportunities for watersports and boat trips to **Scattery Island**, with its medieval round tower and monastic ruins. North from Kilkee stretches a varied coastline of inaccessible cliffs interspersed with fine **beaches**, especially good near Doonbeg and Quilty; north of here lies the village of **Milltown Malbay**, famous for traditional music. Inland does not look so promising. Southwest from Ennis the country flattens out and becomes scrubby and barren: bog, marsh, the odd bit of cotton grass here, the occasional lump of thistles there, with only sporadic pockets of cultivated land. The bald flank of Slieve Callan is to the north and the outline of the Kerry hills to the south across the Shannon.

Kilrush and Killimer

The best reason to stop in **KILRUSH**, 26 miles from Ennis, is for a trip across the broad Shannon estuary to Scattery Island (see opposite). The town itself has a busy marina and one very broad main street; at the top of the street stands the old market house and a statue of the **Maid of Éireann** (see box below). In Toler Street, just off the main street, the spacious **St Senan's Catholic Church** is worth looking in for a view of the Harry Clarke stained-glass windows. The **Vandeleur Walled Garden** (Ⓣ065/905 1760; €2.50) about half a mile out of Kilrush on the Killimer road (N67) features sub-tropical and specialist plants.

At **KILLIMER**, five miles southeast of Kilrush, you'll find **Fortfield Farm**, a small farm zoo (May–Sept Mon–Sat 10am–6pm, Sun 2–6pm; €3) with llamas, red deer, pot-bellied pigs, numerous breeds of rabbits and other domesticated rare animals. It's run by a friendly crowd who encourage children to handle the animals. The farm also does **B&B** (Ⓣ065/905 1457, Ⓔfortfield@eircom.net; ❷; March–Oct); access to the zoo is free if you are staying there.

Practicalities

The **tourist office** in Kilrush is housed in the old market house in the main square (July & Aug Mon–Sat 10am–1pm & 2–6pm, Sun noon–4pm; Ⓣ065/905 1577); ask here for assistance with Bus Éireann information for **buses** to Ennis and around the coast throughout the year, and to Galway and

The Manchester Martyrs

Statues of the Maid of Éireann, commemorating the **Manchester Martyrs**, are scattered around Ireland. In Manchester, England, in 1867, a band of Fenians blew open the back of a Black Maria in an attempt to rescue some of their leaders, who had been arrested after an armed uprising. A police sergeant was killed in the explosion, and three Fenians were hanged as a result. The executions provoked demonstrations throughout England and Ireland, since many considered the sergeant's death to have been an accident and the trials rigged: these monuments are testimony to the strength of those feelings.

Cork during the summer. From the ferry terminal a mile further on from Killimer, you can take the car ferry to Tarbert in Kerry (April–Sept Mon–Sat 7am–9pm, Sun 9am–9pm; Oct–March Mon–Sat 7am–7pm, Sun 10am–7pm; peak season half-hourly sailings from each side, off-peak sailings every hour on the hour from Killimer, return from Tarbert on the half-hour; singles: car €13, pedestrians/cyclists €3; ⓣ065/905 3124). This can cut out 85 miles and the congestion of Limerick city if you are heading to County Kerry from County Clare. The town's **heritage centre** (June–Aug Mon–Sat 10am–1pm & 2–4pm; €3; ⓣ065/905 1596) is also housed in the old market house and town hall, and is, for the most part, a display telling the eighteenth- and nineteenth-century economic and social history of the town. You can **rent bikes** and get camping Gaz from Gleesons, Henry Street (ⓣ065/905 1127) and there's **Internet** access at *The Monastery* in Frances Street (ⓣ065/905 1061).

There's no shortage of **B&Bs** in the town centre. Highly recommended is the very comfortable and friendly *Clarke's* (aka *Bruach na Coille* – "Edge of the Woods"), a family-run Georgian-style house serving a comprehensive breakfast menu, with a garden set back from the road (ⓣ065/905 2250, ⓦwww.clarekilrush.com; ❷). It's easy to find, opposite the Vandeleur Walled Garden. Other **B&Bs** include *Crotty's* (ⓣ065/905 2470; ❷) on Market Square and the bright pink *Hillcrest View*, with en-suite bedrooms, half a mile out of Kilrush on the Doonbeg road (ⓣ065/905 1986, ⓦwww.hillcrestview.com; ❷). *Katie O'Connor's* **hostel**, Frances Street (IHH; ⓣ065/905 1133, ⓔkatieoconnors@eircom.net; closed Jan & Feb), is a decent place, while superior hostel and B&B accommodation is available at *Kilrush Creek Lodge and Adventure Centre*, Cappa Road, just beside the marina (ⓣ065/905 2855, ⓦwww.kcac.nav.to; ❷), where dorms include breakfast, and standard and en-suite rooms are also available. There is an adventure centre alongside where you can enjoy kayaking, canoeing, sailing or wind-surfing, and wetsuits are provided. Though primarily for caravans, *Aylevarroo Caravan and Camping Park* (ⓣ065/905 1102; May to mid-Sept), also caters for **campers** – you'll find it on the N67 Killimer road, less than two miles from Kilrush.

In Henry Street, just off the square in Kilrush, good pub **food** is available at *Kelly's* and *The Haven Arms*. For coffee, cakes and sandwiches there's *The Quayside* on Frances Street. For evening meals, try *Kelly's* mid-range restaurant, above the bar, probably the best alternative to the fast-food outlets around the square. Kilrush is a quiet town, but *Crotty's*, on the square, is a great old **bar**, with traditional sessions most nights during the summer; **Éigse Mrs Crotty** (ⓦwww.eigsemrscrotty.com) is a **traditional music festival** usually held around mid-August, named after the late owner of *Crotty's* bar who was an accomplished concertina player. Other spots for traditional music include *The Haven Arms* (summer Thurs & Fri) and *Gallagher's* (also known as *The Way Inn*), Vaudeleur Street (Sun). *O'Looney's*, John Street, just off the square, is the place to head for rock music (Fri). You can also try the tiny *Buggles* pub on Moore Street, with the red door.

Scattery Island

Scattery Island lies about a mile offshore from Kilrush in the exposed Shannon estuary. It was last inhabited in the late 1970s, and, as you land, you'll notice that the quay before you is dotted with overgrown derelict cottages. Because of its isolation out in the estuary, the island retains a strange sense of timelessness. Walking up the lanes, spongy with moss and bracken, you're likely to disturb rabbits from the burrows that riddle the island. St Senan founded a **monastery** here in the sixth century, and at one time there were seven monastic settlements. The community suffered greatly from Viking raids, but there are still the remains of several churches dating from between the ninth and the fifteenth centuries. Scattery's most impressive feature has to be the **round tower**, perfect in form, the stone made a warm mustardy yellow by the lichen that covers it. Unusually for a round tower, the doorway here is at ground level, as opposed to the more typical raised entrances reached by a ladder that could be withdrawn, making the tower impregnable. The Shannon estuary is also home to a group of bottlenose **dolphins**, one of about five known groups in European waters, and trips from the island to see them are available.

Access to Scattery Island is by small boat from Kilrush; trips take about half an hour and are restricted by tides. Enquire at the Scattery Island Centre, Merchant's Quay, Kilrush, down by the marina (mid-June to mid-Sept daily 10am–6pm; free; ⓣ065/905 2139), where an exhibition recounts Scattery's monastic history. For excursions to the island at other times, and for details of dolphin-watching trips, contact Scattery Island Ferries (ⓣ065/905 1327, ⓦwww.shannondolphins.ie; trips to Scattery Island €8, two-hour dolphin-watching trips €14).

Moyasta and around

At **MOYASTA**, on the N67 Kilrush–Kilkee road, a station house and section of the well-known **West Clare Railway** have been resurrected for short tourist tours (Mon–Sat 10am–6pm, Sun noon–6pm; €6 adults, €3 children; ⓣ065/905 1284, ⓦwww.westclarerailway.com). The railway first opened in 1892 to connect Ennis with the coastal towns of Kilrush and Kilkee and for nearly seventy years it provided the wild landscape of southwest Clare with a lifeline to the outside world. It gained wider recognition four years after opening when the Irish poet and music-hall entertainer Percy French missed an engagement in Kilkee because his train broke down. His poem about the incident, *Are Ye Right There Michael?*, made the railway a national legend although not in the manner it would probably have liked. The "Michael" of the poem was Michael Talty, the head porter at Kilrush station, acting as the guard on French's train that day.

Kilkee and around

KILKEE, over on the Atlantic coast and eight miles northwest of Kilrush, is a small, busy holiday town with all the amenities you'd expect: cheap cafés, restaurants, amusements and nightlife. Popular with the bucket-and-spade brigade, the town comes as a healthy piece of normality if the offbeat romanticism of the west coast has become too much. The westerly tip of the town's magnificent golden beach, set below a dramatic cliff, meets an apron of laminated rock strata known as the Duggerna Rocks, which protects it from the ravages of the Atlantic. Here, when the tide is out, deep, clear pollock holes form, filled with colourful marine life.

Bus Éireann services, departing from outside Neville's just along the Lahinch road, link Kilkee with Ennis and other towns along the coast. The **tourist office** on The Square (mid-May to early Sept daily 10am–1pm & 2–6pm; ⓣ065/905 6112) is very helpful with accommodation, but it's worth bearing in mind that Kilkee is a popular beach resort and often booked out in August. *Kincora* (ⓣ065/905 6250; ❷) on The Square and *Bay View* (ⓣ065/905 6058, ⓔbayview3@eircom.net; ❷) on O'Connell Street, are good bets for **B&B**. Alternatively, you could try *Purtill's Guesthouse*, O'Curry Street, a solid, newly refurbished place (Ⓣ065/905 6771; ❷), or *Dunearn House*, West End (Ⓣ065/905 6545; ❷). The cheapest decent accommodation is at *Kilkee Hostel*, O'Curry Street (IHH; Ⓣ065/905 6209, Ⓔkilkeehostel@eircom.net; ❶; March–Oct), a friendly, family-run **hostel** right in the centre of town. If you want to **camp**, try the large *Cunningham's Holiday Park* (Ⓣ065/905 6430; closed mid-Sept to Easter weekend), reached as you approach town from Kilrush by taking the first left after the petrol station.

Activities available in Kilkee include: pitch and putt, golf on the eighteen-hole championship course (Ⓣ065/905 6048), scuba diving with Kilkee Diving and Watersports Centre (Ⓣ065/905 6707) and pony trekking (Ⓣ065/905 6635). Kilkee Waterworld, at the north end of the beach (June daily noon–8pm; July & Aug daily 11am–9pm, phone at other times; Ⓣ065/905 6855), is a popular family attraction, with geysers, gushers and an exhilarating 200-foot tower slide, and is particularly worth a visit if you are travelling with children, though in fine weather there can be few better places to swim than in the safe waters of the Blue Flag beach.

Lodged in among the bars and chippies you'll find a handful of good **places to eat**, including *The Strand Restaurant* (Ⓣ065/905 6177, Ⓦwww.clareguest-house.com) on the seafront, a popular spot for seafood and *The Pantry*, on O'Curry Street, which does great home baking during the day and restaurant fare in the evening. On the same street, you'll get good bar food at *Myles' Creek* (Ⓣ 065/905 6900). Kilkee has no shortage of **pubs** and *O'Mara's Bar* (Ⓣ065/905 6900), 12 O'Curry St, is a great old bar, with traditional and folk music (summer Mon, Wed & Fri). A younger crowd frequent *Myles' Creek*, to listen to the rock and pop (summer 5 nights a week, winter weekends only) and traditional music (summer Mon). Finally, The *Greyhound* in O'Curry Street is arguably the cutest bar in Clare.

Around Kilkee

The area around Kilkee is a favourite for **scuba diving** and **snorkelling**, but even without equipment, exploration is rewarding. There are exhilarating **walks** for miles along the cliffs both to the north of the town and, more spectacularly, to the south round Loop Head, where you can walk for sixteen miles along the cliff's edge past stack rocks, puffing holes (where the sea spouts up through crevices in the rock) and the natural Bridges of Ross. The other good way to see this peninsula is by **bike**; you can rent them from Williams', Circular Road, Kilkee (Ⓣ065/905 6041; €10 per day).

In the little church at **MONEEN**, near Kilbaha at the tip of the peninsula, you'll find a nineteenth-century curiosity known as **The Little Arc**. In penal times, Catholics were forced to be both ingenious and secret in the practice of their faith. Here they were not allowed to worship on land, and so built a little hut on wheels which was kept on the beach and wheeled down below the high-water mark between tides, beyond the legal grasp of the local Protestant landowner. The priest would then say Mass in it while the congregation knelt around it on the beach. You can **stay** at *The Lighthouse Inn* (Ⓣ065/905 8358), a pub/restaurant and B&B in Kilbaha and enjoy a **drink** in *Keatings* pub.

A couple of pubs in the tiny village of **Cross** are handy for breaking your explorations, but better by far is the unspoilt fishing village of **CARRIGAHOLT**, which has a sliver of beach beside the quays, a ruined castle overlooking the harbour and some very welcoming pubs: *The Long Dock*, for example, does good pub **food** and has **music** several nights a week in summer. Or try the excellent seafood dishes at *Fennells* (Ⓣ065/905 8107), run by the former owner of *The Long Dock*. Carrigaholt is also another place to see Ireland's only known resident group of bottlenose **dolphins** – they're sometimes visible from the shore, but the best way is to take a boat trip with Dolphinwatch (Ⓣ065/ 905 8156, Ⓦwww.dolphinwatch.ie; 2hr boat trip; April–Oct sailings daily, weather permitting; €17 adults, €9 children, advance booking essential).

Miltown Malbay and Spanish Point

The coastline north of Kilkee is one of fine cliffs and sandy beaches, though not all of them are accessible. Those which are include **Doonbeg**, a relaxing spot where you might see seals and otters, and about a mile further north the beautiful **White Strand** – both are Blue Flag beaches and ideal for swimming. Doughmore beach near **Quilty**, eight miles north of Doonbeg, is excellent for experienced surfers, though swimming is not advised here. *Strand Camping* (Ⓣ065/905 5345) is a small family-run site located right by the beach at Doonbeg at the mouth of the Doonbeg River.

The Victorian resort of **MILTOWN MALBAY**, eighteen miles north of Kilkee and situated some way inland, comes alive for the **Willie Clancy Summer School**, held here usually during the first or second week in July, when it's packed with **traditional music** enthusiasts from all over the world (and booking accommodation well in advance is essential). *Clancy's* on Main Street (traditional music summer Fri & Sun) and *Friel's*, The Square (aka *Lynch's*), are likely to be lively any time during the summer, and *The Crosses of Annagh*, about two miles south of Miltown Malbay on the road towards Mullagh, has excellent music sessions (summer Thurs; year-round Sat). For **B&B**, there's *An Gleann* (Ⓣ065/708 4281, Ⓔangleann@oceanfree.net; ❷) and *Malone's* (Ⓣ065/708 4246; ❷), both on the Ennis road, or you could try *The Station House* (Ⓣ065/708 4008; ❷), on the Lahinch road. If you want to try and master the secrets of Irish cuisine check into *Berry Lodge Country House* in Annagh, three miles southeast of Spanish Point (Ⓣ065/708 7022, Ⓔrita.meade@esatclear.ie, ❷–❹), as this Victorian house is also a restaurant and cookery school run by Irish radio cook, Rita Meade.

Two and a half miles from Miltown Malbay you'll find an excellent sandy swimming beach at **SPANISH POINT**, so called because it was here that survivors from wrecked Armada ships swam ashore, only to be executed by the high sheriff of Clare. It's a holiday spot for nuns, and appropriately enough has a very quiet **campsite**, *Lahiff's Caravan and Camping Park* (Ⓣ065/708 4006; April–Sept). Other places to stay include *Atlantic Star* (Ⓣ065/708 4782; ❷), a spacious, modern **B&B** just across from the golf course on the main N67, and a couple of **hotels**: *Armada Hotel* (Ⓣ065/708 4110, Ⓦwww.burkesarmadahotel.com; ❹–❻) and the *Bellbridge House Hotel* (Ⓣ065/708 4038; ❹–❺).

To the east of Spanish Point, **Slieve Callan** rises beside the main road to Ennis. Taking this road you can detour to Knocknalassa, where there's an impressive wedge-shaped **gallery grave**, known as Diarmuid and Gráinne's Bed (after the Irish version of the Tristan and Isolde story). It's quite tricky to find: five miles along the road from Miltown Malbay you will pass a house with a little thatched barn alongside; the grave is about half a mile further east from here, tucked out of sight behind a hummocky rise to the left of the road.

Lahinch and Ennistymon

LAHINCH, eight miles north of Spanish Point, is a busy family holiday resort with a fabulous broad sandy beach. Families aside, Lahinch attracts golfers and surfers, a weird hybrid well served by the town. To get a round at Lahinch **golf course** you will need to book well ahead (Ⓣ065/708 1003); **surfing** is there for the taking. You can hear good music in the bars, especially in the summer months.

B&B accommodation is available at *Seafield Lodge* (Ⓣ065/708 1594, Ⓔitaslattery@eircom.net; ❷; April–Nov) and *Mulcarr House* (Ⓣ065/708 1123; Ⓔmullcarrhouse@esatclear.ie; ❷; mid-March to Nov), both close to the centre on Ennistymon Road. Slightly further out, but offering wonderful views of the bay are *Le Bord De Mer*, (Ⓣ065/708 1454, Ⓔannieobrien@boinet.ie; ❷; March–Oct) and *Nazira*, School Road (Ⓣ065/708 1362; ❷; March–Nov). The resort has several traditional hotels including the newly refurbished *Aberdeen Arms* (Ⓣ065/708 1100, Ⓦwww.aberdeenarms.ie; ❷–❹) and the family-run *Atlantic Hotel* (Ⓣ065/708 1049, Ⓔatlantichotel@eircom.net; ❷–❹; April–Oct) both on Main Street. At the other end of the scale, the *Lahinch Hostel* (IHH; Ⓣ065/708 1040), next door to the church, is a decent budget option, with laundry facilities and bike rental. You can **camp** at *Lahinch Camping and Caravan Park* (Ⓣ065/708 1424; May–Sept), an orderly family site that has a laundry for service washes and a wet-weather shelter. The mighty **meals** served in the bar of *The Shamrock Hotel*, Main Street, will satisfy post-surf hunger. Other bars good for food include *O'Looney's* on the seafront and the nearby *Spinnaker Bar*, both frequented by a lively young crowd. Seafood, good vegetarian fare and fine views are on offer at *The Barrtrá* (Ⓣ065/708 1280), signposted off the road two miles south of Lahinch. For great atmosphere and traditional music head to *The Nineteenth Bar* (summer nightly, winter Sat) or *Kenny's Bar* (summer Mon & Fri–Sun), both on Main Street.

Two miles east of Lahinch, the old market town of **ENNISTYMON**, with its low shopfronts, has a life, albeit a leisurely one, regardless of tourism. Traditional music and ballads are enjoyed year-round in the town's great old **bars**. Try *Phil's Bar*, *Eugene's*, *Cooley's House*, all on Main Street and *Daly's Pub* (Ⓣ065/707 1919) on the same road, has music every night in the summer and Thursday to Sunday all year round. The church at the end of Main Street has been converted into a *teach cheoil* (music house) where you can catch evenings of traditional music. The town's **Traditional Singing Festival** is usually held over the first weekend in June. Ennistymon's setting is surprisingly green; signposted off the main street is the **Cascades Walk** which takes you a short way alongside the River Cullenagh as it rushes over slabs of rock through the heart of the little town. An eighteenth-century church stands on a hill above the town, from where you can see the blue river snaking its way out of the woods and beyond to the sea at Liscannor. Central **B&Bs** include the welcoming *Station House*, on Ennis Road (Ⓣ065/707 1149, Ⓦwww.bb-stationhouse.com; ❷), and the manor-like three-star *Falls Hotel* set in fifty acres of woodland, gardens and glens (Ⓣ065/707 1004, Ⓦwww.fallshotel.net, weekend specials from €100 available; ❹–❻).

The Burren

The **Burren** (Boireann, "rocky land") is a huge plateau of limestone and shale that covers over a hundred square miles of northwest Clare, a highland shaped by a series of cliffs, terraces and expanses of limestone pavement, with little to punctuate the view. Bleak and grey, the northern reaches of the Burren can come as a shock to anyone who associates Ireland with all things lush and

Burren geology and fauna

The Burren is an incredibly stark environment. The grey-rock pavementing stretches before you, split by long parallel grooves known as grykes. Throughout the area, rainwater seeps through the highly porous rock and gouges away at the many underground potholes, caves and tunnels. The only visible **river** is the Caher at Fanore, but there are a multitude of underground waterways, which produce **lakes**, known as turloughs, peculiar to this landscape; they appear only after heavy rainfall, when the underground systems fill up, and vanish once again after a few dry days.

The panorama is bleak, but close up, **wild flowers** burst from the grooves in specks and splashes of brilliant colour, Arctic, alpine and Mediterranean plants growing alongside each other. The best time to see the flowers is late spring, when the strong blue, five-petalled spring gentians flourish. Here, too, are mountain avens, various saxifrages and maidenhair fern. Later in summer, the magenta bloody cranesbill and a fantastic variety of orchids (considered rare elsewhere) bloom: bee orchids, fly orchids and the lesser butterfly orchid. More common flowers look stunning by sheer force of quantity: bright yellow bird's-foot trefoil and hoary rockrose, and milkwort. Obviously flowers must not be picked.

Nobody knows exactly how these plants came to be here, nor why they remain. It has been suggested that some of the Mediterranean flowers have been here since Ireland had a far hotter climate, but how they survived is a source of speculation: it may be the peculiar conditions of moist warm air coming in from the sea, the Gulf Stream ensuring a mild, frostless climate, and very effective drainage through the porous limestone. It's also thought that the bare rock absorbs heat all summer and stores it, so that the Burren land is appreciably warmer in wintertime than areas with a different geology. There's more on the Burren's geology in the **Burren Display Centre** in Kilfenora and at the **Whitethorn Visitor Centre** in Ballyvaughan.

verdant. It's an extraordinary landscape of stark rock, fading to lower green fields, and above all the sky and the ocean. Its cliffs and terraces lean towards the sea in huge steps of wind-pocked pumice. Bone white in sunshine, in the rain the rock becomes darkened and metallic, the cliffs and canyons blurred by mists. A harsh place, barely capable of sustaining human habitation, it was aptly summed up in the words of Cromwell's surveyor Ludlow: "savage land, yielding neither water enough to drown a man, nor a tree to hang him, nor soil enough to bury". There are no sweet rolling fields here, but stick with it and its fascination emerges – there's a raw beauty about the place with its exceptional combination of light, rock and water.

In recent centuries, the Burren has supported a sparse population, living, like most of the west of Ireland, in harsh poverty. It was to this land, west of the Shannon, that Cromwell drove the dispossessed Irish Catholics after his campaign of terror. Few could survive for long in such country. The area's lack of appeal to centuries of speculators and colonizers greedy to cream the fat off Ireland's lusher pastures has meant that evidence of many of the Burren's earlier inhabitants has remained. The place has over sixty **Stone Age** (3000–2000 BC) burial monuments, the most common types being wedge-shaped tombs, cairns and dolmens; over four hundred Iron Age **ring forts** (500 BC–500 AD), which were defensive dwellings; and numerous Christian churches, monasteries, round towers and high crosses. Amongst the most evocative of the Christian ruins is **Corcomroe Abbey**, just outside Bell Harbour, and there are fine **high crosses** at Kilfenora.

You can get to the area by taking a **Bus Éireann** connection from stations at Galway, Limerick or Ennis. There's a direct bus service from Limerick, Ennis

△ Cliffs of Moher

The Burren Way

The **Burren Way** runs through countryside which is quite unlike the rest of the west of Ireland; made up of bare limestone, treeless and exposed, this remarkable area has a weird beauty all of its own. The Way starts at Liscannor and runs parallel to the coast a little way inland; much of this section is close to the road, which is always very busy in high season because of its spectacular views across to the Aran Islands and, on a fine day, the mountains of Connemara. The Way then descends to Doolin and picks up a gradual ascent past Ballynalacken Castle and on across open fields around the shoulder of Slieve Elva. There are no really steep climbs and as the path descends to the Caher River, a valley of classic Burren scenery opens up all around, with stark grey limestone hills and barely a tree in sight. At this point there is the tantalizing option of wandering two and a half miles down the valley to stop over in Fanore, from where you have access to other great walks. The Burren Way itself follows the quiet road southeast through the valley, round past medieval Newtown Castle and down to the silvery shoreline of Ballyvaughan Bay. It's a gentle walk from here into Ballyvaughan, accompanied by fine views across the great expanse of Galway Bay.

Access: It is possible to take the bus from Ennis to Doolin and from Ballyvaughan to Galway, Lisdoonvarna and Doolin.

Accommodation: There are numerous B&Bs and hostels in Doolin, a few B&Bs at Fanore, and B&B accommodation at Ballyvaughan.

Overall distance: 22 miles.

Highest point: Slieve Elva (flank) 980ft.

Maps and guides: The Ordnance Survey map no. 51 (1:50,000) is quite sufficient; *The Burren Way Map and Guide* is available in tourist offices.

and Galway to Doolin and in summer at least one bus a day from Limerick passes through Ennis, Ennistymon and Lisdoonvarna, and at least one a day connects Galway with Lisdoonvarna. To see the Burren's archaeological and ecclesiastical sites, it's best to go by car or bike (**bike rental** is available in the main centres of Doolin and Ballyvaughan, and if cycling in good weather be sure to pack lots of sunscreen as sunshine and Atlantic breezes can be a lethal cocktail). To get to know the landscape and flowers, go on foot. The excellent Tim Robinson **map**, *The Burren* (available in tourist offices and good bookshops), is usefully detailed and will make finding sites easy, though it does not show contours. For walking, the Ordnance Survey map no. 51 (1:50,000) is ideal – and also covers the Aran Islands. There are two north–south routes across the Burren that are of particular archaeological interest; these run from Bell Harbour to Killinaboy and from Ballyvaughan to Leamaneh Castle. If you're doing a lot of walking, a compass is a good idea as there's a shortage of easy landmarks. You're allowed to walk more or less where you want, though do be aware that there are a large number of bulls in the fields. A good start might be to follow the Burren Way (see box above for more details).

Liscannor and the Cliffs of Moher

Once a tiny village, **LISCANNOR** has been swept along by the tide of development that has surged around Ireland's west coast. Despite this, as a base for exploring Clare's most famous tourist spot, the Cliffs of Moher, it makes a good alternative to the busier tourist centre of Doolin. The area is best known for

Liscannor flag, a durable stone used for paving, cladding, fireplaces traditionally, the roofs of dwellings. **Liscannor Stone**, St Brigid's Well (a a mile along the road as you go out of the village towards the Cliffs of Mo is an interesting diversion: an audio-visual display tells the story of the stc and its shop is worth visiting for its dazzling display of exotic crystals and fossils. Be aware that the sandy stretches south towards Lahinch, near the mouth of the river, are unsafe due to quicksand.

Accommodation is mostly at the cheaper end of the scale and includes a caravan site which accepts tents: *Liscannor Caravan and Camping Park*. The *Village Hostel* (IHH; ⓣ065/708 1385; March–Oct) is located right next to the bars on the main street. There are a number of B&Bs: the budget *Cahilly Lodge* (ⓣ065/708 1749; ❷); the modern, spacious *Sea Haven* (ⓣ065/708 1385; ❷; Jan–Nov); and *Seamount* (ⓣ065/708 1367; ❷; mid-March to end Oct), which offers en-suite rooms. You could also try *The Liscannor Bay Hotel* (ⓣ065/7086000, ⓦwww.liscannorbayhotel.com; ❸–❻; closed Nov 1–March 15). For **food**, *The Captain's Deck* (ⓣ065/708 1666) and especially the *Mermaid Restaurant* (ⓣ065/708 1076) offer very good evening meals, after which you could do worse than an evening in *Joseph McHugh's Pub* (ⓣ065/708 1163) on Main Street.

Circling north round the Burren from Liscannor, you arrive almost immediately at the **Cliffs of Moher**. From Hag's Head, just west of Liscannor, the cliffs stretch five miles to a point beyond O'Brien's Tower (a superfluous viewing point with telescope), some four miles south of Doolin. At their highest, they tower 660ft above the Atlantic, and, standing on the headlands that jut over the sheer, ravaged rock face with its great bands of shale and sandstone, you can witness the huge destructive power of the waves. At points, the battering of the water has left jagged stack rocks, continually lashed by white spume. Erosion is constant; during a storm some years ago a section of the cliff fell, taking a picnic table with it. Despite the oppressively commercial **visitor centre** the cliffs are an impressive sight, especially on a summer evening, with the setting sun full on them.

Doolin

The village of **DOOLIN**, four miles north of the Cliffs of Moher and marked as "Fisherstreet" on some maps, is for many the **music mecca** of the "singing county", and, in fact, of Ireland's west. By the time you get here, you may already have met a good few traditional music enthusiasts on their way from across northern Europe, and there are extra buses laid on to bring them here. That said, it is not necessarily the best place for top traditional sessions – these tend to move around – but you are guaranteed to find some kind of merriment in each of Doolin's three **pubs** (*O'Connor's*, *McGann's* and *McDermott's*) every night throughout the year. The music varies enormously and you may come across anything from a bunch of amplified performers doing a medley of Eurovision classics to the kind of fabulous session you'll remember for the rest of your life. Bearing this in mind, the key to getting the best out of Doolin is to remember that if you stumble into a poor session, there are two other bars nearby. Doolin can get very crowded in the summer, so book your accommodation in advance if you want to stay here overnight.

Without the music, Doolin would be a rather forlorn and desolate place, lodged as it is beside a treacherous sandy beach at the tail end of the coast that climaxes with the Cliffs of Moher. Bold shelves of limestone pavement step into the sea by the pier, from which Doolin Ferries (ⓣ065/707 4455) runs to the Aran Islands. If you want more than a couple of hours on the islands – and this is a very good idea – then day-trips are only really feasible to Inisheer. It is possible to sail from Doolin to all three islands and then on to Galway or return to Doolin. See p.473 for more on the Aran Islands.

Music may be Doolin's *raison d'être*, but the village is now ruthlessly geared to providing accommodation for as many visitors as it's possible to squeeze into the place's three pubs. There are plenty of **B&Bs**; all are reasonably priced and offer a decent standard. Highly recommended are the excellent three-star *Doonmacfelim House* (ⓣ065/707 4503, ⓦwww.kingsway.ie/doonmacfelim; ❷) and the centrally located *Cullinan's Restaurant & Guesthouse* (ⓣ065/707 4183, ⓦwww.cullinansdoolin.com; ❷), which has en-suite rooms and a good restaurant. Otherwise, *Seacrest* (ⓣ065/707 4458; ❷), offering wild, blustery views of the coast, and *Atlantic View* (ⓣ065/707 4189; ❷) are situated towards the pier. Behind *O'Connor's* pub are a couple of smart B&Bs: *Fisherman's Rest* (ⓣ065/707 4673, ❶) and *Lane Lodge* (ⓣ065/707 4747; ❷). For a bit of luxury try *Ballinalacken Castle Country House and Restaurant* (ⓣ065/707 4025, ⓦwww.ballinalackencastle.com; ❹–❽). It has good view of the Cliffs of Moher and out to sea, in a comfortable setting with log fires. You could also head for *Aran View House* (ⓣ065/707 4061, ⓦwww.aranview.com; ❹–❻) located on a hill on the coast road out of town, which has great views. Its restaurant specializes in locally caught seafood.

Despite their number, the **hostels** do get awfully packed in July and August, so ringing ahead is essential. *Paddy's Doolin* hostel (IHH; ⓣ065/707 4006) is near *O'Connor's* pub, and is an efficiently run place; further north along the same road is *The Rainbow Hostel* (IHH; ⓣ065/707 4415), which is welcoming and well run. Other hostels include the friendly and laid-back *Aille River Hostel* (IHH; ⓣ065/707 4260), and *Flanagan's Village Hostel* (IHH; ⓣ065/707 4564), a family-run hostel with excellent facilities, comfy beds and great views, five minutes' walk north out of the village. There's **camping** down by the pier at *Nagle's* (ⓣ065/707 4458; May to late Sept) – a great spot to absorb the drama of the landscape – and near the *Aille River Hostel* at *Riverside Camping* (ⓣ065/707 4314; May–Sept).

You'll find a fair selection of places to **eat** here besides the pubs, which all do filling, good-value bar meals. The *Magnet*, near *O'Connor's* pub, serves tasty filled crepes, and nearby is a shop selling filled rolls and other picnic provisions. At the far north end of the village, beyond *Flanagan's* hostel and down a road to the right, is the Doolin Craft Shop and the adjacent café which has an attractive garden and is a good spot to unwind, serving fresh salmon sandwiches, smoked-salmon platters and fine cakes (Easter–Sept). For evening meals there's the moderately priced *Lazy Lobster*, Roadford (ⓣ065/707 4390), specializing in fish; the similarly priced *Doolin Café*, which has a trendy atmosphere; and, a quieter choice, the upmarket *Bruach Na haille* (ⓣ065/707 4120), next door to *McGann's* pub, noted for its seafood and vegetarian meals.

Fanore to Bell Harbour

North of Doolin, the coast remains spectacular but bleak and empty. The first place you'll want to stop is **FANORE**. A number of excellent **Burren walks** are easily accessible from here, the best of which is the magnificent one up to the Caherdoonfergus ring fort and the heights of Dobhach Bhrainin and Gleninagh – a round route of nine and a half miles (contact Burren Hill Walks for more information; ⓣ065/7077168, ⓔburrenhillwalks@eircom.net).

Pleasant **B&B** is available at *Monica's* (Ⓣ065/707 6141; ❷). *O'Donoghue's* pub (Ⓣ065/707 6104) has traditional music on Saturday nights in the summer. **Horse riding** is available at the Burren Riding Centre (Ⓣ065/707 6140).

Beyond, the scenic coast road to Black Head and Ballyvaughan is well worth taking. Beautifully poised between Galway Bay and the Burren, **BALLY-VAUGHAN** is an attractive village with a quay. Its significance as a trading centre has dwindled into tourism, but it makes a calm haven from which to explore the Burren hills, and it's also the northerly limit of the Burren Way (see box on p.442). At the **Whitethorn Visitor Centre**, on the Galway road east out of the village, you can see Burren Exposure (March–May daily 10am–5pm; June–Sept daily 10am–6pm; Ⓣ065/707 7277; €4.45), a 35-minute audiovisual display on the geology, history and flora of the Burren. It gives a good overview and the aerial photographs of ring forts are particularly interesting. There's also a restaurant and a crafts shop at the centre. Further along this road (a mile and a half from the village centre), a signposted lane leads to the tranquil and sandy Bishop's Quarter **beach**. **B&Bs** in the centre of the village include the comfortable *Gentian Villa* (Ⓣ065/707 7042; ❷) and the luxurious and welcoming *Ballyvaughan Lodge* (Ⓣ065/707 7292; ❷). Half a mile east along a quiet green road, there's the peaceful *Dolmen Lodge* (Ⓣ065/707 7202; ❷; mid-March to late Oct), while a short walk beyond *Monk's* pub will take you to *Oceanville* (Ⓣ065/707 7051; ❷). For a secluded Burren location try *Merrijig Farmhouse* (Ⓣ065/707 7120; ❷), three miles inland; head out along the Lisdoonvarna road and take the right fork towards Lismacsheedy Cliff Fort – the farmhouse is on the right after a mile and a half. **Bicycle rental** is available at J. Connole Laundrette.

Whitethorn Restaurant & Crafts (Ⓣ065/707 7044; mid-March to Oct daily 9.30am–6pm), located in the Whitethorn Visitor Centre, is worth calling in on for its stunning setting and offers formal à la carte **dining** in the evening in July and August. You can get tea and snacks at *An Fear Gorta Tearooms*, attractively situated down by the quays. *Monk's* pub (Ⓣ065/707 7003) does good seafood, and the bar meals at *Hyland's Hotel* (Ⓣ065/707 7037) cater for hearty appetites. For an evening meal to remember try the *Tri Na Cheile* restaurant (Ⓣ065/707 7029). **Traditional music** is played several nights a week during the summer in *Hyland's Hotel* and *Monk's* pub.

From Ballyvaughan there are interesting routes south through the heart of the Burren. Within three miles of Ballyvaughan lie Newtown Castle and the Aillwee Cave, both signposted off the R480 towards Corofin. Although the restored sixteenth-century **Newtown Castle** is really a fortified tower house rather than a castle, the guided tour is interesting, telling of the medieval law and bardic schools of the surrounding area. The mile-long guided Newtown Castle Trail takes one hour and covers folklore, botany and history (April–Oct daily 10am–6pm; castle €3, castle and trail €5). The well-lit tour through the two-million-year-old **Aillwee Cave** (six tours daily 10am–6pm; €7.50; Ⓣ065/707 7036, Ⓦwww.aillweecave.ie) will take you past amazing caverns of stalagmites and stalactites and spectacular rock formations.

All along this coast, east of Ballyvaughan, where the Burren borders Galway Bay, short stretches of well-tended farmland reach from the foot of the hills to the shoreline, and water glints through gaps in the high stone walls, while way over Galway Bay the muted cobalt mountains of Connemara lie hazy in the distance. There's a wealth of bird life along these shores: cormorants, guillemots, terns, herons, grebes, fulmars, mallards, teals and swans, as well as sea-otters and seals. Heading towards Galway on the coast road, you pass through **Bell**

Harbour (Beulaclugga), at the southern tip of Muckinish Bay, where the road towards Killinaboy sets off, and further on a turning for the placid **Corcomroe Abbey** signposted on your left. A twelfth-century Cistercian foundation, its considerable remains are beautifully set in a secluded valley.

New Quay, seven miles east of Ballyvaughan, signposted off the main Galway road, is famous for *Linnane's* seafood bar – in fact there is little else there. It's a cosy bar serving delicious seafood year-round and is renowned for its traditional music sessions on Friday.

Lisdoonvarna and the heart of the Burren

Not just the name of an amusing song by Christy Moore, **LISDOONVARNA**, nine miles south of Ballyvaughan and five miles inland from Doolin, is most notable for its month-long **matchmaking festival** (Ⓦwww.matchmakerireland.com) held annually in September. The origins of the festival lie with the farmers who would come down after the harvest from the hills to spend their hard-earned cash and look for a wife in a festival of singing, dancing and drinking. It remains popular with a middle-aged crowd who come along for all manner of merrymaking, so if you want to be here in September, book your accommodation well ahead.

On the whole Lisdoonvarna is probably best enjoyed in spring and early summer as it serves as one of the handiest spots from which to explore the Burren. It's renowned for its **spa** too: the spring waters here contain magnesia, iodine and iron, and reputedly have restorative qualities. The town's principal sulphur spring is in the **Spa Wells Health Centre** (June–Sept daily 10am–6pm; Ⓣ065/707 4023), where you can take the waters in the pump-house, or have a sulphur bath (June–Sept Mon–Fri 10am–6pm, Sat 10am–2pm), a sauna, a shower or a massage. Generally full of elderly holiday-makers, the centre offers an invigorating afternoon for weary cyclists and walkers. The whirlwind tour of the **Burren Smokehouse** (March Mon–Fri 9am–5pm, Sat & Sun 10am–4pm; April, May & Sept–Dec daily 9am–5pm; June–Aug daily 9am–7pm; Ⓣ065/707 4303, Ⓦwww.burrensmokehouse.ie), right in the centre of town, will fill you in on all there is to know about traditional methods of smoking fish: frankly, there's not much to it, but it's worth it for the banter and the sliver of smoked salmon thrown in to tempt you to buy more.

Recommended **B&Bs** here are *St Joseph's*, Main Street (Ⓣ065/707 4076; ❶) and *Ballinsheen House* (Ⓣ065/707 4806; ❷). When it comes to eating, plenty of pubs serve **food**; especially good is *The Roadside Tavern* (Ⓣ065/707 4084; until 8.30pm). All of the pubs have **music** most nights during July and August, some of it pretty mixed, but *The Roadside Tavern* is a good starting point and has traditional music nightly in summer, and on Saturdays in winter.

Kilfenora

The tiny village of **KILFENORA**, four miles southeast of Lisdoonvarna, is a great spot for **traditional music** and is renowned for its year-round music pubs: *Vaughan's* and especially *Linnane's*. Kilfenora's music **festival**, held over the October bank-holiday weekend, is a wonderful and strictly traditional event. The village is also home to the much-publicized **Burren Display Centre** (mid-March to end May & Sept–Oct daily 10am–5pm; June–Aug daily 9.30am–6pm; Ⓣ065/708 8030, Ⓦwww.theburrencentre.ie; €5). The centre explains clearly the basic geography and geology of the Burren with the aid of a landscape model and a film. The **tearoom** makes a good refreshment stop.

Next door stands **Kilfenora Cathedral**, certainly worth a visit for its high crosses, the finest of which is the twelfth-century Doorty Cross, showing three bishops and what is probably Christ's entry into Jerusalem, with beautiful Celtic patterning. Nearby in the churchyard are remains of two other twelfth-century high crosses, one near the northwest corner, another opposite the church door. Wander through the gateway behind the church and you'll see a fourth cross, with a decorated Crucifixion, in the field to the west. The cathedral itself was built in 1190 and altered in the fifteenth century. It has a roofless chancel with a finely carved triple-light east window and two effigies of bishops, possibly fourteenth century.

For **B&B**, try *Mrs Murphy's*, Main Street (Ⓣ065/708 8040; ❷). Alternatively, you can stay at *The Cottage Hostel*, Lissylisheen (Ⓣ086/801 5566), four and a half miles north of here – it's tricky to find so ask locally for directions. It's a small, charming place and also offers **camping**.

Leamaneh Castle and Carran

Heading east from Kilfenora you come to the well-preserved **Leamaneh** ("horse's leap") **Castle**, a fifteenth-century O'Brien stronghold, adjoining which is a four-storey building with mullioned and transomed windows (c. 1640). The area north of here is littered with ancient remains. Take the Ballyvaughan road north at Leamaneh Castle and you will pass the **Poulnabrone dolmen**, the most famous of the Burren's portal dolmens, dating from 2500 BC. It's much smaller than it appears in photographs, but a marvellous place at dusk, when the fading light turns the surrounding fields of stone a vibrant lilac. Alternatively, continue east from Leamaneh Castle and take the left turn north just before Killinaboy. The lane rises steeply through hazel hedgerows and brings you up to a limestone plateau. You will pass two signposted **wedge tombs** on your left and, after another mile or so, come to **Caher Commaun**, a ninth-century triple ring fort. You may have to pay a small fee to walk across the farmer's field. From here, you can wend your way north through a tangle of roads to minuscule **CARRAN**. The hamlet's prime feature is a turlough: in summer it appears as a meadow, in winter a lake. Overlooking the turlough are *Clare's Rock*, a comfortable **hostel** (Ⓣ065/708 9129; May–Sept), and *Croide na boirne* bar and restaurant (Ⓣ065/708 9109), which serves probably the only Burren-themed bar food in the world. Look out for their speciality, *burren mionáin*, organically reared kid. From Carran the road north leads down to Bell Harbour (Beulaclugga) and nearby Corcomroe (see opposite).

Killinaboy and Corofin

Follow the road east from Leamaneh Castle and you'll reach **KILLINABOY**, where a ruined eleventh- to fourteenth-century church has a striking Sheila-na-Gig over the doorway (see box on p.195). There are a handful of pleasant **B&Bs** in the area, of which *Fergus View* (Ⓣ065/683 7606; ❷) is a welcoming option two miles north of Corofin on the Kilfenora road.

From Killinaboy the road winds down into the more substantial village of **COROFIN**, consisting of a handful of houses and a string of cheerful pubs. It makes an excellent base from which to explore the Burren or to enjoy fishing in the abundance of little lakes hereabouts. Lough Inchiquin is particularly scenic and a detour around the lake and up Clifden Hill affords spectacular views – you'll need your own transport for this. The village is also home to the **Clare Genealogical Centre** (9am–5pm; free; Ⓣ065/683 7955, Ⓦwww.clareroots.com). The **Clare Heritage Centre** (May 6–Oct 31 daily

10am–6pm; €4) portrays the traumatic period of Irish history between 1800 and 1860 and fills in the horrors that the Bunratty Folk Park omits: famine, disease, emigration and the issue of land tenure. It also has a genealogy research service for those with origins in the county and holds details of over half a million people, McMahon, Macnamara, Moloney and O'Brien being the most common names. If you want to research your roots in detail, write to or email the centre a few months before your trip and find out as much as possible before you visit (names, dates, marriages, deaths, location, occupation and parish for example). An initial search costs around €50, a full one €150. Alternatively, the new library here is freely available: a morning spent poring over records will probably convince you just why it's worth paying a trained genealogist to do it for you.

You can **stay** here at the friendly, family-run *Corofin Village Hostel* (IHH; ⓣ065/683 7683), with its pleasant campsite. Or for decent B&B accommodation with en-suite rooms try *Lakefield Lodge* (ⓣ065/683 7675, ⓔmcleary.ennis@eircom.net; ❷; April–Oct) on the Ennis road. *Bofey Quinn's* (ⓣ065/683 7321; noon–9pm) does good **bar food** – try their Corofin Smokies, a kind of smoked fish and potato hotpot. For something a little more upmarket head for *Le Catelinas*, Market Street (ⓣ065/683 7425; Tues–Sat 5.30pm onwards, Sun 12.30–4.30pm) which serves all the culinary delights you might expect from a mix of Irish and French owners. **Traditional music** is dished up with tea and brown bread in summer at the village's pleasantly relaxed *teach cheoil* (music house) in Market Street (July & Aug Thurs 9pm; €4; ⓣ065/683 7706), in a lively evening suitable for families, with set dancing. There is also bound to be music on in one of the pubs most nights during the summer (try the *Corofin Arms* and *Inchiquin Inn*, both on Main Street). **Boats** can be hired from Burke's shop.

Travel details

Trains

Ennis to: Dublin (1–2 daily; 3hr); Limerick (1–2 daily; 1hr).

Buses

Bunratty to: Shannon Airport (20 daily; 20min).
Doolin to: Galway (2 daily; 1hr 30min).
Ennis to: Doolin (3 daily; 1hr 15min); Galway (12 daily; 1hr 30min); Kilkee (1–3 daily; 1hr 15min); Lahinch (1–3 daily; 45min); Limerick (8–19 daily; 45min); Lisdoonvarna (summer 1 daily; 1hr 15min); Shannon Airport (14 daily; 45min).
Lisdoonvarna to: Galway (mid-May to mid-Sept 2–4 daily, mid-Sept to mid-May Mon–Sat 2–4 daily; 1hr 20min).
Limerick to: Doolin (summer Mon–Sat 3 daily & 2 Sun, winter 2 daily; 1hr 40min–2hr 20min); Ennis (15 daily; 1hr); Ennistymon (1–3 daily; 1hr 15min); Killaloe (Mon–Sat 1–2 daily; 45min); Lisdoonvarna (1–5 daily; 1hr 55min); Mountshannon (Sat only 1 daily; 1hr 25min); Shannon Airport (20 daily; 45 min).

Galway, Mayo and Roscommon

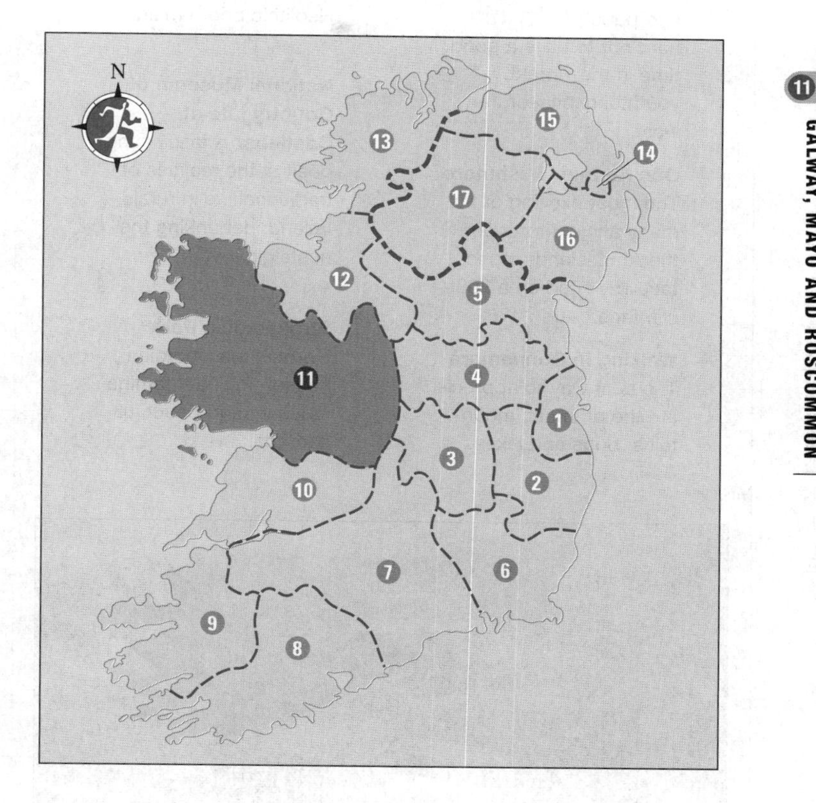

CHAPTER 11 **Highlights**

* **Islands** Choose between the wild beauty of the Arans (p.473), the grandiose scenery of accessible Achill (p.504) and Inishbofin's small-scale charms (p.492).
* **Galway festivals** (p.454) and pubs (p.463) It's hard not to have a good time in the vibrant, youthful capital of the west.
* **Dún Aengus, Inishmore** The most exciting of the many ancient forts on the Aran Islands, spectacularly sited on a 300ft cliff face. See p.478
* **Walking in Connemara** The best way to appreciate the dramatic mountains, bogs and lakes. See p.484
* **Croagh Patrick** A tough climb, enriched by historical and religious associations, and outstanding views. See p.499
* **Céide Fields** Twenty square miles of intriguing Neolithic bog remains. See p.509
* **National Museum of Country Life at Castlebar** A fascinating peek at the realities of traditional life in rural Ireland, debunking the nostalgic myths. See p.514
* **Strokestown Park House** Fine Georgian house, poignant famine museum and beautiful gardens. See p.520

11

Galway, Mayo and Roscommon

Galway, Mayo and Roscommon mark a distinct change in the west of Ireland scene. Coming from the south, **County Galway** may at first seem a continuation of what has gone before in Clare and Kerry. And Galway city is in some ways the west coast town par excellence – an exceptionally enjoyable, free-spirited sort of place and a gathering point for young travellers. But once you get beyond the city things start to change. The landscape is dramatically harsher and far less populous, and there are generally fewer visitors, too.

Lough Corrib, which divides Galway in two, delineates another dramatic split in the landscape of the county, this time between east and west, inland and coast. To the east of the lake lies tame, fertile land which people have farmed for centuries, while to the west lies **Connemara**, a magnificently wild terrain of wind and rock and water. The **Aran Islands**, in the mouth of Galway Bay, resemble Connemara both in their elemental beauty and in their culture; the Galway Gaeltacht – areas where Irish is still spoken – comprises the islands, the moors of Iar-Chonnacht and some scattered communities in north Connemara and on the east shore of Lough Corrib. While it can't compete with the rest of the county, **east Galway**'s medieval monastic sites are well worth taking in as you pass through. Again, **Galway city** straddles the divide. A bridging point both physically and culturally, it's a fishing port, a historic city and the focus of an energetic social and artistic scene.

Further up the coast is **County Mayo**, where the landscape softens somewhat and is even freer of tourists. The pilgrimage centre of **Knock** and the attractions of historic towns like **Westport** aside, it's the coast that is once again the main draw. Physically, it's as exciting and rugged as any in the Republic, and far less exploited, though the downside is that facilities for travellers are less developed. An exception is **Achill**, the largest Irish offshore island and a popular holiday resort, which also provides some of the most spectacular cliffs in the country.

County Roscommon is entirely landlocked and less visited still. There are few real excitements, and the land is for the most part flat and low-lying; nevertheless, the fine detail of this landscape, scattered with small lakes and large houses, has a quiet charm. There are places that merit a look as you pass through, and in the extreme north, around **Lough Key**, there's some very attractive scenery indeed.

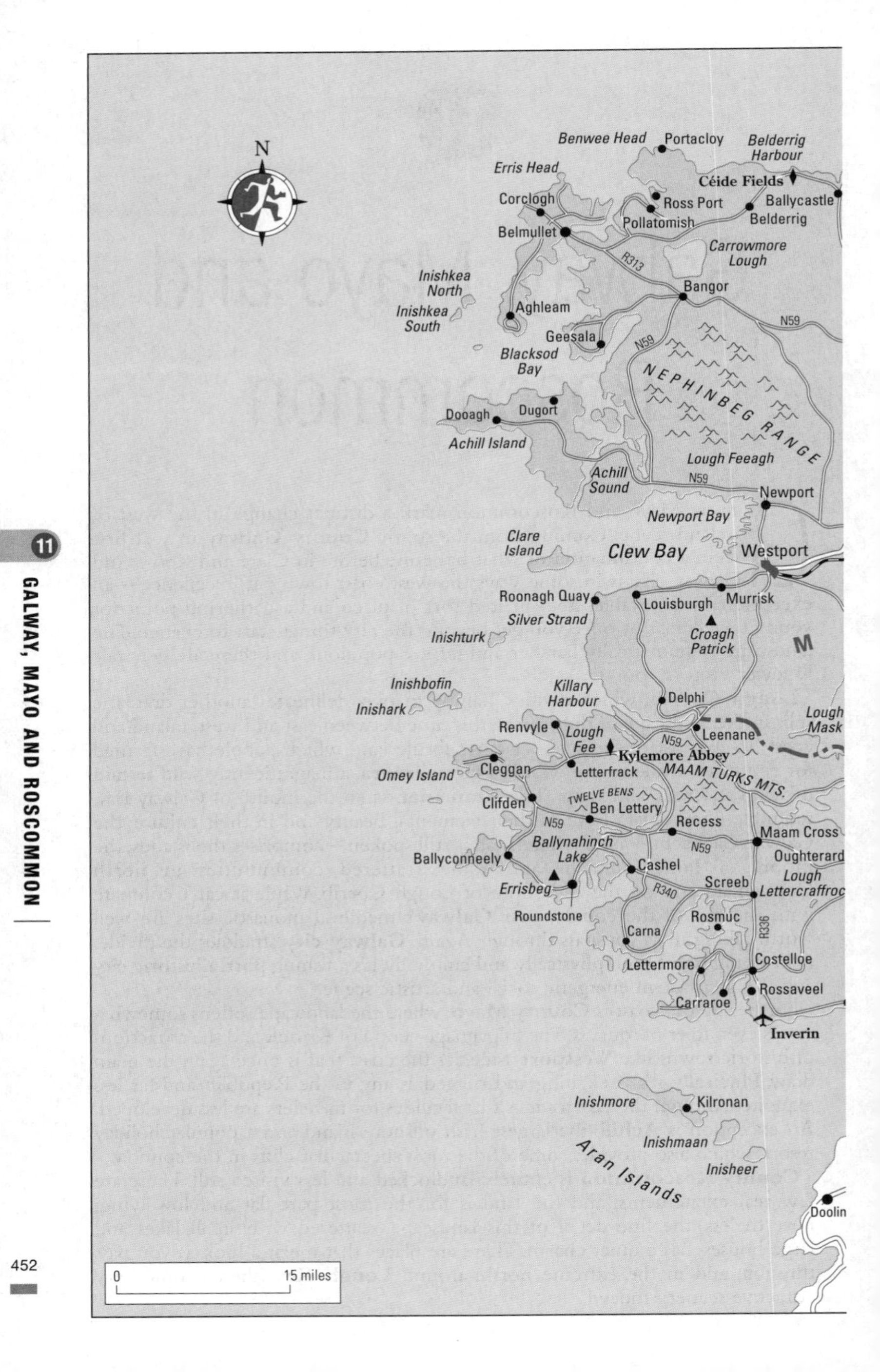

N
Benwee Head
Portacloy
Belderrig Harbour
Erris Head
Céide Fields
Corclogh
Ross Port
Ballycastle
Belmullet
Pollatomish
Belderrig
Carrowmore Lough
R313
Inishkea North
Bangor
Inishkea South
Aghleam
N59
Geesala
N59
Blacksod Bay
NEPHINBEG RANGE
Dooagh
Dugort
Achill Island
Lough Feeagh
Achill Sound
N59
Newport
Newport Bay
Clare Island
Clew Bay
Westport
Roonagh Quay
Louisburgh
Murrisk
Silver Strand
Croagh Patrick
Inishturk
M
Inishbofin
Killary Harbour
Delphi
Inishark
Lough Mask
Renvyle
Lough Fee
Leenane
N59
Kylemore Abbey
Cleggan
Letterfrack
MAAM TURKS MTS.
Omey Island
TWELVE BENS
Clifden
Ben Lettery
N59
Recess
Maam Cross
Ballynahinch Lake
N59
Oughterard
Ballyconneely
Cashel
Lough
Screeb
Lettercraffroc
Errisbeg
R340
Roundstone
Rosmuc
R336
Carna
Costelloe
Lettermore
Rossaveel
Carraroe
Inverin
Inishmore
Kilronan
Inishmaan
Aran Islands
Inisheer
Doolin
0
15 miles

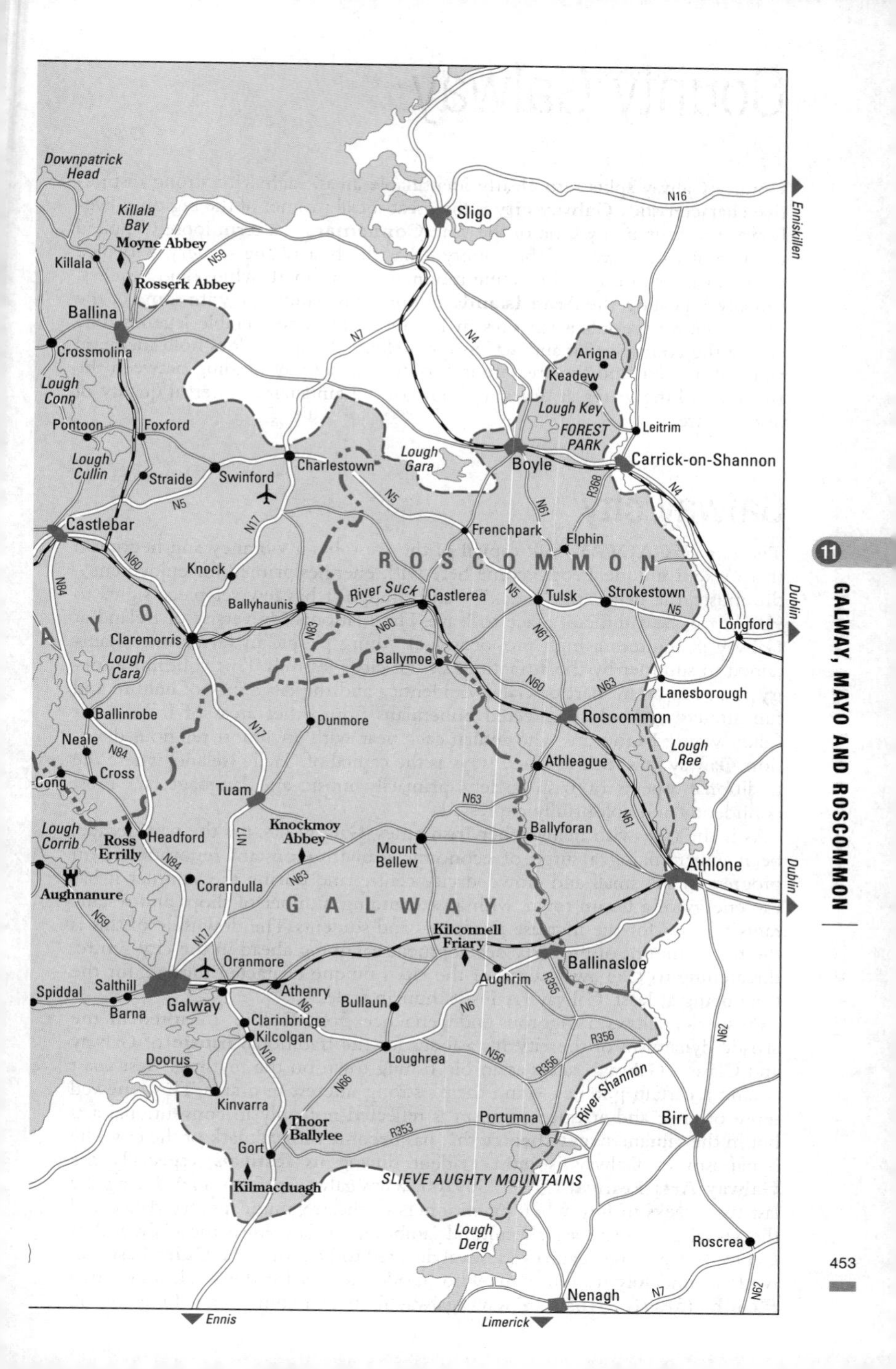
Downpatrick Head
Killala Bay
Moyne Abbey
Killala
Rosserk Abbey
Ballina
Crossmolina
Lough Conn
Pontoon
Foxford
Lough Cullin
Straide
Swinford
Charlestown
Lough Gara
Castlebar
Knock
Ballyhaunis
Claremorris
Lough Cara
Ballinrobe
Neale
Cross
Cong
Lough Corrib
Ross Errilly
Headford
Aughnanure
Corandulla
Tuam
Knockmoy Abbey
Dunmore
Mount Bellew
Oranmore
Salthill
Spiddal
Barna
Galway
Athenry
Clarinbridge
Kilcolgan
Doorus
Kinvarra
Gort
Thoor Ballylee
Kilmacduagh
SLIEVE AUGHTY MOUNTAINS
Loughrea
Bullaun
Kilconnell Friary
Aughrim
Ballinasloe
Portumna
River Shannon
Lough Derg
Nenagh
Roscrea
Birr
Athlone
Ballyforan
Athleague
Roscommon
Lough Ree
Lanesborough
Longford
Ballymoe
Castlerea
River Suck
Tulsk
Strokestown
Elphin
Frenchpark
Boyle
Carrick-on-Shannon
Leitrim
Lough Key
FOREST PARK
Keadew
Arigna
Sligo
MAYO
ROSCOMMON
GALWAY
Enniskillen
Dublin
Dublin
Ennis
Limerick
N16
N59
N7
N4
N5
N17
N60
N84
N83
N61
N63
N6
N18
N66
N56
R356
R355
R353
R368
N62

County Galway

County Galway splits into clearly identifiable areas, each with strong distinctive characteristics. **Galway city** is the great social magnet of the region, a lively place to visit at any time of the year. **Connemara** – a term loosely applied to encompass the west of the county – has the best of the scenery, with vast open expanses of bog, exhilarating mountains and superb white-sand beaches. Equally appealing, the **Aran Islands** combine raw landscape with some of the most exciting pre-Christian sites in Europe – and considerable legends. The east of the county is flat and far less compelling, though it does hold medieval ruins of interest, and the area around south Galway Bay, nestling between the Burren and the water, at times has some of the tantalizing, ethereal quality of north Clare.

Galway city

The city of **GALWAY**, folk capital of the west, has a vibrancy and hedonism that make it unique. People come here with energies primed for enjoyment – the music, the drink, the "crack" – and though it has few set-piece sights to visit, it can be a difficult place to leave. The National University of Ireland at Galway guarantees a high proportion of young people in term time, maintained in summer by the attractions of the city's festivals. This youthful **energy** is an important part of Galway's identity, and the city's mix of culture and fun attracts not only disaffected bohemians from other areas of Ireland but folksy young Europeans who return each year with an almost religious devotion. Galway sees itself in many ways as the capital of Gaelic Ireland, where the traditional aspects of Irish society, primarily music and language, are most confidently and colourfully expressed.

As is the case with many other Irish cities, Galway has, for the past decade, been experiencing a surge of economic growth. Constant renovation is in progress in the small and crowded city centre, and during the summer it has the energy of a boom town, with an expanding number of shops and restaurants to cater for the increase in visitors and students. The downside of this is the huge amount of property development galloping ahead in the city centre, threatening to take away some of the city's unique character, though, for the time being at least, Galway retains its human scale.

Prosperity allows a vigorous independence from Dublin, mirrored in the artistic dynamism of the city. It's a focus for the traditional **music** of Galway and Clare – Galway's status as an old fishing town on the mythical west coast adding a certain potency – and there's strong interest in drama. This renewed sense of civic and artistic optimism is reflected not only in conventional arts but in the vibrant **street theatre** that has become the hallmark of the city. The dynamism of Galway is most evident during its **festivals**, especially the **Galway Arts Festival** (ⓣ091/509700, www.galwayartsfestival.ie) during the last two weeks in July, when practitioners of theatre, music, poetry, dance and the visual arts create a rich cultural jamboree. In late April the Galway Arts Centre (see p.465) organizes a festival devoted to literature, the **Cúirt Festival**, while in mid-July it's film buffs who invade the city for the week-long **Film Fleadh** (ⓣ091/751655, ⓦwww.galwayfilmfleadh.com). The king of all

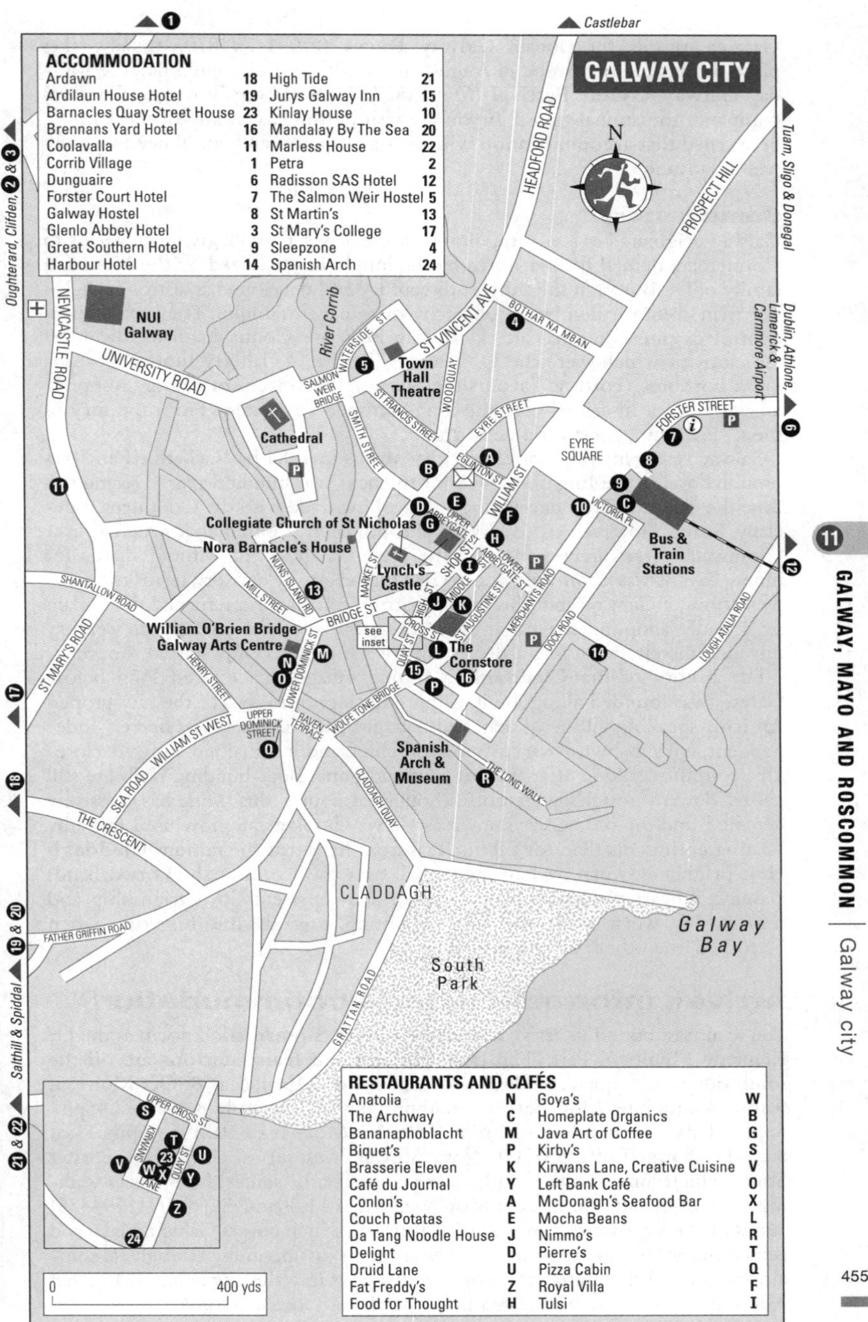
GALWAY CITY
ACCOMMODATION
Ardawn 18
Ardilaun House Hotel 19
Barnacles Quay Street House 23
Brennans Yard Hotel 16
Coolavalla 11
Corrib Village 1
Dunguaire 6
Forster Court Hotel 7
Galway Hostel 8
Glenlo Abbey Hotel 3
Great Southern Hotel 9
Harbour Hotel 14
High Tide 21
Jurys Galway Inn 15
Kinlay House 10
Mandalay By The Sea 20
Marless House 22
Petra 2
Radisson SAS Hotel 12
The Salmon Weir Hostel 5
St Martin's 13
St Mary's College 17
Sleepzone 4
Spanish Arch 24
RESTAURANTS AND CAFÉS
Anatolia N
The Archway C
Bananaphoblacht M
Biquet's P
Brasserie Eleven K
Café du Journal Y
Conlon's A
Couch Potatas E
Da Tang Noodle House J
Delight D
Druid Lane U
Fat Freddy's Z
Food for Thought H
Goya's W
Homeplate Organics B
Java Art of Coffee G
Kirby's S
Kirwans Lane, Creative Cuisine V
Left Bank Café O
McDonagh's Seafood Bar X
Mocha Beans L
Nimmo's R
Pierre's T
Pizza Cabin Q
Royal Villa F
Tulsi I
Castlebar
Tuam, Sligo & Donegal
Dublin, Athlone, Limerick & Carnmore Airport
Oughterard, Clifden, 2 & 3
Salthill & Spiddal
NUI Galway
University Road
Newcastle Road
River Corrib
Waterside St
St Vincent Ave
Headford Road
Prospect Hill
Bothar Na Mban
Town Hall Theatre
Salmon Weir Bridge
Cathedral
Woodquay
St Francis Street
Smith Street
Eyre Street
Forster Street
Eyre Square
Eglinton St
William St
Upper Abbeygate St
Victoria Pl.
Bus & Train Stations
Collegiate Church of St Nicholas
Nora Barnacle's House
Lynch's Castle
Shop St
Lower Abbeygate St
Middle St
St Augustine St
Merchants Road
Market St
Nuns Island Rd
Mill Street
Shantallow Road
Bridge St
William O'Brien Bridge
Galway Arts Centre
see inset
Cross St
High St
Quay St
The Cornstore
Dock Road
Lough Atalia Road
St Mary's Road
Henry Street
Lower Dominick St
Upper Dominick Street
William St West
Raven Terrace
Wolfe Tone Bridge
Spanish Arch & Museum
The Long Walk
Sea Road
The Crescent
Claddagh Quay
Claddagh
Father Griffin Road
Galway Bay
South Park
Grattan Road
Upper Cross St
Kirwans Lane
0 400 yds

Galway festivals, the riotous **Galway Races** (Ⓣ091/753870), usually takes place during the first week in August, and at the end of September, the four-day **Galway Oyster Festival** (Ⓣ091/527282, Ⓦwww.galwayoysterfest.com) completes the annual round. If you are visiting the city at any of these times, be warned that accommodation will be at a premium and you'll need to book well in advance.

Some history

Galway originated as a crossing point on the River Corrib, giving an access to Connemara denied further north by the lough. It was seized by the **Norman** family of De Burgo in the thirteenth century and developed as a strong Anglo-Norman colony, ruled by an oligarchy of fourteen families. They maintained control despite continual attacks by the bellicose Connacht clans, the most ferocious of which were the O'Flahertys. To the O'Flaherty motto "Fortuna Favet Fortibus" (Fortune Favours the Strong), the citizens of Galway responded with a plea inscribed over the long-vanished city gates: "From the fury of the O'Flahertys, good Lord deliver us."

Galway was granted a charter and **city status** in 1484 by Richard III and was proudly loyal to the English Crown for the next two hundred years. During this time the city prospered, developing a flourishing trade with the Continent, especially Spain. However, its loyalty to the monarch ensured that when Oliver Cromwell's forces arrived in 1652 the place was besieged without mercy for ninety days. It was Cromwell who coined the originally derisory term "the fourteen tribes of Galway"; but this didn't worry the Irish, who returned the disdain by proudly adopting the name as a title. From the mid-seventeenth century onwards, the city went into a decline that it has only recently started to reverse.

The history of the **Claddagh**, a fishing village that existed long before Galway was founded alongside it, is quite distinct from that of the city proper. An Irish-speaking village of thatched cottages, the Claddagh was fiercely independent, with its own laws, customs and chief, and it remained a proud, close-knit community long after the cottages had gone. Boat-building skills are still passed down through generations, though of course this work has massively declined, and the old vessels known as Galway hookers are now used more by boating enthusiasts than for fishing. It is from here that the famous **Claddagh ring** originates, worn by Irish people all over the world. It shows two hands clasping a heart surmounted by a crown and represents love, friendship and respect. It's worn with the heart pointing towards the fingertip when betrothed, the other way when married.

Arrival, information and accommodation

You're almost bound to arrive in Galway at **Eyre Square**, also known as the J.F. Kennedy Memorial Park. The **Bus Éireann** and **train stations** are off the south side of the square, while the **tourist office** (April, May & Oct Mon–Sat 9am–5.45pm; June Mon–Sat 9am–6.45pm; July & Aug daily 8.30am–7.45pm; Sept daily 9am–5.45pm; Nov–March Mon–Fri 9am–5.45pm, Sat 9am–12.45pm; Ⓣ091/537700, Ⓦwww.irelandwest.ie) is nearby on Forster Street, which runs from the southeastern corner of the square. It organizes walking tours of the city (June–Sept Mon, Wed & Fri 11.30am; €6; Ⓣ 091/794435) and is the headquarters of Ireland West Tourism, which covers Galway, Mayo and Roscommon. If you arrive by plane, you might just be lucky enough to coincide with the daily bus from **Carnmore Airport** into the city centre (Mon–Sat 1.30pm; €3.50); otherwise a taxi from the airport costs around €15.

Accommodation is plentiful in Galway. There are dozens of **B&Bs** in the city, though most are on the outskirts, including a large concentration in the coastal resort of Salthill (accessible on city buses #1S and #1D from Eyre Square). There are also a large number of **hostels** in Galway, of varying quality (the best are probably *Barnacles*, *Kinlay House* and *Sleepzone*), but they get very full during festival time and throughout August – ring ahead, arrive early or, best of all, book ahead. We would advise ignoring the touts at the station, and only using the hostels which are either listed here or are approved by the tourist office. The number of **hotels** in the city has doubled in recent years, with the new arrivals forcing the more established hotels both to raise their standards and lower their prices. The best local **campsite** is the well-appointed *Ballyloughane Caravan Park*, by a nice sandy beach at Renmore, three miles east of the centre off the Dublin road (Ⓣ091/755338; mid-April to mid-Sept).

Hotels

Ardilaun House Hotel Taylor's Hill Ⓣ091/521433, Ⓦwww.ardilaunhousehotel.ie. Although this hotel is close to the centre off the road to Salthill, its five acres of woodland give it the feel of a country retreat. The hotel boasts all manner of leisure-related extras, including a Jacuzzi, swimming pool and gym, the bedrooms are spacious, and the fine dining room overlooks extensive gardens to the rear. It's worth enquiring about special half-board deals which are offered periodically. ❻

Brennans Yard Hotel Lower Merchants Rd Ⓣ091/568166, Ⓦwww.brennansyardhotel.com. Friendly, excellent-value option housed in a former warehouse near the Spanish Arch, where comfortable, individually designed bedrooms match the characterful nature of the hotel with their antique pine furnishings. ❹

Forster Court Hotel Forster St Ⓣ091/564111, Ⓦwww.forstercourthotel.com. A small but elegant new hotel located in the heart of the city, which offers weekend deals. ❹

Glenlo Abbey Hotel Bushy Park Ⓣ091/526666, Ⓦwww.glenlo.com. Located two miles out of Galway on the Clifden road, the *Glenlo Abbey* is the city's finest hotel. Set in a 138-acre estate on the edge of Lough Corrib, this eighteenth-century country residence offers total comfort in the most atmospheric and tranquil surroundings. ❻

Great Southern Hotel Eyre Square Ⓣ091/564041, Ⓦwww.greatsouthernhotels.com. This rambling Victorian establishment was built as a railway hotel in 1845 and preserves much of its original style and charm. Taking up almost one side of the city's central square, this hotel combines its old-world style with modern facilities such as a rooftop pool. While all the rooms are elegant and spacious, those looking to the front are preferable for their views of the square. Weekend deals offered. ❽

Harbour Hotel The Harbour Ⓣ091/569466, Ⓦwww.galwayharbourhotel.com. Right on the waterfront, this stylish, ultra-modern hotel offers bright rooms, decorated in strong colours and blonde wood, with a choice of city or harbour view. It's busy during the week but can be quiet on weekends, and excellent rates are often offered. ❺

Jurys Galway Inn Quay St Ⓣ091/566444, Ⓦwww.jurysdoyle.com. Ideally located on the banks of the River Corrib near the Spanish Arch, this hotel has all the qualities associated with the *Jurys* chain. The rooms are large and comfortable, and sleep up to four people, making their flat room rate very attractive to families or groups on a budget. ❸

Radisson SAS Hotel Lough Atalia Rd Ⓣ091/538300, Ⓦwww.radissonsas.com. This bright, modern, Scandinavian-run luxury hotel overlooks Galway Bay from a fine position on the northeast side of the train station. A long list of leisure facilities includes swimming pool, gym and, of course, sauna. ❼

Spanish Arch Quay St Ⓣ091/569600, Ⓔemcdgall@iol.ie. A small boutique hotel right in the heart of the action, with individually designed, period-theme rooms, though those facing onto the street can be noisy. ❼

B&Bs

Ardawn 31 College Rd Ⓣ091/568833, Ⓔardawn@iol.ie. A friendly, red-bricked, upmarket B&B ten minutes' walk from the city centre in a quiet part of town. The rooms are well furnished and breakfasts well prepared by the attentive hosts. ❸

Coolavalla 22 Newcastle Rd Ⓣ091/522415. Large, trim family house by the hospital and university, ten minutes' walk west of the centre, with one en-suite and three standard rooms. Closed Dec & Jan. ❷

Corrib Village Newcastle Ⓣ091/527112, Ⓦwww.corribvillage.com. This huge complex on the campus of Galway University offers B&B

accommodation or weekly apartment rentals from June to Sept on the shores of Lough Corrib to the north of town. The village includes laundry facilities and a complimentary shuttle bus to Eyre Square, and guests have access to the university's wide-ranging sports facilities. ❷

Dunguaire 8 Lurgan Park, Murrough, Dublin Rd ⓣ091/757043, ⓔccawley@eircom.net. A friendly place just over a mile to the east of the city opposite the *Corrib Great Southern Hotel* (follow the signs to Galway City East). The house offers two en-suite and two standard rooms, all of which are comfortable, and does decent rates for single travellers. ❷

High Tide 9 Grattan Park, Coast Rd ⓣ091/584324, ⓔhightide@iol.ie. Two miles out of the city on the road to Salthill, this fine house offers four bright, comfortable en-suite rooms overlooking the bay. Closed Dec & Jan. ❷

Mandalay By The Sea 10 Gentian Hill ⓣ091/524177, ⓔmandalay@esatclear.ie. This large, distinctive balconied house, overlooking Galway Bay three miles outside the city in Salthill, is a very comfortable option indeed. The en-suite rooms are large and airy, and the food is excellent. ❷

Marless House Threadneedle Rd ⓣ091/523931, ⓦwww.marlesshouse.com. This large, modern Georgian-style house is situated on the coast two miles from the centre in Salthill. The cosy rooms are large by B&B standards, all are en suite, and the hosts welcome children and will do special family deals. ❷

Petra 201 Laurel Park ⓣ091/521844. This friendly, modern house is located a short distance out of the city centre in the Newcastle area and has three en-suite and two standard rooms. Take buses #4W or #5W from Eyre Square. Closed Dec & Jan. ❸

St Martin's 2 Nuns Island Rd ⓣ091/568286. This is one of the few central B&Bs in Galway. The rooms are comfortable, the food is good, and the owners could not be more obliging. The location is ideal, with the Corrib River running through the house's pleasant garden. ❷

Hostels

Barnacles Quay Street House 10 Quay St ⓣ091/568644, ⓦwww.barnacles.ie. A brightly painted, well-run, security-conscious hostel right in the centre of town; all rooms are en suite, with twins and doubles available, there are laundry and kitchen facilities, and light breakfast is included. This is the place to come if you want to take in Galway's nightlife, but ask for a room at the back if you're looking for a decent night's rest. ❶

Galway Hostel Frenchville Lane, Eyre Square ⓣ091/566959. A good, friendly budget option opposite the station, which also offers twin, double and four-bed rooms, Internet access and self-catering facilities. ❶, including light breakfast.

Kinlay House Merchants Rd, Eyre Square ⓣ091/565244, ⓦwww.kinlayhouse.ie. Large, purpose-built IHH hostel, with many dorms en-suite and double and twin rooms available. It's clean, friendly and efficiently run, with laundry facilities, self-catering kitchens and Internet access available in the shop below. Prices include a simple continental breakfast, bed linen and towel. ❶

St Mary's College St Mary's Rd ⓣ091/527411. Large, summertime An Óige hostel, just over a mile west of the city centre, with family rooms, self-catering facilities, café and bike hire. July & Aug only.

The Salmon Weir Hostel St Vincent's Ave, Woodquay ⓣ091/561133. A small, simple but comfortable IHO hostel with a relaxed, convivial atmosphere suited to those travelling alone who wish to meet up with other people. Private family rooms are available, and there are good laundry facilities.

Sleepzone Bóthar na mBan, Woodquay ⓣ091/566999, ⓦwww.sleepzone.ie. Galway's newest and most modern hostel is a large, well-run establishment five minutes' walk north of Eyre Square. Most rooms are en suite, with singles, twins and doubles available, and there are laundry facilities, self-catering kitchens and Internet access. Prices include a light breakfast. ❶

The City

Galway's centre is defined by the **River Corrib**. Issuing from the lough, it thunders under the Salmon Weir Bridge and wraps itself round the full body of the city, meeting the lively, pedestrianized **Quay Street** at Wolfe Tone Bridge, where it flows into the bay. The quaint old shops and bars that give Galway its villagey appeal are being squeezed on all sides by ugly postmodern facades and bone-headed business development; the area around the bridge has to be one of the most architecturally abused spots in Ireland. Still, Galway is a robust city and somehow its charm pulls through. Over the bridge is the Claddagh, and about a mile and a half west of that is **Salthill**, Galway's commercial seaside town. The **Claddagh** now appears as a small area of modest housing, strangely flanked by a crusting of luxury apartments, but it's worth getting to know for some of its excellent bars and cheap eats. From any of the bridges you can wander beside the pleasant walkways of river and canals, checking out the industrial archaeology, watching salmon make their way upstream, anglers fly-fishing in the centre of the city and cormorants diving for eels, while gawky herons splash through watery suburban back gardens. At the harbour, a walk out around the stone pier places the city in its impressive setting, with a level coastline stretching to the west and the eerie Burren hills washed and etched in half-tones across the bay.

Eyre Square is an almost inevitable starting point. This small park, set in the middle of a traffic interchange, is one of the places to which everyone seems to gravitate. It's used as a performance space during festivals, and outdoor music sessions can start up here at any time, the relaxed atmosphere lending itself to improvisation. Visually, though, the place is a mess. A sentimental statue of the writer Pádraic Ó Conaire, a couple of cannon from the Crimean War and a clutter of disused flagpoles all detract from what should form the focus of the square: Eamonn O'Donnell's splendid sculpture, whose arcs of rusted metal and gushing white fountains evoke the sails of a Galway hooker and the city's nautical history. The distinctive town houses of the merchant class – remnants of which are lightly littered around the city – also hark back to the prosperity of maritime Galway and its sense of civic dignity, with their finely carved doorways, windows and stone slabs bearing armorial carving. Standing forlornly in the middle of Eyre Square, the **Browne doorway** is one such monument, a bay window and doorway with the coats of arms of the Browne and Lynch families, dated 1627. Before you leave the square, it's worth calling into the **Eyre Square Centre**, as the building of this shopping mall in the late 1980s revealed impressive sections of medieval city walls, which are preserved within the complex.

Just about the finest medieval town house in Ireland is **Lynch's Castle** on pedestrianized Shop Street, which, along with its continuations William Street (leading off the west corner of Eyre Square), High Street and Quay Street, forms the town's main commercial thoroughfare. The Lynches were Galway's most prominent family for three hundred years from the late fifteenth century. A local story relates that in 1493 James Lynch Fitzstephen, mayor of the town, found his own son guilty of the jealous murder of a Spanish visitor, and that such was the popularity of the lad that no one in the town would take on the job of hangman – so the boy's father did it himself. Galwegians claim this to be the origin of the term "lynching". The house, which is now home to the Allied Irish Bank, dates from the fifteenth century and features a smooth stone facade decorated with carved panels and medieval gargoyles. The similarly styled **Lynch's Window**, from which Lynch Fitzstephen is said to have hanged his son, can be found on Market Street (further down Shop Street and to the right) just outside the **Collegiate Church of St Nicholas**. The largest medieval church in Ireland, it was built in 1320 and enlarged in the next two centuries. The building – dedicated to St Nicholas of Myra, patron saint of sailors and also revered as Santa Claus – is decorated with finely chiselled gargoyles and contains some mildly diverting tombs (James Lynch Fitzstephen, again), a simply carved sixteenth-century font and various other stone fragments set into the walls. Continuing south along Market Street, and turning off into Bowling Green Lane, you'll come across the house that **Nora Barnacle**, wife of James Joyce, lived in. It's now been converted into a small museum (late May to Aug Mon–Fri & sometimes Sat 10am–5pm; €2.50) and contains, among other Joycean memorabilia, copies of the couple's letters. For arguably the best sense of medieval Galway, take a short walk south from Nora Barnacle's house and make your way through the punters and the pints up to the top floor of **Busker Browne's Bar** on Cross Street. The upper room was the meeting place of the tribes of Galway – its steeply pitched Gothic roof is festooned with their flags – and the building has served as a barracks and as a Dominican convent.

Down by the harbour stands the **Spanish Arch**, a sixteenth-century structure more evocative in name than in reality that was used to protect galleons unloading wine and rum. Adjoining it is a fine piece of medieval wall and the uninspiring **Galway Museum** (May–Sept daily 10am–1pm & 2–5pm; €2), where the only things of real interest are old photographs of the Claddagh and a few examples of sixteenth- and seventeenth-century stone-carving from around the city. Plans are afoot, however, for a much grander civic museum on this site, which will incorporate the Browne doorway and Ó Conaire statue now in Eyre Square.

From the Spanish Arch, you can take a pleasant walk north along a riverside path and across the Salmon Weir Bridge to the **Cathedral of Our Lady Assumed into Heaven and St Nicholas**. Commissioned about thirty years ago and in hideous contrast to the Collegiate Church, its copper dome seeps green stains down its ugly limestone walls. Inside, the horrors continue in a senseless jumble of stone, mahogany and Connemara marble. It's so remarkably awful that it demands attention, and viewed from a distance its sheer bulk does achieve a grandeur of sorts. Nearby, across the bridge, the clean lines of the Neoclassical courthouse are mirrored in the municipal theatre opposite – an assured symbol of contemporary Galway's civic pride.

On the road behind the cathedral is the **university**, now officially known as the **National University of Ireland Galway**(or NUI Galway), a mock-Tudor imitation of an Oxbridge college, which was opened in 1849 at a time when the majority of people in Connacht were starving. The university has the dubious distinction of having conferred an honorary degree on Ronald Reagan. More importantly, it is now UNESCO's base for an archive of spoken material in all Celtic languages, and it runs courses in Irish out in Carraroe (see p.487) in the Connemara Gaeltacht.

The river

If you want to get out onto the water, head for nearby **Woodquay** (cross the Salmon Weir Bridge at the cathedral, turn left and walk a little way along Waterside Street), where you can rent a rowing boat from next to the Galway Rowing Club (book on ⓣ091/564743). Alternatively, from south of the Salmon Weir Bridge, take the Lough Corrib river cruise (daily: July & Aug 12.30pm, 2.30pm & 4.30pm; Sept–June 2.30pm & 4.30pm; ⓣ091/592447; €9), which goes five miles up the river through flat countryside punctuated by derelict castles, out into the open expanse of the lough.

Salthill

Beyond the Claddagh lies **SALTHILL**, Galway's seaside resort, complete with amusement arcades, discos, seasonal cafés and a fairground – as well as scores more hotels and B&Bs. Salthill's **tourist office** is on the front (June, July & Aug daily 9am–5.45pm; ⓣ091/520500). Alongside the tourist office is the **Atlantaquaria** (Mon–Fri 10am–5pm, Sat & Sun 10am–7pm; ⓦwww.atlantaquaria.com; €7, children €4), which, as the name suggests, is an aquarium showcasing Ireland's fresh- and seawater fish. It makes for a fun diversion for children on a wet day, as does the huge **Leisureland** amusement complex, which, apart from being used as a venue for big concerts, has several swimming pools, including a beach pool, bubble pool and a giant waterslide (daily year-round, hours vary according to demand – ☎091/521455; €7, children €4.80). **Lower Salthill** has a long promenade with a series of unspectacular but safe and sandy beaches. Even on a hot summer's day it's never so busy as to be oppressive, and its great asset is the view over a glittering expanse of water to the Burren. West of here, **Upper Salthill** is a mess of a suburb that sits around a golf course, despoiled by huge billboards and caravan parks. Beyond Upper Salthill, probably the nicest of the sandy beaches is the small one at **Silver Strand**, nestling beneath a grassy headland about three miles out of Galway city centre.

Eating

You'll find a wide range of food on offer in Galway with some particularly good upmarket Continental **restaurants** and great seafood. The places listed below are open daily for lunch and dinner except where noted. Prices are indicated by the terms "Cheap" (under €10 for a main course); "Moderate" (€10–15); and "Expensive" (over €15). For daytime eating, a plethora of new **cafés** has appeared recently in the centre of Galway and those listed below are chosen for their atmosphere as well as for their food; plenty of bars also offer good-value meals and snacks, most notably the famous *Busker Browne's* (see pp.460 and 463).

Cafés

Bananaphoblacht 56 Lower Dominick St. Mostly Irish-language café – the name means "banana republic" – which makes a great alternative to the numerous pubs in the area, with backgammon and chess, great coffees and light meals. Open daily till late in the evening.

Café du Journal Quay St. Frequented by arty types languishing in the smoky atmosphere, this place serves a wonderful selection of coffees, omelettes, croissants and desserts; newspapers are available to read.

Delight 29 Upper Abbeygate St. Serves great coffee, breakfasts and pastries, as well as some novel sandwiches, salads and hot dishes, including a daily special tartlet. Closed Sat & Sun.

Food For Thought Lower Abbeygate St. Offers cheap wholefood and vegetarian snacks, sandwiches, light meals and good coffee, to take away or eat in perched on its high stools.

Goya's Kirwan's Lane. Excellent home-baked cakes and coffee, as well as soups, quiches, sandwiches and savoury tarts, to eat in or take away.

Java Art of Coffee 17 Upper Abbeygate St. Good coffee, great ambient tunes and late hours make this a perfect place to hang out.

Left Bank Café Lower Dominick St. Good sandwiches, panini and simple full meals at reasonable prices, often ideal when you want a quiet spot and other places in the more popular Quay and Cross streets area are full.

Mocha Beans Lower Cross St. The aroma of rich roasted coffee and home-baked pastries pervades the air of this little place, where sandwiches, soups and salads are also served.

Restaurants

Anatolia 51 Lower Dominick St. Simple, bright, better-than-average kebab shop and restaurant, serving decent, filling versions of Turkish standards such as Adana kebab, lamb *köfte* (meatballs) with tomato sauce, yoghurt and pitta. Cheap.

The Archway Victoria Place ☎091/563693. A quiet place off the east side of Eyre Square where the owner has been making a reputation for himself by cooking perfect interpretations of classic and modern French dishes. Open Tues–Sat evenings. Expensive.

Biquet's Spanish Parade ☎091/568450. Despite the address, this easy-going wine bar and bistro couldn't be more French. Lunch on tartlets, plates of cheese and charcuterie, or dine on classic dishes such as beef tongue with vinaigrette – sometimes to the accompaniment of a piano or live jazz. Cheap–moderate.

Brasserie Eleven 19 Middle St ☎091/561610. This relaxing restaurant serves up pasta, stir-fry dishes and large salads, as well as more intricate vegetarian and seafood dishes, such as pan-seared bass with sweet potato colcannon. Moderate–expensive.

Conlon's Eglinton St. Popular seafood restaurant,

specializing in oysters, seafood salads and fish and chips in plain but comfortable surroundings. The day's catch is chalked up on a blackboard. Cheap.

Couch Potatas Upper Abbeygate St. This place takes cooking the humble spud to a new level. It claims to demonstrate 101 ways of serving a potato, with all manner of sauces and stuffings – and of course a good selection for vegetarians. Cheap.

Da Tang Noodle House Middle St. One of the few authentic noodle houses in Ireland, this is a real treat. Apart from the mostly northern Chinese noodles – either in soup, sauce or pan-fried – it also serves some excellent sizzling dishes and rice stir-fries. Closed Sun lunchtime. Cheap–moderate.

Druid Lane 9 Quay St ☎091/563015. Relaxed, informal place, with helpful staff and excellent, vaguely French-influenced food, such as duck breast glazed with honey and soya on noodles. Closed lunchtimes & Sun eve. Moderate–expensive.

Fat Freddy's Quay St. Perennially popular place with a buzzy atmosphere, and great pizzas and spaghetti; one of the cheapest places to get an evening meal. Cheap–moderate.

Homeplate Organics Mary St. Serves everything from breakfasts, through sandwiches and ciabatta to main courses such as chicken enchilada; there are organic specials every day. Closed Sun. Cheap–moderate.

Kirbys Upper Cross St ☎091/569404. Joined to the excellent *Busker Browne's* bar is its slightly more upmarket sister restaurant, which offers imaginative cuisine, using local ingredients where possible, in modern but warm and relaxing surroundings; a simpler menu is available at lunchtime. Moderate–expensive.

Kirwans Lane, Creative Cuisine Kirwans Lane, off Upper Cross St ☎091/568266. Very popular restaurant (both locally and with tourists), offering a range of international cuisine, including dishes such as monkfish with chickpeas, beansprouts and Asian salad. The service is good, and evening dining is formal. Booking is advised. Closed lunchtimes in winter (except Dec). Expensive.

McDonagh's Seafood Bar 22 Quay St. A must for seafood lovers; nip in for a thick and creamy chowder, or linger for a full meal. Excellent English-style fish and chips are also on offer, to eat in or take away, and the service is extremely friendly. Cheap–moderate.

Nimmo's Long Walk, Spanish Arch ☎091/561114. Located in a characterful medieval building overlooking the river, *Nimmo's* serves an imaginative Continental menu, with plenty of seafood, in its spacious first-floor restaurant (Tues–Sat eves) and simpler dishes in its ground-floor wine bar, with live music – often jazz – on Sunday evenings. Closed Sun lunchtime & Mon. Moderate–expensive.

Pierre's 8 Quay St ☎091/566066. A haven tucked away within the bedlam that can be Quay Street, this restaurant has a relaxed atmosphere and fine food, and does an excellent early-bird menu, as well as a set three-course menu later in the evening. Evenings only. Moderate–expensive.

Pizza Cabin Upper Dominick St ☎091/582887. Delicious pizzas to take away or eat in, either on the narrow counters here or in *Monroe's* pub next door. Cheap.

Royal Villa 13 Shop St. Popular, successful restaurant serving a mix of simple Chinese, Thai and Malaysian dishes in a central spot above Hynes shoe shop. Moderate.

Tulsi Buttermilk Walk, Middle St ☎091/564831. The city's best Indian, slightly hidden in a small street running off Middle Street, offers excellent vegetarian and meaty food and even tries its hand at Indo-Galwegian fusion dishes such as tandoori mackerel. Moderate.

Drinking, nightlife and entertainment

If the *craic* has eluded you so far on your travels, Galway is where you're going to find it. The **bars** are the social lungs of this town, and even the most abstemious of travellers will find themselves sucked in. **Traditional music** is performed in many of them; some of it will be depressingly over-amplified, but you can hit a great session on any day of the week and at almost any time of the day during the summer months. The bars of Shop and Quay streets are especially good, as are those over the bridge around Dominick Street.

Together with DJ bars, there are numerous **clubs** in Galway, among which *Cuba* and *GPO* stand out; look out for flyers round town to find out what's on, and for concessions being handed out in bars. The main **gay bars** are *Strano* on William Street West (☎091/588219), with a women's night on the first Thursday of every month, and *Zulus* on Raven Terrace (☎091/581204); there's a club, *Bubble Love*, open Thursday to Sunday above *Angels* lap-dancing club at 152 Upper Salthill (take the side entrance). For up-to-the-minute information, call the gay and lesbian information line (see "Listings", p.466).

Listings magazines in Galway come and go frequently, the latest incarnation being the free, fortnightly *Galway Inside Out*; more steadfast is the free newspaper, the *Galway Advertiser*, which comes out every Thursday and goes like hot cakes.

Aras na Gael 45 Dominick St. Irish traditional music venue run and frequented by Irish-speaking enthusiasts, making it feel like a country pub in the middle of the city.

Bazaar Quay Lane. Incongruous Moroccan-themed bar in a venerable, heavy-stoned building that rises to its theme with gusto, with plenty of scattered cushions, carved screens and low lighting.

Blue Note William St West. Despite its name, numerous photos of jazz greats inside and the huge mural outside, this is not a jazz club. DJs play funk, soul and other laid-back sounds into the farthest snugs of this dimly lit, slightly scruffy but fun bar.

Busker Browne's and the Slate House Cross St. This popular bar offers original medieval fireplaces, a lofty, Gothic hall on the third floor hung with the banners of the Galway tribes, and floor upon floor of alcoves and armchairs for comfy eating and drinking. Seafood chowder, salads, open sandwiches and full meals are served daily till late, and there's jazz on Sunday lunchtimes.

The Crane Bar Sea Rd. Busy bar owned by two musicians, with great traditional sessions every night that many regard as the best in the county; the music is especially good on Fridays and Saturdays.

Cuba Eyre Square Ⓦwww.cuba.ie. Three floors of pulse-raising beats and an unobtrusive Cuban theme: the ground-floor bar hosts salsa, a twenty-piece swing jazz band on Mondays and a comedy club on Sundays; the club on the middle floor offers everything from R'n'B and hip-hop to techno; and the top floor is a live venue, which also holds some specialist club nights.

GPO Eglinton St Ⓦwww.gpo.ie. This lively, two-roomed affair, consisting of a main club floor and *The Drum* bar, attracts a young, studenty crowd with a wildly varied programme that occasionally includes top live acts and international DJs; pick up the club's monthly brochure in pubs around town. Look out for the Wednesday night comedy club; your ticket sees you through to *That 80s Club* later.

The King's Head Shop St. A huge three-storey bar featuring live music nightly, including traditional sessions twice a week in summer and Sunday lunchtime jazz. Attracts a young, lively crowd of students in winter and tourists in summer and can be incredibly busy.

Living Room Bridge St. Trendy, popular makeover of the old *Lisheen Bar*, though not strictly bang up-to-date: the place now has a strong Seventies retro feel, heavy on browns, reds and blonde wood, with plenty of padded bench seats and armchairs. There are DJs nightly and decent food during the day.

Massimo William St West. Stylish, modern bar done out with comfy couches, soft lighting, lots of bare wood and primary colours; laid-back DJs nightly and jazz on Sunday evenings.

Monroe's Dominick St. Huge, sociable pub with traditional music nightly. It's worth a visit on Tuesdays for its excellent set-dancing night, and it also has the added attraction of serving delicious pizzas till late from the adjacent *Pizza Cabin*.

Neachtains 17 Cross St. The jewel in the Galway pub crown, in what was once the town house of Humanity Dick (see p.488). Unlike other older pubs, it has resisted the temptation to remove its traditional interior of small rooms and snugs to maximize profits. If you go there with a group, get there early to commandeer a snug for the night.

Nimmo's Wine Bar Spanish Arch. Right on the river, this is a fine place to enjoy one of the many fine wines on offer; especially recommended for its Sunday dinners served to a mellow jazz backdrop.

O'Riada's High Street. Known locally as the *Front Door*, this unusually designed, laid-back pub is often packed with a diverse crowd.

The Quays Quay St. A traditional bar that's become increasingly popular of late. Best to stop in early as it's usually heaving later in the evening, especially when there is live music.

Roísín Dubh 9 Upper Dominick St Ⓣ091/586540. This pub is a Galway institution, and has consistently hosted some of the best musicians to visit the city over the past decade. Expect all kinds of music from folk and traditional to cajun and rock.

The Snug Shop St. Cosy, oak-beamed and flagstoned spot that's worth checking out at weekends for its traditional music.

Taylors Dominick St. Resolutely traditional bar with plain, hard benches and stools and a large beer garden at the back. You might catch the occasional session (usually Sun), though it's more a place to talk than sing.

Tigh Choili Mainguard St. Well-run, central and sociable traditional pub with frequent sessions in the evenings (afternoon and evenings at weekends).

△ Kilmacduagh, County Galway

The arts

Galway is experiencing a real growth in artistic activity, and it's at its most vibrant during the **Galway Arts Festival** (see p.454). There's plenty to detain you year-round, too: Galway's the home of the versatile and highly regarded **Druid Theatre Company** (Ⓦwww.druidtheatre.com), who specialize in new works by Irish authors and undertake extensive tours. If you're lucky enough to be in Galway when they're on, book a ticket in advance, as they play to packed houses. The most exciting artistic development of recent years has been the emergence of the local street theatre troupe **Macnas** (Ⓦwww.macnas.com). This internationally acclaimed group have elevated the art of street theatre to new heights; to watch one of their flamboyant street performances is a truly exhilarating experience and should not be missed. The **Town Hall Theatre**, Courthouse Square, Woodquay (Ⓣ091/569777, Ⓦwww.townhalltheatregalway.com), is the main performance venue, staging drama, dance, music and opera from visiting companies most nights of the year, as well as hosting the local film society (usually Sunday evening). **An Taibhdhearc na Gaillimhe** in Middle St (Ⓣ091/563600) is an Irish-language theatre, while **Siamsa** puts on a well-regarded annual show of traditional dance, music and drama in July and August in the Claddagh Hall (Ⓣ091/755479).

The **Galway Arts Centre** at 47 Dominick St (Ⓣ091/565886, Ⓦwww.galwayartscentre.ie) hosts visual arts exhibitions, workshops and a youth theatre company, and it's also a good place to find out what's going on in the arts locally. There are a few commercial art galleries worth a visit too, notably the **Kenny Gallery** on Middle Street (Ⓣ091/553733).

Crafts shopping

A hugely successful development in Galway is the **Design Concourse Ireland** (Ⓦwww.designconcourseireland.com), down a lane off Cross Street, near *Busker Browne's*. Housed in a beautifully restored medieval town house, it stocks the best of contemporary Irish **design**, including jewellery, furniture and tweed from both the Republic and the North. Dating from the sixteenth and seventeenth centuries, the building once housed a theatre owned by Humanity Dick (see p.488), and it is said that Wolfe Tone performed here.

Further quality contemporary clothing and crafts can be found in **Design Ireland Plus**, housed in the Cornstore (which is also the home of Charlie Byrne's bookshop – see "Listings", p.466) in Middle Street, and in the **Kilkenny Shop** on High Street. A popular local purchase are the chunky woollen **sweaters** people living on the west coast have worn for generations as protection against the notoriously fickle weather. The best places for these are **Faller's Sweater Shop** at 25 High St (Ⓦwww.fallers.com) and **O'Máille's** at 16 High St (Ⓦwww.iol.ie/omaille).

Galway has become something of an attraction of late for couples wishing to become engaged; if you find yourself overcome by romance and want to pledge your heart with a **Claddagh ring**, the place to go is **Dillons** on the corner of Cross and Quay streets, where there's also a small museum with exhibits on Claddagh village itself and the small symbol of eternal devotion associated with it. To complete a crafts tour of Galway, just outside town – follow the N6 to the *Galway Ryan Hotel* and take the first left – is the **Royal Tara china factory** and visitor centre (Ⓦwww.royal-tara.com), while a little further along the N6 is the **Galway Irish Crystal Heritage Centre** (Ⓦwww.galwaycrystal.ie).

Listings

Airport For flight or other enquiries, call ⓣ091/755569 or 1800/491491.
Bike rental Try Europa Bicycles, Earls Island, opposite the cathedral (ⓣ091/563355), or Mountain Trail, Middle St (ⓣ091/569888).
Bookshops Charlie Byrne's, The Cornstore, Middle St, is a good second-hand and discounted bookshop; Eason's, 33 Shop St, is a huge general bookshop with foreign newspapers; Hughes and Hughes, Galway Shopping Centre, is a relaxed bookshop with a wide-ranging stock and pleasant coffee shop; and Kenny's Bookshop, on High St, is regarded by many as one of the best antiquarian bookshops in the country and has a small art gallery attached.
Car rental Avis, by the Galway Shopping Centre on Headford Rd and at Carnmore Airport ⓣ091/530440, ⓦwww.avis.com; Windsor, Monivea Rd, Ballybrit ⓣ091/770707, ⓦwww.galway-guide.com.
Gay and lesbian information lines Gay men ⓣ091/566134 Tues & Thurs 8–10pm, recorded information at other times; lesbians ⓣ091/564611 Wed 8–10pm.
Helplines Samaritans, 14 Nun's Island Rd ⓣ091/561222; Rape Crisis Centre, 3 Augustine St ⓣ1850/355355.
Horse riding Clonboo Riding School, Clonboo Cross, Corrundulla, off the N84 ⓣ091/791362; Rusheen Riding Centre, at the west end of Salthill ⓣ091/521285.
Hospital University College Hospital, Newcastle Rd ⓣ091/524222.
Internet Celtel e.centre, Merchants Rd, Eyre Square, underneath *Kinlay Hostel* ⓣ091/566620, ⓦwww.celtel.ie; Hotlines, 4 High St ⓣ091/562838.
Laundry At the hostels, or try The Bubbles Inn, 18 Mary St ⓣ091/563434.
Left luggage At the train station (Mon–Sat 7.15am–9pm, Sun 10am–9pm; €2.50) or the hostels.
Market For more than just fruit and vegetables, try the Saturday market around St Nicholas' Church, where stalls sell everything from handmade cheeses to sculptured bog oak. There's also a junk and antiques market beneath the medieval walls inside the Eyre Square Centre (Fri & Sat).
Music Mulligan, 5 Middle St (ⓣ091/564961, ⓦindigo.ie/~mulligan), for traditional, world music, jazz, country, folk and blues on tape, vinyl and CD; Wax Factor, 7 Mainguard St (ⓣ091/539149), specializes in dance music on vinyl and CD.
Parking Buy a disc from a newsagent at €0.80 per hour for on-street parking, or use a car park – useful locations include next to the tourist office on Forster St and the multistoreys on Dock Rd and Merchant Rd.
Police Mill St ⓣ091/538300.
Taxis Big-O, 21 Upper Dominick St ⓣ091/585858; Street Taxi, by the *Living Room* bar on Bridge St ⓣ091/563888; and taxi ranks at Eyre Square.
Tours If you're short on time, you might want to sign up for a bus tour of Connemara or the Burren at the tourist office (€20–25 for a full day). Operators include Bus Eireann (ⓣ091/562000, ⓦwww.buseireann.ie), Lally's (ⓣ091/562905, ⓦwww.lallytours.com) and O'Neachtain (ⓣ091/553188, ⓦwww.wombat.ie/pages/oneachtain-tours).
Train enquiries ⓣ091/561444.
Travel agents USIT, Mary St (ⓣ091/565177) and at the New Science Building on the university campus (ⓣ091/524601), is the best agent for youth and student travel.
Wind-surfing At Rusheen Bay, at the west end of Salthill ⓣ086/260 5702.

East Galway

East Galway (ⓦwww.eastgalway.com) cannot rival the spectacular landscapes of west Galway or County Clare, nor their romantic isolation. Nonetheless, to hurry through east Galway without seeing what the place does have to offer would be a mistake. A lot of the land here is low-lying and easily cultivable, attributes which made it attractive to earlier settlers. They've left not only a network of roads and villages, but also a wealth of historic remains, particularly medieval monastic sites. And while the landscape is never exciting, some of it is very pleasant, notably the lakesides of **Lough Derg** at **Portumna** and the delightful southern shore of **Galway Bay**, which becomes particularly special where the heights of the Burren of County Clare become a part of the scene. Added to this is the historical importance of eastern Galway, from the walled town of **Athenry** to the village of **Aughrim**, scene of the bloodiest battle in Irish history.

Galway Bay and the south

The countryside in the south of the county, around the southern shores of Galway Bay and on towards Clare, is some of the prettiest in Galway, and was greatly loved by Yeats, Lady Gregory and others associated with the Gaelic League. The main N18 road round the bay from the city is a busy one, passing through the villages of Galway's "**oyster country**" – Oranmore, Clarinbridge and Kilcolgan (where the main road leaves the water to head south towards Ennis) – and bringing plenty of visitors, particularly during the **Clarinbridge Oyster Festival** (Ⓣ091/796359) over the second weekend in September. The most famous of the **oyster pubs** are *Paddy Burke's Oyster Tavern* at Clarinbridge (Ⓣ091/796226) and *Moran's of the Weir*, a bar-restaurant in a beautiful waterside setting at Kilcolgan (Ⓣ091/796113).

Kinvarra

Set in the southeasterly inlet of Galway Bay, the charming little quayside village of **KINVARRA** is something of a satellite playground for Galway city. Down at the tranquil harbourside, with its smattering of pubs and restaurants, swans drift across the water to **Dunguaire Castle**. The castle (mid-April to mid-Oct daily 9.30am–5pm; €4) was built in 1520 and is a particularly good example of a **tower house**. These tower houses or "castles" were in fact fortified houses, very much a fashion for wealthy landowners from 1450 to 1650, and are found in their greatest concentration in east Clare, east Limerick and south Galway. This is a great one to visit, as the guide delivers a vigorous interpretation of both local history and the political importance of the old building. The castle also hosts medieval banquets, with a literary pageant, a harpist and singers, and decent food (mid-April to mid-Oct twice nightly, subject to demand; €42; Ⓣ061/360788), and, more mundanely, a bureau de change (there's no bank in Kinvarra).

All in all, Kinvarra's a lively spot, and there's enough variety in the area to warrant a reasonable stay between the rigours of Burren-walking and Galway city life. **Bus** #50 serves Kinvarra from Galway city once daily in winter and up to seven times a day in summer. The informative *Kinvarra: A Ramblers Map and Guide*, by Anne Korff and Jeff O'Connell (€2.50), is available in the Londis supermarket and is worth buying for exploration of the immediate countryside.

Locals are not quite sure what to make of a new landmark in the main street: the *Merriman* **hotel** (Ⓣ091/638222, Ⓦwww.merrimanhotel.com; ❹; closed Jan), which claims to have one of the largest thatched roofs in the country (thatch from Turkey, thatchers from England). It has tasteful interiors, comfortable bedroms, a fine restaurant and a pleasant pub with decent bar food, *M'Asal Beag Dubh*. If you would prefer to stay in a **B&B**, *Cois Cuain* (Ⓣ091/637119; ❶; April–Oct), a cottage with a fine garden down by the quays, is hard to beat, while *Fallon's* (Ⓣ091/638088; ❷), above the supermarket, has a less appealing setting but is central, popular and features all en-suite rooms. Also recommended is *Larkin's Barn Lodge* (Ⓣ091/637548; ❷), a friendly country house set back off the road, five minutes' drive from the village towards Kilcolgan. The IHH- and IHO-affiliated **hostel**, *Johnston's*, on Main St (Ⓣ091/637164,

Ⓔchanley@snet.net; closed Sept to mid-July), offers good communal accommodation, as well as family rooms and laundry facilities. To lose yourself in Galway's rugged beauty, however, it's best to make your way a few miles out of town to the hostel in Doorus (see below).

Besides the *Merriman*, good **places to eat** in Kinvarra include *The Pier Head Bar and Restaurant* (Ⓣ091/638188), which has a good reputation locally and fine views of the harbour and bay, and *Rosaleen's*, a little way up Main Street on The Square, a pleasant, inexpensive café-restaurant, which features tasty vegetarian dishes such as carrot and almond loaf. Kinvarra's **bars** are also worthy of exploration: *The Auld Plaid Shawl*, birthplace of nineteenth-century poet Francis Fahy and named after his most famous song, is a good starting point; *Winkles* can be great fun, especially if you join in the set dancing on a Friday night; *Tully's* is a charming place for a civilized pint; and *Greene's* is a lively, old-fashioned spot which frequently has great music sessions. Kinvarra's early spring music **festival**, the *Fleadh na gCuach* (the Cuckoo Fleadh), is held over the May bank-holiday weekend, while the *Cruinniú na mBáid* (the Meeting of the Boats) usually takes place over the second weekend in August, depending on the tides, and involves, along with singing and dancing, the racing of Galway's traditional fishing vessels – Galway hookers – which can often be seen docked in the harbour. Two-hour **hooker trips** are available from the pier in summer for €20 per person (Ⓣ087/231 1779).

The Doorus Peninsula

In addition to all its other attractions, this part of south Galway is closely associated with the poetry of the literary revival group of Yeats, Lady Gregory, Æ and Douglas Hyde; it was in what is now the An Óige hostel on the **Doorus Peninsula**, four miles northwest of Kinvarra, that the idea of a national theatre was first discussed – later to become the Abbey Theatre in Dublin. The hostel was then the home of Count Florimond de Basterot, who entertained and encouraged the group (and also the likes of Guy de Maupassant and Paul Bourget); it's easy to appreciate how the group's romantic nationalist and artistic sensibilities were stirred in this serene location. Given the political implications of the Irish literary revival, it's perhaps ironic that Count Florimond's cash came from French estates which his fleeing aristocratic ancestors had somehow hung onto despite the Revolution.

The small, quiet Doorus Peninsula was an island until the eighteenth century and provides ample opportunity for scenic walks or cycle rides. You can stay at the welcoming An Óige **hostel** (Ⓣ091/637512), which has private rooms (depending on demand; ❶), dorms, a shop and internet access. From Galway, there are 2–5 **buses** a day to Doorus Cross, leaving you with a two-mile walk, and one at 5pm Monday–Friday to the *Travellers' Inn* pub and shop, which will leave a half-mile walk. One of the best local **B&Bs** is *Burren View* (Ⓣ091/637142, Ⓔburrenviewdoorus@eircom.net; ❶; Easter–Oct), set on a farm with great views of the hills. The gentle waters to the south are pleasant, tidal backwaters that contrast sharply with the wide sweep of Traught Blue Flag **beach** to the north, which is stony but safe for swimming and surfing – there's a lifeguard on duty in summer. The beach at Parkmore, to the northeast, however, is dangerous.

Coole Park and around

Back on the Ennis road, the N18, two miles to the north of Gort, you'll find **Coole Park**, the old demesne of the house of Lady Gregory, much visited by Yeats, and the subject of some of his most famous poetry. All that remains of the house itself (another victim of the 1922 Civil War) are some crumbling walls and a stableyard, but the grounds and the lake are now a particularly beautiful forest park, laid out with two signposted nature trails. Sadly, its **autograph tree**, a great copper beech bearing the graffiti of George Bernard Shaw, Sean O'Casey, Augustus John and others, has been railed off to stop the less famous getting in on the act. A visitor centre (Easter–May Tues–Sun 10am–5pm; June–Aug daily 10am–6pm; Sept daily 10am–5pm; €2.50; Heritage Card), with exhibits on Coole, its flora and fauna and Lady Gregory, and a pleasant tearoom have been opened by the stables.

One mile north of here is the small intersection known as **Kiltartan Cross**, immortalized by W.B. Yeats in his much-quoted poem *An Irish Airman Foresees his Death*, in which the hero of the poem, William Greg, a fighter pilot in World War I, reflects on his role in the war and imminent death:

Those that I fight I do not hate, Those that I guard I do not love;
My country is Kiltartan Cross, My countrymen Kiltartan's poor,
No likely end could bring them loss Or leave them happier than before.

The spot is marked by the **Kiltartan Gregory Museum** (April, May, Sept & Oct Sun 1–5pm; June–Aug daily 10am–5.30pm; to arrange a visit at other times call ⓣ091/632346; €2), a small interpretative centre situated in an unusually designed schoolhouse that was built by Greg's father in the style of those he saw while working in India.

A mile further north of here there are signposts for **Thoor Ballylee** (June–Aug daily 10am–6pm; Sept Mon–Sat 10am–6pm; €5), a fourteenth-century tower house which Yeats bought for £35 in 1916, renovated and made his home off and on over the next ten years. A short film tells the story of Yeats's life, rare and first editions of his work are on show, and readings of his verse are relayed into the spartan rooms of the tower. Alongside is a seasonal **tourist office** (June–Sept Mon–Sat 10am–6pm; ⓣ091/631436) and a very cosy tearoom.

Four miles southwest of Gort, just off the Corofin road, lie the remains of **Kilmacduagh**, a monastic settlement founded by St Colman Mac Duagh around 632. The sheer quantity of buildings – dating from the eleventh to the thirteenth centuries – is more impressive than any particular architectural detail: a cathedral, four churches, the Glebe House and a leaning round tower 115ft high, all on one site. And the setting, against the shimmering, distant Burren slopes, lends something magical to the ancient grey stone.

Portumna

PORTUMNA, on the north shore of Lough Derg thirty miles east of Gort on the R353, is a traditional market town and Shannon crossing point, happy to be cashing in on the tourism that drifts its way on the lough cruisers, yet still retaining a friendly and unpretentious character. Close to the shore, where there's a swimming area with changing rooms and showers in the summer, stands the ruin of **Portumna Priory**, for the most part a fifteenth-century Dominican building, though its delicately arched cloisters were built around the remains of a much earlier Cistercian foundation. Nearby **Portumna Castle** (April–Oct daily 10am–6pm; €1.90; Heritage Card), a fine, early seventeenth-century fortified mansion with Jacobean gables (something of a rarity in Ireland), was gutted by fire in 1826 and is currently being renovated. Work is under way to open up the first floor, for a better appreciation of the internal architecture and views of the lake, but currently you're confined to the ground floor, which is arrayed with interesting display boards on the de Burgo family who lived here, the house and its conservation. Look out for the gun holes in the impressively thick walls, reflecting how unsettled life was in seventeenth-century Ireland. In front of the house, the elegant Renaissance garden, one of the first in Ireland, has been recreated, as has the walled kitchen garden to one side. Part of the castle's estate – still home to a large herd of fallow deer – now constitutes the **Portumna Forest Park** (entered from the castle or off the Gort road to the west of town), where you can stroll along marked trails through the woodland to the lakeshore.

From the harbour by the priory, the Portumna Passenger Boat Company (Ⓣ086/391 8364) lays on hour-long **cruises** (June–Aug 4 daily) or trips across to Terryglass on the Tipperary side of the lake (April, May & early Sept 4 daily) for €12 a head. If you're so tempted by the water that you want to live on it for a week or two, contact Emerald Star, which rents cruisers from the marina at the east end of town (Ⓣ090/974 1120, Ⓦwww.emeraldstar.ie).

There are several good **B&Bs** in the centre of Portumna: try Mrs Ryan's *Auvergne Lodge* on Dominic Street (Ⓣ090/974 1138, Ⓔauvergnelodge@eircom.net; ❷), a friendly family home with good child reductions, or the Dolans' *Shannon Villa*, Bridge Road (Ⓣ090/974 1269; ❷), where you can get dinner and relax in the peaceful conservatory. If you fancy something a bit swankier, book into the *Shannon Oaks Hotel and Country Club* (Ⓣ090/974 1777, Ⓦwww.shannonoaks.ie; ❻), which boasts a long list of facilities including a swimming pool and gym. The town's IHH **hostel**, *Galway Shannonside*, St Brigid's Road (Ⓣ090/974 1032, Ⓔgalwayshannonside@eircom.net), is in a restored nineteenth-century schoolhouse and is one of the finest hostels in the country. There are double and family rooms, a laundry, an exceptionally comfortable common room, a generous breakfast of juice, freshly brewed ground coffee, cereal and toast, and the owner offers all manner of guided tours of the locality.

You'll find a couple of very friendly **places to eat** in the main street: *An Bialann*, a reasonably priced café-restaurant serving an impressive and diverse menu; and the *Beehive* (closed Sun lunchtime & Mon), which serves exceptional pizzas and is very popular locally. Although small, Portumna has an astounding twenty-one **pubs**, and there's no shortage of ballad sessions, especially on Saturday nights in summer – the *Corner House* offers regular nights hosted by owner and guitarist John Horan.

Athenry and Loughrea

ATHENRY, thirteen miles east of Galway city, is renowned for the song *The Fields of Athenry*, a poignant indictment of the horrors of the Famine that has mutated into a drunken closing-time song and a football terrace chant. However, the town's history has little to do with the Famine and more to do with its position as a strategic crossing point on the River Clareen (reflected in its Gaelic name Baile Átha an Rí, which means "town of the ford of the king"). Large portions of its Norman town walls have survived, along with a tower gate, five flanking towers and the thirteenth-century **castle** with its stout three-storey keep (April, May & mid-Sept to Oct Tues–Sun 10am–5pm; June to mid-Sept daily 10am–6pm; €2.50), all of which are impressively intact. The narrow streets retain their medieval layout, while the modern town is still contained within the original walls. The town has a good **heritage centre** (daily 10am–6pm; Ⓦwww.athenryheritagetown.com; €3.50), housed in an eighteenth-century church, which itself was built among the ruins of the thirteenth-century St Mary's Church. Walking tours of the town can be arranged at the centre.

LOUGHREA, ten miles southeast of Athenry, is a small lakeside market town that suffers from its position right on the busy N6. In the thirteenth century, Richard de Burgo built a castle and a **Carmelite monastery** here, and the latter still stands in an excellent state of preservation on the north side of the centre. The town's late nineteenth-century **cathedral**, St Brendan's, a product of the Celtic Revival and Arts and Crafts movements, is most notable for its stained glass – an acquired taste, but one that's made more accessible by the church's detailed leaflet and audio tour. Much earlier religious art is on display next door in the **Clonfert Museum** (by appointment only, ⓣ091/841212; free), which includes beautifully simple silver and gold chalices from as early as 1500 and a few rare wood-carvings from the twelfth and thirteenth centuries.

Three miles to the north of Loughrea, next to the Turoe Pet Farm near Bullaun, stands the **Turoe Stone**. This superb, rounded pillar-stone is decorated with the bold swirls of Celtic La Tène art, a style found more typically in Brittany. The finest of its kind in Ireland, it dates from the third or second century BC and was probably a phallic fertility stone. Four miles east of Loughrea off the N6, those of a horsey persuasion might be tempted by the **Dartfield Horse Museum** (daily 9am–6pm; ⓣ091/843968, ⓦwww.dartfieldhorsemuseum.com; €5), to watch equine audio-visual displays, try out a riding machine and go into the stables to admire the beasts. Pony and carriage rides are also on offer, as well as more serious treks and lessons.

For **B&B** accommodation in Loughrea, try Mrs Pauline Burke's *Four Seasons*, Athenry Road (ⓣ091/541414; ②). Alternatively, there's a fine **hotel**, the well-established *O'Dea's*, in a cosy, converted Georgian town house on Bride Street (ⓣ091/841611, ⓦwww.commerce.ie/odeashotel; ⑤). Among the town's **places to eat**, *Catherine's Kitchen*, a bakery on Barrack Road, is a good daytime option, offering good, fresh sandwiches and simple meals.

Aughrim and Kilconnell Friary

Tiny **AUGHRIM**, fourteen miles from Loughrea and just short of Ballinasloe, was the scene in 1691 of a key battle in the Williamite Wars, in which the Irish and French forces, retreating westwards towards the ports of Galway and Limerick, were decisively defeated. The **Battle of Aughrim Interpretative Centre** (June–Aug Tues–Sat 10am–6pm, Sun 2–6pm; €3) explains the significance of the battle – the bloodiest in Irish history with over nine thousand casualties – and places the Williamite Wars in the context of seventeenth-century European power struggles. The adjacent *Hynes* **hostel** (IHH & IHO; ⓣ090/967 3734) has a small number of dorms, twins and family rooms, offers camping and bike rental and is attached to the local pub, which has music at weekends during the summer.

Four miles to the northwest of Aughrim lie the very beautiful remains of the Franciscan **Kilconnell Friary**, which held out successfully against Cromwellian attack in 1651. The ruins are extensive, with additions to the early fourteenth-century building showing that there was increased monastic activity in the later Middle Ages. There's a very pretty arcaded cloister, and in the north wall of the nave are two splendid canopied wall-tombs.

Ballinasloe

BALLINASLOE is the main town in east Galway, important as a crossing point of the River Suck since 1124 when Turlough O'Conor, King of Connacht, built a **castle** here – the remains that can be seen today date mainly from the fourteenth century. You're only really likely to be here if you've come for the famous **horse fair**, which starts on the last weekend in September or the first in October and lasts for eight days. The largest of the ancient fairs left in the country, drawing horse dealers from all over Ireland and England, it gives a fascinating glimpse into a way of life that is slowly disappearing. The bartering is very much a game, though a serious one. Generally, both parties know the value of the horse in question but enjoy the bartering ritual anyway, with its possibilities of outdoing an opponent. The logic seems to be that if you're not up to the bartering, you don't deserve the right price for the animal.

If you intend to visit the fair, you'll have to book accommodation well in advance. The **tourist office**, part of Keller Travel, Main St (July & Aug Mon–Sat 10am–6pm; ⓣ090/964 2131), can give you more information on accommodation around the region and make bookings. The main **hotel** in town is *Hayden's* in Dunlo Street (ⓣ090/964 2347, ⓦwww.lynchotels.com; ❹), which is good value and has a decent self-service restaurant that's a popular and convenient stop for drivers on their way to Connemara. For a **B&B**, try Mrs Ann Quinn's, Harbour Road (ⓣ090/964 3495; ❷).

The east shore of Lough Corrib

The east shore of Lough Corrib provides a gentle passage from Galway city north into County Mayo, far less dramatic than the Connemara roads, whether you follow the N84 to Headford, which would leave you well placed for Cong across the county border (see p.516), or the more easterly but faster N17 via Tuam. The lake shore and the many rivers are popular with fishermen (for trout and salmon in summer, pike in winter), while visitors with no taste for field sports have a number of medieval remains to admire.

Two miles north of Headford, virtually on the border of County Mayo, is **Ross Errilly** (or Ross Abbey), the biggest and best-preserved Franciscan abbey in Ireland. It was founded in the mid-fourteenth century, but the bulk of the buildings belong to the fifteenth – the Franciscan order's greatest period of expansion. The church buildings themselves are impressive, with a battlemented slender tower (typical of Franciscan abbeys) and well-preserved windows, and there's a wonderful tiny cloister, but it's the adjacent domestic buildings and the picture they give of the everyday life of the order that are perhaps the most interesting. Stand in the cloister with your back to the church and you'll see the refectory ahead and to the right, with the reader's window-side desk up in the far northeast corner. Straight ahead is a second cloister (this one without arcading) and behind that the bakehouse. To the northwest of this second courtyard lies the kitchen, where you can see a water-tank used for holding fish and an oven which reaches into the little mill-room to the rear.

Ten miles southeast of Headford off the N84 in the townland of Corrandulla, you'll find one of the area's most unusual **places to stay**: the seventeenth-century *Cregg Castle* (ⓣ091/791434, ⓔcreggcas@indigo.ie; ❻), a place of beautiful faded splendour. Everything here is geared towards relaxation (with breakfast till noon) and conviviality: the owners are garrulous traditional musicians and enjoy evenings with guests around the log fire in the Great Hall.

Tuam and around

Northeast County Galway is served chiefly by the small market town of **TUAM** (pronounced *Choom*). There's little here to detain you, but should you wish to sniff out the scant remnants of the town's historical importance as the seat of an archbishop and a medieval power centre of the O'Conors of Connacht, have a look inside the Church of Ireland **cathedral** on Galway Road. It's primarily a nineteenth-century building, but survivals from the twelfth-century chancel include a magnificent Romanesque arch, showing strong signs of Scandinavian influence, and the accompanying east window.

Tuam's **tourist office** is located in the Mill Museum, which houses the only preserved corn mill in western Ireland (mid-June to mid-Sept Mon–Sat 10am–5.30pm; ⓣ093/25486). If you're stuck for a **B&B**, try Mrs O'Connor's peaceful and spacious *Kilmore House*, Galway Road (ⓣ093/28118, ⓔkilmore-house@mail.com; ❷), on a farm half a mile out of town. For **eating**, the place to go is *Cré na Cille* on High Street (ⓣ093/28232), which serves high-quality food at low prices.

Seven miles southeast of Tuam off the N63 Galway–Roscommon road, it's worth visiting **Knockmoy Abbey**, a Cistercian foundation of 1190. The most remarkable feature of the abbey is on the north wall of the chancel, where you'll see one of Ireland's few surviving medieval frescoes. Extremely faint (only the black outlines retain their original colour), it depicts the legend of the Three Dead Kings and the Three Live Kings. Under the dead kings an inscription reads "We have been as you are, you shall be as we are"; the live kings are out hawking. Underneath this is a picture of Christ holding his hand up in blessing and a barely visible angel with scales.

The Aran Islands

The **Aran Islands – Inishmore**, **Inishmaan** and **Inisheer** – lying about thirty miles out across the mouth of Galway Bay, have exerted a fascination over visitors for centuries. Their geology creates one of the most distinctive landscapes in Ireland, their limestone pavement giving the islands a stark character akin to the Burren of County Clare. This spectacular setting contains a wealth of pre-Christian and early Christian remains and some of the finest archaeological sites in Europe. And it's not only works in stone that have survived out here: the islands are Irish-speaking, and up until the early part of the last century a primitive way of life persisted, a result of the isolation enforced by the Atlantic.

The most detailed **map and guidebook** of the islands is produced by Tim Robinson of Roundstone, available on Inishmore and at bookshops and tourist offices in the Galway and Clare area. In fact the Aran Islands are quite easy to explore and the map isn't essential for finding the major sites. It is, however, of great value to those interested in detailed archaeology and in Irish place names. Although it's possible to do **day-trips** from Galway to the islands, you really need two full days to see the main sites of Inishmore alone, and an overnight stay on Inisheer or Inishmaan adds a priceless dimension to a visit. For more detailed information on transport to the islands see box overleaf.

Some history

The Aran Islands abound with evidence of their **early inhabitants**: the earliest ring forts possibly date from the Iron Age (c. 400 BC–500 AD), though recent research suggests that some of the larger structures may be even earlier, perhaps Late Bronze Age (c. 700 BC). The next group of people to feature are the **Christians**, who came here to study at the foundation of St Enda in the fifth century and went on to found Iona, Clonmacnois and Kilmacduagh. However, the earliest surviving ecclesiastical remains date from the eighth century.

As Galway's trade grew, so the strategic importance of the islands increased, and in **medieval** times control of them was disputed by the O'Flahertys of Connacht and the O'Briens of Munster, the latter generally maintaining the upper hand. In 1565, Queen Elizabeth resolved the dispute by granting the islands to an Englishman on condition he kept soldiers there to guarantee the Crown's interests. In the mid-seventeenth century the islands lost their political usefulness; the Cromwellian soldiers garrisoned there simply transferred to the new regime after the Restoration and became absorbed into the islands' traditional way of life.

After the decline of English interest and influence, the islands fell into poverty, aggravated in the nineteenth century by rack-renting. That rents should be levied on this barren rock suggests a cruel avarice and, not surprisingly, Aranmen were active in the **Land League** agitations: acts of defiance included walking the landlord's cattle blindfold over the Dún Aengus cliff edge. Despite this link with the general political movement on the mainland and the islands' use as a refuge for Nationalists during the War of Independence, it is their isolation, allowing the continuation of a unique and ancient culture that has proved so alluring to outsiders.

Transport to the Aran Islands

Several ferry companies and one airline operate between the mainland and the Aran Islands. As with any of the services to islands off the west coast, it's a good idea to check on the latest schedules (especially for return or inter-island journeys), as they fluctuate according to season and demand – in summer extra services may be laid on, but during winter you're at the mercy of the weather, and there's a chance you'll get cut off from the mainland.

Inismór Ferries In the tourist office or at 29 Forster St, Galway ⓣ091/566535, ⓦwww.queenofaran2.com. The *Queen of Aran II* operates from Rossaveel (Ros an Mhil, around thirty miles west of Galway) to Inishmore (3–4 daily; 35min; €19 return, €10 single), with coach connections to and from Galway for each sailing. This is the only company owned by the islanders, and offers a good hostellers' deal of return fare plus one night, with breakfast, in *Mainistir House* (see p.477) for €20.

Island Ferries Victoria Place, Galway ⓣ091/568903, evenings ⓣ091/572273, ⓦwww.aranislandferries.com. Boats from Rossaveel to Inishmore (2–4 daily; 35min), Inishmaan (1–2 daily; 50min) and Inisheer (1–2 daily; 1hr); returns cost €19 and singles €10, with coach connections to and from Galway for each sailing.

Doolin Ferries Doolin Pier ⓣ065/707 4455, ⓦwww.doolinferries.com. Operates in summer (the season varies) from Doolin to Inisheer (1–2 daily; 40min) and to Inishmore (1–2 daily; duration depends on number of stops on the way), sometimes calling at Inishmaan. Prices range from €15 to €32, depending on the number of islands you take in.

O'Brien Shipping Under the same owners as Doolin Ferries, with a desk in the tourist office in Galway ⓣ091/567283 or 567676. The main cargo and year-round passenger link for all three islands, sailing at least three times a week from Galway to Inishmore (2hr if direct, but 4–6hr if via the other islands), Inishmaan and Inisheer, on a complex and sometimes unreliable schedule. Fares to each island cost €15 for a return and €10 single; single tickets between islands cost €6.

Aer Árann Based at the airstrip at Inverin, west of Spiddal ⓣ091/593034, ⓦwww.aerarann.ie. Runs flights from Inverin to Inishmore (4 daily in winter, up to 8 or more in summer), and to Inishmaan and Inisheer (usually at least 2 daily). All flights take 10min and cost €22.86 single, €44.44 return; coach connections to and from Galway for most flights.

The Gaelic Revival

With the burgeoning fascination for all things Gaelic from the 1890s onwards, the Aran Islands, along with the Blaskets, became the subject of great sociological and linguistic enquiry, the most famous of their literary visitors being J.M. Synge. His writings brought the islands to the attention of other intellectuals involved in the **Gaelic Revival**, and the notion of a surviving community of pure Gaels provided fuel for the Nationalist movement. Ironically, this notion may have been misconceived. The distinct physical type found on Aran – the dark skin, large brow and Roman nose – is, some argue, the legacy of the Cromwellian soldiers who were left on the islands. The islands themselves have produced many fine writers: Liam O'Flaherty from Inishmore wrote several acclaimed novels, most notably *The Informer* (1925) and *Famine* (1937), while Gaelic poet Máirtín Ó'Direáin wrote twentieth-century verse describing the hardship of island life *ag coraíocht leis an gcarraig lom* ("wrestling with the bare rock").

In 1934, Robert Flaherty made his classic documentary *Man of Aran*, which recorded the ancient and disappearing culture he found here. (The film can be seen at the Aran Heritage Centre in Kilronan.) While the **folklore and traditions** recorded in the film have obviously declined, *currachs* – light wood-framed boats covered formerly with hide, now with tar-coated canvas – are still used for fishing and for getting ashore on the smaller islands when the ferry can't pull in, and you may even witness, as in the film, a man fishing with a simple line off the edge of a two-hundred-foot cliff. Fishing and farming are still very much a way of life on Inishmaan, while tourism is the major earner on Inishmore and Inisheer. This means that, though their purpose will change, knowledge of these customs and skills will not vanish, and tourism may even help ensure the language survives, as Irish provides the islanders with a curtain of privacy against the visitors.

Inishmore

Although there's some truth behind the attitude that does down **Inishmore** (Inis Mór, "Big Island", but often referred to simply as "Aran") as the most tourist-oriented and least "authentic" of the Aran Islands, its wealth of dramatic ancient sites overrides such considerations. Increased numbers of minibuses and bicycles can make the main road west across the island to Kilmurvey pretty hectic in high season, but you can still escape what crowds there are by taking the less hilly coast road along the north shore or by walking along the southerly, partly paved "rock road," which cuts across the highest part of the island.

It's a long strip of an island, a great tilted plateau of limestone, with a scattering of **villages** along the sheltered northerly coast. The land slants up to the southern edge, where tremendous **cliffs** rip along the entire length of the island. Walking anywhere on this high southern side, you can see the geological affinity with the Burren of County Clare and visualize the time when these islands were part of a barrier enclosing what is now Galway Bay. As far as the eye can see is a tremendous patterning of stone, some of it the bare formation of the land (the pavementing of grey rock split in bold parallel grooves), some the form of the hundreds of miles of dry-stone walls, which parcel up the man-made fields, painstakingly nurtured out of sand, seaweed and what handfuls of soil there are. The textures blur so that it's impossible to make sense of planes and distances, the only certainties being the stark outline of the cliffs' edges and the constant pounding of the waves below. Across the water the Connemara

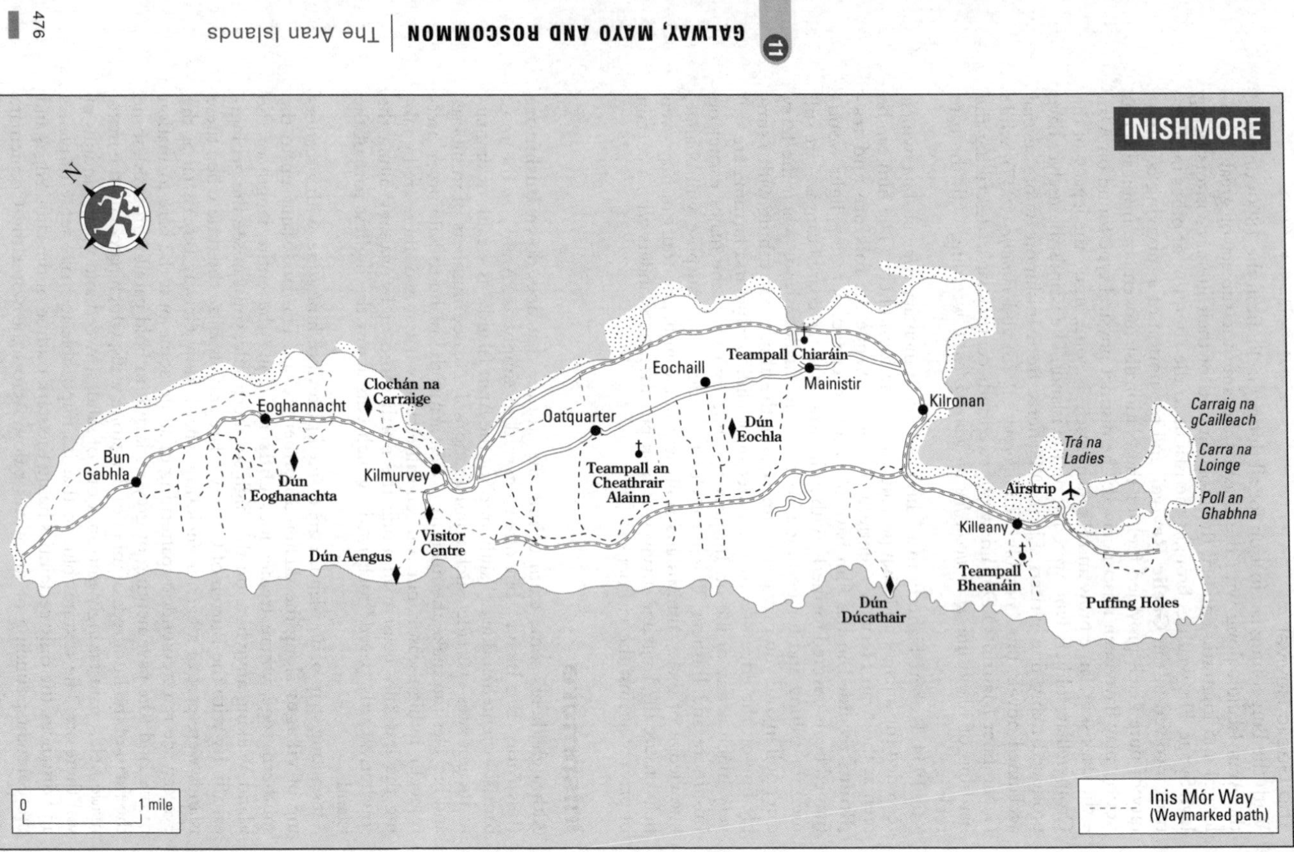
INISHMORE
N
Bun Gabhla
Eoghannacht
Dún Eoghanachta
Clochán na Carraige
Kilmurvey
Visitor Centre
Dún Aengus
Oatquarter
Teampall an Cheathrair Alainn
Eochaill
Dún Eochla
Teampall Chiaráin
Mainistir
Kilronan
Dún Dúcathair
Killeany
Teampall Bheanáin
Airstrip
Trá na Ladies
Carraig na gCailleach
Carra na Loinge
Poll an Ghabhna
Puffing Holes
0
1 mile
Inis Mór Way
(Waymarked path)

mountains stand in contrast, coloured pink and golden and slaty blue in the evening sunlight, while around to the southeast, appearing as just a silvery ridge, are the Cliffs of Moher.

Getting around, information and accommodation

The best way to **get around** Inishmore is by a combination of cycling and walking. You can rent **bikes** from Aran Bicycle Hire, beside the pier in Kilronan, the main village where the ferry docks, or Burkes, next to the helpful **tourist office** (daily: hours variable, rising from 10am–4pm in winter to 10am–6.30pm at the height of summer, with an hour's lunch-break; Ⓣ099/61263), a couple of minutes' walk from the pier. **Pony buggies** will take you on a round tour (about €15 per person in a group of four, depending on how far you go), as will the **minibuses** that line up at the pier waiting for the boats to come in. The latter follow an established route around the island that takes two hours or more, including an hour at Dún Aengus, and charge €10 per person; you could also negotiate with them for a taxi service. There is also a twice-daily public minibus, but limited space means it is best left for the islanders.

There are six **hostels** on Inishmore, two of which are in downtown Kilronan: the IHO-affiliated *Kilronan Hostel* (Ⓣ099/61255, Ⓔkilronanhostel@ireland.com), which has family rooms available and is handy if you want to spend the night in the pub below, but noisy if you don't; and *St Kevin's Hostel* (Ⓣ099/61484; summer only), which offers adequate dorm beds. At the northern edge of Kilronan, the *Artist's Lodge Hostel* (Ⓣ099/61457), which is simple but offers good views of Connemara, and the small *Aharla Hostel* (Ⓣ099/61305) are next to each other at the start of the coast road, just down from *Joe Watty's* pub (see p.480). Away from the hub of Kilronan, one of the most tranquil spots to stay, with a pretty garden and great views, is the well-equipped, spacious IHO-affiliated *Pilgrim Hostel* (Ⓣ099/61393; April–Oct), located just above the village of Killeany, overlooked by Teampall Bheanáin and signposted from the main road. On the main road to Kilmurvey is the *Mainistir House Hostel* at Mainistir (Ⓣ099/61169), a comfortable hostel, which has single and twin rooms and does excellent, mostly vegetarian buffets in the evenings and breakfasts of porridge and freshly baked bread.

Among a dozen or so **B&Bs** in Kilronan, *Seacrest* (Ⓣ099/61292; ❷) is a good bet, with smart en-suite rooms, a spacious living room and hearty breakfasts. The slightly upmarket *Pier House* (Ⓣ099/61417, Ⓕ61122; ❸) occupies a peerless spot by the jetty with panoramic views. One mile east of Kilronan in Killeany is *Tigh Fitz* (Ⓣ099/61213, Ⓦwww.tighfitz.com; ❸), a friendly pub with comfortable rooms above. Towards the west end of the island in Oatquarter, the best-value places to stay are Conneely's *Beach View House* (Ⓣ & Ⓕ099/61141; ❶), overlooking one of the island's idyllic beaches, and *Oatquarter House* (Ⓣ099/61328; ❶), where the friendly Irish-speaking family give a welcome as warm as their bright turf fires. Near the Dún Aengus visitor centre stands *Kilmurvey House* (Ⓣ099/61218, Ⓔkilmurveyhouse@eircom.net; ❸), an impressive 150-year-old country house with a ruined church in its extensive garden. If you have a taste for kitsch, then you'll enjoy staying at the *Man of Aran Cottages* (Ⓣ099/61301, Ⓕ61324; ❷), specifically built for the filming of *The Man of Aran* according to what the film-makers thought traditional Irish cottages should look like.

There is a basic **campsite** (Ⓣ099/61185), with toilets and washbasins but no showers or cooking facilities, a twenty-minute walk from Kilronan – take the main road heading north out of the village and turn right along the coast road in front of *Joe Watty's* pub – but you'd be better off camping in the garden of the *Pilgrim Hostel* (see p.477), where you can share the hostel's facilities. Alternatively, it's just about possible to pitch a tent down by the idyllic beach at Kilmurvey, a lovely sweep of white sand looking out over to the Connemara mountain range, though finding the owner and getting permission is absolutely essential.

There is a surprisingly large and well-stocked Spar **supermarket** in Kilronan, not far from the village **post office**, where the Bank of Ireland opens on Wednesdays (10am–12.30pm & 1.30–2.30pm, 3pm in winter), plus Thursdays in July, August and September. You can also **change money** at the tourist office, the post office and the Aran Heritage Centre, which also offers **Internet** access.

The island

Inishmore's villages are strung along the main road that runs the length of the northern shore, the hub of activity being **KILRONAN**, where the ferry lands. The **Aran Heritage Centre**, *Ionad Árann*, on the right of the main road leading out of Kilronan (daily: April, May, Sept & Oct 11am–5pm; June–Aug 10am–7pm; €3.50 exhibition, €3.50 film, €5.50 for both), provides a fascinating introduction to the island's history, geography and culture and puts on a daily screening of Flaherty's *Man of Aran* (see p.475). There are some great sandy **beaches**: head for the one at **KILMURVEY**, four miles west of Kilronan, which is safe and sheltered with fabulous views of the Connemara mountains, or follow the main road to its eastern extreme and then walk north to get to the safe beaches from Carraig na gCailleach, through Carra na Loinge, down to Poll an Ghabhna. Tucked close to **KILLEANY**, three quarters of a mile to the south of Kilronan, is Cockle Strand, which is also safe for swimming; but beware Tra na Ladies, a little over a mile further on near the airstrip, which looks nice but where you can get caught by tides or sinking sand.

You can **walk** just about anywhere on the island so long as it doesn't look like someone's garden, but be careful when walking on the south of the island in poor visibility, as the cliffs are sheer and sudden. The waymarked **Inis Mór Way** covers the whole of the island on its thirty-mile route, though it can easily be broken up into shorter chunks and satisfying circular walks; a leaflet is available at the tourist office.

Dún Aengus and the forts

The most spectacular of Aran's prehistoric sites is Inishmore's fort of **Dún Aengus** (signposted to the south of Kilmurvey), a massive semicircular ring fort of three concentric enclosures lodged on the edge of cliffs that plunge 300ft into the Atlantic. The inner citadel is a twenty-foot-high, eighteen-foot-wide solid construction of precise blocks of grey stone, their symmetry echoing the almost geometric regularity of the land's limestone pavementing and the bands of rock that form the cliffs. You can still see clearly the *chevaux-de-frise* outside the middle wall, a thirty-foot-wide field bristling with lurching rocks like jagged teeth, designed to slow down any attack.

Daytime access to the site is via the **visitor centre**, built on the site of an early medieval monastery below the fort (daily: April–Oct 10am–6pm; Nov–March 10am–4pm; €1.20; Heritage Card), which compellingly puts Dún Aengus into its historical context based on the results of major excavations carried out here between 1992 and 1995. After hours, you can get up to the fort through the side gate next to the visitor centre.

Prompted by Dún Aengus's extremely exposed location and lack of water, various theories have been put forward over the years about it being a storm temple or some kind of ceremonial theatre, but archaeologists have now returned to the obvious explanation: that it was indeed an inhabited fortress, probably the capital of the Arans, built partly to demonstrate the islands' power when viewed from the sea and located on a site that may have had ritual significance.

The place is tremendously evocative, and it's easy to understand how superstitions have survived on the islands long after their disappearance on the mainland. Visible west of the cliffs of Inishmore under certain meteorological conditions is the outline of what looks like a mountainous island. This is a mirage, a mythical island called *Hy Brasil*, which features in ancient Aran stories as the island of the blessed, visited by saints and heroes – and which was until the sixteenth century actually marked on maps.

Just over a mile west of Kilmurvey, **Dún Eoghanachta** is the smallest of the Aran forts, a perfect circle of rectilinear, almost brick-like stone, settled in a lonely field with the Connemara mountains as a scenic backdrop. The walls of this defended homestead are 16ft thick, and inner steps give access to the parapets. Inside are the foundations of the ancient drystone huts known as *clocháns*.

Dún Dúcathair (the Black Fort) is especially worth visiting for its dramatic location. It's a promontory fort, and what remains is a massive stone wall straddling an ever-shrinking headland precariously placed between cliffs. The eastern gateway fell into the sea early in the last century, leaving the entrance a perilous twelve inches from the sheer drop. Inside are the curved remains of four *clocháns*. It's about a two-mile walk from Kilronan – head south out of the village for three-quarters of a mile, take a turning to the right (signposted to "Cliff House") and follow the lane to the cliffs. If on a bike, be warned: the lane becomes extremely rocky, making cycling impossible. Once at the cliff edge you can see the fort on the second promontory to your left.

The **dating** of these forts is tricky, especially as their functions and significance seem to have varied over the centuries that they were inhabited, but it's clear that all seven forts on the Aran islands were in use around 800 AD, while some are as old as 1100 BC. There's evidence of human activity on the Dún Aengus site from 1500 BC to 1000 AD, with the first enclosure placed around 1100 BC and the most dynamic period of activity around 800 BC. Dún Eoghanachta and **Dún Eochla** (just south off the road to the west of Mainistir) could have been constructed at any time between the first and the seventh century AD – or possibly earlier. The massive buttresses of Dún Eochla are nineteenth-century additions, but the forts have generally been kept in exceptional condition.

Early Christian sites

From the fifth century onwards, the Aran Islands were a centre of monastic learning, the most important of the eremitic settlements being that of St Enda (*Eanna*). At the **seven churches**, just southeast of **EOGHANNACHT** in the far west of the island, there are ancient slabs commemorating seven Romans who died here, testifying to the far-reaching influence of Aran's monastic teaching. The site is in fact that of two churches and several domestic buildings, dating from the eighth to the thirteenth centuries. Here **St Brendan's grave** is adorned by an early cross with interlaced patterns and, on the west side, part of a Crucifixion carving. There are also parts of three high crosses, possibly of the eleventh century, and in the southeast corner of the graveyard, alongside the slabs of the Romans, lie several ninth-century slabs incised with crosses and inscriptions.

The most interesting of the ecclesiastical sites on Inishmore, however, is **Teampall Chiaráin**, a simple twelfth-century church on an old monastic site; take the coast road from Kilronan, opposite *Joe Watty's* pub, and you'll come to it on the left after about a mile. Alongside the church is **St Kieran's Well**, a long U-shaped spring backed by huge blocks of plant-covered stone. It's very pagan-looking – such wells often held sacred significance in pre-Christian times, and were adopted and renamed with the arrival of Christianity. Similarly, some of the tall stones that stand around the site look pre-Christian, even though they have crosses inscribed on them. The one by the east gable has a hole in it that may have held part of a sundial, and nowadays people sometimes pass handkerchiefs through it for luck.

About two miles from Kilronan along the main road across the island, it's well worth breaking your journey at the fifteenth-century **Teampall an Cheathrair Alainn** (the Church of the Four Beauties), named after four saints who are said to have lived and been buried here. This picturesque ruined chapel is reached along a rough, signposted path through grassy fields and over stone walls; water from the well on its south side, hung with crosses and other votive offerings, is believed to cure eye complaints.

Teampall Bheanáin, on the hill behind Killeany, is a pre-Romanesque oratory dating from around the sixth or seventh century, dedicated to St Benen. It's distinguished by its very steep gable ends and its unusual north–south orientation. In all probability, it used to form part of the great early monastic site thought to have been founded by St Enda at Killeany in c. 490, which was torn down by Cromwell's soldiers to build Arkin Castle in the village in 1652.

The finest of Aran's fifty or so *clocháns* is **Clochán na Carraige**, just north of Kilmurvey. This 19ft-long dry-stone hut has a corbelled roof whose arrangement is probably an early Christian design.

Eating, drinking and entertainment

Not surprisingly, **seafood** is the great speciality on the island. The main **restaurant** in Kilronan is the *Dún Aonghasa & Aran Fisherman* (Ⓣ099/61104), which serves quite pricey seafood and meat dishes, plus more reasonable vegetarian options and pizzas. In summer, simpler, better-value lunches and dinners can be had at *The Pier House*. Kilronan also has a fast-food restaurant, *The Ould Pier*, for fish and chips, chowder and other marine delicacies, which you can eat at outdoor tables on fine days. For lunch, your best bet is *Lios Aengus*, a **café** and book exchange by the Spar supermarket, offering good sandwiches, salads and filling daily specials, as well as great coffee.

You can punctuate your cycling or walking with lunch at *Man of Aran Cottages* in Kilmurvey, used as a set in the eponymous film, which also offers upmarket, mostly organic dinners if you book (Ⓣ099/61301); similarly, you could reserve a place for yourself at *Mainistir House Hostel*'s evening buffet (see p.477). While visiting Dún Aengus, you can choose between the sandwiches, soups and cakes at *An Sunda Caoch*, the café by the visitor centre, and the nearby *Tigh Nan Phaid*, a renovated, thatched and whitewashed pub offering seafood and plenty of other refreshments. In the opposite direction, *Tigh Fitz's* at Killeany does daytime bar food.

Tigh Jo Mac's **pub** and *The American Bar* in the centre of Kilronan are convivial enough, but it's still a good idea to wander away from here to sample some of the island's other drinking establishments: *Joe Watty's* on the northern edge of Kilronan, *Cregg's*, a couple of miles west at the top of the main road as it slopes down to the beach at Kilmurvey, and *Tigh Fitz's* in Killeany, are all worth visiting. In addition to these, from June to August there are weekend

céilís in Kilronan parish hall, as well as *Ragús*, a well-regarded show of traditional music and dance (3 shows daily; €12).

Inishmaan

Inishmaan (Inis Meáin, "Middle Island") is the least visited of the three Aran Islands, and locals go about their lives seemingly oblivious to the trickle of tourists who come over. If you've come over from Inishmore, you'll immediately be struck by how much greener Inishmaan is. Brambles and ferns shoot from walls, and bindweed clings to the limestone terraces. Here the warm brown stone walls are remarkably high – up to six feet – and form a stone maze that chequers off tiny fields of lush grass and clover. Yet despite this verdancy, the island still feels dour and desolate. The winter population is only about two hundred, and farming here is almost at subsistence level.

The island is shaped something like an oyster shell. It rises in clear levels from the soft dunes of the north, through stages of flat naked rock, up to minuscule green pastures, then again up to a craggy band of limestone (along which sit the main villages of the island), eventually levelling out on higher ground to meet the crinkled, blowhole-pitted southerly edge.

Inishmaan's most famous visitor was **J.M. Synge**, who stayed here for four summers from 1898, recording the life and language of the people. His play *Riders to the Sea* – which influenced Lorca's *Blood Wedding* – is set here, and his book *The Aran Islands* provides a fascinating insight into the way of life he found. **Synge's Chair**, a sheltered place on the westerly cliffs overlooking St Gregory's Sound, was his favourite contemplative spot, and the thatched, whitewashed cottage he stayed in near Dún Conchúir has been renovated as a small **museum** (May–Sept daily 10.30am–1pm & 2–6pm; €3). Traces of the **culture** he discovered remain. Some of the older women can still be seen wearing traditional brightly coloured shawls; Irish is the main language, though English is understood; and the islanders get on with what they've always done, farming and fishing. There's no hostility to visitors, but tourism isn't the islanders' main concern. If you want to be impressed or entertained, you'll have to look elsewhere.

Synge's Chair, the cottage, all the forts and churches listed below and Trá Leitreach, a safe, sheltered **beach** just north of the pier on the east side of the island, are linked by the **Inis Meáin Way**, a circular, five-mile walking route, which runs across the centre of the island and back and is marked with yellow arrows on limestone plaques.

Forts and churches

One of the most impressive of the Aran forts is Inishmaan's **Dún Conchúir**, situated on elevated ground in the middle of the island and loosely dated between the first and seventh centuries AD, though there may have been a fort on this site as early as 800 BC. Its massive oval wall is almost intact and commands great views of the island, being built on the side of a limestone valley. In myth, Conchúir was the younger brother of Aengus of the Firbolg, commemorated with his own fort on Inishmore, backing up the theory that there was a prehistoric confederation of the islands, with its capital at Dún Aengus.

If you have visited the Hugh Lane Gallery in Dublin (see p.112) and been impressed by the stained glass windows on display there, then you will adore the richly coloured windows from the same workshop of Harry Clarke, in the modern **church** below Dún Conchúir, each depicting a scene from island life amid more traditional Christian iconography.

To the east of Dún Conchúir, the small, rectilinear **Dún Fearbhaí**, probably dating from the ninth century AD or later, looks out over the roofless, eighth-century church, **Cill Cheannannach**, by the shore near the pier.

Practicalities

A **minibus** (Ⓣ087/248 2637) picks up people from the boat, either to ferry them to their accommodation or to give them a tour (price dependent on number of people and extent of tour). Information is available from the **Inishmaan Island Co-operative** (Ⓣ099/73010), near the **post office** in the centre of the island; the Bank of Ireland operates on the second Tuesday of every month.

The small island **hotel**, *Óstan Inis Meáin* (Ⓣ099/73020; ❷), has ten en-suite rooms a short way up from the pier in what's known as Moore Village. If you arrive on spec, you could ask at the pub, about half a mile west of the pier towards the centre of the island, for information about the growing number of **B&Bs**, most of which offer dinner. If you want to book ahead, try the friendly *Ard Álainn* (Ⓣ & Ⓕ099/73027; ❷), a mile or so up the road to Dún Conchúir, the owner of which cooks possibly the most filling breakfast of any B&B in Ireland. Alternatively, *An Dún*, just below Dún Conchúir (Ⓣ & Ⓕ099/73047, Ⓔanduninismeain@eircom.net; ❷), has all en-suite rooms and offers saunas, aromatherapy, good views and pick-ups from the pier; or there's *Tigh Chonghaile*, a spacious, modern house with en-suite bedrooms and views of the Cliffs of Moher, in Moore Village (Ⓣ & Ⓕ099/73085, Ⓔmaireni-chona@hotmail.com; ❷). Most farmers will let you **camp**, but remember to ask them; it's also worth making sure that the knitwear factory is out of earshot before pitching your tent.

There are three **restaurants** – at the B&Bs *An Dún* and *Tigh Chonghaile*, and at the hotel, which also has a bar – and the island's quaint, thatched **pub**, *Teach Ósta*, serves snacks throughout the day during July and August.

There are few other going commercial concerns on the island. Monarcha Cniotála, the **knitwear factory** on the north side of the central village, produces beautifully simple designs in alpaca, linen and wool; it's home, too, to the island's **museum**, a fascinating photographic archive of island history, largely documented in Irish, and a pleasant tearoom. Also based on Inishmaan is the Aran Islands Dive Centre, which organizes **scuba diving** off the Arans in summer (Ⓣ099/73134, Ⓔatlanticdiving@eircom.net).

Inisheer

Inisheer (Inis Oírr, "East Island"), at just under two miles across, is the smallest of the Aran Islands. It doesn't have the archaeological wealth of Inishmore, or the wild solitude of Inishmaan, but regular day-trip ferry services from Doolin bring a constant, if small, flow of visitors. This service also makes for a handy route from County Clare to Connemara. Of course tourism may threaten the very stuff of the island's attraction – the purity of traditions and its romantic isolation – but for the moment Inisheer retains its old character, and for some it's a favourite place.

A great plug of rock dominates the island, its rough, pale-grey stone dripping with greenery. At the top, the fifteenth-century **O'Brien's castle** stands inside an early medieval ring fort, **Dún Formna**. Set around it are low fields, a small community of pubs and houses, and windswept sand dunes.

Half-buried in the sand just southeast of the beach and the pier is the tenth-century **St Kevin's Church**; still in use in the nineteenth century, it is now used only to commemorate him as the patron saint of the island every June 14. Southeast again from here is **Loch Mór**, a pretty lake inhabited by wildfowl.

The six-mile, waymarked **Inis Oírr Way** traces a circular route round the northern half of the island, taking in these sites, and you could easily branch off between St Kevin's Church and Loch Mór to add on a walk down the road to the **lighthouse** at the southeastern tip of the island, which affords fantastic views of the Cliffs of Moher.

Practicalities

If you need information about the island, you can contact the **Inisheer Island Co-operative** near the beach (Ⓣ099/75008, Ⓔccteo@eircom.net), which also offers **Internet** access. There is no bank on the island, but the hotel has a **bureau de change**, and the Bank of Ireland visits every second Tuesday in summer and on the fourth Tuesday of the month in winter. The multipurpose **arts centre**, *Áras Éanna* (Ⓣ099/75150), has a small heritage room and audio-visual material about the island and runs crafts workshops and other courses in the summer.

You should have little trouble finding **accommodation** unless you arrive on the bank-holiday weekends at the end of May or the start of August, which are usually booked up well ahead. The island **hotel**, the *Óstán Inis Oírr* near the pier (Ⓣ099/75020, Ⓕ75099; ❹; Easter–Sept), has cosy, en-suite rooms. Also comfortable is the IHH-affiliated *Radharc na Mara* **hostel** (Ⓣ099/75024, Ⓔmaire.searraigh@oceanfree.net; March–Oct), which offers twin and family rooms, meals and bike hire. Among the island's **B&Bs**, *Radharc an Chláir* by the castle (Ⓣ & Ⓕ099/75019; ❷) has a good reputation for its fine views and great meals; otherwise, try *Uí Chatháin*,a modern, all-en-suite family home to the east in Formna Village (Ⓣ099/75090; ❷). The only place to **camp** is on the official site by the beach, which has hot showers – and plans for a laundry – and is fully serviced from June to September.

The hotel serves filling seafood **meals** in either the bar or the evenings-only restaurant, as does the *Fisherman's Cottage* restaurant (Ⓣ099/75073), which also offers **kayaks** to rent. The hotel bar, *Tigh Ruairí*, and the *Tigh Ned* **pub** have music all week round during the summer.

Connemara

Dominated by two mountain ranges, **Connemara** (Ⓦwww.connemara.net) is exceptionally beautiful. The **Twelve Bens** (or Na Beanna Beola, the "Pins of Beola", a mythical giant) and **Maam Turks** (Mám Tuirc, the "boar pass") glower over vast open areas of bog wilderness, while to the southwest the land breaks up disorientatingly into inshore lakes and myriad tiny islands linked by causeways, slipping out into the ocean.

The whole area has superb **beaches**, with huge sweeps of opalescent white sand washed by clear blue water. Chance upon good weather here and you feel you've hit paradise; even on the hottest of days the beaches are never crowded. Most of Connemara's beaches are safe for **swimming**, including Clifden, Lettergesh, Dog's Bay, Gurteen Bay, Renvyle, Ardmore, Mannin Bay, Aillebrack, Omey, Letterfrack and Spiddal. It is, however, a very varied coast, so, if in doubt, ask about safety locally.

Connemara is country you visit for its scenery rather than its history. There is little evidence of medieval power in the area, either ecclesiastical or secular, beyond a few castles along the shore of Lough Corrib and the occasional one further west. The great exception is the profusion of **monastic remains** dotted over the little islands off the west coast. Mainland settlements up until the nineteenth century were widely scattered, and the area has always been sparsely populated, due to the poverty of the land. There's never been much to attract marauders or colonizers, and any incursions have involved a battle against the terrain as much as against the people. It's easy to see how such a land would remain under the control of clans like the O'Flahertys for centuries, while gentler landscapes bowed to the pressure of foreign rule. In the famine years the area suffered some of the worst of the misery, and a thinly peopled land was depopulated further as people chose to escape starvation by emigration.

Walking in Connemara

If you intend to go **walking** in Connemara, the first thing to bear in mind is that the mountains here, even though they rise to only two thousand feet or so, are potentially **dangerous**, with notoriously fickle weather and the odd lurking precipice – and the nearest rescue team is in Galway.

The Ordnance Survey **maps** have been recently resurveyed at 1:50,000, but if you are doing any serious walking, it's worth getting *The Mountains of Connemara*, which combines a 1:50,000 map derived from aerial photography and fieldwork by Tim Robinson with an excellent guide to eighteen walks of varying length and difficulty by Joss Lynam. It's produced by Folding Landscapes of Roundstone, Connemara, Co. Galway, and can be obtained in bookshops and tourist offices or by post.

A good introduction to the Maam Turks, with fantastic views of the Twelve Bens across Lough Inagh, would be the ascent of **Cnoc na hUilleann** and **Binn Bhriocáin** from the Inagh Valley back road north of Recess, on a three- to four-hour circuit described in *Mountains of Connemara* (part of it on the Western Way). Also described are the high-level **Maam Turks Walk**, which traverses the range from north of Maam Cross to Leenane in around eleven tough hours, and the classic Twelve Bens walk, the seven-hour **Gleann Chóchan Horseshoe**, starting from the Ben Lettery youth hostel and bagging six of the peaks.

Mountains of Connemara also covers the southernmost section of the waymarked **Western Way**, which runs for 140 miles in total from Oughterard to the base of the Ox Mountains on the Mayo–Sligo border; the Ordnance Survey produces a map and guide booklet called *Western Way South*, covering Oughterard to Westport in County Mayo. The varied, low-level Connemara section starts as a pleasant walk beside Lough Corrib from Oughterard, before crossing over from the village of Maam into the dramatic Inagh Valley, which runs between the Bens and the Turks, and finishing in Leenane. The walk can be done in two long days, with an overnight near Maam, where **B&B** is available at *Leckavrea View House* (Ⓣ & Ⓕ094/954 8040; ❷) and *Tiernakill Farmhouse* (Ⓣ091/571181; ❷; April–Oct). There's also a new waymarked route, the **Slí Chonamara**, which runs for 150 miles with quite a few spur trails through the *Gaeltacht* (details from local tourist offices); the main path follows the coast round from Galway through Spiddal, Carraroe and Carna to Recess, with plenty of accommodation options along the way.

The short but very worthy ascents of **Errisbeg** from Roundstone and **Dúchruach** from Kylemore Abbey are described on pp.489 and 495, and the sky road from Clifden and the trails at Connemara National Park on p.494.

Walking tours are organized from Clifden by the Connemara Walking Centre (Ⓣ095/21379 or 1850/266636, Ⓦwww.walkingireland.com), who offer everything from mountain treks and bog trotting to island hopping on day-trips or week-long holidays; and by Connemara Safari Walking Holidays (Ⓣ095/21071 or 1850/777200, Ⓦwww.walkingconnemara.com), who run five- and seven-day walking and island-hopping trips.

Continued economic deprivation and isolation meant that an ancient rural way of life continued for far longer here, so Connemara is still largely Irish-speaking, containing the largest of the Gaeltacht areas. Weekend and one- or two-week **Irish-language courses** for adults, supplemented by cultural activities and singing and dancing workshops, are held under the auspices of NUI Galway at Áras Mháirtín Uí Chadhain (☎091/595101) in **Carraroe**. English is spoken too, however, and the only difficulty for the visitor is that the **signs** on the roads, and on some buses, are often in Irish only (even Galway is sometimes *Gaillimh*). For all its beauty, the dramatic mountain landscape of west Galway is still surprisingly undeveloped in terms of tourism, owing in part to the infamous Irish weather and in part to the fact that walking has not been the popular recreation in Ireland that it is in other, more urbanized European countries. If you're in search of solitude, you won't have to go far to find it.

Bus Éireann services link all villages on major routes between Galway and Carraroe, Carna, Roundstone, Clifden and Leenane. They are reliable, although infrequent, often with only one service daily, occasionally even less frequently. The area is also served by private buses which can be more flexible and cheaper than Bus Éireann.

Hostels and **B&Bs** are both in reasonably good supply throughout Connemara – check with the tourist office for reputable hostel options. You can camp more or less anywhere if you ask permission, but bear in mind that a lot of the area is bog and therefore very wet. Plenty of official **campsites** are listed in the text.

Iar-Chonnacht

Draw a large triangle between Maam Cross, Rossaveel and Galway and you've defined the Gaeltacht area known as **Iar-Chonnacht**, an open and bleak moorland of bog. Occasional white-splotched boulders lie naked on the peat that stretches to the skyline; any grass that survives is coarse and windblown, and, but for small pockets of forestation, the bog has no trees. It's difficult and wet walking country, but numerous lanes and boreens lead to tiny loughs set in the granite hollows of the hills – these are good for fishing for brown trout, sea trout or salmon. The moorland reaches its highest point near Lough Lettercraffoe on the scenic **Rossaveel–Oughterard road**, giving fine views down onto Lough Corrib, whose green and wooded shores are a vivid foil to the barren west.

Oughterard and around

If you're heading for the dramatic walking country of the mountains, or if you plan to base yourself at Clifden, the road to take from Galway is the N59 through Oughterard. It makes the easiest hitch and the most pleasant cycle ride from Galway, avoiding the boring strip development down to Spiddal and taking you instead along the lush shore of island-flecked **Lough Corrib**, past crumbling ruins. These include the main sixteenth-century O'Flaherty stronghold of **Aughnanure Castle**, two miles south of Oughterard (May to mid-June & Oct Sat & Sun 9.30am–6pm; mid-June to Sept daily 9.30am–6pm; €2.50; Heritage Card). Standing on a rock island surrounded by a fast-flowing stream, this well-preserved six-storey tower house was one of the strongest fortresses in the country at the time of Cromwell's blockade of Galway during 1652–54.

OUGHTERARD itself, a small town serving fishing-based tourism, can beguile you into thinking that Connemara is going to be a relatively populous, developed place if you approach from the east. But arriving from the west, it seems a verdant oasis after the barren wilds of the bog, with the banks of the river here lined by luxuriant beech trees.

From Oughterard you can rent boats on the lough or take a trip on the *Corrib Queen* to the uninhabited island of **Inchagoill** (March–Oct; book at the tourist office or call Corrib Cruises on ⓣ087/283 0799, ⓦwww.corribcruises.com; €13 return). The island is a magical place, with a couple of evocative ruined churches: St Patrick's and the twelfth-century Teampall na Naomh (Church of the Saints), which has interesting carvings and a superb Romanesque doorway. If you want a quick route north, you can hop onto the same company's *Lady Ardilaun* at Inchagoill to go across to **Cong** (see p.516) in County Mayo (€16, €20 return from Oughterard).

For a fascinating change from all the glorious scenery hereabouts, head underground at the recently restored **Glengowla Mine** (March–Nov daily 9.30am–6pm; €6.50), two miles west of Oughterard on the N59. This silver and lead mine was worked between 1850 and 1865 and reluctantly yielded from the area's tough marble around three hundred tons of the ore galena. Entertaining guided tours bring to life the hardships of drilling by hand and blasting the rock, often in deep pools of water and always by candlelight.

Practicalities

Oughterard's very helpful **tourist office** is on Main Street (summer daily 9.30am till late; winter Mon–Fri 9.30am–5.30pm, Sat & Sun 10am–2pm; ⓣ091/552808, ⓔoughterardoffice@eircom.net) and has leaflets on walks in the area, including the Western Way (see p.484). **Internet** access is available at the nearby library on Tuesday, Thursday and Friday afternoons, and Wednesday and Saturday mornings.

There's no shortage of **B&Bs** in Oughterard: on the banks of the Owenriff River on the north side of town are Deirdre Forde's pleasant and comfortable *Camillaun* (ⓣ091/552678, ⓔcamillaun@tinet.ie; ❷; April–Oct), where you can rent rowing and motor boats and take dinner, and the more upmarket *River Run Lodge and Restaurant* (ⓣ091/552697, ⓔrivrun@indigo.ie; ❸), with landscaped gardens overlooking the river. To enjoy the impressive countryside, however, it is preferable to stay in one of the fine houses a little further out of town, and the best of these include: the elegant *Waterfall Lodge* (ⓣ091/552168, ⓔkdolly@eircom.net; ❷), which provides private fishing in the grounds, and *Lakeland Country House* (ⓣ091/552121, ⓔmayfly@eircom.net; ❷), just over a mile out of town in Portacarron, which has peaceful gardens running down to the lake and offers dinner. There are three fine **hotels** in Oughterard: the *Connemara Gateway Hotel* (ⓣ091/552328, ⓦwww.sinnotthotels.com; ❺), cosy and welcoming despite its size; the *Corrib House* (ⓣ091/552329, ⓦwww.corribhotel.com; ❸), whose somewhat basic rooms are more than made up for by its warm welcome and open turf fires; and the excellent *Currarevagh House* (ⓣ091/552312, ⓔcurrarevagh@ireland.com; ❻; closed Nov–March), a Victorian country house set in extensive, lush woodland on the Lough Corrib shore. The town's IHH-affiliated **hostel** *Canrawer House*, signposted from the Clifden end of the main street (ⓣ091/552388, ⓔcanrawer@indigo.ie), is popular with fishermen and travellers alike and is of an impressively high standard; dorms, twins and family rooms have en-suite bathrooms, the large well-equipped kitchen is immaculate, and the hostel offers bike and boat rental.

One of the best **places to eat** is *O'Fatharta's*, by the central junction on Main Street (ⓣ091/552692), a smart, stylish restaurant that's strong on fish and seafood dishes, such as wild Corrib trout in brandy and lemon butter. Its main competitor in the summer is the French-run *Le Blason* (☎091/557111; Tues–Sun eve), overlooking the river at the west end of Main Street. The *Boat Inn* is a good fall-back, with sandwiches, Irish stew and fish of the day and other specials in the evening. *Power's*, the thatched and whitewashed **pub** next to the *Boat Inn*, is a good spot for a quiet drink.

West around the coast

The **coast road** is the alternative route west from Galway, passing through the effective capital of the Gaeltacht, **SPIDDAL** (An Spidéal, "the hospital"). Opposite a pleasant Blue Flag beach here, the **Spiddal Craft Centre** (Ceardlann an Spidéil; Mon–Sat 10am–6pm, Sun 2–6pm; reduced hours out of season; ☎091/553376) is a collection of workshops making and selling high-quality pottery, weaving and jewellery. Spiddal can be surprisingly lively for such a small, drive-through town, and you can catch great sessions in the **pubs** here: try *Tigh Hughes*, especially on a Thursday night, or *An Crúiscín Lán*, which also boasts a beer garden and bar food. For **accommodation**, *An Crúiscín Lán* (☎091/553148, Ⓦwww.cruiscinlanhotel.com; ⑤) is a good upmarket option, with large, bright rooms – some with sea-view balconies – and a smart, evening-time restaurant. There are also B&Bs aplenty: if you value friendly service and fine food then head for *Ardmór Country House* (☎091/553145, Ⓦwww.ardmorcountryhouse.com; ②; closed Jan & Feb), where Vera Feeney will take great care of you. Other fine places include *Col-Mar* (☎091/553247; ②; May–Sept), a peaceful country home set in colourful gardens one mile west of town, and Maura Ni Chonghaile's *Caladhgearr* (☎091/593124, Ⓔcgthatchcot@eircom.net; ②; March–Oct), a pretty, thatched cottage, three miles out in the same direction. **Camping** is available at the well-appointed *Spiddal Caravan and Camping Park* (Páirc Saoire an Spidéil; ☎091/553372, Ⓔpaircsaoire@eircom.net); it's one mile off the main road and is well signposted from the centre of the village.

From Spiddal the road continues west to **ROSSAVEEL** (Ros a' Mhíl), departure point for Aran Islands ferries, beyond which the land breaks up into little chains of low-lying islands, linked to one another by natural causeways. These islets, more gentle than the main body of Connemara, make a perfect place to get lost: meandering around the inlets and gullies you experience a happy disorientation.

Across the bay from Rossaveel, **CARRAROE** (An Cheathrú Rua) has a strangely suburban feel to it, but the boulder-strewn coast enjoys magnificent views across to the Aran Islands. Among **places to stay**, *Hotel Carraroe* (☎091/595116; ④) is modern and comfortable though a little soulless. For a feel of the place and its people then, *Réalt na Maidne* (☎091/595193; ②),which has a bar and B&B, is probably a better bet.

North of Rossaveel and Carraroe, you can head straight up the R336 to Maam Cross to join the N59 into Clifden, or you can continue winding round the coast on the R340, which would eventually bring you out near Cashel and Roundstone.

Near **Rosmuc**, a speck of a hamlet at the end of a small peninsula off the R340, is the cottage of the Republican and poet **Pádraig Pearse** (mid-June to mid-Sept daily 10am–6pm; late Sept Sat & Sun 10am–6pm; €1.20; Heritage Card), who signed the 1916 proclamation and was subsequently executed. The cottage is where he held summer schools for his pupils from St Enda's in Dublin and wrote short stories, plays and *O'Donovan's Funeral Oration*, and although there is little of real interest inside, its tranquil setting makes it worth a visit. Further round the R340 at **Carna** you can wander out onto Mweenish Island and look out to St Mac Dara's Island, where the remains of a fine early **church** still stand. Such was the former reverence for the saint that fishermen would dip their sails three times when passing the island. A three-day pilgrimage and **festival**, *Féile Mhic Dara*, is still held here in mid-July.

Maam Cross to Clifden

The main N59 road from Galway and Oughterard takes you through the hamlets of **MAAM CROSS** (Crois Mám), site of the overpowering but uninspiring *Peacockes* complex (Ⓣ091/552306, Ⓦwww.peacockes.net; ❹), consisting of a hotel, restaurant, craft shop, petrol station and pub, and **RECESS**, where all you will find is Joyce's shop, a bar, a petrol station and a post office. Five miles further west, close in under the rugged peaks of the Twelve Bens, is *Ben Lettery* An Óige **hostel** (Ⓣ & Ⓕ095/51136; Easter–Sept), a cosy haven run by friendly wardens, with family rooms available; its location makes it one of the best spots from which to strike off into the mountains. The nearby castle of **Ballynahinch** was once the home of the land-owning Martin family, and later of cricketing maharaja, Ranjit Singhi, and is now a romantic **hotel** with a bar – and food – open to nonresidents (Ⓣ095/31006, Ⓦwww.ballynahinch-castle.com; ❼; closed Christmas & Feb). On Ballynahinch lake are the remains of an old O'Flaherty castle, known as Martin's Prison after the use it was put to by Ballynahinch's most famous son, Dick Martin – aka **Humanity Dick** (1754–1834). The story behind the name is that Richard Martin, originally dubbed "Hairtrigger Dick" because of his duelling prowess, spent his adult life campaigning for animal rights, and any tenant he caught causing suffering to animals was thrown into jail in the castle. Dick was known to have fought duels on behalf of threatened animals, and when asked why he did so replied: "Sir, an ox cannot hold a pistol." More constructively, he pushed various acts through parliament protecting farm animals from maltreatment and was instrumental in founding the RSPCA.

Three miles beyond the *Ben Lettery* hostel, you will come to **Dan O'Hara's Farmstead and the Connemara Heritage and History Centre** at Lettershea (April–Oct daily 10am–6pm; Ⓦwww.connemaraheritage.com; €6), which sounds rather kitsch but is actually very engaging. Fascinating display boards by local archaeologist Michael Gibbons and a twenty-minute video introduce you to the history of Clifden and Connemara, and to Dan O'Hara himself. A tenant farmer whose house was famous for its *céilís* (it was known as the local "ballroom of romance"), O'Hara was evicted in 1845 and eventually found his way to New York, where, having little English, he sold matches and inspired the famous eponymous song. Outside in the grounds, you can view reconstructions of an oratory, a dolmen tomb, a wooden ring fort and a *crannóg*, a thatched dwelling set in a small lake. Guided tours in a tractor-borne bus take you up to Dan O'Hara's refurbished cottage for great views south over the bogs and lakes to Roundstone and Errisbeg and for demonstrations of sheep-shearing and turf-cutting. There's also a daytime café at the centre and **B&B** is available upstairs in bright and airy en-suite rooms (Ⓣ095/21246; ❷, including free entry to the heritage centre).

Roundstone

If you're hugging the coast on the R347, which eventually loops round into Clifden, the next place of interest after Rossaveel is **ROUNDSTONE** (Cloch na Rón, "Seal Rock"), a fishing village at the foot of the Errisbeg Mountain.

Curving its back to the Atlantic, the quaint stone harbour looks across its sheltered waters to the magnificent Twelve Bens. Fishing is the main source of income here, along with an unobtrusive tourism which makes the most of the unique prettiness of the setting and the glorious beach at **Gurteen Bay**, just over a mile to the west, a huge sweep of white sand with lucid blue water that is really very seductive.

In recent years Roundstone has seen percussionists beating a path to the **workshop** of master *bodhrán*-maker **Malachy Kearns** (May, June, Sept & Oct daily 9.30am–6pm; July & Aug daily 9am–7pm; Nov–April Mon–Sat 9.30am–6pm; ⓣ095/35808, ⓦwww.bodhran.com; free) in the old Franciscan monastery on the edges of the village. The workshop shows the techniques Malachy uses to stretch both the eighteen-inch birch drum frame and the treated goatskin that surrounds it; his drums are renowned for their perfect tone, producing the haunting, rolling rhythms that form the backdrop to Irish music. There is also a testing room where the uninitiated can happily clamour, while Malachy's wife paints delicate personalized Celtic ornamentations onto the skins of the drums. The centre also has a fine record shop, **crafts stores** and coffee shop and is highly recommended. The village itself also has several fine crafts shops and galleries; look out for the exquisite linen clothes and kitchenware in the **Dalkey Design Shop** or the pottery and raw naturalist paintings in the **Ivy House Gallery**.

It's an easy couple of hours' **walk** from Roundstone up to the top of **Errisbeg**, just short of a thousand feet above sea level. Follow the fuchsia-flooded lane up the side of *O'Dowd's* bar and then the rough track that it turns into; you'll have to pick your way over often boggy ground and boulders towards the top which, despite appearances from below, turns out to be a ridge of three summits – with a little trial and error, you'll find the one with the scenery you like best. The views are panoramic: the frilly coast of isthmuses and islets runs out to the south; to the west stretch long beaches of white sand – Gurteen, Dog's Bay, Ballyconneely, Bunowen and the coral strand of Mannin Bay – each one echoing the beauty of the last; and towards the Twelve Bens and Maam Turks to the north, a vast and open plain of bog is punctuated only by the irregular glinting surfaces of dozens of little lakes. It's through this wilderness that the **bog road** runs, the source of such superstition that some local people will not travel along it at night. Around the turn of last century, two old women, who lived in the road's only dwelling, robbed and murdered a traveller who'd taken refuge with them, and the road is considered to be haunted.

Practicalities

There's a seasonal **information centre** with irregular hours in the community centre (ⓣ095/35815), which can give information about the village's small **arts festival** in late June or early July. Several places in Roundstone do **B&B**: try *St Josephs* (ⓣ095/35865, ⓔchristinalowry@eircom.net; ❷), a cosy, welcoming place with great breakfasts in the heart of the village, or the comfortable, friendly *Wit's End* (ⓣ095/35951; ❷; June–Aug), painted shocking pink. *Vaughan's Roundstone House Hotel* (ⓣ095/35864, ⓔdiar@eircom.net; ❹; Easter–Oct) is also a good place to stay. There are several **campsites** to the west of Roundstone, including the *Gurteen Caravan Site* beside the beach (ⓣ095/35882; March–Sept), with laundry facilities, a shop and a tennis court. If you don't want to stay in the village itself and feel like splashing out, try one of the two exceptional **hotels** near the village of **Cashel**, about a fifteen-minute drive round the bay towards Carna. The first of these is *Zetland House*

Hotel (☎095/31111, Ⓦwww.zetland.com; ❼), which also has a fine restaurant, but if you want real indulgence, then follow in the footsteps of Charles de Gaulle and pamper yourself at the *Cashel House Hotel* (☎095/31001, Ⓦwww.cashel-house-hotel.com; ❽), set in award-winning grounds (open to nonresidents mid-March to Oct daily 11am–5pm; free) and one of the finest places to stay in the country.

For **eating and drinking** in Roundstone, head for *O'Dowd's*, which has a wonderful atmosphere and serves fine bar food; attached to *O'Dowd's* is an excellent restaurant serving mostly seafood and a café, *Espresso Stop*, offering **Internet** access. Alternatively, try *Vaughan's Hotel*, which has a popular bar and a bright, chic restaurant, *Beola*, specializing in seafood. You can **rent bikes** from Michael Ferron's shop, and go **sailing** from the harbour in a traditional hooker, the *Truelight* (☎095/21034, Ⓦwww.truelight.ie; €40 per person for 3hr, €65 for a full day).

Clifden and around

Because of the dramatic grandeur of the Connemara mountains and the romantic pull of Galway, you expect **CLIFDEN**, the English-speaking capital of Connemara, to be something special. In fact it's a very small place with only three significant streets – Main Street, the continuation of the Galway road, with Bridge Street and Market Street branching off it at either end and meeting to form a triangle. Its great asset is its position, perched high above the deep sides of the boulder-strewn estuary of the River Owenglin. The jumble of the Twelve Bens provides a magnificent scenic backdrop, and the broad streets seem consciously to open out to take in the fresh air of the mountains and the Atlantic. Gimlet spires of matching nineteenth-century churches pierce the sky, giving Clifden a sharp, distinctive skyline.

Clifden seems to be trying hard to cultivate the cosmopolitan atmosphere of Galway. It attracts a fair number of young Dubliners, revving up the life of this otherwise quiet, rural town. Lots of European tourists come here too, but in aiming to serve all tastes, the town somehow misses the mark. The place is at its most interesting when it's busy being Irish: during the annual **Connemara Pony Show**, for example, on the third Thursday in August. This is for the sale and judging of Connemara ponies – tough, hardy animals that are well suited to a harsh bog and mountain existence, yet renowned for their docile temperament. There's also a prestigious and lively **arts festival** (☎095/21644, Ⓦwww.clifden-artsweek.com) in the last week of September.

Information and accommodation

Clifden is an obvious base, especially if you're hostelling, but even though the Connemara mountains *look* magnificent, be warned that they're not particularly accessible from here without your own transport. For information on the town and the whole of Connemara, head for the well-equipped **tourist office**, part of the development around the old station on the Galway road (March–May & Oct Mon–Sat 10am–5pm; June–Sept Mon–Fri 9.30am–6.45pm, Sat & Sun 10am–6.45pm; ☎095/21163). For **bike rental**, try John Mannion, Bridge Street (☎095/21160). **Pony trekking** is organized at Cleggan (see p.492) and at Errislannan Manor (☎095/21134; closed Sun), about a mile beyond the Alcock and Brown Memorial (see p.492), south of Clifden off the Ballyconneely road.

There's plenty of excellent **accommodation** in Clifden, though everything can be very busy in July and August. The best **hotel** in the area is *The Quay*

House down on the harbour (Ⓣ095/21369, Ⓦwww.thequayhouse.com; ❻; mid-March to Oct), set in the early nineteenth-century harbourmaster's house, which later became a Franciscan monastery, then a convent. Rooms are tastefully decorated with antiques and paintings, most overlook the water, and some have working fireplaces and fitted kitchens. Second place would go to the *Ardagh*, a mile south of town on the Ballyconneely road (Ⓣ095/21384, Ⓔardaghhotel@eircom.net; ❻), an informal, family-run hotel, with a relaxed ambience and a good restaurant. Other fine hotels include the large, modern *Station House Hotel* (Ⓣ095/21699, Ⓦwww.stationhousehotel.com; ❺), which often has special deals on, and *Erriseask House* on the road to Ballyconneely (Ⓣ095/23553, Ⓦwww.erriseask.connemara-ireland.com; ❻), with its own private beach on the shores of Mannin Bay.

Good-value **B&Bs** include *Bali Lodge*, Bridge Street (Ⓣ095/22923, Ⓦwww.balilodge.com; ❷), which offers large, tasteful rooms and fine breakfasts; the friendly and very well-appointed *Buttermilk Lodge Guesthouse* (Ⓣ095/21951, Ⓦwww.buttermilklodge.com; ❷), a five-minute walk out on the Westport road; *Bay View*, a mile further out on the same road (Ⓣ095/21286, Ⓦwww.baview.com; ❷; closed Dec & Jan), which offers good discounts for families and lives up to its name with a sweeping panorama of Streamstown Bay; and *Winnowing Hill*, half a mile out on the Ballyconneely road (Ⓣ095/21281, Ⓔwinnowinghill@eircom.net; ❷; mid-March to Oct), set on a peaceful hill with fine views from its conservatory.

The town has an outstanding **hostel** in the shape of the *Clifden Town Hostel*, Market St (IHH; Ⓣ095/21076, Ⓦwww.clifdentownhostel.com), tastefully decorated with prints by Paul Henry and other well-known Irish artists. Family rooms, twins and doubles are available and there are two kitchens, a comfy sitting room and an Internet terminal. If this is full, head further down Market Street, where, near the river, is the less comfortable, though perfectly adequate *Brookside Hostel* (IHH & IHO; Ⓣ095/21812, Ⓔbrooksidehostel@eircom.net). **Camping** and bike rental is possible at *Shanaheever* (Ⓣ095/21018), a mile out of town off the Westport road.

Eating and drinking

There's no problem getting provisions in Clifden, and the town's main streets harbour plenty of **places to eat**. *Walsh's Bakery*, Market St, has a traditional coffee shop, but by far the best daytime option is *Two Dog Café* (Ⓦwww.twodogcafe.ie; closed Sun), on Church Hill, just off The Square at the west end of Main Street. Here you can choose from excellent and imaginative panini, wraps, quiches and soups, finished off with delicious desserts such as lemon and ricotta cake and great coffee; upstairs is a slick communications centre with **Internet** access. *Mannion's* on Market Street is the best pub for food, with daily specials and seafood platters, all in hearty portions. Clifden has, of late, gained a reputation for excellent evening dining, due in no small part to the delicious food served at *O'Grady's*, a slick, minimalist restaurant on Market Street (Ⓣ095/21450; Mon–Sat evenings). Also good is the relaxing *Mitchell's* a few doors along (Ⓣ095/21867; March–Oct), which offers less elaborate dishes, heavily weighted towards fish and seafood.

There are plenty of decent **bars** in Clifden, though it's not renowned for its traditional music: try *E.J. King's*, *Lowry's* or *Mannion's*, all on Market Street. Loud and lively *Malarkey's* at the back of *Foyles Hotel* on The Square is the likeliest spot for modern folk and singer-songwriters, with regular open-mike nights.

Around Clifden

To get into the heart of the **Twelve Bens**, you'll need to cycle, hitch or skilfully manipulate the bus service. For more spontaneous walking, take the westward **beach road** down from The Square to a fine, sandy beach and a path that follows the shore of Clifden Bay. The shell of a nineteenth-century Gothic castellated **mansion** that you pass on the way was the home of John D'Arcy, who founded the town. Running above and roughly parallel to this, what is locally referred to as the **sky road** takes you to more desolate countryside, looping scenically round the narrow peninsula on the north side of Clifden Bay to the long, thin inlet of Streamstown Bay, before hitting the Westport road just north of Clifden (eight miles in total).

On the opposite side of Streamstown Bay, you can get down to the little village of Claddaghaduff, where at low tide you can walk across the beach to **Omey Island**. Three miles north on the same headland is the little village of **CLEGGAN**, where most people go simply to get the ferry to Inishbofin. However, the village is attractive in itself and may be a better place to stay than overcrowded Clifden. There are plenty of **B&Bs**, usually a little cheaper than in Clifden – try the rather grand *Harbour House* (Ⓣ095/44702, Ⓔharbour.house@oceanfree.net; ❷), or a mile out of town, not far from the beach, *Cnoc Breac* (Ⓣ095/44688; ❷; May–Sept). **Horse riding** on the beaches and out to the island is available at Laragan Stables (Ⓣ095/44735) and Cleggan Trekking Centre (Ⓣ095/44746).

To the immediate south of Clifden lies some equally pleasant country. A 14ft aeroplane wing carved in limestone sticks out of the bog four miles from Clifden just off the Ballyconneely road as a melodramatic memorial to the landing of **Alcock and Brown** at the end of their pioneering non-stop transatlantic flight in June 1919. The intrepid aviators circled Clifden twice in celebration, but then nosedived into the bog here, wrecking their plans to continue their triumphal flight to London. On the opposite side of the Ballyconneely road is the site of a telegraph station, where **Marconi** sent the first commercial wireless transmission across the Atlantic in 1907; the station was burnt out by Republicans during the Civil War in 1922 and abandoned, with around a thousand local people losing their livelihoods. Beyond this is the coral strand of **Mannin Bay**, excellent for swimming, and a string of fine beaches stretching around to Roundstone.

Inishbofin

The island of **INISHBOFIN** is a mellow, balmy place, quite different from the mainland. It's more fertile, with sheltered sandy beaches, and there's a general softness to its contours. The only jagged features are the rocky outcrops off the west side, the **Stags**, with a fine vantage point nearby for viewing seals basking on the shore. Even the high, heathery moorland soon gently descends to the placid **Lough Boffin**, rimmed with rustling water iris and bullrushes and inhabited by swans. The lough is the scene of the island's most durable **myth**, a story that explains how it got its name. Several versions of the tale exist, but the basic elements are constant. For eons the island lay shrouded in mist under the spell of an enchantment, but one day two lost fishermen came upon it and lit a fire by the shore, thus breaking the spell. As the mist cleared, they saw an old woman driving a white cow along the strand. She hit it with a stick and was instantly turned to rock. Taking her for a witch, the men hit her and they too immediately turned to rock: *Inis Bó Finne* means "Island of the White Cow".

Transport to Inishbofin

You can visit Inishbofin on a day-trip from Clifden in summer, even without a car. Michael Nee operates three **buses** a day to Cleggan from mid-June to August (plus three a week all the way from Galway) to connect with the ferries; Bus Éireann offers two buses on Wednesdays, year round. **Ferry tickets** are available at the pier in Cleggan or at Clifden tourist office for Kings Ferries (Ⓣ095/44642, Ⓦwww.inishbofinkingferries.com) or on the MV *Galway Bay* (Ⓣ095/45903, Ⓦwww.inishbofinferry.com); both companies make the half-hour crossing from Cleggan between two and five times a day from April to September and charge €15 return. In winter the island all but closes down to visitors, but there's a boat at least once a week.

The known **history** of the island starts in the seventh century, when St Colman arrived here from Iona after a quarrel with Rome over the method of calculating the date of Easter. No remains exist of the monastery he founded, but the ruins of a thirteenth-century **church** stand on the original site in a sheltered vale beside the small lake to the east of the pier. Later the island was taken over by the O'Flahertys, and then Grace O'Malley is supposed to have fortified the place for her fleet. Coming into the island's long protected harbour you'll see the extensive remains of a sixteenth-century **castle**, low on the hummocky terrain and accessible at low tide. It was taken and strengthened yet further by Cromwell, who used Inishbofin – and other west coast islands – as a kind of concentration camp for clerics. The most chilling reminder of his barbarity is the rock visible in the harbour at low tide. Known as **Bishop's Rock**, it was here that Cromwell chained one unfortunate ecclesiastic, then let his troops watch the tide come slowly in and drown him.

You can walk around the island, which is only just over three miles long, in a day, quite easily taking in the sites mentioned above, as well as the small but interesting **heritage museum** by the pier (summer daily noon–5pm; €2.50), the sandy **beach** in the southeast corner, which provides the best swimming, the broad horseshoe of **Rusheen Bay** a little way up the east coast, and **Trá Ghael**, a beautiful beach beneath the island's highest point in the west, where the currents are too dangerous for swimming.

Practicalities

You can get **tourist information** and access the **Internet** at the island community centre in summer (Mon–Sat until 6pm; Ⓣ095/45861 or 45895). **Maps** of the island are available at Clifden tourist office or on the boats over. **Bikes** can be rented at the pier, **boats** from Aidan Day also at the pier (Ⓣ095/45865), and there's an island post office and shop nearby, with exchange facilities and the usual limitations on supplies. The island holds lively **arts festivals** in mid-May and early September.

The pick of the **hotels** on Inishbofin, *Day's Bofin House* by the pier (Ⓣ095/45809), has been flattened but is due to be rebuilt in time for the 2003 season. Its competitor, the *Doonmore Hotel* (Ⓣ095/45804, Ⓦwww.doonmorehotel.com; ❺; Easter–Sept), a mile west of the pier, has fine sea views, a restaurant open to nonresidents and serves decent bar food. If you want to book **B&B**, try *Horseshoe Bay* (Ⓣ095/45812; ❶), a quaint, old-fashioned, white cottage on the shore at Rusheen Bay; the nearby *Galley* (Ⓣ095/45894; ❷), with en-suite rooms in a smart, spacious modern house; or *Emerald Cottage* (Ⓣ095/45865; ❷), a traditional, brightly painted cottage a short way west of the pier, whose friendly owner cooks up crab and baked goods and makes Aran sweaters. The *Inishbofin Island* **hostel** (IHH & IHO; ⓣ & ⓕ095/45855; Easter–Oct) is an extremely friendly and well-run place, with twins, family rooms and space for **camping**.

The daytime **café** at *The Galley* in Rusheen Bay serves delicious smoked fish in various combinations, as well as soups and desserts. Your best bet in the evening is the friendly *Dolphin* **restaurant** (ⓣ095/45992), opposite the hostel, which offers well-cooked fish, meat and veggie dishes in relaxing surroundings. *Day's* **pub** is very friendly and has music sessions any time of the week during the summer season.

Letterfrack and the Connemara National Park

LETTERFRACK is an orderly nineteenth-century Quaker village in a rugged setting around ten miles northeast of Clifden. The village is tiny but it has a post office, shop and bureau de change, and the rambling *Old Monastery* **hostel** (IHH & IHO; ⓣ095/41132, ⓔoldmon@indigo.ie; ❶), with twin and family rooms, **camping**, and great breakfasts included in the price. At the other end of the scale is *Rosleague Manor* (ⓣ095/41101, ⓦwww.rosleague.com; ❼; April–Oct), an elegant, early nineteenth-century country-house **hotel** a mile from the village, with an excellent restaurant and extensive grounds stretching down to the sea. There's good **food** – especially seafood – at *Veldon's*, as well as occasional music sessions. *The Bard's Den* opposite lays on more basic fare such as pizzas, hosts sessions on Thursdays, discos on Saturdays and offers en-suite **B&B** rooms (ⓣ095/41042; ❷). At the east end of the village is the thatched restaurant *Pangur Bán* (ⓣ095/41243), which has an attractive, eclectic menu including delicious tempura. Letterfrack at its liveliest during **Bog Week** (the weekend leading up to the first Monday in June) and **Sea Week** (the weekend leading up to the last Monday in October), when a heady mix of conservationists and musicians descend on the village for field trips, conferences and music sessions.

The **Connemara National Park** covers a thin slice of the northwest sector of the Twelve Bens, stretching east from Letterfrack as far as Benbrack, Bencullagh, Muckanaght and Benbaun, and its chief functions are to promote the area's natural beauty while conserving its bog, heath and granite mountains. The park's **visitor centre** on the west side of the village of Letterfrack (daily: mid-March to May, Sept & Oct 10am–5.30pm; June 10am–6.30pm; July & Aug 9.30am–6.30pm; ⓣ095/41054; €2.50; Heritage Card) is an excellent source of information on the fauna, flora and geology of the area: there is an interesting exhibition on 10,000 years of Connemara, taking in peatland and the changing landscape, and in July and August there are worthwhile, free heritage talks on Wednesday evenings and plenty of activities for kids. Unfortunately, the visitor centre is not the best place to access the mountains, as the multifaceted, granite Diamond Hill immediately to the east is indefinitely closed to walkers due to problems of soil erosion. However, the visitor centre does have three short **nature trails** across the lower slopes, through some natural woodland and over bogland, with free guided walks on Monday and Friday mornings in July and August.

Renvyle and Kylemore

Five miles northwest of Letterfrack, at the end of the Renvyle Peninsula, stands **Renvyle House**, a place of immense interest in Irish literary and political history. At one time it was visited by the great Edwardian comic twosome Somerville and Ross, authors of *Stories of an Irish R.M.*, but the house's most famous owner was Oliver St John Gogarty, the distinguished surgeon, writer and wit. An associate of the Gaelic League, he attended the literary evenings of Yeats, Moore and Æ (George Russell), and is immortalized as "stately plump Buck Mulligan" in Joyce's *Ulysses*. *Renvyle House* is now a relaxing **hotel** (Ⓣ095/43511, Ⓦwww.renvyle.com; ⑧), offering facilities such as golf, tennis, horse riding, boating and a swimming pool; ask about their frequent special deals. About a mile west of the hotel lies a ruined O'Flaherty **castle**, superbly positioned overlooking the sea. Also worth a visit in Derryinver Bay, on the south side of the peninsula, is the **Ocean's Alive Sealife Centre** (daily: May–Sept 10am–7pm; Oct–April 10am–4pm; Ⓣ095/43473; €4.75), which features exhibits of sea life and local maritime history, lots of children's activities and hour-long wildlife cruises to view deserted islands and, hopefully, seals. There are two good, well-signposted **campsites** on the north side of the Renvyle Peninsula, each giving onto an expansive, sandy beach: *Connemara* (Ⓣ095/43406; May–Sept) and *Renvyle Beach* (Ⓣ095/43462; Easter–Sept).

Three miles east of Letterfrack, the Neo-Gothic towers of **Kylemore Abbey** sit in a rhododendron-filled hollow against lush deciduous slopes. Its white castellated outline, perfectly reflected in the reed-punctured lake, has made it the subject of many a postcard. It's home to Irish Benedictine nuns and houses a girls' boarding school, but the library, dining room, morning room and main hall are accessible to visitors, and there are display panels and an audio-visual presentation telling the history of Kylemore (daily 9am–5.30pm; Ⓦwww.kylemoreabbey.com; €5, €10 with the garden).

A walk through the woods by the lake leads to the beautiful Neo-Gothic **church**, which incorporates elements from the great English cathedrals of the late twelfth and early thirteenth centuries. If you follow a steep path up through the rhododendrons from the west side of the abbey, in about thirty minutes you'll reach the white **statue** of the Sacred Heart, which affords a dramatic vista of the valley. If you've still got the legs, it's possible to go on to the sixteen-hundred-foot summit of the hill, Dúchruach, in around 45 minutes for even better views of the Twelve Bens to the south and to the north Killary Harbour, Clare Island and Achill; from the statue, follow an old track eastwards along the slope, before turning sharply to approach the peak over boggy and rocky ground. The abbey also has an impressive **crafts shop** and **restaurant**, and **fishing** on the lake can be arranged at the nearby hut (Ⓣ095/41161, Ⓦwww.kylemorabbeyfishery.com).

You shouldn't leave Kylemore without visiting the abbey's restored **walled garden** (Easter–Oct 10.30am–4.30pm; €6.50, €10 with the abbey), whose entrance is a mile west along the main road. Laid out in the 1860s with no fewer than 21 glasshouses, the huge garden deteriorated after the estate was sold in 1903, but an ambitious project has returned the garden more or less to its former state, using only original Victorian plant specimens. Walking through the walls into the beautifully tended ornamental flower garden is a rather surreal experience, like entering a Victorian English municipal park in the wilds of Connemara. Beyond the flower garden lie stream and fern walks and vast beds of herbs and vegetables, with everything from dill to parsnips (all labelled), divided by a long, pretty herbaceous border. Two of the glasshouses remain, while the head gardener's house and his workers' far more basic bothy have been refurbished, but the most poignant remnants are the very fine, original cabbage trees.

Killary Harbour and Leenane

Instead of speeding inland along the N59 beyond Kylemore, a great route, if you are cycling or driving, to take to the famous hostel at **KILLARY HARBOUR** is along the minor coast road east of Renvyle via some magnificent coastal scenery and lovely beaches. The An Óige **hostel** (Ⓣ095/43417; June–Sept & weekends throughout the year), where Wittgenstein finished writing his *Philosophical Investigations* in 1948, has a deeply ponderous setting at the mouth of Ireland's only fjord, a cold dark tongue of water which cuts eight miles into the barren mountains. Though old-fashioned, the hostel itself is warm and friendly and makes a wonderful sanctuary. Based at nearby **Glasilaun Beach**, Scuba Dive West (Ⓣ095/43922, Ⓦwww.scubadivewest.com) offers courses and **diving** off the coast and nearby islands.

Further east, **LEENANE** (Leenáun) is most famous as a location for shooting *The Field*, and stills from the film hang on the walls of *Gaynor's Bar* here. The town also boasts the **Leenane Cultural Centre** (April–Oct daily 9am–6pm; €2.50), which explores the history of wool, with spinning and weaving demonstrations and a collection of various sheep outside – if you've an interest, it's very enjoyable, and there's a good café-restaurant, too. The **Killary Adventure Centre** (Ⓣ095/43411, Ⓦwww.killary.com) offers all manners of activities and courses, either by the day or residential, from rock-climbing and mountain biking to kayaking and wind-surfing. For a gentler way onto the water, take a ninety-minute **cruise** on the fjord with Killary Cruises (Easter–Sept 4 daily, Oct 2 daily; Ⓣ091/566736, Ⓦwww.killarycruises.com; €16).

Among the town's **B&Bs**, the outstanding choice is the fjord-side *Convent* (Ⓣ095/42240; ❷), which retains some fine stained glass from its previous incarnation as a nunnery, while for somewhere a little more expensive there's the superb *Killary Lodge Country Home* (Ⓣ095/42276, Ⓦwww.killary.com; ❹), an old hunting and fishing lodge down by the harbour. The *Blackberry Café* (Ⓣ095/42240) is a very attractive and welcoming **restaurant**, offering well-prepared and reasonably priced dishes, such as wild salmon with dill sauce.

County Mayo

Often seen as simply a passage between scenic Galway and literary Yeats country, **County Mayo** (Ⓦwww.visitmayo.com) is little visited – though it's hard to see why. Like Galway to the south and Sligo to the north, it has a landscape of high cliffs, lonely mountains and bright fuchsia hedges; in the wild, boggy area to the northwest are the vestiges of a Gaeltacht; and on Lough Conn there's some of the best fishing in Ireland. The Georgian town of **Westport**, an elegantly urban playground for travellers needing a break from the dazzling light and landscapes of the wild west, is the only place that's really on the international tourist trail. **Achill Island**, the biggest of the Irish offshore islands and a traditional Irish family holiday resort, has an oddly fly-blown air that won't suit everyone. Some of the most exciting country, however, is the little-travelled northwest. The interpretive centre at **Céide Fields** holds the key to understanding a landscape that's hardly changed for millennia. The area is easily accessible: the rail line will take you right out to Westport, and there's an international airport at **Knock** (with cheap flights designed for pilgrims to the shrine of the Virgin Mary). Furthermore the whole of the county is magical cycling country. Mayo is bound to become busier, but for the moment it remains wonderfully empty.

The Barony of Murrisk and the islands

If you're travelling by road, you'll probably enter Mayo from Connemara, via the spectacular scenery of Killary Harbour, part of the lobe of land between the Galway border and Westport that's known as the **Barony of Murrisk**. This is country as rugged and remote as anything you'll find in the west, and two ranges of hills, the Mweelrea Mountains and the Sheefry Hills, provide terrain for energetic walking and mountaineering. The coast road passes through the villages of **Delphi** and **Louisburgh**, which, along with the almost-deserted **Clare Island**, are closely associated with the belligerent pirate queen Grace O'Malley (see box on p.503). Before reaching the lively town of Westport the road skirts the foot of spectacular **Croagh Patrick** mountain, the scene of an annual pilgrimage honouring the country's national saint.

Delphi and Louisburgh

The road due north from Killary threads along a narrow valley which opens up, briefly, for a famous salmon and sea-trout lough-fishery with the unlikely name of **DELPHI**. The story behind the name involves the first Marquess of Sligo, whose seat, misleadingly, was at Westport. The flamboyant marquess, a friend of Lord Byron, was caught in the sway of romantic Hellenism and in 1811 set sail for Greece to search for antiquities. He swam the Hellespont with Byron and rode with him overland to Corinth; but when he got to Delphi, he suffered a bout of homesickness, finding that it reminded him of nothing so much as his fishery at home in County Mayo. After numerous adventures, and some pillaging of ancient sites, the marquess returned home to reminisce. Nowadays, there's an **adventure centre** at Delphi (Ⓣ095/42223, Ⓦwww.delphiadventureholidays.ie), running activities and courses in anything from surfing and canoeing to mountain biking and mountaineering. The centre is attached to the *Delphi Mountain Resort and Spa* (Ⓣ095/42987, Ⓦwww.delphiescape.com; ❽), a stylish, new **spa**, offering all kinds of pampering, but especially marine treatments, on package breaks and day programmes. More traditional luxury **accommodation**, excellent cuisine, plus a taste of the area's history, can be had at the *Delphi Lodge* (Ⓣ095/42222, Ⓦwww.delphilodge.ie; ❼; closed Nov), an 1830s sporting lodge by the lake, built for the Marquess of Sligo in a surprisingly austere Neoclassical style.

North of Delphi, the road runs alongside sombre **Doo Lough**, also known as the Black Lake, and over desolate moorland before reaching **LOUISBURGH** (pronounced "lewis-burg"). This is one of the few instances where a town this side of the Atlantic has been named after one on the other: it was renamed after Henry Browne, uncle of the first Marquess of Sligo, had taken part in the capture of Louisburgh, Nova Scotia, in 1758. Louisburgh is essentially little more than a crossroads, but its planned buildings give it an incongruous air of importance, and it's a pleasant enough place to stay. The **Granuaile Centre** (June to mid-Sept Mon–Sat 10am–6pm; rest of the year by appointment; ⓣ098/66341; €3.20) details the exploits of Grace O'Malley, the pirate queen (see box on p.503), and has an audio-visual display and local tourist information (it is advisable to call before arriving as the opening hours can be erratic). There is also an exhibition on the Great Famine, as this area suffered heavily from 1845 to 1849: there's a harrowing tale about the march of six hundred starving locals in 1849 to Delphi Lodge to beg, unsuccessfully, for famine relief; many of them, weak and ill-clothed, died on the return journey amid the uncompromising scenery of Doo Lough. This event is commemorated by a small **memorial** on the Doo Lough road and by the annual Great Famine Walk (enquire at the centre for details).

Louisburgh makes a good base for exploring the sandy **beaches** that run east as far as Murrisk Abbey and south to Killadoon. There are any number of excellent **B&Bs** in the area; try the excellent, family-friendly *Springfield House* (ⓣ098/66289; ❷; closed Dec). One of the best places for **food** is *The Weir House* (ⓣ098/66140), just off the main square on Chapel Street, a cosy spot with an evening-time restaurant offering plenty of fish dishes (daily in summer, Fri & Sat in winter) and simpler bar food all day.

Just outside Louisburgh, at **OLD HEAD** (on the Westport road), there's a **campsite** with plenty of facilities including showers and laundry (ⓣ087/648 6885; June–Aug). Old Head has a good **beach**, though little can compare with **Silver Strand** to the south of Louisburgh, claimed grandiosely in the local tourist leaflets to be second only to Florida's Key West; it is, incidentally, the site of a mass Famine burial. You can reach it by turning southwest at the crossroads just outside Louisburgh on the Killary road along lanes that pick their way through rolling country rich in megalithic monuments. It has several **B&Bs**: *Bay Side* (ⓣ098/68613, ⓔbaysidehouse@altavista.com; ❷) is set on a homely farm on the seafront, ten miles from Louisburgh near the village of Killadoon, with a pleasant garden and light meals available.

Clare Island

Follow the road from Louisburgh west along the strand to the land's tip, and you reach **Roonagh Quay**, where boats leave for the fifteen-minute voyage to **CLARE ISLAND** (May–Sept at least 6 boats a day; in winter there are boats most days, especially at weekends; contact O'Malley's on ⓣ098/25045 or O'Grady's on ⓣ098/26307; €12.70 return). In high summer, a **bus** from Westport runs to the quay to coincide with ferries; otherwise, you're stuck with the Westport–Louisburgh service (Mon–Sat 2–4 daily), leaving you with a four-mile walk (on Thurs, it runs as far as Killadoon, leaving only a two-mile walk).

Although it's tiny – only fifteen or so square miles – Clare Island rises to a height of 1522ft in a massive shoulder of land that dominates everything around. There's not much here besides the hills and some ruins, but there's plenty of **walking** (a leaflet available at the hotel manages to detail five walks); a complete circuit of the island would take about six hours. If you're not up to that, you can rent **bikes** or take a minibus **tour** from O'Leary's by the harbour.

The island is famed above all as the stronghold of **Grace O'Malley** (see box on p.503). Her massive **castle** is at the southeastern tip of the island, and in the middle of the island's south shore, she – or a close relative – is buried in a tomb on the north side of the ruined thirteenth-century Cistercian **abbey**. Towards the lighthouse at the northern tip, there's a **loom shop** and demonstration centre (ⓣ098/25800), where you can watch the weavers spinning and dyeing the wool, and even have a go yourself.

You can **stay** overnight at several places on Clare Island. The *Bay View Hotel*, situated five minutes from the harbour on a cliff face above the island's only beach (Ⓣ098/26307; ❷), has a **bar** and **restaurant**. **B&Bs** include the Morans' *Seabreeze* (Ⓣ098/26746; ❷), just past the beach, and the O'Malleys' *Cois Abhainn* (Ⓣ098/26216; ❷), two miles from the harbour at the island's southwest tip, and the owner will pick you up and make evening meals.

Inishturk

To the south of Clare Island lies the even smaller and less developed island of **INISHTURK**, a tranquil, hospitable, six-hundred-foot-high lump of rock and grass that survives on farming and lobster fishing. **Boats** run over from Roonagh Quay twice a day from May to mid-September (rest of the year once a day most days, especially weekends; 50min; Ⓣ086/202 9670; €20 return). From the tiny harbour, the island's paved road branches north and south: to the north, there's a particularly fine **walk**, veering west off the tarmac around a small lake, before climbing to a ruined watchtower in around 45 minutes. The south road rises to the **community centre** after about fifteen minutes, opposite which a narrow gate points down through the fields to the island's finest sandy **beach**, a gorgeous, sheltered strand with clear, blue water and great views of the mainland.

B&Bs include Delia Concannon's by the pier (Ⓣ098/45610; ❷), which offers brightly coloured rooms, lunch and dinner, and a pretty garden with outdoor tables; and *Tránaun House* (Ⓣ098/45641; ❷), a ten-minute walk up the south road at the **post office**, with en-suite rooms, seafood dinners and pick-ups from the harbour. The community centre prepares light lunches during the day in summer, and doubles up as the island **pub** in the evenings with regular music sessions and *céilís*.

Croagh Patrick

The land between Louisburgh and Westport is dominated by the strange, perfectly conical silhouette of **Croagh** (pronounced "croak") **Patrick**, which at 2513ft is by far the highest mountain in the immediate area. The sandy beaches of the shore peter out at Bertra Strand, just short of Murrisk and the ruins of **Murrisk Abbey**, a house of Augustinian canons set up on the shore of Clew Bay by the O'Malley family in 1457, less than a hundred years before Henry VIII's dissolution of the monasteries.

The starting point if you want to climb the mountain is the excellent new **visitor centre** on the main road in Murrisk (daily: March–June, Sept & Oct, with hours on a sliding scale from noon–5pm; July & Aug 9.30am–6pm; free; Ⓣ098/64114, Ⓦwww.croagh-patrick.com). Here you'll find lockers, showers, advice about the climb and the weather, an excellent **café** and an hour-long video on the **history** of the mountain. In 441, during his long missionary tour of the island, **St Patrick** spent the forty days of Lent on Croagh Patrick in prayer and fasting, and it's from here that he is supposed to have rid Ireland of snakes, sending the reptiles crawling to their doom over the precipice of Lugnanarrib just to the south of the summit. This association with the saint has made the mountain the focus of major **pilgrimages**, which take place three times a year, on March 17 (St Patrick's Day), August 15 (Assumption Day) and – the main event – on the last Sunday in July, Reek Day (which coincides with the pagan harvest festival of Lughnasa). On this day, tens of thousands of pilgrims still make the climb to attend Mass on the summit, some of them fasting and walking bare foot.

The **climb** itself, taking on average 3hr 30min return, is easy to follow though very steep in places – you'll need good walking shoes and preferably a stick, available from the visitor centre. Still, there's a surprise when you get to the top. The summit isn't conical, as it looks from the bottom, but forms a flat plateau, with a little **chapel** that took twelve men six months to build in 1905, and a breathtaking **view**: on a good day you can see right from the Twelve Bens in the south to the mountains of Achill Island in the north, the Nephin Begs to the east of the island and on to the Slieve League in Donegal.

If that doesn't sound strenuous enough, you might consider following St Pat's footsteps along the more advanced pilgrimage trail, the **Tóchar Phádraig**, which runs from **Ballintubber Abbey** to the east (seven miles south of Castlebar off the N84) to the summit of Croagh Patrick, making a very long, twenty-mile day (contact the abbey on Ⓣ094/30934 for information). The **Western Way**, coming up from Leenane on its way to Westport, skirts the mountain and intersects Tóchar Phádraig, allowing a rigorous jaunt up to the peak.

On the shore side of the road opposite the visitor centre is the national **monument** to *an nGórta Mór* (the Great Famine); the bronze sculpture, by John Behan, is of a coffin ship headed for America, its rigging made up of the skeletons of the starving. It is particularly evocative when lit up at night.

If you're relying on public transport for a day-trip to Croagh Patrick, Thursday (the main shopping day in Westport) is the best day to attempt the climb, with four **buses** in each direction between the town and Louisburgh; Tuesdays and Saturdays are also possible, but you won't be able to dawdle on the mountain. For **B&B** in the area, try *Béal-an-t-Sáile* (Ⓣ098/64012, Ⓔwaltbrencole@eircom.net; ❷), overlooking the sea less than a mile from the visitor centre, with great breakfasts – the landlady's the chef at the centre. *The Tavern*, on the main road near the visitor centre, does bar **food** in the evenings.

Westport

"The islands in the bay, which was of gold colour, look like so many dolphins and whales basking there," wrote the English novelist W.M. Thackeray on a visit to Westport in 1842. Set in a picturesque eighteenth-century landscape on the shores of Clew Bay, **WESTPORT** is a comfortable, relaxed town, still recognizably Georgian – it was planned by the architects Richard Cassels and James Wyatt – with a leafy mall, octagonal square, a canalized river and one of Ireland's great stately homes, Westport House. For the past ten years, it has capitalized on its fine architecture and busy urban buzz to offer some elegant town living in the midst of the wild scenery of the remote west. During summer, the place is tremendously lively, with Irish, British, French and German visitors returning annually to resample its charms, and an excellent arts **festival**.

In its heyday the town was extremely prosperous, fattened by the trade in linen and cotton cloth and yarn. However, like many places throughout Ireland, Westport was hit hard by the Act of Union of 1801. Although local landowners like the first Marquess of Sligo supported the Act in the belief that it would be of economic benefit, the reverse was in fact true: Irish hand looms were no competition for the new spinning jennies in Britain's industrial towns, the national linen and cotton industries declined, and Westport's economy was ruined. Mass unemployment forced a choice between reverting to subsistence farming or starting a new life in America.

Its quiet Georgian beauties and its lively modern street life apart, the reason Westport is on the tourist trail nowadays is **Westport House** (Easter–Sept, on a schedule of truly Byzantine complexity; ⓣ098/27766 for full details of this, ⓦwww.westporthouse.ie; €15 per adult, €49 for a family with 6 children), a mile or so out of town towards Clew Bay. Built on the site of one of the castles of the sixteenth-century pirate queen Grace O'Malley (a direct ancestor of the current owner; see box on p.503), Westport House was beautifully designed in 1730 by the ubiquitous Richard Cassels, with later additions by Thomas Ivory and James Wyatt. This was one of the first Irish houses opened to the public – and it's had a go at any and every way of making money. There's a bird and animal park in the grounds, a water slide, bouncy castle and mini-railway for the kids plus horse-drawn caravans for rent, while the dungeons (which belonged to an earlier house) have everything from a trace-your-ancestor service to ghostly sound-effects. On the plus side, though, the delicate response of the house to its luminous surroundings of land, light and water is undimmed and wonderful if you can ignore the commerce – and feel like shelling out the swingeing admission fee.

Inside the house there's a *Holy Family* by Rubens, a violin which used to belong to J.M. Synge and, on the first floor, a room with lovely Chinese wallpapers dating from 1780. A lot of the mahogany in the house was brought back from Jamaica by the first marquess, who was instrumental in freeing slaves during his time as governor there. On the walls of the staircase, a series of paintings of local views by James Arthur O'Connor, commissioned by the second marquess in 1818 and 1819, shows an idyllic nineteenth-century landscape, an overweeningly romantic version of the dramatic scenery at Delphi and bustling activity as sailing boats are unloaded at Westport Quay. This was wishful thinking – Westport in the 1810s was already overshadowed by the changes in the relationship with England, and by 1825 was finished as an industrial centre.

Further out on The Quay, the **Clew Bay Heritage Centre** (April, May & Oct Mon–Fri 10am–2pm; June & Sept Mon–Fri 10am–5pm; July & Aug Mon–Fri 10am–5pm, Sun 3–5pm; ⓣ098/26852; €3) is a chaotic but engaging jumble of photos, old coins, agricultural implements, typewriters, ration books and other documents; it also offers a genealogical service and runs guided **walking tours** of the town (July & Aug Tues & Thurs 8pm; €5).

Practicalities

The informative **tourist office** midway down James Street (Mon–Sat 9am–5.45pm, with some extended hours & Sun opening in June–Aug; ⓣ098/25711) has an abundance of information, a fine selection of local historical and walking books plus a good **heritage centre** downstairs (€3) tracing the development of the town. Daytime activities, sightseeing apart, are plentiful. If you're lucky with the weather, the best **beach** within easy reach of town is at Bertra, six miles out on the Louisburgh road. **Cycling** from Westport is rewarding, if strenuous – there are hills in almost every direction except towards Newport: bikes can be rented from Sean Sammon on James Street (ⓣ098/25471). **Horse riding**, which will let you get right off the road, is available half a mile out of town on the Castlebar road at the Drummindoo Equitation Centre (ⓣ098/25616). The sea **angling** in Clew Bay is magnificent, and there are also good opportunities for salmon and trout fishing in nearby lakes and rivers – details from the tourist office. **Sailing** courses can be arranged through the Atlantic Adventure Centre, out on the Louisburgh road (ⓣ098/64806). For **surfing** instruction, and board and wetsuit hire, contact Surf Mayo on ⓣ087/621 2508.

Accommodation

As evidence of its success as a tourist destination, Westport boasts several new and renovated **hotels**. The most stylish of these in the centre of town is the *Wyatt Hotel* on the Octagon (ⓣ098/25027, ⓦwww.wyatthotel.com; ❻), done out in bare wood and bold colours; ask about its various special deals. At the other end of the style scale is the *Olde Railway Hotel* (ⓣ098/25166, ⓦwww.anu.ie/railwayhotel; ❻), an eighteenth-century coaching inn overlooking the canalized river on the leafy Mall, stuffed with antique furniture and Victorian artefacts. There are also dozens of **B&Bs**: try *Altamont House*, a well-run, flower-strewn place on Ballinrobe Road towards the station (ⓣ098/25226; ❷); the spacious *Carrabaun House* (ⓣ098/26196, ⓔcarrabaun@anu.ie; ❷), with fine views half a mile out of town on the Leenane road; or *Cedar Lodge*, set in colourful gardens five minutes' walk from the centre on Kings Hill (ⓣ098/25417, ⓔmflynn@esatclear.ie; ❷; closed Jan).

The more central of the town's two **hostels** is the fine *Old Mill Hostel* on James St, down from the Octagon (IHH & IHO; ⓣ098/27045, ⓕ21745), converted from part of an eighteenth-century complex of mills and warehouses. The large *Club Atlantic*, opposite the train station on Altamont St, and close to Fair Green where buses stop (ⓣ098/26644, ⓕ26241; mid-March to Oct), is affiliated with both An Óige and the IHH and is very well run and maintained. For **camping**, try the *Club Atlantic* hostel, the Westport Estate *Parklands Caravan and Camping Park* (ⓣ098/27766; mid-May to Aug), or Old Head (see p.498).

Eating

There is a surprising variety of **places to eat** in Westport at all ends of the market. *The Lemon Peel*, just off the Octagon (ⓣ098/26929; Tues–Sun evenings), has deservedly gained a good reputation by imaginatively improvising with local ingredients – the cajun-crusted salmon is especially recommended. Several reasonably priced Italian restaurants with similar menus – pastas, pizzas and more substantial meat and fish dishes – operate on Bridge St, including *Sol Rios* and *Antica Roma*. On the same street is *Orient Aroma*, a superior Chinese restaurant offering some unusual dishes, early-bird set menus and Sunday all-you-can-eat buffet lunches. The *Quay Cottage* (ⓣ098/26412; Tues–Sat evenings), in a quaint stone building near the harbour, is the place to go for seafood and fine vegetarian dishes, while nearby the *Asgard* (ⓣ098/25319) has a delicious bar menu, as well as fancier, mostly fish, dishes in its adjacent restaurant. During the day, try *Tiley's*, opposite the tourist office on James Street, or *McCormack's*, a brightly painted café and art gallery on Bridge Street, which both serve coffee, salads, homemade soup and fine sandwiches; or *The Pentagon*, a bright, modern place in the car park between Bridge and Mill Streets, offering bagels, tasty salads, seafood platters, a wide range of very good coffees and **Internet** access. If you're self-catering, you can find some excellent local produce, much of it organic, at the **Thursday market** at the town hall on the Octagon.

Festivals and nightlife

Westport has developed a real cosmopolitan feel and attracts artistic types from Ireland and beyond. The main focuses for this are the **Arts Festival** towards the end of September (ⓣ098/29551, ⓦwww.westportartsfestival.com), and the public **art studios** which stage temporary exhibitions in the redeveloped area of The Quay, by the entrance to Westport House. In the centre, the best **pubs** are on Bridge Street, where *The West* is hugely popular with a young crowd (arrive early and stay put) and *Matt Molloy's Bar*, owned by the eponymous flautist of The Chieftains, features occasional musical celebrities and gets incredibly crowded for its frequent traditional sessions. If you want to enjoy a quiet drink then *Conway's* on Bridge Street is the place to go.

Newport

The road north out of Westport, bordered by bright fuchsia hedges, follows the shore of Clew Bay for eight miles to **NEWPORT**, a neat, little eighteenth-century town that makes a serviceable base for both the sea and the Nephin Beg Mountains. Newport's main boast is that one of Grace Kelly's ancestors once lived in nearby Drimurla. It's also a centre for sea angling; if you go in the evening to the swanky *Newport House Hotel*, you'll see massive salmon – caught by guests earlier in the day – laid out for the less energetic to admire.

About two miles outside Newport and signposted off the road to Achill is **Burrishoole Abbey**, a Dominican priory in a peaceful setting, lapped by the waters of the bay – at high tide you have to hop across a stepping stone to get in. It was founded in the fifteenth century by Richard Burke – second husband of the pirate queen Grace O'Malley and unfortunately nicknamed "Iron Dick" – who spent the last years of his life here. The abbey has some cloisters still surviving and stands as a symbol of the spread of religious life under the Normans. Another mile or so along the Achill road, the turning labelled "Carrickanowley

Grace O'Malley: the pirate queen

There came to me also a most famous feminine sea captain called Granny Ny Mally and offered her services unto me, wheresoever I would command her, with three galleys and two hundred fighting men, either in Scotland or in Ireland. She brought with her her husband, for she was as well by sea as by land well more than Mrs Mate with him... This was a notorious woman in all the coasts of Ireland.

Sir Henry Sidney, Lord Deputy of Ireland, 1577

Grace O'Malley, or Gráinne Ni Mhaille (often corrupted to **Granuaile**; c. 1530–1600), was the daughter of Owen O'Malley, chief of the west coast islands. Through fearless and none-too-scrupulous warfare and piracy, she made herself queen of the Clew Bay area when he died. She effectively controlled the vigorous trade between Galway and the Continent, as well as running a lucrative business importing Scottish mercenaries for the chieftains' wars against Elizabeth I and their cattle-rustling and plundering activities. She earned her place in Irish legend by being one of the few Irish chiefs to stand up to the English.

In 1575 she visited the St Lawrences of Howth Castle near Dublin (see p.124), expecting to be made welcome in the Irish fashion. When, instead, she was told that the family was eating and that she would have to wait, she responded by abducting the family's heir. When she met Elizabeth I in London in 1593, she insisted on being treated as her regal equal. However, always a canny tactician, Grace switched sides when she realized she couldn't beat the English, and her son was created first Viscount Mayo. Continually mentioned in sixteenth-century dispatches, her exploits included dissolving her Celtic secular marriage to her second husband, Sir Richard Burke of Mayo, by slamming the castle door in his face and then stealing all his castles. At a time when the old Gaelic world was crumbling around her, Grace ensured the continuation of her own dynasty and something of the old culture.

Castle" brings you to **Rockfleet Castle**, a perfect fifteenth- or sixteenth-century tower house that stands with its feet in a quiet outlet of Clew Bay – you'll get your own feet wet stepping up to the door at high tide. An English attack on it was quelled by Grace O'Malley, who subsequently lived here.

For upmarket **accommodation**, there's the gracious *Newport House Hotel*, set in pretty grounds overlooking the river in the centre of town (Ⓣ098/41222, Ⓦwww.newporthouse.ie; ❽; mid-March to Sept). *De Bille House* B&B on the main street (Ⓣ098/41145; ❷; July–Sept) is a handsome stone building offering generously sized rooms that are a good option for families. Good, basic **food** is available from *Kelly's Kitchen* and *The Village Bakery* on the main street, but for sumptuous dining the only place is *Newport House Hotel* which specializes in hearty six-course meals using locally caught fish, seafood and game. There's **Internet** access at *Nevin's Pub*, and the gift shop on the main street has a **bureau de change**. For **horse riding** and pony trekking contact Mulrany Riding School (Ⓣ098/36126); permits for **fishing** are available from the *Newport House Hotel*.

Five miles due north of Newport at the head of Lough Feeagh, high among the powerful outlines of the Nephin Beg Mountains, is the An Óige **hostel** *Traenlaur Lodge* (Ⓣ098/41358; June–Sept), which has family rooms and meals available. The hostel is joined to Newport by the waymarked **Western Way**, which heads north at this stage towards Ballycastle, before looping round to Killala and Ballina. Newport is also the start of the **Bangor Trail** (guidebook available from bookshops and tourist offices), which cuts north-northwest across the wild and lonely Nephin Begs for thirty miles to Bangor.

Achill Island

More than with most places in the west, you need good weather to enjoy **ACHILL ISLAND** (Ⓦwww.achilltourism.com). Although it's the part of County Mayo most developed for tourism, this means no more than a few hotels, B&Bs and hostels, and if it rains there's simply nothing to do but pack up and head for Westport or Sligo. Because of a government tax allowance scheme, Achill has been blighted by a plethora of tourist developments, many of which are modern "cottages" that take no account of traditional architecture or landscape. Against this, however, there's the magnificence of the mountains and cliffs, and in good weather, Achill can be magical, especially for campers who can live at the water's edge. The island's sandy beaches never seem overcrowded, although they attract plenty of tourists in high summer, mostly Irish and Germans, the latter attracted by associations with writer Heinrich Böll, who lived at Dugort in the 1950s. Inland, the bogs and mountains are dotted with ancient relics – standing stones, stone circles and dolmens. The largest of the Irish islands (although it's connected to the mainland by a road bridge), Achill was entirely Irish-speaking until very recently and its eastern half is now a designated Gaeltacht area. Tourism here seems to have had an almost entirely beneficial effect, economically at least: before its arrival, islanders subsisted to a very great extent on remittances sent home by emigrant relatives. The island can be seen at its liveliest during **Scoil Acla**, two weeks of traditional music and cultural programmes at the beginning of August.

Achill Sound

The bridge that crosses to the island will bring you first to **ACHILL SOUND** (Gob an Choire). It's worth noting though, that on the left before crossing the

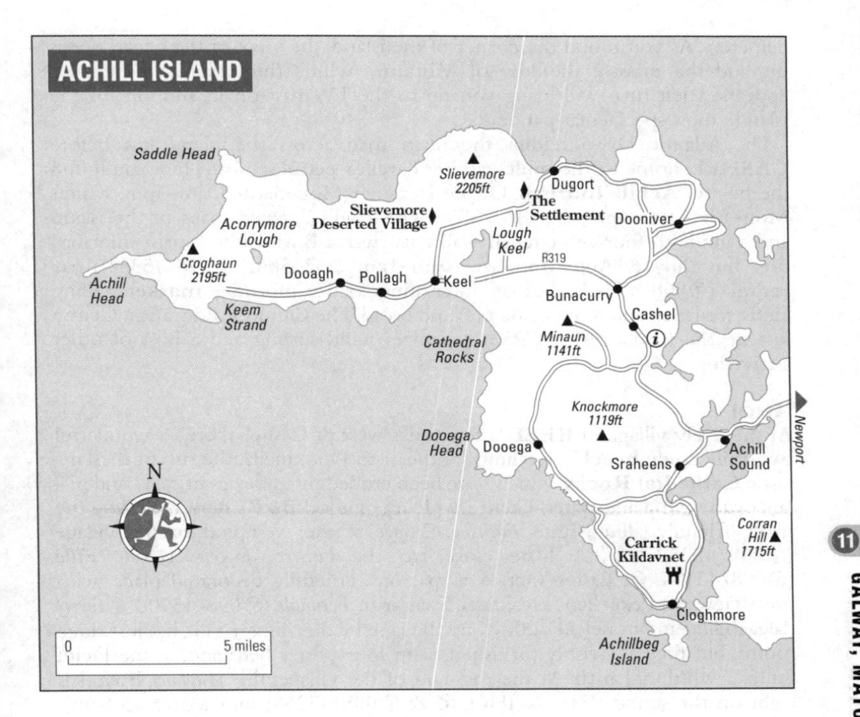

bridge stands a fine new **hotel**, *Óstán Oiléan Acla* (Ⓣ098/45138, Ⓦwww.achillislandhotel.com; ④), which has an excellent bar-restaurant offering fine views of the bay and weekly traditional music in the summer. Also before the bridge, opposite the Garda Station, you'll find the *Railway Hostel* (Ⓣ098/45187) in the old station house, with good rooms, some private or en-suite, two kitchens and big log fires. On crossing the bridge, faded beachballs and plastic buckets hang forlornly outside a cluster of souvenir shops; of more interest may be the island's only **ATM**. Achill Sound really isn't the best base for exploring the island, but if you decide to go no further, it's worth pressing on a few hundred yards and turning left for an excellent **hostel**, the *Wild Haven* (Ⓣ098/45392), which offers the comforts of a warm duvet and an open fire.

Around the island

A combination of **walking** and **cycling** is the most pleasurable way to get to know Achill, although the island can be fairly strenuous going (hitching is a viable alternative, especially in season when the island is full of visitors). The coast road around the eastern part of the island has now been signposted as the "Atlantic Drive". After a left turn at Achill Sound, you'll follow the strait for three miles, before coming to **KILDAVNET**, where the well-preserved tower of the fifteenth-century **Carrick Kildavnet Castle**, once owned by the redoubtable Grace O'Malley, gazes out at the mainland (keys from the house next door). There are also the ruins of an eighteenth-century church and cemetery. As you round the corner of the island, the view of the ocean opens up, and the massive shoulder of **Minaun**, Achill's third highest mountain, appears; a left turn will bring you up to the TV mast on its summit for the island's most spectacular panorama.

The Atlantic Drive rejoins the main road across the island just before **CASHEL**, home to the multi-tasking Lavelle's petrol station. Here you'll find the helpful **Achill Tourism Office** (summer Mon–Sat 9.30am–5pm; winter Mon–Fri 10am–4pm; ⓣ098/47353), which sells detailed maps of the island and a guide to fourteen circular walks; its rival, a Bord Fáilte tourist information hut (July & Aug Mon–Sat 10am–1pm & 2–5pm; ⓣ098/45384); **car rental** (ⓣ098/47242); and an interesting Friday-morning **market**, selling crafts, fresh veg and homemade pies and bread. The Outdoor Education Centre just up the road (ⓣ098/47253) organizes wind-surfing and a host of other **activities**.

Keel

At the lively village of **KEEL**, a few miles west of Cashel, there's a wonderful two-mile sandy **beach** stretching southeast to Dookinella, the site of the fantastic **Cathedral Rocks**, which have been eroded into a series of caves and pillars by the wind and water. There are plenty of good **B&Bs** here, including the small, friendly, all en-suite *Fuchsia Cottage* at the west end of the village (ⓣ098/43350; ❷). A little closer to the centre, *Joyce's Marian Villa* (ⓣ098/43134; ❸; Easter–Oct) is a spacious, tastefully decorated place, with great views and excellent breakfasts. Swiss-run *Ferndale* (ⓣ098/43908, ⓔferndaleachill@eircom.net; ❹), 200yd up the lane by the *Annexe* pub, has just three rooms, but they're lavishly furnished, with four-poster beds and, in the Heidi Suite, a whirlpool bath. At the east end of the village, the *Wayfarer* **hostel** is right on the strand (IHH & IHO; ⓣ & ⓕ098/43266; mid-March to Sept), while *Richview* (IHO; ⓣ098/43462) is run by a friendly musician and set in an attractive old house at the opposite end of the village. There's a swanky caravan park and **campsite** (ⓣ094/903 2054) on the strand.

The best places for **eating** are the *Beehive*, a relaxed café-restaurant and crafts shop, with a bureau de change; *Ferndale* (see above), which offers an ambitious range of world cuisine, an impressive wine list and a huge picture window overlooking the bay; and *Calvey's*, a smart restaurant with comfy banquettes and great views, conveniently next to Calvey's butcher shop for dishes such as fresh Achill mountain lamb. **Drink** at *The Minaun* and *The Annexe*, which are both likely to have traditional-music sessions. The post office and supermarket provides **bike rental** and a bureau de change, and travelling **banks** pitch camp in the centre of Keel on Monday, Tuesday and Wednesday mornings. **Windsurfing** courses and board rental are available from Windwise by the lake at the east end of town (ⓣ098/47968), and **scuba diving** can be arranged through Joseph Carey (ⓣ087/234 9884). You can access the **Internet** at Keel's Achill IT Centre.

Pollagh, Dooagh and beyond

West along the road from Keel is the small settlement of **POLLAGH**, and beyond, overlooking its own sandy beach, **DOOAGH**. Pollagh's *Achill Head* **hotel** (ⓣ098/43108, ⓦwww.achillheadhotel.com; ❸) has smart, recently refurbished rooms, a restaurant, a friendly bar serving very good pizzas to eat in or take away and a weekend nightclub. At Dooagh you'll find a small **folk-life centre** with irregular hours (ⓣ098/43564), and fine **B&B** at the *West Coast House* (ⓣ098/43317, ⓔachwch@anu.ie; ❷), which is signposted from the Keel road and offers amazing views of the bay below. *Croaghan* also offers comfy beds and good breakfasts (Ⓣ098/43301; ❷), as well as an evening-time **restaurant** (weekends only out of season), with great views, set menus and dishes such as catch of the day with sundried-tomato butter.

Beyond Dooagh, the main road ends at the golden sands and, on a good day, sparkling turquoise waters of **Keem Bay**. Often deserted, it's a rewarding place to make for, with impressive views over Clew Bay, but if you're on a bike, be warned: it's tough going (and the sheer drop on the seaward side is vertigo-inducing).

A turning off the Keem road will take you up to **Acorrymore Lough** – surrounded by scree slopes, and now dammed to supply water locally. It's a bleak, rather than poetic, spot and is the best place to embark on an ascent of **Croghaun**, the island's second highest mountain, just a whisker lower than Slievemore at 2195ft. Croghaun's seaward side boasts spectacularly high cliffs, the island's highest, and it is decidedly tough hill-walking country, so you need to be reasonably experienced even to think of attempting it. Once at the top, however, you're rewarded with a magnificent view of the Mullet Peninsula and the scattered islands, while the Croagh Patrick and the Partry mountains rise spectacularly in the southeast. A far easier walk, with only slightly less spectacular views, begins at the Keem Bay car park, heading up to the cliff tops and west along the humped back of **Achill Head** to the end.

Dugort and the north

While **DUGORT**, a clutch of houses nestling at the base of Slievemore Mountain, lacks the arresting open views of the Atlantic on offer at Keel or Dooagh, it does make a quiet, comfortable base. Take the inland road along the west side of the small lough from Keel, and after a mile and a half you'll come to the **Deserted Village**, a strange, linear settlement whose abandonment is still a mystery. Towering to the north is **Slievemore**, Achill's highest mountain at 2205ft – a massive pile of quartzite and mica. A little further east on its southern slopes stands a **dolmen** with a stone circle at each end and a *booley* village of huts formerly used during summer pasturing – a reminder of a much newer, but equally extinct, transhumant way of life. A mile or so further on towards Dugort, some ruined buildings and scattered gravestones are all that's left of a village known simply as **The Settlement**. It was founded in 1834 by a Protestant vicar, the Reverend E. Nangle, who bought up sixty percent of the island and built schools and a printing press in an ultimately unsuccessful effort to evangelize the islanders. At the foot of Slievemore, on the seaward side, are the **Seal Caves**, burrowing way back under the mountain; you can visit them by boat from the tiny pier at Dugort.

You can **stay** on the southern slopes of the mountain at *McDowell's Hotel and Activity Centre* (Ⓣ098/43148, Ⓦwww.achill-leisure.ie; ❹), which does excellent food, including vegetarian, and offers a wide range of outdoor activities, while in Dugort itself you can stay in comfort at *Gray's Guesthouse* (Ⓣ098/43244; ❸), a rambling establishment comprised of several houses, taking up one street of the tiny hamlet. Five miles east, and signposted from all the main roads, is the *Valley House Hostel* (IHO; Ⓣ098/47204, Ⓦwww.valley-house.com), a handsome, crumbling edifice that was once home to the woman whose story is told in J.M. Synge's *The Playboy of the Western World* – her rejected suitor burned down a barn and tossed her onto the flames. The place now operates as a hostel with camping available and the luxury of a bar in the courtyard behind the house. Dugort's other **campsite** is the *Seal Caves Caravan and Camping Park* (Ⓣ098/43262; April–Sept).

Northwest Mayo

Predominantly bogland, **northwest Mayo** is an area that can seem forbidding in bad weather, but when the sun shines and suffuses everything in a hazy glow, you can forgive all. The long, straight bog road west to **Belmullet** is incredibly bleak and desolate, though the village itself is awash with garish, pastel-coloured buildings. East of Belmullet is the county's most interesting sight, the **Céide Fields**, where prehistoric field patterns have been uncovered beneath nearly seven feet of bog, offering a startling view of the unchanging nature of human habitation here over five millennia. The coast road leading from the Céide Fields to the historically resonant town of **Killala**, scene of the 1798 French invasion, is very dramatic. All along the coast from the tip of the Mullet Peninsula to Ballina, you'll spot brown *Tír Sáile* signposts, marking the **North Mayo Sculpture Trail**, a striking series of fourteen modern outdoor sculptures, celebrating the wild beauty and cultural heritage of the area; for further information, contact Ann and Laurence Howard (Ⓣ098/45107) or go to Ⓦwww.mayoireland.ie/tirsaile.htm.

Belmullet and the Mullet Peninsula

Heading up from Achill on the N59 to unremarkable **Bangor**, then along the R313, you'll come to the functional little village of **BELMULLET** (Béal an Mhuirthead, "mouth of the Mullet"), its streets perpetually mired from the mud of the bogs. Like most Irish towns, it's a planned settlement, founded as late as 1825 by the local landlord, William Carter, to "create a home market for produce that did not previously exist nearer than thirty miles by land". Its success was such that it eclipsed the older landlord village of Binghamstown (An Geata Mór), on the peninsula, which was deserted by the late nineteenth century. The attraction of the place lies not so much in its physical charms as in a kind of unpretentious unhurriedness – life goes on, shops stay open until late, and the sun arches slowly toward the horizon over the wide western sea.

There is a small **tourist office** maintained by the Iorras Domhnann Rural Tourism Co-operative on the left side of the main street as you enter the town (July & Aug Mon–Sat 10am–6pm; Ⓣ097/81500, Ⓦwww.belmullet.net), which can give information about the lively **Feile Iorras** in late July, a folk arts festival centred on Belmullet (Ⓦwww.feileiorras.org). You can **stay** in the *Western Strands Hotel* (Ⓣ097/81096; ❷), which has basic rooms, and there are also numerous B&Bs: for good value try *Mill House* in American Street (Ⓣ097/81181; ❷; June–Aug), which also **rents bikes**, or *Drom Caoin* (Ⓣ097/81195, Ⓔdromcaoin@esatlink.com; ❷), which caters well for vegetarians and offers fine views of Blacksod Bay. There are plenty of **bars** and fast-food joints, so take your pick; the liveliest bar is probably the one at the *Western Strands*, where you'll also get a good **lunch** or **dinner**.

A flat slab of land that seems tacked on to the mainland almost as an afterthought, the **Mullet Peninsula** is sparsely populated, but the houses are scattered in the characteristically Irish way (town-dwelling, as well as Ireland's town-planning, was largely an Anglo-Irish invention). Along with this pattern of habitation, you'll also see field systems not much different from the Stone Age ones uncovered at Céide (see opposite).

The seaward side of the peninsula is raked by Atlantic winds to the extent that almost no vegetation can survive. The landward side, overlooking Blacksod Bay, at the southern tip of the peninsula, is much more sheltered and has some good **beaches**, notably at Elly Bay halfway down. To the east and north the land rises; although the cliffs are not hugely spectacular, there's some rewarding walking. The peninsula is one of the locations where the legendary Children of Lir (see box on p.218) were condemned to spend their last three hundred years; they are buried, according to legend, on Inishglora, a tiny island off the west coast. The peninsula is rich in historical remains, too: there are promontory **forts** at Doonamo, Doonaneanir and Portnafrankach. The one at Doonamo, on an impressive cliff-top site, encloses three *clocháns* and a circular fort. Under the waters of Blacksod Bay lies **La Rata**, the largest of three Spanish Armada galleons that sank in 1588.

If you make it down as far as **AGHLEAM** near the tip of the peninsula, call in at the **Ionad Deirble Heritage Centre** (Easter–Sept Mon–Sat 10am–6pm, Sun noon–6pm; ⓣ097/85728; €2.50), which contains some interesting exhibits on subjects such as whaling, Inis Gé and landlordism, has a café and can provide info on local walks. In calm weather, Matthew and Josephine Geraghty run **boat trips** (ⓣ097/85741) out to the islands of Inis Gé (Inishkea North and South) for €16.50 return from nearby Blacksod.

East along the coast from Belmullet

East of Belmullet, the country becomes much wilder: overlooked by the ice-polished shapes of the mountains, it's rough, boggy terrain where many of the remoter villages are still Irish-speaking. Ten miles out towards Ballycastle, you'll see a signpost for the village of **POLLATOMISH** (Poll an Tómais, "Thomas's Hole"), a delightful little place deep in fjord-like country, with a sandy beach, two pubs and two **hostels**. At *Kilcommon Lodge* (IHH & IHO; ⓣ097/84621, ⓦwww.kilcommonlodge.ie), the dorm and twin rooms are excellent, meals and bike hire are available and there's a congenial reading room, heated by a turf fire. The recently refurbished, non-smoking *Old Rectory* (IHO; ⓣ097/84115; April–Sept) also has fine dorms and private rooms, along with panoramic views and a cosy common room. **Diving** and other watersports are laid on at the Cuan na Farraige Dive Centre (ⓣ097/87800).

Around the bay from Pollatomish, a single-track roads lead up to **Benwee Head**; at almost 820ft, this massive cliff has great views of the Donegal cliffs to the northeast and the **Stags of Broadhaven**, a series of seven three-hundred-foot rocks, which stand a mile and a half off the coast. **Portacloy**, where there's a deeply indented bay edged with golden sand, makes a good starting point for walking on the headland. On the road southwest to Rinroe Point at **Carrowteige** (Ceathrú Thaidhg), the other obvious setting-off point for Benwee Head, is the **Donal Turpin** factory shop, an unlikely – not to be missed – outpost of the fashion industry. Here local women work on hand looms to produce designer knitwear in linen, silk and wool at amazingly low prices. The road descends through intricate interlockings of land and sea to golden beaches and the tiny harbour at **Rinroe** itself. East of Portacloy, near Porturlin, the waves have carved the rocks into weird, contorted shapes, including the **Arches**, a thirty-foot opening in the cliff which the brave – or foolhardy – attempt to row through in good weather at low tide.

Céide Fields

In terms of understanding the landscape, the most important site on this stretch of coast is the prehistoric farm that covers some 24 square miles of boggy moorland between Belderrig and Ballycastle. Although signposted from the road, the Belderrig site offers little enlightenment to the untrained eye: for that, carry on another five miles to the main site at **Céide** (pronounced "cage-a")

Fields, five miles short of Ballycastle (daily: mid-March to May, Oct & Nov 10am–5pm; June–Sept 10am–6pm; €3.10; Heritage Card). As Seamus Heaney's poem *Belderg* observes:

They just kept turning up
and were thought of as foreign
one-eyed and benign, they lie about his house
quernstones out of a bog

Under nearly seven feet of blanket bog, archaeologists have unearthed the stone walls of a Neolithic farm system and apparently solved the riddle of how the builders of the great megalithic tombs that run across the northern part of Ireland lived. They were, it seems, farming people who joined the original fishers and hunters of Ireland around five thousand years ago and seem to have lived in harmony with them, and each other: the pattern of settlement is dispersed and shows no defensive features. The fields run longitudinally with the slope of the land and appear to have been used for pasture – as in contemporary Ireland, where the largest single contribution to the national economy still comes from grass-raised livestock.

The faint marks left by these ancient farmers don't look like much to the untrained eye, and the impressive, pyramidal **visitor centre** is, inevitably, heavy on interpretation. The centre includes an exhibition, a viewing platform, an audio-visual theatre (with a romantically narrated show giving some of the area's geological background) and an excellent café. The entrance fee to the site includes a guided tour, usually by one of the archaeological workers on the dig.

Ballycastle

BALLYCASTLE, in the wide valley of the River Ballinglen, is a tranquil village of just one broad, sloping street, with a good swimming **beach**. The **tourist office**, which will be able to offer detailed advice on walking nearby, is based at the Ballycastle Resource Centre (Mon–Sat 10.30am–5pm, Sun 1–4pm; closed for long lunches). Changing exhibitions of works by internationally known artists attached to the local **Ballinglen Arts Foundation** are held at the Courthouse Gallery. For accommodation, try the warm hospitality, great breakfasts and sea views at *Keadyville* **B&B** (Ⓣ096/43288; ❶), or the elegantly refurbished former coastguard station and subsequent convent, the *Stella Maris* **hotel** (Ⓣ096/43322, Ⓦwww.stellamarisireland.com; ❼). There are a handful of relaxed **bars** – try *Healy's* or *Polke's* – and you can eat well at *Mary's* homely **restaurant**.

At **Downpatrick Head** to the northeast of Ballycastle, there are some puffing holes that send up tall plumes of water in rough weather, and a detached stack of rock with a fort perched on it; a plaque commemorates those who were killed in the aftermath of the 1798 Rebellion. There's a profusion of rare birds here and grand views over to Céide Fields and the wild country to the west, eastwards to the Sligo mountains and north across the wide, empty sea.

Killala and around

KILLALA, overlooking Killala Bay as the coast curves back round towards Ballina, is a must, both for the magnificent local scenery and for its historical connections. Scene of one of the most significant events in Irish history – the unsuccessful French invasion organized by Wolfe Tone in 1798 (see box opposite) – it's a pleasantly run-down seaside town, so small it's difficult to believe it's a bishopric, with lovely, wild coasts and some good roads for cycling. As far as sights go, the highlights are an attractive quayside and a fine round tower, but it's the historic atmosphere that's the real attraction here. A couple of miles north there's also a good, sheltered, sandy **beach** for swimming at Ross Point (signposted from the Ballycastle road).

The **tourist office** (July–Sept daily 10am–5pm; ☎096/32166) is in the community centre on the road out of town towards Ballina. Most local newsagents sell Bishop Stock's *Narrative* of the events of 1798 – a surprisingly sympathetic account of the uprising. There are a few comfortable **B&B** options here: nearest to the centre, though still half a mile out on the Crossmolina road, is *Kevin Munnelly's Farmhouse* (☎096/32331; ❷; June–Aug), while *O'Hara's Beach View House* (☎096/32023; ❸) is just under two miles out towards the beach.

The French invasion

On August 22, 1798, three warships flying British colours anchored at Kilcummin, near Killala. The Protestant Bishop Stock, relieved that they were apparently English and not the rumoured French invasion fleet, sent his two sons and the port surveyor to pay their respects. They were immediately taken prisoner; the **invasion** had begun. After a brief resistance, Killala yielded to the French, and at sunset that evening a French soldier climbed to the top of the Bishop's Palace and replaced the British flag with a green flag with a harp in the centre, bearing the words *Erin go Bragh* (Ireland Forever).

Wolfe Tone, the inspirational leader of the United Irishmen, had been working since his exile from Ireland in 1794 to secure foreign aid for his planned insurrection against the British. However, by the time the first French expedition of 1100 men under General Humbert reached Killala, the rebellion had already been all but crushed. Not only was there a military mismatch between the French professional soldiers and the few poorly armed Irish novices who joined them, but there were also ideological clashes. The French had expected that liberation from British rule would appeal to Catholics and Protestants alike, and were further confused to find the Irish volunteers greeting them in the name of the Blessed Virgin and apparently having no idea of the significance of the French Revolution.

The rest of the story is sadly predictable. With some heroic fighting, the Franco-Irish army took Killala, Ballina and Castlebar, but on September 8, near the village of Ballinamuck in County Longford, seriously depleted in both numbers and weapons, it was defeated by the united armies of Lord Cornwallis and General Lake. The French were taken prisoner and returned to France; the Irish rebels were hanged. At Rath Lackan, there's a statue to the first French soldier who fell in the 1798 struggle, as well as a wide bay with golden sands looking over to the Sligo mountains.

A month later, sailing with another French force from Brest, Wolfe Tone was himself captured – along with the French fleet – off the coast of Donegal. He was subsequently court-martialled and condemned to death. Despite his insistence that he should be treated with military honour, and therefore shot, he was sentenced to hang. Before that could be carried out, he cut his throat with a pocketknife and died after seven days of agony. He came to personify the tradition of both revolutionary violence and religious tolerance (he was a Protestant) in the cause of an independent Ireland.

The events of 1798 led directly to the Act of Union with Britain three years later, while the land agitation that spread throughout the country laid the foundations for land reform, Catholic emancipation and, eventually, the long process that led to Irish independence.

Killala is a convivial place with a disproportionate number of **pubs** – *An Granuaile* and *The Village Inn* are two of the most traditional. **Music** is often available at *The Anchor Bar*, as is local seafood and other simple, filling **meals**.

Ballina to Castlebar

The interior of County Mayo can't match the splendour of its sea coasts, and unless you're keen on fishing or walking, you're unlikely to spend much time here. Like all of Ireland's less touristy areas, however, it has a charm of its own if you stick with it. A region of rough moorland – the foothills of the Nephin Beg and Ox ranges – it's strewn with lakes, giving way in the east to flatter, more fertile country. It's dotted, too, with market towns such as **Pontoon**, **Foxford** and **Crossmolina**, each with its own distinctive architecture and character.

The road from Killala to Ballina runs through flat farm country. The minor road that runs closer to the Moy estuary is more interesting, with two abbeys on the estuary, **Moyne** and **Rosserk**, both of them founded in the fifteenth century. Rosserk, with a tower at the water's edge, is the bigger and more poetic of the two – and considered the best Franciscan building in the country – but both have good cloisters. Look out for the sixteenth-century graffiti on the wall at Moyne; the place was burned down by Sir Richard Bingham, the English governor of Connacht, in 1590.

Ballina

The busy town of **BALLINA**, clustered around two graceful bridges on the River Moy, makes a good place to stock up on provisions and information; the town is especially vibrant during the week-long street **festival** that takes place in mid-July. The elegant Victorian and Edwardian pub- and shopfronts testify to a long history of vigorous trading, and this tradition continues in the rebuilding and energetic business activity that's evident everywhere. Stock up on smoked salmon at **Clarke's Salmon Smokery** on O'Rahilly Street, which also displays an impressive range of fresh, whole fish in its windows.

The **tourist office** (Mon–Fri 9.30am–5pm; Ⓣ096/70848) is located between the bridges on the side of the river away from town, and the entrance is guarded by a life-sized picture of Ballina's most famous daughter, former president Mary Robinson. You can **stay** and indulge in some real splendour, with a touch of Gothic-horror excess, at the *Belleek Castle* (Ⓣ096/22400, Ⓦwww.belleekcastle.com; ❼): take Pearse Street eastward from the centre, and follow the signs; a left turn will bring you through an imposing stone gateway and to a long drive through dark forest to a Neo-Jacobean mansion in forbidding grey stone. The *Bartra House Hotel* (Ⓣ096/22200; ❹), a cheerful and friendly place on Pearse Street, is a pleasant, cheaper option. The best of the many **B&Bs** are: *Ashley House* (Ⓣ096/22799; ❷), half a mile out off the Crossmolina road near Belleek Castle, and, four miles out of town on Quay Road, *Jordan's Red River Lodge* (Ⓣ096/22841, Ⓔredriverlodge@eircom.net; ❷; April–Oct). For **camping**, try the well-equipped *Belleek Caravan and Camping Park* (Ⓣ096/71533), a couple of miles north of town on the Killala road.

When **eating**, make sure you try the famous Moy salmon. *Murphy Bros*, a large, well-run pub on the right bank of the Moy, a little downriver from the tourist office, does good seafood platters in the bar and more sophisticated fish and seafood dishes in the upstairs restaurant. *The Broken Jug* – named after John Banville's play – a roomy pub at the top of O'Rahilly Street, offers bar food until 8pm and Indian food in the evening-time restaurant upstairs. For a **drink**, and perhaps a lunchtime sandwich or salad, make for *Gaughans*, a great old-fashioned pub on O'Rahilly St.

Crossmolina

Five or so miles southwest of Ballina, **CROSSMOLINA**, at the top of the renowned fishing lake of Lough Conn, has a place to **stay** that's a sight in itself. Not far south of town on the lakeshore, *Enniscoe House* (Ⓣ096/31112, Ⓦwww.enniscoe.com; ❻; April to Mid-Oct), a Georgian mansion that does B&B, is a good example of easy-going Georgian attitudes to architecture. Originally built in the mid-eighteenth century as a three-storey house, it was extended in the 1790s (and damaged in 1798 when the French army marched down the back avenue) to include a grand facade overlooking Lough Conn. The result inside is two completely different structures whose floor levels and room sizes don't correspond at all; outside, the house's restored Victorian walled and pleasure **gardens** are now open to the public. At the nearby **North Mayo Family Heritage Centre** (June–Sept Mon–Fri 9am–6pm, Sat & Sun 2–6pm; Oct–May Mon–Fri 9am–4pm; Ⓣ096/31809, Ⓦwww.mayo.irish-roots.net) visitors can trace their north Mayo ancestors, browse around the centre's mainly agricultural artefacts and watch demonstrations of traditional crafts.

There is a **tourist office** in the new Enterprise Centre near the statue that marks the middle of Crossmolina (May–Oct Mon–Fri 10am–1.30pm & 2–5pm, Sat 10.30am–1pm & 2–4.30pm). For **accommodation**, *Lake View House B&B* on the Ballina road (Ⓣ096/31296, Ⓔlakeviewhouse@oceanfree.net; ❷) makes for a comfortable alternative to the *Enniscoe*, and you can get good daytime **meals**, as well as homemade cakes and bread, in the *Tea Room*, and evening meals in the lively *Hiney's* **pub** nearby.

Pontoon and Foxford

Sitting on the neck of land that separates Lough Conn from Lough Cullin, **PONTOON** is a good base for exploring both the lakes' shores and the foothills of the Nephin Beg Mountains to the northwest, especially if you check in at creeper-clad *Healy's Hotel* (Ⓣ094/56443, Ⓦwww.healyspontoon.com; ❺). Originally a lakeside coaching inn and hunting lodge and latterly a no-nonsense anglers' **hotel**, it has undergone considerable renovation and is well regarded not only by fishermen but by the many locals who eat at its excellent **restaurant**, renowned for its wholesome, home-cooked Irish food.

FOXFORD, four miles east, is a trim village in the lee of the Ox Mountains which owed its late nineteenth-century survival to the **Foxford Woollen Mill** (Mon–Sat 10am–6pm, Sun noon–6pm; €4, including tour of present-day factory), which now has an elaborate audio-visual presentation to tell its story. There's a gift shop and upstairs a pleasant tea shop; rooms are let to local artists and craftspeople. After the 1840s Famine, the potato crop failed again in the 1870s, resulting in evictions and abject poverty for the people of the town and the peat-cutting districts around. Most families led a precarious existence, relying on their own potato crop and, in the absence of significant cash employment in Foxford, the meagre earnings the men were able to bring back from summers working on big farms in Scotland. Such conditions led to demands for land reform – the Land League was founded in 1879 by **Michael Davitt**, also the bringer of trade unionism to Ireland, who is commemorated in a **museum** at **Straide**, between Foxford and Castlebar, in the church where he was christened and buried (daily 10am–6pm; €1).

The mill at Foxford was founded in 1890 by a far-sighted nun called Marrough Bernard, who called it Providence. At a time when more professionally run mills were failing – so unused were her workers to ideas of productivity that she had to bribe them with cash prizes – the success of the mill could certainly be called providential. Its profits were used to fund schools and a diverse range of cultural activities, of which one, the Foxford Mill brass band, still survives.

The **tourist office**, in one of the mill buildings (Mon–Sat 11am–5pm, Sun noon–6pm; Ⓣ094/925 6488), has useful details of fishing and walking in the area, notably the 53-mile, waymarked **Foxford Way**, which begins at the woollen mill and traces a broad circuit round through Straide and Pontoon, with a branch northeast to meet the Western Way in the Ox Mountains. There are a few **B&Bs** in Foxford – popular with fishermen is the *Foxford Lodge*, Pontoon Road (Ⓣ094/925 7777, Ⓦwww.thefoxfordlodge.com; ❷; closed Dec) – as well as *Gannon's* **hostel** on Providence Rd (IHO; Ⓣ & Ⓕ094/56101), which provides private rooms and facilities for **camping**. *Hennigan's* is a well-run, flagstoned **pub**, with outdoor seats by the river and traditional music at weekends.

Castlebar

CASTLEBAR, the county town of Mayo, offers little reason to hang around in itself but has recently been given a shot in the arm with the opening of the **National Museum of Country Life** at nearby Turlough. Historically, the town is notable for a Franco-Irish victory in 1798, at which General Humbert's army routed a stronger force commanded by General Lake – the event has gone down in history as the "Castlebar Races" because of the speed of the British retreat.

The **tourist office** (June–Aug Mon–Sat 10am–5.30pm; Ⓣ094/902 1207) is in the Old Linen Hall, which was the venue for a celebratory dinner after the rout of the British in 1798. In the same building is the **Linen Hall Arts Centre** (Ⓦwww.thelinenhall.com), which puts on sometimes imaginative shows (including plenty for children) and arthouse films.

You'll find no shortage of **accommodation** here. If you're looking for a **hotel**, head for the friendly and comfortable eighteenth-century *Daly's* (Ⓣ094/902 1961; ❺), which is ideally situated on The Mall in the centre of town. Among **B&Bs** try *Drumshinnagh House* out on the Newport road (Ⓣ094/902 4211, Ⓔberniecollins@oceanfree.net; ❷), or *Millhill House* on the Westport road (Ⓣ094/902 4279; ❷; April–Nov), which allows children to stay for half price. The town's **hostel**, with private rooms and **camping** available, is the *Lonely Planet* (Ⓣ094/902 4822) – unfortunately named, especially given its location way out at the Moneen roundabout on the N5 (though free pick-ups from town are offered).

There's a great choice of **restaurants** in Castlebar. *Café Rua* in New Antrim Street does an excellent range of sandwiches and home cooking for daytime eating, while the *Olive Tree* is a very reasonable Eastern Mediterranean café-restaurant on Newtown Street. *Tulsi*, on Lower Charles Street (Ⓣ094/902 5066), produces some of the finest Indian cuisine in the west of the country, and *Zest*, Rush Street (Ⓣ094/903 5494; closed Mon evening & Sun), serves up dishes such as confit of duck in port jus in a pleasant atmosphere and runs a keenly priced early-bird menu. *McCarthy's Bar* in Main Street is a friendly **pub** with snugs and **traditional music** in summer.

The National Museum of Country Life

The **National Museum of Country Life** (Tues–Sat 10am–5pm, Sun 2–5pm; free) trumpets its theme early on, with a board near the entrance juxtaposing images of romanticism against reality, of a heavily tinted poster for John Wayne in *The Quiet Man* against a roughly contemporary photo of Inisheer men wading in freezing-cold seas to gather seaweed. The aim is to dig beneath the dewy-eyed nostalgia that besets popular images of rural Ireland, to reveal the harsh realities of country life from 1850 to 1950, and the museum achieves this with admirable thoroughness and balance. Even the scenic approach, five miles east of Castlebar off the N5, fits into the picture, the sleek, modern lines of the new building reflected in the beautiful lake of Turlough Park, with a lofty round tower in the background for good measure.

The exhibition works its way downstairs from the entrance, where there's a short introductory audio-visual presentation. **Level -1** includes a brief but very worthwhile history of the period from an ordinary person's point of view and gives examples of the ingenious uses to which twisted hay rope was put: baskets, hens' nests, mattresses and horse collars. The meat of the exhibition is on **Level -2**, which comprehensively chronicles the unremitting work of farming and fishing, of housewives, craftsmen and tradesmen. Nice touches here are a recording of a poignant letter home from an emigrant to America, and footage of men making a coracle on the River Boyne – exactly like weaving a huge basket. Probably the most interesting section deals with the seasons and festivals: churning butter on May Day to ward off evil, leaving food and drink out for dead relatives on Halloween, and grainy footage of Wren Boys, who would knock on doors on St Stephen's Day (Dec 26) with the corpse of a wren, asking for money to bury it while singing songs and telling jokes – the money, of course, would be spent on a party. **Level -3** presents personal reminiscences of the changes in rural life, revealing how horses weren't actually very good at ploughing.

There are free **guided tours** of the museum every day (Ⓣ 1890/687386 for details), as well as a **café** and a shop, and it's possible to look in on two refurbished Victorian rooms in the adjacent **Turlough Park House**.

Knock to Cong

East Mayo is dominated by the devotional shrine at **Knock**, which is easy to visit as an international **airport** was built at nearby Charlestown in 1986. However, if you're not a believer, or religious kitsch isn't a strong enough draw, you're best off heading south to the more engaging and historically rich town of **Cong** and its unique abbey.

Knock

Ever since an apparition of the Virgin Mary, accompanied by St Joseph and St John, was seen on the gable of the parish church of **KNOCK** (Cnoc Mhuire, "Mary's Hill"; www.knock-shrine.ie) in 1879, it has been a place of pilgrimage. As a passer-by in Ireland, it's surprisingly easy to forget the all-pervasive influence of the Catholic Church, but at Knock you're brought slap up against it. Whatever you may believe about the possible authenticity of the apparitions, Knock rates for Catholics, along with Lourdes in France and Fatima in Portugal, as one of the leading modern miraculous confirmations of their faith.

A massive and ugly **church** with a capacity of twenty thousand was opened nearby in 1976, and the pope visited the shrine in 1979.

As a place, Knock is nothing much to look at but if you are interested in religion, or the Marian phenomenon in Irish life, it can prove fascinating. The best place to start is the **Museum of Folk Life** (May–Oct daily 10am–6pm; €3.80), which contains artefacts relating to the apparition and the miracles associated with it. The scene of the apparitions has been glassed in to form a **chapel**, and pilgrims can be seen praying there at all hours. As you might expect, there is no shortage of kitsch plastic religious souvenirs on sale.

When Monsignor Horan, a local priest, first hatched the plan for the international **airport** (Ⓦwww.knockinternationalairport.ie) it seemed a crazy and profligate idea, and there were years of bitter controversy over this apparent waste of public funds. In fact it has proved remarkably successful, and as well as bringing in pilgrims to see the shrine, the airport has had the effect of opening up the northwest of Ireland for travellers – to the extent that Mayo is in reach of London for weekend breaks, and house prices in the county are booming as wealthy inhabitants of southeast England buy their second homes. The airport is situated three miles south of **Charlestown** at the junction of the N17 and N5, but for the moment is not served by public transport – you have to rely on taxis to Charlestown (a major crossroads where you can pick up buses) or Knock. As well as a **bureau de change**, there's a **tourist office** in the airport, open to greet arriving flights, and another in Knock itself (May–Sept daily 10am–6pm; Ⓣ094/938 8193). **Car rental** is available at the airport from National (Ⓣ094/926 7252).

It's unlikely that you'll want to stay in Knock, but if you do, there are three plain **hotels** designed for pilgrims, the *Belmont* (Ⓣ094/938 8122; ❹), *Knock International Hotel* (Ⓣ094/938 8466; ❸; Easter to mid-Oct) and the new *Knock House Hotel* (Ⓣ094/938 8088; ❺); a **campsite** (Ⓣ094/938 8100; March–Oct); and numerous **B&Bs** – try Mrs Carney's *Burren*, Kiltimagh Road (Ⓣ094/938 8362; ❷; June–Sept), or *Carramore House*, Airport Road (Ⓣ094/938 8149; ❷).

Cong and around

CONG lies on the narrow spit of land that divides Lough Mask from Lough Corrib at the point where the dramatically mountainous country of Connemara to the west gives way to the flat and fertile farmland that makes up the east of County Mayo. A picture-book pretty village that caters for plenty of tourists, it's also the site of the ruined **Cong Abbey**, which was founded in around 1135 for the Augustinians by Turlough O'Connor, King of Ireland (though it's probably built on a seventh-century monastic site). The abbey's fine sculpture-work suggests links with western France, though the cloisters look just a little bit too good to be true: they were partially rebuilt in 1860. At its height, Cong Abbey had a population of some three thousand, and the practicalities of feeding such multitudes can be glimpsed in the remains of the refectory and kitchen by the river, where a fishing house over the water contains a fishing hole in the floor; a line ran to a bell in the refectory to let cook know when fish had been caught. The **Cross of Cong**, a twelfth-century ornamented Celtic cross originally made in County Roscommon for the abbey, gives an indication of the wealth and status of the foundation – it's now on show at the National Museum in Dublin. From the abbey there's a pleasant wander through woods down to the river and the lough, although this runs through the grounds of the local big house, **Ashford Castle**, now a luxury hotel (see opposite), which charges for admission to its land in summer (€5).

It's also worth taking a look at the town's **canal**. In the 1840s attempts were made, as a Famine relief project, to dig a canal between Lough Corrib and Lough Mask. The river that links the two runs underground through porous limestone for most of its length, though you can get to it at various points, including the Pigeon Hole, a mile or so north of Cong. This might have been an indication of what would happen to the canal: the porosity of the rock meant that the water just drained away, and Cong is left with a dry canal, complete with locks.

The town is obsessed with *The Quiet Man*, a film that much of the rest of the world may have forgotten but which, shot here in 1951 and starring John Wayne and Maureen O'Hara, is well remembered here; it's a highly romanticized expression of the emigrants' notion of Ireland and Irishness. If you're happy to get into the kitschness of it all, head for the **Quiet Man Cottage Museum** (daily 10am–5pm; €3.75) just around the corner from the abbey and the tourist office, a painstaking replica of the cottage built for the making of the film; the only "real" thing in it is a horse's harness used in the film.

Mostly on the east side of Cong, around the R334 towards Neale, is clustered a sequence of monuments, both ancient and not-so-ancient. They range from a series of stone circles, near Cong, to another of the mysterious monuments that abound in Ireland, a massive stone-stepped **pyramid** in **Neale**, with an almost indecipherable inscription, including the name George Browne and some worn Roman numerals, dating it somewhere in the eighteenth century. The Brownes are the family who occupy Westport House, but the reason for the pyramid remains obscure.

Practicalities

The **tourist office** in the old courthouse building in Abbey Street (March–Oct daily 10am–6pm; ⓣ092/46542) has a **bureau de change** and plenty of books and leaflets about the area, which will guide you round the ancient monuments mentioned above. Undoubtedly the swishest place to **stay** – Ronald Reagan did – is *Ashford Castle* (ⓣ092/46003, ⓦwww.ashford.ie; ❾), which stands at the point where the river meets Lough Corrib and has been converted into a luxury hotel. Although its history goes back to the thirteenth century, what you see now is essentially a Victorian castellated reconstruction. Two other spruce hotels also offer comfortable rooms: pastel green *Danagher's* (ⓣ092/46028; ❹), by the abbey, and terracotta red *Ryan's*, on the main street (ⓣ092/46243; ❸). Among the numerous **B&Bs**, half a mile from the village in Drumshiel is Mrs Coakley's *Hazel Grove* (ⓣ092/46060; ❷; closed Dec & Jan) and, in the same area, O'Connor's *Dolmen House* (ⓣ092/46466; ❷). The *Cong* **hostel**, one mile outside town off the Headford road in Lisloughery (Án Oige, IHH & IHO; ⓣ092/46089, ⓦwww.quietman-cong.com), screens *The Quiet Man* every night, rents out **bikes**, rowing and motor **boats**, and has a **campsite** and a bureau de change. There's more hostel accommodation, camping and bike rental seven miles to the east in **Cross** at the *Courtyard Hostel* (IHH & IHO; ⓣ092/46203, ⓔdowagh@iol.ie), which offers dorms and private rooms in the stable block of an eighteenth-century farmhouse and free pick-ups from Cong. The *Lady Ardilaun* **cruises** from *Ashford Castle* pier to **Inchagoill** island daily in summer, with the possibility of sailing on to Oughterard, on the Connemara shore of the lough, on the *Corrib Queen* (see p.485).

Danagher's offers reasonably priced full **meals**, salads and sandwiches, either in its restaurant or in the sociable **bar**, and the *Quiet Man Coffee Shop* is a friendly daytime place with good home baking. *The Hungry Monk*, a smart little café near the tourist office (closed Mon), serves up salads, pittas and soups, as well as breakfasts and good coffee, and opens Friday to Sunday evenings in summer. For a really special meal, in fabulous surroundings, the culinary star is the *Ashford Castle* restaurant, where meals are served in the stunning Connaught and George V dining rooms.

County Roscommon

Roscommon has the unjust reputation of being the most boring county in Ireland. A long sliver of land running from south to north, it's the only county in Connacht without any sea coast, though it is bounded for almost its entire eastern border by the upper reaches of the Shannon. Although most of the county is either bog or good grassland pasture, the Curlew and Arigna mountains rise high and wild in the north on the Sligo and Leitrim borders. Chances are you'll be approaching the county from the south, which is not its best aspect: the most worthwhile places are **Strokestown**, with its remarkable Georgian mansion and Famine museum, the major Celtic royal sites at nearby **Tulsk** and the historic and congenial town of **Boyle** in the far north.

Roscommon town

More or less in the centre of the county, there's nothing much to **ROSCOMMON**, but it's an oddly pleasant town to spend time and soak up the atmosphere. Its solid tone is set by the heavy, stone buildings in the central Market Square – among them the Bank of Ireland, once the courthouse, and the old **county jail**, now housing a collection of shops and restaurants, its serrated top giving the town a characteristic silhouette, identifiable for miles around. The jail was the scene of all public hangings in the county and used to have a woman executioner called Lady Betty, whose own sentence for murder was revoked on condition that she did her gruesome job for free.

Harrison Hall, a former Presbyterian church in Market Square, houses a slightly higgledy-piggledy **museum of local history** (June–Aug daily 10am–5.30pm; free), the kind of place that museologists are beginning to regard as an endangered species. The building's striking Star of David window was put there by its nineteenth-century Welsh builders in honour of their patron saint.

Roscommon boasts two impressive ruins: on the Boyle road out of town, the enormous and well-preserved **Roscommon Castle** was built by the Normans in 1269, burnt down by the Irish four years later and rebuilt in 1280. Remodelling clearly continued for some time – there are some incongruously refined windows among the massive walls. The other ruin, in the lower part of the town, is the **abbey**. Roscommon takes its name from a Celtic saint, St Coman, who was the first bishop here and under whom the see became well known as a seat of learning, having close ties with the more famous abbey at

Clonmacnois in County Offaly. The priory ruin, however, is Dominican, dating from 1253. Amazingly enough, despite the religious persecution that followed the Reformation and the Plantations, the Dominicans managed to hang on well into the nineteenth century, the last two incumbents, parish priests of Fuerty and Athleague, dying in 1830 and 1872 respectively.

Practicalities

The **tourist office** is in the museum in Market Square (ⓣ0903/26342), and can provide information about the **Suck Valley Way**, a gentle, sixty-mile waymarked trail through woodland and bog which passes to the west of town on a circular route between Mount Talbot and Castlerea. For **accommodation** in the centre of Roscommon, there's *O'Gara's Royal Hotel* on Castle St (ⓣ0903/26317, ⓕ26225; ❷), one of those fine, upstanding inns that still exist in rural Irish towns, comfortable, cheap and good fun, with plenty of locals in the bar; or *Gleeson's* (ⓣ0903/26954, ⓦwww.gleesonstownhouse.com; ❸), an upmarket guesthouse next door to the museum in what used to be the manse of the Presbyterian church. On the southern edge of town, by the **train station** on the Galway road, the *Abbey Hotel* (ⓣ0903/26420, ⓔcmv@indigo.ie; ❺) is a grand alternative, located in an elegant eighteenth-century manor in four acres of gardens. There's also a sprinkling of **B&Bs** to choose from, including the very helpful Mrs Campbell's good-value *Westway* (ⓣ0903/26927; ❷), ten minutes' walk from town on the Galway road. Campers with their own transport should head for the well-equipped *Gailey Bay* **campsite**, Knockroghery (ⓣ0903/61058; May to mid-Oct), six miles from town off the Athlone road and on the shore of Lough Rea.

For **eating**, *Gleeson's*, between its restaurant and simpler café, does everything from breakfast to dinner, with delicious home baking; you can sit outside in good weather. A slightly upmarket option, in the converted jailhouse, is *Knights* (ⓣ0903/25620), serving stylish French-influenced and meat-oriented cuisine. There's also a reasonable Chinese restaurant, the *China Palace*, a little down the hill on Main Street, above the *Lyons Den* bar. *James Harlow's*, a quaint **pub** with a fine long bar and a couple of secluded snugs, lays on traditional music on Wednesdays and Fridays.

Strokestown

In the east of the county is **STROKESTOWN**, a gem of a planned town whose reason for existence is Strokestown Park House, once the centre of the second biggest estate in Roscommon after Rockingham. The enormously wide main street – reputedly the result of an ambition on the part of an early owner to have the widest street in Europe – ends abruptly in a castellated wall with three Gothic arches, behind which lies the big house.

At the other end of the street, the **County Roscommon Genealogy and Heritage Centre** (Mon–Fri 2.30–4.30pm; ⓣ078/33380, ⓦwww.roscommonroots.com) offers a comprehensive research service to people with roots in the county and is located in the elegant St John's Church, designed in 1819 in imitation of a medieval chapter house by the fashionable English architect John Nash (who never visited Ireland).

For **accommodation** in Strokestown, try *Mrs Martin's B&B* (ⓣ078/33247; ❷), centrally located near the heritage centre, or the *Percy French Hotel*, Bridge Street (ⓣ078/33300; ❻). If you have your own transport, your best option is probably Mrs Clyne's *Lakeshore Lodge* (Ⓣ078/33966, Ⓦwww.lakeshorelodgeireland.com; ❷; April–Sept), with gardens running down to Kilglass and dinner available, four miles away in the townland of Clooneen. For a sociable **drink**, head for *Hanley's*, just off the main street on the Longford road, a grocery-cum-pub that hosts occasional **traditional music**. During four days over the bank-holiday weekend in early May, the well-regarded Strokestown **poetry festival** (Ⓦwww.strokestownpoetryprize.com) and associated good *craic* takes over the town.

Strokestown Park House

Strokestown Park House (mid-March to Oct daily 10.30am–5.30pm; rest of year Mon–Fri 9am–5.30pm; Ⓦwww.strokestownpark.ie; €5 each for house, Famine museum and garden, €8.50 for any two, or €12 for all three) is a graceful Georgian residence designed by Richard Cassels on a plan – a central block with two side wings linked by curved arms – whose adaptability as a sort of glorified farmhouse ensures that it turns up again and again throughout Ireland. Sold by the family of the original owners to the local garage in 1979, the house has never gone through an auction and therefore retains everything from furniture to papers relating to the Famine and 1930s school exercise books.

The **house**, which is viewed on entertaining guided tours, makes a good place to get to grips with the Anglo-Irish tradition. Its story is a fairly typical one. The estate was granted to one Nicholas Mahon in reward for his support for Cromwell, and then increased to three thousand acres when Mahon switched his support to Charles II after the restoration of the monarchy. The original building, finished around 1696, was fortified but not particularly grand; only one room of it survives, the stillroom in the cellar. As the family became richer and more secure, with the estate growing to a massive thirty thousand acres at its zenith, they made more grandiose additions, and the current house dates essentially from around 1740, with some early nineteenth-century alterations. In the mid-nineteenth century Major Denis Mahon, who was a particularly nasty piece of work, is believed to have been one of the first landowners to charter less-than-seaworthy vessels (the notorious coffin ships) to take evicted tenants to America during the Famine. His activities were reported and censured in contemporary newspapers both in Ireland and abroad. In 1847 he was shot dead on his own estate.

To give a measure of the interconnectedness of Anglo-Irish society even in comparatively recent times, the lady who sold the house to the garage, the redoubtable Mrs Olive Hales Pakenham-Mahon, married the heir to the Rockingham Estate in 1914, thus uniting the two biggest estates in Roscommon, though the land empire set up by this dynastic marriage ceased to exist very soon afterwards, as did the marriage: the Rockingham heir was killed at the front in the first few days of World War I. The interior of the house gives off a feeling of very comfortable living, but not extraordinary opulence; there's a relaxed living room, and a spacious dining room and library – with a vainglorious portrait of William of Orange over the fireplace – while upstairs you can see the old schoolroom, complete with desks, blackboard and schoolbooks. The north wing contains one of the finest Georgian kitchens left anywhere, which was uncovered when the false modern ceiling and partition walls were knocked through. A gallery runs the length of the kitchen, which allowed the lady of the house to keep an eye on what was happening there without having to venture in; on Monday mornings she would drop the week's menu down from above.

The **Irish Famine Museum** in the stableyards provides a provocative interpretation of the house and its history and explores wider issues of Famine migration, emigration and oppression in a historical context, aiming, in particular, to break the traumatic silence that surrounds the subject. In 1945, a century after the terrible events, the Irish Folklore Commission noted:

I am sorry that this is such a meagre account of what was a dreadful period; but there seems to be very little information or interest left in the minds of the old people about that time. Indeed, it seems there was a sort of conspiracy of silence on the part of their mothers and fathers about it all.

Informed by a sense of outrage at the attitudes, on the part of the British government and the landlords, that allowed this terrible disaster to happen, the exhibition follows the harrowing story of the Famine, juxtaposing it with images of Ascendancy luxury and of present-day famine and emigration. In 1841, Ireland was the most densely populated country in Europe, with a vigorous trading and commercial life. The exhibition shows the tragic results of over-reliance on the potato, which had been introduced into the country in the early eighteenth century; by the 1840s, it was the staple diet of the population. Blight arrived in Ireland in October 1845. In a letter to the British Secretary of the Treasury, a contemporary eyewitness surveyed the devastation:

On the 27th of last month I passed from Cork to Dublin and this doomed plant bloomed in all the luxuriance of abundant harvest. Returning on the third instant I beheld with sorrow one wide waste of putrefying vegetation. In many places the wretched people were seated on the fences of their decaying gardens, wringing their hands and wailing bitterly at the destruction that has left them foodless.

The exhibition traces the poverty and hard-heartedness of the Whig government's laissez faire economic response to the crisis. Its callousness in the face of human suffering on a massive scale – as well as its attitude to Irish ways of life – is indicated by Trevelyan's response, as the Famine deepened:

The great evil with which we have to contend is not the physical evil of famine but the moral evil of the selfish, perverse and turbulent character of the [Irish] people.

The government resolved to make no official intervention to hinder the operation of private enterprise: relief food imports were stopped. Between 1841 and 1851, about 1.4 million Irish people died and another 1.4 million people emigrated – figures almost entirely attributable to the Famine.

A visit to the estate's restored eighteenth-century **vegetable and fruit garden** and adjoining **pleasure garden** may seem a little incongruous after the museum, but they set the Famine story in high relief with their roses and wildflowers, beautifully sited lily pond and the longest herbaceous border in Britain and Ireland; especially poignant are the foundations of an early glasshouse that was used for growing then-fashionable pineapples.

West from Strokestown

Heading west from Strokestown, there are a number of historical attractions that may divert you on your way to Mayo, including an extensive ancient Irish settlement around **Tulsk**; **Frenchpark**, home of Irish-language activist and first Irish president Douglas Hyde; and **Clonalis House**, at Castlerea, the home of one of Ireland's oldest Gaelic families.

Tulsk and Rathcroghani

Paganism has been destroyed though it was splendid and far flung... their old cities are deserts without worship.

Oengus the Culdee, early Christian poet

Centred roughly on the village of **TULSK**, seven miles west of Strokestown on the main N5, is a collection of dozens of barrows, ring forts, enclosures, caves and standing stones that mark one of the great centres of ancient Ireland. Unlike the monuments of, say, County Sligo, they're largely unmarked and unexcavated – most of them are no more to look at than grassy shapes in the fields – and access is generally free and unrestricted. According to legend, this ritual landscape was the home of warrior queen and earth goddess, **Medb**, who was responsible for launching the cattle raid of Cooley, as recounted in the *Taín Bó Cuailnge* (see p.846); the opening and bloody conclusion of the epic were set here. In the historical realm, it was the seat of the **Kings of Connacht**, who as late as the medieval era built a castle in Tulsk that's still visible.

To make sense of the monuments – and perhaps to refuel at the attached café – head first to the imaginative Cruachan Aí (pronounced "crew-han ee") **visitor centre** at the crossroads in Tulsk (Feb–May Tues–Sat 10am–5pm; June–Sept daily 10am–6pm; Oct–Jan Tues–Sat 10am–4.30pm; Ⓦwww.cruachanai.com; €4.50). In terms of an accepted history of its subject, the centre actually has precious little to go on: the sites are probably mostly Iron Age – but even that is not certain – and have never been properly excavated, though they have been the subject of various non-invasive archaeological surveys since the early 1990s (with some of the results yet to be published). However, the stylish, high-tech exhibition more than makes up for all this by revealing the latest theories on the functions of the grassy bumps and lumps and by exploring the powerful myths associated with them, including a lyrical audio-visual presentation on the sites' links with the *Taín Bó Cuailnge*.

The Cruachan Aí leaflet includes a map of the nearby sites, and staff can advise on access to them. The main site is **Rathcroghan**, or Cruachan, three miles northwest of Tulsk on the N5. Set fittingly in a cattle field, it's a ring barrow, the mythical palace of Medb, and traditionally the inauguration place and burial site of the kings of Connacht. The barrow is elevated enough to give good views of the monument-strewn landscape around, and marks the westernmost end of the 365-mile cycling route, the Taín Trail (see p.51).

Frenchpark

Carrying on along the N5, you'll come to **FRENCHPARK** and the **Douglas Hyde Interpretive Centre** (May–Sept Tues–Fri 2–5pm, Sat & Sun 2–6pm; for admission at other times, call Ⓣ0907/70016; donation suggested), housed in an eighteenth-century Church of Ireland church. Hyde (1860–1949), one of the founders of the Gaelic League in 1893 and the leading exponent of the importance of the Irish language and culture in the Nationalist movement, was – like his contemporaries, the poet W.B. Yeats and the playwright J.M. Synge – of Anglo-Irish background. The son of the rector of Portahard, he was sent home from boarding school when he contracted measles, and was brought up here among Irish-speakers, and later did much to record the rich vernacular tradition, as well as writing in the language – he collaborated with Lady Gregory on a number of Irish-language plays, many of which he published under the pen name *An Craoibhín Aoibhinn*, "delightful little branch". Hyde's quixotic aim, to unite all classes in Ireland through the use of Irish language, was bound to end in disappointment and his naive idealism resulted in his disenchantment with the Gaelic League, especially its espousal of revolutionary violence. After resigning from the Gaelic League, Hyde withdrew from public political life until he was elected as first president of Ireland in 1938. With the re-emergence of interest in preserving the language in recent years, there is some sign that Hyde's legacy, which had sometimes seemed a conservative and retrograde form of nationalism, may still be of importance. Hyde was buried in the graveyard of this simple church after a state funeral.

Castlerea

CASTLEREA, south of Frenchpark on the R361, is Roscommon's third most important town after Roscommon and Boyle. It's an unprepossessing place, site of a notorious **prison** and only worth stopping in to visit **Clonalis House** (June to mid-Sept Tues–Sat 11am–5pm; €5.50), just to the west of town on the N60. Clonalis is the ancestral home of the O'Conor clan, which claims to be Europe's oldest family; traditional kings of Connacht and the last High Kings of Ireland, the O'Conors can trace their family back to one Feredach the Just in 75 AD – although an even more fanciful family tree preserved in the house goes back to the fifteenth century BC. If you're expecting the house itself to be ancient, however, you're in for a disappointment – it's a Victorian pile, albeit an engagingly Italianate one, of 1880. Unlike most noble Irish families, the O'Conors always remained Catholic and, although their royal past allowed them to hang onto some of their ancestral lands, they weren't in a position to flaunt their wealth – much of it derived from astute marriages to rich heiresses – until the late nineteenth century.

The house, still very much lived in, is a fascinating jumble of furniture, paintings – many of them portraits charting the family's colourful history at home and abroad – and mementos. There's a modest chapel displaying a chalice, which unscrews into three parts to make it easy to hide. The manuscript room contains the oldest surviving judgement (c. 1580) under the ancient Irish Brehon law system, as well as a number of letters from Douglas Hyde (see opposite). Pride of place, however, is shared between the inauguration stone of the kings of Connacht and the harp of the blind harpist Turlough O'Carolan (1670–1738; see p.556), who numbered the then O'Conor Don among his patrons.

The house aside, there's no need to linger in Castlerea except perhaps to visit *Hell's Kitchen*, a **pub** packed with railway memorabilia on the main street on the corner of the Boyle road, describing itself as "the only national museum with a licence".

Boyle and around

It's disparagingly said that County Roscommon doesn't have any towns. It does, and **BOYLE**, although not the county town, is a fine, upstanding example, which has attracted its fair share of artists, musicians and craftspeople over the last few years. With a couple of diverting historical sights and a pleasant setting on the banks of the River Boyle, there's quite enough here to keep you entertained for a one-night stopover, if you're not hurrying to cross the Curlew Mountains into Sligo. Boyle grew up around the greatest estate in County

Roscommon, **Rockingham**, and although what remained of the estate was disbanded long ago and the house – in what is now the Lough Key Forest Park – was burned down in 1957, the town is still marked by their ghostly presence.

In Boyle itself, the most charismatic building is the Cistercian monastery on the east side of the town, **Boyle Abbey** (April–Oct daily 10am–6pm; €1.20; Heritage Card), consecrated in 1220 and one of the early results of the arrival of foreign monastic orders in Ireland during the medieval pan-European upsurge in spiritual life. In 1142 a group of monks sent to Ireland by the redoubtable Cistercian abbot St Bernard of Clairvaux, at the instigation of St Malachy, established the great abbey of Mellifont in County Louth. Clonmacnois, the important Celtic monastery on the banks of the Shannon in County Offaly, was quickly abandoned, and within twenty years monks from Mellifont had settled at a site beside the River Boyle here at *Mainistir na Buaille*.

The abbey is small and compact, in very pale stone, well enough preserved to let you see how the monks must have lived. You still go in through the gatehouse (a sixteenth- or seventeenth-century addition), and there's a wonderful twelfth-century church. During the sixty-odd years it took to build the place, the Gothic style arrived in the west of Ireland; in a remarkably playful relaxation of their famous austerity, the Cistercian monks allowed themselves to build Romanesque arches down one side, and the new Gothic down the other. Look out, too, for the fantastically ornate (at least, for Cistercians) column capitals.

Boyle's big house may be gone, but the earlier residence of the King family, **King House** in the centre of town (April & late Oct Sat & Sun 10am–6pm; May to mid-Oct daily 10am–6pm; ⓣ079/63242; €4), has been restored and opened to the public with some high-tech exhibits and plenty of activities for kids, plus concerts and other special events, especially in summer. An imposing stone mansion built around 1730, King House, with its pleasure grounds across the river, was home to the family for fifty years before they moved to Rockingham, and it represents the heyday of what was aptly known as the Ascendancy. The original Sir John King, a Staffordshire man, had been granted his land in 1603 for "reducing the Irish to obedience", achieved in part through violent subjugation and by the enforcement of the notorious anti-Catholic Penal Laws. For the King family, establishing themselves in Ireland was a process of determined and successful social climbing: inheriting a baronetcy in 1755, by 1768 Edward King had ensured his elevation to Earl of Kingston.

The first floor of the exhibition details the Kings' colourful family history, including an eighteenth-century crime of passion, a very public nineteenth-century divorce and "How to become an earl in six easy stages". One section deals with the Famine and paints a comparatively rosy picture of Robert King, then Viscount Lorton, who seems to have worked hard to help his tenants, halving the rent for many and paying others to emigrate to America. There's also a section on the house's use as a base from 1793 for the Connacht Rangers, which details their service to the British Army in such conflicts as the Crimean and Boer wars and World War I, culminating in their mutiny at Jullandar in the Punjab in 1920 in protest at the atrocities being perpetrated by the Black and Tans back home in Ireland. Boyle's civic art collection, with some interesting modern pieces, is housed on the ground floor of the building, and there's a pleasant, well-run coffee shop and restaurant by the main gate, much frequented by locals at lunchtime.

Practicalities

The **tourist office** is at the entrance to King House (June to mid-Sept daily 10am–6pm; ⓣ079/62145); as well as the usual services, it can give you details of the area's many summer **festivals**, including the week-long Boyle Arts Festival in late July or early August (ⓦwww.boylearts.com), well worth catching for its ambitious programme of concerts, theatre, poetry readings, lectures and exhibitions. You can also get information from the Úna Bhán Tourism Co-operative and crafts shop, also by the gate of King House (ⓣ079/63033, ⓦwww.unabhan.net), which can arrange guided tours of the area. You can try to **rent bikes** from Brendan Sheerin's bike shop on Main Street, though he's often closed.

Its gardens wedged between the rushing river and the abbey, the ivy-covered, Victorian *Abbey House* is a pleasant **place to stay** (ⓣ & ⓕ079/62385; ❷; closed Nov–Feb), as is the hospitable *Cesh Corran* directly opposite the abbey (ⓣ079/62265, ⓦwww.marycooney.com; ❷), with well-appointed rooms and great breakfasts. The 250-year-old *Royal Hotel* on Bridge Street (ⓣ079/62016; ❹) is a solid country inn where the river rushes by your window. A little outside the town is *Riversdale House* and a **campsite** (see p.526 for details).

Besides the café at King House (see opposite), daytime **places to eat** include the cosy *Stone House Café*, overlooking the bridge and the river in the gatehouse of the now-closed Frybrook House, which offers specials such as fisherman's pie and pasta. For dinner, make for *The Chambers* (ⓣ079/63614), a smart, stone-clad restaurant by the town clock tower on the south side of the bridge, where veggies get plenty of choice and carnivores can tuck into dishes such as beef "Gaelic-style", done in a whiskey cream sauce with roast cherry tomatoes in chutney; or the *Royal*, which serves good Chinese food at very reasonable prices. Tasty and cheap Italian food is dished up daily from noon to 11pm at the simple but well-run *Five Star Restaurant and Take-away* (ⓣ079/64602), in the Supervalu Shopping Centre, up Elphin Street from the clock tower. The **pub** underneath *The Chambers*, *Moving Stairs*, has a strong programme of all sorts of **live music** and is great for a quiet drink at other times, as is *Kate Lavin's* back across the bridge, one that time seems to have forgotten.

Lough Key Forest Park and the Arigna Mountains

The road east out of Boyle towards the **Lough Key Forest Park**, part of the old Rockingham Estate, leads through the gate of the grounds, itself a Gothic fancy, and past a castellated lodge. The park has been thoroughly and relentlessly amenitized, with a hideous wood and glass restaurant at the side of the lake and masses of tarmacked car-parking on the former site of the great house. The estate was abandoned in 1957 after the house – which had been designed by the English architect John Nash, who was also responsible for the Neoclassical mansions in London's Regent's Park – burnt down, but the stable block, church, icehouse and temple, as well as the spine-chilling subterranean passages used to keep the servants out of sight, give an impression of what it must have been like. With hourly **boat trips** in July and August and small boats for rental (ⓣ079/67037, ⓦwww.loughkeyboats.com), a swimming area, walking trails and plenty of ring forts to explore, the lake's a pleasant enough place to spend a sunny day.

You can gaze out, too, at the islands on Lough Key; in a disused castle on Trinity Island W.B. Yeats planned, after his Innisfree days, to base an Irish cult devoted to the occult principles of theosophy and the Order of the Golden Dawn – the idea was to aid the Nationalist cause by trapping the hidden forces of the land. The **circuit** of the lake is well worth doing, particularly the west side, where the road rises to give you a panoramic view. A possible stop on the way is the *Riversdale House* **B&B** (ⓣ079/67012, ⓔjpburke@indigo.ie; ❷; May–Sept), a compact Georgian lodge on a working farm that was once home to film star Maureen O'Sullivan, situated at Knockvicar, where the River Boyle flows out of the lough. There's also a well-equipped **campsite** on the lakeshore, the *Lough Key Caravan and Camping Park* (ⓣ079/62212; April to mid-Sept), where bikes can be rented.

The very north of County Roscommon – hilly terrain where farmland gives way to the moors and lakes of the **Arigna Mountains** – is a good introduction to the more spectacular landscape over the county border in Sligo. You can break your journey northeast of Boyle in the village of **KEADEW**, home to a prestigious harp festival in August, and, outside Keadew by the ruins of the sixth-century **Killoran Abbey**, visit the grave of the famous blind harpist Turlough O'Carolan (see p.556). The waymarked **Arigna Miners Way** (guidebook available from local tourist offices, or call ⓣ078/46702 for further information) runs along tracks used by coal and iron-ore miners for 74 miles through this wild country, crossing into mid-Leitrim and over to Carrowkeel (see p.552) in east Sligo.

Travel details

Trains

Dublin Connolly to: Boyle (3–4 daily; 2hr 20min).
Dublin Heuston to: Athenry (4–5 daily; 2hr 30min); Ballina (3–4 daily, via a connection at Manulla Junction; 4hr); Ballinasloe (4–5 daily; 2hr); Castlebar (3 daily; 3hr 15min); Castlerea (3–4 daily; 2hr 30min); Boyle (3–4 daily; 2hr 20min); Foxford (3–4 daily, via a connection at Manulla Junction; 3hr 45min); Galway (4–5 daily; 2hr 30min–3hr); Roscommon (3–4 daily; 2hr 15min); Westport (3 daily; 3hr 30min–3hr 50min).
Galway to: Athenry (4–6 daily; 15min); Athlone (4–5 daily; 1hr); Ballinasloe (4–5 daily; 45min); Dublin (4 daily; 2hr 30min–3hr); Kildare (2–4 daily; 2hr 15min); Portarlington (4 daily; 2hr).
Westport to: Athlone (3 daily; 2hr); Castlebar (3 daily; 15min); Castlerea (3 daily; 1hr 15min); Dublin (3 daily; 3hr 30min); Portarlington (3 daily; 3hr); Roscommon (3 daily; 1hr 30min).

Buses

Bus Éireann

Ballina to: Aghleam (1–2 daily; 1hr 15min–2hr); Ballycastle (2–3 daily; 30min–1hr); Bangor (1–3 daily; 1hr); Belmullet (1–3 daily; 1hr–1hr 30min); Castlebar (3–8 daily; 1hr); Crossmolina (1–3 daily; 20min); Foxford (2–6 daily; 15min); Killala (2–4 daily; 15min); Pontoon (1–2 daily; 15–30min); Straide (2–6 daily; 20min).
Dublin to: Ballina (6 daily; 4hr 20min); Ballinasloe (hourly; 2hr 40min); Boyle (4–5 daily; 3hr 30min); Castlebar (2–3 daily; 4hr 45min); Galway (hourly; 3hr 40min); Loughrea (hourly; 3hr); Portumna (Mon–Fri & Sun 1 daily; 3hr); Roscommon (2–3 daily; 3hr); Strokestown (6 daily; 3hr); Westport (2–3 daily; 5hr).
Galway to: Athenry (Mon–Sat 4 daily; 35min); Athlone (hourly; 1hr 30min); Ballina (5–6 daily; 2hr 30min); Ballinasloe (hourly; 1hr); Carna (Mon–Sat 1 daily; 2hr); Carraroe (2–6 daily; 1hr 30min); Castlebar (2–5 daily; 1hr 45min); Clarenbridge (hourly; 20min); Clifden (2–5 daily; 1hr 45min–2hr 15min); Cliffs of Moher (summer 2–3 daily, winter Mon–Sat 1 daily; 2hr); Cong (2–5 daily; 1hr); Cork (5 daily; 4hr 15min); Donegal (4–5 daily; 3hr); Doolin (summer 2–5 daily, winter Mon–Sat 3 daily; 1hr 30min); Dublin (5–8 daily; 3hr 45min); Ennis (hourly; 1hr 15min); Gort (hourly; 45min); Kilcolgan (hourly; 30min); Kinvarra (summer 2–7 daily, winter Mon–Sat 1 daily; 30min); Leenane (winter 2 weekly, summer Mon–Sat 2 daily; 1hr 30min–2hr); Letterfrack (winter 2 weekly, summer Mon–Sat 2 daily; 2hr); Letterkenny (4–5 daily; 4hr); Limerick (9 daily; 2hr); Loughrea (hourly; 35min); Oranmore

(at least hourly; 10min); Oughterard (1–6 daily; 40min); Portumna (6 weekly; 1–2hr); Rosmuc (Mon & Fri 1 daily; 1hr 15min); Roundstone (winter 4 weekly, summer 1–2 daily; 1hr 30min); Sligo (5–6 daily; 2hr 15min); Spiddal (2–8 daily; 40min); Tralee (summer 2 daily; 5hr 30min–7hr); Tuam (11 daily; 35min); Westport (4–9 daily; 2hr).
Roscommon to: Athlone (Mon–Sat 1 daily; 40min); Boyle (Mon–Sat 1 daily; 1hr); Castlerea (1–4 daily; 30min); Sligo (Mon–Sat 1 daily; 1hr 30min); Strokestown (Mon–Sat 1 daily; 30min).
Strokestown to: Frenchpark (5 daily; 25min); Tulsk (3–4 daily; 10min).
Westport to: Achill (1–3 daily; 1hr 10min–1hr 50min); Athlone (1–3 daily; 3hr); Ballina (2–7 daily; 1hr); Castlebar (6–12 daily; 20min); Clifden (summer Mon–Sat 1 daily; 1hr 30min); Foxford (1–6 daily; 1–2hr); Knock (1–3 daily; 1hr); Leenane (summer Mon–Sat 1 daily; 45min); Letterfrack (summer Mon–Sat 1 daily; 1hr 15min); Louisburgh (Mon–Sat 2–4 daily; 35min); Newport (1–3 daily; 20min); Roscommon (1–3 daily; 2hr 20min); Sligo (2–4 daily; 2hr 40min).

Private buses

Michael Nee (Ⓣ095/51082) operates several buses a day from Galway City to Clifden, with some continuing to Letterfrack. In winter two a week go on to Cleggan for the Inishbofin ferry, but in summer three buses a day run from Clifden to Cleggan (Bus Éireann can only muster two buses on Wednesdays on this route year-round).

Companies which serve Galway City include: **Bus Nestor** (Ⓣ1800/424248 or 091/797144) and **Citylink** (Ⓣ091/564163, Ⓦwww.citylink.ie), which each run several coaches a day between Galway City (Forster St coach park, beside the tourist office) and Dublin airport and city centre.

Feda O'Donnell Coaches (Ⓣ091/761656, Ⓦwww.fedaodonnell.com) operates daily services between Galway City, Knock, Sligo, Donegal and Letterkenny.

Innisfree (Ⓣ071/53053) runs a weekend service from Sligo to Boyle (1hr), and on to Carrick-on-Shannon (1hr 15min) and Longford (2hr), departing on Fri and returning on Sun.

predominantly Irish, work. Outside, the Garavogue River rushes under Douglas Hyde Bridge, and the revamped riverside paths and cafés provide a pleasant focus away from traffic-choked streets. A fifteen-minute walk east along the south side of the river from here leads to Doorly Park and access to the magical **Lough Gill** (see p.539).

For a taste of the northwest's energetic arts scene, head for **The Model Arts Centre** (Tues–Sat 10am–5.30pm; also April–Oct Sun noon–5.30pm; free; Ⓦwww.modelart.ie) on The Mall, housed in an imposing nineteenth-century stone building. As well as temporary exhibitions, it's home to The Niland Collection, which includes paintings and pencil drawings by Jack Yeats, brother of the poet. His work has a strong local flavour, and his later works such as the semi-abstract *The Graveyard Wall* and the earlier almost symbolist *Sailor Home from the Sea* are especially potent evocations of the life and atmosphere of the area. If you're going to be heading north into Donegal, look out for Paul Henry's *Early Morning in Donegal Lough*, which will give you a taste of things to come. Also worth more than a passing glance are the paintings by George Russell, better known as Æ, the mystical poet and a contemporary of W.B. Yeats, and works by Eva Hamilton and Mainie Jellett – the latter's *4 Elements* has a striking geometry. The centre has a busy annual schedule including three autumn **festivals**: the *Scríobh* literary festival in September, an Early Music festival in October and a contemporary music festival in November as well as weekly traditional music concerts in its theatre during July and August.

If you have children in tow, **Woodville Farm** (June Sat & Sun 2–5pm; July & August daily 2–5pm; adults €4, children €2.50), about a mile west of town off the road to Strandhill, is a useful diversion, with sheep, lambs, free-range hens, peacocks, pigs and a woodland nature trail.

Eating, drinking and nightlife

Aside from the scattering of formal places **to eat**, most of Sligo's large range of pubs seem to serve a bar lunch, and with so much competition the food is great value. You can get **picnic supplies** from *Kate's Kitchen* at 24 Market St or from *Cosgrove's*, a delicatessen on Market Square and something of a tourist attraction in itself, with its nineteenth-century interior and crafts shop attached.

The Ark High Street. A pub serving both bar meals and an extensive *à la carte* menu. Very good value and reasonably priced; popular for Sunday lunches.

Bistro Bianconi 44 O'Connell St Ⓣ071/914 1744. Well-established and understandably popular Italian restaurant generating a warm, convivial atmosphere and serving very good pizza and pasta. Open lunch and evenings Mon–Sat.

Castro's Castle St. Innovative daytime café specializing in Cuban and Creole cuisine.

Coach Lane Donaghy's Pub, 1–2 Lord Edward St Ⓣ071/916 2417. Offers a diverse mix of meat, seafood and vegetarian dishes from around the world and has a pleasant terrace for alfresco summer dining. Daily 5.30–10pm; also Sun 12.30–3pm.

Corianders Stephen St Car Park Ⓣ071/914 4134. Well-furnished, intimate restaurant specializing in modern European fish and meat dishes. June–Sept Thurs–Mon, Oct–May Fri & Sat 6–10pm.

Eurobar Stephen St Car Park. Probably Sligo's best coffee, served in a swish modernist setting.

Garavogue The rear of 15–16 Stephen St Ⓣ071/914 0100. Chic and airy bar and mid-priced restaurant with riverside terrace, serving a tantalizing contemporary menu: choice menu options include crab claws in chilli lime butter, fettucine with smoked chicken, olives and sun-dried tomatoes, and other dishes. Last orders for food daily at 9pm.

Leonardo's 7–8 Market St Ⓣ071/914 7700. An excellent Italian choice for dinner, offering a much broader menu than you might normally expect. June–Sept daily 5pm–11pm; Oct–May Thurs–Tues 5pm–10pm.

The Loft Above M.J.Carr's, Lord Edward St Ⓣ071/914 6770. Lively, informal railway-themed restaurant, serving moderately priced Mexican, vegetarian and fish dishes, with an excellent-value Sunday lunch. Daily 12.30–2.30 & 6–11pm. Bar snacks served daily 12.30–9.30pm.

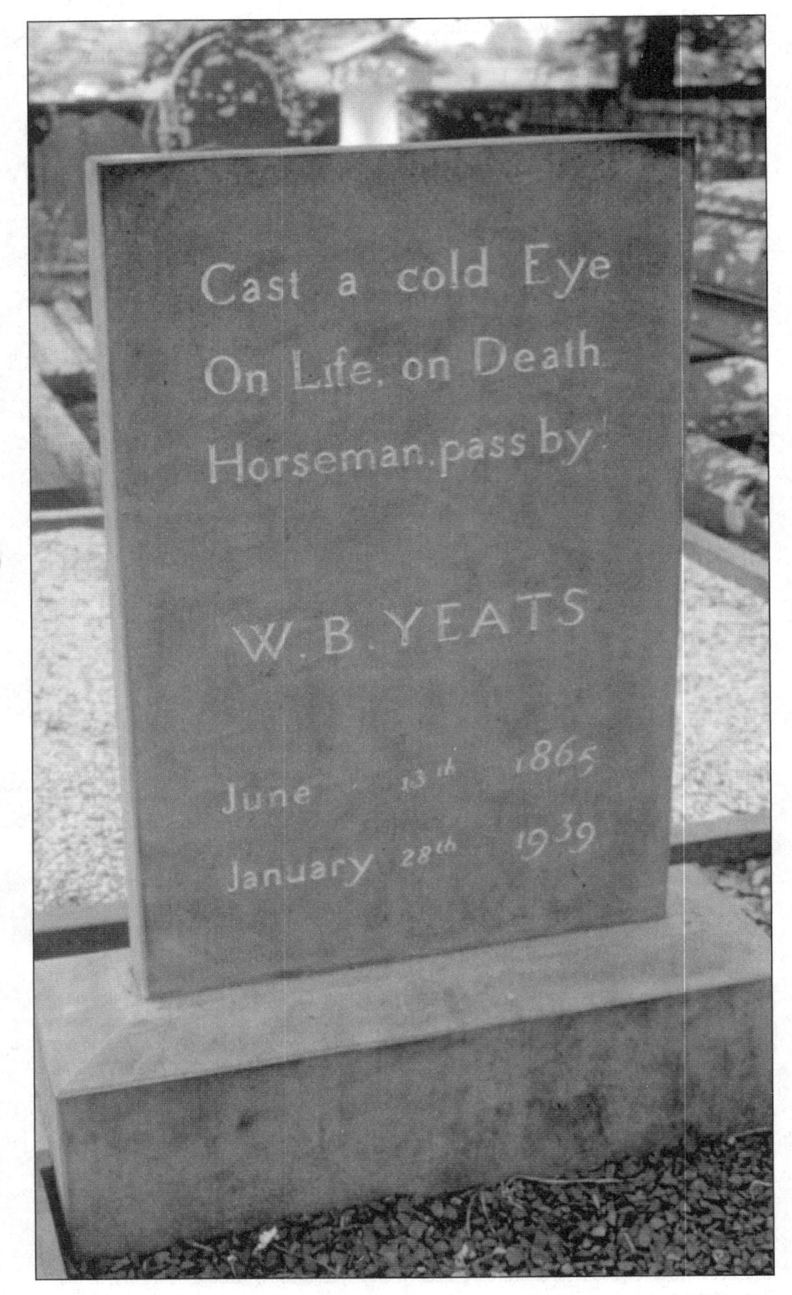

△ Drumcliff, County Sligo

The Penthouse Tobergal Lane ⓣ071/914 5030. One of Sligo's best lunchtime options, with daily specials (fish, meat or pasta dishes) at €6.67 and a more exotic evening menu from €10. Mon–Sat 10am–10pm, Sun noon–10pm.

Nightlife and entertainment

When it comes to **pubs**, Sligo does well. *Hargadon's* on O'Connell Street is one of the most enjoyable places to drink and talk. An exclusively male establishment until the early 1980s, it's a fine old pub, with dark recesses and shut-off rooms, and shelves of nineteenth-century earthenware stout jugs. Note the little swivel windows at the far end of the serving bar, where the whiskey could be slipped through with little fuss by either drinker or landlord.

Sligo is unquestionably one of the best towns in Ireland for **traditional music** and there's a plethora of pubs running regular sessions. *Sheila na Gig*, a characterful bar in Bridge Street, is one of the best spots, thanks in part to its owners, the well-known traditional band Dervish who often play here; there are sessions four nights a week (Mon, Tues, Thurs & Sat). *Earley's*, across the road, is another lively spot with a regular Tuesday night session. Opposite the Lady of Erin statue, *Shoot the Crows*, Grattan Street, is a lively bar with sessions on Tuesdays and Thursdays. *McLaughlin's* on Market Street generally has traditional music on a Tuesday, along with impromptu sessions at other times. *Donaghy's*, Lord Edward Street, runs a popular Sunday night session. As for **clubbing**, the *Clarence Hotel* on Wine Street has DJs (Thurs–Sun) and contains the newly opened *Delicious* club (Tues–Sat 10pm–1.30am). The big **nightclub** in town is *Toff's* at the Embassy Rooms, John F. Kennedy Parade (Thurs–Sun 11pm–2am) and there's also the *Xtreme* disco bar and club (Weds–Fri) on High Street. Check *The Sligo Champion* for details of other events.

The Hawk's Well **theatre** on Temple Street (ⓣ071/916 1518; ⓦwww.hawkswell.com) stages both amateur and professional drama, and also has musicals and classical music concerts, particularly during the Yeats International Summer School (Aug) and the Sligo Arts Festival (May). It's also worth checking to see what's on at The Factory Theatre, Lower Gill Street (ⓣ071/917 0431; ⓦwww.blueraincoat.com), which is home to the movement-based Blue Raincoat Theatre Company; it also acts as a performance space for other cultural events. The Gaiety seven-screen **cinema** (ⓣ071/917 4002) is on Wine Street. The town's **association football** club, Sligo Rovers, plays at The Showgrounds, Knappagh Road (ⓣ071/917 1271 for details of games).

Lough Gill

The twenty-four-mile circuit of **Lough Gill**, a broad lake just east of Sligo with luscious woodland covering the small hills that rise off its indented banks, makes a great day-trip by **bike** from Sligo – or you could break the journey midway in Dromahair (see p.541 and p.560) and allow yourself more time to explore.

A trip out onto the lake – on which sits the isle of **Innisfree**, immortalized by Yeats – is easily accessible from the centre of Sligo: to walk to the lake, set off from Bridge Street east along the south bank of the river for about a mile to **Doorly Park**. Here, short woodland walks give views across the lake and a hint of the beauty that lies beyond. The Wild Rose waterbus from Doorly Park out to Innisfree and Parke's Castle (see overleaf) is a wonderful journey **by boat** across the reed-whipped lake into the heart of Yeats's country (June–Sept daily round trips 2.30 & 5.30pm; €12; ⓣ071/916 4266). From Parke's Castle, the Wild Rose also runs trips to the isle of **Innisfree** on the lake (see opposite). Out of high summer, you should phone in advance, or enquire at the tourist office. Alternatively, you could **rent a rowing boat** from the *Blue Lagoon* pub at Doorly Park (ⓣ071/914 2539; €20 a day), and make your own way onto the water; you'll pass the pub en route to the waterbus jetty.

The northern shore and Parke's Castle

If you have your own transport, head first for **the northern shore**, reached from Sligo by taking The Mall past the hospital, turning onto the R286 at the garage and then following signposts for the **Hazelwood Estate** on the right. A left turn off the road leading into the estate grounds will bring you after half-a-mile to **Half Moon Bay**, where there's a picnic site and a pleasant lakeside walk. Wooden sculptures by various artists are ranged in the woods around – the most stunning is an impressive chariot andteam of horses, arrayed in its own artificial dell.

Back on the R286, a left turn soon after the road forks for the "Lough Gill Loop" will take you up to the **Deerpark Forest**, where a magnificent megalithic court tomb surveys the wild country. Ten minutes' walking on an unpaved road brings you to the top of **Cashelgal Mountain**, where you'll find both the tomb and unparalleled panoramic views.

At the eastern end of the lake – which sticks out into County Leitrim – the road begins to skirt the shore on its approach to **Parke's Castle** (mid-March to Oct daily 10am–6pm; €2.50; Heritage Card), a romantic-looking seventeenth-century fortress only yards from the water. The castle, built by one Robert Parke in the 1620s, is an evocative example of an early planter building and of the talents displayed by the Office of Public Works in restoring the building from a virtual shell to its current state. The foundations discovered in the courtyard of the present castle are thought to be those of the moated tower house of the Irish chieftain Brian O'Rourke, Prince of Breffni. In 1588, O'Rourke sheltered a Spaniard from the wrecked Armada; arraigned for high treason, he was executed at Tyburn in 1591. It seems that Parke used the simplest (and cheapest) method of making a home for himself, by utilizing the outer walls of O'Rourke's castle – and probably completing the demolition of the tower in the process. The reconstruction is clearly a fairly creative one, but it works well as a focus for the surrounding topography. The entrance ticket also admits you to a twenty-minute **audio-visual show**, which, as a quick introduction to the area's built environment, is also worth seeing.

The legends of Lough Gill

A place of such natural beauty as Lough Gill inevitably features in *legend*. The story of the lough tells of a warrior called Romra who had a daughter named Gille ("brightness" in Irish). One day Gille was seen bathing by Omra, a friend of Romra. Omra was captivated by the girl, who wasn't altogether indifferent to him either. However, when Romra learned about it, a fight ensued in which Omra was killed and Romra mortally wounded. Grief-stricken, Gille drowned herself, and the lough was formed from the tears of her doubly grief-stricken nursemaid.

According to another tale, the silver bell from the Dominican Abbey in Sligo lies at the bottom of the lake. Only those free from sin can hear its peals.

The southern shore and the isle of Innisfree

From the eastern end of the lough, the signposted Manorhamilton road leads to the modern, uninspiring **Newtown Manor church**, but the journey, a steep climb through the high wild moorland behind the lake, is exhilarating. The main road around the lake winds on through lush woodland to **DROMAHAIR** in County Leitrim, where, at the end of a short walk on the other side of the rushing River Bonet, lies **Creevelea Friary** (see p.560).

Continuing from Dromahair, the road climbs to offer breathtaking views of the mountains opposite. A signposted lane shortly after the Sligo county border will lead you down to the lakeside where you can gaze out at Yeats's tiny "**Lake Isle of Innisfree**" and breathe in the tranquillity:

I will arise and go now, and go to Innisfree,
And a small cabin build there, of clay and wattles made:
Nine bean-rows will I have there, a hive for the honey-bee,
And live alone in the bee-loud glade.

And I shall have some peace there, for peace comes dropping slow,
Dropping from the veils of the morning to where the cricket sings;
There midnight's all a glimmer, and noon a purple glow,
And evening full of the linnet's wings.

I will arise and go now, for always night and day
I hear lake water lapping with low sounds by the shore;
While I stand on the roadway, or on the pavements grey,
I hear it in the deep heart's core.

The Wild Rose Waterbus runs **boat trips to Innisfree** from Parke's Castle (March–Oct daily 11am, 12.30pm, 1.30pm, 3.30pm, 4.30pm & 6.30pm; ⓣ071/916 4266; €12). **Inismor**, Innisfree's sister island, was the site of the medieval school of poets to the O'Rourkes; unfortunately, its priceless library of manuscripts was destroyed by fire.

Continuing back towards Sligo, the road winds gently through woods with occasional views of the lough. At **Dooney Rock**, a brief stroll through woodlands brings you to a secluded shore where you can view the island opposite and consider swimming over. The road back into Sligo passes **Cairns Hill Forest Park**, where, from the car park, a path leads to the top of Cairns Hill, with a view across to a second cairn on the peak of Belvoir Hill. These are reckoned to be the tombs of Romra and Omra (see box opposite), though another legend makes them out to be the breasts of a monstrous hag, with Lough Gill as her navel.

North of Sligo town

The countryside **north of Sligo town** is dominated by Benbulben, a foreboding plateau that rises steeply from surrounding farmland, its cold grey-green slopes presenting an extraordinary silhouette against the sky. It was much loved by W.B. Yeats, who asked to be buried beneath its slopes. Yeats's grave at **Drumcliff** church is something of a place of pilgrimage, and is well worth visiting to absorb the stark magic of the poet's choice. Immediately south of

Benbulben lies the beautiful **Glencar Lough**, one of the scenic highlights of the area, while to the west lies **Lissadell House**, another essential stopping-off point for fans of Yeats as it was home to the poet's friends Eva Gore-Booth and Constance Markiewicz.

The countryside along this stretch of coast has none of the drama of the inland scenery, but it does conceal some very fine **beaches**, most notably at Rosses Point, Streedagh Strand and at Mullaghmore, where the shoreline swings northwards, capturing fabulous views of the **Donegal mountains**. The island of **Inishmurray** is a prime draw, a desolate place rich in early Christian remains.

Rosses Point

Leaving Sligo along the coast to the north, almost immediately you have the option of a short detour to **ROSSES POINT** (bus #480 from Sligo), around five miles north of town. This (or Strandhill, see p.547) is the place to go for a day at the **beach**, a perfect picture-postcard scene, with the streaks of **Coney Island** (see p.547) and its neighbour Oyster Island guarding the entrance to the bay and the distinctive beauty of Knocknarea and Benbulben behind. A sea marker called the Metal Man marks the deepest part of the channel for Sligo-bound boats; placed there in 1822, it was called by Yeats the "Rosses Point man who never told a lie". The tip of the headland, **Deadman's Point**, took its name from a sailor who was buried at sea here with a loaf of bread thoughtfully provided by his comrades – they weren't sure whether he was really dead but wanted to despatch him quickly so they could make port before the tide turned. Today Rosses Point's Blue Flag beach is good for swimming and for reflecting on the works of Jack B. Yeats, W.B.'s brother, who painted the scene here on many occasions.

For **accommodation** there's the imposing *Yeats Country Hotel* (Ⓣ071/917 7211, Ⓦwww.cisl.ie/sligoaccommodation/yeats; ❸), which looks out across the Atlantic, and several **B&Bs**, too: try *Oyster View* (Ⓣ071/917 7201; ❷), pleasantly situated overlooking the bay, or the comfortable *Coral Reef* (Ⓣ071/917 7245; ❷), a little way back from the seafront. You can **camp** at *Greenlands Caravan and Camping Park* (Easter to mid-Sept; Ⓣ071/917 7113). For seafood, head for *The Moorings Restaurant* (Ⓣ071/917 7112), *The Waterfront* (Ⓣ071/917 7122) or *Austie's Bar and Restaurant* (Ⓣ071/917 7111) – the last-named is a real old-fashioned pub with cosy snugs and excellent bar snacks in summer.

Drumcliff, Benbulben and Glencar Lough

If you stick to the main N15 road out of Sligo you'll bypass the small Rosses Point peninsula, only reaching the sea five miles north of Sligo at **DRUMCLIFF** (bus #480 from Sligo), an early monastic site best known as the last resting place of **W.B. Yeats**. His grave is in the grounds of an austere nineteenth-century Protestant church, within sight of the nearby Benbulben Mountain, as the poet wished. The grave of W.B. and his wife, George, has a simple headstone bearing the epitaph from Yeats's last poem:

Cast a cold Eye
On Life, on Death.
Horseman, pass by!

In 575, St Columba founded a **monastery** here, and you can still see the remnants of a round tower to the left of the road and a tenth-century **high cross** – the only one in the county – on the right. The east face of the cross has carvings of Adam and Eve, Cain killing Abel and Daniel in the lions' den; the west face shows scenes from the New Testament, including the Presentation in the Temple and the Crucifixion. Local excavations have turned up a wealth of Iron and Bronze Age remains, too. Next to Drumcliff church, the former visitor centre houses a good **café** and craft shop. For something more substantial, there's **bar food** at *The Yeats Tavern*, about a hundred yards further along the main road.

At 1730ft, **Benbulben** is one of the most dramatic mountains in the country, and its profile changes constantly as you round it. According to the Fionn Mac Cumhaill legend, it was here that Diarmuid, the ill-fated young warrior, was killed by the wild boar, its bristles puncturing his heel – his one vulnerable point. Access to the slopes is easy, but you need to take care as there are a lot of dangerous clefts into which the unsuspecting walker can all too easily plunge, especially as the mountain is invariably shrouded in mist.

Around four miles east of Drumcliff is **Glencar Lough**, ten miles northeast of Sligo, squeezed between Benbulben and the range of hills known as the Sleeping Warrior. This secluded lakelet is known for its good salmon and trout fishing. To get there from Sligo, take the Manorhamilton bus, ask to be dropped off at the junction for the lake and walk the remaining two miles. With your own transport, follow the road round the northern edge of the lake, passing the recently reopened barium mine sheds on the left, until you see the "Waterfall" signpost. From the nearby car park a path leads up to the fifty-foot-high **waterfall**, especially impressive after heavy rain. There are more waterfalls, visible from the road, in the upper reaches of the valley, although none is quite as romantic as this one. For even better mountain walking, continue along the road to the eastern end of the lake, where a track rises steeply northwards to the **Swiss Valley**, a deep rift in the mountain crowned with silver fir.

Cooldrumman and Lissadell House

North of Drumcliff, the first left turn off the main road (signposted "Lissadell") leads to **CARNEY** village, to the north of which is an area known as **COOLDRUMMAN**, where the **Battle of the Book** took place. This battle followed the refusal of St Columba to hand over a psalm book copied from the original owned by St Finian of Moville, in defiance of the High King, who ruled that just as a calf belongs to its cow so every copy belongs to the owner of the book from which it is made. Columba won the battle at a cost of three thousand lives. Repenting the bloodshed he had caused, he then went into exile on the Scottish island of Iona.

In Carney a signpost to the left indicates the way to **Lissadell House** (June–Sept Mon–Sat tours every 45min: 10.45am–12.15pm & 2.15–4.15pm; €5), an austere nineteenth-century Greek Revival mansion, the popularity of which is mainly due to its Yeats associations. This was the home of the Gore-Booth family, which produced several generations of artists, travellers and fighters for Irish freedom. During the Famine, Sir Robert Gore-Booth, who built Lissadell, mortgaged the place to feed the local people and doled out rations from the hall. His grand-daughters, **Eva Gore-Booth** and **Constance Markiewicz**, were friends of Yeats and took part in the 1916 rising. Constance was condemned to death by the British for her participation but was pardoned and went on to become the first British female MP in 1918 and then Minister of Labour in the Dáil's first cabinet. Bathed in Sligo's luminous marine pastels, the house still has an intimacy that makes it easy to imagine how it looked when Yeats used to visit in 1894:

The light of evening, Lissadell,
Great windows open to the south,
Two girls in silk kimonos, both
Beautiful, one a gazelle.

From *In Memory of Eva Gore-Booth and Con Markiewicz*

During that year, Yeats was in the throes of his unrequited love for Maude Gonne, and much of his time at Lissadell was spent confessing his problems to the "gazelle" Eva, to whom he also briefly considered declaring his love.

It was not only Constance and Eva who espoused radical ideas; their brother, **Jocelyn**, was drummed out of his club in Sligo for his practical encouragement of the early co-operative movement. He was also one of the first landlords to start selling off land to tenants, retaining no more than 3000 acres of the original 31,000 to run a thriving market garden. Among the more eccentric decorative features of the interior are a series of elongated **mural portraits** of Jocelyn and family retainers and a self-portrait in the dining room, all by Constance's husband Count Casimir Markiewicz. They came into being only because bad weather kept the count from shooting during Christmas 1908. One of the rooms has Constance's name scratched on a window, and a photograph shows her playing Joan of Arc in her husband's theatre company: an appropriate role for a woman whose life was soon to turn so completely to politics and propaganda.

The house went through a difficult period after World War II, when the family lost control of the estate to the government. Sligo newspapers were keenly aware of the irony of the Gore-Booth sisters, nieces of Constance – one of the founders of the Irish Free State – being pursued by the police as they protested against the state's inept administration of the property. The experience has left the family with a distrust of government intervention, even in the form of funding, and although plans for restoration are afoot, Lissadell is likely to retain its air of elegant decay for some time.

Walks around Lissadell: Ellen's Pub

The area around Lissadell has some lovely walks and reputedly the warmest patch of sea on the Sligo coast. Worth seeking out is *Ellen's Pub* at **BALLYCONNELL**, around three miles northwest of Lissadell House, whose cottage-home atmosphere draws people from miles around. *Céilís* are sometimes held in the back room at weekends, where musicians gather to belt out tunes on fiddles, accordions and banjos. To find the pub, follow the road past the turning for the Lissadell Estate, bear right away from Maugherow church, turn left at the pub/grocery store at the crossroads and then take the second right; it's another mile straight on. Hitching is easy, because everyone will assume you're headed for *Ellen's* anyway.

From Raghly Point to Mullaghmore

A couple of miles west of Lissadell is **RAGHLY**, a small harbour with a quiet pier and raised beach from where there are spectacular views of the bay and surrounding mountains. On the way there you'll pass Ardtermon Castle (closed to the public), the seventeenth-century fortified manor house once occupied by Francis Gore-Booth, an ancestor of the Lissadell Gore-Booths. In the early 1990s the place was more or less a ruin, but since then it has been well restored by its German industrialist owner – although, in the absence of documentation of the house's original appearance, the resulting garish yellow is rather more Scottish Baronial than Irish.

The next stop along the coast is sandy **Streedagh Strand**, most easily accessible by taking the main road to Grange (served by 3–7 buses daily from Sligo), and following the signposts from there, as roads on the Raghly Peninsula are hard to disentangle. The beach itself is a fantastic stretch of sand, superb for long walks or horse riding by the waves (there are several stables in the district), though bear in mind that offshore currents can be very strong here. When the tide is at its lowest you can walk round to the **caves** at the southern end to do some fossil collecting. At the very north end of the beach is **Carraig na Spáinneach** (Spaniards' Rock), where three ships of the Spanish Armada foundered; there are numerous anonymous burial stones nearby, said to mark the mass graves of some 1100 sailors who either drowned or were butchered by the British and the locals. There's **B&B** at *Shaddan Lodge* right by the strand (Ⓣ071/916 3350, Ⓔshaddan@iol.ie; ❷), which also offers various healing therapies.

Grange, Moneygold and Cliffony

At **GRANGE**, five miles north of Drumcliff, there's not much apart from an old boys' bar off to the right, over the bridge. However, if you venture inland past the pub, you'll get a changing perspective of Benbulben as you approach the Gleniff Horseshoe, a scenic road that runs along a glen on the flank of the Dartry range and gives easy access to the top of Benbulben.

MONEYGOLD, a mile north of Grange, offers basic accommodation at the *Celtic Farm Hostel* (Ⓣ071/916 3337, Ⓦhttp://welcome.to/celticfarm-hostel; phone ahead during low season or if you want a private room). **CLIFFONY**, about three miles north of Moneygold, is remarkable for the **Creevykeel Court Tomb** (just past the village by the roadside), one of the most extensive Neolithic sites in the country, comprising two roofless tombs within a stone court. The graves, which were originally enclosed in a barrow, probably date from between 3500 and 3000 BC, and it's easy to see in this ancient evidence of human presence a reflection of a power in the landscape that has gone on working ever since, right down to the poetry of Yeats and beyond. Cliffony itself houses one of Ireland's premier Italian restaurants, *La Vecchia Posta* (Ⓣ071/917 6777; Tues–Sat 6–10pm, Sun 12.30–3.30pm & 6–10pm), specializing in utterly delicious, authentic Tuscan cuisine (expect to pay around €25 per head plus wine).

Mullaghmore Head

Mullaghmore Head may not have the sense of wild isolation of the other promontories north of Sligo town but it has a charm of its own and, unlike the remoter areas, offers a choice of accommodation and eating places, albeit a limited one. Here the coast faces north, not west, bringing the Donegal mountains into view; Benbulben and the Dartry range are a constant presence behind you.

A left turn at the Cliffony crossroads takes you onto the peninsula, past **Classiebawn Castle** (closed to the public), a construction worthy of Disneyland, but built by Lord Palmerston. It became the home of Lord Mountbatten shortly before he was killed by the IRA in 1979: his boat was blown up in the bay.

MULLAGHMORE is a fine village with a peaceful skiff-filled harbour and an excellent, safe Blue Flag sandy beach. It's an exhilarating spot any time of the year, but take care not to walk on the rocky shelves of Mullaghmore Head at the end of the village; the crashing waves can be very dangerous here. If you're wondering what all the nuns are doing in Mullaghmore, it's because the village has a convent holiday home at which they can relax after the rigours of their parishes. Non-ecclesiastical travellers can **camp** in the sand dunes, as long as they're inconspicuous. **B&Bs** are thin on the ground, but *Seacrest* (Ⓣ071/916 6468, Ⓦwww.seacrestguesthouse.com; ❷) is beautifully appointed and has a wonderful location overlooking the beach. Heading rather more upmarket, there are a couple of comfortable **hotels**: *Pier Head Hotel* (Ⓣ071/916 6171, Ⓦwww.pierheadhotel.com; ❺) and *The Beach Hotel and Leisure Club* (Ⓣ071/916 6103, Ⓦwww.beachhotelmullaghmore.com; ❺), which has a gym and swimming pool. As you would expect, during the summer **seafood** is available in the bars and restaurants of both hotels, and at *Eithna's Seafood Restaurant* (Easter–Nov daily 6.30–9.30pm; Ⓣ071/916 6407). If you fancy catching your own, then you could take a **fishing trip** from the harbour on the *Ellen Louise* (Ⓣ086/828 2782; from €15 per person).

Inishmurray Island

The island of **INISHMURRAY**, about four miles offshore, has been deserted since the 1950s. It's a wonderfully isolated place that is remarkable for its extensive early Christian remains. The crossing from Mullaghmore takes an hour and a half, and allows for several hours in which to explore, but trips are dependent on the weather and the number of people wanting to go. You should expect to pay around €25 per person; book in advance with local boat-owners Rodney Lomax on Ⓣ071/916 6124 or T. McCallion on Ⓣ071/914 2391.

On the island, the remains of the sixth-century **monastery** of St Molaise stand within a massive stone enclosure and include Teampall na bFear (the Men's Church), the much smaller Teach Molaise (St Molaise's church) and a fine corbel-roofed building, probably originally an oratory. Also within the enclosure are three altars, one of which features the **Clocha Breaca**, or "speckled stones". Originally prayer stones, they became known as cursing stones; turned anticlockwise they are said to be effective against one's enemies. Numerous engraved slabs stand both within the enclosure and around the shore of the island, and these were used as stations for prayer. To the north of the enclosure stands a corbel-roofed sweathouse and to the northwest lies the Women's Church.

West of Sligo town

The major sites of interest directly west of Sligo – off the R292 towards Strandhill – are the ancient remains at the **Carrowmore Megalithic Cemetery** and, on top of Knocknarea Mountain, **Medb's Cairn**. Both make for easy day-trips from Sligo town, just to whose west lies **Strandhill**, a popular spot for surfers and lovers of seaweed baths. The main road south and then westward from Sligo (the N59), flanked by the thrilling outlines of the Ox Mountains and the uninspiring coastline of western County Sligo, is rather a mixed bag of a route, yet a few things crop up on the way to Mayo that are worth a mention. If you're not in a hurry, take the road running parallel to, and nearer, the coast.

Strandhill

STRANDHILL, four miles west of Sligo (bus #472), is swiftly becoming something of a city suburb, but does have a wonderful beach and the dramatic Knocknarea Mountain as an ever-present backdrop. As you head out there, a right turn off the road will lead you down to Sligo Bay, where concrete markers delineate a low-tide crossing to **Coney Island** – venture across for plenty of good birdwatching and tranquil sandy beaches. New York's Coney Island is said to have been named after this dot of land by a homesick sea captain from Rosses Point, the headland opposite.

At Strandhill itself there's a fabulous, wild **beach**, with huge breakers rolling in from the Atlantic. It's a great favourite with surfers, but you do need to be completely confident in your abilities: this is a treacherous beach and **swimming is not advised**. The Sligo Open Surfing Championship is usually held here during the first weekend in August, and should you want tuition, head for the Perfect Day Surf School down by the beach (Ⓣ071/916 8464; lessons €20). There is an exhilarating **walk** southwest around the headland to the quieter **Cullenamore** strand where you can take a dip: follow the coast until you are walking back around into a broad bay with Knocknarea Mountain in full view. The bay is home to a colony of two hundred **seals**, so your chances of spotting one are good. As the dunes fall to lower fields you can pick your way back towards Strandhill around the back of the golf course (the walk takes a leisurely hour and a half). Another stroll heads east from Strandhill surf beach towards Sligo airport to catch the sight of small planes coming in over the top of Medb's Cairn. At the end of the airstrip stands the tenth-century **Killaspugbone Church** (access across the beach), where St Patrick allegedly tripped on the threshold and lost his tooth. A beautiful casket in which the sacred tooth was enshrined – the Fiacal Pádraig – is now in the National Museum in Dublin, but the whereabouts of the tooth is a mystery. Strandhill village used to be sited here until drifting sand forced the villagers to move a few centuries ago.

Today, Strandhill sprawls over the best part of a mile from the main Sligo road, with its handful of bars and hotels, down to the beach. It also has the **Celtic Seaweed Baths** (Mon–Fri 10am–9.30pm, Sat & Sun 10am–8pm; Ⓦwww.celticseaweedbaths.com; €14 single; two adults sharing €20) where you can have a steam followed by a seaweedy bath and decide for yourself whether a soak in this slimy organic soup does in fact relieve stress, rheumatism and arthritis. Whatever the claims, it's worth it for the afterglow. The baths also offers therapeutic massages and aromatherapy sessions (from €20–40).

There's an abundance of **B&Bs** to choose from in Strandhill, including *Mardel* (Ⓣ071/916 8295, Ⓔmardel@oceanfree.net; ❷) in an unbeatable seafront position, and *Knocknarea House*, Shore Road (Ⓣ071/916 8313, Ⓔconnollyma@eircom.net; ❷), a short walk from the sea. The latter also runs the adjacent *Strandhill Hostel* (same contact details), if you're counting your pennies, and you can **camp** at *Strandhill Caravan and Camping Park* (Easter to mid-Sept; Ⓣ071/916 8111). A more upmarket choice is the pleasant family-run *Ocean View* **hotel** (Ⓣ071/916 8115, Ⓦwww.ovhotel.com; ❻), at the top end of town. Down beside the sea, the cosy fireside of *The Strand* **pub** is the ideal place to satisfy a well-earned appetite with delicious homemade soup and bar lunches. Its upstairs is occupied by *The Jade Garden* Southeast Asian **restaurant** (Ⓣ071/916 8140), though steaks and salmon are on offer for those wanting more traditional cuisine. Other alternatives are *Shells Café* on the seafront or the restaurant and bar at the *Ocean View Hotel*.

Strandhill is pretty lively during the summer: there is **music** every night in *The Strand* pub (folk, traditional and rock), while *Kelly's*, Top Road, has live music (Thurs–Sun).

Carrowmore Megalithic Cemetery and Medb's Cairn

The **Carrowmore Megalithic Cemetery** lies about two miles southwest of Sligo, signposted off the R292 (Easter–Oct daily 10am–6pm; €1.90; Heritage Card). A field studded with 45 megalithic dolmens, standing stones and stone circles, this is the largest concentration of such tombs in Europe, and possibly the oldest. Analysis of one of the tombs undertaken in 1998 suggested a construction date as early as 5400 BC; this has caused considerable controversy in archaeological circles since this would indicate that it was built well before the introduction of farming in Ireland. Research is ongoing and recent excavations have found yet more tombs, one of which held a large quantity of burned bone, along with stone and antler jewellery. All in all it's an enthralling place, under the eye of the big mother cairn of them all – **Medb's Cairn**, on top of Knocknarea. The easiest ascent of the mountain is along the path that meets the R292 as it skirts its southern flank (the western slopes are too difficult). The sixty-foot cairn on the summit is said to be the tomb of Queen Medb of Connaught, but as she was killed elsewhere it's unlikely that she's buried here. There's a rather unhelpful custom of taking a stone away with you, which is resulting in a shrinkage of the cairn; the authorities are trying to promote an alternative tradition that says if you take a stone with you from the bottom of the mountain and put it on top of the cairn, your wish will come true.

Should you want to go **horse riding**, the Sligo Riding Centre is located right opposite the site (Ⓣ071/916 1353).

Aughris and Dromore West

BALLYSADARE, five miles south of Sligo on the N59, is situated at the head of a beautiful bay with striking views back to Knocknarea and Benbulben. It holds the remnants of a seventh-century monastery and a pre-Romanesque church, but barely justifies a detour.

About ten miles further west and just after **SKREEN**, you can take a turning south for the route through the Ox Mountains (see box opposite), or take the lane north down to the coast and the tranquil harbourside village of **AUGHRIS**, home to an early monastic site and a promontory fort. In the fields you can see remains of *booleys*, the temporary shelters built by the old nomadic herdsmen who brought their flocks to graze in these remote coastal areas. There are several good beaches nearby and the little beach at Aughris is safe for swimming. The cliffs west of the pier are good for birdwatching and dolphin-spotting. You can feast on delicious **seafood** during the summer months at *Maggie's Beach Bar & Restaurant*, an eighteenth-century thatched shebeen down by the pier that is also a venue for traditional music. **Accommodation** is in short supply: the *Beach Bar* does **B&B** (Ⓣ071/916 6703, so8@familyhomes.ie; ❷) and also has a caravan and **camping** site, or you can stay two miles away at *Ave Maria Farmhouse,* Corkamore, Templeboy (Ⓣ071/916 6674, Ⓔammulligan@eircom.net; ❷).

At **DROMORE WEST**, about six miles southwest of Aughris, **Culkin's Emigration Museum** (June–Sept Mon–Sat 11am–5pm, Sun 1–5pm; €3) fills in some of the story behind the deserted buildings that once littered the landscape hereabouts. The museum stands on the site of Daniel Culkin's Shipping

The Ox Mountains

Just after *Skreen*, fifteen miles west of Sligo on the N59, comes the turn-off for the Ladies' Brae Scenic Route, one of only two trails across the vast *Ox Mountains* into south Sligo. Following the course of a tumbling stream between forests of fir, the road ends not far from *COOLANEY*, a one-street village with accommodation at *J.J. O'Grady's* (ⓣ071/916 7211, ⓦwww.jjogrady.com; ❷), a family-run pub on Main Street. *Walking* in the more remote regions of the mountains, where all you'll see are sheep and the odd turf-cutter, can be rewarding – but you need to take care, as the bogs can be treacherous. Much of the Ox range consists of surprisingly undramatic heathery slopes and flat boggy upland, but the second route across the mountains – which starts with a left turn off the road just before Easky – takes you up through the gorgeous setting of *Easky Lough* and then down a dramatic descent of the south-western face of the range into the area surrounding Tubbercurry (see p.553).

and Emigration Agency, which was founded in the nineteenth century and helped many local people on the bitter road to a better life overseas. There's plenty of material on display about emigration and the Famine that fuelled it; most evocative of all is the original shipping agent's shop, a stark reminder of the harsh lives endured by thousands. To get to the museum head west on the N59 towards Skreen and turn left at the third crossroads; the museum is about half a mile further on the right-hand side.

Easky and around

Originally a monastic settlement, **EASKY**, about five miles northwest of Dromore West along the coast road, was a vital link in the anti-Napoleon coastal defensive chain, as two nearby Martello towers attest. With its fine reputation for consistent waves, Easky has become something of a **surfers' paradise**; in the summer months the shore fills up with surfers' camper vans. It hosts the Surfing Association's Tiki Cold Water Classic over the last weekend in September and has also staged the national surfing championships. You'll find the Easky Surf and Information Centre in the middle of the village (July & Aug daily 9.30am–5pm; rest of year Mon–Fri 10am–2pm; ⓣ096/49020), which can provide information about accommodation in the surrounding area, along with **Internet access**. At the mouth of the salmon-rich Easky river stand the ruins of the fifteenth-century **Rosalee Castle**, with a public **shower block** alongside for the convenience of the many surfers who camp rough nearby; tokens are available in the surf centre and local shops.

There's not much **accommodation** on offer. *LJ's* (ⓣ086/815 4400) is a well-equipped hostel attached to a pub in the village centre and *Atlantic 'n' Riverside* (ⓣ096/49001, atlanticriverside@yahoo.com; ❷) is a **B&B** which also does **camping**.

Easky has a busy, if small, summer pub scene: *McGowan's* has **traditional music**, set dancing and rock music; *The Lobster Pot* is a convivial spot; and *The Fisherman's Weir* has a Friday-night disco and live music on Saturdays. **Eating** options include the café in the surf centre, *The Fisherman's Weir*, which serves bar lunches, and snacks at the other pubs.

This coastline offers magical **walks**; the shoreline east of the village is especially rich in fossils. A mile south of Easky, beside the road, is the extraordinary **Split Rock**, a ten-foot-high glacial erratic that's said to have been thrown here by Fionn Mac Cumhaill from the top of the Ox Mountains. Legend also has it that the rock will close on anyone who dares to go through the split three times.

Enniscrone

ENNISCRONE, eight miles southwest of Easky, is a popular, rather ramshackle, seaside resort attracting families during the summer months, with caravan sites hidden away in the sand dunes, and an exceptionally good golf course. There's a sweeping three-mile crescent of **sandy beach** with bath houses, built to exploit the health-giving properties of seaweed and hot seawater. The seaweed bathing tradition continues at the wonderful **Kilcullen's Bath House** (May–Oct daily 10am–9pm; Nov–April Mon–Fri noon–8pm, Sat & Sun 10am–8pm; ⓣ096/36238; bath €12.50, bath & steam €15), a strapping Edwardian establishment where you can experience the slightly strange sensation of lying in fronds of slimy seaweed in an enormous glazed porcelain bath of iodine-rich brown water before finishing off with a cold-water rinse. It is extremely popular, and there is a pleasant **tearoom** alongside where you can wait for your soak. A similarly exhilarating way to spend time in Enniscrone is to take to the waves, which you can do at Seventh Wave Surf School down by the beach; here you can take **surfing** lessons (Tues–Thurs 2–6pm; Sat & Sun 11am–6pm; ⓣ096/49428; €20 for a two-hour lesson).

The town is not short of **B&Bs**: try the *Castle Arms Hotel*, Main Street (ⓣ096/36156, ⓦwww.castlearmshotel.com; ❸), a family-run place offering an excellent carvery and regular live music. Alternatively, there's *Central House* on Main Street (ⓣ096/36234; ❷) or one of the several good options down Pier Road, such as *Enniscrone Lodge* (ⓣ096/36181, ⓔmko@eircom.net; ❷) or *Gowan Brae* (ⓣ96/36396, wwww.gowan-brae.com; ❷). **Camping** is available at *Atlantic Caravan and Camping* (ⓣ096/36132).

South Sligo

The key attractions in **south Sligo** are loosely scattered. Passing through Collooney it's worth calling in to witness the Victorian splendour of Markree Castle, now a hotel, before heading south for Lough Arrow and the area's two prime archaeological sites: the Neolithic passage tomb of Heapstown Cairn and the superb Bronze Age Carrowkeel Cemetery, magnificently sited high above the surrounding countryside. South Sligo is also noted for its **musical** heritage: the great fiddle player Michael Coleman came from here and the heritage centre commemorating him at Gurteen sets out to promote the traditional music of today.

Collooney and Markree Castle

The sight worth stopping for in the village of **COLLOONEY**, five miles south of Sligo where the N4 and N17 separate, is the **Teeling Monument** at the northern entrance to the village, built to commemorate Bartholomew Teeling, hero of the Battle of Carricknagat. The battle was fought nearby during the rebellion of 1798, when a combined Franco-Irish force – on its way from Killala in County Mayo, where the French had landed (see box on p.511), to Ballinamuck in County Longford – was held up by a single strategically placed English gun. Teeling charged up the hill and shot the gunner dead, turning the tide of the engagement. After their defeat at Ballinamuck the French were treated as prisoners of war, but five hundred Irish troops were massacred. Irish-born Teeling, who was an officer in the French army, was later hanged in Dublin. The monument links Teeling and his fallen comrades with subsequent generations of Irish freedom fighters.

Close to Collooney is the battlemented **Markree Castle**, of seventeenth-century origins but with grandiose Victorian extensions, which is still the home of the Coopers, who used to be Sligo's most powerful Anglo-Irish family. It's set in impressive parklands and is now open as a **hotel** (Ⓣ071/916 7800, Ⓦwww.markreecastle.ie; ❾), and also houses an excellent, though expensive, **restaurant** (expect to pay from €37 for a three-course dinner without wine). Midweek, nonresidents can wander in for a drink in the bar.

Heapstown Cairn and Lough Arrow

The more appealing route south from here, to **Lough Arrow** on the Roscommon border, involves a turn east off the N4 at **DRUMFIN** four miles south of Collooney. You can stay just outside the sleepy village of **RIVERSTOWN** in a graceful eighteenth-century Big House, *Coopershill* (April–Oct; Ⓣ071/916 5108, Ⓦwww.coopershill.com; ❼), which has been occupied by the O'Hara family since it was built in 1774. Riverstown itself is home to the **Sligo Folk Park** (May–Oct daily 10am–4.30pm; €4.50; Ⓦwww.sligofolkpark.com) a well-designed collection of buildings which includes a museum devoted to rural history and a collection of farm implements, recreated craft workshops and occasional craft demonstrations, a nature trail along the banks of the Unshin, plus a crafts shop and café. Over the first weekend in August the village is taken over by the **James Morrison Traditional Music Festival** (details from Ⓣ071/916 7560), celebrating the music of the famous fiddler, born in nearby Drumfin in 1893. Around three miles south of the village, **Heapstown Cairn** stands beside the road, a Neolithic passage tomb as large as Medb's Cairn and traditionally the last resting place of Aillil, brother of King Niall of Tara. Many of the cairn stones have been plundered for building material, but even its diminished state remains impressive, best appreciated by climbing it and taking in the view from the top. What's most fascinating about the view is the relationship with the surrounding landscape: the cairn takes a perfect central position in relation to the nearby circle of hills, many with cairns on their peaks.

One option from here is to go down the eastern shore of Lough Arrow, whose blue waters are set with ringlets of isles and whose banks are dotted with ancient landmarks, many of them unmarked on the map. When the sun is shining there are few spots to beat it, especially if you can take a rowing boat onto the tranquil lake – keep your eye out for boats lying by the banks and then ask at a nearby house, or try **Lough Arrow Boats** (Ⓣ071/916 5491), which rents out fibreglass boats. The road round the southern edge of the lake goes through **BALLINAFAD**, at the back door of the Bricklieve Mountains. The road into Ballinafad from the south over the Curlew Mountains of Roscommon gives the most stupendous **view** in the whole of Sligo, right up to Benbulben – it's worth backtracking up the hill to take it in. **Ballinafad Castle** in the village centre near the N4 flyover is a sixteenth-century building remarkable only because its huge circular towers and squat walls are of thirteenth-century design. The charms of the area may well tempt you to **stay** to watch the luminous twilight descend on the lake. You have a choice between the *Rock View Hotel* (Ⓣ071/966 6073, Ⓦwww.rockviewhotel.com; ❷), a down-to-earth angler's hotel halfway down the lough (much further than the signs indicate) – the owners will give plenty of advice on trout fishing in Lough Arrow's limpid waters – and the more upmarket *Cromleach Lodge Country House* (Feb–Oct; Ⓣ071/916 5155, Ⓦwww.cromleach.com; ❾) in Castlebaldwin, close to the northern end of the water, which has splendid views from all its rooms and a very classy restaurant.

Carrowkeel Cemetery and Keshcorran caves

The other route southwards from the Heapstown Cairn takes you back to the N4. Cross the N4 at **CASTLEBALDWIN** and climb the road that forks left behind *McDermot's Pub* for the Bronze Age **Carrowkeel Cemetery** – you can drive all the way up, on dirt roads, or walk: either way, watched over by cairns and (signposted) tumuli, the **panorama** is marvellous, with the whole of County Sligo spread out beneath you. Comprising fourteen cairns, a few dolmens and some fifty-odd pieces of stone foundations, the site is the most important cairn colony west of Sliabh Na Caillighe in northwest Meath. Several cruciform **passage graves** set in the cairns are still roofed, the smaller ones with great lintel stones, the larger with corbelled vaults. You can actually enter Cairn K, one of the roofed tombs: cruciform in shape, with its dry stone roof intact, it's been compared to Newgrange in County Westmeath (see p.201). Here, however, it's lit by the sun on the year's longest day (June 21).

Also of interest in the area are the **caves** on the hill of **Keshcorran**, the cairn-topped summit that faces Carrowkeel to the west, which you can get to by rejoining the main road across the mountains, then turning left down the hill, taking every descending turning until you reach a major road; take a right here towards **KESH**, and a little further on a fingerpost points right – after a couple of hundred yards you'll spot the line of caves cut into the forehead of the mountain. The caves have no depth at all, but the feeling of isolation is immense at this spot. According to legend, this was one of the places where the lovers Diarmuid and Gráinne lived when they fled the anger of Fionn Mac Cumhaill, and it was here that the baby Cormac Mac Airt, later to be the greatest of all the High Kings who ruled at Tara, was reared by wolves. On the last Sunday in July, in a reflection of ancient pagan rituals, locals still gather by the caves for sessions of prayer.

Ballymote

If, instead of taking the Lough Arrow route from Collooney, you follow the N17 **southwest** for three miles, you can make a diversion along the R293 to the small market town of **BALLYMOTE**, five miles further south. Its fourteenth-century castle, built by Richard de Burgo (the "Red Earl of Ulster"), was once the strongest in Connacht but has associations with major defeats – it was O'Donnell's before he was on the losing side at the Battle of Kinsale, and it was James II's possession before he lost at the Boyne. The place has an important and ancient literary connection: it was here, towards the end of the fourteenth century, that the Book of Ballymote was compiled, giving the key to the geometrical ogham letters that are formed on many standing stones of the fourth and fifth centuries; the name comes from the townland of Ogham, outside nearby Tubbercurry, which has plenty of examples of them. Ballymote makes a good centre for both angling and rath-spotting: the low, undramatic countryside all around is covered in ancient ring forts.

For moderately priced **accommodation** you could try *The Millhouse*, Keenaghan (☎071/918 3449; ❷), a very pleasant B&B or there's the *Coach House Hotel*, Grattan Street (☎071/918 3111; ❺), which has a facsimile of pages from the Book of Ballymote on display. The most stylish place to stay in the vicinity, however, is *Temple House* (April–Oct; ☎071/918 3329, ⓦwww.templehouse.ie; ❽), three miles from here on the shores of the lake; take the left fork off the Collooney end of town, and the house is near the N17 towards

Tubbercurry. Founded by the Knights Templar and expanded in 1560, this is one of the grandest and earliest Anglo-Irish houses ever built in Ireland – the bulk of the house was grandly refurbished in 1864 – on a 950-acre estate, with 97 rooms, five of which are for B&B guests. They also do a good dinner for around €30. In the village, *The Stone Park Restaurant* (Ⓣ071/918 3372) serves a good range of moderately priced meals, and *The Corran* next door is a daytime alternative, or there's *The Coach House Hotel*. The village sports a couple of nice old bars, including *Hayden's*. *The Coach House* has a traditional music session on Tuesdays during the summer.

Tubbercurry and around

The district around **TUBBERCURRY** (also spelt Tobercurry), fifteen miles southwest of Collooney – and indeed south Sligo in general – has a strong reputation for traditional music. A good place and time to catch musicians in action is during the **South Sligo Summer School** (Ⓦwww.ssschool.org) which usually runs during the third week in July. There are classes in various instruments, plus traditional singing and set dancing, and lots of concerts and pub sessions. Tubbercurry itself is a spruce market town, with its most scenic attraction being the lovely **Lough Talt**, around four miles to the west. Although the town is usually devoid of tourists, **tourist information** is available in *Killoran's Traditional Restaurant*, Teeling Street – don't miss out on their famous fresh salmon from the River Moy (Ⓣ071/918 5111). During the summer months *Killoran's* has a regular Wednesday night *céilí*. *The May Queen*, May Street, has ballads and country and western at the weekend. **B&B** is available at *The Ox Mountain Lodge*, Teeling Street (Ⓣ071/918 5007; ❷), which is pleasant and good value, and also has a café attached (closes 6pm). *Cawley's* hotel in Emmet Street (Ⓣ071/918 5025, Ⓕ071/918 5963; ❸) is a more formal alternative.

Follow the R294 ten miles or so southeast and you'll reach **GURTEEN**, another thriving centre for traditional music: **Michael Coleman**, one of the greatest of Irish fiddle players, was born in Killavill in 1891, just to the north of Gurteen. The **Coleman Centre** (Mon–Sat 10am–5pm; also April–Sept Sun noon–6pm; €4; Ⓦwww.colemanirishcentre.com) promotes the continuation of the living music tradition with evening classes and weekend workshops and puts on shows of traditional music and dance (April–Oct Weds & Sat). The centre also houses an audio-visual display on the life of Michael Coleman and a series of interactive touch-screens with detailed information on traditional music, instruments and their manufacture. The shop here sells a very good range of traditional music CDs and books. A couple of miles west of Gurteen a further group of buildings includes a replica of the fiddler's home and an archive of south Sligo music. Gurteen is also the focus for the **Coleman Traditional Festival** run over the last weekend in August, and there are a couple of pubs that are likely to have music at other times: *Teach Murray* has a session on Mondays and *Tim's* is another one to try. The best place to **eat** in the village is the *Crossbar*, Main Street, a pub serving a range of bar meals in the evenings. The nearest **B&B** is *San Giovanni*, Gurtygara (Ⓣ71/82038, Ⓦhttp://homepage.eircom.net/~sangiovannigurteenbandb/; ❷), a pleasant farmhouse a mile down the Tubbercurry road.

Lough Gara, tucked away in the southernmost pocket of the county, is not as appealing as the map suggests it might be, having a very undramatic surrounding shoreline. **Moygara Castle**, signposted near the lake, is similarly anticlimactic, with just one of its original four towers left intact.

County Leitrim

The scenery in **County Leitrim** is far more distinctive than it is normally given credit for, especially the lonesome mountains and glens of the north, though it can't compete with Sligo for historical interest. Leitrim stretches fifty miles from County Longford in the southeast to its slim two-mile coastline at Tullaghan in the northwest, and is neatly split into north and south sections by the vast interruption of **Lough Allen**, the first lake on the River Shannon. The southern half is dominated by the presence of the Shannon, while the lake-peppered terrain to the east of the river, with its characteristic drumlins, or hillocks, also merits exploration. The **mountains** of the northern section are grouped around **Manorhamilton**, and Leitrim shares its most beautiful features – Glencar and Lough Gill – with Sligo. Leitrim has the smallest population of all Ireland's counties, a mere 25,000 or so, and has suffered badly from migration, although the 2001 Census marked the first recorded increase since records began in 1841. Its county town, **Carrick-on-Shannon**, has escaped most of the trappings of tourism despite being a popular boating centre and is an enjoyable place to be based.

Carrick-on-Shannon and around

The small county town of **CARRICK-ON-SHANNON**, beautifully positioned on a wide stretch of the Shannon just below Lough Key, is a major **boating** centre, and its marina is full of pleasure boats and Shannon cruisers. The regatta is a lively event, generally held over the first weekend in August (details on ⓣ071/962 0532). It also makes a good base from which to **cycle** round the southern loop of Leitrim or to investigate Lough Key and Lough Boderg in Roscommon, and there's good **coarse fishing** to be had too.

Carrick's received a boost as a tourist centre with the reopening of the Ballyconnell–Ballinamore Canal in the summer of 1994. The canal provides the final link in the **Shannon–Erne Waterway**, 239 navigable miles taking in stretches of still-water canal, canalized river and a sequence of lakes before ending up in Belleek, across the border in County Fermanagh. A latecomer to the canal-building boom that swept the country in the eighteenth and nineteenth centuries, the waterway was completed in 1860, and was used for only nine years before being made redundant by Ireland's growing rail network.

The single item of historical interest the town has to offer is the minuscule **Costello Chapel**, at the top end of Bridge Street. Billed as the second smallest chapel in the world, it was built in 1877 by the fanatically devout businessman Edward Costello as a memorial to his wife, who died young that year. The couple's lead coffins, protected by thick slabs of glass, lie in two sunken spaces on each side of the tiny, beautifully tiled aisle. Opposite the chapel stands the **Market House Centre** which houses, amongst shops and restaurants, the Leitrim Design House (Mon–Sat 9.30am–6pm; also July & Aug Sun 2–6pm; ⓦwww.leitrimdesignhouse.com; free), a showcase for local craftspeople and interior designers. Also worth a visit is Cyril Cullen's pebble-dashed Georgian house and factory shop, **Summerhill**, on the road to St Patrick's Hospital, where he sells porcelain figures and distinctive knitwear designs using wool from his own Jacob sheep.

Arrival and information

The town has good transport connections. **Buses** (Ⓣ071/916 0066) to Athlone, Dublin and Mullingar leave from the main road by the side of *Coffey's Pastry Case* and those to Boyle and Sligo from across the road. The **train station** (Ⓣ071/962 0036), ten minutes' walk southwest of town on the Elphin road, is on the main Dublin–Sligo line, with three or four trains a day in each direction.

Carrick's very helpful **tourist office** (Easter–May, Sept & Oct Mon–Fri 9am–5pm; June–Aug daily 9am–6pm; Ⓣ071/962 0170; Ⓦwww.leitrim-tourism.com) is in the Old Barrel Store, under the bridge on the Leitrim side of the river, offering information on all aspects of holidaymaking in the area, along with an accommodation booking service. Rental of **bikes** and fishing tackle is on offer at Geraghty's on Main Street (Ⓣ071/962 1316; bikes €10 per day). **Internet access** is available at the small cybercafé at the back of Gartlan's newsagents on Bridge Street. The town's **arts festival** is in June (details from Ⓣ071/962 0252) and **traditional music festival**, Session on the Shannon, takes place over the last weekend in October (Ⓣ071/962 0252). Michael Lynch's, on the Roscommon side of the river, has **fishing boats** for rent (Ⓣ071/962 0034), and there are numerous companies that rent out **Shannon cruisers** by the week (two- to ten-berth), such as Emerald Star Line (Ⓣ071/962 0234) or Carrick Craft (Ⓣ071/962 0236). The locks on the Shannon–Erne Waterway – there are sixteen of them in all – are operated electronically with a swipe-card, so you don't need to be an expert to use the canal. For detailed information on Shannon navigation consult Ⓦwww.iwai.ie/maps/shannon-erne/contents.html and to purchase navigation charts call Dúchas, the Heritage Service, in Dublin on Ⓣ01/677 7510. For shorter **excursions**, Moon River organizes various day and evening trips, including party nights with live music, up the river, leaving from the bridge (Ⓦwww.moon-river.net). Another starting point for the waterway is at Ballinamore (see p.559), where you can also rent boats.

Accommodation

There's a fair spread of accommodation in and around the town, including a couple of swanky town-centre hotels and a range of more modest B&Bs. The independent **hostel**, *An Oiche*, Bridge Street (Ⓣ071/962 1848) is a cosy, well-run place right in the town centre offering a couple of small dorms and one four-bed room.

Aisleigh Guest House Dublin Rd Ⓣ071/962 0313, Ⓦhttp://homepage.eircom.net/~aisleigh. A smart, welcoming B&B about a mile out of town, offering a sauna and snooker table along with the rather more usual facilities. ❷

Aisling St Mary's Close, off Main St Ⓣ071/962 0131. A regular B&B in a quiet, central location. Closed Nov–Feb. ❷

The Bush Hotel Main St Ⓣ071/962 0014, Ⓦwww.bushhotel.com. Town-centre hotel with a pleasantly traditional character; rooms vary considerably, but the best are very comfortable indeed. ❺

The Four Seasons Main St Ⓣ071/962 1333. Another decent town-centre option for inexpensive B&B offering en-suite rooms. ❷

Hollywell Liberty Hill Ⓣ071/962 1124, Ⓔholywell@esatbiz.com. A grandiose, comfortable, ivy-clad period house in a riverside setting, offering some of the best accommodation in the area and just a short walk from the centre of town. ❹

The Landmark Hotel Dublin Rd Ⓣ071/962 2222, Ⓦwww.thelandmarkhotel.com. A new modern hotel overlooking the Shannon, offering a wide range of facilities, including an indoor pool. ❽

Eating, drinking and entertainment

Carrick has **pubs** to suit most tastes within a short walk down Bridge Street: starting at the top opposite the clock tower is *Flynn's*, an animated bar with lively conversation; a few paces beyond is *Burke's Bar*, a fairly conservative place for a pint, and then there's *The Oarsman*, an antique-style bar with live music – generally a mix of pop and traditional – from 10pm on Fridays and Sundays. At the bottom of Bridge Street is *Cryan's*, a bar famous for its traditional sessions (Sat & Sun). Two miles out of town on the road towards Elphin is *Anderson's Thatch Pub*, another place with an excellent reputation for traditional music all year round (sessions on Sat, Tues & Weds).

You can get reasonably priced and often huge portions of **food** – lunches and evening meals – at the popular *Cryan's* or *The Oarsman* (see above). Away from the bars, a few other places serve food during the day: try *Coffey's Pastry Case* for light lunches and snacks; *Wheat's*, the Market House Centre, for Carrick's best coffee; *The Bush Hotel* for good roasts, freshly fried fish and similar meals, or the new *Landmark Hotel* overlooking the river for carvery lunches. Carrick's most dynamic restaurant is the *Fusion* brasserie, in the Market House Centre, serving modern European food in an equally modernist setting (expect to pay around €35 for an evening meal). If you are self-catering, it's worth calling into Cheese etc on Bridge Street, for just that.

South of Carrick

As with most of Leitrim, there's little of dramatic interest in the area **south of Carrick**, but if you're passing through, there are a couple of places where you could at least slow down a bit and enjoy the leisurely pace of life around the Shannon. **Mohill** stands as the focus of a patch of lovely rolling countryside, laced with rivers, that attracts plenty of interest from angling folk.

Jamestown and Drumsna

The village of **JAMESTOWN**, just over two miles southeast of Carrick off the N4 Dublin road, is a town dating from James I's "Plantation" of Leitrim in 1622 – its main road passes through a gate, all that's left of the old town walls. Just outside the gate a stone cross leads to the remains of a Franciscan friary while inside the Georgian houses and the wooded river banks create a peaceful atmosphere of planned eighteenth-century living. Jamestown makes a good centre for fishing; if you want to stay, try *Weir View* (☎071/962 4726; ❷). *The Arch* is one of a couple of nice **pubs** right in the centre and, somewhat astonishingly, just out on the road to Carrick, there's a superb Lebanese restaurant, *Al Mezza* (☎071/962 5050; Weds–Mon 6–10pm).

At **DRUMSNA**, about a mile or so east of Jamestown, excavations in the summer of 1989 unearthed huge stretches of a Stone Age wall – one of the oldest artificial structures in the world. It's been estimated that it would have taken a labour force of thirty thousand men ten years to build its full length. The village itself is a single street of neat houses leading down to the river. A plaque on the wall of *Taylor's Lounge* claims that Anthony Trollope began his novel *The MacDermots of Ballycloran* here in 1848. The MacDermots were great Catholic landowners during the eighteenth century who were ruined by the anti-Catholic Penal Laws.

Mohill and around

About six miles east of Drumsna lies **MOHILL**, a trim, busy village reached by turning off the main road south of Drumsna. A sculpture on the main street commemorates Ireland's most renowned harper and composer, the blind **Turlough O'Carolan** (1670–1738), from Nobber, County. Meath, who lived for a time in the area. One of the last of the itinerant harpers, he lived by travelling round the houses of the gentry, often playing tunes composed in their honour. He was also reputed to have been as great with the whiskey bottle as he was on the harp; it's said that on his deathbed he asked for a cup of the stuff, and finding that he hadn't the strength to drink it, touched the cup with his lip, saying that two old mates shouldn't part without a kiss. Mohill was the site of an abbey founded in the sixth century by St Manachan, but today its associations are entirely secular: it's a **coarse-fishing** centre, with fifteen different choices of lake and river in a five-mile radius. You can get B&B **accommodation** on a grand scale at the nineteenth-century stone-built *Glebe House*, set in beautiful parklands a couple of miles north of town on the road to Ballinamore (Ⓣ071/963 1086, Ⓦwww.glebehouse.com; ❸). At a more modest level there's *Coolabawn House*, Station Road (Ⓣ071/963 1033, Ⓔtinaslevin@mohill.com; ❷), a pleasant town house with a very attractive garden. *Fitzpatrick's* and *Clarke's* **pubs** both have live music at the weekends.

Lough Rynn House stands in a fine location on the shores of the lough, south of Mohill, and was first acquired by one Nathaniel Clements, a successful Dublin banker and politician, in 1750. The Clements dynasty, earls of Sligo, built the original Rynn Castle – an exact copy of a house in Ingestry in Staffordshire, England – in 1833, and in 1878 extended it to the Scottish Baronial pile you see now. By this time the house was the centre of an estate that encompassed a massive ninety thousand acres, and the grounds include 1840s' farm buildings, the estate office – a picturesque building by the architect Digby Wyatt, who was also responsible for the Senate Chambers in Leinster House, Dublin – a pretty summer house, as well as the ruins of a seventeenth-century castle and a dolmen. Planned renovation of the house appears to have been shelved at the time of writing, but in the meantime visitors are welcome to walk around the grounds. **Camping** is available on the shore of the lough at *Lough Rynn Camping and Caravan Park* (Ⓣ071/963 1022), two miles south of Mohill.

The area around Mohill, rich rolling pasture land crisscrossed by hedged lanes, makes for good cycling. Further east, the terrain becomes rougher and less interesting, but **CARRIGALLEN**, around eight miles northeast of Mohill, is a pleasant enough eighteenth-century town, with excellent fishing all around and the thriving *Corn Mill* **theatre**, Main Street (Ⓣ049/39612). It's at a point in Carrigallen parish that the three provinces of Ulster, Leinster and Connacht meet, though nothing about the modest demeanour of the town suggests it.

Six miles south of Mohill, the small village of **DROMOD** is the starting point for the little that's left of the **Cavan and Leitrim Railway** (July & Aug Mon–Fri 10am–5.30pm, Sun 1–5.30pm; Sept–June Mon–Fri 10am–2.30pm, Sun 1–5.30pm; train rides April–Sept €5; Ⓦwww.cavanandleitrimrailway.com). Staffed by informative and dedicated enthusiasts, from a station next to the existing Dublin-Carrick main line, this is a fully operational narrow-gauge steam railway with trains running half a mile up the restored track to Clooncolry, though there are plans to continue onward to Mohill whose former station is also being restored.

ROOSKEY, just over the border in County Roscommon, straddles the N4 about seven miles south of Mohill. It's a pleasant riverside village catering for holidaying anglers, with B&B at *Avondale House* (Ⓣ071/963 8095, Ⓔavondalerooskey@eircom.net; ❷), a smart new house set squarely back off the main road, and more upmarket accommodation at the *Shannon Key West Hotel*, a smart and imposing building overlooking the bridge (Ⓣ071/963 8800, Ⓦwww.keywest.firebird.net; ❺). Bar food is on offer at *The Weir Lodge* and you can hear a variety of live music at *Reynolds* bar throughout the summer.

North of Carrick

About four miles **north of Carrick** lies the county's namesake, **LEITRIM** village. It's a tiny place, bisected by the main road, but with a lovely canalside setting – best appreciated from the pub on the bank. From just north of here, the elongated **Lough Allen** stretches northwards, almost touching the Cavan border and dividing Leitrim in two. **Drumshanbo** is the pleasantest base from which to get out onto the water, and there's also countryside around and about that's worth exploring by bike or on foot.

Drumshanbo and around

Though its name translates as "the ridge of the old cow", **DRUMSHANBO**, eight miles north of Carrick, is a neat, cheerful place with an air of briskness, poised at the southern tip of the beautiful **Lough Allen**. The Sliabh an Iarainn Visitor Centre (April–Oct Mon–Sat 10am–6pm, Sun 2–6pm; €2) gives some interesting background on local life, including the use of the sweathouse, a sort of sauna, and the tradition of coal and iron mining, especially around Arigna in Co. Roscommon. The last of the mines in the area closed in 1990.

Drumshanbo has a very strong musical tradition – look out for the plaque in the village centre commemorating the flute player Packie Duignan – and, in July, holds the Joe Mooney Summer School (Ⓦhttp://homepages.iol.ie/~nwoods), a week of **traditional music** classes, concerts and set dancing. You need to be experienced to join most of the music classes, but there is set dancing for novices and plenty of sessions in the bars. Drumshanbo's **tourist office** is based at *Mrs Mooney's* **B&B** on the corner of the High Street and the Carrick Road (Ⓣ071/964 1013; ❶). Other places to stay include *Paddy Mac's* pub and guest-house (Ⓣ071/964 1128, Ⓕ071/964 1703; ❸), High Street, and *Fraoch Bán* (Ⓣ071/964 1260, Ⓔfraochban@eircom.net; ❷), a smart B&B half a mile north on the Dowra road, with lovely views over the lake. You can **camp** at Moorlands Equestrian Centre, at the southernmost tip of Lough Allen (Ⓣ071/964 1500; trekking €15 per hour). Excellent-value **meals** are served all day at *Henry's Haven*, Convent Avenue, and at *An Chrannog*, Church Street, a café during the day and restaurant in the evenings. There are a handful of bars where you might find **music** during the summer: *Conway's*, at the head of the Manorhamilton road, is a cosy favourite, with sessions on Thursdays. Other bars with music worth checking out are *The Mountain Tavern* (Wed), *Paddy Mac's* (Fri) and *Monica's* (Mon).

Music aside, Drumshanbo's finest asset is its proximity to Lough Allen and Slieve Anierin. By car the scenery is not particularly dramatic, but there is plenty of enjoyable walking, cycling and pony trekking. The Leitrim Way from here to Dowra (signposted *Slí Liatroma*, ten miles) affords expansive views across the lake to Corrie Mountain for almost the whole way. You can **rent a bike** for €9 per day from Moran's on Convent Avenue (Ⓣ071/964 1043); a circuit of the lake via Dowra and Drumkeeran is around 25 miles in total. Lough Allen is noted as having the **best pike fishing** in Europe, and rowing boats can be hired from Lough Allen Angling Services (Ⓣ071/964 1648; €20 per day).

East towards Ballinamore

The best move from Drumshanbo is to take the R208 southeast and then head **east** along the R209 into the array of lakes that attracts most of Leitrim's tourism. This route makes a pleasant trip on a **bike**, as many of the lanes skirt the shores as they wind between the hills. Two of these hills have legendary names – **Sheemore** and **Sheebeag** (the Hill of Big Fairies and the Hill of

Little Fairies – and were the subject of the blind harper Turlough O'Carolan's (see p.556) first reputed composition, *Sheebeg and Sheemore*. As with all such enchanted hills, this pair is supposed to open up on *Samhain* (Halloween), when the fairy folk roam the land.

Sheemore lies on the south side of Lough Scur; unfortunately it's not signposted, so you might have to ask a few of the locals for directions. Topped by a cairn and a St Patrick's Cross, the hill commands the best **view** across Leitrim; the cairn is believed locally to be Fionn Mac Cumhaill's (Finn McCool's) grave. On your way along the south of Lough Scur you'll pass a dolmen by the roadside before reaching Sheebeag, which has a gorse-covered cairn but is less exciting than its bigger brother. To get there follow the road straight on rather than turning left into Keshcarrigan, and take a sharp right up the hill and continue for a mile or so.

KESHCARRIGAN, around five miles southeast of Drumshanbo, is one of the places that has been revitalized by the reopening of the Shannon–Erne Waterway. You can **stay** at *Canal View House* (Ⓣ071/964 2056, Ⓔcanalviewcountryhome@eircom.net; ❷), an imposing bungalow a little way out towards Fenagh, overlooking the waterway; it also runs a fairly sophisticated **restaurant** (open to nonresidents, dinner approx €25). For a splendid canalside pint head for *Gertie's Bar*, an amiably relaxed, child-friendly place, decorated with a chaotic mix of ancient beer ads and road signs. About four miles east, **FENAGH** has the ruins of a monastery and two churches founded in the sixth century by St Caillain. The key for the ruins is kept in the first house as you turn off the road for *The Old Rectory* (Ⓣ071/964 4089, Ⓦwww.theoldrectoryireland.com; closed Dec; ❷), whose friendly owners maintain a beautiful Georgian house and serve one of Leitrim's best breakfasts in a superb location overlooking Fenagh Lough, 400yd up the Mohill road.

Ballinamore

Three miles northeast of Fenagh lies **BALLINAMORE**, a wide-streeted former coaching town, which acts as a centre for **angling** in Leitrim's lakes, and for **boating** on the Shannon–Erne Waterway. Canal barges can be rented from Riversdale Barge Holidays (Ⓣ071/964 4122) or you can hire a boat from Ballinamore Boats, 3 Railway Rd (Ⓣ071/964 4881), which also operates a two-hour **river cruise** for €10 (June–Sept only; Ⓣ071/964 4079).

One of the nicest **B&Bs** is *Ardrum Lodge* (April–Oct; Ⓣ & Ⓕ071/964 4278; ❷), a mile towards Fenagh, while *Glenview* (Ⓣ071/964 4157, Ⓔglenvhse@iol.ie; ❸) is a splendid guesthouse with a popular restaurant, two miles south in Aughoo. Central options include *Hamill's* (Ⓣ071/964 4211; ❷), Main Street, and two reasonably-priced modern, family-run **hotels**: the *Commercial and Tourist Hotel* (Ⓣ071/964 4675, Ⓦwww.hotelcommercial.com; ❸) and *McAllisters Hotel* (Ⓣ071/964 4068, Ⓔmcallistershotel@guidetoireland.com; ❸). Probably the best **place to eat** is the cheerful *Smyth's Restaurant*, Main Street, a good spot for tasty homemade food, and there's a surprisingly good Indian here too, the *Taj Mahal* on St Brigid's Street (Ⓣ071/964 5914).

North Leitrim

The **North Leitrim Glens** offer some breathtaking scenery: rugged mountains fall to ribbon lakes, and the area is quiet and as yet undiscovered. **Dromahair** is a quiet base from where you can explore the beauty of Lough

Gill (see p.539), while to its north is the pleasant town of **Manorhamilton** and on the Donegal/Fermanagh border at the northernmost tip of the county sits the peaceful and little-explored **Lough Melvin**.

Manorhamilton

Focal point of the mountainous area north of Lough Allen is **MANORHAMILTON**, lying on the saddle of five valleys some fourteen miles east of Sligo town. The town was founded on top of a strategic plateau by Sir Frederick Hamilton, a Scots colonist, during the seventeenth century; his Plantation castle was destroyed in the 1650s and the ruins lie on the edge of town.

Today, Manorhamilton is a handsome crossroads town, with a sense of self-importance underlined by the sturdiness of its architecture, and it makes a good base for **walking** and **potholing** in the surrounding hills, on both sides of the border. Chief among local sights is the well-preserved megalithic tomb at **Cashel Bir**, on the slopes of Benbo. The newly renovated **North Leitrim Glens Centre** (Mon–Fri 10am–6pm; ⓣ071/985 5833, ⓦhttp://homepage.tinet.ie/~nlgdc), housed in the old Methodist church in the centre of town, serves as a tourism information point and can provide information on local activities. As well as housing temporary exhibitions and supporting local artists, the centre also runs an extensive programme of theatrical and musical events.

The town has a couple of **B&Bs** on the Sligo road, including the welcoming *Cill Chiaráin* (ⓣ071/985 6135; ❷) and, a few hundred yards further on, *Laurel Lodge* (ⓣ071/985 5018; ❷). Sturdy **bar meals** can be had from *The Granary*, Main Street, which advertises itself as a bistro and coffee shop, but is actually a straightforward bar. The best of the many pubs on Main Street is *Heraghty's*, a retro place frequented by the local arts crowd.

Dromahair

The R280 southwest of Manorhamilton leads, after ten miles, to the pretty village of **DROMAHAIR**; if you have transport it makes an excellent base from which to enjoy the rugged valleys and the peerless **Lough Gill** and its environs (see p.539). If you want to **stay** in the centre, head for *Stanfords* (ⓣ071/916 4140; ❸) on the main street, a quaint creeper-clad little pub with quiet rooms which serves bar meals and has a restaurant (dinner around €25). The village also has a top-notch French restaurant, *Cuisto Perigord*, Main Street (ⓣ071/916 4954), open in the evenings and for Sunday lunches (expect to pay around €30 per head plus wine).

A short walk from the centre lies **Creevelea Friary**, its ruined east window turned away from the harsh outlines of the mountains and towards the friendly valley below. This Franciscan friary, founded in 1508, was the last to be built in Ireland before Henry VIII's dissolution of the monasteries. It still has some fine sculptures in the cloister arcade: look out for St Francis with the stigmata, and another of him preaching to the birds from a pulpit.

Kiltyclogher

About ten miles northeast of Manorhamilton, **KILTYCLOGHER**, although trim and pretty, has little to detain you after you've seen its Seán MacDiarmada statue. The dedicated can visit the three-room cottage where MacDiarmada, executed in Dublin in 1916 for his part in the uprising, was born; it is maintained as a kind of national shrine, a short way out of town and signposted off the Manorhamilton road (summer only, by arrangement; ⓣ071/985 3249).

There's nowhere to eat in the village, but you can get a drink at *Meehan's Cosy Corner*, a **bar** that sometimes has traditional music featuring the well-known local fiddler Ben Lennon. *Leitrim Lakes Hostel* (April-Oct; Ⓣ071/985 4044, Ⓔllhostel@gofree.indigo.ie) is a large, well-run affair, but is often filled by groups; it's advisable to phone ahead to reserve.

Heading south, less than a mile from the village, the road passes a well-preserved **gallery grave**, dated between 2000 and 1500 BC, on a tranquil windblown site among the heather-covered slopes of Thur Mountain, overlooking a tiny lough; it's known locally as Prince Connell's Grave.

Around Lough Melvin

Four miles northwest of Kiltyclogher and just outside **ROSSINVER**, at the southern end of **Lough Melvin**, there's a cool, leafy walk along a river that cascades through its valley in a series of waterfalls – a good outing for the baking hot days that happen sometimes, even in the west of Ireland. Immediately outside the village on the Garrison road, Eden Plants (Ⓣ071/985 4122) is one of the growing band of Irish producers of organic herbs and vegetables, and is open to visitors (Tues–Sun 2–6pm; free). Two miles north of Rossinver on the road towards Kinlough is the Organic Centre (May–Sept daily 11am–4pm; €4) whose gardens demonstrate the techniques used in domestic and commercial organic gardening. There's also a children's play area and a shop selling plants, herbs and produce.

The route on up to Kinlough, much less spectacular than the country to the west, runs along the eight-mile western shore of Lough Melvin. A few yards from the northern end of the lake is an islet occupied by the ruin of **McClancy's Castle**. It was here that eight survivors from the three Spanish galleons wrecked off Streedagh Point finally found refuge.

KINLOUGH, near the northwestern tip of the lake, is an unpretentious place worth visiting for the **Dartry Centre** (Mon–Sat 10am–6pm, Sun 10.30am–5pm; free) in the centre of the village. This contains a crafts shop and art gallery alongside a small folk museum with displays on local life and culture and there's also an excellent café, very popular for Sunday lunch. Next door to the centre, *The Tickled Trout* has **traditional music** on Wednesdays. The *Courthouse Restaurant* offers food, based on local produce, in the evenings (Weds–Mon 6.30pm–10pm) and Sunday lunchtime as well as comfortable B&B accommodation (Ⓣ071/984 2391, Ⓔthecourthousetrest@eircom.net; ③).

Around three miles north of Kinlough, **TULLAGHAN**, Leitrim's only outlet to the sea, boasts a ninth- or tenth-century **high cross**, standing forlornly askew on a hummock by the roadside – all in all, a rather dreary resort on a dreary strip of coast.

Travel details

Trains

Carrick-on-Shannon to: Dublin (3–4 daily; 2hr 20min); Sligo (3–4 daily; 1hr).
Sligo to: Ballymote (3–4 daily; 20min); Boyle (3–4 daily; 40min); Carrick-on-Shannon (3–4 daily; 1hr); Collooney (3–4 daily; 10min); Dublin (3–4 daily; 3hr 20min).

Buses

Bus Éireann
Carrick-on-Shannon to: Athlone (2–5 daily; 3hr); Boyle (4 daily; 15min); Dublin (4–5 daily; 2hr 30min–3hr); Jamestown (1 Sat; 5min); Sligo (4 daily; 45min–1hr).

Sligo to: Ballina (1–4 daily; 1hr 55min); Ballymote (1–2 Mon–Sat; 30min); Belfast (2–3 daily; 4hr; change at Enniskillen); Boyle (4 daily; 40min); Carrick-on-Shannon (4 daily; 45min–1hr); Collooney (4–7 daily; 5 min); Coolaney (1 Fri; 30min); Derry (3–7 daily; 2hr 30min); Donegal (3–7 daily; 1hr); Drumshanbo (2 Sat; 40min); Dublin (4 daily; 3hr 15min–3hr 45min); Easkey (1–4 daily; 1hr 15min); Enniscrone (1–4 daily; 1hr 30min); Enniskillen (2–3 daily; 1hr 25min); Galway (4–7 daily; 2hr 30min); Gurteen (2 Sat; 1hr); Manorhamilton (2–3 daily; 35min); Rosses Point (6–8 Mon–Sat; 20min); Strandhill (5–7 Mon–Fri; 20min); Tubbercurry (4–7 daily; 35min); Westport (2–3 daily; 2hr–2hr 40min).

Feda O'Donnell Coaches
Sligo to: Donegal (2–3 daily; 50min); Galway (2–3 daily; 2hr 10min).

13

Donegal

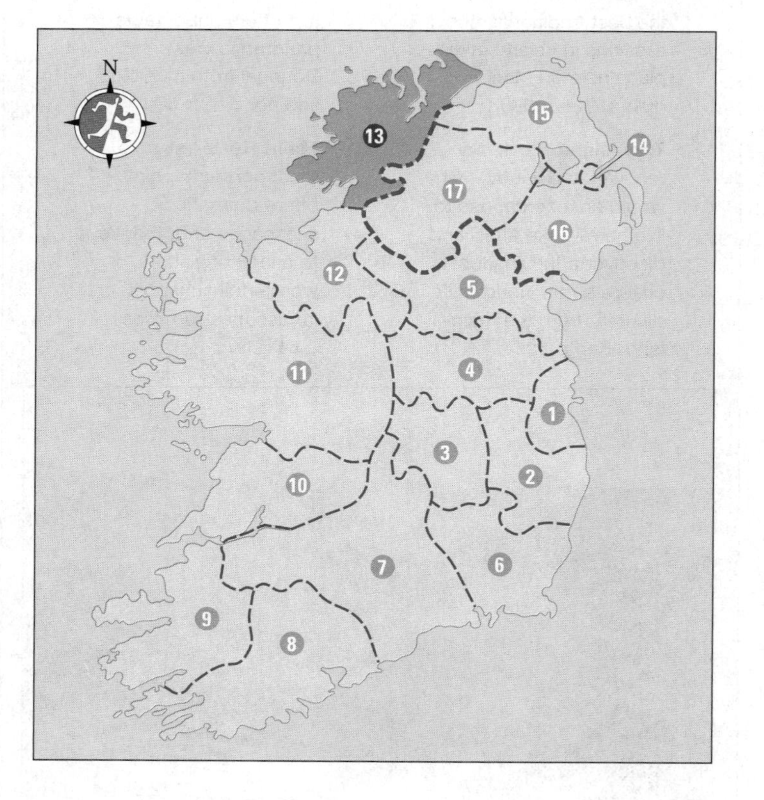

CHAPTER 13 **Highlights**

* **Slieve League** No visit to Donegal would be complete without a walk along the top of this mountain's awesome sea-cliffs. See p.579

* **Húdaí Beag's Pub** Unquestionably one of the best traditional music sessions in Ireland takes place here on Monday nights. See p.590

* **Tory Island** Bleak, barren, wet and windy – why would anyone choose to live here? Take a trip and discover a thriving local culture and a world quite different from the mainland. See p.591

* **Glebe House** Home of the late Derek Hill, Glebe House contains some of the most remarkable modern art in Ireland. See p.595

* **The Grianán Ailigh** This restored circular stone fort offers unbeatable panoramic views of Donegal from its hilltop setting. See p.606

* **Malin Head** Ireland's most northerly point offers dramatic seascapes and, thanks to a lack of visitors, wonderfully unspoilt landscapes too. See p.611

Donegal

Second only in size to County Cork, **County Donegal** has unquestionably the richest scenery in the whole of Ireland, featuring a spectacular two-hundred-mile coastline – an intoxicating run of headlands, promontories and peninsulas rising to the highest sea-cliffs in Europe at **Slieve League**. Inland is a terrain of glens, rivers and bogland hills, of which the best-known parts are the Glencolmcille Peninsula and around Ardara and Glenties in the southern part of the county. The **Glencolmcille** area attracts more visitors than any other, yet the landscape of **northern Donegal** is, if anything, even more satisfying, especially the Rosguill and Inishowen peninsulas and the interior region around Errigal Mountain, Lough Beagh and Lough Gartan. Other noteworthy areas are the **Rosses** and **Gweedore**, which are reminiscent of the more barren stretches of Connemara and make up the strongest Irish-speaking districts in the county.

Donegal's original name was *Tír Chonaill*, which translates as "the land of Conal", who was one of the twelve sons of Niall of the Nine Hostages, reputed to have ruled Ireland in the fifth century. After the Flight of the Earls in 1607, the English changed the name to that of their main garrison *Dún na nGall* ("fort of the foreigners"), which has a certain irony, because Donegal always eluded the grip of English power, thanks to its wild and untillable terrain. Donegal is the most northerly part of Ireland, which confuses some into believing that it is part of Northern Ireland. It has never been so because of the Unionists' belief at the time of Partition in 1922 that Donegal's Catholic population would have threatened the stability of the new statelet by voting the county and the whole of the North back into the Republic at a later stage.

Bundoran and around

Described by the *Sunday People* newspaper in 2002 as like "the back streets of Las Vegas only with cheaper hookers", **BUNDORAN** (Bun Dobhráin, "foot of the River Doran") isn't quite that bad, but it's hard to avoid disappointment if the town is your first sight of Donegal. Lying at the county's southern extreme, this popular, though tacky, seaside resort offers no indication of the pleasures that lie beyond. Although it does have three miles of Blue Flag beaches, packed with Northern holidaymakers in summer, the town itself provides pretty grim fare. The tiny River Doran separates the more genteel **West End** from the **East End** and its rather down-at-heel Main Street, filled with pubs, B&Bs, eating places, and a headland dominated by a **golf course**. Unless you're fond of golf, Bundoran's chief attraction is the lovely golden-sanded **Tullan Strand**, a brac-

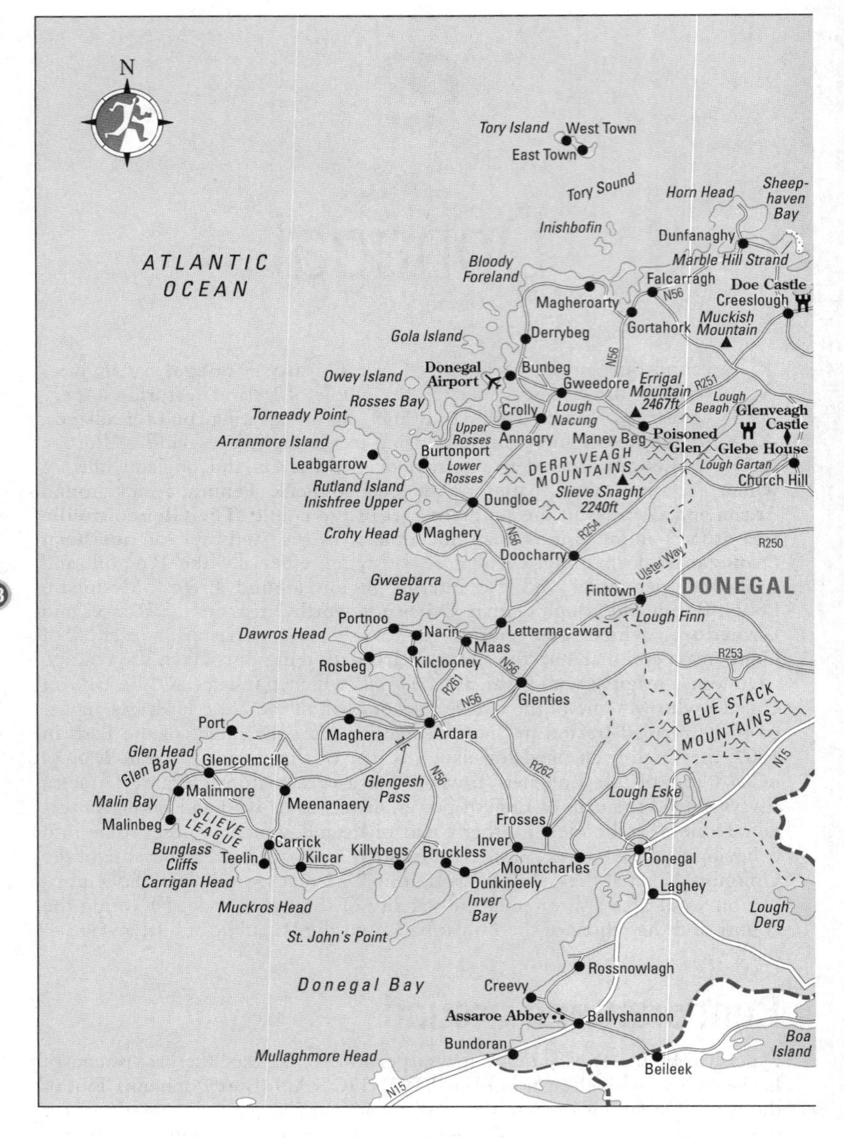

ing stroll along the coastal promenade from the northern end of the town beach. The walk takes in rock formations known as the **Fairy Bridge** and the **Puffing Hole**, with the Atlantic thundering below and appetizing views across to the much more rewarding Glencolmcille Peninsula. Tullan Strand and Rossnowlagh beach (see p.570) are exciting **surfing** spots, and tuition is available from Donegal Adventure Centre, Bayview Avenue (Ⓣ071/42418,

Ⓦ www.donegal-holidays.com). Far safer waters for swimming are to be found at **Waterworld** (Easter week, April, May & Sept Sat & Sun 10am–2pm & 3–7pm; June–Aug daily 10am–7pm; €7; Ⓦ www.waterworldbundoran.com), located on the seafront near the river's mouth, a complex of heated pools with wave machine, water slides and, at the rear, the Aqua Mara seaweed baths (same dates and times €15.20).

Practicalities

The **tourist office** is by the bridge on Main Street (July & Aug daily 9am–8pm; rest of year Mon–Sat 9am–6pm; ⓣ071/984 1350) and there's plenty of **accommodation** if you are intent on staying in Bundoran, the least expensive option being the *Homefield* **hostel**, Bayview Avenue, West End (IHH & IHO; ⓣ071/984 1288, ⓔhomefield@indigo.ie), an activity centre often full of young groups. **B&Bs** are abundant. The best-known of the numerous **hotels** is the huge *Great Northern* (ⓣ071/984 1204, ⓦwww.greatnorthernhotel.com; ❼), right on the headland with its own golf course.

Even if you're not staying, Bundoran has a couple of excellent **restaurants** – the Italian *La Sabbia* (ⓣ071/984 2253), attached to the *Homefield* hostel, and *Le Chateaubrianne*, Sligo Road (ⓣ071/984 2160), which specializes in classic cuisine. There's a plethora of daytime **cafés** and **pubs** with live music, while the hotels often stage major concerts featuring ageing Irish stars. Bundoran is a popular destination for **clubbers** heading at the weekend for *Planet Earth*, Central Avenue, and *The Dome*, Main Street.

Ballyshannon

The lively town of **BALLYSHANNON** (Béal Átha Seanaigh, "ford-mouth of Seanach"), four miles north of Bundoran at the mouth of the River Erne, was the site of a major battle in 1591 when Hugh Roe O'Donnell drove off the besieging English army, but nowadays its hilly streets become most animated during the **Traditional Music Festival** (ⓦwww.ballyshannonfolkfestival.com) on the first weekend in August, featuring major names, such as Donegal's own Altan.

The town stands a few hundred yards upstream from a ford, at the point where the river's fresh waters begin to mingle with the ocean. Most of the interest lies up the steep northern slope and is easily combined in a single, straightforward stroll. The main arteries here form a wishbone, and near the top of the left-hand branch, signposted to the left, is **St Anne's Church** and graveyard, built on the site of the ancient palace of Mullaghanshee. A simple marble slab, inscribed with the word "poet", lies to the left of the church, indicating the burial place of **William Allingham** (1824–89). Allingham was born in Ballyshannon and began work in a bank (the Allied Irish Bank here has a bust of the poet and preserves the words scratched by him on a windowpane. His first volume, *Poems* (1850), contains his best-known work, *The Fairies* ("Up the airy mountain, Down the rushy glen, We daren't go a-hunting For fear of little men…"). Unsurprisingly, such verse attracted him to the Pre-Raphaelites – another work, *Day and Night Songs*, was illustrated by Rosetti and Millais – before Allingham moved onto the more serious poetic subject of his homeland. His posthumous *Diary*, which was edited by his wife, the illustrator Helen Paterson, recounts his friendships with literary contemporaries, most notably Tennyson. Allingham was also a fiddler and balladeer of some skill and contributed to Petrie's collections of "Ancient Irish Music".

From the graveyard there's a marvellous view over the town. Down at the quay, you can see the backs of the tall, old warehouses lined along the river bank, their basement walls dripping with seaweed, and also the ancient isle of **Inis Saimer** just out in the river. The island may have sheltered the first colonists of Ireland, around 3500 BC, offering safety from the ferocious beasts that would have roamed the forests on the mainland, and an ancient Greek coin found there a few years ago has provided evidence of the site's antiquity. There's self-catering **accommodation** on the island, in a nineteenth-century stone house (ⓣ046/903 1106, ⓦhomepage.tinet.ie/~inissaimerisland; sleeps six; €500–760 per week), and the water here teems with fish, so you'll find anglers still trying to bag them well into the night.

A more recently renowned scion of Ballyshannon than Allingham was the blues-rock guitarist **Rory Gallagher**, who was born in 1948 in East Port (head south across the river and roundabout and take the first left). After learning his trade in show bands, he formed the power trio Taste in the 1960s before embarking on a successful solo career. Known as much for his broad-checked shirts as the vivacity of his playing and live performances, Gallagher died prematurely in 1995. Opposite the library in East Port, there's a commemorative plaque, which quotes lyrics from one of his best-known and most appropriate songs, *Going to My Home Town*; a weekend of music celebrates his life at the end of May. Someone who might have come across Gallagher's records is the British Prime Minister **Tony Blair**, whose late mother also hailed from Ballyshannon.

Practicalities

Ballyshannon has a fair number of **B&Bs**. Across the river and over the roundabout, there's the very well furnished and friendly *Elmbrook*, East Port (March–Oct; ⓣ071/985 2615, ⓔelmbrookbandb@eircom.net; ❷) or the adjacent and larger seventeenth-century *Rockville House* (ⓣ071/985 1106l, ⓔrockvillehouse@eircom.net; ❷). Alternatives include the popular *Mullac Na Si*, Bishop Street (April–Oct; ⓣ & ⓕ071/985 2702; ❷), and the recently opened *Forge* (ⓣ071/982 2070, ⓔtheforgeguesthouse@eircom.net; ❸), a very comfortable guesthouse, with a popular restaurant, three miles further down the Rossnowlagh road. More luxurious accommodation can be found at *Dorrian's Imperial Hotel* on Main Street (ⓣ071/985 1147, ⓦwww.dorriansimperialhotel.com; ❻), a refurbished eighteenth-century building whose facilities include a leisure centre, The small but welcoming *Duffy's* **hostel**, a couple of hundred yards up the Donegal road (IHH; March to mid-Oct; ⓣ071/985 1535) has its own secondhand bookshop and **camping** facilities. Waterside camping is available at the *Lakeside Caravan and Camping Park* (ⓣ071/985 2822) off the R230 Belleek road. **Bikes** can be rented from the Erne Cycle Shop, An Mál, off Main Street.

There are several reasonably priced **restaurants** for daytime eating, including the popular upstairs coffee rooms at *Grimes Kitchen Bake* on Main Street, where you can get marvellous fresh cakes and pastries, and *Shannon's Corner*, Bishop Street, for excellent-value breakfast and lunch. In the evening, try *Sweeny's White Horse*, a pub a hundred yards down Bundoran Road, serving a surprisingly imaginative menu, or the Mexican specialities at *El Gringo* by the roundabout.

Ballyshannon's most atmospheric **pub** is *The Thatch*, Bishop Street, with thatched roof and cottage-kitchen interior, which has occasional **traditional music** in summer. More regular music sessions take place at *Sweeny's* on Fridays and *Jimmy Al's* by the bridge early on Sunday evening. Other kinds of music can be found at *Seán Óg's*, and *Dicey Reilly's*, both on Market Street, while the hub of **club** life is *Dino's* on Main Street. The free monthly *On the Move!* magazine provides entertainment **listings** for Ballyshannon and the surrounding area.

As well as its August music festival, Ballyshannon has a number of other events worth investigating. An amateur **drama festival** of mainly Irish plays is held during the week of March 17 (St Patrick's Day); the **Allingham Arts Festival for Writers** takes place over a weekend at the end of November; and the town's traditional **harvest fair** celebrations draw the crowds from the surrounding countryside around the middle of September. The **Abbey Arts and Cultural Centre** at the top of Market Street (ⓣ071/985 2928) hosts a range of musical and theatrical events and has a two-screen **cinema**. At **Ballintra**, four miles along the Donegal road, there's **horse racing** in the open fields on the first Monday in August.

North to Rossnowlagh

Instead of taking the main road to Donegal town, the left turn at the top of Main Street takes you along the more pleasant Rossnowlagh road, where a second signposted left turn leads to the sparse remains of **Abbey Assaroe**, founded by the Cistercians in 1184. Past the abbey and round to the left, you'll come to a restored **mill** beside a bubbling stream. This makes a pretty picture of mill-race and rotating cog-wheels, and there's a small **interpretive centre** (June–Aug daily 10am–6pm; free), explaining the restoration project and the role of the Cistercians in medieval Ireland, as well as an adjacent café. The log gate by the old bridge takes you onto the stream's bank and leads to two artificial **caves**. One is a small grotto known as Catsby's; the other – now around 90ft deep – is said to have once reached all the way under the abbey and run for two miles towards Rossnowlagh. The grotto was once a site for secret Masses, held here to evade the enforcement of the penal laws in the eighteenth century, and you'll find in the Rossnowlagh museum (see opposite) the carved stone known as the Monk's Head that once sat above the entrance. A couple of hundred yards upstream are *Eas Aedha Ruadh*, the **falls** of the chieftain Red Hugh O'Donnell, who reputedly drowned here.

A few yards up the lane from the mill and over a stone stile next to a bungalow, a little track runs down to the shore of the **bay**. St Patrick is said to have once stepped ashore here, and today there are several rusted metal crosses perched on small stony outcrops and a tree covered in assorted weather-beaten thanksgiving mementos. The natural **well** here is said to have sprung up at the spot where the saint's foot touched the shore and its waters, when present, have supposed curative powers. Legend also has it that, having arrived, Patrick was driven away by a local leader named Coirbre and responded by cursing the northern side of the river with a barrenness of fish.

Back on the Rossnowlagh road, two miles on, a turning leads to the tiny seaside hamlet of **CREEVY**. It's a tranquil, though lonely spot, and a memorial on the pier sadly records the death of three local fishermen in 1988, testament to the occasional ferocity of the waters in the bay. Should you fancy **staying**, there's the *Creevy Pier Hotel* (ⓣ071/985 8355, ⓕ985 1236; ❸), where you can watch the waves from the bar and sample the fresh seafood in its restaurant.

Rossnowlagh

ROSSNOWLAGH lies on the coast away from the main Donegal road, with good cliffs for walks overlooking a magnificent expanse of beach that is raked by Atlantic surf and is also, sadly, sometimes blighted by boy-racers. Rossnowlagh has a private **surfing** club beside the swish and elegant *Sandhouse Hotel* (ⓣ071/985 1777, ⓦwww.sandhouse-hotel.ie; ❽), but one of the many surfing buffs will probably be able to help you out with equipment, or at least advise where else to acquire some. The village is also the site of the only **Orange Order parade** (see box on p.734) in the Republic, which takes place on the weekend before July 12. On the cliff-top, there's the excellent *Ard na Mara* **B&B** (ⓣ071/985 1141, ⓔrebeccaashling@hotmailcom; ❸) and the splendidly situated *Smugglers Creek* **inn**, offering excellent seafood and live **music** at weekends.

The Franciscan friary nearby on the Donegal road houses a captivating one-room **museum** (daily 10am–6pm; free), run by the Donegal Historical Society and crammed with Stone Age flints, Bronze Age dagger blades, penal crosses, pistols and other local miscellany. This includes a lovely set of *uilleann* pipes with green felt bag and very handsome regulators, a fiddle that belonged to the great piper Tarlach MacSuibhne (himself buried at Magheragallon cemetery, Gweedore) and a seventeenth-century Flemish painting on glass (*The Christ of Pity*) used as a devotion plate. A mile north of Rossnowlagh towards Ballintra lies **Glasbolie Fort**, a huge earthen rampart 20ft high and nearly 900ft round, said to have been the burial place of a sixth-century High King of Ireland.

Donegal town and around

DONEGAL town is not the most exciting of places, but it's a pleasant enough spot to pass a few hours. It's not even the county town (which is Lifford) but, thanks to a recently built bypass, traffic no longer crams its triangular **Diamond**, the old market place, at the centre. A surprising number of tourists visit the town, but the only real reason to stay long is to explore the surrounding countryside, especially the **Blue Stack Mountains**, which rise at the northern end of **Lough Eske**.

Arrival, information and accommodation

Buses stop outside the *Abbey Hotel* on The Diamond, with timetables available from the **tourist office** on The Quay (Easter–June & Sept Mon–Sat 9am–5pm; July & Aug daily 9am–8pm; ⓣ074/972 1148, ⓦwww.donegal.ie). For details of **walks** in the Blue Stack Mountains, just north of Donegal town (see p.574), and in the rest of the county, pick up a copy of David Herman's excellent *Hill Walkers Donegal* from the tourist office or the Four Masters bookshop on The Diamond. Both also sell Ordnance Survey **maps** of the area.

Donegal has plenty of **accommodation** in all price ranges. The most expensive includes two comfortable **hotels** on The Diamond, the *Abbey Hotel* (ⓣ074/972 1014, ⓦwww.whites-hotelsireland.com; ❺) and the adjacent *Central Hotel* (ⓣ074/972 1027, ⓦwww.whites-hotelsireland.com; ❻). Just out of town is the new *Mill Park Hotel*, The Mullins, Killybegs Road (ⓣ074/972 2880, ⓦwww.millparkhotel.com; ❼), or, if you really want to push the boat out, book in at *St Ernan's House Hotel* (mid-April to Oct; ⓣ074/972 1065, ⓦwww.sainternans.com; ❽), built by Wellington's nephew in 1826 and situated on its own private island, signposted a few hundred yards up the Sligo road. There are dozens of **B&Bs** scattered around the town: central options include *Riverside House* (ⓣ074/972 1083, ⓔkay@tinet.ie; ❷), on Waterloo Place, across the river from the castle, where there are several other nearby B&B possibilities, and the *Atlantic Guesthouse* on Main Street (ⓣ074/972 1187; ❷). For a more atmospheric setting, try *The Water's Edge*, Glebe (ⓣ074/972 1523, ⓔthewatersedgebb2000@hotmail.com; ❷), a short distance up and off the Sligo road, overlooking Donegal Bay, or the similarly situated *Bay View*, Golf Course Road (ⓣ074/972 3018; ❷).

Hostels include the busy, but friendly *Donegal Town Independent Hostel* (IHH & IHO; ⓣ074/972 2805, ⓦwww.donegalhostel.com), half a mile west down the Killybegs road, which has camping facilities; and the secluded but often busy An Óige *Ball Hill Hostel* (Easter–Sept; ⓣ074/972 1174, ⓔmailbox@anoige.ie), about three miles further west in a former coastguard station on the north side of Donegal Bay, which also has camping.

Bikes can be rented from O'Doherty's, Main Street (☎074/972 1119), which also sells **fishing** permits and rents out tackle. The owner is a mine of information on the region, including the best angling spots and hiking routes. Dermo's **laundry** (Mon–Sat 9am–6pm) is in the Millcourt Shopping Arcade on The Diamond.

The Town

Donegal takes its name from *Dún na nGall*, and the original "fort of the foreigners" was thought to have been built on the banks of the River Eske by invading Vikings. There's no doubt, however, that the first Red Hugh O'Donnell, king of Tír Chonaill, had a Norman-style tower house, known as **O'Donnell's Castle**, constructed on its site in the fifteenth century. When the English defeated the second Red Hugh in 1603, Sir Basil Brooke was given command of the town and it was he who rebuilt and extended the old castle, retaining the lower parts of the original tower, which had been razed to the ground by Red Hugh to prevent its capture. This well-restored example of Jacobean architecture sits on Tírconaill Street by The Diamond (mid-March to Oct daily 10am–6pm, last entry 5.15pm; €3.80; Heritage Card). It's a fine marriage of strong defence and domestic grace, featuring mullioned windows, arches, ten gables and no fewer than fourteen fireplaces, over the grandest of which are carved the escutcheons of Brooke and his wife's family, the Leicesters. Brooke topped the tower with a Barbizon turret and added the mansion on the left, with the kitchens and bakery on the ground floor and living quarters on the floor above. Brooke was highly prolific in Donegal and was responsible for the overall design of the town.

On the stone bridge by the castle on the Killybegs road is a plaque commemorating the town's most famous author, the Reverend Dr John Boyce, better known by his pseudonym **Paul Peppergrass**. After ministering for some years in the county, he travelled to America in 1845, concerned for the spiritual welfare of the newly arrived Irish emigrants. Though largely forgotten now, his most popular work was *Shandy Maguire*, a novel describing the tribulations incurred by Irish Catholics in defence of their faith.

In The Diamond stands an obelisk commemorating the compilers of the famed **Annals of the Four Masters**. The Annals were assembled in the town's **Franciscan Friary**, whose ruined remains stand on the left bank of the River Eske, and were a systematic attempt to collect all known Irish documents into a history of the land beginning in 2958 BC and ending at the time of writing, 1616 AD. The friary itself was built in 1474 by the first Red Hugh and his wife Nuala O'Brien of Munster. It was occupied by the English in 1601 and seriously damaged by the besieging O'Donnell army, being finally abandoned after the Flight of the Earls (see p.783). The Annals were completed by friars who had moved to a site by the River Drowes, near Kinlough, Country Leitrim.

Down at the **quay** an anchor is on display, retrieved from the sea near Mountcharles in the 1850s and traditionally believed to have belonged to the French frigate *Romaine*, a member of the fleet supporting Wolfe Tone's rebellion in 1798. On the opposite shore a woodland path known as the **Bank Walk** runs out alongside the bay with a pleasant view towards its many sandy islets and stony shoreline. A **Waterbus** (☎074/972 3666; €8) offers a seventy-minute trip around Donegal Bay starting from the quay.

The County Donegal Railway, which formerly ran from Derry to Ballyshannon, closed in 1959, and its history is told at the **Donegal Railway**

Heritage Centre at the Old Station House on Tírconaill Street (June–Sept Mon–Sat 9am–5pm, Sun 2–5pm; Oct–May Mon–Fri 10am–5pm; €3). Here you'll find a model of the old railway and lovingly restored railcars and carriages from the age of steam.

If you're looking to buy something a little special, it's well worth heading to the **Craft Village** (Mon–Sat 10am–6pm; also June–Aug Sun noon–6pm), three-quarters of a mile south of town on the Sligo road, whose workshops are leased to professional craftspeople, including sculptors, potters, jewellers and designers.

Eating, drinking and entertainment

Eating places are plentiful in Donegal, though it's the pubs as ever that seem to offer most choice. Options include steaks, salmon and pizzas at *The Harbour*, opposite the tourist office, while the restaurant in Magee's store on The Diamond serves light lunches. The carvery in the *Central Hotel* is popular with locals and the *Abbey Hotel's* restaurant serves equally substantial food. Nearby is the new *Dom's Bar & Restaurant*, Quay Street, which also offers an extensive menu. If all you want is a cheap, hearty meal, make for the *Blueberry Tearoom & Restaurant*, opposite the castle, or the *Atlantic Restaurant* on Main Street. Further up Main Street, the *Errigal Chipper* offers fresh fish from Killybegs.

Donegal holds a summer **festival** in late June with plenty of music and street entertainment, while the Donegal Bay and Blue Stacks festival, eleven days of theatre and music, takes place at the beginning of October (Ⓦwww.donegalculture.com). Many of the town's **pubs** offer entertainment year round, and Thursday's *Donegal Democrat* newspaper provides local **listings**. The *Olde Castle* bar, next to the castle, has an excellent restaurant and a cosy bar. Lively *McGroarty's*, a few doors down, has a Thursday night traditional session and other music at weekends, while the nearby *Central Hotel* is the place for home-grown country and western. Options on Main Street include: *i:vibes*, a DJ bar with a lively crowd; the *Star Bar* for sing-songs and live acts at weekends; and, best of all, *The Schooner*, just past the cathedral, with a nautical interior, an original nineteenth-century bar and music on Fridays and Sundays. For a quiet pint, try *Tírconaill*, an old-time bar on The Diamond. *Club N*, on Main Street, holds regular **discos** (Fri & Sat), but the most popular are in the *Abbey Hotel* (Sun 10.30pm–2am; sometimes also on Fridays in summer).

Around Donegal town

Southeast of Donegal town, the landscape is replete with little lakes well stocked for fishing; the largest of these, and a place of pilgrimage, is **Lough Derg**. Less than five miles upriver from Donegal town is another spot of gentle natural beauty, **Lough Eske**, from where you can walk into the wilds of the **Blue Stack Mountains**, which rise to the north.

Lough Derg and Station Island

In the middle of **Lough Derg** ("red lake") is a rocky islet known as **Station Island** or, more popularly, St Patrick's Purgatory, which has long served as a retreat for Catholics needing rigour and solitude to recharge their faith. A national shrine of pilgrimage since the fifth century, it was described by Girardus Cambrensis in *Topography of Ireland* (1186) as "an island, one part of which is frequented by good spirits, the other by evil spirits". Contemporary scholars have argued that as St Patrick never referred to Lough Derg in his writings he probably never visited the island, but nevertheless it still thrives today as a strong centre for **pilgrimage**, especially from June to mid-August. Participants in the three-day retreats abjure sleep and food (apart from black tea and toast) and walk barefoot over rocks, praying at Stations of the Cross. One-day retreats are less austere. Despite the exigencies, it seems particularly popular with Irish students studying for exams – or waiting for the results. *Station Island*, a collection by Seamus Heaney, contains a number of poems dealing with the mystique surrounding this ritual, while Pete McCarthy graphically recounts his experience of a retreat in *McCarthy's Bar* (see p.876).

If want to participate, contact the Purgatory's Prior (Ⓣ071/988 1518, Ⓦwww.loughderg.org). The island is approached via the R233 from **PETTIGO**, six miles south. A bus from Ballyshannon or Enniskillen will drop you in Pettigo village, where there's a small **interpretive centre** explaining the island's background (March–Oct Mon–Sat 9am–5pm; €2.50). Pettigo also has a remarkable number of pubs for such a small village, suggesting an importance placed on spiritual nourishment of a rather different kind.

Lough Eske

Lough Eske ("lake of fish") is no longer a particularly great fishing spot, though it is known as a place to catch char, a tasty nine-inch-long species of the salmon family. They lurk in the depths at the centre of the lake, moving out to the shallower edges around late October, where they can be easily fished using worms. The sandy banks of the River Eske are also known for freshwater oysters – some of which are reputed to contain pearls – but they're a protected species so it's illegal to take them. The ruins of an **O'Donnell tower**, once a prison, stand on one of the small islands on the lake.

The most enjoyable way to get to this area of soft beauty is to take the minor road that runs north of the river, signposted "Lough Eske Drive", half a mile out of Donegal town on the Killybegs road. This leads to a forgotten, forested estate, once belonging to the Brooke family but now owned by the Forestry Commission.

At the southern end of the lough, you'll find *Harvey's Point Country Hotel* (Ⓣ074/972 2208, Ⓦwww.harveyspoint.com; ❻), which offers fine **accommodation** and one of the best **restaurants** in the county (lunch €20, dinner €44 per head). There's also high-quality **B&B** at *Ardnamona* (Ⓣ074/972 2650, Ⓦwww.ardnamona.com; ❺) on the western shore, set in glorious lakeside gardens planted in the 1880s using many seeds and cuttings from the Imperial Gardens in Peking and palace gardens in Kathmandu. Other excellent options in the lough's environs include *Ardeevin* (Ⓣ074/972 1790, Ⓦmembers.tripod.com/~ardeevin; ❷) and *The Arches* (Ⓣ074/972 2029, Ⓦwww.archescountryhse.com; ❷),both on the eastern shore and each set in splendid grounds overlooking the waters.

The Blue Stack Mountains

Carrying on along the western shore of Lough Eske, you'll reach the point where the river flows in at the lough's northern tip. Nearby, a dirt road runs off to the left into the **Blue Stack Mountains**. At the top of the pathway that leads on from the track, there are superb views over the lough and, nearby, the very fine **Doonan waterfall**. From here you can join the waymarked **Bluestack Way**, which passes Lough Belshade (Bhéal Seód, "lake of the jewels"), guarded in legend by a huge black cat. If you're intending to tramp around the mountain range, it's best to keep to the skirts of the hills, for there are many marshy patches on lower ground – and be prepared for misty pockets during bad weather.

West of Donegal town

The most appealing route out of Donegal town heads **west** along the shore of Donegal Bay all the way to Glencolmcille, some 35 miles distant. Leaving Donegal town, the first turning left after the roundabout will lead you down to **Holmes beach** and the *Ball Hill* hostel (see p.571). Further highlights along this coast include the thriving fishing port of **Killybegs**, and the extraordinarily dramatic coastal scenery reaches an apogee in the mammoth sea-cliffs of **Slieve League**. The **Glencolmcille peninsula** is a Gaeltacht, and the attractive villages of Kilcar, Carrick, Teelin and Glencolmcille itself are rich in traditional folklore and music.

Mountcharles to Bruckless

The first village west of Donegal town is the now bypassed **MOUNTCHARLES**, straggling up a steep hillside and taking its name from a seventeenth-century landlord, Charles Conyingham. Near the top of the hill, a bright green pump commemorates the birth nearby of the poet and storyteller **Séamus MacManus**. Mountcharles is a sea-angling centre, and **boats** can be rented from Michael O'Byrne (Ⓣ074/973 5257).

FROSSES (Na Frosa, "the showers"), a mile or so inland off the road between Mountcharles and Inver, is a pleasant, crossroads hamlet that has occasional *céilís* on Sunday nights in the village hall (dancing begins at 10pm), while *Breslin's* **bar** hosts traditional sessions on Saturdays. The **cemetery** here contains the graves of Séamus MacManus and his wife, the very underrated poet, Ethna Carberry. At the end of the nineteenth century, Carberry and Alice Milligan edited the important nationalist literary paper *Shan Van Vocht* (sean bean bocht, "the poor old woman", an oft-used euphemism for Ireland).

Continuing west, the secluded seaside village of **INVER** with its small strand, just a few hundred yards off the road, is a tranquil spot and affords good views over Inver Bay. The recently renovated *Rising Tide* **pub** is good for a pint and was also the birthplace of Thomas Nesbitt, inventor of the harpoon gun.

At **DUNKINEELY** there's the *Blue Moon* **hostel** (IHO; Ⓣ074/973 7284, Ⓦhomepage.eircom.net/bluemoonhostel), with space for camping, and Wednesday night traditional sessions in *McIntyre's*. Another deviation left from the main road takes you first past *Castle Murray House Hotel* (Ⓣ074/973 7022, Ⓦwww.castlemurray.com; ❹), noted for its comfortable accommodation and French gourmet **meals** (dinner around €30 per head), then down a long, narrow promontory to **St John's Point**, where a crumbling castle stands at the tip. As you head south, there are great views over Donegal Bay, especially back towards the narrow entry of Killybegs bay, with **Rotten Island** at its mouth. The waters off the Point are reckoned to offer the best **diving** in Ireland, but you'll need to bring your own boat and equipment. If you decide to stay on the Point, take advantage of the strategically positioned *Sea View* **B&B** (April–Oct; Ⓣ074/973 7252; ❷).

A little west of Dunkineely, at **BRUCKLESS**, there's stylish **B&B** available at Georgian *Bruckless House* (Ⓣ074/973 7071, Ⓦwww.iol.ie/~bruc/bruckless; ❹), and an excellent **hostel**, *Gallagher's Farm Hostel* (IHH; Ⓣ074/973 7057) in

△ Slieve League cliffs

Darney, a mile back towards Dunkineely, with camping facilities. Also in Bruckless is Deane's Open Farm (Easter–Aug; ⓣ074/973 7160; €3), which offers **riding** lessons and trekking. The village **pub**, *Mary Murrin's*, has been splendidly refurbished and provides good-value bar meals, including a children's menu.

Killybegs

Sticking to the coast road west of Bruckless, you'll round Killybegs Bay and arrive in the most successful fishing port in Ireland, **KILLYBEGS** (Na Cealla Beaga, "the little churches"), where tons of top-quality fish are hauled onto the quaysides daily. This marks the halfway point on the route from Donegal town to Glencolmcille, and the mile-long approach road to Killybegs around the bay would be idyllic were it not for a fishmeal processing plant interrupting the view.

Killybegs itself is perched on a slope above the harbour, its gleaming whitewashed buildings huddled around narrow cramped streets. The town is well served by shops and banks and buzzes with traffic in summer, most of it heading down to the quay. A huge international **sea-angling festival** takes place here in the second half of July but you can go fishing any time in one of the boats that go out daily – the **Harbour Store** (ⓣ074/973 1569) has details and sells fishing gear. Picturesque though Killybegs is, it isn't exactly overflowing with interest, and most of the pubs are aimed squarely at working fishermen, though students from the local Tourism College liven the place up in term time. All will change, however, when the **gas rigs** located thirty miles offshore begin functioning over the next couple of years as Killybegs will become their service town.

It's worth visiting the **church** at the top of the hill for a glimpse of the sixteenth-century tombstone of **Niall Mór MacSweeney**, removed from his grave at Ballysaggart Friary on St John's Point and now covered in Celtic carvings and contained in a glass case to the left of the church door. The MacSweeneys originated from the Scottish Hebridean islands and arrived in Ireland as gallow glasses (*gallóglach*, "foreign warrior"), hired by the O'Donnells to drive the O'Neills from the land around the River Foyle. Receiving land in payment, the MacSweeneys became one of Donegal's ruling families prior to the Flight of the Earls, and Niall Mór was head of one branch of the clan.

Practicalities

Accommodation in Killybegs includes the elegant *Bay View Hotel* (ⓣ074/973 1950, ⓦwww.bayviewhotel.ie; ❻), overlooking the harbour, and there are rooms in a number of pubs, including *Cope House*, Main Street (ⓣ074/973 1834, ⓔcopehouse@ireland.com; ❹), and the *Pier Bar* (ⓣ074/973 1045; ❸). The former also has a popular Chinese restaurant and houses the *Lighthouse* **nightclub** (Thurs–Sat). Most of the **B&Bs** are a mile or two out of town on Fintra Road, heading west towards Kilcar, including the comfortable *Bannagh House* (ⓣ074/973 1108, ⓔbannaghhouse@eircom.net) which overlooks the harbour.

Melly's Café, by the harbour, is a local institution and the best place for cheap snacks and fast **food**. Otherwise, you can grab a lunch in most of the **pubs**, including fresh seafood in the *Harbour Bar*; for something slightly more upmarket, try the brasserie at the *Bay View Hotel*. Most of the bars have **music** at weekends.

Kilcar and around

A couple of miles west of Killybegs, signposts point the way to the Blue Flag **Fintragh Beach**. Further on, the road to Kilcar passes *Kitty Kelly's* **restaurant** (summer daily 6–9.30pm; ⓣ074/973 1925), which offers particularly good Irish cuisine. Just after the *Blue Haven Restaurant* (Irish dancing on Thurs), the road divides. For the scenic route, take the road to the left, a narrow switchback ride along the coastline with stupendous views over the ocean, especially from **Muckross Head**, and the looming presence of the hills and mountains to your right.

The roads meet again at **KILCAR** (Cill Charthaigh, "St Carthach's church"), a pleasant village and a centre for the Donegal **tweed industry**: there are several small factories open to visitors. The village has a **sea-angling festival** at the beginning of August, followed shortly afterwards by a raucous **street festival**. **Boats** can be rented from Jim Byrne (ⓣ074/973 8224), while Paddy Clarke (ⓣ074/973 8211) offers guided game angling and hill-walking. Fishing tackle is available from McBrearty's, Main Street. There are five **bars**, including *John Joe's* which stages regular Friday-night sessions. *Teach Barnaí* (ⓣ074/9738160), across the road, is one of Donegal's best **restaurants**, serving superb evening meals and extremely popular Sunday lunches.

Kilcar has **B&B** at *Kilcar Lodge*, Main Street (April–Oct; ⓣ074/9738156, ⓔkilcar-lodge@yahoo.com; ❸), and nearby on the coast road to Carrick at *Hillcrest* (ⓣ074/973 8243; ❷) and *Dún Ulún House* (ⓣ074/973 8137; ❷), which also offers **hostel** accommodation. Alternatively, a little further on is *Derrylahan* (IHH & IHO; ⓣ074/973 8079, ⓦhomepage.eircom.net/~derrylahan), set on a working farm and one of the friendliest and busiest **hostels** in the country; a shorter approach for walkers involves taking the right-hand fork of three options just outside the village and following the green lane over the hill.

Derrylahan is an ideal base for exploring the beautiful countryside around **CARRICK**, especially Teelin Bay and the awesome Slieve League cliffs to the west. In the pretty village of Carrick itself the friendly *Teach Tom* has a regular Friday night traditional session while the *Sliab Liag* **pub** has live music and DJs at the weekend. A mile outside on the Glencolmcille road is **The Gate House** (Easter–Sept daily 10am–6.30pm), built by local landlords in the 1860s and now housing tearooms and a crafts shop. Back on the coast road to Kilcar, the Sliabh League Equestrian Centre (ⓣ074/973 9386) offers **riding and trekking**. If you want to stay in Carrick, there's **B&B** at *Teach Mór* (ⓣ074/973 9137; ❷), up a little lane almost opposite the Teelin turning, and at *Cairnsmore* (ⓣ074/973 9137; ❷), a wonderfully situated bungalow half a mile towards Glencolmcille.

Five miles to the north of Carrick is the village of **MEENANEARY**, dominated by a large crab-processing plant and also home to *Bíalainn na Seab Scoile*, a **café** serving huge portions of food at low prices. Also here is *O'Donnell's* **bar**, which hosts regular **traditional music** sessions (Sat) and is the base for a traditional **music festival** over the first weekend in June (for details call ⓣ074/973 9009).

The southern road from Carrick to **TEELIN** (Teileann, "dish") follows the west bank of the River Owenee, whose rapids and pools are good for **fishing** – licences are available from Teelin Sea Angling Club (ⓣ074/973 9079). Sea-angling and sightseeing **boat trips** to the Slieve League cliffs are provided by Paddy Byrne (ⓣ074/973 9365) and Paddy "Shark Hunter" (ⓣ074/973 9327). Like most of the peninsula, the village is Irish-speaking and rich in folklore,

Climbing Slieve League

There are two routes up to the ridge of **Slieve League** (Sliabh Liag, "mountain of the pillar-stone"). A less-used back route, known as "Old Man's Track", follows the signpost pointing to the mountain just before Teelin and looks up continually to the ridge, while the frontal approach follows the signs out of Teelin to **BUNGLASS**, swinging you spectacularly round sharp bends and up incredibly steep inclines to one of the most thrilling cliff scenes in the world, the **Amharc Mór**. These are claimed to be the **highest marine cliffs in Europe**, and standing here that seems all too likely. The sea moves so far below that the waves appear silent, and the near-two-thousand-foot face glows with mineral deposits in tones of amber, white and red. They say that on a clear day it is possible to see one-third of the whole of Ireland from the summit. **Sightseeing tours** of the cliffs from the waters below are organized from Teelin, weather permitting (see opposite).

If you want to make a full day of it, you can climb up to the cliffs from the Bunglass car park and follow the path along the top of the ridge, which eventually meets "Old Man's Track". From here "One Man's Pass", a narrow path with steep slopes on each side, leads up to the summit of Slieve League. Bear in mind that the route can often be muddy and very windy – it is certainly not advisable in misty weather or if you suffer from vertigo. From the top of Slieve League, you can either retrace your steps back to Teelin or continue west over the crest of the mountain and down the heather-tufted western slope towards the verdant headland village of **MALINBEG**, where there's a sublime, crescent-shaped golden strand enclosed by a tight rocky inlet. Here, Malinmore Adventure Centre (℡074/973 0123) organizes **diving** and other activities, including canoeing and hill-walking. Malinbeg itself is a village of white bungalows, with the land around ordered into long narrow strips. The recently opened *Malinbeg* **hostel** (IHH & IHO; ℡074/973 0006) is well equipped and has space for **camping**. On the cliff edge a ruined Martello tower faces **Rathlin O'Beirne Island**, three miles offshore, a place with many folklore associations. There are occasional boats across (enquire in Teelin – see opposite), but nothing to see beyond some early Christian stone relics and a ruined coastguard station.

Beyond Malinbeg, it's relatively easy to extend your walk through **MALINMORE**, where the large *Glencolmcille* **hotel** (℡074/973 0003, www.glenhotel.com; ❹) serves food, and on to Glencolmcille. The whole distance from Teelin to Malinmore can be comfortably completed in six hours.

which has been recorded over the last half-century by the late Seán Ó'hEochaidh, Donegal's great folklorist. You can **stay** in the village at *Sea Crest* (July–Sept; ℡074/973 9108; ❷), down by the harbour, or *Teelin Bay House* (April–Oct; ℡074/973 9013; ❷) on the way into the village from Carrick. Teelin has a long musical tradition and you're more than likely to catch a session at the weekend in *Cúl a' Dúin*, the village's only **pub**. Part-owned by two members of the internationally successful Donegal traditional group Altan, the pub's cosy lounge is often the venue for dynamic music and traditional song, sometimes featuring the co-owners themselves.

Glencolmcille

As the road from Carrick approaches **GLENCOLMCILLE** ("St Columba's glen"), it traverses desolate moorland that's dominated by oily-black turf banks amidst patches of heather and grass, where not even sheep seem able to subsist. After this, the rich beauty of the Glen, as it's known, comes as a welcome surprise. Settlement in the area dates back to the Stone Age, as testified by the enormous number of **megalithic remains** scattered around the countryside, especially court cairns and standing stones. There's evidence, too, of the Celtic era, in the form of earthworks and stone works. Traditionally, **St Columba** founded a monastery here in the sixth century and some of the **standing stones**, known as the *Turas Cholmcille*, were adapted for Christian usage by the inscription of a cross. Every Columba's Day (June 9) at midnight, the locals commence a barefoot circuit of the fifteen *Turas*, including Columba's Chapel, chair, bed, wishing stone and Holy Well, finishing up with Mass at 3am in the village church. (Columba and Columbcille/Colmcille are the same person – the latter is the name by which he was known after his conversion, and means "the dove of the church").

In more recent times, widespread emigration left the Glencolmcille area a typical example of rural decay. In 1951, however, a new and energetic curate, Father James McDyer, instigated efforts to revitalize the community, while retaining and strengthening its culture. Electricity arrived in the village and road improvements reduced its isolation and allowed new collective enterprises in knitting and agriculture to thrive, simultaneously increasing the area's accessibility to tourism. Thankfully, these developments have not lessened the village's innate attraction. The buildings in **Cashel**, the village centre, are painted in radiant colours – the village church is lavender, there's a whitewashed semi-detached estate, one old pub is a canary yellow, and another a Mediterranean sky-blue.

One of McDyer's major initiatives stands in Doonalt down by the beach – the **Folk Village Museum and Heritage Centre** (hourly tours Easter–Oct Mon–Sat 10am–6pm, Sun noon–6pm; €2.75; Ⓦwww.infowing.ie/donegal/ad/fr), a clustered *clochán* of replica thatched cottages, each equipped with the particular furniture and artefacts of the era it represents. A reception building introduces you to the area's history and cultural heritage, including a reputed visit by Charles Stuart (Bonnie Prince Charlie). There's free access to the **National School** replica, which has a display of informative photographs and research projects, and a section on the American painter Rockwell Kent, who painted marvellous treatments of the area's landscapes. At **Sheebeen** house, you can try seaweed wine and other concoctions, such as honey, fuchsia and elderberry (most much better than they sound). There's also a tea house and crafts shop.

On the way down the main street to the Folk Village is *Foras Cultúir Uladh*, the **Ulster Cultural Centre**. The centre hosts Tapeis Gael, a group of local artists with an innovative approach to tapestry design, and the many **courses** run by Oideas Gael (Ⓣ074/973 0248, Ⓦwww.oideas-gael.com), including Irish language, painting, *bodhrán* playing, dancing, flute and whistle playing, archaeology and hill-walking.

From behind the hostel (see p.581), **cliff walks** steer off around the south side of the bay above a series of jagged drops. Rising from the opposite side of the valley mouth, the promontory of **Glen Head** is surmounted by a Martello tower. On the way out you pass the ruins of **St Columbcille's Church**, with its "resting slab" where St Columba would have lain down exhausted from prayer. North across this headland you can climb and descend again to the forgotten little cove of **Port** a few miles away, a village deserted since the 1940s. Absolutely nothing happens here – although Dylan Thomas once stayed in the next valley at **Glenlough**, renting a cottage for several weeks in a doomed attempt to "dry out" in an area replete in poteen stills.

Practicalities

Glencolmcille's **tourist office** (June–Aug daily 10am–6pm; Ⓣ074/973 0116) is in the Lace House crafts shop on the main street. **B&B** accommodation is available at *Corner House* (April–Sept; ⓣ074/973 0021; ❷) in Cashel. You can catch the sunset at the beautifully positioned *Dooey* **hostel** (IHO; ⓣ074/973 0130, ⓦwww.holidayhound.com/dooeyhostel), set high above the fine shingle strand at the mouth of the valley; it also offers **camping**. To get there on foot, keep on the village road as far as the Folk Village, and then take a path up to the left; in wet weather the longer route by road may be easier (fork left half a mile before the Folk Village). The tea house at the Folk Village does moderately priced **food**, though the most popular place for everything from breakfast to evening meals is *An Cistín*, part of the Ulster Cultural Centre complex. Another option is the *Lace House* **restaurant** above the shop, with freshly baked bread and evening meals. The **bars** here are often quiet during the week, though tend to come alive at weekends, especially if the superb local fiddler James Byrne is present, and during the **fiddle festival** at the beginning of August. Glencolmcille's **community festival** takes place during the middle of August.

Ardara and around

The area around the bustling town of **Ardara** contains some of the most contrasting landscapes in Donegal. Rugged mountains lie to the southwest, traversed by the steeply sinuous **Glengesh Pass** and fringed by the unspoiled expanse of **Maghera** strand. Inland to the northeast sits the stately village of **Glenties**, while to the north the coastline forms peninsulas punctuated by the **Gweebarra** river, which, in turn, leads inland to the tranquil villages of Doocharry and Fintown, virtually surrounded by mountain scenery of an almost lunar quality.

The Glengesh Pass and Maghera

Heading northeast from Glencolmcille, the minor road to Ardara runs through the heart of the peninsula, travelling through the dramatic **Glengesh Pass** (Gleann Gheise, "glen of the prohibition") before spiralling down into wild but fertile valley land. Just before reaching Ardara, a road to the left runs along the northern edge of the peninsula for five and a half miles to **MAGHERA**, with narrow **Loughros Beg Bay** on one side and steep mountains rising from the road on the other. A mile before Maghera you'll pass the transfixing **Assarancagh Waterfall**, from where you can embark on a hardy six-mile waymarked walk uphill to the Glengesh Pass. Maghera itself is an enchantingly remote place, dwarfed by the backdrop of hills and glens and fronted by an expansive and deserted strand (parking €3 in summer) that extends westwards to a rocky promontory riddled with **caves**. One of the largest of these is said to have concealed a hundred people fleeing Cromwell's troops; their light was spotted from across the strand and all were massacred except a lucky individual who hid on a high shelf. Most of the caves are accessible only at low tide and a torch is essential. Beware the **tides**, however, for even experienced divers have been swept away by the powerful currents. Behind the village, a tiny road, unsuitable for large vehicles, runs up to the **Granny Pass**, an alternative route to and from Glencolmcille.

Ardara

Traditionally a weaving and knitwear centre, the bustling little town of **ARDARA** (Ard an Rátha, "height of the fort"), ten miles or so north of

Killybegs on the N56, has heritage town status. The European Union grant that accompanied this award was used to transform the old Law Courts, just past The Diamond in the town centre and next to the bridge, into a **heritage centre** (Easter–Oct daily 10am–6pm; ⓣ074/954 1262; voluntary donation). Inside, there's a coffee shop and a fascinating exhibition on the history of hand-weaving, Aran knitwear and lots of intriguing photographs and equipment, but the real treat is watching the weaver plying away at his loom and supplying his own anecdotes about the industry. There's **tourist information** in the reception area and the friendly staff can answer most questions about the town. Ardara is an excellent place to buy **Aran sweaters**, sometimes at half the price you'll find further south. Molloy's Tweed Factory, a mile or so beyond the southern end of town, is the biggest outlet, but Kennedy's, at the top of the hill, heading north from the heritage centre, is handier (its owner is also a mine of local tourist information), and all the stores are well stocked with hand-loomed knitwear and tweeds.

The Catholic **church** west of The Diamond has a striking stained glass window, *Christ among the Doctors*, by the Modernist-inspired **Evie Hone**, one of the most influential Irish artists of the last century: the authors of the Gospels are depicted symbolically with the infant Christ at the centre and David and Moses above and below.

Accommodation options include the grand old *Nesbitt Arms Hotel* (ⓣ074/954 1103, ⓔnesbitta@indigo.ie; ❺), while a mile east of town off the Donegal road is the stylish, seventeenth-century *Woodhill House* (ⓣ074/954 1112, ⓦwww.woodhillhouse.com; ❻), set in its own extensive grounds. Central **B&B** is available at *Brae House,* Front Street (ⓣ074/954 1296, ⓔbrae-house@tinet.ie; ❷), and *Hollybrook* (ⓣ074/954 1596, ⓔmcnelispo@eircom.net; ❶), half a mile towards Killybegs. For sea views, try *Gort na Greine* (mid-March to Dec; ⓣ074/954 1797, ⓔedohe@eircom.net; ❷) or *Bay View Country House* (ⓣ074/954 1145, ⓔchbennett@eircom.net; ❷), both half a mile up the Portnoo road. There's a small **hostel** on The Diamond, the *Drumbaron Hostel* (IHO; ⓣ074/954 1200). **Bike rental** is available from Don Byrne, just west of the Catholic church (ⓣ074/954 1658).

The best **place to eat** is *Woodhill House*, whose restaurant offers an innovative menu that changes daily and is well worth the asking price of €35 or so per head. It's worth a visit even if you're not hungry as there's a bar, often with music. *Nancy's*, just across the bridge, has excellent bar meals and snacks, while *L'Atlantique* on Main Street (ⓣ074/954 1707; daily 6.30–9.30pm) offers splendid French cuisine. Light meals are available at the heritage centre restaurant and *Charlie's West End Café* on Main Street.

Ardara's L-shaped main street is crammed with **pubs**. Arguably the best is *Nancy's*, a 200-year-old warren of small, cosy rooms run by the same family throughout its history. Equally friendly is the atmospheric *Corner House* bar on The Diamond. For a livelier time, you shouldn't miss *Peter Oliver's*, Main Street, with **traditional music** in the front bar (June–Sept nightly) and **dancing** at the back every Saturday (from 10.30pm or later).

Glenties

Set at the foot of two glens six miles east of Ardara on the N56, **GLENTIES** (Na Gleannta, "the glens") is a tidy village of Plantation grandeur that is reflected in its elegant Neoclassical courthouse, old lodge and *Highlands Hotel*. It also sports one of the largest **clubs** in the northwest, the *Limelight*, at the north end of town (Sat nights), and a host of bars on the main street. Another attraction is a beautiful modern **church** at the Ardara end of town, designed by the Derry architect Liam McCormack; the vast sloping roof reaches down to six feet from the ground, and the rainwater drips off the thousand or so tiles into picturesque pools of water.

Opposite the church, the **St Conall's Museum and Heritage Centre** (June–Sept Mon–Fri 10am–1pm & 2–5pm; €2.50) is one of the best small-town museums in the whole country. The museum displays much material of local interest, focusing on wildlife, Donegal railways, antiquities, household artefacts and the effects of the Great Famine, including a famine pot from the local workhouse. There's a special display on local music, featuring the travelling Doherty family (see box on p.585) and an old 1885 Edison phonograph. Upstairs there are displays on the playwright **Brian Friel**, whose mother hailed from the town – his *Dancing at Lughnasa* bears a dedication to "The Glenties Ladies" – and on the town's most famous son **Patrick MacGill** (1890–1963), who was sold by his parents at a hiring fair for servants. He escaped and fled to Scotland, working as a farm-labourer and a navvy, while at the same time writing poems and attempting to hawk them around. He was lucky to attract patronage and ended up working on the *Daily Express*, was wounded in France fighting for the British in World War II, then returned to Ireland before marrying the American author Margaret Gibbons and emigrating to America. His best-known work is the semi-autobiographical *Children of the Dead End*, which brilliantly recounts the wayward lives of migrant navvies, while *The Rat Pit* parallels this in its tale of young Irish women forced into prostitution. A huge **summer school** is held in his honour annually in mid-August, drawing hundreds of people to its exhibitions, seminars and literary debates (for details, call ⓣ074/955 1103).

Accommodation in town includes the comfortable, family-run *Highlands Hotel* on Main Street (ⓣ074/955 1111, ⓦwww.thehighlandshotel.com; ❸), very much the centre of town life, with a small art gallery displaying the works of its landlord, John Boyle, and, among several **B&B** choices, nearby *Marguerite's*, at the north end of the same street (ⓣ074/955 1113; ❷). Just outside the village on Mill Road, heading towards Ardara, are two very pleasant alternatives: the spacious *Lisdanar House* (April–Nov; ⓣ074/955 1800, ⓦhomepage.eircom.net/~lisdanar; ❷), and, a little further on, *Ardlann* (March–Nov; ⓣ074/955 1271, ⓔardlann@eircom.net; ❷). Next to the museum is the well-equipped *Campbell's Holiday* **hostel** (IHH; March–Oct; ⓣ074/955 1491, ⓦwww.campbellireland.com). **Eating** choices are limited, but the excellent *Highlands Hotel* offers a wide range of food – the gargantuan lunches are exceptional value. Alternatively, try *Maud's Café* on Main Street for grills and fries.

All of the **pubs** are on Main Street and most get crowded at the weekend, with several offering pre-*Limelight* music for clubbers. A quieter alternative is the down-to-earth *Ó Faolain's*, an old-fashioned bar frequented by real characters. For **traditional music**, the *Highlands Hotel* has a Sunday night session and also hosts the **fiddlers' weekend** at the beginning of October; otherwise head for the *Glen Inn*, a bar-cum-grocery three miles out on the Ballybofey road, beautifully situated by the river at the foot of the Blue Stack Mountains; there are sessions most Friday and Saturday nights, often featuring one of the Campbell brothers, well-known fiddlers in these parts and beyond. **Fishing** equipment and advice are available at McDevitt's Tackle Shop, Main Street.

The Dawros Head Peninsula

To the immediate north of Ardara, the **Dawros Head Peninsula** is much tamer than Glencolmcille, with many tiny lakes dotting a quilt of low hills. The terrain of purple heather, fields, streams and short glens makes a varied package for the enthusiastic walker. The first turning to Rosbeg off the R261 Narin road takes you past the **Sheskinmore Nature Reserve**, home to Barnacle and Greenland White-footed geese. The flat sandy coastal plain and patches of short grass are popular too with choughs in late summer and hunted by hen harriers and merlins in winter.

ROSBEG is an isolated village, straggling beside a series of rock-strewn coves, but you can **camp** among the dunes at **Tramore Beach** (Ⓣ074/955 1491). It's even lonelier out at **Dawros Head** itself, but at least there's the welcoming bar at the *Dawros Bay House* to provide succour. In contrast, the caravan sites of Portnoo and Narin, on the peninsula's northern coast, are densely populated with Northern Irish tourists.

If you've headed directly from Ardara towards Narin and Portnoo, in **KILCLOONEY,** just before the pastel-shaded church on the right, is the **Kilclooney dolmen**, probably the best-preserved portal stones in the country. The capstone is over thirteen feet long and the structure is reckoned to date from around 3500 BC. In the centre of the village is the brand-new **Dolmen Eco-Tourism Centre** (call ahead for opening times; Ⓣ074/954 5010, Ⓦwww.dolmencentre.ie), entirely powered by renewable energy. Apart from serving as a local community centre and gym, there's a café and crafts shop here and also a small exhibition on the development of the local landscape.

Continuing onwards towards Narin, the most worthwhile sight on the peninsula is **Doon Fort**, which occupies an entire oval-shaped islet in the middle of **Lough Doon**. To get there turn left at the "Rosbeg/Tramore Beach" signpost a mile before Narin, then head right up the lane just after a school. A few hundred yards later you'll see a sign for **boat rental** leading down to a farmhouse, where you can rent a rowing boat inexpensively to take you across to the island. The idyllic setting, rarely disturbed by visitors, makes the hassle worth it: although its walls are crumbling, the fort has been untouched for over two thousand years. The walls stand 15ft high and 12ft thick; their inner passages were used in the 1950s for storing poteen. Two other lakes nearby, **Lough Birrog** and **Lough Kiltoorish**, also have ruined castles, both built by later Irish chieftains, the O'Boyles. Their stones, however, have mostly been carted away for house building.

NARIN and **PORTNOO** offer the majority of facilities on the peninsula. The spearheaded two-and-a-half-mile-long **Narin Strand** is a wonderful beach, safe for bathing. At low tide you can walk out to **Iniskeel Island**, where St Conal founded a monastery in the sixth century. This has long since disappeared, but there are the ruins of two twelfth-century churches with some cross-inscribed slabs. The villages host a **seafood festival** towards the end of June where you can participate in oyster-opening contests, and all the bars offer seafood specials. In Narin, both *Roaninish* (June–Sept; Ⓣ & Ⓕ074/954 5207; ❷) and *Thalassa Country House* (March–Nov; Ⓣ074/954 5151; ❷) offer good **B&B**. The *Lake House* **hotel** in Clooney, a mile to the east of Narin (Ⓣ074/954 5123, Ⓦwww.lakehousehotel.net; ❹), dates from 1847 and provides a great deal more comfort and a fine restaurant.

Around Gweebarra Bay

The routes north from Ardara and Glenties converge at the hamlet of **Maas**. The road then twists along the edge of **Gweebarra Bay** before one last turn suddenly brings you to a broad iron **bridge** spanning the estuary. Until the first bridge was built in 1890, rarely a year passed by without someone being drowned attempting to ford the river, sometimes home-workers bringing wool back from Glenties.

Across the bridge and west of **Lettermacaward**, a signposted route tours the **Dooey Point** headland, a scenically interesting little detour if you have time to spare. The northern shore, on **Trawenagh Bay**, is the more gratifying, with a fine stretch of beach backed by sand dunes. Classic thatched cottages are the main characteristics. On the southern side is **Cor Strand**, fertile ground for mussels and clams, with a handy nearby bar, *Melly's*.

Doocharry and Fintown

A minor road east from Lettermacaward follows the river Gweebarra five miles inland to **DOOCHARRY**, a tiny place with just a pub and a grocery, which acts as the gateway to some of the most dramatic scenery in the county. From Doocharry, you can head further upstream northeast along a narrow and tortuous lane past **Slieve Snaght**, through the **Glendowan Mountains** and skirting the southern edge of the **Glenveagh National Park** to **Lough Gartan** (see p.594). The desolate, though beautiful countryside bears little sign of human impact and you'll be lucky to see any life beyond the odd sheep or fluttering bird.

Another road heads five miles southeast from Doocharry through rugged, rock-strewn moorland, streaked by turf banks, to **FINTOWN**. On the way, look out for the splendidly set *Glenleighan* **hostel** (IHO; March–Oct; ⓣ074/954 6141). Fintown itself is a simple roadside village set at the foot of towering mountains in the Finn River valley where the river broadens to form an elongated strip of lake. There's little else in the village apart from a few bars and a **traditional music** house, *Teach a' Cheoil* (sessions Thurs & Fri).

The Crohy Head Peninsula

The southern approach to **Crohy Head** curls round the headland's central mountains, looking down to a rocky shelf of coastline from which plumes of spray rise like geysers. As you come round the headland to the final leg, you'll first see the three-storey An Óige *An Chruach* **hostel** (June–Sept; ⓣ074/952 1950, ⓔmailbox@anoige.ie), then the domed outline of **Arranmore Island** comes into view, lying close to the Rosses coast. The hillside below the road can be dangerous at points because of landslips but these, and the great sea stack known as *An Bríste* ("the breeches"), make the headland an even more dramatic experience for the walker.

John Doherty

The greatest Donegal traditional fiddler, **John Doherty** (c.1895–1980), is buried in Fintown **cemetery**. Born in Ardara into a family of travellers and musicians descended in part from the MacSweeney clan, Doherty spent most of his life on the roads between Ballybofey and Glencolmcille, earning his keep by working as a tinsmith and playing the fiddle as a welcome guest at house dances. By his twenties his dynamic, yet intricate style of playing guaranteed his living, but for the first fifty or so years of his life his reputation remained firmly within the environs of his travelling beat. In the 1950s he began to be sought out by music collectors and folklorists (he was a grand man for recounting the tale of a tune's genesis) and subsequently he made commercial recordings (several excellent CDs of his work are commercially available). Many of the tunes played in Donegal today owe their origins to the repertoire of John Doherty and his brothers Mickey and Simon, and despite more than twenty years passing since his death he remains a major influence upon the region's driving style of fiddle playing.

The one-pub fishing village of **MAGHERY** lies at the foot of the north side of the headland. Its most unusual feature is the tall wall that runs by the abandoned mansion house at the far side of the short strand: called the **Famine Wall**, this windbreak was built by the villagers for the landlord, who devised the task so that he could pay them a wage as famine relief.

The Rosses

The **Rosses**, a vast expanse of rock-strewn land and stony soil, is a strong Gaeltacht area. Dotted with over one hundred and twenty tiny lakes, the crumpled terrain stretches from **Dungloe** in the south to **Crolly** in the north, but the forbidding nature of much of the landscape meant most settlements could only survive near the sea, so following the shoreline route around the Rosses is far more rewarding than the more direct road north.

Dungloe

An Clochán Liath is the name you'll see on signposts as you approach **DUNGLOE**, referring to the grey-coloured stepping-stones that were once used to cross the river here. The modern anglicized version comes from *Dún gCloiche*, the name of a stone fort situated on a rock a few miles off shore. When the fair that was held at the fort moved in the eighteenth century to the village of An Clochán Liath which had grown up around the stepping-stones, the fort's name stuck, though Irish-speakers still refer to the town by its original name.

For most of the year, there's little to detain you in Dungloe apart from entertainment in the **pubs**. At the beginning of August, however, the **Mary From Dungloe festival** (Ⓦwww.maryfromdungloe.info), centred around a rather wholesome beauty pageant, provides a good pretext for general festivities, plenty of music and street events and almost certainly at least one concert featuring local singing legend Daniel O'Donnell. There's no antiquity behind the festival's origins or name – it dates from 1968 and the title comes from a hit single by the Emmet Spiceland band (including the now notable traditional musician Dónal Lunny whose mother hails from the Rosses village of Rannafast, see p.588).

Dungloe is also synonymous with the rejuvenating work of **Paddy 'the Cope' Gallagher** (1871–1966), who envisaged the salvation of these then poor communities through cooperative ventures, in particular by reducing their dependency on moneylenders. Oddly enough, the enterprise's practical origins lay in Paddy's discovery that the price of manure was reduced when purchased by societies. As a result, he founded the Templecrone Co-operative Agricultural Society (the "Cope") in 1906, and its central branch still stands proudly on Dungloe's main street with branches throughout the Rosses.

The very helpful **tourist office** (June–Aug Mon–Sat 10am–1pm & 2–6pm; Ⓣ074/952 1297) is just off Main Street, to the left as you go downhill towards the bridge. Upmarket **accommodation** is provided by *Ostan Na Rosan*, Mill Road (Ⓣ074/952 2444, Ⓦwww.ostannarosann.com; ❻), which has its own leisure centre and pool. On the same road are the **B&Bs** *Roninnis House* (April–Sept; Ⓣ074/952 1094; ❷) and *Sea View* (March–Nov; Ⓣ074/952 1353; ❷), both well-equipped places offering seaviews, while in the centre, there's *Atlantic House,* Main Street (Ⓣ074/952 1061, Ⓔjcannon@iol.ie; ❷), which also has a bar and provides meals. *Greene's Holiday* **hostel** (IHH & IHO; Ⓣ074/952 1021) on Carnmore Road is a modern building with **camping** in its grounds.

There's a handy **laundry** nearby on the Gweedore road (Tues–Fri 9am–1pm & 2–6pm).

Eating options on Main Street include the *Coffee Dock* for excellent-value lunches, the *Lite Lunch* café in the Dungloe Centre for fine coffee and sandwiches and *Doherty's Restaurant*, a good low-priced chipper and grill. The *Riverside Bistro* (☎074/952 1062), near the bridge, serves more upmarket, though reasonably priced modern Irish cuisine. The *Tírconnaill* **bar** near the top of the hill is a genuine old-timers' pub with not a note of music interfering (even during the festival) and a fabulous view of the ocean. Further down Main Street, *Beedy's Bar* has traditional sessions on Tuesdays, and there's assorted entertainment in the *Bayview Lounge* at weekends. **Fishing** tackle and permits for local fisheries are available from Bonner's, Main Street, and further advice and information on **boat hire** can be obtained from the Rosses Angling Association (☎074/952 1163).

Burtonport and Arranmore Island

Lying half a mile off the coastal route north from Dungloe, **BURTONPORT** (signposted **Ailt an Chorráin**, "curved gully") is the embarkation point for **Arranmore Island** and, if you can find someone to take you out, for other smaller islands. In the late eighteenth century, the founder of Burtonport, William Burton, attempted to establish **Rutland Island** as a major trading centre and, consequently, this area became the first English-speaking district in the whole of Donegal. During the 1798 Rebellion James **Napper Tandy** landed on the island with French troops, but became somewhat inebriated on hearing of Wolfe Tone's capture and had to be carried back on board. More recent English connections have included the Screamers, a post-hippie commune with a belief in primal scream therapy and sexual liberation whose leaders departed some years ago for Colombia, and, in the 1990s, the Silver Sisters, a trio of apparently demure Victorian-dressed ladies who fled Burtonport once it became clear that the disciplined life they espoused had more to do with sado-masochism than moral rectitude.

Apart from busy activity at the harbour, Burtonport has little to say for itself, but should you want to stay, there's **B&B** at *Campbell's Pier House* (☎ & ⓕ074/954 2017; ❷), near the harbour, or *Teac Hughie Bán* (☎074/954 2104; ❶), a quarter of a mile back towards the main road. **Hostel** accommodation is available at *Cois na Mara* (IHO; ☎074/954 2079, ⓔtimothydoherty@hotmail.com), a hard-to-miss yellow-fronted house half a mile down the coast road towards Dungloe. For **eating**, *The Lobster Pot* specializes in delicious seafood and the *Harbour* provides bar meals. There's little nightlife here, though the *Skipper's Tavern* offers occasional traditional music, but all changes during the boisterous local **festival** held over the last week in July. There are plenty of **fish** in the nearby waters and you can rent a boat from West Donegal Sea-Angling Charters (☎074/954 8403) or Dónal O'Sullivan (☎074/954 2077).

Arranmore Island

There's a year-round **car ferry** (Mon–Sat 5–8 sailings, Sun 3–7 sailings; ☎074/952 0532; €9 return, €26 for car plus driver) for the twenty-minute trip from Burtonport to **Arranmore Island**, which passes through the straits between the nearest cluster of islands (Rutland, Edernish, Inishcoo and Eighter), and then across an open expanse of water to the main village on Arranmore, **LEABGARROW**. There's little **accommodation** on the island apart from the *Glen Hotel* (☎074/952 0505; ❷) and *Bonner's* (☎074/952 0532; ❷) by the pier. However, the old An Óige **hostel** has been refurbished as the new *Arranmore Hostel* (IHH; ⓣ074/952 0015), though it's often full with young people visiting the island during the summer months, so ring ahead. The island's permanent population of around eight hundred people is almost entirely concentrated along the eastern and southern coastlines. The high centre-ground of bogland and lakes reaches a greater altitude than anywhere else in the Rosses and it's well worth hiking a few hundred yards upland for great views back across the water to Burtonport.

A circuit of the whole island takes around six hours and the terrain isn't especially taxing. Much of it consists of blustery cliff-top views of the Atlantic, but there are a few intriguing spots to investigate or ponder on. The island's greatest tragedy occurred off the very southeastern tip during the stormy night of November 9, 1935, when a sailing ship carrying returning islanders ran aground on the rocks. Nineteen people died, including seven from the same family – the eighth member on board, Patrick Gallagher, was the only survivor. Many ships have foundered in the choppy seas hereabouts, but, in 1983, the lone American yachtsman, Wayne Dickenson, landed on the island's west coast after 142 days at sea in the smallest boat ever to cross the Atlantic. In the cliffs below St Crone's Church on the southern shore is **Uaimh an Áir** (the "cave of slaughter"), where seventy hiding islanders were massacred in the seventeenth century by a certain Captain Conyngham, in an action which lay somewhat outside his remit from Charles I to rid the Rosses of "rogues and rapparees". Two islanders took revenge by killing the captain in Dunfanaghy. Uninhabited **Green Island**, at the southwestern tip, is now a **bird sanctuary** and rare species have been spotted hereabouts, including the Snowy Owl in 1993. The most dramatic of the several **beaches** is at the northwestern end of the island, on the way to the lighthouse and approached by a set of steps down the side of a perpetually crumbling cliff.

Facilities on Arranmore are limited, but the half-dozen **pubs** are blessed with a 24-hour fishing port licence, which is helpful as there is little nightlife apart from the *Glen Hotel*'s nightclub, though *Pally's* bar has regular entertainments. A few of the pubs have small shops attached, and you can eat at the *Bonner's Ferryboat* **restaurant** or, more expensively, the *Glen Hotel,* while *Phil Ban's* bar serves snacks all day. **Football** (soccer) is the sport here and Arranmore is the only Irish island to have a team playing in a mainland competitive league.

Crolly and around

The road up through the Rosses to Gweedore cuts through a wild and crazed terrain of granite boulders and stunted vegetation. **Cruit Island**, three miles north of Burtonport and accessible by bridge, has beautiful beaches and a cluster of thatched **cottages** available for rental (ⓣ071/917 7197, ⓦwww.donegalthatchedcottages.com; €255–830 per week). A little further along the coast you'll come to **Kincasslagh** (Cionn Calach, "head of the sea-inlet"), birthplace of the renowned Irish singing star **Daniel O'Donnell**. Off the coast road, a further three miles on is the small **Carrickfinn Peninsula**, which boasts a fine strand and **Donegal Airport** (2 daily flights to Dublin by Celtic Airways; ⓣ074/954 8284, ⓦwww.donegalairport.ie). About a mile further along the coast road is **ANNAGRY**, where *Teac Jack's* **pub** serves fine food, and, if you wish to spend rather more, *Dannie Minnie's* **restaurant** (ⓣ074/954 8201) offers superb seafood specialities. There's **B&B** in Annagry at *Bayview House* (April–Oct; ⓣ074/954 8504, ⓔjns@eircom.net; ❷), while the local *feile*, one of the biggest in the Rosses, takes place here at the beginning of June.

A short detour north of Annagry leads to **RANNAFAST** (Rann na Feirste, "peninsula of the sand-bank ford"), a village with an astonishing Irish literary heritage. The oral tradition has always been strong in the Rosses, but its writers only came to prominence once the school system was improved early in the twentieth century. Foremost among them were three brothers from Rannafast's **Clann Mhic Grianna** (*clan* being Irish for "family"): Séamus Ó'Grianna, the author of 27 books under the pseudonym Máire, and a popular choice for School Leaving Certificate examinations; Seosamh Mac Grianna, whose most famous works are *An Druma Mór* and his autobiography, *Mo Bhealach Féin*; and Séan Bán Mac Grianna, the youngest of the lot and the poet of the family. The village also hosts a large **Irish-language college**. All its pubs were closed to prevent students from undermining their studies.

In the townland of **MEENALECK**, just before Crolly, look out for a sign pointing to **Leo's Tavern**. The proprietors, Leo and Baba Brennan, were both well known on the dance-band circuit in the 1950s and 1960s, but other family members have achieved greater fame. Three of their children (Máire, Pól and Ciarán) were members of the group **Clannad** and another is the celebrated singer/musician Eithne, better known as **Enya** – the pub's walls are decorated with a variety of awards and mementos. The *Tavern*, which has just been rebuilt from scratch and now serves food, is hugely popular with tourists, and the nightly singalong sessions, often featuring Leo himself on piano accordion, are usually adapted to suit their tastes. You're more likely to meet the locals at *Tessie's* across the road, one of the friendliest bars in the county, with an excellent **traditional music** session on Sundays.

If you take the main N56 road from Dungloe to Crolly, look out for the small signs to your left marked "**Kerrytown Shrine**". In January 1939, some residents of this townland four miles south of Annagry claimed to have witnessed an apparition of the Virgin Mary on a rock, and once the newspapers had reported the story, large crowds began to gather nightly for prayer meetings. Pilgrimages arrived from all over the country and continue to this day, especially on August 15, the Feast of Assumption. A couple of miles further north on the N56 is **LOUGHANURE** (Lough an Iúir, "lake of the yew tree"), pleasantly set beside the lough from which it takes its name. The local Anglers' Club (☎074/954 8689) has **boats** for rent and **fishing** permits, with further information available in the village shop. The thatched *Casad na Tsúgáin* is a popular **bar-restaurant** with sessions in summer.

CROLLY (Croithli, "shaking bog") marks the end of the Rosses and the beginning of neighbouring Gweedore. The large *Teach Phaidí Óg* **pub** has bar food, camping and laundry facilities and occasional live music. From here a narrow road on the right, just after the bridge, leads up into the **Derryveagh Mountains** (see p.593). This passes lovely **Lough Keel** and its deserted village before reaching its highest point by an abandoned school and swinging sharply right to return to Dungloe. If you head straight on instead, you'll arrive at the most wonderfully situated and very congenial **hostel**, *Screag an Iolair* (IHO; March–Oct; ☎074/954 8593), with cosy rooms, an open fire, traditional music and lots of advice on walking. Nestling in beautiful semi-wild gardens on the side of **Cnoc na Farragh Mountain**, the hostel (whose name means "eagle's nest") provides magnificent views of mountains, lakes, distant Arranmore Island and spectacular sunsets.

Gweedore and Tory Island

Like its southern neighbour, the Rosses, the interior of the **Gweedore** district is largely desolate and forbidding country, and settlements again cling to the shoreline. To the southwest lie the villages of **Bunbeg**, **Middletown** and **Derrybeg**, their cottages sprinkled across a blanket of gorse and mountain grasses. It's a dispiriting kind of landscape and the ruggedness intensifies as it continues up the coast and round the Bloody Foreland to Gortahork and Falcarragh in the Cloghaneely district. Yet surprisingly, there has been significant house-building across the area and it's said to be the most densely populated rural area in Europe.

BUNBEG (An Bun Beag, "the little river-foot") has a gorgeous little harbour, packed with smallish trawlers, a mile from the village along an enchanting rollicking road. There's a regular year-round **ferry** service to Tory Island (see box opposite), and it's possible to negotiate a boat trip from the pier to other, mainly uninhabited, offshore islands such as Gola, Inishmeane and Inishsirrer. The **beach** further up the coast is approached by taking any track off to the left from the road running north from the harbour crossroads towards **DERRYBEG**.

For **accommodation**, there are two luxurious hotels in Derrybeg: *Ostan Gweedore* (Ⓣ074/953 1177, Ⓦwww.ostangweedore.com; ❻) and *Ostan Radharc na Mara* (Ⓣ074/953 1159, Ⓔostanradharcnamara@eircom.net; ❺). At Bunbeg harbour, there's excellent **B&B** at *Bunbeg House* (Ⓣ074/953 1305; ❸), with pleasant waterside views from its restaurant. You can also **eat** extremely well in Bunbeg at the two hotels, while nearby *Sergeant Pepper's* offers decent fast food. The best **bar** is *Teach Húdaí Beag*, by the harbour crossroads, which hosts a famous Monday night traditional session, sometimes involving as many as thirty musicians. *Seán Óg's* pub has a Wednesday night session and other music throughout the week. Both the *Ostan Gweedore* and *Ostan Radharc na Mara* hotels hold regular weekend **discos**. Summer **Irish-language courses** are run by An Chrannóg in Derrybeg (Ⓣ074/953 2188, Ⓦwww.crannog.ie).

At **GLASSAGH**, about four miles north of Derrybeg, the road climbs abruptly to Knockfola, loosely translated as the **Bloody Foreland**, a grim, stony, almost barren zone, crisscrossed by stone walls, and so called because of the red hue acquired by its heather from the light of the setting sun. If you fancy lingering a while, the best **place to stay** is *Teac Jack* (Ⓣ074/953 1173, Ⓦwww.teacjack.com; ❷), which has a fine restaurant and a bar often hosting traditional music. From Knockfola, the road turns eastwards hugging the side of the mountain, with the bogland and its hard-worked turf banks stretching below towards the Atlantic. You should be able to spot the distinctive shape of **Tory Island** far out to sea and, at **MAGHEROARTY**, five miles east of Derrybeg, a road runs down to the pier, where you can pick up a ferry to the island (see opposite). Rather nearer offshore lies **INISHBOFIN**, largely deserted but now home to a new independent **hostel**, *Teach Jonny* (IHO; June–Sept; Ⓣ087/669 5984, Ⓦwww.teachjonny.com); ring ahead to arrange collection by boat. There's little to do on the island except relax and wander or perhaps muse on the strange fate of **Arthur Kingsley Porter**. A Harvard professor and owner of Glenveagh Castle (see p.594), Kingsley Porter was living in a small house on the island when he failed to return from a walk in July 1933. Though he probably drowned, rumours concerning his whereabouts flourished, some even suggesting that he had been sighted at continental art galleries. Whatever the case, his inquest was the first in Ireland to take place without a body, and a verdict of misadventure was recorded.

Tory Island

With its ruggedly indented shores pounded by the ocean, **TORY ISLAND** (Toraigh, "place of rocky heights"), though only eight miles north of the mainland coast, is notoriously inaccessible. Yet despite the island's barren landscape and the ferocity of the elements, the Tory islanders are thriving, a situation no one could have predicted after the events of 1974 threatened to curtail thousands of years of settlement. During that winter the harshest of **storms** battered Tory for over eight weeks, severing all communications and preventing helicopters from landing. When it finally abated, two dozen families applied for mainland housing, ten of them eventually moving to Falcarragh. It later transpired that Donegal County Council had drawn up a full-scale evacuation plan. As in Glencolmcille (see p.579), the arrival of a new priest, **Father Diarmuid Ó Péicín**, stimulated a transformation. Arriving on a day-trip in 1980, he ended up staying for four years as the island's pastor. Conditions were poor and the islanders dispirited. Essential amenities such as a water supply, proper sanitation and reliable electricity were lacking. There was no ferry service and, even if there had been, the harbour was unfit to receive it. Rallying the islanders, the pastor began to lobby every possible target, securing support from such disparate characters as the US senator Tip O'Neill (who had Donegal ancestors) and Ian Paisley. The campaign attracted media attention and, despite Ó Péicín's replacement, conditions gradually began to improve thanks to the eventual support of the embarrassed state and the financial assistance of an American philanthropist. Nowadays, around 120 people live permanently on the island and 25 children attend the local junior school, a happy sign of the island's revival (older children spend term times in Falcarragh).

Tory's inaccessibility has long reinforced its remoteness, ensuring the retention of a powerful culture that has almost vanished from the mainland, referred to by islanders as "the country". Only two and a half miles long and less than a mile wide, its vulnerability to the elements means little can grow here, and what does has to be protected from the salty winds behind stone walls. The Irish-speaking islanders have a deep respect for the island and its landscape, both as inspiration for their musicians, story-tellers and artists and as powerful sources of legend. According to local mythology, Tory was the stronghold of the **Fomorians**, who raided the mainland from their island base and whose most notable figure was the cyclops **Balor of the Evil Eye**, the Celtic god of darkness. Intriguingly, the local legend places his eye at the back of his head. There's also said to be a crater in the very heart of the island that none of the locals will approach after dark, for fear of incurring the god's wrath.

Ferries to Tory Island

Ferries to Tory Island are operated by Turasmara Teo (☎074/953 1320), whose offices are at the harbour crossroads in **Bunbeg**. There's a daily sailing between April and October, which leaves Bunbeg at 9am and heads back from Tory soon after dropping off (Nov–March sailings Mon–Fri only). There are additional sailings from **Magheroarty** (June & Sept daily 11.30am & 5pm; July & Aug daily 11.30am, 1.30pm & 5pm). The price of a return trip on both services is €15. Departure times may be affected by the tides and the weather, so always call ahead to check. Whatever the weather, be prepared for sudden changes and for a forced overnight stay on the island.

In the sixth century, **St Columba** landed on Tory with the help of a member of the Duggan family. In return, the saint made him king of the island; the line has been unbroken ever since and you're more than likely to meet the present king, **Patsy Dan Rodgers**, who regularly greets arriving ferries at the newly expanded harbour. Some monastic relics from St Columba's time remain on Tory, the most unusual of which – now the island's emblem – is the **Tau Cross**. Its T-cross shape is of Egyptian origin, and is one of only two such monuments in the whole of Ireland. It has now been relocated and set in concrete on Camusmore Pier in West Town, one of the island's two villages. There are other mutilated stone crosses and some carved stones lying around, several by the remains of the **round tower** in West Town, which is thought to date from the tenth century and is uniquely constructed from round beach stones. Another superstition focuses on the **wishing stone** in the centre of the island, three circuits of which will supposedly lead to your wish being granted. It was utilized to defeat invaders by wrecking their ships: the British gunboat *Wasp*, sent to collect taxes, was caught in a sudden storm that killed all but six of its crew.

Tory islanders are famed for their **painting**, a development that originated in a chance encounter between the English painter Derek Hill and one of the island's fishermen, **James Dixon**, in 1968, both now deceased. Dixon had never lifted a brush before the day he told Hill that he could do a better job of painting the Tory scenery, but he went on to become the most renowned of the island's school of **primitive painters** – Glebe House has a remarkable painting by him (see p.595). You can view the islanders' work and, more than likely, meet the artists, at the **James Dixon Gallery**, the originator's former home, a little way to the east of the harbour.

Of Tory's two villages, **EAST TOWN** and **WEST TOWN**, you'll find most of the amenities in the latter. There are a couple of shops, and the *Caife an Chreagáin* serves hearty snacks and meals. Alternatively, there's the restaurant at the *Ostan Thoraigh*, which provides comfortable **accommodation** (ⓣ074/913 5920, ⓦwww.toryhotel.com; ④), has one of the only two bars on the island and organizes a range of summer events, including traditional music, *sean-nós* singing, painting and birdwatching weekends. For **B&B**, try *Graceanne Duffy* (ⓣ074/913 5136; ②) in East Town. The **Social Club** in West Town is one of the hubs of island life, with a bar and regular traditional music and dancing. The island has also recently become popular for **diving**, and the Tory Diving Centre (ⓣ074/913 5920) offers a sample dive for €28 or two-day breaks, featuring four dives, for €120–130, including accommodation.

The Derryveagh Mountains and Glenveagh

Inland from Gweedore lies some of the most dramatic scenery in Donegal, an area dominated by mountains such as **Errigal** and **Slieve Snaght** and loughs of startling beauty. This is popular hill-walking country, especially along the Poisoned Glen, part of the much-visited **Glenveagh National Park**. Further on, towards Letterkenny, the countryside becomes gentler and increasingly verdant, especially in the environs of **Lough Gartan**, an area rich in associations with St Columba.

Lough Nacung, Dunlewy Lough and the Derryveagh Mountains

Heading east on the N56 from Gweedore, the imposing and starkly beautiful mass of **Errigal Mountain** becomes increasingly prominent. From a distance the mountain appears to be snow-covered, but as you skirt the northern shore of **Lough Nacung** it becomes apparent that the white colouration has geological, rather than meteorological, causes. You can **stay** very comfortably near the lough at the recently built *An Chuirt* hotel (ⓣ074/953 2900, ⓦwww.anchuirt-hotel.ie; ⑥) or, if you want to press on, the minor R251 road leads to **MONEY BEG** (sometimes referred to as Dunlewy after the name of the nearby lough), where the *An Earagail* An Óige **hostel** (ⓣ074/953 1180, ⓔmailbox@anoige.ie) sits at the foot of the mountain. Here too, in the former *Dunlewy Hotel*, is the independent *Lakeside Hostel* (March–Oct; ⓣ074/953 2133). Quite often the area is shrouded in mist, but on a clear day the beauty of Errigal is unsurpassable, its silvery slopes resembling the Japanese artist Hokkusai's images of Mount Fuji. A hike up to the top is a must, and there's a waymarked trail from the road, a mile and a half past the Poisoned Glen turn-off, up the southeast ridge. The climb to the summit is well worth it for the stupendous **views**: virtually all of Donegal, and most of Ulster, is visible and you could easily spend several hours just sitting and absorbing the contrasts provided by coastline, loughs and mountains.

Back down in Money Beg village, there's a post office, shop and *McGeady's* **bar**. The lane next to the *Lakeside Hostel* runs south for about half a mile to the narrow strip of land which divides Lough Nacung from Dunlewy Lough. On the way there's the **Dunlewy Lakeside Centre** (Easter–Oct Mon–Sat 10.30am–6pm, Sun 11am–7pm; tour of farm and outbuildings €4.50, boat trip €4.50, combined ticket €7), an impressive visitor centre on the lough shore. There's an excellent **restaurant** here and a book-cum-crafts shop, with maps of the area on sale. It's very child-friendly outside with a small farmyard 'zoo', adventure playground and pony rides on offer. For adults the highlight is the re-creation of the home of the notable local weaver, Manus Ferry, and the **boat trip** around Dunlewy lough is a pleasure for all ages. The centre hosts a superb series of traditional music concerts, *Trad Trathnóna*, on Tuesday evenings and other nights during the summer, and is also the focus for one of Ireland's biggest **traditional music** events, the Frankie Kennedy Winter School (commemorating the late Altan flute player) over the New Year.

Glenveagh National Park

According to legend, the **Poisoned Glen**, east of Dunlewy Lough is where the cyclops Balor of the Evil Eye (see p.591) was slain by Lugh, poisoning the ground on which his single orb fell. There are many other explanations for the origins of its name, from the darkly conspiratorial (the glen's waters were polluted to kill English soldiers) to the purely botanical (poisonous Irish spurge used to grow here).

To reach the glen, head a little way further east of Money Beg on the R251 and take the signposted lane leading downhill to the right. Just below the ruined church at the eastern end of Lough Nacung turn off to the left and follow the track over the old bridge. The path dwindles away and you should follow the left bank of the river deep into the gorge until it turns sharply left. Walk through the water here to the opposite bank and climb up towards a granite crest. From here walk beside the small stream through a gully and finally you'll emerge on a ridge. It's not an easy tramp, for a lot of the ground is marshy, but the views are fantastic, with the River Glenveagh flowing into Lough Beagh down below. You're now in the **Glenveagh National Park** and may well see deer hereabouts. If you don't want to retrace your tracks and are prepared for a longer hike, you have a number of options. However, it's vital to follow all the basic rules of hill-walking (see p.52) and essential to keep to the designated roads and paths during the winter deer-culling season (Sept–Feb), or you run the risk of being **shot**. Experienced hill-walkers will probably be tempted by the sight of **Slieve Snaght**, the highest point in the park, off to the southwest. Alternatively, if you head downhill to the southeast, the Glendowan road at the bottom leads eastwards to **Lough Gartan** (see below) and westwards to **Doocharry** (see p.585). If you take this road east towards Gartan for a short distance, an old disused vehicle track to the left will lead you down the barrel of the glen alongside the river to Lough Glenveagh.

A less arduous approach to Glenveagh is to follow the R251 alongside the mountains until it curves to meet Lough Beagh's northern tip. A little further on is the official National Park **visitor centre** (mid-March to early Nov daily 10am–6.30pm; last admission 5pm; €2.50; Heritage Card). The centre has detailed and interactive displays on the area's ecology and geology, and there's also a reasonably priced restaurant. Free minibuses ply between here and **Glenveagh Castle** (same hours; €2.50; Heritage Card), built on a small promontory for George Adair between 1870 and 1873. Adair was the creator of the estate that now forms much of the park, but while you might admire the end-product it's impossible to condone the means by which it was achieved. Though some land was obtained through purchase, Adair despicably evicted 244 tenants during the bitterly cold April of 1861 – the **Derryveagh Evictions** – forcing many into the workhouse and others to emigrate to Australia. The rhododendron-filled gardens surrounding the castle were very much the work of Adair's wife, Cornelia, who also introduced the herds of red deer to the estate. The steep ascent to the viewpoint behind the gardens is more than worthwhile for the wonderful views down to the castle and along the lough deep into the glen. Guided tours of the castle focus on the collection of furniture and artwork collected by the millionaire Irish-American, Henry McIlhenny, the last owner of Glenveagh, who bequeathed the castle and its contents to the nation. An earlier proprietor was Arthur Kingsley Porter who disappeared in mysterious circumstances on Inishbofin island (see p.590).

Lough Gartan and around

The environs of **Lough Gartan** are one of the supreme beauties of Ireland. **St Columba** was born into a royal family here in 521; his father was from the House of Niall of the Nine Hostages and his mother belonged to the House of Leinster. If you walk over from Glenveagh you'll pass his **birthplace** – take the first road right at the first house you see at the end of the mountain track, and you'll come to a colossal **cross** marking the spot; the site is also signposted from the road running along the lough's southern shore. Close by is a slab locally known as the **Flagstone of Loneliness**, on which Columba used to sleep, thereby endowing the stone with the miraculous power to cure the sorrows of those who also lie upon it, though nowadays it's bestrewn with coins. During times of mass emigration, people used to come here the night before departure in the hope of ridding themselves of homesickness. Archaeologically, it's actually part of a Bronze Age gallery tomb and has over fifty cup marks cut into its surface.

Going back to the track leading downhill will bring you to the lakeside road, where a left turn leads to the remains of a church known as the **Little**

Oratory of St Colmcille. It's an enchanting ruin, no larger than a modern living room, with a floor of old stone slabs with grass growing up through the cracks. A holy well is here too and nearby the Natal Stone, where the baby Columba first opened his eyes; to this day pregnant women visit the slab to pray for a safe delivery.

Glebe House and around

Glebe House (Easter weekend & mid-May to Sept Mon–Thurs, Sat & Sun 11am–6.30pm; €2.50; Heritage Card) is a gorgeous Regency building set in beautiful gardens on the northwest shore of Lough Gartan. Richly decorated both inside and out, it owes its fame to the time of its tenure by the English artist Derek Hill (1916–2000), though it's now run as a **gallery** by Dúchas, the Heritage Service. The converted stables house some of Hill's paintings and are used for visiting exhibitions, while the rooms of the house itself display a rich collection of paintings and sketches, including works by Kokoschka, Yeats, Renoir and Picasso. The study is decked out in original William Morris wallpaper, and there are Chinese tapestries in the morning room. The kitchen has various paintings by the Tory Island group of primitive painters (see p.592), most remarkably James Dixon's impression of Tory from the sea. It's well worth buying the guidebook and taking the tour.

Moving on round the northeast of the lake, in the direction of Church Hill, a right turn immediately after crossing the bridge will take you down to the modern **Colmcille Heritage Centre** (Easter week & May–Sept Mon–Sat 10.30am–6.30pm, Sun 1–6.30pm; €2), on the opposite shore from Glebe. The exhibition space is devoted to St Columba's life and the spread of the Celtic Church throughout Europe. If you have no interest in ecclesiastical history, there are other intriguing items, including very beautiful stained glass windows of biblical scenes by Ciaran O'Conner and Ditty Kummer and a step-by-step illustration of vellum illumination and calligraphy.

The road to the heritage centre continues a little further on to the **Gartan Outdoor Adventure Centre** (☎074/913 7032), which runs a range of outdoor activities, including courses in mountain skills and leadership (prices start at €100 for a mountain skills weekend). Continuing east from here towards Letterkenny, you ascend from the northern shore to the village of **Church Hill**, with superb cross-country views as far north as the peninsulas.

The Rock of Doon and Kilmacrennan

Lying a few miles northeast of Lough Gartan, **The Rock of Doon** and **Doon Well** are signposted off the R255 shortly after the village of **Termon** (An Tearmann, "the sanctuary") on the way to Kilmacrennan. Following the directions will lead you to a rural cul-de-sac right next to the well. A path from here ascends to a large bushy outcrop that is the Rock of Doon. From 1200 to 1603 this was the spot where the O'Donnell kings were crowned, standing above a huge gathering of their followers. The inauguration stone on the summit is said to bear the imprint of the first Tír Chonaill king, a mark into which every successor had to place his foot as his final confirmation. Doon, an ancient pagan healing **well**, is still a place of pilgrimage, marked out by a bush weighed down with personal effects left behind by the sick, hoping for a cure. You're meant to take off your shoes as you approach and be well intentioned before taking the water. You'll probably pick up a story or two of dramatic conversion and miracles effected by the water, which is sent to Irish émigrés all over the world.

KILMACRENNAN is a sweet-looking inland village on the road southeast to Letterkenny. A quarter of a mile down the Ramelton road from here is yet another site with Columba connections, **Cill Mhic n-Eanain**, where Columba was fostered and educated by Cruithnechan in around 528. A monastery stood here from the sixth century to 1129, and it was also the site of the O'Donnells' religious inauguration following the rites at Doon. The ruins on the left are of a sixteenth-century Franciscan **friary**, while the Church of Ireland building to the right dates from 1622 and fell into disuse around 1845. Back in the village, both the *Angler's Haven* and the *Village Tavern* **pubs** have reasonably priced food.

The north Donegal coast

Running from the Cloghaneely district, which adjoins Gweedore, the **north Donegal coast** holds some of the most spectacular scenery in the whole country, where the battle between the elements is often startlingly apparent. Overshadowed at first by the bleak beauty of **Muckish Mountain** to the south, the main road from **Gortahork** in the west to **Milford** passes through verdant countryside as it meanders around the deep bays and inlets and alongside the glorious and often deserted beaches which punctuate the shoreline. The coast itself is dominated by three contrasting peninsulas: **Horn Head**, with its rugged, sea-battered cliffs; **Rosguill**, almost circumscribed by the marvellous Atlantic Drive; and the more sedate **Fanad** for lonely walks and tremendous views across Lough Swilly to Inishowen.

Falcarragh and around

The first place you'll come across in the **Cloghaneely** area to the east of the Bloody Foreland is **GORTAHORK** (Gort an Choirce, "field of oats"), an Irish-speaking village with a strong cultural history. Ireland's first Irish-language **summer school** was established here in 1912 and the village is home to perhaps the country's greatest contemporary Gaelic poet, **Cathal Ó Searcaigh**. *Teac Maggie Dan's* (ⓦwww.maggiedans.ie; daily 10am–midnight) is a kind of all-purpose **café**, bar and crafts shop and has its own **theatre**, *Amharclann Uí Shearcaigh*, in honour of the poet. For Irish **music**, head to *Teac Billie*, an old man's drinking place with Tuesday night sessions, or on Thursday nights to *Teach Ruarí*, a splendid pub with an astonishingly good restaurant a couple of miles south in **BELTANY**. You can **stay** comfortably just down the road at *Teach Beltaine* (ⓣ074/916 5681; ❷), while back in Gortahork, the renovated *Ostan Loch Altan* (ⓣ074/913 5267, ⓔostanaltan@esatclear.ie; ❹) offers good-value weekend and midweek breaks, and serves bar meals as well as a reasonably priced Sunday carvery lunch.

Two miles east of Gortahork, **FALCARRAGH** (An Fál Carrach, "the rocky field") is livelier and better supplied with pubs, shops and other amenities. As you enter the village from Gortahork, there's **B&B** at *Ferndale* (May–Sept; ⓣ074/916 5506; ❷). **Eating** options are limited: *John's Café*, at the Gortahork end of the main street, or the upstairs restaurant at the *Gweedore* bar are the best, and the latter has **music** of varying kinds most nights in summer. The *Shamrock Pub* and *The Loft* also have live music and the *Errigal* runs Friday **discos**. Falcarragh **beach** is reached by heading north at the village crossroads and turning right about a mile further on, then continuing east for a couple of miles; eventually the dunes will appear behind a car park. This is one of the more beautiful strands on this northwest coast, but a strong undercurrent makes it **unsafe for swimming**.

The road south from Falcarragh to Glenveagh passes through **Muckish Gap**. The slate-grey mass of **Muckish** ("pig's back") **Mountain** dominates the view all the way; the hillsides are pitted with old workings where quartzite sand was extracted for the manufacture of optical glass. It's a relatively easy climb from the roadside shrine at the Gap up a grassy ridge to the **summit** and, on a clear day from here, the entire coastline from the Bloody Foreland, with distant Tory, to Malin Head is splendidly visible.

Heading east out of Falcarragh, the road to Dunfanaghy opens up a significantly milder landscape, with the green grass beginning to outstrip the ruggedness, and the odd reed-fringed lake with swans sitting prettily alongside the road.

Dunfanaghy and around

The small resort of **DUNFANAGHY** (Dún Fionnachaidh, "fort of the white field), seven miles east of Falcarragh, is the gateway to the **Horn Head Peninsula**. It's an aristocratically self-conscious Plantation town, whose strongly Presbyterian atmosphere contrasts vividly with settlements to the west or south. On the western outskirts of town is the impressive **Workhouse** (March–Oct Mon–Sat 10am–5pm, Sun noon–5pm; €3; Ⓦwww.theirishfamine.com), sympathetically restored as a local history and community centre. It was originally built in 1845 on the eve of the Great Famine and at first had only five inmates, but by 1847, as the Famine intensified, over six hundred people were crowded inside. The Famine story is recounted upstairs, through the tale of one local inmate, 'Wee' Hannah Herrity, who lived until 1926 – though the narrative method (a distinctly dull and disappointing series of tableaux) undermines the power of her story. The centre also displays work by local artists and has a coffee shop.

There are two **hotels** in Dunfanaghy – *Arnolds* (Ⓣ074/913 6208, Ⓦwww.arnoldshotel.com; ❻; mid-March to Oct), which also has a riding stables (Ⓦwww.irish-trailriding.com), and *Carrig Rua* (Ⓣ074/913 6133, Ⓔcarrigruahotel@eircom.net; ❺) – both of which also serve food. There are plenty of **B&Bs**, including *Rosman House* (Ⓣ074/913 6273, Ⓦcome.to/rosmanhouse; ❷) and *The Whins* (Ⓣ074/913 6481, Ⓦwhins.businessdot.com; ❷), both of which are a cut above the average. As a less expensive, though comfortable, alternative, the excellent *Corcreggan Mill* **hostel** (IHH; Ⓣ074/913 6409, Ⓦwww.corcreggan.com) is a mile or so west towards Falcarragh and also has private rooms in a converted railway carriage and **camping**.

As for **places to eat**, *Danny Collins* pub offers soups and pricey but delicious seafood, and the upmarket *Danaa's* (Ⓣ074/913 6150) serves lobster and turbot dishes from €25. *McGilloway's Oyster Bar* is light and airy, and a grand place for enjoying a pint, enhanced by the Derry artist John McCandless's tremendous portraits of musicians and writers, from Sinead O'Connor to Brendan Behan. There's occasional **live music** here, too (from traditional to blues), and sessions also at *Michael's Bar* up the street.

Moving east from Dunfanaghy, the road follows the edge of **Sheephaven Bay**; signposted turn-offs run to the popular holiday spots **Portnablagh** and **MARBLE HILL STRAND**. The latter is a vast sweep of sand and the location for the *Shandon Hotel* (March–Oct; Ⓣ074/913 6137, Ⓦwww.shandonhotel.com; ❼), equipped with pool, tennis courts and pitch-and-putt. You can also learn to **wind-surf** here or rent boards from Marble Hill Windsurfing (Ⓣ074/913 6231; July & Aug only). Overlooking the strand, Marble Hill House was once owned by **Hugh Law**, TD for Donegal in the first Irish Parliament of 1922, who entertained all manner of celebrities here, including

W.B. and Jack Yeats. Nearby, **Ards Forest Park** occupies the former demesne of the Capuchin friary of Ard Mhuire; a mile-long avenue alongside Lough Lilly takes you into its centre, where there are fine walks through the woodland.

The Horn Head Peninsula

Horn Head is magnificent, a six-hundred-foot rock face scored by ledges on which perch countless guillemots and gulls. Puffins are also returning in significant numbers. The best view of the cliffs, sea-stacks and caves is from the water, but the cliff road is vertiginous enough in places to give you a good look down the sheer sides. To get there take the slip road at the western end of Dunfanaghy village; it descends to skirt the side of a beautiful inlet before rising steeply to go round the east side of the head. A spectacular vista of headlands opens up to the east – Rosguill, Fanad and Inishowen – but none can match the drama of Horn Head's **cliffs**, their tops clad in a thin cover of purplish heather. Alternatively, you can walk from Horn Head bridge, half a mile from Dunfanaghy on the Horn Head road, and head west across the dunes to **Tramore Beach**. Then follow the sheep track north, passing two small blowholes called the **Two Pistols** and then a much larger one, **McSwyne's Gun**, so called because of the power of the sonic boom produced by the explosion of compressed air from the cavern. Erosion has occurred over the years, however, and you'll be lucky to hear anything these days. Continuing onwards, you'll come to **Pollaguill Bay** and beach. The next wondrous site is the seventy-foot high **Marble Arch**, cut by the sea through the base of Trawbreaga Head. Horn Head itself soon becomes visible as you ascend the next headland. The walk as far as here takes around three hours from Dunfanaghy and you can either complete the whole circuit of the peninsula or head back by road.

Creeslough and around

The sleepy village of **CREESLOUGH** (An Craoslach, "the gorge") stands on a slope commanding gorgeous views across the head of Sheephaven Bay. Partway down its main street is a **church** designed by Liam McCormack, its whitewashed whorl and back-sloping table roof reflecting the thickly set Muckish Mountain nearby. You can see the mountain from within the church – it's usually swathed in mist, or what's known locally as the Donegal *smir*. There are pubs and grocery stores in the village, but little to detain you for long.

The coastal road northward towards the Rosguill Peninsula offers a couple of worthwhile diversions. To the left, just before Lackagh Bridge, **Doe Castle** is currently closed to the public as a result of ongoing restoration. The tall central keep, standing within a *bawn* and rock-cut fosse, was the original fortress of **McSwyney Doe**, whose grave slab is now fixed to its wall, and was the base for the O'Dohertys' raids on Derry in 1608. The carving on the stone is faint, but its intricacy makes it historically important; the seven-speared fleur-de-lis at the top represents the close family connections with Scotland, while other carvings show a fox, cow, dolphin and eagle, as well as Celtic tracery.

Lackagh Bridge offers a tremendous viewpoint of Sheephaven Bay, the curving silty shoreline lying downstream and a ginger-brown picture of rushes and heather reaching deep into the hills. Immediately after the bridge there's a turn-off running for two miles to **GLEN** on a circuitous route to Carrigart that's worth taking for the scenery and the opportunity to drop in at the *Olde Glen* **bar**. This is a low-ceilinged place, smoky and atmospheric, with music at weekends and other nights too. If solitude is what you want, this is a good area to explore: apart from Lough Glen, there are several other small lakes in the district, all enclosed in a silent, rocky landscape.

Carrigart

CARRIGART is the back-door entrance to the Rosguill Peninsula. It's a beguiling village, whose **bars** define the essence of the place: *P. Logue's*, at the west end of town, is a welcoming sort of hideaway. **Accommodation** is available in the village centre at *Hol-Tel Carrigart* (April–Sept; ⓣ074/915 5114, ⓦwww.carrigarthotel.com; ❺) or at *Mevagh House* (ⓣ074/915 5693, ⓔmevaghhousebedbreakfast@hotmail.com; ❷) by the turn-off to Rosguill. There are plenty of stores for stocking up on provisions or you can **eat** economically at *Weavers Restaurant*. The only **bank** on the peninsula is in Carrigart (July & Aug Mon–Fri 10am–noon; rest of year Mon, Tues, Thurs & Fri 10am–noon).

The Rosguill Peninsula

The route onto the extremely beautiful and very manageable **Rosguill Peninsula** starts by the side of Carrigart church; follow this road for a little, then fork left, and you'll pass the rabbit-infested dunes at the back of a tremendous and usually deserted **beach**. The three-mile strand runs in a scimitar's curve all the way back round to the southern end of **Sheephaven Bay** – it's a marvellous four-hour walk to Doe Castle, though when the tide comes in, you might have to do a mile or so of the journey on the lanes.

At the top of the strand is **DOWNINGS** (Na Dúnaibh, "the forts"), a small and sprightly holiday centre patronized mainly by Northern Irish tourists, with caravan sites hogging the rear end of the beach and holiday chalets creeping up the hillside behind the village. The one **pub** you should head for is *Downings Bar* (also known as the *Harbour Bar*), uphill at the far end of the village, a welcoming place with an open fire, lots of *craic* and music at weekends. The most luxurious **place to stay** is the *Rosapenna Hotel* (mid-March to Oct; ⓣ074/915 5301, ⓦwww.rosapenna.ie; ❻), next to its own eighteen-hole golf course. Alternatively, there's the *Beach Hotel* (April–Oct; ⓣ074/915 5303, ⓕ915 5907; ❸) or **B&B** at *Mrs McBride*'s, Bay Mount (April–Aug; ⓣ074/915 5395; ❷), up above the village. You can **camp** at *Casey's Caravan Park* (ⓣ074/915 5301).

Downings' main street runs on round the west side of the headland to become the panoramic **Atlantic Drive**, first passing by the harbour slip road, on which, just before the pier, is McNutt's tweed shop with a daytime coffee shop attached offering superb home baking. The Atlantic Drive runs right round the headland and also makes a stupendous eight-mile walk. The range of views encompasses the essence of Donegal – rugged landscapes in constant tussle with the Atlantic Ocean. About halfway round, a turning leads to **Melmore Head**, where you'll find, perfectly placed at **TRÁ NA ROSANN** beach at the northeastern corner of the headland, an Alpine-style An Óige **hostel** (June–Sept; ⓣ074/915 5374, ⓔmailbox@anoige.ie). A quicker way to get here is to take the right-hand fork on the way into Downings from Carrigart.

South of the Melmore Head road you'll pass the congenial *Singing Pub* (traditional music on Sat), sited on a turning up to the left. Opposite this turning and down to the right is **Mevagh Church** graveyard. It has an early Christian cross and an intriguing slab into which some cup-like cavities have been carved. And there's one gravestone that cannot but raise a smile: *Pat MacBride 1910–86, Shoemaker and Philosopher.*

The Fanad Peninsula

The road from Carrigart to the **Fanad Peninsula** passes close to Mulroy Bay before arriving in **MILFORD**, a village with amenities but little attraction, though the *Milford Inn*, out on the Ramelton road, is a popular venue at weekends, usually for **country and Irish music** (the national adaptation of country and western).

From Milford, the road up the **western** side of the peninsula leads to **KERRYKEEL**. The *Village Inn* at the northern end of the village has a somewhat expensive but wide-ranging menu and *Mr Ed's* serves huge portions of fish and chips. *McGettigan's* **bar** has almost nightly entertainment in summer.

From Kerrykeel the road north runs along the water's edge up to **TAMNEY**, where there's **B&B** at *Avalon House* (March–Oct; ⓣ074/915 9031; ❷). Further on, the landscape flattens and the ubiquitous "Fanad fences" begin to appear, agricultural wire barriers that scythe across the countryside and deter adventurous walking. A left turn at the *Fanad Lodge* bar will take you to the large **Ballyhiernan Strand** or you can take a right turn to **Fanad Head** (see p.602).

Ramelton and Rathmullan

The road crawling up the **east** side of the peninsula is a much more interesting approach to Fanad Head. It starts at **RAMELTON** (Ráth Mealtain, "Mealtan's fort"), a quaint and sedate little town which sits attractively on the eastern bank of the broad black flow of the salmon-rich River Leannan. Despite the town's appeal, wander uphill and you'll encounter boarded-up buildings (including the eighteenth-century *Sweeney's Tavern*) and other signs of decay. Fortunately, rejuvenation is under way and its most obvious sign is **Donegal Ancestry** (April–Sept daily 10am–5.30pm; ⓣ074/915 1266, ⓦindigo.ie/~donances),occupying the old Steamboat Store, built in 1853, on The Quay. The building houses a genealogical research centre (fees dependent upon the amount of work undertaken) and the **Ramelton Story** (€3.80), which recounts through interesting audio-visual material the story of the town from its role as the seat of the O'Donnell's in the twelfth century through to the Plantation and Georgian periods.

Should you decide to stay in Ramelton, there's fine **B&B** at *Ardeen* (ⓣ074/915 1243, ⓔardeenbandb@eircom.net; ❷; April–Oct), overlooking Lough Swilly, or right in the centre of town at *Crammond House*, an eighteenth-century town house in Market Square (ⓣ074/915 1055; ❷; April–Oct). The best **food** can be found at *Mirabeau* (ⓣ074/915 1138), a popular restaurant serving steaks and seafood. For **entertainment**, try the *Bridge Bar*, where you can hear R&B, jazz or rock (Wed & Fri–Sun).

The next stop north, **RATHMULLAN** (Ráth Maoláin, "Maolán's fort") is a pretty place, with its long row of multicoloured houses facing Lough Swilly. The **beach** here is classed among the cleanest in Europe – note the Blue Flag at the pier, where **boats** can be rented from Rathmullan Enterprise Group (ⓣ074/915 8131), based at the *Pier Hotel*. In 1587 **Red Hugh O'Donnell** was lured onto a British merchant ship here, on the pretext of a merry drink, and ended up in Dublin jail for six years; and in 1607 Rathmullan was a departure point for the **Flight of the Earls**, the event that marked the end of the Gaelic nation. **Rathmullan Heritage Centre** (Easter to mid-Sept Mon–Sat 10am–5pm, Sun noon–5pm; €2.50) recounts this event and the impact of the flight, as well as providing information on local accommodation and leisure activities. In October 1798 the French frigate *Hoche*, with Wolfe Tone on board, was intercepted in the lough nearby and Tone was captured and taken to Dublin for trial.

The view across to Fahan on the Inishowen Peninsula is enticing, but otherwise the only thing to delay your passing through is **Rathmullan Friary**, one of the better-preserved historical ruins in Donegal. The original part of it was built by Rory MacSweeney in 1508 and then presented to the Carmelites. George Bingham plundered it in 1595 and used it as a barracks, and in 1618 it was further adapted as a castle residence by Bishop Knox. Only the chancel area continued to serve as a church until its eventual abandonment in 1814. Today you can see traces of Gothic doorways and narrow window apertures.

Accommodation in the village is offered by the comfortably old-fashioned, though soon-to-be-redeveloped *Pier Hotel* (ⓣ074/915 8115, ⓦwww.rathmullancottages.com; ❷), which serves excellent fresh salmon for a fraction of what you'd pay at the upmarket *Rathmullan House* nearby (ⓣ074/915 8188, ⓦwww.rathmullanhouse.com; ❼; closed Jan to mid-Feb). The only other place to stay is the *Fort Royal Hotel* (ⓣ074/915 8100, ⓦwww.fortroyal.com; ❻; April–Oct). On the way into Rathmullan, there's very good **food** at the *Water's Edge* restaurant (ⓣ074/915 8182), while gourmets and wine lovers are also catered for by *An Bonnan Buí* (ⓣ074/915 8453) on Pier Road. You can savour the Lough Swilly view over a pint in the friendly *Beachcomber* **bar**.

Towards Portsalon

Two miles north of Rathmullan, on the coast road, a signpost to the left indicates a little track that leads towards the tenth-century **Drumhallach cross slab**, only four and a half feet high. It has delightful carvings of two figures sitting on the arms of the cross sucking away at their thumbs. This curiosity is linked by local folklore with **Fionn Mac Cumhaill**, who one day burned his thumb while tending to the salmon of knowledge, and immediately stuck it in his mouth – thereafter doing the same whenever he needed to be wise. The lower figures on this front face are harder to discern but are meant to represent bishops.

Back on the main route, the road climbs to give great views across to **Dunree Head** and the **Urris** range of mountains on the Inishowen Peninsula to the east. About seven miles north of Rathmullan is *Bunnaton House* **hostel** (IHO; March–Oct; ⓣ074/915 0122, ⓦwww.bunnaton.com), sited in an old coastguard station with pleasant views of a small cove with a rocky beach. The hostel can provide details of the great walks nearby, both beside the lough and inland through the Irish-speaking **Glenvar valley** to Kerrykeel on the western side of the peninsula. Further on the road towards Portsalon is the *Knockalla Caravan and Camping Park* (mid-March to mid-Sept; ⓣ074/915 9108).

Continuing north, the road rises until you're running along the cliff-top approach to **Saldanha Head**. Here you'll witness the most spectacular views on the entire peninsula, looking across to Inishowen and down onto the three-mile stretch of golden sand at Ballymastocker Bay. The tiny village of **PORTSALON** (Port an tSalainn, "port of the salt"), on the other side of the strand, was once a great holidaying spot, but there's little sign of this now, apart from a courtyard of holiday chalets. The highlight is **Rita's Pier Stores** by the tiny harbour, with its 1950s-style decor, wooden bar counter and shelves for sweets and bottled drinks. For **B&B**, try the award-winning *Croaghross* (March–Oct; ⓣ074/915 9548, ⓦwww.croaghross.com; ❹), which also serves excellent dinners. The Portsalon **golf course** (ⓣ074/915 9459) has one of the most picturesque settings in the country.

Fanad Head

Though some stretches are forested, most of the five-mile route north from Portsalon to **Fanad Head** (Fánaid, "sloping ground") is through humpy and barren land, with clusters of granite pushing through marshy ground. Before reaching the Head, there is one other curiosity worth taking in – the rock formation known as the **Seven Arches**, created by the constant erosive battering of the waters. To get there, follow the signpost on the right of the road, then take the path down to the new house, and finally cross the fields to the rocky strand. Alternatively, there's private access to the arches from **Ballydaheen Gardens**, a gorgeous six-acre spread of flora, herbs and vegetables (May–Sept Mon, Thurs & Sat 10am–3pm; €4).

Returning to the main road, you'll find that it leads straight on to **Fanad Head**, where it reaches a dramatically placed cliff-edge **lighthouse** and its namesake **pub**, the *Lighthouse Tavern*. The road runs on from here down to the low rocky coast and a pebble beach.

East Donegal

The rich farming land of **East Donegal** may seem bland in contrast to other parts of the county and, certainly, it's the area's urban communities that offer the greater attractions. **Letterkenny** is Donegal's boom town, seemingly increasing in size and prosperity daily; it's also the hub of the county's public transport network. To its south lie **Ballybofey** and **Stranorlar** (known as "the twin towns"), the border town of **Lifford** and the former ecclesiastical centre of **Raphoe** with its nearby **Beltany stone circle**, one of Ireland's major Neolithic remains.

Letterkenny

LETTERKENNY is the largest town in Donegal by some way, with a current population exceeding eleven thousand and the only traffic lights in the whole of the county. It has been the county's commercial focus ever since Derry was partitioned into the North and has undergone massive redevelopment in recent years with a refurbished town centre, huge new shopping malls and a growing industrial sprawl beyond its boundaries. Although it sits at the mouth of Lough Swilly, there's no water in sight, and the most notable visual element is the huge nineteenth-century **Cathedral of Saints Eunan and Columba** at the top of Church Street, with its intricate stone-roped ceiling, flying buttresses and gaelicized Stations of the Cross. The only other place of interest in town is the **Donegal County Museum** (Mon–Fri 10am–noon & 12.30–4.30pm, Sat 1–4.30pm; free), housed in part of the old Letterkenny workhouse on High Road. Temporary exhibitions occupy the downstairs area while upstairs is a typical display of artefacts from megalithic to more recent times, including the keys and lock of the old Lifford jail, and an account of the old Donegal County Railway, which ran to and from Letterkenny. If you're heading west on the R250 Fintown road, look out for the restored **Newmills Corn and Flax Mills** (June–Sept daily 10am–6.30pm; last admission 5.45pm; €2.50; Heritage Card), in a pleasant setting by the River Swilly and, naturally, powered by its waters. The mill closed as recently as 1982 and much of the old machinery is still present.

Arrival and information

The **bus station** is by the roundabout at the bottom of Port Road; both Bus Éireann (Ⓣ074/912 1309) and Lough Swilly (Ⓣ074/912 2863) operate services from here. The brand new **tourist office** (June–Aug Mon–Sat 9am–6pm, Sun noon–3pm; Sept–May Mon–Fri 9am–5pm; Ⓣ074/912 1160) is on Neil T. Blaney Road, half a mile out of town towards Derry at the Milford roundabout. There's a **bureau de change** in the tourist office (daily 11am–6pm) and plenty of **banks** and a **post office** on Main Street. **Internet** access is available at *Cyberworld*, below the *4 Lanterns* café on Main Street.

Accommodation

Letterkenny's boom has been matched by a staggering increase in the numbers of **hotels** and **B&Bs**, although there are still relatively few in the town centre. Apart from the places listed below, the greatest preponderance of accommodation can be found along or near the R245 Ramelton road.

Castle Grove Country House Ballymaleel Ⓣ074/915 1118, Ⓦwww.castlegrove.com. A couple of miles out on the Ramelton road, this elegant seventeenth-century house, set in large grounds overlooking Lough Swilly, offers splendidly furnished rooms and an excellent restaurant. ❻

Gallagher's Hotel 100 Main St Ⓣ074/912 2066, Ⓕ912 1016. A Letterkenny institution: friendly and comfortable with 27 en-suite bedrooms and excellent breakfasts. ❼

Glencairn House Ramelton Rd Ⓣ074/912 4393, Ⓔglencairnbb@hotmail.com. A spacious B&B in a bungalow just over a mile from town, with pleasant gardens offering great views of the surrounding countryside. ❷

Gleneany Guesthouse Port Rd Ⓣ074/912 6088, Ⓦwww.gleneany.com. Pleasant, well-kept rooms characterize this comfortable, family-run guesthouse with its own popular restaurant. ❸

Holiday Inn Derry Rd Ⓣ074/912 4369, Ⓦwww.holidayinnletterkenny.com. An imposing, modern structure a couple of miles out towards Derry, featuring large bedrooms and its own 20m swimming pool and sauna. ❽

Oaklands 8 Oaklands Park, Gortlee Rd Ⓣ074/912 5529, Ⓦwww.bandbdonegal.net. A comfortable, modern B&B in a quiet setting off the Ramelton road, ten minutes' walk from town. ❷

Quality Court Hotel 29–45 Main St Ⓣ074/912 2977, Ⓦwww.irishcourthotels.com. Opened in 1999, this stylish town-centre hotel offers luxurious accommodation in its apartment-style suites and en-suite bedrooms. Bedrooms ❺, suites ❽

Eating, drinking and entertainment

There are plenty of places **to eat** in Letterkenny, most of which are on Main Street. At the top of the hill, *Galfees* has a wholesome daytime buffet and serves excellent cakes and coffee. Nearby *The Quiet Moment* tries to epitomize the ambience of Dublin's *Bewley's* with some success. *Pat's On The Square*, 9 Market Square, is an excellent family-run **restaurant** specializing in appetizing home-made pasta and ice cream, freshly ground coffee and desserts to die for, while *Rico's*, opposite the library, is another grand coffee house. Many of the pubs along Main Street serve lunches, too, including an excellent carvery at *Dillon's Bar* and specials too at *McGinley's* and *The Brewery* on Market Square. On Lower Main Street, there's *The Lemon Tree* (Ⓣ074/912 5788; daily 5–10pm) and *The Yellow Pepper* (Ⓣ074/912 4133; daily noon–10pm), both specializing in reasonably priced fish and meat dishes, with several **vegetarian** options.

Letterkenny has enough **bars** to defeat even the hardiest pub-crawler and almost all are on Main Street; a fair few offer Irish music, too. Both *McGinley's* and the *Cottage Bar* are popular with students, and the latter has a Tuesday session. *Nellie's* currently offers music four nights a week. *The Brewery*, in the Market Square, with its striking brass interior, is very popular and has music nightly, including the occasional session. Lower down Main Street, *Mono* is a massive new DJ bar, claiming to be able to hold more than a thousand punters at once, while, further down the hill, *The Cavern* is equally popular, if rather smaller. Letterkenny also has several **clubs**, of which *Pulse*, on Port Road, is currently the most fashionable, attracting up-and-coming and well-established DJs. *The Old Orchard Inn* on High Road has three floors packed at weekends thanks to music in its *Fubar* and DJs in the top-storey club. If you just want a quiet pint, then *Blake's* or *McLafferty's* on Upper Main Street will satisfy.

The local **theatre**, An Grianán (Ⓣ074/912 0777, Ⓦwww.angrianan.com), on Port Road, offers an impressive drama programme and has a reputation as one of Ireland's best **music** venues (from traditional to classical). On Pearse Road is the six-screen Century **cinema** (Ⓣ074/912 5050). Letterkenny also hosts two **festivals**: the Donegal International Car Rally in mid-June and the two-week Errigal Arts Festival in mid-July (details on Ⓣ074/912 9186).

South of Letterkenny

The gently rolling countryside **south of Letterkenny** is probably the least visited of any area in the county. A glance at a map shows a roughly triangular area, delineated by the major roads to and between **Ballybofey** and Strabane (see p.754), which includes the small town of **Raphoe**, with its striking **stone circle**.

Raphoe and the Beltany stone circle

Almost at the centre of this triangle is the small town of **RAPHOE**, set trimly around one of the largest diamonds in the county. Its erstwhile importance as an ecclesiastical centre is still indicated today by its inclusion in the Church of Ireland bishopric of Derry and Raphoe, though it was once a see in its own right. The town has had its own **cathedral**, dedicated to St Eunan, since the ninth century, but the present plain Gothic cathedral church dates merely from 1702. Transfixed in the inner wall is a stone block with some peculiar and indecipherable carvings, and there's a very impressive and resonant wooden baptismal chapel. The former Bishop's Palace lies in ruins to the rear.

The major reason for visiting the area, however, lies two miles to the south – **Beltany stone circle**. To get there, follow the signs from the south of The Diamond in the centre of Raphoe and eventually you'll arrive at the entrance to a farm. The circle is a quarter of a mile up the bridle path to the right, over a stile and across a field full of sheep. This is one of the best-preserved circles in the country, consisting of approximately sixty stones, varying in height between one and four feet. It's easy to comprehend one of the reasons for its construction, as there's a marvellous panoramic view of the local valleys and the distant mountains.

Raphoe town makes a pleasant overnight stop, though there's little in the way of **accommodation**: choices are limited to *The Central Hotel* (Ⓣ074/914 5126; ❷), a grand old place on The Diamond, and Mrs Chambers' B&B, Strabane Road (April–Oct; Ⓣ074/914 5410; ❷). There are quite a few **pubs** in or just off The Diamond – *Tirconnail House* serves a good pint and *The Diamond Bar* has the best traditional music session in the area (Thurs). Surprisingly, Raphoe has one of the biggest **clubs** in the county, *Frankie's*, just west of The Diamond, with very popular dance nights.

The Twin Towns and Lifford

Heading southwest towards Donegal town, you're certain to pass through the twin towns of **STRANORLAR** and **BALLYBOFEY**, separated only by a bridge over the River Finn. There's little remarkable about either, though the latter is by far the livelier. **Isaac Butt**, one of the founders of the Irish Home

Rule Party, is buried in the Stranorlar church graveyard. Ballybofey is home to Donegal's only League of Ireland **football** (soccer) team, Finn Harps, and also to the successful and innovative **Balor Theatre** (ⓣ074/913 1840), which has its own local company and entertains touring companies from all over Europe. The municipal **tourist office** (Mon–Fri 9am–5pm; ⓣ074/913 2337) is inside the Balor Theatre building. Surprisingly, there's some top-notch **accommodation** here at *Jackson's Hotel*, Ballybofey (ⓣ074/913 1021, ⓦwww.jacksons-hotel.ie; ❻), just out on the road to Glenties, and *Kee's Hotel*, Main Street, Stranorlar (ⓣ074/913 1018, ⓦwww.keeshotel.ie; ❻), plus the new *Villa Rose Hotel*, Main Street, Ballybofey (ⓣ074/913 2266, ⓦwww.villarose.net; ❹). There's a **hostel**, *Finn Farm* (IHH & IHO; ⓣ074/913 2261), two miles west of Ballybofey off the Fintown road, which also offers **camping**, horse riding and trekking. There are plenty of **bars** in both towns: *The Claddagh* in Ballybofey's Main Street is the current favourite and has music at weekends. The best **place to eat** is the *Villa Rose* offering a popular lunchtime carvery and splendid evening meals.

If you've entered Donegal from Strabane, across the border in County Tyrone, you'll almost certainly bypass the small border town of **LIFFORD**, though it does have a couple of sights for which it's worth dallying. The town was formerly Donegal's legal centre and the County Council is still based here. The graceful **Old Courthouse**, dating from 1746, was designed by Michael Priestley, and nowadays houses a **visitor centre** (Easter–Oct Mon–Sat 9am–4.30pm, Sun 12.30–4pm; ⓦwww.infowing.ie/seatofpower; €4), which tells the story of the O'Donnell clan and notable events in Donegal's history. The building's former legal use has not been forgotten and models re-enact old trials, including that of Napper Tandy (see p.587), with the assistance of new technology. Down in the basement cells, there's a pretty gruesome re-creation of the conditions experienced by prisoners. A couple of miles northwest of Lifford off the N14 is **Cavanacor House** (Easter–Sept Tues–Sat noon–6pm, Sun 2–6pm; €2.50), a fine seventeenth-century mansion where James II dined in 1689. It was also the ancestral home of **James Knox Polk**, US president from 1845 to 1849. A small museum reflects on both these notables, but the real treat is its **art gallery**, displaying a changing array of work by contemporary painters.

The Inishowen Peninsula

The **Inishowen Peninsula** in the northeast of County Donegal is perhaps the great overlooked treasure of the Irish landscape (and certainly has the longest signposted scenic drive – the "Inishowen 100"). Few tourists come here, perhaps because of its proximity to the North, but those who do discover a diverse and visually exciting terrain, where the views usually encompass the waters of the loughs or the Atlantic waves. Virtually every aspect of the landscape is superb – the beaches (especially Kinnego Bay, Culdaff, Tullagh and Pollan), the towering headland bluffs (Malin, Inishowen, Dunaff and Dunree) and the central mountain range, with **Slieve Snaght** (Sliabh Sneachta, "mountain of snow") at the centre of it all.

The peninsula derives its name from **Eoghán**, who was made First Lord of the island by his father Niall, High King of Ireland. Phases of the peninsula's history before and after Eoghán have left a legacy of fine antiquities, from the **Grianán Ailigh** fort to a host of beautiful early **Christian crosses** (Cloncha, Mura, Carrowmore and Cooley).

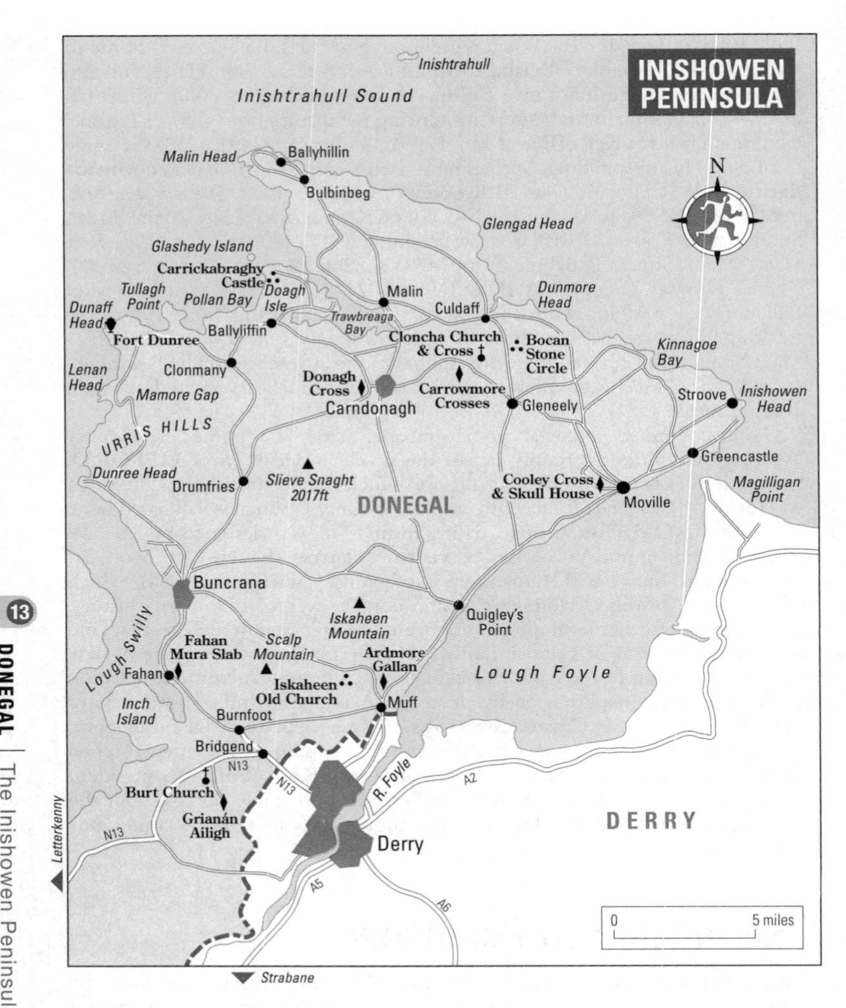

Burt Church and the Grianán Ailigh

The approach to the most stimulating of all Inishowen's sights, the ancient fort known as the Grianán Ailigh, passes the Liam McCormack-designed **Burt Church**, near Bridgend on the N13 Letterkenny–Derry road. This is probably the most beautiful modern church in all Ireland, and like other McCormack designs in Donegal, its structure is evocative of the mystical landmark nearby. The seating is set concentrically, under a whitewashed ceiling that sweeps up into a vortex to allow sunlight to beam down directly upon the altar; the allusions in every detail to Neolithic sepulchral architecture (especially Newgrange – see p.200) are fascinating and very atmospheric. In a recent survey of architects the church was voted Ireland's building of the twentieth century.

The origins of the **Grianán Ailigh**, a mile up the hill from the church, date back to 1700 BC, and it's thought to be linked to the Tuátha Dé Danann, pre-Celtic invaders. It was sufficiently significant to be included by Ptolemy, the Alexandrian geographer, in his second-century AD map of the world, and was the base of various northern Irish chieftains. Here in 450, St Patrick is said to have baptized Eoghán, the founder of the O'Neill clan that ruled the kingdom of Ailigh for more than five hundred years. In the twelfth century, the fort was sacked by Murtagh O'Brian, King of Thomond, in retribution for a raid on Clare, and a large amount of its stone was carried away. Today's impressive building was largely reconstructed in the 1870s by Walter Bernard from Derry and is the only remaining terraced fort in Ireland. It's enclosed by three earthen banks, but its most stunning asset is the view across the primordial jumble of mountains and hills far away to the west and the loughs to each side of Inishowen immediately to the north. You can discover more about the fort at the **Grianán Ailigh Centre** (daily: June–Aug 10am–7pm; Sept–May noon–4.30pm; Ⓦwww.griananailigh.ie; €5.25), half a mile west of the Burt Church back on the main road towards Letterkenny. The ticket price includes a return minibus journey to the fort itself (handy if you don't have your own transport) and an exhilarating audio-visual journey through Celtic history. There's also the superb, innovative *Old Church* **restaurant** (daily 10am–10pm; Ⓣ074/936 8000), serving Lough Neagh eels and wild boar.

Western Inishowen

The lane on the opposite side of the N13 from the Burt Church leads to **western Inishowen** (or you can head east to Bridgend and turn onto the R238). Whichever you choose, a couple of miles past Burnfoot is a signposted turning to **INCH ISLAND**, connected to the mainland by a causeway. This was once a strategic O'Doherty base, guarding Lough Swilly and the clan heartlands, and has a ruined **castle** to boot. If you have time for a detour, there are great views of the lough and the Inishowen coastline from the pier at the north of the island, while wetland habitats to the west of the island attract vast colonies of Whooper and Bewick swans and other waterfowl. Inch Island Stables (Ⓣ074/936 0335, Ⓦwww.eiremall.com) organizes **riding** holidays around the Inishowen 100.

The village of **FAHAN**, next stop on the mainland, has impressive monastic ruins. The first abbot was St Mura (one of six saints in the same family), and surviving from his time is the seventh-century **St Mura cross slab**, a spellbinding example of early Christian stone decoration. Long-stemmed Latin crosses are carved on both faces with typical Celtic interlacing. There's said to be a rare Greek inscription on the edge, but it's hard to locate. Eighteenth-century *St John's Country House* (mid-March to Oct; Ⓣ074/936 0289, Ⓦeircom.net/stjohnscountryhouse; ❼), as you enter the village, offers stylish **accommodation** and local seafood specialities in its **restaurant** (dinner €38 per head plus wine), while the *Railway Tavern* cooks its food on an open wood-burning firebox and has regular Friday night traditional **music**.

Buncrana

BUNCRANA (Bun Cranncha, "foot of the river Crana"), a few miles north of Fahan, is the largest town on the peninsula and its high street is a long cavalcade of shops and bars. The town is packed out during the summer, for this is the Derry people's unrivalled seaside resort, and the streets are especially thronged during the annual **music festival** during the last week of July (details on ⓣ074/936 1397). To escape the crowds, take the left turn that runs down to the pier at the north end of the main street and you'll reach the coastal path to **Stragill Strand**, a beautiful and isolated stretch of golden sand. The view across **Lough Swilly** here is delightful, as if the waters were those of a large mountain lake. Also well worth visiting is the community-run **Tullyarvan Mill** (May–Sept Mon–Sat 10am–5pm), a mile north of town off the Drumree road, which has a crafts shop and café and hosts regular exhibitions and musical events.

Buncrana has surprisingly few places to stay. The brand new **tourist office**, Railway Road (March–May Thurs–Sat 10am–5pm; June–Sept Mon–Fri 9am–5pm, Sat 10am–2pm, Sun noon–3pm; ⓣ074/936 2600), should be able to help, but rooms are in especially short supply during the music festival. For **B&Bs**, try the pleasant *Marine Lodge*, Barrack Hill (ⓣ074/936 2866, ⓦhttp://homepage.tinet.ie/~marinelodgehouse; ❷), overlooking both the town and Lough Swilly, or *Ross na Rí*, Old Road (March–Oct; ⓣ074/936 1271; ❶). There are a couple of **hotels**: the Victorian and cosy *Lake of Shadows*, Grianan Park (ⓣ074/936 1005, ⓦwww.lakeofshadows.com; ❹), overlooking the lough, and, the larger, modern *Inishowen Gateway*, Railway Road (ⓣ074/936 1144, ⓦwww.inishowengatewayhotel.com; ❺), as you enter the town from Fahan.

For **eats** in Buncrana, there are the lunchtime specials at the *Cranberry Café* or, for more substantial fare, the more upmarket *Ubiquitous*, both on Main Street, where you'll also find The *Town Clock Restaurant* offering everything from breakfasts to evening meals. *The Drift Inn*, Railway Road, is a popular choice for pub lunches and has an attached restaurant, while the *Stranagor Restaurant*, Swilly Road (ⓣ074/936 1050), specializes in wonderful seafood dishes and offers views across the lough to Fanad.

Buncrana's Main Street is jam-packed with **pubs**. If you're looking for a plain and unpretentious bar, try *Hutton's* or *Roddens*. More upbeat venues include *O'Flaherty's*, which has traditional music in summer (Weds), and *McCallion's* music bar, which includes the *Zone* club. At the weekends, car- and coach-loads of northerners pour over the border to dance into the small hours at **clubs** such as *Liberty's* in the *Inishowen Gateway Hotel*.

North of Buncrana

Perched on a headland overlooking the mouth of Lough Swilly, just past the tiny village from which it takes its name, **Fort Dunree** began life as a Martello tower and stands near the spot where Wolfe Tone was brought ashore in 1798. The tower was subsequently enlarged into a fortress to guard against the possible return of the French and was further developed in the late nineteenth century. It now has a **museum** of predictable military memorabilia (June–Sept Mon–Sat 10.30am–6pm, Sun 1–6pm; ⓦwww.dunree.pro.ie; €4), though the interactive displays at least provide an insight into the fort's former use. North out of Dunree village, the road climbs steeply past a scattering of weather-beaten thatched cottages before crossing a small bridge close to the **Mamore Gap** (Mám Mór, "the great mountain pass"), which seems like a chunk bitten out of the Urris Hills. From the top of the Gap the road spirals steeply downwards, each bend providing an ever-wider and more spectacular view of the flat foreground to **Dunaff Head**. The mile-long **Tullagh Strand**, to the east of Dunaff Head, is a safe bathing beach, with *Tullagh Bay Camping and Caravan Park* just behind it (ⓣ074/937 6289). *The Rusty Nail* **pub**, by the roadside, has music at weekends and offers good-value bar food and Sunday lunch.

The route from here works its way inland between the mountains to

CLONMANY, a village of predominantly cream-coloured terraced houses, a few shops and several bars, quiet for most of the year, but almost hyperactive during its week-long **festival** at the beginning of August (Ⓦwww.clonmany.com), featuring everything from crisp-eating contests to music concerts. *The Square Bar* has a **traditional music** session on Sundays and the best **place to stay** in the area is *Four Arches* (Ⓣ074/937 6561; ❷), a modern bungalow in a splendid setting near the Mamore Gap.

The holiday village of **BALLYLIFFIN** (Báile Lifin, "halfpenny farm") is more geared to tourism, and has several places to stay. The *Strand* (Ⓣ074/937 6107, Ⓔstrandhotel@ballyliffin.com; ❸) is a family **hotel** whose restaurant's Sunday lunch is hugely popular; there's also the new *Pollan Beach Hotel* (Ⓣ074/937 8991, Ⓦwww.pollanbeachhotel.com; ❻), overlooking Pollan Bay a mile north of the village in Ardagh. **B&B** options include *Carrickabraghey House* (Ⓣ074/937 6977, Ⓔmofflin@eircom.net; ❷), *Castlelawn House* (Ⓣ074/937 6600; ❷) and the more upmarket *Rossaor House* (Ⓣ074/937 6498; ❸). Apart from **golf** – the Glashedy course here (Ⓣ074/937 6119) is reckoned to be one of the toughest in Ireland – the other main local draw is the traditional **song festival** held on the last weekend in March (Ⓦpages.prodigy.net/folkmusic/inishowenseminar). Should you want to explore the area, **bikes** can be rented from McEleney's Cycles (Ⓣ074/937 6541) on the road to Clonmany.

The minor road heading north from Ballyliffin leads to the entrancing **Pollan Strand**, at the northern tip of which stands the ruin of **Carrickabraghy Castle**, an O'Doherty defence built in the sixteenth century. Weathered by centuries of spray and sea salt, the stones of the tower show colours ranging from the darkest hues through oranges and reds to golden yellows. The strand itself has wonderfully wild breakers, which unfortunately make it dangerous to swim. The castle sits on the western side of **DOAGH ISLE**, another former island, linked to the mainland through centuries of silt accumulation, which you can drive onto by a road a couple of miles east of Ballyliffin. The **Doagh Visitor Centre**, well signposted from the Ballyliffin turn-off (Easter–Oct daily 10am–5.30pm; €4), is an intriguing attempt to tell the story of the Great Famine, drawing parallels with the contemporary situation in Africa, while also providing a wealth of information about local customs. You'll discover a re-created farm cottage (including a remarkably small "kitchen" bed), the fairy house home of Fergus McArt and mannequins posed in various symbolic tableaux. Before Christmas the centre transforms itself into "Ireland's Lapland", complete with a podgy Santa getting stuck down the chimney. From here you can head out further east for **Trawbreaga Bay** (Trá Bréige, "the treacherous strand"), an exquisite piece of coastline. The mouth of the bay is bewitching: if you walk onto the beach here you'll find the sea has fashioned the rocks into myriad shapes and colours.

Carndonagh

Just before you turn into **CARNDONAGH** town, coming from the Ballyliffin direction, there's a church on the corner against whose wall is the elegantly shaped and decorated seventh-century **Donagh Cross** (Domhnach, commonly "Sunday", but also "church founded by St Patrick"), with two diminutive pillar stones to its right and left. The pillar stones show figures with rather large heads, while the cross depicts evil little characters jumping out of its Celtic interlacing – all of which harks back to the druidic religion. A few other decorated stones stand by the entrance.

The buildings of Carndonagh town are stacked up the hillside, near the crown of which stands the omnipresent Catholic **church**. Most of the activity here occurs in the environs of The Diamond and this is the place to stock up on supplies. Near the corner of Chapel Street is the **Inishowen Tourist Office** (Mon–Fri 9.30am–5.30pm; July & Aug also Sat & Sun same times; ⓣ074/937 4933, ⓦwww.visitinishowen.com), whose friendly staff can supply you with information on the whole peninsula. You can rent **bikes** from Bikes and Toys (ⓣ074/937 4084; €9 per day, €40 per week), three miles northwest of town on the Ballyliffin road – handily, they'll deliver to anywhere on the peninsula for an additional fee.

For **accommodation**, try *Ashdale Farmhouse* (Easter–Oct; ⓣ074/937 4017, ⓔashdalehouse@eircom.net; ❷), half a mile north on the Malin road, or *An Caisléan* (ⓣ & ⓕ074/937 4537; ❶), a mile south in Millbrae. For **food**, there's *The Corncrake*, Millbrae (ⓣ074/937 4534), a mile out on the Derry road, specializing in seafood and Donegal lamb (from €25 for dinner), or *Donagh Lodge* (ⓣ074/937 4137), out towards Ballyliffin, serving fine steaks and seafood for around €30 a head plus wine. Other alternatives include the restaurant at *Trawbreaga Bay House* on The Diamond, while on Malin Street *The Quiet Lady* has extremely good-value lunches. *The Persian Bar* on The Diamond has **live music** (Fri & Sat) and *The Quiet Lady* has DJs on Fridays and live music on Sundays. *Tul-na-ri*, out on the Culdaff road, attracts the crowds to its weekend **discos**.

Culdaff and the ancient sites

Not far to the east of Carndonagh is a neighbouring set of historical remains – the Carrowmore high crosses, the Cloncha cross, the Bocan stone circle and the Temple of Deen.

To get to the **Carrowmore high crosses**, take the Moville road out of Carndonagh for four miles, then turn right forty yards after the signposted turning for Culdaff: the two plain crosses are 80yd up the lane, one on each side, the northern cross undecorated, while its partner has a figure, supposedly of Christ. These and a few meagre building stones are all that remain of the ancient monastery of St Chonas, husband of Dareaca, a sister of St Patrick.

For the **Cloncha cross and church**, return to the Culdaff turning and follow it for a couple of miles until you see a bungalow with a garden hedge of small firs; the site is up a path alongside. This was once the most important monastic foundation in Inishowen, a status reflected in the beautiful designs carved on the cross's stem. Inside the ruined sixteenth-century church are a few more carved stones, the outstanding piece being a tenth-century tombstone.

For the other two sites, continue onwards towards Culdaff,. When you reach a church standing at a T-junction, instead of heading left to Culdaff, turn right and then first left; the **Bocan stone circle** is through the first field gate on the left, commanding a fine view of the surrounding ring of hills and it's believed that the stones were deliberately aligned on an east–west axis between Slieve Snaght and the Paps of Jura in the Scottish Hebrides. On the other side of the main road from the circle is a gallery tomb known as the **Temple of Deen** (go a little further along the road towards Moville and take a right up as far as the wire barrier – you'll spot it from there). It's nothing special, but it's possible that what is exposed today is only the central chamber of an immense cairn.

CULDAFF (Cúil Dabhcha, "corner of the vat") is the nearest base for all of these places, a cosy village set around an ancient stone bridge whose nearby

beach forms a stunning natural crescent. There's a major **sea-angling festival** here at the end of July and, in mid-October, a cultural weekend commemorates the eighteenth-century actor, **Charles Macklin** (call ⓣ074/937 9104 for details). However, for the rest of the year, it's *McGrory's* **bar** that's the centre of attention. It may be hard to credit, considering its isolated location, but the back room here is one of the best venues in Ireland for **live music**, with traditional sessions on Tuesdays and Fridays. Equally excellent are its bar meals, featuring delights such as Donegal rock oysters, and its more upmarket **restaurant**. You can also **stay** very comfortably here (ⓣ074/937 9104, ⓦwww.mcgrorys.ie; ❹), as well as at *Ceecliff House*, Bunnagee Road (ⓣ & ⓕ074/937 9159; ❷). Summer **boat trips** to Inishtrahull Island (see below) leave from the pier (ⓣ074/937 0605).

Malin and Malin Head

Four miles north of Carndonagh, and approached via a ten-arched bridge, is **MALIN** (Málainn, "sloping ground") village, tucked picturesquely into the side of Trawbreaga Bay. A Planter settlement with a charming grassy Diamond, it has two **pubs**, *McClean's* and *McGonnigle's*, as well as the refurbished *Malin* **hotel** (ⓣ074/937 0645, ⓦwww.inishowen.com; ❸), which hosts a variety of entertainments.

A little way north of Malin, a signpost shows the way to **Five Fingers Strand**, across the bay from Doagh Isle – it's worth the diversion to experience the ferocity of the breakers on the beach and the long walks on its sands, though the strand has undergone recent severe coastal erosion. Following the "Inishowen 100" signs will next lead you around **Knockamany Bens**, from which there are tremendous views of the strand and, occasionally at low tide, of the wreck of the *Twilight*, which sank in 1889 en route to Newfoundland.

Twelve miles north of Malin village, **Malin Head**, the northernmost extremity of Ireland, might not be as stupendous as other Donegal headlands but is nevertheless excellent for blustery, winding coastal walks – and for ornithologists: choughs, with their glossy black plumage and red legs and bill, inhabit the cliffs, and the rasping cry of the rare corncrake can be heard in the fields. The tip of the headland is marked by **Bamba's Crown**, a ruined signal tower, built in 1805. The western path from Bamba's Crown heads out to **Hell's Hole**, a 250-foot chasm in the cliffs, which roars with the onrushing tide.

Five miles offshore is **INISHTRAHULL ISLAND**, deserted since the last families left in 1928, though boats from the pier at **BULBINBEG** (a half-mile walk from *Farren's* bar; see overleaf) will take you there in summer. Some say its name translates as the "island of yonder strand", though others claim its meaning derives from a legendary murder – "island of the bloody strand" or even "shore grave". Whatever the case, the island is composed of the oldest rock in Ireland – 2-billion-year-old Lewisian gneiss.

On the headland, there's **B&B** at *Barraicín* (Easter–Oct; ⓣ & ⓕ074/937 0184; ❶), overlooking the Atlantic. There are a couple of excellent **hostels** here, too. The *Malin Head Hostel* (IHH & IHO; ⓣ074/937 0309), on the way into Bulbinbeg, is well equipped and has private rooms, and the owner, who also offers reflexology and aromatherapy and has an organic garden, is a mine of information on the area; you can hire bikes here too. Alternatively, *Sandrock Holiday Hostel* (IHH & IHO; ⓣ074/937 0289, ⓦwww.cardonagh.com/sandrock) at Port Ronan Pier – fork left at the *Crossroads Inn*, just north of the *Malin Head Hostel* – has dormitory accommodation, wonderful sea views and bikes for rent. Just about the only place to eat is the **restaurant** at *Seaview Tavern* (with a tiny public bar-cum-hardware shop); take the right fork heading north at the *Crossroads Inn* and then the first turning on the right – while *Farren's* **bar** in Bulbinbeg is a cosy place to sit and chat to the locals.

Eastern Inishowen

Though still attractive country, the coastline of **eastern Inishowen** holds less interest than the west. Its proximity to Derry also means that it is substantially busier, especially at the weekends when the city's clubbers hit the area's night-clubs. Nevertheless, it's still possible to find isolated spots, especially to the west of Inishowen Head, and there are lots of pleasant places to visit.

Muff and around

The tiny village of **MUFF** (Magh, "plain"), just a few minutes' drive north of the Derry border, is not quite as moribund as it may at first appear. *Finnegan's* serves superb bar **meals** while *The Flough* is a traditional Irish cottage with music sessions and dancing to match. There's a lively **festival** here on the first weekend in August. Lenamore Stables (Ⓣ074/938 4022) offers **riding** and **trekking** in the vicinity and beyond. Just north of Muff, there are also a couple of lively **bars** in **TURE**: *The Ture Inn* and *Mary Deeney's* both offer great food throughout the week and live music at weekends.

The countryside immediately around Muff is scattered with several interesting remains. Uphill from Muff in **ISKAHEEN**, opposite St Patrick's Church, a plaque in the wall of the ruined church in the graveyard marks the burial place of **Eoghán**, son of Niall of the Nine Hostages. Of greater antiquity is the Bronze Age **Ardmore Gallan** stone, a striking monument heavily carved with symbolic forms. There are forty small cup dents and a large vertical valley down the middle of one face. To get to it, take a left off the Moville road about half a mile north of Muff, then up the lane at the side of a red-doored house; follow the road straight up and turn right to the farmyard at the end. The stone is in the far side of the field in front of the yard.

Also recommended is the fourteen-mile trip across the mountains through **Gráinne's Gap** and on to Buncrana on the western side of the peninsula (see p.607). There are spectacular views back down onto the Foyle estuary from the gap, and the inland scenery is all trickling burns, heathery boggy slopes lined with turf banks and rocky granite outcrops.

Moville and around

Set on a gentle hillock beside the Foyle, **MOVILLE** (Magh Bhile, "plain of the sacred tree") is an agreeable seaside resort and was once a port of call for transatlantic liners, though there's little activity in today's compact harbour. It's handy for a rocky shoreline **walk** that you can pursue as far as Greencastle without too much difficulty, although at a few points you'll have to walk circumspectly across the bottom of a few private gardens. The village rarely stirs itself to offer anything more than the odd tingle of excitement. Nevertheless, there are several **places to stay**. *McNamara's Hotel* (Ⓣ074/938 2010, Ⓕ938 2564; ④) is the grandest and has *Club Max!* attached. For B&B try *Naomh Mhuíre*, Main Street (April–Oct; Ⓣ074/938 2091; ①), or the larger *Carrownaffe Admiralty House* (May–Sept; Ⓣ074/938 2529; ①), overlooking the bay, five minutes' walk north of town. *Barron's* café, Lower Main Street, offers economical daytime **meals**, while *Rosatos*, Malin Road, is the best place for an evening meal. There are traditional sessions at *Rawdon's Bar and Grocery*, Malin Road, on Fridays, while the *Hair of the Dog* **pub** by the pier has live music at weekends.

The most notable historical remains in the district are the **Cooley Cross** and **Skull House**, approached by taking the left turn just before the petrol station on the way into Moville. Follow the turn-off up the steep hill for about a mile, always bearing right, and you'll discover an ancient Celtic wheel-cross guarding the entrance to a walled graveyard. There are very few examples of this kind of cross with the pierced ringhole in its head – the hole was once a pagan device used to clinch serious treaties, the hands of the opposing parties being joined in amity through it. The Skull House, in the graveyard, is in the form of the beehive huts of early monks and it was once possibly an oratory before becoming an ossuary. Any bones that were stored here have long since vanished.

Greencastle and around

The harbour village of **GREENCASTLE** has a pleasant view across to the extensive golden sands of Magilligan Strand on the Northern Irish side of Lough Foyle. At dusk you'll see the area across the water begin to sparkle with lights like a ship at sea – these are the lights of the prison camp, just hidden behind the dunes. A highlight of village life are the regular visits by cruise ships, though a more recent innovation is the Greencastle-to-Magilligan **ferry** service operated by Lough Foyle Ferry Co., The Pier (Ⓣ074/938 1901, Ⓦwww.loughfoyleferry.com; April–Sept Mon–Sat 7.20am–9.50pm, Sun 9am–9.50pm; Oct–March service ends two hours earlier; pedestrians €1.60 single, €2.60 return, cars €8 single, €13 return). Next to the harbour, in the old coastguard station, is the **Maritime Museum and Planetarium** (June–Sept Mon–Sat 10am–6pm, Sun noon–6pm; Ⓦhomepage.eircom.net/~greencastlemaritime; museum €4, museum, planetarium and laser shows €8), which recalls maritime travel from a bygone era through a range of Irish boats from six to fifty feet in length. Amongst the range of maritime memorabilia, pride of place goes to a nineteenth-century rocket cart used to fire flares to aid survivors of wrecked ships. The new state-of-the-art planetarium takes you on exhilarating trips through the universe, while laser light shows feature a soundtrack ranging from Led Zeppelin to traditional music.

Next to the road to Stroove (see overleaf) are ruins of a fourteenth-century Richard de Burgo **castle**, built on a rocky knoll to allow the Anglo-Normans to guard the narrowest part of the lough. It was briefly captured in 1316 by Edward Bruce of Scotland, who had himself crowned King of Ireland. The castle was retaken shortly afterwards and remained in De Burgo's hands until 1333, when his grandson William, the Brown Earl, was murdered and Anglo-Norman control of the northwest ended. Later the castle fell into the hands of the O'Dohertys, but it was badly damaged by an attack by their rival Calvagh O'Donnell. Though there were subsequent attempts at renovation, by 1700 the castle was a complete ruin and has remained so ever since. Nearby is **Greencastle Fort**, a lookout post built during the Napoleonic Wars, which unsurprisingly affords good views across the estuary, though nowadays it houses a bar and restaurant with **B&B** (Ⓣ074/938 1279; ❸). You can also stay right next door to De Burgo's ruin in the *Castle Inn* (Ⓣ074/938 1426; ❸), which also has a reputable restaurant, and at *Tardrum Country House* (Ⓣ074/938 1051, Ⓦwww.iol.ie/~tardrum; ❷), a Victorian house overlooking the sea near the golf course on the way to Stroove. As you'd expect, seafood is available in abundance and, in addition to the **restaurants** above, the place to aim for is *Kealy's* (Ⓣ074/938 1010), reckoned to be one of the best in Donegal (around €30 per head plus wine). The village also has an active local drama centre, the **Cairn Theatre**, Stroove Road (Ⓣ074/938 1104), which mounts a variety of productions during the summer.

At **STROOVE** (pronounced "shroove"), the scenery jumps into a more exciting gear, with lovely clambering walks along its coastline to the lighthouse. There you'll have to return to the road to reach the small beach, from where doughtier walkers can resume the clamber as far as the cliffs of the awesome **Inishowen Head**. An easier way to the head is simply to follow the road until it turns left, at which point you carry on straight on up the hill; a car can make it the first couple of miles, but after that you run the risk of getting stuck in a rut. From the head, it's a beautiful but tiring walk to isolated **Kinnagoe Bay**, one of the most secluded sandy beaches around, tucked between the rocky walls of headland against which the waves throw spray as delicate as lace. The alternative route here entails going back to the main road and following it to the right turn by the thatched cottage in Stroove – this will take you along the narrowest of roads over the headland and through two beautiful glens. A plaque by the roadside at Kinnagoe Bay records the sinking of *La Trinidad Valencera* from the Spanish Armada and other ships around the coast. Forty of its crew died in the water, and most of the remaining three hundred survivors were killed outside Derry by an English army. *Kinnagoe Bay House* (ⓣ074/938 1280, ⓦwww.iol.ie/~kinnagoebayhouse; ❷; April–Oct) is a fine, isolated **place to stay** with wonderful views of the bay. Back in Stroove, the *Drunken Duck Seafood Bar* (ⓣ074/938 1362) is well worth a visit for its good **food** and fantastic views.

Travel details

Donegal has no trains, but there's a plethora of **bus** services, divided here between public and private companies. Apart from express services, few companies operate on Sundays and many services are much reduced in winter.

Public bus companies

Bus Éireann

Donegal town ⓣ074/972 1101; Letterkenny ⓣ074/912 1309; Stranorlar ⓣ074/913 1008; ⓦwww.buseireann.ie.

Ardara to: Donegal (July & Aug Mon–Sat 2 daily; Sept–June Mon, Wed & Fri 1 daily; 1hr 15min); Dungloe (July & Aug Mon–Sat 2 daily; 1hr 15min); Glenties (July & Aug Mon–Sat 2 daily; Sept–June Mon–Fri 1–2 daily; 20min); Killybegs (July & Aug Mon–Sat 2 daily; Sept–June Mon, Wed & Fri 1 daily; 25min); Narin (July & Aug Mon–Sat 2 daily; 35min).

Ballybofey to: Derry (3–7 daily; 1hr 05min); Donegal (3–7 daily; 30min); Letterkenny (3–7 daily; 20min); Strabane (Mon–Sat 5 daily; 55min).

Ballyshannon to: Bundoran (5–9 daily; 10min); Donegal town (8–10 daily; 20min); Sligo (Mon–Sat 5–8 daily, Sun 3 daily; 1hr 05min).

Donegal town to: Ardara (July & Aug Mon–Sat 2 daily; Sept–June Mon, Wed & Fri 1 daily; 1hr 15min); Ballybofey (3–7 daily; 30min); Ballyshannon (8–11 daily; 15min); Belleek (3–5 daily; 45min); Bundoran (5–9 daily; 30min); Derry (3–7 daily; 1hr 25min); Dublin (3–5 daily; 3hr 30min); Dungloe (July & Aug Mon–Sat 2 daily; 2hr 30min); Enniskillen (3–5 daily; 1hr 05min); Frosses (2–4 daily; 20min); Galway (3–5 daily; 3hr 45min); Glencolmcille (2–3 daily; 1hr 15min); Glenties (2 daily; 1hr 30min); Glenveagh (July & Aug Mon–Sat 1 daily; 1hr 45min); Killybegs (Mon–Sat 3-5 daily; 30–45min); Letterkenny (3–7 daily; 50min); Sligo (6–8 daily; 1hr 20min).

Glencolmcille to: Donegal (1–2 daily; 1hr 15min).

Killybegs to: Ardara (July & Aug Mon–Sat 2 daily; Sept–June Mon, Wed & Fri 1 daily; 25min); Dungloe (July & Aug Mon–Sat 2 daily; 1hr 40min); Glencolmcille (2–3 daily; 45min); Glenties (July & Aug Mon–Sat 2 daily; Sept–June Mon, Wed & Fri 1 daily; 40min); Malinmore (Sat only 1 daily; 1hr).

Letterkenny to: Ballybofey (3–7 daily; 20min); Derry (3–7 daily; 35min); Donegal (3–7 daily; 50min); Lifford (Mon–Sat 4 daily; 50min); Raphoe (Mon–Sat 5 daily; 35min); Strabane (Mon–Sat 5 daily; 55min).

Ulsterbus

Belfast ⓣ 028/9033 3000.
Ballyshannon to: Belleek (1–7 daily; 15min); Enniskillen (1–7 daily; 1hr 10min).
Pettigo to: Ballyshannon (Mon–Sat 1 daily; 45min); Belfast (2–3 daily; 3hr 15min); Belleek (Mon–Sat 1 daily; 30min); Enniskillen (Mon–Sat 5 daily; 50min).

Private bus companies

Patrick Gallagher

ⓣ 074/953 1107.
Annagry to: Belfast (1 daily; 3hr 50min); Letterkenny (1 daily; 1hr).

Lough Swilly

Derry ⓣ 028/7126 2017; Letterkenny ⓣ 074/912 2863.
Bunbeg to: Knockfola (Mon–Fri 2 daily; 15min).
Buncrana to: Ballyliffin (Mon–Sat 3 daily; 35min); Carndonagh (Mon–Sat 3–4 daily; 25–50min); Clonmany (Mon–Sat 3 daily; 30min); Derry (3–13 daily; 35min); Letterkenny (Mon–Fri 3–4 daily; 40min).
Carndonagh to: Ballyliffin (Mon–Sat 3 daily; 15min); Buncrana (Mon–Sat 3–4 daily; 25–50min); Clonmany (Mon–Sat 3 daily; 20min); Derry (Mon–Sat 4–5 daily; 55min); Malin Head (Mon, Wed & Fri 2 daily, Sat 3 daily; 30min).
Dunfanaghy to: Derry (Mon–Sat 3–4 daily; 2hr); Dungloe (Mon–Sat 1–3 daily; 1hr 20min–3hr); Letterkenny (Mon–Sat 5 daily; 50min).
Dungloe to: Annagry (Mon–Sat 2 daily; 30min); Burtonport (Mon–Sat 2 daily; 10min); Crolly (Mon–Sat 2 daily; 15min); Derry (Mon–Sat 1–2 daily; 3hr 10min); Derrybeg (Mon–Sat 2 daily; 30min); Dunfanaghy (Mon–Sat 2 daily; 1hr 15min–1hr 25min); Falcarragh (Mon–Sat 2 daily; 1hr); Kincasslagh (Mon–Sat 2 daily; 20min); Letterkenny (Mon–Sat 1–2 daily; 2hr 05min–2hr 20min).
Greencastle to: Derry (Mon–Sat 5 daily; 55min).
Letterkenny to: Buncrana (Mon–Fri 2–3 daily; 40min); Derry (Mon–Sat 11 daily; 30–55min); Dunfanaghy (Mon–Sat 2–3 daily; 55min); Dungloe (Mon–Sat 2-3 daily; 2hr 15min–3hr 55min); Fanad (Mon–Sat 2 daily; 1hr 40min); Ramelton (Mon–Sat 3-4 daily; 20min); Rathmullan (Mon–Sat 2–3 daily; 35min); Portsalon (Mon–Sat 1 daily; 1hr 25min).
Malin Head to: Carndonagh (Mon, Wed & Fri 2 daily, Sat 3 daily; 30min); Derry (Mon, Wed & Fri 2 daily, Sat 3 daily; 1hr 25min).
Moville to: Derry (Mon–Sat 5–6 daily; 50min); Greencastle (Mon–Sat 5 daily; 10min); Stroove (Mon–Sat 4 daily; 20min).
Muff to: Derry (Mon–Sat 8–11 daily; 20min).
Portsalon to: Letterkenny (Mon–Sat 1 daily; 1hr 55min).
Ramelton to: Letterkenny (Mon–Sat 3–4 daily; 20min).
Stroove to: Derry (Mon–Sat 4 daily; 1hr 10min).

McGeehan Coaches

ⓣ 074/954 6150, ⓦ www.mgbus.com.
Dungloe to: Dublin (2 daily; 5hr) via Glenties, Ardara, Donegal town, Enniskillen and Cavan.
Glencolmcille to: Dublin (2 daily; 4hr 50min) via Carrick, Kilcar, Killybegs, Ardara, Donegal town, Enniskillen and Cavan.

John McGinley

ⓣ 074/913 5201.
Crolly to: Dublin (1–2 daily; 5hr 25min) via Bunbeg, Dunfanaghy, Letterkenny, Omagh and Monaghan.
Letterkenny to: Belfast Airport (1 daily; 2hr 45min); Glasgow (1 daily; 11hr).
Milford to: Dublin (1 daily; 4hr 30min) via Ramelton, Letterkenny, Omagh and Monaghan.
Moville to: Dublin (1 daily; 5hr 15min) via Carndonagh, Buncrana, Letterkenny, Omagh and Monaghan.

Northwest Busways

ⓣ 074/938 6219.
Buncrana to: Ballyliffin (Mon–Sat 2-4 daily; 25min); Carndonagh (Mon–Sat 2-4 daily; 35min); Clonmany (Mon–Sat 2–4 daily; 20min); Letterkenny (Mon–Sat 2–4 daily; 45min); Moville (Mon–Sat 2–4 daily; 55min).
Carndonagh to: Culdaff (Mon–Sat 2 daily; 15min); Derry (Mon–Sat 3–4 daily; 35min).
Culdaff to: Carndonagh (Mon–Sat 2 daily; 15min); Derry (Mon–Sat 2 daily; 50min).
Greencastle to: Derry (Mon–Sat 3 daily; 1hr).
Letterkenny to: Ballyliffin (Mon–Sat 2–4 daily; 1hr); Buncrana (Mon–Sat 2-4 daily; 45min); Carndonagh (Mon–Sat 2–4 daily; 1hr 20min); Clonmany (Mon–Sat 2–4 daily; 1hr 05min); Moville (Mon–Sat 2–4 daily; 1hr 40min).
Moville to: Ballyliffin (Mon–Sat 2-4 daily; 30min); Buncrana (Mon–Sat 2–4 daily; 55min); Carndonagh (Mon–Sat 2–4 daily; 20min); Clonmany (Mon–Sat 2–4 daily; 35min); Derry (Mon–Sat 3 daily; 40min); Greencastle (Mon–Sat 3 daily; 20min); Letterkenny (Mon–Sat 2–4 daily; 1hr 40min); Stroove (Mon–Sat 3 daily; 25min).

O'Donnell

Ⓣ 074/954 8356.

Dungloe to: Belfast (1 daily; 4hr 40min) via Burtonport, Annagry, Bunbeg, Dunfanaghy, Letterkenny and Derry.

Feda ó Donnell

Ⓣ 074/954 8114, Ⓦ www.fedaodonnell.com.

Crolly to: Galway (2–3 daily; 5hr 50min) via Dunfanaghy, Letterkenny, Donegal town, Sligo and Knock.

14

Belfast

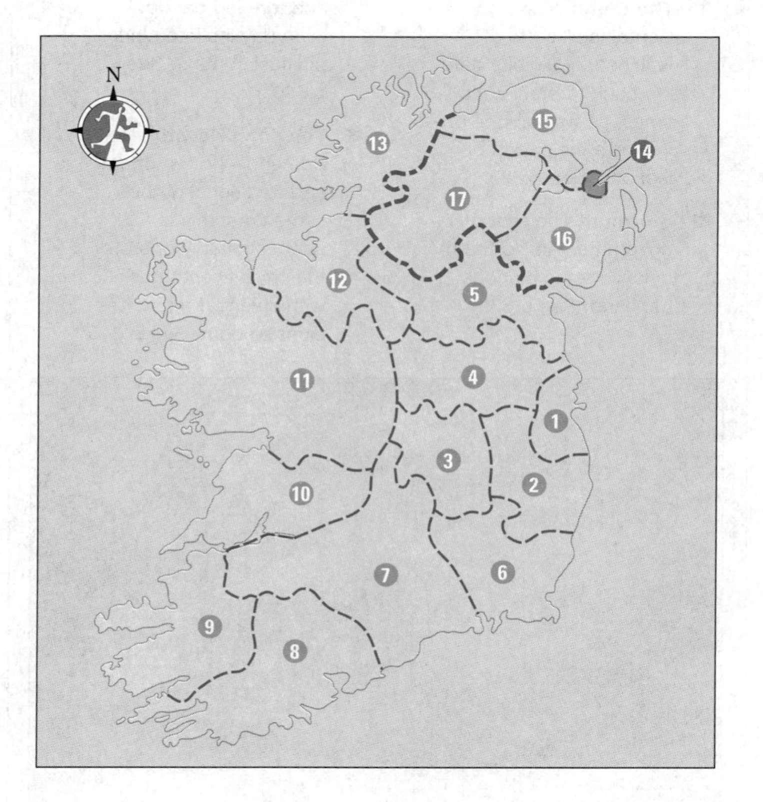

CHAPTER 14 Highlights

* **The Laganside** Nowhere has the city seen more recent change than in its harbour and docklands, revitalized by developments such as the Odyssey Arena and the Waterfront Hall. **See p.634**

* **The Ulster Museum** Contains all sorts of fascinating exhibits dating back to prehistoric times, as well as one of Ireland's major art collections. **See p.638**

* **Stormont** The seat of government in Northern Ireland, set in glorious parkland. **See p.639**

* **Cave Hill** The best spot for a panoramic view of the city and Belfast Lough spread out below. **See p.640**

* **West Belfast** An essential part of any visit to the city: the murals, Peace Line, cemeteries and fortified bars put everyday life into stark political context. **See p.640**

* **The John Hewitt** Somehow both modern and traditional at the same time, this is unquestionably one of the city's finest pubs, with splendid music sessions to boot. **See p.645**

Belfast

BELFAST is the capital of Northern Ireland and its largest city by some way. More than a third of the province's population live within the Belfast conurbation and, consequently, there's a pace and bustle about the place that you'll find almost nowhere else in Northern Ireland. For many, however, Belfast will always be remembered as the focus of the **Troubles** that have dominated Northern Ireland's politics and so many people's personal lives since 1969, and the city continues to bear the scars.

In appearance Belfast closely resembles Liverpool, Glasgow or any other industrial port across the water, and, similarly, its largely defunct **docklands** – in which, famously, the *Titanic* was built – are undergoing massive redevelopment. Though the city centre is still characterized by numerous elegant **Victorian** buildings, there's been an enormous transformation here, too, and the streets leading northwards from the hub of Belfast life, **Donegall Square**, are packed with chain stores and shopping precincts. Yet this prosperity is not reflected in every aspect of Belfast life. The number of rough sleepers has increased and some areas of the city evince obvious economic decline, most notably North Belfast and the once-thriving, now-tarnished **Golden Mile** where restaurants that appeared during the boom years during the second half of the 1990s have closed and remain boarded up. On week nights the city centre resembles a ghost town, though there's no doubt that Belfast continues to thrive culturally. Music, theatre and the visual arts are all flourishing, and traditional Irish culture is rapidly being rediscovered.

Belfast is a place for getting out and about, and has plenty to experience. This need not take more than a couple of days in the city itself, although Belfast is a good base from which to visit virtually anywhere else in the North. In the centre, concentrate on the glories brought by the Industrial Revolution: grandiose **architecture** and magnificent Victorian **pubs**. To the south are the lively and influential **Queen's University** and the extensive collections of the **Ulster Museum**, set in the grounds of the **Botanic Gardens**. A climb up **Cave Hill**, to the north, rewards you with marvellous views of the city spread out around the curve of its natural harbour, **Belfast Lough**. Security measures in the city have been considerably relaxed and most of the barriers and controls have been removed. However, the iron blockade known as the **Peace Line** still bisects the Catholic and Protestant communities of **West Belfast**, a grim physical reminder of the city's and country's sectarian divisions – and there are certain **flashpoints** such as the Short Strand and the Ardoyne which it is inadvisable to visit.

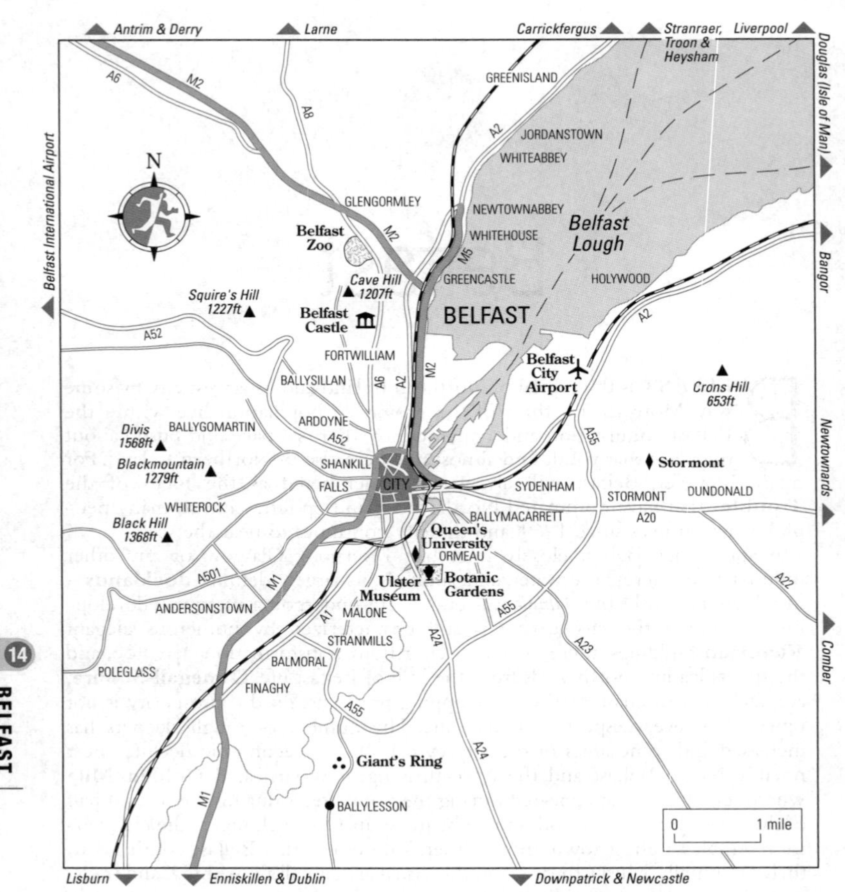

Some history

Belfast began life as a cluster of forts built to guard a ford across the **River Farset**, which nowadays runs underground beneath the High Street. The Farset and Lagan rivers form a valley that marks a geological boundary between the basaltic plateau of Antrim and the slaty hills of Down: the softer red Triassic sandstones from which their courses were eroded are responsible for the **bright red** colour of Belfast's brickwork.

Belfast developed slowly at first and, indeed, its history as a city does not really begin until the seventeenth century. A **Norman castle** was built here in 1177, but its influence was always limited, and within a hundred years or so control over the Lagan Valley had reverted firmly to the Irish, under the O'Neills of Clandeboye, who had their stronghold to the south in the Castlereagh Hills. Theirs was the traditional Irish pastoral community, their livestock and families spread between the hills and valley plain. Then, in 1604, **Sir Arthur Chichester**, a Devonshire knight whose son was to be the first Earl of Donegall, was "planted" in the area by James I, and shortly afterwards the tiny settlement was granted a charter creating a corporate borough. By the restoration era of 1660 the town was still no more than one hundred and fifty houses in five or six streets, and **Carrickfergus** at the mouth of the lough held the monopoly on trade.

By the end of the seventeenth century, things were looking up. French Huguenots fleeing persecution brought skills that rapidly improved the fortunes of the local linen industry – which, in turn, attracted new workers and wealth. In 1708, the town was almost entirely destroyed by **fire**, but it was only a temporary setback: throughout the eighteenth century the **cloth trade** and **shipbuilding** expanded tremendously, and the population increased tenfold in a hundred years. Belfast was a city noted for its **liberalism**: in 1784 Protestants gave generously to help build a Catholic church and, in 1791, three Presbyterian Ulstermen formed the society of **United Irishmen**, a gathering embracing Catholics and Protestants on the basis of common Irish nationality. Belfast was the centre of this movement, and thirty Presbyterian ministers in all were accused of taking part in the **1798 Rebellion**. Six were hanged.

Despite the movement's Belfast origins, the rebellion in the North was in fact an almost complete failure, and the forces of reaction backed by the wealthy landlords quickly and ruthlessly stamped it out. Within two generations most Protestants had abandoned the Nationalist cause, and Belfast as a sectarian town was born. In the **nineteenth century**, Presbyterian ministers like the Reverend Henry Cooke and Hugh "Roaring" Hanna began openly to attack the Catholic Church, and the **sectarian divide** became wider and increasingly violent. In 1835, several people were sabred to death in Sandy Row, and sporadic outbreaks of violence have continued from that day on. Meanwhile, the nineteenth century saw vigorous commercial and industrial expansion. In 1888, Queen Victoria granted Belfast **city** status; the city fathers' gratitude to her is stamped on buildings throughout the centre. By this time the population had risen to 208,000 and, with the continued improvement in both the linen and shipbuilding industries, the population exceeded even that of Dublin by the end of the century.

The twentieth century to the present

Partition and the creation of Northern Ireland with Belfast as its capital and Stormont as its seat of government inevitably boosted the city's status, but ultimately ensured that it would become the focus for much of the **Troubles**. This became first apparent in March 1969 when Loyalists from the UVF and UPV bombed the Castlereagh electricity sub-station in East Belfast in an attempt to undermine the government of Terence O'Neill and followed up their action by several attacks on Belfast's water supply. Serious **rioting** followed that year's July 12 Orange Order parades, with many families being forced to leave their homes (the beginnings of Belfast's modern demographic reorganization), and British troops entered West Belfast in August as a result of further disturbances caused by the Battle of the Bogside (see p.684) in Derry. The first "**peace line**" was constructed to separate Catholic and Protestant areas, while Catholics who had at first welcomed the British Army now began to establish "no-go" areas.

Serious rioting again occurred in March 1970 following Orange parades and continued in Ballymurphy for a further few days, while a major gun battle took place in June in the Short Strand between the IRA and Loyalists. The following day five hundred Catholic workers were forced to leave the Harland & Wolff shipyard by their Protestant colleagues, many never returning. Continued violence led to the introduction of **internment** on August 9, 1971, a day followed by some of the worst violence in the city's history in which seven thousand people were forced to flee their homes. While now targeting the security forces in addition to Loyalist paramilitaries, the IRA's response was **Bloody Friday**, when 22 bombs exploded during 75 minutes in Belfast's city centre on July 21, 1972, killing nine people and seriously wounding a further 130. This triggered the army's **Operation Motorman**, a massive attempt to smash the "no-go" areas. In return, the IRA attacked various army undercover units.

Government attempts to introduce power-sharing via the **Sunningdale agreement** led to the May 1974 strike called by the Ulster Workers Council (see p.796), which thoroughly paralysed Belfast before the British gave in. While the remainder of the 1970s was characterized by the IRA's bombing campaigns on mainland Britain, Belfast was the scene of vicious internecine disputes. In 1975 alone, the UVF and the UDA killed 120 Catholics, many the victims of the notorious **Shankill Butchers**. Partly in retaliation, the IRA bombed the *Bayardo Bar* on the Shankill Road, though it still maintained its prime aim of removing the British from Ireland.

One of those allegedly leading the IRA's West Belfast brigade was **Gerry Adams**, who was elected MP for the area in 1983. While he has never taken up his seat in Westminster, Adams was and to this day remains a dominant figure in Belfast and the North's politics – so much so that in March 1987 a solo UDA operative, **Michael Stone**, attempted to kill both Adams and another significant political figure, Martin McGuinness, while they were attending the funeral of three IRA members shot in Gibraltar by the British. Stone missed, but was successful in killing three others. As the funeral of one of these victims was making its way to Milltown, a car driven by two army corporals inexplicably drove into the cortege. Mourners dragged the men out of the car and away to waste ground where they were shot. The initial moments were filmed by a television crew and were subsequently widely broadcast, heightening tension even further.

Although political machinations were leading eventually to the IRA's 1994 declaration of a ceasefire, the Loyalists were still regarded as fair game, and one of the last major bombings of the Troubles took place in October 1993 when the IRA bombed a fish shop on the **Shankill Road**, believing that Johnny Adair and other leaders of the UDA were attending a meeting above the premises. The bomb detonated prematurely, killing the bomber himself and nine Protestants in the shop at the time. The UDA response was to bomb a bar in Greysteel, Country Derry.

Even before the Troubles, German bombing in World War II had destroyed much of the city, so by the time the IRA declared a **ceasefire** in 1994, much of it resembled a battle site. The end of IRA activities marked a sea change in the city's fortunes, and significant rebuilding has taken place in the intervening period, especially in West Belfast. Billions of pounds of money poured in from Britain and the European Union for **revitalization** in the hope that economic growth might help to bring about a more hopeful future. Major shopping centres were built, swish hotels, bars and restaurants seemed to spring up almost overnight, and buildings such as the Waterfront Hall and Odyssey Arena have fundamentally altered the city's skyline. Young Belfast partied like never before – and continues to do so – while the atmosphere of the whole city centre has changed irrevocably.

Nevertheless, feuding has continued to hit the headlines over the last couple of years, particularly over incidents at **Holy Cross School** in North Belfast, where Protestants sought to prevent Catholic parents from taking their children to school through a Loyalist area, and in the **Short Strand** area of East Belfast, where a small Catholic enclave sees itself as the victim of a deliberate squeezing-out policy by Loyalists. On a constitutional note, Belfast's first **Sinn Féin mayor**, Alex Maskey, took office in 2002.

Arrival, information and transport

Belfast is served by two **airports**. Most flights arrive at **Belfast International Airport**, nineteen miles west of the city in Aldergrove; from here, there are airport buses to Europa Buscentre (Mon–Sat every 30min 7.10am–11.20pm; Sun hourly 6.50am–11.20pm; £5 single, £8 return). A taxi costs around £25. An increasing number of carriers use the tiny **Belfast City Airport**, three miles northeast of the centre, from where Citybus #600 runs to the Europa Buscentre (Mon–Fri every 40min 6.25am–10.20pm, Sat every 40min 6.25am–1.50pm, Sun every 40min 1.10–7.10pm; £2) and the regular #21 bus runs to City Hall on Donegall Square (Mon–Sat every 20–30min 6am–10.20pm; on Sun the route is served by buses #101 and #102 hourly 9.35am–9.35pm; Mon–Sat £1.30, Sun 80p). Alternatively, trains run from Sydenham Halt, a short walk from the City Airport terminal, to Central Station (Mon–Fri every 30min, less frequently at weekends; £1.20). A taxi from City Airport to the centre costs around £6.

Ferries from Britain arrive at various dockside termini. The Seacat services from Heysham, Troon and the Isle of Man use **Donegall Quay**. From here to the city centre is about a fifteen-minute walk, or a £3.50 taxi ride. Stena high-speed ferries from Stranraer dock a little further north at **Corry Road** – a taxi from here will cost around £5. Norse Irish Ferries from Liverpool dock even further north on **West Bank Road**; expect to pay a taxi fare from here of at least £6. P&O ferries from Cairnryan dock at the town of **Larne**, twenty miles north (see p.660), which is connected by Ulsterbus to the Laganside Buscentre and by train to Yorkgate and Central stations.

The majority of **trains** call at **Great Victoria Street Station** in the centre, with the exception of trains from Dublin and Larne, which terminate at **Central Station** near the Waterfront Hall on East Bridge Street, a little way east of the centre. From Central Station you can hop on a connecting train to Great Victoria Street Station, which stops midway at Botanic and City Hospital stations – both of which are useful if you're staying in the university quarter.

Express **buses** arrive at one of Belfast's two stations. The **Europa** bus station, alongside Great Victoria Street train station in Glengall Street behind the *Hastings Europa Hotel*, handles services to Armagh, west Derry, west Down, Fermanagh and Tyrone as well as to the Republic, the airports and the ferry terminals. The **Laganside Buscentre** in Queen's Square near the Albert Clock serves Antrim, east Derry and east Down. Both of them are very central and well served by Citybus services.

The **Centrelink** bus #100 runs every twelve minutes on a very useful circular route from and to Central Station, via Donegall Square, the Europa Buscentre and the Laganside Buscentre.

Information

The new **Belfast Welcome Centre** at 47 Donegall Place, just north of Donegall Square (Mon–Sat 9am–5.30pm; ⓣ028/9024 6609, ⓦwww.gotobelfast.com), stocks a vast range of information on the city and the rest of the North, provides an accommodation booking service (£2) and sells tickets for events. It also has an Internet café (£4 per hour) and the only left-luggage facilities in the city. There are **tourist offices** at both airports – Belfast International (daily 24hr) and Belfast City (daily 5.30am–10pm; Sat closes 9pm). **Bord Fáilte**, which supplies tourist information for the Republic, is located at 53 Castle St (Mon–Fri 9am–5pm; March–Sept also Sat 9am–12.30pm; ⓣ028/9032 7888).

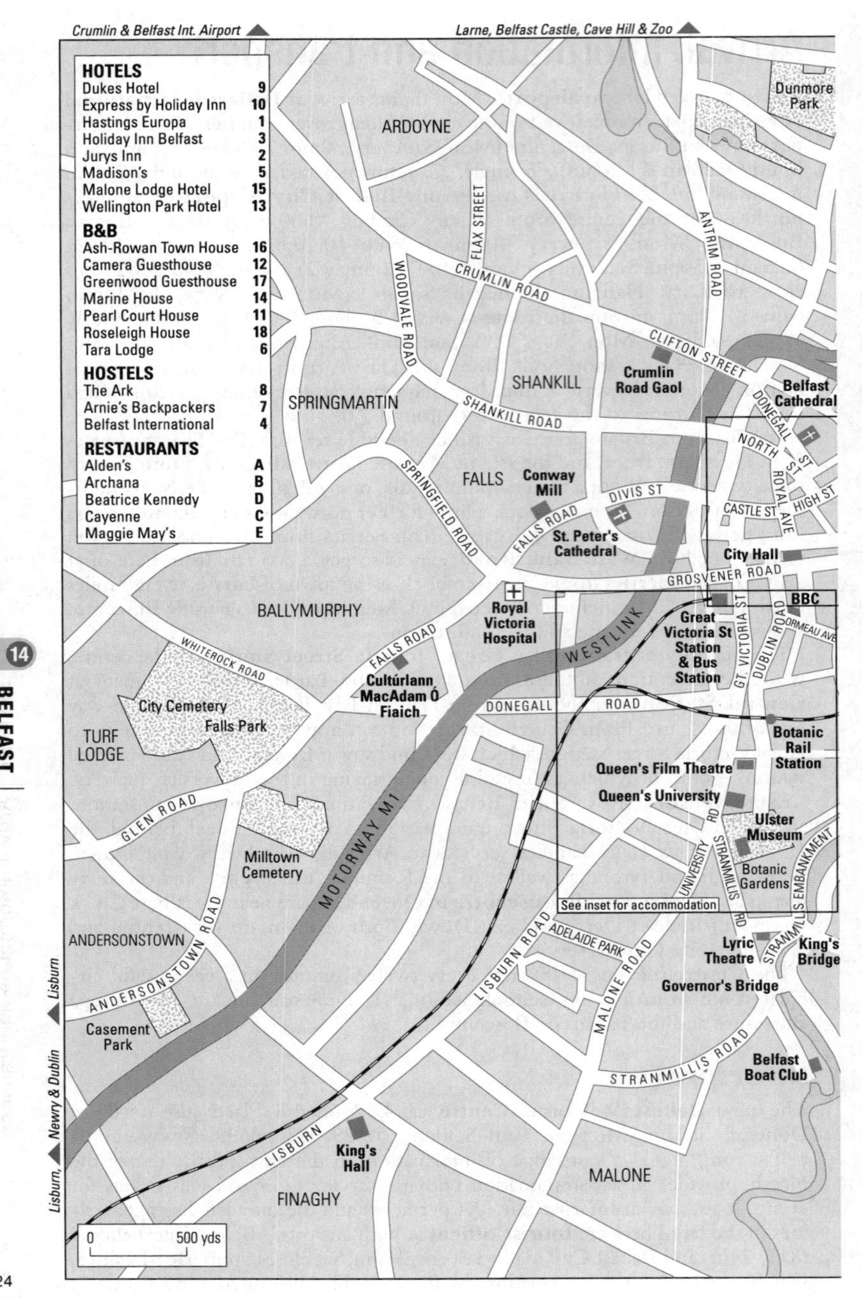

Crumlin & Belfast Int. Airport
Larne, Belfast Castle, Cave Hill & Zoo
HOTELS
Dukes Hotel 9
Express by Holiday Inn 10
Hastings Europa 1
Holiday Inn Belfast 3
Jurys Inn 2
Madison's 5
Malone Lodge Hotel 15
Wellington Park Hotel 13
B&B
Ash-Rowan Town House 16
Camera Guesthouse 12
Greenwood Guesthouse 17
Marine House 14
Pearl Court House 11
Roseleigh House 18
Tara Lodge 6
HOSTELS
The Ark 8
Arnie's Backpackers 7
Belfast International 4
RESTAURANTS
Alden's A
Archana B
Beatrice Kennedy D
Cayenne C
Maggie May's E
ARDOYNE
Dunmore Park
FLAX STREET
WOODVALE ROAD
CRUMLIN ROAD
ANTRIM ROAD
CLIFTON STREET
Crumlin Road Gaol
SHANKILL
SPRINGMARTIN
SHANKILL ROAD
Belfast Cathedral
DONEGALL ST
NORTH ST
ROYAL AVE
HIGH ST
CASTLE ST
SPRINGFIELD ROAD
FALLS
Conway Mill
DIVIS ST
FALLS ROAD
St. Peter's Cathedral
City Hall
GROSVENER ROAD
Royal Victoria Hospital
BALLYMURPHY
BBC
Great Victoria St Station & Bus Station
GT. VICTORIA ST
DUBLIN ROAD
ORMEAU AVE
WESTLINK
WHITEROCK ROAD
FALLS ROAD
Cultúrlann MacAdam Ó Fiaich
DONEGALL ROAD
City Cemetery
Falls Park
TURF LODGE
Botanic Rail Station
Queen's Film Theatre
Queen's University
GLEN ROAD
Milltown Cemetery
MOTORWAY M1
UNIVERSITY RD
STRANMILLIS RD
Ulster Museum
Botanic Gardens
EMBANKMENT
See inset for accommodation
ANDERSONSTOWN ROAD
ANDERSONSTOWN
ADELAIDE PARK
LISBURN ROAD
MALONE ROAD
Lyric Theatre
STRANMILLIS
King's Bridge
Governor's Bridge
Lisburn
Casement Park
Newry & Dublin
STRANMILLIS ROAD
Belfast Boat Club
LISBURN
King's Hall
Lisburn,
MALONE
FINAGHY
0 500 yds

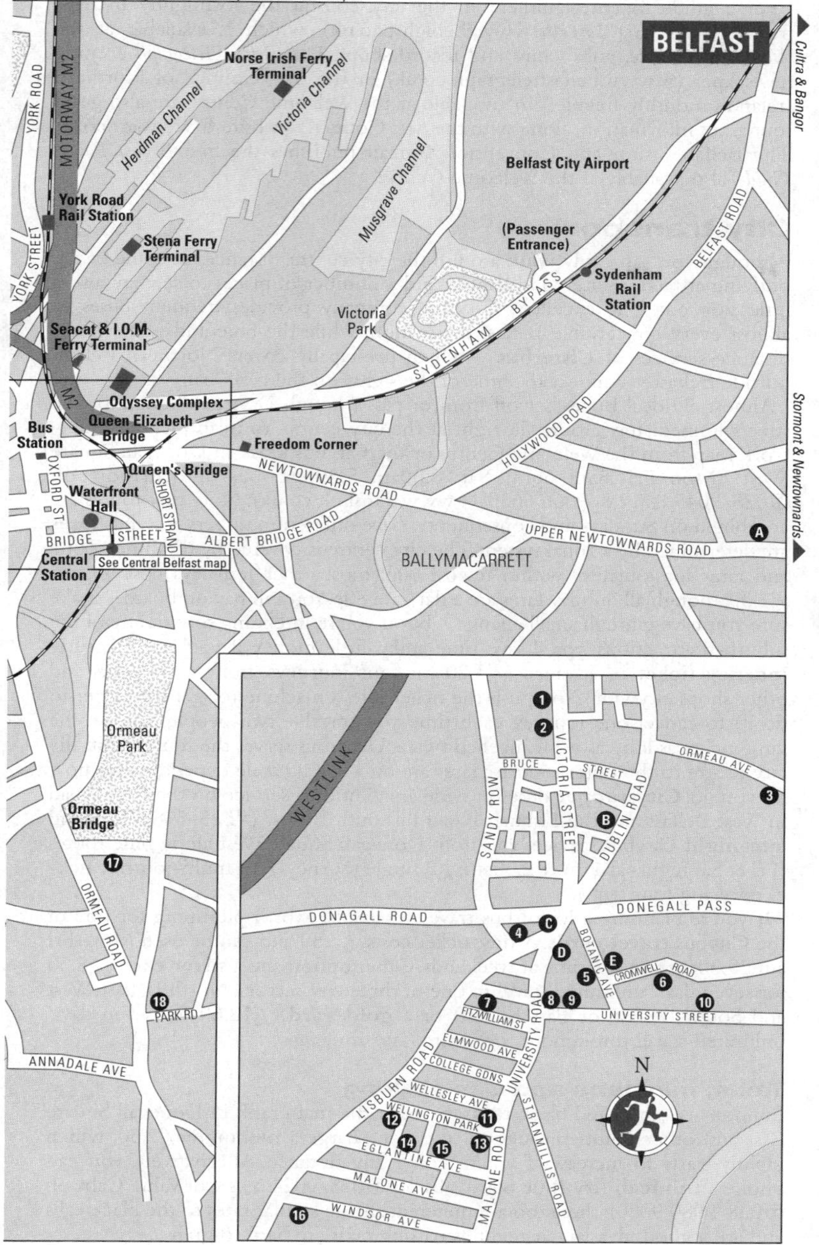
Carrickfergus, Larne, Derry & Belfast Int. Airport
BELFAST
Cultra & Bangor
Stormont & Newtownards
Norse Irish Ferry Terminal
Victoria Channel
Herdman Channel
Musgrave Channel
MOTORWAY M2
YORK ROAD
YORK STREET
York Road Rail Station
Stena Ferry Terminal
Belfast City Airport
(Passenger Entrance)
Sydenham Rail Station
BELFAST ROAD
Victoria Park
SYDENHAM BYPASS
Seacat & I.O.M. Ferry Terminal
M2
Odyssey Complex
Queen Elizabeth Bridge
Bus Station
Freedom Corner
HOLYWOOD ROAD
Queen's Bridge
NEWTOWNARDS ROAD
OXFORD ST
Waterfront Hall
SHORT STRAND
ALBERT BRIDGE ROAD
UPPER NEWTOWNARDS ROAD
BRIDGE STREET
Central Station
See Central Belfast map
BALLYMACARRETT
Ormeau Park
Ormeau Bridge
ORMEAU ROAD
PARK RD
ANNADALE AVE
WESTLINK
BRUCE STREET
SANDY ROW
VICTORIA STREET
DUBLIN ROAD
ORMEAU AVE
DONAGALL ROAD
DONEGALL PASS
BOTANIC AVE
CROMWELL ROAD
UNIVERSITY STREET
FITZWILLIAM ST
UNIVERSITY ROAD
ELMWOOD AVE
COLLEGE GDNS
LISBURN ROAD
WELLESLEY AVE
WELLINGTON PARK
EGLANTINE AVE
MALONE AVE
WINDSOR AVE
MALONE ROAD
STRANMILLIS ROAD
N

For a guide to entertainment in the city, consult the fortnightly **listings** freesheet *The Big List* (Ⓦwww.thebiglist.co.uk), which is available at the Welcome Centre, pubs, clubs and record shops. The *Belfast Telegraph* evening newspaper (Ⓦwww.belfasttelegraph.co.uk) or the Arts Council of Northern Ireland's monthly freebie, *Art*, available at the Welcome Centre, are also good sources of information, along with the Arts Council's website Ⓦwww.art.co.ni. The Belfast Visitor and Convention Bureau publishes the free *Belfast Pocket Guide*, also available at the Welcome Centre.

City transport

Although you can easily **walk** around the city centre, distances to some of the outlying attractions are considerable, and a number of places to stay are also a little way out. The excellent **Citybus** company provides frequent buses to almost every conceivable Belfast destination, while the blue and white long-distance services of **Ulsterbus** – which principally covers Northern Ireland outside Belfast – connect to some of the sights on the city's fringes.

Almost all local **buses** set off from or pass through Donegall Square or the streets immediately around it, right at the city centre. You can pick up a network map from the Welcome Centre or the Citybus kiosk in Donegall Square West (Mon–Fri 8am–6pm, Sat 8.30am–5.30pm; bus information on Ⓣ028/9045 8484 & 9066 6630, Ⓦwww.translink.co.uk). Note that routes are combined on Sundays and consequently have different numbers. Citybus **fares** are determined by a zonal system. The city centre is covered by the Inner Zone and fares for journeys within it cost 60p; most other journeys cost 90p or £1.30, though all Sunday fares are a flat-rate 80p. You can pay on board – make sure you have enough small change – but if you're intending to visit any of the suburban attractions, you'll save time and a little money if you buy a **multi-journey ticket** in advance (£3.20 for four journeys, from newsagents and other shops citywide). You push the ticket into a machine (or get the driver to do it) to cancel one journey each time you travel – two people can use the same ticket as long as it is cancelled twice. Ulsterbus serves the routes from the city centre to the outer suburbs; fares are on a sliding scale depending on how far you go. **Citystopper** buses provide an additional service on the Falls Road in West Belfast and the Lisburn Road in South Belfast (#523–538). Weekend **late-night** Citybus services run from Donegall Square West along nine routes (Fri & Sat nights at 1am & 2.30am; £3 single journey, £10 multi-journey ticket covering four trips).

If you're planning a lot of bus travel, it may be worth plumping for one of the Citybus **travel cards**. A **day** ticket costs £2.80 and can be used Mon–Fri after 9.30am and any time at weekends. Other options are a **silver card** (£8.30 for seven days' unlimited travel in one of three city sectors: North Belfast, West and South Belfast, or East Belfast) or a **gold card** (£12.60 for seven days' unlimited travel throughout the entire City zone).

Taxis, minicabs and car-parking

London-style metered black **taxis**, based at the main rank in Donegall Square East and other points throughout the city, charge a minimum £2.50, which rapidly starts to increase if you're going any distance. Alternatively, you can phone a **minicab** (try Blue Star Cabs on Ⓣ028/9024 3118, or Value Cabs on Ⓣ028/9080 9080); these too are metered, charge similar rates to the black cabs and are a good idea late at night as passing taxis are hard to grab

If you're **driving**, you need to be careful about where you **park**: there are still a few city-centre **control zones** (clearly marked with black and yellow signs), where parking is not permitted for security reasons, although these have almost all been phased out throughout the North. You'll find plenty of car parks, however, and pay-and-display parking operates in many of the streets. Following several arson attacks, if you're driving a car with **Republic of Ireland plates** you'd be strongly advised to seek secure, off-street parking at night.

Guided tours

Citybus operates a couple of **guided tours** by bus of Belfast which can save time and shoe leather; both leave from Castle Place, run from May to September, cost £9 and last for an hour and a half (call ⓣ028/9045 8484 for details). The City Tour (Mon–Sat 11am) takes in Belfast's architectural highlights, while the Living History Tour covers more recent history, including visits to both West and East Belfast (daily 2.30pm). Johnston's Bus Tours (ⓣ028/9064 2264, ⓦwww.belfastours.com) also offers a ninety-minute tour of the major sites from Castle Place (May–Sept Mon–Sat 9.30am, noon & 2.30pm; £9), while Minicoach (ⓣ028/9032 4733, ⓦwww.minicoachni.co.uk) runs minibus tours of the city departing from the Belfast International Hostel (Mon–Fri 10.30am & 2pm, Sat & Sun 10.30am; 2hr; £7.50).

West Belfast is one of the features of both **Black Taxi Tours** (ⓣ0800/052 3914 or 028/9064 2264, ⓦwww.belfasttours.com) and **Original Black Taxi Tours** (ⓣ0800/032 2003, ⓦwww.tobbtt.com), which provide ninety-minute tours of the Falls and Shankill roads (including the murals and the Peace Line), plus Milltown Cemetery, the docks and the university. Tours operate daily year round, must be pre-booked and cost from £7.50 per person.

There are a variety of **walking tours** available. The Titanic Trail (Thurs 7pm; 1hr 30min; £4) focuses on the characters of the *Titanic* era and the streets they frequented, while The Old Town 1660–1685 (Sat 2pm; 1hr 30min; £4) concentrates on the city's foundations. The City Centre Walk (Fri 2pm; 1hr 30min; £4) does exactly what is says and the Blackstaff Way (Sat 11am; 1hr; £2) explores the heart of the old city. All these tours depart from the Belfast Welcome Centre, where tickets can be purchased in advance. In addition, there's the Baileys' Historical Pub Tour (May–Sept Thurs 7pm & Sat 4pm; 2hr; ⓣ028/9268 3665; £6), which begins at *Flannigan's*, upstairs in the *Crown Liquor Saloon*, Great Victoria Street, and features six pubs. Advance tickets can be obtained at the Belfast Welcome Centre.

For something a little more strenuous, there's the Belfast city **cycling tour**, run by Irish Cycle Tours, which meets in the foyer of the *McCausland Hotel*, Victoria Street, before embarking on a two-and-a-half-hour ride around the sights (May–Sept Mon–Fri 6.30pm, Sat & Sun 10am & 2pm; ⓣ028/9064 2222, ⓦwww.irishcycletours.com; £18 individuals, £30 couples); tours are limited to six persons and bikes are provided.

Accommodation

The 1994 ceasefire resulted in a huge growth in the number of tourists visiting Belfast and, although this has waned in more recent years, the number of places offering **accommodation** has continued to increase, especially at the top end of the range. However, there's still a relative dearth of budget places and it's worth booking ahead in the summer season.

Much of the city's accommodation is concentrated south of the centre in the **university quarter** on Botanic Avenue, Eglantine Avenue and the Malone Road. Many hotels and guesthouses are geared towards business travellers and so frequently offer significant reductions for weekend breaks.

Hotels

Dukes Hotel 65–67 University St ⓣ028/9023 6666, ⓦwww.dukeshotelbelfast.com. Smart, modern redevelopment of a fine Victorian building, featuring twenty elegant bedrooms, a small gym and sauna, a fashionable bar and a restaurant serving Glenarm salmon. ❼

Express by Holiday Inn 106 University St ⓣ028/9031 1909, ⓦwww.holidayinn.Ireland.com. The smaller and slightly cheaper sister to the Ormeau Ave branch (see below) is another grand modern hotel with swish decor and many facilities. ❼

Hastings Europa Great Victoria St ⓣ028/9032 7000, ⓦwww.hastingshotels.com. Often bombed in the past, this massive city-centre hotel near the Opera House has recently been even further extended to offer new, lavish executive suites. The bar, with its huge windows overlooking the city's main drag, is a poseur's paradise. ❾

Hilton Belfast 4 Lanyon Place ⓣ028/9027 7000, ⓦwww.hilton.com. Huge and extravagant dock-land addition to the Belfast skyline with staggering views across the city and prices to match. ❽

Holiday Inn Belfast 22 Ormeau Ave ⓣ028/9027 1706, ⓦwww.holidayinn.com. The latest addition to the city's hotels is another huge modern edifice, offering air-conditioned bedrooms and a health and leisure centre. ❽

Jury's Inn Belfast Fisherwick Place, Great Victoria St ⓣ028/9053 3500, ⓦwww.jurysdoyle.com. A gargantuan, 190-bed branch of the Dublin chain, with rooms capable of taking up to three adults or two adults and two children – handily, prices are per room no matter how many stay. ❻

Madison's 59–63 Botanic Ave ⓣ028/9030 9800, ⓦwww.madisonshotel.com. A plush, economically priced hotel with spacious rooms and a popular bar/nightclub. ❻

Malone Lodge Hotel 60 Eglantine Ave ⓣ028/9038 8000, ⓦwww.malonelodgehotel.com. Welcoming, completely refurbished hotel near Queen's, with off-street parking, pleasantly decorated rooms and a notable restaurant. ❼

McCausland Hotel 34–38 Victoria St ⓣ028/9022 0200, ⓦwww.mccauslandhotel.com. Installed in elegant, long-unused buildings and ideally situated near the Albert Clock and Laganside Buscentre, the *McCausland* offers spacious and well-furnished rooms, plus an excellent restaurant and bar. ❾

Wellington Park Hotel 21 Malone Rd ⓣ028/9038 1111, ⓦwww.mooneyhotelgroup.com. Comfortable, four-star business hotel in the university area, with a bar probably best known as a cruising ground for singles. ❽

B&Bs

Ash-Rowan Town House 12 Windsor Ave ⓣ028/9066 1758, ⓦwww.eyp.co.uk/adverts/1016459. Grand guest-house off Malone Road, once home to Thomas Andrews, designer of the *Titanic*; the breakfasts are stupendous. ❻

Camera Guest House 44 Wellington Park ⓣ028/9066 0026, ⓔpauldrumm@hotmail.com. Very luxurious and elegantly decorated town house offering en-suite and standard accommodation. ❸

Greenwood Guesthouse 25 Park Rd ⓣ028/9020 2525, ⓦwww.greenwoodguesthouse.com. Adjacent to Ormeau Park, this excellent guest-house has friendly owners, well-appointed rooms and a wide choice for breakfast. ❹

The Kitchen Bar 16 Victoria Square ⓣ028/9032 4901. Cosy accommodation bang in the city centre above one of Belfast's best bars; facilities are self-catering. ❸

Marine House 30 Eglantine Ave ⓣ028/9066 2828, ⓔmarine30@utvinternet.co.uk. A large Victorian guesthouse in a quiet setting offering attractive, spacious rooms. ❸

Pearl Court House 11 Malone Rd ⓣ028/9066 6145, ⓦwww.pearlcourtguesthouse.com. Large house with spacious bedrooms, including some family and triple rooms, offering a fine breakfast. ❸

Roseleigh House 19 Rosetta Park ⓣ028/9064 4414, ⓦwww.roseleighhouse.co.uk. Deluxe accommodation in a quiet area at the bottom of the Ormeau Road. ❸

Tara Lodge 36 Cromwell Rd ⓣ028/9059 0900, ⓦwww.taralodge.com. This guesthouse off Botanic Avenue has swish decor and excellent facilities. ❹

Hostels

The Ark 18 University St ⓣ028/9032 9626, ⓦwww.arkhostel.com. Clean, cosy, well-equipped IHO hostel in a welcoming terraced house, with 36 beds, laundry and cooking facilities.

Arnie's Backpackers 63 Fitzwilliam St ⓣ028/9024 2867. Friendly IHH-affiliated hostel with 22 beds in five dorm rooms, plus laundry and cooking facilities. Closed Dec 31.

Belfast International Hostel 22–32 Donegall Rd ⓣ028/9031 5435, ⓦwww.hini.org.uk. Modern 124-bed hostel with some double rooms near the Protestant enclave of Sandy Row. There's year-round 24-hour staffing and a restaurant, but no self-catering. Booking ahead is advisable.

The Linen House Hostel 18–20 Kent St ⓣ028/9058 6400, ⓦwww.belfasthostel.com. Modern, wheelchair-friendly 130-bed IHH hostel bang in the city centre near the tourist office; also has eight private rooms and offers bike rental.

The City

The physical core of Belfast is **Donegall Square**: in its centre stands the City Hall, and buses and taxis depart for every part of the city from the sides of the square. The main shopping area lies a stone's throw north and the prime areas for entertainment and accommodation are immediately south. Most of the grand old Victorian buildings that characterize the city are in the north and east, towards the river.

Further out, **North Belfast** boasts Cave Hill, with its castle and zoo, and **South Belfast** is home to the **Golden Mile**, leading down to the university, Botanic Gardens and Ulster Museum. The River Lagan flows towards Belfast Lough along the eastern side of the city centre and offers riverside walks. The riverside is also the focus for the most radical development in the last few years, the **Laganside**. In **East Belfast**, across the river beyond the great cranes of the Harland & Wolff shipyard, lies suburbia and very little of interest apart from **Stormont**, the former Northern Irish parliament and home to the modern Assembly. Working-class **West Belfast**, by contrast, seems almost a separate city in its own right, divided from the rest by the speeding traffic of the Westlink motorway, pierced by the Catholic Falls Road and Protestant Shankill Road, and providing many insights into Belfast's turbulent political history.

The city centre

Belfast's **city centre** is fairly compact and easy to wander around. The heart of the old city can be found in the narrow atmospheric lanes of the former commercial district, the **Entries**, about five minutes' walk northeast of Donegall Square. On a grander scale, many of Belfast's most handsome buildings, evidence of the city's transformation during the Industrial Revolution, are concentrated further north and east, between **St Anne's Cathedral** and the River Lagan. Right by the river you'll find the Lagan Weir and a little further south, the huge new Laganside development, currently focused on the **Waterfront Hall**.

Donegall Square

City Hall dominates Donegall Square and the entire centre of Belfast. Completed in 1906, it's a smug-looking building of bright white Portland stone, quadrangular and squat, and with its turrets, saucer domes, scrolls and pinnacle pots is representative of all the styles absorbed by the British Empire. In front of the building stands an imposing statue of Queen Victoria, the apotheosis of imperialism, her maternal gaze unerringly cast across the rooftops towards the Protestant Shankill area. At her feet, sculpted in bronze, stand proud figures representing the city fathers' world-view: a young scholar, his mother with spinning spool and his father with mallet and boat, the three of them representing "learning, linen and liners", the alliterative bedrock of Belfast's heritage.

The City Hall offers the only opportunity to be shown around one of Belfast's many Neoclassical buildings; guided **tours** last 45 minutes (June–Sept Mon–Fri 10.30am, 11.30am & 2.30pm, Sat 2.30pm; Oct–May Mon–Sat 2.30pm; advance booking necessary on ⓣ028/9027 0456; free) and access is through a security entrance at the rear, opposite Linenhall Street. Inside, the **main dome**, with its unreachable whispering gallery, arches 173ft above you. Modelled on St Paul's Cathedral in London, the dome is adorned around its rim with zodiac signs, both painted and in stained glass windows. The marbled **entrance hall** itself is palatial, with staircase pillars, colonnades and bronze and

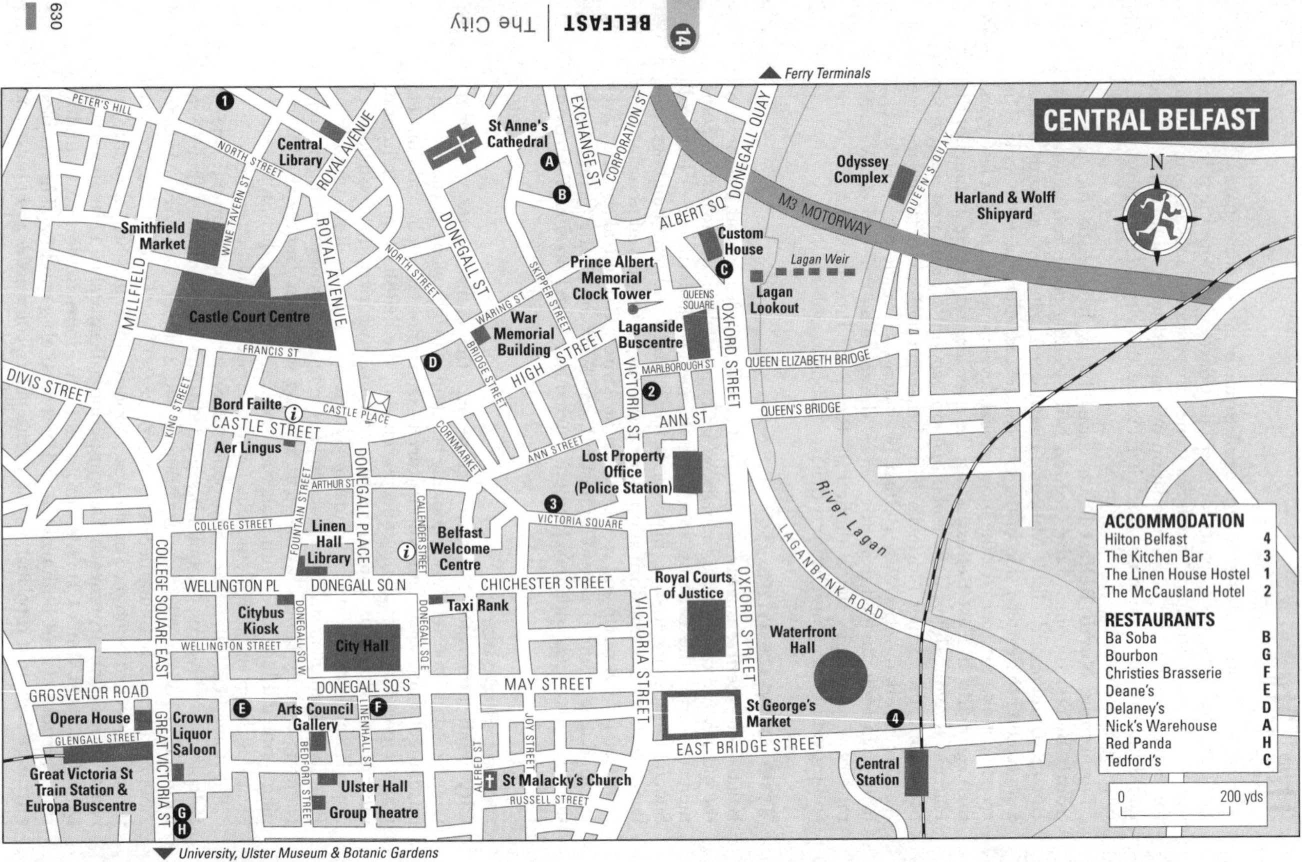
CENTRAL BELFAST
ACCOMMODATION
Hilton Belfast 4
The Kitchen Bar 3
The Linen House Hostel 1
The McCausland Hotel 2
RESTAURANTS
Ba Soba B
Bourbon G
Christies Brasserie F
Deane's E
Delaney's D
Nick's Warehouse A
Red Panda H
Tedford's C
0 200 yds
N
Ferry Terminals
Falls Road
University, Ulster Museum & Botanic Gardens
Harland & Wolff Shipyard
Odyssey Complex
M3 MOTORWAY
QUEEN'S QUAY
DONEGALL QUAY
Custom House
Lagan Weir
Lagan Lookout
River Lagan
LAGANBANK ROAD
QUEEN ELIZABETH BRIDGE
QUEEN'S BRIDGE
Waterfront Hall
Central Station
St George's Market
EAST BRIDGE STREET
OXFORD STREET
Royal Courts of Justice
VICTORIA STREET
VICTORIA ST
Lost Property Office (Police Station)
ANN ST
ANN STREET
MARLBOROUGH ST
QUEENS SQUARE
Laganside Buscentre
Prince Albert Memorial Clock Tower
ALBERT SQ
CORPORATION ST
EXCHANGE ST
St Anne's Cathedral
DONEGALL ST
SKIPPER STREET
WARING ST
War Memorial Building
HIGH STREET
BRIDGE STREET
CORNMARKET
VICTORIA SQUARE
CHICHESTER STREET
MAY STREET
JOY STREET
RUSSELL STREET
ALFRED ST
St Malacky's Church
Belfast Welcome Centre
CALLENDER STREET
Taxi Rank
DONEGALL SQ E
DONEGALL SQ N
DONEGALL SQ S
DONEGALL SQ W
City Hall
LINENHALL ST
BEDFORD STREET
Ulster Hall
Group Theatre
Arts Council Gallery
Linen Hall Library
DONEGALL PLACE
ARTHUR ST
FOUNTAIN STREET
COLLEGE STREET
WELLINGTON PL
WELLINGTON STREET
Citybus Kiosk
COLLEGE SQUARE EAST
GREAT VICTORIA ST
Crown Liquor Saloon
GROSVENOR ROAD
Opera House
GLENGALL STREET
Great Victoria St Train Station & Europa Buscentre
Aer Lingus
CASTLE STREET
CASTLE PLACE
Bord Failte
KING STREET
DIVIS STREET
FRANCIS ST
Castle Court Centre
MILLFIELD
Smithfield Market
WINE TAVERN ST
NORTH STREET
ROYAL AVENUE
Central Library
PETER'S HILL

marble statues. Two of the statues portray Frederick Robert Chichester, Earl of Belfast (1827–53): the first, upright and stern, stands on the principal landing, while the other, Frederick embraced by his mother on his deathbed, has been hauled out of the rain into the Octagon entrance porch. Also on the principal landing is a **mural**, executed in 1951 by John Luke, that celebrates Belfast's now mostly defunct traditional industries – rope-making, shipbuilding, weaving and spinning. Oddly though, the central position in the picture is occupied by the Town Crier, a cryptic reference perhaps to Belfast having the oldest continuously published newspaper in the world – *The Newsletter*, founded in 1737. The tour also takes in the **robing room**, where the trick is to ask to try on one of the civic cloaks for a snapshot. The building's highlight is the oak-decorated **council chamber** with its hand-carved wainscoting and councillors' pews as well as a visitors' gallery (open only on the first of the month). Council meetings are often stormy, but, in their absence, it's a very urbane scene with a backdrop of portraits of British royalty and aristocracy. The seating arrangement puts the majority Unionists on the far side, with the rest of the parties on the near side, while the ever-present press sit in between as a kind of firebreak.

At the northwest corner of Donegall Square stands Belfast's oldest library, the **Linen Hall Library** (Mon–Fri 9.30am–5.30pm, Sat 9.30am–4pm; Ⓦwww.linenhall.com; free), established in 1788. The library has recently been substantially revamped and is now entered via 52 Fountain St, just around the corner from the square. The library has a huge array of Irish literature, language and reference books as well its Political Collection, a unique accumulation of over 80,000 publications dealing with every aspect of Northern Irish political life since 1966, encompassing every election poster printed since then, as well as documents ranging from party political ephemera, doctoral theses sent in from all over the world, to prison letters smuggled out of Long Kesh. This radical approach is not a new departure for the Linen Hall: one of the institution's librarians was Thomas Russell, executed in Downpatrick in 1803 for inciting an uprising in sympathy with Robert Emmett's 1798 Rebellion down south. The Linen Hall is an independent institution and visitors are free to examine its collection (tours on request daily except Sat; free): there's a computerized catalogue on the first floor, use of which is free, though a donation is welcome. The library also boasts excellent facilities for tracing family trees and stocks all the daily newspapers.

Between the back of the City Hall and the BBC, on Alfred Street, look out for the turrets of the strange and wonderful Catholic **St Malachy's Church** (1844), the finest Victorian building in Belfast. The interior resembles nothing so much as an inverted wedding cake, and the fan-vaulted ceiling is modelled on that of Henry VII's chapel in London's Westminster Abbey. Other elaborate features are the canopied pulpit and carved marble altar, both dating from a 1926 restoration.

The Entries and the High Street

The streets north from Donegall Square lead you into downtown Belfast. The main shopping street, **Donegall Place**, continues into **Royal Avenue** and houses familiar chain-store names. Castle Place, off Donegall Place, was once the hub of Victorian Belfast, and the grand old department stores here, in creams, pinks and browns, have only recently been transformed into a plethora of voguish shops, though happily only the ground floors have been converted, leaving the lofty grandeur of the storeys above undisturbed. New structures, too, have risen swiftly, but they at least tend to reflect the rhythm and sheer bulk of their nineteenth-century forebears. Much of this zone is pedestrianized (though buses go through), and nearly every conceivable shopping need can be supplied in this relatively small area.

The pedestrianized **Cornmarket**, marked by a cap-hooded red bandstand, is a regular gathering place for the city's youth, though most prevalent are the religious ranters. This spot – or near enough to it – is where Henry Joy McCracken was hanged after leading the Antrim rebels in the ill-fated (and in the North almost farcically unsuccessful) 1798 Rebellion.

Nearby, along Ann Street, and off down any left or right turning, you're among the narrow alleyways known as the **Entries**. You'll stumble across some great old saloon **bars** down here, like *The Morning Star* in Pottinger's Entry, with its large frosted windows and Parisian café-like counter; *The Globe* in Joy's Entry; and *White's Tavern* in Winecellar Entry (off High Street), which dates from the seventeenth century. Crown Entry was where the Society of United Irishmen was born; it was led by the Protestant triumvirate of Wolfe Tone, McCracken and Samuel Nielson. Nielson also printed his own newspaper in this area, the *Northern Star*. Heavily influenced by the French revolutionary ideals of liberty, equality and fraternity, the newspaper's inflammatory material led to him being hounded out of town.

Across the **High Street** to the north, a similar set of Entries used to run through to Waring Street, but was destroyed by bombing in World War II. Still, this end of the High Street, with the River Farset running underground, is the oldest part of the city, its atmosphere in places redolent of the eighteenth century.

On Waring Street itself stands the **War Memorial Building**, containing a small exhibition (Mon–Fri 9am–5pm; free) commemorating the role of Northern Ireland in World War II. At the rear is the **Royal Ulster Rifles Museum** (Mon–Fri 10am–12.30pm & 2–4pm, Fri closes 3pm; £1), which features the usual array of insignia, uniforms and weaponry, as well as Billy, a rather despondent-looking regimental dog, stuffed in 1901. The currently vacant building at **2 Waring Street** was originally built as a market house in 1769, but is more renowned as the venue for the 1792 Belfast Harp Festival: by the end of the eighteenth century, the old Gaelic harping tradition had reached almost terminal decline and the convention was a deliberate attempt by its organizers, the United Irish Society, to record some of the harpers' airs for posterity. The transcriber, Edmund Bunting, was stimulated to tour Ireland collecting further airs, 77 of which were published in his illustrious collection of 1809.

St Anne's Cathedral and around

Down Waring Street, a couple of hundred yards off to the left on Donegall Street you'll find the most monolithic of all the city's grand buildings, the Protestant **St Anne's Cathedral** (Mon–Sat 10am–4pm; Ⓦ www.belfastcathedral.org; free), a Neo-Romanesque basilica started in 1899. Entrance is via the huge west door, immediately to the right of which is an intricately designed representation of the Creation on the baptistery ceiling, consisting of 150,000 tiny pieces of glass. Most significant, however, is its only tomb, marked by a simple slab on the floor of the south aisle, which contains the body of **Lord Edward Henry Carson** (1854–1935). His is a name that Ulster has never forgotten: the bodily symbol of Partition, he's seen either as the hero who saved Ulster or the villain who sabotaged the country's independence. A Dubliner of Scots-Presbyterian background, Carson took the decision in 1910 to accept the leadership of the opposition to Home Rule, which in effect inextricably allied him to the Ulster Unionist resistance movement, an association which is

△ City Hall

about the only thing for which he is remembered. Yet his personality and integrity went far deeper than this. He abhorred religious intolerance, and behind the exterior of a zealous crusader was a man who sincerely believed that Ireland couldn't prosper without Britain and only wished that a federalist answer could have involved a united Ireland. Nonetheless, this was the same man who, as a brilliant orator at the bar, and in the role he loved the most, brought about the humiliating destruction of Oscar Wilde at Wilde's trial in 1895.

As it continues north, Donegall Street becomes Clifton Street, which takes its name from **Clifton House** (built 1771–74; not open to the public). Better known as the "Poor House", or the "Charitable Institute for the Aged and Infirm", it's built in handsome Georgian style, of pedimented brick with an octagonal-based stone spire at its rear and symmetrically projecting wings to its sides. This is one of the simpler but more effective buildings that Belfast has to offer, yet was designed by an amateur architect and local paper merchant, Robert Joy, uncle of the hapless Henry Joy McCracken. The Institute was built at a time of much poverty and unrest, brought about by the Donegalls' eviction of tenants when their leases started running out – the very same Donegalls whose name is tagged to so many of Belfast's streets.

A little further along is the **Clifton Street Graveyard**, which contains the graves of Robert Joy and Mary Anne McCracken, Henry Joy's sister, along with several United Irishmen, including Dr William Drennan, reputed to have been the originator of the phrase "Emerald Isle".

Along the riverfront

At the eastern docks end of the High Street stands the **Prince Albert Memorial Clock Tower**, built in 1867–69 and tilting slightly off the perpendicular as a result of its construction upon gradually sinking wooden piles. It's a strange memorial, especially as Prince Albert never had anything to do with Belfast, but it's a handy landmark.

North of the Albert Memorial, along Victoria Street, you'll come across a series of grand edifices inspired by the same civic vanity as that behind the design of the City Hall. The restored **Custom House** on Donegall Quay is a Corinthian-style, E-shaped edifice designed between 1854 and 1857 by Charles Lanyon, who was responsible for several of the city's finest buildings. Unfortunately, it's not open to the public, leaving you unable to verify rumours of fantastic art masterpieces stored in its basements – though it is known that Anthony Trollope, the nineteenth-century novelist (and not-so-well-known inventor of the pillar box), once worked here as a surveyor's clerk.

Just beyond the Custom House on Donegall Quay is the ambitious **Laganside** development project, the first component of which to be completed was the **Lagan Weir**, designed to protect the city against flooding. Millions of pounds have been pumped into dredging the river to maintain water levels and revive the much depleted fish population – successfully it seems: there was salmon fishing on the weir's inauguration day.

You can find out more about the weir project at the **Lagan Lookout** (April–Sept Mon–Fri 11am–5pm, Sat noon–5pm, Sun 2–5pm; Oct–March Tues–Fri 11am–3.30pm, Sat 1–4.30pm, Sun 2–4.30pm; £1.50), a raised, circular visitor centre on the riverfront. It also explores the river's crucial role in the successful development of the city as a centre for industries as diverse as linen, tobacco, rope-making and shipbuilding – a glance across the river to the Harland & Wolff shipyard confirms that the last-named still survives. Windows all round the centre match Belfast landmarks to explanations of their significance, interwoven with fascinating potted histories of local characters.

In summer, **boat trips** on the Lagan (June–Sept Mon–Fri 2pm & 3pm; Ⓦwww.laganboatcompany.com; £4) leave from opposite the Laganside Buscentre just south of the Lookout – the company also operates a weekend **Titanic** tour of the harbour (same times and price). If the sea air's twitching your nostrils, head further north towards the Seacat terminal, where you'll find the restored **Harbour Office** and nearby **Sinclair Seamen's Church** (Sun services 11.30am & 7pm; visits Wed 2–5pm) on Corporation Square. The latter is yet another Lanyon design, but it's the contents that are most intriguing. Sailors must have felt truly at home among the cornucopia of maritime equipment – an old-fashioned wooden wheel, the bell from *HMS Hood*, assorted navigation lights and a ship's prow for a pulpit.

The most obvious changes to the city's skyline can be seen from almost any river viewpoint: further south along Oxford Street sits the glittering two-thousand-seater **Waterfront Hall** concert venue, a housing development and a *Hilton* hotel. The gargantuan **Odyssey** leisure complex opened on Queen's Quay across the river with much pomp in late 2000, featuring a ten-thousand-seater indoor arena, cinemas and a complex of bars, restaurants and shops. Also here is the **Whowhatwherewhenwhy** scientific discovery centre, known as **W5** (Mon–Fri 10am–6pm, Sat & Sun noon–6pm; last admission 5pm; Ⓦwww.w5online.co.uk; adults £5.50, children £3.50) with over a hundred interactive exhibits aimed primarily at children. Best of these is the See/Do section in which you can create your own animated cartoon and have a go at composing on a laser harp. From mid-July to August W5 also runs a series of special workshops for children (£2.50 each) – the subjects change annually. The Odyssey centre also boasts the **Sheridan IMAX cinema** (Ⓣ028/9045 2515, Ⓦwww.belfastimax.com for times of shows; £4.50), featuring a massive 62ft by 82ft screen, ten times larger than a normal cinema, and a 12,000-watt digital surround-sound system; current shows include the space exploration in *Blue Planet* and mountaineering in *Everest*. To get to Odyssey, cross the river via Bridge Street (opposite Ann Street) and immediately take the first street left, or catch Citybus #600 from Donegall Square East.

South Belfast

The university area occupies part of the stretch of **South Belfast** known as the **Golden Mile**, which starts at the Opera House on Great Victoria Street and continues south past the **university**, up into the Lisburn, Malone and Stranmillis roads. You're likely to spend much of your time in the area, since it's littered with eating places, pubs and bars, B&Bs and guesthouses. Near the university are the lush **Botanic Gardens**, within which sits the vast **Ulster Museum**, displaying everything from dinosaur bones to contemporary art.

The Golden Mile

Though it continues to thrive at both its city centre and university ends, much of the **Golden Mile** is now a depressing stretch of boarded-up shops and restaurants, punctuated by the odd extant business. It begins at the grandiose, turn-of-the-century **Grand Opera House**, which sits just a short distance west of Donegall Square at the northern end of Great Victoria Street (not to be confused with Victoria Street out east near the Albert Memorial).

At the northern head of the street, almost opposite the *Europa Hotel*, stands one of the greatest of Victorian gin palaces, the **Crown Liquor Saloon**. It's now a National Trust property but is still open for drinking. The saloon has a

Belfast murals

As much of a marker of an area's allegiances as painted kerbstones or fluttering flags and bunting, the politically inspired **murals** of Northern Ireland are among the most startling sights in the country, and not least in Belfast. This ephemeral art form, which recycles the images and slogans of the Troubles, characterizes the violent struggles of the last few decades. New murals are painted over old ones or the houses that they adorn are demolished; consequently, some of the slogans and murals mentioned here may have vanished by the time of your visit.

Loyalist murals

For most of the twentieth century, mural-painting in Northern Ireland was a predominantly **Loyalist** activity. The first mural appeared in East Belfast in 1908 and, like many of its successors, celebrated **King Billy**'s victory at the **Battle of the Boyne**. Loyalist murals have tended to use imagery symbolic of power, such as the clenched scarlet fist, known as the **Red Hand of Ulster**, or flags, shields and other heraldic icons. However, the Loyalist response to the Troubles translated into what is now the most common form of painting, the militaristic mural. If King Billy appears at all, it is often with a guard of balaclava-clad, weapon-toting **paramilitaries**, accompanied by a threatening slogan. Inspired by the desire for "**no surrender**" and preservation of the status quo, Loyalist mural-painting is certainly less dynamic and diverse than its Republican counterpart. A typical example, on the Shankill Road, is of two masked gunman kneeling in front of the furled flags of England and Scotland, with a bronze shield between them, the Red Hand at its centre, surrounded by the words "UVF [Ulster Volunteer Force] for God and Ulster". In a mural on the Woodstock Link in East Belfast four gunman guard the UVF badge, captioned simply with "East Belfast 1912–2000". Despite the Loyalist ceasefire there has been no diminution in the production of militaristic images, although in recent years cartoons have been added to the repertoire. One famous example, now removed, had an aggressive Spike the dog grabbing Jerry the cat by the scruff of his Glasgow Celtic football shirt (for more on sectarianism in sport, see p.649).

The greatest concentration of Loyalist murals is to be found on and around the Shankill Road, especially the Shankill Estate, to the right, and Percy Place, off Dover Street, to the left. Nearby Crumlin Road has its fair share too. Other areas are Sandy Row and Donegall Pass in South Belfast, and Newtownards Road, Martin Street and Severn Street in East Belfast.

Republican murals

Republican murals were at first limited to simple sloganeering or demarcation of territory, the best-known example being the long-standing "You are now entering Free Derry" in the Bogside (see p.690). As with much else in Republican politics, however, the 1981 **hunger strikes** had a significant influence. Murals in support of the ten hunger strikers abounded and the (usually smiling) face of **Bobby Sands** – the IRA commander in the Maze prison who led the strike – remains an enduring image. Murals soon became a fundamental part of the Republican propaganda campaign and an expression of the community's current cultural and political concerns, though militaristic images have never really dominated Republican murals as much as they have done Loyalist ones. Prominent themes have been **resistance** to British rule, the call for the **withdrawal of troops** and questioning the **validity of the police**.

More recently, however, Republican muralists have turned increasingly to **Irish legends** and history as their sources of inspiration and it now can be difficult to find militaristic images except in flashpoints such as the Ardoyne. Other main areas where you can find Republican murals are on the Falls Road or nearby streets such as Henry Street, Beechmount Avenue, Shaw's Road and Lenadoon Avenue in West Belfast, and New Lodge Road in North Belfast.

glittering tiled exterior – amber, carmine, rouge, yellow, green, blue and smoke-grey – resembling a spa baths more than a serious drinking institution. The rich, High Victorian stuccowork continues inside, too: the scrolled ceiling, patterned floor and the golden-yellow and rosy-red hues led John Betjeman to describe it as his "many coloured cavern". Once armed with drinks (and if it's not too crowded), grab a snug and shut the door. It's like sitting in a railway carriage compartment, with snatches of conversation floating over from the neighbouring snugs. There's no let-up in decoration here either, what with the painted mirrors, the oak panelling sporting flourishes of frieze-work (like the heraldic beasts guarding each snug entry) and the mounted gun-metal plates provided for striking matches. The push-button bell activates an indicator on a board above the bar, though it's just as much of an experience to order at the bar from the white-aproned and black-bow-tied staff – the bar counter is a gorgeous S-curve of tile work, with exotically carved timber dividing screens. The pub featured in the 1946 British movie, *Odd Man Out*, starring James Mason as a wanted IRA gunman, and the film was used as a model for the *Crown*'s restoration (it had suffered from the repeated bombing of the *Europa Hotel* in the 1970s).

Before heading into the university quarter, sidestep off Great Victoria Street into **Sandy Row**, which runs parallel to the west. A strong working-class Protestant quarter (with the tribal pavement painting to prove it), it's one of the most glaring examples of Belfast's divided worlds, wildly different from the Golden Mile's cosmopolitan sophistication, yet only yards away. In Blythe Street and Donegall Road, off to the west, are some of the murals that characterize these sectarian areas (see box opposite). Sandy Row used to be the main road south, and although hard to credit today, it was once a picturesque stretch of whitewashed cottages.

The university quarter

Back on the Golden Mile, just past the southern end of Sandy Row (about three-quarters of a mile south of the Opera House), stand three churches – Moravian, Crescent and Methodist – whose distinctive steeples frame the entrance into the **university quarter**. It's a highly characteristic area; many of the terraces leading up to the university buildings represent the final flowering of Georgian architecture in Belfast. The **Upper Crescent** is a magnificent curved Neoclassical terrace, built in about 1845 but sadly neglected since and now used mainly for office space. The **Lower Crescent**, perversely, is straight.

Queen's University, however, is the architectural centrepiece, flanked by the most satisfying example of a Georgian terrace in Belfast, University Square, where the red brickwork mostly remains intact, with the exception of a few bay windows added in the Victorian era. The terrace now houses various faculty buildings and the **Queen's Visitor Centre** (Mon–Fri 10am–4pm; May–Sept also Sat 10am–4pm; Ⓦ www.qub.ac.uk/vcentre; free), which has displays on the university's history and hosts occasional exhibitions. The Italianate **Union Theological College**, nearby on College Park, was temporarily the site of the Northern Ireland Parliament until Stormont was built in 1932. Both this and **University College** itself are Lanyon designs, the latter built in 1849 as a mock-Tudor remodelling of Magdalen College, Oxford. Across the road from here is the Students' Union, a white 1960s design. A little further south down University Road, the university **bookshop** is especially good for Irish history and politics and, oddly enough, for its collection of Beat poetry.

The Botanic Gardens and Ulster Museum

Just below the university are the popular **Botanic Gardens** (daily 8am–sunset; free), first opened in 1827 and well protected from the noise of the surrounding traffic. Within the gardens is the **Palm House** (Mon–Fri 10am–noon & 1–5pm, Sat & Sun 2–5pm; Oct–March closes 4pm; free), a hothouse predating the famous one at Kew Gardens in London, but very similar in style, with a white-painted framework of curvilinear ironwork and glass. It was the first of its kind in the world, another success for Lanyon, who worked in tandem on this project with the Dublin ironfounder Richard Turner. The nearby **Tropical Ravine** (same hours as the Palm House) is a classic example of Victorian light entertainment – a hundred-year-old sunken glen chock-full of "vegetable wonders" extracted from far-flung jungles and replanted for the delight of the visiting Belfast public.

Also in the Botanic Gardens, you'll find the **Ulster Museum** (Mon–Fri 10am–5pm, Sat 1–5pm, Sun 2–5pm; Ⓦ www.ulstermuseum.org.uk; free except for special exhibitions; buses #69, #70 & #71 from Donegall Square East), re-sited here in 1929 and expanded in 1972 with a concrete extension that subtly matches the original Portland stone. You'll need a fair bit of stamina to get round the museum, since it's a monster of a collection covering over two thousand square feet. Displays run from a dinosaur show through reproductions of early Irish Christian jewellery to the history of the post office in Ireland, water wheels and steam engines, local archaeological finds, Irish wildlife, rocks, fossils and minerals. The fascinating **Early Ireland** exhibition traces the development of the prehistoric population. Among the many explanatory displays you'll find the earliest remains yet discovered in Ireland (eel bones and burnt water lily seeds), some remarkable gold lunulae and a couple of polished stone axes dug up on nearby Malone Road. Interesting though this is, the museum's undoubted showpiece is the **Girona exhibition**, containing treasures from the Spanish Armada ships that foundered off the Giant's Causeway in 1588, salvaged by divers in the 1960s. In addition, the new **Habitas** gallery concentrates on biodiversity and allows computer access to issues relating to Northern Ireland's botany, geology and zoology.

The top two floors of the museum house the **art galleries** and are nowadays dedicated to temporary exhibitions featuring works from both the museum's own extensive collections of national and international artwork and from other sources. The bright and airy spaces of the topmost floor are often used for substantial and challenging exhibitions of modern art.

Further south: the Lagan Towpath and the Giant's Ring

Beyond the university area lie the glades of middle-class suburbia. From the Botanic Gardens, a ten- to fifteen-minute stroll south down Stranmillis Road (Struthán Milis, "sweet stream"), turning left into Lockview Road, will take you back to the river and to the start of the **Lagan Towpath**, where the *Cutter's Wharf* pub draws thirsty crowds for Sunday lunch and jazz. From here, follow the signs to the Lagan Meadows. The tarmacked towpath can be tramped for about eight miles south to Lisburn, passing old locks and lock-houses, rapids, woodland and marshes on the way. The waterway opened in the late 1790s, ready to carry the newly discovered coal from Lough Neagh, but its utility declined with the advent of the railway in 1839. Today, it's been harnessed as part of the Ulster Way, for rambling and canoeing enthusiasts.

Travelling south under the ring road, you'll pass by **Malone House** (Mon–Sat 10am–4.30pm; free). It's well worth climbing up the hill for the views of the surrounding area and to see the house itself, an almost pristine white bow-fronted late-Georgian mansion, built for William Wallace Legge, a prominent local merchant. The house was rebuilt by Belfast Council following a devastating fire in 1976 and is now mainly used as a conference centre, though you can visit the Higgin Gallery, which hosts regular art exhibitions, and there's a fine restaurant here, too. A little further south along the towpath, you'll find the internationally renowned **Mary Peters Track**, part of the Malone Playing Fields, which is just off the Upper Malone Road. Set in what amounts to a natural amphitheatre, with the Castlereagh Hills in the distance, the track, established by Olympic gold medallist Mary Peters, is regarded as one of the best in Europe.

Alternatively, if you leave the towpath at Shaw's Bridge (the ring-road crossing), it's a mile-long signposted walk along country lanes to the **Giant's Ring** (free access dawn to dusk), a colossal, two-hundred-yard-wide earthwork thought to be a burial ground or meeting place. You wouldn't be far wrong in thinking that its inwardly sloping wall would make an excellent speed-track circuit, for in the eighteenth century it was used for horse racing: six circuits made a two-mile race, with the punters jostling for position on the top of the rampart. Most captivating of all is the huge dolmen at the central hub of this cartwheel structure. As a single megalithic remain, it is immediately more impressive than even the great structures of the Irish High Kings at Tara, though here there's little information concerning its origins and usage. The ground chosen for the site, high above the surrounding lowlands (probably once marshy lake), is impressive – there's a powerful feeling that the great dramas and decision-making of the ancient northeast must have been played out here. To save you walking the whole way back, you can catch Ulsterbus #13 back to the city from Shaw's Bridge; it runs every half-hour or so to Laganside.

East Belfast

The Lagan Lookout near the Custom House (see p.634) is a good position from which to view the world's second- and third-largest cranes, Goliath and Samson, across the river in East Belfast's **Harland & Wolff shipyard**. This is the city's proudest international asset: the ill-fated *Titanic* was built here, and the shipyard is nowadays said to possess the largest dry dock in the world – over 600yd long and 100yd wide. Unfortunately, the area is very security-conscious, as its workforce has always been predominantly Protestant, and access is impossible without making a formal application.

East Belfast (Ⓦ www.eastbelfast.com) is trying hard to attract interest in its few attractions, though headlines have recently been dominated by sectarian clashes in the Short Strand. There are notable **murals** at **Freedom Corner** near the beginning of the Newtownards Road, and the area does have some well-known scions. The theologian and author of the *Narnia* chronicles **C.S. Lewis** was born in Dundela Villas, and there's a plaque commemorating him at Dundela Flats, which stand on the site where the house once stood, off Dundela. Another plaque on Burren Way in the Cregagh estate commemorates the childhood home of footballer **George Best**. And **Van Morrison** fans might get a thrill from seeking out his birthplace, a private house at 125 Hyndford St, off Beersbridge Road, and the many streets that feature in his songs (Cyprus Avenue, Castlereagh Road and others).

Four miles east of the centre, off the Newtownards Road, is **Stormont** (bus #16 and #17 from Donegall Square West), the home of the Northern Ireland Parliament until the introduction of direct rule in 1972, and now housing the Assembly, elected in June 1998 and due for re-election in 2003. You can't visit the house itself, but it's an impressive sight, a great white Neoclassical mansion crowning a rise in the middle of a park at the end of a magnificent long, straight drive, near whose end stands a statue of Lord Edward Carson. You can wander freely in the grounds, a popular place for a walk. Also here, though obviously not open to the public, is **Stormont Castle**, the office of the British Secretary of State for Northern Ireland.

North Belfast

North Belfast's attractions amount to no more than a castle and the city's zoo, both out on the Antrim Road and conveniently alongside one another on the slopes of Cave Hill, served by a welter of buses (#45–#51) from Donegall Square West.

Belfast Castle (daily 9am–6pm; free) and its wooded estate are open to the public. The castle was restored and refurbished in 1990 but, sadly, is virtually empty of Victorian period accoutrements, though the cellars have been redesigned in an attempt to re-create a typical Victorian Belfast narrow street and contain a bar and restaurant. It stands on the former deer park of the Third Marquis of Donegall, whose wish was for the sandstone castle to be built here to the designs of Lanyon and his associates, in 1870. Consequently, the exterior is in the familiar Scottish Baronial style, inspired in part by the reconstruction of Balmoral Castle in Aberdeenshire in 1853, with a six-storey tower, a series of crow-stepped gables and conically peak-capped turrets. The most striking feature of all, however, is the serpentine Italianate stairway that leads down from the principal reception room to the garden terrace below. Upstairs a modest **visitor centre** is best visited for a look through its remote-controlled camera on the roof.

Adjoining the castle is the Bellevue Estate, the old pleasure gardens laid out by the Belfast Street Tramway Company, but functioning since 1934 as **Belfast Zoo** (daily: April–Sept 10am–5pm; Oct–March 10am–2.30pm; Ⓦwww.belfastzoo.co.uk; adults £6, children £3, Oct–March adults £5, children £2.50), set in well-landscaped parkland stretching up towards Cave Hill. A now-completed fifteen-year renovation programme and an investment of £10 million has left the zoo looking much less like an animal prison than it once did. Within, you'll find spider monkeys, Malayan tapirs, penguins and sea lions, and a free flight aviary, where rare species have room to breed.

Castle and zoo aside, though, it's **Cave Hill** itself that should be your target in the area. Several paths lead up from the castle estate to the hill's summit – a rocky outcrop known as "Napoleon's Nose" – which affords an unsurpassable overview of the whole city and lough. From here you can't help but appreciate the accuracy of the poet Craig Raine's aerial description of the city in his *Flying to Belfast*: like "a radio set with its back ripped off". Cave Hill was once awash with Iron Age forts, for there was flint (for weapon-making) in the chalk under the basalt hill-coverings. In 1795, Wolfe Tone, Henry Joy McCracken and other leaders of the United Irishmen stood on the top of Cave Hill and pledged "never to desist in our efforts until we have subverted the authority of England over our country and asserted our Independence".

West Belfast

Like many other cities, Belfast's population expanded dramatically during the nineteenth century as people flocked from the countryside to work in the booming new flax and linen industries. Many of these migrants were crammed into jerry-built housing in the grids of streets which still today define **West**

Belfast (Ⓦwww.westbelfast-failte.com). Conditions were deplorable and did nothing to ease tensions between Catholic and Protestant residents. There were numerous sectarian riots – the worst was in 1886, during the reading of the Home Rule Bill, when 32 people died and over 370 were injured – leading to the almost inevitable creation of two separate neighbourhoods. In 1968 and 1969, this division was pushed to its limit when sectarian mobs and gunmen evicted over eight thousand families from their homes, mainly in Catholic West Belfast. The then Royal Ulster Constabulary, or RUC, called for government assistance, and British troops arrived on the streets on August 15, 1969. A month later the makeshift barrier dividing the Catholic **Falls** from the Protestant **Shankill** had become a full-scale reinforced "peace line". British intervention may have averted a civil war, but it failed to prevent an escalation in sectarian conflict. Indeed, the army soon came to be viewed as an occupying force and a legitimate target for a reviving IRA. In return, Loyalist paramilitaries sought to avenge Republican violence, often through indiscriminate acts of aggression. Over the next 25 years, West Belfast remained the major battleground of the Troubles. The busy **Westlink motorway** separates West Belfast from the rest of the city, and at the height of the conflict, the various overhead bridges and roundabouts were used by the police and army as virtual border crossings to control access to and from the area.

Today, however, West Belfast is completely safe for strangers to the city to stroll around in. There's little of architectural note among the mainly residential streets and most of the "sights" are associated with the area's troubled past. Much of the old terraced housing has been replaced in recent years by rows of modern Housing Executive homes, but it's impossible to miss examples of the partisan **mural paintings** which decorate walls and gable ends in both Catholic and Protestant areas (see box on p.636).

The Falls

Divis Street, a westward continuation of Castle Street, leads to the **Falls Road**, which continues for a further two miles west past Milltown Cemetery (see overleaf) and into Andersonstown. The first part of the Falls Road is known as the **Lower Falls** where most of the land to the left (south) consists of recently built red-brick terraced housing estates. The right-hand side of the road is more of a hotchpotch and features some of the local landmarks: the bright blue swimming baths, a recently built railing-secured shopping plaza, the DSS (the Department of Social Security, known as "the Brew" – a corruption of "bureau") cooped up in an awning of chicken-wire, a weary-looking Victorian library and a Worshippers of Peace convent. Down Conway Street (by the DSS), stands the old **Conway Mill**, revitalized by a concerted community effort, spearheaded by local activist Father Des Wilson. Inside you can buy the wares of the few small businesses that operate from here. All the way along the Falls Road you'll spot, blocking the ends of the streets to the right, walls of iron sheeting. These comprise the "**Peace Line**", and directly behind them is the Protestant working-class district of Shankill.

Further on, you'll pass the red-brick buildings of the **Royal Victoria Hospital**, at the junction with Grosvenor Road. Since the Troubles began, the Royal, as it's known locally, has received international acclaim for its ability to cope with the consequences of the violence. Just beyond it, in a disused Presbyterian church at 216 Falls Rd, is the **Cultúrlann MacAdam Ó Fiaich**, a cultural centre for Irish-speakers, housing an extensive bookshop (also selling traditional music CDs), an excellent café and a thriving theatre, often the host to musical events. The Irish language is thriving in Catholic areas of Belfast and throughout the North; the first Irish-speaking primary school is over twenty years old, and the first secondary school was opened in 1991. A year earlier, the Ultach Trust was set up, a group that aims to broaden the appeal of Irish among Unionists. Although you are unlikely to hear any Irish being spoken on the streets or in most pubs, the language has a growing presence in the city.

The **Springfield** area to the northwest is the focus for a massive new £80 million campus jointly run by the University of Ulster and the Belfast Institute, geared towards offering opportunities in further education to the local population.

Milltown Cemetery

Follow the Falls Road west for another mile and you'll come to **Milltown Cemetery**, the main Republican burial ground in Belfast, situated opposite a fortified RUC station. Enter through the stone arch and you're immediately surrounded by a numbing array of Celtic and Roman crosses. If you're in search of the Republican plots, continue directly on from the entrance for about 100yd, then veer right, heading towards a corrugated warehouse shed just outside the perimeter of the cemetery. Along the way are two plots, marked off by a low green border fence. The nearer one holds a large memorial tablet listing the Republican casualties in the various uprisings from 1798 to the present day, behind which lies an empty plot still awaiting the body of Volunteer Tom Williams, hanged in Belfast Jail in 1942. The far plot contains a modern granite-block sculpture, and also the graves of Bobby Sands, Mairéad Farrell, Seán Savage and others. Once you start to look, it's not difficult to spot the graves of many other victims of the Troubles, a devastatingly long list of (usually young) men and women.

The M1 motorway runs along the bottom of the burial park. It was onto this stretch of road in 1988 that Michael Stone (see p.622) was pursued after he'd opened fire and hurled grenades at mourners attending the funeral of Seán Savage, one of the IRA members (along with Mairéad Farrell and Danny McCann) who was killed that year by a British SAS unit in Gibraltar.

Shankill

The Protestant population of West Belfast lives in the area abutting the Falls to the north, between the **Shankill** Road and the Crumlin Road. As with the Falls, there's little here of special interest, apart from an array of Loyalist murals (some now even including Web addresses) and street names familiar from news bulletins. Along the **Crumlin Road**, in particular, are a number of evocative sites symbolizing the worst years of the Troubles. From the Westway you'll pass between the courthouse and the notorious **Crumlin Road jail**, the two connected by an underground tunnel; the jail is no longer in use, and is being developed as a new arts centre. Nearby is the bizarre sight of a completely fortified betting shop, standing in grim isolation in the centre of a patch of wasteland.

Despite many obvious signs of redevelopment and renovation – the most apparent being the new leisure centre – the area is in decline, its population shrinking in inverse proportion to the Catholic population the other side of the Peace Line. Yet Shankill (Sean Cill, "the old church") does have a rich history, though you'll have to travel almost out of town to learn more about it. A two-mile journey on bus #63 from Wellington Place will convey you to the end of Glencairn Road; a further ten-minute stroll down here will take you to **Fernhill House: The People's Museum** (daily 10am–4pm; £2), a recreated 1930s Shankill house. Here you'll find displays on the history of the Shankill district, with particular focus on the 1886 Home Rule crisis and the world wars. Fortunately, there's a café here to restore your spirits for the return trek.

Eating

By the end of the 1990s **eating out** had become one of young Belfast's favourite evening pastimes and an astonishing number of fashionable cafés and chic restaurants sprang up around the city centre. But the last couple of years has been marked by a major number of closures, and estate agents' signboards can often be seen on those businesses still operating. Other cafés and restaurants have moved to the Odyssey Complex. Unlike Dublin, where tourism constantly refuels the restaurant trade, there were simply too many places – and too many pricey places – to survive. Nevertheless, there's still a fair choice, from modern Irish and European cuisine, with French and Italian especially popular, to a smattering of Indian and Chinese restaurants. Standards are generally high and often exceptionally good value for money. The choice is limited for **vegetarians**, and there's a complete dearth of wholefood restaurants, but many more restaurants now include vegetarian dishes on their menu. Bear in mind that restaurants are often still fully booked on Friday and Saturday evenings, so you need to reserve a table unless you are prepared to eat early.

There are plenty of places for **daytime eating** in the centre and at the southern end of the Golden Mile, from new cafés to traditional pubs (many of the latter serve excellent lunches); most of the city's well-established restaurants are around Donegall Square or in the university area.

Cafés

Bewley's Donegall Arcade. Welcoming branch of the much-loved Dublin coffee house. Mon–Sat 8am–5.30pm, Thurs until 8.30pm.

Bookfinders 47 University Rd. Secondhand bookshop with a café at the back serving healthy lunches. Mon–Sat 10am–5.30pm.

Bronco's Web 122 Great Victoria St. Internet café serving paninis, sandwiches and soup. Mon–Fri 8am–10pm, Sat 10am–10pm, Sun 11am–7pm.

Café Paul Rankin 12–14 Arthur St & 27–29 Fountain St. Modernist interiors, gourmet coffees and, best of all, choice Mediterranean breads. Mon–Sat 7.30am–6pm, Thurs until 9pm.

Café Vincents 78 Botanic Ave ⓣ028/9024 2020. Known to all as *Vincents*, this place does excellent breakfasts, value-for-money high teas and plenty of pizzas. Daily 9am–11pm, Fri & Sat until midnight.

Coffee Works 11 Arthur Square, The Cornmarket. City-centre café serving everything from a full breakfast to filled ciabatta sandwiches. Mon–Sat 8am–6pm, Thurs until 9pm, Sun 1–5pm.

Conor's Cafe Bar 11a Stranmillis Rd ⓣ028/9066 4714. Opposite the Ulster Museum, this café has an interesting, affordable Mediterranean-style menu in the artist Willie Conor's former studio. Good for brunch. Daily 9.30am–11.30pm.

Equinox 32 Howard St. One of the recent bloom of café society hangouts, at the back of the Equinox interiors shop. As you'd expect, it looks good, with food to match. Mon–Sat 9.30am–4.30pm.

Queen's Espresso 17 Botanic Ave. Good coffee and all sorts of snacks, from toasted sandwiches to tasty salads. Mon–Sat 8am–5.30pm.

Revelations 27 Shaftesbury Square. Internet café with a range of coffees and sandwiches on offer. Mon–Fri 10am–10pm, Sat 10am–6pm, Sun 11am–7pm.

Restaurants

Alden's 229 Upper Newtownards Rd ⓣ028/9065 0079. This East Belfast outpost is well worth the trek for its top-quality fish and seafood menus. Mon–Sat noon–2.30pm & 6–10pm, Fri & Sat until 11pm.

Archana 53 Dublin Rd ⓣ028/9032 3713. Possibly Belfast's finest Indian restaurant, serving spicy curries and balti dishes upstairs and vegetarian meals below in its *Little India* offshoot (which has a bargain lunchtime *thali* special at £2.50). Mon–Sat noon–2pm & 5pm–midnight, Sun 5pm–midnight.

Ba Soba 38 Hill St ⓣ028/9038 6868. Belfast's first and immensely popular noodle bar, packed even at lunchtime. Mon noon–3pm, Tues–Sat noon–11pm.

Beatrice Kennedy 44 University Rd ⓣ028/9020 2290. Serves an ever-changing and innovative cosmopolitan menu at around £25 per head with an early-bird (5–7pm) two-course special for £10. Tues–Sat 5–10.30pm, Sun 12.30–2.30pm & 5–8.30pm.

Bourbon 60 Great Victoria St ⓣ028/9033 2121. Flavoursome cajun cooking brings New Orleans to

Belfast. Daily noon–3pm & 5–11pm.
Cayenne Ascot House, Shaftesbury Square ☎028/9033 1532. Founder of the acclaimed and erstwhile *Roscoff*, Paul Rankin's latest venture in the style of club-meets-bistro offers everything from oysters to the best of modern Irish cuisine, heightened by adroit use of spices. Mon–Fri noon–2.15pm & 6–11pm, Sat 6–11pm.
Christies Brasserie 7–11 Linenhall St ☎028/9031 1150. Popular French-style brasserie with an extensive menu from seafood to steaks, plus live music at weekends. Mon–Fri noon–2.30pm & 6–10.30pm, Sat 6–10.30pm.
Deane's 34–40 Howard St ☎028/9033 1134. Belfast's only Michelin-starred restaurant is an elegant venue for stunning modern Irish cuisine with a strong French influence, but expect to pay at least £25 for the pleasure. Wed–Sat 7–9.30pm, also Fri 12.15–2pm. There's also a brasserie here with a more affordable menu (Mon–Sat noon–2.30pm & 5.30–11pm, Sat opens 12.30pm).
Delaney's 19 Lombard St. Economical, wholesome food from a restaurant handily placed in the main shopping area. Mon–Sat 9am–5pm, Thurs until 9pm.
Maggie May's 45 Botanic Ave ☎028/9032 2662. Huge, economically priced portions of wholesome Irish cooking with lots of veggie choices. Be prepared to queue and bring your own wine. Daily 7.45am–11pm.
Nick's Warehouse 35 Hill St ☎028/9043 9690. Chic, pricey restaurant upstairs and an atmospheric wine bar and less expensive menu downstairs. Mon 10am–5pm, Tues–Fri 10am–10pm, Sat 6–10pm.
Red Panda 60 Great Victoria St ☎028/9080 8700 & the Odyssey Pavilion ☎028/9046 6644. Very pleasant establishments specializing in dim sum and other authentic Chinese dishes. Daily noon–3pm (Sun until 4pm) & 5–11.30pm.
Tedford's 5 Donegall Quay ☎028/9043 4000. A piscivore's paradise with fresh seafood, lobsters and king scallops; offers a theatre menu in keeping with its handiness for the Waterfront Hall. Mon–Sat noon–3pm & 5–11pm.

Drinking, nightlife and entertainment

Belfast has a myriad of excellent **pubs** concentrated in the city centre and the **club** and **music** scenes continue to thrive, although Sundays can be quiet, with many bars closing early or remaining shut all day. To tap into the pulse of the city, your best bet is to wander around the Entries or up Donegall Street, while there's plenty of action at each end of the Golden Mile. For the latest **information** on what's going on in the city, the fortnightly listings freesheet *The Big List* is essential, though the *Belfast Telegraph* also features extensive, if somewhat disorganized, listings.

Pubs and bars

As always in Ireland, the **pubs** are the heart of the city. The liveliest in the evenings are on Great Victoria Street, on and near Donegall Street and around the university, and if you start drinking at the famed *Crown Liquor Saloon* (see p.635 & below) you can manage a substantial pub crawl without moving more than a few hundred yards. In addition to the handful of places mentioned here, there are dozens of pubs around the city that double up as venues for live music of one sort or another; we've listed these separately below.

If you're short of time, you could always join the **Historical Pub Tour**, covering six of Belfast's best-known bars (see p.627).

Crown Liquor Saloon 46 Great Victoria St, opposite the *Europa Hotel*. The most famous and spectacular pub in Belfast, with a clientele that thinks itself intellectual (there's no music). Good repertoire of Ulster food – champ, colcannon and the like – and also Strangford oysters in season, which usually go by early afternoon.
Flannigan's 19 Amelia St, above the *Crown*'s side entrance. Sedate, cosy alternative to the packed bar below. Closed Sun.
Kelly's Cellars 30 Bank St. Belfast's oldest surviving continually run pub and, according to legend, a frequent meeting place for the United Irishmen behind the doomed 1798 Rebellion – Henry Joy McCracken hid under the bar counter from British soldiers. Good lunches, including

thumping portions of homemade Irish stew and steak pie.
The Monico 17 Lombard St. Tiled floors, wood panelling and snugs galore characterize this traditional pub.
Morning Star 17 Pottinger's Entry. Fine old-fashioned bar, busy in the day, quiet at night. Its upstairs restaurant is one of Belfast's best.
Morrison's 21 Bedford St. Completely revamped retro-bar, tastefully refurbished and serving value-for-money food.
Wetherspoon's 35–37 Bedford St. Undoubtedly Belfast's cheapest pint of stout and a range of economically priced meals on offer all day.
White's Tavern Winecellar Entry, High St. Atmospheric old Entries bar, offering enormously popular "pile your plate" self-service lunches.

Live music

The best Belfast entertainment is **music** in the pubs. The range on offer covers excellent traditional and folk, blues, country, jazz and indie music, and the number of visiting international performers has increased dramatically since the opening of the Waterfront Hall and Odyssey Arena. The local scene is thriving too and, despite the absence of any real music industry infrastructure, there are always good up-and-coming bands playing in the city, just waiting to get noticed. While traditional music usually comes **free** with your pint, rock venues may charge between £3 and £6 depending on the act's reputation. Pre-booked tickets for the biggest names playing in purpose-built halls will usually cost much more – between £10 and £30.

Traditional

The Hatfield 130 Ormeau Rd. Richly restored, ornate South Belfast bar with a fine Sunday night session (9pm).
The John Hewitt 53 Donegall St. Light and airy pub run by the Belfast Unemployed Resource Centre, with newspapers, paintings by local artists on sale, plus excellent traditional sessions (Mon–Wed & Sun 9.30pm, Sat 5pm) featuring musicians who used to play at the sadly defunct *Liverpool*. Also serves healthy, reasonably priced meals.
The Kitchen Bar 16 Victoria Square. A long, narrow bar and one of the city's finest pubs, featuring superb-value lunches and a brilliant Sunday evening session.
Madden's Berry St. Wonderful, unpretentious, atmospheric pub, with lots of locals drinking in two large rooms, one upstairs, one downstairs. Serves cheap stew and soup and there are excellent traditional sessions (Fri & Sat 9.30pm).
Pat's Bar 19–22 Prince's Dock St. Located in the north of the city by the docks, off York Rd, and most easily reached by taxi, *Pat's Bar* was recently renovated in traditional style, with a choice of two bars (one large, one small) and open fires. Sessions Wed 9pm.

Rock, indie, blues and jazz

Aunt Annie's Porterhouse Dublin Rd ⓣ028/9050 1660. Large drinking emporium with music on two floors most nights (singer-songwriters downstairs; rock, indie and DJs upstairs).
Cutters Wharf Stranmillis Embankment. Excellent Laganside pub with a regular jazz session on Sunday afternoons.
The Duke of York 11 Commercial Court, off Donegall St ⓣ028/9024 1062. Live music most nights, with a traditional session on Thursdays.
The Empire Bar & Music Hall 42 Botanic Ave. Cellar bar in a former church just up from the station, with a boisterous beer-hall atmosphere. Good-value food and bands (Thurs, Fri & Sun) and a "pre-club strut" (Sat), plus a traditional session on Wednesday.
The Errigle Inn 320 Ormeau Rd. A little way out, but serves great-value food, if you're in the area, especially its all-day Sunday lunch. Features occasional and splendid blues and rock gigs run by The Real Music Club (ⓦwww.realmusicclub.com).
The Front Page 106 Donegall St. Packed with journalists from the nearby *Belfast Telegraph* and *Irish News* during the day; there's live music featuring local bands (Mon, Wed, Fri & Sat).
The Hercules 61 Castle St. Fine city-centre bar with food at lunchtime and regular traditional jazz bands (Fri & Sat).
Katy Daly's 17 Ormeau Ave. Cavernous and popular bar-cum-club featuring singer-songwriters or acoustic rock (Tues & Sat), local bands (Wed) and an innovative experimental music club night (Sat).
King's Hall Balmoral Showgrounds ⓣ028/9066 5225, ⓦwww.kingshall.co.uk. The city's main stage for the biggest, though increasingly occasional pop and rock concerts.
McHugh's 29–31 Queen's Square. Belfast's oldest

surviving building features live rock, blues and indie bands (Wed–Sat).

The Menagerie 103 University St. Near the Ormeau Rd, this retro-kitsch bar, run by escapees from the *Rotterdam*, hosts gigs by some of the North's most innovative up-and-coming bands and musicians plus a variety of DJs and music.

Mercury Bar & Grill 451 Ormeau Rd. Hosts a popular Sunday afternoon live jazz band, plus traditional music the same evening, alongside live bands (Wed & Thurs) and DJs (Fri & Sat).

The Odyssey Arena 2 Queen's Quay ⓣ028/9076 6000, ⓦwww.odysseyarena.com. Rapidly supplanting other venues as the place for the biggest rock and pop singers and bands to play.

Robinson's 38 Great Victoria St. Theme bar spread over four floors and overshadowed by the *Crown* next door. Packed at lunchtimes with local workers taking advantage of the cheap menus. Live music (5–7pm most nights), plus a traditional session on Sundays (9.30pm) and DJs upstairs (Fri–Sun 9pm–midnight).

Rotterdam Bar 54 Pilot St ⓣ028/9074 6021. A dockland institution, with bands most nights, leaning towards blues, rock and new country, and a traditional session on Thursdays.

Clubs and DJ bars

Belfast's **club scene** is buzzing – dance culture is big, so are celebrity DJs – and there are plenty of pre-club **DJ bars** around, too. Check *The Big List* for who's on when; you'll find most venues run different clubs on different nights. Venues are scattered fairly evenly around the city centre; students – not surprisingly – tend to dominate those closest to the university area. Admission may be free early in the week and as low as £1 or £2 up to Thursday nights, while weekend prices are usually around £5 to £7.

Apartment 2 Donegall Square. Describing itself as "urban living made easy", this swish, newly renovated bar is rapidly usurping the *Europa* and *Fly* as the place for bright young Belfast to be seen; DJs most nights.

Bar Red 1 Linenhall St. Popular DJ bar in the centre with a live jazz session on Fridays (5–7.30pm).

Basement Bar & Grill 16 Donegall Sq East ⓣ028/9033 1925. DJs Fri & Sat with an emphasis on current chart hits.

Benedicts Hotel Bradbury Place ⓣ028/9059 1999. Bands and/or DJs nightly; strict dress code – no sportswear – and over-21s only.

The Botanic Inn 23 Malone Rd. Perhaps inevitably known as the "Bot", this place caters almost entirely to students and has plenty of atmosphere. There are DJs Wed–Sun from 9pm until late, playing mainly chart-oriented dance music.

Culpa 1 Bankmore Square, Dublin Rd ⓣ028/9023 3555. Nightly mayhem at a club whose dress code is "sinfully deadly at all times". Mon–Thurs 9pm–1am, Fri 9pm–2am, Sat 9pm–3am, Sun 9pm–midnight.

Dempsey's Terrace 45 Dublin Rd. Popular hang-out for the younger set, with DJs most nights and even on Friday afternoon. Tues–Sat 9pm–2am.

East 2–14 East Bridge St ⓣ028/9024 0055, ⓦwww.east-online.co.uk. Highly rated, European-flavoured bar serving meals from noon onwards and hosting great club nights (10pm–late), including R&B (Fri) and commercial dance (Sat).

The Edge May's Meadow, Laganbank Rd. Recent waterside development off East Bridge Street near Central Station, featuring a grand, if rather pricey, à la carte menu and DJs at weekends.

The Eglantine Inn 32 Malone Rd. Located opposite the "Bot" (see above), this place is known to the students who pack it out as the "Eg". Very crowded, with DJs most of the week and a regular Tuesday night quiz.

The Fly Bar 5–6 Lower Crescent ⓣ028/9023 5666. Intensely hip three-storey venue, which was undergoing renovation at the time of writing and was due to reopen in 2002.

La Lea 43 Franklin St ⓣ028/9023 5942. Claiming to be the city's "most prestigious nightclub" and with entry prices to match, the key night to be seen is Sunday's R&B club, often featuring major international DJs. Weds–Sun 9pm–2am.

Lavery's Gin Palace 14 Bradbury Place. Snazzy outside but a regular pub within. The Back Bar has DJs virtually every night while the Top Bar has Club Heaven for dancers (Sat).

The Limelight 17 Ormeau Ave. A serious dance club with various club nights, including Shag for students (Tues), Planet Earth for Eighties sound (Thurs), Disco-a-Go-Go (Fri) and the mixed indie-dance club Helter Skelter (Sat). 10pm–2am.

Madison's 59–63 Botanic Ave ⓣ028/9050 9800. Be seen, but wear the right threads at this thirty-somethings' hotel bar and nightclub, the latter featuring DJs in Club 33 (Fri–Sun until 2.30am).

M Club The Manhattan, 23 Bradbury Place

Gay and lesbian Belfast

The **gay scene** in Belfast is small, and there's much travel back and forth to Dublin. The main resource is Queerspace, part of Cara-Friend, Cathedral Buildings, Donegall St (Ⓦwww.queerspace.org.uk), a collective aiming to serve the needs and raise the profile of the gay, lesbian, bisexual and transgendered community of Belfast and Northern Ireland; Queerspace holds a weekly drop-in session on Saturday afternoons (3–6pm). **Helplines** include Cara-Friend (Ⓣ028/9032 2023; Mon–Wed 7.30–10pm) and Lesbian Line (Ⓣ028/9023 6668; Thurs 7.30–10pm). Belfast's **Gay Pride** week begins on the last Saturday in July.

For details of the gay nightlife scene, check Ⓦwww.glyni.org.uk. While there are a few gay-friendly **bars**, such as the *John Hewitt* (see p.645), current **venues** and regular **events** catering specifically for the gay community include:

The Custom House 22 Skipper St Ⓣ028/9024 5558. Formerly *The Crow's Nest*, this place offers a range of entertainment throughout the week and is a popular pre-club spot; Belfast's sole women-only disco takes place here once a month (phone Lesbian Line for details).

Forbidden Fruit At the *Milk Bar Club* (see below). A long-standing, regular Monday night bash (9.30pm–2.30am), featuring plenty of on-stage entertainment, including drag acts.

Howl At *Orpheus & the Underworld* (see below). Takes place the first Friday of each month and features a mixed bag of funk, indie, hip-hop and rock music.

Kremlin 96 Donegall St Ⓣ028/9080 9700, Ⓦwww. kremlin-belfast.com. Voted Ireland's best gay venue in 2001, the *Kremlin* is firmly focused on dancing till you drop – popular nights include Thursday's Metrosexuality and Sunday's Ball Busting Bingo. Daily 7.30pm–3am; happy hour 7.30–9.30pm.

The Parliament Bar 2 Dunbar St Ⓣ028/9023 4520, Ⓦwww.theparliament.co.uk. Belfast's longest-established gay bar has events on three floors, including karaoke early Friday and Saturday evening, plus DJs at the weekend and the frenetic Club Heat on Saturday nights.

Slosh At *White's Tavern* (see p.645). Every Wednesday 9.30pm–2am, a gay club night featuring a mix of chart hits and dance music.

Ⓣ028/9023 3131. Different themes (Mon & Thurs–Sat 9pm–2am), such as the Groovy Train 70s retro night on Fridays, flares essential.

Milk Bar Club Tomb St Ⓣ028/9027 8876, Ⓦwww.clubmilk.com. Ever-popular and ever-packed club offering dance music to suit all tastes every night of the week (9pm–2.30am).

Northern Whig 2–10 Bridge St. Massive new bar in the premises of the old newspaper, featuring pre-club DJs every night except Wed.

Orpheus & the Underworld University St Ⓣ028/9020 5005. Hugely popular bar-club with students, thanks to its low prices, and Tuesday night retro club; more DJs and live acts on Fri & Sat.

Shine Mandela Hall, Queen's Student Union Ⓣ0870/241 0216, Ⓦwww.shine.net. Saturday student bash featuring differently themed nights (£10); also live local bands on Fri (free). Student ID required.

Thompson's Garage 3 Pattersons Place, Arthur St Ⓣ028/9032 3762. Once a garage owned by aviation freak Harry Ferguson – an addiction commemorated with a mural of an aeroplane in mid-flight – this place now hosts a variety of club nights featuring R&B, house, garage and Old Skool classics, the US house night on Saturdays being the big draw. Thurs–Sat 9pm–3am.

Classical music and opera

Classical music concerts are thin on the ground and almost all take place in the Ulster Hall or Waterfront Hall. **Opera** fans are catered for at the Grand Opera House. Tickets for the Ulster Orchestra's performances at the Waterfront and Ulster Halls are available from Elmwood Hall, Queen's University Belfast, 89 University Rd (Ⓣ028/9066 8798).

Grand Opera House Great Victoria St ⓣ028/9024 1919, ⓦwww.goh.co.uk. Belfast's most prestigious venue, featuring regular operatic performances as well as many of London's West End productions.

Ulster Hall Bedford St ⓣ028/9032 3900, ⓦwww.ulsterhall.co.uk. Most of the city's classical music performances are given by the Ulster Orchestra; the hall is also used for big rock and pop concerts.

Waterfront Hall Lanyon Place, Laganside ⓣ028/9033 4455, ⓦwww.waterfront.co.uk. Hosts classical music and ballet, mainstream jazz and occasional big names from the moribund world of middle-of-the-road pop and rock.

Whitla Hall Queen's University ⓣ028/9024 5133. Stages some professional and amateur classical concerts.

Theatre, cinema and art

Most of Belfast's **theatres** and **cinemas** are concentrated in the south of the city. Although the choice for both is relatively limited, there is enough of a range to please most tastes. Recently, the city has seen a rapid expansion in the number of **art galleries**, and there's now an interesting selection to choose from, showing the best of modern and contemporary Irish art.

Theatres and arts centres

Crescent Arts Centre 2–4 University Rd ⓣ028/9024 2338, ⓦwww.crescentarts.org. A focus for much of Belfast's leftfield arts and performance activities and home to the Fenderesky Gallery (see below).

Group Theatre Bedford St ⓣ028/9032 3900. Tends to be used mainly by local drama companies, with varying degrees of success.

Lyric Theatre 55 Ridgeway St, Stranmillis ⓣ028/9038 1081, ⓦwww.lyrictheatre.co.uk. Stages more serious contemporary drama, and gave actor Liam Neeson an early platform.

Old Museum Arts Centre 7 College Square North ⓣ028/9023 5053, ⓦwww.oldmuseumartscentre.org. The place to go for experimental or fringe productions; also hosts regular art exhibitions.

Cinemas

Mainstream **cinemas** showing the usual general-release movies include the monster ten-screen UGC on Dublin Rd (ⓣ0870/155 5176), Belfast Cineplex in the Kennedy Centre, Falls Rd (ⓣ028/9060 0988), the Movie House, Yorkgate on York St (ⓣ028/9075 5000), and the Warner Village in the Odyssey complex (ⓣ0870/240 6020). Alternatively, Queen's Film Theatre, 7 University Square Mews off Botanic Ave (ⓣ0800/328 2811, ⓦwww.qub.ac.uk/qft), has two screens showing arthouse movies and late-night shows at exceptionally good prices.

Art galleries

Arts Council Sculpture Park 180 Stranmillis Rd ⓣ028/9038 1591. Alfresco exhibition of works by local contemporary sculptors.

Eakin Gallery 237 Lisburn Rd ⓣ028/9066 8522. A family-run terraced house gallery, which highlights Belfast's star painters.

Fenderesky Gallery Crescent Arts Centre, University Rd ⓣ028/9024 2338. Presents important Irish moderns – Barrie Cooke, Patrick Hall, Felim Egan – and the Ireland-based Mexican printmaker Alfonso Monreal.

Ormeau Baths Gallery Ormeau Ave ⓣ028/9032 1402. Set in what was once a public baths, this is the hippest venue on the arts scene, with four exhibition spaces spread over two floors. Hosts exhibitions of contemporary Irish and international artists' work.

Ulster Museum Stranmillis Rd ⓣ028/9038 3000, ⓦwww.ulstermuseum.org.uk. Has a wide-ranging collection of international and national art, but increasingly allocates space to temporary, yet ever-absorbing, exhibitions.

Waterfront Hall Lanyon Place, Laganside ⓣ028/9033 4455, ⓦwww.waterfront.co.uk. Regularly mounts shows for viewing while you wait for the main performance to commence.

Spectator sports

Though watching, discussing and betting on **sport** is as much of a pastime in Belfast as anywhere else, you'll find very few locals expressing particularly passionate opinions about the city's teams and players, with the notable exception of boxing. Indeed, when people watch sport here, it's usually the televised variety, and attendances for most events are relatively small, an indifference that applies equally to the North's national teams. Nevertheless, if you're interested in attending a match of whatever kind, there are plenty of opportunities, and the *Belfast Telegraph* usually has the details.

The Northern Ireland **football** (soccer) team has not seen anything approaching glory since its astonishing performance at the 1982 World Cup finals in Spain when it defeated the home country 1–0 in Valencia. Sadly, the superb George Best, from the Cregagh Estate in East Belfast, who was the toast of Manchester United in the 1960s, never graced such a stage. Internationals are played at **Windsor Park** (the home ground of the **Linfield** club) near the Lisburn Road (bus #58 and #59 to Lower Windsor Ave). The biggest club sides in Belfast – paradoxically enough – are Glasgow's Celtic and Rangers, supported respectively by Catholics and Protestants, as well as Liverpool and Manchester United; the city's pubs are packed out for major televised games. If you'd like to see the local teams in action, bear in mind that Irish League football is a major sectarian bastion, despite efforts to reduce bigotry – the Northern Ireland captain, Neil Lennon, who committed the crime of playing for Glasgow Celtic, was forced to retire from international football in 2002 after receiving a death threat. The last regularly successful Catholic side, Belfast Celtic, resigned from the league in the late 1940s after players were assaulted on the pitch, the result of one fulfilled threat too many. More recently, the police refused to allow local amateur side Donegal Celtic to play a cup match against Linfield (whose supporters are known as the Billy Boys) on their own ground for fear of sectarian violence. Other Belfast league clubs and their grounds are **Crusaders** (Seaview, off Shore Rd; bus #7–#11), **Glentoran** (The Oval, Redcliffe Parade; bus #16, #20–#22, #24 down the Newtownards Rd to Dee St) and the Catholic-supported **Cliftonville** (Solitude, Cliftonville Rd; bus #35).

Since football is the Belfast sport, success at both **hurling** and **Gaelic football** has been lacking, and County Antrim (which in this case includes Belfast for sporting purposes) has never won either All-Ireland Senior Final. Nevertheless, hurling is undergoing something of a revival, with the county winning the All-Ireland Junior championship for the first time in 2002. You can see both sports most weekends at Roger Casement Park, on Andersonstown Road (bus #14, #15 & #90), where the Ulster Hurling Final is held in July.

Belfast's **rugby** hero was Mike Gibson, capped 69 times for Ireland, and top-class games are played by the Malone club at the park named after him off Woodstock Road (bus #33 & #34) and by Collegians at Deramore Park, Malone Road (bus #70 & #71). Major **athletics** meetings take place at the Mary Peters Track (see p.639), and in early May the streets are cleared for the Belfast **Marathon**. For many, Belfast's **boxing** success will always evoke 1980s memories of Barry McGuigan (actually born in Monaghan); big fights take place at the King's Hall, Upper Lisburn Road.

Listings

Airlines Aer Lingus, 46 Castle St ⓣ0845/973 7747; British European ⓣ0870/567 6676; British Midland ⓣ028/9024 1188; easyJet ⓣ0870/600 0000; Gill Airways ⓣ0191/214 6666.
Airports Belfast City ⓣ028/9093 9093, ⓦwww.belfastcityairport.com; Belfast International ⓣ028/9448 4848, ⓦwww.belfastairport.com.
Banks Most of the major UK banks are allied to the following Northern Irish ones, all of which have city-centre branches: Bank of Ireland, 54 Donegall Place ⓣ028/9023 4334; Northern Bank, 8 Donegall Square North ⓣ028/9032 7477; Ulster Bank, 47 Donegall Place ⓣ028/9024 4112. Their ATMs accept a wide range of debit and credit cards.
Bike rental Bike-It, 4 Belmont Rd ⓣ028/9047 1141; McConvey Cycles, 182 Ormeau Rd ⓣ028/9033 0322.
Books Bookfinders at 47 University Rd has secondhand books; there's also the University Bookshop on University Rd, Waterstones on Royal Ave and Fountain St, and branches of Eason's on Ann St, Botanic Ave and in the Castlecourt Centre, Royal Ave. No Alibi, 83 Botanic Ave, specializes in crime books.
Buses For all enquiries call Translink (ⓣ028/9066 6630, ⓦwww.translink.co.uk).
Car rental Avis, 69–71 Great Victoria St ⓣ028/9024 0404 & Belfast City Airport ⓣ028/9045 2017. There are many other big names at the airports and local firms such as McCausland Car Hire (ⓣ028/9033 3777), which also has a city-centre depot at 21–31 Grosvenor Rd, plus Holmes Motors, 2–20 Beersbridge Rd (ⓣ028/9045 1850).
Exchange As well as banks try Thomas Cook, 11 Donegall Place (ⓣ028/9055 0030), the Belfast Welcome Centre, 47 Donegall Place (ⓣ028/9024 6609), and the post offices at Castle Place, Donegall Square and Shaftesbury Square.
Ferries Norse Merchant Ferries, West Bank Rd ⓣ0870/600 4321; P&O, Larne Harbour ⓣ0870/242 4777; Seacat, Donegall Quay ⓣ0870/552 3523; Stena Line, Corry Rd ⓣ0870/570 7070.
Festivals The Belfast International Festival at Queen's University (ⓦwww.belfastfestival.com), which lasts for two to three weeks from late October to November, claims to be Britain's second-biggest arts festival after Edinburgh. Others are the Between the Lines – Belfast Literary Festival in mid-March (ⓣ028/9024 2338); the Cathedral Quarter Arts Festival for ten days in early May (ⓦwww.cqaf.com); the Ulster Drama Festival at the Lyric Theatre for a week in mid-May; the Greater Shankill Community Festival for two weeks in late June (ⓣ028/9031 1333); Orange Parades on July 12 (and marching season from Easter onwards); the Belfast Film Festival in late September; and the Royal Ulster Academy Annual Exhibition at the Ulster Museum for three weeks in October. In addition, early August sees the West Belfast Féile An Phobail (ⓦwww.feile-belfast.com), a week-long music and dance festival, which was originally a Republican event but increasingly includes Unionist voices.
Hospitals In an emergency, call ⓣ999. Belfast City Hospital, Lisburn Rd ⓣ028/9032 9241; Royal Victoria Hospital, Grosvenor Rd ⓣ028/9024 0503.
Internet access Belfast Welcome Centre, 47 Donegall Place (Mon–Sat 9am–5.30pm); Bronco's Web, 122 Great Victoria St (Mon–Sat 7.30am–10pm); the Linen Hall Library, Donegall Square (Mon–Fri 9.30am–5.30pm, Thurs until 8.30pm, Sat 9.30am–4pm); Revelations, 27 Shaftesbury Square (Mon–Fri 10am–10pm, Sat 10am–6pm, Sun 11am–7pm). Internet booths are also available at some hostels.
Laundry Globe, 37–39 Botanic Ave ⓣ028/9024 3956.
Left luggage Belfast Welcome Centre, 47 Donegall Place.
Libraries Central Library, Royal Ave (Mon–Fri 9.30am–5.30pm, Mon & Thurs until 8pm, Sat 9.30am–1pm).
Lost property Musgrave police station, Ann St ⓣ028/9065 0222.
Markets The huge St George's Casual Retail Market (also known as the Variety Market) in May St (Tues & Fri mornings) is the liveliest: the Friday food and variety market is by far the more popular, with about 200 traders taking part; on Tuesday it's more of a fleamarket-type affair, selling new and secondhand clothes and a variety of junk. The Smithfield Retail Market, at the back of the Castlecourt development on West St/Winetavern St, is also pretty good; it operates from about thirty shop units and sells new and secondhand goods and clothes.
Motoring organizations 24-hour breakdown services for members: AA ⓣ0800/887766; RAC ⓣ0800/828282.
Newspapers Two daily newspapers for all of Northern Ireland are published in Belfast: the Nationalist *Irish News* and the Unionist *News Letter*. The city's local daily paper, the *Belfast*

Telegraph, has adopted an increasingly liberal, pro-Agreement stance in recent years.
Police In an emergency, call ⓣ999. The main city-centre police station is in North Queen St.
Post office General Post Office, Castle Place (Mon–Sat 9am–5.30pm).
Shopping hours Mon–Sat 9.30am–5.30pm. Many city-centre stores stay open until 8pm or 9pm on Thursdays and an increasing number open on Sundays (1–5pm).
Trains For information, call Central Station on ⓣ028/9089 9411.
Travel agents Thomas Cook, 11 Donegall Place ⓣ028/9088 3900; USITNow, 13B Fountain Centre, College St ⓣ028/9032 4073.

Travel details

Trains

Belfast to: Antrim (4–11 daily; 30–55min); Ballymena (4–10 daily; 50min–1hr 20min); Bangor (12–36 daily; 35min); Carrickfergus (7–37 daily; 25min); Coleraine (4–10 daily; 1hr 15min–2hr); Derry (4–8 daily; 2hr 05min); Drogheda (4–7 daily; 1hr 30min); Dublin (5–8 daily; 1hr 45min); Dundalk (4–7 daily; 1hr 10min); Larne Harbour (5–14 daily; 55min); Larne town (6–21 daily; 50min); Lisburn (11–38 daily; 10–20min); Newry (4–9 daily; 50min); Portrush (1–2 daily; 2hr 10min); Whitehead (7–30 daily; 35min).

Buses

Only details of direct services from Belfast are listed. Call **Ulsterbus** on ⓣ028/9033 3000 to get details of bus connections to places not given here. The **Antrim Coaster** service runs from Belfast to Coleraine via Larne, the Glens of Antrim and Ballycastle; see p.700 for full details.
Belfast (Bridge St) to: Carrickfergus (8–37 daily; 30min); Whitehead (4–12 daily; 45min).
Belfast (Europa) to: Armagh (4–13 daily; 50min–1hr 25min); Athlone (Mon–Sat 1 daily; 4hr 50min); Banbridge (9–31 daily; 1hr 05min); Cavan (1 daily; 2hr 40min); Derry (6–15 daily; 1hr 40min); Downpatrick (5–26 daily; 1hr); Dublin (6–7 daily; 2hr 50min); Dublin Airport (6–7 daily; 2hr 35min); Dungannon (7–16 daily; 50min); Dungiven (6–19 daily; 1hr 10min); Enniskillen (4–10 daily; 2hr 15min); Hillsborough (10–34 daily; 45min); Monaghan (1–4 daily; 1hr 45min); Newcastle (11–15 daily; 1hr 20min); Newry (4–6 daily; 1hr 20min); Omagh (6–10 daily; 1hr 30min–1hr 45min).
Belfast (Laganside) to: Antrim (10–40 daily; 35–50min); Ballycastle (3–4 Mon–Sat; 1hr 30min); Ballymena (5–22 daily; 1hr–1hr 20min); Bangor (8–31 daily; 45min); Carrickfergus (8–24 daily; 35min); Coleraine (5–7 daily; 1 hr 45min); Comber (7–22 daily; 30min); Cookstown (1–4 daily; 1hr 40min); Donaghadee (9–22 daily; 1hr); Holywood (8–34 daily; 25min); Killyleagh (1–8 daily; 1hr); Larne (2–13 daily; 55min–1hr 25min); Magherafelt (1–5 daily; 1hr 10min); Newtownards (12–60 daily; 40min); Portaferry (4–14 daily; 1hr 30min); Portrush (4–6 daily; 2hr 05min); Portstewart (4–6 daily; 1hr 55min); Whitehead (4–10 daily; 50min).
Belfast (Upper Queen St) to: Lisburn (28–43 daily; 25min).

Antrim and Derry

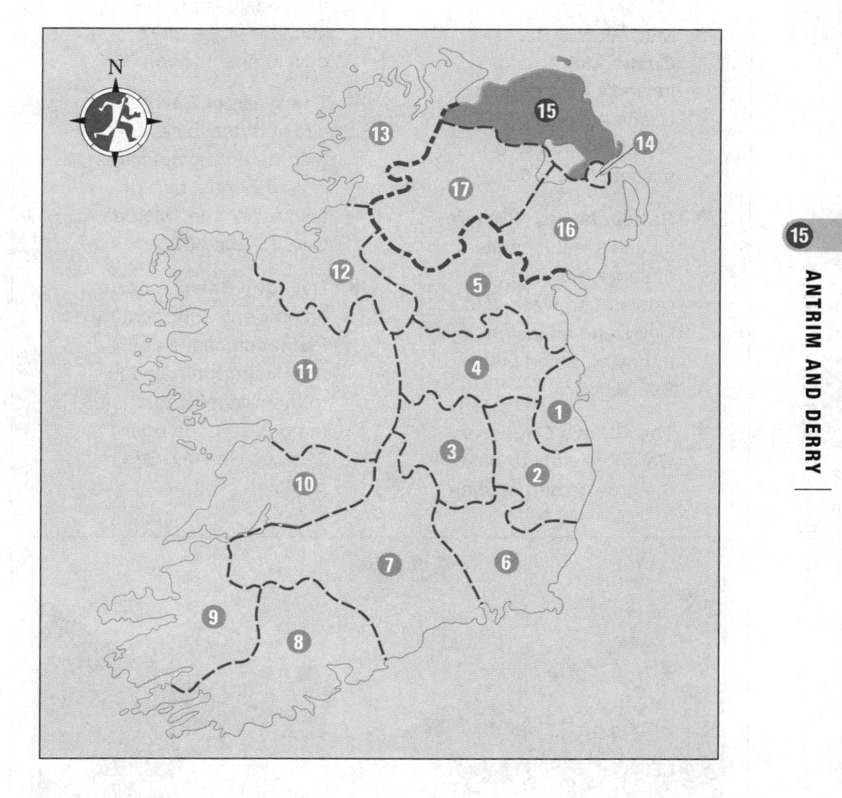

CHAPTER 15

Highlights

* **The Antrim Coast Road** The route from Larne to Portrush skirting the Glens of Antrim is one of Ireland's most scenic, with magical seascapes, staggering cliff-top walks and some of the North's prettiest villages. See p.660

* **McCollam's Bar, Cushendall** One of Ireland's best pubs for traditional music sessions – not to be missed! See p.664

* **Rathlin Island** Northern Ireland's last inhabited offshore island offers exhilarating walks and views and an insight into a thriving island culture. See p.669

* **The Giant's Causeway** Get there early to beat the crowds and marvel at one of the strangest geological formations in Europe. See p.673

* **The Tower Museum, Derry** One of the best local history museums in Ireland, the Tower provides a profound and thoroughly enjoyable account of the city's development. See p.686

* **The Walls of Derry** A circuit of these seventeenth-century defences is an essential part of any visit to the "Maiden City". See p.688

* **Bellaghy Bawn** A beautiful seventeenth-century Plantation castle and now, in part, a homage to the village's most famous son, the poet Seamus Heaney. See p.695

Antrim and Derry

Much of the coastline of counties **Antrim** and **Derry** is as spectacular as anything you'll find in Ireland and, consequently, unlike other parts of the North, it has always attracted an abundance of tourists. On fine days, the Mull of Kintyre and the islands of Islay and Jura are clearly visible across the water, and much of the predominantly Protestant population derives originally from Scotland.

County Antrim's major attractions are the nine **Glens of Antrim** in the northeast corner, green fertile fingers probing inland from high cliffs, almost immediately followed by the weird geometry of the **Giant's Causeway**. Along this part of the coast the **Ulster Way** and the inland **Moyle Way** offer great opportunities for short walks and long hikes, and the former passes some wonderful deserted beaches. As you follow the coast road (A2) further west, you'll come to two of the North's great seaside resorts, **Portrush** and, across the border in County Derry, **Portstewart**, popular holiday spots with sandy beaches and waves perfect for surfing. Modern **Derry city** sprawls around the old steep, walled town and spills over the banks of the River Foyle. A border town, with a substantial Catholic majority, it was traditionally the starting point for emigrants from Donegal and around on their journey to the Americas. Derry is a more alternative city than Belfast and its forward-looking council has encouraged the arts with great success.

If you're not driving, **transport** around the coastline can be a problem. **Buses** are infrequent, although there are summer specials to the various sights. **Hitchhiking**, though, is easy enough hereabouts, or you can take the **train**, which cuts a less interesting inland route through bland farming country. Trains from Belfast run to both Larne and Portrush, but most of the stops along the way to Derry are at some fairly grim inland towns: **Antrim**, **Ballymena** and **Coleraine**. The other route inland is the A6 road from Antrim to Derry, passing through and near some of the Plantation towns, and ascending steeply through the northeastern fringe of the Sperrins by means of the **Glenshane Pass**.

If transport is somewhat scarce, then at least finding **accommodation** is usually easy. There are some fine hotels and plenty of unpretentious, reasonably priced B&Bs where you're generally assured of a friendly welcome and a cup of tea. Hostels have grown in number and improved in quality and there's a fair smattering of campsites. Keep in mind, though, that this is where Northerners also holiday, so accommodation may be hard to come by in July and August and at festival times.

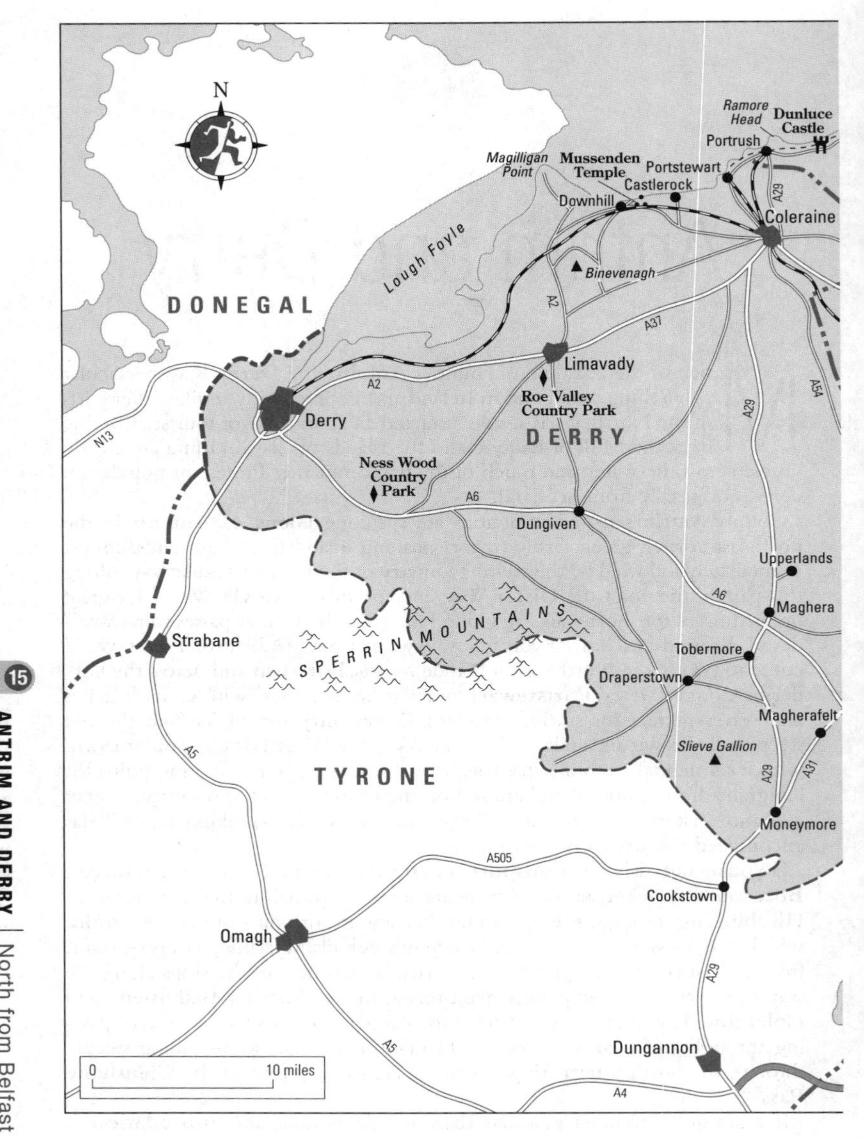

North from Belfast

The coastal strip from Belfast to Larne is largely unprepossessing countryside, although there are a few spots to detain you as you head towards the Antrim glens further north.

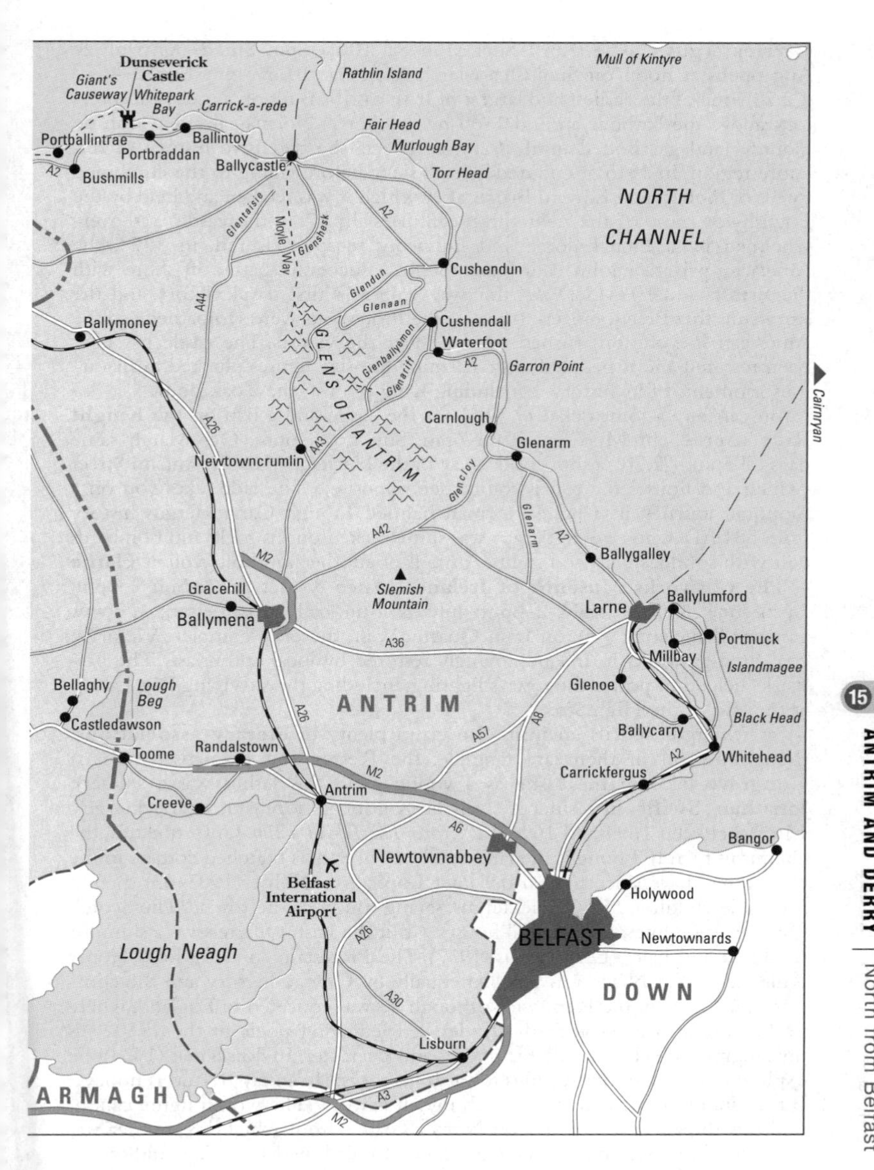

Carrickfergus

Heading past Belfast's northern suburbs, the A2 skirts the edge of Belfast Lough before reaching **CARRICKFERGUS** (Carraig Fhearghasa, "Fergus's rock"), an unremarkable seaside town (though with a recent reputation for Loyalist violence) whose seafront is dominated by its only real point of interest,

Carrickfergus Castle (April–Sept Mon–Sat 10am–6pm, Sun 2–6pm; July & Aug opens at noon on Sun; Oct–March Mon–Sat 10am–4pm, Sun 2–4pm; £2.70), one of the earliest and largest of Irish castles. Built on a rocky promontory above the harbour around 1180 by the Anglo-Norman invader John de Courcy (and garrisoned until 1928), it reflects the defensive history of this entire region. In 1315, it endured a year's siege before falling to the combined forces of Robert and Edward Bruce, after which it was retaken and held by the English for most of the next three centuries. In 1760, the castle was overwhelmed by a French force and hurriedly recaptured, and, in 1778, the American privateer John Paul Jones fought a successful battle off-shore with the British vessel *HMS Drake*; this was America's first naval victory, and the story runs that Belfast citizens (most of the Protestants were sympathetic to the American Revolution) rushed out to cheer the victors. The castle has now been restored and is peopled with alarming life-size figures plucked from various moments of its history – including King John in the cloakroom.

You can buy a joint ticket (£4.85) for the castle and a trip on the **Knight Ride** (April–Sept Mon–Sat 10am–6pm, Sun noon–6pm; Oct–March same days till 5pm; £2.70), a short walk away in the Heritage Plaza on Antrim Street (which also houses the tourist office, see opposite). The ride takes you on a monorail journey in a huge Norman helmet through Carrickfergus history from 581 AD, when noble Fergus was shipwrecked on his rock, and bombards you with sound, smells and sights. A smell of another kind hits you at **Flame – The Gasworks Museum of Ireland** (March & Oct Sat & Sun 2–6pm; April–June & Sept daily 2–6pm; July & Aug daily 10am–6pm; Ⓦwww.gasworksflame.com; £2), on Irish Quarter West, the only complete Victorian coal-fired gasworks in Ireland, lovingly restored by local enthusiasts. The gasworks helped to power the town's lighting, including the surviving **Big Lamp** at the end of the High Street.

Carrickfergus and its environs also claim plenty of **literary associations**, though not all of them are tangible: the Restoration dramatist **William Congreve** lived in the castle as a young child (his father was a soldier); **Jonathan Swift**'s first sinecure was at Kilroot, just outside Carrickfergus, where, between 1694 and 1696, he wrote *The Tale of a Tub*. Unfortunately, the chemicals firm ICI bought the land and levelled Swift's thatched cottage in the 1960s; they have since moved on. Poet **Louis MacNeice** (1907–63) spent a miserable childhood in Carrickfergus, saying sourly of the town: "The Scotch Quarter was a line of residential houses / But the Irish Quarter was a slum for the blind and halt" (*Carrickfergus*, 1937). The Protestant son of a local Home Rule cleric, MacNeice was repelled equally by Orange bigotry and the complacency found in the Republic. Although he was educated in England, where he became associated with the Auden-led left-wing poets of the 1930s, his upbringing indelibly tinged his poetry and character. In *Valediction* (1934), he explored his ambiguous feelings towards his roots: "I can say Ireland is hooey... But I cannot deny my past to which myself is wed / The woven figure cannot undo its thread". The rectory on North Road – from which his mother was committed to an asylum – no longer stands. Instead the MacNeice Fold on the same spot offers sheltered accommodation and a plaque on its walls proclaims the connection.

In the town centre overlooking Market Place, the **Church of St Nicholas**, patron saint of mariners and children, where MacNeice's father ministered (open mornings only), was built by John de Courcy in 1205 – like many of the castles and historic buildings hereabouts – but extensively reworked in 1614. Some interesting features set it apart: a leper's window, a "skew", or crooked aisle, symbolizing Christ's head on the cross falling to the right and, in the porch, a Williamite bomb fired in 1689.

Still, none of these claims to fame is as tenuous as that concerning the American president Andrew Jackson, whose parents emigrated from Carrickfergus in 1765. The **Andrew Jackson Centre** (April, May & Oct Mon–Fri 10am–1pm & 2–4pm, Sat & Sun 2–4pm; June–Sept Mon–Fri 10am–1pm & 2–6pm, Sat & Sun 2–6pm; £1.20), two miles north of Carrickfergus on the Larne Road, isn't even their home, but rather a reconstruction of an eighteenth-century thatched cottage stocked with appropriate period furniture and displays on Jackson and Northern Ireland's connections with the United States. Next door is something slightly more substantial – the **US Rangers' Centre** (same hours and ticket), which celebrates the formation of the first battalions of this American commando force in 1942 from US troops based in the North and trained at Carrickfergus.

One reason to give Carrickfergus a little more time might be the **annual fair**, Lughnasa, which is tackily medieval – with wrestlers, archers, minstrels and people dressed up as monks – but great fun nonetheless. It's held at the end of July; check the dates with the **tourist office** at the Heritage Plaza on Antrim Street (April–Sept Mon–Fri 9am–6pm, Sat 10am–6pm; July & Aug also Sun noon–6pm; Oct–March Mon–Fri 9am–5pm; Ⓣ028/9336 6455, Ⓦwww.carrickfergus.org).

If you want **to stay**, there's a scattering of hotels around, including the central, family-run *Dobbins Inn Hotel*, 6 High St (Ⓣ028/9335 1905, Ⓦwww.dobbinshotel.co.uk; ❹), and the Mediterranean-style *Quality Hotel*, 75 Belfast Rd (Ⓣ028/9336 4556, Ⓔinfo@qualitycarrick.co.uk; ❻), while for B&B there's *Langsgarden* on the seafront at 70 Scotch Gardens (Ⓣ & Ⓕ028/9336 6369; ❷) or *Tramway House*, 95 Irish Quarter South (Ⓣ028/9335 5639; ❷), a Victorian town house opposite the Marina, both providing comfortable facilities. The hotels offer the best **eating** options, though other good bets include *Ecu*, 63 North St, a café-bar serving modern European cuisine and the *Central Bar*, High Street, a Wetherspoon's pub.

This is also **golf** and **fishing** country. Carrickfergus Golf Club (Ⓣ028/9336 3713), on North Road west of the town centre, is an eighteen-hole parkland course with great views to Scotland and over the Mourne Mountains. Whitehead Golf Club (Ⓣ028/9335 3792), half a mile north of town at McCrea's Brae, also offers distracting views and a challenging course over varied terrain.

Whitehead and Islandmagee

The small seaside village of **WHITEHEAD**, three miles further up the coast from Carrickfergus, marks the entry point to the narrow peninsula of Islandmagee. There's little to detain you here, apart from a bracing stroll along the promenade or onto the Black Head path and its cliff-top views of the Down coast to the south. However, the village provides a base for visiting the **Railway Preservation Society of Ireland** (Ⓦwww.rpsi-online.org) at the end of Castleview Road. There's a collection of steam locomotives for viewing and riding (June–Aug Sun afternoons), and the society runs a number of summer excursions from Belfast Central to Portrush, Derry and Dublin (call Ⓣ028/2826 0803 for details).

Seven miles long and two wide, **ISLANDMAGEE** is a predominantly rural strip of land with the blatant exception of the Ballylumford power station at its northern tip. In the seventeenth century, the "island" was held by the Bissett family in return for an annual payment of goshawks, which breed on the cliffs. The most notable of these cliffs are the **Gobbins**, halfway along the eastern seaboard, which were once much visited but are now remembered more for a notorious incident in 1641 when the local inhabitants were hurled into the sea by soldiers from the Carrickfergus garrison. You can approach the cliffs via a gate on Gobbins Road, but the paths and bridges constructed to guide tourists have long since fallen into disrepair and in places are decidedly unsafe.

Further north of the Gobbins lies the tiny harbour village of **Portmuck**, named after the apparently pig-shaped island it faces (*muc* being Irish for "pig"), and a sandy beach at **Brown's Bay**, where there's a caravan park that allows camping (Ⓣ028/9338 2497). At **Ballylumford**, at the tip of the peninsula, you can catch a ferry across the water to Larne (Mon–Sat hourly 7.30am–5.30pm; £1). On the road west from here to **Millbay** you can spot the 4000-year old Ballylumford dolmen, known locally as the "Druid's Altar", sitting incongruously in the front garden of a house. There are few bars on the peninsula, but one, the *Millbay Inn*, in Mill Bay, offers en-suite **B&B** (Ⓣ028/9338 2436, Ⓕ9338 2152; ❸).

Ballycarry

Back on the A2, **BALLYCARRY** (Baile Cora, "townland of the causeway"), just off the main road, is the site of the remains of the first Presbyterian church ever to be built in Ireland, **Templecorran**, with a memorial to its first minister, who was ordained in 1613. The **church**'s graveyard contains the tombs of some of the supporters of the 1798 Rebellion, including that of James Burns, whose cryptic gravestone can only be deciphered using the following key: the numbers 1, 2, 3 and 4 represent the vowels "a", "e", "i" and "o" respectively, and 5 and 6 the letter "w". Another United Irishman, James Orr – better known as the Bard of Ballycarry, Ulster's answer to Robbie Burns – is also buried here, and some ringing verses in dialect are carved into his tombstone. There's also a grand Masonic memorial of 1831, which bears a patriotic poem about Ireland: "Erin, loved land! From age to age, Be thou more great, more famed and free."

Larne

Seven or so miles north of Ballycarry, the A2 enters **LARNE**, the last town of any size for a considerable distance on the coastal route. Larne is an important freight centre and is also one of the main ports of entry for visitors to Northern Ireland, served by P&O **ferries** from Cairnryan in Scotland. Although the town's seaside position is impressive and its main street bustles with shoppers most of the week, it is, in reality, a grim and ugly place, paint-splattered with Loyalist slogans, symbols and insignia. The town's **history** is inextricably linked to its convenience as a landing stage. Norse pirates used Larne Lough as a base in the tenth and eleventh centuries; Edward Bruce, brother of Robert, landed here in 1315 with a force of six thousand men to urge the Irish to overthrow the English; and in 1914, the Ulster Volunteers, opposed to the Irish Home Rule Bill, landed German arms here – one April night, some 140 tons, consisting of an astonishing 35,000 rifles and five million rounds, were unloaded and rapidly distributed to supporters throughout Ulster by a waiting motorcade of several hundred vehicles. The racket was such that local residents believed an invading army had arrived.

History apart, though, Larne is not a place to hang around in. The only real landmark is the **round tower**, at the entrance to the port, and even that's an 1888 reproduction – a memorial to James Chaine MP, the driving force behind the development of Larne's sea routes to Scotland and the Americas. The other sight is the ruined sixteenth-century **Olderfleet Castle**, which cowers amid the industrial wasteland of the harbour.

The coast around Larne, stretching from Garron Point in the north to Black Head in the south, is of great **geological** interest, with examples of just about every rock formation and period, from the earth's original crust to raised beaches and glacial deposits. At **Curran Point**, just south of the harbour, flint bands, frequently found in the chalk of this coast, provided useful material for Stone Age people, and many arrow heads and other artefacts have been found. Three-quarters of a mile out on the Antrim Coast Road, north of Larne, beyond Waterloo Cottages, stands a large **monument** to the engineer of this road, William Bald, and his stalwart workers, who blasted their way through, over and round this route in the 1830s. Here, at low tide, bands of fossil-rich Lias clay are exposed – even **dinosaur remains** have been discovered – and beneath the black basalt boulders, the mollusc shell, *Gryphea*, known locally as the Devil's Toenail, is common. Check at the Larne tourist office (see below) for geological tours and their useful guidebook to the rock formations of this part of the coast.

Practicalities

Ferry information for P&O services to Cairnryan can be obtained on ⓣ0870/242 4777; see p.18 for fares and further details. For local **bus** information, call ⓣ 028/2827 2345.

If you really must stay in Larne, the **tourist office** in Narrow Gauge Road (Mon–Fri 9am–5pm; Easter–Sept also Sat 9am–5pm; ⓣ028/2826 0088), will book B&B **accommodation** for you, and there is plenty to choose from. Close to the ferry terminal is the comfortable *Manor Guest House*, 23 Olderfleet Rd (ⓣ028/2827 3305, ⓦwww.themanorguesthouse.com; ❷), or

Amanda M'Kittrick Ros

In contrast to Larne's lack of vigour is the work of the town's best-known author. **Amanda Malvina Fitzalan Anna Margaret McLelland M'Kittrick Ros** – her signature gives some indication of the embroidery of her prose style – has gone down in history as the world's worst novelist. Born in 1860 in Ballynahinch, twenty miles south of Belfast, she was a true child of the Victorian era. She came to Larne as a schoolteacher and married the stationmaster, Andrew Ros. On their tenth wedding anniversary he gave her a present that generations of fans must be grateful for – the publication of her first fantastical alliterative work, *Irene Iddlesleigh* – and a stream of feverish hyperbole followed. Take, for instance, a passage from *Helen Huddleston* about its eponymous heroine:

She had a swell staff of sweet-faced helpers, swathed in stratagem, whose members and garments glowed with the lust of the loose, sparked with the tears of the tortured, shone with the sunlight of bribery, dimpled with the diamonds of distrust, slashed with sapphires of scandal and rubies wrested from the dainty persons of the pure...

Mark Twain and Aldous Huxley swooped on her work with delight and formed appreciative societies, reading circles and dining clubs dedicated to her "unintentional enormities". She became a cult figure, never, it seems, realizing what inspired such devotion. "My works," she said, "are all expressly my own – pleasingly peculiar – not a borrowed stroke in one of them." Quite. She also wrote excruciating verse.

there's the *Seaview Guest House*, 154–156 Curran Rd (Ⓣ028/2827 2438, Ⓔseaview@talk21.com; ❷), near the harbour. There's a **campsite** at *Curran Caravan Park*, 131 Curran Rd (Ⓣ028/2827 3797; April–Sept), but you're better off at Carnfunnock Country Park on the way to Ballygalley (see below).

The Glens of Antrim and Rathlin Island

Northwest of Larne lie the nine **Glens of Antrim**, cutting back from the sea to wild country behind. It's a curious landscape, with enormous contrasts between the neat seaside villages and the rough moorland above, and its well-defined topography gives first-time visitors the strange sensation that they know it well already. The best base for exploration of the area is **Cushendall**, a charming village 26 miles northwest of Larne in the heart of the Glens.

Despite their proximity to the Scottish coast, the Glens were extremely isolated until the completion of the coast road in the 1830s. As a consequence, they were also one of the last places in Northern Ireland where Irish was spoken. **Transport** is still a problem here and the only service to run from one end of this coast to the other is the daily Belfast–Coleraine Ulsterbus express, called the Antrim Coaster (see p.700). If you have time, you can dawdle along on a series of local buses; check the times with local tourist offices. **Hitching** is generally fine, but don't expect lifts to take you very far, while **cycling** is heady but strenuous (and bikes are best rented in Belfast – see p.650). One alternative means of getting about is **pony trekking**, which can be a delight in good weather: the main centre is at **Ballycastle**, at the northern extremity of the glen-fractured coast (see p.666).

Ballycastle is also the departure point for the ferry to rugged **Rathlin Island**, Northern Ireland's last inhabited offshore island, in one of whose caves Robert the Bruce of Scotland acquired a legendary lesson in patience from a spider spinning and re-spinning its web.

Ballygalley and Glenarm

The impressiveness of the coast road builders' achievement becomes apparent the moment you leave Larne's dull suburbs. The view expands to take in the open sea and, beyond it, the low outline of the Scottish coast. About three miles north of Larne, **Carnfunnock Country Park** (daily 9am–dusk; car-parking charge related to length of visit) is a good walking stop with a maze in the shape of Northern Ireland, a walled garden, a time garden with a collection of sundials ranging from the simple to the arcane, and a nine-hole golf course. You can also **camp** here (Ⓣ028/2827 0541; Easter–Sept).

The first settlement you come to north of Larne is **BALLYGALLEY** (sometimes "Ballygally"), with a wide, wild bay and a sandy beach embraced by hills. There's something about the sobriety of the architecture that makes it look more like Scotland, an impression heightened by the crow-stepped gables of **Ballygally Castle**, built by seventeenth-century Planters. You can call in here for a drink or stay – it's now a plush **hotel** (Ⓣ028/2858 3212, Ⓦwww.hastingshotels.com; ❼) with, they tell you, a ghost in the dungeon bar – although the building is more impressive from the outside.

The southernmost of the glens, **Glenarm** ("glen of the army"), is headed by a village of the same name, which grew up around a hunting lodge built by Randal MacDonnell after Dunluce Castle, further up the coast, was abandoned (see p.675). Glenarm became the major seat of the Earls of Antrim, something that might lead you to expect that **Glenarm Castle** (open days in July; ⓣ028/2884 1203 for details) would be worth seeing, but major rebuilding in the eighteenth and nineteenth centuries has left it an architectural mishmash of conflicting styles. **GLENARM** village itself, though, is a delight and very much a taste of what's to follow, with a narrow main street of colour-washed buildings broadening out as it approaches an imposing gateway, the old estate entrance, which now provides access to the glen itself. The lower part of the glen is blighted with Forest Service conifers, but carry on and you reach National Trust land, with far better walking. Back in the village, you'll find a few cosy bars, a couple of cafés and a salmon-processing plant on the outskirts with a shop where you can inspect the wares. There's a **tourist office** here in the Community Hall on the bridge (Mon 1–5pm, Tues, Thurs & Fri 9.30am–5pm, Sat 1–4pm, Sun 1–6pm; ⓣ028/2884 1087) and a smattering of comfortable and affordable **places to stay**, including *Riverside House*, 13 Toberwine St (ⓣ028/2884 1474; ❷), and *Nine Glens*, 16 Toberwine St (ⓣ028/2884 1590, ⓕ2884 1590; ❶), which both offer en-suite accommodation.

Carnlough and Waterfoot

Shortly after leaving Glenarm, you'll pass through the hamlet of **Straidkilly**, the "sliding village", so named because its houses move about an inch annually towards the sea. Rounding the next bay, you'll arrive at **CARNLOUGH** (Carnlach, "place of cairns"), standing at the head of **Glencloy**, the "glen of the stone". The village's most striking feature is its sturdy, white limestone buildings: until the 1960s, Carnlough's way of life was linked to its limestone quarries. The shining white buildings in the centre of the village were constructed by the Marquess and Marchioness of Londonderry in 1854. Over the main road there's a solid **stone bridge** that once carried a railway bringing material down to the **harbour** – which itself has an impressive breakwater, clock tower and courthouse of limestone. A mile north of the village, at the front of a cottage garden on the Ballymena road, there's an ever-changing, alfresco "**scrap museum**", consisting of an astonishing range of cleaned-up *objets trouvés*, ranging from Roman coins to tin baths, all bedecked with various humorous slogans and philosophical statements from the owner.

Back in Carnlough, on the seafront, the solid *Londonderry Arms Hotel* (ⓣ028/2888 5255, ⓦwww.glensofantrim.com; ❻), once briefly owned by Winston Churchill, is a comfortable **place to stay**; you can also sample the smoked salmon fished in Glenarm here, or just go for a drink and admire the bizarre collection of mementos of the 1960s champion steeplechaser Arkle. For cheaper B&B, there are rooms above the *Bridge Inn* in Bridge Street (ⓣ028/2888 5669, ⓦwww.mcauleyscarnlough.com; ❷). If you're **camping**, the *Bay View Caravan Park* (ⓣ028/2888 5685; April–Sept) and *Ruby Hill Caravan Park* (ⓣ028/2888 5692; March–Oct), both on Largy Road, have spaces for tents. This is also a good place to attack the **Ulster Way**, with walks up behind the village to forests and waterfalls along the Carnlough River.

From Carnlough the road skirts round a gaunt shoulder of land and on to **WATERFOOT**, a short strip of houses with a couple of bars that comes to life in the evenings. There's plenty of **B&B** around, including the welcoming and comfortable *Glenhaven*, 38 Bayview, Garron Road (ⓣ028/2177 2839, ⓦwww.glenhaven.co.uk; ❷), and farmhouse accommodation at *Dieskirt Farm*, 104 Glen Rd (ⓣ028/2177 1308, ⓦwww.dieskirt.8k.com; ❷; April–Dec).

It's **Glenariff**, though, Waterfoot's "glen of arable land", that is the real attraction here, a wide, lush and flat-bottomed valley that is abruptly cut off by the sea. A few miles up the glen is the **Glenariff Forest Park** (daily 10am–dusk; car £3, pedestrians £1.50), which has a **campsite** (☎028/2955 6000; contact the head forester in advance) and a number of waymarked trails. Opt for the Waterfall Trail to see a spectacular series of **cascades** skirted by a timber walkway, first built a hundred years ago. You'll pass Altnagowna, the highest waterfall of all, as you travel up the Glenariff road from Waterfoot, and you can see some of the others by turning left at the sign for the *Manor Lodge* restaurant (a popular spot for Sunday lunches), a mile up the road, and stopping at the restaurant car park.

To the north, between Waterfoot and Red Bay, there's a series of **caves** with an odd history. The so-called "School Cave" was where lessons were conducted for the children of Red Bay in the eighteenth century, a practice made necessary by the oppressive penal laws that outlawed Catholic education. One such pupil was Dr James McDonnell, founder of the Belfast Medical School. The largest of the caves, "Nanny's Cave", 40ft long, was the home of the redoubtable distiller of illicit poteen, Ann Murray, who died, aged 100, in 1847.

Cushendall and around

CUSHENDALL (Cois Abhann Dalla, "foot of the River Dall"), which lies at the head of three of the nine Glens of Antrim, is a delightfully understated village with a predominantly Catholic population, its charming colour-washed buildings grouped together on a spectacular shore. The red sandstone **tower** at the main crossroads was built in 1817 by one Francis Turnley, an official of the East India Company, as "a place of confinement for idlers and rioters". Down the road on Mill Street, sharing premises with the Glens of Antrim Historical Society, is Cushendall's **tourist office** (July–Sept Mon–Fri 10am–1pm & 2–5.30pm, Sat 10am–1pm & 2–4.30 pm; Oct–June Tues–Sat 10am–1pm; ☎028/2177 1180), where you can check for details of **dancing and traditional music** in local pubs: *McCollam's*, known to all as *Johnny Joe's*, a cottage-style pub also on Mill Street, is not to be missed, sessions usually taking place on Friday and Sunday throughout the year plus Mondays and Tuesdays in high season. Another great session takes place every Wednesday at *The Skerry Inn* in **Newtowncrumlin**, eight miles southwest off the Ballymena road. Cushendall itself comes alive during the **Glens of Antrim festival** in the middle of August, one of the area's oldest events, replete with traditional music, sporting events and much merriment, culminating in a huge street *céilí* on the Sunday.

Cushendall is probably the best base for exploring the Glens of Antrim, and accordingly it's well provided with **accommodation**. For B&B right in the centre, there's the cosy and congenial *Irené*, 8 Kilnadore Rd (☎028/2177 1898; Easter–Oct; ❷), or, heading towards Waterfoot, try *The Meadows*, 81 Coast Rd (☎028/2177 1130; ❷), friendly and spacious, with disabled access, too. Alternatively, there's the welcoming *Cullentra House*, 16 Cloghs Rd (☎028/2177 1762, Ⓔcullentra@hotmail.com; ❷), a mile northwest of the village off the Cushendun road, with its wonderful views. The municipal **campsite** is at 62 Coast Rd (☎028/2177 1699; Easter–Sept), next to Cushendall Boat Club, three-quarters of a mile towards Waterfoot. The nearest **hostel** accommodation is the isolated *Ballyeamon Camping* Barn (IHO; ☎028/2175 8541, Ⓦwww.taleteam.demon.co.uk), five miles up the Ballymena road; it's handily placed if you're walking the Moyle Way, and the owner is one of the North's best-known story-tellers.

Eating options include *Gillan's* friendly café on Mill Street during the day, *Harry's* almost next door, which offers exceptional, good-value meals in both its downstairs bar and restaurant upstairs, and *dPizza*, serving deep-pan delights on the corner of Mill Street and Coast Road. **Fishing** licences are available from O'Neill's Country Sports on Mill Street.

Layde Old Church and Ossian's Grave

Beyond Cushendall, the land rises sharply and the main road swings away from the coast, which is good news for **walkers**. A cliff-top path, running northwards from the beach, takes you to the ruins of the **Layde Old Church**, chief burial place of the MacDonnells, which originally dates from the thirteenth century. The local historical society has published a catalogue of the gravestones here – an interesting read in itself, but more so if you have Glens ancestry.

The other trip from Cushendall is to **Ossian's Grave**, signposted a couple of miles along the main road to Cushendun. There's a double fake involved here. Ossian, the legendary son of Fionn Mac Cumhaill, was the supposed author of the popular Ossianic cycle of poems, though these were in fact largely fabricated by James Macpherson in the 1760s. The poems inspired the early Romantic movement, particularly in Germany, where Goethe quoted Ossian at length in *The Sorrows of Young Werther*. However, the tomb doesn't actually have anything to do with either legendary or poetic incarnation as it's really a Neolithic court grave. All the same, standing in a sloping field above the valley, with views to Glendun, Glenaan and, in the distance, Scotland, it oozes spirit – as good a place as any to reflect on the shaky origins of the first Celtic literary revival. The stone cairn here commemorates a more substantial literary figure, **John Hewitt**, known as the poet of the Glens.

Beyond the grave runs **Glenaan** ("glen of the burial-chamber"), one of the smallest of the glens, which soon peters out to little more than a dip of red reeds and black seams of peat between two hills of heather and cotton grass.

Cushendun to Fair Head

The once-fashionable resort of **CUSHENDUN** ("foot of the River Dun") is an architectural oddity almost entirely designed by Clough Williams-Ellis, the stylish architect of Portmeirion in Wales, between 1912 and 1925. However, it has nothing of Portmeirion's twee Italianate style, which was used famously as the setting for the 1960s TV serial *The Prisoner*. Built to a commission from Ronald McNeill, the first (and last) Lord Cushendun, and his Cornish wife, Maud, Cushendun's houses are of rugged, rough-cast whitewash with slate roofs – a Cornish style that clearly weathers the Atlantic storms as efficiently here as in Cornwall. The town was home to Agnes Nesta Shakespeare Higginson (1870–1951), who crafted folksy, sentimental ballads under the far more apposite adopted name of **Moira O'Neill**. Very popular in her day, she's now better known as the mother of Mary Nesta Skrine (1904–1996), who went one better than Agnes and wrote under two pen-names, Molly Keane and M.J. Farrell. *Good Behaviour*, written by Molly Keane in her seventies after a thirty-year silence, is a piercingly witty novel of family life in the Big House tradition.

All of Cushendun is National Trust property, and it shows. It's a tiny and well-tended place where tourists – and everyone else – seem peculiarly out of place. The high spot of the village calendar is unquestionably its **festival week** towards the end of July, with plenty of music, competitions and sporting events. Otherwise it's a place for summer strolls and watching the fishing boats.

The village is blessed with one of the county's best **bar-restaurants**, *Mary McBride's*, whose homemade chowder and more substantial fish lunches and dinners are well worth sampling, if a touch pricey at around £15 for two courses (excluding drinks). **B&Bs** include: the award-winning *Sleepy Hollow*, 107 Knocknacarry Rd (Ⓣ & Ⓕ028/2176 1513; ❸); *Drumkeerin*, out towards Torr Head at 201a Torr Rd (Ⓣ028/2176 1554, Ⓔdrumkeerin@zoom.co.uk; ❸), which also has **hostel** accommodation (IHO; same contact details); and *Villa Farmhouse*, 185 Torr Rd (Ⓣ028/2176 1252, Ⓔmaggiescally@amserve.net; ❸). The council caravan park at 14 Glendun Rd (Easter–Sept; Ⓣ028/2176 1254) has space for **camping**.

The main road from Cushendun northwest to Ballycastle runs inland, traversing some impressively rough moorland, and passes **Loughareema**, the "vanishing lake", so termed because of its tendency to drain away completely in hot weather. A mile further on, **camping** is available at *Watertop Open Farm* (July & Aug; Ⓣ028/2076 2576, Ⓦwww.watertopfarm.co.uk), a working farm that can also arrange pony trekking and fishing. However, if you take the main road, you'll be missing some of the best of the northern coastline. The narrow, winding **coastal road**, edged with fuchsia and honeysuckle, switchbacks violently above the sea to **Torr Head**, the closest point on the Irish mainland to the Mull of Kintyre in Scotland. You can also pick up the signposted **Ulster Way** around here, although it swings inland immediately after Cushendun, joining the coast again at Murlough Bay.

Murlough Bay and Fair Head

Perhaps because of the absence of a main road, **Murlough Bay** is the most spectacular of all the bays along the northern coast. From the rugged cliff-tops, the hillside curves down to the sea in a series of wildflower meadows that soften an otherwise harsh landscape. As much as anywhere else on the Irish coastline, this is a place for just spending time and drinking it all in.

The last headland before Ballycastle is **Fair Head**, whose massive six-hundred-foot cliffs offer a truly spectacular view across the North Channel to Scotland – the Mull of Kintyre and further to Islay and the Paps of Jura – a proximity that sheds light on the confusion of land ownership between Ireland and Scotland. Nearby Rathlin Island (see p.669) was hotly contested right up to the seventeenth century, while the MacDonnells owned land both here and on Kintyre (which was considered dangerous enough to English interests to be settled, or "planted", with people from elsewhere in Scotland during the seventeenth century, just as Ireland was). **Lough na Cranagh**, one of three lakes in the hinterland behind the cliffs, has an oval island that is actually a *crannóg*, a lake dwelling, encircled by a parapet wall. A walk from the Fair Head car park to Murlough Bay takes about 45 minutes, but muddy paths and changeable weather make walking boots and a waterproof essential.

Ballycastle

The lively market town and port of **BALLYCASTLE** sits at the mouth of the two northernmost Antrim glens, **Glenshesk** ("barren glen") and **Glentaisie** ("Taise's glen"), and makes a pleasant base for exploring the Causeway Coast or the glens themselves, especially if you find yourself passing through at the time of the *Fleadh Amhrán agus Rince* three-day music and dance **festival** in June or the **Ould Lammas Fair** held on the last Monday and Tuesday in August. This last event is more than just a tourist promotion: Ireland's oldest fair, it dates from 1606 when the MacDonnells first obtained a charter, and has sheep and pony sales as well as the obligatory stalls and shops. Stallholders do a roaring trade in **dulse**, an edible seaweed, and **yellowman**, a tooth-breaking

Sir Roger Casement

A stone cross in the car park at Murlough Bay commemorates **Sir Roger Casement**, who was, extraordinarily, both a successful administrator for the British and later a martyr for the Nationalist cause. Born in Dublin in 1864, Casement moved to Antrim following the death of his parents, to live with his guardian and, initially at least, espoused the Loyalist views that characterized his Anglo-Irish upbringing. His brilliant diplomatic career included a stint in the Belgian Congo, where he fearlessly exposed all manner of colonial exploitation, and Peru, which he called the "Devil's Paradise of the Amazon". He was knighted in 1911, but, influenced by his foreign experiences, on his return to Ireland became increasingly involved with the Sinn Féin movement. Believing that World War I offered Ireland the opportunity of achieving independence from Britain, he negotiated military aid from Germany and arranged for a shipment of arms to be landed at Banna Strand on the Kerry coast. His plans were discovered and he was captured before the crucial 1916 Easter Rising and tried.

Seemingly set on martyrdom, at his trial he asserted: "I committed high treason with my eyes open – and for a cause I love above all else. I must some day pay the penalty – I do not mind if I have helped Ireland." However, aside from treason, Casement's homosexuality played a part in his fate. His diaries – the notorious "black diaries", supposedly recording his sexual exploits – were confiscated by the British government after his arrest and circulated unofficially. Their contents were said to be so damning that the chance of a reprieve was out of the question, despite campaigning behind the scenes by Conan Doyle, George Bernard Shaw and others, and he was hanged in Pentonville Prison, London, in 1916. Debate still rages today over the authenticity of Casement's diaries and whether they were a British fabrication designed to sully Casement's reputation as a champion of the colonially oppressed. Whatever the case, it's more likely that Casement's sexuality compounded his treachery in the eyes of the British establishment and made it determined to exact revenge on one of its own. A further twist to the tale has come with the release of once-secret MI5 papers in which Casement admits the futility of the uprising, once Germany had refused to send troops in support, but that he would be branded a coward and traitor to the Irish cause if he did not complete his part in the plan.

yellow toffee that's so hard it needs a hammer to break it up. Both of these delicacies feature in a sentimental song that originates locally:

Did you treat your Mary Ann
To dulse and yellowman
At the Ould Lammas Fair in Ballycastle–O?

Ballycastle has a solid, prosperous feel about it that derives from the efforts of an enlightened mid-eighteenth-century landowner, Colonel Hugh Boyd, who developed it as an industrial centre, providing coal and iron ore mines, a tannery, a brewery and soap, bleach, salt and glass works. The town's prosperity, though, really depended on its **coal mines**; lignite was mined at Ballintoy on the coast a few miles further west, an enterprise which came to an abrupt end in the eighteenth century when the entire deposit caught fire and burned for several years. More recently, the **harbour** area was redeveloped to cater for the now-defunct ferry to Campbeltown on the Mull of Kintyre, though, fortunately, Morton's fresh fish shop has been left intact. There's still a regular ferry service to Rathlin Island (see p.669) and there are also evening and all-day **fishing** trips operated by Ballycastle Charters (Ⓣ028/2076 2074).

At the seafront there's a memorial to **Guglielmo Marconi**, the inventor of the wireless, who in 1898 made his first successful radio transmission between Ballycastle and Rathlin. From the seafront, Quay Road leads gradually uphill past houses and shops to the **Diamond**, the town's focus. Up the steeper Castle Street hill, the town's tiny **museum** (July & Aug daily noon–6pm; free) occupies the old eighteenth-century courthouse. Temporary exhibitions are hosted upstairs, while downstairs in the former cells, there's a small and somewhat poignant collection of artefacts produced by the pre-World War I Irish Home Industries Shop. Pride of place goes to the Glentaisie banner for the first *Feis na nGleann* ("festival of the Glens") in 1904.

A little way out of town, on the main road to Cushendall, are the ruins of **Bonamargy Friary**, founded by the dominant MacQuillan family around 1500. One family member, Julia, insisted on being buried in the main walkway, so that she might be humbled by the stepping feet of others even in death. A number of the rival MacDonnell family are also buried here, including the hero of Dunluce Castle, Sorley Boy MacDonnell, and his son Randal, first Earl of Antrim (see p.675). An indication of the strength of the Irish language in these parts is that the tomb of the second earl, who died in 1682, is inscribed in Irish as well as the usual English and Latin: the Irish inscription reads, "Every seventh year a calamity befalls the Irish", and, "Now that the Marquis has departed, it will occur every year". The **River Margy**, on which Bonamargy Friary stands, is associated with one of the great tragic stories of Irish legend, that of the Children of Lir (see box on p.218), whose jealous stepmother turned them into swans and forced them to spend three hundred years on the Sea of Moyle (the narrow channel between Ireland and the Scottish coast). Also on the stretch of shore near Ballycastle is **Carraig Uisneach**, the rock on which the mythical Deirdre of the Sorrows, her lover Naoise and his brothers, the sons of Uisneach, are said by some to have come ashore after their long exile in Scotland (see p.672).

Practicalities

If you're going to **stay** in Ballycastle, the **tourist office** in Sheskburn House on Mary Street (July & Aug Mon–Fri 9.30am–7pm, Sat 10am–6pm, Sun 2–6pm; Sept–June Mon–Fri 9.30am–5pm; ⓣ028/2076 2024) can point you in the right direction. If your budget is generous, the *Marine Hotel*, at the bottom of Quay Road on the waterfront (ⓣ028/2076 2222, ⓦmultamarine.net; ❺), is very comfortable. Otherwise opt for the stunning seascape views from comfortable *Kenmara House*, 42 North St (ⓣ028/2076 2600; ❸), uphill from the front, the very place where Marconi conducted his tests. Alternatively, there's the larger *Hilsea*, 28 North St (ⓣ & ⓕ028/2076 2385; ❸; closed Dec & Jan), also overlooking the sea, plus several other options on Quay Road. The independent *Castle Hostel* is at 62 Quay Rd (IHH; ⓣ028/2076 2337, ⓔinfo@castlehostel.com), while round the corner on North Street is the smaller *Ballycastle Backpackers Hostel* (ⓣ028/2076 3612). There are also several caravan sites that allow **camping**, but the most pleasant is six miles east of town at *Watertop Open Farm* (see p.666).

The usual range of fast **food** and tea shops can be found around town: both *Donnelly's Coffee Shop* and *Herald's Restaurant* on Ann Street are excellent for daytime meals, and there are good bar lunches at nearby *McCarroll's* and at the *Marine Hotel*, which also incorporates the *Legends* nightclub. *Wysner's* **restaurant**, 16 Ann St (closed Sun), has an adventurous and inexpensive menu, often including salmon from Carrick-a-rede (see p.671), and is located next door to the famous butcher of the same name. The *Anzac Bar*, 5 Market St, also has a deserved reputation for its splendid meals. You'll find Ballycastle's **pubs** surprisingly lively: *McCarroll's* has **traditional music** on Thursdays; the *House of McDonnell* (also known as *Tom's*), on the main street, is young and buzzy, with music on Fridays; and the *Central Bar* opposite has sessions on Wednesdays. For a quiet pint, *The Diamond Bar* is the place to go, while down on the seafront, the friendly *Angler's Arms* is a great place to end the evening.

Rathlin Island

Northern Ireland's last remaining inhabited offshore island, **RATHLIN ISLAND**, lies five miles north of Ballycastle and just twelve miles west of the Mull of Kintyre in Scotland. Shaped like a truncated figure seven, Rathlin is an impressive, rugged place, with a coastline consisting almost entirely of cliffs and a lighthouse at each tip. As the island's width is never more than a mile, the sea dominates the landscape and its salty winds discourage the growth of vegetation – wind turbines harness this energy source for electricity generation. The presence of dry-stone walls and numerous ruined cottages indicates a time when the population was far larger than the hundred or so current inhabitants concentrated around **Church Bay**.

A stroll around the island will reveal relics of far greater antiquity. Halfway to the West lighthouse is the site of a **Stone Age** axe factory, and, to its north, earthworks known as **Doonmore** (Dún Mór, "great fort"). In the early Christian period, the island was a haven for **monks**, who have left evidence of their presence in the form of a sweathouse (a kind of primitive sauna) at Knockans, back towards Church Bay. In 795 AD Rathlin was the first place in Ireland to be raided by the **Vikings**. Subsequent raids saw three bloody massacres, one by the Scots and two by the English. In 1575, the mainland MacDonnells sent their women, children and old people to Rathlin for safety from the English, but that didn't stop the invading fleet, under the Earl of Essex (whose soldiers included Sir Francis Drake), from slaughtering the entire population. Later, in 1642, the MacDonnells were again butchered by their Scottish enemies, the Campbells; Rathlin was deserted for many years afterwards. You can discover more about the island's history and culture in the Boathouse, down by Church Bay's harbour, which has been converted to house a **visitor centre** (May–Aug daily 10am–4pm; free).

The island's cliffs make superb **birdwatching** country, particularly **Bull Point**, on the western tip, part of a large RSPB nature reserve. The **viewpoint** at the west lighthouse (April–Aug; contact warden in advance on ⓣ028/2076 3948) provides wonderful views of Northern Ireland's largest colony of seabirds – a minibus plies between here and Church Bay in summer. The foot of the cliff is riddled with **caves**, many of them accessible by boat only in the calmest of weather, and many also filled with detritus from wrecked ships, brought to the surface by storms.

Bruce's Cave, on the northeast point of the island, below the lighthouse, is a cavern in the black basalt where, in 1306, so the story goes, the despondent Robert the Bruce retreated after being defeated by the English at Perth. Seeing a spider determinedly trying to spin a web gave him the resolve to "try, try and try again", so he returned to Scotland and defeated the English at Bannockburn.

Practicalities

Caledonian MacBrayne **ferries** (ⓣ028/2076 9299, ⓦwww.calmac.co.uk) make the 45-minute trip from Ballycastle harbour to Rathlin four times daily

△ Bushmills barrels

between June and September; a return ticket costs £8.40. Outside these months services are reduced to twice daily but in winter the wreck-filled waters in the "race" (as the stretch of water is known locally) can become too treacherous for the boat to sail at all or make the return trip, so it's worth booking ahead to make sure you find a bed on the island, as **accommodation** is strictly limited.

There's **B&B** by the harbour at the *Rathlin Guest House* (April–Sept; ⓣ028/2076 3917; ❷) or at the National Trust-owned *Manor House* (ⓣ028/2076 3964, ⓦwww.nationaltrust.org.uk; ❸), a restored late-Georgian home with its own excellent tearoom. Overlooking Mill Bay ten minutes' walk to the south is the tiny *Soerneog View Hostel* (IHO; ⓣ028/2076 3954, ⓦwww.n-irelandholidays.co.uk/rathlin), which also rents **bikes**. **Campers** can pitch their tents for free on the east side of Church Bay.

Life on the island is simple and uncomplicated, but not entirely basic: you'll find a **bar-restaurant**, *McCuaig's*, lunches and teas at the *Manor House* and a couple of shops at Church Bay. Rathlin is a good place for **fishing**, and you can **rent a boat** in Church Bay (ⓣ028/2076 3154 or 2076 3922). The island's two major events are the week-long **festival** in mid-July, with everything from *céilís* to model yacht racing, and the **regatta** on the last weekend in August.

The north Antrim coast and northeast Derry

The north coast of County Antrim, west of Ballycastle, is dominated by Northern Ireland's most famous tourist attraction, the strange formation of basalt columns at the legend-wrapped **Giant's Causeway**. On the way, around the town of **Ballintoy**, there are several pleasant diversions, not least the precarious rope bridge to **Carrick-a-rede Island**. West of the Causeway, you can sample some whiskey at **Bushmills** and visit the imposing and well-preserved remains of **Dunluce Castle**, the stronghold of the local MacDonnell clan.

The coastline west of Dunluce is another major holiday spot, with the twin resorts of **Portrush** and **Portstewart** filled with tourists in July and August and students the rest of the year. Inland lies the dull manufacturing town of **Coleraine**, which you're only likely to visit en route to the coast.

To Ballintoy and Dunseverick Castle

As you draw level with **Carrick-a-rede Island**, not far outside Ballintoy on the coast road west from Ballycastle, you'll see the island's **rope bridge**. Strung 80ft above the sea, the rope-connected planks lead to a commercial salmon fishery on the southeast side of Carrick-a-rede (the name means "rock in the road": the island stands in the path of migrating salmon) – but its main function seems to be to scare tourists, something it does very successfully. Walking its sixty-foot length, as the bridge leaps and bucks under you, is enough to induce giggles and screams from the hardiest of people. The bridge is up from mid-March to the end of September (daily 10am–6pm; July & Aug until 8pm; car park £3), when the salmon fishing season ends.

BALLINTOY itself has a dramatic harbour, much loved by artists, with a dark, rock-strewn strand contrasting oddly with the neat pale-stone breakwater. It's lively with boats in the summer, when visitors pack the **café**, *Roark's Kitchen*, but in winter it's bleak and exposed. In good weather you can rent boats from fishermen at the harbour for angling and trips along the coast and, in the summer,

boat trips run out from Ballintoy, past **Sheep Island**, the bizarre rocky column standing just offshore, which is home to a colony of cormorants, to Carrick-a-rede (£2). At the top of the harbour road stands a little white **church**, which replaced an earlier one in which local Protestants took refuge from Catholics in 1641 before being rescued by the Earl of Antrim. A landlord of Ballintoy in the eighteenth century, Downing Fullerton, founded Downing College in Cambridge; the staircase and oak panelling from the castle at Ballintoy were removed when it was demolished in 1795 and taken to the Cambridge college.

If you're tempted to **stay** in the village, try the refurbished *Fullerton Arms*, 22 Main St (Ⓣ & Ⓕ028/2076 9613; ❸), or, for seaviews, *Portcampley House*, 8 Harbour Rd (Ⓣ028/2076 8200, Ⓦwww.portcampley.8k.com; ❷). **Hostel** accommodation is available at the recently built and well-equipped *Sheep Island View Hostel*, 42a Main St (IHH & IHO; Ⓣ028/2076 9391, Ⓔsheepisland@hotmail.com), which has space for **camping** and rents out **bikes**. Traditional music fans should head for the *Carrick-a-Rede* **bar** and its Tuesday, Friday and Sunday night sessions.

Continuing west along the coast, **Whitepark Bay** is a delightful, mile-long sweep of white sand with a HINI **hostel** (Ⓣ028/2073 1745, Ⓦwww.hini.org.uk) that will organize pony trekking, canoeing, pub trips and parties and is the sort of place where you arrive for one night and stay several. A footpath from Ballintoy leads past here to **PORTBRADDAN**, a tiny hamlet of multi-coloured houses, next to one of which is St Gobban's, a slate-roofed little church, which, at twelve feet by six and a half, is supposedly the **smallest church in Ireland**. Needless to say, there are other contenders: the ruins of an even smaller one, St Lasseragh's, stand on the cliff above.

Dunseverick Castle

From Portbraddan the coast path leads round a headland, through a spectacular hole in the rock and then, by degrees, up to the cliffs of **Benbane Head**. The road and path almost converge at **Dunseverick Castle**, now no more than the ruins of a sixteenth-century gatehouse. This was once the capital of the old kingdom of Dalriada, which spread over north Antrim and Scotland, and the terminus of one of the five great roads that led from Tara, the ancient capital of Ireland. Its location, naturally enough, made it one of the main departure points for the great Irish colonization of Scotland that took place from the fifth century onwards, and the castle was stormed by the **Danes** in the ninth and tenth centuries. Dunseverick also features in one of the great Irish love stories, the ninth-century *Longas mac n-Usnig* ("The fate of the children of Uisneach"). Deirdre, the betrothed of King Conor, falls in love with his bodyguard, Naoise. Together with Naoise's two brothers, the sons of Uisneach, they flee to Scotland. Fergus, one of Conor's soldiers, believes the king has forgiven them and persuades them to return home. Landing at Dunseverick (or, some say, Ballycastle), they take the high road to Conor's court at Armagh, but the king kills the brothers and seizes Deirdre, who dashes her head against a stone and dies. And Fergus, outraged, destroys Conor's palace (though not, apparently, the king himself). Down in postcard-picturesque Dunseverick harbour, there's a tiny **museum** (June–Aug Mon–Sat 10am–4pm; £1), focusing on objects salvaged locally and elsewhere, including lumps of coal from the *Titanic*.

The Giant's Causeway

Ever since 1693, when the Royal Society first publicized it as one of the great wonders of the natural world, the **Giant's Causeway** has been a major tourist

Fionn Mac Cumhaill: The Causeway legends

According to the romantic version of the legend, the Causeway is the everyday story of a love affair between giants. The Ulster warrior **Fionn Mac Cumhaill** (Finn McCool) became infatuated with a female giant who lived on the island of Staffa, off the Scottish coast (where the Causeway resurfaces), and built the great highway to bring his lady love to his side. Some have added fanciful embellishments to the story, such as an estimate of Fionn's height calculated on the basis of a large shoe-shaped stone that's known as his boot. A more robust version has Fionn involved in a row with a Scottish giant. He built the Causeway to go over to Scotland for a punch-up, but on seeing the size of the other giant, lost his nerve and fled home. Safe in Ireland, he had his wife tuck him up in an outsize cot. When the Scots giant arrived in pursuit he saw the size of Fionn's "baby" and in turn took fright and fled, never to be heard of again.

attraction. The highly romanticized pictures of the polygonal basalt rock formations by the Dubliner **Susanna Drury**, which circulated throughout Europe in the eighteenth century, did much to popularize the Causeway: two of them are on show in the Ulster Museum in Belfast (see p.638). Not everyone was impressed, though. William Thackeray ("I've travelled a hundred and fifty miles to see *that*?") especially disliked the tourist promotion of the Causeway and would loathe it even more vehemently today, claiming in 1842 that "the traveller no sooner issues from the inn by a back door which he is informed will lead him straight to the causeway, than the guides pounce upon him." Although the Causeway is probably less overtly money-making than it used to be, it still attracts hundreds of thousands of visitors annually, filling the visitor centre (see overleaf) and the minibus that scurries back and forth. But even in high season it's easy to escape the crowds by taking to the cliffs.

For sheer otherworldliness, the Causeway can't be beaten. Made up of an estimated 37,000 black basalt columns, each a polygon – hexagons are by far the most common, with pentagons second, though sometimes the columns have as many as ten sides – it's the result of a massive subterranean explosion, some sixty million years ago, that stretched from the Causeway to Rathlin and beyond to Islay, Staffa (where it was responsible for the formation of Fingal's Cave) and Mull in Scotland. A huge mass of molten basalt was spewed out onto the surface, which, on cooling, solidified into what are, essentially, crystals. Though the process was simple, it's difficult, when confronted with the impressive regular geometry of the columns, to believe that their production was entirely natural. The Irish folk versions of their creation (see box above) are certainly more appealing.

Undoubtedly the best way to **approach** the Giant's Causeway is along the cliffs, preferably on a wet and blustery day when you're scared you'll lose your footing along the muddy way. The waymarked **North Antrim Cliff Path**, cut into the cliff side alongside the black geometric configurations, runs all along this stretch of coast. **Public transport** to and from the Causeway is well organized in summer: the "open topper" **bus** runs in July and August four times daily between Coleraine (where the stop is opposite the train station) and the Causeway, stopping at Portstewart, Portrush, Portballintrae and Bushmills; you can flag it down anywhere along the way. If you're travelling by **train** from Belfast, the line ends at Portrush, from where you can catch either the open topper or the regular bus #172 towards Ballycastle; for more details phone ⓣ028/7034 3334. Alternatively, a restored **narrow-gauge railway** now runs between Bushmills and the Causeway (mid-May to Sept 3–5 times daily plus some days in other months; 20min; single £2, return £3.50). If you want to **stay** close to the Causeway, there's the *Causeway Hotel* (Ⓣ028/2073 1226, Ⓕ2073 2552; ❹) near the visitor centre or the *Carnside Farmhouse*, 23 Causeway Rd (Ⓣ028/2073 1337, Ⓔcarnsideguests_giantscauseway@hotmail.com; ❷; March–Oct), which has superb views.

Visiting the Causeway

The Causeway's **visitor centre** (daily: June 10am–6pm, July & Aug 10am–7pm, Sept–May 10am–5pm; free) was severely damaged by fire in March 2000 and continues to be housed in temporary accommodation on the clifftop while Moyle Council determines its future. As well as providing tourist information, the centre offers the usual range of "Celtic" gifts and a café, while regular announcements are made for the frankly ignorable twelve-minute Causeway audio-visual presentation in the adjacent theatre (£1) and the unnecessary guided tours (£2). If you want to avoid paying the council's extortionate car-park charge (£5), then park on the road by the narrow-gauge railway station and walk up the hill.

Resist the temptation to follow the crowds on the ten-minute walk along the road straight down to the Causeway from the visitor centre and dodge the minibus that runs every fifteen minutes (£1 return), the only form of transport allowed along the road except cycles; instead take a better route that's a round trip of roughly two miles. Follow the cinder path up behind the visitor centre and round the edge of several promontories – among them **Weir's Snout** – from which you can gasp at the Causeway from above, and watch the eider and gannets wheeling across from Ailsa Craig, thirty miles away in Scotland. If you're here in autumn and in luck, you may sight the Aurora Borealis bouncing in the sky northwards. A flight of 162 steps takes you down to sea level and a junction in the path, leading further along to the forty-foot basalt columns known as the **Organ Pipes**. Many of the formations have names invented for them by the guides who so plagued Thackeray and his contemporaries – the Harp, for example – but at least one, **Chimney Point**, has an appearance so bizarre that it persuaded the crew of the *Girona*, a ship of the Spanish Armada, to think it was Dunluce Castle, a couple of miles further west, where they might get help from the MacDonnells: instead, their vessel was wrecked on the rocky shore. Before you reach Chimney Point, **Port-na-Spánaigh** is the place where the ship foundered in September 1588. The treasure it was carrying was recovered by divers in 1968, and some of the items are on show in the Ulster Museum in Belfast. Sadly, extensive cliff erosion prevents any further exploration and prohibitive costs are likely to deter future reparation.

Tucked into the coastline, inaccessible from land, are some spectacular **caves**: Portcoon Cave, 450ft long and 40ft high; Leckilroy Cave, which you can't go into; and Runkerry Cave, an amazing 700ft long and 60ft high. Your best option, if you want to explore, is to persuade a fisherman in Portballintrae (see opposite) or Dunseverick harbour (see p.672) to take you; £50 is considered a persuasive sum.

If the weather is inclement, you can warm yourself up by playing with the whipping tops and skipping ropes in the museum of the Williams-Ellis designed **Causeway School** (July & Aug daily 11am–5pm; 75p), next to the centre car park, or sit at an ink-splotched desk in the recreated 1920s classroom.

Bushmills and Dunluce Castle

The next stop on the main road beyond the Causeway is **BUSHMILLS**, whose foremost attraction is the **Old Bushmills Distillery** on the outskirts of town. Whiskey has been distilled here legally since 1608, making it the oldest licit distillery in the world, and it's well worth making the **tour** (April–Oct Mon–Sat 9.30am–5.30pm, Sun noon–5.30pm, last tour 4pm; Nov–March Mon–Fri tours at 10.30am, 11.30am, 1.30pm, 2.30pm & 3.30pm; £3.95). Bushmills whiskey is distilled three times, once more than Scotch; but perhaps the biggest surprise is just how unsubtle a business the industrial manufacture of alcohol is, despite all the lore that surrounds it. The distillery is a massive factory where an extraordinary range of (mostly unpleasant) smells assail your nostrils, making it difficult to imagine that the end product really does delight the taste buds. All the same, at the end of the tour you're offered a tot of the hard stuff. The best bet is the unblended malt, representative of what goes on in Bushmills itself, as the grain whiskey that goes into the blend is almost all distilled in Cork; alternatively ask for a tot of Coleraine whiskey, only a tiny amount of which is still produced. They also serve hot toddies, which may be more in order in winter. To find the distillery, follow the signs from the cenotaph in the centre of town – it's barely a quarter of a mile.

Accommodation in the town includes the *Bushmills Inn*, 9 Dunluce Rd (Ⓣ028/2073 2339, Ⓦwww.bushmillsinn.com; ❽), a former coaching inn with cottage-style interior, complete with gas-lit bar, secret library and turf fires, and a superb **restaurant** featuring such delights as beef fillet flamed in (naturally) Bushmills whiskey; allow at least £25 per head. The new HINI **hostel**, 49 Main St (Ⓣ028/2073 1222, Ⓦwww.hini.org.uk), is equipped with small, en-suite dorms, and for **B&B** there's *Ardeevin,* 145 Main St (Ⓣ028/2073 1661; ❸), on the road out to the distillery. Out of town *Ahimsa*, 243 Whitepark Rd (Ⓣ028/2073 1383; ❷), with an organic garden and good **vegetarian meals**, offers inexpensive accommodation in a modernized cottage. There's more luxury at *Killen's*, 28 Ballyclough Rd (Ⓣ028/2074 1536, Ⓦwww.killens.com; ❻), a converted nineteenth-century schoolhouse four miles southwest of town off the Coleraine road; it's well equipped with a swimming pool, sauna and solarium and a restaurant with excellent local produce.

A detour westwards along the minor coast road from Bushmills will take you past the **narrow-gauge railway** station for trips to the Giant's Causeway (see p.673) to the decorous little village of **PORTBALLINTRAE** about a mile away. Here, you'll find **accommodation** at the very comfortable *Bayview Hotel*, 2 Bayhead Rd (Ⓣ028/2073 4100, Ⓦwww.bayviewhotelni.com; ❼), and seaside B&B at nearby *Manor House*, 51 Beach Rd (Ⓣ028/2073 2002, Ⓦwww.portballintrae.com; ❸). There's **camping** at the caravan park on Ballaghmore Avenue (Ⓣ028/2073 1478; April–Oct) and good **fishing** from the tiny harbour, which you can watch from the conservatory of *Sweeney's Wine Bar*, 6B Seaport Ave (Ⓣ028/2073 2405), housed in converted stables dating from the seventeenth century and serving tasty, reasonably priced **meals**.

Dunluce Castle

The main road rejoins the coast a couple of miles west of Bushmills. Here you'll see the most impressive ruin on this entire coastline, the sixteenth-century **Dunluce Castle** (April–Sept Mon–Sat 10am–6pm, Sun 2–6pm, June–Aug opens noon on Sun; Oct–March closes at 4pm; £1.50). Perched on a fine headland, high above a cave, it looks as if it only needs a roof to be perfectly habitable once again. Its history is inextricably linked to that of its original owner, **Sorley Boy MacDonnell**, whose clan, the so-called "Lords of the Isles", ruled northeastern Ulster from this base. English incursions into the area culminated in 1584 with Sir John Perrott laying siege to Dunluce, forcing Sorley Boy ("Yellow Charles" in Irish) to leave the castle. But as soon as Perrott departed, leaving a garrison in charge, Sorley Boy hauled his men up the cliff in baskets and recaptured the castle, later repairing the damage with the proceeds of the salvaged wreckage of the *Girona* and arming the fort with three of its cannons. Having made his point, Sorley Boy agreed a peace with the English, and his son, **Randal**, was created Viscount Dunluce and Earl of Antrim by James I. In 1639, Dunluce Castle paid the penalty for its precarious, if impregnable, position when the kitchen fell off the cliff during a storm, complete with cooks and dinner. Shortly afterwards, the MacDonnells moved to more comfortable lodgings at Glenarm, and Dunluce was left empty.

However, it remains an extraordinary place. The MacDonnells' Scottish connections – Sorley Boy's son continued to own land in Kintyre – are evident in the **gatehouse**'s turrets and crow-step gables and the tapering chimneys of the seventeenth-century **Great Hall**. There's a strange touch of luxury in the **loggia** that, oddly, faces away from the sun. A spectacular scramble, particularly in wild weather, takes you down to the **cave** below the castle that pierces right through the promontory, with an opening directly under the gatehouse.

Portrush

The town of **PORTRUSH** ("port of the promontory"), on the Ramore Peninsula, has sandy beaches backed by dunes, running both east and west, and everything you'd expect from a seaside resort, including summer drama in the Town Hall and plenty of amusements for children. Many students from the University of Ulster at Coleraine live here and make it a considerably livelier place than you might expect, even out of season. The huge popularity of the local dance scene draws clubbers from all over the North and the town can have a distinctly raucous feel at weekends. The **beach** is long and sandy, ending towards eastern Dunluce at the **White Rocks**, where the weather has carved the soft limestone cliffs into strange shapes, most famously the so-called "Cathedral Cave", 180ft from end to end.

Portrush's wide range of activities and entertainments for children and wet afternoons include: the all-weather **Waterworld**, by the harbour (April, May & Sept Sat & public hols 10am–7pm, Sun noon–7pm; June Mon–Sat 10am–7pm, Sun noon–7pm; July & Aug Mon–Sat 10am–8pm, Sun noon–8pm; £4.50), with water flumes, slides, sauna, Jacuzzis, aquarium and restaurant; the **Fantasy Island** indoor adventure playground on the promenade (Easter–Sept Mon–Sat 10am–8pm, Sun noon–8pm; Oct–March Fri & Sat 10am–8pm, Sun noon–8pm; £3.25); and the summer-only **Barry's Fairground** just behind the seafront. The controversially expensive **Dunluce Centre**, 10 Sandhill Drive (April & May Sat & Sun noon–7pm; June Mon–Fri 10am–5pm, Sat & Sun noon–7pm; July & Aug daily 10am–8pm; Sept–March Sat & Sun noon–5pm; Ⓦ www.touristnetuk.com/ni.dunluce; £2.75 per attraction, £7 combined ticket), houses the tourist office (see opposite), a viewing tower and a variety of interactive and cinematic experiences, including a simulated ghost train, a high-tech treasure hunt and an interactive adventure playground. The former bath-house for the well-heeled patrons of the *Northern Counties Hotel* on the seafront is now the **Portrush Countryside Centre** (June–Sept daily Mon–Fri 10am–6pm, Sat & Sun noon–8pm; Ⓦ www.nics.gov.uk/ehs; free), with an indoor sea-creature-filled rock pool, local natural history displays and staff who will happily name your rock samples or flower specimens.

There is rewarding **surfing** off West Strand and White Rocks: you can rent boards and gear at one of the surf shops in Portrush or further along the coast in Portstewart, but first check the safety of the waves (Ⓣ090/6133 7770). Safety considerations are seemingly jettisoned, however, during the annual **raft race** at the beginning of June, when participants race each other across the harbour on homemade rafts.

The main sporting attraction here is the **Royal Portrush Golf Club** (Ⓣ028/7082 2311), the North's premiere club, which boasts one nine-hole and two eighteen-hole courses, though in fact most of the coast seems to be covered in greens and fairways – eighty in all – whose vistas offer a welcome distraction from your handicap. Demand is high in the summer, especially in good weather, and it's wise to **book ahead**. A detailed list of green fees, course lengths and standard scratch scores is available from the tourist office.

Practicalities

The friendly and efficient **tourist office** (March & Oct Sat & Sun noon–5pm; April to mid-June & Sept Mon–Fri 9am–5pm, Sat & Sun noon–5pm; mid-June to Aug daily 9am–7pm; Ⓣ028/7082 3333) is in the Dunluce Centre on Sandhill Drive, a little south of the town centre. **Bikes** can be rented from Thompson's Cycles, 77B Main St (Ⓣ028/7082 9606).

Note that **accommodation** fills up quickly in high season and also in May during the **North West 200** motorbike road races and July during major golf championships. Top-of-the-range options in the town centre include the new and appropriately named *Comfort Hotel*, 73 Main St (Ⓣ028/7082 6100, Ⓦwww.comforthotelportrush.com; ❼), and the pleasant *Peninsula Hotel*, 15–19 Eglinton St (Ⓣ028/7082 2293, Ⓦwww.peninsulahotel.com; ❻), near the station. There are dozens of **B&Bs**, too, most of them very friendly and welcoming: try *Glenkeen Guest House*, 59 Coleraine Rd (Ⓣ028/7082 2279, Ⓦwww.glenkeenguesthouse.co.uk; ❸), which has won tourist board awards, or the Victorian *Harbour Heights*, on the seafront at 17 Kerr St (Ⓣ028/7082 2765, Ⓦwww.harbourheightsportrush.com; ❸). For superb farmhouse B&B, there's also the award-winning *Maddybenny Farmhouse* (Ⓣ028/7082 3394, Ⓦwww.maddybenny.freeserve.co.uk; ❸), out of town on Loguestown Road; the breakfasts here are sumptuous and there's an attached **riding school** and self-catering cottages (£350–450 per week). **Campsites** abound in the area, though most of them are actually fairly unattractive caravan parks that also take a few tents; closest to town is the municipal *Carrick Dhu Caravan Park*, 12 Ballyreagh Rd (Ⓣ028/7082 3712; April–Sept), a mile west of town on the A2, or there's the *Ballymacrea Caravan and Camping Park*, 220 Ballybogy Rd (Ⓣ028/7082 4057), a mile and a half down the B62 Ballymoney road.

At the harbour, the *Ramore Restaurant* (Ⓣ028/7082 4313; reservations essential) serves good **food** for at least £25 a head, while its revamped wine bar offers a less pricey menu. Alternatively, try the excellent Italian *Don Giovanni's*, 9 Causeway St, or *Darcy's*, 94 Main St, an excellent spot for pub lunches. There are also plenty of cheap cafés and takeaways. The town has a few convivial **pubs** – the nicest bar in town is the *Harbour Inn* – but if you're hoping to hear traditional music your best option is to head to Ballycastle (see p.666). **Nightlife** is quite a serious business here: *Lush!* in *Kelly's Golf Links Hotel* on Bushmills Road (Ⓣ028/7082 3539) attracts major DJs and, consequently, clubbers from far and wide, while *Traks*, 16C Eglantine St (Ⓣ028/7082 2112), has an equally loyal following.

Portstewart

Across the border in County Derry, **PORTSTEWART**, like Portrush, is full of Victorian boarding houses. Of the two, Portstewart is decidedly more sedate and has always had more airs and graces: the train station is said to have been built a mile out of town to stop hoi polloi from coming. In terms of sheer location, though, Portstewart wins hands down. Just west of the town is **Portstewart Strand**, a long sand beach firm enough to drive on (£4) – which the locals delight in doing – with some of the best **surfing** in the country. It's a grand place, too, if you hit fine weather and feel like getting out your bucket and spade. The best way to take the sea air is the bracing **cliffside walk**, which runs between the beach and the town, passing battlements and an imposing Gothic mansion, now a Dominican college.

The **tourist desk** in the library on The Crescent (July & Aug Mon–Sat 10am–1pm & 2–4.30pm; ⓣ028/7083 2286) can help with **accommodation** bookings if you have any problems – there's less choice here than in Portrush. **B&Bs** are mostly along the promenade or nearby and include the large and comfortable three-star *Anchorage Inn*, 87–89 The Promenade (ⓣ 028/7083 2003, ⓦwww.theanchorbar.com; ❹) or the cosy, family-run *O'Neill's*, 31 High Rd (March–Sept; ⓣ028/7083 2774). **Hotel** accommodation is available at the *Edgewater Hotel*, 88 Strand Rd (ⓣ028/7083 3314, ⓦwww.edgehotel.com; ❻), which has breathtaking views from its lounge bar. There's also the good independent *Rick's Causeway Coast* **hostel** at 4 Victoria Terrace (IHH; ⓣ028/7083 3789, ⓔrick@causewaycoasthostel.fsnet.co.uk; closed Jan & Feb) and the municipal *Juniper Hill Caravan Park* at 70 Ballyreagh Rd (ⓣ028/7083 2023; April–Sept), a mile down the A2 towards Portrush, which offers **camping**. *Morelli's*, 53–58 The Promenade, is justly famous for its ice cream, and also serves snacks and Italian **food**. The busy local haunt *Shenanigans*, 78 The Promenade (ⓣ028/7083 6000), is a mid-priced restaurant on the main drag, while *Ashiana*, 12A The Diamond (ⓣ028/7083 4455), serves the best tandoori in these parts and isn't too expensive. However, the most innovative food is served at *Smyths*, Lever Road (ⓣ028/7083 3564), a popular brasserie with a deservedly high reputation. In the evenings, *Nero's* **nightclub**, part of *Nelly's Complex* on Coleraine Road, is the place for late-nighters, and has a pleasant pub attached. The *Anchorage Inn* is the place to try for traditional music, while the Flowerfield **Arts Centre**, 103 Coleraine Rd (ⓣ028/7083 3959), runs a variety of courses and stages occasional exhibitions, but was due to be closed for rebuilding work until November 2003.

Coleraine

COLERAINE (Cúil Raithin, "ferny nook") is County Derry's second-largest town, a lively enough manufacturing and shopping centre during the day, but a depressingly empty, pedestrianized wasteland at night. Most of the interesting action here takes place down by the River Bann, where there are pleasant walks and a thriving marina, and at the **University of Ulster** campus, with its excellent **Riverside Theatre** (ⓣ028/7032 3232) on Cromore Road.

A mile south of Coleraine, on the eastern bank of the river, **Mountsandel** is a two-hundred-foot mound, apparently the earliest-known dwelling place in Ireland, though the discoveries in Boora Bog in County Offaly must run a fairly close second. The post-holes and hearths of the wooden houses that once stood here have been dated at around 7000 BC.

The helpful **tourist office** on Railway Road by Coleraine's train station (Mon–Sat 9am–5pm; ⓣ028/7034 4723, ⓦwww.colerainebc.gov.uk) will attempt to convince you of the town's attractions: there's a mildly diverting "Historical Trail" to follow, and in summer it's worth enquiring about the environmental **walks** regularly conducted in the area.

B&Bs are mostly out of town: try the remarkable *Greenhill House*, 24 Greenhill Rd in Aghadowey (Ⓣ028/7086 8241, Ⓔgreenhill.house@btinternet.com; ❸; March–Oct), an award-winning Georgian country house seven miles south of Coleraine on the B66; or *Camus House*, 27 Curragh Rd in Castleroe (Ⓣ028/7034 2982; ❸), a seventeenth-century listed country house overlooking the River Bann, two miles south of Coleraine. The University of Ulster campus provides cheap rooms during the summer vacation (Ⓣ028/7034 4141; ❷).

Though Coleraine has plenty of daytime cafés, there are few **eating** choices available at night. *Little Caesars*, 45 Railway Rd (Ⓣ028/7032 9991), is a worthwhile Italian option, while *The Water Margin* (Ⓣ028/7034 2222), on the river, is the best-known Chinese. Coleraine's **pubs** are particularly dire, with the exception of *The Old Courthouse*, a Wetherspoon's place across the river on the corner of Lower Captain Street, which also serves food all day.

The northwest Derry coast and Limavady

West of the Bann estuary, the remaining northern coastline of County Derry sees relatively few visitors, but makes a pleasant detour. There are marvellous beaches here all the way from **Castlerock** to **Magilligan Point** and stunning views from the cliffside **Mussenden Temple** and around **Mount Binevenagh**. Inland, **Limavady** retains a few relics of Georgian times.

Castlerock and around

Five miles or so west of Coleraine, at the Castlerock crossroads, is **Hezlett House** (mid-March to May & Sept Sat, Sun & public hols noon–5pm; June–Aug Mon & Wed–Sun same times; £2.50), built in 1690 and restored after a fire in 1986. The house is a fine example of cruck-truss construction, an early method of prefabricated building using wooden frames filled with clay and rubble that was common in England but is enough of a rarity here to warrant preservation by the National Trust. The last owner of the house is buried in the graveyard at Downhill (see overleaf), where his gravestone quaintly bears both his own version of the spelling of his name and that of his father, a Mr Hazlett.

Lying almost a mile north, the small resort of **CASTLEROCK** has a long strand reaching eastwards to the Barmouth, where the River Bann's estuary draws flocks of migratory birds and stationary watchers. Unless you're a surfer, there's not much else to tempt you, apart from the renovated but still cosy *Bertha's Bar* (known locally as *Love's*) at the beginning of the promenade.

Two miles west of the Castlerock crossroads, a pair of huge ornate Pompeian gates alongside the main A2 road mark the main entrance to **Downhill Palace** (daily 9am–dusk; free), built in the 1780s by **Frederick Augustus Hervey**, Anglican Bishop of Derry and fourth Earl of Bristol. Hervey was an enthusiastic grand traveller, after whom all the many *Hotel Bristols* throughout Europe are named, and was also an art collector and great sportsman, once organizing a pre-prandial race between Anglican and Presbyterian clergy along the strand. His palace, accessed through pleasant gardens, lies in ruins and was last occupied by US troops, billeted there during World War II. Across fields at the back of the house is the diminutive **Mussenden Temple** (mid-March to May &

Sept Sat, Sun & public hols 11am–6pm; June–Aug daily same times; free, car parking £3), which clings precariously to the eroding cliff-edge and offers stunning sea views. Its classic domed rotunda was apparently modelled on the Roman temple of Vesta and was built by Hervey in honour of his cousin Mrs Frideswide Mussenden, who died aged 22 before it was completed. It was subsequently used as a summer library. Later, with characteristic generosity and a fairly startling lack of prejudice, Hervey allowed a weekly Mass to be celebrated in the temple, as there was no local Catholic church. The inscription on the temple frieze translates rather smugly as: "It is agreeable to watch, from land, someone else involved in a great struggle while winds whip up the waves out at sea." The bishop's other constructions include a **folly** in the grounds of the palace, and the **Bishop's Road**, which runs from Downhill and across Mount Binevenagh on its way to Limavady.

The main A2 road continues down the hill a few hundred yards to **DOWNHILL** hamlet, where you'll find the excellent and spacious *Downhill* **hostel** (IHO; ⓣ028/7084 9077, ⓦwww.angelfire.com/wa/downhillhostel), also a working pottery, on the edge of the hugely long, car-accessible **beach**, which is itself overlooked by Mussenden Temple on the cliff-edge above. There is neither a shop nor a pub in Downhill, so stock up on provisions in advance if you intend staying here.

Magilligan Point to Limavady

West of Downhill the road hugs the cliffs, while the seven-mile stretch of beach curves around to **MAGILLIGAN POINT**, passing **camping** opportunities at the *Benone Tourist Complex* (ⓣ028/7775 0555) and the adjacent *Golden Sands Caravan Park* (ⓣ028/7775 0324; March–Oct). The road to the point runs across the dunes, skirting the edge of an open prison (once an army base and later an internment camp) before reaching the tip of the peninsula. Here, at the narrow entrance to Lough Foyle, stands a **Martello tower**, dating from the Napoleonic Wars, with walls more than nine feet thick. There's the *Point Bar* too (open summer only) to provide succour, and a new regular daily **ferry** service to **Greencastle** across the water in County Donegal (pedestrians £1 single, £1.60 return, cars £5 single, £8 return; see p.613 for details).

One of Ireland's most famous harpers, Dennis Hempson, was from the Magilligan townland and attended the great Belfast Harp Festival of 1792 (see p.632), where he played the *Londonderry Air*. Hempson was one of the last harpers to play the then brass-strung instrument with long fingernails. The Ordnance Survey project to **map** the whole of Ireland began at Magilligan Strand in 1824 when Lt Col Thomas Colby established a baseline here for a network of imaginary triangles covering the whole country, from which measurements could be calculated using trigonometry.

From the peninsula, the road cuts south along the foot of **Mount Binevenagh** before reaching **BELLARENA**. The land around the mountain is now a conservation park, dedicated to the preservation of birds of prey, in particular falcons and kestrels. In the village itself lies **Bellarena House**, an old Plantation mansion, dating back in parts to the seventeenth century. This was once the home of Sir John Heygate, a minor novelist now long out of print, who achieved some notoriety when he travelled with his more famous Fascist-sympathizing colleague Henry Williamson (author of *Tarka the Otter*) to pay homage to Adolf Hitler in the 1930s. Unfortunately, the house is no longer open to the public, but it is visible from the common ground banks of the River Roe.

LIMAVADY (Léim an Mhadaidh, "leap of the dog") was once a major settlement, its old site lying two miles further south down the valley of the River Roe across whose steep gorge, legend has it, a dog owned by an O'Kane chieftain once leapt to take a warning message to a nearby castle. The town was refounded as Newtown Limavady in the early seventeenth century by Thomas Phillips, speaker of the Irish House of Commons, and promptly spent the next three hundred and fifty years or so in relative obscurity. However, in recent years, Limavady has undergone major economic expansion and most roads to the centre now pass through industrial estates. Although the town's population has consequently increased, there's still relatively little to do or see here. The six-arch **bridge** spanning the river was built in 1700, and Main Street, which runs down from it, is still recognizably Georgian. Number 51 Main Street was once the home of **Jane Ross**, who noted down the *Londonderry Air* from a travelling fiddler in 1851 (the tune later formed the base for Ireland's most popular ballad, the tear-jerking "Danny Boy", penned by an English lawyer, Fred E. Weatherley, in 1912). A more modern musical event is the town's excellent jazz and blues **festival** in mid-June. Limavady's only other recent claim to fame is as the birthplace of William Massey, Prime Minister of New Zealand from 1912 to 1925.

Tourist information is available from the council offices at 7 Connell St (July & Aug Mon–Fri 9am–5.45pm; rest of year Mon–Fri 9am–5pm; April–Sept also Sat 9.30am–5.30pm; ⓣ028/7776 0307). There are some lively **bars** in the centre of town, including the atmospheric *Owen's* on Main Street, and a few **B&B** options, including *Gorteen House Hotel*, 187 Roemill Rd (ⓣ028/7772 2333, ⓦwww.gorteen.com; ❸).

The **Roe Valley Country Park**, a couple of miles south of Limavady, preserves Northern Ireland's first hydroelectric power station, opened in 1896, with much of the original equipment intact, as well as a small **weaving museum** and visitor centre (Easter–Aug daily 10am–6pm; rest of year closes 5pm; free).

Derry city

DERRY lies at the foot of Lough Foyle, immediately before the border with the Republic. It's a crossroads city in more ways than one; roads from all cardinal points arrive here, but it was also a major point of emigration from the eighteenth century onwards, an exodus that reached tumultuous proportions during the Great Famine. Derry is the fourth-largest town in Ireland and the second biggest in the North, but it has a markedly different atmosphere from Belfast, being two-thirds **Catholic**. While entrances to the city are now marked by signs in Irish welcoming visitors to Derry, the city still appears as "**Londonderry**" on many road maps and signs, a preference adhered to by the British government, Unionists and television news bulletins. Indeed, it has also acquired the nickname "**Stroke City**" – a reference to the tactful placating of both Nationalist and Unionist traditions by entitling it "Londonderry/Derry" on signs and in radio and television broadcasts. Whatever the case, locals of both persuasions now generally refer to their city as "Derry". Within Ireland, Derry is highly regarded for both its characteristically caustic humour – best caught in the busier bars and at the football matches at the Brandywell – and its musical pedigree, having produced names as diverse as Dana, Dáithí Sproule (of Altan), Phil Coulter, The Undertones and many other less well-known artists.

Approached from the east in winter twilight or under a strong summer sun, the city presents a beguiling picture, with the spread of the **River Foyle** and the rise of the city's two hillsides, terraced with pastel-shaded houses and topped by the hueless stone spires of the ever-present religious denominations. With its rich history, Derry has several worthwhile attractions, mostly enclosed within the seventeenth-century **walls**, themselves the most significant reminder of the city's past. And four miles or so west of the centre, across the County Donegal border on the Letterkenny road, is the unmissable **Grianán Ailigh** (see p.607), a stone fort and the oldest habitation left standing in Ireland.

Outside Ireland, the name of Derry recalls the Troubles of recent years and savage events like the **Bloody Sunday** massacre. Nonetheless, under no circumstances be deterred from visiting, for, unlike Belfast, the cutting edge of violence had receded considerably here even before the ceasefires, and the city

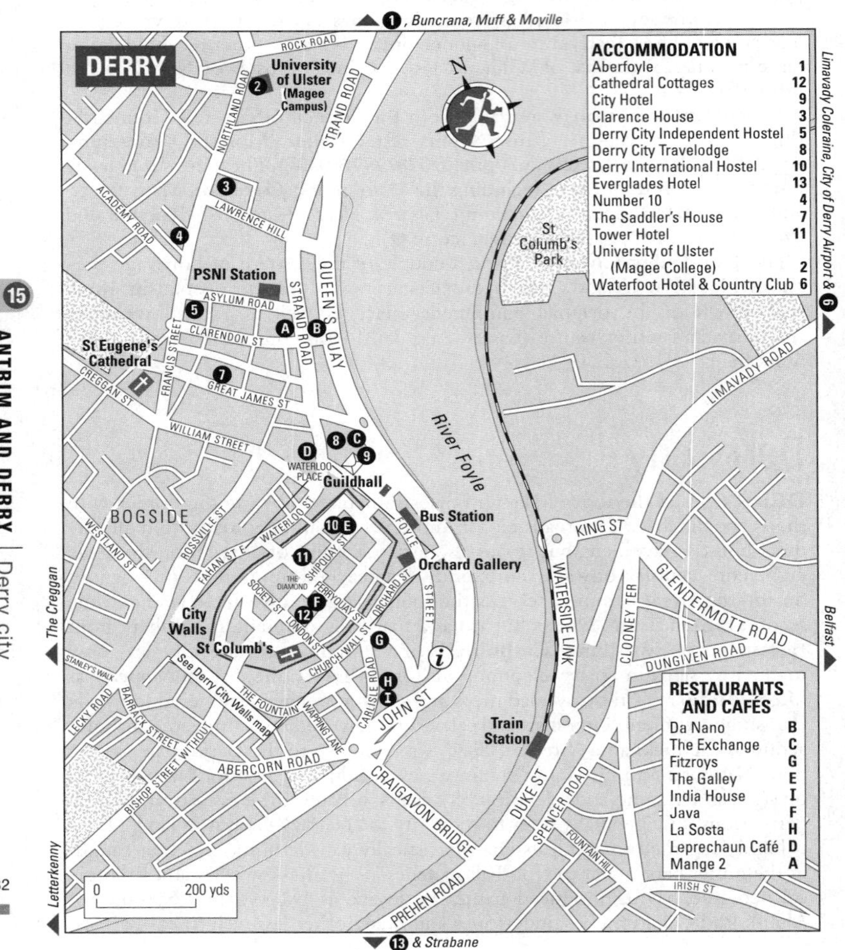

is still imbued with a real sense of optimism, despite its losing much trade to nearby Letterkenny thanks to the declining value of the old Irish punt against sterling.

Some history

Derry's original name was Doire Calgaigh ("oakwood of Calgach"), given for a legendary warrior who led the Caledonians at the battle of the Grampians. Some time after **St Columba** founded a monastery here in 546 AD, the spot was renamed Doire Cholm Cille. The monastic settlement must have been relatively unimportant for, although **Vikings** settled around Loughs Foyle and Swilly, only one actual attack was made on Doire. By the twelfth century, however, the Mac Lochlainn dynasty, based in Inishowen, had taken control and a small township began to develop. However, decline had set in by the beginning of the fourteenth century when it was granted to the Anglo-Norman de Burgos, builders of the fortress at Greencastle, Inishowen (see p.613). By 1500, the power of the O'Dohertys had spread from Inishowen and they constructed a tower house which was later absorbed into the seventeenth-century walls.

In 1566, **Elizabeth I** of England sent a small task force in a failed attempt to pacify such troublesome Irish chieftains as Shane O'Neill, but at the end of the century the uprising of Hugh O'Neill, Earl of Tyrone, provoked another English invasion. Doire's strategic position on the River Foyle was quickly appreciated and the town was soon captured and the resident population expelled, though an accidental explosion led to the evacuation of the garrison soon afterwards. The military presence was not restored until 1600 when an English army of four thousand troops under **Sir Henry Docwra** landed at Culmore Point. Doire was soon recaptured and Docwra began fortifying the remains of the medieval town, using it as a base for incursions against the O'Neills and O'Donnells, gaining the support of the O'Dohertys in his ventures. When the war ended in 1603, the town began to develop as a small trading centre and Doire became **anglicized** as "Derry" when it was incorporated as a city in the following year. However, in 1608, Sir Cahir O'Doherty rebelled against Docwra's successor, Pawlett, and burnt Derry to the ground. This destruction made the city ripe for the "**Plantation**" of English and Scottish settlers, and the financial assistance of the wealthy businessmen of the City of London was obtained to achieve this. A new walled city was constructed and renamed "**Londonderry**" in 1613 in honour of its backers, the Twelve Companies of the Corporation of London.

The 1688–89 siege and its aftermath

The **seventeenth century** was the most dramatic phase of the city's evolution. The city walls withstood successive sieges, the last of which, in 1688–89; played a key part in the Williamite army's final victory over the Catholic King James II at the **Battle of the Boyne** (see p.785), the Derrymen's obduracy crucially delaying the plans of James and his ally Louis XIV. James's accession had seen the introduction of a policy of replacing Protestants with Catholics in leading positions in the Irish administration and army. In December 1688, a new garrison attempted to enter the city, but was prevented when a group of young **apprentices** seized the keys and locked the city's gates. Eventually, after negotiation, an all-Protestant garrison under Governor Robert Lundy was admitted. Over the following few months the city's resident population of two thousand swelled to thirty thousand as people from the surrounding area took refuge from Jacobite forces advancing into Ulster. Fearing that resistance against the Jacobite army was futile, Lundy departed; his effigy is still burnt each December by Protestants. Around seven thousand Protestants died during the fifteen-week **siege** that followed (the longest in British history), the survivors being reduced to eating dogs, cats and rats. The suffering and heroism of those weeks still have the immediacy of recent history in the minds of Derry's citizens, who commemorate the siege with a skeleton on the city coat of arms, and the lyrical tag "maiden city", a reference to its unbreached walls.

After the siege, many Derry people **emigrated** to America to avoid harsh English laws, and some of their descendants, such as the pioneer frontiersman **Daniel Boone**, achieved fame there. George Farquhar (c.1677–1707), a Derryman who chose to stay, achieved fame as a playwright. Derry's heyday as a **seaport** came in the nineteenth century, a period in which industries such as linen production also flourished. It was a Derry weaver, **William Scott**, who established the world's first industrialized shirt manufacturers, cutting the shirts in Derry and sending them to the cottage women of Donegal for stitching. After **Partition**, the North–South dividing line lay right at Derry's back door, and the consequent tariffs reduced much of its traditional trade.

Civil rights and the Troubles

Though Derry remained relatively peaceful, its politics were among the North's most blatantly discriminatory, with the substantial Catholic majority denied its civil rights by gerrymandering geared towards ensuring the Protestant minority's control of all important local institutions. On October 5, 1968, a two-thousand-strong **civil rights march** – led by a Protestant, Ivan Cooper, and a Catholic, John Hume (later to lead the SDLP) – demanding equality of employment and housing, and other political rights, set off on a route through the walled city. Confronted by the batons of the Protestant police force and the notorious B Specials, rioting spilled over into the Catholic **Bogside** district and over eighty people were injured. The clash is seen by many as the catalyst for the modern phase of the Troubles: faith in the impartiality of the Royal Ulster Constabulary was destroyed once and for all, and the IRA was reborn a year or so later.

The Protestant **Apprentice Boys' March** in August 1969 was a further step. The infamous "Battle of the Bogside" ensued when the RUC attempted to storm the area (from where stones were being thrown at the march), which for several days afterwards lay in a state of siege. The Irish Prime Minister, Jack Lynch, moved units of the army to the border and set up field hospitals for injured Bogsiders. In the mounting tension that ensued, British troops were for the first time widely deployed in the North, and many of the demands of the civil rights movement were forced on Stormont by Westminster. Then, on January 30, 1972, came **Bloody Sunday**. Thirteen people were shot dead when British paratroopers (who subsequently claimed that they had been shot at first) opened fire on another unarmed civil rights march. In 1999, after years of mounting pressure for a full investigation, the British government established the Saville Inquiry, which conducted its proceedings in Derry's Guildhall until moving to Westminster in 2002 to continue its investigation.

While 2000 saw the election of Cathal Crumley, the first **Sinn Féin mayor** in Northern Ireland, the city has been controlled for some time by the Social Democratic and Labour Party (SDLP), which attempts to operate in a scrupulously non-sectarian fashion. In this they seem to have been successful (at least in Northern Irish terms), and they also pursue an enlightened policy towards the **arts**, which has succeeded in making Derry a lively and unexpectedly entertaining place to visit. The city's fabric has also undergone dramatic changes, with the construction of huge new developments such as the Foyleside, Quayside and Richmond shopping centres and the Millennium Forum theatre, plus the development of pleasant riverside walks along the Foyle.

Arrival and information

The tiny **City of Derry Airport** (ⓣ028/7181 0784, ⓦwww.cityofderryairport.com), seven miles northeast of town on the A2 road, is served by Ryanair flights from London Stansted and British Airways from Dublin, Glasgow and Manchester. There's a small tourist office here (Mon–Fri 8am–9pm, Sat 8am–4pm, Sun 4–9pm), and the airport is connected by Ulsterbus #143 (£2) to the train station and Foyle Street bus station; a taxi from the airport to the city centre costs £8.

Derry's **train station** (ⓣ028/7134 2228) is situated across the River Foyle from the town centre in the Waterside district, with a free connecting bus service to the **bus station** on Foyle Street. The latter is served by Ulsterbus (ⓣ028/7126 2261) for all the main Northern Ireland destinations and Bus Éireann (information from Ulsterbus), which operates buses to Dublin, Donegal town, Galway and Sligo. In addition, Lough Swilly (ⓣ028/7126 2017) and Northwest Busways (ⓣ077/86219) run services from across the border in north Donegal. Local city buses leave from stops along Foyle Street. The Airporter coach service (Mon–Fri 6am–6pm every 2 hours; Sat & Sun less frequently; ⓣ028/7126 9996, ⓦwww.airporter.co.uk) runs from outside 3 Lower Clarendon St, off Strand Road to and from Belfast International and Belfast City airports; journey times are ninety minutes to Belfast International (single £14.50, return £20) and two hours to Belfast City Airport (single £15, return £25). **Black taxis** operate from Foyle Street; or call Co-op Taxis (ⓣ028/7137 1666) or the Derry Taxi Association (ⓣ028/7126 0247).

The main **tourist office** is at 44 Foyle St (mid-March to June Mon–Fri 9am–5pm, Sat 10am–5pm; July–Sept Mon–Fri 9am–7pm, Sat 10am–6pm, Sun 10am–5pm; Oct–June Mon–Fri 9am–5pm; ⓣ028/7126 7284, ⓦwww.derryvisitor.com), which also houses a **Bord Fáilte** office (Mon–Fri 9am–5pm; ⓣ028/7136 9501) and a **bureau de change**. Grab a free pocket *Visitor Guide* for up-to-date information about the city's attractions and facilities. The Nationalist *Derry Journal* newspaper (Tues & Fri) is good for entertainment listings, while the monthly free magazine *The Beat* concentrates on music listings. **Walking tours** of the historic centre leave from the tourist office (July & Aug Mon–Fri 11.15am & 3.15pm; Sept–June Mon–Fri 2.30pm; ⓣ028/7128 7284; £4). Foyle Cruise Line (ⓣ028/7136 2857) operates a **river cruise** from a pier behind the Guildhall to Culmore Bay (June–Aug 2pm & 4pm; 1hr 15min; £5) and an evening cruise up the lough to Greencastle (June–Aug 8pm; 4hr; £10).

Accommodation

Although Derry has plenty of **accommodation** at the top end of the price range, finding a more economically priced room in the centre can be difficult, especially in high season. It's worth **booking in advance**, or calling in at the tourist office when you arrive.

Hotels and B&B

Aberfoyle 33 Aberfoyle Terrace, Strand Road ⓣ028/7128 3333, ⓔaberfoyle@ntlworld.com. Pleasant Victorian house offering en-suite B&B just a little way north of the Queens Quay roundabout. ❷

City Hotel City Quay ⓣ028/7136 5800, ⓦwww.greatsouthernhotels.com. Huge new monument to elegant minimalism with views of the Foyle and all the leisure facilities imaginable, including a dance studio. ❾

Clarence House 15 Northland Rd Ⓣ & Ⓕ028/7126 5342). Mostly en-suite, well-equipped guesthouse ten minutes' walk from the city centre. ❸

Derry City Travelodge 22 Strand Rd Ⓣ028/7127 1271, Ⓦwww.travelodge.co.uk. Modern, if somewhat functional rooms in a prime city-centre location. ❻

Everglades Hotel 41–53 Prehen Rd Ⓣ028/7134 6722, Ⓦwww.hastingshotels.com. Top-of-the-range, high-quality accommodation on the southern banks of the Foyle. ❽

Number 10 10 Crawford Square Ⓣ028/7126 5000. Small but popular guesthouse in a quiet location just off Francis Street. ❷

The Saddler's House 36 Great James St Ⓣ028/7126 9691, Ⓦwww.thesaddlershouse.com. Stylish and well-furnished Victorian town-house B&B very near the city centre, off Strand Road. Its friendly, knowledgeable owners also run the equally grand Georgian *Merchant's House* at 16 Queen St nearby. ❸

Tower Hotel Butcher St Ⓣ028/7137 1000, Ⓦwww.towerhotelgroup.com. A large new establishment just inside the city walls, comprising ninety bedrooms plus three executive suites, with a flash bistro and excellent café-bar. ❼

Waterfoot Hotel & Country Club 14 Clooney Rd Ⓣ028/7134 5000, Ⓦwww.thewaterfoothotel.co.uk. Across the river and approached via the Caw roundabout on the Limavady road, this well-appointed hotel features a restaurant and leisure centre. ❻

Hostels and self-catering

Cathedral Cottages 14 & 16 London St Ⓣ028/7126 9691, Ⓦwww.thesaddlershouse.com. These two eighteenth-century houses in the centre of the old city are run by the owners of *The Saddler's House* B&B and make the ideal place for a week-long stay. No. 14 sleeps 5–6 and no. 16 sleeps 4; both cost £300 per week.

Derry City Independent Hostel 4 Asylum Rd Ⓣ028/7137 7989, Ⓦwww.derry-hostel.co.uk. Also known as Steve's Backpackers, this friendly IHO hostel is based in a small terraced house off Strand Road by the PSNI station and offers sixteen beds in private rooms and smallish dorms, free breakfast and Internet access, plus all-you-can eat barbecues for £1.50 in summer.

Derry International Hostel 4–6 Magazine St Ⓣ028/7128 0280, Ⓔderrycitytours@aol.com. Efficient but slightly impersonal 150-bed independent hostel inside the city walls, with an economical restaurant, bureau de change and Internet access. At the time of writing its future was uncertain, so calling ahead is advised.

University of Ulster (Magee College) Northland Road Ⓣ028/7137 5255, Ⓦwww.ulst.ac.uk/accommodation/vacation. Accommodation in study bedrooms available from June to mid-September at £14.10 per night or £140 for a week-long stay in a two-bedroom unit.

The City

Since the removal of the security blanket of metal barricades and barbed wire following the ceasefire, it has once again been possible to walk the entire circuit of Derry's **city walls**. One of the best preserved defences in Europe, a mile in length and never higher than a two-storey house, the walls are reinforced by bulwarks and bastions and a parapeted earth rampart as wide as any thoroughfare. Within their circuit, the original medieval street pattern has remained, with four **gateways** (Shipquay, Ferryquay, Bishop and Butcher) surviving from the original construction, albeit in slightly revised form.

You're more than likely to make your approach from the Guildhall Square, once the old quay, east of Shipquay Gate. The Neo-Gothic ecclesiastical appearance of the **Guildhall** (Mon–Fri 9am–5pm; free) belies its true function as the headquarters of the City Council. Inside, the city's history is depicted in a series of stained glass windows. Most of the city's cannons are lined up opposite here, between **Shipquay Gate** and Magazine Gate, their muzzles peering out above the ramparts. A reconstruction of the medieval **O'Doherty Tower** here (June–Sept Mon–Sat 10am–5pm, Sun 2–5pm; rest of year closed Sun & Mon; Ⓦwww.derry.net/tower; £3.65) is home to a prize-winning **museum** telling the city's history over the past four centuries. Entered via a re-creation of an old tunnel serving as a stores passage, the combination of tableaux and audio-

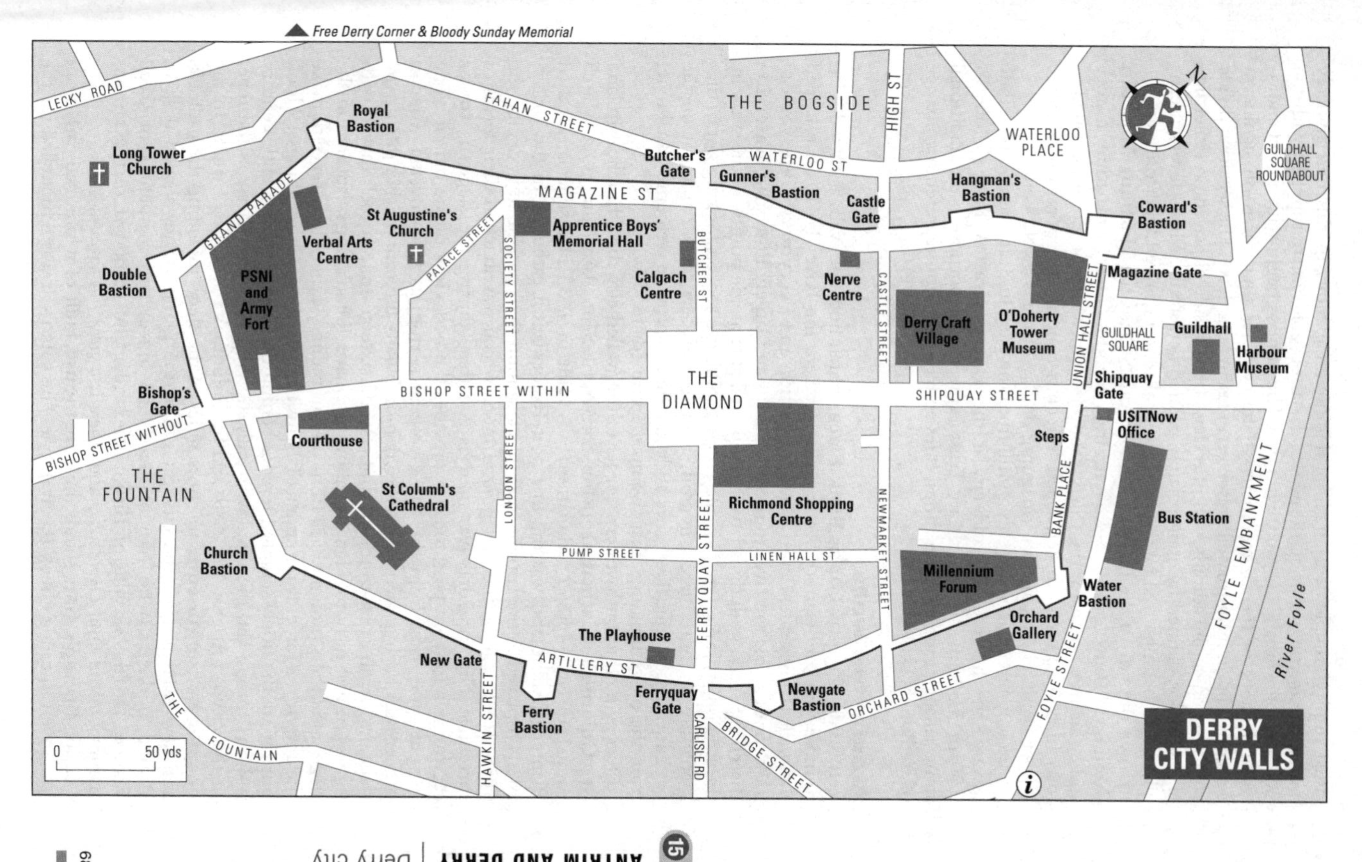

Free Derry Corner & Bloody Sunday Memorial
DERRY CITY WALLS
THE BOGSIDE
THE FOUNTAIN
THE DIAMOND
LECKY ROAD
FAHAN STREET
WATERLOO ST
WATERLOO PLACE
HIGH ST
MAGAZINE ST
GRAND PARADE
PALACE STREET
SOCIETY STREET
BUTCHER ST
CASTLE STREET
UNION HALL STREET
GUILDHALL SQUARE
GUILDHALL SQUARE ROUNDABOUT
BISHOP STREET WITHIN
BISHOP STREET WITHOUT
SHIPQUAY STREET
LONDON STREET
PUMP STREET
LINEN HALL ST
FERRYQUAY STREET
NEWMARKET STREET
BANK PLACE
FOYLE EMBANKMENT
River Foyle
ARTILLERY ST
HAWKIN STREET
CARLISLE RD
BRIDGE STREET
ORCHARD STREET
FOYLE STREET
THE FOUNTAIN
Long Tower Church
Royal Bastion
Butcher's Gate
Gunner's Bastion
Castle Gate
Hangman's Bastion
Coward's Bastion
Magazine Gate
Guildhall
Harbour Museum
Shipquay Gate
USITNow Office
Steps
Bus Station
Water Bastion
Orchard Gallery
Millennium Forum
Newgate Bastion
Richmond Shopping Centre
Ferryquay Gate
The Playhouse
Ferry Bastion
New Gate
Church Bastion
St Columb's Cathedral
Courthouse
Bishop's Gate
Double Bastion
PSNI and Army Fort
Verbal Arts Centre
St Augustine's Church
Apprentice Boys' Memorial Hall
Calgach Centre
Nerve Centre
Derry Craft Village
O'Doherty Tower Museum
N
0
50 yds

visual displays supplements traditional museum exhibits in this determinedly non-sectarian gallop through time – as far as possible, you're supplied with the facts and left to make up your own mind. The displays begin with a brief audio-visual account of the development of the city and then focus on significant developments in its history, all presented in fascinating detail. The sectarian divide is covered especially adroitly, with the views of each side displayed on either side of a corridor, defined by appropriately painted kerbstones. Music lovers, meanwhile, will be impressed by the museum's collection of rare Undertones singles.

Down the side of the Guildhall in Harbour Square, the **Harbour Museum** (Mon–Fri 10am–1pm & 2–4.30pm; free) recounts Derry's maritime history and contains a replica of the thirty-foot *currach* in which St Columba sailed to Iona in 563 AD and an actual late fifteenth-century longboat found in the Upper Bann. There's also an intriguing display of maps of old Derry.

Shipquay Street slopes steeply uphill from the gate. Just off it as you penetrate towards the heart of the old city is the **Derry Craft Village** (Mon–Sat 9.30am–5.30pm), an Inner City Trust project in a purpose-built traditional stone village complex, with shops, cafés and a crafts shop representing a range of traditional skills.

Around the walls

Left inside Shipquay Gate is **Bank Place**, which hugs the walls as they dogleg round at the southeastern Water Bastion, where the River Foyle once lapped the walls at high tide. On to Newgate Bastion and **Ferryquay Gate**, you can look south across the river to the prosperous and largely Protestant **Waterside district**. Several sculptures have been placed at strategic points on the walls by the English artist Antony Gormley, their gaping eye sockets looking out in diametrically opposite directions from a single body – a frank comment on the city's ideological split. Aesthetics aside, the figures provide welcome visual relief from the office buildings that swamp the immediate view.

Occupying the southwestern corner of the walled city, the Church of Ireland **St Columb's Cathedral** (Mon–Sat: April–Sept 9am–5pm; Oct–March 9am–1pm & 2–4pm; £1 donation) was built in 1633 in a style later called Planters' Gothic and was the first post-Reformation cathedral in the British Isles. Displayed in the entrance porch is a cannon shell catapulted in during the 1688–1689 siege by the besieging army, to which was attached their terms of surrender. The cathedral was used as a battery during the siege, its **tower** serving as a lookout post; today it provides the best **view** of the old city. The present spire dates from the late Georgian period, its lead-covered wooden predecessor having been stripped to fashion bullets and cannon shot during the siege. Inside, an open-timbered roof rests on sixteen stone corbels carved with figures of past bishops. Hanging above the nave, French **flags** captured in the siege, and others brought back from various military expeditions, serve to make the interior a forceful reminder of British imperialism. Other things to look out for are the finely sculpted reredos behind the altar, the eighteenth-century bishop's throne and the window panels showing scenes as diverse as the relief of the city on August 12, 1689, and St Columba's mission to Britain. In the **chapter house museum** are more relics of the siege, including the padlocks and keys used to lock the city gates, plus the grand kidney-shaped desk of Bishop Berkeley (who only visited Derry once) and mementos of Cecil Frances (1818–95), wife of Bishop Alexander and composer of the famous hymns *Once in royal David's city* and *There is a green hill far away*.

Inside **Bishop's Gate** stands the **courthouse**, built of white sandstone from Dungiven in crude Greek Revival style. The gate itself was remodelled for the first centenary of the siege and reopened in 1789. Immediately outside the walls here is the **Fountain** area, named after the freshwater source that once supplied the city, though there are few remnants of any antiquity here apart from the immediately visible remaining tower of the old Derry jail, jammed up against the grim modern houses. The Fountain is a Protestant housing estate that sticks into the Catholic west bank like a sore thumb and is of interest solely for its Union Jack kerb paintings and huge **murals**, which read as direct responses to the more famous Catholic "Free Derry" mural in the next valley. Until recently, the Fountain area had the **oldest mural** in the North. Painted in the early part of the twentieth century by Bobby Jackson, it showed the Siege of Derry and the Battle of the Boyne, and was repainted every year. In the 1970s, when the area was redeveloped, the wall was painstakingly dismantled, moved, reassembled and repainted, but it finally disintegrated in 1994. A replica was painted in 1995 on a special Bobby Jackson memorial wall. Other Loyalist murals are to be found in Bond Street in the Waterside.

Continuing north from Bishop's Gate, you reach the **Double Bastion**, where the "Roaring Meg" cannon sits. During the siege, it was said that "the noise of the discharge was more terrifying than were the contents of the charge dangerous to the enemy." Just by here is the **Verbal Arts Centre** (Ⓦwww.verbalartscentre.co.uk), a unique project aimed at sustaining and promoting forms of communication and entertainment once central to Irish culture: legend, folklore, *sean-nós* – a nasalized and unaccompanied narrative form of singing (see p.833) – and story-telling performed by a *seanachie* (story-teller). The centre, incorporating designs by Louis De Brocquy, commissions works from writers, hosts poetry readings and story-telling and has its own resident *seanachie*. It also visits schools and community centres and has a determinedly non-sectarian ethos, influenced by its understanding of the importance of the oral tradition in all cultures. Every year at the beginning of April, it promotes an international **story-telling festival**; and there are also plenty of events year-round, so drop in and check out what's on the programme.

The nearby **Royal Bastion** was constructed between 1826 and 1828 and used to be topped by a nine-foot high statue of Reverend George Walker, the defender of Derry "against an arbitrary and bigoted monarch" (to quote the still-legible inscription). The statue was blown up in 1973 and the surrounding area remains a significant flashpoint every August 12 when the Apprentice Boys march in Walker's and their predecessors' memory (see box on p.734). The view from here across the Bogside district (see below) is expansive.

Just inside **Butcher's Gate** is **The Fifth Province** in the Calgach Genealogy Centre, an overblown multimedia "journey" through Ireland's heritage (shows Mon–Fri 11.30am & 2.30pm; £3). The trip begins in a stone chamber, "Departure Lounge", where the late actor Richard Harris provides a video introduction to the history of Derry. Next it's off to the module and a trip into space to meet Calgach, founder of ancient Derry, who regales you with tales from the past. Finally, your senses are bombarded with a panoply of images celebrating Irish culture.

A little further downhill, on the south side of Magazine Street, is another focus of Derry's dynamic cultural world, **The Nerve Centre** (Ⓣ028/7126 0562, Ⓦwww.nerve-centre.org.uk), which contains all manner of sound, film and video studios and editing suites, alongside an arthouse cinema, music venue and coffee bar.

The Bogside

In the valley below the northern city walls is the Catholic **Bogside** district, where, at the start of the Troubles, young Catholics were caught up in an advancing disarray of army and police, who replied to bricks and petrol bombs with tear gas, rubber bullets and careering Saracen armoured cars. The area at the foot of the escarpment has been redeveloped in the form of a dual carriageway, a new estate of tenement flats and empty concrete precincts. But clinging to the opposite hillside is a classic urban landscape, with turn-of-the-century terraces of stucco facades, blue tile roofs and red chimney stacks.

Most eye-catching in this panorama is a gable-end **mural** showing the former independent Republican MP and one of the organizers of the People's Democracy movement Bernadette Devlin, megaphone in hand, in front of the old "You are now entering Free Derry" mural. Other murals visible nearby include a massive hunger-strike mural featuring one of the blanket-clad participants, Raymond McCartney, while another, the "Death of Innocence" mural commemorates a 14-year-old girl, Annette McGavigan, who died in 1971, caught in crossfire between the British Army and IRA. There are also striking murals featuring a gas-mask-clad petrol bomber and a British soldier smashing down a door with a sledgehammer during Operation Motorman. These and the nearby Bloody Sunday murals were painted by the Bogside Artists – Kevin Hasson, Tom Kelly and William Kelly – who have recently published an illustrated book on their work, available from Bookworm (see p.692).

For the first two years of the Troubles, the territory beyond the original Free Derry mural was the notorious "no-go area", the undisputed preserve of the IRA. This autonomy lasted until 1972, when Operation Motorman was launched; the IRA men who had been in the area were tipped off, though, and got across the border before the invasion took place. Further across to the right of the Bernadette Devlin mural stands the memorial pillar to the thirteen Catholic civilians killed by British paratroopers on **Bloody Sunday**, January 30, 1972 (a fourteenth died later of his wounds). The soldiers immediately claimed they had been fired upon, an assertion that was later disproved, though some witnesses have come forward to report seeing IRA men there with their guns. The bitter memory of the subsequent Widgery Commission's failure to declare anyone responsible for the deaths has festered in Catholic Derry, and pressure has been maintained on successive governments to reopen investigations. A new inquiry was finally announced in spring 1998 and opened in 1999, but at the time of writing, it had yet to declare its findings. To the right of this area once stood the Rossville flats, by far the most infamous part of the Bogside – Derry's equivalent of the Divis flats in Belfast.

Eating, drinking and entertainment

Although **eating out** in Derry has improved dramatically in recent years, you still won't be faced with a bewildering choice. *The Galley*, within the walls at 12A Shipquay St, is a good daytime choice, with quality pizzas and home baking, while *Java*, 37 Ferryquay St, probably serves the city's best coffee. Otherwise, try the very sociable *Leprechaun Café* on the Strand Road. As ever, you can also get lunch in many of the pubs: *Badgers*, in Orchard Street, has recently won awards, while the *Metro* in Bank Place, the *Linenhall* in Linenhall Street and the *Monico Lounge* opposite the main post office are also worth checking out. Alternatively, try the two Wetherspoon's pubs *The Diamond*, exactly where you'd expect it to be on The Diamond within the city walls, and the *Ice Wharf* on Strand Road. All of the large hotels also have their own restaurants.

Restaurants

Da Nano 2–4 Lower Clarendon St ⓣ028/7126 6646. A very popular spot for pizza and pasta.
The Exchange Exchange House, Queens Quay ⓣ028/7127 3990. This new wine bar is currently the spot to be seen and offers a cosmopolitan menu too.
Fitzroys 2–4 Bridge St ⓣ028/7126 6211. A modern, city-centre brasserie just outside Ferryquay Gate, open for both lunch and evening meals.
India House 51 Carlisle Rd ⓣ028/7126 0532. The city's best Indian restaurant, offering a reasonably priced menu.
La Sosta 45A Carlisle Rd ⓣ028/7137 4817. Authentic Italian food in a pleasant, family-run establishment.
Mange 2 2 Clarendon St ⓣ028/7136 1222. Arguably the city's most stylish restaurant, and certainly one of its most popular, serving a variety of meat and fish dishes. Open daily for lunch and Wed–Sun for dinner.

Bars and music

What Derry lacks in restaurants, it makes up for, inevitably, in **pubs**. Congenial and conversational places include *The Clarendon Bar*, 44 Strand Rd; *Badgers*, 18 Orchard St (for an older clientele); and *Mullins* on Sackville Street.

Traditional music in the city is not as exciting as it once was. The venues that remain are mostly grouped in and around Waterloo Street, just outside the northern section of the walls, a Catholic working-class area. The *Dungloe Bar* has a Tuesday night traditional session and rock music on other week-nights. Other sessions take place at the *Rocking Chair Pub* and the *Gweedore Bar*, which has a function room upstairs with good music and dancing; it often stays open until 1am and is connected to *Peadar O'Donnell's* next door, a retro pub that has traditional music every night in summer. Elsewhere, *Beckett's*, on Foyle Street, offers music five nights a week, including salsa and DJs, and *Sandinos*, around the corner in Water Street, has a mixed bag, including traditional music and jazz. The *Anchor Inn*, 38 Ferryquay St, has live music every night except Monday and a traditional session on Wednesdays.

For livelier **nightlife**, head for Shipquay Street, where *Downey's* claims to be "Ireland's largest R&B club" and has music most nights. Other clubs include *Fusion*, Strand Road (Fri–Sun), and *Earth* in the *Le Roc* complex at the junction of Strand and Rock roads (Fri–Tues). Also worth checking out for DJs are the *Strand Bar* and the *Carraig*, both on Strand Road. A popular choice for Friday and Saturday nights is to cross the border, to nightclubs in Letterkenny, Carndonagh and Buncrana.

Arts and other entertainment

Classical music thrives in the city through the Londonderry Arts Association (ⓣ028/7126 4481), with around a dozen concerts a year held in the Great Hall of the University of Ulster's Magee Campus on Northland Road. Orchestral concerts by the Ulster Orchestra are held much less regularly in the Great Hall of the Guildhall. The university's Arts Development Office also organizes a broad year-round programme of cultural activities (ⓦwww.ulst.ac.uk).

One of the latest additions to the city landscape is the huge Millennium Forum **theatre** on Newmarket Street (ⓣ028/7126 4455, ⓦwww.millenniumforum.co.uk), a controversially expensive development that offers a broad, if somewhat middle-of-the-road programme, including ballet and opera. More innovative theatre and dance can often be found at The Playhouse on Artillery Street (ⓣ028/7126 8027). However, theatre in Derry since the early 1980s is still associated, despite its current inactivity, with the polemical and hugely controversial Field Day Theatre Company, whose principal members have included, at one time or another, the poet Seamus Heaney (see box on p.696), the academic Séamus Deane, actor Stephen Rea and playwright Brian Friel. **Film** buffs are catered for by the seven-screen Strand cinema in the Quayside Centre (ⓣ028/7137 3000) and the Orchard Hall cinema, Orchard Street (ⓣ028/7126 2845), as well as by The Nerve Centre (see p.689).

The **visual arts** are also attracting a lot of international attention, thanks largely to the highly innovative contemporary art programming of the Orchard Gallery in Orchard Street (Tues–Sat 10am–6pm). A visit there is a must – as is the community-based Context Gallery in The Playhouse, Artillery Street. The Heritage Library on Bishop Street also occasionally has local artists' work on display.

Several **arts festivals** take place at regular times throughout the year (see "Listings" below). In addition, **Halloween** is traditionally an excuse for riotous celebration, with fireworks, fancy dress and partying in the streets. The tourist office has details of all events.

Listings

Airlines British Airways ⓣ0845/773 3377; Ryanair ⓣ0870/156 9569.
Banks Principally situated on Shipquay Place, Shipquay Street and Strand Road.
Bike rental Happy Days Cycle Hire, 245 Lone Moor Rd (ⓣ028/7128 7128, ⓦwww.happydays.ie), rents bikes from £9 per day and £35 a week.
Bookshops Bookworm, 18–20 Bishop St (ⓣ028/7128 2727), is one of the best bookshops in Ireland, with comprehensive coverage of contemporary and historical Irish works. Books in Irish can be found at Ogmios, 34 Great James St (ⓣ028/7126 4132, ⓦwww.gaelaras.ie).
Car rental Desmond Motors, 173 Strand Rd (ⓣ028/7136 0420), and several companies based at City of Derry Airport, including Avis (ⓣ028/7181 1708), Europcar (ⓣ028/7130 1312), Hertz (ⓣ028/7181 1994) and Abe King (ⓣ028/9335 2557).
Exchange Available from all banks, the main tourist office and Thomas Cook, 34 Ferryquay St (Mon–Sat 9am–5.30pm; Thurs opens 10am; ⓣ028/7185 2500).
Festivals City of Drama Festival – a week of theatre in early March (ⓣ028/7136 5151); *Guth an Earraigh* – an Irish-language festival in mid-March (ⓣ028/7126 4132); the Walled City Festival – lots of outdoor events in early June (ⓣ028/7126 7284); Maiden City Festival – various events culminating in the Apprentice Boys' march around the walls in early August (ⓣ028/7126 6677); Halloween Carnival – four days of mayhem culminating in a massive firework display on October 31; the Foyle Film Festival in November (ⓣ028/7126 7284).
Hospital Accident and emergency department, Altnagelvin Hospital, Belfast Road (ⓣ028/7134 5171); call this number also for dental emergencies after working hours or at weekends.
Internet access *Bean-There.Com*, 20 The Diamond (Mon–Sat 9am–7pm, Sun 2pm–7pm; ⓣ028/7128 1303, ⓦwww.bean-there.com; £4.50 per hour).
Laundry and dry cleaning Smooth Operators, Sackville Street (Mon–Sat 9am–5.30pm; ⓣ028/7136 0529)
Library The Central Library, 35 Foyle St, has a good selection on Irish studies and local history.
Market Bottom of William Street – stalls most days, but busiest on Saturday.
Newspapers The Nationalist *Derry Journal* (Tues & Fri; ⓦwww.derryjournal.com) has a good run-through of what's on in the city; the Unionist local paper is the *Londonderry Sentinel* (Wed).
Police The main police station is on Strand Road (ⓣ028/7136 7337).
Post office Custom House Street (Mon 8.30am–5.30pm, Tues–Fri 9am–5.30pm, Sat 9am–12.30pm; ⓣ028/7136 2563) and 3 Bishop St (Mon–Fri 9am–5.30pm, Sat 9am–12.30pm).
Radio BBC Radio Foyle (93.1 FM) and the commercial station Q102.9 FM.
Records and CDs Sounds Around, 24 Waterloo St (ⓣ028/7128 8890), has one of the best selections of music in Ireland, including plenty of rare traditional albums.
Travel agents Premier Travel, 35 Carlisle Rd ⓣ028/7126 2261; Thomas Cook, 34 Ferryquay St ⓣ028/7185 2500; USITNow, 4 Shipquay Place ⓣ028/7137 1888.

Southern County Derry

South of the Derry–Antrim A6 road, the landscape settles down into a pattern more familiar to the Republic: fertile farming land rising to the **Sperrin Mountains**, punctuated by small planned towns. The pattern in the North is subtly different, though, because the grants of land here were not made to individuals but to various London guilds or companies. Consequently, there isn't the strange, late-flowering feudalism that you see in the Republic, with its repeated archetype of Big House and surrounding town, but rather entirely **planned towns**, such as **Magherafelt** and **Moneymore**, often built on green-field sites selected by professionals who specialized in doing just that. The huge expanse of Ireland's biggest lake, **Lough Neagh**, laps against the county's southeastern corner and here too is one of the must-see sites of the entire North, **Bellaghy Bawn** castle.

The road to Dungiven

Seven or so miles east of Derry, a turning leads to **Ness Wood Country Park**, a pleasant place to stop and stroll through a mixture of natural and imported woodland. The centrepiece is **Shaun's Leap waterfall**, the highest in the North, whose waters cascade into a small glen below a thirty-foot wide chasm, across which the outlaw Shaun Crossan is said to have leaped to evade capture.

DUNGIVEN (Dún Geimhin, "fort of the cattle hide"), ten miles further on, is a fairly unremarkable town, though it does harbour one or two ruins of interest. Originally an O'Cahan stronghold, Dungiven was given to the Skinners' Company to settle in the seventeenth century. The remains of the O'Cahan fortifications are incorporated into the newly restored **castle**, whose battlemented outline gives Dungiven a particular flavour when approached from the south. The castle dates back to 1839 and is set in 22 acres of parkland with views across to the Sperrins. During World War II, it was used as a dance hall by American troops, and it was later the scene of an attempt in 1971 to set up an independent Northern Ireland parliament. By the 1980s, it had fallen into disrepair but, following the restoration work, it now houses en-suite hostel-style **accommodation**, including double and family rooms (Ⓣ028/7774 2428, Ⓦwww.dungivencastle.com; ❷).

Dungiven Priory, signposted down a footpath half a mile out of the town towards Antrim, gives a taste of the pioneering life of the early Plantation settlers, and of the continuity of tradition. No more than a ruin, the Augustinian priory stands on an imposing site on a bluff above the river. Founded in 1100 by the O'Cahans, it belongs to the first wave of European monastic orders that arrived in Ireland to supplant the Celtic Church. The priory contains what is rated as the finest **medieval tomb** in Northern Ireland, that of Cooey na Gall O'Cahan, who died in 1385: beneath the effigy are six bare-legged warriors in kilts, presumably denoting Scotsmen, who represent the O'Cahan chieftain's foreign mercenaries, from whom he derived his nickname "na Gall", or "of the foreigners". At some point, the O'Cahans added a defensive tower to the west end of the church, and later – when Dungiven was granted to the Skinners' Company, in the person of Sir Edward Doddington – this was enlarged to become a two-and-a-half-storey defensive manor house. There's an evocative artist's impression on the site of what that building looked like. Although the church hasn't been used since 1711, Dungiven Priory remains a religious site of sorts. A tree knotted with rags – handkerchiefs, torn-off bits of summer dresses, socks – stands over a deeply hollowed **stone**, originally used by the monks for milling grain and now an object of pilgrimage for people seeking cures for physical illness. There's little to tempt you to stay, although if you fancy a night in a converted stone mill, aim for *The Flax Mill*, Mill Lane (IHH; ⓣ028/7774 2655), an independent **hostel** three miles north of town and signposted off the Limavady road.

The ruined **Banagher Old Church**, a couple of miles southwest of Dungiven, was founded in the twelfth century by St Muiredach O'Heney, who is buried in the well-preserved mortuary house built on a sandhill in the churchyard. Banagher sand is said to bring good fortune to the founder's line and perhaps did so to a famous modern bearer of the saint's name, **Seamus Heaney**, who is known to have visited for the explicit purpose. The ruins themselves are sedately impressive, as are the walks around the nearby Banagher Glen **nature reserve** (June–Sept daily 9am–9pm; free).

The Plantation towns

South of Dungiven, well into the Sperrin Mountains, are more of the **Plantation towns** of the London companies, most of them characteristically planned around a central diamond. **DRAPERSTOWN** is essentially a junction, with well-mannered houses facing each other in a very grand street design. The **Plantation of Ulster Visitor Centre** on the High Street (Easter–Sept Mon–Sat 10am–5pm, Sun 1–5pm; rest of year closed Sat & Sun; £3.50), as its name suggests, recounts the Plantation story and that of the Flight of the Earls in more detail, using multimedia technology. At **UPPERLANDS**, three miles northeast of Maghera, which itself lies seven miles northeast of Draperstown, you can get some idea of the impact of the new eighteenth-century technology on the area at the **Old Mill Museum**, a private textile museum owned by the Clark family. In 1740, Jackson Clark dammed the river to provide power and installed linen-finishing machinery here. If you want to look around, phone William Clark & Sons in advance to arrange a guided tour (Wed 10am–4pm; advance booking necessary on ⓣ028/7954 7200; free). *Ardtara Country House*, a nearby **guesthouse** at 8 Gorteade Rd, offers a taste both of Victorian elegance and wild boar in its excellent restaurant (ⓣ028/7964 4490, ⓕ7964 5080; ❽).

Heading south, **MAGHERAFELT** (Machaire Fíolta, "Fiolta's plain"), granted to the Salters' Company by James I, has another wide, sloping main street and an increasingly successful **arts festival** in March. The town makes a reasonable base for exploring Lough Neagh and the Bellaghy area and has an amenable **tourist office** (Mon–Sat 9am–5pm; ⓣ028/7963 1510) in The Bridewell, 2 Churchwell Lane. There's **accommodation** at *Laurel Villa*, 60 Church St (ⓣ028/7963 2238, ⓦwww.laurel-villa.com; ❸), which also organizes heritage and angling breaks, and at the comfortable *Hostel 56*, 56 Rainey St (IHO; ⓣ028/7963 2096; ⓦwww.hostel56.club24.co.uk), complete with its own roof garden. There's also plenty of **eating** choices, including *Mary's*, an exceptionally pleasant old-time pub on the Market Square, which serves substantial bar meals and has an upstairs carvery

At one time a real gem, **MONEYMORE** (Muine Mór, "large hill"), about five miles further south, had until recently degenerated into a run-down, traffic-choked disgrace but is thankfully undergoing renovation to reinvigorate some of its once-graceful pedimented buildings. Originally constructed by the Drapers in the early seventeenth century (and restored by them in 1817), these buildings face each other across a wide main street topped by an Orange Hall; there are plenty of red, white and blue kerbstones here indicating the continuing strength of local Loyalism. Moneymore was the first town in the North to have piped water – amazingly enough, as early as 1615. The new **Heritage Centre** in the Manor House on the High Street (mid–March to Sept daily 10am–6pm; rest of year closed Sat & Sun; £3) explores the town's history, with a model village showing its original layout and constituents.

Just outside town, **Springhill** (mid–March to June & Sept Sat, Sun & public hols noon–6pm; July & Aug daily same times; £3.50) is a grand Plantation manor house built between 1680 and 1700 by William "Good-Will" Conygham in order to fulfil a marriage contract with the father of his bride-to-be, Anne Upton. Elegant both without and within, its sober whitewashed architecture houses fine rooms, equipped with original period furniture and paintings belonging to William and his descendants, who occupied the house until 1959. Upstairs, the Blue Room is believed to be haunted by the ghost of Olivia Lenox-Conyngham, whose husband George was found shot here in 1816. Outside the house, the stables house a **costume collection**, which adopts a specific theme each year, drawing upon three thousand items collected from the mid-seventeenth century to the 1970s. There are also delightful gardens, a tower dating from the 1730s, which was probably originally part of a windmill, and a pleasant walk through beech and yew trees.

Lough Neagh and Bellaghy

East of Magherafelt and Moneymore are the fish-filled waters of the biggest lake in Ireland, **Lough Neagh**. Tributaries flow from every point of the compass: the Lower Bann, which drains the lake and runs north to **Lough Beg** (finally reaching the sea north of Coleraine), contains some huge **trout**, including the rare *dollaghan*, the Lough Neagh trout; the best **fishing** is from mid-July to October. Similar to salmon – which are also common – *dollaghan* grow by three pounds every year and can be caught by spinning, worming and fly-fishing: the Ballinderry Black and the Bann Olive are famous flies derived from this region. To fish in the lough or the river, all anglers require a Fisheries Conservation Board Rod; however, while this entitles you to carry a rod it doesn't mean that you can fish unless you have a **permit** from the Department of Culture, Arts & Leisure (Ⓣ028/9025 8861). The angling clubs that control much of the water let day tickets at reasonable rates. For details of licences and permits, ask at local tackle shops, the nearest being Heuston's Sport, Main Street, **Castledawson** (Ⓣ028/7966 8282) and Hamilton's Sport, Burn Road, **Cookstown** (Ⓣ028/8676 6541; see p.758).

Like many of the Plantation settlements in the area, **BELLAGHY** (Baile Eachaidh, "Eochaidh's townland"), just west of Lough Beg, has a history which reflects the divisions between communities. Indeed, no fewer than two of the ten 1981 hunger strikers (see p.797) – cousins Francis Hughes and Thomas McElwee – came from the village, and Orange Parades have been a regular flashpoint. Bellaghy is neatly laid out around a T-junction, and if you wander south past the whitewashed terraces on Castle Street, you'll come to one of the best examples of a surviving Plantation castle, **Bellaghy Bawn** (Easter–Sept daily 10am–6pm; Oct–Easter Tues–Sat 9am–5pm; £2), built in 1618 by the Vintners' Company. Most of its fortifications were lost in 1641, but it still retains an impressive circular flanker tower. Inside you'll find fascinating interpretive displays explaining the 7000-year-old history of the settlements in this area, the Vintners' construction of the village – today's houses still occupy the same original allocated plots of land – and the diverse ecology of the Lough Beg wetland area. The real treasure here, however, is the dedication of much of

Seamus Heaney

There was a sunlit absence.
The helmeted pump in the yard
heated its iron,
water honeyed

in the slung bucket
and the sun stood
like a griddle cooling
against the wall
of each long afternoon.

(From *Mossbawn: 1. Sunlight*)

It's impossible to conceive of a contemporary poet, Irish or otherwise, whose works are more evocative of time and place than **Seamus Heaney**. He was born, the eldest of nine children, on the family farm of Mossbawn (itself the title of two poems in his fourth collection *North*), in the townland of Tamniarn, near Bellaghy, on April 13, 1939. Heaney's family background, his Catholic upbringing and his study of Irish at school imbued him with a strong sense of being Irish in a state that considered itself British, a paradox that would form a major motif in his work during the 1970s. While at Queen's University, Belfast, he was further influenced by the literature he discovered in Belfast's Linen Hall library, especially the works of John Hewitt, the Antrim-born "Poet of the Glens", and the English "naturalist" poet Ted Hughes, in whose work he found an "association of sounds in print that connected with the world below". The rural Monaghan setting of Patrick Kavanagh's poetry further echoed his own experience and vision.

Heaney's first poem, *Tractors*, was published in the *Belfast Evening Telegraph* in 1962. His first significant collection, *Death of a Naturalist*, followed in 1966 and was immediately recognized for its earthiness and command of diverse metrical forms. While lecturing at Queen's, his career expanded into journalism and television and

the Bawn's space to a most notable local man, **Seamus Heaney**, one of the world's greatest living poets, who was born and brought up nearby (see box above). Heaney himself is the star of a unique and atmospheric video showing in the Bawn, "A Sense of Place", in which he recounts the influence of his upbringing, local character and landmarks on his poetry. His father, for instance, rented grazing rights on the strand at Lough Beg and, in his poem *Ancestral Photograph*, Heaney recalls helping to herd the cattle that grazed there down Castle Street on their way to market. Prints of other poems are displayed on the walls of various rooms, and the Bawn's library contains the ultimate collection of his works, including first drafts and extremely limited editions. The Bawn's helpful curators are very knowledgeable and there's a small **café** here too.

You can see the shimmering Lough Beg from the windows of the flanker tower, and a stroll down to the lake is well worthwhile. In summer, the lake's waters recede and **Church Island** becomes accessible from the strand. Besides a walled graveyard, you'll find the ruins of a medieval church here, said to have been founded centuries before by the ubiquitous St Patrick, with a tower and spire added in 1788 by the eccentric Frederick Augustus Hervey, Anglican Bishop of Derry and fourth Earl of Bristol (see p.679), to improve his view from Ballyscullion House on the mainland nearby. He commissioned Lanyon to build a huge replacement for the original house which stood here, with, he became increasingly involved in the **Civil Rights movement**. His response to the Troubles saw him seeking for "images and symbols adequate to our predicament" and he began to see poetry as a mode of resistance. Eventually, though, the violence so disturbed him that he moved with his family to County Wicklow, prompting Ian Paisley's *Protestant Telegraph* to bid farewell to "the well-known papist propagandist" on his departure to his "spiritual home in the popish republic". While his 1970s collections *North* and *Field Work* had mixed receptions – some saw the strong influence of Robert Lowell on the former – Heaney found himself turning increasingly to his Irish heritage as a source of inspiration, particularly the long medieval poem *Buile Suibhne (The Madness of Sweeney)*, and published his own *Sweeney Astray* collection in 1983. The following year's *Station Island* drew upon his experiences as a participant in St Patrick's Purgatory.

The hunger strikes of the early 1980s brought a new urgency to Northern politics and a revival of Heaney's polemicism. Prompted by the staging in Derry in 1980 of Brian Friel's play *Translations*, which showed English surveyors travelling through eighteenth-century Ireland anglicizing all the place names, Heaney co-founded the **Field Day Theatre Company** with Friel, his old friend and fellow-academic Séamus Deane, the actor Stephen Rea and others. While the group's theatrical activities were themselves controversial, it was their publications that engendered the most antipathy. Their pamphlets were criticized as attempts to over-intellectualize the Troubles and the 1991 *Field Day Anthology of Irish Writing* was decried for its under-representation of work by women writers.

Heaney's reputation, however, has remained largely unsullied, maintained not merely by the sheer literary strength of his work and its ready accessibility, but by his undoubted "presence" and a lack of pomposity – his nickname "Famous Séamus" notwithstanding. In 1995, his abilities were more widely recognized by the award of the **Nobel Prize for Literature**. Heaney's recent works include a translation of the Anglo-Saxon epic poem *Beowulf*, his dramatic retelling of this tale of monster- and dragon-slaying managing to breathe new life into a work that was long considered too dense and metaphorical for a modern readership.

apparently, 365 windows, but died abroad before ever moving in. You can view the ruins from one of the *Lough Beg Coach Houses* (Ⓣ028/7938 6235, Ⓔrichard@mulholland.com; £200–380 per week), which offer good **self-catering accommodation** and also run coarse-fishing and birdwatching weekends.

South Antrim: Ballymena to Lisburn

South Antrim consists mainly of rolling and bland farmland, with the exception of **Slemish Mountain**, though the larger population centres, such as **Ballymena**, **Antrim** and **Lisburn** possess a few items of cultural interest.

Ballymena and around

BALLYMENA (An Baile Meánach, "the middle townland") is a predominantly Protestant town that could have been transplanted straight from the Scottish lowlands. Indeed, most of its Plantation settlers came from the south-west of Scotland, and the Ballymena accent still retains traces of Scottish lowlands speech. Like many Northern Irish towns, its prosperity derived from the linen trade; the alleged tightfistedness of its residents earned it the sobriquet of the "Aberdeen of Ireland". Ballymena is the home base of the Reverend **Ian Paisley**, despite the fact that he originates from Armagh; this demagogic leader of the Democratic Unionist Party, who has dominated local politics since the late 1970s, remains the most outspoken Loyalist opponent to the Good Friday Agreement. Ballymena's Saturday **market** is a lively affair and its streets are often thronged with shoppers and crammed nose to tail with traffic, but significant redevelopment has left little surviving from the pre-Victorian era. The **tourist office** is at 76 Church St (Mon–Fri 9.30am–5pm; Ⓣ028/2563 8494, Ⓦwww.Ballymena.gov.uk), just behind which, at 3 Wellington Place, is the local **museum** (Mon–Fri 10am–1pm & 2–5pm, Sat 10am–1pm; free), offering plenty of information on the area's history and housing a variety of temporary exhibitions. The town's biggest attraction, however, is the **ECOS Environmental Centre**, Kernohans Lane, Broughshane Road (Easter–Sept Mon–Sat 10am–4pm, Sun noon–5pm; rest of year closes 4pm; £3.75), a mile from the town centre, featuring high-tech interactive galleries focusing on biodiversity, energy sustainability and alternative energy sources, as well as walking and cycling trails around its 150 acres of parkland.

A mile and a half west of Ballymena is **GRACEHILL**, a reminder of the curious mixture of religious oppression and tolerance that has characterized Northern Ireland's history: at the same time as Ireland's Catholics were suffering heavy penalties, the country was welcoming dissenting Protestant groups, among them the Moravians (the United Brethren), who founded a model settlement at Gracehill in 1746. The elegant town square survives, with separate buildings for men and women, whose main trade was making lace and clocks. Segregated in life, the sexes remained divided in death, and in the graveyard you can walk down the long path that separates the graves of the men from those of the women.

For miles around Ballymena the landscape is dominated by one of County Antrim's most mystical reference points, **Slemish Mountain**, best approached from the village of **Buckna**, eight miles or so east. This extinct volcano is said to be the place where St Patrick herded swine as a slave-boy after being captured and brought to Ireland, and, consequently, is a place of pilgrimage on March 17 – though others claim his writings indicate that the place of his captivity was Killala, County Mayo. Whatever, the mountain is a steep climb of about 700ft from the car park to the summit, but the **views** are well worth the effort; to the north, you can see the ruins of **Skerry Church**, the ancient burial place of the O'Neills of Clandeboye.

Antrim town and around

ANTRIM is a largely undistinguished town whose centre demonstrates all the typical decay that follows the construction of out-of-town shopping developments. If you've time to kill, there's a tenth-century **round tower** in Steeple Park, a mile north of town, indicating the site of an important monastery that flourished between the sixth and twelfth centuries, and a pretty, if unremarkable, eighteenth-century cottage, **Pogue's Entry**, on Church Street (call Ⓣ028/9442 8000 for opening times; free), the preserved childhood home of Alexander Irvine, author of *My Lady of the Chimney Corner*, which recalled his boyhood years before the Famine; the tiny **tourist office** nearby at 16 High St (May, June & Sept Mon–Wed 9am–5pm, Thurs & Fri 9am–6pm, Sat 10am–1pm; July & Aug Mon–Fri 9am–6pm, Sat 10am–3pm; Oct–April Mon–Fri 9am–5pm; Ⓣ028/9442 8331, Ⓦwww.antrim.gov.uk) will let you in. If you pop through the Castle Gate on Dublin Road, you'll find yourself in the pleasant gardens of the old **Antrim Castle**. The building itself was totally destroyed by fire in 1922, but the carriage house and stables now house the **Clotworthy Art Centre** (Mon–Fri 9.30am–5pm, Sat 10am–5pm; July & Aug also Sun 2–5pm; free), which is worth a look for its galleries of work by local artists and occasional international exhibitions.

West of Antrim, Lough Neagh's northern shores are easily accessible by taking the road from **Randalstown** to **CREEVE**, from where a minor road leads down to Churchtown Point and the lough. The ruins of an ancient Irish **church** lie here as well as a still-extant **holy well** close by. This was formerly the site of an annual pilgrimage on May 1 that involved walking barefoot thirteen times around both church and well before drinking the waters and then bathing in them. The lough's waters are rich in **eels** here and, if you're lucky, you might find a fisherman willing to sell you a few before he takes his catch off to the processing plant at Toomebridge. If not, the nearby *Cranfield Inn* serves eel. Back in Creeve, the *Creeve House Country Guest Inn*, 115 Staffordstown Rd (Ⓣ028/9447 2547, Ⓔaconnolly@btconnect.com; ❷) is a friendly **pub** and **guesthouse** and an ideal base for soaking up the atmosphere of this tranquil spot.

Lisburn

LISBURN, eight miles southwest of Belfast, is basking in its newly acquired city status, its busy, pedestrianized shopping streets and packed car parks indicating ongoing commercial success, perhaps unknown since its days as an important linen town. After the revocation of the Edict of Nantes in 1685, which removed French and Dutch Huguenots' freedom of worship, large numbers of them were persuaded to come to Ulster, where they founded the local linen trade. Bleach greens were set up along the banks of the River Lagan, the first of which started in 1626 at **Lambeg**, a mile downstream from Lisburn. Lambeg has given its name to the big drums that appear in the Orange marches, deriving from the military drums of Prince William's army.

Lisburn's one major attraction is the **Irish Linen Centre and Museum** (Mon–Sat 9.30am–5pm; Ⓦwww.lisburn.gov.uk; free) in the eighteenth-century assembly rooms in the Market Square. A permanent exhibition, "Flax to Fabric", recounts the industry's history, and you can watch weavers plying away in the purpose-built hand-loom workshop, while the museum also mounts regular temporary exhibitions. The building's modern annexe contains the **tourist office** (same times; Ⓣ028/9266 0038), plus a café and shops, and there are often art displays and lunchtime recitals. There's been a Tuesday **market** in Lisburn since 1627, but little of architectural note survived a catastrophic fire in 1707. The seventeenth-century **cathedral** opposite the Linen Centre was rebuilt after the fire, and you'll find a number of Huguenot graves in its churchyard. Down by the river is the new **Island Arts Centre**, Lagan Valley Island (Ⓣ028/9250 9509), which hosts a varied programme of musical and artistic events. The best place for a **drink** in town is the *Tuesday Bell*, Lisburn Square, a Wetherspoon's pub with the usual range of reasonably priced food.

A mile northeast of Lisburn in the village of Hilden, the **Hilden Brewery** (Tues–Sat 10.30am–4pm; tours 11.30am & 2.30pm; £4.50, including beer tasting) is one of only two real-ale breweries in Northern Ireland (the other is Whitewater in Kilkeel, County Down). It was established in 1981 in the courtyard of a former linen baron's mansion. A visit is an olfactory treat, the whiff of malted barley and hops leaving you eager to slake your thirst with a taste of the amber-coloured Hilden Ale or the hoppy Scullion's Irish. You can lunch here, too, in the attached *Tap Room* **restaurant**.

Travel details

Trains

Antrim to: Belfast (4–11 daily; 30min–1hr); Derry (3–8 daily; 1hr 35min).
Ballymena to: Belfast (4–10 daily; 1hr 25min); Derry (3–8 daily; 1hr 20min).
Carrickfergus to: Belfast (7–36 daily; 25min).
Coleraine to: Belfast (4–10 daily; 1hr 50min); Derry (4–9 daily; 40min); Portrush (10–21 daily; 15min).
Derry to: Ballymena (7 Mon–Sat, 3 Sun; 1hr 20min); Belfast (7 Mon–Sat, 3 Sun; 2hr 40min); Castlerock (8 Mon–Fri, 6 Sat, 3 Sun; 35min); Coleraine (8 Mon–Fri, 6 Sat, 3 Sun; 40min).
Larne to: Belfast (6–21 daily; 50min).
Lisburn to: Belfast (10–40 daily; 20min).
Portrush to: Coleraine (10–21 daily; 15min).

Buses

(all Ulsterbus unless stated otherwise)
The **Antrim Coaster** (Goldline Express Service #252) operates from Belfast all the way around the Antrim coast to Portrush (via Larne, the Glens, Ballycastle and the Giant's Causeway), then calls at Portstewart before terminating at Coleraine. The summer service (June–Sept) leaves Belfast Europa Buscentre Mon–Sat at 9am, calling at Laganside Buscentre ten minutes later. A Sunday service operates at the same times in high summer (July–Sept). An all-year service also runs from Larne to Coleraine, departing Mon–Sat at 3pm (July–Sept also Sun). The return service departs from Coleraine all year Mon–Sat at 9.40am (July–Sept also Sun) and June–Sept daily at 3.40pm.
The **Bushmills Bus** (Ⓣ 028/7032 5400) is an open-top service running from Coleraine through Portrush to the Giant's Causeway, weather permitting, five times daily during July and August.
Antrim to: Belfast (6–39 daily; 35–55min); Staffordstown (3 Mon–Fri; 25min).
Ballycastle to: Ballymena (5–6 Mon–Sat; 55min); Bushmills (4–8 daily; 40min); Coleraine (4–5 Mon–Sat; 1hr); Cushendall (1 Mon–Fri; 50min); Cushendun (1 Mon–Fri; 40min); Giant's Causeway (5–7 daily; 35min); Portrush (5–7 daily; 1hr).
Ballymena to: Belfast (4–19 daily; 1hr–1hr 20min); Bellaghy (5–7 Mon–Sat; 50min); Carnlough (4 Mon–Sat; 1hr); Cushendall (3–4 Mon–Sat; 55min); Cushendun (4–5 Mon–Sat; 1hr 10min); Larne (4–5 Mon–Sat; 50min).
Carrickfergus to: Belfast (8–34 daily; 35min).
Coleraine to: Armagh (1 daily; 2hr); Ballycastle (3–4 Mon–Sat; 1hr); Belfast (4–8 daily; 1hr 45min); Bushmills (3–8 Mon–Sat; 25min); Castlerock (7–9 Mon–Sat; 15min); Derry (2–14 daily; 1hr 15min–2hr); Limavady (2–15 daily; 25min–1hr); Portrush (Mon–Sat every 30min–1hr, Sun hourly; 20min); Portstewart (Mon–Sat every 30min–1hr, Sun hourly; 30min).
Derry to: Ballybofey (*Bus Éireann*; 4–5 daily; 1hr 10min); Belfast (6–15 daily; 1hr 40min); Buncrana (*Lough Swilly*; 3–12 daily; 35min); Carndonagh (*Lough Swilly*; 4–5 Mon–Sat; 45min); Coleraine (2–12 daily; 1hr 25min); Derry Airport (6 daily; 20min); Donegal (*Bus Éireann*; 3–5 daily; 1hr 30min); Dublin (*Bus Éireann*; 4–5 daily; 4hr 30min); Dunfanaghy (*Lough Swilly*; 2–3 Mon–Sat; 2hr 10min); Dungiven (6–25 daily; 30min–1hr); Dungloe (*Lough Swilly*; 1–3 Mon–Sat; 3hr 15min–5hr); Enniskillen (4–7 daily; 2hr–3hr 30min); Galway (*Bus Éireann*; 3–4 daily; 5hr 10min); Greencastle (*Lough Swilly*; 5 Mon–Sat; 55min); Letterkenny (*Bus Éireann*; 3–6 daily; 35min & *Lough Swilly*; 11–12 Mon–Sat; 30–55min); Limavady (2–13 daily; 35–55min); Magherafelt (1 Mon–Fri; 2hr 50min); Malin Head (*Lough Swilly*; 2 Mon, Wed & Fri, 3 Sat; 1hr 25min); Moville (*Lough Swilly*; 5–6 Mon–Sat; 50min); Muff (*Lough Swilly*; 9–11 Mon–Sat; 20min); Omagh (5–9 daily; 1hr 10min); Sligo (*Bus Éireann*; 4–5 daily; 2hr 30min); Strabane (5–21 daily; 25–40min); Stroove (*Lough Swilly*; 4 Mon–Sat; 1hr 10min).
Draperstown to: Maghera (1 Mon–Fri; 15min); Magherafelt (3–8 Mon–Sat; 30min); Omagh (via the Sperrins); 2 Mon–Sat; 1hr 10min).
Dungiven to: Belfast (6–15 daily; 1hr 10min); Derry (6–19 daily; 30min–1hr); Limavady (3–8 daily; 25min).
Larne to: Belfast (2–16 daily; 55min–1hr 35min); Carnlough (3–9 daily; 40min); Cushendall (2–4 daily; 1hr 15min); Cushendun (2–4 daily; 1hr 30min); Glenarm (3–9 daily; 30min).
Limavady to: Belfast (3–5 daily; 1hr 40min); Castlerock (6–7 Mon–Sat; 45min); Coleraine (2–13 daily; 25min–1hr); Derry (3–17 daily; 35–55min); Dungiven (3–7 daily; 25min).
Magherafelt to: Antrim (3–7 daily; 50min); Bellaghy (4–7 daily; 15 min); Cookstown (3–13 daily; 30min); Toome (3–11 daily; 20min).
Portrush to: Belfast (4–7 daily; 2hr); Giant's Causeway (5–6 daily, plus additional open-top service in July & Aug; 25min).
Whitehead to: Belfast (4–14 daily; 1hr); Islandmagee circular service to Mill Bay, Brown's Bay and Portmuck (2–4 Mon–Sat; 20–30min).

Down and Armagh

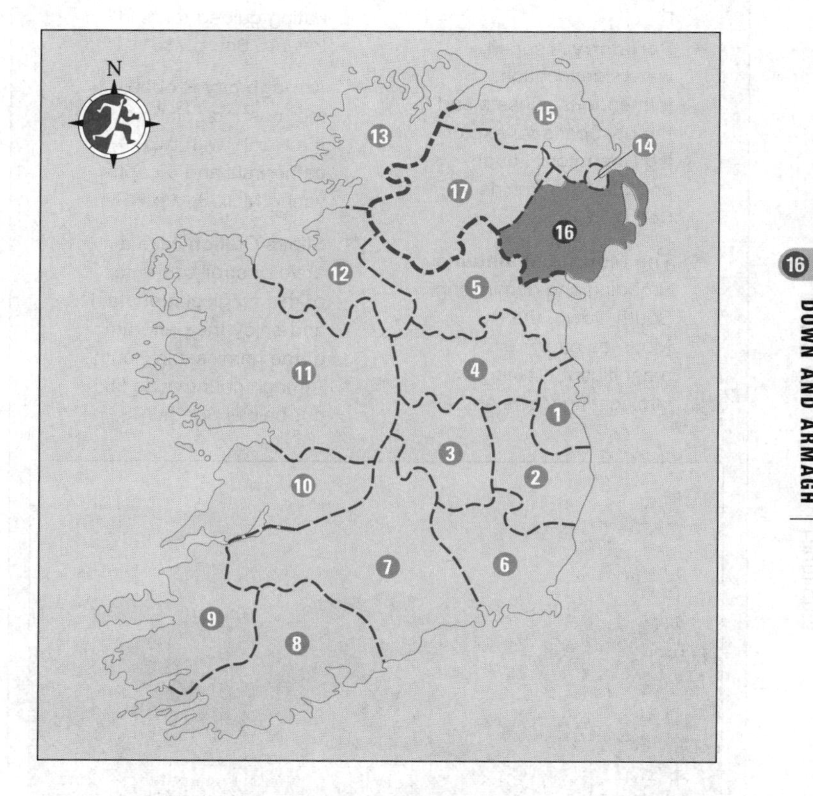

CHAPTER 16

Highlights

* **The Ulster Folk and Transport Museum** Possibly the best museum in Northern Ireland – it consummately encapsulates much of the North's cultural and industrial history. **See p.707**

* **Portaferry** A superb waterside location, tremendous sunsets and the best base for exploring Strangford Lough and the Ards Peninsula. **See p.713**

* **The Mourne Mountains** Brooding and dominating South Down, the Mournes offer magnificent walking, intoxicating views and a total escape from the contemporary world. **See p.724**

* **The Argory** A magnificent nineteenth-century mansion, set in gorgeous grounds and featuring one of the most illuminating guided tours in Ireland. **See p.736**

* **Armagh city** Probably the most graceful city in the North, with two cathedrals and a captivating Mall. **See p.737**

* **Slieve Gullion** Take a drive or stroll to the top of this magical mountain and enjoy the panorama of the unmissable South Armagh countryside laid out below. **See p.743**

16

Down and Armagh

Counties **Down** and **Armagh** occupy the southeastern corner of Northern Ireland, between Belfast and the border. It's a region where all too many of the place names are familiar from the news, and certainly the border areas, especially South Armagh, have borne more than their share of the Troubles. But it's also very attractive country, especially around the coast, and you're never far away from associations with **St Patrick**, who sailed into Strangford Lough to make his final Irish landfall in County Down, founded his first bishopric at Armagh and is buried at either Downpatrick or Armagh, depending on whose claim you choose.

Heading south from Belfast, the glowering **Mourne Mountains** increasingly dominate the panorama, and it's in this direction that most of the attractions lie. If you simply take the main roads in and out of Belfast – the A1 for Newry and the border, or the M1 motorway west – you'll come across very little to stop for: it's in the rural areas, the mountains and coast, that the charm of this region lies. Probably the best option is to head east from Belfast around the Down shore – past the **Ulster Folk and Transport Museum**, one of the best in the North, and the blowsy suburban resort of **Bangor** into the **Ards Peninsula** or along the banks of **Strangford Lough**. There are plenty of little beaches, early Christian sites, defensive tower houses and fine mansions to visit on the way towards **Newcastle**, the best base for excursions on foot into the Mourne Mountains. Beyond the Mournes a fine coast road curves around to **Carlingford Lough** and the border.

Inland there's less of interest, certainly in County Down. **Armagh city**, though, is well worth some of your time for its ancient associations, cathedrals and fine Georgian streets. South Armagh has some startlingly attractive country, especially around the peak of **Slieve Gullion**.

County Down

The coast and the **Mourne Mountains** at the southern extremity are the major attractions of County Down. The big towns in the north, **Newtownards** and **Bangor**, are much less appealing, but beyond them the A2

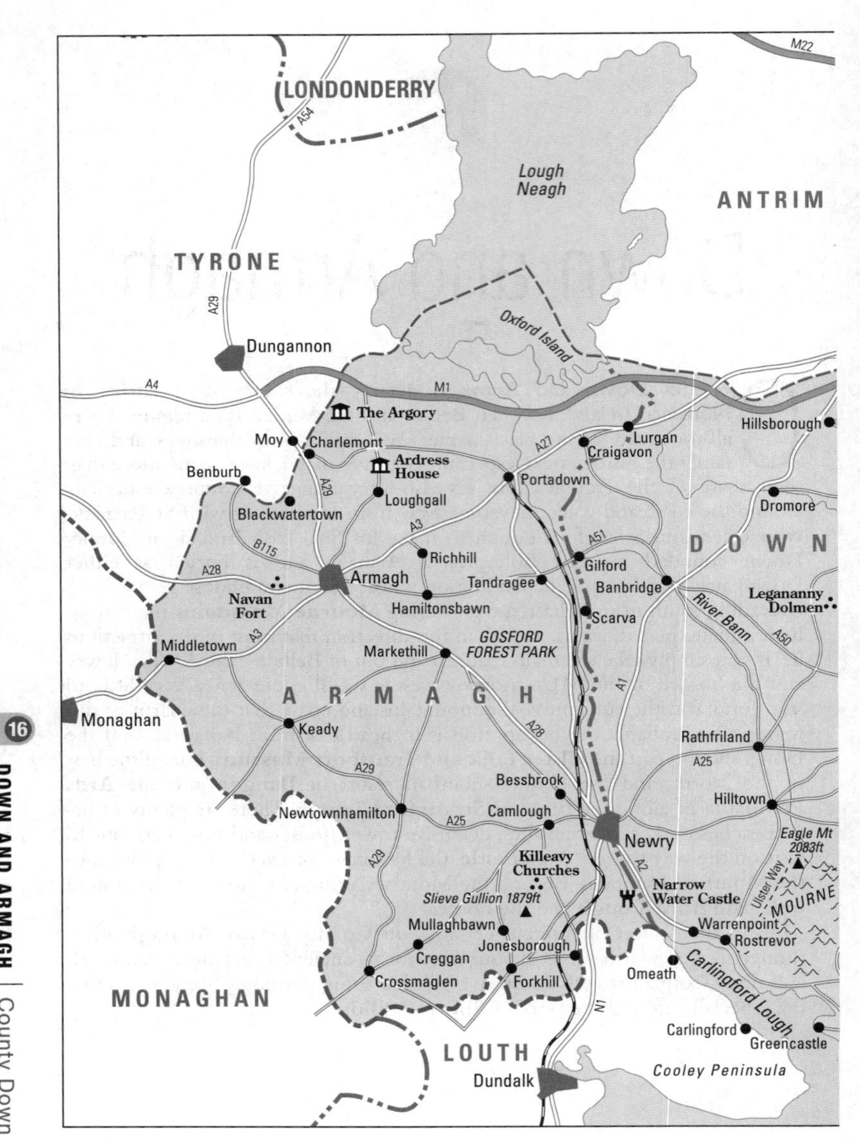

road clings to the coast for much of the way down the **Ards Peninsula** and, via the Strangford ferry, all the way to **Newry**. Other routes follow the shores of **Strangford Lough** towards **Downpatrick** and its associations with the arrival of St Patrick. There are numerous small resorts around the coast, but **Newcastle** is the biggest, and in many ways the most enjoyable. It's also the ideal place to start your exploration of the mountains.

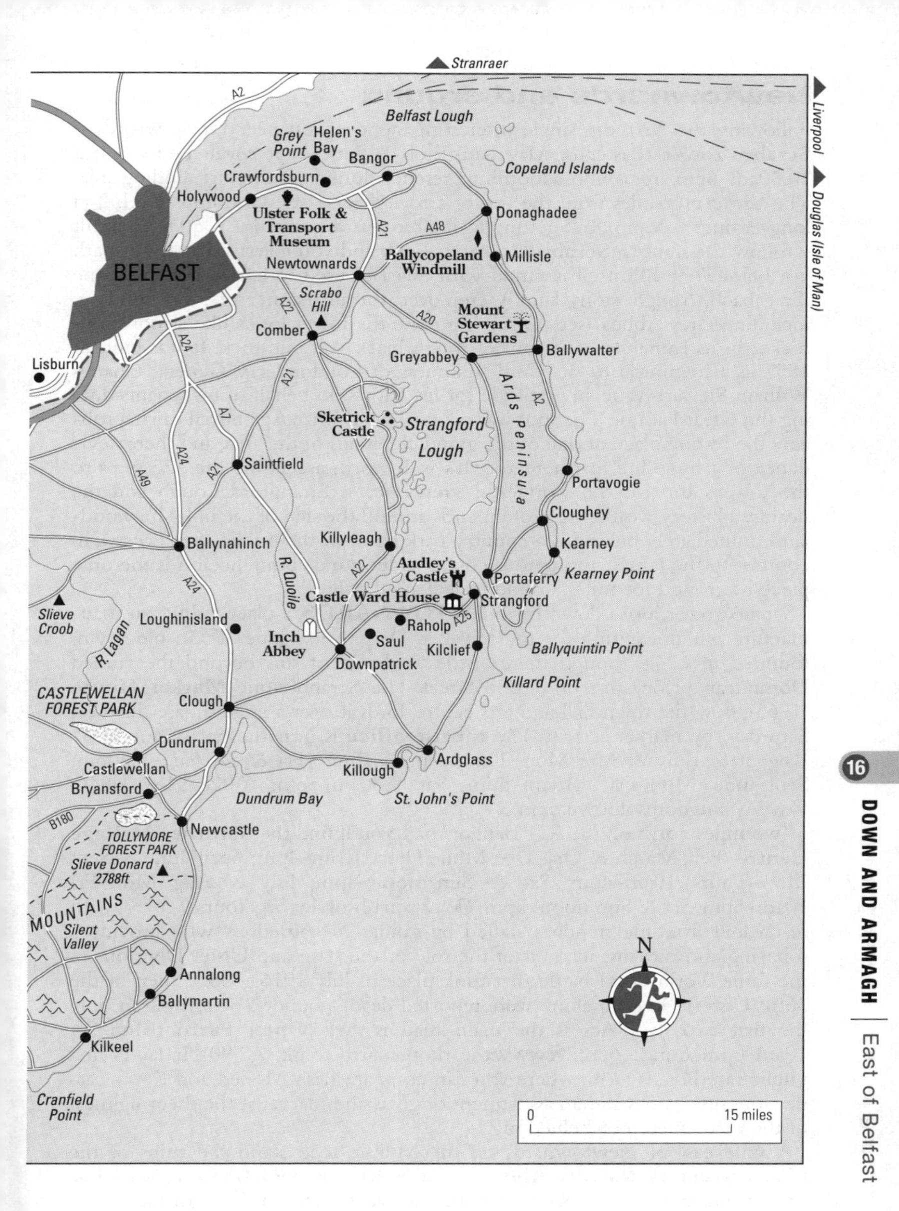

East of Belfast

Heading east into County Down from Belfast, you've a choice of two routes: the A20, which heads due east past Stormont (see p.639) to **Newtownards**, at the head of Strangford Lough; or the A2, which heads northeast past the excellent Ulster Folk and Transport Museum to **Bangor**.

Newtownards and around

Following the A20, the single interesting sight as you near Newtownards is **Scrabo Tower** (Easter & May bank hols & June–Sept Mon–Thurs & Sat 10.30am–6pm; free), whose looming presence dominates the surrounding area. The tower protrudes from the top of a rocky, gorse-strewn hump of a hill (a long-extinct volcano), but getting to it after you've spotted it is quite a circuit – follow the signs to **Scrabo Country Park** and you'll arrive in the car park just below. The hill itself is pitted with quarries used to extract Scrabo stone (Screabach, "rough, stony land"), employed for all manner of local building, including Grey Abbey (see p.712). Up close the tower looks like a monstrous rocket in its launcher, hewn out of rough black volcanic rock. It was built in 1857 as a memorial to the third Marquess of Londonderry, General Charles William Stewart-Vane, in gratitude for his efforts on behalf of his tenants during the Great Famine. The spot was originally a Bronze Age burial cairn, probably the resting place of one of the grand chieftains of the area, and there's evidence of a huge hill fort here, too. It's well worth ascending the 122 steps to the tower's top for the wonderful **views** across Strangford Lough and the healthy, blustery weather that often curls around the side of the hill. The woodland immediately behind is a country park open to the public (free access); in contrast to the tamed, prosperous countryside round about, Scrabo is the only piece of ground for miles around to feel at all wild.

Scrabo Tower looks down on **NEWTOWNARDS**, a place strong on manufacture but unexciting for the traveller. Despite its name, it's an old town, founded in 1244, though there's little evidence of this beyond the ruined Dominican priory just off Castle Street. The Scrabo stone **Market House** (1765), now the town hall and arts centre, lords it over a large square filled on Saturdays by market activity. The **tourist office** is near the bus station at 31 Regent St (July & Aug Mon–Thurs 9am–5.15pm, Fri & Sat 9am–5.30pm; Sept–June Mon–Fri 9.15am–5pm, Sat 9.30am–5pm; ⓣ028/9182 6846, ⓦwww.kingdomsofdown.com).

Two miles north on the A21 Bangor road, you'll find the **Somme Heritage Centre** (Feb, March & Oct–Dec Mon–Thurs 10am–4pm; April–June & Sept Mon–Thurs 10am–4pm, Sat & Sun noon–4pm; July & Aug Mon–Fri 10am–5pm, Sat & Sun noon–5pm; ⓦwww.irishsoldier.org; tours £3.75), with re-created frontline trenches staffed by guides in battledress who provide a sobering and moving account of the role of the Irish and Ulster Divisions in the futile World War I battle that took place in July 1916 – 5500 men of the 36th (Ulster) Division alone were reported dead, wounded or missing in only the first two days. Across the main road is **Ark Open Farm** (Mon–Sat 10am–6pm, Sun 2–6pm; ⓦwww.thearkopenfarm.co.uk; £2.90), Ireland's first public rare breeds farm, where you can compare Irish Moiled and Kerry cattle alongside llamas and an assortment of goats and marvel at the sheer ugliness of the Vietnamese pot-bellied pig.

A mile east of Newtownards on the Millisle road stand the ruins of the fifteenth-century **Movilla Abbey**. It's a largely disappointing site, but some ancient grave slabs in its north wall hint at what once was here. In the cemetery next door there's the more recent grave of James Francis, a Greyabbey man who fought in the Irish Brigade on the Union side in the American Civil War. The Brigade suffered heavy casualties during two of the war's bloodiest actions, the Battle of Cold Harbour and the Siege of Petersburg, but Francis survived both and later returned to Newtownards, dying there in 1921.

The Ulster Folk and Transport Museum

The A2 towards Bangor is both more scenic and more interesting than the A20, and still within easy reach of a day-trip from Belfast. There's a lovely fifteen-mile walk from **HOLYWOOD** (pronounced "hollywood") to Helen's Bay (see below), along a mildly indented estuary coast with some beautiful silvery sand beaches, especially the small crescent-shaped ones at Helen's Bay itself. The **train** line runs between the path and the road, with a couple of stations where you can pick up services on towards Bangor.

At Cultra station you can alight for the one of the most fascinating museums in the North, the **Ulster Folk and Transport Museum** (March–June Mon–Fri 10am–5pm, Sat & Sun 11am–6pm; July–Sept Mon–Sat 10am–6pm, Sun 11am–6pm; Oct–Feb Mon–Fri 10am–4pm, Sat 10am–5pm, Sun 10am–4pm; Ⓦ www.nidex.com/uftm; museums £4 each, combined ticket £5) – also served by Ulsterbus #B1 from Belfast's Laganside Buscentre. The main site is an open-air **museum village** where about thirty typical buildings from all over the North, some dating from the eighteenth century, have been taken from their original sites and rebuilt complete with authentic furnishings, including an entire street from Dromore and Belfast terraces. Conceptually, you can walk from one part of Northern Ireland to another, amid appropriate scenes. Traditional **farms** have also been created and assorted livestock roam between the buildings. The starting point is a gallery on Ulster's social history and an introduction to the buildings themselves. From here you walk around the grounds, visiting the various buildings, including a small village street with church and rectory, two schools, various typical farm dwellings, a forge and other buildings used in light manufacture. Each of these is "inhabited" by a member of staff, garbed in period costume and informative about the building and its origins. Such historical realism is impressive, though sometimes a little disquieting: the Kilmore Church graveyard contains real tombstones donated by family members.

On the far side of the main road, across a bridge, are the **transport galleries**, where the exhibits include every conceivable form of transport, from horse-drawn carts to lifeboats and a vertical take-off plane, but especially veteran cars, motorcycles and trams. You'll also meet *Old Maeve*, the largest locomotive ever built in Ireland, and a De Lorean sports car from the infamously defunct factory, while the *Titanic* exhibit documents the origins and fate of the Belfast-constructed liner. "The Flight Experience" examines the history of aviation through films, models and interactive displays. Outside the galleries there's a miniature railway that runs on summer Saturdays, and back in the main section there's a handy **restaurant**, located in the Education Centre. The museum also regularly stages temporary exhibitions and occasional cultural events.

Helen's Bay and around

If you're not walking, follow the signpost off the A2 to reach **HELEN'S BAY**, which is also a stop on the Belfast–Bangor **train** line. It's a rather twee but restful little place, with a red-painted Scots Baronial-style station. Down at the bay itself, a walking path leads east to **Grey Point Fort** (April–Sept Mon & Wed–Sun 2–5pm; Oct–March Sun 2–5pm; free), positioned to command the mouth of Belfast Lough, along with its sister fort at Kilroot on the other side. The fort has what you'd expect by way of quarters and stores, as well as an impressive battery of gun emplacements, ready to challenge the shipping that entered the lough during the two world wars. In the event, the two six-inch breech-loading guns were never fired except in practice (local residents had to be warned to open their windows and doors to prevent blast damage), apart from one occasion in World War II, when a merchant ship failed to respond to the signal "heave to or be sunk" and received a warning shot across its bows. The guns were sold for scrap in 1957 when the Coast Artillery was disbanded. After the fort was opened to the public in 1987, an identical six-inch gun was relocated here from the prison on Spike Island in Cork harbour. The Battery Observation Post and Fire Command Post are today staffed by dressed-up mannequins, like stills taken from a war movie – though they're now staring straight into a growth of trees that have sprung up to obscure the view. There's also a selection of photos showing the original guns and their positions; but it's really as a viewpoint with an atmosphere of military history, rather than the other way round, that the fort is worth visiting nowadays.

Should you want to stay, there's a classy **B&B** in Helen's Bay: *Carrig-Gorm*, 27 Bridge Rd (Ⓣ028/9185 3680, Ⓦwww.kingdomsofdown.com/carrig-gorm; ❹).

Crawfordsburn Country Park

The short stretch of coast from Helen's Bay to Grey Point, including the fort, is actually part of the **Crawfordsburn Country Park** (April–Sept 9am–8pm; Oct–March 9am–4.45pm; free), an estate handed down from the Scottish Presbyterian Crawford family, then acquired by Lord Dufferin (whose mother Helen gave her name to the bay) and now in public hands. Its glens and dells are replete with beeches, cypresses, exotic conifers, cedars, the usual burst of rhododendrons and also a Californian giant redwood, but the park's best features are the wild-flower meadow and the woodland planted with native species. Perhaps the most scenic walk (well marked by green arrows) is to follow the pathway back from Grey Point to the top of the bay's beaches and turn inland by the trickle of Crawford's Burn. This will take you up through the best of the woodland, under a fine – and still used – nineteenth-century railway viaduct, and up to a waterfall at the head of the glen. The **Park Centre** (daily 10am–5pm; free) has a café and an incredible amount of information on local ecology and wildlife. **Helen's Tower**, which can be seen from a considerable distance, was built by Lord Dufferin in the nineteenth century to honour his mother, and as a famine relief project.

CRAWFORDSBURN village is on one of Ireland's most ancient highways, a track that ran from Holywood to Bangor Abbey (now the B20), and has a nice but (like many things in this part of the world) twee early seventeenth-century **pub**, *The Old Inn*, 15 Main St (Ⓣ028/9185 3255, Ⓦwww.theoldinn.com; ❻), a partly thatched coaching inn offering elegant en-suite accommodation and an excellent, if pricey, **restaurant** serving specialities such as Portavogie scampi.

Bangor

BANGOR probably takes its name from its curving bay set between a pair of symmetrical headlands (beanna chor, "curved peaks"), and its sheltered position made it ideal for exploitation as a holiday resort. The town has been hugely popular with Belfast people since the railway came in the 1860s, but today it's as much a suburb of Belfast as a holiday spot. It still possesses a tawdry charm, stuck in a 1960s time warp with all the appropriate bucket-and-spade paraphernalia – giant swan boats to paddle around a mini-lake in the fun park, a miniature railway and amusement arcades. There's also a 500-berth marina, which makes Bangor a good place for stocking up on provisions or exploring the coast, while for the land-based the town is well equipped as a stop-off point for dinner and a stroll along the promenade.

Bangor's period of greatest historical significance was almost entirely associated with its **abbey**, which was founded by St Comgall in 586 AD, and from which missionaries set forth to convert pagan Europe. Though the abbey remained powerful for eight hundred years, there's not a trace of the building left. The only vestige of its fame is the Antiphonarium Benchorense, one of the oldest-known ecclesiastical manuscripts, consisting of collects, anthems and some religious poems; the original now lies in the Ambrosian Library in Milan, but you can view a facsimile of it in the **North Down Heritage Centre** (July & Aug Mon–Sat 10.30am–5.30pm, Sun 2–5.30pm; rest of year closes 4.30pm & all day Mon; Ⓦwww.north-down.gov.uk/heritage; free), tucked away at the back of the town hall. Other displays trace the rise of the Ward family (see p.720), who were largely responsible for the town's development and built Bangor Castle (now the town hall). There's also a fascinating collection of Eastern *objets d'art* collected by a local-born diplomat, Sir John Jordan, and a collection of archaeological discoveries, featuring the Ballycroghan swords, a wonderful pair of bronze weapons dating from 500 AD.

Practicalities

The only building of any antiquity in Bangor is the seventeenth-century **Old Custom House and Tower** on the seafront, now occupied by the **tourist office** (June & Sept Mon 10am–5pm, Tues–Fri 9am–5pm, Sat 10am–4.30pm, Sun 1–5pm; July & Aug Mon & Sat 10am–7pm, Tues–Fri 9am–7pm, Sun noon–6pm; Oct–May Mon 10am–5pm, Tues–Fri 9am–5pm, Sat 10am–4pm; Ⓣ028/9127 0069, Ⓦwww.northdown.gov.uk), which also has a bureau de change.

As you'd expect, there are dozens of **places to stay** here. The two most luxurious **hotels** are on Quay Street – the *Marine Court* (Ⓣ028/9145 1100, Ⓦwww.marinecourthotel.net; ❻) and the *Royal* (Ⓣ028/9127 1866, Ⓦwww.the-royal-hotel.com; ❻) – but you'll find plenty of less expensive **B&Bs** on Queen's Parade and Princetown and Seacliff roads. The nearest **camping** is at Donaghadee, six miles south along the coast.

Most of Bangor's **restaurants** are dotted along the seafront or up nearby side streets. Overlooking the marina, *Genoa's*, 1A Seacliff Rd (Ⓣ028/9146 9253), is the place for classy seafood and Mediterranean dishes. *Café Brazilia*, 13 Bridge St, serves numerous varieties of espresso plus an imaginative and cheap lunchtime menu. At the west end of the esplanade, *Knuttel's Restaurant*, 7 Gray's Hill (Ⓣ028/9127 4955; Wed–Sat 6.30–9pm) – named after and decked out in paintings by the owner – offers a good-value four-course dinner. Other relatively inexpensive restaurants are at the *Marine Court Hotel* and the *Avant-Garde Café Bar*, 132 Main St, a bar-bistro-cum-restaurant offering cosmopolitan cuisine.

Most of the **pubs** opt for DJs or rock bands, but you'll find regular **traditional music** at Friday night sessions at *Fealty's* (also known as the *Ormeau Bar*) on the High Street. The *Jenny Watts*, also on the High Street, has traditional sessions (Tues) as well as Sunday lunchtime jazz. A few doors down, *Café Ceol* is a lively and popular place with a varied music programme. Purple Heather (Ⓣ07050/608036) runs regular **fishing trips** from the harbour to various destinations, such as the Copeland Islands (see overleaf), and short **boat trips** around the bay from the Pickie Fun Park.

Ards Peninsula

The **Ards Peninsula** (Aird Uladh, "peninsula of the Ulstermen") stretches out an arm to enclose the waters of Strangford Lough, with only the narrowest of openings to the sea in the south. The eastern seaboard coast south of Bangor is far from the most attractive hereabouts, but, if you have the time for a detour, there are still some pleasant spots.

Donaghadee

East of Bangor's sprawling suburbs, the first place of any size is **DONAGHADEE**, a small market town whose origins lie in its proximity to the Scottish coast – on a clear day, it's easy to see Galloway across the water if you climb up the little hill to **The Moat**, the remains of a nineteenth-century folly. From the seventeenth century until the middle of the nineteenth century, ferries ran between here and Portpatrick in Galloway, the shortest sea-crossing available. Various notables arrived in Ireland by this route, including, in 1818, **John Keats** on his walking tour of the British Isles. He was reputedly so depressed by the poverty he saw on his way to Belfast, and the mockery attracted by his fancy London clothes, that he soon returned to Scotland. *Grace Neill's Inn*, on the High Street, dates back to 1611 and claims to have put up Peter the Great of Russia during his European tour. Donaghadee's decline began when the ferry service was transferred to Larne in 1849. Nowadays, apart from watching the dulse-gatherers at low tide or fishing activity at the harbour, there's little going on here, and the town's only other claim to fame is that its lighthouse received a lick of paint from Brendan Behan when he was employed after the war by the Commission for Irish Lights. More enticing is the possibility of visiting the three **Copeland Islands**, a mile or so offshore and uninhabited since the 1940s. The middle one, Cross Island, is now a bird sanctuary run by the RSPB, which arranges cruises to it (Ⓣ028/9049 1547); Nelson's Boats in Donaghadee run regular trips to the other two (Ⓣ028/9188 3403, Ⓦwww.kingdomsofdown.com/nelsonsboats; June–Sept).

There are a few small **B&B**s around town, including *Herdstown House* (Ⓣ028/9188 3773, Ⓦwww.kingdomsofdown.com/herdstownhouse; ❷), a listed farmhouse on Hogstown Road. **Camping** is available at *Donaghadee Caravan Park* (April–Oct; Ⓣ028/9188 2369) on Millisle Road. The **bistro** in *Grace Neill's* is a popular upmarket option for meals, or there's *Pier 36*, The Parade, a **pub** by the pier serving generous helpings of seafood.

South to Ballyquintin Point

Unless you're a caravan devotee, you'll want to give the villages of **Millisle** and, further down the coast, **Ballywalter**, a complete miss – each is swamped by half a dozen sites. Just about the only place of interest around here is the late eighteenth-century **Ballycopeland Windmill** (May–Sept Tues–Sat 10am–6pm, Sun 2–6pm; Ⓦwww.kingdomsofdown.com/ballycopelandwindmill; £1), a mile west of Millisle. This claims to be the only windmill in working order in Ireland, though it hasn't ground grain on a regular basis since 1915. An electrical model in the miller's house demonstrates its functions.

If you leave the A2 in Ballyhalbert and stick to the coast road, you'll pass **Burr Point**, the most easterly place in Ireland, before reaching **PORTAVOGIE**, a fishing port famous for its catches of giant prawns, which can be bought ready-peeled in the village or sampled at *The Quays Bar* on New Harbour

Road. From here the coast road curves inland, taking you around Cloghy Bay and past **Kirkistown Castle**, a tower house built in 1622 by one of the Savage family, the Anglo-Norman landlords of the peninsula; unfortunately it's on private land, so you can't inspect the remains any more closely. The next stop, **KEARNEY**, is a charming village, consisting almost entirely of whitewashed cottages and now mostly owned by the National Trust. You can walk from here to **Kearney Point**, an often blustery ten-minute stroll with panoramic views across the Irish Sea. Instead of heading directly to Portaferry from Kearney, choosing the road around **Ballyquintin Point** will take you past the entrance lane to **St Cowey's Wells**, where the faithful optimist is spoilt for choice: there's a drinking well, a wishing well and a well for bathing sore eyes. Look out for the rock nearby – the indentations are supposed to mark the places where the saint's hands and feet rested as he prayed.

Strangford Lough

Ancient annals say that **Strangford Lough** was formed around 1650 BC by the sea sweeping in over the lands of Brena. This created a beautiful, calm inlet, the archipelago-like pieces of land along its inner arm fringed with brown and yellow bladderwrack and tangleweed, and tenanted by a rich gathering of bird life during the warmer months and vast flocks of geese and waders in the winter. It's an attractive haven for small boats and yachts, and several picturesque halts for the land-bound make the road along the lough's western shore the most interesting route leading south from Belfast.

The eastern shore

The eastern edge of Strangford Lough is not as indented as its opposite shore but betters it in having a major road (the continuation of the A20) that runs close to the water virtually all the way down. Also the scenery is delightful, and there are two places to stop off en route to Portaferry – the **Mount Stewart** gardens and **Grey Abbey**.

Mount Stewart

Five miles southeast of Newtownards, served by Ulsterbus #9 and #10 from Belfast's Laganside Buscentre, is the former family home of the Londonderry family, the National Trust-owned **Mount Stewart House and Gardens** (opening times differ, see below; £4.75 for house, gardens and temple, £3.75 for gardens only).

The 98 acres of **gardens** (April daily 10am–4pm; May–Sept daily 10am–5pm; Oct Sat & Sun 10am–4pm) were laid out by Lady Londonderry, wife of the seventh marquess, in the 1920s – and a thorough job she made of it: among others, there are Spanish and Italian gardens, a Space Garden and the Shamrock Garden (with a topiary harp and an appropriately leaved Red Hand of Ulster). The trees and shrubs here are no more than seventy to eighty years old, but they've grown at such a remarkable rate that they look twice that. The principal reason for this is the unusually warm and humid microclimate: the gardens catch the east coast sun, causing a heavy overnight dew, and the Gulf Stream washes the shores only a stone's throw away. Despite the northerly latitude, conditions here rival those of Cornwall and Devon.

Although the gardens are the highlight, the **house** is also worth viewing (April & Oct Sat & Sun noon–6pm; May & Sept Mon & Wed–Sun noon–6pm; June–Aug daily noon–6pm). The family was a leading member of the Protestant Ascendancy and its members included Lord Castlereagh, who was Foreign Secretary under Pitt the Younger and is best remembered for guiding the Act of Union into operation. Among the splendid (and occasionally eccentric) furniture inside is a set of 22 Empire chairs used by the delegates to the Congress of Vienna in 1815, who included the Duke of Wellington and Talleyrand; the chairs were a gift to Castlereagh's brother Lord Stewart, another high-ranking diplomat of the time. The Continental connection is flaunted further in bedrooms named after various historically important cities: Rome, St Petersburg, Madrid, Moscow and Sebastopol (from the time of the Crimean War). The house contains a number of paintings, particularly portraits of Castlereagh's political contemporaries, but the most notable and largest is *Hambletonian* (1799) by George Stubbs, showing the celebrated thoroughbred being rubbed down after a victory at Newmarket.

A little to the east of estate's main entrance, the octagonal **Temple of the Winds** (April–Oct Sat & Sun 2–5pm) is a remodelling by James "Athenian" Stuart (1713–88), one of the pioneers of Neoclassical architecture, of Athens' Tower of Andronicus Cyrrhestes. The temple is set on a promontory overlooking Strangford Lough, making it a great place for birdwatching.

Grey Abbey

A couple of miles south on the shore road, **Grey Abbey** (April–Sept Tues–Sat 10am–6pm, Sun 2–6pm; Oct–March Sat 10am–1pm & 2–4pm, Sun 2–4pm; Ⓦ www.kingdomsofdown.com/greyabbey; free; Ulsterbus #9 & #10) lies half a mile to the east of the village which later developed around it. The abbey was founded in 1193 by Affreca, daughter of Godred, King of Man, and wife of John de Courcy, as a thanksgiving for having made a safe sea-crossing during a storm. Typical of the **Cistercian** order, of which Mellifont was the mother house in Ireland, the abbey sits in once-remote parkland beside a rivulet, which would have been a source of fresh water and fish – self-reliance was crucial to Cistercianism. Even today, that setting is barely disturbed, and reason in itself to visit, with a substantial set of ruins to complete the picture. The abbey was burnt in 1572 by Brian O'Neill to prevent the English turning it into a fort and was subsequently granted to the Montgomery family in 1607 – slabs in the walls of the church designate the tombs of various family members.

Following the standard design of Cistercian abbeys, it has a church at one end and the living and working quarters of the monks ranged around a **cloister**, a plain structure without distracting embellishments. Grey Abbey is unusual for Ireland, though, in showing early Gothic features at a time when late Romanesque work was still common here. Among the best-preserved remains are the **west door**, much of whose carved decoration can still be made out, and the fine lancet windows in the east end. Another unusual feature is that the church is a simple hall, with no aisles. Outside the church there's a re-created "physic garden" and the notes on display help you to imagine the elongated cloister when it was overshadowed on three sides by the chapter house, dormitories and refectory, which are now no more than stumps. The gatehouse also now houses a small **museum** recounting the abbey's history and the role of the Cistercian order in Ireland.

GREYABBEY village is renowned for its numerous **antiques** shops. The *Wildfowler Inn* on Main Street is a popular choice for its bar meals and **restaurant**. Nearby **B&Bs** offering pleasant en-suite accommodation are *Brimar*, 4 Cardy Rd (Ⓣ028/4278 8681; ❸), and, out towards Kircubbin, *Mervue*, 28 Portaferry Rd (Ⓣ028/4278 8619, Ⓦ www.kingdomsofdown.com/mervue; ❷).

Portaferry

PORTAFERRY, at the mouth of the lough, is the home of the **Exploris** aquarium (April–Aug Mon–Fri 10am–6pm, Sat 11am–6pm, Sun 1–6pm; rest of year closes 5pm; Ⓦwww.ards-council.gov.uk/exploris/exploris.htm; £5.40), which has a touch tank for the brave to stroke a stingray and an open sea tank where you can view the odd roaming shark and basking seals. However, the town's main attraction is the marvellous **sunset** looking across the "Narrows" to Strangford, a view enhanced by a ten-minute climb to the stump of the old windmill just behind the town. In July the **Galway Hookers Regatta** livens the place up – the traditional boats sail round from Galway to be welcomed by the Portaferry Yacht Club, and every pub has virtually 24-hour music sessions.

Ferries leave every half-hour for the five-minute ride across the lips of the lough to Strangford (Mon–Fri 7.45am–10.45pm, Sat 8.15am–11.15pm, Sun 9.45am–10.45pm; £1 single, £1.60 return; car £4.80 single, £7.70 return). The **tourist office** is in The Stables, Castle Street (Easter–June & Sept Mon–Sat 10am–1.15pm & 2.15–5pm, Sun 2–6pm; July & Aug Mon–Sat 10am–5.30pm, Sun 1–6pm; Ⓣ028/4272 9882), next to the ruined tower house. Should you be looking for somewhere to **stay**, the *Portaferry Hotel*, 10 The Strand (Ⓣ028/4272 8231, Ⓦwww.portaferryhotel.com; ❻), is relatively luxurious and has a popular **restaurant** specializing in fish meals; or try the brilliantly designed *The Narrows*, 8 Shore Rd (Ⓣ028/4272 8148, Ⓦwww.narrows.co.uk; ❻), where every room has a stupendous view across the lough. There's super food here too and all manner of special craft and activity weekends on offer. For good-value **B&B** try *Adairs*, 22 The Square (Ⓣ028/4272 8412; ❷), or the rooms above the *Fiddlers Green* pub, 10 Church St (Ⓣ028/4272 8383; ❸). Bear in mind that accommodation may be hard to find during the Castle Ward opera season in June (see p.720). Portaferry also has the independent **hostel** *Barholm*, 11 The Strand (Ⓣ028/4272 9598, Ⓦwww.barholmportaferry.co.uk), handily placed next to the ferry. The nearest **campsite** is *Tara Caravan Park*, three miles southeast on Ballyquintin Road (Ⓣ028/4272 8459), by a long, sandy beach.

As for **food**, there's little on offer outside the hotels and the chipper, though for coffee and good cakes try the *Harlequin*, Castle Street. The **pubs** are good at just about any time of year, with nightly singalong folk sessions led by the landlord and traditional music at the *Fiddler's Green* most nights; another popular session pub is the *Saltwalter Brigg*, six miles north of Portaferry towards Kircubbin, on Friday evenings.

The western shore

Leaving Scrabo Tower just east of Belfast on the A22, you'll pass through **COMBER** – famous for its potatoes – before reaching a turning east to **Castle Espie Wildfowl and Wetland Centre** (March–Oct Mon–Sat 10.30am–5pm, Sun 11.30am–6pm; Nov–Feb Mon–Sat 11.30am–4pm, Sun 11.30am–5pm; Ⓦwww.wwt.org.uk; £3.65), where admission earnings are ploughed back into conserving the wetlands area for the seven thousand birds that visit it and the resident population of waterfowl. The centre also has a coffee shop and art gallery.

From Castle Espie, you can wind along the very edge of the lough on a series of minor roads. Travelling this scenic route is enjoyable in itself, but there are a couple of spots worth making for. First of them is **Mahee Island**, named for St Mochaoi, supposedly the first abbot of the island, and reached via a twisting lane and several causeways. Heading past the crumbling remains of Mahee Castle at the entrance to the island, and over the final causeway, you come to the Celtic **Nendrum Monastic Site**, a few hundred yards further on. It's a marvellously isolated spot, surrounded by drumlins and the lough's waterways. Annals and excavations indicate that a sizeable community lived here from the seventh century onwards, but the remaining ruins probably date from the twelfth century at the very earliest. It was clearly a substantial establishment, with church, round tower, school and living quarters all housed in a cashel of three concentric wards. Today, the inner wall shelters the ruined church, and a reconstructed sundial uses some of the original remnants. There's an illuminating reconstruction map at the site and a helpful **visitor centre** (April–Sept Tues–Sat 10am–1pm & 1.30–6pm, Sun 2–6pm; Oct–March Sat 10am–4pm, Sun 2–4pm; Ⓦwww.kingdomsofdown.com/nendrummonastery; 75p).

Back on the road along the lough, follow the signs to Ardmillan, Killinchy and then Whiterock to reach **Sketrick Island** (which itself is not signposted). As with Mahee Island, there's a castle to guard the entrance, now no more than a shattered reminder. *Daft Eddie's Pub and Restaurant*, behind the castle, offers bar snacks as well as a more elaborate restaurant menu. An equally daft competition known as the **Hen Island race** takes place here in October, when craft constructed from oil drums and crates are ridden and paddled between Sketrick and the nearby Hen Island.

The tiny coves and inlets at the feet of little drumlins continue as far as Killyleagh, almost any of them worth exploring. A good way to do this is to take one of the **cruises** organized by Strangford Charter (Ⓣ028/9754 1564), which operates from Sketrick Island at weekends during June to August from noon until 6pm, and cost £6 per person for a one-hour trip.

Killyleagh

Approaching **KILLYLEAGH**, what looks like a huge Gothic fantasy comes into view, a sight wholly out of character with the area: the **oldest inhabited castle** in Ireland, it was erected by John de Courcy in the late twelfth century, but was rebuilt by the Hamilton family in 1648 and again in 1850 to give it the Bavarian *Schloss* appearance it has today. It's still a private house, and when viewed close up it's much more gaunt, with a squat mixture of crenellations, turrets and cones. The stone outside the castle gates commemorates the town's most famous son, Hans Sloane (1660–1753), physician to King George II and founder of both the British Museum and Kew Gardens – London's Sloane Square is named after him. The gatehouse towers themselves have been adapted for **holiday letting** (Ⓣ028/4482 8261, Ⓦwww.fjordlands.org/strngfrd/kilapts; £210–360 per week). A little way back down the hill, the *Dufferin Arms* coaching inn (Ⓣ028/4482 8229, Ⓦwww.dufferincoachinginn.co.uk; ❹) offers extremely comfortable **B&B** and organizes a wide range of activity breaks.

Two miles south of Killyleagh is **Delamont Country Park** (daily: April–Sept 9am–dusk; Oct–March 9am–5pm; Ⓦwww.delamontcountrypark.co.ni; car £2.50), a pleasant spot with grand views over the lough, a heronry and Ireland's longest miniature railway.

The Lecale region

Jutting into the southern reach of Strangford Lough, the **Lecale Peninsula** is above all **St Patrick** country. Ireland's patron saint was a Roman Briton, first

△ Strangford, County Down

carried off as a youth from somewhere near Carlisle in northern England by Irish raiders. He spent six years in slavery in Ireland before escaping home again and, at the age of thirty, decided to return to Ireland as a bishop, to spread Christianity. Christianity had already reached Ireland a while earlier, probably through traders and other slaves, and, indeed, St Patrick was not in fact the first bishop of Ireland, but he remains easily the most famous. He arrived in Ireland this second time, according to his biographer Muirchú (also his erstwhile captor, converted), on the shores of the Lecale region, and his first Irish sermon was preached at **Saul** in 432. Today the region commemorates the association with sites at Struell Wells and Saul, as well as at **Downpatrick** town.

The **Lecale Trail** is a thirty-mile tour of the peninsula starting from in front of the Down County Museum in Downpatrick (further information and trail maps can be obtained from the town's tourist office). If you've had enough of St Patrick and his seeming connection with nearly every landmark, alternative ways of exploring the peninsula are the **nature rambles** and **horse rides** available at the Quoile Countryside Centre just outside Downpatrick.

Downpatrick and around

DOWNPATRICK (Dún Pádraig, "St Patrick's fort"), 23 miles south of Belfast, is a pleasant enough place of little more than ten thousand people, and its compact size and the proximity of its rich and well-preserved historical sites make for an easily negotiable day's visit.

The **Hill of Down**, at the north of the town, was once a rise of great strategic worth, fought over long before the arrival of St Patrick made it famous. A **Celtic fort** of mammoth proportions was built here and was called first Arús Cealtchair, then later Dún Cealtchair ("Celtchar's fort"). Celtchar was one of the Red Branch Knights, a friend of the then King of Ulster, Conor MacNessa, and, according to the Book of the Dun Cow, "an angry terrific hideous man with a long nose, huge ears, apple eyes, and coarse dark-grey hair." The Dún part of the fort's name went on to become the name of the county, as well as the town.

By the time the Norman knight **John de Courcy** made his mark here in the late twelfth century, a settlement was well established. Pushing north out of Leinster, and defeating Rory MacDonlevy, King of Ulster, de Courcy dispossessed the Augustinian canons who occupied the Hill of Down to establish his own **Benedictine abbey**. He flaunted as much pomp as he could to mark the occasion, and one of his festive tricks was to import what were supposedly the disinterred bodies of St Brigid and St Columba to join St Patrick, who was (allegedly) buried here. One of the earliest accounts of Patrick's life asserts that he's buried in a church near the sea; and since a later account admits that "where his bones are, no man knows", Downpatrick's claim seems as good as any.

The Town

Downpatrick thrives upon its association with the saint, and the new and extremely expensive **St Patrick Centre** (April, May & Sept Mon–Sat 9.30am–5.30pm, Sun 1–5.30pm; June–Aug Mon–Sat 9.30am–6pm, Sun 10am–6pm; Oct–March Mon–Sat 10am–5pm; March 17 9.30am–7pm; last admission 90min before closing; Ⓦ www.stpatrickcentre.com; £4.50), just off the main drag Market Street, aims to recount his life and influence in extensive detail. Its hagiographic, multimedia approach is pretty arid, however, and by the time you've been round its maze of interactive displays and sat through the five-screen 180-degree virtual helicopter ride through Christian history, you might even wish you'd never heard of the saint.

Signposts next to the centre point the way uphill to the elegant, spacious Mall, at the end of which stands Downpatrick's **Cathedral** (Mon–Sat 9.30am–5pm, Sun 2–5pm; Ⓦwww.cathedraldown.Anglican.org; free). The site of the three graves of Columba, Patrick and Brigid is meant to be just to the left of the tower entrance and is marked today by a rough granite boulder, put there around 1900 to cover a huge hole created by earlier pilgrims searching for the saints' bones. The cathedral built by de Courcy was destroyed in 1316 during Edward Bruce's invasion, and a new abbey erected in the early sixteenth century was even more short-lived. Today's cathedral dates basically from the early 1800s, though it incorporates many aspects of earlier incarnations. Its unique feature is the private box-pews, characteristic of the Regency period and the only ones remaining in use in Ireland.

Leaving the cathedral and retracing your steps a little down English Street, which is crowded with Georgian buildings, you come to the eighteenth-century jail, home to the **Down County Museum** (Mon–Fri 10am–5pm, Sat & Sun 1–5pm; free), which used to house an excellent account of St Patrick's life until usurped by the new centre. The three-storey Georgian **Governor's House** in the centre of the walled courtyard houses a somewhat lacklustre local history gallery, though there are often more interesting temporary exhibitions elsewhere on the site. The cell block at the back of the enclosure once held the United Irishman Thomas Russell, who had already survived the 1798 Rebellion but was found guilty of complicity in Robert Emmett's uprising and was duly hanged in 1803 from a sill outside the main gate of the jail.

Turn downhill between the jail and the barricaded courthouse and, inauspiciously tucked behind a secondary school, you'll find the **Mound of Down**, a smaller prominence than the Hill of Down and half-submerged in undergrowth. It's in fact 60ft high and inside its outer ditch is a horseshoe central mound of rich grass. Once a rath, or round hill fort, it was considerably altered and enlarged to create a Norman motte-and-bailey fortification, with a *bretasche* (a wooden archery tower) at the centre. Its view of the Hill of Down clearly displays the attractions the hill had for its earliest settlers; it's believed by some to be the site of the palace of the kings of Ulster.

At the rear of the market car park on Market Street, the **Downpatrick Railway Museum** (Mon–Fri 9am–4pm, Sat 10am–4pm; £2.50), offers tours of the restored station and workshops and occasional train rides along a restored section of the Belfast–Newcastle main line (details on Ⓣ028/4461 5779). A little further along Market Street is **Downpatrick Race Course** (Ⓦwww.kingdomsofdown.com/downpatrickraceclub), the second-oldest in Ireland and home to the Ulster National. Nowadays, race meetings happen here relatively infrequently, so it's best to enquire at the tourist office for dates.

Practicalities

The **bus station** (Ⓣ028/4461 2384) is on Market Street, a hundred yards south of the St Patrick Centre, where you'll find the **tourist office** (July & Aug Mon–Sat 9.30am–8pm, Sun 2–6pm; Sept–June Mon–Sat 9.30am–5pm; Ⓣ028/4461 2233, Ⓦwww.downdc.gov.uk). The best and most central of the town's **B&Bs** are *Denvir's*, 16 English St (Ⓣ028/4461 2012, Ⓦwww.kingdomsofdown.com/denvirs; ❸), which offers en-suite accommodation in one of Ireland's oldest coaching inns, and *Hillside*, 62 Scotch St (Ⓣ028/4461 3134, Ⓦwww.kingdomsofdown.com/hillside; ❷), in a listed Georgian town house. Out of town, try the newly converted *Mill at Ballyduggan*, Drumcullen Road (Ⓣ028/4661 3654, Ⓦwww.ballyduganmill.com; ❹), dating from 1792, or the splendid *Pheasant's Hill Country House*, 37 Killyleagh Rd (Ⓣ028/4461 7246,

Ⓦ www.pheasantshill.com; ❹), offering one of the best breakfasts in the North and a pleasant rural setting. If you're **camping**, your best bet is to go to Castle Ward Park (see p.720), six miles northeast on the A25 towards Strangford.

Downpatrick boasts a number of fine **cafés**, including the *Iniscora Tea Rooms* in the Down Civic Arts Centre (see below), for soups, salads and imaginative sandwiches, and *Harry Afrika's*, in the new shopping centre on Market Street, for its phenomenal breakfasts and vast Sunday brunches. *Denvir's* (see p.717) serves superb lunches and evening meals, while good **pub** lunches are also easy to find: try *Brendan's Pub* or *Rea's* on Market Street, or the *Forge Bar* on Church Street. The best **traditional-music** session is on Friday nights at *Speedy Mullan's* on Church Street. There may be occasional performances in the excellent **Down Civic Arts Centre**, 2–6 Irish St (Mon–Fri 10am–4.30pm, Sat 9am–4pm; Ⓦ www.kingdomsofdown.com/downcivicartscentre), which has an art gallery and performance space.

Around Downpatrick

A mile northwest of Downpatrick, on the other side of the Quoile Marsh, lie the remains of the Cistercian **Inch Abbey** (free access). The exquisite setting is temptingly visible from the town, but the river's intervention means that the only access is a mile out along the Belfast road, taking the left turn down Inch Abbey Road just before the *Abbey Lodge Hotel*, followed by another signposted left turn shortly afterwards. The site was once an island, and its early church was replaced by de Courcy in the 1180s with the Cistercian abbey, whose monks were shipped over from Furness Abbey in Lancashire with the intention of establishing a strong centre of English influence. Little of it is now left standing – it was burnt in 1404 and monastic life was completely over by the mid-sixteenth century. Still, its setting, among small glacial drumlins and woodland, is picturesque, and strolling up the valley sides is a pleasant way to pass time.

About two miles northeast of Downpatrick, off the A25 Strangford road, the **Quoile Countryside Centre** (April–Aug daily 11am–5pm; Sept–March Sat & Sun 1–5pm; free) focuses attention on the natural habitats created by the building of a tidal barrier to prevent local flooding. It organizes **nature rambles**, seal watches in Strangford Lough, dawn chorus walks on Quoile River and even butterfly trips. Tullymurray Equestrian Centre on Ballydugan Road organizes **trail rides** to the local big houses – Tollymore, Castlewellan and Castle Ward – or along the coast, with beach rides to Newcastle and Tyrella (details from Ⓣ 028/4481 1880).

On the trail of St Patrick

About four miles west of Inch Abbey (take the B2 to Annacloy and then the first turning on the left), **Loughinisland** is probably the most worthwhile of all the sites in the area associated with St Patrick, and indeed one of the most idyllic spots in County Down. It comprises a reed-fringed lake contained by ten or so little drumlin hills, one of which forms an island in the lake. Here, across a short causeway, are the ruins of three small churches, set next door to each other. The most interesting of these churches is the smallest one, **MacCartan's Chapel** (1636), which has an entrance door no taller than four or five feet. The larger northern church was used by both Catholics and Protestants until they quarrelled on a wet Sunday around 1720 over which camp should remain outside during the service. The Protestants left and built their church at Seaforde instead.

The next St Patrick landmark is at **SAUL** (Sabhall, "barn"), a couple of miles northeast of Downpatrick off the Strangford road. St Patrick is said to have landed nearby, sailing up the tiny River Slaney, and it was here that he first preached, immediately converting Dichu, the lord of this territory. Dichu gave Patrick a barn as his first base and the saint frequently returned here to rest from his travelling missions – legend has it that he died here in 461. Today a **memorial chapel** and round tower in the Celtic Revival style, built of pristine silver-grey granite in 1932 to commemorate the 1500th anniversary of the saint's arrival, is open daily to visitors. Two cross-carved stones from between the eighth and twelfth centuries still stand in the graveyard, though there's not a trace of the medieval monastery built here by St Malachy in the twelfth century.

A short distance further south, between Saul and Raholp, **St Patrick's Shrine** sits atop Slieve Patrick, a tract of hillside much like a slalom ski-slope, with the Stations of the Cross marking a pathway up. This huge Mourne granite statue, clad at the base with bronze panels depicting Patrick's life, was erected in the same year as Saul church. The summit is no more than a twenty-minute climb and offers a commanding view of the county, a vista of the endless little bumps of this drumlin-filled territory.

At **RAHOLP** is the ruined church of **St Tassach**, named for the bishop from whom the dying Patrick received the sacrament. Patrick gave Raholp to Tassach as a reward for crafting a case for Christ's crozier, the *Bachall Isú*, one of Ireland's chief relics until its destruction in 1538. The ruins here were mainly restored in 1915 from the rubble that lay around, but their material is thought to date from the eleventh century. If you're eager for the complete St Patrick experience, it's a mile from the car park of the *Slaney Inn* (which serves superb bar meals) in Raholp to the spot on the lough shore where he is believed to have first landed: head towards Strangford, then left down Myra Road; cross the main Strangford road and turn left at the first fork; at the bottom of the hill, take the track on the right to the shore.

The easiest way to find the last St Patrick site, **Struell Wells**, is to return to Downpatrick. Take the Ardglass road southeast, turn left just past the hospital, then right down a narrow track into a secluded rock-faced valley and you'll come to the wells. The waters here, believed to be the wells referred to in early accounts of Patrick's mission, have been attributed with healing powers for centuries. In 1744 Walter Harris described the scene: "Vast throngs of rich and poor resort on Midsummer Eve and the Friday before Lammas, some in the hopes of obtaining health, and others to perform penance." The site contains a small eye well, a drinking well and men's and women's bath houses. Mass is still said here on midsummer night, and people bring containers to carry the water home with them.

Strangford and the Lecale coast

If you're following the A2 round the coast of the Ards Peninsula, your arrival on Lecale will be at tiny **STRANGFORD** village, directly opposite Portaferry and linked by a regular ferry service (see p.713). The earlier name of this inlet was Lough Cuan (*cuan* being Irish for "harbour" or "haven"), but it was renamed Strangfiord by the Vikings over a thousand years ago because of the strong eight-knot current in the narrows. Its small harbour makes a pleasant setting for watching the to and fro of the ferry boats, and the *Lobster Pot* **inn**, on the front, has a welcome pub garden and middle-of-the-range prices for fine evening meals. The only **place to stay** is the elegantly furnished *Cuan* (ⓣ028/4488 1222, ⓦwww.thecuan.com; ❹), which has a deserved reputation for its splendid restaurant and equally friendly bar. There's **camping** at *Strangford Caravan Park*, Shore Road (ⓣ028/4488 1888).

Immediately around Strangford are a few houses and castles worth visiting, the first of them on the road back towards Downpatrick. **Castle Ward** (mid-March to April, Sept & Oct Sat, Sun & public hols noon–6pm; May Wed–Sat 1–6pm; June daily 1–6pm; July & Aug daily noon–6pm; house £4.50, grounds £3 per car) is Ireland's Glyndebourne: for three weeks every June, **opera** enlivens the house and grounds, and *bon viveurs* flock here with picnic hampers, starched napkins and candlesticks (tickets £25–40; for information call ⓣ028/9066 1090). The house, which was the eighteenth-century residence of Bernard and Anne Ward, later Lord and Lady Bangor, is now owned by the National Trust. It's a positively schizophrenic building, thanks to the opposed tastes of its creators (they later split up): Bernard's half is in the Classical Palladian style, Anne's Neo-Gothic, a split carried through into the design and decor of the rooms inside. Outside there are pleasant **gardens** (daily 10am–dusk) and preserved farm buildings. There's also a sixteenth-century tower house (Old Castle Ward) inside the grounds; the fifteenth-century **Audley's Castle** just outside on the lough shore, with a superb view across the lough – though there's a better example of a tower house just south of Strangford at Kilclief (see below); and the **Strangford Lough Wildlife Centre** (same hours as Castle Ward house; no extra charge), housed in a restored barn. If you want to stay, you can **camp** in the castle estate (ⓣ028/4488 1680).

South from Strangford to Ardglass

A signposted turning one mile south of Strangford directs you to the **Cloghy Rocks** observation point. The rocks themselves are 20yd or so out in the lough and for most of the day look decidedly inconsequential, but at low tide you can spot basking **seals**. They're well camouflaged against the seaweed, so a pair of binoculars would be handy.

Further south, **Kilclief Castle** (July & Aug Tues & Fri–Sun 2–6pm, Wed & Thurs 10am–1pm; 75p) is one of Ireland's earliest tower houses, a well-preserved fifteenth-century example that was originally the home of John Cely, Bishop of Down – until he was defrocked and thrown out for living with a married woman.

The next stop is **St Patrick's Well**, set on a wonderful rocky shore between Ballyhornan and Chapeltown. You can get to within a few hundred yards of the well by road, but the best approach is to start from Ballyhornan – where you'll see a narrow strip of water separating the village from Guns Island, accessible at low tide and still used for grazing – and follow the foreshore path for about a mile. The well is easily spotted: it looks rather like a sheep dip with concrete walls, but with a crucifix at its head. Its holy water has turned into something closer to stagnant consommé than an ever-youthful source of new life.

Half a mile or so before you reach Ardglass, the ruin of fifteenth-century **Ardtole Church** is well signposted just a few hundred yards east of the road. It's set on the spur of a hill, which gives it a fine perspective out to sea and back across the undulating flat of Lecale. Once dedicated to St Nicholas, patron saint of sailors, the church was used by English fishermen until a quarrel broke out with the Irish around 1650. The story goes that the fishermen tied a sleeping Irish chief to the ground by his long hair so that he couldn't get up when he awoke. Tradition has it that Swift derived the similar episode in *Gulliver's Travels* from this tale, and certainly the Ardtole region runs amok with tiny drumlins – very much like the description of the Lilliputian mountains.

Ardglass

ARDGLASS (Ard Ghlas, "green height") is set on the side of a lovely natural inlet. Its domestic buildings, rising steeply from the harbour, are interspersed with seven fortified mansions, towers and turrets, dating from a vigorous English revival in the sixteenth century, when a trading company first arrived to found a colony here. The best preserved of the fortifications, and the only one open for visits, is **Jordan's Castle**, next door to the *Anchor* pub on the Low Road (July & Aug Tues & Sat 10am–1pm, Wed & Thurs 2–6pm; 75p), the most elegant and highly developed of all the Down tower houses. The tall, crenellated building with white plaster trimming up on the hill was once **King's Castle**; its nineteenth-century renovation is obvious, as is modern work to turn it into a nursery. The lone ornamental-looking turret on the hilltop is **Isabella's Tower**, a nineteenth-century folly created by Aubrey de Vere Beauclerc as a gazebo for his disabled daughter.

In the nineteenth century, Ardglass was the most thriving **fishing** port in the North; and even today, aside from the prawns, herrings and whitefish brought in by the fishing fleet, there's very good rod-fishing to be had off the end of the pier for codling, pollack and coalfish. The supermarket on the quay is wonderfully stocked with a vast range of **seafood** (scallops, monkfish, oysters, salmon and more), enough in itself to entice a quick shopping visit. It's also sometimes possible to buy direct from fishing boats or from the cannery on the quay. The old **inn**, the very convivial *Commercial*, on the main street, has a well that is still in use; it's covered over with glass on the lounge floor. You can eat well at the popular *Aldo's* Italian **restaurant**, 7 Castle Place (Ⓣ028/4484 1551; closed Tues), which serves evening meals, or sample the huge portions of fresh fish and chips and vast range of ice cream at *The Quayside* restaurant on The Quay. There's very comfortable **B&B** at *Burford Lodge*, 30 Quay St (Ⓣ028/4484 1141, Ⓦwww.kingdomsofdown.com/burfordlodge; ❷), a Georgian house on the seafront, and the cosy *Margaret's Cottage* (Ⓣ028/4484 1080, Ⓦwww.margaretscottage.co.uk; ❷), next door to *Aldo's*.

West from Ardglass to Clough

KILLOUGH, a few miles west of Ardglass, is a tranquil village stretching around a harbour that is much larger than its neighbour's but is now silted up. The A2 passes through Killough's main street – a fine French-style avenue of sycamores with a string of picturesque cottage terraces at its southern end, making an unlikely major thoroughfare. It was the Wards of Castle Ward who built the harbour in the eighteenth century, and there's still a direct road running inland, virtually in a straight line, from Killough to Castle Ward. Untouched by tourism, there is no accommodation in the village.

From the southern end of Killough you can head out to **St John's Point** – much favoured by birdwatchers – on which lie the ruins of one of the North's best examples of a **pre-Romanesque church**; it's an enjoyable two-and-a-half-mile walk. The tiny west door of the tenth-century church has the distinctive sloping sides, narrowing as the doorway rises, that were a common feature of these early churches. Also still apparent are the *antae*, enclosures created by the extension of the west and east walls to give extra support to the roof. Excavations in 1977 showed up graves that extended under these walls, indicating that an even earlier church existed in the early Christian period, probably made of wood. There's a black-and-gold-striped **lighthouse** on the nail of the point.

From Killough, the A2 heads west past long, sandy beaches at Minerstown and Tyrella Strand before reaching **CLOUGH**, a crossroads village midway between Downpatrick and Newcastle. Tucked behind the petrol station at the northern end of the village is a Norman motte-and-bailey earthwork **castle**, as pristinely preserved as a carpet of fresh grass, though marred by the remains of a thirteenth-century stone keep stuck in the middle. Despite its low-lying position the site has surprisingly good views across Dundrum Bay inlet towards the Mournes and back over to Slieve Croob in central Down.

It's worth taking a short detour north at Clough on the A24 to the **Seaforde Tropical Butterfly House** (April–Sept Mon–Sat 10am–5pm, Sun 1–6pm; Ⓦwww.seafordegardens.com; £2.50, or £4.50 including gardens). There's a flight area swarming with hundreds of giant, vividly coloured butterflies, quails running underfoot and a ferocious collection of large and fast-moving insects and reptiles, fortunately kept in glass cases. Best of all, though, is the overgrown walled **garden**, whose maze leads to a rose-covered pavilion that shelters a statue of the goddess Diana. Nearby, *Drumgooland House* on Dunnanew Road (Ⓣ028/4481 1956, Ⓦwww.activityholidaysireland.com; ❸) does a great **B&B**, and offers fishing in its own lake and riding. Loughinisland (see p.718) is three miles further north.

Dundrum

Although it's not officially in the Lecale region, whose inland ending is at Clough, **DUNDRUM**, just a few miles down the Newcastle road, has some quite spectacular ruins of a large Norman **castle** (April–Sept Tues–Sat 10am–6pm, Sun 2–6pm; Oct–March Sat 10am–4pm, Sun 2–4pm; Ⓦwww.kingdomsofdown.com/dundrumcastle; 75p). The town lies beside a hammer-headed tidal bay, with the ruins sitting dramatically above, a steep fifteen-minute walk uphill from the village. The castle has a central circular donjon (with a fine spiral stairway in its walls), a fortified gateway and drum towers, all set upon a motte and bailey. In its time it was described as the most impenetrable fortress in the land, yet it was captured on several occasions and partly dismantled by Cromwell's soldiers in 1652. Some say it was a de Courcy fortress, designed for the Knights Templar, but the circular keep, a rarity in Ireland, is unlike the other fortresses de Courcy built to defend the stretch of coast from Carlingford right up to Carrickfergus. De Courcy's successor, de Lacy, is a more likely candidate – his Welsh connections tie in with the castle's similarity to the one at Pembroke in west Wales.

Newcastle and the Mourne Mountains

Newcastle, with its lovely stretch of sandy beach, is the biggest seaside resort in County Down – packed with trippers from Belfast on bank holidays and summer weekends – and, with Slieve Donard rising behind the town, it's by far the best base if you want to do any serious walking or climbing in the **Mourne Mountains**. On busy days the main drag can feel like nothing more than a soulless strip of amusement arcades, fast-food outlets and tacky souvenir stores, but the town's more sedate qualities can be appreciated when the trippers have gone.

The Mournes are a relatively youthful set of granite mountains, which explains why their comparatively unweathered peaks and flanks are so rugged, forming steep sides, moraines and occasional sheer cliffs. Closer up, these give sharp, jagged outlines; but from a distance they appear much gentler, like a sleeping herd of buffalo. The wilder topography lies mostly in the east, below

Newcastle, although the fine cliff of **Eagle Mountain** (2083ft), to the southwest, is wonderful if you can afford the time and effort to get there, and the tamer land above Rostrevor has views down into **Carlingford Lough** that rival any in Ireland.

In summer at least (winters can be surprisingly harsh), there are plenty of straightforward hikes in the Mournes that require no special equipment, with obvious tracks to many of the more scenic parts. For further information, and maps, go to the Newcastle tourist office or the Mourne Countryside Centre (see box on p.724). There are also, of course, more serious climbs: **climbing courses** in the Mournes are run by the Tollymore Mountain Centre in Bryansford (Ⓣ028/4372 2158, Ⓦwww.tollymoremc.com), but they must be booked well in advance.

Newcastle

NEWCASTLE isn't exactly exciting, but it's well equipped for a range of outdoor activities, including **walking** in the Mourne Mountains southwest of town (see box on p.724), **pony trekking** and **fishing** on the river. Golfing enthusiasts may be tempted by Newcastle's Royal County Down **golf course** (Ⓣ028/4372 3314, Ⓦwww.royalcountydown.org), which has a reputation as one of the most challenging links worldwide. For the inevitable rainy day, the town also has indoor alternatives at the **Newcastle Centre and Tropicana Complex** on the promenade (summer only), with swimming pools, water slides and playgrounds.

Newcastle has a few literary connections: **Seamus Heaney** was a waiter in the 1950s at the long-gone *Savoy Café*; Brook Cottage (now a hotel), on Bryansford Road, was home to the dramatist and dialect-poet Richard Valentine Williams, better known as Richard Rowley; and a fountain on the Promenade commemorates the popular Irish songwriter Percy French, composer of *The Mountains of Mourne* and numerous comic songs. Behind the Newcastle Centre, a plaque celebrates one of the first powered flights in Ireland, undertaken in 1910 by **Harry Ferguson** to win a £100 prize – he was later to become famous through the success of the Massey Ferguson tractor.

The **bus station** (Ⓣ028/4372 2296) is on Railway Street at the eastern end of Main Street, which, a couple of hundred yards west, becomes the Promenade. Here you 'll find the very helpful **tourist office** at 10–14 Central Promenade (July & Aug Mon–Sat 10am–7pm, Sun 2–7pm; rest of year Mon–Sat 10am–5pm; Ⓣ028/4372 2222, Ⓦwww.Newcastle.tic.org). There's a wide choice of **places to stay**. The best of the more upmarket **hotels** is the *Slieve Donard Hotel*, Downs Road (Ⓣ028/4372 3681, Ⓦwww.hastingshotels.com; ❽), though it's closely followed by the *Burrendale Hotel & Country Club*, 51 Castlewellan Rd (Ⓣ028/4372 2599, Ⓦwww.burrendale.com; ❼). Cheaper central **B&Bs** with seaviews include *Marine Villa*, 151 Central Promenade (Ⓣ028/4372 5030, Ⓦwww.kingdomsofdown .com/marinevilla; ❷), in a pleasant Victorian house, or the congenial *Dacara*, 47 South Promenade (Ⓣ028/4372 6745, Ⓦwww.kingdomsofdown.com/dacara; ❷). Three miles northwest of town, in **BRYANSFORD** village, opposite Tollymore Forest Park, is the cordial and comfortable *Briers Country House*, 39 Middle Tollymore Rd (Ⓣ028/4372 4347, Ⓦwww.thebriers.co.uk; ❸), with a popular restaurant serving wholesome meals at reasonable prices. Newcastle's HINI **hostel** is in a town house on the seafront at 30 Downs Rd, near the bus station (Ⓣ028/4372 2133). There are also several **caravan and camping sites** around Newcastle, though the best are located in the forest parks (see box overleaf).

Walks in the Mournes

There's little to see in Newcastle itself, but the **Mourne Mountains** offer some beautiful walks close to the town, and, for more serious walking, plenty of good hiking routes throughout the range. Before you set off it's worth visiting the **Mourne Countryside Centre**, 87 Central Promenade in Newcastle (Mon–Fri 9am–5pm; June–Aug also Sat & Sun 9am–4pm; ⓣ028/4372 6493), for information on walks, access and the local ecology.

The climb up **Slieve Donard**, just south of Newcastle, is the obvious first choice. Although at 2796ft it's the highest peak in the Mournes – and in all Ulster – the ascent is a relatively easy one on a well-marked trail that starts three miles out of town on the Annalong road at Bloody Bridge (see opposite) and ends at the massive hermit cell on the summit; from here the views across the whole mountain landscape are quite spectacular.

For gentler local walking, there are several pleasant **parks** created from the estates of old houses in the vicinity. The nearest is **Donard Park** (free access) on the slopes of Slieve Donard. There's a good meander along the River Glen from Newcastle town centre to the park, and if you keep following this path uphill you'll emerge on the other side and eventually come to the Saddle, a col between the two mountains of Slieve Donard and Slieve Commedagh. If you want to carry on further into the mountains from here, a good route is via **Trassey Burn** towards the **Hare's Gap**, where minerals have seeped through the rock to form precious and semi-precious stones – topaz, beryl, smoky quartz and emeralds – in the cavities of the **Diamond rocks** (hidden behind an obvious boulder stone on the mountainside). Around this point in spring, you might hear the song of the ring ouzel, a bird that migrates from Africa to breed in these upland areas.

Two miles inland from Newcastle, along the Bryansford Road, **Tollymore Forest Park** (daily 10am–dusk; car £4, pedestrians £2) is considerably bigger and better equipped than Donard, and has a **campsite** (for details, call the ranger on ⓣ028/4377 2252). The park creeps up the northern side of the Mournes, and its

Mario's Italian Restaurant, 65 South Promenade, on the front towards the harbour is the best place for evening **meals** and Sunday lunches, unless you go out of town towards Castlewellan (take the A50) for the *Burrendale Hotel & Country Club*, whose *Vine Restaurant* is extremely popular. The *Donard Hotel* on Main Street also does reasonable lunches. The *Pavilion* on Downs Road does everything from snacks to steaks, while the *Percy French*, also on Downs Road, offers reasonable à la carte. Otherwise there are plenty of cafés, chip shops and fast-food outlets along the Promenade.

The landward slopes of the Mournes

The landward side of the Mourne Mountains is a patchwork of fields divided by dry-stone walls: attractive, especially in the morning light, but with nothing of pressing interest. **HILLTOWN** has a main street well provided with pubs – supposedly because it was once a smugglers' hideaway, where the spoils would be divided – and it's still a crossroads where numerous roads meet. There's a pretty parish church, which was founded in 1776, a Georgian market house opposite and a fortnightly market, but most of the time it's as quiet as a ghost town. Little over a mile east of Hilltown on the Newcastle road is the handsome **Goward dolmen**, known locally as "Pat Kearney's big stone". It's well signposted off the road, though the last quarter-mile of track is severely potholed.

picturesque trails wind through woodland and beside the river. You enter the park by one of two ornate Gothic folly gates – there are more follies in Bryansford nearby – and there's an **information centre** and café in an elaborate stone barn.

Castlewellan Forest Park (same hours and prices) is also inland about five miles further north, outside the elegant market town of Castlewellan. The estate lies in the foothills of the Mournes, and from the highest point in the forest, **Slievenaslat**, you get panoramic views over the mountain range. A wonderful **arboretum**, dating originally from 1740 but much expanded since, is its outstanding feature: the sheltered south-facing slopes of its hills, between the Mournes and the Slieve Croob range, allow exotic species to flourish. There's trout **fishing** in its main lake and coarse fishing in the smaller lakes (enquire at the Newcastle tourist office for details of this and other local fisheries). There's a pleasant **campsite** in the park here, too (call the forest officer on ⓣ028/4377 8664). Nearby **riding schools** offering trekking through the forest parks include Mount Pleasant Riding and Trekking Centre, 15 Bannanstown Rd, Castlewellan (ⓣ028/4377 8651, ⓦwww.mountpleasant.com), and Mourne Trail Riding Centre, 96 Castlewellan Rd, a couple of miles out of Newcastle on the A50 (ⓣ028/4372 4351, ⓦwww.mournetrailridingcentre.com).

If you're planning on more serious hiking in the Mournes, heights worth chasing include **Slieve Binnian**, beyond the Hare's Gap, reached through the Brandy Pad passes by the Blue Lough and Lough Binnian; **Slieve Commedagh**, with its Inca-like pillars of granite; and **Slieve Bearnagh**, up to the right of the Hare's Gap. Also, try and cross the ridge from **Slieve Meelmore** to **Slieve Muck**, the "pig mountain", descending to the shores of Lough Shannagh, where there's a beach at either end – useful for a dip, though the water's freezing. In the panorama beyond the Hare's Gap, the places not to miss are the eastern slopes of the **Cove Mountain** and **Slieve Lamagan**. If you're sticking to the roads, all you can really do is circle the outside of the range, though there is one road through the middle, from Hilltown to Kilkeel.

Drumena Cashel, two miles southwest of **Castlewellan** on the A25, is one of the better-preserved ring forts, or defended homesteads, in the area. It has a T-shaped underground chamber intended to give shelter from the Vikings – though this is only twelve yards long and seems better suited to its peacetime function of providing cold storage for food. The stone foundations of a few circular beehive huts (known as *clocháns*) also remain. The puzzling aspect of the cashel is its position below the summit of the hill: possibly a compromise between the needs of defence and those of comfort, so there would be some shelter from the harsh winds that curl through the area.

The Mourne coast

The A2 south along the coast from Newcastle is a beautiful drive, trailing the shore around the edge of the mountains. It takes you past the chasm known as **Maggie's Leap**, after a local woman who jumped to avoid the attentions of an unwanted suitor, and over the **Bloody Bridge**, reputedly so called because of a nearby massacre during the 1641 Rebellion. Further along the way, the fishing harbour towns of **Annalong** and **Kilkeel** are alternative bases for **walking** or exploring the mountains.

Annalong and Silent Valley

The small fishing harbour of **ANNALONG** (Áth na Long, "ford of the ships") is a pleasantly relaxed seaside town during the summer, with a stony beach and

Slieve Binnion providing a grandiloquent backdrop. In the harbour, pleasure craft are tied up alongside the fishing boats and small trawlers; the whiff of their herring catches sometimes permeates the whole town. Just off the main road in Marine Park stands an early nineteenth-century **cornmill**, still in working order and open for visits (June–Sept Tues–Sat 11am–5pm; £1.85).

B&Bs here include a former farmhouse, *The Sycamores*, 52 Majors Hill (Ⓣ028/4376 8279, Ⓦwww.kingdomsofdown.com/thesycamores; ❷), and luxurious country house accommodation at *Glassdrumman Lodge*, 85 Mill Rd (Ⓣ028/4376 8451, Ⓔglassdrumman@yahoo.com; ❼), which has its own stylish restaurant. There's little in the way of other **places to eat**, but right on the harbour, the refurbished *Harbour Inn* serves hearty lunches and evening meals, while the *Halfway House*, north of town on the A2, offers bar meals and Sunday lunches.

Inland a mile or so from Annalong, signposts point to the **Silent Valley** (daily: Easter–Sept 10am–6.30pm; Oct–Easter 10am–4pm; car £3), where you'll find Belfast and County Down's **reservoir**, a huge thirty-year engineering project that was completed in 1933. There's a car park by the lower reservoir, bounded by the Mourne Wall, a sturdy 22-mile-long granite boundary to the catchment area that links the summits of fifteen mountains along its route. The views out to Slieve Binnian and Ben Crom, behind it to the west, are worth the effort of the three-mile circular **Viewpoint Walk** (starts at the car park). Less energetic, but still superb, is the half-mile Sally Lough stroll (or you can take the shuttle bus; £1.50) up to the dam at Ben Crom; again the views are spectacular.

Kilkeel

Continuing south, **KILKEEL** ("the church of the narrows") is a much grander version of Annalong, remarkable mainly for the even heftier stench of fish from the canneries on the harbour; the town is home to nearly a hundred trawlers. The biggest excitements here are the fish auctions that take place on the quayside when the fishing boats come home, and the annual summer **harbour festival**. Bang next to the harbour is the **Nautilus Centre** (Easter–Sept Mon–Sat 10am–9pm, Sun noon–6pm; rest of year Mon–Sat 10am–6pm, Sun noon–6pm), which contains a small exhibition on the fishing industry, a fish shop (if you're subsequently tempted), a gift shop, café and conference centre.

The ruined "narrows" **church**, built in the fourteenth century, stands in the centre of Kilkeel in a ring fort. Kilkeel is a prosperous, predominantly Protestant place, but behind the village on the banks of its river memories of less happy days remain – small grave markers identify where the inmates of Kilkeel workhouse are buried. One of those buried here is the infamous **William Hare**, who murdered sixteen people in the space of a year in Edinburgh. Hare owned a lodging house, and when an old lodger died owing rent, he and his accomplice William Burke decided to sell the body to a medical school. The £7.10 they were paid spurred them on to greater efforts; however, their enthusiasm eventually raised the neighbours' suspicions and their profitable venture came to an end. Hare turned king's evidence and got his freedom, while Burke was hanged. Deciding to lie low, Hare came to Kilkeel and soon landed in the workhouse; his identity was only revealed to the locals when a Dr Reid, a former medical student from Edinburgh, recognized him.

There's a small **tourist office** in Kilkeel at 28 Newcastle St (Mon–Sat 9am–5.30pm; Ⓣ028/4176 2525), which can help you to find **places to stay** in town. The grandest **hotel** is the *Kilmorey Arms*, 41 Greencastle St (Ⓣ028/4176 2220, Ⓦwww.kilmoreyarmshotel.co.uk; ❺), whose **restaurant** has an à la carte menu, but the most atmospheric place to stay is *Morne Abbey Guest House*, 16 Greencastle Rd (Ⓣ028/4176 2426, Ⓦwww.kingdomsofdown.com/morneabbeyguesthouse; ❷), set a couple of miles south of town on a mixed farm. If you're **camping**, take your pick of the seven campsites hereabouts – the best are along Cranfield Point, a flat piece of grassy land jutting out at the entrance to Carlingford Lough: try *Sandilands Caravan Park* on Cranfield Road (mid-March to Oct; Ⓣ028/4176 3634) or *Chestnutt Caravan Park*, next to the beach on Grange Road (March–Oct; Ⓣ028/4176 2653). **Restaurants** in Kilkeel are thin on the ground, but *The Fisherman*, 68 Greencastle St (Ⓣ028/4176 2130), has an extensive, though pricey, fish menu, and *Jacob Hall's*, 8 Greencastle St, at the other end of the price scale, does tasty grills and fish and chips.

Carlingford Lough

The eastern shore of **Carlingford Lough**, which borders the Mournes to the south, offers some wonderful views back to the mountains and across the lough itself. Driving round to **Warrenpoint**, though, the villages become increasingly politicized as you approach the border, Republican slogans alternating with Union Jacks.

Greencastle Fort

Guarding the mouth of the lough, **Greencastle Fort** (July & Aug Tues & Fri–Sun 2–6pm, Wed & Thurs 10am–1pm; Ⓦwww.kingdomsofdown.com/greencastlefort; 75p) sits in brooding isolation about four miles southwest of Kilkeel, and its views alone are worth a diversion. The fort is a comparatively well-preserved Anglo-Norman edifice, with a unique rock ditch, built in the same year (1261) as Carlingford Castle on the southern side of the lough. After succumbing to several attacks from the local Magennis clan, and falling to Edward Bruce in 1316, it collapsed into complete ruin after the Cromwellian invasion and now only guards the farm across the road. It's hard to imagine the fort's great fireplaces providing a counterblast to the buffeting winds that sweep across from the lough – you can feel their full force by climbing up the corner turrets to the top storey, where you can look down on the sandy beach below and enjoy tremendous views of the lough.

Rostrevor

If you take the main road inland from Kilkeel (cutting behind Greencastle Fort), four or five miles out of Kilkeel a signpost points to the **Kilfeaghan dolmen**, a mile inland then a short walk through a couple of fields and kissing gates. Its capstone is enormous and could only have arrived here during the retreat of the glacial drift.

Further up the lough, the village of **ROSTREVOR** (Ros Treabhair, "Trevor's wood") lies at the point where the bay waters dramatically begin to narrow towards Newry – and where the population and political climate turn more in favour of the Nationalist communities of County Armagh and those across the ever-nearing border. Rostrevor is a charming and sleepy village of Victorian terraces and friendly pubs, meandering up the lower slopes of **Slieve Martin**. There are a few small **B&Bs**, including *An Tubar*, 2 Cherry Hill (Ⓣ028/4173 8712, Ⓦwww.kilbroney.net; ❷), and *Glenbeigh*, 18 Victoria Square (Ⓣ028/4173 8025, Ⓦwww.glenbeighbedandbreakfast.com; ❸). **Camping** is available at *Kilbroney Park*, Shore Road (April–Oct; Ⓣ028/4173 8134), where you can hike up the hill to the thirty-ton **Cloughmore** ("big stone") for views across the lough to the Cooley Mountains over the border; geologists reckon the stone is a remnant of the Ice Age, but locals prefer a more spectacular story involving Fionn Mac Cumhaill. Opposite the church, *The Kilbroney Inn* is deservedly acclaimed for its wondrous **food**, including specialities such as roast monkfish, while *The Healthy Choice Cafe* provides hearty lunches and home baking. The **Fiddler's Green Festival** in the last week of July is a big, enjoyable event, attracting folk and traditional musicians from across Europe.

Warrenpoint

WARRENPOINT is as picturesque as Rostrevor, with a colourful esplanade of seafront housing and a spacious central square. It's a much more traditional seaside resort than its neighbour and has been attracting visitors since the early nineteenth century, when an enterprising local man advertised warm baths for the "gentry, nobility and public". There are handy **boat trips** across to Omeath on the opposite shore of Carlingford Lough in the Republic, which leave from the pier on Osborne Promenade (June–Sept daily 1–6pm every 30min, tides permitting; £3 return).

Less than a mile northwest of Warrenpoint along the Newry Road is the **Narrow Water Castle** (guided tours: July & Aug Tues, Fri & Sat 10am–1pm, Wed & Thurs 2–6pm; free). The original was built in 1212 by Hugh de Lacy to guard against access to Newry via the river, but this was burnt down during the 1641 Rebellion and the ruins here are of a building erected some twenty years later; there are very slight remains of the earlier castle nearby.

Warrenpoint's **tourist office** (Mon–Fri 9am–5pm; ⓣ028/4175 2256) is in the town hall on Church Street. You shouldn't have any trouble finding **accommodation** here, except during the **Maiden of the Mournes festival** in August, a local version of the Rose of Tralee (see p.417). Lough-shore **B&Bs** include the tiny *Lough View*, 10 Osborne Promenade (ⓣ028/4177 3067; ❷), the nearby *Mournes*, 16 Seaview (ⓣ028/4177 2610; ❷), and the more lavish *Whistledown & Finns*, 6 Seaview (ⓣ028/4175 4174, ⓦwww.whistledown.co.uk; ❹).

For **food**, you can dine sumptuously at *Aylesforte House* on the outskirts towards Newry, while for cheaper eating, try *Diamond's* on the main square, which has a choice of low-priced specials. Wholesome food is also available at several **pubs**, including *Bennett's* on Church Street and *Jack Ryan's* on the square. Many of the pubs, including *The Victoria* on the square, and the *Duke Bar*, Duke Street, have music of the ballads and rock variety. The **disco** activity is at *Club Chéri* in the *Marine Tavern*, Marine Parade, and *Shenanigans* in the nearby *Boathouse Inn*.

Newry

Although **NEWRY** (An tIúr, "the yew tree"), astride the border of Down and Armagh, is this region's most important commercial centre, bustling with urban vibrancy and its recently gained city status, it has little to sustain more than a short visit. Traditionally, it was the place for people from the Republic to come and shop, and the town still thrives economically, its already traffic-clogged streets suffering gridlock on **market day** (Thurs). Given its key position, you're highly likely to pass through here, and it does make a possible base for exploring Slieve Gullion and the South Armagh district, but you're unlikely to be tempted to stay.

Newry was founded by Cistercian monks in 1144, but for most of its history has been a **garrison**, guarding the borders of Ulster at the narrow point between hills on either side known as the Gap of the North. There's no trace at all of the bitterly contested early fortresses; what you see dates mostly from the eighteenth and nineteenth centuries, when a canal to Lough Neagh (cut in 1742, the first in the British Isles) brought the produce of the inland towns to the markets here.

Perhaps the most interesting building in town is the **Catholic Cathedral** on Hill Street, in the pedestrian precinct. Despite an unpromising granite exterior, the rich mosaic pattern along its interior walls gives a Byzantine feel, and there's also a striking vaulted ceiling of decorative sweeping plaster arcs and vivid stained-glass windows. Nearby, there's a strange bronze totem pole by sculptor Paddy McElroy, which depicts, in tortured relief, scenes from Newry's past. Not far away, the **Town Hall** is remarkable mainly because it's built on a bridge over the River Clanrye – it's half in Down, half in Armagh. Just opposite, the **Newry and Mourne Arts Centre**, 1A Bank Parade, hosts exhibitions of local artists' work, plays and all types of music in the auditorium, as well as housing the **Newry and Mourne Museum** (Mon–Fri 10.30am–1pm & 2–4.30pm; free). The museum contains Nelson's table from *HMS Victory*, as well as plenty of information on local history and a re-created eighteenth-century Panelled Room, featuring period furniture and locally carved panelling salvaged from a house on North Street.

Another recent archaeological find is **Bagenal's Castle**, the remains of which were discovered within the former McCann's Bakery on Abbey Way. This one-time Cistercian abbey was confiscated during the Reformation of 1548, and the premises were leased to a certain Nicholas Bagenal, who had apparently earlier fled his native Staffordshire to escape indictment for murder. After acting as a secret agent infiltrating the O'Neill clan, he was granted a pardon and subsequently became marshal of the English army in Ireland and established a garrison in Newry. While Bagenal was largely successful in defending the area against the O'Neills, his daughter Mary eloped and married Hugh O'Neill, a story that became the subject of Brian Friel's play *Making History*. At the time of writing, further archaeological investigations of the site were taking place, and Newry and Mourne Council were planning to restore the castle and open it to the public as a heritage centre, funding permitting.

Practicalities

Newry's **bus station** (T 028/3026 3531) is on The Mall alongside the canal, while the **train station** (T 028/3026 9271) is a mile west of town on Millvale Road and connected to the centre by local bus #341C (daily except Sun).

The **tourist office** is in the town hall (Mon–Fri 9am–1pm & 2–5pm, Sat 10am–1pm & 2–4pm; T 028/3026 8877, W www.newryandmourne.gov.uk). If you have to stay, the most luxurious **accommodation** is provided by the canalside *Canal Court Hotel*, Merchants Quay (T 028/3025 1234, W www.canalcourthotel.com; 7), which is equipped with a gym and sauna. There are a fair number of **B&Bs** scattered around town. Newry's best **food** is at the *Brass Monkey* bar, 16 Trevor Hill, opposite the courthouse, which specializes in steaks. *The Cove* on Hilltown Road has a renowned Tuesday night **traditional music** session.

Central County Down

Heading west from Belfast, the M1 motorway offers very rapid access to Armagh and Tyrone, while the A1 road cuts southwest towards Newry. On the former route there's little to stop for until you're in County Armagh; on the latter there are contrasting attractions in picturesque **Hillsborough** and the bustling town of **Banbridge**, while the pleasant local countryside can be explored by following the **Brontë Homeland Drive** or taking a trip to the **Legananny dolmen**.

Hillsborough

The historic village of **HILLSBOROUGH**, just a mile off the main A1 road and twelve miles southwest of Belfast, merits a quick detour. Its main street has a chintzy, Middle English ambience, reinforced by a sprinkling of tearooms and antique shops. You get the best of Hillsborough by following a route that starts from the **war memorial** (where regular Ulsterbus services from Banbridge and Belfast stop) and heads up the magnificent approach to the eighteenth-century Gothic **parish church**. Bear right here for the main entrance to Hillsborough's elegant but ruined **fort** (April–Sept Tues–Sat 10am–7pm, Sun 2–7pm; Oct–March Tues–Sat 10am–4pm, Sun 2–4pm; free), constructed by Colonel Arthur Hill (after whom the village is named) in 1650 and remodelled in the eighteenth century as a fun palace. Beyond this, a deciduous **forest** opens up, curving around a **lake** stocked with brown and rainbow trout. Footpaths meander through the trees in all directions – a circuit of the lake takes around an hour.

Exiting via the car park, a driveway brings you out near the *White Gables Hotel* (Ⓣ028/9268 2755, Ⓕ9268 9532; ❻) on Dromore Road, beyond which you'll notice a statue on a raised column, master of all it beholds – the third Marquis of Downshire, erstwhile owner of the estate. A right turn at the end of the drive brings you back into town, with **Hillsborough Castle** (tours: April–Sept Sat 10am–4pm; castle £5, gardens £2.50) on your left. The mansion itself dates from 1797, and from 1925 to 1973 was the residence of the governor of Northern Ireland. Since then it's been used mainly to house visiting diplomats, although it hit the headlines when the Anglo-Irish Agreement was signed here in 1985. More recently, Tony Blair stayed here during the April 1997 peace settlement talks, and the castle is now the official residence of the British secretary of state for Northern Ireland. Tours take you through the State Drawing and Dining Rooms, replete with Georgian furniture and silver from *HMS Nelson*, while the gardens are particularly lovely in May and June, when the many roses and Europe's largest rhodedendron bush are in bloom.

Hillsborough's **tourist office** (Mon–Sat 9am–5.30pm; July & Aug also Sun 2–6pm; Ⓣ028/9268 9717, Ⓦwww.kingdomsofdown.com/hillsboroughvillage) is housed in the elegant Georgian **courthouse** on The Square at the top of Main Street. There's a mildly interesting exhibition on the court system here and the tourist office can provide details of **walking tours** of Hillsborough (June to mid-Sept Sat 2pm; £2.50). The village has several excellent options for **food**, including *The Plough Inn*, opposite the courthouse, and, just down the hill, the seventeenth-century *Hillside Inn*, both of which serve bar meals and more substantial fare in their restaurants. If you want to **stay** in the area, try *Fortwilliam*, 210 Ballynahinch Rd (Ⓣ028/9268 2255, Ⓦwww.fortwilliamcountryhouse.com; ❸), a pleasant country house a couple of miles southeast of the village.

Banbridge and around

Follow the A1 south from Hillsborough and you'll pass through **BANBRIDGE** on the River Bann, once a major linen centre and also a stop on the old coach route to the Mourne Mountains. However, the steep hill – now the main street – to the south of the river presented problems to horse-drawn mail coaches. A threat to bypass the town was enough to initiate drastic action – and the result is the town's best-known feature. In 1834 the wide main street was divided into three with an **underpass**, known to locals as "the cut", carved out in the middle to lower the hill, and the **Downshire Bridge** was built over the gap. The town's most famous offspring is **Captain Crozier**, a pioneer of the Northwest Passage (the sea route from the Atlantic to the Pacific via Arctic Canada), who was born in 1796 in a house on Church Square. The house now overlooks the Crozier Memorial, on which four polar bears stare at the captain, who in turn gazes to the northwest.

The **tourist office** is a couple of miles south of town at 200 Newry Rd (June & Sept Mon–Sat 10am–5pm, Sun 2–6pm; July & Aug Mon–Sat 9am–7pm, Sun 2–6pm; Oct–May Mon–Sat 10am–5pm; ⓣ028/4062 3322). The best **B&B** in the area is four miles northwest, just beyond Gilford at *Mount Pleasant*, 38 Banbridge Rd (ⓣ028/3883 1522, ⓔmuriel.butler@talk21.com; ❶), a vast, castellated Georgian linen house sitting on a grassy knoll with a fine view, and with bedrooms the size of tennis courts. *Harry's Bar*, on Dromore Street in Banbridge, serves great pub **food** and (a real rarity for Ireland) specializes in draught ales. There's little **nightlife** in the town, although occasional club nights at the *Coach Inn*, Church Square, draw the crowds. Banbridge's proximity to the Bann offers numerous **angling** opportunities: advice, equipment and licences are available from James Coburn & Son, 32 Scarva St (ⓣ028/4066 2207).

The area around Banbridge contains a number of sites of varied antiquity and importance. **Lisnagade Fort**, three miles west on the Scarva road, is an

The Bronte Homeland Drive

The start of the **Brontë Homeland Drive** is best approached by taking the A50 from Banbridge southeast to Moneyslane and thence to Ballyroney. If you've followed the signs correctly, you should end up at the Drumballyroney interpretive centre (mid-March to Sept Tues–Fri 11am–5pm, Sat & Sun 2–6pm; £2), a minuscule place with a mock schoolroom. The drive itself is justified by a rather tenuous link – the Brontës in question are not the famous sisters, or even Branwell, their brother, but father Patrick Brontë and his parents. Nor is there any evidence that the literary daughters ever visited Ireland, though there is a story that one of the uncles took his shillelagh and headed to England to sort out a reviewer critical of *Jane Eyre*. This is more the story of a local boy made good. Patrick obviously dragged himself up by his bootlaces, working in the linen works by day and reading the classics by night, and with help from a local rector, he won a place to read theology at Cambridge. In 1806 he came back to preach his first sermon at Drumballyroney church, but eventually moved to Yorkshire, where he married Maria Branwell and had his six children – all of whom he outlived. Little remains of Patrick's birthplace at Emdale but a few feet of stone wall. And several of the other sights are specious: Knockiveagh, a hilltop stopping point, seems to be on the signposted route mainly to give you a chance to get your bearings. But if the drive doesn't yield nuggets of literary history, it does offer a route – however difficult to follow – through lovely hillocky countryside that you might not otherwise explore.

impressive circular earthwork, consisting of three massive ditch-separated banks. The diameter of the inner circle is a good thirty metres, but while bronze artefacts have been recovered from the site, little is known about its occupants. A little more is understood about the **Loughbrickland crannóg**, three miles southwest of Banbridge near the village of Loughbrickland (take the A1, then the B3 Milltown road). Constructed sometime around 500 AD, this artificial island was inhabited in the seventeenth century by the Magennis family, who had vacated a castle that's thought to have been located on the lough shore. Lastly, and most notably, the **Legananny dolmen** is worth a considerable detour; it's signposted at the A50–B7 crossroads nine miles southeast of Banbridge, and also at the village of Leitrim, three miles north of Castlewellan. Whichever your approach, you'll find yourself on narrow humped lanes, gradually ascending the southern edge of the Slieve range, and feeling increasingly distant from modern realities. You may also experience a sense of déjà vu when you arrive at the site, for the dolmen is a popular choice of guidebook and tourist-board photographers. There's no doubting the impressiveness of the structure, looking for all the world like a giant stone tripod. Not too far away on the Castlewellan road to the east is a welcome oasis, the *Slieve Croob Inn* (Ⓣ028/4377 1412, Ⓦwww.slievecroobinn.com; ❹), a wonderfully situated **hotel** whose bistro and **restaurant** serve mouth-watering meals.

County Armagh

Recent history has hardly heightened **County Armagh**'s appeal for tourists. The villages of **South Armagh** – a predominantly Catholic area – were the heartland of violent Republicanism, so much so, in fact, that it has often been referred to as "Bandit Country" or "The Killing Fields", even by locals. On the other side of the sectarian divide, the name of **Portadown** has become synonymous with recalcitrant Unionism thanks to the stand-off at Drumcree church between the authorities and the Orange Order (see box on p.734). Yet the county does warrant exploration, for it has some luscious landscapes and a history as rich as any county in Ireland: **Armagh city** has strong associations with St Patrick and early Christianity, while the sedately rural areas harbour some sites that are redolent of the island's legendary past, notably **Navan Fort** and **Slieve Gullion**.

North Armagh

Below **Lough Neagh**, the north of County Armagh is dominated by the developed industrial strip containing the almost connected towns of **Lurgan**, **Craigavon** and **Portadown**. There is little in this urban hinterland to attract you – and, indeed, Portadown's reputation as the most vehemently bigoted Loyalist town in the North is in itself deterrent enough. Outside the towns,

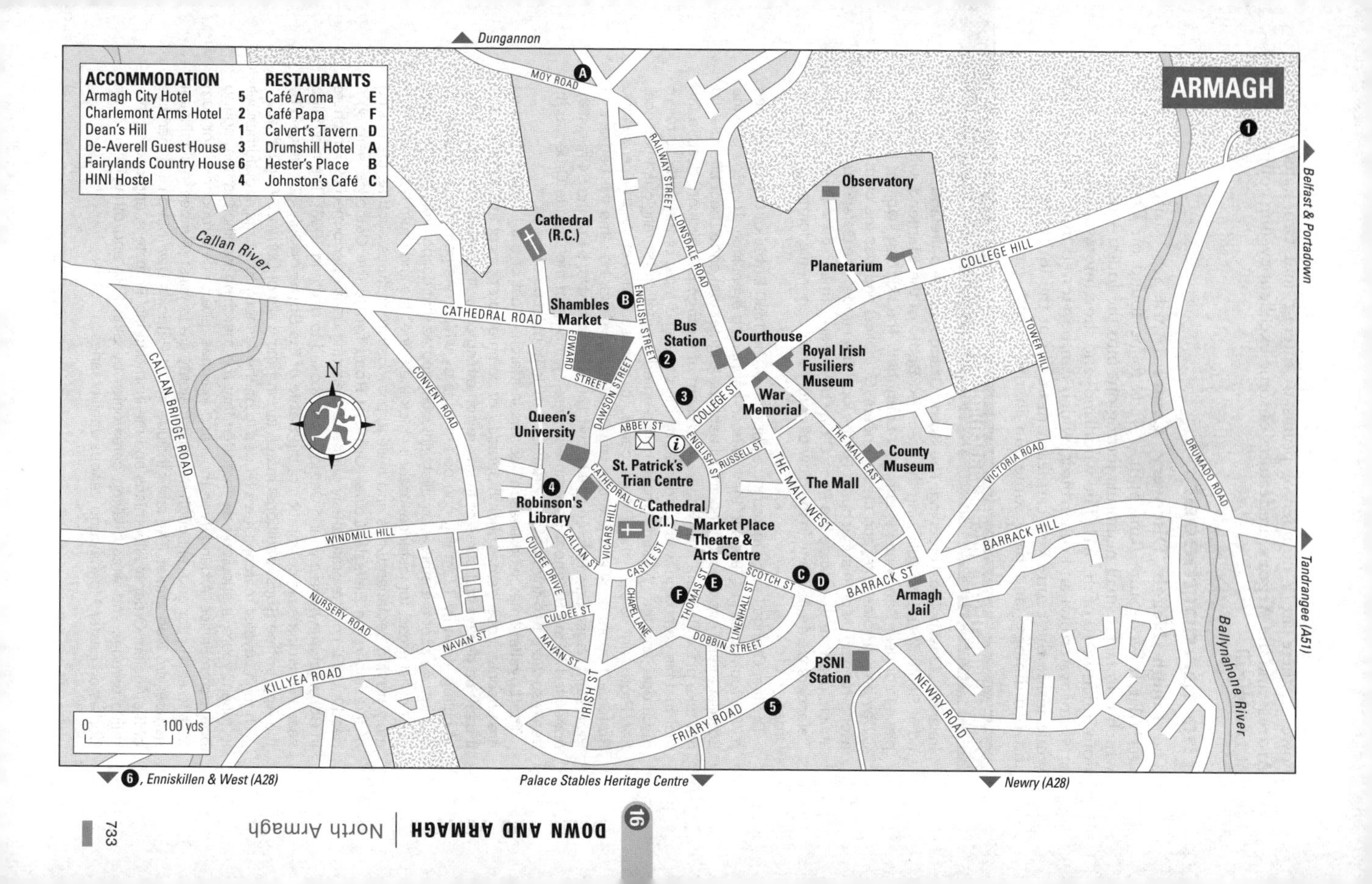

ACCOMMODATION		RESTAURANTS	
Armagh City Hotel	5	Café Aroma	E
Charlemont Arms Hotel	2	Café Papa	F
Dean's Hill	1	Calvert's Tavern	D
De-Averell Guest House	3	Drumshill Hotel	A
Fairylands Country House	6	Hester's Place	B
HINI Hostel	4	Johnston's Café	C

however, there are a number of points of interest, and two stately homes, **Ardress** and the **Argory**, are features of some excellent cycling country north of **Loughgall**.

The far northeast

The **Lough Neagh Discovery Centre** (April–Sept daily 10am–7pm; Oct–March Wed–Sun 10am–5pm; £4) is to be found on **Oxford Island**, which is in fact a small peninsula jutting out into the lough – best approached from junction 10 of the M1. The woodlands and shoreline swamps draw a multitude of waterfowl and other birds, which can be viewed from various hides, while inside the centre you can learn more about the lough, its management and ornithology (and have some fun in the Ecolab games room). You can

The Orange Order and the marching tradition

Ireland's oldest political grouping, **The Grand Orange Lodge of Ireland**, was founded in September 1795 following the so-called **Battle of the Diamond**, which took place in or near Dan Winter's farm near **Loughgall**. The skirmish involved the Peep O'Day boys (Protestants) and the Defenders (Catholics) and was the culmination of a long-running dispute about control of the local linen trade. The Defenders attacked an inn, unaware that inside the Peep O'Day boys were armed and waiting. A dozen Defenders were killed, and in the glow of victory their opponents formed the Orange Order.

The first Orange Lodge march in celebration of the 1690 **Battle of the Boyne** (see p.785) took place in 1796, and they've been happening ever since. The Boyne is the Loyalist totem, even though the actual battle at Aughter that ended Jacobite rule did not take place until the following year. **William of Orange** is their icon, despite the fact that his campaign was supported by the pope and most of the Catholic rulers of Europe, and that William himself had a noted reputation for religious tolerance. For Protestant Ulster, the Boyne came to represent a victory that enshrined Protestant supremacy and liberties, and the Orange Order became the bedrock of Protestant hegemony. Between 1921 and 1969, for example, 51 of the 54 ministers appointed to the Stormont government were members of the Orange Order; at its peak, so were two-thirds of the Protestant male population of the North.

The **Loyalist** "marching season" begins in March. Most of the Loyalist marches are uncontentious – small church parades, or commemorations of the Somme – but it can't be denied that some of them are something other than a vibrant expression of cultural identity. Marching can be a means by which one community asserts its dominance over the other – Loyalists selecting routes that deliberately pass through Nationalist areas, for instance, or their "Kick the Pope" fife and drum bands deliberately playing sectarian tunes and making provocative gestures such as the raising of five fingers on Belfast's **Lower Ormeau Road** (where five Catholics were shot dead in 1992) or the gratuitously offensive stamping dance performed by marchers in **Portadown** (where a young Catholic was kicked to death in 1998). The marching season culminates in celebration of the **Battle of the Boyne** on July 12, followed by the **Apprentice Boys'** traditional march around the walls of Derry on August 12.

Though Loyalist marches have tended to be the flashpoints for major disturbances in recent years, it shouldn't be forgotten that the marching tradition is common to both communities. Around three thousand marches take place throughout Northern Ireland each year and, although the vast majority are Loyalist parades, a significant number are **Nationalist**. The latter include the St Patrick's Day (March 17) marches of the Ancient Order of Hibernians and the Irish National Foresters, and commemorative parades and wreath-laying ceremonies by Sinn Féin and other Republican bodies on Easter Monday and various anniversaries.

explore more a little to the east at **Kinnego Bay**, where there's a marina, boat trips, specialist powerboat and sailing courses, and **hostel** accommodation available in *Waterside House Activity Centre* (Ⓣ028/3832 7573; closed Dec), which also offers a range of activities, including canoeing and wind-surfing.

Further on to the west, the M1's junction 13 is the access point for **Peatlands Park** (daily 9am–dusk), where the visitor centre (Easter–May & Sept Sat & Sun 2–6pm; June–Aug daily 2–6pm) can tell you everything you ever wanted to know about peat. A narrow-gauge **railway** (£1) runs for a mile along part of the track once used by the previous owners, the Irish Peat Development Company, to transport extracted peat.

The roach-filled upper section of the River Bann, south of Portadown, is the place for coarse anglers to head, and another watery attraction is the **Newry**

The Drumcree church parade

In the 1990s, it became clear that the Orangemen's march to the beat of the Lambeg drum was falling increasingly out of step with the political realities of Northern Ireland. What may well come to be seen as the turning point in the political fortunes of the Orange Order arrived during the summer of 1998.

For several years the **Drumcree church parade** in Portadown on the Sunday before the "Glorious Twelfth" (July 12 – the anniversary of the Battle of the Boyne) had been the focus for the Orange Order's assertion of their political identity, their march from the church down the Nationalist **Garvaghy Road** constituting a massive statement of the permanency of their power in Northern Ireland. Opposed to the peace settlement and the formation of the new Assembly, the Order made Drumcree its rallying cry, and was provoked to even greater stridency when the 1998 march was banned by the **Parades Commission**, a body formed specifically to limit the fractiousness (and cost) of marches by controlling or stopping them. The Order expected a massive security operation preventing their march, but failed to anticipate the subsequent Protestant violence that swept across the North, fuelled by Orange rhetoric and catalysed by the hard-line Loyalist Volunteer Force (LVF). Every day saw petrol bombings, vehicle hijacks, Catholic areas besieged and, hardest for the patriotic Orangemen to stomach, attacks on the RUC and troops. Early on the morning of Sunday July 12, 1998, a **petrol bomb** was thrown into a Catholic family's house on a largely Protestant estate in Ballymoney, County Antrim, killing three young brothers. The reaction of some Orange Lodge members, who seemed more concerned about maintaining their "traditional right to march" than with condemning the murder of innocent children, outraged people of both communities and exacerbated the divisions in the Order. Its chaplain called for Drumcree to be abandoned, and many Orangemen resigned. The RUC raided the protesters' camp and found weapons and explosives; the Protestant **Church of Ireland** then barred the protest from its grounds, forcing the abandonment of the Drumcree parade. The death of a policeman wounded by a blast bomb at Portadown further diminished the Orange Order's standing.

Subsequent years have again seen the Parades Commission refuse permission for the Garvaghy Road parade. While 1999 saw the Orange Order make only a symbolic protest, July 2000 witnessed a return to the demonstrators' more provocative stance, fuelled by the presence of paramilitaries from the LVF and the UDA (Ulster Defence Association). While 2001 and 2002 saw little more than a stand-off between would-be paraders and a massive security presence, Drumcree remains a profoundly politicized gathering, and the events of 1998 will be recorded as a crucial episode in the modern political history of Ireland.

Canal, which flows into the river through a natural trough in the landscape, running through fourteen locks on the way. One of these features the restored **Moneypenny's Lockhouse** (April–Sept Sat & Sun 2–5pm; free), named after the family who kept the lock for 85 years – it's a two-mile stroll along the towpath from Shillingford Quay in Portadown.

Loughgall and around

LOUGHGALL, a tranquil and pretty estate village about five miles west of Portadown (and the same distance north of Armagh along the B27), lies in the middle of apple orchard country, beautiful in the spring, and is worth visiting mainly for its historical connections. Like many of its neighbours in Armagh's rural north, Loughgall is strongly **Protestant**. It was three miles northeast of the village at Diamond Hill that the Battle of the Diamond took place in 1795, which led to the foundation of the first Protestant **Orange Order** (see box on p.734) in the home of Dan Winter nearby. Unfortunately, two cottages claim the distinction of being the birthplace of the Order, and matters are confused further by the fact that much of the land around the Diamond crossroads was leased by members of the Winter family. The first claimant, **Dan Winter's Cottage** (May–Sept Sat & Sun; call ⓣ028/3885 2777 for times; free) at the Diamond crossroads, was probably damaged during the battle, according to carbon-dating of charred rafters found during restoration, and contains period furniture and an original 200-year-old weaving loom. Its rival – generally believed to be the more likely candidate – is **Dan Winter's House** (Mon–Sat 10.30am–5.30pm, Sun 2–5.30pm; free), in a nearby farmyard just down Derryloughan Road, which displays maps and relics from the battle alongside seventeenth-century furniture; the cottage roof still contains original lead-shot.

Back in Loughgall, off Main Street, you'll find the **Loughgall Country Park** (daily 10am–dusk; car £2.50), which offers waymarked trails and children's play areas. Main Street also features a couple of fine antique shops, while, two miles east on Ballyhagan Road (off the B77 to Portadown), is *The Famous Grouse*, a lively **bar** with the best **restaurant** for miles around plus regular live music.

Five miles or so north of Loughgall are two National Trust stately homes a few miles apart that are worth visiting if you're spending more than a day in the area. **Ardress House** (mid-March to May & Sept Sat, Sun & public hols 2–6pm; June–Aug Mon & Wed–Sun 2–6pm; £2.70) is a seventeenth-century manor house with ornate plasterwork by Michael Stapleton, a good collection of paintings, a sizeable working farmyard and wooded grounds. More enticing, however, is **The Argory** (mid-March to May & Sept Sat, Sun & public hols noon–6pm; June daily 1–6pm; July & Aug daily noon–6pm; £4), a fine Neoclassical building dating back to 1824 and set in 350 acres by the River Blackwater. The splendid grounds (daily 10am–dusk; car £2) include very pleasant gardens, but it's the house that's the real attraction. Built of Caledon stone, its entrance hall features a fine, cantilevered staircase, and the rooms contain Victorian and Edwardian furniture among many other period items, including a fabulous cabinet barrel organ. The house is still lit by an original 1906 acetylene gas plant in the stable yard, and during the summer it stages musical events and organized garden walks (details from ⓣ028/8778 4753).

Armagh city and around

ARMAGH is one of the most attractive places in the North, and the rich history of the city and its surroundings has plenty to keep you occupied for a day or two. The city offers **cathedrals, museums** and a **planetarium** set in handsome Georgian streets, and two miles west is the ancient site of once-grand **Navan Fort**. Armagh has been the site of the **Catholic** primacy of All Ireland since St Patrick established his church here, and has rather ambitiously adopted the title of the "Irish Rome" for itself – like Rome, it's positioned among seven small hills. Paradoxically, the city is also the seat of the **Protestant** Church of Ireland's archbishop of Armagh.

Armagh has a number of **events** during the year, but the biggest concentration occurs during the early May **Apple Blossom** festival, when there are daily entertainments and activities, blues and dance festivals. As you'd expect, the local **St Patrick's Day Parade** (March 17) is one of the largest in the country. The County **Fleadh** (traditional music and dancing festival, usually with plenty of sessions around town) takes place in June, while November sees the **Bard of Armagh** poetry competition and one of Ireland's major *uilleann* piping events, the **William Kennedy Piping Festival**.

Some history

Armagh (Ard Macha, "Macha's height") was named after **Queen Macha**, wife of Nevry, who is said to have arrived in Ireland 608 years after the biblical flood. She built a fortress on the main hill where the Church of Ireland cathedral now stands and is supposed to be buried somewhere in the hillside. The claim that Armagh is one of the oldest settlements in Ireland is supported by the city's position on one of the most ancient roads in the land, the Moyry Pass, which once stretched from the extreme south of Ireland, through Tara, to the north. In about 300 BC, the centre of power shifted westward across the River Callan to where another queen (of the same name, Macha) built the legendary **Navan Fort**.

After nearly seven hundred years, the ruling dynasty at Navan was defeated by the Collas brothers, and the new rulers re-established their main base back on the hill of Armagh. A hundred years later, in 445 AD, **St Patrick** declared the hill the site of his primacy and first bishopric and built his cathedral here (having first converted the local chieftain, Daire, a descendant of the Collas brothers). Other churches grew up around the cathedral, and Armagh became a pre-eminent centre of learning during the Dark Ages, the period when Ireland was known as the "Isle of Saints and Scholars". The settlement developed around three distinct districts (*Trians),* their boundaries still reflected today by English, Irish and Scotch Streets. Armagh strongly challenges Downpatrick's claim to be the **burial place** of St Patrick; locals argue that since the relics of Patrick's book, bell and staff are here, his body must be too (though the burial site is not identified).

Between the ninth and the eleventh centuries, the city was repeatedly pillaged by the **Vikings**, mainly from the Norse settlements at Lough Neagh. The Irish king who claimed final victory over the Norsemen, **Brian Boru**, was killed at the Battle of Clontarf in 1014, and was buried in Armagh cathedral. The arrival of the **Normans** in the twelfth century saw the city become a constant battleground as the O'Neills sought to maintain their control. Despite this, Armagh's ecclesiastical power did not waver until the **Reformation**. Further local conflict ensued and it was not until the end of the Williamite wars that peace finally broke out. The arrival of Richard Robinson as archbishop in 1765 saw a final flourish of building work, much of which survives today, despite the encroachment of recent supermarket developments. Modern Armagh is a predominantly Catholic city, strong on Gaelic sports (indeed the county won the All-Ireland Senior Gaelic football championship for the first time in 2002), and although physically it has borne up well to the Troubles (certainly in comparison to Newry and Derry), it has not avoided them.

Arrival, information and accommodation

The **Ulsterbus** station (Ⓣ028/3752 2266) is on Lonsdale Road, just north of the centre. An excellent way to get around is the 1940s-style **bus** (June–Sept daily 10am–5.20pm; £4), which operates a hop-on-and-off service calling at all the major attractions.

The **tourist office** is in the Old Bank Building, in front of the St Patrick's Trian Centre at 40 English St (June–Aug Mon–Sat 9am–5.30pm, Sun 2–5.30pm; rest of year closes 5pm; Ⓣ028/3752 1800, Ⓦwww.armagh.gov.uk); **walking tours** of the city operate from here during the summer (June–Sept Sat 11am & 2pm, Sun 2pm; 90 min; £4).

The huge new *Armagh City Hotel*, Friary Road (Ⓣ028/3751 8888, Ⓦwww.mooneyhotelgroup.com; ❼), offers the plushest **accommodation** in the city. More central options include the friendly and well-equipped *De-Averell Guest House*, 47 English St (Ⓣ028/3751 1213, Ⓦwww.deaverellhouse.com; ❹), and the nearby and newly refurbished *Charlemont Arms Hotel*, 63–65 English St (Ⓣ028/3752 2028, Ⓦwww.charlemontarms.hotel; ❺). The best **B&Bs** include *Dean's Hill*, College Hill (Ⓣ028/3752 4923, Ⓕ3752 4923; ❹), an eighteenth-century building in wooded grounds up past the Observatory, and *Fairylands Country House*, 25 Navan Fort Rd (Ⓣ028/3751 0315, Ⓦwww.fairylands.net; ❷), a congenial place in a quiet rural setting a mile from the centre. There's a recently built HINI **hostel** (Ⓣ028/3751 1800), superbly situated near the Church of Ireland cathedral at 39 Abbey St. The nearest **camping** is at *Gosford Forest Park*, seven miles southwest along the A28 near Markethill (Ⓣ028/3755 1277), with fine facilities set in wooded grounds around a castle.

The City

The best way to get your bearings is to walk up the steps of **St Patrick's Roman Catholic Cathedral** (Mon–Sat 10am–5pm; free), built on a hillside just northwest of the Shambles Market. The view of the town from here is impressive, and you should be able to identify most of the key sites spread out below. The cathedral's foundation stone was laid in 1840, but completion was delayed by the Famine and a subsequent lack of funding. Whilst the pope and local nobility chipped in, money was also raised by public collections and raffles – one prize of a grandfather clock has still not been claimed. On the outside, the cathedral first appears little different from many of its nineteenth-century Gothic Revival contemporaries, but it is impressively large and airy. Inside, as befits the seat of the cardinal archbishop, every inch of wall glistens with **mosaics**, in colours ranging from marine- and sky-blue to terracotta pinks and oranges. Other striking pieces include the white granite "pincer-claw" **tabernacle holder**, reflected in a highly polished marble floor, and a **statue** of the Crucifixion, which suggests (deliberately or otherwise) the old city's division into *Trians*. Armagh is known for its **choral music**, and the annual Charles Wood Summer School (check with the tourist office for dates) is worth catching.

Heading south along Dawson Street, you'll soon reach Cathedral Close and **St Patrick's Church of Ireland Cathedral** (daily: April–Oct 9.30am–5pm; Nov–March 9.30am–4pm; tours June–Aug Mon–Sat 11.30am & 2.30pm; Ⓦ www.stpatrickscathedral-armagh.org; free). This lays claim to the summit of the principal hillock, Drum Saileach, where St Patrick founded his first church in 445 AD. It commands a distinctive Armagh view across to the other hills and down over the clutter of gable walls and pitched roofing on its own slopes. A series of churches occupied the site after 445 and, although the core of the present one is medieval, a nineteenth-century restoration has coated the thirteenth-century outer walls in a sandstone plaster of which Thackeray remarked, "It is as neat and trim as a lady's dressing room." Many of the ancient decorations were removed, leaving the Spartan interior you see today. Just as you enter from the highly distinctive timber porch, you'll see a few remnants of an eleventh-century **Celtic cross** and a startling **statue** of Thomas Molyneux. Inside, high up, you should be able to sight the medieval carved heads of men, women and monsters. One other unusual feature is the tilt of the chancel, a medieval building practice meant to represent the slumping head of the dying Christ. The **chapter house** has a small collection of stone statues (mostly gathered from elsewhere), the most noticeable of which are the Stone Age **Tandragee Idol** and a Sheila-na-Gig with an ass's ears. Outside the north transept a plaque on the west wall commemorates the burial of **Brian Boru**.

Just down the hill from the cathedral, the **public library** (known locally as Robinson's; Mon–Fri 10am–1pm & 2–4pm; free but donations welcomed) has, among many rare tomes, a first edition of *Gulliver's Travels* annotated by Swift himself, and an early edition of Raleigh's *History of the World* (1614), as well as a collection of engravings, including some by Hogarth. The library was founded in 1771 by Archbishop Richard Robinson, who was described as converting Armagh "from mud to stone" and who is responsible for almost all the older buildings in the city – the nearby infirmary was one of his, too, though it's now occupied by the university.

Cathedral Close leads downhill to the main shopping area, where an entry leads into the narrow winding lane of **McCrum's Court**, where the rock-walled *Hole in the Wall* pub is well worth a visit. Walking back and a little way north up English Street, you'll come to **St Patrick's Trian Centre**, an ambitious complex containing the tourist office and three separate **exhibitions** (Mon–Sat 10am–5pm, Sun 2–5pm; joint ticket £4). The first of these, peopled with figures representing the Land of Lilliput and Jonathan Swift's connection with Armagh, occupies the former Presbyterian Meeting House, which was partly constructed from the ruined abbey of St Peter and St Paul – Swift is reputed to have commented that the masons were "chipping the popery out of the stones". The second installation, "The Armagh Story", is a multimedia account of the town's growth and the nature of belief, while the third, "Patrick's Testament", is an interactive account of the saint's association with Armagh.

The Mall

Russell Street leads down to **The Mall**, an elegant tree-lined promenade fringed to the east by two terraces of handsome Georgian houses designed by the Armagh-born architect Francis Johnston, who worked primarily for Archbishop Robinson. Johnston was responsible for many of Dublin's best Georgian buildings, and you'll encounter more examples of his work around town, including the classical **courthouse** at The Mall's northern end; the former **jail** occupies the southern end. In its late eighteenth-century heyday The

Mall was a racecourse; nowadays there's nothing more athletic than the occasional jogger and Saturday cricket matches.

A former schoolhouse on the east side of The Mall houses the **County Museum** (Mon–Fri 10am–5pm, Sat 10am–1pm & 2–5pm; free), an old-style museum with all the usual local miscellany on display, including an alarmingly vivid collection of stuffed wildlife, plus a little **art gallery** tucked away on the upper floor. Here there are twenty or so mystical pastels, oils and cartoon sketches by the Irish turn-of-the-century poet **George Russell**, a much-neglected companion to Yeats, who acquired the alias Æ as a result of a Dublin newspaper misprinting a letter that he had signed "Aeons". The prolific local artist J.B. Vallely is also represented with a superb oil showing five musicians enjoying a session; the theme of traditional music figures in more than three thousand of Vallely's canvases and, with his wife Eithne, he currently runs the town's Armagh Pipers' Club (their children are all well-known traditional musicians). Elsewhere, a display devoted to railway history recounts the story of Ireland's worst railway disaster, when two passenger trains collided outside Armagh in 1889, killing 89 people, many of whom are buried in nearby St Mark's churchyard.

Further north along The Mall is the **Royal Irish Fusiliers Museum** (Mon–Fri 10am–12.30pm & 1.30–4pm; free), built from the leftovers of the courthouse. It's pretty much as you'd expect: tons of weaponry, uniforms, medallions and silverware from the regiment formed in 1793 in response to the Napoleonic crisis and subsequently known as the "Faughs" from their battle-cry *Faugh a Ballagh!* ("Clear the way!"). The Fusiliers subsequently fought in the Crimean and Boer wars (where they relieved the Siege of Ladysmith) and in both world wars before amalgamating with the Inniskilling Fusiliers (see p.766) and Ulster Rifles in 1968.

The Observatory and Planetarium

College Hill, the road that heads east from The Mall alongside the Fusiliers museum, will take you to the **Observatory** (dome open April–Sept Mon–Fri 9.30am–4.30pm; free) – an ancient institution that celebrated its second centenary in 1990, but is still at the forefront of European astronomical research, with a ten-inch telescope. The nearby **Planetarium** (Mon–Fri 2–4.45pm; Ⓦwww.armagh-planetarium.co.uk; £2) is currently undergoing major restoration and the only features available are the **star theatre** shows (Mon–Fri 3pm), where you whizz through the universe from the safety of a reclinable seat, and twice-monthly evening public telescope sessions.

Armagh Friary

The ruins of **Armagh Friary**, founded by the Franciscans in 1263, lie within easy walking distance south of the city centre, just off Friary Road by the entrance to the grounds of the Archbishop's Palace (now the District Council offices). The ruins are those of the church alone, and the site is an unfortunate example of how atmosphere can be destroyed when a major road runs alongside. The focus now is the **Palace Stables Heritage Centre** (May–Aug Mon–Sat 10am–5.30pm, Sun 1–5pm; Sept–April Mon–Sat 10am–5pm, Sun 2–5pm; £3.75), where tableaux of life-sized figures depict July 23, 1776, the day on which Archbishop Robinson entertained the notable English agriculturalist and writer Arthur Young – his *Tour of Ireland* was published in 1780 – and you're guided around the exhibits by living history interpreters garbed in contemporary costumes. From here you move into the main part of the palace, which dates from around 1770, though the final storey was added in 1825, and was inhabited by subsequent archbishops until 1975, when the private Primate's Chapel next door was deconsecrated. In the grounds there's a well-preserved **ice house**, a curious **tunnel** by which servants accessed the basement kitchens, a stimulating **sensory garden** and, somewhat incongruously, the municipal dog pound.

Eating, drinking and entertainment

Many of Armagh's pubs will serve bar **food** at lunchtime, but eating in the evening can be more problematic. Pick of the pubs with food is the lively *Calvert's Tavern*, 3 Scotch St, while you can always get a reasonably priced full meal at the *Drumsill Hotel*, Moy Road. The basement **restaurant** at *De-Averell Guest House* is splendidly innovative, and the *Charlemont Arms Hotel* and *The Market Place* restaurant in the theatre and arts complex (see below) are both highly recommended. *Hester's Place* on Upper English Street and *Johnston's Cafe*, Scotch Street, both serve good-value lunches. The best coffee and sandwiches in the city are to be had at *Cafe Papa*, 15 Thomas St, which also opens as a bistro on Friday and Saturday evenings, while *Café Aroma*, 45 Thomas St, is another good spot for caffeine addicts.

The most atmospheric **pub** for a pint is the *Hole in the Wall Bar* in McCrum's Court (see p.739). The top end of English Street is a good area to pub-crawl in search of **music**; weekends are best but many places have sing-songs on Tuesdays and Thursdays. Traditional music is surprisingly scarce in the city, and your best bet is to head for the villages of Mullaghbawn and Forkhill in the south of the county (see p.744). The *Northern Bar*, 100 Railway St, is the place for blues and rock. For **nightclubs**, your options are limited – locals head to nearby Keady, Moy or across the border to Castleblaney – but try *The Met* complex on Moy Road for weekend club nights.

The **Market Place Theatre and Arts Centre** (Ⓣ028/3752 1821, Ⓦwww.marketplacearmagh.com) features a four-hundred-seat auditorium, a smaller studio theatre, gallery, bars, coffee house and bistro, and has an imaginative programme of theatrical and musical events. Also on the Market Place is the

Road bowls

The sport of **road bowls** is popular in Holland and Germany and was once played throughout Ireland, but is now limited mainly to Cork and Armagh, where it's also known as "road bullets".

The game's principle is simple: a pair of rival contestants each propels a 28oz (800g) solid iron ball along a course of country roads (usually about two and a half miles long), the winner being the player who reaches the finishing line with the **fewest number of throws**. In practice, it's a complicated business. The Armagh roads twist and turn, up and down, and bowlers are assisted by a team of camp followers, including managers and road guides who advise on the most advantageous spots to aim and the force of the throw. Traditionally a male sport, it's become increasingly popular with women, who've held their own championship since 1981. Roads around Armagh where you're likely to catch sight of the game – usually on Sunday afternoons – include Cathedral Road, Napper Road, Blackwater Town Road, Rock Road, Tassa Road, Keady Road, Newtonhamilton Road and Madden Road. The most reliable information on forthcoming games is probably to be had in local pubs. One of the biggest competitions, **Ból Fada**, takes place in Keady, South Armagh, towards the end of April, with the **Ulster Championship** in Armagh city in August.

Armagh City Film House (Ⓣ028/3751 1033), a four-screen cinema with a regular late show on Friday and Saturday nights. There's a small Saturday **market** in Market Place Square, and the bigger **Shambles Market**, just off Cathedral Road, is open Tuesdays and Fridays from 9am to 5pm.

Navan Fort

For nearly seven hundred years **Navan Fort** (open access; free) was the great seat of northern power, rivalling Tara in the south. It was here that the kings of Ulster ruled and Queen Macha built her palace on the earthwork's summit. It's a site of deeply mystical significance, but one also of enormous archaeological interest. The court of the **Knights of the Red Branch**, Ireland's most prestigious order of chivalry, was based here too. The knights, like those of the Round Table, are historical figures entirely subsumed into legend, their greatest champion being the legendary defender of Ulster, **Cúchulainn**. The stories of these warriors' deeds are recited and sung in what's now known as the *Ulster Cycle*. Their dynasty was finally vanquished in 332 AD, when three brothers (the Collas), in a conquest known as the Black Pig's Dyke, destroyed Navan Fort, razing it to the ground and leaving only the earthen mounds visible today. The defeated Red Branch Knights were driven eastwards into Down and Antrim, and were little heard of again.

The only approach to the fort (two miles west of Armagh on the A28; bus #73) is via the road entrance to the now-defunct, multimillion-pound Navan Centre which once housed multimedia displays on the site and its history. Skirting this building, you'll discover that the site area is defined by a massive bank with a defensive **ditch**. When you reach the fort, you'll find an **earthen mound**, which gives a commanding view but no hint of its past. Excavation of the mound took place over a ten-year period (1961–71) and revealed a peculiar structure, apparently unique in the Celtic world. Archaeologists reckon that around 100 BC the buildings that had existed since the Neolithic period were cleared, and a huge structure 108ft in diameter was constructed. An outer wall of timber surrounded five concentric rings of large posts, 275 in all, with a massive post at the very centre. This was then filled with limestone boulders and **set on fire**, creating a mountain of ash that was then covered with sods of clay to make a high mound. It is anybody's guess what the purpose of the structure was – possibly a temple, or maybe a monumental funeral pyre.

Nearby you can visit for free other ancient archaeological structures: a second fort, the earliest known artificial lake in Ireland and a large natural lake that has yielded various archaeological finds.

South Armagh

The **South Armagh** (Ⓦwww.south-armagh.com) countryside is amongst the most attractive in the North, yet many visitors are deterred from coming here by the area's notoriety. Proximity to the border and a predominantly Catholic population have resulted in this being a nucleus of resistance to British rule, and evidence of military occupation is everywhere – from the hilltop surveillance posts to the constant whirring blades of helicopters monitoring the ground from above. Since the first ceasefire, however, many of the border controls and barriers have been removed, and South Armagh has remained a safe and remarkably welcoming place for tourists.

The Ring of Gullion

Most of South Armagh's attractions are concentrated in and around the area known as the **Ring of Gullion**, a naturally formed ring-dyke of low-lying hills that encircles (and pre-dates) the mountain at its core. People have lived here for more than six thousand years, and there's a rich heritage of remains and monuments. On the ring's western fringe is the **Dorsey Enclosure**, two huge earthen banks and ditch ramparts dating from the Iron Age, running for a mile either side of the old route to Navan Fort. Elsewhere are numerous dolmens and cairns, Christian relics and monuments from the Plantation era.

Slieve Gullion (Sliabh gCuillinn, "mountain of the slope"), which dominates the southeastern corner of County Armagh, is one of the most mysteriously beautiful mountains in the country. A store of romantic legends is attached to it, especially concerning **Cúchulainn**, who took his name here after slaying the hound (Cú) of the blacksmith Culainn. Due south at Glendhu is where Cúchulainn single-handedly halted the army of Queen Medb of Connaught, who was intent on capturing the great bull of Cooley. **Fionn Mac Cumhaill**, who founded the *Fianna*, a mythical national militia whose adventures are told in the *Fenian Cycle*, also appears in stories here.

A scenic way to approach the mountain is from the north, passing the turning to **BESSBROOK**, a nineteenth-century model village developed by a Quaker linen entrepreneur; the Cadbury family's Bourneville estate in Birmingham, England, followed a very similar layout. Just outside the village stands **Derrymore House** (May–Aug Thurs–Sat 2–5.30pm; £2.25), an eighteenth-century thatched manor house built for Isaac Corry, Chancellor of the Exchequer of the last Irish Parliament before the Act of Union, which was drafted in his drawing room here. After **CAMLOUGH** ("crooked lake"), where the Irish Tricolour flutters, turn off the main road to go down by the eastern slopes of Camlough Mountain and you'll see the beautiful **lake**, set like a jewel within its green banks. A little further on, between Camlough Mountain and Slieve Gullion, are the ruined **Killeavy churches** (Cill Shléibhe, "church of the mountain"). Two churches of different periods share the same gable wall: the west church is pre-Romanesque and one of the most important survivors of its kind in the country; the other, larger church dates from the thirteenth century. A granite slab marks the **grave of St Bline**, the founder of a fifth-century nunnery sited here – there's a holy well dedicated to her a little further up the slopes of Slieve Gullion, which pilgrims visit on her feast day (the Sunday nearest to July 6).

The official, tarmacked entrance up into Slieve Gullion is on the mountain's forested southern face, after you've passed through the village of **KILLEAVY**. You'll find a small **forest park** (Easter–Sept daily 10am–dusk; free), fronted by the **Courtyard Centre**, where there's a café and crafts shop. From the centre it's an eight-mile winding drive up to the summit (or you can follow a walking trail), where there's a couple of megalithic **cairns**. Fionn Mac Cumhaill was legendarily bewitched here by Miluchra, and local superstition holds that bathing in the small summit **lake** will turn your hair white; another tale states that under certain conditions a visitor to the site will be given the power to foresee everything that will happen that day. Various vertiginous viewpoints offer spectacular **views** over the Ring of Gullion and the surrounding countryside for miles around.

Jonesborough and around

JONESBOROUGH, east of the mountain, is the venue each Sunday for a vast open-air **market** (11am–5pm), drawing traders and customers from both sides of the border. The range of goods on offer is equally enormous and it's well worth experiencing. The excellent *Flurrybridge Inn* serves lunches Thursday to Sunday and holds occasional sessions.

Two miles south of Jonesborough is the **Pillar Stone of Kilnasaggart**, a beautifully inscribed monument dating from 700 AD, which marks the site of an early Christian cemetery. Several small crosses are marked within circles on its back face, and the defaced markings on its edges are possibly *ogham* writing. It's surrounded by several other tiny stones with similar cross markings, all held within a pentagonal enclosure three fields away from the roadside, behind a farmhouse. Less than a mile west of here, on the other side of the train line, you should be able to see the ruins of **Moyry Castle** on a hill. This is a timid affair and not really worth even this slight detour, but among its interesting features are several musket loopholes. It was built in 1601 by Lord Mountjoy, Queen Elizabeth I's deputy, as the defence for the Gap of the North.

Forkhill and Mullaghbawn

You might expect **FORKHILL** to lie in an elevated position, but this tiny village nestling in the southwestern foothills of Slieve Gullion derives its name from the Irish *foirceal* ("trough"). It's a simple, quiet and remote-looking place, though dominated by the massive army encampment stacked upon the crown of an overlooking hill. The village is strong on traditional culture: O'Neill's *Welcome Inn* has a well-known **story-teller**, John Campbell, and **sessions** most Tuesday nights (and other music at the weekends); there's weekend music, too, at *The Forge*. Neighbouring **MULLAGHBAWN** (An Mullach Bán, "the white summit"), to the north, has *O'Hanlons' Bridge House*, which holds regular sessions on Fridays and Saturdays, and the innovative *Tí Chulainn* **cultural activities centre** (Ⓣ028/3088 8828, Ⓦwww.tichulainn.ie), dedicated to the promotion of the area's culture and literary heritage. South Armagh has a powerful **song tradition** and the centre hosts both the *Stray Leaf* singers' club (every second Saturday) and a number of annual events, including the Tommy Makem International Song School in the second week of June. The **Slieve Gullion Festival of Traditional Singing** takes place in both villages on the first weekend in October. Notable local singers to look out for include Patricia Flynn and Pádraigín Ní Uallacháin and her husband Len Graham.

If you want to stay, there are a couple of **B&Bs** in Forkhill: *Lakeview Cottage*, 34 Church Rd (Ⓣ028/3088 8382; ❷), with fine views of the mountain, and *Greenvale*, 141 Longfield Rd (Ⓣ028/3088 8314; ❶), which also offers **pony trekking**. In Mullaghbawn, there's *Lar Na Tuaithe*, 89 Maphoner Rd (Ⓣ028/3088 8897; ❸), very close to the *Tí Chulainn* centre. Near here, the Ring of Gullion Centre on Lough Road (Ⓣ028/3088 9311, Ⓦwww.rogequestrian.com) also provides pony trekking and **riding lessons**.

Crossmaglen and around

In the far southwestern corner of Armagh just inside the border, **CROSSMAGLEN** (Crois Mhic Lionnáin, "MacLennon's cross") has reputedly the largest market square in Ireland, the scene of a fortnightly Friday **market**. Face south and it's impossible to ignore the huge PSNI/British army barracks here with its outcrops of aerials, cameras and sangars (small pillbox-like fortifications). During the Troubles the town's reputation for armed struggle against the British was fearsome, and, in truth, it has been a cauldron of activity ever since Partition. Indeed, had the 1924 Boundary Commission's proposals been fully implemented, the town and surrounding countryside would have been transferred to Dublin rule rather than staying inside the North. All this said, on arrival you'll find the pubs much friendlier than you might have expected and you're very unlikely to brush up against any trouble.

The extremely helpful **tourist office** (Mon–Fri 9am–5pm, extended to 6pm and weekends in summer; ⓣ028/3086 8900) is in Ó Fiaich House on The Square. There's **B&B** at *Murtagh's Bar*, 13 North St (ⓣ028/3086 1378, ⓔaidmur1964@aol.com; ❷), and at *Cnoc Mhuire*, 40 Annaghmare Rd (ⓣ028/3086 1896; ❶), the latter a hilltop farmhouse a mile or so north on the Newtownhamilton road. Lunches are available at *Murtagh's*, while several of the other bars, including *The Cartwheel*, serve evening **meals**. *Keenan's* bar on The Square hosts a notable **traditional-music** session on Thursdays. Crossmaglen is at the forefront of the local revival of interest in Gaelic games, and the town's **Gaelic football** team have been recent All-Ireland club champions as well as providing the backbone of the 2002 Senior Championship-winning county team.

A couple of miles east of Crossmaglen on the B30 Newry road is **CREGGAN** and its **Poets' Graveyard**, so named because three eighteenth-century Gaelic poets are buried there: Art Mac Cooey, Patrick Mac Aliondain and Séamus Mór Mac Murphy (who was also an outlaw of some notoriety). The inscription on Mac Cooey's stone is taken from his most famous poem, *Úr-Chill an Chreagáin* – "That with the fragrant Gaels of Creggan I will be put in clay under the sod."

East of Creggan, a turning off the main road leads to **GLASSDRUMMOND** and **Hearty's Folk Cottage** (Sun 2–6pm) where you can admire the arts and crafts collections and enjoy excellent afternoon teas to the accompaniment of traditional music.

Travel details

Trains

(*services are far less frequent on Sundays*)
Bangor to: Belfast (every 30min; 30min); Lisburn (every 30min; 1hr 10min).
Helen's Bay to: Belfast (every 30min; 20min).
Newry to: Belfast (5–12 daily; 50min); Dublin (4–7 daily; 1hr 15min); Dundalk (4–7 daily; 20min).

Buses

The **Mourne Rambler** (ⓣ028/4372 2296) is a circular service running in July and August from Newcastle to the Silent Valley and back. Buses depart Newcastle (Mon–Sat) at 10.10am, 11.35am, 2.05pm & 3.30pm; the return fare is £3.60. All other buses are run by **Ulsterbus** unless otherwise stated.
Armagh to: Belfast (4–11 daily; 1hr–1hr 20min); Benburb (2–3 Mon–Sat; 25min); Caledon via Navan Fort (4–10 Mon–Sat; 20min); Castleblaney (1–5 daily; 50min); Cavan (1–4 daily; 1hr 30min); Dublin (1–2 daily; 2hr 30min); Dungannon (4–7 Mon–Sat; 40min); Enniskillen (1 daily; 1hr 45min); Loughgall (1–7 Mon–Sat; 15min); Markethill (5–9 Mon–Sat; 20min); Monaghan (4–12 daily; 30–45min); Newry (5 Mon–Sat; 1hr); Portadown (5–25 Mon–Fri; 30min).
Banbridge to: Belfast (11–30 daily; 45min–1hr 15min); Newcastle (3–4 Mon–Sat; 1hr); Newry (9–24 daily; 30min).
Bangor to: Belfast (8–32 daily; 45min); Donaghadee (5–19 daily; 25min); Newtownards (7–31 daily; 15min).
Donaghadee to: Bangor (5–17 daily; 25min); Belfast (7–20 daily; 55min).
Downpatrick to: Ardglass (2–10 daily; 25min); Ballyhornan (2–6 daily; 50min); Belfast (6–26

daily; 1hr); Kilkeel (1–12 daily; 1hr 20min); Killough (2–10 daily; 15min); Killyleagh (1–8 daily; 20min); Newcastle (5–17 daily; 35min); Newry (2–4 daily; 1hr); Raholp (4–5 Mon–Sat; 15min); Strangford (5–7 Mon–Sat; 25min).
Hillsborough to: Belfast (12–30 daily; 45min).
Kilkeel to: Annalong (7–16 daily; 15min); Downpatrick (1–13 daily; 1hr 20min); Greencastle (2 Wed & Sat; 20min); Newcastle (7–14 daily; 40min); Newry (4–10 daily; 50min); Rostrevor (4–10 daily; 30min); Warrenpoint (4–10 daily; 35min).
Newcastle to: Annalong (6–15 daily; 25min); Banbridge (2 Mon–Sat; 1hr); Belfast (10–19 daily; 1hr 20min); Bryansford (2–3 daily; 10min); Castlewellan (7–23 daily; 10min); Downpatrick (5–15 daily; 35min); Kilkeel (6–15 daily; 40min); Newry (via Hilltown: 2–4 daily; 40min; via Kilkeel: 2–8 daily; 1hr 50min).
Newry to: Armagh (5–7 Mon–Sat; 1hr); Banbridge (9–24 daily; 30min); Bessbrook (16–24 Mon–Sat; 10min); Crossmaglen (4–6 Mon–Sat; 55min); Downpatrick (2–4 daily; 1hr); Dublin (Bus Éireann 4–7 daily; 2hr); Forkhill (4–6 Mon–Sat; 35min); Jonesborough (3–5 Mon–Sat; 15min); Mullaghbawn (4–6 Mon–Sat; 30min); Newcastle (via Hilltown: 2–4 daily; 40min; via Kilkeel: 2–8 daily; 1hr 50min); Rostrevor (7–18 daily; 20min); Warrenpoint (10–21 daily; 15min).
Newtownards to: Bangor (7–33 daily; 10min); Belfast (every 10–20min Mon–Sat, 12 Sun; 15min); Comber (7–16 daily; 15min); Greyabbey (8–14 daily; 20min); Portaferry (8–14 daily; 50min–1hr 15min).

Tyrone and Fermanagh

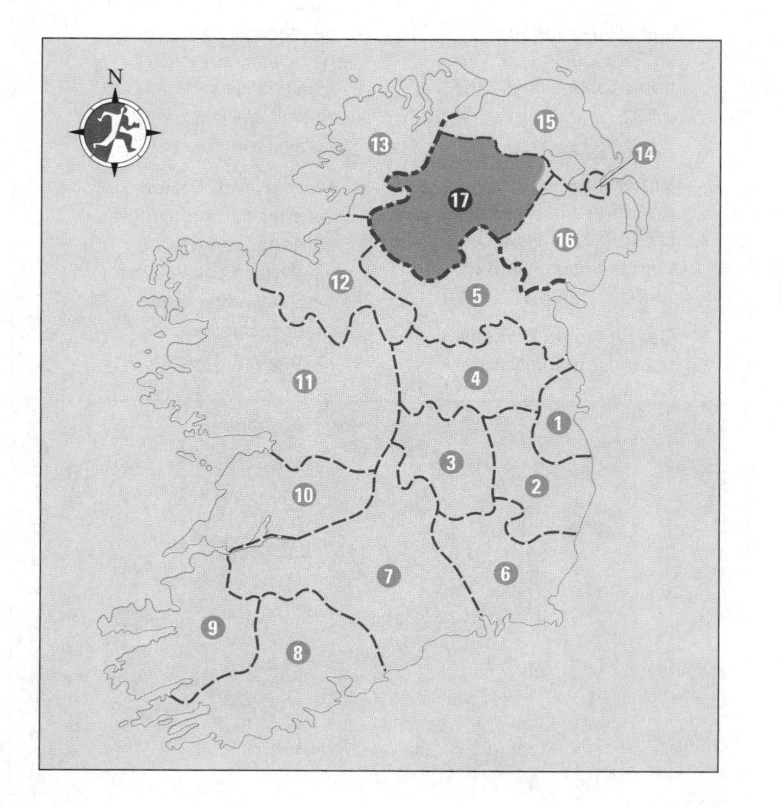

CHAPTER 17

Highlights

* **The Sperrin Mountains** Arguably even more picturesque than the Mourne Mountains, the Sperrins offer a splendid variety of hikes and trails. See p.755

* **Beaghmore Stone Circles** Seven Bronze Age stone circles and numerous other relics set in a lonely spot with tremendous views. See p.757

* **Lough Neagh** Ireland's largest lake – and indeed the biggest in the British Isles – is best viewed from the churchyard at Ardboe. See p.758

* **Castle Coole** Perhaps the most magnificent building of its kind in Northern Ireland, this gorgeous eighteenth-century mansion is richly decorated inside and set in wonderful grounds. See p.767

* **Devenish Island** Getting out on the water is an essential part of any trip to Fermanagh, and there's no better place to do it than at this former monastic settlement in Lower Lough Erne. See p.768

* **Marble Arch Caves** Take a boat trip along a subterranean river to view these caves filled with stalactites and other marvellous rock formations. See p.774

17

Tyrone and Fermanagh

Much of inland Northern Ireland is formed by neighbouring **Tyrone** and **Fermanagh**, predominantly rural counties whose few sizeable towns lie at the eastern and western fringes of the region. The chief scenic attractions of County Tyrone are to be found in the wild and desolate **Sperrin Mountains** in the north, and a scattering of castles, archaeological sites and heritage centres, including the excellent **Ulster American Folk Park**, close to the town of **Omagh**.

In contrast to Tyrone, County Fermanagh attracts plenty of visitors – chiefly for the watersports, boating and fishing that are widely available. At its core is **Lough Erne**, a huge lake complex dotted with islands and surrounded by richly beautiful countryside. Fermanagh's biggest town, **Enniskillen**, evinces a strong sense of history, while the remnants of the medieval past – along with those of the seventeenth and eighteenth centuries – are found all over the region, on islands and mainland alike. As in Tyrone, sights of interest are dispersed, and buses can be very infrequent away from the main routes; but the key to enjoying Fermanagh is to get out onto the water – and this is easy enough from Enniskillen and a number of the villages that rest on the lakes' shores.

County Tyrone

Stretching from the shores of the vast Lough Neagh (the largest lake in the British Isles) in the east to the border of the Republic and Donegal in the west, County Tyrone lies bang in the middle of Northern Ireland. Its northeastern limits are high in the desolate and beautiful **Sperrin Mountains**, and in the south it reaches towards the lakes of County Fermanagh. This is first and foremost farming country, with little evidence of industrialization apart from the

starchily neat Planters' villages that grew up with the linen industry and a smattering of heavier industries in the towns near Lough Neagh.

The Sperrin range offers major scenic attractions; it's rich in wildlife and is an excellent target for determined, lonesome walking. The place to head for is **Gortin**, a village on the **Ulster Way** footpath and the most easily accessible overnight stop in the area. Tyrone also has no shortage of archaeological remains, the most remarkable being the **Beaghmore Stone Circles**, in the southeast of the Sperrins. The towns, though, are not much of a draw. **Omagh** is the county's largest town, agreeable enough but with little to warrant a stop. **Cookstown** and **Dungannon** in the east, and **Strabane** on the Donegal border, are similarly places to pass through, with minimal points of interest scattered around. The nearest the county's settlements get to being picturesque are the villages and tiny hamlets of the Sperrins. There's little else in the way of sights around the county beyond the heritage centres that celebrate the historic connections between the Ulster province and the US. Of these, the **Ulster American Folk Park** near Omagh is by far the best.

The only **local transport** in the region is Ulsterbus, which is reliable along main routes but infrequent elsewhere. So, if this is your only way of getting around, it makes sense to pick up a timetable in a major bus station before you head off into the country. However, so scattered are Tyrone's attractions that you're likely to see little of the most interesting parts without a car or a bike. The one exception, of course, is in the Sperrins, where **hiking** is the best way to get around.

Omagh and around

On the afternoon of Saturday August 15, 1998, a five-hundred-pound **car bomb**, planted by the dissident Republican group the Real IRA, exploded on Market Street in the centre of Tyrone's largest town, **OMAGH** (An Ómaigh, "the virgin plain"). Twenty-six people were killed outright (a further three died later) and more than two hundred were injured. It remains the worst single atrocity in the history of the Troubles and drew outrage and condemnation from every quarter. Much of the eastern part of Omagh's main street was devastated by the bombing and has since undergone major reconstruction. The area uphill to the west, originally thought to be the bombers' target on the basis of their misleading warning, remained unscathed and contains two adjacent buildings that would grace any town – the fine classical **courthouse** and the irregular twin spires of the Catholic **Sacred Heart Church**.

Practicalities

Omagh's **bus station** (ⓣ028/8224 2711) is just across the river from the town centre in Mountjoy Road (north off the High Street). The **tourist office** is right in the centre at 1 Market St (April–June & Sept Mon–Sat 9am–5pm; July & Aug open until 5.30pm; Oct–March closed Sat; ⓣ028/8224 7831); it has a **bureau de change**, a small exhibition space and sells tickets for local events. You'll need your own transport to see most of the region it promotes: you can rent **cars** from Johnson King Motors, 82 Derry Rd (ⓣ028/8224 2788), and **bikes** from Conway Cycles (ⓣ028/8224 6195) on Old Market Place.

If you're hiking the Sperrins, a better bet might be to base yourself in Gortin (see p.756), but within Omagh, *Silverbirch Hotel*, 5 Gortin Rd (ⓣ028/8224 2520, ⓦwww.silverbirchhotel.com; ❻), offers relatively luxurious **accommodation**, while *Hawthorn House*, 72 Mountfield Rd, signposted to Killyclogher off the A505 (ⓣ028/8225 2005, ⓦwww.hawthornhouse.co.uk; ❹), is friendly, comfortable and has a very popular restaurant. The nearest **B&B** to the town centre is *Ardmore*, 12 Tamlaght Rd (ⓣ028/8224 3381, ⓔirismccann@hotmail.com; ❷), up the left fork in front of the Sacred Heart and along the second turning on your right. Also near the centre is *Bridie's*, 1 Georgian Villas, Hospital Rd (ⓣ028/8224 5254; ❷); go down the main street away from the courthouse and, once across the river, turn to the right. The *Omagh Independent* **hostel** is two and a half miles north, at 9A Waterworks Rd (IHH; ⓣ028/8224 1973, ⓦwww.omaghhostel.co.uk), signposted off the B48 and A505; the hostel managers will pick you up from Omagh bus station.

Omagh is a good place to stop for **food**, particularly during the daytime. The *Pink Elephant* in the High Street is a local favourite, serving breakfast and lunches in huge helpings, and there's also *Coffee@Grinders*, Anderson House, Market Street, for snacks and a caffeine buzz. Plenty of pubs serve food, though the best is undoubtedly the *Coach Inn*, 1 Railway Terrace, offering tasty lunchtime specials and an extensive evening menu. *Hawthorn House* (see above) is extremely popular in the evenings, specializing in lobster and other seafood and steaks (allow £35 per head including wine). *Molly Sweeney's*, 28 Gortin Rd (Ⓣ028/8225 2595), has an excellent fish menu and *Grant's*, 29 George St (Ⓣ028/8225 0900), offers a bistro menu or snacks in the wine bar.

For **nightlife**, head for the Dún Úladh Cultural Heritage Centre of Ulster, just outside town on the B4 Carrickmore road (Ⓣ028/8224 2777), the provincial branch of the national organization Comhaltas Ceoltóirí Éireann, which promotes Irish **traditional music** and culture. There's all manner of events running here, including a traditional session on Saturday nights. **Bars** offering traditional music sessions include *Sally O'Brien's*, 35 John St (Thurs), and *Grant's* (see above; Sat), while *Bogan's*, near the tourist office, is a pleasant place for a pint. Most of the hotels have live music at weekends, often of the country and Irish kind, while **clubbers** head for *Taste*, 30 Castle St, or *Utopia*, 55–57 Market St.

The Ulster American Folk Park

The most successful of Northern Ireland's American heritage projects is the **Ulster American Folk Park** (April–Sept Mon–Sat 11am–6.30pm, Sun 11.30am–7pm; rest of year Mon–Fri 10.30am–5pm; last admission 90min before closing; Ⓦwww.folkpark.com; £4), three miles north of Omagh in Camphill, a short hop on one of the regular Strabane-bound buses. The Folk Park makes a good afternoon out from Omagh and a fine day-trip if combined with the Ulster History Park near Gortin (see p.756).

The first significant **emigration** from Ireland to North America was that of Ulster men and women in the early eighteenth century, many of whom were of Scottish Protestant origin. Of all the immigrant communities in the United States, it was the Irish who most quickly – and profoundly – made their mark: the three first-generation **US presidents** were all of Ulster stock, and a further nine presidents could trace their roots to here. Throughout the eighteenth and nineteenth centuries thousands of people left to establish new lives in North America, a steady flow of emigrants that became a torrent during the Famine years.

You can find detailed information on the causes and patterns of migration in the Folk Park's indoor **gallery**, but the real attractions lie outside in the park itself, where **original buildings** have been transplanted or replicas constructed to provide a sense of Ulster life in the past. The disparity in living conditions is represented by a typical pre-Famine **single-room cabin** from the Sperrins, which you'll pass on your way to the **Mellon Homestead**, a significantly more substantial dwelling from which the local Mellon family migrated in 1818. There's an austere **Presbyterian meeting house** and the squat **Tullyallen Mass House**, a Catholic chapel dating from 1768. A re-created Ulster street, including the impressively authentic Reilly's Spirit Grocers from Newtownbutler, leads to the *Union*, a full-size **brig** reconstructed to demonstrate the gruelling conditions endured during the voyage across the Atlantic. An American street leads to edifices constructed by the **Pennsylvanian settlers**, including a multipurpose log barn and massive six-roomed log farmhouse. There are plenty of other buildings, and you'll meet costumed guides and craftworkers ready to explain their activities and answer questions, augmenting the Folk Park's attention to authenticity.

The complex also houses the **Centre for Emigration Studies** (Mon–Fri 9.30am–4.30pm), a major reference and research library that contains an enormous variety of material, such as emigrants' letters, passenger lists and contemporary newspaper articles.

There's a **café** on the site, but for more substantial fare head up the road to the *Mellon Country Inn* (Ⓣ028/8166 1224, Ⓔmelloncountryinn@utvinternet.com; ❻), which serves traditional Irish food in a cosmopolitan style and has stylish, recently renovated **accommodation**; they can also provide you with walking routes and **maps** for the nearby Ulster Way, which enters the scenic Gortin area to the northeast.

Northwest Tyrone

The northwestern part of Tyrone is seldom visited by tourists yet has some of the county's most attractive towns and countryside. The fastest route through the area is the A5 north to Derry or Letterkenny via **Newtownstewart**, **Sion Mills** and **Strabane**. A quieter alternative is the route via **Castlederg** along minor country roads and across the border to Castlefinn in County Donegal.

Castlederg

The market town of **CASTLEDERG** sits around a spruced-up square beside the River Derg, across whose waters lie the ruins of a Plantation **castle**, built in 1619 and destroyed by Sir Phelim O'Neill during the 1641 Rebellion. Modern Castlederg retains something of its traditional flavour as a staging-post for travellers and a watering-hole for pilgrims on their way to St Patrick's Purgatory on Lough Derg (see p.573). The town's bars and cafés make this a good place to stop for refuelling, and the **Castlederg Visitor Centre**, 26 Lower Strabane Rd (April–Oct Tues–Fri 11am–4pm, Sat 11.30am–4pm, Sun 2–5pm; Ⓣ028/8167 0795), will give you lots of information on local sites of interest. **Davy Crockett**'s family came from the Castlederg area and the visitor centre has a small display (£1.30) containing a model of the Alamo Fort where the celebrated frontiersman made his last stand. Close to each other one mile north of the village off the Lurganboy road are two large **megalithic tombs** that stand as memorials to the area's pre-Christian past: Todd's Den is a cairn with a portal stone, but more impressive is the Druid's Altar, a chambered grave with two portal stones and capstones, one inscribed with *ogham* runes.

Accommodation in the town itself is limited to the en-suite rooms at the *Derg Arms*, 43 Main St (Ⓣ028/8167 1644, Ⓔdergarms@aol.com; ❷). A few miles west off the Killeter road is *Ardmourne House and Stables*, 36 Corgary Rd (Ⓣ028/8167 0291, Ⓦwww.hiking-n-biking.com; ❷), with comfortable B&B and **riding** and trekking, too. Surprisingly, the **nightlife** in Castlederg can often be quite lively, with various musical entertainments, from singalongs to discos, at bars such as the *Castle Inn* and *Gallen's*.

Newtownstewart and Sion Mills

The quicker route north from Omagh passes through rich farmland to **NEWTOWNSTEWART**, which, surprisingly for its size, boasts remnants of two **castles**. In the main street a gable wall is all that remains of the Stewart castle burned down on the orders of James II; squatting in isolation on a hill to the southwest are the ruins of the fourteenth-century Harry Avery's castle, another O'Neill stronghold. But Newtownstewart's real draw is the gem of a **museum** housed in the tiny **visitor centre** (May–Sept Tues–Fri 11am–4pm, Sat 11.30am–5pm, Sun 2–5pm; £1.30) a couple of hundred yards down the Omagh road from the main street. Local historian Billy Dunbar, a walking encyclopedia, donated his collection of vintage packaging, man traps, stereoscopes and war memorabilia to the museum when he could no longer navigate from one end of his house to the other. Highlights include a bordalous (a mini-chamberpot named after a French priest renowned for his over-long sermons) and a threepenny bit engraved with the Lord's Prayer.

The linen industry of the eighteenth century made a big impact in Tyrone, as it did all over Ulster, but its traces are mostly faint ones – such as the disused mills along the Ballinderry River near Cookstown. **SION MILLS**, a planned linen village seven miles north of Newtownstewart, is the obvious exception. The quaint village, which belies the gruesome conditions of nineteenth-century factory work, is designated a conservation area, though the Herdman's linen works still operates here amidst security fences and cameras. You can skirt around it on foot and down to the Mourne River, where there's good **fishing**, but there's little other reason to stay here.

Strabane and around

Present-day **STRABANE**, north of Omagh, is pretty grim and often traffic-congested, and there's no reason to linger here when both Derry city and County Donegal are so close. In the eighteenth century, however, Strabane was an important printing and publishing centre. John Dunlap emigrated from here and went on to print the broadsheets of the American Declaration of Independence in 1776, as well as the *Pennsylvanian Packet*, America's first daily newspaper. All that is left in Strabane of these times is the cute, bow-windowed frontage of **Gray's Printing Press**, 49 Main St (April–Sept Tues–Sat 2–5pm; £2.50), owned by the National Trust. It contains a small printing **museum** with a selection of nineteenth-century presses, displays of compositing and an audio-visual show on print history.

One of Strabane's most famous sons was Brian O'Nolan, a multifaceted writer better known as the surreal and comic novelist **Flann O'Brien** and the brilliantly zany *Irish Times* columnist Myles na Gopaleen. Born in 1911 into an Irish-speaking household at 15 Bowling Green, he had a glittering academic career at University College Dublin and spent much of his working life as a civil servant. An irascible character with a fondness for drinking, he was unfortunate enough to produce his best work, *At Swim-Two-Birds*, just before the outbreak of World War II. Since his death in 1966 his absurdist novels have been republished and – much to his annoyance, no doubt – he has become a cult figure (for more on his work see p.853). Another scion of Strabane is the well-known singer-songwriter **Paul Brady**, while a less entertaining individual to have his roots in the area is the American president **Woodrow Wilson**. Head east of Strabane two miles down the Plumbridge road and you'll find the Wilson ancestral home in the village of **DERGALT** (July & Aug Tues–Sun 2–5pm; £1); this small, traditional farmer's cottage was home to the president's father, a printer in Strabane. Stuffed with furniture and effects belonging to the family, it's now a target for American tourists, who dutifully meander through the hallowed rooms.

Strabane's **tourist office**, in a glass pagoda on Abercorn Square (April–June & Sept Mon–Fri 9am–5pm, Sat 10am–4pm; July & Aug Mon–Fri 9am–5.30pm, Sat 9am–4.30pm; Oct Mon–Fri 9am–5pm; Ⓣ028/7138 3735, Ⓦwww.strabanedc.com), will help with finding **accommodation**, should you really need to stay here. Top of the range is the *Fir Trees Hotel*, Dublin Road (Ⓣ028/7138 2382, Ⓕ7138 3116; ④), which also has a fine restaurant, or try the central **B&B** *Bowling Green House*, 6 Bowling Green (Ⓣ028/7188 4787; ②). Wholesome daytime **meals** can be found at *Dempsey's*, 74 Lower Main St, while piscophiles should head for *Oysters Restaurant*, 37 Patrick St (Ⓣ028/7138 2690; closed Mon), for lunch and evening fish specialities.

The Sperrins

The impressive, undulating **Sperrin Mountains** form the northeastern limits of County Tyrone. Wild, empty and beautiful, they reach 2240ft at their highest, yet the smooth and gradually curving slopes give them a deceptively low appearance. The covering of bog and heather adds to this effect, suggesting nothing more than high, open moorland. For all this, views from the summits are panoramic, and the evenness of texture can make these mountains sumptuous when bathed in evening light. Once in the mountains, it's impossible not to catch sight of the **wildlife**. Sparrowhawks and kestrels hover above, and you might see buzzards or the far rarer hen harrier. They're attracted by rich prey in a landscape mostly undisturbed by development – the mountains teem with assorted rodents, rabbits, badgers and even the Irish hare. One threat to this delicately balanced ecosystem has been the rediscovery of **gold** in the mountains. Their future is in the balance, but for the moment at least, the Sperrins offer a wilderness to be enjoyed.

For local sheep-farming communities, however, the depopulation of the Sperrins is a real problem, and their traditional way of life is now slowly dying. The sparseness of the population and the lack of focal centres make it difficult for an outsider to key into this culture. For the same reason, hitching isn't easy, and walkers should bear in mind that there's a shortage of places to buy food, so **planning ahead** is essential. Rely only on large villages for provisions of any sort; hamlets often have nothing.

The **Sperrin Heritage Centre** (April–Oct Mon–Fri 11.30am–5.30pm, Sat 1.30am–6pm, Sun 2–6pm; £2.20) lies between Cranagh and Sperrin, nine

Walking the Sperrins

The forty-mile-wide range of the Sperrin Mountains offers good long-distance **walking**, without necessarily involving steep inclines. You can ramble wherever you like, but remember that – despite appearances – these are high mountains, and changeable weather makes them potentially dangerous. A map and compass are essential for serious walking.

For those not equipped for the high ground, the **Glenelly** and **Owenkillen** river valleys run through the heart of this stunning countryside from Plumbridge and Gortin respectively, and are particularly enjoyable for cyclists.

The **Central Sperrins Way** is a new 25-mile waymarked trail, which begins and ends at Barnes Gap, a few miles southeast of Plumbridge. The two-day walk takes in a variety of countryside with spectacular views of the mountains, moorland and Glenelly valley. The exposed moorland can often be very wet and boggy underfoot, and, as there is no accommodation en route, taking a tent is essential.

The official **Ulster Way** footpath takes an arduous 34-mile route – the steepish Glenelly Trail – from Dungiven up over Glenshane Mountain to Goles Forest. From Gortin a second stage of the Way leads to the Ulster American Folk Park, a ten-mile trek. Various guidebooks to the Ulster Way are available, but it's always advisable to ask locals about the state of the path.

The Countryside Access and Activities Network for Northern Ireland (Ⓣ028/9038 3848, Ⓦwww.countrysiderecreation.com) has a detailed website providing information on these and other waymarked routes in the region.

miles east of Plumbridge (see below), and lets you explore the area's environmental and cultural issues without getting your feet wet. The video games and audio-visuals of this welcoming interpretive centre are quite a surprise – particularly the holographic story-teller and the quaint 3-D slide shows – and they also organize gold-panning expeditions or can rent you a pan (65p). Its pleasant **tearoom** serves homemade food and real coffee. The centre is tricky to reach without your own transport, although the Mon–Sat **Sperrin Rambler bus** passes by (see p.775).

Gortin and around

If you're tackling the Sperrins to the north of Omagh, there are really only two villages that can offer you any amenities at all – Gortin and its near-neighbour Plumbridge. And even these are comatose for much of the year.

GORTIN (An Goirtín, "the little field"), ten miles north of Omagh and served by three buses daily, is a long one-street village with a surprising number of **pubs**, one of which, the *Badoney Tavern*, offers lunches and evening **meals**. Alternatively, there's an innovative menu at *The Pedlar's Restaurant*. **Accommodation** is available at the new HINI **hostel**, 62 Main St (Ⓣ028/8164 8346, Ⓦwww.gortin.net), whose rooms are all en suite; it also has four self-catering houses (sleeps 4–6; £180–275 per week). Alternatively, there's the *Gortin Hostel and Outdoor Centre*, 198 Glenpark Rd (Ⓣ028/8164 8083, Ⓦwww.gortinhostel.com), in a converted school 50yd down the road to Omagh. For **camping**, head to the *Gortin Glen Caravan Park* (Ⓣ028/8164 8108), three miles south on the Omagh road (5 buses Mon–Sat). Just opposite is the **Gortin Glen Forest Park** (daily 10am–dusk; pedestrians £1, cars £2.50), which offers a five-mile forest drive and various trails leading to viewpoints of the area, en route to which you may encounter members of the park's herd of Sitka deer.

A little over three miles south of Gortin is the **Ulster History Park** (April–Sept daily 10am–5.30pm; July & Aug open till 6.30pm; Oct–March Mon–Fri 10am–5pm; last admission 1hr before closing; Ⓦwww.omagh.gov.uk/uhpindex; £3.75), which features full-scale reconstructions of buildings in Ireland from 7000 BC up to the seventeenth century. Inside there are videos and displays that serve to distract in bad weather, but far more rewarding is the **interactive tour**, on which a guide talks you round such authentic traditional dwellings as a stinking deerskin-covered tepee, shows you how to chip flint, explains ancient symbols and answers questions expertly, no matter how daft they are. The rath, *crannóg* and medieval castle are particularly interesting, and the latest addition is a seventeenth-century Plantation settlement.

PLUMBRIDGE, three and a half miles north of Gortin, sits clustered prettily on the banks of the Glenelly River. Apocryphally, it gets its name from the building of the village bridge: the engineer in charge didn't have a plumb line and so, from his scaffolding, spat in the water, using his spit to take the perpendicular. There's little here beyond a few bars and a couple of shops, and the liveliest times are during the annual Glenelly **sheepdog trials** in August. However, you might encounter the odd optimistic gold panner, convinced that the river's waters hold the key to his or her fortune.

Three and a half miles east of Gortin on the B46 Creggan road is the tiny village of **ROUSKEY**, with the ruins of a "**sweat lodge**", an early form of sauna (after the steam treatment, the luckless invalid was plunged into the icy stream nearby). Widespread use of sweat lodges died out after the Famine years, possibly because the experience of typhoid that accompanied the Famine dealt a severe blow to people's confidence in traditional medicinal treatments, but some were still functioning up to the 1920s. Also in the village is *Teach Ceoil* (Ⓣ028/8164 8882), a restored stone barn worth investigating for its regular evenings of **traditional music** and dancing.

Prehistoric remains and the Beaghmore Stone Circles

County Tyrone is peppered with archaeological remains: there are more than a thousand standing stones in the Sperrins alone and the county as a whole has numerous chambered graves. The **Lough Macrory** area, just east of Mountfield on the A505 Omagh–Cookstown road, is particularly rich in dolmens and megaliths, though many of these are hard to find and of specialist interest only.

The uninitiated will get most out of the Bronze Age **Beaghmore Stone Circles**, in the southeast of the Sperrins. From Gortin, take the B46 east onto the A505, from where they're well signposted up a track three and a half miles north off the road. Although most of the stones on this lonely site are no more than three feet high, the complexity of the ritual they suggest is impressive: there are seven stone circles, ten stone rows and a dozen round cairns (burial mounds, some containing cremated human remains). All of the circles stand in pairs, except for one, which is filled with over eight hundred upright stones, known as Dragon's Teeth. The alignments correlate to movements of the sun, moon and stars; two of the rows point to sunrise at the summer solstice.

An Creagán Visitor Centre

Just off the A505, roughly halfway between Omagh and Cookstown, is the **An Creagán Visitor Centre** (April–Sept daily 11am–6.30pm; Oct–March Mon–Fri 11am–4.30pm; Ⓦwww.ancreagan.com; £2), modelled on the many cairns that surround it – 44 of them in a five-mile radius. The centre is circular and built from local stone on the land of one of the last native Irish-speakers in the district, Peadar Joe Haughey, who died in the 1950s. Staff in the centre speak Irish, and the place is actually more of a cultural centre than a museum, with locals coming along to the **traditional-music** sessions, dancing, storytelling and singing events. But An Creagán also explores the rare raised bog terrain all around, with interpretive displays and signposted **rambling and cycling routes** over the countryside (they also rent bikes). The farmers driven to these bogs in the eighteenth century made huge efforts to reclaim the soil; there are limekilns from which they treated the reclaimed land, and you can still see their **potato ridges**: these grassed-over Copney spade ridges – a form of cultivation that maximized production – point back to the devastating Famine of 1845–49 and the farmers' desperate attempts to survive. You can organize self-catering **accommodation** here (Ⓣ028/8076 1112; £110–330 per week) in the traditional *clachán* settlement, with open turf fires supplemented, fortunately, by central heating.

Eastern Tyrone

The only places in the east of County Tyrone that could be described as anything more than villages are the rather drab towns of **Cookstown** and **Dungannon**. The dominant feature is the eastern shore of **Lough Neagh**, and there are a number of relics of both the region's historical heritage, such as high crosses at **Ardboe** and **Donaghmore**, and its more recent industrial past at **Coalisland** and the **Welbrook Beetling Mill**. The village of **Benburb**, to the south, is one of the most attractively situated in the North.

Cookstown and the Lough Neagh shore

A planned Planters' town, **COOKSTOWN** boasts the longest main street in Ireland, the site of an extensive Saturday **market**. The **tourist office** is at The Burnavon, Burns Road (Mon–Fri 9am–5pm, Sat 10am–4pm; ⓣ028/8676 6727). The pick of the local **accommodation** is the very plush *Tullylagan Country House* (ⓣ028/8676 5100; ❹), set in thirty acres of grounds in Sandholes, four miles south of the town.

The **Wellbrook Beetling Mill**, four miles west of Cookstown off the A505, is a National Trust-owned eighteenth-century water-powered linen mill (mid-March to June & Sept Sat, Sun & public hols noon–6pm; July & Aug daily noon–6pm; £2.50). "Beetling" was the final stage of production whereby linen was given a sheen and smoothness by hammering with heavy wooden "beetles". Though it ceased operation in 1961, the mill is excellently preserved, and all the engines still work.

For more monumental interest, head two miles south of Cookstown on the B520 to **Tullaghoge Fort**, the erstwhile headquarters of the O'Hagans, chief justices of Ireland, who undertook the coronations of the O'Neill kings from the twelfth to the seventeenth century. From the road, the fort appears to be simply a copse of beech and Scots pine on top of a very gentle hill, but in fact these are very clear earthworks of the early Christian period – a circular outer bank with an inner oval enclosure. It was in Tullaghoge forest that O'Neill tribesmen hid after the Flight of the Earls.

It seems even the legendary Fionn Mac Cumhaill was unimpressed by east Tyrone's low-lying terrain. Legend has it that he took a massive lump of land from Ulster and hurled it across the Irish Sea. It landed and became the Isle of Man, and the hole it left behind became **Lough Neagh** (pronounced "nay"). The lough's shores form the county's eastern boundary and provide excellent **fishing** and plenty of bird life, but, beyond this, both land and lake are almost featureless. Small settlements house eel fishermen, whose catches go to the Toome Eel Fishery at **Toome**, sometimes known as Toomebridge, (at the northern tip of the lake), the largest eel fishery in Europe.

Slight relief is to be found at **ARDBOE**, ten miles east of Cookstown, where there's a tenth-century **high cross**. The elements have eroded the various biblical scenes carved onto the sandstone almost beyond recognition, but its exceptional size – 18ft high – is impressive. The cross stands in the grounds of an early monastery associated with **St Colman**, but the ruined church nearby dates from the seventeenth century and is of little interest. On a humid day in early summer, you'll also not fail to be impressed by the swarms of black Lough Neagh mayflies, a particularly pointless insect which, lacking a mouth, is born merely to copulate and die.

Ruined **Mountjoy Castle** lurks behind a farm eight miles south of here near Washing Bay. Built in 1602 as part of the English campaign against Hugh O'Neill, it was strategically important, but, sadly, the setting is disappointing.

If you pass through the town of **COALISLAND** on the way to Dungannon, check out the **Cornmill Heritage Centre** on Lineside (Mon–Fri 10am–5pm; £1.50), a mélange of artefacts and exhibits from the area's industrial past, particularly coal-mining, and photographs of local luminaries (including **Dennis Taylor**, the former world snooker champion). The mill itself ground to a halt in 1978 after providing employment for more than seventy years. Coalisland is a sleepy place, but becomes more animated during its annual **international music festival** in July.

Dungannon and around

DUNGANNON, about ten miles south of Cookstown, is a dreary town with no trace of its illustrious past as the hilltop seat of the O'Neills, from which they ruled Ulster for over five centuries. Outside town, on the A45 Coalisland Road, is the **Tyrone Crystal factory** (Mon–Sat 9am–6pm, Sun 1–5pm; Ⓦwww.tyronecrystal.com; £2), where you can see demonstrations of glass-blowing and hand-cutting. There's excellent **B&B** and home cooking in the Georgian *Grange Lodge*, 7 Grange Rd (Ⓣ028/8778 4212, Ⓔgrangelodge@nireland.com; ❺), and surprisingly good lakeside **camping** in *Dungannon Park* on Moy Road (Ⓣ028/8772 7327).

At **DONAGHMORE**, three miles northwest, there's another **high cross** dating from the tenth century in front of the parish church, though whoever reassembled it in the nineteenth century clearly botched the job as there's an obvious join halfway down the shaft. Four hundred yards up the Pomeroy road the local **heritage centre** (Mon–Fri 9am–5pm; free) occupies a converted school and has an interesting collection of photographs and documents related to the area.

A couple of miles southwest in **CASTLECAULFIELD** lie the ruins of a fortified **mansion** built by Sir Toby Caulfield in 1619, while the village **church** has a plaque commemorating the poet Charles Wolfe (1791–1823), author of *The Burial of St John Moore* and curate of Donaghmore for a few years.

Between Dungannon and Armagh, the picturesque village of **BENBURB** (An Bhinn Bhorb, "the prominent cliff") merits a detour. The tiny cottages in Main Street were once apple-peeling sheds, and the parish **church**, dating from 1618, is one of the oldest still in regular use in Ireland. The church stands next to the gates of a **Servite priory** – the monastic order of Servants of the Virgin, founded in Florence in 1233, but which did not establish itself in Ireland until 1948. The priory grounds offer a pleasant stroll, but far better are the walks along the Blackwater River in **Benburb Valley Park** (daily 10am–dusk), where, perched on a rock a hundred feet or so above the water, are the substantial remains of a **castle** built by Viscount Powerscourt in 1615.

A mile south of Benburb village in the canalside hamlet of **MILLTOWN** is the **Benburb Valley Heritage Centre** (Easter–Sept daily 10am–5pm; £2), housed in a nineteenth-century weaving factory and containing a range of old linen-making machinery and a scale model of the 1646 Battle of Benburb, at which a Scottish army suffered catastrophic losses in an encounter with Owen Roe O'Neill. There's a **café** here, too.

The Clogher Valley

Ten miles or so west of Benburb, the Blackwater River forms the **Clogher Valley**, a twenty-mile stretch running from the market town of Aughnacloy (near the Monaghan border) through the villages of **Ballygawley**, **Augher** and **Clogher** to **Fivemiletown**. There's nothing here of special interest, but the pleasantly rolling countryside is sufficient in itself to justify a diversion.

Three miles east of Ballygawley, to the north of Aughnacloy, is the **Grant Ancestral House**, signposted off the A4 Dungannon road (April–Sept Tues–Sat noon–5pm, Sun 2–6pm; £1.50). The land here was once a smallholding farmed by the maternal ancestors of the eighteenth US president, **Ulysses S. Grant** (1822–85), whose life and exploits during the American Civil War are depicted in the visitor centre. A tiny two-roomed cottage has been restored and refurnished in typical nineteenth-century style, while the surrounding working farm displays agricultural implements from the same period and is stocked with traditional breeds. Three miles west of Ballygawley, and signposted to the north, is a hill known as **Errigal Keerogue**, where there is an unfinished high cross and a ruined fifteenth-century church dedicated to St Ciaran.

At one time a railway connected the valley's villages, and at **AUGHER** you can sample home baking in the old station, which now houses *Rosamund's Coffee Shop*. The village makes much of its connection with the writer **William Carleton** (1794–1869), whose most notable novel was *Black Prophet*, a sombre tale of the Famine years. A summer school celebrates his life and work each August. The cottage where the author was born is a mile south in **Springtown** (signposted from Augher) and is part of the longer of two Carleton Trails, which start and finish at Clogher.

A couple of miles northwest of Augher lies **Knockmany Forest**, where a cairn on the top of a steep wooded hill protects a Bronze Age passage tomb, said to be the resting place of Ainé, the mother-goddess with whom Fionn Mac Cumhaill was infatuated. The stones in the tomb are inscribed with complex swirling patterns, but you can merely peer at them from a distance through a locked grille.

CLOGHER, further west, is a little livelier, its main street climbing gently upwards to its eighteenth-century Church of Ireland **cathedral**. The village lays claim to the oldest bishopric in Ireland – its first bishop was St MacCartan, a disciple of St Patrick – and there is also evidence of the place's earlier significance. In the park behind the cathedral is a recently excavated Iron Age **hill fort**, thought to be the seat of the old kings of Oriel. Inside the cathedral is the "golden stone", a slab cross dating from the ninth century, and a gallery of portraits of former bishops bearing expressions of appropriate solemnity. On the main street, *The Rathmore* and *The Trident Inn* pubs provide **meals**, and you can also dine in the evenings at *Corick House*, 20 Corick Rd (Ⓣ028/8554 8216, Ⓔcorickhousehotel@netscapeonline.co.uk; ❺), which offers the best **B&B** in the area. Alternatively, there's **camping** at the *Clogher Valley Country Caravan Park* (Ⓣ028/8554 8932; mid-March to Oct) in Fardross Forest, a mile west on the A4.

The **Clogher Valley Scenic Drive** is ideally accessed from **FIVEMILETOWN**, seven miles west of Clogher, though the lack of signposts at certain crucial junctions means it's best tackled with an Ordnance Survey map. The complete circuit runs for about 25 miles in a loop either side of the A4, but the southerly section is easily the more enjoyable and takes you into the most isolated part of the county outside the Sperrins. Head south from the crossroads in Fivemiletown and once you've picked up the first sign you'll find yourself on narrow woodland lanes gradually ascending towards **Slieve Beagh**. It's more than likely that sheep will be your only company unless you encounter the odd hiker on the Ulster Way, which you'll traverse as the route enters moorland. The whole valley can be surveyed from the car park viewpoint before you descend into **Fardross Forest**. The only other site of note is a few miles on. Look out to your left for a bizarre, three-tiered hilltop tower known as **Brackenridge's Folly**, named after George Brackenridge, who had the tower constructed as his mausoleum – thus compelling the squirearchy who had looked down on him during his lifetime to look up to him once he was dead. Fivemiletown has a couple of **hotels** on the main street: the *Valley* (Ⓣ028/8952 1505; ❹) and *Four Ways* (Ⓣ028/8952 1260, Ⓔfourwayshotel@lakelands.net; ❹). There's also **camping** at *Round Lake Caravan Park* (Ⓣ028/8776 7259), half a mile north off the Fintona road.

County Fermanagh

Fermanagh is justly famous for the intense beauty of its **lakes**. Much of the landscape is dominated by their waters, which, along with numerous rivers, constitute more than a third of the county's area. Though there are several attractive smaller loughs, it's the two interconnected parts of **Lough Erne** that draw the most visitors – Lower Lough Erne in the northwest and Upper Lough Erne in the southeast. Surrounding hills are wooded with oak, ash and beech, producing a scene of fresh, verdant greens in spring and rich and rusty colours in autumn. The water's rippling surface reflects whatever light there is, mirroring the palest of skies through to the ruddiest of magenta sunsets. It's a breathtaking landscape, where land and water complement each other in a resonant, stately harmony.

In winter **Lower Lough Erne** has the character of an inland sea, dangerous waves making even the locals wary of sailing. Fabulous vistas reach across to the shores of richly wooded, mostly uninhabited islands, on which are scattered early Christian ruins and evidence of earlier pagan cultures. The **Upper Lough** is quieter and less spectacular. The waterway here is a delightful muddle of little inlets and islands, where waters are shallower and shorelines reedy. Fields have shocks of bristly marsh-grasses; definitions between land and water are blurred. There are plenty of opportunities for **watersports**, and the less energetic can get out onto the lakes by renting a boat or taking one of the lough cruises. **Walkers** will find the countryside to be mostly gentle hills and woods, which rise to small mountains in the south and west of the county, made accessible by the Ulster Way. For **cyclists**, there are well-surfaced, empty roads (though routes around the Upper Lough are harder to negotiate, with little lanes often leading only to some empty reed-infested shore).

The county town of **Enniskillen** sits at the point where the Upper and Lower loughs meet. Long a strategic bridging point, it has more amenities than the rest of Fermanagh put together and, consequently, is a good base for exploring the region. With your own transport you can easily access Fermanagh's impressive series of Planters' castles, while the county's two stately houses, **Florence Court** and **Castle Coole**, are both open to the public.

Public transport in the county is limited to Ulsterbus – although reliable enough, only the main routes from Enniskillen are served with any frequency. County Fermanagh is as friendly as anywhere in the North, but it is one of the few remaining areas still patrolled by the British Army.

Fishing in Fermanagh

There are countless opportunities for **angling** in Fermanagh, with the two Lough Ernes, Upper and Lower Lough Macnean, Lough Melvin, thirty smaller lakes and numerous rivers. A good move is to get a copy of *Fishing in Fermanagh* from the tourist office in Enniskillen (see p.765), which can also tell you of any temporary restrictions and allow you to secure particular waters in advance. Most of the waters of Lough Erne are suitable for **coarse fishing**, and you can obtain a rod licence for this from tackle shops or the tourist office; if you're fishing for salmon or trout you'll need a **game licence** too. Note that a game licence must be held if you're fishing from a boat on Lower Lough Erne. There are signs at virtually all the designated fisheries providing information on the fish available and whether you'll need a permit from the water's owner.

As you'd expect, there are plenty of angling **boats for rent** and several **tackle shops**, including, in Enniskillen, Home, Field and Stream on Church Street (☎028/6632 2114) and Mullen's Pet and Shooting Supplies on Sligo Road (☎028/6632 4975). Other outlets are the Carlton Fishing Centre, Main Street, Belleek (☎028/6865 8181), and Erne Tackle, Main Street, Lisnaskea (☎028/6772 1969).

Some history

The region's early history was dictated by the intricacies of the Lough Erne waterways, once even more confused and forested than today. Recorded history begins with the **early Christians**, who slowly permeated Celtic culture and established religious foundations, especially on islands in the lough. Ruins of several **medieval monasteries** remain, and it is likely they were visited by pilgrims on their way to St Patrick's Purgatory, the shrine on Lough Derg, across the border in Donegal. More brutal invaders found the lough complex difficult to infiltrate. Neither Vikings nor Normans ever managed to control the region, and throughout the medieval and Tudor periods, the **English** similarly failed to subdue it.

The land was unruly and hard to govern even for the Irish. The **Maguires**, who ruled the west of the kingdom of Oriel (Fermanagh, Monaghan, south Tyrone and Louth) from 1250 until 1600, were originally based at **Lisnaskea**, but the cattle raids of neighbouring chiefs forced them to move to **Enniskillen** in the early fifteenth century. The town was to become strategically crucial as the determination of the English to dominate Ireland increased during the sixteenth century. As the crossing point through the waterways it was one of only three land routes into Ulster available to the invaders, the others being over the river near Ballyshannon and the Moyry Pass between Dundalk and Newry. So Enniskillen and the Maguire castle became the focus of **Irish resistance** to the Tudors. It was taken in 1594, although shortly afterwards retaken by the Maguires. After its recapture in 1607, the Planters arrived.

The usurpers were obliged to build a **ring of castles** around the lough in order to maintain control of their domain: Crom, Portora, Tully, Castle Archdale, Crevenish and Caldwell. Most importantly of all, the old Maguire castle at Enniskillen was enlarged and fortified. Given sizeable grants from the English Crown, the planters of Enniskillen built an Established church, a fort and a royal school, turning the place into a British colonial town. It became a **Loyalist** stronghold, which successfully defended itself against the Irish during the Great Rebellion of 1641 and against an attack by James's troops in 1689. The Loyalists of Enniskillen formed a regiment that William of Orange chose as his personal guard at the Boyne. In the late eighteenth century, Enniskillen

△ Castle Coole, County Fermanagh

proved to be of key military importance, with the threat of a **French invasion** through the northwest of Ireland. By now the town had two royal regiments – a unique phenomenon.

At **Partition**, Fermanagh became a part of Northern Ireland, despite its predominantly Catholic population and their cultural affinities with neighbouring Leitrim and Cavan in the Republic. In 1921, the county returned a Nationalist majority in local government elections, an undesirable state of affairs for the British. The abolition of proportional representation in 1922, and the **gerrymandering** that followed, ensured the subsequent Unionist majority. With a history of such blatant injustices, a large Catholic population and a lengthy border with the Republic, Fermanagh was a nucleus of **Republican** activity and today still has strong Sinn Féin sympathies. It was the constituency of Fermanagh and South Tyrone that in April 1981 returned **Bobby Sands** as MP to Westminster. At the time of the election Sands was serving a fourteen-year prison sentence at the Maze prison for possession of weapons and was leading a **hunger strike** (see p.797) for political status for IRA prisoners. His death from starvation after 66 days made him one of the most famous IRA heroes, and he appears iconically in Republican murals (see box on p.636), while also being remembered as a songwriter of no little merit thanks to Christy Moore's recordings of his songs *Back Home in Derry* and *McIlhatton*.

Today Fermanagh remains largely sustained by agricultural subsidies and its **tourist industry** centred on Enniskillen and Lough Erne. It is the furthest of the Northern Irish counties from Belfast and many of its people feel a closer affinity to the four Southern counties it borders, with which it has much cultural interplay, not least through traditional music.

Enniskillen and around

A pleasant, conservative little town of around eleven thousand people, **ENNISKILLEN** sits on an island like an ornamental buckle, two narrow ribbons of water passing each side connecting the Lower and Upper lough complexes. The strategic strength of this position has long been recognized – indeed, the town takes its name from *Innis Ceithleann*, "the island of Kathleen", wife of Balor (see p.591), who sought refuge here after a defeat in battle. Later the island became a Maguire stronghold before William Cole, a Planter from Cornwall, was appointed governor in 1607. The town played a major role in the 1641 Rebellion and the later Williamite wars, the latter leading to the formation of its two famous regiments, the **Inniskilling Dragoons** and the **Royal Inniskilling Fusiliers**, which played a significant role in the victory at the Battle of the Boyne.

With its historic **castle** and proximity to the elegant **Castle Coole**, plus a town centre relatively unspoilt by shopping developments, Enniskillen is worthy of a day's visit in its own right. It's also ideally situated as a base for exploring Lough Erne and touring the attractive local countryside. However, the name Enniskillen is still associated primarily with one of the most devastating atrocities of the Troubles. On Remembrance Day 1987, an IRA **bomb** killed eleven and injured 61 people as they gathered to commemorate the dead of the two world wars. The resulting widespread outrage was instrumental in directing parts of the Republican movement towards seeking a political solution to the Troubles.

Arrival and information

Enniskillen's **bus station** (☎028/6632 2633), on Wellington Road a block south of the High Street, has services from Belfast, Derry, Dublin, Dungannon, Omagh and Sligo, as well as local buses. Next door is the **tourist office** (Easter–June & Sept Mon–Fri 9am–5.30pm, Sat 10am–6pm, Sun 11am–5pm; July & Aug Mon–Fri 9am–7pm, Sat 10am–6pm, Sun 11am–5pm; Oct–Easter Mon–Fri 9am–5.30pm; ☎028/6632 3110, Ⓦwww.fermanagh-online.com). You can get **fishing licences and permits** here, and book a place on one of the summer guided **tours** of the town or Lough Erne. The Round "O" Jetty for **lough cruises** is signposted off the Derrygonnelly road northwest of town – see box on p.768 for more details of boat rental.

Bike rental is available from the Lakeland Canoe Centre, an outdoor activity centre on Castle Island (☎028/6632 4250; £10 per day) – the island is served by free ferries (8am–midnight), which leave from the Lakeland Forum leisure centre just behind the tourist office. Two **car-rental** outlets are Lochside Garages, Tempo Road (☎028/6632 4366), and M & N Motor & Tyre Co, 101 Irvinestown Rd (☎028/6632 2727). Aside from the banks, the **post office** on East Bridge Street will change money.

Accommodation

Among the few **places to stay** in the town centre are the family-run *Railway Hotel*, 34 Forthill St (☎028/6632 2084, Ⓦwww.railwayhotelenniskillen.com; ❹), the grander *Fort Lodge Hotel*, 72 Forthill St (☎028/6632 3275, Ⓦwww.lakelands.net/fortlodgehotel; ❹), and the spacious, modern *Ashberry Hotel*, 14–20 Tempo Rd (☎ & Ⓕ028/6632 0333; ❹). Alternatively, try the *Killyhevlin Hotel* (☎028/6632 3481, Ⓦwww.killyhevlin.com; ❼), a mile south of town on the Dublin road, which offers luxurious rooms in a lakeside setting.

There are plenty of **B&B** options but most are some distance from the centre – pick of the bunch is *Mountview Guesthouse*, 61 Irvinestown Rd (☎028/6632 3147, Ⓦwww.mountviewguests.com; ❸), a grand house set in spacious grounds half a mile north of the centre. A good alternative is the *Lackaboy Farm Guesthouse*, Tempo Road (☎028/6632 2488, Ⓕ6332 0440; ❷), a mile northeast. If you're driving, you could stay at one of two splendid country houses: *Killyreagh* (☎028/6638 7221, Ⓕ6638 7122; ❹), a couple of miles southeast of town on the A4 in Tamlaght, and *Tempo Manor* (April–Oct; ☎028/8954 1953, Ⓦwww.templemanor.com; ❻), a Gothic fantasy in Tempo, about six miles northeast on the B80.

The Kingfisher Cycling Trail

Enniskillen is a good starting point for the 192-mile **Kingfisher Cycling Trail**, which skirts Lower Lough Erne before running through the Leitrim lakelands to Carrick-on-Shannon (see p.554), then east to Belturbet in County Cavan (see p.254 and back via Clones in County Monaghan (see p.251) around the Upper Lough to Enniskillen. The route passes through a wonderful variety of countryside, and the hills are rarely too arduous to deter cyclists, though some are pretty steep. You can either bring your own bike and plan your own accommodation or take advantage of various **tour packages** available (contact ☎028/6632 0121 or visit Ⓦwww.cycletoursireland.com for details). Tours include two- or three-day short breaks and longer six- to eight-day casual, active or challenging rides. Accommodation is usually in B&Bs (though you can choose to stay in hotels or hostels), 18-speed bikes and essential equipment are provided, and your luggage is transported to and from each night's stop.

There's a new and intriguingly Modernist-designed HINI **hostel** right in the centre on Belmore Street (Ⓣ028/6634 0110, Ⓔinfo@hiniorg.uk), with all en-suite accommodation and a restaurant on site. Otherwise, try the Lakeland Canoe Centre (Ⓣ028/6632 4250), on Castle Island just offshore of Enniskillen (behind the bus station), which has hostel-style accommodation and a **campsite**. All the other campsites are well out of town: *Blaney Caravan and Camping Park* (Ⓣ028/6864 1634, Ⓦwww.blaneycaravanpark.com), eight miles to the northwest off the A46, directly behind the Blaney service station, is a beautifully situated and well-equipped site.

The Town

Waterways loop their way around the core of Enniskillen, their glassy surface imbuing the town with a pervasive sense of calm and reflecting the mini-turrets of **Enniskillen Castle**. Rebuilt by William Cole, it stands on the site of the old Maguire castle damaged by siege in 1594, next to the island's westerly bridges. Cole's additions show obvious Scottish characteristics in the turrets corbelled out from the angles of the main wall. The castle houses the **Watergate History and Heritage Centre** (May, June & Sept Mon & Sat 2–5pm, Tues–Fri 10am–5pm; July & Aug Mon, Sat & Sun 2–5pm, Tues–Fri 10am–5pm; Oct–April Mon 2–5pm, Tues–Fri 10am–5pm; £2), depicting life in the fifteenth to seventeenth centuries through models and audio-visual exhibits, archaeological displays in the arcaded barracks and, in the keep, the **Regimental Museum of the Royal Inniskilling Fusiliers** (same ticket), a proud and polished display of the uniforms, flags and paraphernalia of the town's historic regiments.

The centre invites strolling: the main street undulates gently, lined with confident Victorian and Edwardian town houses, thriving shops and smart pub fronts. This street changes its name five times between the bridges at either end, running from Ann Street to East Bridge Street: lanes fall to either side down towards the water, and clustered together are three fine **church** buildings – Church of Ireland, Catholic and Methodist. Much of Enniskillen's character comes from wealth based on the care of a colonial presence. Evidence of British influence is widespread: on a hill to the west, the stately **Portora Royal School** overlooks the town, carrying a discreet reminder of the continued elitism in the social order. The school was founded by Charles I in 1626, though the present building dates from 1777; old boys include **Oscar Wilde** – the pride of the school, until his trial for homosexuality – and **Samuel Beckett**. Over on a hill to the east, **Cole's Monument**, a statue commemorating one of Wellington's generals, keeps an eye on the town from Forthill Park; catch the park-keeper and pay to ascend to the viewing gallery (May–Sept daily 2–6pm; 70p). Immediately below is the war memorial, scene of the 1987 bombing.

On Down Street, just off the High Street, the **Buttermarket** is a craft and design centre with a range of artisans working on site all year round. These wonderfully renovated dairy market buildings date from 1835, and during the summer you'll find music and theatrical displays in the enclosed, yet airy courtyard. You can buy direct from the craft workers or from the shop attached to *Rebecca's* excellent coffee shop. For something less sedate, Thursday's general street **market** on Forthill Street is worth a trip.

Eating, drinking and entertainment

Enniskillen has a handful of good cheap **places to eat**. The best of the bunch is unquestionably *Oscar's*, 29 Belmore St (Ⓣ028/6632 7037; Mon–Sat

5–10.30pm), which serves a range of East Asian and European dishes in a child-friendly setting. Alternatively, the adjacent *Scoff's Wine Bar*, 17 Belmore St, offers a variety of fish and meat dishes, while *Franco's* (ⓣ028/6632 4424; Mon–Sat noon–11.30pm, Sun noon–10pm) in Queen Elizabeth Road serves mouth-watering pizza, pasta and seafood. A lot of the bars along the main street also do decent **pub food**, particularly *Mulligan's* on Darling Street, and, on Townhall Street, *The Linen Hall* and *Pat's Bar* – above which the *Melvin House* **restaurant** offers lunches, grills and dinners. The restaurant at the Ardhowen Theatre, a mile east of town on the Dublin road (ⓣ028/6632 5440; Mon–Sat 11am–3.30pm), is worth visiting for its waterside setting (you can also enjoy the view from an excellent bar), should you be hungry after a traipse around Castle Coole (see below).

Enniskillen is also well served for **cafés**, many of which do excellent, inexpensive meals. These include the *River Café*, in the HINI hostel on Belmore Street, and the pleasant *Café Cellini*, at the bottom of East Bridge Street. *Leslie's*, 10 Church St, is a fine place for home-bakes and salads.

There's no shortage of cheerful **pubs** in town, and bar extensions until 1am are commonplace in summer. **Rock bands** or **DJs** play at *The Crow's Nest* in the main street every night and on Fridays and Saturdays at *Mulligan's* on Darling Street. On Forthill Street, the *Fort Lodge Hotel* has a variety of rock and pop (Wed–Sat) and the *Railway Hotel* has live music at the weekends. **Traditional music** options are limited; your best bet is to try *Blake's of the Hollow* on Church Street at the weekends, a traditional Victorian bar with original fittings, fine pints and a chatty crowd. At the west end of town, the *Tippler's Brook* is the place for a quiet drink or to play cards with local farmers in town for the night.

The hub of Enniskillen's **arts scene** is the Ardhowen Theatre (see above), which has a year-round programme of top-quality drama, film and ballet, and hosts a great range of music events – traditional Irish, jazz, opera, country, classical – as well as productions by local community groups and an annual **theatre festival** in March. Check with the tourist office for dates of the Fermanagh *feis* in March – lots of traditional music, dancing, drama and crafts – and the Fleadh, the competitive traditional music festival, in June. The Enniskillen Omniplex, on Factory Road (ⓣ028/6632 4777), is a seven-screen **cinema** showing the usual range of general release films.

Castle Coole

Evidence of how the richest of the Enniskillen colonists lived is found about a mile southeast of the town centre at **Castle Coole** (mid-March to May & Sept Sat, Sun & public hols noon–6pm; June Mon & Wed–Sun noon–6pm; July & Aug daily noon–6pm; last tour starts at 5.15pm, grounds open all year; £3.50, car £2 extra), designed by James Wyatt and completed in 1798 as the lakeside home of the Earls of Belmore. The castle can be approached either from the Dublin road (signposted just opposite the Ardhowen Theatre) or across the golf course from the Castlecoole road. A perfect Palladian-fronted building of silver Portland stone, set in a beautiful landscaped Garden and part of a huge seven-hundred-acre estate, the castle features such delights as scagliola columns, exquisite plasterwork, a cantilevered staircase, a state bedroom decorated for George IV (who never actually arrived – the room was never subsequently used), Hogarth prints and an elegant library stocked with Regency furnishings and fireplaces. The informative guided tour is well worth taking.

Lough Erne

Lough Erne has had a profound effect on the history of Fermanagh. The earliest people to settle in the region lived on and around the two lakes; many of the islands here are in fact *crannógs* (early Celtic artificial islands). The lough's myriad connecting waterways were impenetrable to outsiders, protecting the settlers from invaders and creating an enduring cultural isolation. Evidence from stone-carvings suggests that Christianity was accepted far more slowly here than elsewhere: several pagan idols have been found on Christian sites, and the early Christian remains to be found on the islands show the strong influence of pagan culture. Here, Christian carving has something of the stark symmetry and vacancy of expression found in pagan statues. Particularly suggestive of earlier cults is the persistence of the human head motif in stone-carving – in pagan times a symbol of divinity and the most important of religious symbols.

Devenish Island and **White Island**, the most popular of the Erne's ancient sites, are on the Lower Lough, as is **Boa Island** in the far north, which is linked to the mainland by a bridge at each end. The **Upper Lough** is less rewarding, but has interesting spots that repay a leisurely dawdle. Aside from **cruising** the waterways (see box below) and visiting the islands, there are a number of minor attractions around the loughs that are worth dropping into during your stay. Perhaps the most impressive are the early seventeenth-century Planters' **castles** scattered around the shoreline.

Devenish Island

Heading around the eastern shores of Lower Lough Erne, if you don't have transport of your own, the easiest place to visit from Enniskillen is **Devenish Island** (Daimhinis, "ox island"). **Ferries** run continuously to the island from Trory Point, three miles north of Enniskillen off the A32 Irvinestown road (Easter–Sept daily 10am–6pm, Sun 2–6pm; £2.25), though it's advisable to check times with the tourist office before setting out, as poor weather can

Lough Erne cruises and rentals

The *MV Kestrel*, run by Erne Tours (☎028/6632 2882, Ⓦwww.fermanaghlakelands.com/m.v.kestrel), sails from the **Round "O" Jetty** northwest of Enniskillen (see p.765) around the Lower Lough, calling at Devenish Island (May & June Sun & public hols 2.30pm; July & Aug daily 10.30am, 2.15pm & 4.15pm; Sept Tues, Sat & Sun 2.30pm; morning cruises £6, afternoons £7). There are also additional evening dinner cruises to the *Moorings Restaurant* in Bellanaleck on the Upper Lough shore (July & Aug Sat 7pm; £13).

The *Inishcruiser* sails around the Upper Lough from the Share Holiday Village at **Smith's Strand**, signposted off the Lisnaskea–Derrylin road (Easter–June & Sept Sun 2.30pm; July & Aug Thurs–Sun 2.30pm; ☎028/6722 2122; £7).

Renting your own boat is another possibility, and there are a number of operators. Most offer open rowing boats, with or without outboard motor, though some have larger twenty-foot boats available. Prices range accordingly from £10 to £100 for a full day, depending on the operator and boat size. The tourist office in Enniskillen has lists of rental companies and, if you fancy something grander, of cruisers available for rent (weekly prices in high season range from £600 for smaller boats to £1325 for 8-berth specials). Unless you're going out on a small lake you should always let the boat owner know where you're going and ask to borrow navigation charts – Lough Erne can be dangerous, especially outside the summer months.

sometimes delay or cancel departures. To get to Trory Point from Enniskillen, take the Omagh bus and ask to be set down at the Kesh turn-off.

A monastic settlement was founded on Devenish by St Molaise in the sixth century and became so important during the early Christian period that it had 1500 novices attached. Though plundered by Vikings in the ninth century and again in the twelfth, it continued to be an important religious centre up until the Plantation period. It's a delightful setting, not far from the lough shore, and the ruins are considerable, spanning the entire medieval period. Most impressive are the sturdy **oratory** and perfect **round tower** (currently closed for health and safety reasons), both from the twelfth century; **St Molaise's Church**, a century older; and the ruined **Augustinian priory**, a fifteenth-century reconstruction of an earlier abbey. The priory has a fine Gothic sacristy door decorated with birds and vines. To the south is one of Ireland's finest **high crosses**, with highly complex, delicate carving. Other treasures found here – such as an early eleventh-century book shrine, the Soiscel Molaise – are now kept in the National Museum in Dublin, while the island's own small **museum** (same hours as ferry; joint ticket with ferry, or 75p if you've arrived in your own boat) includes other less notable relics and detailed information about Devenish itself.

Killadeas, Irvinestown and Castle Archdale

In **KILLADEAS** churchyard, seven miles north of Enniskillen on the eastern side of the lough (take the B82), stands the **Bishop's Stone**, carved some time between the ninth and eleventh centuries. It's one of the most striking examples of the appearance of pre-Christian images in early Christian culture, having a startled pagan-style face on one side and a bishop with bell and crozier on the other. There are other interesting carved stones in the graveyard, too, including two cross slabs and a rounded pillar, possibly a pagan phallic stone. If you want to get out onto the water from here, Manor House Marine (Ⓣ028/6862 8100) rents six-seater **motor boats** for £45 for a half-day, £60 for a full day.

The only site of any interest in **IRVINESTOWN**, a few miles northeast and inland, is Dr Patrick Delany's **church**, built in 1734, though the clock tower and pinnacled battlements are all that remain. Jonathan Swift played an unlikely cupid to the rector, introducing him to court favourite and London society hostess Mary Granville. They married, and Delany later became dean of Down, while she left a revealing record of eighteenth-century Anglo-Irish society and gossip, gathered during their visits to the Big Houses. Irvinestown has a few **B&B**s, including the central *Harlows*, 60–62 Main St (Ⓣ028/6862 1241, Ⓦwww.harlowsfermanagh.com; ❸), and the more rurally set *Lettermoney House*, on the Enniskillen–Omagh road (Ⓣ028/6638 8347; ❶). Just outside town, there's accommodation and **equestrian** activities in the splendid, woodland-situated *Necarne Castle* (Ⓣ028/6862 1919, Ⓕ6862 8382; ❸); to get there, take the road behind the town-centre clock and turn right at its end.

To immerse yourself thoroughly in the beauty of the lough scenery, you could hardly do better than stay in the HINI **hostel** (March–Oct; Ⓣ & Ⓕ028/6862 8118) set in the **Castle Archdale** Country Park near Lisnarick, about five miles west of Irvinestown. If you're relying on public transport, the Pettigo **bus** (4 daily) will drop you a mile away at the park entrance; otherwise take one of the buses from Enniskillen to Kesh (4 daily) as far as Lisnarick and walk or hitch. The hostel is perfectly placed for getting out to the lough and is a stone's throw from a large caravan park and **campsite** (Ⓣ028/6862 1333), which has a small supermarket and a fast-food outlet in high season. The **ferry** to White Island (see below) leaves from nearby, and you can also **rent boats** and **bikes** (£10 per day) here in July and August. And, should you fancy exploring the area on **horseback**, Drumhoney Riding Stables (Ⓣ028/6862 1892) is handily adjacent too.

White Island

Mounted on the wall of a **ruined abbey**, the seven early Christian carvings of **White Island** look eerily pagan. Found early last century, they are thought to be caryatids – columns in human form – from a monastic church of the ninth to eleventh centuries. The most disconcerting statue is the lewd female figure known as a **Sheila-na-Gig**, with bulging cheeks, a big grin, open legs and arms pointing to her genitals. This could be a female fertility figure, a warning to monks of the sins of the flesh or an expression of the demoniacal power of women, designed to ward off evil. (In the epic *Taín Bó Cúailnge*, Cúchulainn was stopped by an army of 150 women led by their female chieftain Scannlach. Their only weapon was their display of nakedness, from which the boy Cúchulainn had to avert his face.)

Less equivocal figures continue left to right: a seated **Christ** figure holding the Gospels on his knees; a hooded figure with bell and crozier, possibly **St Anthony**; **David** carrying a shepherd's staff, his hand towards his mouth showing his role as author and singer; **Christ the Warrior** holding two griffins by the scruff of their necks; and another **Christ** figure with a fringe of curly hair wearing a brooch on his left shoulder and carrying a sword and shield – here he is the King of Glory at his Second Coming. There is an unfinished seventh stone and, on the far right, a carved head with a downturned mouth, which is probably later than the other statues. The **church** of White Island also contains eleventh-century gravestones; the large earthworks round the outside date from an earlier monastery.

A **ferry** from Castle Archdale Country Park marina (Ⓣ028/6862 1892) runs to White Island on the hour (Easter Sat & Sun 11am–6pm; April–June & Sept Sun 2–6pm; July & Aug daily 11am–6pm; £3).

Kesh

KESH (An Cheis, "the wickerwork causeway"), four miles north of Castle Archdale Country Park, is a possible overnight stop. **Accommodation** options in the village include the *Lough Erne Hotel*, Main Street (Ⓣ028/6863 1275, Ⓦwww.loughernehotel.com; ❺), in a fine riverside setting with a restaurant and weekend entertainment, while **B&B** is available at *Roscolban House*, on the Enniskillen road (Ⓣ028/6863 1096, Ⓔsales@mni.co.uk; ❷). If you have transport, there's also the option of staying at *Ardess House* (Ⓣ028/6863 1267, Ⓦwww.fermanaghcraft.com/ardesscraft; ❸), housed in a fine Georgian rectory, which offers day and residential courses in various crafts (from £25 per day); take the Enniskillen road out of Kesh, turn left just before the police barracks, take a hard right, then follow the road for a mile and a half.

There are a few **places to eat** in Kesh, including the excellent *Riverside Restaurant*, 9 Main St (Ⓣ028/6863 2342; Tues–Sun 5–9.30pm & Sun lunch), serving specialities such as duckling, and, further up the street, *Sarah Jane's Diner and Bakery* (daily 9am–11pm), offering fine, inexpensive home cooking.

Kesh's chief recommendation is its position on the lough. You can rent **rowing boats** (with or without outboard engines) here from Erinona Boats at Boa

Island Bridge, a little way out of town on the way to Belleek (Ⓣ028/6863 2328; £40 a day, lesser rates for shorter periods), while Drumrush Watersports, Boa Island Road (Ⓣ028/6863 1578, Ⓦwww.drumrush.co.uk), offers everything from canoeing to jet-ski rental and banana-boat rides; it also has its own guesthouse (❸) and offers **camping** at its *Lakeland Caravan Park*.

Boa Island and around

One of the most evocative of the carvings of Lough Erne is the double-faced Janus figure of **Boa Island**, six miles west of Kesh at the northern end of the Lower Lough – barely an island at all these days, as it's connected to the mainland by bridges. The landmark to look out for is **Caldragh cemetery**, signposted off the A47 about a mile west of Lusty Beg Island. Follow the signs down a lane and the graveyard is through a gate to your left.

This ancient Christian burial ground of broken moss-covered tombstones, shaded by low, encircling hazel trees, has an almost druidic setting. Here you'll find the **Janus figure**, an idol of yellow stone with very bold symmetrical features. It has the phallus on one side, and a belt and crossed limbs on the other. The figure was probably an invocation of fertility and a depiction of a god-hero, the belt being a reference to the bearing of weapons. Alongside it stands the smaller "**Lusty Man**", so called since it was moved here from nearby Lustymore Island. This idol has only one eye fully carved, maybe to indicate blindness – Cúchulainn had a number of encounters with war-goddesses, divine hags described as blind in the left eye. Boa Island's name has nothing to do with snakes, but comes from Badhbh, a Celtic war-goddess.

Quiet **Lusty Beg Island** just off Boa Island is a popular weekend retreat for Enniskillen people: you'll find luxury **log cabins** with saunas (Ⓣ028/6863 2032, Ⓦwww.lustybegisland.com; sleep 4–6; £310–370 a week), **B&B** in *The Courtyard* guesthouse (same phone & website; ❺), **canoeing**, gentle **walks** and a **restaurant**. A free car ferry will take you across; dial Ⓣ0 from the telephone on the pier.

Castle Caldwell Forest and Belleek

Continuing along the northern shore, the **forest of Castle Caldwell**, on the A47 near the western extremity of Lower Lough Erne, is formed by two narrow promontories, which make it a natural breeding site for waterfowl such as the common scoter (a species of duck) and a habitat of rarities such as the hen harrier, peregrine falcon and pine marten. However, its seventeenth-century **castle** has long since fallen into dilapidation, and the surrounding estate is now a commercial, state-owned forest of spruce, pine and larch. At the castle's entrance, look out for the giant stone fiddle in front of the gate lodge, the sobering memorial to Denis McCabe, a local musician who in 1770 tumbled from the Caldwells' barge while drunk and drowned. Its inscription "DDD" supposedly stands for "Denis died drunk"!

Lively **BELLEEK** (Béal Leice, "ford-mouth of the flat rock"), five miles further west, holds the **Fiddle Stone Festival** every June in McCabe's memory. Its other main attraction is the famous **Belleek Pottery** (tours every 20min: Mon–Fri 9.30am–12.15pm & 2.15–4.15pm; Ⓦwww.belleek.ie; £2.50), which offers interesting tours of the works and a chance to buy the rather fussy products. On Main Street you'll find **Fermanagh Crystal** (Mon–Sat 10am–5pm; free), where you can watch the creation of glassware and even, funds permitting, commission your own piece. Across the river on the main A46 Enniskillen Road is the **Erne Gateway Centre**, which houses a **tourist office**

(June–Sept daily 11am–5pm; ⓣ028/6865 8866) and the **Explore Erne Exhibition** (same hours; £1), where a giant video wall screens an explanation of how the lake was formed and how it moulded the lives of lakeside dwellers over the centuries.

Belleek has grand **accommodation** at the riverside *Hotel Carlton* (ⓣ028/6665 8282, ⓦwww.hotelcarlton.co.uk; ❺), at the bottom of Main Street, and **B&B** further up the road in *The Fiddlestone* pub (ⓣ028/6865 8008; ❷). The village has a couple of cafés, and *The Black Cat Cove* provides excellent bar **meals** in an atmospheric setting. **Bikes** can be rented from Belleek Bicycle Hire on Main Street (ⓣ028/6865 8181) and **rowing boats** from Belleek Angling Centre, The Thatch, Main Street (ⓣ028/6865 8181; £10 per day, £30 with outboard motor).

Monea Castle to Lough Navar Forest

Monea Castle (free open access), seven miles northwest of Enniskillen off the B81, is a particularly fine ruin of a Planters' castle in a beautiful setting at the end of a beech-lined lane. Built around 1618, it bears the signs of Scottish influence in its design, with similar features to the reworked Maguire castle in Enniskillen. It was destroyed by fire in the Great Rebellion of 1641 and by Jacobite armies in 1689, and was eventually abandoned in 1750 after another fire. Five miles further north, beyond Derrygonnelly, the fortified house and *bawn* of restored **Tully Castle** (April–Sept Tues–Sat 10am–6pm, Sun 2–6pm; £1), itself burned by the Maguires in 1641, sits down by the lough shore. Further to the west, there are tremendous views of the lough and surrounds from **Lough Navar Forest** (daily 10am–dusk; car £2.50).

Upper Lough Erne and Lisnaskea

Upper Lough Erne holds nothing like the interest of the Lower Lough, nor the scenic splendour, although it does have the best-preserved of the Planters' castles nearby. The most you're really likely to do around the lough is disturb the anglers or get lost among its crazy causeways and waterways – fun on a boat, but frustrating on dry land.

Should you be tempted to venture further into the maze of reeds and water, there are **cruises** (see box on p.768) from the **Share Holiday Village** (Easter–Oct; ⓣ028/6722 2122, ⓦwww.sharevillage.org) at Smith's Strand, signposted off the Lisnaskea–Derrylin road, where they also offer water-based activity holidays with facilities for disabled travellers, B&B (❷), self-catering chalets (sleep 6–10; £540–£570 per week) and a campsite.

The National Trust **Crom Estate** (mid-March to Sept Mon–Sat 10am–6pm, Sun noon–6pm; July & Aug open till 8pm; car or boat £4), three miles west of Newtownbutler on the eastern shore of the lough, has the largest surviving area of **oak woodland** in Northern Ireland, home to rare species such as the purple hairstreak and wood white butterflies. There's a café and interpretive centre here, and you can rent **rowing boats** too. Unfortunately, the modern Crom Castle is privately occupied and not open to the public, though you can visit the ruins of the **old castle**. The estate has renovated courtyard **cottages** (ⓣ08704/584442, ⓦwww.nationaltrustcottages.co.uk; £195–508 per week for 2–6 people).

The elegantly chiselled gravestones on **Galoon Island**, three miles southwest of Newtownbutler and accessible by both car and boat, with their reliefs of skull and crossbones, hourglass and coffin, are worth a detour if you have transport. *Ports House*, right by the waterside at Ports, not far from Newtownbutler, offers **B&B** (ⓣ & ⓕ028/6773 8528; ❷).

Almost five miles north of Newtownbutler, **Castle Balfour** (free access) at **LISNASKEA** (Lios na Scéithe, "fort of the shield") was built for Sir James Balfour, a Scottish Planter, in the early seventeenth century and shows strong Scottish characteristics in the turrets and parapets, high-pitched gables and tall chimneys. Lisnaskea itself is one of Fermanagh's few towns – and a small one at that. Its tiny nineteenth-century Cornmarket yard has an early Christian **carved cross** depicting Adam and Eve beneath a tree, and the library up the road towards Enniskillen contains a diminutive but interesting **folk museum** (Mon, Tues & Fri 10am–5.30pm, Wed 10am–7.30pm, Sat 10am–1pm; free), with displays on local traditions and festivals, including plenty of detail on the making of poteen. The town has several lively **bars** along Main Street, including the wonderfully named *Shoe the Donkey*, while the best place to **eat** is unquestionably the *Donn Carragh Hotel*, which specializes in seafood and provides the only local **accommodation** (Ⓣ028/6772 1206, Ⓔdonncarragghhotel@btclick.com; ❹), in a recently renovated setting. There's a **campsite** two miles north of Lisnaskea at Mullynascarthy (April–Oct; Ⓣ028/6772 1040).

Western Fermanagh

The stretch of countryside on the western edge of the county offers some good **walking** opportunities, particularly in the hills to the south. The **Ulster Way**, which runs northwest from the Upper Lough and east towards Tyrone, makes the riches of the terrain easily accessible.

This region also has two attractions that are well worth seeking out. The magnificent eighteenth-century **Florence Court** is the most assured achievement of the colonists, built 150 years after the initial defensive Planters' castles. If you have your own transport, a visit to the house can be combined with an hour or so at the **Marble Arch Caves**, the finest cave-system in Northern Ireland. Walkers can reach both along the Ulster Way, accessible from the A4 near Belcoo; the path runs four miles south past Lower Lough Macnean to the Marble Arch Caves and then a further five miles east to Florence Court.

Florence Court

The magnificent three-storey mansion of the National Trust-owned **Florence Court**, about eight miles southwest of Enniskillen (April, May & Sept Sat, Sun & public hols noon–6pm; June Mon–Fri 1–6pm, Sat & Sun noon–6pm; July & Aug daily noon–6pm; £3.50; grounds and forest park open all year 10am–dusk; £2 per car), was commissioned by John Cole, one of the Earls of Enniskillen, and named after his wife. The house, completed around 1775, is notable for its restored rococo plasterwork and rare Irish furnishings; the dining room is especially lavish, its ceiling hosting a cloud of puffing cherubs with Jupiter disguised as an eagle in the centre, all flying out of a duck-egg blue sky. Unfortunately, the top floor of the house was completely destroyed by a fire in 1955 and has never been renovated internally. To get to the house from Enniskillen, follow the A4 Sligo road for three miles, branching off on the A32 Swanlinbar road and taking the signposted right turn four miles further on. The Swanlinbar-bound **bus** passes this last junction, from where it's a mile walk to the house.

You can **stay** in the pretty *Rose Cottage* in the Florence Court walled garden (Ⓣ028/9571 0721; sleeps 5; £325–575 per week), which is well equipped and

The Ulster Way in western Fermanagh

From Marble Arch Caves the **Ulster Way** heads past Lower and Upper Lough Macnean before taking you through the bog and granite heights of the Cuilcagh Mountains to **Ballintempo Forest**, where there are fabulous views over the loughs. The Way then continues north, through the **Lough Navar Forest**, a well-groomed conifer plantation with tarmacked roads and shorter trails. Although a great deal of fir-plantation walking is dark and frustrating, this forest does, at points, provide some of the most spectacular **views** in Fermanagh, looking over Lower Lough Erne and the mountains of Tyrone, Donegal, Leitrim and Sligo. The Lough Navar Forest also sustains a small herd of red deer, as well as wild goats, foxes, badgers, hares and red squirrels.

Before setting out, it's well worth obtaining a copy of *The Ulster Way: Southwest Section* from the tourist office in Enniskillen (see p.765). This describes in detail the five connected trails constituting the Way's route through the county.

Accommodation along the Way is limited. There are half a dozen B&Bs near **BELCOO**, two and a half miles west from the trail's ascent to the Ballintempo Forest: try *Bella Vista*, Cottage Drive (Ⓣ028/6638 6469; ❷), or *Corralea Lodge*, 154 Lattone Rd (March–Oct; Ⓣ028/6638 6325; ❸). There's also *Meadow View*, Sandhill (Ⓣ028/6864 1233; ❷), half a mile north of **DERRYGONNELLY** on the B81. A bit further away from the route of the Way, west near the border at **GARRISON** (take the minor road from Derrygonnelly), the *Lough Melvin Holiday Centre* (Ⓣ028/6865 8142, Ⓦwww.loughmelvinholidaycentre.com) offers archery, caving, canoeing, windsurfing and hill-walking courses and has a **restaurant**, hostel-style accommodation and camping, although you should ring ahead to check on space if you want to stop here. Finding **places to eat** can be tricky: the *Waterside Bar* in Belcoo serves food all day (or there are alternatives in Blacklion, just across the bridge; see p.256), but you'll only come across fast food and basic bars in Derrygonnelly (though often great **traditional music** at weekends).

has two double bedrooms. There's award-winning accommodation nearby at *Arch Tullyhona*, 59 Marble Arch Rd (Ⓣ028/6634 8452, Ⓦwww.archhouse.com; ❷), whose **restaurant** offers hearty daytime meals.

The Marble Arch Caves

Fermanagh's caves are renowned, and while some are for experts only, the most spectacular system of all, the **Marble Arch Caves**, five miles west of Florence Court, is accessible to anyone. A tour of the system lasts around an hour and a quarter, beginning with a boat journey along a **subterranean river**, then on through brilliantly lit chambers, calcite-walled and dripping with stalactites and fragile mineral veils. **Tours** of the caves (daily: mid-March to June & Sept 10am–4.30pm; July & Aug 10am–5pm; Ⓣ028/6634 8855; £6) are sometimes booked out by parties, so it makes sense to call ahead to check that your journey won't be wasted; in a steady Irish downpour the caves can be flooded, so check weather reports as well. You'll need to wear sturdy walking shoes and bring warm clothing as the temperature can drop significantly.

From whichever direction you approach the caves, you'll travel along the **Marlbank Scenic Loop**, with tremendous views of Lower Lough Macnean, and on either side you'll see limestone-flagged fields, much like those of the Burren in County Clare. It was fifty thousand years of gentle water seepage through the limestone that deposited the calcite for the amazing stalactite growths in the caves below.

Almost opposite the caves' entrance is the **Legnabrocky Trail**, which runs through rugged limestone scenery and peatland to the shale-covered slopes of **Cuilcagh Mountain**. This forms part of an environmental conservation area and offers a strenuous six- or seven-hour walk to the mountain's summit and back (be prepared to turn back if the weather turns sour). A part of the Marble Arch Caves centre is now devoted to exhibits and displays describing the restoration of the mountain park's damaged peatland and bogland habitats.

Travel details

Buses

(*all Ulsterbus unless stated otherwise*)

The **Sperrin Rambler** runs twice daily from Omagh (Mon–Sat 10am & 1.45pm) via Gortin and Plumbridge through the Sperrins and on to Draperstown, Magherafelt and Castledawson (the return service operates Mon–Sat 10.10am & 1.40pm from Castledawson).

Cookstown to: Coalisland (1–9 daily; 30min); Dungannon (1–9 daily; 45min); Magherafelt (3–13 daily; 30min); Moneymore (2–12 daily; 15min).

Dungannon to: Armagh (4–7 Mon–Sat; 45min); Belfast (8–15 daily; 50min); Coalisland (4–21 daily; 15min); Cookstown (1–9 daily; 45min); Omagh (5–8 Mon–Sat; 1hr 15min).

Enniskillen to: Armagh (2 Mon–Sat; 1hr 50min); Ballyshannon (3–5 daily; 1hr); Belfast (6–9 daily; 2hr 20min); Belleek (3–5 daily; 45min); Bundoran (3–5 daily; 1hr 10min); Clones (2–5 daily; 50min); Derry (4–7 daily; 2hr 40min); Derrygonnelly (5 Mon–Sat; 25min); Donegal (*Bus Éireann*; 5–6 daily; 1hr 10min); Dublin (*Bus Éireann*; 4–5 daily; 3hr 05min); Fivemiletown (3 Mon–Sat; 45min); Irvinestown (4–7 Mon–Sat; 25min); Kesh (3–5 Mon–Sat; 40min); Lisnarick (3–6 Mon–Sat; 30min); Lisnaskea (2–7 daily; 30min); Monaghan (2 Mon–Sat; 1hr 20min); Omagh (4–7 daily; 1hr 10min); Pettigo (3–4 Mon–Sat; 1hr); Sligo (2–3 daily; 1hr 25min).

Omagh to: Belfast (7 Mon–Sat, 5 Sun; 1hr 50min); Castlederg (5 Mon–Fri, 1 Sat; 50min); Cookstown (1 daily; 1hr 10min); Cranagh (2 Mon–Sat; 55min); Derry (5–8 daily; 1hr 10min); Draperstown (2 Mon–Sat; 1hr 10min); Dublin (*Bus Éireann*; 4–5 daily; 3hr); Dungannon (7 Mon–Fri, 5 Sat; 1hr 15min); Enniskillen (1–7 daily; 1hr 10min); Gortin (5 Mon–Sat; 35min); Kesh (2 Mon & Thurs; 45min); Letterkenny (*Bus Éireann*; 5–6 daily; 1hr); Plumbridge (2 Mon–Sat; 45min); Strabane (6–14 daily; 35min); Ulster American Folk Park (13 Mon–Fri, 11 Sat, 6 Sun; 15min).

Strabane to: Belfast (7 Mon–Sat, 4 Sun; 2hr 30min); Castlederg (3–7 Mon–Sat; 40min); Derry (5–19 daily; 25–40min); Dublin (5 Mon–Sat, 3 Sun; 4hr); Enniskillen (1 daily; 3hr); Newtownstewart (5–15 daily; 25min); Omagh (5–16 daily; 35min).

Contexts

History

An understanding of Ireland's history is essential in order to make sense of its troubled present. In these few pages, we cannot do more than provide a brief outline of that history, but ideas for further reading are suggested later in this section (see p.860).

Earliest inhabitants

During the last Ice Age, when most of the country was covered by an ice cap, low sea levels meant that Ireland was attached to Britain, and Britain to the European continent. As the climate warmed (from about 13,000 BC), and the ice gradually retreated, sea levels rose and the broad land connection between Ireland and Britain began to recede to one or more narrow land bridges. The first human inhabitants arrived over these routes, probably from Scotland, sometime after 8000 BC. By about 7000 BC the land bridges were submerged and Ireland geographically isolated, while Britain remained connected to continental Europe for much longer.

The first inhabitants, **Mesolithic** (middle Stone Age) hunter-gatherers, found a densely forested land that could only be penetrated easily along its waterways, and, for the most part, they seem to have lived close to the sea, rivers and lakes (flint work from the period has been found in Antrim, Down, Louth and Dublin). Their way of life continued undisturbed until, from about 3500 BC, **Neolithic** (late Stone Age) farmers began arriving by sea, probably from Britain. With skills in animal and crop husbandry, weaving and pottery, the new arrivals used their stone axes to clear large tracts of forest for cultivation. The hunter-gatherer and agricultural economies were, however, complementary, and it is thought the two peoples co-existed for many centuries before the older way of life was gradually assimilated by the new.

The Neolithic people were the creators of Ireland's **megalithic remains**. There are more than 1200 such burial sites scattered throughout the country, with the greatest concentrations in the north and west. Such sites are also found all along the Atlantic seaboard of Europe, from Spain to Scandinavia – a sign of Ireland's ancestral and cultural links with the rest of Europe at this time and, in particular, with the peoples of Britain and Brittany.

The most dramatic and best-known megalithic remains in Ireland are the great **passage graves** at Knowth and Newgrange in County Meath, with their elaborate spiral engravings, cut into the stone entirely without the use of metal tools. It is thought that the function of these tombs was not purely religious or ceremonial; they were also territorial markers, which at times of population pressure staked a communal claim to the surrounding lands. Little is known of the people themselves, although their civilization was long lasting, with thousands of years separating the earliest and the latest megalithic constructions. Only rarely have skeletons been found in the graves (in most cases only the cremated remains of bones are discovered), but what few there are seem to indicate a short, dark, hairy people with a life expectancy of little more than 35 years.

Around 2000 BC the use of bronze spread to Ireland, though it is uncertain whether this was the result of the commercial contacts of the existing population or the migration of a new people. The next significant technological development, generally associated with the arrival of the Celts, was the introduction of iron around 700 BC.

The Celts

The **Celts** were an Indo-European group called Keltoi by the Greeks and Galli by the Romans, who spread south from central Europe into Italy and Spain and west through France and Britain. By 500 BC, Celtic language and culture were dominant in Ireland, but there is no evidence of any large-scale invasion or social upheaval. It is probably more accurate to think of their arrival as a gradual and relatively peaceful process that took place over hundreds of years.

Their settlements took the form of ring forts (or raths), and they divided the island into about one hundred small **kingdoms** or *Tuátha*, each with its own king. The *Tuatha* were grouped into the Five Fifths or provinces, which were Ulster (*Ulaid*), Meath (*Midhe*), Leinster (*Laigin*), Munster (*Muma*) and Connacht (which retains its Irish spelling). In theory, the High King (*Ard Rí*) ruled over all from his throne on the Hill of Tara – a place long associated with mysterious power – although only rarely did any one figure of sufficient strength emerge to lay undisputed claim to that title.

It is hard to separate the truth about the Celts from the stories they told of themselves. Theirs was an oral culture in which the immortality to be gained from being the hero of an epic tale was highly prized. With an enthusiasm for war little short of bloodthirsty, they celebrated battles decided by the single combat of great champions, guided and aided by the unpredictable whims of the gods. They also appropriated the religion and beliefs already current in Ireland and, although they had nothing to do with their building, megalithic sites continued to have great symbolic significance for them.

The two greatest heroes of the Irish epics, **Cúchulainn** and **Fionn Mac Cumhaill** (Finn McCool), have been tentatively identified as warrior champions of the second and third centuries AD, transformed by legend into semi-divinities in much the same way as King Arthur was in England.

The coming of Christianity

The christianization of Ireland began as early as the fourth century AD, well before the arrival of St Patrick (whose existence is now the subject of some controversy). Vestiges did survive of the previous religion of the Celts, but after the collapse of the Roman Empire, Ireland assumed a position at the very forefront of European Christianity. (Also around this time the people of Ireland took the name Goidil – Gaels – for themselves, from the Welsh "Gwyddyl".)

In the sixth century, the early Christian leaders successfully adapted the established pattern of church organization to suit the scattered and tribal nature of Gaelic society by setting up monastic foundations. The country became a haven for religious orders, the only sources of learning at this time. The sheer impassability of much of the landscape supported monastic development, and many of the great Irish monasteries, such as St Enda's on the Aran Islands, Clonmacnois in County Offaly and Clonard in County Meath, date from this period. **Ogham**, the Celtic line-based writing system seen on standing stones, was rapidly supplanted by the religious scholars, who introduced Latin. The first – and best-known – of their richly illuminated Latin manuscripts, the **Book of Kells**, can be seen in the Library of Trinity College, Dublin.

The traditional view of these times as "Dark Ages" of terror and chaos throughout Europe is not supported by events in Ireland. Although intertribal warfare was constant, the country enjoyed relative cultural and religious stability. Alongside this, well-established diplomatic and trading contact along the Atlantic seaboard encouraged the development of a strong missionary impulse in Irish Christianity. Between 500 and 800 the Irish Church spread the gospel widely across the Continent. The most prominent of the many missionaries was St Columban, who founded monasteries in France, Switzerland, Germany and Austria, and at Bobbio in Italy – where he died in 615.

Invasion: Vikings and Normans

From 795, Ireland was increasingly plagued by destructive **Viking raids**, in which many of the great monasteries were plundered and burned (though many more were destroyed as a result of indigenous intertribal warfare in the eighth and ninth centuries). The instability of the period led to the development of the round towers, which were used as lookout posts and places of sanctuary – and which characterize early Irish architecture. The Viking raids culminated in a full-scale invasion in 914 and the subsequent founding of walled cities, usually at the mouths of rivers, such as Dublin, Wexford, Waterford, Youghal, Cork, Bantry and Limerick. The decisive defeat of the Danes by the High King Brian Boru at the Battle of Clontarf in 1014 at least spared Ireland from becoming a Viking colony. However, the death of Brian Boru in the battle, and the subsequent divisions among his followers, meant that his victory was never consolidated by the formation of a strong unified kingdom. The Vikings that remained soon merged fully into the native Irish population.

From the time of the **Norman Conquest** onwards, the kings of England coveted Ireland. The first of the Anglo-Normans to cross over to Ireland was a freelance adventurer, Richard FitzGilbert de Clare, more usually known as Strongbow. He came in 1169 at the invitation of Dermot MacMurrough, the exiled king of Leinster, who sought help to regain his throne. Henry II of England, however, was concerned that Strongbow might establish a threatening power base and therefore went personally to Ireland as overlord. He had earlier secured papal support and authorization over all powers – native, Norse and Norman – from, as chance would have it, the only English pope in history, Adrian IV.

In 1172, Pope Alexander III reaffirmed Henry II's lordship. This seemed to open the prospect of Anglo-Norman rule in which Gaelic tribal kingdoms would be reshaped into a feudal system on the English model, but the Irish resisted so effectively that royal authority outside the "English Pale" (an area surrounding Dublin) was little more than nominal (and gave rise to the pejorative English expression "beyond the pale", signifying a lack of civilization).

The Statutes of Kilkenny

By the fourteenth century, the Anglo-Norman settlers had integrated with the native Irish population to such an extent that the Crown, eager to regain control, sought to drive a permanent wedge between the natives and the colonists with the introduction of the **Statutes of Kilkenny** (1366). This legislation prohibited intermarriage with the Irish, forbade the Irish from entering walled cities and made the adoption of Irish names, dress, customs or speech illegal. The ineffectiveness of these measures allowed Gaelic influence to increase until, by the end of the fifteenth century, the "Pale" had been reduced to just a narrow strip of land around the capital.

The Tudors and the Stuarts

The continued isolation of Irish politics from English and Continental influence during the fifteenth century, and England's preoccupation with the Wars of the Roses, helped Ireland's most powerful Anglo-Norman family – the Fitzgeralds of Kildare – to establish and consolidate control of the east and southeast of the country. For the most part, their growing authority was left unchallenged by the early **Tudor monarchy**, whose policy towards Ireland was based mainly on considerations of economy; it was cheaper to accept Kildare's rule than establish an English deputy who would need expensive military backing and security. Irish discontent with English rule should also not be allowed to take forms that might be exploited by England's foreign enemies.

The Reformation

Henry VIII was able to retain his attitude of expedient caution until his break with Rome introduced several new factors. The clergy began to preach rebellion against the schismatical king, while Henry was able to reward his supporters with the spoils from the dissolution of religious houses. Convinced that his family's power was under threat, Kildare's son, Lord Offaly ("Silken Thomas"), staged an insurrection in the summer of 1534. Aid from the pope – who for the first time was seen as a potential supporter of opposition to England – was expected, but never came. Henry, inevitably, reacted forcibly and exchanged his policy of prudence for one of aggression. War dragged on until 1540, by which time Kildare and his supporters, their power all but crushed, were forced to submit to the Crown.

The Dublin Parliament enacted legislation accepting Henry's **Act of Supremacy**, which made the king head of the Church. At least three distinct factions emerged in Ireland: the "Old English", who were loyal to the king but denied him spiritual primacy; the independent-minded and staunchly Catholic Gaelic Irish; and the new Protestants, many of whom had benefited materially by acquiring Church property. (At this stage, those "recusants" who refused to swear the oath acknowledging Henry as head of the Church were not yet subject to discrimination.) In an attempt to bind the chiefs and nobles of Ireland more closely to its authority, the Crown forced them to surrender their lands, only to return them again with the reduced status of landlords. Central to Henry's policy was the wish to rule Ireland cheaply, with least risk of foreign intervention, through Irish-born "deputies" whose loyalty was assured.

But such loyalty could not be counted on, and after Henry's death the authority of the English Crown was again challenged.

Elizabeth I and James I

During the reign of **Queen Elizabeth I** (1558–1603), a growing number of adventurers, mainly younger sons of the aristocracy, arrived from Protestant England to pillage Ireland. For the first time, the supposed moral imperative to turn the Gaelic Irish away from the papacy was used as an excuse to invade and dispossess. This justification for the suppression of Irish culture, religion and language was to be the trademark of English occupation of Ireland for many years to come.

Elizabeth's aim was to establish an English colony. This policy of **Plantation** had been started, albeit unsuccessfully, some thirty years earlier during the reign of Mary I, when Laois – renamed "Queen's County" – and Offaly – "King's County" – were confiscated from their native Irish owners and given into the possession of loyal Old English. Elizabeth's first attempt, in the 1570s, to "plant" northeast Ulster, which was then the most Gaelic area of the country, failed miserably. However, the colonization process, when eventually completed, was the principal instrument in subjugating the entire country.

At least three major Irish **rebellions** were prompted by Elizabeth's policies. Two of these, led by the Desmonds of Munster, were easily put down; the Desmond lands were confiscated and given to English settlers. The third, last, and most serious was in Ulster, and was led by **Hugh O'Neill**. O'Neill, originally a protégé of the English court, participated in crushing the revolt of the Desmonds, and had long been groomed to become chief of Ulster. He'd always imagined the role to be that of an autonomous Gaelic chieftain; he turned against his queen in 1595 when he began to appreciate the extent to which he would be the pawn of English Protestantism. His forces won a major victory over the English at the Battle of the Yellow Ford in 1598, but were defeated at **Kinsale** in December 1601 after failing to link up effectively with the Spanish reinforcements that had arrived there.

The Tudor conquest of Ireland was completed when O'Neill signed the **Treaty of Mellifont** in 1603, ignorant of the death of Elizabeth just a few days before. Half a million acres of land were confiscated from the native Irish, including all the estates of O'Neill and his fellow rebel Hugh O'Donnell, king of *Tír Chonaill* (Donegal). English plans to redistribute the land supposedly included generous endowments to the "natives". However, an abortive and unplanned insurrection was enough to frighten them into abandoning any such idea, and English and Scottish "Planters" – many of whom were ex-soldiers – were brought over to be ensconced in fortified "*bawns*". Chiefs such as O'Neill were still nominally landlords but, unable to accept the loss of their ancient authority, and living under constant suspicion that they were plotting against the Crown, many chose instead to leave their country as exiles. Their mass departure to continental Europe in 1607 became known as the **Flight of the Earls**, an event that many identify as the beginning of the end for the old Gaelic order.

It was at this time that the character of Ulster began to change. James VI of Scotland had just become **James I** of England, and he encouraged many, largely Protestant Scots to migrate the short distance to Ulster where so much newly confiscated land awaited them. There was a great deal of bitterness on the part of the dispossessed native people, and little intermarriage with the newly arrived Planters, so that the whole country, and above all Ulster, became divided along Catholic and Protestant lines.

Charles I and the English Civil War

The widespread belief in England and Ireland that James's successor, **Charles I**, harboured pro-Catholic sympathies was one of the spurs for the armed rebellion in Ulster in 1641. Terrifying stories circulated in England of the torture and murder of Protestant Planters, and the rebels' (bogus) claim that they were acting with Charles's blessing did much to provoke the **English Civil War**. The origins of the current situation in the six northeast counties of Ulster can in many respects be traced to the policy and events of this period.

During the Civil War, the Old English in Ireland allied with the native Irish in the **Confederation of Kilkenny**, supporting the Royalist cause in the hope of bringing about the restoration of Catholicism. It was an uneasy alliance, characterized by inadequate leadership and personal rivalries, in which the Irish felt they had nothing to lose in pursuit of liberty, whereas the Old English lived in fear of a Protestant invasion should the forces of **Oliver Cromwell** achieve victory. The war did indeed end with the establishment of Cromwell's Protectorate and the execution of the king; and the conquest of Ireland became Cromwell's most immediate priority.

Cromwell and the Act Of Settlement

Cromwell's ruthless campaign in Ireland remains a source of great bitterness to this day. He arrived in Dublin with 12,000 men of the New Model Army in August 1649, and was soon joined by another force under General Ireton. **Drogheda** was stormed in September, and thousands, including civilians and children, were slaughtered. Cromwell continued south and quickly took Wexford and New Ross, whereupon the towns of Cork, Youghal and Kinsale in the southwest (all in the hands of Royalists) swiftly capitulated. Although Waterford held out for several months, it was not long before Cromwell's forces had overrun the entire country and broken the backbone of resistance.

By the time the struggle was over, almost two years on, one-quarter of the Catholic population was dead and those found wandering the country orphaned or dispossessed were sold into slavery in the West Indies. The **Act of Settlement** drawn up in 1652 confiscated land from the native Irish on a massive scale. All "transplantable persons" were ordered to move west of the River Shannon by May 1, 1654, on pain of death; in the notorious phrase, it was a matter of indifference whether they went "to Hell or to Connacht". The mass exodus continued for months, with many of the old and sick dying on the journey. Cromwell's soldiers were paid off with gifts of appropriated land, and, remaining as settlers, constituted a permanent reminder of English injustice.

King Billy and King James

Irish hopes were raised once more by the **Restoration** of Charles II in 1660. He had regained the English throne, however, only after lengthy negotiations with the Protestant parliamentarians of London and Dublin, and was in no position to give expression to any Catholic sympathies which he may have held.

Things changed only when Charles's brother James II succeeded him in 1685. He appointed a Catholic viceroy in Ireland and actually got as far as repealing the Act of Settlement. However, the Whigs and the Tories in England united to invite the Protestant William of Orange to take the throne. James fled and was soon raising an army in Ireland. He was successful in controlling the spread of this "Glorious Revolution" to Ireland until 1689, when he came to lay siege to the city of Derry in Ulster; young trade apprentices, known thereafter as the **Apprentice Boys**, shut the gates of the city in the face of James's troops – an event still celebrated today during the annual marching season.

However, arguably the most significant victory of Protestant over Catholic was on July 12, 1690, when William's army defeated that of James at the **Battle of the Boyne**. The repeal of the Act of Settlement was therefore never implemented – but the very idea that the Catholics still had claims to their old property that they might one day be able to reassert became established in the Protestant consciousness. As William's victory was consolidated, measures were taken to ensure irreversible Protestant control of the country.

The penal laws to the Act of Union

In 1641, 59 percent of the land in Ireland was owned by Catholics. In 1688, the figure was 22 percent, and by 1703 it was fourteen percent. The Protestant population, about one-tenth of the total, lived in fear of an uprising by the vast majority of dispossessed and embittered Catholics. In order to keep them in a position of powerlessness, a number of Acts were passed, collectively known as the penal laws. Not only were Catholics forbidden to vote or join the army or navy, but it became illegal to educate a child in the Catholic faith; they could not teach, open their own schools or send their children to be educated abroad. Catholics could neither buy land nor inherit it, other than by the equal division of estates between all sons. There were vast rewards for turning Protestant; a male convert was entitled to all his brothers' inheritance, a female to her husband's property. Irish language, music and literature were banned, as was the saying of the Mass. The intention was to crush the identity of the Irish people through the suppression of their culture. However, clandestine "hedge schools" developed where outlawed Catholic teachers taught Irish language and music; Mass was said in secret, often at night in the open countryside, and although the erosion of the culture had begun, for the time being it remained strong (it wasn't until the devastating effects of the Famine that the culture went into serious decline).

Grattan's Parliament

The next turning point in Irish history came in the late eighteenth century, when the increasingly prosperous merchant class ceased to identify its own interests exclusively with those of the British Crown. The British, in their turn, were forced to realize that the best guarantee of stability was the country's economic strength. This was an age of bourgeois revolution, and the events of the **American War of Independence** attracted much attention in Ireland. As early as 1771, Benjamin Franklin was in Dublin suggesting future transatlantic cooperation. Although the rebellion of the American colonies threatened Irish commercial interests, opposition to the war did not mean opposition to the American cause. Thus far, the bulk of Irish emigrants to the American colonies had been Ulster Presbyterians, Catholic emigration being subject to legal restrictions, and the Protestants of Ireland felt a deep sympathy with Washington's campaign. The demand for "no taxation without representation" struck an emotional chord with the parliamentarians of Henry Grattan's Patriot Party

– although Ireland was not taxed directly by the British Parliament, the Irish Protestants felt, increasingly, that their interests were not properly represented in the politics and policies of the British Isles as a whole.

One increasingly significant factor was the formation of the United Volunteers by Grattan and his patron the Earl of Charlemont to replace the British militia which had been withdrawn from Ireland to fight in America. Eighty thousand Protestant men were recruited and organized into groups to defend Ireland from the now increased threat of a French invasion. While declaring allegiance to George III, the Volunteers also pressed for economic equality with Britain and an independent Irish legislature.

Protestants and Catholics (though legally disbarred from joining the Volunteers) made common cause to the extent that Grattan declared "the Irish Protestant could never be free till the Irish Catholic had ceased to be a slave". Its resources stretched to the limit by war, the British Government was sufficiently intimidated by the thought of Irish rebellion to be in the mood for concessions. The land stipulations of the penal laws were repealed in 1778, and in 1782, **Grattan's Parliament** achieved what was felt at the time to be constitutional independence for Ireland, beyond the interference of the London Parliament, although still subject to the veto of the king. In the **Renunciation Act** of 1783, the British Parliament declared that the executive and judicial independence of Ireland should be "established and ascertained forever, and ... at no time hereafter be questioned or questionable".

As it turned out, the independence of the Dublin Parliament lasted for just eighteen years, and even those were long on dissent and short on achievement. Economic measures certainly benefited the merchants, but such issues as the extension of voting rights to Catholics – despite Grattan's personal support – were barely addressed. A major reason for its failure was the influence of the **French Revolution** in 1789.

Wolfe Tone and the United Irishmen

For Irish nationalists of all persuasions the French Revolution transformed the thought of a French invasion from a menace to be feared to a prospective means of national liberation. **The Society of United Irishmen**, led by Wolfe Tone and built on the foundations of the Protestant Volunteers but attracting, if anything, more support from Catholics, rallied to the call of Liberty, Equality and Fraternity. Tone himself was a Protestant barrister, who saw equal rights for Protestants and Catholics in Ireland as the only route to independence from England. The United Irishmen were originally disposed towards nonviolence, but for Tone the possibility of French aid was too appealing to resist. The British, and the majority of Ulster Protestants, were by contrast so alarmed by tales of the bloodshed in France that they also prepared for war; it was at this juncture that the Protestant Orange Society, later the Orange Order, was established (1795). Although influenced by revolutionary ideas from France, its main aim was to oppose Catholic emancipation and thus maintain Protestant power in Ireland, particularly in the Ulster province where the Order had been formed and was at its strongest (for more on the Order, see box on p.734).

The uprising came in **1798** (see pp.272 & 511); disorganized fighting broke out in different parts of the island well before the French fleet – and Tone himself – arrived, and the scattered rebels were swiftly and bloodily suppressed. Tone was sentenced to be hanged, but committed suicide by cutting his own throat before his execution. The limited advances Henry Grattan had won for Catholics were withdrawn as a result of the rebellion.

The Act of Union

The destiny of Ireland during the period following the uprising was largely subject to the whim of political factions in England, ever ready to make an emotional cause célèbre of the latest developments. The rebellion of 1798 provoked Prime Minister William Pitt into support for the complete legislative union of Britain and Ireland and the dissolution of the Dublin Parliament. Pitt argued that this offered the most hopeful road towards Catholic emancipation while also ensuring the perpetuation of the Protestant Ascendancy. In 1801, the **Act of Union** came into force, abolishing the 500-year-old Irish Parliament and making Ireland part of the United Kingdom.

All hopes of independence seemed crushed. Ireland itself housed an utterly divided people, a minority Protestant ruling class and a politically powerless Catholic majority. **Robert Emmet**, a romantic figure in Irish history, inspired by Wolfe Tone, made one last stand for independence, and attempted a rising in 1803. His followers, however, were small in number and disorganized. The rising failed, and Emmet was executed.

Daniel O'Connell

The quest for Catholic emancipation by peaceful constitutional means was the life's work of **Daniel O'Connell** (1775–1847), the lawyer who became known as "The Liberator" and whom Gladstone called "the greatest popular leader the world has ever seen". He founded the Catholic Association in 1823, which attracted a mass following in Ireland with its campaign for full political rights for Catholics. O'Connell himself was elected to the British House of Commons as the member for Ennis, County Clare in 1828. As a Catholic, he was forbidden to take his seat in Westminster, but the moral force of his victory was such that a change in the law had to be conceded. Royal assent was given to the Catholic Emancipation Bill on April 13, 1829, granting voting rights to some Catholics. Stringent property qualifications, however, ensured that the Catholic vote remained a small one.

At the height of his success, O'Connell's popularity was phenomenal. He was elected Lord Mayor of (Protestant) Dublin for the year of 1841, and two years later embarked on an ambitious campaign for the **repeal of the Union** with England. O'Connell addressed a series of vast "monster meetings" throughout Ireland; according to the conservative estimate of *The Times*, over a million people – one-eighth of the Irish population – attended the meeting symbolically held at the Hill of Tara.

The climax of O'Connell's campaign was to be a meeting at Clontarf (where Brian Boru had defeated the Danes in the eleventh century) on October 8, 1843. All Ireland was poised and waiting, conscious of the sympathy that O'Connell's profoundly peaceful movement had won from around the world. The pacifism which had led him to say that "no political change is worth the shedding of a single drop of human blood", and his determination always to act within the law, were, however, exploited by the British. One day before the Clontarf meeting it was declared to be an illegal gathering and O'Connell, remarkably, obliged by calling it off. The crowds that had already gathered, and the population at large, were baffled that O'Connell backed down from direct confrontation. His moment passed and the stage was left to those who, having seen pacifism fail to secure independence, believed that armed struggle would prove the only way forward. The **Young Ireland movement**, once aligned with O'Connell, attempted an armed uprising in 1848, but by then there was little chance of mass support. The country was already undergoing a national disaster.

The Famine

The failure of the Irish potato crop from 1845 to 1849 plunged the island into appalling **famine**. Elsewhere in Europe, the blight was a resolvable problem but Irish subsistence farmers were utterly dependent on the crop. No disease affected grain, cattle, dairy produce or corn and throughout the disaster Irish produce that could have fed the hungry continued to be exported overseas. Millions were kept alive by charitable soup kitchens, and some individual landlords were supportive to their tenants; for millions more, the only choice lay between starvation and escape.

Between 1841 and 1851, census returns suggest that 1.4 million people died in Ireland and 1.4 million emigrated to the United States and elsewhere – though the exact numbers in each case were probably higher. Many emigrants were too ill to survive the journey on what became known as "coffin ships", some drowned when overcrowded ships sank, and still more died on arrival in the United States, Canada, Britain, Australia and New Zealand.

One consequence of **mass emigration** was the creation of large Irish communities abroad, which henceforth added an international dimension to the struggle for Irish independence. Financial support from the Irish overseas became crucial to such Nationalist organizations as the Irish Republican Brotherhood, also known as the **Fenians** (a name derived from the Fianna of Irish mythology; see p.846). Their attempted uprising in 1867 was little short of a fiasco, but they nonetheless retained a loyal following both in the States and in England (where a number of bombings were carried out in their name).

The legacy of the Famine was such that the long-standing bitterness instilled by the British connection now deepened to a new level of emotional intensity. Resentment focused on the failure of the British Government to intervene, and more specifically on the **absentee English landlords** who had continued to profit while remaining indifferent to the suffering of their tenants. Such landlords had little or no contact with the realities of life on their estates; rents were far higher than most tenants could pay, and evictions became widespread, most notoriously at Derryveagh in Donegal (see p.593).

Parnell and the Home Rule

The second half of the nineteenth century was characterized by a complex interplay of political and economic factors, which exacerbated religious differences. The most important of these was the struggle for land and for the rights of tenants. A coherent Nationalist movement with modest aims began to emerge, operating within British parliamentary democracy.

Charles Stewart Parnell (1846–91; see p.156), a Protestant who was elected to Westminster in 1875 and became leader of the **Home Rule Party** two years later, was the tenants' champion. He insisted that only the establishment of an Irish Parliament in Dublin could be responsive to the needs of the people and, to that end, consistently disrupted the business of the British House of Commons. Parnell also organized the Irish peasantry in defiance of particularly offensive landlords, adding a new word to the English language when the first such target was a Captain Boycott.

A breakthrough seemed to be approaching when Parnell won the support of the prime minister, Gladstone, but the **Phoenix Park** murders in Dublin in 1882 (see p.118) again hardened English opinion against the Irish. Three Home Rule Bills were defeated in the space of ten years and instead the Prevention of Crimes Act was brought in which (temporarily) abolished trial by jury and increased police powers. The transparent honesty of Parnell's denials of complicity in the murders for a while served to boost his career, but public opinion finally swung against him in 1890, when he was cited in the divorce case of his colleague Captain O'Shea.

The attitude of many Irish Protestants to the agitation for Home Rule was summed up by the equation "Home Rule = Rome Rule"; such a threat was enough to unite the Anglican (broadly speaking, conservative gentry) and Presbyterian (liberal tradesmen) communities. These were certainly the people who were doing best from a modest boom in Ireland's economic fortunes, with Ulster, and specifically Belfast, having been the main beneficiary when the Industrial Revolution finally arrived in the country. Large-scale **industrialization**, in export industries such as shipbuilding, linen manufacture and engineering, gave the region an additional dependence on the British connection, while the fact that these industries were firmly under Protestant ownership increased social tensions.

The end of the nineteenth century saw a burst of activity aimed at the revival of interest in all aspects of Irish culture and identity. Ostensibly non-political organizations such as the **Gaelic League** and the Gaelic Athletic Association were founded to promote Irish language, music and traditional sports, and these inevitably tended to attract the support of politically minded Nationalists. As well as those who sought to encourage the use of Irish, a body of writers, with W.B. Yeats in the forefront, embarked on an attempt to create a national literature in English.

In 1898, Arthur Griffith, a printer in Dublin, founded a newspaper called the *United Irishman*, in which he expounded the philosophy of **Sinn Féin**, meaning "We, Ourselves". His was a nonviolent and essentially capitalist vision, arguing that the Irish MPs should simply abandon Westminster and set up their own parliament in Dublin, where, with or without the permission of the British, they would be able to govern Ireland by virtue of their unassailable moral authority. Such political freedom was a prerequisite for Ireland to achieve significant economic development. Sinn Féin incorporated itself into a political party in 1905. Meanwhile, socialist analyses of the situation in Ireland were appearing in the *Workers' Republic*, the newspaper of **James Connolly**'s Irish Socialist Republican Party, pointing out that Ireland's frail prosperity rested on a basis of malnutrition, bad housing and social deprivation.

Reaction and counter-reaction

In reaction to the declared intentions of Asquith's Liberal government in Britain in 1911 to see through the passage of yet another (exceptionally tame) Home Rule Bill, the Protestants of Ulster mobilized themselves under the leadership of **Sir Edward Carson**. A Dublin barrister who at first glance had little in common with the people of Ulster, a region he barely knew, his one great aim was to preserve the Union, in the face of the "nefarious conspiracy" hatched by the British Government. To that end he declared that, in the event of the Home Rule Bill becoming law, the Unionists would defy it and set up their own parliament. In preparation for that eventuality, they organized their own militia, the **Ulster Volunteers**.

James Connolly, who had spent the years from 1903 to 1910 in disillusionment in the United States, found himself on less fertile ground when he tried to convert the workers of Belfast to socialism. He was impressed, however, by the example of the Ulster Volunteers, and the brutal police suppression of a protracted and bitter strike in Dublin, organized by James Larkin's Irish Transport Workers Union, gave him the opportunity to form the **Irish Citizen Army**. Other militant Republicans had also resolved to create an armed force in the south to parallel the Ulster Volunteers, and almost simultaneously, in November 1913, the **Irish Volunteers** came into being. The Gaelic League and Gaelic Athletic Association acted as prime recruiting places and provided such leaders as Pádraig Pearse (see p.111). The movement should not, however, be seen in strictly sectarian terms; at least two of its most prominent leaders were Ulster Protestant.

Rebellion and civil war

The British Parliament eventually passed the Home Rule Bill of 1912, and for a while the conditions appeared to exist for Ireland to erupt into civil war. Before this could happen, however, the outbreak of World War I dramatically altered the situation. An immediate consequence of war was that enactment of the Bill was indefinitely postponed.

For the majority of the Irish Volunteers, the primary aim of their movement was to safeguard the postwar introduction of Home Rule. Not simply to that end, but also out of loyalty to the British Crown, many of them joined the British Army. Some, however, led by Eoin MacNeill, in part supported the British war effort but were reluctant to commit too much of their strength towards defending Britain without a pledge of concrete rewards. These in turn fell under the domination of a small and secret militant faction, the revived **Irish Republican Brotherhood** (after 1916 they became the Irish Republican Army, or IRA), to whom "England's difficulty was Ireland's opportunity". They made tentative overtures for German support (and even contemplated installing a German prince as King of Ireland) but went ahead with preparations for armed insurrection regardless of whether or not they received foreign aid – indeed all but regardless of the virtual certainty of defeat.

The Easter Rising

The outbreak of fighting on the streets of Dublin on Easter Monday in 1916 was expected by neither the British nor the Irish Army, and was a source of bemusement to the Dubliners themselves. Republican forces swiftly took over a number of key buildings, although they missed an easy opportunity to capture the castle itself.

The leaders of the rising made their base in the General Post Office in O'Connell Street, and it was from there that Pádraig Pearse emerged to read the "Proclamation from The Provisional Government of the Irish Republic to the People of Ireland":

Ireland, through us, summons her children to the flag and strikes for her freedom ... The Irish Republic is entitled to, and hereby claims, the allegiance of every Irishman and Irishwoman. The Republic guarantees religious and civil liberty, equal rights and equal opportunities to all its citizens ... cherishing all the children of the nation equally, and oblivious of the differences carefully fostered by an alien Government, which have divided a minority from the majority in the past.

To these fine democratic sentiments Pearse in particular added a quasi-mystical emphasis on the necessity for blood sacrifice; although potential allies such as Eoin MacNeill declined to join them with so little prospect of success, these were men prepared to give their lives as inspiration to others.

So weak was the rebel position that they only held out for five days; at the time of their surrender they were even less popular with the mass of the nation than when they began, as a result of the terrible physical damage Dublin had suffered.

And yet, as the leaders of the rising were systematically and unceremoniously executed by the British – the wounded James Connolly was shot tied to a chair – sympathy did indeed grow for the Republicans and their cause. Yeats expresses the sentiment in *Easter 1916* with the words "... changed, changed utterly: A terrible beauty is born".

War with Britain

When the British Government felt able once again to turn to Irish affairs, it found a dramatically altered situation. Sinn Féin won a resounding victory in the elections of 1918 and refused to take its seats at Westminster. Instead the newly elected MPs met in Dublin as the Dáil Éireann (Assembly of Ireland) and declared independence. Leadership passed to Eamon de Valera, the sole surviving leader of the Easter Rising, whose sentence of death had been commuted. Michael Collins, the Minister of Finance in the new government and its most effective military organizer, began mobilizing the IRA for war. In January 1919, the killing of two members of the Royal Irish Constabulary (RIC), the main instrument of British power in Ireland, marked the beginning of the hostilities, which were to last for two and a half years.

The RIC experienced severe difficulties in recruiting sufficient new members (other than from Ulster). Newly demobilized British soldiers were therefore brought over from England, and by virtue of their distinctive uniforms became known as the **Black and Tans**. The Irish Republicans, fighting on home territory, were well able to hold their own in guerrilla fighting across the country, while the Black and Tans acquired an infamous and enduring reputation for brutality.

The **Government of Ireland Act** of 1920 created separate parliaments for "Northern Ireland" (Derry, Antrim, Fermanagh, Down, Tyrone and Armagh) and "Southern Ireland" (the 26 counties of the present-day Republic), to remain under the nominal authority of the British Crown. Elections were held for the two bodies in 1921, but the members elected to the Southern Parliament constituted themselves instead as the **Dáil Éireann**, with de Valera as their president. With the Protestants of Ulster still firmly pledged to the Union, and the fighting at a stalemate, a negotiated settlement seemed the only way out. A truce was called in July 1921 and de Valera sent emissaries to London, including Arthur Griffith and Michael Collins, to negotiate a treaty. Lloyd George persuaded them to agree to peace terms based on the partition of the island along the lines set out by the Government of Ireland Act. The 26 southern counties would become not a republic but an independent nation within the British Commonwealth – the Irish Free State. The northern border, Lloyd George suggested, would be so small as to preclude the North from being a viable entity, thus bringing about eventual unity. The alternative to the treaty was, he said, "immediate and terrible war".

Civil War

The **Anglo-Irish Treaty** was signed in London on December 6, 1921, and hailed by Lloyd George as "one of the greatest days in the history of the British Empire". A provisional government was formed in Ireland in January 1922, pending elections. The link with Britain had been broken at last – but not completely or cleanly enough for a militant minority in Ireland. During the negotiations, Griffith and Collins in London and de Valera in Dublin had failed to agree a clear line on an acceptable outcome. On the negotiators' return, de Valera rejected the treaty as it veered too far from the Republican ideal. He resigned from office and left the Dáil; by July he and his military supporters had plunged Ireland into a squalid and economically devastating **civil war**.

Men who had been fighting alongside each other the year before were now pitched into a bitter conflict: the supporters of the treaty, the "Free Staters", against Republicans fighting for a united Ireland. In the North, the understandably alarmed Protestant community created the Ulster Special Constabulary, including the "**B Specials**" drawn from Carson's Ulster Volunteers, ostensibly to control the rioting which persistently broke out in response to events south of the border.

De Valera and his supporters were eventually forced to capitulate in May 1923; as he put it, "military victory must be allowed to rest for the moment with those who have destroyed the Republic."

The Irish Free State

With the death of Michael Collins and Arthur Griffith during the civil war, the leadership of the Irish Free State fell to William T. Cosgrave, and finally in the summer of 1923 the new government began to reconstruct Ireland as an independent nation. A civil service was set up, along with a police force and the hydroelectric scheme on the River Shannon, which was to lead to the establishment of the ESB (Electricity Supply Board).

Meanwhile Eamon de Valera, still an important political force, abandoned Sinn Féin's post-civil war policy of boycotting the Dáil to form his own political party in 1926. This took the explicitly mythological name of **Fianna Fáil** (Soldiers of Destiny) and was victorious in the 1932 general election. Under de Valera other state bodies were set up, including Coras Iompair Éireann (road and rail transport), Aer Lingus (air transport) and Bord na Mona (peat production). In 1933, the rival **Fine Gael** (Tribes of Gaels) party was founded.

The recession of the 1930s was made considerably worse for Ireland by the **economic war**. De Valera had withheld repayments to England of loans made to tenants to buy their holdings; the British responded by imposing heavy duties on Irish goods.

In 1938, a new **constitution** came into effect, which finally declared Ireland's complete independence by renouncing British sovereignty. The Free State, under the new name of **Éire**, was to be governed by a two-chamber parliament (the Dáil and the Seanad), with a president (the Uachtarán), and a prime minister (the Taoiseach).

Ireland remained officially neutral during World War II, although considerable informal help was given to the Allies. De Valera, on the other hand, was the only government leader in the world to offer his commiserations – to a Nazi German minister in Dublin – on the suicide of Adolf Hitler.

The Republic

The **Republic of Ireland** finally came into being in 1949, following legislation in the Dáil the previous year, severing residual economic ties with Britain and removing Ireland from the Commonwealth. It took a further twenty years, however, to recover from the economic stagnation brought on by the war. Vast numbers of people, disproportionately drawn from among the young and talented, moved across to fill Britain's labour shortage. Not until a break was made with the past, with the accession to the premiership in 1959 of the vigorous and expansionist Sean Lemass, was a sufficient level of prosperity achieved to slow down the process of chronic emigration. Foreign enterprises began investing heavily in Ireland, unemployment fell by a third, and the way was paved for the country's successful application to join the European Economic Community in 1972. The immediate benefits were enjoyed by those employed in agriculture (twenty percent of the working population), although Irish fishing waters had now to be shared with other EEC members.

Ireland's and Britain's membership of the **EEC** did not, however, bring the Republic and Northern Ireland closer together. Their membership was made official on January 22, 1972; eight days later came Bloody Sunday (see p.690), and on February 2 the British Embassy in Dublin was destroyed by an angry mob.

The international recession hit Ireland very severely in the 1980s. Emigration rocketed once again and unemployment remained consistently high. Referenda on abortion in 1983 and divorce in 1986 (both remained illegal) reflected the Catholic Church's considerable influence.

Charles Haughey

The 1987 general election, fought principally on the issues of taxation and unemployment, resulted in accession to power of the Fianna Fáil party, led by the resilient and wily **Charles Haughey**. In the summer of 1989, Mr Haughey called another election with the intention of increasing his majority. The result, however, was a Fianna Fáil/Progressive Democrat alliance, in which Haughey's hold on power always seemed tenuous.

The presidential election of 1991 yielded a surprise result when the feminist lawyer **Mary Robinson**, an independent candidate supported by Labour and The Workers' Party, was elected. Some in Haughey's party (and outside) accused the Taoiseach of sabotaging the campaign of his own party's candidate, Brian Lenihan (an old rival), but whatever the causes of her success, there can be no doubt that the president breathed new life into the office and into Irish politics in general: as a woman, and as a representative of causes outside the old two-party stalemate. In particular, her election gave hope to many that a new era of greater integrity and **liberalism** in politics, and perhaps some easing of positions on the intractable problems of the North, was about to dawn.

Early in 1992, Charles Haughey, whose government was weighed down by constant (and later to be proven) allegations of financial mismanagement and even corruption, resigned. The final straw came when Sean Doherty, speaker of the Seanad and a former minister under Haughey, claimed that he personally had delivered tapes of tapped phone calls, made by journalists unfriendly to Fianna Fáil, to Mr Haughey in 1982. Although Haughey denied any knowledge of such tapes, the threat of his coalition falling apart finally forced him to step down.

From Albert Reynolds to Bertie Ahern

The new prime minister, **Albert Reynolds**, took over the leadership of a seemingly exhausted Fianna Fáil party. His downfall, however, less than three years later, was due to a moral issue – as so often is the case in Irish politics. Reynolds' years as prime minister were plagued by scandal and the powerful influence of the Church in public and political life. An early case was that of the 14-year-old rape victim whom the Irish High Court at first refused to allow to go to Britain to seek an abortion. In May 1992 came the dramatic confessions of an American woman, former lover of Dr Eamonn Casey, the Bishop of Galway, who had apparently been using church funds to bring up his teenage son. Then, in 1993, it emerged that warrants from Belfast for the extradition of the paedophile priest Father Brendan Smyth had been ignored for several months. The government – under pressure from the Church – continued to cover up the scandal, but in November 1994, after questions in the Dáil, the prime minister's part in the affair came to light and he was forced to resign. It didn't help that at the same time a 68-year-old priest, Liam Cosgrave, died in a Dublin gay sauna club; this spate of clerical scandals caused disarray among Irish Catholics and would appear to have irrevocably undermined the Church's authority on moral issues.

Since 1994, there has been a series of coalition governments. The current one is Fianna Fáil-led, under their leader **Bertie Ahern**. Ahern's term in office has been dogged by damaging **financial scandals**, involving leading figures in his party, notably Charles Haughey and Foreign Minister Ray Burke. Haughey was found guilty in 1997 of taking a "gift" of £1.3 million from top Irish businessman, Ben Dunne. Shortly afterwards, Burke resigned when it was revealed he had received £30,000 from a company wanting to develop land in his constituency. The **Flood Commission's** subsequent investigations pulled further skeletons from their closets, but one positive outcome of these scandals has been the passing of an Ethics in Public Office Act – evidence that Ireland is developing into something approaching a mature democracy.

The election in October 1997 saw a second successive female president, **Mary McAleese**, elected to the post. Her politics, however, differ fundamentally from her predecessor's. Born in Belfast, President McAleese's politics are Nationalist and influenced by her strongly held Catholic beliefs (she is ardently pro-life). However, it was the greenness of her Nationalism not her social conservatism that caused concern for some southerners during her election campaign. There were fears that she might alienate Ulster Unionists at a delicate time in the peace process (she had once described Northern Ireland as "the archetypal police state"). Other critics worried that her campaigning zeal, most in evidence in her role as vice-chancellor of Queen's University, Belfast, would be inappropriate for the apolitical position of president. These fears, however, have not been realized.

One of the most significant developments in Irish society over the last dozen years has been the staggering growth of the country's GDP, earning it the epithet **Celtic Tiger**. The reasons for this impressive performance are manifold, but are chiefly due to the granting of generous tax concessions to multinationals, economic support from Europe and a young, highly educated workforce. However, there are doubts over the sustainability of this growth. Concentrated in five high-tech sectors, owned by multinationals, the real growth of the economy has not included that of indigenous industries. These two sides of the economy have been left sitting uncomfortably side by side. There are also concerns that only certain sectors of society are benefiting from the recent wealth-creation and that social inequalities are growing.

In recent years, however, there has been marked resistance to Ireland's drive towards globalization. The arrival of numbers of refugees and asylum-seekers has challenged perceived notions about Ireland's homogeneity and, in some urban areas, catalysed ugly forms of racist intolerance. Additionally, in 2001, the Irish people narrowly voted against the adoption of the Nice Treaty which proposed an expansion in the number of member countries in the EU. As a supporter of the Treaty, Bertie Ahern's standing was weakened internationally, and he was undermined at home by the defeat of a proposal to tighten even further the country's already stringent laws on abortion. Nevertheless, the absence of any viable political alternative saw Ahern's Fianna Fáil make significant gains in the May 2002 general election, albeit continuing to rely on the support of Mary Harney's Progressive Democrats to retain power. The following month Ahern secured victory in a rerun referendum on the Nice Treaty.

Northern Ireland from 1921

On June 22, 1921, the new political entity of **Northern Ireland** came into existence with the opening of the Northern Irish Parliament in Belfast's City Hall. In order to understand the present situation in the North it is necessary to grasp the political background to this development. Since the settlements of the seventeenth century, the Protestant descendants of the settlers had been concentrated in the northern part of the island; they rarely intermarried with local people or assimilated into native culture, feeling both superior to and threatened by the Catholics, who formed the vast majority of the population of Ireland as a whole. The economically dominant group in the northern counties was essentially Protestant, and when an industrial base developed in this part of the island, the prosperity of the region was inextricably tied to the trading power of Britain. In negotiating for their exclusion from the new Irish state, Carson and the Unionist Council decided to accept just six counties of Ulster out of a possible nine, because only in this way could a safe Protestant majority be guaranteed. Thus Westminster gave political power into the hands of those whose pro-British sympathies were certain.

The Unionists were not slow to exploit their supremacy: a Protestant police force and military were set up, and "gerrymandering" (the redrawing of boundary lines in order to control the outcome of elections) was commonplace, so securing Protestant control even in areas with Catholic majorities. Thus Derry city, with a two-thirds Catholic majority, returned a two-thirds Protestant council. Nothing was done to rectify the situation for several decades. The Catholic community was to benefit from the British welfare state, but they were discriminated against in innumerable ways, most notoriously in jobs and also in housing, an area controlled by Protestant local authorities.

Civil Rights

In 1967, inspired by the civil rights movement in America, the Northern Irish **Civil Rights Movement** was born, a non-sectarian organization demanding equality of rights for all. Massively supported by the Catholic community, the campaign led to huge protest marches, some of which were viciously attacked by Loyalist mobs. The **RUC** (Royal Ulster Constabulary) rarely intervened, and when they did take action, it was generally not to protect the Catholics. The Apprentice Boys' march of 1969 proved to be the flashpoint. This triumphalist procession, commemorating the city's siege in 1689 (see p.785), annually passed through Derry's Catholic areas (in recent times it has been truncated, first by the Parades Commission and subsequently by mutual agreement with the city council). The 1969 march provoked rioting that ended with the Catholic community barricading themselves in and Jack Lynch, the Irish prime minister, mobilizing Irish troops and setting up field hospitals on the border.

On August 14, British troops were sent to Derry to protect the besieged minority, and at first they were welcomed by the Catholics, who were relieved to see the troops pushing back the RUC and B Specials. Belief in the neutrality of the British Army did not last long, as escalating violence between the two communities across the North forced the army into a more interventionist role, but confusion arose as to whether **Stormont** (the Northern Parliament) or Westminster was giving the orders. Before long the army was acting not as a protective force but as a retaliatory one, and it was clear that retaliation against the Catholics was far harsher than measures taken against the Protestants. With the Catholics again vulnerable, the resurgent IRA quickly assumed the role of defenders of the ghetto areas of Derry and Belfast. Within a few months the **Provisional IRA**, now stronger than the less militant Official wing of the organization, had launched an intensive bombing and shooting campaign across the North.

At the request of Northern Ireland's prime minister, Brian Faulkner, **internment without trial** was introduced in 1971, a measure which was used as an indiscriminate weapon against the minority population. Then, on Sunday, January 30, 1972, thirteen unarmed civil rights demonstrators were shot dead by British paratroopers in Derry, an event that shocked the world and was to become known as **Bloody Sunday**. The Irish Government declared February 2 a national day of mourning; on the same day an angry crowd in Dublin burned down the British Embassy. Stormont was suspended and direct rule from Westminster imposed.

Power-sharing and its aftermath

In 1973 a conference was held at **Sunningdale** between representatives of the British and Irish governments and both sections of the community in Northern Ireland, a meeting that led to the creation of a power-sharing executive for the province representing both Unionists and Nationalists, as well as proposals for a Council of Ireland, a non-executive body bringing together politicians from both North and Republic. An elected executive took office in January 1974, but Ulster Unionist opposition to the Council of Ireland forced Faulkner's resignation. More significantly, inspired by the Reverend Ian Paisley and his Democratic Unionist Party's vehement opposition to the end of majority rule, the Ulster Workers' Council responded to the proposition of power-sharing by organizing a massive strike in May 1974 which, enforced by the roadblocks of the UDA (Ulster Defence Association), crippled the power stations and other essential services run by a strongly Unionist workforce. In the same week as the strike, three car bombs planted by the UDA exploded during rush hour in Dublin without warning – 33 people were killed, the highest death toll since 1969. By the end of the month, the Sunningdale executive – the first ever to have Catholic representation – was disbanded, and direct rule from Westminster continued until the implementation of the Good Friday peace agreement in 1999 (see p.800).

Throughout 1973 and 1974 the IRA had been conducting a **bombing campaign** in Britain, aimed at destabilizing the government by provoking public revulsion. Twenty-one people were killed in a pub bombing in Birmingham in 1974, and in the same month seven people died in simultaneous pub bombings in Woolwich and **Guildford**. However, a ceasefire was declared in late December, at a time, it subsequently emerged, when the IRA leadership was involved in secret negotiations with the British Government. Though some concessions were made, the British refusal to consider the question of Irish unity saw a resumption of the bombing campaign early in 1975. The British responded by introducing the **Prevention of Terrorism Act**, permitting lengthy detention without charge. Four people were arrested for the Guildford bombings and convicted on the basis of confessions and forensic evidence which even at the time were thought by many people to be unreliable. After fifteen years in jail, the prisoners were released when the judiciary finally conceded, with no hint of regret for the injustice, that they were indeed innocent. Six Irish people were given life sentences for the Birmingham attack, and their convictions, too, were finally overthrown in 1991.

In 1976 Special Category Status was abolished for future prisoners in Northern Ireland. Previously those arrested for offences connected with what had become known as the Troubles enjoyed the status of political prisoners. The abolition of status provoked the 1981 **hunger strikes**, in which Republican inmates of Long Kesh (also known as The Maze) demanded the reinstatement of their political status. The prison housed hundreds of activists, Loyalist and Republican, interned without trial by the British government. Originally all inmates had Special Category Status, in accordance with the Emergency Powers legislation under which they had been convicted, but when the British government phased out internment in late 1975, special status went with it. From March 1, 1976, the prison was in the peculiar position of housing the last of these special category prisoners as well as – in the H-blocks – those convicted after this cut-off date, who were now classified, and treated, as ordinary criminals.

The IRA campaign for the reinstatement of status began when Kevin Nugent, in refusing to wear prison clothes, initiated what became known as the "**blanket protest**" (quite simply, draping a blanket around himself instead of wearing prison clothes). By 1978, this had escalated into the famous "**dirty protest**", in which Republican prisoners refused to undertake ordinary prison duties such as emptying chamber pots, resorting instead to smearing the cells with their own excrement in order to get rid of it. In 1978 Britain was found guilty by the European Court of Human Rights of "inhuman and degrading treatment" of Republican prisoners. In 1981, a concerted **hunger strike** led to the deaths of ten men, including Bobby Sands, provisional commander of the IRA men inside the prison, who had, significantly, been elected MP for Fermanagh and South Tyrone six weeks into his fast. None of this succeeded in budging the government, which steadfastly refused to back down in the face of what it believed was nothing more than moral blackmail, and the deaths brought widespread condemnation of British intransigence.

The Anglo-Irish Agreement and the Downing Street Declaration

The year 1982 saw the British Government make a timid attempt to break the impasse, introducing the **Northern Ireland Assembly**, a power-sharing body with some legislative but no executive powers. It was boycotted by the Nationalists, and survived only until 1985, by which time the final stages had been reached in the negotiations over the **Anglo-Irish Agreement**. Largely drafted by John Hume, the leader of the moderate Nationalist SDLP, and signed in 1986, it instituted official co-operation between Dublin and Westminster on security and other issues, and strengthened the consultative part played by Dublin in Northern affairs. Unfortunately, the agreement was weakened by the non-participation of the Ulster Unionists, who had not been involved in its preparation, in the processes it inaugurated.

Throughout the early 1980s Republicans had increasingly become involved in the democratic process. **Gerry Adams** was elected MP for West Belfast in June 1983 and became Sinn Féin's president in November that year. Three years later, the party ended its policy of refusing to take up seats in the Dáil following election gains in the South, though significantly Adams and fellow-MP **Martin McGuinness** have always abstained from attending at Westminster. For many this combination of armed and political Republican activity was encapsulated in ex-internee and Sinn Féin member Danny Morrison's famous question to his party conference, "Would anyone here object if, with the ballot paper in this hand and an Armalite in this hand, we take power in Ireland?" However, despite increased Republican political activity, by the early 1990s the IRA had intensified the pressure through a series of bombing campaigns in both Northern Ireland and England (the latter including an audacious attempt to mortar-bomb the British prime minister, John Major, and his Cabinet while meeting in 10 Downing Street). Loyalist reprisals in Northern Ireland, featuring their old speciality, the random attack, were so widespread that, for the first time since 1975, deaths from their activities were more numerous than those resulting from the actions of Republican paramilitaries.

The next major step in addressing the stalemate in the North came with the **Downing Street Declaration** of December 1993. Brokered courageously, once again, by John Hume, and issued jointly by the Irish and British premiers, Albert Reynolds and John Major, it signalled a new readiness for dialogue with all sides involved in the Troubles – including Sinn Féin and the IRA. Previously, the Republican movement had been "psychopaths, godfathers, crypto-fascists", and worse; now, in a remarkable volte-face, they were people who could be reasoned with. They were repeatedly assured of their place at a negotiating table if they embraced the Downing Street Declaration and if the violence stopped.

The Irish Government's ban on broadcast of interviews with, or direct statements by, representatives of Sinn Féin, the IRA and other organizations associated with militant Republicanism or militant Loyalism fell due for renewal just a month after the Downing Street Declaration. This ban, which provided the inspiration for a similar, though less restrictive, prohibition in Britain, had been consistently opposed by civil liberties organizations and media professionals, and the government had it under review for months before the Downing Street Declaration. In a rare example of liberal leadership to Britain, the Irish Government decided not to renew the ban, and was subsequently followed by the British Government.

The ceasefire, the peace process and the Good Friday Agreement

In July 1994, a Sinn Féin conference rejected the Downing Street Declaration, but with continued political bargaining by Albert Reynolds and lobbying by Irish-American groups the party was eventually persuaded of the virtues of participation in a Nationalist coalition. On August 31, 1994, the IRA declared a "complete cessation" of military activities. Loyalist paramilitaries announced their own **ceasefire** two months later.

After further negotiation, in February 1995, the London and Dublin governments produced a framework document which attempted to satisfy some of the Republicans' constitutional demands, including provision for an all-Ireland authority with far-reaching executive powers.

Major's precondition that the IRA should commence decommissioning its weaponry before Sinn Féin be allowed to participate in the all-party talks proved a huge stumbling block. Seen by Republicans as a demand for the IRA's unconditional surrender, the deadlock was not broken until the establishment of an international commission in November 1995 to advise on the decommissioning process. Chaired by the US senator George Mitchell, it recommended that talks should go ahead in tandem with the handing over of weapons. Crucially, the report detailed six conditions for participation in such talks. Known as the **Mitchell Principles**, these included an overriding commitment to peaceful and democratic principles and all-party consensus and acceptance of the outcome of the political process. However, in the absence of any weaponry being yielded, and bowing to Unionist pressure, the British Government unilaterally announced its intention to hold elections in May 1997 for participation in the all-party talks which would commence in June if the IRA maintained its ceasefire.

The patience of Republicans, however, was being severely tested by what they saw as British intransigence. Sinn Féin's insistence on the whole of the Irish people's right to national self-determination meant that it could not accept the principle of majority consent in Northern Ireland. The IRA's ceasefire was itself essentially fragile and its threats of a return to violence if the political process did not achieve its desired ends became reality with the explosion on February 9, 1996 of a massive **bomb** near London's **Canary Wharf**, killing two people, injuring many more and causing several hundred million pounds of damage to buildings.

Many feared this was the end of the process, but support for political change in Northern Ireland remained powerful and vociferous. The key players remained active, not least the SDLP leader, John Hume, who saw negotiation in the absence of Sinn Féin as redundant and resumed contact with Gerry Adams, seeking a restoration of the IRA's ceasefire. This call was reiterated by **Bill Clinton** whose support for the peace process had become much greater than a simple desire to target the Irish-American vote. Adams was permitted entry to the United States, and the White House became a vital intermediary, risking the displeasure of its traditional ally. Signs that the political stalemate might be over came with the election of new parties and leaders in both Britain and the Republic. Elected by an enormous majority, the first Labour prime minister for eighteen years, **Tony Blair**, made clear his commitment to the Northern Ireland peace process in his visit to Belfast less than two weeks after his election in May 1997. **Mo Mowlam** was his inspired choice as Northern Ireland Secretary. As the first woman to hold the post, her bluff no-nonsense "matey" approach was to undermine significantly the suspicions of many involved in the peace process. The following month, Bertie Ahern's Fianna Fáil won the Republic's general election. **Ahern**, along with Foreign Secretary **Dick Spring**, was to play a major role in subsequent events, not least in becoming the first Taoiseach to meet the leader of the Ulster Unionists, David Trimble. It was Ahern's securing of Trimble's trust which was to have huge significance in later events.

The elections for the **all-party talks** took place at the end of May 1997. Sinn Féin had obtained a large enough vote to participate, but could not do so because of the IRA's refusal to return to a state of ceasefire. However, intense lobbying within Republican circles resulted in the IRA's announcement of "an unequivocal restoration of the ceasefire of August 1994" on July 19, 1997. Though Sinn Féin was now actively engaged and **Gerry Adams** was to make a historic visit to **Downing Street**, at Blair's invitation, on December 9, 1997, little demonstrable progress was made until the following year. Violation of the principles set out by George Mitchell, who had been appointed chair of the talks, led to representatives of the Loyalist paramilitaries and, later, Sinn Féin being suspended. Moreover, the radical Republican INLA's assassination of the Loyalist paramilitary LVF's leader, **Billy Wright**, in The Maze just before Christmas 1997 threatened a full-scale return to the violence of the past. The IRA's and Loyalist groups' ceasefires seemed increasingly precarious, especially once dissident Loyalists embarked on a spree of random sectarian attacks. In March 1998, two close friends were shot dead in the Railway Bar in **Poyntzpass**, County Armagh, a village regarded as one of the friendliest and most integrated in Northern Ireland. That one of the pair was Catholic and the other Protestant enhanced the general outrage at the killings and the increasing pointlessness of violence as a solution to the Troubles. Blair seized the impetus by declaring that the all-party talks had to reach a compromise by April 9, 1998 or the process was finished for the foreseeable future.

As the deadline loomed nearer, the chances of a successful conclusion seemed to recede and the day and night of April 9 saw a frenzy of activity and frantic negotiation. Finally, a settlement was somehow negotiated and the accord, known as the **Good Friday Agreement**, was signed on April 10, 1998. It was, without doubt, the most important development in the political history of Northern Ireland. The agreement committed its signatories "to partnership, equality and mutual respect as the basis of relationships within Northern Ireland" and reaffirmed the participants' dedication "to exclusively democratic and peaceful means of resolving differences on political issues". The principle of "consent" lay at the agreement's core. Hugely significant in securing Unionist and Loyalist support, this categorically stated that both governments would respect the legitimacy of the wishes of the majority of the people of Northern Ireland, whether that be to remain part of the United Kingdom or, at some later date, to become part of a united Ireland. In reinforcement, the two governments also agreed to make legal changes – the British Government to repeal the Government of Ireland Act 1920 asserting the sovereignty of the United Kingdom's Parliament over Ireland, and the Irish to hold a referendum on Articles Two and Three of its constitution, claiming territorial sovereignty over the North.

Further provisions included the establishment of a 108-member **Assembly**, elected by proportional representation to ensure the rights of Nationalists, and with a twelve-strong executive committee of ministers appointed on a cross-community basis. The Assembly would have legislative and executive authority over six departments previously run by the British Government's Northern

Ireland ministers. An intergovernmental Council of the Isles was also to be established, with membership from the Assembly, Dáil, Commons and the new devolved Welsh and Scottish assemblies. The signatories also committed themselves to the incorporation of the European Convention of Human Rights into Northern Ireland law and the establishment of a new Northern Ireland Human Rights Commission. Apart from the consent principle, the most controversial aspects of the agreement dealt with the accelerated release of political prisoners (an issue that divided the Ulster Unionist Party) and the establishment of an independent commission to review the RUC and the future of policing in the North. In addition, the agreement's signatories "reaffirmed their commitment to the total disarmament of all paramilitary organizations". However, the issue of the decommissioning of terrorist weaponry remained the most thorny part of the agreement, until the IRA's surprise announcement early in 2000 (see p.803).

On May 22, 1998, the people of Northern Ireland took part in a **referendum** on the agreement while, simultaneously, the people of the Republic voted on the proposal to amend the Irish constitution. There were strong divisions within the Unionist camp with both Ian Paisley's DUP and Robert McCartney's United Kingdom Unionist Party (a body which seemed largely to consist of Mr McCartney himself) urging opposition to any potential loosening of the bonds with the United Kingdom. The turnout in the North was an unprecedented 81 percent, of whom 71.12 percent supported the settlement, enough to suggest that Trimble had been backed by a majority of Unionist voters. Though the Republic's turnout was lower, a massive 94.4 percent ratified the deal. In the consequent Assembly elections in June, enough pro-Agreement Ulster Unionists and Progressive Unionists were returned to guarantee Trimble a working majority over dissident Unionist parties, while the SDLP and Sinn Féin both received handsome support. For the first time since 1972, Northern Ireland had its own form of government and, for the first time ever, one that largely represented the composition of the electorate. **David Trimble** was elected its **First Minister** and the SDLP's **Seamus Mallon** his **deputy**.

Drumcree and Omagh

The first test for the new political order in Northern Ireland came in July 1998, the traditional climax of the Orange Order's marching season. Since 1995, the Orangemen's march on the Sunday before the "Glorious 12th", commemorating victory at the Battle of the Boyne, from **Drumcree church** to its lodge in Portadown, County Armagh, via the predominantly Catholic Garvaghy Road, had become a focus for the assertion of traditional Unionist rights and identity. The **July 1998 parade** took on extra significance in the light of the peace agreement and the asserted intention of many dissident Unionists to embody the spirit of their opposition in the march. However, when the march was banned by the Parades Commission, Orangemen reacted by employing a strategy of brinkmanship, calling Unionists and Loyalists from all over Northern Ireland to assemble at Portadown, knowing full well that the RUC and army had already set up blockades to prevent them marching down the Garvaghy Road. Mass demonstrations at the barricades inspired an astonishing wave of violence throughout Northern Ireland. There were numerous attacks on Catholics and their property and, much to the horror of more conservative Unionists, on members of the RUC itself. Then a tragic event in County Antrim led to many Orangemen abandoning their protest. Early in the morning of July 12, the home of Chrissie Quinn, a Catholic woman living on the mainly Protestant Carmany estate in Ballymoney, County Antrim was firebombed. In the resulting conflagration, three of her four young sons were burned to death. Condemnation of this outrage brought to the boil divisions within the Orange Order which had already been simmering over the tactics employed at Drumcree. The Church of Ireland refused the Order permission to camp on its land and the demonstration gradually fizzled out, leaving residual questions about the continued relevance of the Orange Order to the new Northern Ireland.

Many hoped that the tragic deaths of the Quinn children in Ballymoney would be the last politically motivated killings in Northern Ireland, but this illusion was shattered by events on Saturday, August 15, 1998 in the County Tyrone town of **Omagh**. A dissident Republican group calling itself the **Real IRA** had embarked upon a campaign of town-centre bombings to express its opposition to the Good Friday Agreement and jeopardize continued Republican involvement in the peace process. Misleading telephone warnings led the RUC to evacuate people to the very area where a bomb had been planted, and 29 people were killed and hundreds injured when the device exploded. It was the worst single atrocity in the entire thirty years of conflict in Northern Ireland. Politicians acted frantically to deter a Loyalist backlash, but were aided by an unprecedented statement by Gerry Adams who, visiting Omagh, declared his unequivocal condemnation of the bombing. Both Irish and British governments announced their intention of strengthening existing legislation against terrorism and, two weeks later, the Real IRA declared a ceasefire.

The Real IRA's announcement helped to ease the tension surrounding the historic first **face-to-face meeting** between David Trimble and Gerry Adams at the beginning of September 1998. They may have stopped short of shaking hands, but their very contact demonstrated just how much progress had been made towards a lasting settlement. The international community's recognition of this came in October 1998 with the award of the **Nobel Peace Prize** to Trimble and John Hume.

The Assembly and the IRA Statement

Most of 1999 passed quietly in the wake of the Omagh bombing, as politicians prepared for the opening of the Assembly while paramilitaries maintained their ceasefires (with the exception of the small breakaway Continuity IRA which had never declared one). However, while general optimism remained in place, the ramifications of the implementation of parts of the Good Friday Agreement became apparent. Army numbers were reduced and many of their security installations, including some notable Belfast landmarks, were demolished or removed. However, the two key issues, interrelated in the eyes of many Unionists, were the release of political prisoners and the decommissioning of weaponry.

Around the turn of the year, David Trimble found himself conducting two acts of political brinkmanship, first persuading his party to vote narrowly in favour of participation in the Assembly (but only until the end of February 2000, if the IRA had not announced its decommissioning plans) and, secondly, just defeating a leadership challenge from the Rev Martin Smyth, an anti-Agreement Unionist. The UUP's concerns were further exacerbated by the report of the **Patten Commission** into the future of the **Royal Ulster Constabulary**. Chaired by the former Tory minister, Chris Patten, who, in his role as governor of Hong Kong, had overseen the protectorate's return to China, the report astonished Unionists by proposing the RUC's abolition and replacement by a body called the Police Service of Northern Ireland which would recruit its members equally from both Catholic and Loyalist communities. The loss of the words "Royal" and "Ulster" from the new organization's title were impossible for Unionists to accept, and the new secretary of state, **Peter Mandelson** (who had replaced Mo Mowlam), bowed to pressure by rejecting many of the Commission's findings, despite strong Nationalist and Republican protest.

The Assembly began functioning on December 1, 1999 and Sinn Féin's two ministers took up their executive positions, most notably, Martin McGuinness as the new education minister, an appointment which alarmed Unionists. Their concern did not persist for long, however, as the row over decommissioning boiled over in early 2000 and Mandelson suspended the Assembly after a mere few months in operation. Sinn Féin's leadership was aghast at this new development, arguing that, as a political party, it had met all the conditions of the Good Friday Agreement and had no powers over decommissioning. Many now worried for the future of devolution, fearing that this apparent dead end in the political process would see many IRA members defecting to the increasingly active Real IRA, based on the belief that the Adams-McGuinness strategy for political progress had been a mistake. If Gerry Adams could not persuade the IRA to decommission, they reasoned, then nobody could, while the absence from the political arena of John Hume, who had fallen seriously ill the previous Christmas, represented another significant vacuum.

As Mandelson resumed the mantle of power in Northern Ireland, the next two months saw last-ditch attempts to save the agreement. While the process saw Adams and McGuinness invited by Tony Blair for talks at Chequers, his weekend residence, attention focused increasingly on the key figure of John Taylor, deputy leader of the Ulster Unionists, whose continued support for Trimble was essential if devolution were to remain a reality. Yet, suddenly, on May 6, 2000 came an event which even the most hardened participants in Northern Ireland's political roller-coaster ride would have found hard to predict. It came in the unexpected form of **a statement from the leadership of the IRA** which, while not renouncing its avowed aim of securing a united Ireland, declared its continued commitment to the peace process. While this itself was of extreme significance, another part of the statement immediately changed the whole context of political debate in Northern Ireland by declaring that "the IRA leadership will initiate a process that will completely and verifiably put IRA arms beyond use". A number of its arms dumps were to be sealed and inspected by agreed third parties, and the IRA had already identified its two favoured inspectors, Cyril Ramaphosa (former secretary-general of the African National Congress) and the ex-president of Finland, Martti Ahtisaari. The IRA's statement had not so much moved the decommissioning goal posts, but marked out an entirely new pitch.

Unionism's troubled waters had still to be calmed, however, and efforts now concentrated on securing backing for the acceptance of the IRA's proposals. The DUP had no intention of doing so, but David Trimble was successful in persuading the Ulster Unionists' ruling council to comply. Devolution was now back in business and the Assembly was reinstated, despite the renewed efforts of the Real IRA to undermine Republican faith in the process. Their campaign, allegedly co-ordinated from Dundalk in the Republic by the Provisional IRA's ex-quartermaster, set out to prove that the armed struggle was not over, and their most notable success was the bombing of

Hammersmith Bridge in London – a target selected simply because the IRA's own bomb, a few years previously, had failed to detonate. Later that year, in September, in a grim reminder of its prowess, the Real IRA mortared an RUC station in Armagh and bombed an Army training camp at Magilligan, County Derry, at the very time that the inquest into the Omagh bombing was in session.

Loyalist marching remained a contentious issue. The 2000 Drumcree parade saw opponents of the agreement determined to make a stand, both within the Orange Order and beyond. Yet again, permission to march down the Garvaghy Road was refused by the Parades Commission and once more barricades were mounted by the RUC, bolstered by a huge British Army presence. Observers were concerned to see many Loyalist paramilitaries present at the protest, most notably the recently released leader of the UDA, **Johnny Adair**. However, while order was largely maintained, subsequent months in Northern Ireland were characterized by a formidable **feud between Loyalist paramilitary groups**. The UDA, joined by the closely linked UFF, embarked on a campaign against its rival, the UVF, which included murder, arson, reprisals and the wounding of an eleven-year-old girl in Coleraine. The battle precipitated an increased army presence in areas such as the Falls Road, in Belfast, and the return to incarceration of Johnny Adair, the first released political prisoner to be sent back to his cell.

At the end of 2000 John Hume stepped down from the leadership of the SDLP (to be subsequently replaced by Mark Durkan), while January 2001 saw not only a Real IRA mortar attack on an army post in Derry but also the resignation of Peter Mandelson over his alleged role in the Hinduja passport affair in London. John Reid, the first Catholic to hold the post, was appointed his successor. Trimble meanwhile continued to demand total IRA disarmament – the Real IRA's reaction was to explode a bomb outside the BBC Television Centre in West London in March and further bombs in Post Office depots in the city over the following months.

A new sectarian feud commenced in June 2001 when the RUC had to protect parents and young children from attack as they tried to enter the Catholic Holy Cross Girls' School in North Belfast. The **Loyalist blockade** of the route to the school continued until the end of the month and was reinitiated when term began again in September and continued until late November. While TV footage of adults hurling sectarian abuse at children as young as four years of age did nothing for the Loyalist cause, the area remained a significant flashpoint for trouble throughout the period of the blockade.

On July 1, 2001, **David Trimble resigned** as First Minister over the IRA's lack of movement on disarmament, immediately leading to John Reid's announcement of a decision to suspend the Assembly, though this was a tactical device to allow further discussions about the future of the Good Friday Agreement to take place. July 12 saw the worst rioting for many years in Belfast with a senior RUC officer claiming that the IRA had orchestrated violence against Orange Order parades in the Ardoyne area of North Belfast. An implementation plan, published on August 1 and jointly produced by the British and Irish governments, addressed the remaining issues of the agreement – the Real IRA responded by setting off a car bomb in the London suburb of Ealing the following day. Shortly afterwards, the head of the Independent International Committee on Decommissioning, General John de Chastelain, announced that the IRA had made an acceptable proposal to put its arms "completely and verifiably beyond use". The UUP responded by rejecting both the implementation plan and the IRA statement.

An event of increasingly vital significance occurred in August 2001 when three Irishmen were arrested at Bogota airport in Columbia for travelling on false documents. Allegations then surfaced that the three were members of the IRA who had been training Columbian left-wing guerrillas in weaponry. At the time of writing, the trio are still in jail in Columbia awaiting the conclusion of their trial. Equally significant at the time was the fact that the IRA rescinded its plan to put its weapons out of use. However, after pressure from Gerry Adams and Martin McGuinness, it announced in October 2001 that it had in fact reverted to its original plan and had begun decommissioning its weaponry. This ultimately led to the re-establishment of the Assembly, though because of splits in his own party, David Trimble only secured the position of First Minister through the actions of the moderate Alliance Party.

The new **Police Service of Northern Ireland** (PSNI), replacing the RUC, came into existence in November 2001 while the remainder of the year was dominated by the Police Ombudsman's report on the Omagh bombing in which Nuala O'Loan described serious misgivings concerning the RUC's handling of the affair – an inquiry has subsequently been established.

January 2002 saw anti-sectarian **rallies** taking place in a number of towns and cities in the North in response to increasing levels of violence, especially in North Belfast while a rally was also held in Belfast to commemorate the thirtieth anniversary of Bloody Sunday (the inquiry into whose events still continues at the time of writing; see p.796). In March, David Trimble gave a speech to the Ulster Unionist Council in which he described the Republic of Ireland as a "pathetic sectarian, mono-ethnic, mono-cultural state", calling at the same time for a referendum to be held on the question of a united Ireland.

The remaining months of 2002 witnessed **increased violence** in a number of areas – most notably the Ardoyne and Short Strand districts of Belfast – and further Unionist pressure upon Trimble to withdraw from government, protagonists of this view arguing that Unionists should not sit with Sinn Féin in the Assembly while there was little significant evidence of the IRA undertaking its promised decommissioning. Matters came to a head when several Republicans were arrested in connection with papers stolen from the **Castlereagh** police station and then, in October, when four members of the Sinn Féin staff at Stormont were arrested in connection with an alleged spy ring. Secretary of State John Reid once again suspended the Assembly while the IRA reacted once more by withdrawing its proposals. In a British Cabinet reshuffle in November Paul Murphy replaced Reid, becoming the first Irish Catholic to hold the post. The future, however, remains utterly uncertain, a situation that has characterized Northern Ireland's politics for the last thirty years or so.

Environment and wildlife

Ireland conjures up images of a romantic wild territory unscarred by human activity – a somewhat rosy picture, but with more than a little truth to it. Genuine wilderness may be scarce, but centuries of economic deprivation have ensured that much of Ireland is a rural landscape in which the only intervention has come from generations of farmers.

The topography of Ireland is fairly homogenous: there are few high mountain ranges and most of the centre of the country is covered by a flat boggy plain. And with only four degrees of latitude from north to south, it lacks extremes of weather, the enveloping Atlantic Ocean producing a mild, damp climate. Summers are rarely hot, winters rarely cold, and in parts of the west it rains on two days out of every three.

In these conditions you'd expect to find broad-leaved woodland, but intensive pressure on the landscape during the centuries leading up to the Famine of 1845 to 1849 denuded the country of its original tree cover. It has been replaced mostly by a patchwork of small grass fields divided by wild untidy hedgerows – long lines of trees acting as refuges for the former woodland community of plants and animals. The small population in Ireland today means that over much of the country the intensity of land use is lower than in many other European countries. Mixed farms are still more common than specialized intensive units.

Natural habitats such as peat bogs, dunes and wetlands still survive here, having all but disappeared elsewhere under the relentless pace of modern development. However, the pressures are growing: the great midland bogs are being rapidly stripped for fuel; mountainsides are disappearing under blankets of exotic conifers; shoals of dead fish are becoming all too frequent a sight in Irish waterways; and rapid housing developments threaten some of Ireland's most valuable habitats, most notably in coastal regions.

Flora

Certainly for anyone travelling from Britain only a few of the common species in Ireland are going to be unfamiliar, and on the whole it is in the sheer **abundance of habitats** in which the interest lies, rather than any particularly unusual plants. The flowers of the Irish countryside are impressive perhaps more in their profusion than in their variety.

Woodlands

At one time Ireland was covered in oakwoods. This great forest canopy also included elm and alder, and holly grew beneath the tall trees. The first major clearances of woodlands were in the late Stone Age (5000 years ago), but vast areas of forest survived well into the medieval period. By the eighteenth century felling for housing, shipping and smelting had been so extensive that wood actually started to be imported. Today only six percent of Ireland is woodland (the lowest percentage of any European country), and afforestation in recent decades has tended to be coniferous, doing immense damage to natural habitats. As a result, **indigenous oak forests** are extremely rare, though good examples can still be seen at Glengarriff and in the National Parks at Killarney and Glenveagh.

Throughout the country strong westerly winds keep the treeline low (about 150m in the west to 350m in the east) and small trees growing diagonally towards the east as if swept by one almighty blast are a common sight in exposed areas, particularly in the west. The limited range of flowers found in forests includes **foxgloves**, **violets** and **primroses** – this last growing in abundance, and flowering from March to May.

Bogs and other wetlands

Bogs – or peatland – cover around one-sixth of Ireland's total landmass, a proportion in Europe topped only by Finland. Now that they have been recognized internationally as providing habitats of great ecological value, considerable progress has been made in the conservation of blanket bogs, but there's no room for complacency.

Bogs have formed over the last 10,000 years: at the end of the last Ice Age retreating glaciers and ice sheets left central Ireland covered by shallow lakes that filled with vegetation, which then dried and partly decomposed. Today they form a remarkable legacy, not only in terms of biodiversity, but also as a living repository of cultural history. The bog is a great natural preservative, and as well as providing botanists with a calendar of plant history over the past nine thousand years, it has bequeathed a great deal to archaeologists – dugout canoes, gold and silver artefacts, shoes, amber beads and, of course, bodies in extraordinarily good condition. Bog pools were revered during the Bronze Age, and votive offerings such as weapons and ornaments placed there. The Iron Age saw the construction of *tochair*, or wooden pathways, to cross the bog, and these too have been discovered.

The **exploitation of bogs** has been going on for centuries. Dried peat sods have always been used for fuel; the top layer of matted vegetation was once used to insulate thatched roofs; preserved timbers dug from the bog – some of them 5000 years old – provided lintels; and the lime-rich marl below the peat was used to fertilize the land. Bogs have a unique place in folk history too and the annual ritual of "saving the turf" is well represented in stories, poetry and song, carrying with it traditions as strong as any other form of harvest.

Blanket bogs are characterized by a layer of peat between two and six metres thick spreading over large areas of land, and are found in both low-lying and mountainous areas. Connemara, Mayo and Donegal provide particularly dramatic landscapes, with huge expanses of open countryside, wild, treeless and exposed, and blanket bogs are also found in Cork, Kerry and the Wicklow Mountains. But it's the Slieve Bloom Mountains, straddling counties Laois and Offaly, which offer the finest examples of relatively undamaged blanket bog, and the two mountain roads that divide the range rise to 1300ft, with wonderful views in every direction. Somewhat smaller, and favoured by commercial operators, **raised bogs** are found in the central lowlands, domed in shape, with an average peat layer of seven metres, though they can develop to nearly twice that. To see a raised bog of international importance, go to Mongan Bog in County Offaly.

Bogs support a range of **plant life**: black bog rush, purple moor grass, sphagnum mosses and milkwort are all commonly found on blanket bogs. On raised bogs you are likely to find bog cotton, sphagnum moss, sundew, ling heather, cranberry and cladonia lichen. **Peatland World**, nearby in Lullymore, County Kildare, provides an excellent introduction to Irish bogs (see p.270).

Fens are found in waterlogged areas and lakesides and are different to blanket and raised bogs in that the layer of peat is only about two metres deep and plants are fed by mineral-rich water as opposed to just rainwater. Pollardstown Fen, two miles northeast of Newbridge, is a fine expanse of fen. The **plant life** in fens includes fen rush, bog bean, saw sedge and pond weed. Fens also support various **orchids**, particularly marsh helleborine and the marsh orchid, and the **marsh marigold** and **flag iris** are both fairly common.

Alongside many rivers are **callows** – areas of meadow which are flooded during periods of high rainfall, producing nutrient-rich soil where **herbs** such as **meadowsweet**, **loosestrife** and **marsh pea** thrive.

Turloughs, found most readily in the Burren of County Clare, are hollows which appear as meadows for most of the year, but become lakes after flooding. Generally found in areas of limestone, they support a range of grasses, but you may also find cinquefoil, creeping buttercup and various sedges.

The West

County Kerry and the peninsulas of west Cork benefit from a damp climate which, because of the Gulf Stream, is far warmer than elsewhere in the country. Consequently it's here that you'll find Ireland's limited number of fairly exotic plant species, including palm trees, the Mediterranean **strawberry tree** (or arbutus) and very rare Lusitanian plants including Irish spurge and **St Patrick's Cabbage**, the latter found nowhere else in Europe. In the valleys of Killarney National Park you can also see **holly** and **rowan trees**, and common on the mountainsides are various heathers, forming a beautiful purple cloak when in bloom in September. Hedgerows throughout the southwest are commonly full of the brilliant purple-red bulbs of **fuschia**, and musky-scented **honeysuckle** clambers over walls and hedges. A shock of bright orange **mont bretia** is a common sight along many quiet laneways in the west, as are the dramatic pink spears of foxgloves that grow throughout the country. Other species which you may come across include the Kerry butterwort, the Kerry lily and occasionally Cornish moneywort.

The karst region called **the Burren** in County Clare forms an extraordinary landscape (see also p.439). From a distance its virtually treeless slopes appear completely barren, but the long cracks and grooves in the limestone support and shelter an astonishing array of both **Alpine**, **Mediterranean** and **Arctic plants**: hart's tongue and maidenhair ferns grow well, and the profusion of wild flowers include the blue spring gentian and mountain avens, saxifrages and a number of orchid species; the best times to visit are spring and early summer.

Further north, the mountains of Connemara have a somewhat colder climate and here the plant life is more spartan, but you will find **St Dabeoc's heath** and, in the west of the region, wild **London pride**.

In some counties, notably Donegal, Mayo and Kerry there are extensive **sand dunes**. In summer these are clothed in a profusion of wild flowers such as the yellow **bird's-foot trefoil** and pink sea bindweed. Prickly leafed sea-holly, sea-pansy and kidney vetch are common, and the exotic-looking **bee orchid** is one of the rarities sometimes found in the dunes. Sea pinks thrive on cliffs and in sandy places, and on coastal cliffs in Donegal you will find wild lovage and dwarf willow. The shoreline is always worth exploring for the splendid varieties of **seaweed** that flourish, including kelp, bladderwrack and thong weed.

Mammals

Ireland, like many islands, has a relatively small number of mammal species; besides its famous lack of snakes, there are no moles, for example. However, the largely undeveloped landscapes mean that there are plenty of opportunities for observing mammals in the wild, particularly in remote areas.

The coasts

Ireland's **marine life** is particularly impressive. The remoteness of the islands off the west coast makes them havens for wildlife: **grey seals** breed on island beaches and in caves during the autumn months. Due to lack of disturbance, nocturnal animals like **otters** can be seen during daylight, hunting for food among rocks and pools. Herds of **common seals** can be seen basking on sand banks in numerous locations all around the coast, especially in the west and at Strangford Lough in the northeast, where there are literally hundreds of them in late June when the new pups are born.

Patient sea-watching from a western headland may also be rewarded with a school of **dolphins** or porpoises, or the occasional **whale** feeding in the rich inshore waters. Whales might also be seen off the east coast of the Ards Peninsula, and if you're lucky you may see basking sharks.

Inland

Inland there's far less of interest. Small mammals include both grey and red squirrels in Ireland's diminished woodlands; stoats, rabbits and foxes are common, as is the pygmy shrew, and the **Irish hare** is a wonderful sight spotted from time to time running across huge areas of bog. You may well see **badgers** late at night scuttling along a country lane away from car headlamps. The rare **pine marten**, a furry brown weasel-like creature with cream markings on its throat and ears, is occasionally sighted darting amongst the rocks of the Burren in County Clare, near low hazel scrub.

Around a quarter of all land mammals in Ireland are **bats**, which tend to roost in undisturbed buildings, old trees and the cracks of old stone bridges, certain species moving to underground sites such as caves and cellars during the winter months. Bats can be spotted at night as they flit through the air hunting for insects, and are especially easy to see when flying low over water.

The only mammals of any size that you are likely to encounter are wild **goats**, which generally keep to remote hillsides – though on occasion they have been known to explore Mayo villages – and herds of **red deer**, which roam in the remote valleys of the Glenveagh National Park.

Birds

What Ireland may lack in mammals it more than makes up for in bird life. The spectacular coastline provides superb opportunities for spotting seabirds and, in season, flocks of migrating species. There's interest inland too, with wetlands providing largely undisturbed habitats for a great range of water birds and mountainous areas harbouring birds of prey.

The coasts

Ireland has over two thousand miles of **coast**, most of it undeveloped, and hundreds of **islands**, providing an environment that sustains a rich diversity of birds. It's the wild coasts of the west and the north that have the most dramatic scenic appeal and it's here you'll find some of the best opportunities for observing **seabirds**.

Kerry has Ireland's largest concentration: the Blasket Islands, the Skelligs and Puffin Island are home to impressive colonies of puffins, and Little Skellig is also home to around twenty thousand pairs of gannets, a fabulous sight as they dive for food from heights of around 120ft. Kerry's islands also have a great number of Manx shearwaters and the world's largest colonies of stormy petrels.

Clear Island, off the west Cork coast, has an important observatory recording the patterns of **migratory birds**, and here you can see huge numbers of Manx shearwaters, particularly during July and August. Other species in abundance include stormy petrels, gannets, cormorants, fulmars and kittiwakes.

In the southeast the Wexford Slobs are the wintering ground for around ten thousand Greenland white-fronted geese – over a third of the world population – and along with these there are mute and Bewick swans, godwits, oystercatchers and coots. At Tacumshane Lake further south wintering wildfowl include brent geese and scaups.

A trip to the bird sanctuary on the Saltee Islands off the Wexford coast, especially in late spring or early summer, is rewarded with the sight of puffins, razorbills, cormorants, auks and kittiwakes. The nearby Hook Head Peninsula also makes an exhilarating spot from which to observe migrating seabirds in spring and autumn.

In the northeast, Strangford Lough has all the characteristics of a marine environment, despite the fact that its opening to the sea is extremely narrow. It's most famous as a wintering ground for migrating birds: the annual arrival of the pale-bellied brent geese from Arctic Canada is expected in late August and by the end of October their population can reach twelve thousand. The sheer variety of bird life on the lough is stupendous: Icelandic whooper swans, wigeon, pintail and shoveler are all common here, and overwintering waders include golden plovers and oystercatchers. In the summer huge numbers of terns arrive from their winter residences in Africa.

The spectacular cliffs of Horn Head, County Donegal, has Ireland's largest colony of razorbills, and the magnificent Antrim coast offers excellent opportunities for observing **cliff-breeding birds**, especially at Rathlin Island with its colonies of fulmars, guillemots, puffins, kittiwakes and Manx shearwaters.

Ireland's low coasts, especially to the east and south, are punctuated by estuaries, some with vast, lonely mudflats. Despite their bare appearance, below the surface they harbour countless shellfish and other burrowing animals, attracting feeding **waders** and **wildfowl**. From October to April the estuaries are alive with the calls of curlews, redshanks, godwits, widgeon, teal and shoveler.

Ireland's absence of tree cover means few breeding birds, but cuckoos are a special feature of Irish sand dunes, as they exploit the nests of the ubiquitous meadow pipits. The chough, a comparatively rare crow, breeds extensively on the south and west coasts and can be seen in large flocks feeding in sand-dune systems.

Wetlands

Travellers in the midlands and west of Ireland will encounter numerous small lakes and reed-fringed marshes. High rainfall and poor drainage ensure

Useful contacts

ENFO 17 St Andrew Street, Dublin 2 ☎01/679 3144.
Invaluable resource centre for information on environmental issues and campaign groups in the Republic; personal visits welcome, and a wealth of literature available.

Northern Irish Tourist Board 59 North Street, Belfast, BT1 1NB ☎028/9024 6609.
Detailed information on birdwatching in Northern Ireland.

plentiful surface water, especially in winter, and breeding **water birds** are extremely common as a result. Every waterway has its resident pair of swans, moorhens and herons. Wetlands of international importance include Lough Neagh, which supports a dozen species of duck, large numbers of Bewick and whooper swans, terns and grebes, and the **Shannon Callows** near Clonmacnois, where in late summer you can listen for corncrakes as they search for mates. For Ireland's biggest corncrake population, however, you will need to travel to Inishowen – and most particularly Malin Head.

Mountains

Mountainous regions provide rocky crags and cliffs for **birds of prey**: the little-visited Sperrin Mountains are noted for buzzards, hen harriers and sparrowhawks, and both here and in the Mourne Mountains you can see peregrine falcons and kestrels. In the uplands of the Wicklow Mountains hen harriers are easily sighted, and other species include ouzel and red grouse, typical of heather-clad moorland. The wild mountains of Cork were Ireland's last habitat for golden eagles, but today you can still see merlins and sparrowhawks.

Architecture

Despite the predominantly rural character of Ireland outside the major cities you will find that the landscape bears the rich patina of a complex architectural inheritance. In Dublin and Belfast, confidence and prosperity, born of the extraordinary economic boom of the 1990s has given rise to a new adventurousness in building projects, both public and private.

Beginnings

The most tangible legacy left by the inhabitants of prehistoric Ireland are the numerous stone tombs, found throughout the country. The earliest of these date from the Neolithic period (3700–2000 BC) and the simplest form is the **dolmen**. Resembling a tripod, this is usually formed by several standing stones supporting one or two capstones, the largest of which can be as much as 20ft long. While these simply marked a grave, the **court-cairn** was more complex, consisting of a rectangular burial chamber, again built with large stones, and covered by a mound of earth. Conceptually similar, though most advanced of all, however, are the **passage tombs**, of which the best-known examples are clustered near Drogheda, in the valley of the River Boyne, at Newgrange, Howth and Dowth. As the name suggests, a passage from the edge of the mound provides access to one or two burial chambers. The **Newgrange** grave is positioned inside a circle of standing stones; its 280-foot-diameter mound is almost 35ft high and the passage is 60ft long. The burial chamber's roof shows its builders' grasp of the technique of corbelling where layers of flat stones are placed on top of each other, each layer projecting gradually outwards below the next. Most striking here, however, is that an opening in the stonework was created to allow sunlight to penetrate the tomb on the winter solstice, December 21, the shortest day of the year, evidence of a society sophisticated in its understanding of the calendar.

The **Bronze Age** (2000–500 BC) saw further tomb building, though the constructions were generally smaller. Most tombs surviving from this period were plain compartments of stone, though some more elaborate chambers were covered by a wedge-shaped mound. Domestic structures are thought to have been constructed of wood and daub and the most significant development, circular fortified enclosures built on hilltops, came towards the end of the period. However, the finest examples of these **hill forts** date from the **Iron Age**. The huge fortress of **Dún Aengus** on the Aran Island of Inishmore sits spectacularly on the cliff-top, while the partially restored **Grianán of Aileach**, near Derry, affords staggering views down to Inishowen and for miles around in all directions. There is evidence of many other smaller ring forts, built of stone or earth, which were probably fortified dwellings. The Iron Age also saw the building of **crannógs**, artificial islands, set in defensive isolation in the middle of lakes.

Early Christian and Medieval period

Christianity arrived in Ireland in the fifth century and, consequently, most of the architectural remains from this period until medieval times are **ecclesiastical**. Ireland was divided into bishoprics which resulted in a system of scattered monasteries. Most buildings were constructed of wood and daub and none, whether religious or domestic, has survived. The stone churches you now see when visiting early monastic sites were constructed during a later era. However, among the ruins of **St Fionan's Abbey** on the rocky crag of Skellig Michael off the Kerry coast is a group of six dry-stone beehive huts, built according to the corbel technique. **Stone churches** began to be built in the ninth century, and an exceptional example dating from this time is **Gallarus Oratory** on the Dingle Peninsula, which represents a transition from the round beehive shape to the later rectangular church. The remains of **round towers** are often found on early monastic sites. These slender, stone, tapering structures, sometimes more than 100ft high, are a specifically Irish phenomenon. The entrance is usually several feet above ground level and it is believed that this signified a defensive purpose. However, others claim that they were used as bell towers and the doorway's elevation was a question of engineering, designed to ensure that the structure had a strong and stable base. One of the best-preserved towers is part of the St Molaise monastic complex on **Devenish Island** in Lower Lough Erne, near Enniskillen, County Fermanagh.

Increasing contact with England and continental Europe saw the introduction of the highly decorative **Romanesque** style to Irish ecclesiastical architecture from the twelfth century onwards. Built between 1127 and 1134, the beautiful, twin-towered **Cormac's Chapel** in Cashel, County Tipperary is the earliest and best surviving example, though much smaller in scale than its European counterparts. Gradually, the simple box style of church architecture began to be superseded by the **basilica** style, characterized by a nave, side aisles and a round apse at the eastern end. Often, church doorways and chancel arches were decorated with intricate sculpture using traditional Celtic motifs, such as interlacing and animal patterns, seen to tremendous effect in the wonderful six-arched doorway of **Clonfert Cathedral**, County Galway.

Further changes resulted from the arrival of monastic orders, such as the Cistercians, Dominicans and Benedictines. They favoured large cruciform churches, and their settlements, typified by the Cistercian **Boyle Abbey**, County Roscommon, were very European in their layout of a cloister surrounded by church, chapter house and domestic buildings.

Much of Ireland was under **Norman** subjugation by the end of the twelfth century and the invaders constructed fortifications to protect their new domains. The earliest of these were earthworks surmounted by wooden forts. However, soon more substantial **stone castles**, distinguished by a massive keep, began to be constructed, such as those at **Carrickfergus**, County Antrim and **Trim**, County Meath. The fifteenth-century castle at **Cahir** in County Tipperary, surrounded by high enclosing walls and defended by eight towers, is the most impressive of the surviving feudal strongholds.

Simultaneously, the Anglo-Normans, as they came to be known, introduced **Gothic** architecture to Ireland. The huge new **cathedrals**, constructed in the main towns, were characterized by high-pointed arches and clustered columns.

Dublin's two thirteenth-century cathedrals, **St Patrick's** and **Christ Church**, are among the finest examples of this innovation.

Later Anglo-Norman fortifications tended to be smaller in size, typified by the **tower houses** which began to be constructed during the fifteenth century and continued to be built over the next two hundred years. There are the remains of hundreds of these rectangular, fortified multistorey residences across the island, several in relatively close proximity and varying states of ruin around **Strangford Lough**, County Down. In the west, two such houses which have been restored and are open to the public are elaborate **Bunratty Castle**, County Clare and the sixteenth-century **Dunguaire Castle**, County Galway.

The seventeenth and eighteenth centuries

Few purely domestic residences constructed before the **seventeenth century** have survived. One such, **Rothe House** in Kilkenny, built in 1594, is a unique example of an Irish merchant's home from the prosperous Tudor period and is now open as a museum. Most domestic buildings from the seventeenth century show some evidence of fortification, reflecting a turbulent time in Irish history. The first **unfortified mansion** is claimed to be **Beaulieu House**, County Louth, built in the 1660s following Cromwell's departure. A red-brick, hipped-roof dwelling, it closely follows the **Dutch style** popular in contemporary England. This century also saw the first **thatched cottages**, constructed of clay, whitewashed both inside and out, and consisting of merely one or two rooms poorly illuminated by small windows. Though these may have suited the damp Irish climate, the humble conditions reflected the continuation of a repressively feudal social system in which the rights of the landlord held sway.

Classical buildings began to appear in Ireland in the late seventeenth century, the finest example of this period being the **Royal Hospital Kilmainham**, Dublin, built between 1680 and 1687. It was designed by Sir William Robinson who used as his model Les Invalides in Paris, the home for retired soldiers. The building's core is an arcaded courtyard around which are ranged a great hall and chapel on one side and living quarters on the other three. During the 1980s, the then derelict building was fully restored at a cost of £20 million and reopened in 1991 as the Irish Museum of Modern Art.

The following century witnessed massive developments in public and private building. The Irish ruling class, known sometimes as the Protestant Ascendancy, drew its prosperity in part from lands granted or acquired during the 1600s and consolidated its position on them through the construction of mansions. The presence of an Irish Parliament in Dublin, though still subject to Westminster, gave the city a new confidence, and evidence of its consequent wealth is present in the many fine public buildings and elegant squares that still exist today. The Ascendancy's dominance was reinforced through the enactment of the repressive penal laws which prevented Catholics from holding public office, owning property or practising their religion. As a result, hardly a Catholic church was constructed during this period, though a notable example is the South Parish Church in Cork, built in 1766.

The architectural style favoured by the Ascendancy was influenced by the work and publications of the sixteenth-century Italian architect, Andrea

Palladio. Equally popular in England, **Palladian** designs first appeared in Ireland in the 1720s and the largest and most palatial Palladian country house is **Castletown** in County Kildare, completed in 1732 and designed by Alessandro Galilei and Sir Edward Lovett Pearce. Elsewhere, the Palladian style was utilized in the construction of simpler houses built as much for utility as for ostentation, such as **Hazelwood**, County Sligo and **Ledwithstown**, County Longford. Pearce was also responsible for the design of the great **Parliament House** (now the Bank of Ireland) in Dublin's College Green, constructed between 1729 and 1739. It is the earliest large-scale Palladian public building in all of Ireland and England, and the model, a century later, for the British Museum in London. Another notable architect of the period was the German, Richard Cassels, responsible for **Leinster House** (1745), commissioned as a town house for the Dukes of Leinster, and now the seat of the Dáil.

Towards the end of the eighteenth century, **Neoclassicism** became the prevailing architectural style, taking ancient Greece and Rome as even more direct influences than its predecessor. A refined Neoclassical creation is the **Casino** at Marino, just northeast of Dublin, designed during the 1760s by Sir William Chambers as a country house for Lord Charlemont. **Castle Coole**, near Enniskillen, County Fermanagh, was designed by James Wyatt and is unarguably the best Neoclassical house in Ireland. The house is now owned by the British National Trust and has been lavishly restored.

The great architect of this period was undoubtedly **James Gandon** (1743–1823) who designed some of the most important public buildings in Dublin, including the **Custom House** and the **Four Courts**, both dating from the 1780s. Each building has an impressive columned riverside facade, topped by a magnificent dome.

Sadly, however, much of Ireland's Georgian architecture has vanished. As late as the 1950s, Dublin was still one of the most perfectly intact eighteenth-century cities in Europe, but much has since been lost (for more on this see p.92). Irish independence and the subsequent civil war led to a decline in the fortunes of the **Anglo-Irish Ascendancy**, resulting in the sale of many estates and **Big Houses**. Many of the houses themselves still lie in ruins following their destruction by a people who had long been repressed by a political system completely identified with their erstwhile owners. In recent years, however, there has been something approaching a *rapprochement* and the Anglo-Irish heritage is beginning to be seen as something inherently Irish. A good example of this change is **Strokestown Park House**, County Roscommon, an outstanding Palladian dwelling which has been meticulously restored by a local garage business and is now open to the public.

The nineteenth century

Although the Act of Union (1801) dissolved Ireland's independent government and diminished localized power and prosperity, architecture continued to flourish throughout the nineteenth century. Indeed the expansion in numbers of Irish-born members of the profession led to the establishment of the **Royal Institute of the Architects of Ireland** in 1839. At the same time, many English architects continued to be commissioned.

Perhaps feeling further isolated from their English contemporaries after Dublin ceased to be a centre of power, the Anglo-Irish Ascendancy embarked on a spate of building during the first few decades. Neoclassicism remained the predominant style, exemplified by such buildings as the **General Post Office** in Dublin's O'Connell Street, designed by Francis Johnston and completed in 1818, and William Morrison's **courthouse** in Carlow, dating from 1828.

The nineteenth century was also notable for the revival of the Gothic style, the catalyst for which was Catholic emancipation in 1829, leading to the construction of numerous **new churches**, influenced by the French style of slender towers and pointed spires surrounded by smaller pinnacles. Examples include **St Finbarr's Cathedral** in Cork and **St Colman's Cathedral**, Cobh, both begun in the 1860s. The similarly aged **Ashford Castle**, County Mayo demonstrates the adaptation of the Gothic style to domestic architecture. Elsewhere, there are many examples of the architectural eclecticism which characterized the nineteenth century. **St Mary's Pro-Cathedral** in Dublin, started in 1814, shows a marked **Greek Revival** influence, a style more often associated with large-scale public building. **Tudor** and **Oriental** styles were also popular and it was almost as though architects saw the rapid development of the **railway system** as an opportunity to test the limits of their imagination in the design of station buildings.

Towards the end of the century, the **Celtic revival**, associated with the Gaelic literary movement, had a limited impact on architectural design, most noticeably in church building. The favoured style was Hiberno-Romanesque and examples of its influence are visible in the design of the **Honan Chapel**, University College Cork, and **Spiddal Church**, County Galway.

To the present

A history of Ireland's twentieth-century architecture is as much about what has been lost as about what was built. Any post-colonial country necessarily inherits a complicated relation to its past, and buildings are one of the most tangible reminders of past eras. After independence in 1922, the country entered a state of dormancy, from which it has only begun to emerge in the last four decades. The great public buildings of the colonizer continued to function as intended under the new order. Country-house architecture fared badly with only a few hundred period houses left intact (see p.815), and Dublin's elaborate Georgian squares and domestic architecture have been vandalized as much by central government as by the property developers. The eminent English architectural historian Sir John Summerson was employed by the Electricity Supply Board in the 1960s to justify the demolition of a range of Georgian houses on Fitzwilliam Square, Dublin. Sir John said he believed that the interjection of some modern buildings would greatly relieve the monotony of red brick.

This is not to say that nothing notable was built between 1922 and 1960. The dominant influence during this period was **Art Deco**. While a restrained use of the style was invoked to good effect in the construction of institutions such as hospitals, it barely disguised their sombre debt to the workhouses of the mid-nineteenth century. As in the development of the visual arts, **modernism** reached Ireland relatively late in the twentieth century. Indeed, the first significant modern construction was the **Dublin Airport terminal**, designed by Desmond Fitzgerald, in 1940. One of the first postwar constructions to express this modernity with comfort was the **Busáras** station in Store Street, Dublin, which contains a theatre and was designed in 1953 by Michael Scott, later to become one of the leading exponents of modern architecture in Ireland.

The economic boom of the 1960s and 1970s saw considerable expansion in architecture, though the demands of industry paid little heed to the heritage of the past. Systematic and effective legislation preserving buildings and monuments presupposes a buoyant economy and a sort of uncomplicated approach to the past which had not developed. Innately conservative, Irish society had yet to discover any meaningful understanding of the importance of preservation and the rapid changes to the urban landscapes of Dublin and other cities took place without hindrance of debate or planning. For instance, it was only in the 1970s that **factory builders** began to consider the impact of such construction on the aesthetic nature of the local environment. Carroll's cigarette factory in Dundalk, designed by Ronald Tallon, is a worthy example of attractive development.

Similar modernist trends became visible in **school building**, for example, Birr School by Peter and Mary Doyle, built in 1980, which applied new designs to accommodate contemporary educational theory. The most significant work in **ecclesiastical architecture** has been undertaken by Liam McCormick from Derry, whose style is marked by a consideration of the natural landmarks which overshadow his projects. Fine examples of his church designs are to be found in the Donegal villages of Burt, Creeslough and Glenties.

The recession of the 1980s reduced building activity, and increasing worldwide awareness of environmental issues stimulated debate among architects about the cultivation of a new Irish architecture. Greater concerns for context and progressive town planning came to dominate new architectural theory. Postwar barbarism gradually became subsumed by desires to maintain the remnants of the country's built heritage, and considerable state funding was provided for the restoration of buildings such as the **Custom House**, **Dublin Castle**, the **Casino** at Marino and the **Royal Hospital Kilmainham**, which was converted into the Irish Museum of Modern Art.

The grim public housing style of the 1960s, deck-access low- and high-rise blocks, was abandoned in favour of schemes such as **City Quay**, Dublin, and **Share Housing** in Cork. These 1980s developments paid far greater attention to street pattern and context and set the template for future designs. Similarly, private housing has undergone radical changes, though the virtual absence of planning regulations has resulted in a blight of **bungalow construction** which mars the landscape all the way from Kerry to Donegal. Conversely, many rural areas are equally sullied by dilapidated properties which have been deliberately allowed to fall into ruin.

Sadly, Dublin's cityscape is also marred by far too many examples of retarded **modernist building**. One of the worst examples of this trend is the Civic Offices at Wood Quay. Commonly known as the "bunkers", these ugly structures are all the more offensive for being constructed on the most important early Viking archaeological site in Europe before it was fully excavated. In contrast, an especially fine example of the juxtaposition of old and modern buildings can be seen at New Square in Trinity College, Dublin.

Ireland has been the beneficiary of considerable funding since the 1970s, resulting from its membership of the European Union. At the same time, tax incentives have encouraged private investment in the redevelopment of rundown areas in the major urban centres and towns. As a direct consequence, the country has witnessed a building boom of a magnitude similar to the accelerated urban expansion of the eighteenth century. The most significant changes have again taken place in the city centres, most notably in the construction of massive new shopping centres and in adaptations of Ireland's industrial and commercial past. Redevelopment of the semi-derelict **Temple Bar** area of Dublin was the subject of a competition. Revitalized as Dublin's answer to Paris's Left Bank or London's Covent Garden, the streets have been cobbled and pedestrianized, public sculptures installed, and a host of cultural institutions and fashionable bars and shops occupy the restored or newly constructed premises. The gains are there for all to see, but the downside is that Dublin's appearance is edging nearer and nearer to that of any other European city.

Much state funding has also been directed towards tourism. Virtually every town now seems to have its own heritage or interpretive centre, no matter the level of justification. While existing buildings are, for the most part, converted to accommodate these attractions, several new buildings have been constructed. The Office of Public Works is at the forefront of this trend. Several large-scale interpretive centres have already been completed by them, including **Dunquin**, County Kerry and **Ceíde Fields**, County Mayo, and others have been developed through heritage funding, such as **Ardara**, County Donegal. The marketing of the past in the service of economic recovery has touched every country town. Fake timber shopfronts abound, creating an illusory but gentler version of the past, which has more to do with cultural stereotypes than with the grim historical realities of the subsistence of the majority of Irish people. The development of hotels and holiday homes has also become a contentious issue in small rural communities, with provision of accommodation for visitors for a couple of months of the year overriding social, aesthetic and ecological concerns.

Ireland is in the grip of a **property pricing boom** comparable to the worst excesses of London in the 1980s. The cost of housing in Dublin and the most popular tourist and holiday-home areas has risen to levels that prohibit all but the wealthiest from purchase. Though prices in the North remain relatively low, certain areas have also seen a dramatic escalation. Homelessness has become a way of life for some in the Republic, and there have been significant changes in the landscape, resulting from an apparently ever-broadening commuting range. Ugly new housing developments have sprung up around towns even as far as eighty or ninety miles from Dublin, and, if you drive around, large areas of the country can sometimes seem like one constant road-widening or resurfacing scheme. But there are benefits too. The booming economy has spawned a new confidence in cultural expression particularly manifest in a number of major public building works. The Millennium Wing of the National Gallery in Dublin and the Ussher Library in Trinity College demonstrate a new public monumentalism, and there are numerous signs of a fresh **adventurousness** in architectural projects dotted around the country. Noteworthy examples include The Mermaid arts centre in Bray, *The Bridges Hostel* in Enniskillen and the National Museum of Country Life in Castlebar. Balancing the needs of the country's growing economy and precarious ecological and social environments will be a major challenge for Ireland as the twenty-first century progresses.

Art

Irish art has long been overshadowed by the island's literature and, to some extent, its music. For the lay majority, Irish art is generally associated with the products of a Celtic culture in the centuries preceding and following the arrival of Christianity, and few, if pressed, are able to name a single Irish artist of the modern period. There is, however, a significant body of modern Irish work that deserves broader recognition.

The Stone, Bronze and Iron Ages

The oldest art works in Ireland available to us can be found in the Stone Age tombs of the Boyne Valley, especially the passage grave at **Newgrange** (see "Architecture", p.812). The stones and slabs of this 5000-year-old burial chamber are adorned with basic, but impressive whorls, zigzags and geometric forms whose purpose has long since been lost to us. The site has also yielded stone balls and beads as well as the remains of some rudimentary pottery.

Other decorative work on stone has survived from the **Bronze Age** (2000–500 BC), an epoch more notable for some startling work in goldsmithery. The National Museum of Ireland in Dublin houses a stunning collection of artefacts and jewellery, including a variety of lunulae (crescent-shaped collars of beaten gold), earrings and torques (twisted gold necklaces and armbands). One of the finest examples is the **Gleninsheen Gorget**, an elaborate gold neck ornament with roundel fastenings, dating from around 800 BC.

The subsequent **Iron Age** witnessed continuing developments. There are a number of fine examples of figurative stone-carving scattered around the country. Among the most notable are the **Janus statue**, two conjoined and grotesque figures carved back to back, in Calgach Cemetery on Boa Island, County Fermanagh, and the **Tandragee Idol**, now in the Church of Ireland Cathedral, Armagh city. Linear designs of flowing tendrils, typical of the La Tène style of Celtic art found in continental Europe, are visible on a number of surviving works, including the well-known **Turoe stone** in County Galway (see p.471). The National Museum holds several good examples of this style, including the **Somerset box lid** (also from Galway) and the so-called **Petrie Crown** gold collar, part of a hoard unearthed in 1896 in Broighter, County Derry, which also included a wonderful miniature sailing boat complete with oars.

Early Christian art

In Ireland, the early Christian era (432–1170 AD) is often described as the **Golden Age**. Irish society remained unscathed by the turmoil in the centuries following the fall of the Roman Empire and its society based on small tribal units was not disturbed radically by the advent of Christianity. Indeed, artists and craftworkers retained a privileged status, continuing to develop skills in metalwork and other areas. The period attained its zenith with the production of justifiably famous illuminated manuscripts such as the **Book of Kells**, but other wonderful artefacts have also survived from this era and a visit to the magnificent **high crosses** will take you to some of the most beautiful parts of the country.

Illuminated manuscripts

The first of the surviving manuscripts is an early seventh-century book of psalms known as **the Cathach** (pronounced "kohok"), now housed in the library of the Royal Irish Academy in Dublin. Only the initial letter of each paragraph of Latin text is decorated and such illustration consists of scrolls and animals in a limited range of colours. These motifs set the style for the greater books that followed.

The first of the truly magnificent illuminated texts is the **Book of Durrow**, dating from around 675 AD, and displayed alongside the Book of Kells in the Old Library in Trinity College, Dublin. The Book of Durrow was produced by the monastery of the same name in County Offaly and consists of a copy of the four Gospels. Though the artist's palette was limited to red, yellow and green, the three major stylistic components of spirals, animals and interlacing bands, typical of the great books, are plainly evident. These bands, like the dots which surround some of the initial letters in the Cathach, suggest a stylistic link with Coptic or other Middle Eastern sources. The Book of Durrow is also notable for its full-page illustrations (called carpet pages) devoted entirely to ornamentation or a depiction of the saint whose gospel follows.

Other books were produced during the next hundred and fifty years. Two others displayed in Trinity College are the **Book of Armagh**, commissioned in 807 by Torbach, Bishop of Armagh, and the **Book of Dimma**, typical of a smaller pocket format designed to be carried around. Similar illuminated manuscripts, such as the Lindisfarne Gospels, can be found in museums and libraries abroad, reflecting the travels of many of the monks of the period. St Columba, for example, spread the Gospels and founded monasteries around Britain and Europe.

However, it was in the **Book of Kells** that this art form found its highest expression in Ireland. Again a copy of the Gospels in Latin, this glorious manuscript is a perfect synthesis of all the motifs and styles – both imported or developed locally – used in earlier books. Its origins are obscure and some suggest that it was produced by monks from Iona, St Columba's first Scottish base. Created around 800 AD, it takes its name from the Columban monastery at Kells, County Meath, where it was kept for centuries until it was transferred to Trinity in 1654 for protection during the Cromwellian wars. The beauty of the book's illustrations defies description, from the vividly ornamental geometric and floral patterns to the human and animal forms gracing the page margins. It is no wonder at all that the Book of Kells is easily Ireland's most popular visitor attraction and queueing for a view is an essential part of a trip to the island.

Metalwork and jewellery

The decorative style of the illuminated manuscripts is reflected in the best of the period's metalwork, including two impressive chalices. The first is part of the eighth- or ninth-century **Derrynaflan Hoard**, discovered in County Tipperary in 1980, while the second, a century older, was found at **Ardagh**, County Limerick. Both chalices are roughly eight inches high and similar in shape, with a rounded cup and a conical base, though the elaborately engraved Ardagh Chalice is technically more refined than its plainer successor. However, for evidence that secular art also flourished during this period, look no further than the eighth-century bronze **Tara Brooch**, found on the seashore near Bettystown, County Louth in 1850. Covered with gold and decorated with amber, glass and fine metalwork, intricate designs on both its sides bear close similarities to patterns in the Book of Kells. Both chalices and the brooch are on view in the National Museum, Dublin.

The development of metalwork over the following centuries showed the increasing influence of Romanesque and Viking styles. While the latter is apparent in numerous examples of brooches and other jewellery, the former is best exemplified by the magnificent **Cross of Cong**. The cross was made around 1123 in order to contain and protect a chip from the True cross, presented by Pope Calixtus II to the King of Connacht, Turlough O'Connor. It is made of oak, encased in gilt bronze, copper and silver, and the arms are decorated with fine gold filigree. There is a central bronze boss into which is set a polished crystal.

High crosses and Sheila-na-Gigs

The Cross of Cong pre-dated by several centuries another great, but also relatively short-lived, genre of Irish art, the **high crosses**. An early simple, but gloriously executed example is the seventh-century **Donagh Cross**, near Carndonagh, County Donegal. The interlaced design of the head of the cross is typical of many and, while each face is decorated, the east face depicts a number of biblical scenes, including the Crucifixion. A pair of more elaborate crosses is to be found at **Ahenny**, County Tipperary. Here the arms of each cross are joined by a circle, a form that served as a prototype for subsequent sculptures.

The best of the later scriptural crosses can be ranked amongst Ireland's finest artistic achievements. One such is the **Cross of Moone**, County Kildare. Although its setting is less picturesque than others, there is an instant appeal about this long, narrowly proportioned cross with its almost naive flat figures depicting biblical scenes.

Other more striking examples are to be found at the beautiful locations of **Clonmacnois**, County Offaly and at **Monasterboice**, County Louth. The former's Great Cross unusually includes a secular scene, while, at Monasterboice, the graphic biblical scenes of St Muiredach's Cross have survived a thousand years of Ireland's inclement climate. Elsewhere, various examples can be seen in **Kells**, County Meath and at **Donaghmore** and **Ardboe** in County Tyrone. Sadly, many crosses were carved from local sandstone and their decorations have not withstood the elements, but the granite **Castledermot Crosses**, in County Kildare, have fared better than many.

Crosses continued to be carved in stone right up to the twelfth century, although there were significant changes in style. For instance, the White Cross of Tola at **Dysert O'Dea**, County Clare, where large figures in relief of Christ and a bishop have replaced flatter charactered biblical panels. The arms of this cross are not joined by a circle.

Evidence that Irish Christianity retained some idiosyncrasies is provided by the stone sculptured **Sheila-na-Gigs** found on some early church decorations and in castle walls (see box on p.195). A pair of these pagan fertility symbols are exhibited in the National Museum, but to see one *in situ*, a visit to **White Island** in Lower Lough Erne, County Fermanagh, is essential (see p.770). The figures are undeniably female, but what is also indisputable is the sheer provocative lewdness of their representation. The White Island figure grins lasciviously, her cheeks bulging, legs wide open and arms pointing towards her genitalia.

Norman and Medieval art

Until the dissolution of the monasteries in the sixteenth century, virtually all Irish art was religious in context and content and the Church was the principal patron. Following the Norman invasion in the twelfth century, the earliest stone figure carvings were of bishops, such as those still visible in the Norman cathedrals of **St Patrick** and **Christ Church** in Dublin. Not to be outdone, some Norman knights also had effigies carved of themselves: that of Strongbow in Christ Church was reckoned to be one of the best until it was destroyed by the collapse of a wall and replaced by an anonymous earl.

The most notable achievement of this period was probably the refinement of stone-carving techniques, and there are numerous surviving examples. The fifteenth-century cloister carvings at the important Cistercian monastery of **Jerpoint,** near Thomastown, County Kilkenny, were the work of the nearby Callan carvers, who were also responsible for the tomb of Piers Fitz Oge Butler in **Kilcooly Abbey**, County Tipperary. New stones were used by the craftworkers and a startling example from the sixteenth century is the beautiful black marble effigies of Piers Butler and Lady Margaret Fitzgerald, his countess, in **St Canice's Cathedral**, Kilkenny.

Fortunately, examples of the woodcarver's art have survived too. The earliest is thought to be the thirteenth-century **Kilcorban Madonna and Child**, displayed in the Loughrea Museum, County Galway, while, in Dublin, the National Museum has the **St Molaise of Inishmurray** and **God the Father** from Fethard, County Tipperary. St Mary's Cathedral in Limerick has the only set of misericords in the country – black oak choir seats, carved with various animals, both fabulous and real, in bold relief. Limerick's Catholic cathedral, **St John's**, is worth visiting for its fifteenth-century mitre and carved crozier, thought to be the finest religious artefacts of the Middle Ages in Ireland.

Protective shrines or casings in metalwork have survived from the first millennium, and some of these were reworked in medieval style. **The Cathach Shrine**, for example, has work dating from about 1050, but the most impressive panels are possibly fifteenth century. This, the **Breac Maodhóg** and the **Domhnach Airgid** shrines can all be seen in the National Museum. Each is lavishly decorated with bronze or silver-gilt illustrations of the Crucifixion, the saints or other religious themes.

Seventeenth- to nineteenth-century art

Following the models of England and continental Europe, guilds of urban craftworkers began to form during the later medieval period. A new "professionalism" produced significant technical advances in the decorative arts of goldsmithery, plasterwork, silver, glass and furniture. The visual arts were stimulated by the desire of the new Anglo-Irish ruling class to display images of itself, and many such works were commissioned from painters and sculptors. Easel-based portrait painting thus became the dominant mode and a painters' guild was formed in 1670. Later prominent members included **Garrett**

Morphey, noted for his portraits of the martyred Oliver Plunkett, and **James Latham**, probably the first Irish artist of major ability. Latham had studied at Antwerp, and the depth of perception displayed in his work, especially his portrait of the philosopher Bishop George Berkeley, influenced Irish art for decades.

Drawing schools were founded in Dublin around 1740 and many artists, such as **Robert Healy**, were trained in charcoal and chalk techniques. Both his and **Hugh Hamilton**'s work can be seen in the National Gallery. Hamilton, a pastelist, also became a distinguished painter in the Neoclassical style, which was popular later in the century. The greatest stimulus to the visual arts, however, came from **Edmund Burke**'s theory of aesthetics, described in *A Philosophical Enquiry into the Origins of our Ideas of The Sublime and Beautiful*, published in 1756. Two major painters of the period, **George Barret** and **James Barry** were protégés of Burke and attempted to embody his aesthetic principles in their work. Influenced by such ideas as the excitement of pain or danger (the sublime) or love (the beautiful), the subject-matter of Irish painting broadened to include historical and some landscape work, often with classical or mythological allusions. Barry later became Professor of Painting at the Royal Academy, London, a position he held from 1782 until he was sacked in 1795 following an altercation with colleagues. Two paintings in the National Gallery, his *Self-Portrait* and *Adam and Eve*, are typical of his style.

Another influential artist of the period was **Nathaniel Hone**, the first painter of note in a family that would much later produce other major artists. He was known for his portraits of children and miniatures, but his most famous work, *The Conjurer*, now in the National Gallery, Dublin, was a satire on Sir Joshua Reynolds' attempts to emulate the Old Masters. Unsurprisingly, it was rejected for exhibition by the Royal Academy in London in 1775 and Hone defiantly held his own one-man show instead.

George Barret adapted Burke's principles to his landscapes and these paintings, together with **Robert Carver**'s, were often characteristically Romantic. However, a later Classical school developed, deriving much from the Frenchman Claude Lorraine and including landscapists such as **Thomas Roberts** and **William Ashford**. Paintings of this genre typically featured a green and brown foreground, green middle-distance and often, further back, a Gothic-style ruin set against a lighter, blue background. Topography, too, gradually became an important concern and its finest proponent was **James Malton**, a former draughtsman in the architect James Gandon's practice. His series of line drawings, *Views of Dublin*, drawn in 1790 to 1791, include some marvellous aspects of contemporary Irish architecture.

Classical and Rococo styles were also seen in the applied arts in the eighteenth century, particularly in stuccowork. Dublin's **Powerscourt Townhouse**, recently restored as an imaginatively designed shopping centre, has a magnificent ceiling by **Michael Stapleton** (also responsible for the plasterwork at Trinity) and a staircase by **James McCullagh** and **Michael Reynolds**, which have been decorated with motifs of urns, scrolls and heads. The rich Baroque ceiling of the **chapel** in the Rotunda Maternity Hospital by **Bartholomew Cramillion** is unlike anything else in the country. Life-size figures by the Swiss-Italian **Francini brothers**, the foremost contemporary stuccoists, and detailed birds and musical instruments by Robert West decorate **Newman House** at 85–86 St Stephen's Green. The extraordinary beauty of these make it all the more poignant that heartless town "planners" and "developers" have allowed the wanton destruction or neglect of many equally fine interiors in Ireland's principal city.

The eighteenth century was also noted for heavy, deep-cut glasswork and for high-quality silverware, some of which, such as three-legged sugar bowls, were made in characteristically Irish shapes. Sculpture in Classical and Neoclassical styles can be seen on a number of buildings such as the **Custom House**, the **City Hall** and the **Casino** at Marino, Dublin.

During the early years of the nineteenth century, following the 1801 Act of Union, many artists emigrated to London. Those who remained formed new organizations aimed at consolidating art in Ireland. The leading body was the Royal Hibernian Academy, established in 1823, and directly modelled on its London equivalent, holding annual exhibitions and seeking to stimulate debate on the direction and concerns of painting.

Nineteenth-century Irish art is dominated by the landscapists, led by **James Arthur O'Connor**. Though he was partially influenced by seventeenth-century Dutch works, the persistence of Classical and Romantic styles is visible in his *Homeward Bound* and **Edwin Hayes**' seascape *The Emigrant Ship*. The landscape tradition was further developed by **George Chinnery**, **William Sadler**, **Cecilia Campbell** and **Henry O'Neill** working in a variety of media – watercolour, gouache and oil. **George Petrie**, a distinguished archaeologist who was for some time attached to the Irish Ordnance Survey, also produced many topographical illustrations for travel books, a popular publishing genre of the time.

Portrait painting continued, though occasionally it followed the Victorian English trend for cloying sentimentality, as in **Richard Rothwell**'s *The Young Mother's Pastime*. Beginning as a pencil portraitist, Cork-born **Daniel Maclise** went on to produce historical frescoes, such as *The Meeting of Wellington and Blücher* and *The Death of Nelson*, both of which are displayed in the House of Lords' Royal Gallery; he also illustrated works by Dickens and Tennyson. His contemporary, **William Mulready** from Ennis, also studied at the Royal Academy and had an equally significant impact on English art through his studies *Barber's Shop* and *Boys Fishing*. **Francis Danby** was also notable for his large historical and biblical paintings, characterized by the Romanticism still popular among Irish painters.

John Henry Foley, **John Lawlor** and **Samuel Ferris Lynn** collaborated with British sculptors to produce the Albert Memorial in London. Foley was also noted for his Classical-style busts, but his major works were the commissions he received for **public monuments**; several examples of his work still stand in Dublin, such as the memorials to Oliver Goldsmith and Edmund Burke in College Green, and to Daniel O'Connell in O'Connell Street. There is some fine stuccowork from this time, too, such as that in the hall of Ballyfin House, County Laois by **Richard Morrison**.

From Impressionism to the present day

Developments in European art had a marked influence on Irish painting from the late nineteenth century onwards. The landscapes of **Nathaniel Hone**, the great-grandnephew of his namesake, and early paintings of **Walter Osborne** were inspired by the rustic realism of Jules Bastien-Lepage, though Osborne became one of many native artists stimulated by Impressionism, its influence visible in such works as *Tea in the Garden*. His *St Patrick's Close* depicted the griminess of working-class Dublin. Post-Impressionism had a powerful impact on the work of **Roderic O'Conor**, and his *Field of Corn* in the Ulster Museum, Belfast, is reminiscent of Cézanne and perhaps Van Gogh.

Other notable artists of the period include **William Orpen**, a precociously talented draughtsman who began training at the Dublin Metropolitan School of Art at the age of eleven. Later, as a young instructor at the school, he painted some marvellous coastal scenes with figures near Howth, but he is better known for his sketches and paintings at the front during World War I and at the subsequent Paris Peace Conference, where he was official painter. His portraits are worth seeing simply for their vitality and feeling for character. Similarly adept was **John Lavery**, many of whose works are displayed in the Ulster Museum in his home town, Belfast. In his early career, he too was influenced by Bastien-Lepage. Lavery studied in Glasgow, London and Paris and became a significant portraitist, especially during the 1920s when he painted many of the leading contemporary Irish political figures, including Carson and Collins.

Most prominent among artists of this period were **Jack Butler Yeats** and **Paul Henry**. Son of a successful portraitist and brother of the poet W.B. Yeats, Jack B. Yeats is probably the best-known Irish twentieth-century painter, though he worked originally as an illustrator, sketching horses for *Paddock Life* magazine and drawing the first cartoon-strip version of Sherlock Holmes, *Chubblock Homes*, for *Comic Cuts*. Like his father, he was a fine portraitist, although he later developed a highly personal Expressionist style, marked by extremely vivid colour and loose brush technique. Yeats's subjects were Celtic mythology and everyday Irish life, yet though he undoubtedly contributed to the upsurge of nationalist sentiment in the arts, following Irish independence, his influence on Irish art was largely osmotic, for he took no pupils and was never seen at work. Paul Henry studied first at his native Belfast School of Art before continuing his education in Paris. Like Yeats, he was originally an illustrator, working with high competence through the medium of charcoal. His early paintings were heavily influenced by Millet and, while living on Achill Island, County Mayo, he produced a number of works on Irish country life in which Millet's characteristic "peasant" poses were apparent. Later, Henry fell under the spell of Whistler and studied at his new Paris studio. Returning to Dublin he became active in the local arts world and, along with his wife, Grace Mitchell Henry, and a number of other painters, including Yeats, formed the **Society of Dublin Painters** in 1920. He had already developed his own characteristic style which remained hardly altered for the rest of his life and it is for his Connemara landscapes that he is most remembered. Using a palette of matt blues and greys, his paintings commonly consist of a few elements, natural or man-made, set in bold composition against a cloud-filled sky. *Lakeside Cottages* (c. 1930) is a typical example. In the 1920s, some of Henry's works were reproduced as posters and were also used in tourist literature and government publications. Such was the demand for similar pictures, that Henry's subsequent work almost sank to the level of romantic caricature.

In contrast to Post-Impressionism, abstract art was relatively late in arriving in Ireland. Some artists, such as **Seán Keating**, **Maurice MacGonigal** and **Sean O'Sullivan**, continued to work in the landscape tradition. Other young Irish artists travelled abroad to absorb the advances of Cubism and Futurism; the most influential on their return were **Mainie Jellett** and **Evie Hone** who had both trained under André Lhote and Albert Gleizes in Paris. Interestingly, early Modernism's masculinist avant-garde was given little credence in Ireland, leaving space for women like Jellett and Hone to be the main proponents of

Irish Modernism. Evie Hone was best known as a distinguished member of An Túr Gloine, a school for stained glass founded by the painter Sarah Purser, and her best works include windows in the chapel at Eton College in England and the CIÉ headquarters in O'Connell Street, Dublin. In 1943, along with fellow abstract artists Louis Le Brocquy and Norah McGuinness, Hone and Jellett, founded the **Irish Exhibition of Living Art** as an alternative showcase for Modernist work rejected by the compilers of the Royal Hibernian Academy's annual exhibitions.

Postwar Ireland saw major advances in sculpture. **Clíona Cussen**, **Hilary Heron** and **Oisín Kelly** pioneered the use of new casting techniques and developed the concept of an Irish vernacular sculpture. Kelly's *Children of Lir*, inspired by the Celtic legend, stands in Parnell Square, one of a number of public monuments placed around the capital by the Dublin Corporation. Sculptors of achievement have included **Michael Bulfin**, **John Behan**, **Edward Delaney**, **Conor Fallon** and **John Burke**. More recently, sculptors such as **Christopher Keaney** and **Jill Crowley** have produced remarkable figures, the latter wittily caricaturing Irish men.

One Expressionist painter using a uniquely Irish context for his work is the prolific Armagh artist and *uilleann* piper, **J.B. (Brian) Vallely**, who has produced more than four thousand canvases. Many of these centre on his love of traditional music, often showing musicians in action, and demonstrate an extraordinary dynamism and vitality.

The influence of the Exhibition of Living Art developed during the 1950s, serving as a focus for the works of artists like **Barrie Cooke**, **Cecil King**, **Nano Reid** and **Camille Souter**, while the landscape tradition was maintained by **Patrick Collins** and **Tony O'Malley**. Le Brocquy's contorted human shapes dominated abstract art, and an idiosyncratic school of primitive artists developed on **Tory Island** off the coast of Donegal (see p.591). Partly as a result of government funding, the visual arts have flourished in Ireland since the 1970s, and, in more recent years, in the North. In the 1980s, Living Art opened its doors to video and performance artists, exhibiting the works of **Aileen MacKeough**, **Nigel Rolfe**, **Eilis O'Connell** and a host of others. A strong new Expressionist movement has emerged from the Independent Artists group, represented by **Michael Kane**, **Patrick Hall**, **Brian Maguire**, **Patrick Graham**, **Eithne Jordan**, **Michael Mulcahy** and **Michael Cullen**.

Along with increased support, there has been a steady expansion in the number of **exhibition spaces**. In Dublin, the Irish Museum of Modern Art, opened in 1991, and the Douglas Hyde Gallery, in Trinity College, both offer opportunities for new experimentalism. More recent additions include the New Galleries at the Irish Museum of Modern Art and the Millennium Wing of the National Gallery in Dublin. The transportation of the interior of Francis Bacon's London studio to the Hugh Lane Gallery is yet further evidence of the increased investment in the visual arts. There's a host of commercial galleries here too, such as the Kerlin and Green on Red, ensuring that a steady stream of contemporary Irish art is always on show. Around the country there are numerous local art centres and galleries such as the Triskel in Cork, the Model Art Centre, Sligo and The Mermaid in Bray. In Northern Ireland, the Orchard Gallery in Derry has a long history of top-quality exhibitions, and the Ormeau Baths Gallery in Belfast regularly presents an equally strong contemporary Northern Irish programme. Names to watch out for include John Carson, Brian Connolly, Rita Duffy, Philip Napler and Louise Walsh. Animated debates in the pages of *Circa* testify to the continued revitalization of the Irish arts.

The profile of **conceptual art** has been raised by the Irish Museum of

Modern Art and the arrival of the Nissan Arts Project, which gives an artist the chance to create a temporary piece in a public space. Perhaps the most celebrated of contemporary Irish conceptual artists is **Dorothy Cross** whose work demonstrates an extraordinary versatility and imagination, fashioning artefacts and collective experiences from a huge range of materials.

Additionally, recent years have seen major developments in **contemporary applied arts and design**, especially in such fields as jewellery, glass, furniture and ceramics. In the Republic, such work has been supported by a government agency, the Craft Council of Ireland. The two capitals are the best locations for viewing, though there are plenty of others dotted around the island. In Dublin, there is the **Crafts Council gallery** in the Powerscourt Townhouse Centre and several outlets in **Temple Bar**, including DESIGNyard. Kilkenny Design Centre, with outlets in Kilkenny and Dublin is especially noted for ceramics, while in Belfast, work can be viewed in the **Craftworks gallery** in Bedford Street.

Film

The international profile of **film-making** in Ireland has been well established for over a decade as a result of financial incentives for foreign film-makers. Government funding for indigenous film-makers has spawned a thriving film community, catapulted onto the world stage largely thanks to the activities and successes of directors Neil Jordan and Jim Sheridan.

The Irish have always been conscious of the stereotypical images of Irishness in foreign, particularly American, pictures: the country as a pastoral idyll, its people a good-humoured mix of priests and nuns, fiery redheads and hard-drinking and violent men. More recently, however, films made in and about Ireland have started to explore broader themes, reflecting the changing state of Irish society and giving the world a very different image of Irishness: urban, diverse and outward-looking.

The films below are listed in chronological order, each title followed by the director and year of release.

Knocknagow (Fred O'Donovan, 1917). Set in the post-Famine years of the 1840s, this sprawling landlord/tenant silent drama, produced by the largely Nationalist Film Company of Ireland, is effectively a call to arms and was considered propagandist by the British authorities.

Willie Reilly and his Colleen Bawn (John McDonagh, 1920). Political drama set in the 1740s in which the rights of the landowning classes are upheld regardless of religion. Protestant squire's daughter Helen and Catholic gentleman Willie Reilly fall in love; rival suitor and anti-Catholic bigot Sir Whitecroft attempts to use the penal laws to dispossess Reilly, burning down his house in the process. Sympathetic Protestants come to the beleaguered Willie's assistance and ultimately justice prevails.

Irish Destiny (George Dewhurst, 1926). The first fictionalized film about the War of Independence and the civil war, with plenty of horrific detail including footage of the burning of Cork city and the Custom House, and the brutality of the Black and Tans. The film was banned by the British Board of Censors in 1926, but was received enthusiastically in Ireland and America.

Mother Machree (John Ford, 1928). Silent movie made for the Irish-American market in which an impoverished Irish immigrant is forced to surrender her son for adoption and devote her energies to raising the child of her employer, only to find both son and the girl fall in love in adult life.

Man of Aran (Robert O'Flaherty, 1934). Landmark documentary about life on the Aran Islands. Long criticized as portraying the islanders' primitive struggle against the elements in an overly romanticized, epic form that runs contrary to its documentary status, it nonetheless remains a thrilling film.

The Quiet Man (John Ford, 1952). US film included here because it represents the pinnacle of Hollywood "Oirishness". This romantic comedy stars John Wayne as the prize fighter who has hung up his gloves and returned to the auld sod from the States, and focuses on his courtship of the feisty Maureen O'Hara and the hostility he encounters from her pugilist brother.

Shake Hands With the Devil (Michael Anderson, 1959). The first international production to be made at Ardmore Studios in Bray, County

Wicklow. Melodrama starring James Cagney in which an IRA man develops a taste for violence as an end in itself.

Saoirse? ("Freedom?", George Morrison, 1961). Documentary account of the emergence of the modern Irish state, focusing on events from 1918 to the civil war.

Ryan's Daughter (David Lean, 1970). Set amid the gorgeous scenery of the Dingle Peninsula in 1916, the adulterous affair between a British officer (Christopher Jones) and the local schoolteacher's wife (Sarah Miles) is common knowledge by the time a boatload of IRA guns arrive to be intercepted by British forces. The locals set upon Miles, believing her to be responsible for the treachery. For all this, a rather lacklustre film.

Down the Corner (Joe Comerford, 1974). The first urban working-class film shot in Ireland by an Irish director; the action centres around the escapades of five adolescent boys. Their surrounding adult world is characterized by alcoholism, unemployment and memories of the 1916 Rising.

Withdrawal (Joe Comerford, 1974). Film dealing with mental illness and drug addiction in an uncharacteristically raw manner.

On a Paving Stone Mounted (Thaddeus O'Sullivan, 1978). A tale of the lives of Irish emigrants in London, significant not just for its subject-matter, but also for the improvisational scope given to its actors. The film deploys a mix of drama and documentary styles and presents a dislocated collage of memory and experience.

Our Boys (Cathal Black, 1981). Iconoclastic milestone in Irish film history which combined documentary and drama to highlight the inequities of Irish Christian Brothers' schools. "The Brothers" were notorious for their insensitivity and the outbursts of savage brutishness which they inflicted on pupils. It was deemed so subversive that RTÉ, one of the film's backers, refused to broadcast it for the best part of a decade after its release.

Angel (US title "Danny Boy", Neil Jordan, 1982). Fine revenge thriller set in Northern Ireland, in which a saxophonist pursues the murderer of a mute girl and is thus drawn into a world of violence.

Cal (Pat O'Connor, 1984). Fatalistic love story set in the context of the Troubles in Northern Ireland. Cal, an IRA volunteer, seeks redemption for his part in the murder of a policeman, from the dead man's widow. Love blooms all too briefly and their relationship is destroyed when the past catches up with them.

Eat the Peach (Peter Ormrod, 1986). Droll and quirky movie in which protagonists Arthur and Vinnie set out to build a motorcycle wall-of-death to relieve the unrelenting tedium of their bleak and desolate bogland home.

Reefer and the Model (Joe Comerford, 1987). Highly enjoyable thriller in which an ex-prostitute heroin user, now pregnant, and an ex-IRA man meet up and rampage through Connemara, rob a mobile bank and effect a getaway of sorts.

My Left Foot (Jim Sheridan, 1989). A fine and touching film based on Christy Brown's best-selling autobiography. Brown, almost entirely paralyzed by cerebral palsy, except for his left foot, retells the story of his courageous battle with disability.

December Bride (Thaddeus O'Sullivan, 1990). Family drama set at the beginning of the twentieth century, beautifully shot on location at Strangford Lough. Central to the film is one pregnant woman's refusal to marry at the behest of the local minister, and her growing understanding of the sacrifices that must be made for the sake of future generations. The film was commended at the 1990 European Film Awards for its rich and varied portrayal of Northern Protestants.

The Field (Jim Sheridan, 1990). Sentimentalized story about one man's fight to keep the field he's created and tended over the years. A crude allegory of land ownership and the dignity of toil.

The Commitments (Alan Parker, 1991). One of the most popular film treatments of working-class Dublin. Adapted from Roddy Doyle's novel, the film follows the rise of the eponymous soul band and is chiefly enjoyable for its rather obvious comedy and R&B/soul classics.

Hear My Song (Peter Chelsom, 1991). Engaging light comedy in which Liverpool night-club manager Micky O'Neill hopes to revive his fortunes by luring legendary tenor Josef Locke to perform in his ailing club. However, O'Neill has underrated the complexities of Locke's past and things do not run smoothly.

The Crying Game (Neil Jordan, 1992). Excellent thriller in which an IRA man becomes haunted by his part in the death of a British hostage and subsequently develops an intimate relationship with the dead man's lover. However, things are not that simple, and this gripping film comes to an unexpected ironic conclusion.

Into the West (Mike Newell, 1992). Clichéd but nonetheless charming contemporary working of the Tír na nÓg myth – the quest for the Land of Eternal Youth. The film focuses on the horseback adventures of two young boys and their father's struggle to accept the death of their mother. The film fuses gritty Dublin realism with the magical landscape of the west.

In the Name of the Father (Jim Sheridan, 1993). Based on the true story of the Guildford Four who were wrongfully imprisoned for the 1974 IRA Guildford pub bombing in which five people died. The film focuses on the imprisonment of Gerry Conlon and his father Guiseppe, and the attempt to clear the family name. Although marred by historical inaccuracies and a ludicrous final courtroom scene, this remains a powerful drama, thanks chiefly to the towering performance of Daniel Day Lewis as Gerry.

Korea (Cathal Black, 1994). Set in the border country of the 1950s. An adolescent boy's romance forces his father to confront a changing world and put local enmities dating back to the civil war behind him.

A Man of No Importance (Suri Krishnamma, 1995). Light movie in which gay bus conductor Alfie Byrne, played by a delightful Albert Finney, attempts to loosen up the travelling public in a repressive Dublin of the 1960s. Action revolves around his efforts to stage a production of Wilde's *Salome* in a church hall.

Circle of Friends (Pat O'Connor, 1995). Light, chocolate-box tale of young romance and betrayal in 1950s Ireland. This adaptation of a Maeve Binchy novel remains cosy and warm-hearted throughout.

Guiltrip (Gerard Stembridge, 1995). Adultery, impotence and frustration drive squaddie Liam, an army corporal, to extremes in this tense small town drama.

Nothing Personal (Thaddeus O'Sullivan, 1995). Action-packed

Troubles movie in which innocent individuals are caught up in the terrorists' war. Criticized as having pro-Republican sympathies, the film can be credited with some honest scrutiny of the motivations and inner tensions of Loyalist organizations. As the film comes to its awful conclusion, the inevitability that violence begets violence is made horribly clear, and so too is the message that this is a war in which everyone loses.

The Run of the Country (Peter Yates, 1995). The quiet, forgotten border country is the setting for this adolescent rite of passage, the drama centring around a cross-border romance and an unwanted pregnancy. Fine scenery and pale shadows of IRA activity provide a modicum of local colour.

The Boy From Mercury (Martin Duffy, 1996). Slight, amusing film about a boy's obsession with science fiction, in particular Flash Gordon movies. The young James Cronin pulls through the trials of boyhood with the help of his wide-eyed imagination and the outer-space fantasies of the local cinema.

Michael Collins (Neil Jordan, 1996). Hugely important biopic in which Republican leader Collins, played by Liam Neeson, is portrayed as a heroic figure in the struggle against imperial Britain. The film includes a powerful dramatization of the 1916 Easter Rising and, although it skirts over the details of the Treaty negotiations of 1921, follows Collins through the founding of the Free State to the civil war and his assassination.

Some Mother's Son (Terry George, 1996). Enthralling and moving film about the 1981 Irish hunger strikers in The Maze prison, focusing on the effect of their endeavour on two mothers of differing political beliefs. Despite occasional lapses into sentimentality, this is a convincing evocation of those times and includes superb performances by Fionnula Flanagan and Helen Mirren.

The Van (Stephen Frears, 1996). Based on Roddy Doyle's novel, this Dublin working-class comedy revolves around protagonist Bimbo's attempt to launch a chip van business in time for Ireland's World Cup games.

The Boxer (US title "Hell's Kitchen", Jim Sheridan, 1997). Circles of violence explored as ex-con boxer returns to his Republican community to discover the continuing demands of sectarianism are as restricting as life inside. A very convincing portrayal of the men of violence's stranglehold on a community.

The General (John Boorman, 1998). Based on the true-life story of a notorious Dublin art thief. The "general" becomes fatally caught up in the complexities of the political underworld when the UVF proves to be the only organization capable of buying his haul. A magnificent performance by Brendan Gleeson in the central role.

The Butcher Boy (Neil Jordan, 1998). Powerful, dark comedy set in small-town Ireland in which a young boy's failure to cope with the dysfunctional society that surrounds him leads to violence. From the Patrick McCabe novel of the same name.

Divorcing Jack (David Caffrey, 1998). Pacey comic thriller in which a Belfast journalist (David Thewlis) finds himself caught up in both murder and political scandal. Taken from the novel by Colin Bateman, the film uses the social backdrop of the Troubles to, at times, hilarious effect.

Angela's Ashes (Alan Parker, 1999). Moving and faithful adaptation of

Frank McCourt's international best-seller based on his Limerick childhood. Despite the child deaths, the father's drinking and above all the unrelenting poverty, this is a tale suffused with humour.

Nora (Pat Murphy, 1999). Biopic following the courtship and early married life of Nora Barnacle and James Joyce. The title suggests Murphy's feminist agenda: we find Nora portrayed here as a robust and down-to-earth character, with tensions between the couple generated by Joyce's sexual jealousies and insecurities. An especially powerful performance by Susan Lynch in the leading role.

The Last September (Deborah Warner, 1999). Set in 1920, the film explores some of the contradictory impulses of the Anglo-Irish Ascendancy at this critical period in their history. Upper-class Lois is drawn to stereotypical IRA rebel Peter – brooding, attractive and misogynous – despite the advances of an eligible English captain with whom, arguably, she has more in common. An atmospheric portrait of a fading world.

When the Sky Falls (John MacKenzie, 1999). Fictionalized account of the investigations into Dublin's drug world by journalist Veronica Guerin and her subsequent murder. Guerin actually assisted Jim Sheridan in the development of an early screenplay. Criticized for its sympathetic portrayal of the IRA.

I Could Read the Sky (Nicola Bruce, 1999). An old Irish man reflects on his life as a labourer on a London building site in this moving piece about the experiences of loneliness and regret that were common to many Irish emigrants. Based on Timothy O'Grady's book of the same name.

The Borstal Boy (Peter Sheridan, 2000). Set during World War II, the film is based on the early years of notorious playwright Brendan Behan who, at 16, was arrested carrying explosives from Ireland to Liverpool. Once in prison, Behan comes to see the enemy somewhat differently in this intelligent film.

Country (Kevin Liddy, 2000). Set in rural Ireland in the 1970s, *Country* tells the story of a motherless family of men shaken by the arrival of an estranged aunt from England. The theme of the outsider is continued in the social backdrop of a community of travellers.

H3 (Les Blair, 2001). An important and highly focused feature about the 1981 H-Block hunger strike in The Maze prison in which ten men died in their attempt to have their political status reinstated by the British Government. Written by ex-prisoners, it tells the story from their perspective and is set solely within the confines of the prison.

Music

Ireland and **music** are as inseparable as fish and chips. Traditional music may form the well-known cultural backbone, but there is also an important, though often ignored, body of classical composition. Artists such as Van Morrison, Thin Lizzy, U2, The Corrs and Sinéad O'Connor have ensured Ireland's prominence in the world gazetteer of rock while also carving out a niche in the pop world through a succession of successful boy bands such as Boyzone and Westlife and their girl counterparts B*witched, and the disco diva Samantha Mumba.

Traditional music

Kept alive by a combination of historical, political and cultural forces, Irish **traditional music** remains one of the richest musical cultures in the Western world. In Ireland itself, the growing interest in traditional music is further evidence of a national maturity that allows Irish people to be more relaxed about aspects of their traditional culture. Consequently, traditional music is neither seen as backward, rural and something shameful, nor is it a stick of cultural purity for fending off the twenty-first century. Long after much traditional music in the industrialized West has ceased to exist in any meaningful way, Irish music continues to refashion itself, not as introverted, stagnant, and nationalistic, but as an evolving and progressive part of a common, universal oral folk tradition.

Most of the instrumental music the visitor will hear in Ireland is **dance music** (such as reels, jigs and hornpipes), originally played in kitchens, barns and at crossroads dances, usually to mark an occasion, such as a wedding or a wake. The melody of any dance tune is but bare bones to a traditional musician; it's dependent on performance for flesh, blood and soul. Through ornamentation, decoration and embellishments the performer breathes life into the music and this controlled extemporization allows the player to re-create a tune with each rendition.

Sean-nós and the vocal tradition

Songs in the Irish language are at the heart of Irish music and the most important belong to a tradition known as **sean-nós** (literally "old style"). An unaccompanied singing style of great beauty and complexity, it is thought to derive in part from the bardic tradition which died out in the seventeenth century with the demise of the old Gaelic order, though other recent research has suggested links to North Africa. Hugely demanding for both singer and listener, it requires the skill of the former to vary the interpretation of each verse by means of subtle changes in tempo, ornamentation, timbre and stress, while the latter needs to possess the knowledge and discrimination to appreciate fully the singer's efforts. To the untutored ear it can easily "sound all the same", with its slightly nasal tone and unemotional manner of performance, but perseverance

Instruments and players

We've included mention of some of the best instrumentalists on the Irish music scene in this round-up of **traditional instruments**. If you get the chance to see any of them at the festivals, don't miss it.

Uilleann pipes

"Seven years learning, seven years practising, and seven years playing" is reputedly what it takes to master the *uilleann* (pronounced "illun" or "illyun", depending on local dialect) pipes. Perhaps the world's most technically sophisticated bagpipe, it is highly temperamental and difficult to master. The melody is played on a nine-holed chanter with a two-octave range blown by the air from a bag squeezed under the left arm, itself fed by a bellows squeezed under the right elbow. As well as the usual set of drones, the *uilleann* pipes are marked by their possession of a set of regulators, which can be switched on and off to provide chords. In the hands of a master, such as the late **Leo Rowsome**, they can provide a sensitive backing for slow airs and an excitingly rhythmic springboard for dance music.

The pipes arrived in Ireland in the early eighteenth century and reached their present form in the 1890s. Taken up by members of the gentry, who became known as "gentlemen pipers", they were also beloved by the Irish tinkers or travellers, and two different styles evolved: the restrained and delicate parlour style exemplified by the late **Séamus Ennis**, and the traveller style (known as "open" or "legato") which, designed as it was to coax money from the pockets of visitors to country fairs, is highly ornamented and often showy.

Some of the most acclaimed musicians of recent years have been pipers: Séamus Ennis, **Willie Clancy** and travellers **Johnny** and **Felix Doran**, all alas now dead. Today **Liam O'Flynn** is regarded as one of the country's foremost practitioners and has pushed forward the possibilities for piping through his association with classical composer **Shaun Davey** and with the band Planxty. Other contemporary pipers worth catching include **Paddy Keenan**, one-time star of the Bothy Band, and **Davy Spillane**, who learned much of his technique from travelling pipers.

Flutes and whistles

It's the wooden flute of a simple type that is mainly used in Irish music, played mostly in a fairly low register with a quiet and confidential tone which means that it's not heard at its best in pub sessions. Played solo by such musicians as **Matt Molloy** or **Desi Wilkinson**, its clear flow of notes displays a gentler side to the rushing melodies of jigs and reels.

While anyone can get a note, though not necessarily the right one, out of its little cousin the tin whistle, it can take a long time to develop an embouchure capable of producing a beautiful flute tone, and so piper Finbar Furey has introduced the low whistle, which takes the place of the flute when there is no proper flute player around. In the right hands – those of **Paddy Moloney**, **Seán Ryan**, **Mary Bergin** or the young and phenomenal **Gavin Whelan**, for example – the tin whistle itself is no mean instrument, but it's also suitable for the beginner. If you're interested, make sure you get a D-whistle, as much Irish music is in this key.

Fiddles

The fiddle is popular all over Ireland, and each area has its own particular characteristics: Donegal breeds fiddlers with a smooth melodic approach but lively, attacking bowing techniques, whereas the Sligo style, exemplified in the playing of the great **Michael Coleman**, is more elaborate and flamboyant. Alongside his Sligo contemporary, **James Morrison**, Coleman's 1920s recordings in America still wield an incredible influence on contemporary fiddling. Currently worth catching are the US-based Clare fiddler **Martin Hayes**, who works as a duo with guitarist Dennis Cahill, the semi-legendary Donegal fiddler **Tommy Peoples** and, of the younger breed, **Dezi Donnelly**, **Oisín Mac Diarmada** and **Liz Doherty**.

Melodeons, accordions and concertinas

Squeeze-boxes come in a variety of shapes and sizes in traditional music. The simplest is the one-row button accordion, usually known as a melodeon to Irish ears. Now rarely seen, one of its true masters is the Connemara box player **Johnny Connolly**, generally regarded as the acme of accompanists for dancing. The far more popular two-row button accordion comes in a variety of tunings, usually either B/C (favoured by the highly influential **Joe Burke**) which produces a more rolling and frilly style of play, or the C#/D variety (whose well-known exponents include **Dermot Byrne** and **Séamus Begley**). Also well worth seeking out are **Jackie Daly** and **Máirtín O'Connor**, both of whom play boxes in a variety of tunings. The piano accordion is less well favoured, though there are some cracking musicians using it, including **Alan Kelly** and **Mirella Murray**.

The smaller concertina was once thought of as primarily a women's instrument and was especially popular in County Clare (for too many reasons to list here). Again, it's ideal for accompanying dancers and probably the best-known exponents are **Mary Mac Namara**, **Noel Hill** and **Micheál Ó Raghallaigh**.

The bouzouki

At first sight it might seem odd to include the bouzouki on a list of traditional Irish instruments. Nevertheless, its light but piercing tone makes it eminently suitable both for melodies and providing a restrained chordal backing within an ensemble, and since its introduction to the island by **Johnny Moynihan**, in the late 1960s, and subsequent popularization by **Dónal Lunny**, it has taken firm root. In the process it has lost much of its original Greek form, and with its flat back the Irish bouzouki is really closer to a member of the mandolin family. Along with other string instruments like the guitar and banjo, which provide supporting harmonies in a "folky" idiom, bouzoukis crop up at sessions all over the country, and some of the best accompanists are bouzouki players.

The bodhrán

The *bodhrán* (pronounced "bore-run") is an instrument much in evidence at traditional sessions and a relatively recent addition to the dance music line-up. It is not universally welcome, partly because it looks like an easy way into playing – and it isn't. The great piper Séamus Ennis, when asked how a *bodhrán* should be played, replied "with a penknife". The *bodhrán* is a frame drum usually made of goatskin and originally associated with "wren boys" or mummers who went out revelling and playing music on Wrens Day (Dec 26). It looks like a large tambourine without jingles and can be played with a small wooden stick or with the back of the hand.

When played well by the likes of famed Galway musician **Johnny "Ringo" McDonagh**, or **Colm Murphy**, **Mel Mercier, John Joe Kelly** and **Tommy Hayes**, the *bodhrán* sounds wonderful, a sympathetic support to the running rhythms of traditional music. Since it was introduced into mainstream traditional music in the 1960s by the great innovator Seán Ó Riada, it has come on by leaps and bounds, and new techniques are constantly being invented. Many traditional ensembles now regard it as *de rigueur*.

will lead to great rewards. *Sean-nós* remains strongest in the Gaeltacht areas, especially Connemara, while the marvellous **Iarla O'Lionáird** (from west Cork) has taken the art form to international audiences, especially through his work with the roots-dance fusion outfit Afro Celt Sound System.

The session: music and craic

Travellers to Ireland will most likely come across traditional music in a pub setting and these quasi-impromptu musical get-togethers are known as "**sessions**". These are the life-blood of traditional music, accompanied by the associated notion of **craic** (or crack) whereby music, conversation and drink combine to produce an evening of fun. A session is not strictly a performance, but more of a dynamic of musician and listener – a group of people enjoying the *craic* together. While sessions take place all year round in the major cities, summer is the optimal time for sessions in traditional music's heartland, the west of Ireland, and a few enquiries locally will point you to the best. A comprehensive listing is also included in the monthly *Irish Music* magazine, available from newsagents in Ireland.

The instrumental repertoire mainly consists of dance tunes, but there are also slow airs played without accompaniment and usually to hushed attention. Most are laments or the melodies of songs, some so old that the words have been lost. The *uilleann* pipes (see box on p.834) are particularly well suited to the performance of airs, as their plaintive tone and ability to produce complex ornamentation cleanly allows them to approach the style of *sean-nós* singers (see p.833).

Playing in groups or with accompaniment is a prominent feature of traditional music performance today. One of the most exciting exponents of this style is the band **De Dannan**, which in its heyday featured three women singers who went on to have solo careers in commercial rock: **Mary Black**, **Dolores Keane** and **Maura O'Connell**. Ireland's best-known traditional band, **The Chieftains**, carry on the virtuoso tradition, too. This group was the spearhead of the 1960s revival of Irish traditional music, which itself was largely due to the efforts of the composer and arranger, **Seán Ó Riada**. While working as musical director of the Abbey Theatre Ó Riada hit on the idea of ensemble music-making using traditional instruments like the pipes, fiddle and whistle, forming the group Ceoltóirí Chualann to put theory into practice. It was a brilliantly obvious innovation and, over the past four decades, The Chieftains, originally featuring musicians from Ceoltóirí Chualann, and led by whistler and piper **Paddy Moloney**, have developed the concept of ensemble playing to the point where it has become universally accepted and adopted. In addition, Ó Riada brought his genius for interpretation to bear on choral, liturgical and orchestral music.

A widely known musician exploring the ensemble format is **Sharon Shannon**. Playing furiously energetic dance music, Shannon is a mesmerizing button-accordion player who can also turn her hand to the fiddle and spent some time with The Waterboys before forming her own band. Her first solo album mixed well-known and much-played tunes like *The Silver Spire* and *O'Keefe's* with cajun, Swedish, and new material in traditional style. Her profile was further enhanced by her involvement with the 1992 *Woman's Heart* album combining with Maura O'Connell, Frances and Mary Black, Dolores Keane and Eleanor McEvoy to produce one of the most successful Irish albums of all time, while her more recent releases, *Each Little Thing* and *The Diamond Mountain Sessions,* are less traditional but exude the ebullience that has become her trademark. Donegal-based **Altan** derive their energy from a twin-fiddle attack led by **Mairéad Ní Mhaonaigh** and **Ciarán Tourish** coupled with the phenomenal accordion work of **Dermot Byrne**, while their earlier recordings feature the exquisite flute playing of the late **Frankie Kennedy** – all can be appreciated on their stunning album *Island Angel*. **Dervish**, based in neighbouring Sligo, are another effervescent grouping and feature the extraordinary range of singer Cathy Jordan, a dab hand on bones and *bodhrán* too. Other bands to look out for include **Danú**, from County Waterford, who create a mighty musical confection, enhanced by another remarkable *sean-nós* singer, **Ciarán Ó Geabháin**, and the trio **Cran**, featuring the three terrific musicians, singer **Seán Corcoran**, piper **Ronan Browne** and flute player **Desi Wilkinson**. **Coolfin**, led by traditional alumnus, **Dónal Lunny**, brings together some staggering talent, including singer **Maighread Ní Dhomhnaill** and piper **John McSherry**, who himself was a one-time member of **Lúnasa**, a band which harnesses the instrumental prowess of fiddler **Seán Smyth**, flute player **Kevin Crawford** and piper **Cillian Vallely**. Perhaps the nearest thing to a supergroup is **Patrick Street** (featuring **Andy Irvine** from Planxty, **Kevin Burke** from the Bothy Band and the astounding accordionist **Jackie Daly**), while the American band **Solas** represent a marvellous dynamic between aggression and tenderness, drawing on the skills of multi-instrumentalist **Seamus Egan**, fiddler **Winifred Horan** and singer **Deirdre Scanlan**.

Folk meets traditional

Singing **folk songs** to instrumental accompaniment became enormously popular in Ireland in the 1960s with the triumphal return from America of **The Clancy Brothers and Tommy Makem** (three brothers from Tipperary joined by a member of a well-known Armagh musical family). The Clancys and Makem had taken New York's Carnegie Hall and the networked *Ed Sullivan Show* by storm, and they were welcomed home to Ireland as conquering heroes. Their heady blend of rousing ballads accompanied by guitar, harmonica and banjo revitalized a genre of folk song that had all but vanished. Hundreds of sound-alike ballad groups sprang up, decked out in a motley selection of ganseys – The Clancys' and Makem's hallmark was the Aran sweater. Before the ballad-group fashion petered out, it had laid the foundations for a revival of interest in popular folk singing that endures to this day. Still going strong is another great group of this era, **The Dubliners**. With an uncompromisingly urban image, in contrast to the rather twee Oirishness of The Clancys, their work was often bawdy and their ribald spirit was captured in the most popular song of this era, *Seven Drunken Nights* (although The Dubliners only sang about five of these nights, it still managed to be banned from Irish radio). Earthiness may have been part of the reason why their true musical accomplishment was never fully appreciated because, as well as fielding two unique singers, **Luke Kelly** (who died in 1984) and **Ronnie Drew**, they boasted two fine instrumentalists, banjoist **Barney McKenna** and fiddler **John Sheahan**. In many ways they helped lay the groundwork for the fusion of the traditional/ballad genre explored by bands such as **Sweeney's Men**, **The Johnstons**, **The Bothy Band** and, most influential of all, Planxty.

Planxty was formed from the musicians recording Christy Moore's *Prosperous* album, and the evolution of traditional music can be traced through the band members' post-Planxty recordings. The band consisted of **Liam O'Flynn**, **Dónal Lunny**, **Andy Irvine** and **Christy Moore**, and their self-titled first album (known as "The Black Album") mixed traditional, modern folk and ballad singing through harmonies backed by O'Flynn's superlative pipe playing. They recorded three albums before their split and a selection from each is available on the 1976 album *The Planxty Collection*. The band reformed again in 1978, adding the former Bothy Band and currently Chieftains' flute player, **Matt Molloy**, to their ranks. Their best work in this period is *The Woman I Loved So Well* but the band split finally when Lunny and Moore moved on to stretch the traditional genre even further with the formation of Moving Hearts.

Moving Hearts radically attempted to fuse traditional and rock music and almost succeeded. Consisting of two pipers, saxophone, bass and lead guitars, electric bouzouki, drums and percussion, their gigs were memorable feasts of exciting music, seeming simultaneously familiar and new. Too large to survive financially, the band sadly folded in 1984. Since then there have been a few reunions which have played to crowds of fans old and new. Released after their break-up, their 1985 album *The Storm* is a landmark in its pioneering use of rock and jazz idioms to redefine the harmonic and rhythmic foundations of Irish music.

Moore has since moved on to become possibly Ireland's best-loved singer, recording a number of highly successful and acclaimed albums. In his first recordings, such as the album *Prosperous*, he was overtly political in the style of Woody Guthrie or the early Bob Dylan. This commitment is also evident in his recordings with Moving Hearts, such as his protest against state repression *No Time for Love* and, in the mid-1980s album *The Time has Come,* his song *Section 31* which criticized the Republic's media censorship of Sinn Féin. Though Moore has become less politically engaged, his popularity has been maintained through stunning live performances, including regular mainstays such as the comic *Lisdoonvarna* and the ballad *Ride On*. Finally, in 1996, after years of singing others' songs, he released a self-penned album *Graffiti Tongue*. In 1998 he announced his retirement on the grounds of ill-health, but returned at the end of the following year with a grand new album and has recently started touring again, albeit on a much smaller scale.

Moore's brother Barry records under the name **Luka Bloom** (a combination of Suzanne Vega's song and the protagonist of *Ulysses*). Early on he backed his brother who recorded some of Bloom's work, most notably *The City of Chicago*. With a reputation himself for magnificent live performances he has also made some fine albums including *Turf* and *Salty Heaven*.

Of the other musicians recording crossover traditional music and folk in the 1960s, **Paul Brady** continues to produce music of an exceptional standard. From Strabane in County Tyrone, Brady became involved in the Dublin folk renaissance while studying there. His first recordings were made with The Johnstons with whom he made seven albums before leaving for London and New York, returning in 1974 to join Planxty for a short time. In 1976 he teamed up with Planxty member Andy Irvine, and the album they produced, with its unique and sensitive interpretations of songs such as *Arthur McBride*, is one of the finest albums in the traditional canon. His work in the late 1970s was of an equally high standard, culminating in arguably his best solo album, *Welcome Here Kind Stranger*, in 1978, featuring his benchmark rendition of *The Lakes of Ponchartrain*. The 1980s saw Brady move away from his traditional roots through *Hard Station* (1981), which included the passionate exposé of anti-Irish racism, *Nothing but the Same Old Story*. Subsequent albums have further highlighted his tremendous songwriting talents – he's been recorded by Tina Turner and Eric Clapton among many others and the best way of sampling these is his remastered compilation *Nobody Knows*.

Contemporary bands striving for new ways to express the tradition are the excellent **Kíla**, whose latest album *Lemonade & Buns* mixes traditional singing with African rhythms, the superb **Afro Celt Sound System** and **Anúna**, a vocal group spanning classical, folk, traditional and contemporary. Other experimental outfits include **Flook**, featuring the astonishing young *bodhrán* player **John Joe Kelly** and a twin flute attack, and the **Mike McGoldrick/John McSherry Band** who explore traditional music through a variety of fusion contexts. The Belfast acoustic guitarist **Colin Reid** has also produced a couple of startlingly original CDs, including 2001's *Tilt*.

Any examination of Irish traditional music must include a reference to **The Pogues**. Originally known as Pogue Mahone ("kiss my arse" in Irish), this London-Irish band emerged in the early 1980s playing a chaotic set of "Oirish" standards and rebel songs. Iconoclasts to the core, they brought a punk energy to the Irish ballad. They were also blessed with one of the finest Irish songwriters of recent years, **Shane MacGowan**. His songs captured the casualties and condition of Irish exile in London and, said fan and producer Elvis Costello, "saved folk from the folkies". Certainly they helped bring a new audience, and a new generation of musicians, back to look at its roots. MacGowan subsequently formed his own band The Popes and released three albums, though none matched the glorious exuberance of The Pogues' *Red Roses for Me* or *Rum, Sodomy and the Lash*. The influence of The Pogues remains strong and currently is incarnate in the music of the raucous **Blood and Whiskey** and the more refrained **Dúchas**.

Rock, pop and dance music

Naturally, Ireland's rock scene has always borne close similarities to Britain's. Physical proximity, the permeation of British mass media, especially radio and the influential rock press, and British stars' use of Dublin as a tax haven have all facilitated a musical currency between the two. What happens in London, Liverpool or Manchester tends to be mirrored in Belfast and Dublin and, occasionally, vice versa. However, there are two significant exceptions. First, apart from mavericks like Richard Thompson or the Oysterband, British rock and pop bear little indication of any traditional folk origins, whereas Irish rock culture is steeped in it – a hardly surprising conclusion considering the number of Irish musicians who learn a traditional instrument and its associated tunes at an early age. Secondly, the overwhelmingly mono-cultural nature of Irish society means that important components of the British scene – reggae, ragga, bhangra, black dance and soul music in its many variations – are rarely experienced first-hand or develop from cultural traditions. Two Tone, for instance, could never have happened in Dublin, just as a host of Clannad clones is never likely to appear in Coventry. Nevertheless, the country's rock heritage is a rich one and, for every dozen bands trying to be the new Coldplay, there's always something happening in the pubs and clubs of Dublin, Cork, Belfast and Derry.

Showbands and beat

For most of the 1960s and the following decade, live music was dominated by that peculiarly Irish phenomenon, the **showband**. These groups of neatly coiffed, shiny-suited cover-version merchants toured the country, playing their selections in vast ballrooms (barely a few of which survive today). Enthusiasm tended to supersede talent, but their regimentation did provide a training ground for future stars such as Rory Gallagher and Eric Bell (Thin Lizzy's first guitarist).

The showbands' dominance was undermined by the arrival of **beat music**, conveyed by radio and, like Liverpool, by sailors bringing American R&B records to the ports of Dublin and Belfast. By the mid-1960s Dublin was awash with beat groups, the majority of whom are long- (and perhaps best-) forgotten, though you can hear examples of the recordings of The Greenbeats, The Movement, Purple Pussycat and a horde of others on the Sequel collection *Ireland's Beat Groups: 1964–69*. The most successful group was **Bluesville**, led by Ian Whitcomb, an American studying at Trinity College, which had a US top ten hit with *You Turn Me On*. Meanwhile, in Belfast, George Ivan Morrison had got together with guitarist Billy Harrison to form **Them**. **Van Morrison** (see p.639) had toured with another Belfast band, The Monarchs, since 1959, when he was only 14, but Them's successes with *Baby, Please Don't Go* (the B-side was the wonderful *Gloria*) and *Here Comes the Night* established musical credentials which he has never relinquished. Dissatisfied with his management, constant personnel changes and the quality of the band's first two albums, Morrison left and moved to the US. After disastrous experiences with the Bang label, he signed with Warner Brothers; his first two albums with them achieved astonishing critical, if not entirely commercial, success and established the hallmarks of his style. The marvellously atmospheric *Astral Weeks* was recorded in only two days, consisting of apparent improvisation by an adept band adroitly working around Van's range of vocal stylings and poetic lyrics. *Moondance* followed two years later, in 1970, revealing his ability to construct compact songs characterized by a sense of relaxation, though driven by extremely tight instrumentation. Since then Morrison has released numerous albums, of late almost annually, but while none has attained the excellence of the early pair, he remains the consummate professional and a tremendous experience live.

Morrison's love of the blues was shared by the Donegal-born guitarist **Rory Gallagher** (see p.569). Extracting himself from the showband scene, Gallagher was first successful as leader of the progressive blues band **Taste** where he developed a reputation for his powerful rolling guitar licks. Taste split acrimoniously in 1970, citing the then popular "musical differences" and Gallagher launched a creditable solo career, using a variety of bassists and drummers, notable for his range of checked shirts and the intensity of his live performances (captured semi-successfully on *Irish Tour* and *Live! in Europe*). His later career was bedevilled by health problems and, sadly, he died in 1995.

The Seventies

Ireland dabbled with psychedelia and for a time the music scene was dominated by bands such as Granny's Intentions, Dr Strangely Strange and Eire Apparent. However, it was **Skid Row**'s more straight-out-the-barrel rock which was to have a lasting impact. The original band featured the bassist **Brush Shiels** (still playing regularly in Dublin), an astonishingly young Belfast lad, **Gary Moore**, on guitar and, for a while, **Phil Lynott** as singer. Skid Row released two progressive albums in the early 1970s, after which Moore left – he later played with a variety of other bands running the gamut of rock to heavy metal before establishing himself as a major solo performer and interpreter of the blues.

Phil Lynott, however, formed **Thin Lizzy**, the first Irish band to crack the world market which led to Lynott becoming the first black Irish superstar. Initial success came with a reworking of the traditional *Whiskey in the Jar* in 1973. Then followed a series of albums, dominated by Lynott's romantic lyrics and a characteristic twin lead guitar sound. The 1976 album *Jailbreak* retains its initial impact, even if the macho posturing of its biggest hit, *The Boys are Back in Town*, jangles raucously in an era of more considered sensibilities. Lynott later produced a couple of fine, though sadly overlooked, solo albums (*Solo in Soho* is the better), before dying from kidney and liver failure in 1986.

Elsewhere, two more folk-oriented bands enjoyed a modicum of popularity in the early 1970s. The acoustic duo **Tír na nÓg** supported virtually everybody and made a couple of whimsical albums for Chrysalis. Meanwhile, **Horslips** were almost single-handedly responsible for Celtic Rock. Retrospectively, their Irish legend-based concept albums such as *The Táin* (1973) and *The Book of Invasions* (1976) seem clumsily contrived in context and obscure in content – as many such albums were – but their use of traditional instruments in a rock setting was of durable influence and they blazed a trail for later bands to follow, such as **Moving Hearts** (see p.838), **In Tua Nua** and **Lick the Tins**.

There may have been fewer Irish dinosaurs to be declared extinct, but the advent of punk and new wave in the second half of the 1970s reinvigorated the home scene. However, the initial success of **The Boomtown Rats**, led by **Bob Geldof**, relied on their ability to produce powerful three-minute pop songs such as *Rat Trap* (1978) and *I Don't Like Mondays* (1979). For a while the Dublin scene thrived through bands such as **The Radiators from Space** (featuring later Pogues guitarist Philip Chevron), **The Virgin Prunes**, **The Blades** and a very young bunch of hopefuls called **The Hype**. Perhaps the greater successes, however, were in the North. **Stiff Little Fingers** first came to notice in 1978 with their astonishingly powerful debut single *Suspect Device*, a song whose driving beat struggled to contain an equally powerful lyric of political discontent. Meanwhile, **The Undertones** had been formed in Derry in 1974, but failed to achieve any success until the BBC Radio One disc jockey John Peel adopted their *Teenage Kicks* as a virtual personal anthem. Four albums of finely crafted perceptive songs followed, mixing in perfect harmony the **O'Neill Brothers**' songs of adolescent yearning, **Feargal Sharkey**'s idiosyncratic tremolo voice and a pumping beat. After their split in 1983 Sharkey had a couple of solo hit singles while Damien and John O'Neill formed **That Petrol Emotion** whose initial releases were marked by powerful political sentiments questioning the continued British presence in Ireland. The Undertones (albeit without Feargal) have recently reformed and are wowing Derry audiences once again.

U2 to The Corrs

The Hype, having changed their name to **U2**, went on to become the biggest rock band in the world. Listening to their first album *Boy* (1980), it's just about possible to understand the reason. Then, as now, U2's ability to try their hand at a range of styles is very much apparent, even if their original efforts lacked their subsequent polish and grasp of studio technique. Nevertheless, the key elements have remained the same: a tight rhythm bedrock of **Adam Clayton** (bass) and **Larry Mullen** (drums) setting the framework for **Dave Evans**'s innovative chordal guitar stylings and **Bono**'s soaring voice. Their anthems proved ideal American stadium fodder and the video of *Under a Blood Red Sky* (1983) brought them an even wider audience. *The Joshua Tree (*1987), however, was their major breakthrough, despite the bleakness of songs such as *Where the Streets Have No Name* and *I Still Haven't Found What I'm Looking For*. The album even spawned a notable group of Dublin parodists, The Joshua Trio, featuring one of the future authors of *Father Ted*. The release of subsequent U2 albums and their associated tours have become major international events and Bono has become Ireland's greatest living love-hate figure, derided for his occasional pomposity (such as his on-stage telephone calls to political leaders), but revered for his undeniable care for his country (such as his appearance at Ash's 1998 peace settlement gig with the politicians David Trimble and John Hume). The year 2000 saw the band return to their musical roots with an album, *All You Can't Leave Behind*, which exudes the style, confidence and distinctive rock melodies that won them such acclaim in the 1980s.

Following U2's ascent to glory, Dublin's bars and clubs were awash with agents and talent scouts trying to sign "the next big thing". Most of the recordings of these bands have sunk without trace and few now recall Cactus World News, Cry Before Dawn or Light a Big Fire, though Aslan reformed in the late 1990s. A couple are worth noting – the country-tinged **Stars of Heaven**, who sadly split before the talent displayed in their debut *Sacred Heart Hotel* could evolve further, and the continued efforts of **Gavin Friday** (first with the Virgin Prunes and later solo) to gain the audience he deserves for his original confection of the baroque and bizarre. A significantly successful signing, however, was the then shaven-headed young singer, **Sinéad O'Connor**, first with her Prince-written single *Nothing Compares 2 U* and later with the album *I Do Not Want What I Haven't Got* (1990). Yet it was her outspoken public pronouncements on Ireland, abortion and papal power which brought her even greater attention. Oppressed by her fame, she left Ireland and moved to London to rear her children, only to return after undergoing a much-publicized religious conversion, which she claimed to be the inspiration behind her disappointing album *Faith and Courage* (2000). Ever courting controversy, Sinead's latest album, *Sean-Nós Nua* (2002) is a reinterpretation of many well-known traditional ballads. At the time of writing, Sinead had also just recorded tracks with Massive Attack for their forthcoming album *100th Window*.

Every musical genre seems to be represented in twenty-first-century Ireland. There are plenty of solo singers ploughing their lonely furrows. Apart from Paul Brady and Christy Moore (see p.838), those currently popular include **Sinéad Lohan**, **Eleanor McEvoy**, **Kieran Goss**, **Paddy Casey**, **Damien Rice, Gemma Hayes, Damien Dempsey, John Spillane** (formerly of the traditional band Nomos) and the ethereally voiced **Cara Dillon**. Also worth seeking out are the sporadically released albums by **Pierce Turner** (quirky avant-garde meets Irish sensibility), the blues and jazz of the smoky-voiced **Mary Coughlan**, while *Metropolis Blue* (2000) has seen the sublime **Jack Lukeman** receive the recognition he has long deserved. **The Cranberries**, after enjoying brief global success in the mid-1990s, attempted to re-establish themselves with *Bury the Hatchet* (1999) – the critics promptly threw one instead. In contrast, still going strong are **The Saw Doctors** whose whimsical and bucolic take on rock has been immensely popular ever since they first hit the heights back in 1991 with *I Useta Lover*. At one time it seemed as though the film *The Commitments* would sire a host of spin-off bands; only one, Glenn Hansard's **The Frames** has had any lasting impact, with their 2000 album *Dance the Devil* hugely popular in the alternative music scene. Other bands to enjoy success have included **Hothouse Flowers** (led by Liam O'Maonlai), **The Frank and Walters**, **A House**, **An Emotional Fish**, **Something Happens**, **The Sultans of Ping FC** and two notable results from the break-up of the wonderfully angry 1980s band **Microdisney** – the raw psychopathy of Cathal Coughlan's **Fatima Mansions** and the Beach Boys-inspired work of **The High Llamas**, led by Sean O'Hagan. **Coughlan** has since released a highly impressive solo album *Black River Falls* (2000). Mention must also be made of the traditional-inspired "Celtic hush" music of Donegal's now defunct **Clannad** and the more ambient, but exceedingly popular, doodles of their fellow family member **Enya**. There's a thriving dance scene in Ireland, too, with the most innovative and universally acclaimed work being produced by **David Holmes** from Belfast. *Stop Arresting Artists*, a box set of 12-inch remixes, was released in 1999, followed in 2000 by arguably the finest Irish album of the year, *Bow Down to the Exit Sign*, which succeeds in capturing the seedy underside of New York City where the album was recorded. 2002 saw the release of *Come Get It I Got It* and *David Holmes presents The Free Association*. Ethereal electronica can be found in *My Fault* (2000) the debut album of **Metisse** fronted by sensual French vocalist Aida.

At the forefront of the resurgence of Northern Ireland as a hotbed for young talent are **Ash** from Downpatrick who, having showed precocious polish on their debut album *1977*, have come of musical age with a succession of powerful albums. One-man band, **Neil Hannon**, better-known as **The Divine Comedy**, gained a loyal following with quirky recordings such as *Casanova* (1995) which evoke the sharp-suited romance of a James Bond movie. Other bands worth looking out for are **Watercress**, who hit the mark with their infectiously poppy *Bummer* album (1999) and **Snow Patrol** (originally from Belfast though now based in Glasgow). In the Republic, bands with significant potential include **Cyclefly** (fronted by the pink-haired Declan O'Shea), **Romolos Pop**, **Horizon**, **The Devlins** and **Crayonz**. Ireland's only rock paper, the superb *Hot Press*, is the place to look for information.

However, apart from the old reliables (Moore, Morrison and so on), the favourite Irish artistes of the moment, naturally, come from the more mainstream areas. The teen market is catered for by bands fathered by Ireland's pop impresario Louis Walsh, the man responsible for boy-bands **Boyzone** (who spawned the solo careers of **Ronan Keating** and **Stephen Gately**) and **Westlife**, though the lads are being outshone of late by his latest teen (now twenties) sensation **Samantha Mumba**. For a time in the late 1990s the girl-band **B*witched** also dominated the UK pop charts. The middle-aged, of course, are not left out and their darling is **Daniel O'Donnell**, the homely Donegal singer of standards, country and western and gospel who broke a million hearts by getting married in 2002. Lastly, tapping the sensitivities of *Rumours*-period Fleetwood Mac, albeit with a strong Irish traditional influence, are the family foursome, **The Corrs** (three sisters, one brother), whose bright good looks and anodyne, but catchy, songs have been recorded on two hugely popular albums *Forgiven not Forgotten* (1997) and *Talk on Corners* (1998) which have guaranteed them global popularity and healthy bank accounts for years to come.

Classical music

As in the visual arts, Ireland has a strong classical music tradition, though it's little known outside the island. The dominant instrument of early music was the **harp**, though we know little of how it was played since no written record has survived. However, more than two hundred works by the poet, harper and composer **Turlough O'Carolan** (1670–1738) have survived. His work, together with the performances of the participants at the 1792 **Belfast Harp Festival**, transcribed and published by **Edward Bunting**, were the prime sources of the airs which have formed a major component of Irish music since that time.

During the eighteenth century, Dublin became an important musical centre and attracted many European composers, including **Handel**, who staged the premiere of the *Messiah* in the capital in 1742. The first native classical composer of note was **John Field** (1782–1837), who, as a child prodigy, was apprenticed to Clementi to demonstrate pianos. He taught in Europe for several years and produced a significant body of keyboard work, especially his *19 Nocturnes* which considerably influenced Chopin and other Romantics.

Another precocious child was **Michael Balfe** (1808–70), who made his debut as a violinist at the age of nine, though he had already begun composing two years earlier. During the 1820s, he studied under Rossini and became converted to the opera form. Numerous compositions followed and his *The Bohemian Girl* was a success of the time. From 1846, he was conductor of the London Italian Opera. Similarly popular were the operas of Waterford man **Vincent Wallace** (1813–65), particularly *Maritana* and *Lurina*. This Irish operatic tradition was continued by **Victor Herbert** (1859–1924), a cellist who played in the orchestras of Joseph Strauss before emigrating to the US to join the New York Metropolitan Opera Company. His forte was the comic opera and he became popular for songs such as *Sweet Mystery of Life* before settling down to pen more serious work. Most prolific in this period, however, was **Charles Villiers Stanford** (1852–1924), who was organist at Trinity College, Cambridge. After a stint teaching at the Royal College of Music he became Professor of Music at Cambridge and taught numerous young British composers of the era. In his own right he adapted Tennyson's poetry to choral settings and wrote a number of operas and religious pieces. His origins are reflected by his *Irish Symphony* and *Six Irish Rhapsodies*.

In the first half of the twentieth century, **Hamilton Harty** (1880–1941), from Hillsborough, County Down, attained a degree of fame through his conducting of the Hallé Orchestra from 1920 to 1933 and revived Handel's popularity through his arrangements of the *Fireworks* and *Water Music* suites. However, his own work, including an *Irish Symphony* utilizing the strains and melodies of traditional songs, is less well known. **A.J. Potter** (1918–80), the son of a blind Belfast piano-tuner, was Professor of Composition at the Royal Irish Academy of Music for almost twenty years and his own eclectic style influenced many of his students. Other notable figures have included the popular conductor **Brian Boydell** (b. 1917) whose works for orchestra and string quartet are influenced by Bartok and Hindesmith, and **Gerard Victory** (1921–1995), who became well known via his work with the RTÉ Symphony Orchestra from 1967 onwards. Head of Music at the RTÉ for some of the same time was **John Kinsella** (b. 1932) until he resigned in 1988 to devote himself to full-time composition, subsequently producing a number of influential works. **Seóirse Bodley** (b. 1933) has written five full symphonies and numerous other works revealing influences ranging from the European avant-garde to traditional song. **Gerald Barry** (b. 1952) studied composition under Stockhausen and has had many works commissioned by the BBC, additionally penning operas for the ICA and Channel 4. The flautist **John Buckley** (b. 1951) has produced a range of works for solo instruments and various ensembles. Intriguingly, the latest generation of composers producing influential work includes a significant number of **young women**, including Elaine Agnew, Rhona Clarke, Siobhan Cleary and Deirdre Gribbin – a trend which bodes well for the future.

Finally, the more popular end of the home market has come to be dominated recently by composers experimenting with adaptations and reformulations of Irish traditional music. Notable exponents include **Patrick Cassidy**, **Michael Alcorn** and **Shaun Davey**, while **Michael Ó Súilleabháin**'s recordings in this genre, such as *The Dolphin's Way* and his most recent album *Templum* (featuring the Irish Chamber Orchestra), have attained considerable success. However, without any doubt, the most famous (or notorious, depending on your viewpoint) is **Bill Whelan**, responsible for the *Riverdance* phenomenon and a huge increase in the sale of dancing shoes.

Literature

Oscar Wilde once sighed to Yeats that "we Irish have done nothing, but we are the greatest talkers since the Greeks"; Samuel Beckett claimed that Irish writers had been "buggered into existence by the English army and the Roman pope". **Irish writing** has always flouted and challenged, experimented and fantasized, from the great anti-novel, Joyce's *Ulysses*, to what some see as the great anti-play, Beckett's *Waiting for Godot*. Much Irish writing concerns the dysfunction of real life, but this is usually laced with wild, fantastical and spiritual imaginings; one of the country's great contemporary novelists, Patrick McCabe, claims, in a typical Irish inversion, this should be deemed "social fantastic" not "poetic realism". Authors from Swift to Roddy Doyle present us with the conflict between high ideals and sordid reality, a conflict captured by Beckett when he claimed he wanted to "sit around, scratch my arse and think of Dante". Tension has also come from writing in a language that belongs, essentially, to another tradition. This is most clearly articulated by Nobel laureate Seamus Heaney who sees the conflict between his folk background, what he deems "hearth culture", and expressing himself in poetry, the most formal genre in English, as the central dynamic in his work. Thus any study of Irish literature must begin with an examination of the folk culture and tradition to which Irish writers belong.

The Gaels

Irish writing first appeared in the fifth century AD when monastic settlers brought Classical culture into contact with a Gaelic civilization that had a long and sophisticated oral tradition. Faced with the resistance of the pagan bards, the newcomers set about incorporating the Celtic sagas into the comparatively young system of Christian belief. These ancient tales told of war and famine, madness and love, death and magical rebirth – story sequences from deep in the folk memory. One of the earliest of these, the **Taín Bó Cuailnge** (Cattle Raid of Cooley), deals with a rumpus between **Cúchulainn**, a prototypical Celtic superman, and the mighty Queen Medb, over the theft of a prize bull. The best translation of the epic is, without doubt, Thomas Kinsella's *The Taín* (1969), which has an excellent introduction and a map of areas relating to the tale. The series of tales concerning Cúchulainn, known as the **Ulster Cycle,** were, from the eighth century, superseded by those concerning the exploits of **Fionn Mac Cumhaill** and his posse, the Fianna, known as the **Ossianic Cycle**. Fionn was a more disturbing and sophisticated figure, not only a warrior but a poet, sage and mystic; in the most prominent tale in the cycle, *Tóraigheacht Dhiarmada agus Ghráinne* (Pursuit of Diarmaid and Gráinne), Fionn is represented as a jealous, ageing warrior, irate at being cuckolded by the young Diarmaid and chasing him and his former lover Gráinne around Ireland.

Later Irish artists made much of the early tales, sometimes with less than proper reverence; in Beckett's novel *Murphy* (1938), for instance, a character attempts suicide by banging his head repeatedly against the bronze buttocks of the statue of Cúchulainn, which adorns the lobby of Dublin's GPO. Another tale which has proved an inspiration to many writers is *Buile Suibhne* (Frenzy of Sweeney), a twelfth-century text detailing the adventures of the king **Sweeney** who, driven mad by the noise of incessant warfare, seeks refuge in the tree tops of Ireland, where he writes lyrical nature poetry. This tale was one of the inspirations behind Flann O'Brien's novel *At Swim-Two-Birds* (see p.867), while Seamus Heaney's *Sweeney Astray* (1983) is a lyrical translation of the mythical wanderings of the mad king.

Fairy tales from this Celtic era reveal a world of witches, imps and banshees, all jollying around in a Manichaean struggle with the forces of love, wisdom and goodness – which, refreshingly, do not always triumph. Check out Kevin Danaher's *In Ireland Long Ago* (1962) for full-blooded retellings.

A literature of resistance

The first of many incursions from England took place in the twelfth century, when gangs of Norman adventurers invaded at the invitation of an Irish king. But it wasn't until four centuries later that the English presence found its way into the literature, when the excesses of English rule began finally to provoke an early literature of resistance.

The high point of this Irish-language tradition is the long poem by **Eibhlín Dhubh Ní Chonaill** (1748–1800), *Caoineadh Airt Uí Laoghaire* (A Lament for Art O'Leary). A traditional *caoineadh*, or lament, infused with a new political awareness, it deals with the execution of the poet's lover, who had refused to sell his prized white horse to the Sheriff of Cork and was therefore hunted down and killed; even in translation this has a sparse and chilling beauty.

Other marvellous laments include the anonymous *Donal Óg*, Lady Gregory's translation of which was included with cheeky but effective licence in the 1985 John Huston film of Joyce's short story, *The Dead*. But the early written tradition wasn't all tears, and some pieces harked back to a pre-Christian earthiness. One such text from the later Irish-language era is **Brian Merriman**'s satirical *aisling* (vision poem), *Cúirt an Mheán Oíche* (The Midnight Court; 1967), a trenchant attack on the sexual inadequacy of the Irish male.

Despite persecution, the Irish language persisted as a majority tongue well into the nineteenth century, and Seán Ó Tuama and Thomas Kinsella's book of translations, *An Duanaire: Poems of the Dispossessed*, records the voices of those marginalized by foreign rule and famine. However, defying both economic realities and the ineptitude of successive Irish governments, the Irish language has survived, and in recent years has produced an impressive canon of its own, far removed from the rural preoccupations it is often associated with. Such preoccupations were exemplified by story-teller **Peig Sayers** (1873–1958) – still perhaps the most famous Irish-language author in the country – whose recounting of the misery of life on one of Ireland's westerly outposts was the set text in Irish schools and which, not surprisingly, turned bored urban schoolchildren against the language for life. Far preferable is **Pádraig Ó Conaire** (1883–1928), whose *Scothscéalta* reads like Maupassant, capturing the stark cruelty of the Irish landscape and the petty malices of rural life.

The first step towards modernity in Irish writing was, in many ways, the wickedly satirical and hilariously funny *An Béal Bocht* (The Poor Mouth; 1941) by **Myles na Gopaleen**, aka Flann O'Brien (see p.853), which satirized such classic Gaelic works on the difficulty of life on Ireland's western seaboard. **Seán Ó Ríordáin** (1916–77) from west Cork drew heavily on both the Gaelic and Modernist traditions in his poems, while the poetry of **Máirtín Ó Díreáin** (1910–88) from the Aran Islands explored the themes of deracination and the anonymity of urban life. This modernist tradition greatly influenced a group of poets working out of University College Cork, the **Innti** group, whose writing embraced all manner of urban and popular cultural references. The most prominent of this group is **Nuala Ní Dhomhnaill**, whose work marks an engagement between the feminist and Gaelic traditions and is well received both in Irish and English translation. **Gabriel Rosenstock** and **Cathal Ó Searcaigh** are prolific writers and translators, working closely with Seamus Heaney; the latter's *Out in the Open* (1997) causing a stir because of its sexual candidness. Other contemporary poets writing in Irish are **Michael O'Siadhail** whose collected poems were published in 1999 and **Michael Davitt** whose work, heavily influenced by American Beat poetry, can be read in *Selected Poems 1970–98.*

The start of the literary tradition

Between the 1690s and the 1720s the hated penal laws were passed, denying Catholics rights to property, education, political activity and religious practice. British misrule created widespread poverty which devastated the countryside and ravaged the population. It's in this period that **Anglo-Irish literature** began.

One of the most prominent of the early pamphleteers and agitators was **John Toland** (1670–1722), to whom the authorities gave the dubious distinction of being the first Irish writer to have his work publicly burned. But the first big-league player arrived in the angry little shape of **Jonathan Swift** (1667–1745; see also p.106), Dean of St Patrick's Cathedral, Dublin. Swift was a cantankerous but basically compassionate man who used his pen to expose viciousness, hypocrisy and corruption whenever he saw it, which in eighteenth-century Dublin was pretty often. Swift was a master of satire; in one of his 75 pamphlets, *A Modest Proposal*, he proposed that the children of the poor should be cooked to feed the rich, thereby eliminating poverty and increasing affluence, and his masterpiece, *Gulliver's Travels*, is as terrifying now as it ever was. He died a bitter man, leaving in his will an endowment to build Dublin's first lunatic asylum, adding in a pithy codicil that if he'd had enough money he would have arranged for a twenty-foot-high wall to be built around the entire island. He is buried in the vault of St Patrick's, where, as his epitaph says, "fierce indignation can no longer rend his heart".

The other great satirist of the eighteenth century was **Laurence Sterne** (1713–1768). A tremendous wit with more mad whimsy than venom, his greatest work *Tristram Shandy* was once memorably described as "the greatest shaggy dog story in the language".

The elegant prose of **Edmund Burke** (1729–97) – graduate of Trinity College, philosopher, journalist and MP – argued for order in all things, decrying the French Revolution for its destruction of humanity's basic need for faith. He is a complex and difficult figure, and his ideas are claimed in Ireland both by the civil-liberties-trampling Right and by elements of the progressive Left.

1780–1880: the Celtic revival

Towards the end of the eighteenth century, a Europe-wide vogue for all things Celtic prompted a renaissance in Irish music and literature. This period also saw the birth of that misty, ineffable Celtic spirit, which was to influence Yeats a century later. A couple of important books appeared, including **Joseph Cooper Walker**'s *Historical Memoirs of the Irish Bards* (1786) and **Edward Bunting**'s *A General Collection of the Ancient Irish Music* (1796).

Dublin at the time of the Act of Union with Britain (1801) had long been a truly European city, frequently visited by French, German and Italian composers. Indeed, Handel's *Messiah* was first performed in Dublin's Fishamble Street. One Irish composer and writer who thrived under the European influence was the harpist **Turlough O'Carolan**, who met and traded riffs with the Italian composer Geminiani.

At the turn of the century a series of Irish harp festivals began, their purpose being to recover the rapidly disappearing ancient music. With their evocation of the bardic tradition they became a focus not just for nifty fingerwork but for political agitation. The harpists continued into the nineteenth century until **Thomas Moore** (1779–1852) finally stole many of their traditional airs, wrote words for them, published them as *Moore's Irish Melodies* and made a lot of money.

The concomitant literary revival entailed a resurrection of the Irish language too, and although few went so far as to learn it, it became a vague symbol of a heroic literary past that implied a fundamentally nationalist world view. John Mitchell's Fenian movement, provoked by Britain's callous response to the Famine, was at least as influenced by the Celtic revival as it was by the new revolutionary ideas being imported all the time from Europe. The Fenians were to provide a bridge between the heroic past and the demands of modernism and had a huge impact on the thinking of Yeats and other leaders of the Celtic revival. One of their supporters, **James Clarence Mangan** (1803–49), inaugurated in *My Dark Rosaleen* the image of suffering Ireland as a brutalized woman, awaiting defence by a heroic man. In a country where visual and literary imagery of the Virgin Mary is ubiquitous, the symbolism escaped nobody.

The nineteenth-century novel

The unease generated among the aristocracy by the growth of Irish Nationalism and the Fenian Rebellion of 1848 found expression in novels showing the peasantry plotting away in their cottages against their masters up in the mansion – the "Big House" sub-genre of Anglo-Irish writing, represented by such writers as **Lady Morgan** (1775–1859). Typically, such a book would involve an evil-smelling Irish hoodlum inheriting the mansion and either turning it into a barn or burning it to the ground. *Castle Rackrent* by **Maria Edgeworth** (1776–1849) is one of the few good Big House novels, its craftily resourceful narrator telling the story of the great family's demise with a subtle glee.

The Irish fought back, appropriating the well-made novel for themselves. **Gerald Griffin** (1803–40), **John Banim** (1798–1842), **William Carleton** (1794–1869) and **Charles Lever** (1806–72) emerged as the voice of the new middle class, protesting at the stereotyping of the Irish as savages, and demanding political and economic rights.

This period also saw the entry of the Anglo-Irish into the crisis that would haunt them until their complete demise in the 1920s, as they struggled between the specifically "Anglo" and "Irish" sides of their identity. This kind of angst can be found running throughout the work of **Sir Samuel Ferguson** (1810–86), **Standish O'Grady** (1846–1928) and **Douglas Hyde** (1860–1949), the founder of the Gaelic League in 1893 who went on to become Ireland's first president in 1937.

The writing of **E.O. Somerville** (1858–1949) and **(Violet) Martin Ross** (1861–1915) – cousins and increasingly impoverished daughters of the Ascendancy – is typical of nineteenth-century Anglo-Irish confusion. Their work, such as *The Irish RM* and the powerful novel *The Real Charlotte*, is imbued with a genuine love of Ireland and the ways of the Irish peasantry, yet occasionally there's a chilling sense that the status quo is in danger. The peasants, previously marginalized in the tradition, now seem to keep intruding in unwelcome ways, sneaking into the upstairs rooms, interrupting their betters or conspiring behind the bushes in the estate's well-kept gardens.

Meanwhile **Bram Stoker** (1847–1912) was busily writing his way into the history books with a work that would enter modern popular culture in all its forms, from the movies to the comic book. *Dracula* is a wonderful novel, more of a psychological Gothic thriller than a schlock horror bloodbath, and its concerns – the nature of the soul versus the bestial allure of the body, for instance – are curiously Irish. But even this had political implications. With its pseudo-folkloric style and its pitting of the noble peasants against the aristocratic monster debauching away in his castle, its symbolism is inescapably revolutionary and romantic.

The story of the stage Irishman

It's one of the delicious twists of fate which seem to beset Irish literary history that the country's most important early dramatist only took up writing by mistake. One evening a young Derry actor named **George Farquhar** (1677–1707) was playing a bit part in the duel scene of Dryden's *Indian Emperor* at the Dublin Smock Alley theatre when, in a moment of tragic enthusiasm, he accidentally stabbed a fellow actor, almost killing him. Understandably shaken, Farquhar gave up the stage for good and went off to London to write plays instead.

Farquhar is often credited with the invention of the stage Irishman, the descendants of whom can still be seen in many soap operas and situation comedies on British television to this day. Effusive in his own way, but basically sly, stupid and violent, this stock character stumbled through the dramas of **Steele** (1672–1729), **Chaigneau** (1709–81), **Goldsmith** (1728–74) and **Sheridan** (1751–1816), tugging his forelock, bumping into the furniture and going "bejayzus" at every available moment. In fact Irish stereotypes had existed in the British tradition for many centuries before these dramatists had at least the good sense to make some money out of them. The stage Irishman was brought to his ultimate idiocy by **Dion Boucicault** (1820–90), whose leprechaunic characters seemed to have staggered straight out of the Big House novel and onto the London stage. Boucicault, however, has undergone something of a revival in recent years, with a few critics arguing that his unstable and unpredictable dramas were subversive attacks against the version of colonial reality imposed upon Ireland in the nineteenth century.

Boucicault's chum, **George Bernard Shaw** (1856–1950), turned out to be the kind of stage Irishman the English couldn't patronize out of existence. A radical socialist and feminist, he championed all kinds of cranky causes and some very admirable ones, and lived long enough to be a founder member of CND. His cerebral and often polemical plays, of which *Saint Joan* is perhaps the best, have remained a mainstay of theatre repertoire (see also box on p.92).

Yet even Shaw paled in comparison to the ultimate king of the one-line put-down, **Oscar Wilde** (1856–1900). After a brilliant career at Oxford – during which he lost both his virginity and his Irish accent – Wilde went on to set literary London alight, creating the smiling resentment that would finally destroy him. In *The Picture of Dorian Gray* he expanded on the Gothic tradition of Stoker and **Sheridan Le Fanu** (1814–73) to explore the fundamental duality of the romantic hero. But it was in his satirical plays, particularly *The Importance of Being Earnest*, that he was at his most acerbic. A brilliant and gentle man, he poured scorn on his critics, openly espoused home rule for Ireland and lived with consummate style until the debacle of his affair with Lord Alfred Douglas. This self-obsessed bimbo persuaded Wilde into a foolish libel action against Douglas's thuggish father, the Marquess of Queensbury, which Wilde lost. Immediately afterwards he was arrested for homosexuality, publicly disgraced and privately condemned by his many fair-weather friends. He served two years in prison where he wrote his finest works, *The Ballad of Reading Gaol* and *De Profundis* (published in 1905 after his death). In early 1900 one of Ireland's greatest, and most tragic, writers, died alone and distraught in Paris. "I will never live into the new century", he declared. "The English would just not allow it."

Irish Modernism: poetry and drama

Shortly before Wilde's death, the myth of the fallen hero had entered the vocabulary of Irish literature with the demise of Charles Stewart Parnell, Protestant hero of the Irish Nationalist community. Savaged from the pulpit and the editorial page for his adulterous involvement with Kitty O'Shea, Parnell had resigned in disgrace, defended by only a few lonely voices in the literary world. He died shortly afterwards, and Irish constitutional politics died with him.

The changed atmosphere of Irish life is caught in the work of **J.M. Synge** (1871–1909) and **George Moore** (1852–1933), who wrestled to accommodate a tradition they now saw rapidly slipping into the hands of the priests. Synge's *The Playboy of the Western World*, with its parricidal hero, is the last and perhaps the most brilliant attempt at a fundamentally English view of Irish peasant life, and was greeted by riots when it opened at the Abbey. His friend George Moore identified Catholicism as a life-denying and authoritarian creed, and his extraordinary volume *The Untilled Field*, published in 1903, in many ways anticipates much later writers.

William Butler Yeats (1865–1939), one of the most written about but most elusive characters in Irish literature, was a Protestant aristocrat who argued for Irish independence and helped found the world's first national theatre, the

Abbey, before the nation even existed. He wrote early lyrical ballads about gossamer fairies and stunning sunsets until, stricken with desire for the beautiful Maude Gonne, he began reaming out some of the century's greatest poetry of unrequited love. Much of the work of his middle period lambasts the Dublin middle class for its money-grabbing complacency – *September 1913* is well worth a read if white-lipped rage is your thing. In 1923 Yeats was awarded the Nobel Prize for Literature, though he had become somewhat disillusioned with the world, expressed in his bleak poem *The Second Coming*, part of the collection *Michael Robartes and the Dancer*, published in 1921. Yeats's later period is more problematic, however, producing a series of spare, lucid but complex meditations on the artist's task. The influence of Yeats, in many ways the father of modern Irish literature and one of the most important English-language poets of all time, cannot be underestimated.

Until the 1920s Yeats kept up a friendship with **Sean O'Casey** (1884–1964), who was that rarest of things, a working-class Irish writer. The Dublin slums in which he was born were later immortalized in his trilogy of plays, *Shadow of a Gunman* (1923), *Juno and the Paycock* (1924) and *The Plough and the Stars* (1926). As with Synge, O'Casey's first nights were occasions for rioting and were usually attended by more policemen than punters – *The Plough and the Stars'* overt criticism of Irish nationalism particularly enraged the Dublin audience. It was actually Yeats who had to lead the coppers' charge into the stalls to break up the fracas and he later harangued the audience, screeching that the very fact they had broken up his play meant that O'Casey was a genius, and that "this was his apotheosis"; O'Casey's journal records that while he smiled nervously and twiddled his thumbs backstage he couldn't wait to get home so that he could look up the word "apotheosis" in the dictionary. In 1928, after the rejection of his play *The Silver Tassie*, dealing with World War I, O'Casey moved to England, eventually settling in Devon, where he wrote several plays on the subject of workers' struggles and injustice.

Irish Modernism: fiction

As the tide of history turned towards Nationalism and Republicanism, and Yeats wondered glumly whether the tradition would die with the aristocracy, one of the seminal figures of literary Modernism was emerging in Dublin. While still a student at the new University College – established in 1908 as a college for Catholic middle-class youth along lines suggested by Cardinal John Henry Newman – **James Joyce** (1882–1941) set himself against the world of politics and religion, and announced that he would become, in his own phrase, "a high priest of art". His subsequent career was to be the epitome of obsessive dedication.

Dubliners (1914), his first book, continued where George Moore had left off, evoking the city as a deathly place, its citizens quietly atrophying in a state of emotional paralysis. *A Portrait of the Artist as a Young Man* is largely autobiographical and deals with Stephen Dedalus's decision to leave Ireland, criticizing the country as a priest-ridden and superstitious dump. After ten years of trying to get it published, Joyce finally had the bad luck to get it printed in 1916, the year of the Easter Rising. Perhaps understandably, lack of patriotism was not fashionable. Joyce was condemned by just about everyone who mattered and quite a few people who didn't.

His next novel, *Ulysses*, came out in 1922, another flashpoint in Irish history, as the new Irish government went to war with its former comrades. Modelled on Homer's *Odyssey*, the book follows Stephen Dedalus and Leopold Bloom through one day and one night of Dublin life, recording their experiences with a relish and precision that repulsed the critics, including Virginia Woolf and D.H. Lawrence. The book was widely banned and its self-exiled author was condemned as a pornographer. *Ulysses* is a kaleidoscope of narrative techniques; Joyce's last work, the vast *Finnegans Wake* (1939), is the only true polyglot novel, a bewitching – and often impenetrable – stew of languages, representing the history of the world as dreamed by its hero, Humphrey Chimpden Earwicker (alias "Here Comes Everybody", "Haveth Childers Everywhere" etc). Critics of different persuasions see it as either the pinnacle of literary Modernism or the greatest folly in the history of the novel.

The other great Irish Modernist, **Samuel Beckett** (1906–89), emigrated to Paris and became Joyce's secretary in 1932. One writer has remarked that while Joyce tried to include everything in his work Beckett tried to leave everything out, and that's a pretty good summary. Beckett is bleak, pared down, exploring the fundamental paradox of the futility of speech and yet its absolute necessity. A Modernist in his devotion to verbal precision, Beckett is on the other hand a dominant figure in what has been termed the Postmodern "literature of exhaustion". As he said shortly before his death – "I have never been on my way anywhere, but simply on my way." Despite his reputation for terseness, Beckett was a prolific writer – the best places to start are the trilogy of novels, *Molloy*, *Malone Dies* (both 1952) and *The Unnamable* (1953), and the play *Waiting for Godot* (1949).

The absurd prose and hilarious satire of **Flann O'Brien** (real name Brian O'Nolan; 1912–66) has earned him the reputation of being Ireland's greatest comic writer. His comic vision of Purgatory, *The Third Policeman*, includes the famous molecular theory, which proposes that excessive riding of a bicycle can lead to the mixing of the molecules of rider and machine – hence a character who is half-man, half-bike. O'Brien's other great book, *At Swim-Two-Birds*, is a weird mélange of mythology and pastiche that plays around with the notion that fictional characters might have a life independent of their creators. Under one of his several other pseudonyms, Myles Na Gopaleen (Myles of the Little Horses), he wrote a daily column for the *Irish Times* for many years, and his hilarious journalism is collected in *The Best of Myles* and *Myles Away from Dublin*.

Traditional fiction continued, of course – for instance, **Brinsley MacNamara** (1890–1963) devastatingly portrayed small-town life in *The Valley of the Squinting Windows* in 1918. But many writers had moved away from social observation and into a kind of modernist fantasy that had its roots way back in the Celtic twilight. **James Stephens** (1882–1950), a writer with an unjustly insignificant international reputation, used absurdity as a route to high lyricism. His *The Crock of Gold* (1912) is a profoundly moving fantasy on the Irish mythological tradition, part fairy story and part post-Joycean satire.

Postwar literature

Ireland in the late 1940s and 1950s suffered severe economic recession and another wave of emigration began. Added to this, the people had in 1937 passed a constitution – still operational today – which enshrined the Catholic Church's teachings in the laws of the land. Intolerance and xenophobia were bolstered by an economic war against Britain and a campaign of state censorship which was truly Stalinist in its vigour. Books which had never been read were snipped, shredded and scorched by committees of pious civil servants.

No history of postwar Irish literature would be complete without at least a mention of *The Bell*, a highly influential but now defunct literary magazine. In its two runs, 1940–48 and 1950–54, it was a forum for writers like **Frank O'Connor** (1903–66), **Seán Ó Faoláin** (1900–91) and **Liam O'Flaherty** (1897–1984), all of whom were veterans of the independence war, and all of whom became outstanding short-story writers. They chronicled the raging betrayal they felt at state censorship and social intolerance – O'Connor's *Guests of the Nation* (1931) is perhaps the most eloquent epitaph for Ireland's revolutionary generation, a terrifying tale of the execution of two British soldiers by the IRA that enormously influenced Brendan Behan's *The Hostage*. *The Bell* also opened its pages to writers like **Peadar O'Donnell** (1893–1985), a radical socialist who, only six months before he died, publicly burned his honorary degree from the National University of Ireland on the occasion of a similar honour being conferred on Ronald Reagan.

In an infamous speech President Eamon de Valera envisaged a new rural Ireland full of "comely maidens dancing at the crossroads and the laughter of athletic youths". But writers such as **Denis Devlin** (1908–59), **Francis Stuart** (1902–90), **Mary Lavin** (1912–96) and **Brian Moore** (1921–99) took up the fight for truth against propaganda. Their youths and maidens didn't dance. They were too busy packing their bags, or wandering in bewilderment across the desolate pages of an Ireland that had failed to live up to its possibilities. In their poetry **Austin Clarke** (1896–1974) and **Thomas Kinsella** (b. 1928) mourned the passing of hope into despair and fragmentation.

Patrick Kavanagh (1906–67) was an exception to all the rules. His poetry is almost entirely parochial, celebrating what he called "the spirit-shocking wonder of a black slanting Ulster hill", and his contemplative celebrations of the ordinary made him perhaps Ireland's best-loved poet. But as time went on, the harshness of reality began to press in on his work. His long poem *The Great Hunger* (1942) portrays rural Ireland – the same Ireland he had formerly extolled – as physically barren, with the blasted landscape an incisive metaphor for sexual repression. Its publication was widely condemned and the writer was even questioned by the police, an event he discussed with customary venom in his own short-lived journal, *Kavanagh's Weekly*.

The forces of reaction were again about to wage war on Irish literature. O'Casey's anti-clerical play *The Drums of Father Ned* was produced in Dublin in 1955 and received aggressive reviews. Three years later there was a proposal to revive it for the new Dublin Theatre Festival. The Catholic Archbishop of Dublin, John Charles McQuaid, insisted that the plans be dropped, and when the trade unions stepped into the fray on his behalf, he succeeded. The year before, the young director Alan Simpson had been arrested and his entire cast threatened with imprisonment for indecency following the first night in Dublin of Tennessee Williams's play *The Rose Tattoo*. Now the doyen of Ireland's novelist **John McGahern** (b. 1935) lost his teaching job in a Catholic school in 1966 following the publication of his second book, *The Dark*, which was immediately banned. It's a marvellous novel, dealing tenderly with adolescence and clerical celibacy.

A more celebrated literary victim – in this case a self-destructive one – was **Brendan Behan**, who died in 1964, only six years after the publication of his first book, *Borstal Boy*. He spent the last years of his life as a minor celebrity, reciting his books into tape recorders in Dublin pubs, drunk and surrounded by equally drunk admirers, some of whom sobered up for long enough to try to save him from becoming the victim of his own myth.

Contemporary writing

It was only in the 1970s that the post-revolutionary climate of repression began to lift, and a sophisticated and largely progressive generation began having their works published. **Seamus Heaney** is the leading light of an unofficial group of Northern Irish poets who combine sophistication of technique with self-conscious political commitment. Heaney's first work, *Death of a Naturalist* (1966), is easily accessible and is firmly rooted in his childhood experiences in south Derry. *Door into the Dark* (1969) and *Wintering Out* (1972) see Heaney trying to find a voice to deal with the increasing sectarian violence in the North. *North* (1975) was Heaney's most controversial work, with many commentators criticizing the lack of condemnation when dealing with the violence of the Troubles. In 1995 Heaney's poetic world changed: not only did he become Ireland's fourth **Nobel literary laureate** (after Yeats, Shaw and Beckett), but, with the emergence of the peace process in the North, he found a refreshed poetic voice. His most recent works have been *Beowulf* (1999), a widely acclaimed translation of the Anglo-Saxon epic into his native south Derry vernacular, and a dazzling collection, *Electric Light* (2002).

John Banville is another writer who prefers to remain at a tangent to the national identity, taking Ireland (when he writes of it at all) as the means rather than the end of his artistic vision. His first book, *Long Lankin*, appeared in 1970, a precocious debut that has been followed by a string of extraordinarily inventive novels, the most recent being *Shroud*.

The Irish Writers' Co-op produced novelists such as **Desmond Hogan**, **Ronan Sheehan** and **Neil Jordan**, the last of whom has gone on to major international success as a film director (see p.831). Jordan's work (much like Banville's) is located firmly within the counter-tradition of the novel coming out of Joyce. Owing something to the fantastic narratives of the sagas, this counter-tradition was also a rejection of the traditional novel form, which Joyce saw as having an in-built British view of the world. The 1970s also saw the establishment of courageous publishing companies founded by writers, including Peter Fallon's Gallery, Dermot Bolger's Raven Arts Press, and Steve McDonogh's Brandon.

At the end of the decade **Paul Durcan** emerged as the inheritor of Kavanagh's mantle. He is a quirkily witty and profoundly religious poet, whose work encompasses social issues such as IRA bombings and Ireland's prohibition, until recently, of divorce and its continuing ban on abortion, but always addresses them in personal terms. Other important poets include **Padraic Fiacc**, **Ciaran Carson**, **Pat Boran**, **Michael Hartnett**, **Brendan Kennelly** and **Derek Mahon**. **Michael Longley** seems doomed always to be cited as the husband of the major revisionist critic Edna Longley, but his poetry is innovative and striking, and the last decade has seen him publish three exceptional volumes, *Gorse Fires* (1991), *The Ghost Orchid* (1995) and *The Weather in Japan* (2000). Two poets having close relations with the US, **Paul Muldoon**, born in Mayo but now living in New York, and **John Montague**, born in Brooklyn of Irish parents but brought up in Tyrone, explore the relations between different poetic traditions on the island. **Christopher Nolan**, a severely disabled writer, has proved to be an amazing talent, employing a rich language reminiscent of Dylan Thomas. His first book of poetry, *Damburst of Dreams* (1988), received great acclaim, and he later won the Whitbread Prize for his autobiographical novel *Under the Eye of the Clock* (1988).

Perhaps the most exciting contemporary verse in Ireland is being written by women writers who, in the absence of civic or political opportunities, have turned to poetry to express their experiences of the modern state. Up and down the country poetry groups and workshops turn out collections that deal with the realities of being an Irish daughter, wife or mother. In this they receive support from established poets such as **Eiléan Ní Chuilleanáin**, **Eavan Boland**, **Paula Meehan** and **Medbh McGuckian**. Boland, especially, has explored the complexities of modern Irish female experience in particularly enabling ways. McGuckian's poetry is tremendously imaginative, creating ephemeral worlds where language is fluid, meaning forever shifting.

Without doubt, the most successful theatre company and cultural initiative on the island in recent times has been **Field Day**, a Northern-based team founded by **Seamus Deane**, **Tom Paulin**, **Brian Friel**, Seamus Heaney and actor Stephen Rea. As well as being established poets, Deane and Paulin are also insightful critics who from their locations in the US and England continue to do battle with all comers over the rights to Irish literary history. Friel, who turned from short-story writing to the theatre in the 1960s, wrote some of Ireland's best-loved plays, including *Philadelphia Here I Come!* (1964), *The Loves of Cass Maguire* (1966) and *Lovers* (1967).The outbreak of violence in the North drew a response from Friel in two plays, *The Freedom of the City* (1973), loosely based on the events in Derry on Bloody Sunday, and *Volunteers* (1975) which treated Irish history in a more symbolic manner. It was Friel's play *Translations* (1980), broaching the subject of rewriting history, which provided Field Day with their greatest success, a subject he came back to with his last play for the company *History* (1988). However, after giving his hugely popular work, *Dancing at Lughnasa* (1990), to Dublin's Abbey Theatre, he left the group and has continued to write highly acclaimed works such as *In Wonderful Tennessee* (1993), *Give Me Your Answer, Do!* (1997) and *Two Plays After* (2002).

Any list of Ireland's innovative theatre writers must include **Tom Murphy** who is celebrated in many corners as Ireland's greatest living playwright. Murphy's plays are hugely critical of contemporary Ireland, yet continue to be met with universal acclaim, including his latest offering, *Bailegangaire* (2001). While many cite Murphy as Ireland's leading dramatist others point to Ulsterman, **Frank McGuinness**. His play *Observe the Sons of Ulster Marching Towards the Somme* (1995) focuses on the participation of a group of Northern Loyalists in the battle of the Somme and exploits the symbolism of the whole Irish tradition, permitting a range of readings, in which the Somme represents the current situation in the North, or the battlefield of the Boyne, or the slaughters of the early sagas. It was his 1987 piece, *Carthaginians*, set in Derry city, which had thrust him into the major league of Irish writers. The play found a vocabulary in which to explore ancient Irish themes – the nature of political allegiance, death and resurrection, the relationship between Britain, Ireland and the North, sexuality, religion – in a way that seems to sum up the whole tradition while simultaneously threatening to demolish it. Never afraid to articulate the unfashionable, he asks questions of nationalism in a manner that demands attention: his *Someone To Watch Over Me* (1992) starts out appealing to our readiness to accept crude national stereotypes, but ultimately becomes, among other things, a homage to the English literary tradition. McGuinness's work provides, if not some hope of unifying the various strands of Ireland's long cultural histories, at least the imperative to understand what divides them; in this act of enquiry lies great humanity.

The Irish stage has produced numerous exciting new dramatists in recent years. **Sebastian Barry** is one of the finest, producing plays that combine moral depth with astonishing poetic intensity. Barry often takes figures from his recent ancestry and weaves plays from their unique junction with history, the finest example being *The Steward of Christendom* (1995). The plays of **Conor McPherson** are set in contemporary Ireland and have met with critical acclaim: in *This Lime Tree Bower* (1996) he brings pace and pathos – at times with acute hilarity – to stories of provincial life; *The Weir* (1998) and *Port Authority* (2001) have confirmed his reputation as a compelling dramatist. Belfast writer **Gary Mitchell** has produced some fine work, most notably *In a Little World of Our Own* (1997) and *As the Beast Sleeps* (1998), plays which centre around a Loyalist housing estate, the latter dealing with militants trying to come to terms with the encroaching ceasefire, while *Tearing the Loom* (1999) explores the political complexities of the 1798 United Irish rebellion.

One of the freshest voices in Irish drama at the moment is **Marina Carr**, whose plays *Portia Coughlan* (1996), *On Raftery's Hill* (2000) and *Ariel* (2002) deal with the dark side of human poverty and feature powerfully written, energetic dialogue, often in the voice of her native midlands. Arguably the most successful dramatist to be writing plays in an Irish context right now is in fact English: **Martin McDonagh**, the Jack Charlton of contemporary Irish theatre, sets his work in an Irish west coast of the imagination, managing to both exploit and explode its associated myths. Heavily reminiscent of Synge, he deploys the traditional themes of murder, ignorance, familial hatred and isolation with swift, dark humour. McDonagh is a gifted story-teller, and *The Beauty Queen of Leenane*, *The Cripple of Inishmaan*, *The Lieutenant of Inishmore* and *The Lonesome West* have all proved immensely popular. Other exciting dramatists to emerge in recent years are **Mark O'Rowe**, whose *Howie the Rookie* took the Edinburgh Festival by storm in 1999 and Corkman **Enda Walsh**, whose powerful one-act plays *Disco Pigs* (1997), *Misterman* (1999) and *Bedbound* (2001) have been hugely popular with audiences more familiar with clubbing than theatre-going.

It is perhaps in the novel and in autobiography that the richest seam of contemporary Irish literature is to be discovered. Over the past decade or so, writers like **Colin Bateman**, **Philip Casey**, **Dermot Healy**, **Eoin McNamee**, **Glenn Patterson**, **Eamon Sweeney** and **Robert MacLiam Wilson** have begun to turn the accepted version of Irish literary tradition on its head. **Dermot Bolger**, as well as being a gifted poet and playwright, has produced hard-hitting yet lyrical novels of contemporary Dublin. **Colm Tóibín** has written two deceptively understated novels of Irish experience at home and abroad in *The South* (1990) and *The Heather Blazing* (1992); in *The Story of the Night* (1996), set in Argentina at the time of the generals, he achieves a work of breathtaking poise, while his latest novel *The Blackwater Lightship* (1999) tells the story of an AIDS victim. *The Butcher Boy* (1992) by **Patrick McCabe** won numerous awards as well as being shortlisted for the prestigious Booker Prize, and the grisly comedy of that novel reappeared in even grimmer form in *The Dead School* (1995). In the novel *Breakfast on Pluto* (1998), McCabe's mordant humour shifts its focus to a violent, seedy London underworld, while *Mondo Desperado!*(2000) is a hilarious and at times absurd ride into small-town Irish life.

Without doubt, the most successful of this new generation of novelists has been **Roddy Doyle**, a writer who, along with Bolger and others, disdains the critical title of "Northside realist" (referring to the north side of the River Liffey where most of their work is set). All three novels of *The Barrytown Trilogy*, *The Commitments* (1987), *The Snapper* (1990) and *The Van* (1991), have been made into successful films, and Doyle snapped up the Booker Prize in 1993 for *Paddy Clarke Ha Ha Ha*; this book was followed in 1996 by *The Woman Who Walked Into Doors*, which tackles the darker theme of domestic violence. Doyle's fiction makes deceptively easy reading, while the enormous sales figures for his books must compensate somewhat for the criticism that he merely reproduces modern urban variations on the stage Irishman. Perhaps with this in mind Doyle spent three years researching and writing *A Star Called Henry* (1999), a historical novel set around the struggle for Irish independence from 1916 to 1921. This novel, like all of Doyle's work is highly accessible but, unlike some of his previous works, is of huge literary significance in its powerful critique of the accepted ideologies that underpin the Irish state.

Younger writers such as **Joseph O'Connor**, **Keith Ridgway** and **Emma Donoghue** tend to work in other genres besides the novel, and their writing responds to the new Ireland of sex and drugs and rock 'n' roll in which they grew up. Ridgway presented an unusually edgy take on Dublin, often negotiating the city's gay life, in his collection of short stories *Standard Time* (2001) and novel *The Long Falling* (1998), while Donoghue produced, in her first two novels *Stir-fry* (1994) and *Hood* (1995), perhaps the first happy lesbian love stories in Irish fiction. Other new female writers worth reading are **Mary Morrissey**, whose acclaimed first novel *Mother of Pearl* (1998) has been followed by the equally enjoyable *The Pretender* (2000) about a Polish factory worker who thinks she is the daughter of the last Russian tsar. **Antonia Logue** from Derry wrote the most exciting first novel in recent years, *Shadow Box* (1999), which deals with the relationships between black heavyweight boxer Jack Johnston, a white Modernist poet and one of the foremost figures in the Dadaist movement in the States. **Anne Enright** has recently cemented her reputation with the stylish and ambitious *The Pleasure of Eliza Lynch* (2002), which, with its sharp eye for the subtleties of despair and failure, has been described as "*Heart of Darkness* written by a woman". Other young Irish writers have a resolutely international outlook, notably **Colum McCann**, whose work has ranged from New York to Spain and whose new novel, *Dancer* (2003), is based on the life of dancer Rudolf Nureyev.

From the 1980s on, novelists gave short shrift to the hackneyed themes of the traditional canon: the Catholic Church, the lure of the land, the repression of sexuality. Irish novels and short stories began to anatomize social change rather than conservatism, revealing an Ireland populated by women as well as men, Protestants as well as Catholics, fervent atheists as well as true believers, gays as well as straights, people who feel British as well as people who feel Irish and writers for whom Ireland is no longer a necessary subject. It is interesting then that after such a great loosening of the soil, there emerged in the late 1990s a couple of writers who returned to explore these themes via personal memoir, and in so doing found that their experiences of repression, denial and acute poverty struck a deep resonance in the consciousness of an older generation. **Nuala O'Faolain**'s *Are You Somebody?*(1996), an autobiography which deftly portrays the desolate marginalization of women, and **Frank McCourt**'s *Angela's Ashes* (1996), an extraordinary book showing the degradation and poverty of an entire class of Irish people, were both enormously popular, and perhaps cathartic, in an Ireland moving to publicly come to terms with huge areas of deprivation in its immediate past. McCourt's follow-up *'Tis* (1999) had none of the warmth or humour of *Angela's Ashes* and was a great disappointment.

Less emotively, but no less successfully, in the North, too, childhood has proved fertile ground for novelists. **Seamus Deane**'s semi-autobiographical *Reading in the Dark* (1996) stands as a powerful, myth-spectred work, a child's world full of half-gleaned tales of superstition, political reprisals and fear, and **Ciaran Carson**'s *The Star Factory* (1997) delivers a Belfast ringing bright with poetic imagery, fresh and full of life. Childhood Belfast is also the subject of **Bernard MacLaverty**'s *The Anatomy School* (2001), an exuberantly funny story of male adolescence, and of **Eugene McEldowney**'s endearing novel The *Faloorie Man* (2000), an intimate portrait of childhood life from an author more generally associated with the thriller genre. King of the Irish thriller at the moment is **John Connolly**, whose *The White Road* (2002) is a pulsating read. The last few years have seen some novels of great inventiveness too. Ciaran Carson's *Last Night's Fun* (1996) is an astonishing book conjuring up the spontaneous magic of the world of traditional music. **Deirdre Madden** has moved away from grim novels of life in the North with *Authenticity* (2002), an ambitious love story and meditation on what it is to be an artist. **Ann Haverty**'s *One Day As a Tiger* (1997) is a delightfully mischievous tale drawing us in to consider the emotional and romantic possibilities of life in an age of genetic engineering, while *The Beauty of the Moon* (1999) is a collection of delicately crafted poems. **Sean O'Reilly**, a Derryman who graduated from Trinity College Dublin's creative writing MA, conjured up cruel and dreamily surreal cityscapes, full of menace and poetry, in his short-story collection *Curfew* (2000) and novel *Love and Sleep* (2002).

Books

Most of the **books** listed below are in print and in paperback – those that are out of print (o/p) should be easy to track down in second-hand bookshops or on the Internet.

History and politics

John Ardagh *Ireland and the Irish: Portrait of a Changing Society*. Comprehensive and lively, this is an excellent anatomy of Irish society and its efforts to come to terms with the modern world.

★ **Jonathan Bardon** *A History of Ulster*. A comprehensive account from early settlements to the current Troubles.

J.C. Beckett *The Making of Modern Ireland 1603–1923* (o/p). Concise and elegant, this is probably the best introduction to the complexities of Irish history.

David Beresford *Ten Men Dead*. Revelatory account of the 1981 hunger strike, using the prison correspondence as its basic material; a powerful refutation of the demonologies of the British press.

Peter Berresford Ellis *Hell or Connaught*; *The Boyne Water* (o/p). Vivid popular histories of Cromwell's rampage and of the Battle of the Boyne.

★ **Angela Bourke** *The Burning of Bridget Cleary*. Impeccably researched account of nefarious goings-on in Tipperary in the 1890s, describing the sensational case of a young woman supposedly taken by the fairies, tortured and murdered, and the subsequent trial of her husband, father, aunt and four cousins.

★ **Terence Brown** *Ireland: A Social and Cultural History 1922–1985*. Brilliantly perceptive survey of writers' responses to the dog's breakfast made of post-revolutionary Ireland by its leaders.

★ **Max Caulfield** *The Easter Rebellion*. Recently revised account of the events of 1916, originally published in 1963, brought to life with interviews with those involved.

Michael Collins *In His Own Words*. A collection of extracts from the revolutionary's writings and speeches.

S.J. Connolly (ed) *The Oxford Companion to Irish History*. A massive introduction to almost every aspect of Irish history, revised and updated in 2002.

★ **Tim Pat Coogan** *The Troubles: Ireland's Ordeal 1966–1996 and the Search for Peace*. The former *Irish Press* editor's popular-history writing has many followers, and his *The IRA* is a contemporary classic. His biographies of two icons of modern Ireland, *Michael Collins* and *De Valera: Long Fellow, Long Shadow*, are also essential reading. His latest, *Wherever Green is Worn: The Story of the Irish Diaspora*, is a ground-breaking account of Irish emigration and the impact of the émigrés on culture throughout the world.

Sean Duffy *The Atlas of Irish History*. A good introduction to Irish history, rich with maps, diagrams and drawings.

Garret FitzGerald *All in a Life*. The first former Taoiseach to write his memoirs has produced an extraordinary book, characteristically frank, and full of detail on the working of government. His new *Reflections on the Irish State* offers perceptive insights and challenging theories on the big issues of Irish public life.

David Fitzpatrick *Oceans of Consolation: Personal Accounts of Migration to Australia*. Using over a hundred unedited letters largely written around the 1850s and 1860s, this book brings to life the experiences of loss and longing of Irish emigrants to Australia.

★ **R.F. Foster** *Modern Ireland 1600–1972*. Superb and provocative book, generally reckoned to be unrivalled in its scholarship and acuity, although it has been criticized for what some feel to be an excessive sympathy towards the Anglo-Irish. Not recommended for beginners. Foster also edited *The Oxford History of Ireland*, a succinct, yet never wavering summation of Ireland's development from prehistory to modern times; Declan Kibberd's chapter on the relationship between Irish literature and history is characteristically incisive.

Kathleen Hughes and Ann Hamlin *The Modern Traveller to the Early Irish Church*. The remains of monastic settlements are found all over Ireland and this revised edition enhances the visitor's appreciation by reconstructing the daily religious and secular life of Ireland in the Early Christian Period; also includes a detailed list of recommended sites.

★ **Robert Kee** *The Green Flag* (3 vols). Scrupulous history of Irish Nationalism from the first Plantations to the creation of the Free State. Masterful as narrative and as analysis.

Dáire Keogh and Nicholas Furlong (eds) *The Women of 1798*. Women are often "hidden" in Irish history, and this collection of essays reasserts the vital role many played in the 1798 rebellion, from Matilda Tone (wife of Wolfe) who redefined the role of woman as patriot, to the Belfast revolutionary Mary Anne McCracken.

★ **Christine Kinealy** *This Great Calamity: The Irish Famine*. Unravels fact from fiction through systematic analysis of primary source material related to the Great Famine.

F.S.L. Lyons *Ireland Since the Famine*. The most complete overview of recent Irish history; either iconoclastic or revisionist, depending on your point of view.

★ **Eamonn Mallie and David McKittrick** *Endgame in Ireland*. Hugely detailed yet very readable account of the Northern Ireland peace process.

★ **Susan McKay** *Northern Protestants: An Unsettled People*. Utterly grim but absolutely essential account of the North's Protestant community and its disparate views, based on numerous interviews, simultaneously offering hope for the future and sheer desperation.

David McKittrick and David McVea *Making Sense of the Troubles*. Clear, dispassionate and authoritative crash-course on the conflict over the past thirty years.

T.W. Moody and F.X. Martin (eds) *The Course of Irish History*. Highly readable collection of essays on the various eras of Irish history.

★ **Ed Moloney** *A Secret History of the IRA*. Authoritative account, with Gerry Adams as its sinisterly intriguing central character, of the struggle within the Republican movement over the last thirty years.

George Morrison *The Irish Civil War*. A powerful collection of photographic images of the civil war, accompanied by commentary by Tim Pat Coogan.

R.J. Scally *The End of the Hidden Ireland: Rebellion, Famine and Emigration*. History revealing the strategies deployed by one particular Roscommon peasant community in their struggle to avoid eviction and emigration; the book also details their exploitation by Irish Catholic middlemen.

David Sharrock and Mark Prendergast *Man of War, Man of Peace? The Unauthorised Biography of Gerry Adams*. Lengthy, detailed account of the Sinn Féin leader's rise to prominence.

A.T.Q. Stewart *The Narrow Ground*. A Unionist overview of the history of the North from 1609 to the 1960s, providing an essential background to the current situation. In his recent *The Shape of Irish History*, Stewart sets out to open up the closed shop of academic research on Irish history to the general reader.

Ruth Taillon *Women of 1916*. Key documentation of the part played by women in the struggle for independence.

★ **Peter Taylor** *Provos: The IRA and Sinn Féin*, published in USA as *Behind the Mask*. Study of the historical development of the Provisional IRA, including fascinating interviews with IRA members by a noted TV journalist. His *Loyalists* and *Brits: The War against the IRA* shed further welcome light on the Northern Irish political mindset.

★ **Alan Titley** *A Pocket History of Gaelic Culture*. Titley's brief, iconoclastic and often very witty account of the development of Gaelic culture from prehistory to the twentieth century is stimulating reading.

★ **Colm Tóibín and Diarmaid Ferriter** *The Irish Famine: A Documentary*. Highly readable and thought-provoking analysis of the 1845–49 Famine, which takes an incisive look, both at the complex issues surrounding the failure of the potato crop, and the inadequacy of previous historical accounts of the crisis.

Kevin Toolis *Rebel Hearts: Journeys within the IRA's Soul*. Highly acclaimed and topical account of what makes the IRA tick by this journalist and screenwriter.

Cecil Woodham Smith *The Great Hunger: Ireland 1845–1849*. The classic history of the Famine, superseded by recent research, but still a superb and harrowing narrative.

Gaelic tales

★ **Kevin Danaher** *In Ireland Long Ago*. The best volume on Irish folklore, recorded with a civil servant's meticulousness and a novelist's literary style.

Myles Dillon (ed) *Irish Sagas*. An excellent examination of Cúchulainn, Fionn Mac Cumhaill and the other mythical heroes in literary and socio-psychological terms.

★ **Seamus Heaney** *Sweeney Astray*. A modern reworking of *Buile Suibhne*, the ancient Irish saga of the mad king Sweeney.

Pádraig Ó Conaire *Finest Stories* (o/p). Ó Conaire's dispassionate eye roams over the cruelties of peasant life.

Frank O'Connor *Kings, Lords and Commons*. Translations of Irish-language poems from the seventeenth to the nineteenth century, preserving the earthiness of the originals.

Tomás Ó Criomhtháin (sometimes Thomas O'Crohan) *An tOileánach*, available in an authoritative new edition by Seán Ó Coileáin; in English, *The Islandman*. Similar to Ó Conaire but nonfiction and, if possible, even more raw.

Maurice O'Sullivan *Twenty Years A-Growing*. The story of O'Sullivan's youth and the traditional way of life on the Blasket Islands in the early twentieth century, in a style derived from folk tales.

★ **Seán Ó Tuama and Thomas Kinsella** *An Duanaire: Poems of the Dispossessed*. Excellent translations of stark Irish-language poems on famine and death. See also *The Táin*, Kinsella's translation of one of the earliest sagas, the *Táin Bó Cúailnge*.

Peig Sayers *An Old Woman's Reflections*. Unfortunately, Sayers' complacent acceptance of her own powerlessness is still held up as an example to Irish schoolchildren. Still, in spite of itself, a frightening insight into the eradication of the Irish language through emigration, poverty and political failure. A funny deconstruction of the Sayers style is Myles na Gopaleen's *An Beál Bocht* (in English, *The Poor Mouth*).

William Butler Yeats (ed) *Irish Fairy and Folk Tales*. Yeats gets all misty-eyed about an Ireland that never existed.

Prose fiction

★ **Peter Ackroyd** *The Last Will and Testament of Oscar Wilde*. Witty re-creation of the life of the tragic, abused artist in exile; a superb parody and an absolute must for anyone so familiar with Wilde's epigrams, they wish he'd written more.

★ **John Banville** First-rate Irish novelist, nominated for the Booker Prize in 1989 for *The Book of Evidence*, a sleazy tale of a weird Dublin murder. *The Untouchable* is a superb fiction based on the life of Anthony Blunt, full of deception and treachery, while in *Eclipse* an actor plays out his own psychological crisis by a return to his childhood home. Banville's talents show no sign of waning in his most recent novel, *Shroud*, a beautifully written mystery about an ageing academic forced to confront the secrets of his past.

Sebastian Barry *The Whereabouts of Eneas McNulty*. Tremendously moving, tragic account of one of Barry's ancestors who fought for the British in both world wars, and the life he then had to lead as a consequence.

Colin Bateman *Divorcing Jack*; *Cycle of Violence*; *Of Wee Sweetie Mice and Men*; *Empire State*; *Murphy's Law*; *The Horse with My Name*. A selection of sparkling and fast-paced tales of violence and men in crisis by one of the North's most successful novelists, who has been described as a cross between Roddy Doyle and Carl Hiaasen.

★ **Samuel Beckett** *More Pricks Than Kicks*; *Beckett Trilogy*, including *Molloy*, *Malone Dies* and *The Unnamable*. Beckett's early short stories, grotesque tales set around the eccentric character of Belacqua

Shuah, were followed by his wonderful and increasingly bleak trilogy of breakdown and glum humour.

Brendan Behan *Borstal Boy*. Behan's gutsy *roman à clef* about his early life in the IRA and in jail.

★ **Dermot Bolger** *The Journey Home*. Dublin unforgettably imagined as both heaven and hell. *A Second Life* is an assured novel about a man who, miraculously given a second chance at life, sets out to find out the truth about his adoption. The psychological thriller *Father's Music* is set in Dublin's criminal underworld. Bolger's latest, *The Valparaiso Voyage*, deals with themes of political corruption and alienation in contemporary Ireland, in a tale of a violent homecoming.

Elizabeth Bowen *The Death of the Heart* and *The Last September*. The former is a finely tuned tale of the anguish of unrequited love, generally rated as the masterpiece of this obliquely stylish writer. In the latter, the immense political change of 1920s Cork forms the setting for a tale of an upper-class woman's coming of age; now a film by Neil Jordan.

Clare Boylan *Room For a Single Lady*; *Beloved Stranger*; *Collected Stories*. *Room for a Single Lady* features 1950s Dublin and a cast of eccentric lodgers, while *Beloved Stranger* is a comic and moving account of marriage and depression.

Philip Casey *The Fabulists*. Deftly woven tale of love and story-telling; a fine first novel. *The Water Star* is a similarly compassionate novel about a group of people rebuilding their lives in postwar London. Casey's latest, *The Fisher Child*, examines a family thrown into crisis by the birth of a baby.

John Connolly *The White Road*. The latest blend of horror and suspense from Ireland's leading crime writer.

Michael Curtin *Sing!* A deft comic novel which movingly touches on themes of loss and compromise.

Seamus Deane *Reading in the Dark*. A turbulent semi-autobiographical tale set in Derry in the 1950s and 1960s, full of ghosts, fear and political enmities.

★ **J.P. Donleavy** *The Ginger Man*. Outlandish exploits of a consummate bounder; semi-autobiographical, it was banned in Ireland for some time.

Emma Donoghue *Stir-fry*. Well-wrought love story from young Irish lesbian writer. *Hood* is a painful and at times funny story about overcoming bereavement. *Slammerkin*, Donoghue's latest novel, is a vivid and harsh historical tale from the underbelly of eighteenth-century London.

★ **Roddy Doyle** *Paddy Clarke Ha Ha Ha*. Hilarious and deeply moving novel of Dublin family strife that won the Booker Prize in 1993. The earlier *Barrytown Trilogy*, including *The Commitments*, *The Snapper* and *The Van*, is lighter and funnier and made Doyle's reputation. In *The Woman Who Walked Into Doors*, Doyle shifts to the darker theme of domestic violence, while *A Star Called Henry* is an irreverent romp through early twentieth-century Irish history.

Maria Edgeworth *Castle Rackrent*. Best of the "Big House" books, in which Edgeworth displays a subversively subtle sympathy with her peasant narrator. Would have shocked her fellow aristos if they'd been able to figure it out.

★ **Anne Enright** *The Portable Virgin*. Highly original stories of life on the outside. *The Wig My Father Wore* is a tale of sex, death and reproduction. *The Pleasure of Eliza*

Lynch, which is Enright's latest, is a historical novel, based on the true story of the nineteenth-century Irish courtesan, who became the richest woman in the world, and her adventures in Paraguay.

Oliver Goldsmith *The Vicar of Wakefield*. An affecting celebration of simple virtue.

Anne Haverty *One Day as a Tiger*. Delightful, arcadian tale of love and genetic engineering which twists as the betrayals set in. A sentimental journey for our times.

Dermot Healy *A Goat's Song*. Dark and deep novel which convincingly weaves a study of obsessive love into a fresh view of the Northern conflict. *The Bend for Home* is a touching memoir of the author's family life, while *Sudden Times* is a rich tale of paranoia, innocence and the tragedy of the working-class Irish in England.

Aidan Higgins *Flotsam & Jetsam*; *Langrishe, Go Down*; *Lions of the Grunewald*. The most European of Irish writers, whose later works play with language in a mordantly humorous and deeply personal way.

Desmond Hogan *The Ikon Maker*. Impressive, impressionistic first novel from one of Ireland's most lyrical prose writers, about angst-ridden adolescence in the 1970s, before Ireland was hip. *A Farewell to Prague* (o/p) is an intense, episodic, autobiographical novel that wanders lonely through late-twentieth-century Europe.

Neil Jordan *Night in Tunisia* (o/p). Film director Jordan first made his name with this impressive collection, which prefigures treatments and themes of his films. His later novel, *Sunrise with Sea Monster* (o/p), is a delicate, powerful study in love and betrayal.

★ **James Joyce** *Dubliners*; *Portrait of the Artist as a Young Man*; *Ulysses*; *Finnegans Wake*. *Dubliners* evokes the city as a deathly, sterile dump, while *Portrait* is the tale, largely autobiographical, of Stephen Dedalus's decision to leave Ireland. No novel written in English last century can match the linguistic verve of *Ulysses*, Joyce's monumental evocation of 24 hours in the life of Dublin. From the time of its completion until shortly before his death – a period of sixteen years – he laboured at *Finnegans Wake*, a dream-language recapitulation of the cycles of world history. Though indigestible as a whole, it contains passages of incomparable lyricism and wit – try the "Anna Livia Plurabelle" section, and you could be hooked.

Molly Keane *Good Behaviour*. Highly successful comic reworking of the "Big House" novel.

Mary Lavin *In a Café: Selected Stories*. Collection of previously published stories by one of the great short-story writers, in the Chekhov tradition.

★ **Antonia Logue** *Shadow Box*. This extraordinary novel is an exhilarating mix of surrealism and boxing inspired by the life of Dadaist poet Mina Loy.

★ **Bernard MacLaverty** *Cal* and *Lamb*. Two novels of love beset by crisis; the first deals with an unwilling IRA man and the widow of one of his victims, while *Lamb* is the disturbing tale of a Christian Brother who absconds from a borstal with a young boy. *Grace Notes*, a finely crafted novel about grief, love and creativity, has been followed by *The Anatomy School*, an exuberantly funny story of male adolescence in 1960s Belfast.

Deirdre Madden *Hidden Symptoms*; *The Birds of the Innocent Wood*;

Remembering Light and Stone; *Nothing is Black*. Evocatively grim novels of life in the North. Madden's most recent novel, *Authenticity*, is more ambitious, a love story and a reflection on being an artist in contemporary society.

Eugene McCabe *Death and Nightingales*. Powerfully relevant novel of love, land and violence, set in late-nineteenth-century Ireland.

★ **Patrick McCabe** *The Butcher Boy*; *The Dead School*. Scary, disturbing, but funny tales of Irish small-town life. *Breakfast on Pluto* is a camp and macabre satire in which McCabe's protagonist takes his cross-dressing from his sleepy parochial home to a sleazy London underworld. There's a crop of absurd short stories in *Mondo Desperado*, while the funny and inventive *Emerald Germs of Ireland* is a dark fairy tale for adults.

Colum McCann *This Side of Brightness*. McCann's breakthrough novel, a multiracial story set in New York, about survival and redemption, and the rise and fall of America.

Eugene McEldowney *The Faloorie Man*. Pleasantly understated autobiographical novel set in pre-Troubles Belfast, enjoyable chiefly for the affectionate nature of the reminiscences.

★ **John McGahern** *The Barracks*; *The Leavetaking*; *Amongst Women*; *Collected Stories*; *That They May Face the Rising Sun*. A selection of works by the man regarded in many quarters as Ireland's greatest living novelist. *The Barracks* is classic McGahern: stark, murderous and not a spare adjective in sight. *Amongst Women* tells of an old Republican and the oppression of rural and family life, while in *The Leavetaking* a teacher in a Clontarf national school reviews his life on the day he expects to be sacked for marrying an American divorcée. *That They May Face the Rising Sun*, McGahern's latest novel, is a dark and elegiac narrative set in rural County Leitrim (published as *By the Lake* in the US).

★ **Robert McLiam Wilson** *Ripley Bogle*. Very funny first novel in which the irrepressible and precocious down-and-out Bogle tells his tale in wonderfully extravagant tones. *Eureka Street* is acerbic, irreverent humour in both pre- and post-ceasefire Belfast.

Eoin McNamee *Resurrection Man*. A darkly poetic and gripping tale of sectarian killings and the minds of the perpetrators, loosely based upon the Shankill Butchers. *The Blue Tango* is a stylish, assured reconstruction of the dark motives behind the true-life murder of a young woman.

Brian Moore *The Lonely Passion of Judith Hearne*. Moore's early novels are rooted in the landscape of his native Belfast; this was his first, a poignant tale of emotional blight and the possibilities of late redemption by love. The somewhat Cartlandesque *The Magician's Wife* is a tale of pernickety sexual repression at the court of Napoleon III, while *Black Robe* re-creates an extraordinary culture clash between seventeenth-century missionary Jesuits and native North Americans.

Mary Morrissey *A Lazy Eye* (o/p); *Mother of Pearl*. Impressive stories and a novel by one of the new generation of women writers. Her *The Pretender* (o/p) tells the story of the Polish factory worker who claimed to be Anastasia, daughter of the last tsar of Russia.

★ **Christopher Nolan** *Under the Eye of the Clock*. Extraordinary and explosive fiction debut: the largely autobiographical story of a handicapped boy's celebration of the power of language. *The Banyan Tree* is an evocative tale, chock-full of poetry, about an elderly woman's love for her family and the land.

Edna O'Brien *The Country Girls; Down by the River. The Country Girls* is a sensitively wrought novel from a top-class writer sometimes accused, unjustly, of wavering too much towards Mills and Boon. In *Down by the River*, incest and bigotry in parochial Ireland is dealt with head-on and delivered with brutal poetry.

★ **Flann O'Brien** *The Third Policeman*. O'Brien's masterpiece of the ominously absurd and fiendishly humorous. *At Swim-Two-Birds* is a complicated and hilarious blend of Gaelic fable and surrealism; essential reading. Also see "Memoirs and Journalism", p.874, under Myles na Gopaleen.

Frank O'Connor *Guests of the Nation*. Arguably the best Irish political fiction of the twentieth century. *My Oedipus Complex & Other Stories* is a collection of witty short stories from a master of the genre, especially enjoyable for Catholics.

Joseph O'Connor *True Believers; Cowboys and Indians; Desperadoes; The Salesman; Inishowen; Star of the Sea*. The first two titles deal with life on the peripheries in London and Dublin: love and loss, madness and redemption. *Desperadoes* is a love story ranging from 1950s Dublin to modern Nicaragua, while *The Salesman* is a pacey revenge thriller in which a man hunts the thief who has left his daughter in a coma. *Inishowen*, a comic novel set in small-town Donegal, has been followed by *Star of the Sea*, a historical thriller set on a refugee ship bound for New York in 1847.

Peadar O'Donnell *Islanders* (o/p). Evocative, mesmerizing prose from important Republican figure.

Julia O'Faolain *No Country for Young Men* (o/p). Spanning four generations, this ambitious novel traces the personal repercussions of the civil war.

Seán Ó Faoláin *Midsummer Night Madness*. A master of the short-story form and the juiciness of rural dialect.

Liam O'Flaherty *The Informer*. Finest of the postwar generation of former IRA men turned writers. His best-known work is a racy tale of Gypo Nolan, a former Republican, who betrays a colleague to the Garda and is hunted down by his erstwhile associates.

Jamie O'Neill *At Swim-Two-Boys*. Commanded the highest ever advance for an Irish literary work, but this epic love story set against the background of the 1916 Rising – eloquent and Joycean or just plain overwrought – divided the critics.

Sean O'Reilly *Love and Sleep*. A bleak, distinctive first novel set in Derry, blending hard-edged realism with vivid, dream-like qualities.

Glenn Patterson *Burning Your Own*. Distinctive young Northern writer gives Protestant child's-eye view of late-1960s Northern Ireland just about to explode. *Fat Lad* (o/p) follows a man giving up a promising career to return to Belfast, in an uncompromising yet positive portrayal of the city. *The International*, a fine novel set in pre-Troubles Belfast, is based around the lives of staff and guests of what was then just an ordinary provincial hotel.

Keith Ridgway *The Long Falling*. Ridgway's often harrowing debut novel is both a love story and murder story, set in a Dublin that is dangerous and alienating.

Frank Ronan *Home*. A funny and poignant tale of a boy torn between New Age inanities and Catholic pieties.

E.O. Somerville and (Violet) Martin Ross *The Irish RM*. Hilarious tales in which the locals always outwit the resident magistrate. The "begorra" factor is a little too heavy here and there, but Somerville and Ross write with witty flair and their tales are significant for what they unwittingly reveal about a dying class.

James Stephens *The Crock of Gold; The Charwoman's Daughter; The Demi-Gods* (o/p). Three fabulous masterpieces from the country's most underrated genius.

Laurence Sterne *The Life and Opinions of Tristram Shandy; A Sentimental Journey Through France and Italy*. Essential reading from an eighteenth-century comic genius.

Bram Stoker *Dracula*. Stoker woke up after a nightmare brought on by a hefty lobster supper, and proceeded to write his way into the nightmares of the twentieth century.

Francis Stuart *Black List Section H*. Once a protégé of Yeats, Stuart consistently maintained a stance of opposition, in his life and his art. *Black List Section H*, his masterpiece, depicts the life of an Irishman in wartime Germany.

Eamon Sweeney *Waiting for the Healer*. A single father's bleak descent into drink handled with wry humour. *There's Only One Red Army* is a fictional memoir of a life led through alcoholism and an obsession with a third-rate football team, Sligo Rovers. *The Photograph* is Sweeney's latest witty and erudite novel which takes on the big issues of religion and politics, and their role in Irish culture.

Jonathan Swift *Gulliver's Travels; The Tale of a Tub and Other Stories*. Acerbic satire from the only writer in the English language with as sharp a pen as Voltaire.

Colm Tóibín *The South; The Heather Blazing; The Story of the Night; The Blackwater Lightship*. In *The South* a woman turns her back on Ireland for Spain and returns thirty years later to resolve her life, and to die. A powerfully understated novel, *The Heather Blazing* explores themes of personal and political loss, while his *Story of the Night* is a haunting love story set in Argentina at the time of the generals. *The Blackwater Lightship* follows the grim journey of an ordinary family confronting AIDS.

William Trevor *Collected Stories*. Five of Trevor's short-story collections in one volume from Penguin, revealing more about Ireland than many a turgid sociological thesis. Often desperately moving, these stories confirm Trevor as one of the true giants of Irish fiction. *Two Lives* included the novella *Reading Turgenev*, a sensitive account of an unhappy marriage which was shortlisted for the 1991 Booker Prize. Trevor's latest novel, *The Story of Lucy Gault*, beginning in rural Cork during the troubles of 1921 and telling the story of the disasters that ensued for one family, was also nominated for the Booker.

Oscar Wilde *The Picture of Dorian Gray*. Wilde's exploration of moral schizophrenia. A debauched socialite maintains his youthful good looks, while his portrait in the attic slowly disintegrates into a vision of evil.

Poetry

Samuel Beckett *Poems 1930–1989.* The most complete collection of Beckett's poetry, in both English and French (with his own translations), and including translations of major twentieth-century French poets such as Rimbaud and Eluard.

★ **Eavan Boland** *Collected Poems*; *The Lost Land*; *Code.* Thoughtful, spare and elegant verse from one of Ireland's most significant poets.

Pat Boran *The Unwound Clock*; *As the Hand, the Glove.* Wry, insightful poems of contemporary Irish life.

★ **Ciaran Carson** *The Twelfth of Never.* Richly allusive poetry that will baffle those not steeped in Irish history and politics. Carson's prose works offer a more accessible taste of one of Ireland's most musical literary voices, but include highly experimental pieces that probably belong best alongside his poetry: *Fishing for Amber* is a "long story" that pulls together Irish fairy tales, Ovid's *Metamorphoses* and the history of the Dutch Golden Age into the form of a magic alphabet; *Shamrock Tea* is a wildly imaginative fantasy based on a herbal remedy infiltrating a Belfast reservoir which can cleanse the windows of perception.

Austin Clarke *Selected Poems.* Clarke's tender work evokes the same stark grandeur as the paintings of Jack B. Yeats.

★ **Patrick Crotty** (ed) *Modern Irish Poetry: An Anthology.* This anthology covers a broad range of poetry from 1922 onwards, includes Irish and English translations of a number of poems, and provides highly accessible introductions to both the period and the individual poets represented.

Denis Devlin *Collected Poems.* Pre-eminent Irish poet of the 1930s, owing allegiance to the European Modernist, rather than the prevailing Yeatsian, tradition.

★ **Paul Durcan** *A Snail in My Prime*; *O Westport in the Light of Asia Minor*; *The Berlin Wall Café*; *Greetings to our Friends in Brazil*; *Cries of an Irish Caveman.* Ireland's most popular and readable poet. *Berlin Wall* is a lament for a broken marriage, recounted with agonizing honesty, dignity and, ultimately, forgiveness. His later *Greetings to Our Friends in Brazil* is somewhat mellower, with many of the poems centring on a priest who, far from being repressive and hypocritical as in his earlier works, is honourable and truly spiritual.

Peter Fallon *News of the World.* Reflections on a reassuring landscape, the present consciously linked to the past, punctuated by the petty rivalries and discreet madnesses of country life.

Padraic Fiacc *Missa Terribilis* (o/p); *Ruined Pages: Selected Poems.* Fiacc's work is informed by the political and social tribalisms of Northern Ireland, and explores personal relationships in these contexts.

Michael Hartnett *Collected Poems.* A richly lyrical and rhythmical collection covering Hartnett's 40-year career, compiled by Gallery Press since his recent death.

★ **Seamus Heaney** The most important Irish poet since Yeats. His poems are immediate and passionate, even when dealing with intellectual problems and radical social divisions. The title of *The Spirit Level*, winner of the 1997 Whitbread Prize, alludes to the delicate balances of private and political life following the ceasefire; cool, reassuring poetry with its own quiet music. *Opened Ground: Poems 1966–96*, a massive selection from all his previous published work, has been followed by his recent collection, *Electric Light*. *Finders Keepers* is an anthology of his energetic prose, consisting of essays and lectures written between 1971 and 2001.

★ **Patrick Kavanagh** *The Complete Poems*. Joyfully mystic exploration of the rural countryside and the lives of its inhabitants by one of Ireland's most popular poets, perhaps most famous for *The Great Hunger*, in which he attacked sexual repression in 1940s Ireland. See also his autobiographical novel, *Tarry Flynn*.

Brendan Kennelly *Cromwell*. Speculative meditation on the role of the conqueror in Irish history. *Poetry My Arse* is an epic poem which "sinks its teeth into the pants of poetry itself", while *Begin* presents an accessible and highly enjoyable selection of Kennelly's "echopoems". See also his *Penguin Book of Irish Verse*.

Thomas Kinsella *Collected Poems: 1956–2001*. The full variety of Kinsella's work is on display here, employing modernist and traditional elements, on subjects ranging from love to political satire, social commentary and metaphysical speculation. See also his first-rate anthology *The New Oxford Book of Irish Verse*.

Michael Longley *Gorse Fires*; *The Ghost Orchid*; *The Weather in Japan*. Three fine collections which show Longley as a highly skilled poet with a strong moral voice.

Shane MacGowan *Poguetry*. Powerful and pungent lyrics by the former Pogues' bardperson. Not for Yeats fans.

Louis MacNeice *Collected Poems*; or *Selected Poems*. Good chum of Auden, Spender and the rest of the "1930s generation", Carrickfergus-born MacNeice achieves a fruitier texture and an even more detached tone.

Derek Mahon *Selected Poems*; *Collected Poems*; *The Hudson Letter*; *The Yellow Book*. A selection of works from one of the finest contemporary Northern Irish poets. See also his *Penguin Book of Contemporary Irish Poetry* (ed with Peter Fallon).

★ **Medbh McGuckian** *Venus in the Rain*; *Selected Poems*; *The Face of the Earth*. Trawling the subconscious for their imagery, McGuckian's sensuous and elusive poems are highly demanding and equally rewarding.

Paula Meehan *The Man who was Marked by Winter*; *Pillow Talk*; *Dharmakaya*. Memorable work, often concerned with women's lives, issues of family, gender and sexuality and rooted in the inner-city experience.

John Montague *Collected Poems*. Terse poetry concerned with history, community and social decay. See also his anthology, *The Faber Book of Irish Verse*.

Paul Muldoon *Poems 1968–98*. Muldoon's own selection of his more accessible, witty and inventive poetry taken from work spanning thirty years. Moving between Ireland and the US, his latest collection, *Moy Sand and Gravel*, is equally playful and assured.

Eileán Ní Chuilleanáin *The Rose Geranium*; *The Brazen Serpent*. Manages to carve something new, purposeful and whole from the iconography and language of religion; quietly impressive.

★ **Nuala Ní Dhomhnaill** *The Astrakhan Cloak*; *The Water Horse*. Good introductions to her work, in Irish and English, with translations in the former by Paul Muldoon, in the latter by Medbh McGuckian and

Eileán Ní Chuilleanáin. Haunting translations of her modern erotic verse by the fine poet Michael Hartnett are included in *Raven Introductions 3* and in Frank Ormsby's anthology of love poetry (see below).

Frank Ormsby (ed) *The Long Embrace: Twentieth-century Irish Love Poems* (o/p). Excellent anthology with major chunks from the work of almost every important twentieth-century Irish poet from Yeats to the present day. *A Rage To Order* (ed; o/p) is an impressive anthology of poetry born of the Troubles. Horror, pain, anger and pity somehow all wrestled into some sense of form; an absorbing book. See also his *Poets from the North of Ireland* anthology.

Tom Paulin *Fivemiletown*; *The Strange Museum*; *Walking a Line*; *Selected Poems 1972–90*. Often called "dry" both in praise and accusation, Paulin's work reverberates with thoughtful political commitment and a sophisticated irony. His latest, *The Invasion Handbook*, is an ambitious and varied work, setting out to recount the origins of World War II.

★ **William Butler Yeats** *The Poems* (published as *The Collected Poems* in the US). They're all here, poems of rhapsody, love, revolution and eventual rage at a disconnected and failed Ireland "fumbling in the greasy till".

Drama

Sebastian Barry *Our Lady of Sligo*; *Plays 1*. Characters from Barry's family history are central to his plays, all brought to life by a rich use of language. In the latter collection, *The Steward of Christendom*, relating the story of the Catholic head of the Dublin Metropolitan Police before the change in regime in 1922, is particularly compelling. His latest, *Hinterland*, a portrayal of a disgraced former Taoiseach not wholly unlike Charles Haughey, met with such harsh reviews that Barry threatened to leave Ireland.

★ **Samuel Beckett** *The Complete Dramatic Works*. Bleak hilarity from the laureate of the void, including his seminal masterpiece *Waiting for Godot* and other absurdist treats such as *Endgame*.

Brendan Behan *The Complete Plays*. Flashes of brilliance from a writer destroyed by alcoholism. His *The Quare Fellow* takes up where Wilde's *Ballad of Reading Gaol* leaves off.

Marina Carr *Portia Coughlan*; *On Raftery's Hill*; *Ariel*. Three plays by one of Ireland's leading playwrights, including her most famous, *On Raftery's Hill*, a harsh tale of three generations of the same family living in a close-knit farming community in the midlands.

George Farquhar *The Recruiting Officer*. The usual helping of cross-dressing and mistaken identity, yet this goes beyond the implications of most Restoration comedy, even flirting with feminism before finally marrying everyone off in the last scene.

★ **Brian Friel** *Plays: Two*. A selection of the Derry playwright's later work, including probably his most famous play, *Dancing at Lughnasa*, a family drama which examines the tensions between Catholicism and paganism in Irish society. *Plays: One* includes *Translations* and *Faith Healer*.

Oliver Goldsmith, *She Stoops to Conquer*. Sparky dialogue, with a more English sheen than Farquhar.

Augusta, Lady Gregory *Collected Plays*. The Anglo-Irish writer who understood most about the cadences of the Irish language. This gives not only her translations, but also her original drama an authenticity lacking in the work of others.

Martin McDonagh *Plays Volume 1* (published as *The Beauty Queen of Leenane and Other Plays* in the US); *The Cripple of Inishmaan*; *The Lieutenant of Inishmore*. Festering familial hatred, murder and isolation on the west coast of Ireland, dished up with aplomb by this wickedly funny, abrasive young dramatist.

★ **Frank McGuinness** *Plays*; *Plays 2*. Collections of the major works from one of Ireland's most important playwrights. The former includes *Observe the Sons of Ulster Marching towards the Somme*, an examination of the Ulster Protestant experience of World War I, and the latter *Someone To Watch Over Me*, an exploration of the cultural resources that sustain three hostages – one English, one Irish and one American – in the Middle East.

Conor McPherson *McPherson: Four Plays* (published as *The Weir and Other Plays* in the US). A collection including *This Lime Tree Bower*, a very funny play in which the lives of three men change in the course of a weekend; and *The Weir*, an eerie, compelling drama set in an isolated village in the west of Ireland.

Gary Mitchell *Tearing the Loom & In a Little World of our Own*; *Trust*; *The Force of Change*; *As the Beast Sleeps*. Fine plays from one of Belfast's leading playwrights, chiefly focusing on the changing lives of the Loyalist community.

★ **Tom Murphy** *Famine*; *The Gigli Concert*; *Bailegangaire*. Along with Friel and McGuinness, Murphy is one of the three outstanding contemporary Irish playwrights.

★ **Sean O'Casey** *Three Plays*. Contains the socialist playwright's famous Dublin trilogy *Juno and the Paycock*, *Shadow of a Gunman* and *The Plough and the Stars*, which powerfully challenged the revolutionary rhetoric and political orthodoxies of the day.

★ **John Millington Synge** *The Complete Plays*. Lots of "begorras" and "mavourneens" and other dialogue kindly invented for the Irish peasantry by Synge, but *The Playboy of the Western World* is a brilliant and unique work, greeted in Dublin by riots, threats and moral outrage.

★ **Oscar Wilde** *The Complete Works of Oscar Wilde*. The full emotional range, from the glittering, profound and subversive satire of *Lady Windermere's Fan* and *The Importance of Being Earnest*, to the moving verse of *The Ballad of Reading Gaol*, written during his imprisonment.

Biography and criticism

Anthony Cronin *Samuel Beckett: The Last Modernist*. Accessible, anecdotal biography, good on the Irish background. *No Laughing Matter: The Life and Times of Flann O'Brien* (o/p). Witty and insightful biography, and particularly interesting on 1950s Dublin.

★ **Seamus Deane** *Short History of Irish Literature*. Deane brings a poet's sensitivity to a massive and sometimes unwieldy tradition, with skill and a profound sense of sociopolitical context. See also his shorter analysis of modern writing in *Irish Writers*.

Ruth Dudley Edwards *James Connolly*. A short, direct biography of the socialist leader, which gathers pace around the time of his relations with Larkin, the 1913 Lock-Out in Dublin and the 1916 Rising.

★ **Richard Ellmann** *James Joyce*; *Oscar Wilde*. Ellmann's wonderful biography of Joyce is a literary masterpiece in its own right. His work on Wilde was, unfortunately, unfinished when he died, but is still an excellent insight into the work of this often misunderstood writer.

Christopher Fitz-Simon *The Boys*. Frank and conscientious biography of the founders of Dublin's Gate Theatre, Micheál Mac Liammóir and his equally mysterious lifelong lover, Hilton Edwards.

★ **R.F. Foster** *W.B. Yeats – A Life – The Apprentice Mage*. Volume One of two volumes (Volume Two due out in 2003). This is a superb biography – dispassionate, scholarly, and bound to augment your understanding of, though not necessarily your feelings for, the great man. *The Irish Story: Telling Tales and Making it up in Ireland* is a provocative, witty deconstruction of myth-making and clichés in Ireland's telling of its own history.

Michael Holroyd *Bernard Shaw*. Unfairly slammed by the critics, this is actually a pretty successful stab at understanding one of the most difficult and complex authors of the Anglo-Irish canon; made more accessible to the general reader in this abridged, one-volume edition.

Robert Kee *The Laurel & the Ivy: The Story of Charles Stewart Parnell*. Illuminating account of the life and times of the great statesman by one of Ireland's most respected historians.

★ **Declan Kiberd** *Inventing Ireland*. A massively scrupulous assessment of modern Irish literature from Yeats to Friel, set against a background of flux and turmoil. The universally praised follow-up, *Irish Classics*, presents an accessible discussion of the greatest Irish works since 1600 in English and Irish.

★ **James Knowlson** *Damned to Fame: The Life of Samuel Beckett*. Stunning biography, by one of the world's pre-eminent Beckett experts: thorough, balanced and scholarly.

Brenda Maddox *Nora: A Biography of Nora Joyce* (published in the US as *Nora: The Real Life of Molly Bloom*). Eminently readable story of the funny, irreverent and formidable Nora Barnacle and her life with James Joyce – an interesting complement to Ellmann's Joyce biography.

Ulick O'Connor *Brendan Behan*. Moving account of the dramatist's life.

Antoinette Quinn *Paddy Kavanagh: A Biography*. Astute and often gently paced account of the life and poetry of County Monaghan's favourite son.

★ **Margaret Ward** *Hannah Sheehy Skeffington: A Life*. Fascinating, scholarly biography of a militant suffragist; co-founder of the Irish Women's Franchise League in 1908, Skeffington was one of the most important political activists of her day.

Robert Welch (ed) *Oxford Companion to Irish Literature*. This encyclopedic tour through who's who and what they've written fills a long-standing need.

Memoirs and journalism

★ **Christy Brown** *My Left Foot*. Born with cerebral palsy, Brown painstakingly typed out this unsentimental autobiography, published in 1954 when he was 22, focusing on his upbringing in a huge Dublin family, dominated by the remarkable endurance and character of his mother.

Dr Noel Browne *Against the Tide*. Tremendously important autobiography and account of Irish political life by one of Ireland's key twentieth-century radicals, and particularly illuminating on the role of Catholicism in Irish politics.

★ **Ciaran Carson** *The Star Factory*. Magical account of growing up in 1950s and 1960s Belfast; Carson has a poetic ingenuity reminiscent of Dylan Thomas.

Liam Fay *Beyond Belief*. Hilarious, irreverent look at the state of religion in Ireland.

★ **Myles na Gopaleen** *The Best of Myles*. Priceless extracts from a daily humorous newspaper column by Flann O'Brien's alter ego.

Hugh Leonard *Home before Night*; *Out after Dark*. Beautifully written evocations by the noted playwright of, respectively, his childhood and his adolescence in south Dublin around the 1940s. At times moving, often hilarious.

★ **Frank McCourt** *Angela's Ashes*. Stunning memoir of a Limerick childhood; a tale of bleak, desperate poverty, laced with astonishing moments of humour and a deep respect for the lives led. In the disappointing sequel, *'Tis*, McCourt finds both escape and a sense of purpose through education in New York.

Nuala O'Faolain *Are You Somebody?* Despite a life rich in ideas and experience, this memoir reveals an Ireland that until recently treated women with, at best, indifference. Neat sketches of literary Dublin in the 1950s, puncturing one or two cosy myths along the way.

Colm Tóibín *The Sign of the Cross: Travels in Catholic Europe*. Novelist Tóibín uses his journalistic skills to find the old-time religion in Ireland and elsewhere. *Bad Blood* is a perceptive account of a journey along the line that divides Northern Ireland from the rest of the island.

John Waters *Jiving at the Crossroads*. Curiously engaging autobiography by the *Irish Times'* gadfly columnist, which traces a fascination with Fianna Fáil politics through the formative years of a western youth in the 1970s and 1980s. *An Intelligent Person's Guide to Modern Ireland* is a controversial examination of Ireland's self-styled progression, arguing that the Irish have lost their cohesiveness in the drive for a "perverse and lonely" prosperity.

Art and music

★ **Bruce Arnold** *Irish Art: A Concise History*. This updated edition provides a fuller account of Irish Modernism. See also his biography of *Jack Yeats*.

The Bogside Artists *Murals* A lavish A4 illustrated explanation and analysis of Derry's famous murals, penned by the painters themselves.

Breandán Breathnach *Folk Music and Dances of Ireland*. Breathnach's classic developmental account and analysis of the structure of Irish music is essential reading. A companion CD features all the songs and tunes from the book's closing section.

★ **Helen Brennan** *The Story of Irish Dance*. Not just a fascinating history of the development of traditional dancing in Ireland, but a (literally) step-by-step guide to some of the most popular set dances.

Ciaran Carson *The Pocket Guide to Irish Traditional Music*. Useful introduction to the world of traditional music, while *Last Night's Fun* is a wonderful evocation of the elusive pleasures of traditional music sessions.

Victoria Mary Clarke and Shane MacGowan *A Drink with Shane MacGowan*. Shane's long-time – now former – partner takes the singer and songwriter through his personal history and several large martinis on the way.

Tony Clayton-Lea & Richard Taylor *Irish Rock*. Popular account of the growth of the Irish music scene, particularly good on the punk and new-wave years.

P.J. Curtis *Notes from the Heart*. Criminally ignored on first publication, P.J.'s opening chapters provide an admirable overview of the music's twentieth-century developments, while the remainder focuses on major figures in County Clare's music.

Brian Fallon *Irish Art 1830–1990*. The development of art in Ireland and its reflection of questions of national identity and culture.

Caoimhín MacAoidh *Between the Jigs and Reels: The Donegal Fiddle Tradition*. A marvellous book which truly captures the richness of the county's musical heritage through a detailed analysis of its history, informative biographies of many musicians and valuable descriptions of their various techniques.

★ **Christy Moore** *One Voice*. Not just a scintillating account of Moore's own life through song, but a hard-hitting analysis of Ireland over the last thirty years.

Nuala O'Connor *Bringing It All Back Home*. Detailed account of the history of traditional Irish music written to accompany a 1991 BBC TV series and recently revised to encompass the last decade's developments.

Dáibhí Ó Cróinín *The Songs of Elizabeth Cronin*. Ultimately flawed, thanks to a lack of biographical detail, but still fascinating study of one of Ireland's most important traditional singers, accompanied by two CDs of her singing.

Francis O'Neill *The Dance Music of Ireland*. Known as "O'Neill's 1001" or to some musicians simply as "the book", this compiles a 1001 of the best-known traditional tunes.

Donal O'Sullivan *Carolan: The Life, Times and Music of an Irish Harper*. Original 1958 masterpiece reissued to glorious effect, combining O'Sullivan's biography with scores of all Carolan's compositions.

Mark J. Prendergast *Irish Rock: Roots, Personalities and Directions*. Dated, but still the best in-depth account of the development of Irish rock music.

★ **Fintan Vallely** (ed) *The Companion to Irish Traditional Music*. Provides constant delight in its copious accounts of the music's form, style and qualities, and brief biographies of many key participants; required reading.

Fintan Vallely and Charlie Piggott *Blooming Meadows: The World of Irish Traditional Musicians.* The authors' fascinating biographical snapshots of a broad range of singers and musicians are enhanced by Nutan's evocative photographs of their subjects.

★ **Geoff Wallis and Sue Wilson** *The Rough Guide to Irish Music.* A quintessential account of the roots and current state of traditional music in Ireland, containing a comprehensive directory of more than four hundred singers, musicians and groups and details of the best places to see them in action.

Landscape, topography and travel

★ **Aalen, Whelan and Stout** (eds) *Atlas of the Irish Rural Landscape.* Wholly absorbing collection of essays, maps and illustrations revealing and analysing the changing landscape of Ireland; a must for all concerned with its history and future. The recent *Newgrange and the Bend of the Boyne*, by Geraldine Stout, is the first of several planned offshoots of the atlas.

Deirdre Flanagan and Lawrence Flanagan *Irish Place Names.* Expertly researched account of the origins of virtually everywhere on the island – a dipper's delight.

Breandán & Ruarí ó hEithir *An Aran Reader.* A fascinating anthology of writings about the Aran Islands, including the works of early travellers, anthropologists, poets and islanders.

★ **Pete McCarthy** *McCarthy's Bar.* Runaway bestseller by the former travel-show presenter and stand-up comedian. An extended crawl around the McCarthy's Bars of Ireland provides occasion for insight and plenty of irresistible humour.

Mark McCrum *The Craic: A Journey Through Ireland.* Though perhaps a little too fascinated by the remnants of the Anglo-Irish aristocracy, McCrum's travels still offer plenty of amusement and analysis.

Patrick McKay *A Dictionary of Ulster Place-Names.* Not just a cornucopia of etymological derivations but a veritable treasure trove of information about almost every single place in the province of Ulster.

H.V. Morton *In Search of Ireland.* Originally published in 1930, this still offers profound insights into the character of Ireland's people and is as wonderfully written as Morton's other travelogues.

Eric Newby *Round Ireland in Low Gear.* Enjoyable account by the doyen of travel writers of a leisurely cycle trip around the country.

Tim Robinson *The Stones of Aran: Pilgrimage.* Treats the largest of the Aran Islands to a scrutiny of Proustian detail. *The Stones of Aran: Labyrinth* completes the project, to form a uniquely challenging travel book.

Guides

Kevin Corcoran *West Cork Walks*. A good, accessible guide to ten, mostly circular, day-walks including a wealth of interesting material on the history and natural history of the county. *West of Ireland Walks* covers fourteen circular day-walks in Clare, Galway and Mayo in a similar vein.

Cycling in the Southwest of Ireland; Cycling in the Southeast of Ireland; Cycling in the North of Ireland Collins guides, fully mapped in colour, each covering 25 routes ranging from short rides suitable for families to regional tours.

Paddy Dillon *Twelve Walks in Glendalough*. A lightweight, easy-to-use guide to walks around Glendalough, ranging from short and easy to long and very strenuous. Colour photographs and clear maps are included.

David Herman *Hill Walkers' Donegal*. Over thirty walks in the county described in excellent detail.

★ **Pat Liddy** *Secret Dublin*; *Walking Dublin*. Two beautifully written walking guides to the city, replete with historical insights and up-to-date information.

★ **Joss Lynam** (ed) *Best Irish Walks*. Seventy-six walks through some of the most beautiful and remote parts of the country. *Easy Walks near Dublin*. An excellent guide to forty walks, many in the Wicklow Mountains, and several with details about access by public transport from Dublin.

Sally and John McKenna *Bridgestone Traveller's Guide*. The best in an almost non-existent field of Irish food writing. The same authors' guide for vegetarians and annual round-up of Ireland's hundred best restaurants are also popular.

Jennifer Miller and Ann Bracken *Healthy Getaways and Complementary Health Centres throughout Ireland*. For those seeking a healthier holiday, a comprehensive guide to the country's spas and healing centres.

Patrick Simms and Tony Whilde *West of Ireland Walk Guide*. Detailed descriptions of west and northwest walks from counties Clare to Derry.

Alan Warner *Walking the Ulster Way*. The first man to walk the entire five hundred miles describes his journey in detailed and sometimes whimsical diaries.

Language

Language

Language

A visitor to Ireland will probably have little or no contact with the Irish language, unless they seek to do so in the **Gaeltacht** (Irish-speaking areas mostly in the west of the country). However, the legacy of the language still pervades many aspects of Irish life, be it in the rhythms of speech patterns in English, the town and townland names throughout the country or in traditional poetry or song. It has been said for decades that Irish is a dying language and although there is little chance of it becoming the first tongue of more than a small minority of the people of Ireland, the recent rebirth of interest has ensured that it will not follow in the linguistic footsteps of its deceased Celtic cousins.

The **Celtic settlement** of Ireland probably began in the seventh century BC; the later migration of Irish tribes to the Isle of Man and to Scotland established Irish-speaking kingdoms in those areas. With the rise of Rome the Celtic languages survived only in the peripheral western areas – today, Celtic languages are limited to parts of Scotland, Wales and Brittany in addition to Ireland. Cornish, another Celtic derivative, died out in the eighteenth century and, in the twentieth century, Manx ceased to be a community language.

The earliest form of script in Celtic Ireland, known as **ogham**, is found on standing stones dating from the fourth to seventh centuries. Employing a twenty-character alphabet derived from Latin, the letters were represented by varying strokes and notches, and read from the bottom upwards. Following the establishment of monasteries, a written form of the language, more closely resembling its modern-day form, evolved, with monks recording significant events in the areas in which they were based. The best-known non-religious text of this period is the *Táin Bó Cúailgne* (The Cattle Raid of Cooley), which dates back to the seventh century. With the first Viking raid of 795, the world of the monastery was thrown into chaos and the thread of the language, now known as **Old Irish**, was cut, giving way to a less scholastic and more vernacular-based written language referred to as **Middle Irish**. It was in the later part of this era that the Fenian Cycle emerged, charting the exploits of Fionn Mac Cumhaill and his Fianna (band), tales which were very popular with the peasantry.

The period from 1200 to 1600 is considered the **Classical Period** in the development of the language, when the grammatical chaos of Middle Irish was brought under control. A succession of invaders speaking Norse, French and English were assimilated into the population, with a resulting cross-fertilization of languages. There were, however, concerted attempts to stamp out the use of the language, one example being in 1367 when the Statutes of Kilkenny declared that, among other things, "the English may not entertain or make gifts to Irish minstrels, rhymers or story-tellers". Despite these attempts to preserve an English-speaking culture, the first Anglo-Norman aristocracy became thoroughly Gaelicized, and even as late as 1578 the Lord Chancellor could report that "all English, and most part with delight, even in Dublin, speak Irish and greatly are spotted in manners, habit and conditions with Irish stains".

However, after the Battle of Kinsale in 1601, the Gaelic aristocracy disappeared, as did the king's court, the Brehon system of law and the bardic schools. Poets soon became a class of wandering minstrel, known as "rakarees" (from the Irish *recaire* – "one who recites") and were persecuted since they represented "the old way".

Although the use of Irish was still widespread in the nineteenth century, the language was further weakened by the establishment of the **National School System** in 1831, which decreed that all children should be educated through the medium of English, despite the fact that many of their parents only spoke Irish. A further blow to the language was the **Great Famine** which hit hardest in many Irish-speaking areas. Even mass-movement politics of a vaguely nationalistic nature eschewed the use of Irish, and Daniel O'Connell, despite being a fluent speaker, preferred to use English both at his rallies and in his propaganda.

Despite the language's decline in the nineteenth century, some organizations sprang up to preserve its use: ironically, considering today's political climate, it was northern Protestants who spearheaded this campaign, the most prominent being the Revd William Nelson. In the late nineteenth century, a catalyst for the revival of Irish was the poet **Thomas Davis** who promoted the use of Irish as a living language. His efforts were followed by the formation of the **Gaelic League** that works to this day in the field of language promotion.

Immediately after **Independence** in 1921, Irish was installed as the first national language and steps were taken to revive it as a community tongue. Apart from an intensive education programme, the government attempted in other ways to "Gaelicize" Ireland, the most obvious example being the planting of Gaelic-speaking communities in the heart of English-speaking areas (one such community still remains at Rathcairn, County Meath). This enthusiasm has, however, in postwar years, given way to apathy and governments' efforts at promoting the language have been tokenistic at best; Article 8 Section 1 of the Constitution states that Irish is the first language, though this is viewed in most political circles as anachronistic and irrelevant.

Despite these factors militating against the survival of the language, it is still estimated that 80,000 people live in the designated Gaeltacht (Irish-speaking) areas – in counties Donegal, Mayo, Galway, Kerry, Cork, Waterford and Meath – of which between 20,000 and 30,000 are fluent Irish speakers. In parallel to this, there is growing **grassroots interest** in the promotion and use of Irish. It is in many ways evidence of an increasing national confidence that instead of seeing Irish as backward, it is nowadays embraced by some of the most progressive elements in society. 1972 saw the establishment of the **Irish-language radio station**, Raidió na Gaeltachta, and the latter half of the twentieth century has seen many fine writers writing in Irish about subjects that are far removed from the rural preoccupations some associate with Irish-language literature: the first staging-post towards modernity in Irish writing was *An Béal Bocht* by Myles na Gopaleen, followed by the poetry of Seán Ó Ríordáin and Máirtín Ó Díreáin, and latterly by the contemporary poetry of Nuala Ní Dhomhnaill, Gabriel Rosenstock, Cathal Ó Searcaigh and Michael O'Siadhail. In the North, the rise in the use of Irish has been both cultural and political: in the 1970s, Republican prisoners began to learn Irish, though owing to the insular nature of its usage and the lack of professional teaching, it mutated into a kind of pidgin that was known as "jailic". Perhaps the most conspicuous evidence of this revived interest came in the form of the **national television station**, TG4 (Teilifis na Gaeilge Cathair), which, through its progressive and inventive programming and its energetic youth-oriented presentation, offers the contemporary face of the Irish language.

Irish words commonly found in place names

abhainn/abha - river
achadh - field
aileach - rocky place
ais - back, ridge
árd - height
áth - ford
baile - town
bán - white
barr - top
beag - small
béal - mouth (of a river)
beann - peak, headland, cliff
bearna - gap
bel - beautiful
bó - cow
bóthar - road
bruach - bank
buí - yellow
bun - base
cabha - hollow, slope
caiseal - stone ring fort
caisleán - castle
caol - narrow
carn - cairn
carraig - rock
ceann - head, headland
cill - church
cloch - stone
cluain - meadow
cnoc - hill
coill - wood
cos/cois - foot
dearg - red
doire - oak wood
droichead - bridge
dubh - black
dún - fort
eaglais - church
eanach - marsh
eas - waterfall
eó - yew tree
fál - hedge
fiodh - wood
fionn - white, fair
fraoch - heather
gall - foreigner
gaoth - estuary
garbh - rough
garraí - garden
geal - bright
glas - green or grey; stream
gleann - valley
gort - field
grian - sun; gravel
inis - island, peninsula, river meadow
iúr - yew tree
lag/log - hollow
lann - church
leaba - bed, burial chamber
leath - half
léim - leap
leitir - hillside
loch - lake
machaire - plain
mainstir - abbey, monastery
maol - bare, bald
móin - peat bog
muc - pig
mullach - summit, hilltop
nead - nest
nua - new
ráth - ring fort
rua - red
sagart - priest
sean - old
sí - fairy
sliabh - mountain
sneachta - snow
sráid - street
suí - seat
teach, tí - house, monastery
teampall - church
tír - country, land
tobar - well, spring
trá - beach
tulach - small hill
uaimh - cave
uisce - water

Basic pronunciation of Irish

Irish **pronunciation** is notoriously difficult for outsiders, bearing little resemblance to English pronunciation. A few basic, simplified pointers are given below. Bear in mind, also, that the language has **three distinct dialects** which differ in pronunciation and grammar. These dialects are commonly referred to as Connacht Irish, spoken in the Gaeltacht areas of Galway and Mayo, Munster Irish, found mostly in Cork, Kerry and, to a lesser extent, Waterford, and Ulster Irish spoken in the western areas of Donegal.

Vowels

Irish uses an accent known as a *fada* to lengthen vowel sounds.

a as in "bat", or like the "o" in "slot"
á as in "saw"
e as in "met"
é as in "hey"
i as in "sit"
í as in "machine"
o as in "son"
ó as in "bone"
u as in "book"
ú as in "rule"

Consonants

Irish distinguishes between slender **consonants** – when beside an e or i – and broad consonants – when beside an a, o or u. For many consonants the slender pronunciation is different from the broad one.

bh broad, mh broad - "w" or "v"
bh slender, mh slender - "v"
c - always hard, as in "cat"
ch - the glottal sound found in English words with Gaelic origins such as "loch"
d broad - "th" as in "this"
d slender - sharp "d", almost a "j" as in "jelly"
dh broad, gh broad - "gh", like a voiced version of "ch" in "Bach"
dh slender, gh slender - "y" as in young
fh is silent
g - always hard, as in "gift"
ph - as in "phone"
s broad - "s" as in "some"
s slender - "sh" as in "sugar"
sh, th - "h" as in "hop"
t broad - aspirated, resembling "th" in "thin"

Language books and resources

Gaeilge agus Fáilte An up-to-date (2002), easy-to-follow combination of book and two cassettes aimed at adult beginners, produced by Gael Linn (see opposite).

Irish for Beginners A. Wilkes and J. Shackell. Humorous illustrations and puzzles help make learning more fun; no cassettes but websites recommended to help with pronunciation.

Learn Irish – CD ROM Words and Phrases for Beginners Not the greatest CD ROM ever but is as good a place to start as any.

Learning Irish Mícheál Ó Siadháil. Modern guide to language through speaking, with four cassettes available. Strong on grammar; Connacht dialect preferred.

Now You're Talking Based on the RTÉ–BBC Northern Ireland television programme of the same name, this is a good resource for both the beginner and those wishing to brush up on their language, with five cassettes available.

Teach Yourself Irish Miles Dillon and Donncha Ó Cróinín. Revised and updated course for beginners, with two cassettes; southern dialects are favoured.

Courses

For information about Irish-language classes, try contacting Conradh na Gaeilge, 6 Harcourt St, Dublin 2 (Ⓣ01/475 7401, Ⓦwww.cnag.ie). For books relating to the language, Siopa Leabhar (Book Shop) at the same address is the best place in Dublin. Well-respected **courses** are run by Gael Linn, 35 Dame St, Dublin 2 (Ⓣ01/675 1200, Ⓦwww.gael-linn.ie), whether non-residential in Dublin or staying in the Donegal, Cork or Mayo Gaeltachtaí; and by the excellent Oideas Gael (Ⓣ074/973 0248, Ⓦwww.oideas-gael.com; see also p.580), based in Glencolmcille in Donegal, where you can combine language learning with cultural activities such as walking, *bodhrán* playing and dancing.

Glossary

Alliance Party A moderate, centrist, non-sectarian Northern Ireland party.
bawn A castle enclosure or castlefold.
bodhrán (pronounced "bore-run") A hand-held, shallow, goatskin drum.
B Specials Auxiliary police force of the Stormont government; disbanded in 1971.
céilí/ceilidh An evening of Irish traditional dancing usually accompanied by a band.
cashel A kind of rath (see opposite), distinguished by a circular outer stone wall instead of earthen ramparts.
Celtic Tiger The Republic seen in terms of its extraordinary growth during the 1990s.
clochán A beehive-shaped, weatherproof hut built of tightly fitted stone without mortar. Clocháns date from the early Christian period.
The Continuity IRA Small breakaway organization maintaining the armed struggle against British rule and now thought to have amalagamated with the Real IRA.
"craic/crack" Good conversation, a good time, often accompanying drinking. "What's the crack?" means "what's the gossip?" or "what's going on?"
crannóg An artificial island in the middle of a lake, dating from the Bronze Age.
currach/curragh Small fishing vessel used off the west coast; traditionally made of leather stretched over a light wood frame, modern currachs are of tar-coated canvas.
The Dáil Lower house of the Republican parliament.
dolmen (or "portal tomb") A chamber formed by standing stones that support a massive capstone. The capstone often slopes to form the entrance of the chamber. Dates from the Copper Age (2000–1750 BC).
drumlin Small, oval, hummocky hill formed from the detritus of a retreating glacier.
DUP The Democratic Unionist Party. A traditionalist, anti-Republican right-wing party founded by Ian Paisley and Desmond Boal in 1971. Paisley has remained leader since then and is the only European political leader in modern times to have founded his own church. The DUP is fundamentally opposed to the Good Friday Agreement and any loosening of the bonds with the United Kingdom.
Éire Irish name for Ireland, but officially indicates the 26 counties.
esker A long, winding ridge, as sometimes found above a bog.
Fenian The name of a member of a nineteenth-century revolutionary organization which fought for an independent Ireland.
Fianna Fáil The largest and most successful of the Republic's two main political parties since Independence. Essentially a conservative party, it has its origins in the Republican faction of Sinn Féin, and fought against pro-Treaty forces in the civil war. During the 1930s, the party did much to assert Ireland's separateness from Britain.
Fine Gael The Republic's second largest political party, Fine Gael sprang from the pro-Treaty faction of Sinn Féin which formed the first Free State government in 1921. Since that time it has not been able to gain a strong majority, and periods in office have been in coalitions. It advocates more liberal policies than Fianna Fáil in terms of social welfare, but in fact there is very little to distinguish the two main parties.
Fir Men (sign on men's public toilets).
Gaeltacht Any region in Ireland in which Irish Gaelic is the vernacular speech; these are chiefly in the west.
gallery grave A simple burial chamber of squared stones, generally found under a long mound.
Garda Siochána The police force of the Republic of Ireland.
INLA Irish National Liberation Army. Extreme Republican paramilitary group. Its aim is the creation through physical force of a united socialist 32-county republic.
IRA Irish Republican Army. The upholders of the Irish Fenian tradition, dedicated to the establishment of a united 32-county republic by whatever means possible and

notorious both for its bombing campaigns and the extreme sophistication of its organizational structure.

IRSP Irish Republican Socialist Party. The most revolutionary, if small, party in Northern Ireland and the political wing of the INLA.

lough A commonly used term for lake; also a narrow coastal bay.

LVF Loyalist Volunteer Force. Paramilitary organization based in and around Portadown, led by Billy Wright until his assassination by the INLA in The Maze prison, December 1997.

Loyalist Hardline Northern Irish Protestant loyal to the British Crown.

Martello tower Circular coastal tower once used for defence.

Mná Women (sign on women's public toilets).

motte A circular mound, flat on top, which the Normans used as a fortification.

Nationalists Those who wish to see a united Ireland.

The North Term referring to Northern Ireland, used by many people.

ogham (rhyming with poem) The earliest form of writing used by the Irish (fourth to seventh centuries), and found on the edge of standing stones. Employing a twenty-character alphabet derived from Latin, the letters were represented by varying strokes and notches, and read from the bottom upwards.

Orange Order A Loyalist Protestant organization, found throughout Northern Ireland, which promotes the Union with Britain. The name comes from William of Orange ("King Billy"), the Protestant king who defeated the Catholic James II at the Battle of the Boyne (1690) and at the Battle of Aughrim (1691). Most Unionist MPs are Orangemen, and outside of Northern Ireland, Orange Lodges (branches) are found amongst Loyalist expats. See also box on p.734.

passage grave A megalithic tomb from the Neolithic period. A simple corridor of large, square, vertical stones leads to a burial chamber, and the whole tomb is covered with earth. The stones are decorated with simple patterns: double spirals, triangles, zigzag lines, and the sun symbol.

plantation The process of colonization of Ireland by the English Crown by which land was confiscated from the indigenous people and given to English and Scottish Protestant settlers.

poteen/poitín (pronounced "potcheen") Highly alcoholic (often toxic) and illegal spirit, usually distilled from potatoes.

PUP Progressive Unionist Party. Northern Irish party seen as the political wing of the UVF. Many of its leading lights are former Loyalist paramilitaries, including David Ervine, a major player in ensuring Loyalist support for the Good Friday Agreement.

rath or **ring fort** A farmstead dating from the first millennium AD. A circular timber enclosure banked by earth and surrounded by a ditch formed the outer walls, within which roofed dwellings were built and, in times of danger, cattle were herded. Today raths are visible as circular earthworks.

The Real IRA Breakaway faction which rejects the political process and maintains the armed struggle; responsible for the Omagh bombing, the Real IRA has attacked RUC and British Army installations and exploded bombs in England, most notably at Hammersmith Bridge and outside the BBC's headquarters in Shepherd's Bush.

Republicans Supporters of the ideals incorporated in the 1916 Proclamation of the Republic, the overthrow of British rule in Ireland and the promotion of Irish language and culture.

round tower Narrow, tall (65–110ft) and circular tower, tapering to a conical roof. Built from the ninth century onwards, they are unique to Ireland. They are found on the sites of early monasteries, and served to call the monks to prayer. The entrance is usually a doorway 10–15ft above the ground, which was reached by a wooden or rope ladder that could be pulled up for safety.

RUC Royal Ulster Constabulary. Northern Ireland's regular, but armed, police force up until 2001, when it was replaced by the Police Service of Northern Ireland.

SDLP Social Democratic and Labour Party. The largest Northern Irish Nationalist party, centrist left, founded in 1970.

Sinn Féin ("We, Ourselves") Sinn Féin's history has been colourful, eventful and characterized by splits. Re-emerging in the

1970s, it subsequently became a major political force in Northern Ireland, aiming to achieve national self-determination and the formation of a 32-county socialist republic, based on the principles of the Proclamation of 1916 and the beliefs of Tone, Pearse and Connolly. It has been labelled by some as the political wing of the IRA. Its leader since 1983 has been Gerry Adams who has gradually steered Republicanism towards democratic resolution of its goals.

The Six Counties Nationalist/Republican name for Northern Ireland.

souterrain Underground passage that served as a hiding place in times of danger; also used to store food and valuables.

Taoiseach Prime minister of the Republic of Ireland.

TD Teachta Dála. Member of the Republic's parliament.

townland An area of land, similar to a parish, but not necessarily a village.

tricolour The green, white and orange flag of the Republic.

The 26 counties The Republic of Ireland (Éire).

UDA Ulster Defence Association. A Loyalist paramilitary organization, the largest in Northern Ireland.

UDP Ulster Democratic Party. Political wing of the UDA.

Ulster One of Ireland's four provinces, often erroneously used by Unionists and journalists as a synonym for Northern Ireland, thus ignoring the counties of Cavan, Donegal and Monaghan which Ulster also comprises.

Unionists Those (predominantly Protestant) who wish to keep Northern Ireland in union with the rest of the United Kingdom.

UUP Ulster Unionist Party. Founded in 1905 by Edward Carson, the UUP was in power in Northern Ireland from 1921 until the dissolution of Stormont in 1972. Also known as the Official Unionists, the party is led by David Trimble.

UVF Ulster Volunteer Force. A Protestant paramilitary organization.

Index

and small print

Index

Map entries are in **colour**

C

D

E

F

G

L

M

INDEX

N

O

P

Q

R

S

T

U

V

W

Y

Twenty Years of Rough Guides

In the summer of 1981, Mark Ellingham, Rough Guides' founder, knocked out the first guide on a typewriter, with a group of friends. Mark had been travelling in Greece after university, and couldn't find a guidebook that really answered his needs.There were heavyweight cultural guides on the one hand – good on museums and classical sites but not on beaches and tavernas – and on the other hand student manuals that were so caught up with how to save money that they lost sight of the country's significance beyond its role as a place for a cool vacation. None of the guides began to address Greece as a country, with its natural and human environment, its politics and its contemporary life.

Having no urgent reason to return home, Mark decided to write his own guide. It was a guide to Greece that tried to combine some erudition and insight with a thoroughly practical approach to travellers' needs. Scrupulously researched listings of places to stay, eat and drink were matched by careful attention to detail on everything from Homer to Greek music, from classical sites to national parks and from nude beaches to monasteries. Back in London, Mark and his friends got their Rough Guide accepted by a farsighted commissioning editor at the publisher Routledge and it came out in 1982.

The Rough Guide to Greece was a student scheme that became a publishing phenomenon. The immediate success of the book – shortlisted for the Thomas Cook award – spawned a series that rapidly covered dozens of countries. The Rough Guides found a ready market among backpackers and budget travellers, but soon acquired a much broader readership that included older and less impecunious visitors. Readers relished the guides' wit and inquisitiveness as much as the enthusiastic, critical approach that acknowledges everyone wants value for money – but not at any price.

Rough Guides soon began supplementing the "rougher" information – the hostel and low-budget listings – with the kind of detail that independent-minded travellers on any budget might expect. These days, the guides – distributed worldwide by the Penguin group – include recommendations spanning the range from shoestring to luxury, and cover more than 200 destinations around the globe. Our growing team of authors, many of whom come to Rough Guides initially as outstandingly good letter-writers telling us about their travels, are spread all over the world, particularly in Europe, the US and Australia. As well as the travel guides, Rough Guides publishes a series of dictionary phrasebooks covering two dozen major languages, an acclaimed series of music guides running the gamut from Classical to World Music, a series of music CDs in association with World Music Network, and a range of reference books on topics as diverse as the Internet, Pregnancy and Unexplained Phenomena. Visit **www.roughguides.com** to see what's cooking.

Rough Guide credits

Text editor: Sally Schafer
Series editor: Mark Ellingham
Editorial: Martin Dunford, Jonathan Buckley, Kate Berens, Ann-Marie Shaw, Helena Smith, Olivia Swift, Ruth Blackmore, Geoff Howard, Claire Saunders, Gavin Thomas, Alexander Mark Rogers, Polly Thomas, Joe Staines, Richard Lim, Duncan Clark, Peter Buckley, Lucy Ratcliffe, Clifton Wilkinson, Alison Murchie, Matthew Teller, Andrew Dickson, Fran Sandham (UK); Andrew Rosenberg, Yuki Takagaki, Richard Koss, Hunter Slaton (US)
Production: Susanne Hillen, Andy Hilliard, Link Hall, Helen Prior, Julia Bovis, Michelle Draycott, Katie Pringle, Zoë Nobes, Rachel Holmes, Andy Turner, Dan May
Cartography: Maxine Repath, Melissa Baker, Ed Wright, Katie Lloyd-Jones
Cover art direction: Louise Boulton
Picture research: Sharon Martins, Mark Thomas
Online: Kelly Martinez, Anja Mutic-Blessing, Jennifer Gold, Audra Epstein, Suzanne Welles, Cree Lawson (US)
Finance: John Fisher, Gary Singh, Edward Downey, Mark Hall, Tim Bill
Marketing & Publicity: Richard Trillo, Niki Smith, David Wearn, Chloë Roberts, Demelza Dallow, Claire Southern (UK); Simon Carloss, David Wechsler, Megan Kennedy (US)
Administration: Julie Sanderson, Karoline Densley

Publishing information

This seventh edition published June 2003 by
Rough Guides Ltd,
80 Strand, London WC2R 0RL.
345 Hudson St, 4th Floor,
New York, NY10014, USA.
Distributed by the Penguin Group
Penguin Books Ltd,
80 Strand, London WC2R 0RL.
Penguin Putnam, Inc.
375 Hudson Street, NY 10014, USA.
Penguin Books Australia Ltd,
487 Maroondah Highway, PO Box 257,
Ringwood, Victoria 3134, Australia.
Penguin Books Canada Ltd,
10 Alcorn Avenue, Toronto, Ontario,
Canada M4V 1E4.
Penguin Books (NZ) Ltd,
182–190 Wairau Road, Auckland 10,
New Zealand.
Typeset in Bembo and Helvetica to an original design by Henry Iles.

Printed in Italy by LegoPrint S.p.A

912pp includes index
A catalogue record for this book is available from the British Library

ISBN 1-84353-059-7

Help us update

We've gone to a lot of effort to ensure that the seventh edition of **The Rough Guide to Ireland** is accurate and up to date. However, things change – places get "discovered", opening hours are notoriously fickle, restaurants and rooms raise prices or lower standards. If you feel we've got it wrong or left something out, we'd like to know, and if you can remember the address, the price, the time, the phone number, so much the better.

We'll credit all contributions, and send a copy of the next edition (or any other Rough Guide if you prefer) for the best letters. Everyone who writes to us and isn't already a subscriber will receive a copy of our full-colour thrice-yearly newsletter. Please mark letters: "**Rough Guide Ireland Update**" and send to: Rough Guides, 80 Strand, London WC2R 0RL, or Rough Guides, 4th Floor, 345 Hudson St, New York, NY 10014. Or send an email to **mail@roughguides.com**

Have your questions answered and tell others about your trip at **www.roughguides.atinfopop.com**

Acknowledgements

Margaret Greenwood would like to thank John Lahiffe and Katrina Doherty at Tourism Ireland; Sally-Ann Whittaker and Fleur; Robin and Rory Stephenson, Nicole Matthews and family; Colin Harrison; Helen Stuffins and Adrian; Mary Corcoran; Jack and Cathy, and of course Nick, John, Anne and Frank Greenwood.

Geoff Wallis would like to thank Finbar Boyle, Dermot Byrne and Mairéad Ní Mhaonaigh, P.J. Curtis, Dublin Tourism, Malachy Finnegan and the Northern Irish Tourist Board, Hugh Gallagher, Independent Holiday Hostels Ireland, Éamonn Jordan and Mireille Cambier, Henry King and all Harrington Hall, Hertz Belfast, John Lahiffe and Tourism Ireland, Seán MacLoskey, Joanie McDermott, Gerry Murphy, the National Trust, North West Ireland Tourism, Joan Pyne, Mary Reynolds, Paddy "Sharkhunter", and all at *Tessie's Bar*, Meenaleck.

Paul Gray would like to thank Bord Fáilte staff around the country, especially Mary Cosgrave in Dublin; Mary Fleming at IHH; Enda McLoughlin at Inis Mór Ferries; Larry and Fionnuala O'Connell; Julia, Delphine, Nick, Niamh, Andy, Alexia and all the Gurkleys.

In addition the editor would like to thank all those involved in producing this book, including Rachel Holmes for expert typesetting and layout; Joe Mee for excellent picture research; Sam Kirby, Katie Lloyd-Jones and Ed Wright for their cartographic expertise; Louise Boulton for the superb cover; Jennifer Speake for meticulous proofreading; Sam Thorne for additional editing; David Quin and the Ennis Tourist Board for last-minute help and especially Helena Smith and Clifton Wilkinson for all their advice.

Readers' letters

Thanks to all the readers who took the trouble to write in with their comments and suggestions (and apologies to anyone whose name we've misspelt or omitted):

Richard Allen, Barbi Arnaud, Bruce Baron, Leszek and Renata Bojanowska, Autumn Brennan, Lynne Brighton, Colin and Mary Brockington, Lyn Brookes, Pierre-Jean Chandes, Mark D. Cole, Christine Collett, Brendan Connolly, Dave Crookes, Lydie Daunay, Antoine de Vermouthier, Chris Deane, John Dennis, Caroline Evans, Brian Farrington, Mark Farrington, Rev. John Fowler, Joseph Gannon, Jean Gaskarth, B. Gordon, Pat Graham, Liam Harkin, Irene Hennessy, M.R. Hillside, Lotta Holmberg, Celia James, Helen James, A.M. Harvey-Jamieson, Tim Johnson, Sian Jones, Mary Lamb, Peter Maxwell, Carmel McCann, Pádraig McCarthy, Will McCarthy, Helen McClory, Carol Mitteldorf, Mike Moir, Pauline O'Donovan, David Oram, M. Pendsay, Poortenga, Rosemarie Pundsack, W. Ruxton, Paul Shanley, Anthony Smith, Bryan Stevens, Sarah Suggs, Jennifer Taranto, Peter Taylor-Gooby, Mary Thompson, Chris Turner, Chris and Penny Turner, John Watts and Anja Mundt, David Wild.

Photo credits

Cover credits

Main (front picture) Carrick © Aspect Photo Library
Front (small top image) Co. Clare © Robert Harding
Front (small lower image) Dunluce Castle, Co. Antrim © Robert Harding
Back (top image) Ancient beehive © Robert Harding
Back (lower image) Doolin, Co. Clare © Robert Harding

Colour introduction

Dublin Custom House © H.P. Merten/Robert Harding
Moon over Croagh Patrick © R.Drury/Trip
Atlantic Puffin © Ralph A. Clevenger/Corbis
Book of Kells © The Board of Trinity College, Dublin/Bridgeman Art Library
Irish fiddler © Adam Woolfitt/Corbis
Inside a passage grave, Newgrange, Co. Meath © Adam Woolfitt/Robert Harding

Inishmore, Aran Islands, Co. Galway © David Lomax/Robert Harding
Fishing harbour, Ring of Kerry © Chris Coe/Axiom
Green postbox, Killarney National Park, Co. Kerry © Angela Hampton/Travel Ink
Ormond Castle, Carrick-on-Suir, Co. Tipperary © K. McLaren/Trip
High cross at Monasterboice, Co. Meath © Philip Craven/Robert Harding
Beehive hut, Blasket Islands, Co. Kerry © N. McDiarmid/Trip
Hurling sticks against a wall © Collections/ Michael Diggin
Carrying a *curragh* to the sea, Inisheer, Aran Islands © Michael S. Yamashita/Corbis

Things not to miss

01 Upper Lake and Macgillycuddy's Reeks, Killarney, Ring of Kerry © Roy Rainford/ Robert Harding
02 White Island, Co. Fermanagh © Michael Jenner/Robert Harding
03 *The Liffey Swim* (detail), Jack B. Yeats © The National Gallery of Ireland
04 *Doheny & Nesbitt*, Dublin © Abbie Enock/ Travel Ink
05 Boat on Lough Gill, Co. Sligo © Chris Coe/Axiom
06 St Patrick's Day parade, Dublin © Paul Quayle/Axiom
07 Surfing © Richard Cummins/Corbis
08 Georgian doorway, Dublin © Roy Rainford/Robert Harding
09 Dún Aengus, Aran Islands, Co. Galway © Michael St. Maur Sheil/Corbis
10 Drinking a pint © Jenny Acheson/Axiom
11 Saloon at Castle Coole © The National Trust Photographic Library/Patrick Prendergast,
12 Slea Head, Dingle Peninsula, Co. Kerry © Roy Rainford/Robert Harding
13 The Crown Liquor Saloon, Belfast © Abbie Enock/Travel Ink
14 Newgrange passage graves, Co. Meath © Adam Woolfitt/Robert Harding
15 Bantry House, Co. Cork © Paul Gray
16 Basket of seafood © Sylain Grandadam/ Robert Harding
17 Walls of Derry © Chris Coe/Axiom
18 The Burren, Co. Clare © Roy Rainford/ Robert Harding
19 Rock of Cashel, Co. Tipperary © Michael Jenner
20 Horses on the shoreline, Connemara © Chris Coe/Axiom
21 Bogside mural, Derry © Touhig Sion/ Corbis Sygma
22 Book of Kells © The Board of Trinity College, Dublin/Bridgeman Art Library
23 The Twelve Bens Mountains, Co. Galway © B. Woods/Trip
24 Old fishing boat in Kinsale harbour, Co. Cork © Ian Cumming/Axiom
25 Sperrin Mountains, Co. Tyrone © Geray Sweeney/Corbis
26 Macnas Parade, Galway Arts Festival © Joe Shaughnessy/Galway Arts Festival
27 Musicians in a pub, Dublin © Ian Cumming/Axiom
28 Giant's Causeway, Co. Antrim © K. McLaren/Trip

Black & white photos

Broighter Boat in the National Museum, Dublin © National Museum of Ireland p.60
James Joyce Statue, Dublin © Roy Rainford/ Robert Harding p.73
Wicklow Mountains, Co. Wicklow © K. McLaren/Trip p.144
Powerscourt Estate © Fraser Hall/Robert Harding p.165
Birr Castle, Co. Offaly © Richard T. Nowitz/ Corbis p.177
Trim's Anglo-Norman castle © Farrell Grehan/Corbis p.194
High cross at Kells, Co. Meath © Michael Jenner p.213
Carlingford village and the hills of the Cooley Peninsula, Co. Louth © Geray Sweeney/ Corbis p.228
Patrick Kavanagh © National Library of Ireland p.251
Scene from Straszny Dwor at Wexford Opera © Clive Barda/ARENA-PAL p.260
Jerpoint Abbey, Co. Kilkenney © Michael Jenner p.275
Beverly Crosier © The Hunt Museum p.288
Cahir Castle, Co. Tipperary © Philip Craven/ Robert Harding p.311
River Lee estuary, Co. Cork © Angela Hampton/Travel Ink p.334
Mending a boat beside a waterway, Cork city © Michael Jenner p.353
Skellig Michael, Co. Kerry © Michael Jenner/ Robert Harding p.382
Dún Beag, Dingle Peninsula, Co. Kerry © Martin Barlow p.392
The Burren, Co. Clare © Roy Rainford/ Robert Harding p.422
Cliffs of Moher © Michael Jenner p.441
Climbing Croagh Patrick, Co. Mayo © Jiri Rezac/Axiom p.450
Round tower at Kilmacduagh © Chris Coe/ Axiom p.464

Benbulben Mountain, Co. Sligo © Roy Rainford/Robert Harding p.530
Grave of W. B. Yeats, Drumcliff, Co. Sligo © Jody Denham/Trip p.538
Lough Doon, Co. Donegal © Michael Jenner p.564
Slieve League cliffs, Co. Donegal © Gavin Hellier/Robert Harding p.576
Botanic Gardens, Belfast © Eitan Simanor/ Axiom p.618
Belfast City Hall © C. Bowman/Robert Harding p.633
Giant's Causeway, Co. Antrim © K.Murray/ Trip p.654
Barrells of Bushmills whiskey, Co. Antrim © Andy Lovell/Travel Ink p.671
Early morning mist, Mourne mountains, Co. Down © H. Roger/Trip p.702
Boat at Strangford, Co. Down © Michael Jenner p.715
Florence Court, Co. Fermanagh © National Trust Photographic Library/ Patrick Prendergast p.748
Castle Coole, Co. Fermanagh © National Trust Photographic Library/Matthew Antrobus p.763

The Famine Cottage
"atmospheric, haunting, moving, authentic, a time capsule of 19th century Ireland"
Maurice O'Keeffe, Historian & Antique Expert
Slea Head Drive, Fahan, Dingle
Tel: 066-9156241 ~ 087-7622617
E-mail: managh@indigo.ie
www.faminecottage.com
Open 7 Days
From 9.00am

NORTH
SOUTH
TRAVEL

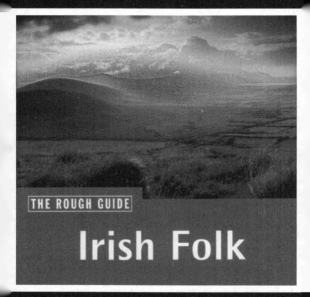